LAW AND BUSINESS OF THE ENTERTAINMENT INDUSTRIES

DONALD E. BIEDERMAN
Southwestern University School of Law and Pepperdine University School of Law

ROBERT C. BERRY
Boston College Law School

EDWARD P. PIERSON
University of Denver College of Law

MARTIN E. SILFEN
New York Law School

JEANNE A. GLASSER
Pace University School of Law

Auburn House Publishing Company
Dover, Massachusetts

ACKNOWLEDGMENTS

This book had its beginnings in separate efforts by the various authors to assemble materials pertaining to the legal and business aspects of the entertainment industries. Several years have passed since each of us began to work and write in the field. During that time, numerous individuals and institutions have aided us with invaluable support and comments. We would like to recognize the following in particular.

Special thanks goes to Southwestern University School of Law, and its faculty and staff, for unstinting support of the project over many years. Among others, Professors Darrell Johnson and Robert Lind of Southwestern provided critical comments and wonderful assistance.

Special recognition is accorded Professor Lon Sobel of Loyola—Los Angeles for his extensive comments and supply of materials, and to Mark Fischer of Boston for his great contributions to one set of materials that was consulted in writing this volume.

Various individuals provided needed comments on our efforts over time, including Alvin Deutsch, Alan Hartnick, and Harriet Dorsen of New York; Gerald Weiner and Michael Painter of Los Angeles; Richard Frank and W. Robert Thompson of Nashville; and Robert Loventhal of Braintree, Massachusetts. Professor Edward Rubin of the University of California at Berkeley also provided valuable reactions and comments.

Another group of individuals worked on our materials, suggesting useful refinements. Our thanks to Jan Suzukawa, Alan Gutman, Lisa Christopher, Esther Burns, Carol Wernik, and Kevin Yeam.

Finally, we are most grateful to the authors and publications who kindly granted permission for the inclusion of their important articles in this volume. We note authors and publications as they appear, and so do not repeat them here.

THE AUTHORS

Library of Congress Cataloging in Publication Data

Law and business of the entertainment industries.

Includes index.
1. Performing arts—Law and legislation—United States. 2. Entertainers—Legal status, laws, etc.—United States. 3. Artists' contracts—United States.
I. Biederman, Donald E.
KF4290.L39   1987   343.73'0787902   87-1131
                        347.303787902

ISBN 0-86569-153-3

Printed in the United States of America

FOREWORD

When I first started practising entertainment law in 1956, record contracts and actors' contracts were three to ten pages in length, publishing contracts were printed on two sides of one piece of paper, and management contracts were three pages at most. There were no videos for recording artists to make, and movies were distributed principally to theatres, not via cable, pay television, pay-per-view, video or laser disc. Audio recordings were sold primarily in the form of LPs and 45s, and limitedly in the form of 8-track tapes; but cassettes had yet to make an impact on the market and there were no such items as CDs, CDVs, 12-inch singles, or digital audio tapes.

The people producing motion pictures really did not understand the music business and, of course, were not adept at using either the talent or the music audience for their own purposes. The same was true of the music industry when it came to understanding or dealing with motion pictures. Motion picture companies used a certain few film composers to write and in-house orchestras to perform the music for their movies, and rarely, if ever, went outside to pop or rock and roll stars to write or perform music for motion pictures. Record companies did not participate in the making of soundtracks, and it was rare that a motion picture company released a film soundtrack on records.

The entertainment world today is not even remotely similar to the one of thirty years ago. The video clauses alone in today's average record contract are longer than the entire record contract originally was. One cannot deal in the current record industry without being fully cognizant of all aspects of the motion picture and television industries; similarly, one cannot deal in motion pictures and television without being intimately familiar with the music business. The terms of a contract for a record deal could affect an artist's future employment in film and television. For example, every record contract today contains substantial exclusivity provisions restricting the right of the artist to appear in any video not exclusively owned and distributed by the record company. Should that same artist in the future wish to do a movie, the motion picture company would require the right to distribute the movie, or excerpts therefrom, incorporating that artist's performance in video form. The resulting conflict, which may or may not have been avoided by appropriate negotiation of the record contract in the first in-

v

stance, could result in the artist's loss of substantial income and/or career momentum.

Such instances of overlapping and conflicting rights within the record and motion picture industries are growing daily. Whereas at one time the record industry dealt almost exclusively in audio product and the movie and television industries dealt almost exclusively in visual product, today all these industries deal in "audio-visual" product and are in direct competition. As a result, the legal and business knowledge required for today's deal-making is enormous.

Further, the growing sophistication in the delivery systems of entertainment product requires the negotiator to be aware of all possible avenues of maximizing income for the client. Additionally, the increased sophistication of artists makes it incumbent upon the legal practitioner to be aware of the seemingly endless possibilities of solving negotiation and contractual problems. That same sophistication which has made artists and companies more aware of their rights and potential has given rise to longer and more complicated contracts and to an exten-

sive increase in litigation over the past twenty years. The results of such litigation are, in turn, responsible for even longer and more complicated contracts.

These many changes in the entertainment industries constitute, in themselves, sufficient reason for this extraordinary book. *Law and Business of the Entertainment Industries* will bring the user up to date on the problems the practitioner faces every day and the vital cases that affect every aspect of contract negotiation in the entertainment industry. Uniquely qualified by their broad range of experience throughout the entertainment industries, the authors draw upon that experience in presenting to the reader a clear and concise compendium of significant materials.

Broad in scope, yet meticulous in its detail, this book arms one with the most recent and significant information essential to successfully negotiating or properly advising clients in the entertainment field. It is, in short, indispensable for anyone working in the area of law and entertainment, as well as for students preparing for a law career in related areas.

JAY L. COOPER
*Past Chairman, The Forum Committee
on Entertainment and Sports,
American Bar Association*

CONTENTS

INTRODUCTION

Change is the theme of this book. For changes occur all the time in the various entertainment industries. All too often, a practitioner who deals exclusively in one industry will be unaware of cases in other industries which may affect what he or she is doing. For example, several cases in this book deal with the question of whether subsequent changes to the work of a creator constitute "mutilation" actionable under Section 43a of the Lanham Trademark Act. (See Secs. 2.50, 4.60, 7.30.)

But is "colorization" mutilation? Colorization of movies has become a "hot" issue in the entertainment world. Proponents cheer and opponents cringe at the thought of *Casablanca, Maltese Falcon,* and *Yankee Doodle Dandy* being turned from black-and-white into color through the marvels of a computer. Supporters of colorization assert it is simply a business decision. If enough people want to see Humphrey Bogart and Ingrid Bergman bid farewell in colored mist, so be it. Opponents cry "illegal" when it comes to tampering with the original (now revered) black-and-white imagery. One thing is clear—when John Houston directed *Treasure of the Sierra Madre,* he never envisioned that he would live to see, almost a

half-century later, the development of a process that could take his black-and-white print and more or less faithfully transform it into color. If he had, one must assume that he would have had his lawyer do something about it in his contract.

The role of law in the entertainment industries is often one of anticipation. A contract today should cover events well into the future. Antitrust decisions should deal with current disputes by providing reasonable business guidelines for future advances. Copyright revisions by Congress should address current and future states of the arts. Labor relations, communications laws, corporate and tax regulations, and concepts of privacy, publicity, unfair competition and libel should be similarly directed.

No one pretends that anticipation in these areas has been perfect. In fact, the analysis of law as applied to the entertainment industries is often one of assessing how incomplete and inadequate the anticipation has been. From that vantage point, the entertainment lawyer must assay the damage and construct a method of dealing with the inadequacies to obtain the best result in an imperfect system.

The colorization issue brought the reclusive Woody Allen from New York City to

Washington, D.C., to testify at a Congressional committee holding hearings on the legal issues involved. To Allen, the moral issues were fully as important as the legal. As he said in an interview:

> Fifty percent of the issue, I think, is that in any area—whether it's landmarks preservation or fine arts—one wants to preserve a treasury of things. And the other 50 percent of it is that, you know, it's just morally unacceptable to come in and simply destroy an artist's work or change an artist's work without that artist consenting.

At the conclusion of the hearings, Congressman Richard Gephardt introduced a bill that would require the principal director and screenwriters to approve any "material alteration" in a movie. As of this writing, the fate of the bill is uncertain. It might well not pass Congress, and if it does, its retroactive applicability to the scores of old black-and-white movies is doubtful. In the meantime, the proponents of colorization, such as Turner Entertainment, which spent billions to purchase the vast MGM and Warner Brothers libraries, fight for their right to bring "new" entertainment to the public. The company also seeks to copyright its "new" color films, so that it can control them for another 75 years. The U.S. Copyright Office is currently studying whether colorization is a creative reinterpretation that qualifies the color-added film for copyright.

The colorization issue illustrates the dynamics of the entertainment industries. Change—or at least the appearance of change—is vital. Consumer interests have limited lifespans. The same old fare offered again and again inevitably suffers declining audiences. The dilemma is that basic entertainment does not change that much. Drama, comedy, sports and games, music, art, and (arguably) news and current events are the basics, probably now and forever.

How these are packaged and delivered are the real subjects of change.

Colorization of movies is only one small wrinkle on an entertainment map that over the past decades has witnessed the development of "moving" pictures; the harnessing of sound and later visual transmissions over the air, even unto satellites thousands of miles above the earth; the capture of sounds on vinyl, tape and disc; and the emergence of the computer as a progenitor of various types of entertainment vehicles. Minds struggle to discover new methods of repackaging our entertainment to make it appear novel and unique.

This need for change plunges the entertainment industries into high-risk ventures. The potentials for huge payoffs are accompanied by the possibilities of economic disasters. While profits from a *Star Wars* and its technological imageries soared over a $100 million, almost the entire $40 million invested in *Heaven's Gate* and its production calamities was lost, and a major motion picture company reeled under the blow. Michael Jackson's "Thriller" album helped to revive the lagging sales in the recording industry, but countless albums and tapes continue to languish in stores and warehouses—unsold, unheard, unwanted.

To read the factual backgrounds of the people involved in the legal disputes that are chronicled in this book is to ask, "How could they have done it that way? Why risk what they did?" The answers are complex. Perhaps it was the lure of easy money that begat carelessness. Perhaps it was pride that put fame ahead of common sense. Perhaps it was the experienced and powerful taking advantage of the weak and naive. Whatever the reasons—and, as with *Heaven's Gate*, it is often a combination of circumstances gone awry—the lessons to be learned are often overshadowed by the uncomfortable knowledge that misjudgments will undoubtedly occur in the future.

This book attempts to pinpoint the principal areas of controversy in each of the major entertainment industries. A description of what has caused problems in the past will surely warn of what to avoid in the future. We do not attempt to present a seemingly coherent theory of so-called entertainment law, since we doubt such a concept really exists. Instead, we view transactions in the entertainment industries and invite inspection as to what was right and what went wrong, from both a legal and a business perspective. We hope thereby to encourage speculation on what should have been done to avoid the debacles that ensued.

The transactions discussed must be placed in an overall context of certain realities that face most, if not all, entertainment industries. First, escalating production costs often outstrip earning potential for all but a handful of fortunates who somehow climb to the top of the heap and exclaim, "Look at me!" Second, in the glamorous and alluring world of entertainment, new forms of delivering entertainment are conceived all the time, and competition for the consumer dollar is fierce and growing. Third, actual opportunities to break into some fields of entertainment are shrinking. As competition intensifies, the weak drop out or are absorbed. Retrenchment occurs. Caution grows. Opportunities shrivel.

These realities demand examination in the context of the individual industries. We begin, in Chapter 1, with an overall examination of contract dealings and principles in various entertainment contexts. We then turn to individual industries in Chapters 2 through 8. Chapter 2 discusses literary publishing—its business background and the legal and business developments. Many of these themes are repeated and new issues raised in music publishing (Chapter 3), recording (Chapter 4), live theatre (Chapter 5), motion pictures (Chapter 6), television (Chapter 7), and such advancing technologies as cable, videocassettes, and video games (Chapter 8). We believe this organization makes the most practical and, ultimately, logical sense. It forces the analysis of problems in a factual context. We avoid painting the "big picture" because that picture, we think, would be somewhat vacuous and definitely misleading. However, that is not to say there should be an absence of looking at similar problems across industries. Comparative study of these contractual provisions, or the lack thereof, in different industrial settings is not only helpful, but essential. This should be done, though, only after these provisions are first examined in the context of the precise business situations in which they first arose.

Each industry has its own idiosyncrasies. These are described in the introductory sections to Chapters 2 through 8. A few recent developments should be noted at this point, as they underscore the futility of discussing legal problems in the entertainment industries without basing them in the context of ongoing business concerns.

Literary publishing has been marked by multiple takeovers and mergers of old line companies in the past few years. In some instances, one publishing company has absorbed another. In others, outside media and even nonmedia companies have entered the publishing field, all with substantial ramifications. Literary publishing is projecting itself as a glamor business as it doles out large sums for top-name authors. In 1985, a previously unheralded writer received a $1 million advance for her first novel, and noted Latin American author Jorge Amado netted a record $250 thousand for a translation. Of substantial legal significance in the publishing industry is the fact that courts have imposed limitations on a publisher's previously unfettered right to reject a manuscript on the grounds that it is not "satisfactory in form and content." The extent to which such limitations will extend to submitted screenplays, teleplays, and work in other industries must be monitored.

Music publishers have been successful in defeating the claim of the Association of Independent Television Stations that blanket licensing of music for performance in syndicated TV shows through ASCAP (the American Society of Composers, Authors and Publishers) and BMI (Broadcast Music, Inc.) violated the federal antitrust laws. (See *Buffalo Broadcasting*, Section 3.10.) In response, broadcasters persuaded key Congressmen and Senators to introduce bills in the 1986 and 1987 Congresses. These bills would require music publishers to license performances to program producers and would prohibit licensing by performing rights societies such as ASCAP or BMI. To date, hearings have been conducted, but no action has been taken. In the meantime, TV performance royalties continue to escalate through the fees charged by the societies.

Quite obviously tied to music publishing, the record industry was an outlet for music and for years seemed to have unlimited growth potential. Observers were surprised, therefore, by the recession that hit the industry between 1978 and 1983. The hard times spurred rethinking of methods of doing business. One result was that unknown singers or groups had fewer opportunities to break into the field with a contract from a major recording label. Although the tide eventually turned, mainly because of a few extremely successful albums by stars such as Prince and Michael Jackson, new marketing techniques such as MTV, and the introduction of the compact digital disc, the cutbacks

introduced into the industry continued for the most part. A tough field to enter has become even tougher.

The Broadway stage seems ever on the brink of disaster. Even so, while it staggers along, changes are afoot. Most notable is the new pact between the Dramatists Guild and the League of American Theatres and Producers. The "Approved Production Contract" has replaced the "Minimum Basic Production Contract," which was the standard form used between authors and producers for more than 30 years (see Section 5.10). It has altered the economic relationships between authors and producers significantly. Another significant change is the increase in touring (road), regional, and local theatres, all of which now gross far more than the Broadway stage. Off-Broadway and Off-Off-Broadway are also experiencing success as alternatives for new plays.

Film production, distribution, and exhibition have undergone significant changes during the past decade. For example, United Artists (UA) merged with Metro Goldwyn Mayer (MGM), only to be split again in 1986 when TV's Ted Turner bought MGM and UA was spun off to former MGM majority owner Kirk Kerkorian and the former MGM/UA stockholders. Twentieth Century–Fox went private under the ownership of Denver oil magnate Marvin Davis, who first sold half, then complete ownership, to international newspaper giant Rupert Murdoch. The other major studios, such as Paramount, Universal, Disney, Warner, and Columbia also have had their ups and downs; one or two box office hits per year made the difference. And new players arrived, as Orion, Cannon, New World, and Tri-Star (a joint venture of Columbia Pictures, HBO, and CBS) challenged the major studios. Wall Street became deeply involved when major stockbrokerage houses floated hundreds of millions in limited partnership shares in such specific ventures as Silver Screen, Delphi, Omega, and Balcor. In some instances, four or five offerings originated from the same sources. The past decade also saw an increase in the number of screens in the country to a high of nearly 20,000, after several years' steady decline.

During this same period, the three major TV networks faced increased competition from independent local TV stations; from pay-TV services such as HBO and Showtime/The Movie Channel; from "superstations" such as WTBS in Atlanta and WWOR–TV in New York; and from a home video explosion. The network share of prime time audiences dwindled from nearly 90 percent to the low 70s. In addition, the networks continued to battle with film and TV producers over the FCC's "financial interest and syndication" rules, under which the networks were essentially prohibited from ownership of prime time entertainment programming and from the increasingly lucrative syndication market (where a hit such as M*A*S*H could command over $200 million in syndication fees). Networks also had to contend with producers' demands for increased license fees for network programming.

The FCC amended its rules to allow an entity such as a network to own as many as 12 TV stations and 12 AM radio and 12 FM radio stations. This led to a number of expensive acquisitions and takeovers. In 1985, ABC was acquired by Capital Cities Communications, and RCA (which owned NBC) agreed to be acquired by General Electric. Rupert Murdoch completed his acquisition of Twentieth Century-Fox and added as well the Metromedia "owned and operated" TV stations—all powerful independents in major markets.

From these comments, it can be seen that entertainment concerns are no longer the exclusive province of California and New York. Other localities and business interests have entered the industries vigorously and effectively. For example, in film production, California has faced "runaway" productions which, according to one estimate, have cost California residents and businesses some $1.5 billion in revenues per year. Studios abound in New York, Texas, North Carolina, and South Carolina. Other states have established agencies to attract film and television production. There are now approximately 70 state and local film commissions and bureaus aggressively seeking a share of the action. The recording industry faces similar competition. Recording activity has expanded beyond the traditional centers of Los Angeles, New York, Nashville, and San Francisco to such places as Minneapolis (where Prince emerged) and Muscle Shoals, Alabama.

The business opportunities and the economic risks associated with the entertainment industries make this topic a fascinating one to examine. When placed in a legal-business context, each transaction assumes a life of its own. The average adult, according to U.S. government data, spends 64.5 hours per week, or 9.2 hours per day, as leisure time. The breakdown is 29 hours per week watching television, 23 listening to radio, 3.8 reading newspapers, 3.7 listening to records and tapes (and now compact discs), 2.3 reading magazines, 1.2 reading books, and only miniscule amounts watching live spectator sports, movies, and other entertainment. Maintaining or increasing their share of the entertainment pie is what the industries examined in Chapters 2 through 8 are seeking.

The concerns addressed in the final chapters relate to *all* entertainment industries. Chapter 9 considers the roles that certain professionals perform—lawyers, managers, agents, and promoters. Of course, the roles in each industry are not identical, and this we note. Of special interest are instances in which a person assumes more than one role—for example, acting as both a lawyer and a promoter. This duality of roles is a trend in some entertainment industries. Our focus is on the pitfalls that confront one who attempts too many tasks.

The final considerations in Chapter 10 are directed at the rights of the individual, particularly the celebrity who is cast in the public glare. Performers, artists, and authors are central characters in the entertainment industries. Without their creative talents and public personalities, these businesses would not be show businesses as we know them.

Where there are stars, however, predatory practices are sure to follow. Therefore, it is fitting that we conclude with an analysis of the growing areas of rights of privacy and publicity, and protections against unfair competition, deceptive practices, and libel.

The various analyses in this book emphasize one theme: No single approach, in business or law, is necessarily conclusive in the entertainment industries with multiple actors and varying problems that do not fit neatly into categories of contracts, antitrust, copyright, or publicity. Therefore, approaching entertainment industry problems with flexibility and comprehensiveness is essential.

CONTRACT CONSIDERATIONS AND SPECIAL STATUTES

1.00   Contracts in the Entertainment Industries

Entertainment is a document-intensive business. In all the industries, a finished entertainment property is delivered to the public only after extensive contract negotiations and drafting between many related parties. The transactions are complex and vital. For example, a motion picture deal may include lengthy negotiations and hopefully eventual agreements involving the following parties: investors, the producer, banking institutions, the director, actors and actresses, stunt persons, choreographers, film composers, music publishers, record labels owning recordings used in the film, the owner of the underlying work, screenwriters, persons whose lives may be portrayed in the film, and the film distribution company.

Much of the practice of law in motion pictures, television, recording, music publishing, video, and literary publishing contemplates an involved negotiation, execution, and enforcement of personal services contracts. Unlike other industries, the entertainment industries are, to a large degree, based on the unique, intangible, and highly subjective talents of an individual performer or artist. Without the individual songwriter and acquisition of certain rights in and to the song which he or she composes, the music publishing company cannot do business. Likewise, the motion picture studio is in need of personal services contracts for the actors, actresses, directors, producers, screenwriters, cinematographers, choreographers, and composers in order to produce a motion picture today. For these reasons, a basic understanding of contract law is essential to the practice of entertainment law, and an in-depth understanding of the unique aspects of personal services contracts and the interpretation and enforcement of those contracts is necessary.

In the motion picture industry, beginning in the 1920s, there developed what was known as the "star system." Specific artists, actors, actresses, and directors were employed by a studio through long-term personal services contracts. For example, in *De Haviland v. Warner Brothers Pictures* note the terms and conditions under which Olivia De Haviland entered an exclusive personal services contract with Warner Brothers Pictures (see Section 1.30).

1

Beginning in the 1940s, as major studios witnessed a decline in motion picture attendance, the studio system declined to the extent that studios were left unable or unwilling to negotiate long-term personal services contracts with various actors, actresses, producers and directors, and since that time the trend has been toward short duration or nonexclusive personal services contracts. Accordingly, the major actors and actresses today—the Robert Redfords, Jessica Langes and Dustin Hoffmans—are not signed exclusively to an individual studio, but rather enter into personal services contracts on a film-by-film basis.

However, exclusive long-term personal services contracts still exist in the television industry; they are used by both the networks and by independent television producers who are engaged by the studio to produce and deliver certain television shows. Likewise, the record industry today utilizes exclusive long-term personal services contracts. Recording artists regularly sign agreements that may consist of an initial term of one year, with four one-year options exercisable by the record company to bind the recording artist for long periods of time.

The following issues are essential in evaluating personal services contracts:

- Existence of a formal contract between the parties.
- Personal services exclusive or nonexclusive.
- Term of the agreement.
- Statutory restrictions on the term of the agreement.
- Provisions for extension of the term of the contract.
- Consideration flowing to the artist.
- Services to be performed by the artist.
- Duration for a fixed term or a fixed term with option.
- Options in the agreement, and how exercised.

- Effect of a breach of the agreement by either the company or the artist.
- Availability and type of injunctive relief.
- Controlling state laws and possible exclusivity of the forum hearing any disputes as to the contract.

State laws may dictate whether a formal contract exists between parties, under what terms and conditions that contract may be enforced, and the duration of the contract. The great majority of entertainment contracts negotiated today are entered into and performed in the states of New York and California. Because the entertainment industries are so firmly entrenched in those states, extensive regulations of the entertainment industries exist in those jurisdictions. Accordingly, a firm understanding of the statutes of these jurisdictions is essential in determining the ultimate validity or invalidity of a contract. Likewise, a significant number of personal services contracts in entertainment are with minors, and the enforceability of such contracts is specifically contingent upon the applicable statutes of the jurisdiction.

Chapter 1 examines personal services contracts in light of these issues. We examine whether contracts need to be in writing and other problems in making a binding agreement. We then consider the terms and conditions of the personal services contract and the remedies available under that contract.

1.10 Contract Formality

The entertainment industries exist on ideas turned into deals. When an idea is "hot," immediate action is desired. Parties rush to agree, and in the process, desire at times outraces common sense. The "deal," as it turns out, is strictly verbal, or there are scattered memos but no single, final, formal written agreement.

Did the parties actually reach agreement?

Is there really a contract, with the final writing only a memorial of the deal already concluded? Is there a sufficient writing to satisfy the applicable statute of frauds? If the production proceeds as envisioned, these questions are moot. There is no problem because the idea becomes a deal that produces a success. Everyone is happy. But at other times, dreams die early, the deal sours, and the parties go to war. This is when the questions become pressing inquiries.

Metro-Goldwyn-Mayer, Inc. v. Scheider, 352 N.Y.S.2d 205 (App.Div. 1st Dept. 1974)

. . . In September, 1971, plaintiff, a producer of films, and ABC, a television broadcaster, made an agreement, pursuant to which plaintiff was, at ABC's option to be exercised after receipt of a script, to make a pilot film to be the precursor, if ABC exercised a second option to that effect, of a television series to be broadcast by ABC either in the fall of 1972 or the next mid-season. By trade custom, if ABC opted for the series for fall (September) commencement of broadcast of the series, filming would be required to start no later than June; if for mid-season (January) commencement, then filming would start in November. Plaintiff then entered into an oral agreement, the basic terms of which were arrived at on or about September 30, 1971, with defendant, an actor, to play the lead in both the pilot, should ABC opt to have it made, and in the making of the series, and possible yearly series for five years, should ABC decide to proceed. As requested by defendant to relieve him of unnecessary commitments, it was further agreed that, if ABC decided not to proceed and so advised plaintiff, plaintiff's option to command defendant's services would cease. Agreed sums were to be paid defendant, depending on the extent of the work.

In February, 1972, the pilot having been made, and accepted, ABC decided to proceed. Defendant was notified by plaintiff to report no later than June 5, 1972, to start filming in time for commencement of broadcast by September 15. Defendant refused. Plaintiff promptly instituted this action to enjoin defendant from working for others, and for damage for the breach. Defendant interposed a defense of Statute of Frauds, claiming the contract not to be performable within a year (section 5–701[1], General Obligations Law). Trial Term sustained the defense. We hold the agreement by its terms to have been performable within a year. ABC controlled the cutoff date and could have terminated the agreement at any option stage. Nor is it unusual for a third party to govern the possibility of performability of a contract. . . . In any event, as the dates turned out, as chosen by ABC and ordered by plaintiff, performance for this series would have been complete before the first broadcast date, less than a year from the first agreement. And ABC retained an option to stop then or to go on from year to year thereafter. Thus, the contract was terminable at any time within a year whenever ABC chose. . . . The Statute of Frauds is not applicable and cannot serve to defeat plaintiff's claim.

NOTES

1. The preceding *MGM* case can be contrasted with *Sawyer v. Sickinger*, 366 N.Y.S.2d 435 (1975), in which the plaintiff sued for injunctive relief to compel the defendant to specifically perform an oral agreement which allegedly granted to the plaintiff the exclusive option to acquire the defendant's motion picture and the related motion picture rights in a novel and to pay 1.5 percent of the producer's share of net profits from that motion picture. Such an agreement would seem to be incapable of performance within one year, and thus unenforceable under the statute of frauds. In the *Sawyer* case, correspondence of the attorney for the plaintiff distinguished ongoing negotiations with a view toward a possible contractual relationship from the actual existence of a bona fide contract. The court, referring to New York law, found that the alleged obligation to pay a percentage of profits was continuing, was not subject to termination by either party, and, accordingly, could not be performed within one year.

2. If it is established that the parties did not intend their agreement to be binding until in writing and signed, there is no enforceable oral agreement. See *Scheck v. Francis*, 26 N.Y.2d 466, 311 N.Y.S.2d 841 (1975).

3. However, a course of conduct may create a contractual obligation, even where a formal written contract is contemplated, especially if the party desiring to enforce the contract has taken action in reliance on the agreement with knowledge of the other party. See

GLG, Inc. v. ALF Productions, Inc., reported in *New York Law Journal*, Fein, J., Sup.Ct.N.Y., May 23, 1975.

4. Under certain circumstances, a court may determine that a basic agreement has been entered on the understanding of the parties with various terms to be agreed on at a later date. A court may rule the agreement to be enforceable and require that the parties reasonably negotiate those additional terms. Contrast the ruling in *Scheider* with the ruling in *De Laurentiis* (see Section 1.20) and the ruling in *American Broadcast Company, Inc. v. Wolf* (see Section 1.53).

5. Entertainment agreements that deal with the transfer of copyright ownership, including certain publishing agreements, screenplay agreements, and recording contracts, have additional requirements under copyright statutes that they be reduced to writing. The Copyright Act of 1976, 17 U.S.C. 204(a) provides:

> A transfer of copyright ownership, other than by operation of law, is not valid unless an instrument of conveyance, or a note or memorandum of the transfer, is in writing and signed by the owner of the rights conveyed or such owner's duly authorized agent.

The new law defines a "transfer of copyright ownership" as:

> an assignment, mortgage, exclusive license, or any other conveyance, alienation, or hypothecation of a copyright or of any of the exclusive rights comprised in a copyright, whether or not it is limited in time or place of effect, but not including a nonexclusive license. 17 U.S.C. 101

An exclusive license will be treated as an agreement for purposes of requiring a written instrument.

Jillcy Film Enterprises, Inc. v. Home Box Office, 593 F. Supp. 515 (S.D.N.Y. 1984)

MOTLEY, CHIEF JUDGE

Plaintiff, Jillcy Film Enterprises, Inc., is a Canadian corporation that was formed for the purpose of producing the film documentary in question in this case. Defendant, Home Box Office, Inc. (HBO), is a New York corporation which operates a cable television network in the United States. Jillcy has sued HBO for breach of contract and HBO has moved to dismiss the complaint pursuant to Fed.R.Civ.P. 12(c) and 56. . . .

HBO and a Canadian corporation not a party to this suit had made arrangements for a feature-length film entitled "The Terry Fox Story" to be made and broadcast on HBO's nationwide pay-television network. The principals of the then-unformed Jillcy Film Enterprises, Inc., approached HBO with a proposal to make a film documentary of the making of "The Terry Fox Story."

Jillcy was formed and executed a letter agreement with HBO on July 21, 1982. The relevant terms of the letter agreement were:

(a) HBO gave Jillcy the right to film a documentary of the filming of "The Terry Fox Story."

(b) Within six weeks after the commencement of the film, Jillcy was to submit some rough footage of the documentary that had been filmed up to that point.

(c) For a period of up to 90 days after the delivery of that rough footage, the parties agreed to "negotiate exclusively and in good faith with respect to the terms and provisions relating to the distribution, exhibition or other exploitation of the documentary."

(d) Finally, the parties agreed that "in the event that you and we do not reach agreement," Jillcy would not use the documentary in the United States for the duration of the copyright in the documentary.

On October 5, 1982, both parties executed another letter agreement extending the delivery date of the first assemblage of rough footage until November 5, 1982. The rough footage was delivered on November 4, 1982. Negotiations took place for some time, although it is not clear when they began, with respect to a long term production and licensing agreement.

On December 1, 1982, a handwritten memo appeared on a page from a note pad with the name "Meg Louis" printed on the top. The memo was neither signed nor addressed to anyone. On it appears the date and the words "deal closed" and notes concerning some terms.

Mr. Spivak, Jillcy's counsel, sent a letter dated December 27, 1982, to Margret Louis, HBO's associate director of business affairs, containing 67 proposed changes in a draft production and licensing agreement. Among them was included one proposal that Jillcy receive its initial payment regardless of whether or not the Agreement was executed. The letter closed with a request that Louis call Spivak "so that we may expeditiously consummate the Agreement."

Jillcy contends that on January 7, 1983, an oral agreement was reached, the terms of which were embodied in the Production and License Agreement. HBO denies this contention, but assumes it to be true only for the purpose of its motion and argument based on the statute of frauds.

On January 17, 1983, another handwritten memo appeared on a page from the note pad of "Meg Louis." To it was attached a copy of the unexecuted agreement. The memo was signed "Meg" and addressed to "Janet" directing her to "make payment . . . as soon as possible" pursuant to a specified provision of the Agreement which provided for payment upon "approval by HBO of selected footage." On the bottom of the memo appears another handwritten notation, "1/18 Meg says don't pay—deal being *pulled*." (Emphasis in original.) This notation is neither signed nor initialed and its author is therefore unidentified.

Louis sent a letter dated January 18, 1983 to Mr. Saperia, another counsel for Jillcy, in which she indicated she was enclosing three unexecuted copies of the agreement with revisions pursuant to recent conversations. She requested their prompt signature by Jillcy and return to HBO, "after which I will forward a fully executed copy. . . ." The agreement did not contain Jillcy's proposal referred to in its December 27, 1982 letter but rather provided that Jillcy's initial payment be made no more than 10 days after execution and delivery of the agreement to HBO. That same day, Jillcy delivered more rough footage to HBO where it was screened but received an unfavorable review by HBO employees.

The next day, on January 19, 1983, an HBO employee called one of Jillcy's attorneys and told him that the deal was off. This oral notice to Jillcy apparently was given prior to the receipt by Jillcy of the January 18, 1983, transmittal letter and execution copies of the agreement which had been sent by Louis. Approximately two weeks after the receipt by Jillcy of the oral notice and the unexecuted agreement, Jillcy nevertheless executed the agreement and returned it to HBO. HBO has never executed the agreement.

Jillcy thereafter sued HBO seeking damages caused by HBO's alleged breach of the purported oral agreement of January 7, 1983, and damages caused by HBO's alleged breach of the July 21, 1982 letter agreement to negotiate in good faith. HBO has moved to dismiss both claims. . . .

The New York statute of frauds provides in pertinent part:

(a) Every agreement, promise or undertaking is void, unless it or some note or memorandum thereof be in writing, and subscribed by the party to be charged therewith, or by his lawful agent, if such agreement, promise or undertaking:

1. By its terms is not to be performed within one year from the making thereof or the performance of which is not to be completed before the end of a lifetime.

N.Y. General Obligations Law § 5–701. It is undisputed by Jillcy that the agreement contains several provisions which, by their terms, will require more than a year to fully perform. It would appear, therefore, that because the contract is not capable of full performance within a year, it is within the statute of frauds and is unenforceable.

The issue is complicated, however, by the existence of termination clauses in the agreement. For example, either party has the option to terminate the agreement in the event of "accidents, riots, strikes, epidemics, Acts of God, or any other legitimate conditions beyond the affected party's control (hereinafter 'force majeure')." HBO has the option to terminate the agreement in the event Jillcy's property is attached or comes under the possession of a trustee, receiver, or assignee for the benefit of creditors, or upon the filing of proceedings for bankruptcy, dissolution, or liquidation, or if Jillcy is insolvent.

The legal effect of such clauses with respect to the statute of frauds is a controversial area of law. New York has adopted the approach that, in certain circumstances, a termination clause may operate to take the contract out of the statute of frauds. The cases are not altogether clear, however, with respect to the precise circumstances under which such clauses operate in this way. There is, nevertheless, a line of cases which indicates that the types of termination clauses contained in the unexecuted agreement in this case do not operate to take the contract out of the statute of frauds.

The New York rule was expressed by the New York Court of Appeals in *Blake v. Voigt*, 134 N.Y. 69, 31 N.E. 256 (1892). In that case, the oral agreement required the plaintiff to obtain consignments of goods to the defendants for a year and required the defendants to pay plaintiff commissions therefore, but permitted either party to terminate the agreement seven months after its commencement. The court observed that the contract thus "could be performed in either of two ways." 134 N.Y. at 72, 31 N.E. 256. It could be performed continuously for one year, or for seven months, by exercising the option. Exercising the early termination option "did not *defeat* the contract, but simply advanced the period of fulfillment." *Id*. (Emphasis added.)

In *Radio Corp. of America v. Cable Radio Tube Corp.*, 66 F.2d 778 (2d Cir. 1933), the Second Circuit observed that in *Blake* the option to terminate was an "absolute option" which could be exercised at the "mere wish" of either party. 66 F.2d at 784. In contrast, contingencies such as bankruptcy, insolvency, or appointment of a receiver were ones over which the defendant "had no control." *Id*. Therefore, the court held: "The existence of such an option does not take the case out of the statute of frauds for the contingency upon which its exercise depends is one over which the [defendant] cannot hasten or retard." 66 F2d at 784–85.

These criteria for an option taking an agreement out of the statute of frauds, that it be in the control of the party as expressed in *Radio Corp. of America* and that it not defeat the contract as expressed in *Blake*, have been applied in subsequent cases. . . .

In *North Shore Bottling Co., Inc. v. C. Schmidt & Sons, Inc.*, 22 N.Y.2d 171, 292 N.Y.S.2d 86, 239 N.E.2d 189 (1968), the New York Court of Appeals held the statute of frauds inapplicable to an agreement that: "included an event"—*within the defendant's control*, i.e., its decision to cease selling beer in the New York area—"that [would] end the contractual relationship of the parties," and by that token, the defendant's possible liability "within a year." 22 N.Y.2d at 178, 292 N.Y.S.2d at 91, 239 N.E.2d at 193 (emphasis added). Elsewhere in the opinion the court noted that the contingency giving rise to termination was "unquestionably within the defendant's power to take at any time." 22 N.Y.2d at 176, 292 N.Y.S.2d at 90, 239 N.E.2d at 191.

Unlike the options in *Blake* and *North Shore*, the contingencies giving rise to the option to terminate in the purported agreement between Jillcy and HBO are not ones over which the defendant has "absolute control." Rather, they are exactly the same as those in *Radio Corp. of America* over which the defendant has no control. Furthermore, the agreement does not establish anything like a continuous course of business between two parties which simply can be ended early as in *Blake* and *North Shore*. Its purpose is the production of a film documentary to be aired on television. The contingencies giving rise to termination are those that would frustrate Jillcy in its ability to produce that documentary. They do not establish alternative methods of performance or fulfillment but, instead, clearly defeat the purpose of the contract. The termination clauses in the purported agreement between Jillcy and HBO, therefore, do not operate to render the statute of frauds inapplicable.

Jillcy alternatively argues that the writing requirement of the statute of frauds has been satisfied by the existence of the unexecuted written agreement, together with the signed memo from Louis dated January 17, 1983, directing payment to Jillcy.

It is settled in New York that the writing requirement of the statute of frauds may be satisfied by several writings which, taken together, may be construed as a single enforceable contract. *Crabtree v. Elizabeth Arden Sales Corp.*, 305 N.Y. 48, 110 N.E.2d 551 (1953).

It is also settled, however, that if the parties intend not to be bound until a written contract is fully executed, they will not be bound until that event takes place. . . .

This is true even if the parties have agreed to all the terms. . . .

The question of whether or not the parties intended to be bound is a triable issue of fact. . . .

In this case, HBO claims that the parties did not intend to be bound until execution of the written agreement. It points to the language in the contract that provides that Jillcy's first payment on the total contract price be paid only after execution. During negotiations, Jillcy had expressly proposed that its first payment not be dependent on execution of the agreement. This proposal, however, was not contained in the final draft agreement.

Jillcy, on the other hand, claims that the parties did intend to be bound and it points to the January 17, 1983, memo signed by HBO's Louis while the agreement remained unexecuted which directs that Jillcy be paid pursuant to a specified provision of the draft agreement. This memo is dated a day before HBO sent Jillcy execution copies of the agreement for its signature.

As the cases indicate, the question of intent is central to determining whether the parties are bound by the unexecuted agreement. . . . The evidence presented to the court indicates that there is a dispute concerning intent. The resolution of that issue would therefore be improper on a motion for summary judgment. . . .

Jillcy's second claim is breach of the July 21, 1982 letter agreement to "negotiate exclusively in good faith with respect to the terms and provisions relating to the distribution, exhibition or other exploitation of the Documentary." HBO has moved to dismiss this claim on the ground that such a claim is unenforceable. There has been conflict within this district concerning the enforceability of such a clause under New York law.

Jillcy cites *Thompson v. Liquichimica of America, Inc.*, 481 F. Supp. 365 (S.D.N.Y. 1979). In that case the court held that an agreement "to use best efforts to reach an agreement" constituted an enforceable agreement. 481 F. Supp. at 366. . . .

However, in *Candid Productions, Inc. v. International Skating Union*, 530 F. Supp. 1330 (S.D.N.Y. 1982) (Weinfeld, J.), the court held that a contract that provided that a defendant "will not negotiate any further contract [] without first negotiating in good faith with [plaintiff]" was unenforceable. In a lengthy analysis of the issue, the court observed: "An agreement to negotiate in good faith is even more vague than an agreement to agree. An agreement to negotiate in good faith is amorphous and nebulous, since it implicates so many factors that are themselves indefinite and uncertain that the intent of the parties can only be fathomed by conjecture and surmise." *Id.* at 1337. In *Pinnacle Books, Inc. v. Harlequin Enterprises, Ltd.*, 519 F. Supp. 118 (S.D.N.Y. 1981), the court expressed similar concerns when it held unenforceable a contract providing that "if, after extending their best efforts, the parties are unable to reach an agreement" regarding an option to renew, one party would be free to offer rights to nonparties. . . .

The most recent pronouncement by New York courts indicates that the position of the courts in *Candid* and *Pinnacle* is the proper interpretation of New York law. In *Mocca Lounge, Inc. v. Misak*, 94 A.D.2d 761, 462 N.Y.S.2d 704 (2d Dep't 1983), the court held that courts can enforce a definite and certain duty to negotiate in good faith, but: "even when called upon to construe a clause in a contract expressly providing that a party is to apply his best efforts, a clear set of guidelines against which to measure a party's best efforts is essential to the enforcement of such a clause." 94 A.D.2d at 763, 462 N.Y.S.2d at 706. The court cited both *Candid* and *Pinnacle* with approval. . . .

Because no definite, objective criteria or standards against which HBO's conduct can be measured were provided in the July 21, 1982 letter agreement, the provision is unenforceable on the grounds of uncertainty and vagueness and should be dismissed.

Rock Tours, Ltd. v. Kiss (a partnership) and Kiss Organization, Ltd., 84 Civ. 0011-CLB (U.S. Dist. S.D.N.Y. 1985)

BRIEANT, J.

Plaintiff commenced this diversity action to recover money damages claimed to be a result of defendants' alleged breach of contract. The complaint asserts two claims for relief, one of which was decided on the record by this Court following a non-jury trial held in November, 1984. This first claim, on which a partial final judgment has been entered, was for an amount due as a credit against an advance paid by plaintiff according to the terms of a validly executed agreement dated December 10, 1982, between plaintiff and defendants.

The second claim for relief is based upon plaintiff's theory that the parties formed another contract, or that they agreed to a binding oral modification of their December 1982 contract, such that defendants' nonperformance places them in breach. As to this second claim, the Court reserved decision at the conclusion of the trial and permitted the parties to submit post-trial memoranda of law. There follows the Court's findings of fact and conclusions of law.

Rock Tours, Ltd. is a Michigan corporation engaged in the merchandising business, specifically, sales associated with musical groups which perform concerts on "rock tours." Plaintiff and its agents sell goods such as T-shirts, programs, hats and posters, usually at a booth near the concert site. Defendants are a partnership and a New York corporation, both made up of the individual members of the rock music group known as "Kiss."

On December 10, 1982, plaintiff and Kiss entered into a valid contract which granted an exclusive license to Rock Tours. The license agreement in substance granted to Rock Tours the right to use the Kiss names and likenesses on articles to be sold during a Kiss tour which was to run from December 27, 1982 until on or about June 15, 1983. For reasons best known to defendants, the Kiss tour ended early, and the band performed its final concert on April 3, 1983. . . . Rock Tours was left in possession of many licensed products which it had manufactured or purchased for distribution at the anticipated concerts which were never held.

Thereafter, plaintiff and defendants at various times expressed their desire to continue a business relationship. Their discussions and correspondence focused on the probability that Kiss would resume its tour, or begin another tour, and that in either event Kiss would be interested in contracting for the same sort of merchandising. By July and August, 1983, negotiations had proceeded to the point where counsel for the parties began to exchange draft agreements. . . . On October 12, 1983, defendants' counsel sent five "execution copies" of a contract to counsel for Rock Tours with a letter which stated: "Kindly have four (4) copies signed by your client and returned to me for countersignature. (The fifth copy is for your records). I will then return two (2) executed copies for your files." . . .

Rock Tours signed this Agreement under date of October 7, 1983. Kiss neither signed the writing nor performed any of its terms. In fact, Kiss contracted with another merchandising company to sell the Kiss paraphernalia during the band's subsequent tour, from about December 1983 until April 1984. During this latter tour, Kiss appeared onstage "unmasked" for the first time in its history, apparently creating a furor in the world of rock music, as well as creating an arguably wider market for sales of T-shirts, programs and the like. . . .

According to the Complaint, ¶ 7, and the arguments presented at and after trial, plaintiff contends that the parties entered into a binding contract on or about October 7, 1983. This contention is the basis for plaintiff's second claim for relief on which this Court took evidence and reserved decision. For its second claim, plaintiff seeks judgment in the amount of $250,000.00 "as consequential damages proximately related to defendants' repudiation of the agreement." . . . Defendants deny that a contract was ever formed.

The issue tendered to this Court for resolution is in essence whether the parties in 1983 ever formed a binding agreement. As in most contract disputes, the issue can be subdivided. Plaintiff's legal theories are (1) that the 1983 contract was an oral modification of the December 10, 1982 contract; (2) that this oral modification was not required to be in writing because the parties' conduct establishes partial performance sufficient to remove the contract from the statute of frauds; and (3) that defendants are equitably estopped from invoking the statute of frauds because defendants induced plaintiff's significant and substantial reliance upon the oral modification. These theories present a mixed question of law and fact, and the parties are in agreement that New York law applies.

We begin our discussion by noting that New York law not only contains a traditional statute of frauds, it also has expressed a related state policy in the situation where one party claims that a written contract was modified at a date after its formation.

A written agreement or other written instrument which contains a provision to the effect that it cannot be changed orally, cannot be changed by an executory agreement unless such executory agreement is in writing and signed by the party against whom enforcement of the change is sought or by his agent. N.Y. General Obligations Law § 15–301(1).

The December 1982 contract in this case which

is said to have been modified, invokes that rule, since it expressly states that "None of the terms of this Agreement can be waived or modified except by express agreement in writing signed by both parties."

In the face of this mandate by the New York Legislature and the expressed intent of the parties, we cannot find that the parties agreed to any binding modification of the 1982 contract absent a writing unless one of two recognized exceptions is present: there must either be partial performance of an oral modification sufficient to take the modification out of the writing requirement, or there must be circumstances to support a finding of equitable estoppel. . . .

Plaintiff argues that modification occurred when the parties continued to have friendly discussions after the end of Kiss' first tour, and when they eventually negotiated the terms of the "modification" as expressed in the October 7, 1983 writing signed by Rock Tours but not by Kiss. Plaintiff contends that the testimony of Rock Tours' president establishes performance "unequivocally referable to the oral modification." The testimony was that the president, Mr. Kravetz, kept a truck he had purchased specifically for the vendors to use during the first tour, and that he ordered a new van for use during the upcoming Kiss tour. Neither the truck nor the new van were specifically manufactured according to any needs peculiar to the rock group Kiss. . . . In addition, Mr. Kravetz testified that he retained in his employ a crew chief, and that he kept and stored all of the Kiss merchandise left over from the first tour which had been cancelled by Kiss. Had he not anticipated the relationship with Kiss to continue for the second tour, Mr. Kravetz testified that he would have tried to sell the truck and would have refrained from buying a new van. He also would have refrained from incurring further debt and would have tried to dispose of the licensed Kiss products in the possession of Rock Tours. . . .

The Court also has considered testimony by the attorneys and/or agents who were negotiating the alleged modification on behalf of Rock Tours and Kiss. Plaintiff argues that the written and oral assurances supplied by Kiss' agents were an expression of intent to be bound, and that these repeated assurances lulled plaintiff into believing that an oral modification had been accepted. The performance cited by plaintiff is the defendants' "energetic participation in the negotiating process," together with the assurances communicated by defendants until October 1983. Finally, plaintiff places great weight on the fact that the October 12, 1983 letter of transmittal contained no language reserving defendants' right to alter the contract terms, whereas all earlier cover letters had contained such expressions of an intent not to be bound.

This Court is not persuaded that these instances of conduct constitute part performance sufficient to take the oral modification out of the statutory requirement of a writing, nor do they provide a basis for an equitable estoppel. In *Spa Realty*, the case relied upon by Rock Tours, the Court of Appeals found that "the conduct of the parties evidence[d] an indisputable mutual departure from the written agreement." In that case the modification was of a quantity term in a sales contract. Both parties *acted* as if they had agreed to change the quantity term and go ahead with the sale. In contrast, the evidence in this case fails to establish that both parties took steps to effect a change in their 1982 agreement, or that they began to perform any new, modified terms. Mr. Kravetz' conduct reveals some level of forebearance, but the defendants' conduct shows no more than a desire to keep their options open as long as possible. This is both a natural result and the intended benefit of a clause requiring that modifications be in writing.

Furthermore, plaintiff's characterization of these events as an oral modification of a prior written agreement is not an accurate reading of the law. The rule of *Spa Realty* is that "a partial performance unequivocally referable to the oral modification" does not create an enforceable contract unless the actions of the parties are *not* compatible with their prior written agreement. Here, Mr. Kravetz' actions appear to be compatible with the 1982 contract, if it can be said that the 1982 contract survived after Kiss cancelled its first tour ahead of schedule. In our view, the 1983 negotiations were aimed at the formation of a new contract rather than the modification of any existing contract. Nevertheless, even under this theory, there is no writing sufficient to overcome the statute of frauds, N.Y. General Obligations Law §

5–701. The signed cover letter by counsel for Kiss dated October 12, 1983, together with the enclosure of the unsigned "execution copies" of the agreement would not satisfy the rule of *Crabtree v. Elizabeth Arden Sales Corp.*, 305 N.Y. 48, 110 N.E.2d 551 (1953). There is insufficient evidence of an intent to be bound before the completion of the final signed writing.

If defendants' counsel by forwarding the proposed agreement were intending to bind their clients, without the client's signature, something which I find that counsel had no actual or apparent authority to do, no purpose would be served for counsel to require the return of four copies for "countersignature." There can be no valid inference that attorneys who are exchanging documents for clients intend that their clients be bound when they send a proposed contract for signature by the other party, accompanied by the express direction that it be "returned to me for countersignature." . . . Such a paper, under the circumstances of this case, remains only an offer or counteroffer until actually countersigned and delivered by the client Kiss.

The requirement of a signed writing controls this case. Just as there is inadequate evidence on which to find Kiss' intent to be bound to the final draft of the writing, the record lacks sufficient evidence upon which to find that defendants are equitably estopped from invoking the statute of frauds. The detrimental reliance claimed by plaintiff is primarily the purchase of a van, the sort of vehicle good for any number of useful purposes apart from servicing defendants, and presumably worth its purchase price. Estoppel against invocation of the statute of frauds generally requires proof of a fraudulent oral promise by the defendant upon which the plaintiff justifiably relies. . . . While it may have been unfair or sharp practice to make the encouraging statements to plaintiff relied on here, there is no evidence of conduct rising to the level of a "fraudulent oral promise," nor do we find sufficient unconscionability to be actionable. . . .

The Clerk of the Court is directed to enter a final judgment for defendants that all relief be denied on the second claim, and in all other respects, except as set forth in the prior judgment entered pursuant to Rule 54(b) herein on December 3, 1984.

1.20   Other Problems in Contract Formation

The previous section considered several examples of free and loose dealing in the entertainment industries. We reviewed deals made on a handshake, which often proved to be an invitation to later disputes. Even when the deal is in writing, problems occur. Language is slippery, and proper care is not always taken to ensure all contingencies are covered. Dimensions of the age-old problem of indefiniteness of terms, now applied to the entertainment context, are examined in Section 1.21.

Another important problem in entertainment is contracting with minors. A child artist, whether *ingenue* or *enfant terrible,* is often vital to the success of a production. The services of the minor must be obtained, and it is essential that the contract promising those services be binding. All states have general provisions dealing with minors' contracts. In Section 1.22 we consider the special entertainment applications in California and New York.

1.21   Indefiniteness of Terms

When courts face ambiguous language in a contract, several possibilities exist. In some instances, a court will conclude that the parties never agreed on an essential term, since the language was patently ambiguous and the parties, by their objective manifestations, obviously "intended" different consequences. In this case, the court will rule a contract was never concluded; there was no mutual assent.

The circumstances under which a court rules a contract's terms fatally indefinite are increasingly rare. A more likely result is for the court to use interpretative aids to resolve the ambiguities and save the contract. These include (1) the express language of the contract as understood in a legal context; (2) the extent to which the parties performed under the agreement and the understandings under which they performed, both stated and implied; (3) the parties' dealings in past transactions; and (4) custom and usage in the specific entertainment industry involved. The prevailing judicial view is that if the parties can reduce their understandings to writing, ambiguities will be resolved if at all possible. A deal should not be voided if its terms can be saved by interpretation.

The two cases that follow (*De Laurentiis* and *Miller*) examine how courts set the stage for dispute resolution, resolve ambiguities, and determine the duties owed by each side.

De Laurentiis v. Cinematografica de Las Americas, 215 N.Y.S.2d 60, 9 N.Y.2d 503 (1961)

DESMOND, CHIEF JUDGE

We granted petitioner leave to appeal so that we might consider certain problems in the law of arbitration.

In 1957 petitioner De Laurentiis, an Italian producer of motion pictures, respondent Cinematografica, a Panamanian corporation which distributes films, and respondent Enrique Campos Menendez, an author (herein called "Campos"), made a written agreement whereby the three parties covenanted to do what was necessary for the production and distribution of a motion picture to be based on Campos' biography of the South American patriot Bolivar. De Laurentiis, as producer, was to begin photography within 15 months from the date of the writing and was to complete production within 8 months more and was to devote to the enterprise the major part of his time and effort beginning at the date of the agreement. He was required to engage a writer or writers of the first rank to prepare a story outline, a "screen treatment" and thereafter a final scenario. Campos and De Laurentiis were to consult during the preparation of the story outline and scenario. De Laurentiis was to complete a scenario in final form within three months from the date of the agreement and if Cinematografica did not approve that script De Laurentiis was to

revise it. De Laurentiis undertook to make all necessary arrangements for financing, for the hiring of actors and a director and for world distribution of the completed picture, all this to be subject to the prior approval of Cinematografica which promised not to withhold such approval unreasonably. Cinematografica made certain other commitments as to financing and distribution. Other provisions required De Laurentiis and Cinematografica to share expenses up to a total of $150,000. Campos was to act as consultant and give his consent to the use of his book for a fee of $75,000. There were in the contract elaborate provisions whereby, if the final scenario should be unacceptable to De Laurentiis, Cinematografica should have the right to take over the whole project by reimbursing De Laurentiis for his expenditures.

Paragraph 14 of the contract required that any dispute arising thereunder should be submitted to arbitration in New York City under the rules and regulations of the American Arbitration Association and the laws of New York State, and in connection thereto each of the parties designated residents of New York City to act as their respective agents for the receipt of process in the State of New York. The motion picture has never been produced and respondents charge that De Laurentiis has never engaged a writer for the scenario or performed any of his other obligations under the agreement. On June 20, 1960 New York City attorneys who had been designated as representatives of respondents sent on their behalf to American Arbitration Association a demand for arbitration of the disputes which had arisen out of the contract between their clients and De Laurentiis and sent a copy of this demand to the agent (Serpe) designated by De Laurentiis.

The letter which demanded arbitration charged De Laurentiis with having failed to perform any of the obligations undertaken by him. In the letter of demand, damages of Cinematografica were claimed in a total of $1,105,000 broken down as follows: advanced to De Laurentiis, $75,000; expenditures for travel and other necessary expenses, $85,000; legal expenses, $20,000; loss of business reputation of Cinematografica, $150,000; and loss of its profits, $600,000. Damages of respondent Campos (Menendez) were set forth as: loss of his $75,000 fee as consultant and $100,000 damage to his business and professional reputation.

De Laurentiis responded to this demand for arbitration by commencing the present proceeding for a stay. His petition says that his agreement with Cinematografica and Campos was unenforceable because the promises therein contained were illusory. Also, says he, even assuming the agreement to be valid, the issues and the damages should be limited by the court to those arising directly out of the alleged breach of the agreement. . . .

. . . The present agreement, as petitioner points out, does leave to future agreement the approval of the story outline and scenario and failure to approve might put an end to all the obligations. However, De Laurentiis and Campos expressly promised each other to consult at reasonable times and places during the preparation of the outline and of the scenario "to the end that both De Laurentiis and Campos may make every effort in good faith to cause to be created, within the period specified herein a story outline, screen treatment and final scenario acceptable to both." Thus, in addition to the implication of good faith read into every contract (see Wood v. Lucy, Lady Duff-Gordon, 222 N.Y. 88, 118 N.E. 214), we had an express promise of consultation and of good-faith effort to bring to completion a scenario of such form and quality as to be acceptable. It is for the arbitrators to decide what, under all the circumstances, these covenants contemplated and whether petitioner did all that he was thereby required to do.

As his other ground for a stay petitioner attacks the sufficiency of the demand for arbitration, arguing that the issues and damages are stated in much too general terms and that some of the round figure damage items are outside any possible scope of the arbitration clause. We are told that the claim for "Loss of business reputation" and "Damage to personal and business reputation" as well as the items for legal expense and travel and secretarial expenditures describe purely consequential damages not recoverable. . . . As to the alleged failure of the demand for arbitration to set forth with definiteness any dispute or disputes, we think the demand (plus the affidavits) is to be read as alleging that petitioner took none of the steps required of him by the agreement and did none of the things he had promised to do. As to whether damages of the kind listed are recoverable, it must be remembered that the parties agreed not only to arbitrate their differences but to do so under the rules of the American Arbitration Association, one of which rules (No. 42) says that the arbitrator in his award "may grant any remedy or relief which he deems just and equitable and within the scope of the agreement of the parties." The arbitration agreement here called for the submission of "Any dispute arising under this agreement" and was not otherwise limited. When we incorporate rule 42 into that clause we have a grant of power to the arbitrators so broad that it would be inappropriate to determine in advance of an arbitration that there must be eliminated from any award any items of damage which the arbitrators might consider "just and equitable" under the facts as developed before the arbitrators. . . .

The order should be affirmed, with costs.

FROESSEL, JUDGE (CONCURRING)
I concur in the result. In my opinion, the contract is not illusory, and arbitration is, therefore, the appropriate remedy. As to any consequential damages, the arbitrators are bound by our decisions in Marchant v. Mead-Morrison Mfg. Co., 252 N.Y. 284, 169 N.E. 386 and De Lillo Const. Co. v. Lizza & Sons, 7 N.Y.2d 102, 195 N.Y.S.2d 825.

VAN VOORHIS, JUDGE (DISSENTING)
It is familiar law that courts will not permit arbitrators to change unambiguous contracts nor to make awards of damages which are of so speculative a nature as to be outside of the province of a court of law. There has to be an arbitrable dispute in order to permit arbitration. . . .

NOTES

1. For further discussion of obligations of good faith and fair dealings, see MacNeil, "Power of Contract and Agreed Remedies," 47 *Cornell Law Quarterly* 495 (1962); Burton, "Breach of Contract and the Common Law Duty to Perform in Good Faith," 94 *Harvard Law Review* 369 (1980); Comment, "Has the Right of First Refusal Been Thrown to the Wolves? *American Broadcasting Co. v. Wolf*," 1 *Cardozo Arts and Entertainment Law Review* 137 (1982).

2. An agreement entered into between a television production company and the sponsor of an ice skating championship for exclusive North American television rights provided for a good-faith negotiation clause to the extent that the sponsor would not negotiate any further contracts for television rights without negotiating "in good faith" with the television network. The clause was held to be vague and indefinite and thus unenforceable. *Candid Productions, Inc. v. International Skating Union,* 530 F. Supp. 1330 (S.D.N.Y. 1982).

3. In *Sellers v. American Broadcasting Co.,* 668 F.2d 1207 (11th Cir. 1982), the United States Court of Appeals dismissed an action in which the plaintiff attempted to enforce an "exclusive story" agreement he had made with Geraldo Rivera of ABC on contract and misappropriation grounds. The exclusive story involved information that Elvis Presley had died from an overdose of drugs, a theory which the Court found neither novel, unique, nor original so as to afford the plaintiff protection under the misappropriation doctrine. Furthermore, the "contract" of the plaintiff was unenforceable as it was too vague and indefinite as to the information which Sellers was to provide regarding Elvis's death.

The plaintiff's entire contract read as follows:

> I, Larry L. Sellers, do hereby agree not to release this exclusive story to any reporter other than Geraldo Rivera or any network other than ABC until the network has first released said story within a reasonable period of time or thirty days. Once the story has been released, other media forms may be contracted by Larry Sellers.
>
> I, Geraldo Rivera, do hereby agree to grant Larry Sellers all copy-write [*sic*] privileges of the exclusive Elvis Presley story and full claim for the discovery of the story by acknowledgement in any media use made of it from this day forth.
>
> If the story is accepted for further investigation, all expenses incurred by Larry Sellers will be reimbursed by ABC.
>
> Should the story be proven false, this contract is hereby null and void.

In re Miller, 447 A. 2d 549 (N.J. 1982)

CLIFFORD, J.

This appeal questions a trial court decision, affirmed by the Appellate Division, that an interest in royalties terminated on a specific date. The issue turns on interpretation of the contract granting that interest. The Chancery Division determined that a transfer by the widow of Alton Glenn Miller (Glenn Miller) to the appellant's father, David Mackay, now deceased, of a one-third interest in certain royalties accruing from the sale of recordings of the Glenn Miller Orchestra terminated on March 15, 1967. The Appellate Division affirmed substantially for the reasons expressed by the trial court. We granted Mackay's petition for certification, 87 N.J. 407, 434 A.2d 1084 (1981), and now affirm. . . .

Because our holding is based principally upon inferences drawn from the circumstances surrounding the parties' dealings with each other, a recitation of the somewhat complicated facts is necessary. Beginning in 1939 David Mackay served as attorney and advisor to Glenn Miller. Until Miller's disappearance in 1944 while on a military flight, Mackay performed various legal services for Miller and assisted him in the negotiation and execution of several performance and recording contracts. Miller paid Mackay for these services. After the War Department officially declared Miller dead in 1945, Mackay served as attorney for Miller's estate. Under Miller's will, which was admitted to probate in Probate Division of the Bergen County Court (Miller having died a domiciliary of New Jersey), Miller's wife, Helen D. Miller, was named the sole beneficiary and executrix.

Although Helen Miller was executrix, Mackay handled all the finances of the estate. The estate's income, principally from royalties from the sale by RCA Victor (RCA) of recordings made by the Glenn Miller Orchestra before Miller's death, was sent to Mackay, who deposited it in the estate account. Mackay prepared any checks written on the estate account and mailed them to Mrs. Miller for her signature. During the years immediately following Miller's death the income from the RCA recording royalties declined steadily, from approximately $54,000 in 1948 to slightly less than $14,500 in 1951.

In response to this decline Mackay discussed with Mrs. Miller a proposal for a project that would increase the estate's earnings. This proposal involved the possible use of recordings of radio broadcast performances of the Glenn Miller Orchestra. These recordings, known as library reference recordings or "air checks," were made directly from the broadcasts and were intended by Miller to be used solely to evaluate the broadcasts and to improve the orchestra's performance. The sound quality of these recordings was poor, owing both to the static and noise attendant to the radio broadcasts and to the low level of technology in the recording process. Mackay had preserved these air checks after Miller's death.

In 1951 Mackay suggested to Helen Miller that perhaps RCA could do something with the air checks to "clean them up" and make commercial quality recordings from them. When Mrs. Miller agreed to this proposal, Mackay catalogued the air checks and later monitored their recording—a task characterized by an expert witness as "a monumental job." RCA determined that it was feasible to make commercial quality recordings from the air checks.

As a result Helen Miller, as executrix of the Glenn Miller estate, entered into a contract with RCA dated August 8, 1951. The contract provided that RCA would release one album a year for three years, each album to contain eight selections recorded from among 250 of the air checks. RCA agreed to pay the estate a six percent royalty on 91.5 percent of all sales, to be paid semi-annually. The contract gave RCA the perpetual right to manufacture and release records of the selections made under the contract.

On the same day that she signed the RCA contract, August 14, 1951, Mrs. Miller signed a document, handwritten by Mackay, the legal effect of which is the issue in this appeal. The document stated:

> For value received the undersigned hereby sells, assigns, transfers and sets over unto David Mackay a sum equivalent to one-third of the royalties to accrue to the undersigned from the agreement of August 14, 1951 entered into simultaneously herewith between the undersigned and Radio Corporation of America covering the recordings and releasing of phonograph records to be made from Glenn Miller radio broadcast library reference recordings.

The recordings released pursuant to the 1951 contract met with greater commercial success than any of the parties had anticipated, wherefore the parties entered into a new agreement in 1954. Significantly, this agreement, and all later agreements discussed below, did not contain the distinctive feature of the 1951 contract that gave RCA a perpetual right to manufacture and release air check recordings. Indeed, Mackay acknowledged at trial that the earlier contract had been "superseded" and that the 1954 document be-

came the "controlling agreement." The 1954 agreement provided that the estate would turn over to RCA all recordings of the Glenn Miller Orchestra, in any form, that had not previously been released. RCA agreed that between 1954 and 1959 it would re-record and release a minimum of 80 performances from these recordings and would pay the estate six percent of 90 percent of all sales. The new agreement also modified the method of payment, apparently to create a tax advantage to the estate. RCA agreed to pay the estate $50,000 a year from 1955 to 1959. Any income exceeding that amount would be retained by RCA as a reserve fund against future payments. Whenever the reserve fund exceeded $250,000, however, RCA would pay the estate the excess semi-annually as earned.

When she signed the 1954 RCA contract, Mrs. Miller also executed, at Mackay's request, a document nearly identical in wording to the 1951 document that granted Mackay a one-third interest in monies accrued under the 1951 RCA contract. This new document gave Mackay a one-third interest in monies accruing under the 1954 RCA contract with the exception, however, that his percentage would be computed and paid only after the estate received the first $15,000 each year. The reason for this change was that Mrs. Miller believed that since the estate was earning about $15,000 per year in royalties before Mackay had arranged for releases based on the air checks, Mackay was not entitled to receive one-third of that amount.

The RCA releases continued to meet with commercial success. In 1955 the parties again entered into a new contract. RCA now agreed to release a minimum of 120 selections in the period between 1954 and 1962. The $50,000 per year minimum payment was continued, but the reserve fund ceiling was increased to $400,000. In all other respects the 1955 contract with RCA continued the terms of the 1954 contract. Once again Mackay requested that Mrs. Miller execute a document entitling him to one-third of the proceeds, after the first $15,000 per year, accruing under the 1955 RCA contract, but this time Mrs. Miller balked. The record contains several letters written by Mackay in 1955 wherein he requests that Mrs. Miller execute such a document. There is also a letter from Mackay to Mrs. Miller, dated

April 15, 1958, wherein he refers to her wish that rather than having a blanket assignment related to each RCA contract, she would prefer to grant Mackay his one-third interest on a year-to-year basis. Mackay told her, however, that such a plan would have an adverse tax effect on the estate. For whatever reason, sometime after April 15, 1958, Mrs. Miller signed the document transferring to Mackay one-third of the income accruing under the 1955 RCA contract.

Meanwhile, in January 1958, RCA and Mrs. Miller had again amended their agreement. Other than an adjustment in the royalty rate for record club sales, the only changes were that the yearly payments were extended through 1964, the annual minimum payment was increased to $100,000, and the reserve fund ceiling was increased to $700,000. After some prodding in the previously discussed April 15, 1958 letter from Mackay, Mrs. Miller executed a document giving Mackay a right to one-third of the proceeds of the January 1958 amendment to the 1955 RCA contract.

There were three subsequent amendments to the 1955 RCA contract: 1960, 1962, and 1963. In each, the annual minimum payments were extended through 1965, 1966, and 1967 respectively. The reserve ceiling was modified in the 1960 and 1962 amendments. In all other respects the 1955 contract, as amended in 1958, remained in effect. As to the transfer of one-third of the proceeds to Mackay in 1960, Mrs. Miller signed a document that was identical to those already discussed, save in one important aspect. This document stated that Mackay was to receive one-third of the monies to accrue under the 1955 RCA contract "and any amendments thereof." Mackay subsequently took the position that this additional language obviated the need for similar documents in connection with the 1962 and 1963 amendments.

None of the documents in which Mackay was given one-third of the royalties made any mention of how long he would continue to collect that amount. He continued to collect one-third of the royalties up to and through the time of Helen Miller's death on June 2, 1966.

In her will, Mrs. Miller left her entire estate in two testamentary trusts, one for each of her children, Steven Miller and Jonnie Soper, the respondents in these proceedings. Mrs. Miller's will appointed David Mackay as executor of the estate and trustee of the trusts. Mackay received executor's fees under this appointment. In addition, under Glenn Miller's will Mackay was named, along with one Chalmers MacGregor, as successor co-executor. When MacGregor decided not to serve as co-executor (in response to Mackay's assurances that Glenn Miller's estate was almost completely settled and MacGregor was not needed), Mackay became sole successor executor under Glenn Miller's will and began to take executor's commissions. As indicated above, Mackay was also still receiving one-third of the royalties that accrued under the 1963 payment schedule on the RCA contract, which was due to expire on March 15, 1967.

In letters to Steven Miller and Jonnie Soper, dated June 20, 1968, Mackay explained the arrangements that he had with Mrs. Miller concerning his receipt of one-third of the RCA royalties, after the $15,000 exclusion each year. He also explained that he had been receiving annual fees of $5,000 from the Glenn Miller estate for legal services. Mackay proposed that in the future the $15,000 exclusion be eliminated, thereby entitling him to one-third of all royalties, and also that the $5,000 legal services fee be eliminated. Although it would appear that this would make no difference in Mackay's income unless the royalties fell below $15,000 in any year, in which case Mackay would earn less than he had before, it is worth observing that if Mackay had closed the Glenn Miller estate by December 31, 1967, as the trial court found that he should have, he would no longer have received the annual $5,000 for legal fees to the estate. As it was, both Miller and Soper agreed to Mackay's proposal, and Mackay continued to receive one-third of the royalties thereafter.

Sometime in 1975, after a disagreement between respondents and Mackay, respondents initiated an investigation into Mackay's dealings in relation to the estate. As a result of that investigation respondents brought an action for an accounting and to surcharge Mackay for certain monies that they alleged he wrongfully took. After a fourteen day trial, the trial court issued an opinion containing several findings.

The court found that Mackay had improperly computed certain executor's commissions. It refused to find, however, that Mackay had improperly charged attorney's fees to the Glenn Miller estate. Although these findings were the subject of appeal and cross-appeal in the Appellate Division, the parties do not raise them before us.

The sole issue that we face is whether there is sufficient credible evidence to support the trial court's conclusion that the documents executed by Mrs. Miller did not entitle Mackay to receive one-third of the income of the RCA royalties after March 15, 1967. . . .

On their face the documents that granted Mackay a one-third interest in the proceeds of the RCA royalties do not give any indication of how long Mackay was to continue to receive that interest. The trial court's task then was to resolve the ambiguity as to the duration of Mackay's interest by examining the intent of the parties in the context of well-settled principles of law. Perpetual contractual performance is not favored in the law and is to be avoided unless there is a clear manifestation that the parties intended it. . . . The documents themselves contain no words that would indicate such intent. The trial court was unable to find any clear manifestation in the record that Mrs. Miller intended to give Mackay an interest that would last in perpetuity, nor did Mackay ever testify that Mrs. Miller acknowledged at any time that he had such an interest.

The parties' conduct, in fact, could reasonably be interpreted to indicate the opposite. Each time the payment schedule was extended, Mackay insisted that Mrs. Miller execute a new document. If, as appellant now argues, the original transfers gave an interest in royalties as long as they accrued, it would not have been necessary to modify those transfers merely because the payment schedule was modified. Also of importance is the fact that Mrs. Miller expressed a desire to give Mackay an interest in the royalties on a year-to-year basis. Only when Mackay convinced her that such an arrangement would have an adverse tax effect did she sign the transfers as written by Mackay. Her attempt to pay Mackay yearly is a strong indication that Mrs. Miller never intended Mackay's interest to be perpetual.

In short, after canvassing the entire record, we conclude that there is sufficient support for the trial court's finding that Mrs. Miller did not intend Mackay to continue to receive a one-third interest in the RCA royalties for as long as they continued to accrue. . . .

The trial court next found that "the parties intended that Mackay's right to participate in the royalties run only as long as the period of the guaranteed payment for the royalties in the underlying contracts between RCA and the Glenn Miller estate." Those guaranteed payments ended on March 15, 1967, and, therefore, so did Mackay's interest. . . . Considering the effort that Mackay expended in connection with the RCA recording contracts and the return that he received for that effort (more than $400,000 between 1952 and 1967), there is adequate evidence buttressing the trial court's finding that March 15, 1967 was a reasonable termination date for Mackay's interest in royalties.

Moreover, if a definite period of time can be inferred from the conduct of the parties and the surrounding circumstances, then that time period should govern the duration of the agreement. . . . Several facts support the inference that Mrs. Miller intended that Mackay's interest would end on March 15, 1967. Of greatest importance is the close link between the RCA royalty contracts and the documents transferring an interest in those royalties to Mackay. The 1954 and 1955 RCA contracts, and the subsequent amendment to the latter, contained fixed periods during which guaranteed payments were to be made. Each time the payment schedule was modified and extended, Mackay asked Mrs. Miller to sign a new document that gave him an interest pursuant to the new RCA agreement. Surely this supports the inference that Mrs. Miller understood that the interest she was assigning to Mackay was limited in time to the payment schedules in the underlying RCA contracts. If it were otherwise, there would be no reason for her to sign a new document every time the payment schedule—and only the payment schedule—was changed. Mrs. Miller's attempt, mentioned above, to put Mackay's interest on a year-to-year basis further supports this inference.

Additional support for the March 1967 termination date is manifest from what the parties believed would be the revenues under the RCA contracts. Mackay admitted that none of the parties realized how profitable the sale of the RCA records would be. In his first intermediate accounting as successor executor of the Glenn Miller estate, dated September 10, 1970, Mackay stated that it was anticipated that the amounts paid under the RCA contract would have decreased until there was no probability of further income. If this is so, it is unlikely that Mrs. Miller contemplated that Mackay would go on receiving payments indefinitely. It seems more likely that she believed that by the time the last payment schedule expired, *i.e.,* March 15, 1967, the Glenn Miller estate, and as a result David Mackay, would no longer be receiving income from RCA.

Finally, there are the writings themselves. Where an ambiguity appears in a written agreement, the writing is to be strictly construed against the draftsman. . . . It is undisputed that Mackay drafted the documents giving him an interest in the RCA contracts. The 1951 document is in his handwriting. If he wanted to ensure that his interest in the royalties would continue as long as royalties accrued, it would have been simple so to word the documents. Mackay's failure to do so must be construed against him and in favor of Helen Miller. . . .

All of this evidence lends ample support to the trial court's conclusion that the circumstances give rise to a compelling inference that Helen Miller intended Mackay's interest to terminate when the final guaranteed payment under the RCA agreement was made, *i.e.,* March 15, 1967. . . .

1.22   Contracts with Minors

Additional considerations arise when a personal service contract involves a minor. Although definitions of a minor vary, a majority of state statutes now provide that a minor is any person under 18 years of age. Our concerns are with minors entering contracts involving the entertainment industries. The following sections explore problems of contracts with minors in California and New York.

1.22–1   California Provisions on Minors

The age of majority in California has been 18 since 1971, under California Civil Code § 25. It is incumbent on the employer to make an actual determination of whether or not the employee is a minor. A minor's misrepresentation of age does not alter the consequences of dealing with the minor. See *Lee v. Hibernia Savings & Loan,* 171 P2d 677 (Cal. 1946), and *Williams v. Leon T. Shettler Co.,* 276 P. 1056 (Cal. 1929).

The major risk in entering a contract with a minor is that generally the contract is voidable at the option of the minor at any time, either before the minor's majority or within a reasonable time thereafter. The power to disaffirm a contract, including a personal services contract, is embodied in California Civil Code § 35.

When a valid contract is approved by the superior court in California (see California Civil Code § 36), significant limitations are then placed on the ability of a minor to disaffirm. Court-approved contracts apply to agreements in which a person is employed "to render artistic or creative services" in virtually any realm of the entertainment industry.

In California, a court-approved contract may extend to option periods. In *Warner Bros. Pictures v. Brodel,* 192 P.2d 949 (Cal. 1948), a minor attempted to disaffirm the option period on an otherwise valid contract that had previously been approved by the superior court. However, the superior court's approval of the contract was upheld, the option period was binding, and the minor's later attempt to disaffirm was denied.

A contract in California between a minor and a talent agency is controlled by the California Labor Code. An agreement cannot be disaffirmed if the talent agency has complied with the necessary licensing provisions of the Labor Code.

A company which enters a personal services or literary property contract with a minor may also wish to contract with the minor's parents. The provisions of such an agreement may well include clauses in which the parents relinquish the custody, control, or earnings of a minor, covenant that they will not interfere with the performance of a minor's services under the contract and, in certain circumstances, guarantee the obligation of performance by the minor.

1.22–2   New York Provisions on Minors

In New York, until 1983, a general statute provided for minors' contracts, including judicial approval of certain types of contracts (see old New York Obligations Law, § 3–105). Under this statute, if a contract met the statutory requirements and was duly approved by a court, the minor could not disaffirm during his minority or upon reaching his majority. In 1983, § 3–105 was repealed and replaced by New York Arts and Cultural Affairs, § 35.03. The scope was narrowed to focus on minors entering entertainment, arts, and sports contracts. (For contracts involving employment of children as models, see N.Y. Arts and Cultural Affairs, § 35.05.)

The means by which courts in New York approve minors' contracts and the consequences flowing therefrom are sufficiently important to set forth basic provisions of § 35.03, as follows:

> § 35.03. *Judicial approval of certain contracts for services of infants; effect of approval; guardianship of savings*
>
> 1. A contract made by an infant or made by a parent or guardian of an infant, or a contract proposed to be so made, under which (a) the infant is to perform or render services as an actor, actress, dancer, musician, vocalist or other performing artist, or as a participant or player in professional sports, or (b) a person is employed to render services to the infant in

connection with such services of the infant or in connection with contracts therefor, may be approved by the supreme court or the surrogate's court as provided in this section where the infant is a resident of this state or the services of the infant are to be performed or rendered in this state. If the contract is so approved the infant may not, either during his minority or upon reaching his majority, disaffirm the contract on the ground of infancy or assert that the parent or guardian lacked authority to make the contract. A contract modified, amended or assigned after its approval under this section shall be deemed a new contract.

> 2. . . . (c) No contract shall be approved unless (i) the written acquiescence to such contract of the parent or parents having custody, or other person having custody of the infant, is filed in the proceeding or (ii) the court shall find that the infant is emancipated.

> (d) No contract shall be approved if the term during which the infant is to perform or render services or during which a person is employed to render services to the infant, including any extensions thereof by option or otherwise, extends for a period of more than three years from the date of approval of the contract. If the contract contains any other covenant or condition which extends beyond such three years, the same may be approved if found to be reasonable and for such period as the court may determine.

> (e) If the court which has approved a contract pursuant to this section shall find that the well-being of the infant is being impaired by the performance thereof, it may, at any time during the term of the contract during which services are to be performed by the infant or rendered by or to the infant or during the term of any other covenant or condition of the contract, either revoke its approval of the contract, or declare such approval revoked unless a modification of the contract which the court finds to be appropriate in the circumstances is agreed upon by the parties and the contract as modified is approved by order of the court. . . .

> 3. (a) The court may withhold its approval of the contract until the filing of consent by the

parent or parents entitled to the earnings of the infant, or of the infant if he is entitled to his own earnings, that a part of the infant's net earnings for services performed or rendered during the term of the contract be set aside and saved for the infant pursuant to the order of the court and under guardianship as provided in this section, until he attains his majority or until further order of the court. Such consent shall not be deemed to constitute an emancipation of the infant.

(b) The court shall fix the amount or proportion of net earnings to be set aside as it deems for the best interests of the infant, and the amount or proportion so fixed may, upon subsequent application, be modified in the discretion of the court, within the limits of the consent given at the time the contract was approved. . . .

6. At any time after the filing of the petition the court, if it deems it advisable, may appoint a special guardian to represent the interests of the infant. . . .

8. (a) The infant shall attend personally before the court upon the hearing of the petition. Upon such hearing, and upon such proof as it deems necessary and advisable, the court shall make such order as justice and the best interests of the infant require.

(b) The court at such hearing or on an adjournment thereof may, by order:

(i) determine any issue arising from the pleadings or proof and required to be determined for final disposition of the matter, including issues with respect to the age or emancipation of the infant or with respect to entitlement of any person to his earnings;

(ii) disapprove the contract or proposed contract or approve it, or approve it upon such conditions, with respect to modification of the terms thereof or otherwise, as it shall determine;

(iii) appoint a limited guardian as provided in subdivision seven of this section.

(c) If the contract is approved upon condition of consent that a portion of the net earnings of the infant under the contract be set aside, the court shall fix the amount or proportion of net earnings to be set aside and if the court shall find that consent or consents

thereto have been filed as provided in subdivision three of this section, shall give directions with respect to computation of and payment of sums to be set aside.

The case of *Prinze v. Jonas*, 345 N.E.2d 295 (N.Y.Ct.App. 1976), suggests a cautionary note be added about the exclusivity of judicial approval (or lack thereof) of a minor's contract under New York law. Although *Prinze* was decided under the New York Obligations Law, cited above, the provisions of that law are not materially different from those of the recently enacted Arts and Cultural Affairs, particularly § 35.03. Thus, there is no reason to believe that future New York courts will deviate from the *Prinze* holdings.

In *Prinze*, the court recognized that a contract with a minor, even though it could not be approved by a court under the then-prevailing § 3–105, could nevertheless still be found to be "reasonable and provident" to the minor, and thus enforceable under N.Y. General Obligations Law § 3–101. Judicial approval, therefore, was not necessarily a requisite for an enforceable contract against a minor.

The *Prinze* court went even further in its evaluation of the enforceability of an arbitration clause that was in the contract in dispute. The court held that its function was merely to review whether the arbitration clause was reasonable. If it was reasonable, the arbitrator, not the court, should rule on the ultimate validity of the contract itself. Thus, an arbitrator, called into the dispute only because of the contract clause, could then rely on that clause to establish jurisdiction over the dispute and resolve the validity of the contract. The arbitrator could uphold or void the contract; even in voiding, the arbitrator was still empowered to act because of the contract clause.

No New York court has faced this same conundrum under current law, but there is little reason to believe *Prinze v. Jonas* is anything other than binding precedent. Under the Arts and Cultural Affairs statutes, § 35.01 tracks the old § 3–101 as to "reasonable and provident" contracts in a minor's business, and § 35.03 tracks the old § 3–105 as to the grounds for judicial approval of a contract. A New York court reviewing an arbitration clause in a minor's contract would face essentially the same statutory reconciliations as were analyzed and resolved in *Prinze*.

1.30 Contract Duration: Special Issues Under California Statutes

In the 1920s and 1930s, Hollywood movie moguls developed the "star" system, which involved promotion of actors and actresses into something larger than life. At heart, it was a way to exploit the public by heightening interest in the stars and increasing the box office. As it developed, it was exploitation of the "stars" as well. The trick was to find young talent, sign them to exorbitantly long contracts, and then hope that promotion and luck would make them "stars" in the public perception.

The usual vehicle through which a young actor or actress entered the system was a "studio" contract. In agreeing to a contract, the talent might be bound for ten years or more, at a salary that would later prove to be well below market value. At length, the California legislature tempered "studio" contracts by enacting a seven-year limit on personal service contracts. Other protections, to both employer and employee, were added.

Today, California is unique with its limitations on the duration of personal service contracts. Since so many entertainment transactions come under California legal aegis, the California enactments require thorough analysis. We begin with §§ 2855, 2924, and 2925 of the California Labor Code; then we discuss important cases that have applied this legislation.

§ 2855. Enforcement of contract to render personal service; time limit

A contract to render personal service . . . may not be enforced against the employee beyond seven years from the commencement of service under it. Any contract, otherwise valid, to perform or render service of a special, unique, unusual, extraordinary, or intellectual character, which gives it peculiar value and the loss of which can not be reasonable or adequately compensated in damages in an action at law, may nevertheless be enforced against the person contracting to render such service, for a term not to exceed seven years from the commencement of service under it. If the employee voluntarily continues his service under it beyond that time, the contract may be referred to as affording a presumptive measure of the compensation.

§ 2924. Employment for a specified term; grounds for termination by employer; discharge for garnishment

An employment for a specified term may be terminated at any time by the employer in case of any willful breach of duty by the employee in the course of his employment, or in case of his habitual neglect of his duty or continued incapacity to perform it. . . .

§ 2925. Employment for specified term; grounds for termination by employee

An employment for a specified term may be terminated by the employee at any time in case of any wilful or permanent breach of the obligations of his employer to him as an employee.

DeHaviland v. Warner Brother Pictures, 153 P.2d 983 (Cal.App. 1944)

Shinn, J.

Defendant has appealed from a judgment declaring at an end its contract for the services of plaintiff as a motion picture actress. The ground of the decision was that the contract had run for seven years, the maximum life allowed such contracts by former Civil Code, section 1980, now section 2855 of the Labor Code. It was executed April 14, 1936, for a term of fifty-two weeks and gave the employer the right to extend the term for any or all of six successive periods of fifty-two weeks each. These options were exercised from time to time by the employer so as to cover the entire contract period. The services commenced May 5, 1936, and, except as interrupted by certain periods of suspension, were continued to August 13, 1943. The present action was commenced August 23, 1943. The contract gave the producer, defendant, the right to suspend plaintiff for any period or periods when she should fail, refuse or neglect to perform her services to the full limit of her ability and as instructed by the producer and for any additional period or periods required to complete the portrayal of a role refused by plaintiff and assigned to another artist. Plaintiff was to receive no compensation while so suspended or thereafter until she offered to resume her work. It was provided that the producer had the right to extend the term of the contract at its option, for a time equal to the periods of suspension. There were several such suspensions after December 9, 1939, and one suspension of thirty days which plaintiff agreed to and which was occasioned by her illness. In each instance defendant exercised its right to extend the term of the agreement. The several periods of suspension totaled some twenty-five weeks. The facts as to the suspensions are not in dispute; defendant's right to impose them is not questioned. Plaintiff's reason for refusing the several roles was that they were unsuited to her matured ability and that she could not faithfully and conscientiously portray them. Her good faith and motives are not in issue, but according to the contract the producer was the sole judge in such matters and she had to do as she was told. The sole question is whether the provisions for suspension, and for extension of the term of the agreement, were lawful and effective insofar as they purported to bind plaintiff beyond seven years from the date her services were commenced. If they were lawful, plaintiff still owes twenty-five weeks of service; otherwise the contract came to an end May 5, 1943. . . .

If we are to accept defendant's construction of [§ 2855] as amended, we must add words to the phrase used in the proviso so that it would read "for a term not beyond a period of seven years *of actual service* from the commencement of service under it." In fact, the words "of actual service" could have been used appropriately after the word "term" and also after the words "seven

years" if it had been the intention to do away with the limitation of seven calendar years from the commencement of service. It is true that the exception in the first clause of contracts for exceptional services, to which the proviso relates, suggests a possible intention to take such contracts out of the general rule, but the proviso itself is the enacting clause and the controlling one. It is the clause which determines whether the general limitation was intended to be removed as to contracts for exceptional services. Defendant's contention is that there could have been only one purpose in amending the section, namely, to allow the enforcement against employees of contracts for personal services to the extent of seven years of actual service, regardless of the time over which such services might extend. With this we cannot agree. The difficulty with the argument, and which we think is insurmountable, is that the Legislature has not used the words "of service," and the failure to use those or equivalent words is far more significant as indicating the purpose of the enactment than the entire amendment as written. We cannot believe that the phrase "for a term not beyond a period of seven years" carries a hidden meaning. It cannot be questioned that the limitation of time to which section 1980* related from 1872 to 1931 was one to be measured in calendar years. It is conceded that contracts for general services are limited to seven calendar years. The substitution of years of service for calendar years would work a drastic change of state policy with relation to contracts for personal services. One would expect that such a revolutionary change, even as applied to a particular class of contracts, would be given expression in clear and unmistakable terms. . . .

Although as a rule legislative enactments are drawn under expert guidance and with much care, it is inevitable that ambiguity will be encountered occasionally. But the ambiguities found in the 1931 amendment amounted to no more than imperfections of phraseology and fell far short of working any change in the substantive law. The language of section 1980, Civil Code, was carefully revised in the drafting of the Labor Code section. The ambiguous language which was suggestive of a possible meaning that con-

---

*The forerunner of § 2855.

tracts of artists might be enforced for seven years of actual service was eliminated. The result, we think, was to state in the Labor Code section the true meaning of amended section 1980 and to state it in more carefully chosen terms. Again the phraseology which was used clearly indicated that the limitation applied to calendar years; otherwise the phrase "term of service" or "years of service" would have been used. The later enactment, we think, may be regarded as an interpretation by the Legislature of the meaning of section 1980, that is to say, that the phrases which were eliminated from that section were merely redundant and had added nothing to its meaning.

What we have said does not fully answer the question why section 1980 was amended, if it was not to make a special rule for the enforcement of contracts of artists. Defendant's argument is that if it did not serve that purpose it served no purpose at all. The amendment would seem to have been unnecessary, for it worked no change in the substantive or procedural rights of either the employer or the employee. It is not questioned by either party that before the amendment was adopted, employers who had contracted for the exclusive services of artists could enforce their contracts for the term limited by section 1980 by means of injunction restraining the rendering of services of their employees to others. Both plaintiff and defendant cite *Lumley v. Gye* in support of this proposition. Prior to 1919, section 3423 of the Civil Code provided that an injunction may not be granted to prevent the breach of a contract which would not be subject to specific performance. In 1919 the section was amended so as to except contracts for exceptional services such as the one in issue, which provide a rate of compensation of not less than $6,000 per annum. But even though the amendment of section 1980 did not enlarge the rights of employers to enforce such contracts other than to extend the term to seven years, the amendment was nevertheless desirable because it constituted a statement of a well established rule of equity and there is a good purpose served by the codification of established rules of law or equity. Even after the 1919 amendment of section 3423, there was in the codes no specific, affirmative statement of the right of an employer

to enforce any kind of contract for personal services, by injunction or otherwise. The amendment of section 3423 inferentially gave the employer the right to an injunction in certain cases. The amendment of 1980 states the right in affirmative terms. It had the effect at least of correlating the two sections and removing any doubt as to what was intended by the amendment of section 3423, which, by inference only, extended the right of injunction in certain cases to the contract rights of the employers of artists. It was undoubtedly to the advantage of all those who might be affected, to have the law put in statutory form. These were sufficient reasons, and we believe the real reasons, for the amendment of section 1980.

We have not overlooked the earnest arguments of counsel as to whether a producer of motion pictures should or should not have the right to the exclusive services of an artist for a period of seven years of service. It is to be presumed that the Legislature considered such matters in legislating upon the subject, but the arguments do not aid us in determining what the code sections mean. While the purpose sought to be accomplished in the enactment of a statute may be considered as an aid to interpretation, the question whether the Legislature has acted at all in a given particular must find answer in the statute itself. We think the expressions of the various enactments cannot be bent to a shape that will fit defendant's argument, and that the several extensions of plaintiff's contract due to her suspensions were ineffective to bind her beyond May 5, 1943, seven years after her services commenced.

A second contention is that if defendant had not the right under the code to demand seven years of service, plaintiff has waived the right to question the validity of the extensions, which carried beyond the seven-year period. By her breaches of the contract, it is claimed, she brought into operation the provisions for extension and is now estopped to avoid them. Defendant relies upon section 3513 of the Civil Code, reading as follows: "Anyone may waive the advantage of a law intended solely for his benefit. But a law established for a public reason cannot be contravened by a private agreement." Defendant insists that the limitations of said sections 1980 and 2855 were enacted solely for the benefit of employees and not for a public reason, and may be waived. . . .

The fact that a law may be enacted in order to confer benefits upon an employee group, far from shutting out the public interest, may be strong evidence of it. It is safe to say that the great majority of men and women who work are engaged in rendering personal services under employment contracts. Without their labors the activities of the entire country would stagnate. Their welfare is the direct concern of every community. Seven years of time is fixed as the maximum time for which they may contract for their services without the right to change employers or occupations. Thereafter they may make a change if they deem it necessary or advisable. There are innumerable reasons why a change of employment may be to their advantage. Considerations relating to age or health, to the rearing and schooling of children, new economic conditions and social surroundings may call for a change. As one grows more experienced and skillful there should be a reasonable opportunity to move upward and to employ his abilities to the best advantage and for the highest obtainable compensation. Legislation which is enacted with the object of promoting the welfare of large classes of workers whose personal services constitute their means of livelihood and which is calculated to confer direct or indirect benefits upon the people as a whole must be presumed to have been enacted for a public reason and as an expression of public policy in the field to which the legislation relates. . . .

The power to restrict the right of private contract is one which does not exist independently of the power to legislate for the purpose of preserving the public comfort, health, safety, morals and welfare. The power to provide for the comfort, health, safety and general welfare of any or all employees is granted to the Legislature by article XX, section $17\frac{1}{2}$ of the state Constitution. Enactments exercising the power have been upheld in many instances. . . . The rights of employees as now declared by section 2855 of the Labor Code fall squarely within the prohibition of section 3513 of the Civil Code, that rights created in the public interest may not be contravened by private agreement.

Finally, it may be pointed out that the construction of the code sections contended for by defendant would render the law unworkable and would lead to an absurd result. If an employee may waive the statutory right in question by his conduct, he may waive it by agreement, but if the power to waive it exists at all, the statute accomplishes nothing. An agreement to work for more than seven years would be an effective waiver of the right to quit at the end of seven. The right given by the statute can run in favor of those only who have contracted to work for more than seven years and as these would have waived the right by contracting it away, the statute could not operate at all. It could scarcely have been the intention of the Legislature to protect employees from the consequences of their improvident contracts and still leave them free to throw away the benefits conferred upon them. The limitation of the life of personal service contracts and the employee's rights thereunder could not be waived. . . .

NOTES

1. An important aspect of the De Haviland decision is the unreported facts in the case. The original contract with the studio was for a period of less than seven years. De Haviland was a minor at the time of its execution, and accordingly, the contract was approved by the Los Angeles Superior court as being "just, fair and conscionable and to be in the best interest of Olivia De Haviland." The extensions of the term of the contract were occasioned by her own breaches and refusals to perform. Warner Brothers, in its unsuccessful appeal, argued:

> On one occasion, Respondent [De Haviland] signed a written agreement approving the suspension dates; on another occasion Respondent herself requested and received an extension of the contract in order that she might absent herself from the studio for a period of four consecutive weeks commencing February 16, 1942. . . . Respondent alone is responsible for the term of her service extending one day beyond seven calendar years. She asked for it on February 16, 1942. She benefitted by it.
>
> If the statute can be waived, or if she can be estopped from hiding behind the statute, whatever its meaning may be, then in this case that statute has been waived and the estoppel exists. . . . Only a holding that L.C. 2855 is mandatory, absolute, and represents an expression of public policy and was established for a public reason, can in this case justify the granting of any relief herein to the artist.

2. In an unreported decision of the Los Angeles

Superior Court filed in 1973, *Lukas aka Susan St. James v. Universal*, No. C54945, a mid-term extension was litigated under § 2855. The employment contract with Universal provided for an initial term of 26 weeks, with options for a possible total of seven years. Six months later, another employment agreement of seven-year potential was executed, with a condition that the first contract was terminated upon execution of the second. The issue raised by St. James and never resolved in that case was whether she was obligated to perform beyond the initial seven-year period under a second agreement, which she claimed was not negotiated "at arm's length."

3. In *Foxx v. Williams*, 244 Cal. App. 2d 223, 52 Cal. Rptr. 896 (2d Dist. 1966), which is also discussed in Section 1.54 with reference to Civil Code § 3423, an issue arose under § 2855. Dootone Records contended that § 2855 was inapplicable to its recording contract with comedian Red Foxx because Foxx was an independent contractor, while § 2855 applies only to an "employee." Dootone had never withheld taxes on Foxx or paid Social Security taxes or state disability assessments for him. Nor had Dootone exercised any control over the creative aspects of Foxx's material or performance. The court nonetheless found § 2855 applicable.

The first two contracts between Dootone and Foxx had been denominated "contract for your personal services between Dootone Records as the employer, and you as the vocalist, and we hereby employ you for the purpose of making phonograph records." Foxx recorded in the same manner under all three of his contracts, even though the last contract did not contain the quoted language. However, Dootone selected the times and places of recording, whether to invite an audience (and, if so, whom to invite), and the equipment to be used in recording (which it operated). The court distinguished *Ketcham v. Hall Syndicate, Inc.* (see below), because Ketcham turned in completed cartoon strips, whereas Foxx's efforts were not complete until worked on by Dootone. The language of the earlier contracts, plus the consistent pattern of involvement of Dootone in the recording process, was sufficient to permit the court to find an employer-employee relationship which triggered the application of § 2855.

4. Lawyers have argued for years as to whether or not a mid-term renegotiation will serve to start the California seven-year statute running anew. One school of thought holds that only a "moment of freedom"—a release given under noncoercive circumstances—will suffice. In other words, the artist must be free to walk out of the room without signing a new contract so that the act of re-signing is perceived to be

totally voluntary. Another view holds that a renegotiation involving substantial new consideration, entered into toward the end of a deal and for an independent business reason, should be sufficient to restart the seven-year period.

In the case of *Melissa Manchester v. Arista Records, Inc.*, No. CV 81–2134–RJK, in the U.S. District Court for the Central District of California, the court suggested (in an unpublished—and later withdrawn—opinion by Kelleher, J. in 1981) that if the latter criteria were met, the statute could indeed be restarted.

Manchester, a popular singer, signed with Arista in 1973 while a resident of New York. She later moved to California. In 1976, in order to obtain monies with which to fund a settlement with her manager and terminate their agreement, Manchester entered into a further contract with Arista for an additional year at Arista's option, to follow the end of the term of the original agreement.

Due to late delivery of recordings by Ms. Manchester, Arista suspended the term of her agreement on several occasions so that, by the time Arista purported to exercise its one-year option under the 1976 agreement, Arista claimed that Manchester owed it three LPs, two under the original agreement and one under the additional agreement. Manchester refused to perform further, citing Labor Code § 2855.

The various contracts contained forum selection and/or choice-of-law clauses referring the matter to New York. Ms. Manchester, however, contended that to uphold these would violate the strong public policy of California underlying § 2855. The court, however, was not persuaded and held that the forum selection clause of the 1973 agreement should be enforced. The 1976 contract specified New York law but did not contain a forum selection clause. As to this, the court stated:

> Manchester takes the position that the 1976 agreement is not an independent contract. . . . [that] it must necessarily be an extension of the 1973 contract and thus also invalid pursuant to § 2855. She argues that it cannot be anything but an invalid extension because of the prohibition of waiver of employees' rights under § 2855. This argument is unpersuasive. It would effectively prevent an employee from entering into a new contract with his or her current employer until after the completion of all obligations between them. The better course is to consider the circumstances surrounding the formation of the new contract in each situation. If the new contract was entered into at or near the time of formation of the earlier contract, and if the two contracts appear to have been entered into to avoid the application of § 2855 to a single agreement, then they should be considered a single contract for the purposes of § 2855. However, if the latter contract was entered into toward the end of the first contract, it should be treated as a separate agreement for

purposes of § 2855. Each employment situation will necessarily be interpreted according to its unique facts. The interpretation of the two contracts should be made in light of the policy consideration underlying § 2855 to protect employees, rather than by principles of formal contract law. . . .

. . . The 1976 contract was entered into after the 1973 agreement was partially completed. It was an integrated agreement that differed in several material respects from the 1973 agreement. It did not have a forum selection clause; it materially altered the royalty provisions; and it was entered into to pay the debt that Manchester owed [to her ex-manager] and was thus supported by different considerations. The only significant factor that supports treating the two contracts as one is that the 1976 agreement is an option contract that Arista could exercise only if it had exercised all of its options under the 1973 contract.

Upon consideration of all of these undisputed facts, it is the determination of the Court that the 1976 contract was separately entered into and that it was not entered into with the purpose of evading the seven-year employment limitation of § 2855. Accordingly, the Court will treat the 1976 contract as a separated agreement for purposes of § 2855. Since the 1976 agreement has not been in effect for seven years, the provisions of § 2855 are not yet applicable to it. The claim of Manchester with respect to the 1976 contract must be dismissed on its merits.

Although withdrawn from publication (and therefore uncitable), this decision is well known throughout the entertainment industry and is the subject of frequent discussions among entertainment lawyers.

5. A California bill (Senate Bill 469) was introduced in the California legislature to amend § 2855 of the California Labor Code. Basically, the bill would have allowed an extension of a renegotiated contract another seven years. The proposed statute, after various amendments by the senate and assembly, was passed by both houses but vetoed by California Governor George Deukmejian in 1986.

In amendments to the bill, it was proposed that the bill be applicable to record companies only if the employee gave written notice, in which case the record company would still be entitled to seek damages for breach of contract. Another draft provided that an employee who renegotiated after three years had run on the original contract could not invoke the statute unless the renegotiation failed to provide the employee with significantly improved contract terms. The issue still remains, in light of the veto of Senate Bill 469, whether a record company can sue for damages in California against an employee who invokes the seven-year provisions of § 2855.

6. For additional analysis of problems arising under California's seven-year statute, see Bushkin and Meyer, "The Enforcement of Mid-Term Extensions of Employment Agreements Under California Labor Code § 2855," 15 *Beverly Hills Bar Journal* 385 (1980).

Ketcham v. Hall Syndicate, Inc., 236 N.Y.S.2d 206 (N.Y.S.C. 1962)

On January 24, 1951 the plaintiff (the creator of the cartoon panel entitled "Dennis The Menace") and the defendant, then known as the Post-Hall Syndicate, Inc., entered into an agreement for the syndication by Hall of the cartoon panels.

The contract provided that the panels were to be delivered to Hall's office in the City of New York at least six weeks prior to the scheduled date of release.

The agreement further provided that its duration should be for the period of one year with automatic renewals from year to year without notice unless the plaintiff's share from syndication did not equal certain minimum stipulated weekly payments, in which event either party had the right to terminate it.

There is no claim that the minimum returns have not been met. In fact, the evidence is quite to the contrary, and it is uncontradicted that the payments are now over five times the required minimum.

The parties performed under the contract from the date thereof until December 18, 1961 when the plaintiff wrote a letter to the defendant in which he purported to cancel and terminate the contract as of March 11, 1962. However, the plaintiff is still performing under the contract by reason of the provision in the aforesaid letter of December 18, 1961, that if the cancellation were not recognized then the plaintiff would continue to perform until such right of cancellation and termination should be established by litigation.

In answer to the plaintiff's letter, on March 8, 1962, the defendant advised the plaintiff that by reason of the payment of the minimum provided by the terms of the contract that it would deem the contract renewed for the further period of one year and that it would also deem it renewed from year to year thereafter provided the stipulated payments had been made.

The plaintiff's complaint seeks a declaratory judgment determining whether the plaintiff has the legal right to terminate the contract on the grounds (a) that it is for an indefinite term and that there is no mutuality; (b) that section 2855 of the Labor Code of the State of California provides that such a contract may not be enforced beyond seven years from the commencement of the services; and (c) that if the contract is governed by the laws of the State of California it may be cancelled and terminated since it is no longer enforceable under the aforesaid section of the Labor Code.

The questions of law are clearly defined and are (1) is the contract governed by the laws of the State of New York or of the State of California; (2) if the contract is governed by the laws of California, is it terminable by reason of section 2855 of the Labor Code; and (3) is the contract, which calls for automatic renewals upon the payment of certain minimums, voidable either by reason of indefiniteness or lack of mutuality.

The California statute (Labor Code § 2855) provides as follows:

> 2855. Enforcement of contract to render personal service; time limit. A contract to render personal service, other than a contract of apprenticeship as provided in Chapter 4 of this division, may not be enforced against the employee beyond seven years from the commencement of service under it. Any contract, otherwise valid, to perform or render service of a special, unique, unusual, extraordinary, or intellectual character, which gives it peculiar value and the loss of which can not be reasonably or adequately compensated in damages in an action at law, may nevertheless be enforced against the person contracting to render such service, for a term not to exceed seven years from the commencement of service under it. If the employee voluntarily continues his service under it beyond that time, the contract may be referred to as affording a presumptive measure of the compensation.

There is no decision of the California courts which has determined whether a contract such as the one in question is governed by the above-quoted statute. Defendant contends that the contract in question established a relationship not of employer-employee but one of the status of an independent contractor and that therefore the section relied on does not apply.

Section 2750 of Article 1 of Chapter 2 of said Code defines a contract of employment as one "by which one, who is called the employer, engages another, who is called the employee, to do something for the benefit of the employer or a third person."

Edwin S. Pillsbury, Esq., plaintiff's expert on California law, testified on cross-examination that the contract in question "does not establish, in my opinion, the relationship of employer and employee in the strict sense"; and further testified that this contract would fall within the category of "an independent contractor relationship," and that Mr. Ketcham was an independent contractor by reason of the fact that there was no "right of supervision, direction and control."

Mr. Pillsbury, however, testified that section 2855 of the California Labor Code applied to independent contractors. That the second sentence of section 2855 relating to contracts to "render service of a special, unique, unusual, extraordinary, or intellectual character, which gives it peculiar value" had reference to independent contractors and that Mr. Ketcham's contract was of this type. However, he never stated the basis for his opinion, except that there was a strong public policy (in California) "to the effect that an employee should be protected by law against improvidently contracting his services away for a longer period than seven years."

Reliance is also placed by plaintiff on De Haviland v. Warner Bros. Pictures, 67 Cal. App. 2d 225, 153 P. 2d 983. However, in that case the acting was performed by the employee at the direction of her employer at places designated by her employer. In this case, however, plaintiff's performance was delivery by him at the defendant's New York office of six daily cartoon panels per week. There was no supervision, plaintiff worked where he pleased. The provision regarding the quality of the panels is usual in certain types of sales or building contracts and does not imply supervision.

Sidney Justin, Esq., defendant's expert witness on California law, testified that he was "very intensively" acquainted with the provisions of section 2855 by reason of his employment in the legal department of Paramount Pictures Corp. because the section involved all of the employment contracts of the studio. He testified that the contract was one "to furnish materials" and similar to contracts between motion picture producers and distributors, whereas the contract in the De Haviland case, supra, was "a typical employment contract." He testified that the sole purpose of section 2855 "was to protect employees" and that there were no provisions of the

Labor Code which he could find which govern independent contractors. He testified that although the word "employee" was not used in the second sentence of section 2855 (relating to unique services) it must be read into it. Since the third sentence commences: "If the employee voluntarily continues his service under it . . .," the conclusion is inescapable that the word employee must be read into the second sentence.

Furthermore, it should be noted that the first sentence of section 2855 refers to "employee." "Employee" is defined by the same Labor Code in section 350(b) as follows:

(b) "Employee" means every person including aliens and minors, rendering actual service in any business for an employer, whether gratuitously or for wages or pay and whether such wages or pay are measured by the standard of time, piece, task, commission, or other method of calculation and whether such service is rendered on a commission, concessionnaire, or other basis.

It should also be noted that the defendant is not an "employer" as defined by section 350(a) of the Labor Code as follows:

(a) "Employer" means every person engaged in any business or enterprise in this State, which has one or more persons in service under any appointment, contract of hire, or apprenticeship, express or implied, oral or written, irrespective of whether such person is the owner of the business or is operating on a concessionnaire or other basis.

The above definitions add additional weight to the conclusion of the defendant's expert, whose opinion seems more compelling. The court adopts his interpretation of the statute that the sentence is only intended to include employees and would exclude independent contractors.

It is obvious that under the usual rules of statutory interpretation the provisions of section 2855 would apply only to the normal employer-employee relationship and not to situations where one of the parties was an independent contractor.

Since the second sentence was not interpreted by the California courts, I believe that we can accept our own definition of an independent contractor as laid down by our Court of Appeals in Hexamer v. Webb, 101 N.Y. 377, 385, 4 N.E. 755, 757:

The test to determine whether one who renders service to another does so as a contractor or not is to ascertain whether he renders the service in the course of an independent occupation, representing the will of his employer only as to the result of his work, and not as to the means by which it is accomplished. Shearm. & Redf., Neg. § 76. In Blake v. Ferris, 5 N.Y. [48] 58, within the rule last stated, it is held that when a man is employed in doing a job or piece of work with his own means, and his own men, and employs others to help him or to execute the work for him, and under his control, he is the superior who is responsible for their conduct, no matter for whom he is doing the work. To attempt to make the primary principal or employer responsible in such cases would be an attempt to push the doctrine of *respondeat superior* beyond the reason on which it is founded. . . .

The evidence also establishes that the parties by their own conduct never considered the relationship to be that of employer-employee. There was never a withholding by the defendant for income taxes or social security; the plaintiff paid all the expenses of producing the cartoons; and the plaintiff in filing his Federal income tax return paid the "self-employment tax" which was measured by the income received from the defendant.

The contract provides that: "Should Ketcham become incapacitated or unable to deliver the material . . . or in the event of the decease of Ketcham, he or his executors shall have the privilege of employing substitute services to prepare the materials" or that the defendant "shall have the privilege of securing substitute services."

In either event Ketcham (or his estate) was still to receive the benefits of the contract (less the cost of the substitute).

Ketcham was not an employee and the contract is at best one for his services as an independent contractor. Indeed in most of its aspects is is more a contract of sale or a contract to supply a product rather than services.

There is yet another reason for holding the California Statute inapplicable. The New York Conflict of Laws rules require a finding that the contract is governed by New York Law, under the theory of "center of gravity" or the "grouping of contacts." Defendant's office is and was in New York, all of its operations (other than traveling salesmen) are conducted in New York, including the mat makers, the editorial work, financial work, photo-engravers, etc. Performance of the contract by plaintiff was to be by delivery of the panels at defendant's New York office. The contract was signed in New York by defendant and by "Kennedy Associates, Inc. by John J. Kennedy as agents for Hank Ketcham." The verified complaint sets forth that Kennedy Associates, Inc. "executed the contract as agent for the plaintiff." Plaintiff prepared the panels at various residences during the years following the execution thereof. Indeed the place where plaintiff or his substitute was to prepare the panels was of absolutely no significance. The most important contact was the place of delivery, the fixed place where all of defendant's work had to be performed. New York was the place of most significant contact when the contract was signed, was so during the intervening years and is today, and therefore New York law governs. . . .

The first, second and third affirmative defenses have been proven and therefore the California statute will not be applied.

Since we have decided that the California law is inapplicable, the remaining questions to be determined are whether the contract is indefinite and does it lack mutuality.

The issue of mutuality poses no problem. Plaintiff's argument that the contract lacks mutuality of obligation is adequately answered by a comparison of the facts in this case and those in Wood v. Lucy, Lady Duff-Gordon, 222 N.Y. 88, 118 N.E. 214. In this case, the defendant was expressly obligated to produce certain minimum payments to keep the contract in force, whereas in the Wood case, supra, the court merely implied an obligation on plaintiff's part to use its best efforts. There is thus certainly more basis for finding mutuality than existed in Wood, where the Court of Appeals found mutuality.

Whether or not the contract is indefinite presents a more difficult question and is probably the most important problem to be resolved in this case. The question, however, is not whether the contract is for an *indefinite term*, it is whether the contract, by its terms, *is indefinite as to its duration*. If it is, then judicial construction is necessary and thus plaintiff should prevail because it is well settled in New York, that a contract will not be construed to require perpetual performance where another construction is available. . . .

Absent a fixed or *determinable duration* or an express provision that the duration is perpetual, the contract is one terminable at will. . . .

The contract in the case at bar is not indefinite as to duration. Paragraphs 4, 5 and 6 provide specifically for termination by either party upon the happening of certain events. The contract provides that it "shall be for a period of one year . . . and shall renew itself automatically from year to year for additional periods of one year each without the giving of notice by either party to the other, except that each of the parties shall have the right to terminate this agreement at the end of any one year period hereof . . . in the event" that plaintiff's share fell below the stipulated amount and the defendant at its sole discretion, to avoid a termination of this agreement, failed to advance the difference in the minimum stipulated amount.

The plaintiff asserts that these provisions render the contract indefinite because they include no specific date for the termination of the contract. This, however, is not the kind of indefiniteness which renders the contract voidable, since specific provision is made for termination. It is this specificity which destroys the plaintiff's case. The contract is for one year and renewable from year to year, but this, from the terms of the contract itself, appears to have been the intention of the parties. The paragraphs regarding termination clearly provide for automatic renewal and just as clearly give the defendant the right to keep the contract alive in the event certain requirements for automatic renewal are not met. It was the intention of the parties that the contract should run so long as the minimum receipts were realized and that during such period that neither party should be able to desert the other. The strip started as an idea and both parties were to be integral parts of its development, the plaintiff by his creative ability and the defendant by his promotion and salesmanship. The terms of the contract are clear and unambiguous and freely signed by the plaintiff and his agent.

That contracts providing for perpetual performance are not invalid is undoubtedly the law of New York, although no precise holding on this point can be found among the New York cases. . . .

For contracts which had no calendar fixed date

of termination but were held as contracts for a definite term, see Matter of Exercycle v. Maratta, 11 A.D.2d 677, 201 N.Y.S.2d 885, affd. 9 N.Y.2d 329, 214 N.Y.S.2d 353; Ehrenworth v. George F. Stuhmer & Co., 229 N.Y. 210, 214, 215, 128 N.E. 108, 109; Deucht v. Storper, City Ct., 44 N.Y.S.2d 350, 351. In Exercycle, the contract provided for continuation until the employee voluntarily leaves the employ of Exercycle. In Ehrenworth, the contract was for "as long as the plaintiff . . . remained in business." In Deucht, the employment was to be for so long a time as defendant "continued to employ workers, trained, developed and gathered by plaintiff." (See Warner-Lambert Pharmaceutical Company Inc. v. John J. Reynolds, Inc. [S.D., New York, 1959] 178 F. Supp. 655, 661.) . . .

The defendant, therefore, must prevail. Contracts which are vague as to their duration generally will not be construed to provide for perpetual performance, but where, such as the case here, the contract is not vague, no judicial construction is necessary. . . .

1.40   Termination of Contract and Performance Breach

Circumstances change, and the initial intents of parties to a transaction shift as well. When one party to a contract believes another party is not fulfilling the bargain, the simmering dispute begins a perceptible movement toward the courts. The pages of *Variety* constantly chronicle the filing of breach of contract lawsuits. Stars walk out. Producers renege. Directors revolt.

While most suits are settled, some go the legal distance. These provide guidelines to advise others what to expect if their later disputes find a legal forum. As the following cases suggest, settling a dispute may be a good deal less painful than vindicating one's rights in court. However, if a legal fight it will be, it is best to have had competent contract drafting in the first place. That is the starting point. If that fails, then some of the

limitations under which courts operate must be confronted.

This section on the circumstances of breach is a natural lead-in to the following sections that examine the remedies each side can realistically seek when the other party is in breach. Since breach and remedies for breach go hand in hand, this section examines remedies as well.

Warner Brothers Pictures, Inc. v. Bumgarner, 17 Cal.Rptr. 171 (Ca.App. 1961)

FOURT, JUSTICE

This is an action by Warner Bros. Pictures, Inc., hereinafter referred to as "Warner," for a declaration determining the status of a contract between Warner, as the employer, and James Bumgarner, also known as James Garner, hereinafter referred to as "Garner," as the employee. Garner cross-complained for damages for breach of the contract. The judgment declared the contract terminated as of March 10, 1960, and allowed Garner as damages the sum of $1,750.00. Both parties have appealed. Warner appeals ". . . from the judgment . . . and from the whole thereof." Garner appeals ". . . from that part of the judgment . . . to wit, Subdivision 3 providing that plaintiff and cross-defendant pay to defendant the sum of $1,750.00, with interest thereon at the rate of 7% per annum from March 10, 1960 up to the date of the judgment. Defendant and cross-complainant does not appeal from the rest of the judgment as set forth in Subdivisions 1, 2 and 4 thereof."

A résumé of some of the facts is as follows:

Warner is a producer of motion pictures of different types for showing in theatres or on television. Garner is an actor who had been employed by Warner since 1955 under successive contracts, the latest of which, and the one with which we are here concerned, was made February 27, 1959, hereinafter referred to as "Garner Contract." The Garner Contract, among other things, contained a so-called *force majeure* clause.

Effective mid-January, 1960, the Writers Guild of America, West, Inc. declared a strike against

Warner and many other producers. The writers' guild is an organization or union composed of the writers of scripts or screen plays for both theatrical and television motion pictures. The strike continued from January until June 20, 1960.

The present controversy arose when Warner, on March 2, 1960, regarded the situation as of that time as a casualty within the *force majeure* clause and notified Garner that as of March 3, 1960, his compensation would be discontinued by reason thereof.

The chronology of significant dates is as follows:

January 16, 1960—Television and feature writers struck against many feature and television producers, including Warner.

March 2, 1960—Warner elected to suspend payment of compensation to Garner alleging existence of a "casualty period" under the employment contract.

March 8, 1960—Garner objected to suspension claiming that no casualty period existed and demanded payment of salary.

March 9, 1960—Warner refused to pay salary after Garner's demand.

March 10, 1960—Garner informed Warner that Warner was in breach of contract and that he elected to treat employment contract as terminated.

June 20, 1960—Writers' guild strike ended.

When the writers' strike commenced Warner was producing ten television programs or series. A series consisted of successive episodes involving the same main characters and exhibited on television at weekly or other regular intervals. One of such series was known as "Maverick," with Garner as one of the main characters therein.

Each television episode was a motion picture filmed from a script. A script is in the form of a play with dialogue, and of the correct length to make the required episode. Scripts are written from stories, the latter being basic literary material. A script is the working tool. Scripts are the product of screen writers, and practically all of such script writers are members of the screen writers' guild. Stories are furnished to such writers by the producing company and form the basis of the required script. . . .

The preparation of motion pictures by plaintiff was not prevented, materially hampered or interrupted by reason of the writers' strike; the production of motion pictures by plaintiff was not prevented, materially hampered or interrupted by reason of the writers' strike; and the completion of motion pictures by plaintiff was not prevented, materially hampered or interrupted by reason of the writers' strike.

A large amount of statistical data was introduced to show the effect of the writers' strike on the preparation, production, and completion of theatrical and television motion pictures. The evidence shows and Warner concedes that ". . . there was at all times during the strike, both before and after March 3rd, some activity at the Studio, and some preparation, production or completion of motion pictures were at all times going on in some way and to some extent and with respect to some pictures or series." The evidence supports the finding. . . .

As already pointed out, the provisions of paragraph 15 of the contract are in the disjunctive and contain several alternatives. The first alternative relating to Warner's general activity has heretofore been discussed. Another alternative contained in paragraph 15 is that ". . . if the production of any motion picture or other production to which Artist is assigned hereunder shall be suspended, interrupted or postponed by any such cause, . . . (the continuance of any such event being hereinafter designated as the 'casualty period'), then, during the continuance of such casualty period, Producer shall not be obligated to make any weekly payments to Artist. . . .

The trial judge in his "Memorandum Decision" made it clear that he construed the above alternative provision of paragraph 15 as not being applicable to Maverick (i.e. any Warner's production). The memorandum provides in pertinent part as follows:

> The court will find that the provision "or if the production to which Artist is assigned hereunder shall be suspended, interrupted or postponed by any such cause" means the lending or assignment of the services of Artist pursuant to Paragraph 13 to a producer other than Warner Bros. and does not mean "assignment" of the Artist to one of Warner Bros. productions.

Initially it must be noted that there was no finding made concerning whether Garner was "assigned" to a production by Warner. The court did find (Finding XV) that "The production by plaintiff of the 'Maverick' series was *not* suspended, interrupted or postponed by reason of the writer's [sic] strike." (Emphasis added.) . . .

An examination of the record discloses that there is substantial evidence to support the trial court's determination (Finding XV) that "The production by plaintiff of the 'Maverick' series was not suspended, interrupted or postponed by reason of the writer's [sic] strike."

As of March 2, 1960, Warner had completed production on the Maverick series for 1959–1960 and had filmed one "extra" episode which was not scheduled to be telecast until September 25, 1960. In the past, Warner had not started production until May or June or later, with respect to the next air date season, and producer Trapnell testified that when he took over as Maverick producer on June 15, 1969, there was not a single completed script for the 1959–1960 season, yet Warner met its September 12 air date. Warner's executives knew that production on the Maverick series for the 1960–1961 season would ordinarily not begin until May, at the earliest, and that May production would, as the trial court found (Finding XVII), allow the maximum time necessary to meet the 1960–1961 air date commitments. The facts must be related to the manner by which Warner conducted its business.

On March 3, 1960, Warner had approximately 14 "Hermanos"* writers available in its television department; at least one of the 14 had done work on a Maverick script previously. Warner had at least two stories suitable for development into Maverick scripts and, judging by both past and subsequent events, it could write a Maverick script in 15 days, or possibly rewrite an old script in as little as five days. Furthermore, the head of the television department indicated on direct examination that Warner ". . . may have had other [Maverick and Cheyenne] scripts in at this point but I don't think so."

We believe that the evidence, taken as a whole, shows that Warner was able to obtain scripts when Warner wanted them and that production of Maverick was not suspended, interrupted or postponed by reason of the writers' strike. . . .

---

*pseudonymous—Ed.

At the conclusion of the arguments by counsel, the Reporter's Transcript discloses that the trial judge made the following statement:

The Court: Well, I am satisfied from the evidence that Warner Bros. did not have justification for laying Mr. Garner off on March 2nd. I think that is indicated by the testimony even of the plaintiff's witnesses and particularly Mr. Warner.

The trial judge in his "Memorandum Decision" stated in pertinent part as follows:

The court will find that plaintiff was not justified in stopping the payment of defendant's salary, under the provisions of paragraph 15 of the contract, for the reason that the preponderance of the evidence does not establish that a "casualty period" in fact existed; and for the further reason that the refusal to pay Garner's salary was in bad faith as evidenced, in part, by the manner in which the Bob Hope Show transaction was handled. Plaintiff's act in refusing to pay defendant's salary justified Garner in treating the refusal as a total breach of the contract.

When the dispute arose as to the rights of Warner Bros. to suspend Garner's salary, it could have protected itself by paying the salary and recouping the amount paid—if the suspension was justified—under the provisions of the second paragraph of numbered paragraph 17 of the contract.

A reasonable inference can be drawn from all of the evidence that Warner knew that it would not be in any trouble with respect to Maverick unless it could not start preparing another episode by May 1, 1960 (at the very earliest, since one 1960–1961 episode was already completed). Warner did in fact start preparation on two episodes in late April and by June 15 (at least three months prior to the first air date and still before the end of the writers' strike) had completed "preparation" and "production" on four "Maverick" episodes, was filming a fifth, and had four scripts in preparation.

Finally, Warner asserts as its last contention that "If Warner erroneously interpreted the contract, its action did not constitute a serious and total breach justifying a termination by Garner."

Warner's contention cannot be sustained. When Warner informed Garner that it elected not to pay Garner the stipulated weekly salary, Warner's act constituted a refusal, without cause, to pay an employee his compensation. The employee's right to *terminate* the contract where there has been a wrongful refusal to pay compensation is established by both the statutory and case law of this jurisdiction.

Labor Code section 2925 provides that "An employment for a specified term may be terminated by the employee at any time in case of any *wilful* or permanent breach of the obligations of his employer to him as an employee." (Emphasis added.) As set forth above, the trial judge in his "Memorandum Decision" stated that the "breach in this case was wilful."

In May v. New York Motion Picture Corp., 45 Cal.App. 396, the court defined "wilful" in connection with what is now Labor Code section 2924, and stated at page 404 in part as follows, 187 P. 785, at page 788.

> In civil cases, the word "willful," as ordinarily used in courts of law, does not necessarily imply anything blamable, or any malice or wrong toward the other party, or perverseness or moral delinquency, but merely that the thing done or omitted to be done was done or omitted intentionally. It amounts to nothing more than this: That the person knows what he is doing, intends to do what he is doing, and is a free agent. Benkert v. Benkert, 32 Cal. [467] 470; Towle v. Matheus, 130 Cal. [574] 577, 62 Pac. 1064; 40 Cyc. 944. . . .

Having disposed of Warner's contentions raised on its appeal from the judgment, we now turn to Garner's contentions on his limited appeal from the judgment. . . .

Garner, on April 26, 1960, filed an "Amended Cross-Complaint (Damages for breach of contract; Injunction)." As set forth above Garner was awarded the sum of $1,750 plus interest, and Garner's appeal is from that award.

The basis for the trial court's determination that Garner was entitled to judgment in the sum of $1,750 is succinctly set forth in his "Memorandum Decision" as follows:

> This brings us to the question of Garner's right to recover damages.
> *It must be remembered that Garner was not discharged.* (Emphasis added.)
> As was said in Percival v. National Drama Corp., 181 Cal. 631, p. 638 [185 P. 972]: "The evidence does not show that the defendant refused to permit the plaintiff to render any services. The most that can be said of it is that defendant did not require any services of plaintiff. This fact, unless accompanied by some affirmative act indicating a discharge, is not sufficient proof thereof."

When Warner Bros. notified Garner his salary would be suspended he (underlining shown) treated it as a breach of the contract. Warner Bros. was still anxious for him to render services under the contract.

The law is that if an employee is discharged his remedy is an action for damages. Where he has not been discharged but merely has been prevented by the employer from working, he need not treat the contract as broken but may sue on the contract and recover the agreed compensation. But in order to recover the agreed compensation he must be ready, able and willing to perform.

In this case, after declaring a breach of the contract, Garner refused to recognize it and refused to render services to or for Warner Bros.

Therefore, while Garner had the right to terminate the contract, he does not have the right to recover damages. The right he had was the option to quit his employment and sue for the salary then due, or of continuing in the employ of Warner Bros., and sue for his salary as it accrued.. . . .

Garner terminated the contract about one week after the commencement of the term, and he is entitled to be paid for that period. (Emphasis added.)

In accordance with the foregoing the court will find and conclude: that the conditions that would have warranted Warner Bros. to suspend Garner's salary did not exist; that Garner was justified in terminating the contract; that Garner does not have the right to recover damages for breach of contract because he terminated the contract and was unwilling to perform further; that Garner has the right to recover one week's salary, i.e., $1,750.00, and his costs of suit. . . .

In the light of the evidence, the findings of fact based thereon and the conclusions of law which flow from the findings, it is clear that the trial court correctly determined the amount of damages to which Garner was entitled, unless this court holds as a matter of law that Warner's suspension of Garner's salary payments constituted a "wrongful discharge."

It is stated in Percival v. National Drama Corp., 181 Cal. 631, 637–638, 185 P. 972, 974:

> A discharge cannot be effected by a secret, undisclosed intention on the part of the master. It must be done by some word or act communicated to the servant. "No set form of words is necessary; but any words or acts which show a clear intention on the part of the master to dispense with the servant's services, and which are equivalent to a declaration to the servant that his services will be no longer

accepted, are sufficient." (26 Cyc. 987.) . . . *[T]he authorities declare that mere failure of the master to pay wages to the servant does not amount to a discharge.* (Citations.) *Such failure or refusal to pay merely gives the servant the option of quitting his employment and the right to sue for the salary then due and unpaid, or of continuing in the service, with the corresponding right to require and enforce payment of the salary as it accrues.* (Emphasis added.)

Even when the refusal to pay is accompanied by a refusal to permit the servant to perform the duties it has been held that no discharge was shown. . . .

The Percival case has been cited in later cases as authority to the effect that: (1) nonpayment of compensation in itself is not a discharge. . . . (2) no set words or language are necessary to constitute a discharge provided the circumstances show a disclosure of an unequivocal intention on the part of the employer to dispense completely with the services of the employee. . . . and (3) one of the factors entering into determining such intent would be whether the employer has gone out of business. . . .

We are not prepared to hold as a matter of law that the suspension by Warner constituted a discharge. Without belaboring the point we believe that the trial court, upon the evidence presented, was correct in its determination.

For the reasons stated, the judgment, and the whole thereof, is affirmed.

NOTE ⎯⎯⎯⎯⎯⎯⎯⎯⎯⎯⎯

1. The following provisions for the title "Force Majeure: Defaults and Remedies" appear in a current record company/music production agreement:

(a) If Company's performance hereunder is delayed or becomes impossible or commercially impracticable by reason of any force majeure event, including, without limitation, any act of God, fire, earthquake, strike, civil commotion, acts of government or any order, regulation, ruling or action of any labor union or association of artists affecting Company and/or the phonograph record industry, Company, upon notice to Producer, may suspend its obligations hereunder for the duration of such delay, impossibility or impracticability, as the case may be. In the event any force majeure suspension exceeds six (6) consecutive months, Producer may terminate the term of this agreement upon ten (10) days written notice to Company; provided, that any such termination by Producer shall be effective only if the force majeure event does not affect a substantial portion of the United States recording industry, in no way involves Producer's or Artist's acts or

omissions, and Company fails to terminate the suspension within ten (10) days after its receipt of Producer's notice. Company shall not withhold payment or royalties during any such suspension unless the force majeure event materially impairs Company's ability to calculate and/or pay royalties.

(b) Each of the following shall constitute an event of default hereunder:

(i) Artist's voice and/or playing ability becomes impaired as determined by a physician reasonably designated by Company and Producer (provided that Producer shall not thwart Company's rights under this paragraph 11(b) by failing to designate a physician) or Artist ceases to seriously pursue Artist's career as an entertainer or Producer attempts to assign this agreement except as permitted hereunder or Producer and/or Artist fails, refuses or neglects to fulfill any of their respective material obligations hereunder.

(ii) In the event Producer or Artist commences a voluntary case under any applicable bankruptcy, insolvency or other similar law now or hereafter in effect or consents to the entering of an order for relief in any involuntary case under such law or consents to the appointment of or taking possession by a receiver, liquidator, assignee, trustee or sequestrator (or similar appointees) of Producer or Artist or any substantial part of Producer's or Artist's property or Producer or Artist makes any assignment for the benefit of creditors or takes any act (whether corporate or otherwise) in furtherance of any of the foregoing.

(iii) If a court having jurisdiction over the affairs or property of Producer or Artist enters a decree or order for relief in respect of Producer or Artist or any of Producer's or Artist's property in an involuntary case under any applicable bankruptcy, insolvency or other similar law now or hereafter in effect or appoints a receiver, liquidator, assignee, custodian, trustee or sequestrator (or similar appointee) or Producer or Artist or for any substantial part of Producer's or Artist's property or orders the winding up or liquidation of Producer's or Artist's affairs and such decree or order remains unstayed and in effect for a period of fifteen (15) consecutive days.

(c) On the occurrence of any event of default, Company, in addition to its other rights or remedies, may, by notice to Producer, elect to (i) suspend its obligations to Producer hereunder for the duration of such event (except that Company shall not suspend its obligation to pay royalties earned hereunder if Producer's failure to perform Producer's obligations is caused by reasons beyond the reasonable control of Producer), (ii) terminate the term of this agreement by written notice to Producer given at any time (whether or not during a period of suspension based on such event or based upon any other event), and thereby be relieved of all liability other than any obligations hereunder to pay royalties in respect of Masters delivered prior to termination and/or (iii) require Artist to render Artist's exclusive recording services (and Artist's services as an individual Producer to the extent required hereunder) directly to Company in accordance with Artist's inducement letter.

(d) Producer acknowledges that its performance and the services of Artist hereunder, and the rights granted Company herein, are of a special, unique, extraordinary and intellectual character which gives them peculiar value, the loss of which cannot be reasonably or adequately compensated in damages in an action at law, that a breach by Producer or Artist hereunder from, or to render performances due to Producer hereunder for, any party or person other than Producer, including, without limitation, any successor in interest to Producer. Company shall be entitled to seek injunctive and/or other equitable relief to prevent a breach of this agreement by Producer and/or Artist, which relief shall be in addition to any other rights or remedies which Company may have, whether for damages or otherwise.

Goudal v. Cecil B. De Mille Pictures Corp., 5 P.2d 432 (Ca.App. 1931)

FRICKE, JUSTICE PRO TEM

This is an appeal from a judgment for plaintiff in the sum of $34,531.23 in an action to recover damages for breach of a contract of employment entered into in April, 1925. Under this agreement respondent was employed by appellant as a motion picture actress for one year beginning May 19, 1925, with the option to appellant of four yearly extensions of the contract, each yearly extension to be at a specified substantial increase in compensation. Respondent entered upon her duties, and appellant twice exercised its option, extending the period of employment to May 18, 1928. On September 10, 1927, respondent was discharged by appellant. The basic question in this case is whether such termination of the employment of respondent was wrongful or whether it was justified by acts of the respondent violative of the terms of the contract. The trial court found that respondent had not violated the contract, and that her discharge was not justified.

Many of the alleged violations of the employment contract set forth in appellant's brief are either not supported by the references to the transcript due either to counsel drawing inferences not justified by the testimony or to the fact that the references are to the testimony of Cecil De Mille as to what he told respondent had been reported to him, testimony which, while perhaps admissible on another theory, is pure hearsay so far as its being proof of the conduct of respondent

is concerned. As an example of the misinterpretation of the evidence may be cited appellant's statement that "Mr. Howard testified that in two specific instances she refused to follow the directions of the director." When we examine the reference to the transcript, we find the testimony of Mr. Howard to be that in one scene Miss Goudal appeared disturbed, and did not perform the scene as he thought her capable of performing it, and that, in another instance, "She played the scene in a manner well enough for me to accept it and put it in my picture as a part of the picture but not in a manner I think fully as good as she was capable of playing it." Even the viewing of the testimony through the rose-colored glasses of the advocate can hardly justify counsels' statement that this was a refusal to perform a part of the contract.

The claim that respondent failed or refused to perform her parts as requested is based upon many incidents set forth in detail in the record. They relate to occasions when the respondent, instead of unquestioningly performing as directed by the director in charge, called attention to inconsistencies, inaccuracies, possible improvements, or lack of artistic quality in the performance called for as they appeared to her. In some instances this resulted in the suggested change being made by the director without argument; in other cases the change was made after some argument between them. In most instances where the director did not make the suggested change it appears that respondent took the question up with the president of the appellant corporation, and in a substantial number of instances he agreed with her and the changes were made. In other instances he did not agree. This presents the question, Was respondent compelled by the contract to go through her scenes as a mere puppet responding to the director's pull of the strings, regardless of whether or not he pulled the right or the wrong string, or was she called upon by the language and spirit of the contract to give an artistic interpretation of her scenes, using her intelligence, experience, artistry, and personality to the ultimate end of securing a production of dramatic merit? We believe that the latter is the correct interpretation. Suggestions and even objections as to the manner of enacting the various scenes, when made in good faith, were in the interest of the employer; in fact, it appears from the testimony that they were welcomed and encouraged in many instances, and, prior to commencing work, the president of appellant informed respondent that he did not want mannikins to work for him, that he wanted thinking people, and that, if she would explain to him why she wanted to do a thing in a particular way, he would appreciate it. By the very wording of the contract "it is agreed that the services of the artist herein provided for are of a special, unique, unusual, extraordinary and intellectual character." Even without the evidence contradicting that of appellant, the trial court was more than justified in finding that it was not true that respondent had refused or failed to perform her part of the contract.

Some of the incidents, stressed by appellant as instances of a failure of respondent to perform her contract, turn out, when reference is had to the transcript, to be dependent upon the opinion of the director as to whether respondent performed to the best of her ability; others were dependent upon the feeling of the particular director as to whether he was or was not satisfied. The declarations of several of the directors as to their dissatisfaction with the work of respondent is rather inconsistent with the testimony elsewhere of one of them that the picture "White Gold," in which respondent performed under his direction, was "the best picture I ever will make," and the testimony of the director of her last picture, that he considered it one of his best American pictures. When considering the testimony of the directors who expressed dissatisfaction with the performance of her parts by respondent, one may well wonder who was temperamental and out of step when we note in connection therewith that in the picture in which Cecil De Mille directed Miss Goudal there was no trouble whatever. There is, furthermore, a conflict in the evidence as to whether the performance given by respondent was to the best of her ability and of an artistic character. In this conflict the trial court was fully sustained in its findings against appellant.

The remaining ground urged as justifying her discharge is that respondent on certain occasions was late in arriving on the sets at the time designated by her employer. The instances cited were explained by the testimony for respondent as being due, not to any neglect or intentional absence, but to duties relating to costumes which had been voluntarily assumed by respondent with the approval of appellant, though not required by the contract, delays in appearing on the set due to the necessary consumption of time in the donning of a special wig, and, in the last picture, the only one made after the exercise of the last option by appellant to re-employ respondent for another year, delays due to the large number of costumes used, in one instance, a failure of her maid who forgot an article of clothing, and the delay of appellant in delivering to respondent the script, which determined the costumes required. It should also be noted that as to this last picture the director in charge, when respondent expressed regret at being late, stated to her that he understood, and that never before had he had as little trouble as he had with her. The case of May v. New York Motion Picture Corporation, 45 Cal. App. 896, 187 P. 785, so strongly relied upon by appellant, is easily distinguishable from the case at bar. The fact that the maximum salary under the contract of the plaintiff there was $125 per week as compared to the maximum salary of respondent of $5,000 per week sufficiently discloses the comparative skill of the respective artists. In that case also the plaintiff repeatedly was from one and a half to two hours late in arriving at the place of employment, on at least one occasion failed to appear after she had been notified by telephone, and on the three days preceding her discharge failed to appear for work at all, her reason for not appearing on those days being that her contract did not require her presence, a reason not sustained by the court's interpretation of the contract. The May Case involved the willful disobedience of a reasonable order incident to the employment justifying the plaintiff's discharge. There is in the case at bar no willful tardiness nor invalid excuse for absences, the instances of tardiness here being covered by the general description that those delays were occasioned by the requirements of the scenes to be enacted on those particular days, delays while respondent was actually engaged in performing her employer's business.

It may also be noted that the references to alleged breaches of the contract consist largely of incidents prior to May, 1927, when appellant, for the second time, had exercised its option to continue and extend the contract for another year, and by which time respondent had completed seven of the eight pictures in which she performed for appellant. It is rather difficult to reconcile as sincere the appellant's criticism and faultfinding as to respondent's services in the pictures made during the two years prior to May, 1927, with the fact that in that month appellant voluntarily availed itself of its option to secure the talents and services of respondent for another year. Particularly is this significant when we consider that the salary under the latter option would amount to $39,000 more than respondent's salary for the preceding year. This circumstance alone would fully justify the trial court in considering as of little or no weight the testimony as to alleged breaches of contract prior to May, 1927. The exercise of the option not only evinced a desire on the part of appellant to retain respondent's services, but expressed an approval of the manner in which she had performed her services in the past, and was an indication that a continuation of the former services was desired. Having thus placed the stamp of approval upon respondent's conduct and services as rendered prior to May, 1927, it is not reasonable that a continuance of such services and conduct was unsatisfactory, and, from appellant's viewpoint, constituted a breach of the contract warranting respondent's discharge. Furthermore, the exercise of the option may be considered as a declaration by act that the past conduct of the artist was not such conduct as was intended by the contracting parties as a justification for the termination of the contractual relations. This would be particularly true where, as here, the duties of the performing party are described in the contract by such general phraseology as that the artist shall render the services "conscientiously" and "artistically." It might well be said that an artist who performed her part as directed without remonstrance or suggestion, in spite of the fact that the action was inartistic, crude, and illogical, would not be rendering services either conscientious or artistic in character, while the artist who made an effort to secure a change in the action to produce an artistic result would be complying with the letter and spirit of the contract. These matters and the intent and

good faith of the respondent were matters of fact to be passed upon by the trial court, and, since their decision adversely to appellant is sustained by the evidence, the findings of the trial court are not subject to review here.

To constitute a refusal or failure to perform the conditions of a contract of employment such as we have here, there must be, on the part of the actress, a willful act or willful misconduct (May v. New York Motion Picture Corp., 45 Cal. App. 396, 187 P. 785; Ehlers v. Langley & Michaels Co., 72 Cal. App. 214, 221, 237 P. 55), a condition which is absent when the actress uses her best efforts to give an artistic performance and to serve the interests of her employer. The trial court was fully warranted by the evidence in finding that respondent neither failed nor refused to perform the services required of her under the contract.

Even in the most menial forms of employment there will exist circumstances justifying the servant in questioning the order of the master. Would the discharge of a ditch digger be justified if, instead of immediately driving his pick into the ground at the point indicated, he in good faith suggested to the employer that the pipes they were to uncover lay on the other side of the highway? And when the employment is of the services of "a special, unique, unusual, extraordinary and intellectual character," as is agreed by the contract here under consideration, to be rendered "conscientiously, artistically and to the utmost of her ability," sincere efforts of the artist to secure an artistic interpretation of play, even though they may involve the suggestion of changes and the presentation of argument in favor of such changes, even though insistently presented, do not amount to willful disobedience or failure to perform services under the contract, but rather a compliance with the contract which basically calls for services in the best interests of the employer. What may in the case of the extra girl be rank insubordination because of a refusal to do exactly what she is ordered to do by a director may be even praiseworthy co-operation in the interests of the employer when the refusal is that of an artist of the exceptional ability expressly stipulated in the contract here before us.

Appellant's final point is that respondent is precluded from recovery because, after her discharge, she failed to seek other employment. The testimony of respondent is that, after her discharge, she held herself in readiness to perform her part of the contract, and did not try to secure employment elsewhere. We are referred to no evidence, and appellant's brief concedes that there is none, that respondent could, with reasonable diligence, have secured other suitable employment during the remaining period of the agreement other than, as found by the trial court, that, after the 1st day of January, following her discharge, it should have become evident to her that appellant would not accept her services and that the circumstances showed that she did not diligently seek other employment which she could have obtained. Under this finding the trial court limited the recovery to the period ending January 1, 1928, and, pursuant to a stipulation, deducted therefrom the sum of $3,000 received by respondent from other employment.

"The measure of recovery by a wrongfully discharged employee is generally and primarily . . . the agreed wage for the unexpired part of the term; and the burden is upon the employer to rebut this presumption by proof that the damages sustained were actually less." Gregg v. McDonald, 73 Cal. App. 748, 757, 239 P. 373, 376. "The measure of damages in such cases is the amount of the salary agreed upon for the entire period of service, less the amount which the servant has earned or with reasonable effort might have earned from other employment." Boardman Co. v. Petch, 186 Cal. 470, 484, 199 P. 1047, 1051; Seymour v. Oelrichs, 156 Cal. 782, 801, 106 P. 88, 97, 134 Am. St. Rep. 154. The case last cited calls attention to the fact that, where the action is brought before the expiration of the period of employment provided by the contract, the action is not to recover wages due, but for damages for breach of contract, and that: "The measure of damages is, therefore, prima facie, the contract price." The burden was on the defendant to show, not only that respondent remained unemployed, but also that she could by diligence have secured suitable employment elsewhere. Rosenberger v. Pacific Coast Ry. Co., 111 Cal. 313, 318, 43 P. 963. Conceding that the proof would warrant the inference that respondent did not seek other employment, such proof would not establish that respondent could have

secured other employment. Appellant failed to sustain the burden placed upon it by the law, and there is no proof which would warrant a reduction in the amount of damages awarded by the judgment.

Appellant has moved this court for an order of diminution of the record to bring before this court the order of the trial judge that: "The defendant's answer is ordered amended to conform to the proof by inserting therein an allegation that since January 1, 1928, the plaintiff did not diligently seek other employment which she might have obtained at the same salary." As the judgment of the trial court did not allow to the plaintiff any amount for damages after January 1, 1928, it becomes immaterial here whether such amendment was ordered or not, and the motion is denied.

The judgment is affirmed.

Loew's, Inc. v. Cole, 185 F.2d 641 (9th Cir. 1950)

POPE, CIRCUIT JUDGE

In the month of October, 1947, the Committee on Un-American Activities of the House of Representatives conducted a public hearing, at Washington, for the purpose of inquiring into alleged Communist infiltration into the motion picture industry. Among dozens of witnesses called, beginning October 20, and concluding October 30, were the appellee, Lester Cole, and a number of the executives of the appellant, Loew's, Incorporated, a Delaware Corporation, engaged, under the trade name of Metro-Goldwyn-Mayer, in the production and distribution of motion pictures. Cole had been employed by Loew's as a writer of screen plays since 1945. He was currently employed under a written contract to which we shall presently refer.

At the hearing Cole, and some nine other screen writers, who came to be known in the current newspaper accounts of the hearing (which had extremely wide notice in the press and on the radio) as the ten "unfriendly" witnesses, were accompanied by counsel who challenged the validity of the investigation and the power of the Committee to conduct the inquiry or to issue the subpoenas served, by a so-called motion to "quash the subpoenas." When Cole was called to the stand he was asked "Are you now or have you ever been a member of the Communist Party?" The statement he then made was interpreted by the committee as a refusal to answer, and he was cited on November 24, 1947, by the House of Representatives for contempt, and was thereafter indicted for contempt of Congress.

Cole's employment contract contained a paragraph 5 which read: "The employee agrees to conduct himself with due regard to public conventions and morals, and agrees that he will not do or commit any act or thing that will tend to degrade him in society or bring him into public hatred, contempt, scorn or ridicule, or that will tend to shock, insult or offend the community or ridicule public morals or decency, or prejudice the producer or the motion picture, theatrical or radio industry in general."

Cole was the last of the eleven "unfriendly" witnesses called. He testified on October 30. On December 2, following, he was sent a notice of suspension reading as follows:

Dear Mr. Cole: At a recent hearing of a committee of the House of Representatives, you refused to answer certain questions put to you by such committee. By your failure to answer these questions, and by your statements and conduct before the committee and otherwise in connection with the hearings, you have shocked and offended the community, brought yourself into public scorn and contempt, substantially lessened your value to us as an employee, and prejudiced us as your employer and the motion picture industry in general. By so doing you have violated your obligations under your contract of employment with us and your legal obligations to us as our employee. Accordingly, and for good and sufficient cause, this is to notify you that we have elected to suspend your employment and payment of your compensation under your contract of employment with us dated December 5, 1945, as amended, commencing as of December 3, 1947, and continuing until such time as you are acquitted or have purged yourself of contempt of the Congress of the United States and you declare under oath that you are not a Communist. This action is taken by us without prejudice to, and we hereby reserve, any other rights or remedies which we may have. Very truly yours, Loew's Incorporated, by Louis K. Sidney, Asst. Treasurer.

Cole then filed this action, alleging the existence of a controversy arising out of this notice, and as to the right of Loew's to suspend Cole from his employment, and praying declaratory and other relief. The answer admitted the existence of a controversy, the written agreement between the parties, and the notice, denying other allegations of the complaint, and demanded a jury trial.

A form of special verdict, containing four questions, was submitted to the jury. Although no general verdict was called for, the court gave extensive instructions. The verdict was as follows:

Question 1: Did the plaintiff Lester Cole by his statements and conduct before the House Committee on Un-American Activities, in connection with the hearing held by said Committee, bring himself or tend to bring himself into public hatred, contempt, scorn, or ridicule? (Answer "yes" or "no.") Answer: No.

Question 2: Did the plaintiff Lester Cole, by his statements and conduct before the House Committee on Un-American Activities, in connection with the hearing held by said Committee, tend to shock, insult or offend the community? (Answer "yes" or "no.") Answer: No.

Question 3: Did the plaintiff Lester Cole, by his statements and conduct before the House Committee on Un-American Activities in connection with the hearing held by said Committee, prejudice the defendant Loew's Incorporated as his employer or the motion picture industry generally? (Answer "yes" or "no.") Answer: No.

Question 4: Did the defendant Loew's Incorporated by its conduct towards the plaintiff, subsequent to the hearing, waive the right to take action against him by suspending him? (Answer "yes" or "no.") Answer: Yes.

The court adopted the findings of the jury and made additional ones of its own; that what Cole did before the Committee was within his rights; that he did not breach his contract; that prior to the time Cole testified, Loew's led Cole to believe that if he conducted himself before the Committee as he did, he would not thereby become liable to suspension; and that after Cole had appeared before the Committee, Loew's with full knowledge of the facts, by choosing to retain him in their employ, elected to keep the contract in full force. Judgment was entered adjudging that Loew's had no right to suspend Cole's employment or compensation, ordering his reinstatement, and awarding Cole $75,600 in back pay, and retaining jurisdiction to see to it that subsequently maturing payments of wages should be made when due.

Appellant specifies numerous asserted errors

in instructions given and refused, and in the admission and rejection of evidence. Before we have occasion to deal with the points thus made, we must consider two other contentions. . . .

It is argued that what Cole did at the hearing was not a violation of his contract. Thus the court found that "The acts and conduct of the plaintiff before said House Committee were within the plaintiff's rights and did not constitute any breach on the part of the plaintiff of his contract of employment with the defendant." Further, appellee says that a fair reading of paragraph 5 of the employment contract, quoted above, (and which he calls the "morals clause") will disclose that it was not intended to prohibit the sort of thing done by Cole when he was called to testify; that his conduct there was "political," and citing the sections of the California Labor Code, which forbids the employer to use his power as such to coerce or influence the political action or activity of his employees, Cole says that if paragraph 5 is not to be held void under those sections, it must be construed as he contends.

There is no room for doubt as to just what Cole did before the Committee. A transcript of his testimony is a part of the pre-trial order. This discloses that the Committee sought to elicit from him answers to two questions: "Are you a member of the Screen Writers' Guild?" and "Are you now or have you ever been a member of the Communist Party?" All that need be said is that although Cole stated he would be very happy to answer these questions, the Committee did not succeed in getting an answer from him to either one.

It is not seriously contended that he did not refuse to answer. It was for such refusal he was cited and indicted. His general attitude with respect to answering the inquiries is somewhat illuminated by a statement which he had prepared and sought to read into the record and which he distributed to the press. In this he stated: "From what I have seen and heard of this hearing, the House Committee on Un-American Activities is out to accomplish one thing, and one thing only, as far as the American Motion Picture Industry is concerned; they are going either to rule it, or ruin it."

If, as a jury might well find, he wilfully refused to answer these questions, he was guilty of con- tempt of Congress, a misdemeanor under Title 2 U.S.C.A. § 192, and subject to fine and imprisonment. . . .

The first clause of paragraph 5, quoted above, says that "The employee agrees to conduct himself with due regard to public conventions and morals . . ." We think it rather elementary that one who, for whatever motive, chooses to conduct himself in such manner as to be guilty of a misdemeanor as serious as this one can hardly be said to be doing so "with due regard to public conventions." . . .

The conduct of the employee during this period adds up to an attitude of definite hostility and unfriendliness to the Committee hearings, which the producers apparently feared was headed in the direction of censorship of the screen. Thus Cole may have felt that he was justified in carrying a torch for freedom of speech, and in protesting against the proceedings. But we cannot think that as a matter of law this gave him the implied consent of the employer to go so far as to subject himself to a misdemeanor charge. He was plainly ill advised to go to the extreme which he did. A more reasonable course of conduct would have enabled him to trumpet his protest without danger to himself. Thus Mr. Mayer, in his testimony as to his talk with Cole following the meeting, suggested what was patently the more reasonable alternative for Cole, when he asked him why he did not first protest and then answer. . . .

Throughout the hearing the industry representatives had been undertaking to demonstrate to the Committee that their product contained no Communist propaganda. In the face of this obvious effort to play down the so-called Communist infiltration, Cole (evidently in concert with others), by his tactics of evasion, reasonably construed to be a refusal to answer, and calculated to carry the sting of contempt even more than a mere "I refuse to answer," chose in effect to broadcast to a listening world that it might place what construction it chose upon his refusal to answer whether he was or had been a Communist party member. We cannot say that as a matter of law such action was sanctioned by the prior conduct of his employer. . . .

. . . As soon as Cole left the witness stand his conduct was fully known to his employer. Are we to conclude that any use of his services thereafter, no matter how brief, destroys any defense? Another question is whether all the facts, of which the party charged with election must have knowledge, were in the possession of the employer prior to the time when it had an opportunity to examine and appraise the great flood of adverse criticism of Cole, his associates, and the film industry which followed the testimony. Or, if that may not be considered, does the party charged with election have a reasonable time within which to make his choice?

There is substantial evidence to show that Cole was informed that his testimony had put him in a predicament from which his employer might have difficulty in extricating him. . . .

Here it can be said that immediately following the Washington hearings the employer did not then know all the facts having a bearing upon the effect and the results of Cole's conduct. True, it was known exactly how he had performed, but it was as yet obviously impossible to evaluate the extent to which Cole had destroyed his own usefulness, or the effect which his continued employment might have upon Loew's and its public relations.

But even if it could be said that all the facts were then known, we think the appellant should not be denied a reasonable time to arrive at a course to be pursued. Whether this action, taken 33 days after Cole's testimony, was within a reasonable time is a question of fact, and for the jury. To paraphrase what was said in the Compania-Constructora Bechtel-McCone case, supra, competent managers do not formulate personnel policies on the basis of a hurried or partial consideration of the factors involved. Cole knew that his status had not been decided upon, for if his testimony first given is correct, he was informed that Mr. Mayer "was terribly upset particularly about the effect of this on Mr. Trumbo and myself," and Cole testified concerning Mayer: "He was angry and he said there had to be some way found to straighten out this situation." A jury, if it believed this statement was made, might well find it disproved any "intentional relinquishment of a known right."

The theory upon which Cole's counsel tried this aspect of the case was that until after the Congressional hearing the employer was entirely satisfied if not actually pleased with what Cole had done, that he was put back to work and his services used without any idea of discharging him, and that only after a public uproar arose in consequence of the action of the writers who testified did the executives of the industry, in their surprise and chagrin, determine to try to save themselves by throwing these "unfriendly" witnesses to the wolves.

The verdict of the jury indicates that it may have adopted this view. Plainly this theory made much progress with the court, for a considerable portion of the court's opinion is devoted to an exposition of Cole's claim that Loew's agreed to a policy which involved suspending Cole, only after being persuaded, against its initial desires, to take such action in concert with similar action by other producers. We think that the manner in which appellant came to be persuaded to take the action which it obviously did is wholly without bearing on the case. As respects the action taken, and the right to take it, such matters are as irrelevant as would be a transcript of the debates in its director's meetings.

Finally, it is said Cole should have judgment as a matter of law for the reason that even if we assume Loew's could have discharged him, yet it had no right to suspend him.

The written contract between the parties contained extensive provisions relating to the employee's "suspension" and to "periods in which the employee is not entitled to compensation." It provided in part as follows:

> In the event of the failure, refusal or neglect of the employee to perform his required services or observe any of his obligations hereunder to the full limit of his ability or as instructed, the producer, at its option, shall have the right to cancel and terminate this employment, may refuse to pay the employee any compensation for and during the period of such failure, refusal or neglect on the part of the employee, and shall likewise have the right to extend the term of this agreement and all of its provisions for a period equivalent to all or any part of the period during which such failure, refusal or neglect continues. . . . During the period of any such suspension, refusal to pay or leave of absence the employee shall not have the right to render his services to or for any person, firm or corporation other than the producer without the written consent of the producer first had and obtained. . . . During any period or periods in which the employee is not entitled to compensation pursuant to

the provisions of this paragraph, he shall be deemed to be laid off without pay, and during such periods, of course, the employee shall not have the right to render his services for any person, firm or corporation without the written consent of the producer first had and obtained.

Cole asserts that the hardship worked upon him by suspension is such that it could not have been the intent of the contract that he could be suspended for violation of paragraph 5. He says that the effect of the suspension is that he may not work for the employer, who is relieved from payment of his salary; that the employer may extend the term of the contract for the term of the suspension, and that during the period of suspension he is prohibited from working for anyone else.

Further, he says that these hardships were multiplied in the present case through the attachment to the notice of suspension of illegal and impossible conditions, namely, that the suspension would continue until Cole had been acquitted or purged of contempt, and until he declared under oath that he was not a Communist. He states that the net effect of all this would be to leave him in an impossible position where he could not comply with the notice and could never accept employment elsewhere.

We think that the notice left Cole in no worse position than that he would have occupied had he received a notice of discharge. The provisions of the contract quoted above which purport to forbid Cole from practicing his profession during the period of suspension are manifestly void under the California Code. Presumably Cole was so notified by his attorneys whose advice the record shows was constantly available to him and who have called our attention to the same provision in their briefs. When this is borne in mind, it is apparent that the notice of suspension was not so drastic as would have been a notice of discharge, for the notice of suspension permitted Cole to resume his employment if he complied with the conditions, and he was at the same time at liberty to seek employment elsewhere should he choose not to conform.

It is contended that compliance with these conditions was impossible; that he had no control over procuring an acquittal and there were no means by which he could be purged of contempt.

As for the required non-Communist oath, it is said that the employer was without power to demand it.

While the securing of an acquittal was, of course, not a matter within Cole's control, we think that Cole is in no position to assert that he was without power to purge himself of contempt. Had he sought from the Committee an opportunity to reappear before them with notification of his desire to purge himself of contempt, and had he then been refused that privilege, his argument of impossibility would have weight. It does not lie in his mouth to say that he could not have purged himself of contempt for he made no effort to do so.

We think that at the time notice of suspension was given him, the demand that he purge himself of contempt was not an unreasonable one. By that time the widespread and adverse reaction in the press and other organs of public opinion had become so violent that the executives of the industry had reason for genuine concern lest drastic action in the form of legislation or boycott might be taken. This had come about mainly because of the attitude of Cole and the other "unfriendly" witnesses at the hearing. We think it not unreasonable that the employer should attach the condition that Cole, to the extent possible, undo the harm he had succeeded in accomplishing. As for the non-Communist oath, if the employer was justified in believing Cole's own statement that he was not a Communist, the taking of the oath was likewise within Cole's power.

If it be argued that perhaps he was a Communist and therefore unable to take such an oath, and that therefore attaching such condition was the equivalent of notifying Cole that if he was a Communist he could no longer work for his employer, we think that under the circumstances the demand for the declaration under oath, even if it amounted, as suggested, to a notice of discharge if he be a Communist, was not outside the rights of appellant. It is our view that at the time the notice was given the employer would be fully within its rights in giving Cole just such a notice—that if he was a Communist his services were ended. For the situation had changed entirely from the time when Mannix, the manager, had said he did not care whether Cole was a Communist or not so long as he did good work.

When Mannix made that statement there was no occasion to suspect that the public generally had reason to suppose that Cole was a Communist or that the industry was generally employing writers who were Communists. The conduct of Cole and the other witnesess completely changed the situation. A film company might well continue indefinitely the employment of an actor whose private personal immorality is known to his employer, and yet be fully justified in discharging him when he so conducts himself as to make the same misconduct notorious.

The net effect of the hearing was to make Cole a distinct liability to his employer. We think that the insertion of these conditions, which were calculated to furnish Cole with an opportunity to undo a portion of what he had succeeded in accomplishing, was not beyond the power of the employer.

But even if it were to be said that the employer might discharge but not suspend Cole, we think the contention of the appellant correct when it says that if it be found that Cole acted in violation of the requirements of paragraph 5 he could not, having thus breached the conditions of his contract, recover from the employer.

We thus hold that Cole was not entitled to judgment as a matter of law and that his rights must be determined in accordance with the facts as found by a jury. We therefore must deal with the specifications of error relating to the instructions given and refused, and the evidence received and excluded.

We think that a number of the specifications of error relating to the instructions given are well taken. In general we think the court fell into error by undertaking to give instructions upon matters with which the jury were not concerned.

Thus the court instructed the jury at length upon the rights of Congressional committees to subpoena witnesses and ask questions, and upon the rights of the witnesses to decline to answer questions. As we have previously disclosed, the question of whether Cole was guilty of contempt was not one of the issues submitted to this jury. There was therefore no occasion to instruct them upon the subject, except to advise them that the Committee had the right to propound the questions and that it was the duty of Cole to answer

them. Instead, this portion of the charge contained such comments as that the witness "may decline to answer certain questions in order to secure from the courts a final determination of the right of the Committee to ask the particular question"; that "when a question is asked of a witness before a committee he may give either a direct or an irresponsive answer"; that "the citizen when interrogated about his private affairs has a right before answering to know why the inquiry is made; and if the purpose disclosed is not a legitimate one, he may not be compelled to answer"; that "a witness rightfully may refuse to answer where the bounds of the power are exceeded or the questions are not pertinent to the matter under inquiry." The instruction concluded with the statement: "And even the alien in our midst, if he be a legal resident, has certain rights and privileges which he may assert and which it is the duty of a legislative committee to respect and of the courts to protect."

We think this portion of the charge erroneous, misleading and prejudicial in that it could not but have the effect of leading the jury to believe that it was for them to decide as to the propriety of the questions, as to whether Cole had the right to refuse to answer, and their answers to the questions submitted were undoubtedly influenced accordingly.

As for the suggestion that Cole had the right to refuse to answer in order to test the right of the Committee to ask the questions, the instruction was particularly misleading, for he who chooses to test the validity of a statute of this kind acts at his peril. "He was bound rightly to construe the statute. His mistaken view of the law is no defense." . . .

The court also instructed the jury at considerable length upon the California law of libel.

> You are instructed that in California it is libelous to call a person a Communist. This for the reason that such a charge would expose a person to the hatred, contempt and ridicule of many persons. . . . I have stated that in California an accusation of Communism against a person is libelous. This is so because, under California law, every false and unprivileged publication which exposes a person to hatred, contempt, ridicule or obloquy or causes him to be shunned or avoided, or which has a tendency to injure him in his occupations, is libelous per se. . . .

The person who libels another has the burden of proving that the charge is true. He who repeats a libelous statement, if he wishes to justify it, must prove not that another has made the statement, but that the statement is true. These principles should be borne in mind by you in considering the testimony in this case in which reference was made as to certain accusations made against the plaintiff in certain publications and before the Committee which were repeated and discussed in the presence of some of the defendant's representatives. You were admonished at the time when these accusations were repeated here and I admonish you again now that they are to be considered only as having been made and that no one has proved in this lawsuit that these accusations are true. Indeed the truth of these accusations is not an issue in the case. And the reason, as already stated, is that the defendant has not charged the plaintiff is a Communist or a member of the Communist Party.

To the lawyer a discussion of the law of libel might well be understood, as we have no doubt the court intended it, as a statement that the court and the jury may take judicial notice that the public generally looked with scorn and contempt on persons believed to be Communists. Appellant requested such an instruction which the court refused, choosing apparently to discuss the subject by way of reference to the law of libel, and trusting the jury to perceive that the allusion was purely be way of analogy. Lawyers understand such reasoning but we think a jury would not. We are of the opinion that what a jury would most likely believe the judge was driving at was that he was suggesting to the jury that the Congressional Committee was guilty of attempted defamation of Cole, particularly in view of his reference in the instruction to "certain accusations made against the plaintiff in certain publications and before the Committee." We think the court erred in giving this instruction and in not giving the instruction relating to judicial notice requested by appellant.

The court charged the jury at length upon the general subject of "the acts of the employer considered as waiver." The greater portion of this instruction related to the question of whether the acts and statements of the defendant prior to Cole's testimony before the Committee were such as to give rise to a belief on his part that the employer was not concerned about whether he

was a Communist and therefore he had the employer's permission to act as he did when he appeared before the Committee.

No question relating to any such issue was submitted to the jury. In question No. 4, the court made inquiry of the jury as to whether defendant waived its right to suspend Cole by its action *subsequent* to the hearing. This was the only issue relating to waiver that was before the jury. Not only were the matters just referred to wholly inappropriate but we think even if it had been related to a matter submitted to the jury, the charge was inadequate and misleading in giving undue emphasis to the earlier statements made by Mayer and Mannix while omitting evidence as to testimony of Mayer and Johnston with regard to their desire not to hire known Communists, given prior to Cole's testimony. While it raised the question as to whether the employer's actions and statements "led the plaintiff Lester Cole to believe that they were not concerned about charges that he was a Communist," it failed to state that Cole's belief in that regard must have been reasonably justified by what the employer did and said.

The remainder of the instruction related to waiver arising out of the subsequent conduct of defendant. In respect to this the court said:

> To put it into a brief sentence: An employer knowing of an employee's conduct which might warrant suspension or termination of employment may not continue employing him thereafter and at a later date treat the employee's conduct as a breach of his obligations. So, here, if you find that when Cole came back from Washington, Loew's knew of Cole's statements and conduct before the House Committee in Washington in connection with the particular hearings, but nevertheless, put him back to work, and accepted his services with the intention of accepting Cole as its employee under the employment contract, then I instruct you that Loew's waived the right to rely upon such conduct in taking action against Cole.

The substance of this language was that if the employment was continued at all, a waiver by election resulted. The vice of this is that it wholly overlooks the circumstances to which we have heretofore alluded which might well require a different result. It overlooks the question of defendant's right to a reasonable time for evaluation of the results of Cole's testimony and to evolve a personnel policy, and the question whether viewed as a whole its conduct evinced an intentional relinquishment of a known right. . . .

Another portion of the charge which we think was not relevant to any issue before the jury, dealt with the status of the Communist party. The court charged:

> At the same time, I instruct you that in California it is lawful for a person to be a member of the Communist Party, and to register with the Registrar of Voters of a county as a member of such party. In California, the Communist Party is entitled to participate in elections, including primary elections, and to nominate candidates. And, while, under the California law, any party which carries on or advocates the overthrow of the government by unlawful means or which carries on or advocates a program of sabotage may not participate in primary elections, the courts of California have ruled that the courts do not take judicial notice of the fact that the Communist Party advocates the overthrow of the government by force or violence, and they have also ruled that a registered Communist is not guilty of a violation of the State law by the mere fact of membership in the Communist Party. . . . [B]ear these facts in mind in judging whether the conduct of the plaintiff was as charged by the defendant.

If it were to be an issue before the jury as to whether the Communist Party was lawful or unlawful, whether it was in fact not a political party but a "conspiratorial and revolutionary junta," "dominated and controlled by a foreign government," seeking to attain its goal by "violent and undemocratic means," and whose members are agents of a foreign power "to execute the Communist program," then evidence of these matters should have been received, since, at least in 1947, they were not matters of which the court might take judicial notice. . . .

Appellant sought unsuccessfully to introduce such proof. The offer was rejected on the ground as stated by the court, that "I do not think the question was material or that the question is one that is the subject of proof in this case."

This brings us to a discussion of appellant's specification of error relating to this rejection of its offered proof. Even if it may be assumed that such evidence would be logically relevant to the issues in this case, it does not follow that it was error to reject the offer.

This is a case which has primarily to do with the question of whether Cole violated his employment contract, and whether Loew's had the right to take the action which it did in consequence of such violation. While that inquiry necessarily touches upon the question of the effect of Cole's conduct upon public opinion generally, we think that the true character of the Communist Party and the true nature of membership therein, is far from being a primary issue in this case. It is relatively remote. We think that if in the trial of this case evidence of the character here offered were to be received, the result might well be to produce undue confusion in the minds of the jurors. The issues relating to an alleged breach of contract might be lost from sight behind a mass of testimony relating to the purposes of the Communist Party.

We think it was properly within the discretion of the trial court to exclude such testimony under the principle which gives rise to what Mr. Wigmore calls "the simplificative rules of evidence." This principle, which results in the exclusion of evidence otherwise relevant, is stated by Mr. Wigmore as follows:

> (a) If the use of certain evidential material tends to produce undue confusion in the minds of the tribunal—i.e. the jurors—by diverting their attention from the real issue and fixing it upon a trivial or minor matter, or by making the controversy so intricate that the disentanglement of it becomes difficult, the evidence tends to the suppression of the truth and not to its discovery; and there is good ground for excluding such evidence, unless it is so intimately connected with the main issue that its consideration is inevitable. (b) So also, if certain evidential material, having a legitimate probative value, tends nevertheless to produce also, over and above its legitimate effect, an unfair prejudice to the opponent, . . . there is good ground for excluding such evidence, unless it is indispensable for its legitimate purpose. Wigmore on Evidence, Third Ed., § 1864.

Evidence as to the true character of the Communist Party having been thus properly excluded, it was improper and misleading for the court to charge the jury, as it did, upon this matter.

Upon cross-examination of Cole, appellant sought to inquire whether Cole was in fact a member of the Communist Party. Objection to the inquiry was sustained.

In the context of the instructions as given this inquiry should have been permitted, for the court not only instructed the jury that the violation of contract charged must have been done "wilfully and intentionally," but as we have indicated, told the jury that a witness before the committee "also has rights. He may decline to answer certain questions in order to secure from the courts a final determination of the right of the Committee to ask the particular question." Thus the court indicated that Cole's motive in refusing to answer was material. If it was, appellant should have been permitted to show the possibility of a different motive—a motive to conceal his actual party membership.

But since his motive is not material, Sinclair v. United States, supra, we think the error lay, not in rejecting the inquiry, but in giving the instruction, as we have previously stated.

We do think that the true import of Cole's behavior on the witness stand should not be judged without considering it in the light of what his associates, the other "unfriendly" witnesses, had done when they preceded him upon the stand. The record contains his own admission that what he did was in consequence of his agreement with the others. We think the jury were entitled to know what this concerted action was, for only by observing all of it could Cole's conduct be judged in its actual setting, and in its entirety. The court erred in excluding evidence of the conduct of these other witnesses.

For reasons which we have previously stated, we think that if the question of waiver or election by subsequent conduct is to be submitted to the jury, the actual effect of Cole's conduct upon public opinion generally becomes material. We think the court unduly restricted the scope of the evidence upon this point, and that appellant's offers of proof to this end should have been received. If the offered evidence is to be credited, it would indicate that when the employer's officers acted to suspend Cole, they knew the industry, and its standing with the public, had been dealt a heavy blow. The evidence which brought this knowledge to them they should have been permitted to present to the jury.

We think these errors require us to reverse the judgment and to remand the cause for a new trial.

It is so ordered.

NOTE _____

1. The use of "morals" clauses in entertainment contracts is widespread. Employers argue that the performer who appears before the public is under constant scrutiny. Any questions raised about the performer's character can badly damage that person and, in turn, those who hire the performer. One veteran actor who has always been considered a paragon of virtue nevertheless found himself signing a motion picture employment contract that contained several "morals" clauses. Following are excerpts from a 1948 contract that Roy Rogers signed with Republic Productions:

(a) He (Roy Rogers) shall not use or authorize or willingly permit the use of his name, likeness, or voice in connection with alcoholic beverages, tobacco, laxatives, deodorants, or articles of feminine use, or any other product with which, at the time of such use, authorization or permission, it reasonably might be considered to be detrimental or prejudicial to associate artist or inconsistent with or harmful to his position as a motion picture star, particularly with reference to his youthful fan audience.

(b) In connection with publications (including so-called "comic" magazines), phonograph records, transcriptions and the like, artist shall, from and after the date of his contract, insert or cause to be inserted in all contracts and agreements appertaining thereto, a clause substantially as follows: "The artist shall not be depicted, described, shown or mentioned, in any form whatsoever, in the character of a villian, thief, or other despicable or derogatory character, or as consuming, dispensing or handling alcoholic beverages, tobacco of any kind or form, laxatives, deodorants, articles of feminine use or any other product with which it reasonably might be considered to be detrimental or prejudicial to associate artist, or as engaging in any mental or physical dissipation, or in any manner which will appeal to the sensual emotions of the reader, but all material shall star artist, and depict, describe, show or mention artist or any character described by the name of Roy Rogers or Rogers, in a decent and virtuous manner, and as champion of right and the enemy of wrong." . . .

5. Artist agrees to conduct himself with due regard to public conventions and morals, and further agrees not to do or commit any act or thing that will reasonably tend to degrade him or to bring him into public hatred, contempt, scorn or ridicule, or that will reasonably tend to shock, insult or offend the community or offend public morals or decency, or to prejudice producer of the motion picture industry in general.

1.50 Injunctive Relief

The entertainment industries exist on great enthusiasm and high expectations. Everything seems turned up a notch, and the principals' expectations become increasingly difficult to satisfy. When these circumstances are coupled with other parties waiting in the wings to join the action and perhaps lure stars to other attractions, trouble looms. The personal service contract is jeopardized, as the performer becomes dissatisfied with the present situation and yearns to move on.

A keystone to the entertainment industries is the ability to thwart the star from walking. While the normal legal response to contract breach in other situations is damages for loss incurred, how does one accurately measure the loss of a star attraction? The lost profits from a proposed, but unfulfilled, venture may be too speculative to prove to a court's satisfaction. While damages are an effective remedy in some situations, the employers of talent have often turned to another weapon to deal with the defecting performer. That weapon is the negative injunction.

The enforcement of the personal services contract through a negative injunction dates to the landmark English case decided in 1852, *Lumley v. Wagner*, 1 De G.M.&G 604, 42 Eng. Rep. 687 (1852). A young opera singer, Johanna Wagner, was under contract to Her Majesty's Theatre of London. When she attempted to breach that contract and join a rival troupe, Her Majesty's Theatre sued both her and her new employer. As to Ms. Wagner, the court pointed to the provision in her contract where she was to render her exclusive services to Her Majesty's Theatre for a number of months. The Chancellor granted a negative injunction preventing Wagner from performing for the rival company with the stated reasoning that, while a court could not specifically enforce the contract, an injunction preventing her performing elsewhere might cause the defendant to return and perform her prior contractual obligations. While the Chancellor's reasoning was unavailing in Wagner's case, in that

she did not return to Her Majesty's Theatre, the grounds for a negative injunction were established.

Other 19th-century English cases expanded on *Lumley v. Wagner*. In *Webster v. Dillon*, 30 L.T.R.(n.s.) 71 (1857), the court held that it was not necessary to include a specific clause in a contract specifying that injunctive relief was permissible. It was sufficient that the contract terms made it clear the services were to be exclusive, and that it could be determined, from the nature of the services, that they were unique and difficult to obtain from a substitute.

A second case, *Grimston v. Cunningham*, (1894) 1 Q.B. 125, involved an English actor who was in a road company touring the United States. Dissatisfied with the roles assigned him, he abandoned the tour and returned to England, only to face a day in court when he signed with another company. He was enjoined from performing in England during the time his contract with the road company in the United States was still running. This rather extensive restriction meant it was not necessary for an employer to show competitive harm in order to obtain a negative injunction; the loss of a performer's unique services was enough. Even so, under concepts that an injunction cannot be unduly harsh or burdensome (see Section 1.53), the absence of competitive harm may cause a court to deny an injunction. Yet another English case that dealt with competitive harm, or the lack thereof, was *Marco Prod., Ltd. v. Pagola*, (1945) K.B.111.

Early entertainment cases in the United States involving the negative injunction looked to the English precedents for support. Both *Daly v. Smith*, 38 N.Y.Sup.Ct. 158 (1874) and *Mapleson v. Del Puente*, 13 Abb.N.Cas. 144 (N.Y. 1883) noted the availability of the injunction when conditions paralleled those examined in the English cases just cited. Thus, the negative injunction was effectively transferred to U.S. jurisdictions and has been a principal deterrent to contract jumping ever since.

NOTES _____

1. The negative injunction in performer contracts has been analyzed in numerous articles, including the following:

(a) Tannenbaum, "Enforcement of Personal Service Contracts in the Entertainment Industry," 42 *California Law Review* 18 (1954).

(b) Berman & Rosenthal, "Enforcement of Personal Service Contracts in the Entertainment Industry," 7 *Journal of the Beverly Hills Bar Association* 49 (Sept. 1973) and 24 (Nov.–Dec. 1973).

(c) Steinberg, "Injunctions—Unjust Restraint on Entertainers in California," 1 *Loyola Entertainment Law Journal* 91 (1981).

2. Professional athletes seeking to "jump" to teams in rival leagues have also found themselves fighting negative injunctions. The special twists in negative injunctions in the sports context are reviewed in Berry & Wong, *Law and Business of the Sports Industries,* Vol. I, *Professional Sports Leagues* (Auburn House: Dover, Mass., 1986), pp. 67–90.

3. A comparison between negative injunctions in entertainment and sports contexts can be found in Berry & Gould, "A Long, Deep Drive to Collective Bargaining: Of Players, Owners, Brawls and Strikes," 31 *Case Western Reserve Law Review* 685, 713–725 (1981).

4. While our deliberations here focus on the ability of an entertainment company to obtain injunctive relief against a breaching performer, we should note other remedies potentially available to the company. In particular, the company may seek damages for advances or salaries made to the breaching employee and may also seek lost profits. However, lost profits in particular are difficult to prove, and the attempt to recover them may fail.

In a book publishing agreement, the author's breach of the satisfactory manuscript clause often allows for the recovery of advances paid the author, as held in *Random House Inc. v. Gold* (see Section 2.20). In *Doubleday v. Curtis* (see also Section 2.20), the publisher recovered a $50,000 advance as damages paid to the celebrity author of a novel, where that author rejected editorial assistance.

Beyond the advance, damage recoveries are rare. For example, damages for future profits lost by a company against the author or artist are seldom recovered. In *J.B. Lippincott Co. v. Lasher* (see Section 2.20), when a publisher was granted recovery of advances, its additional claim for "future profits" was dismissed as "far too speculative."

Because of the limited extent of recovery in these cases, the injunction looms as a company's principal weapon against the defecting performer.

5. When a performer attempts to "jump" his or her contract and go with another company, the suspicion is often that it is the other company, as much as the performer, that is responsible for the attempted switch. Thus, it is not unusual for a second lawsuit to be brought against the other company under a theory of interference with a contractual, business, or advantageous relationship (the exact nature of the tort varies from state to state). In fact, in the first English case on the matter, *Lumley v. Wagner,* discussed earlier, a companion suit was brought against the rival company seeking Johanna Wagner's services. The action is recorded in *Lumley v. Gye,* 2 El.&Bl. 216, 118 Eng.Rep. 749 (1853). The interference torts are considered at several points throughout this book.

1.51 Standards for Injunctive Relief

The sports area provides one of the earliest articulations of the standards for obtaining a negative injunction in U.S. courts. However, the precedents for the use of the negative injunction in the entertainment context should be heeded as well. In *Metropolitan Exhibition Co. v. Ewing,* 42 F. 198 (S.D.N.Y. 1890), the court held the following to be necessary inquiries:

1. The breach must be one for which damages would be inadequate compensation.
2. The party seeking the injunction must have "clean hands."
3. The injunction sought must not be unduly oppressive to the defendant.
4. The contract must have mutuality and be founded on adequate consideration.
5. The terms of the contract must be definite.

These standards were also applied in such early sports cases as *Metropolitan Exhibition Co. v. Ward,* 9 N.Y.S. 779 (Sup.Ct. 1890) and *Philadelphia Ball Club, Ltd. v. Lajoie,* 51 A. 973 (Pa. 1902).

Today, the articulation of standards for a negative injunction concentrates initially on the inadequacy of the legal remedy and irreparable harm to the nonbreaching party. In addition, the defenses listed in *Ewing* of unclean hands, lack of mutuality, undue oppressiveness, and indefiniteness of contract terms are still available to the performer fighting the injunction. Undue oppressiveness in particular is an important defense (see Section 1.53).

The party who loses the performer's services will often first seek a preliminary injunction barring the defecting performer from working elsewhere pending a full trial on the merits. This is often a decisive stage in legal maneuvering. The party who wins the battle can often force a settlement on favorable terms. For a preliminary injunction, the party must show not only lack of an adequate legal remedy and irreparable harm, but a likelihood of success on the merits as well. Thus, the hearing on a preliminary injunction is far more than a motion; it is generally the trial in miniature, with key evidence introduced to sustain the basis of the complaint. The court's decision is often determinative of the eventual results.

Harry Rogers Theatrical Enterprises v. Comstock, 232 N.Y.S. 1 (1928)

FINCH, J.

The question presented by this appeal is the right to an injunction pendente lite enjoining a theatrical performer from rendering services to another than his employer and enjoining the third party from so employing him. The injunction was denied at Special Term. . . .

The plaintiff corporation or its assignor had a five-year contract, starting in 1923, with the defendant Comstock, professionally known as "Billy House." Before this contract expired and in 1927, a new contract for four years, or until 1931, was entered into by the plaintiff with the defendant Comstock. Defendant Shubert and defendant Shubert Theatrical Corporation wished to obtain the services of Comstock for a musical show which was in preparation. Defendant Shubert, together with one Lyons, the booking agent of Shubert, saw Rogers for the purpose of obtaining a release of Comstock or a transfer of Rogers' contract to Shubert. After various negotiations, the proposed deal fell through, and then Shubert engaged Comstock. Shubert now attempts to justify this action and urged various grounds of defense.

The defendants urge as their first ground of defense that no written contract existed between the plaintiff and the defendant Comstock. The record shows that the existence of the written contract is clear, and the attempt to raise an issue as to its existence is well-nigh ludicrous. The best argument that can be used to show the existence of the contract is the following statement taken from the affidavit of this defendant: "I thereupon checked myself and now, although I have made a true and sincere effort to remember, I cannot recall if the agreement was in fact signed by me, although I do not believe that it was." This defendant certainly knew whether he signed what was to him the most important contract up to this time in his career and under which contract and continuation thereof he had been working for the last five years. In fact, this whole record is pregnant with this contract because of the attempt to evade the same.

The principal item of the second ground of defense urged by the defendants is an alleged estoppel, based upon a written offer by the plaintiff's predecessor to release Comstock upon certain terms. This offer was declined, and it is elementary that no estoppel can be based thereon. Moreover, the making and declination of this offer, together with other evidence in this record, afforded ample notice to the defendants that the defendants were not proceeding in accordance with the rights of the plaintiff, but in direct violation thereof.

The third ground of defense urged by the respondents is that there was nothing unique, special, or extraordinary about the services of the defendant Comstock, but that said services were ordinary and could easily be replaced. Therefore, urge the respondents, these services fall within the principle that ordinary contracts for personal services are not enforceable in equity . . . and that damages at law afford an adequate remedy. The record is replete with the usual conclusory opinion affidavits, pro and con, alleging and denying the uniqueness of the services. Facts when present, however, are always more persuasive than opinions. In the case at bar the contract whose existence is attacked admits the services of Comstock to be unique and extraordinary. While such recital is not controlling, it reflects upon the affidavit later made by Comstock, when his interest was to the contrary, swearing that his services were not unique. Next we have the uncontroverted fact that the ability of Comstock is regarded as unique upon the Albee-Keith circuit and that a substitute will not be accepted. Hence in this well-known vaudeville office Comstock cannot be replaced. Again, Comstock is now admittedly receiving a salary of $1,000 a week, which, in his work, is very large and compares most favorably with that received by the leaders in the scientific, artistic, and political world. In Winter Garden Co. v. Smith, 282 F. 166, where two plaintiffs were to receive a joint salary of $1,100 a week, the Circuit Court of Appeals of the Second Circuit said: "When, therefore, actors such as these have been successful for many years because of individual characteristics, and command salaries of a size rarely known in the liberal arts and sciences, their peculiar ability in the field in which they perform is almost res ipsa loquitur."

It seems unnecessary to go further with a recital of facts when the defendant Shubert, who knew Comstock was under a contract with the plaintiff, was willing to risk a lawsuit and pay $1,000 a week to secure the services of Comstock. The conclusion is therefore sustained that defendant Comstock has that personality which denotes the unusual and unique artist and enables him to pick up the attention of an audience and hold it interested, amused, or in pathos until released. Where, therefore, the services of the actor are shown to be unusual, unique, or extraordinary, and that the damage to the plaintiff will be irreparable and unascertainable, the latter may enjoin the performer from appearing elsewhere during the period of his contract, and, even though a negative covenant not to appear elsewhere may be lacking, such will be implied and enforced not only against those who are

parties to the contract, but also restraining third parties from doing those acts which induce and continue the breach. This has been the law since the well-known early case of Lumley v. Wagner, 1 De G.M.&.G. 604, and has been repeatedly applied in this court and elsewhere. . . .

It is obvious that a court of equity is governed by principles of law impartially applied to the facts in the particular case, and that the facts, when accurately and truthfully ascertained, are alike masters of bench and bar. If the time shall ever come when a court of equity must stand helplessly by while unique and unusual theatrical performers may be induced to breach contracts with impunity, except for such damages as a jury may see fit to award at some distant date, theatrical corporations will find their business hampered by intolerable conditions. It follows that the order appealed from should be reversed with $10 costs and disbursements, and the motion granted with $10 costs.

Order reversed with $10 costs and disbursements, and motion granted with $10 costs. Settle order on notice. All concur.

King Records, Inc. v. Brown, 252 N.Y.S.2d 988 (1964)

MCNALLY, JUSTICE

The question presented is whether plaintiff-appellant is entitled to an injunction *pendente lite* restraining violation of an express negative covenant not to "perform for the purpose of making phonograph records for any person other than us."

Defendant James Brown is a vocalist, musician and orchestra leader. On June 23, 1960 plaintiff and Brown entered into a written agreement whereby his "exclusive professional services in connection with the production of phonograph records" were engaged by plaintiff for the period of five years commencing July 1, 1960. Thereby substantial payments and royalties were required to be and were paid by plaintiff to Brown. Brown covenanted during the contract period not to make recordings for any other person; the contract recites his "services are unique and extraordinary." Two extensions of the original term of the basic agreement have been entered into, the effect of which we do not now decide since the original term of five years has not expired.

On January 20, 1964 Brown entered into a recording agreement with Fair Deal Records, the predecessor of defendant Fair Deal Record Corp. Fair Deal was organized by Brown and his manager. On February 28, 1964 Fair Deal granted to defendant Mercury Record Corporation the exclusive right to distribute and sell Brown's recordings. Fair Deal warranted to Mercury that it had an exclusive recording agreement with Brown. Mercury's president admits knowledge "that Brown's recordings had appeared on the label of the plaintiff." Mercury received assurances from Brown's manager that "Brown was not under any obligation to record for King." Mercury's president knew that Brown and his manager had formed Fair Deal. Mercury's attorney inquired of American Federation of Musicians as to the existence of any contract between Brown and the plaintiff; he was informed no such contract had been filed with the Federation. No attempt was made by the corporate defendants to ascertain from the plaintiff whether it had or claimed a contract with Brown. We conclude on this record that the corporate defendants had knowledge of plaintiff's contract with Brown for his exclusive recordings.

The 1960 contract expressly provides Brown's services are unique and extraordinary. The nature and extent of the recordings made by Brown under plaintiff's contract and the large quantity thereof publicly sold substantiate the contract characterization of Brown's services as unique and extraordinary. Mercury's president verifies that within two months of the contract with Fair Deal it paid $27,500 to Fair Deal and advanced costs of recordings to the extent of $10,000. Thereby is confirmed Mercury's appraisal of Brown's services as unique and extraordinary. . . .

Brown and Fair Deal cross-moved for a stay of proceedings pending arbitration. On March 18, 1959 plaintiff entered into a collective bargaining agreement with American Federation of Musicians of the United States and Canada relative to members of the Federation denominated "musicians." The collective bargaining agreement incorporates the provisions of the constitution and by-laws of the Federation. The said constitution and by-laws provide for arbitration of any claim arising from any agreement relating to services of a musician member of the Federation; also, that no contract with a musician member of the Federation shall be effective unless approved by its executive board.

Plaintiff argues with great force that its contract with Brown pertains to his professional services as a vocalist, not as a musician within the meaning of the collective bargaining agreement. It is unnecessary to decide that issue, although the practical interpretation of said agreement would seem to sustain the plaintiff's view. Plaintiff also argues that the contract with Brown does not itself contain provision for arbitration and does not adequately incorporate the arbitration provisions of the Federation's constitution and by-laws. An agreement to arbitrate must be direct and the intention made clear without "implication, inveiglement or subtlety." . . . The agreement relied on herein is neither clear nor direct.

If it be assumed, arguendo, for the purpose of this appeal that Brown is a musician and that the provision for arbitration applies, nevertheless, Brown may not avail himself of arbitration, a right which is vested exclusively with the collective bargaining agent, the Federation. . . . The application for a stay pending arbitration constitutes an exercise of the right to arbitration since the stay is the exclusive remedy in respect of an action allegedly in violation of the provision for arbitration. . . .

We note defendants' claim that plaintiff's contract was not approved by the Federation as provided in the collective bargaining agreement. We need only observe that the provisions of the collective bargaining agreement are not available to Brown and that the Federation, the collective bargaining agent in whom is vested the rights under said agreement, is not a party and makes no claim thereon. Moreover, the corporate defendants are not parties to and have no rights under the said agreement.

The various defenses pleaded by the defendants are factually unsupported.

The order should be modified, on the law, on the facts and in the exercise of discretion and the motion for an injunction *pendente lite* granted to the extent of restraining defendant Brown from vocal phonograph recordings and restraining the corporate defendants from causing or providing such recordings or manufacturing, distributing or selling any vocal phonograph recordings of defendant Brown; the cross-motion of defendant Brown denied; and, as so modified, the order should be affirmed. Settle order providing for bond.

Order, entered on June 11, 1964, modified, on the law, on the facts and in the exercise of discretion, and the motion for an injunction pendente lite granted to the extent of restraining defendant Brown from vocal phonograph recordings and restraining the corporate defendants from causing or providing such recordings or manufacturing, distributing or selling any vocal phonograph recordings of defendant Brown; the cross-motion of defendant Brown denied; and, as so modified, the order is affirmed with $30 costs and disbursements to appellant. Settle order on notice providing for bond. . . .

EAGER, JUSTICE (CONCURRING)

I would hold that the plaintiff was bound by the provisions for arbitration contained in the constitution and by-laws of the American Federation of Musicians. The collective bargaining agreement between plaintiff and the Federation contained the express provision that "[a]ll present provisions of the Constitution, By-Laws, rules and regulations of the Federation . . . are made a part of this agreement." Clearly, plaintiff as a knowledgeable employer in the recording business was well aware of the provisions for the arbitration of employee grievances contained in the said constitution and by-laws and expressly made a part of the collective bargaining agreement.

There is, however, no showing by the defendants that the grievance procedure, as agreed upon, has been invoked by the plaintiff or the Federation or that the defendant Brown, as an alleged employee of the plaintiff, has the right to initiate such procedure. I agree with Mr. Justice McNally that, on the record here before the court, it does not appear that the alleged contractual provisions for arbitration are directly enforceable by the defendant Brown or his co-defendants. Generally speaking, "[a]n individual member of a labor union has no right to compel arbitration under a collective labor agreement signed by the union and the employer." . . . On

this basis, I concur in the modification of the order appealed from to grant an injunction *pendente lite* to plaintiff and to deny cross-motion of defendants to stay the action.

VALENTE, JUSTICE (DISSENTING)

I dissent and would affirm the order on the opinion of Justice Loreto at Special Term. I would add, however, that I am in agreement with that portion of the concurring opinion of Justice Eager which would hold that plaintiff was bound by the arbitration provisions in the constitution and by-laws of the American Federation of Musicians.

Where I part company with Justice Eager and the majority of this Court is on the ground on which they rest the denial of the application to stay the action, viz., that an individual member of a labor union has no right to compel arbitration under a collective labor agreement between a union and employer. That rule of law . . . has no relevancy to the case at bar. Injection of that principle in the instant case fails to recognize the true nature of the defendant's motion—which is merely to stay the pending action—and to distinguish such an application from one to compel arbitration.

A party seeking a stay of an action does not have to move, at the same time, to compel arbitration. . . . The plaintiff, who is thus stayed, may then initiate arbitration proceedings against the appropriate party. . . .

Reason and consistency require that if an employee is precluded from suing an employer who has a collective agreement with a union, or may not compel the employer to arbitrate, then the employer should be equally barred, in contravention of the collective agreement from asserting a claim against the employee in an action, where the employer has agreed to arbitrate such disputes with the union. It would seem that the same impediment preventing the employee to sue his employer would likewise stand in the way of a suit by the employer against the employee. All the employee is asking here is that plaintiff's suit be stayed. He is not demanding that the employer arbitrate the dispute with him. The granting of a stay of the action would then relegate the plaintiff to resort to arbitration with the proper party to resolve the dispute if the plaintiff were still inclined to press the demand for an injunction. Under the circumstances, defendants were within their rights to seek a stay of the action.

Beverly Glen Music, Inc. v. Warner/Elektra/Asylum/Nonsuch Records, and Anita Baker, 86 Daily Journal, D.A.R. 997 (Cal.App. 1986)

The Plaintiff appeals from an Order denying a preliminary injunction against the Defendant, Warner Communications, Inc. We affirm.

In 1982, plaintiff Beverly Glen Music, Inc. signed to a contract a then-unknown singer, Anita Baker. Ms. Baker recorded an album for Beverly Glen which was moderately successful, grossing over one million dollars. In 1984, however, Ms. Baker was offered a considerably better deal by defendant Warner Communications. As she was having some difficulties with Beverly Glen, she accepted Warner's offer and notified plaintiff that she was no longer willing to perform under the contract. Beverly Glen then sued Ms. Baker and sought to have her enjoined from performing for any other recording studio. The injunction was denied, however, as, under Civil Code section 3423, subdivision Fifth, California courts will not enjoin the breach of a personal service contract unless the service is unique in nature and the performer is guaranteed annual compensation of at least $6,000 which Ms. Baker was not.

Following this ruling, the plaintiff voluntarily dismissed the action against Ms. Baker. Plaintiff, however, then sued Warner Communications for inducing Ms. Baker to breach her contract and moved the court for an injunction against Warner to prevent it from employing her. This injunction, too, was denied, the trial court reasoning that what one was forbidden by statute to do indirectly, one could not accomplish through the back door. It is from this ruling that the plaintiff appeals. . . .

From what we can tell, this is a case of first impression in California. While there are numerous cases on the general inability of an employer to enjoin his former employee from performing services somewhere else, apparently no one has previously thought of enjoining the new employer from accepting the services of the breaching employee. While we commend the plaintiff for its resourcefulness in this regard, we concur in the trial court's interpretation of the maneuver.

"It is a familiar rule that a contract to render personal services cannot be specifically enforced." (Foxx v. Williams (1966) 244 Cal. App. 2d 223, 235.) An unwilling employee cannot be compelled to continue to provide services to his employer either by ordering specific performance of his contract, or by injunction. To do so runs afoul of the Thirteenth Amendment's prohibition against involuntary servitude. (Poultry Producers Etc. v. Barlow (1923) 189 Cal. 278, 288.) However, beginning with the English case of Lumley v. Wagner (1852) 42 Eng. Rep. 687, courts have recognized that, while they cannot directly enforce an affirmative promise (in the Lumley case, Miss Wagner's promise to perform at the plaintiff's opera house), they can enforce the negative promise implied therein (that the defendant would not perform for someone else that evening). Thus, while it is not possible to compel a defendant to perform his duties under a personal service contract, it is possible to prevent him from employing his talents anywhere else. The net effect is to be denying him the means of earning a living. Indeed, this is its only purpose, for, unless the defendant relents and honors the contract, the plaintiff gains nothing from having brought the injunction.

The California Legislature, however, did not adopt this principle when in 1872 it enacted Civil Code section 3423, subdivision Fifth, and Code of Civil Procedure section 526, subdivision 5. These sections both provided that an injunction could not be granted: "To prevent the breach of a contract the performance of which would not be specifically enforced." In 1919, however, these sections were amended, creating an exception for: "a contract in writing for the rendition or furnishing of personal services from one to another where the minimum compensation for such service is at the rate of not less than six thousand dollars per annum and where the promised service is of a special, unique, unusual, extraordinary or intellectual character. . . ."

The plaintiff has already unsuccessfully argued before the trial court that Ms. Baker falls within this exception. It has chosen not to appeal that judgment, and is therefore barred from questioning that determination now. The sole issue before us then is whether plaintiff—although prohibited from enjoining Ms. Baker from performing herself—can seek to enjoin all those who might employ her and prevent them from doing so, thus achieving the same effect.

We rule that plaintiff cannot. Whether plaintiff proceeds against Ms. Baker directly or against those who might employ her, the intent is the same: to "deprive Ms. Baker of her livelihood and thereby pressure her to return" to plaintiff's employ. Plaintiff contends that this is not an action against Ms. Baker but merely an equitable claim against Warner to deprive it of the wrongful benefits it gained when it "stole" Ms. Baker away. Thus, plaintiff contends, the equities lie not between the plaintiff and Ms. Baker, but between plaintiff and the predatory Warner Communications company. Yet if Warner's behavior has actually been predatory, plaintiff has an adequate remedy by way of damages. An injunction adds nothing to plaintiff's recovery from Warner except to coerce Ms. Baker to honor her contract. Denying someone his livelihood is a harsh remedy. The Legislature has forbidden it but for one exception. To expand this remedy so that it could be used in virtually all breaches of a personal service contract is to ignore over one hundred years of common law on this issue. We therefore decline to reverse the order.

The order is affirmed.

1.52 Uniqueness

The uniqueness of the performer's talents is a central issue in obtaining a negative injunction against the performer. Uniqueness is largely an element of proving irreparable harm, but it bears on the issue of inadequacy of legal damages as well. Uniqueness to the extent that the performer is impossible to replace is not required. A showing of great difficulty and inconvenience in finding a substitute performer of similar talents is generally sufficient. Other important questions remain, as the following case and note illustrate.

Wilhelmina Models, Inc. v.. Abdulmajid, 413 N.Y.S.2d 21 (1979)

Order, Supreme Court, New York County, entered May 19, 1978, granting plaintiff's motion for preliminary injunction, is unanimously reversed, on the law and the facts, and in the exercise of discretion. . . .

Coming now to the merits of the preliminary injunction, as Special Term said, "plaintiff has not clearly shown at this point that it will be irreparably harmed in the absence of injunctive relief." The court nevertheless granted the preliminary injunction, primarily in reliance upon the decision of this Court in *King Records, Inc. v. Brown*, 21 A.D.2d 593, 252 N.Y.S.2d 988 (1st Dept. 1964), and the fact that the contract in the present case as in the *Kings Records v. Brown* case recited that the defendant Iman Abdulmajid's (hereinafter "defendant model") services are extraordinary and unique and that there is no adequate remedy at law for the breach of the agreement and that in the event of breach or threatened breach, plaintiff should be entitled to equitable relief by way of injunction or otherwise. We do not think that *King Records v. Brown*, *supra*, requires the grant of preliminary injunction merely because of these circumstances.

The uniqueness of defendant model's services would seem to be somewhat diluted by the fact that plaintiff apparently requires all of the models it manages to sign contracts with such recitations; the contract is obviously a form contract. Insofar as defendant model's services are "unique," in the sense that she looks like herself and not somebody else and is very popular, that uniqueness is not vis-a-vis plaintiff but vis-a-vis the photographers and commercial organizations who hire the model. Vis-a-vis plaintiff, defendant model is simply one of a number of models whom plaintiff manages, some of whom are in the same price category as defendant model, and as to whom plaintiff's interest is not in having the model render services to plaintiff but rather in plaintiff's receiving commissions from the compensation for the services that defendant model renders to third persons. Furthermore, unlike *King Records v. Brown, supra*, the defendant model does not render any services to plaintiff nor does plaintiff pay the defendant model. It is quite the other way around. Plaintiff renders services to defendant model as manager and defendant model pays plaintiff. Thus damages would appear to be an adequate remedy.

1. It must be proved that a performer has unique talents in order to show irreparable harm will befall the other party. How to prove the uniqueness of talents? Lawyers have been innovative in adducing evidence as to uniqueness. In *Shubert Theatre Co. v. Rath*, 271 F. 827 (2d Cir. 1921), expert testimony from fellow producers was used; in *Harry Hastings Attractions v. Howard*, 196 N.Y.S. 228 (1922), newspaper articles were offered as evidence.

1.53 Undue Oppressiveness and Restraint

A court will not issue a negative injunction if it feels it will be unduly harsh or burdensome. The court is influenced by the length of time the injunction is to run, the extent of geographical area in which the defendant is to be prohibited from seeking alternative work, the types of work prohibited by the requested injunction, and the likelihood that the injunction will produce positive results.

The time left under the original contract is important, although courts have issued injunctions that effectively prohibit important types of alternative employment for three or more years. In *Warner Bros. Pictures, Inc. v. Nelson*, (1937) 1 K.B. 209, actress Bette Davis was enjoined from making films or appearing on stage in England for the remainder of her contract or three years, whichever was shorter. The court did refuse plaintiff's request that, during this time, the actress be barred from all entertainment work. Even so, the length of time preventing her pursuit of her chief career was formidable.

The Davis case involved another issue of harshness of a negative injunction. When it appeared that Davis would not make further films for Warner Brothers, she was suspended from the company payroll and was still not being paid under her studio contract when suit was brought against her. The court indicated it would not order an injunction unless the company indicated a firm willingness to lift the suspension. In other words, one cannot both suspend a performer and restrain the performer from working elsewhere.

The following cases delve into further issues of harshness and undue restraints.

Machen v. Johansson, 174 F. Supp. 522 (S.D.N.Y. 1959)

KAUFMAN, DISTRICT JUDGE

In this action tried to me without a jury the plaintiff seeks to enjoin the defendant from engaging in a boxing match with Floyd Patterson, the heavyweight champion of the world, scheduled to be held in New York City on June 25, 1959, approximately two weeks from today. He asks that this injunction continue until the defendant shall have engaged in a return boxing match with the plaintiff.

Plaintiff's claim for an injunction is grounded upon the contention that the defendant had agreed to a rematch with the plaintiff and had also agreed not to engage in any fights in the United States and specifically not to fight Floyd Patterson anywhere in the world before the rematch with the plaintiff had been held. At this juncture a brief statement concerning the factual contentions is in order.

In 1958 and until September 14, 1958, the plaintiff was recognized by the National Boxing Association and "Ring Magazine" (a recognized publication in the boxing world) as the Number One or Number Two challenger for the world's heavyweight title. The defendant was the European heavyweight champion and ranked 6th or 8th.

In the latter part of April, 1958, negotiations for a boxing match between plaintiff and defendant to be held in Sweden were begun between the Swedish promoter Edwin Ahlquist and Eddie Machen's manager, Sidney Flaherty, or his designated agents.

After preliminary negotiations the plaintiff mailed and Ahlquist received a letter dated June

7, 1958, containing a plaintiff's terms for a boxing match in Sweden. The letter stated among other things "one of the conditions of Eddie Machen meeting Ingemar Johansson is that should Johansson win then he agrees to a rematch with Machen, said rematch to take place in San Francisco at a date to be agreed upon when we arrive in Sweden."

On June 27th Flaherty telegraphed Ahlquist urging a reply to his letter of June 7th. Here, a serious cleavage in the facts develops. Ahlquist insists that sometime between June 12th and 15th, or in that vicinity, he replied to Flaherty advising him that Johansson would not agree to a rematch provision. A copy of the purported letter was produced at the trial and it was asserted by Ahlquist that he had prepared the letter in handwriting and then gave it to an employee to type and mail, his regular secretary being absent because of illness. In this letter and in his testimony at the trial Ahlquist insisted that the declination of a return match was the direct result of specific instructions received by him from Johansson.

In a subsequent telegram, dated July 18th, Ahlquist agreed to arrange a contest pursuant "to your terms in previous letter." There was a further exchange of letters ultimately leading to the signing of an agreement, dated August 3rd, between Ahlquist as "promoter" and Western Promotions, Inc., a corporation of which Flaherty was President, as "manager." This document (Exhibit 10–A) does not contain any provisions for a rematch. Plaintiff's explanation is that he did not expect such a provision in a contract between a promoter and plaintiff's manager and, therefore, did not insist upon the provision in this agreement. Ahlquist, plaintiff claims, was acting in two capacities. He urges that by Ahlquist's telegram of July 18th accepting all of the terms contained in the letter of June 7th, defendant had already agreed to the rematch. Plaintiff asserts that Ahlquist was the promoter of the Swedish fight as well as Johansson's manager and agent. Defendant, on the other hand, points to this agreement as containing all of the terms agreed upon and the absence of the rematch provision as indicating that it was never consented to.

The fight between plaintiff and defendant was scheduled to take place on September 14, 1958, in Gothenburg, Sweden. Plaintiff, his manager and party arrived in Sweden in late August 1958. It is plaintiff's contention that on the day of his arrival his manager Flaherty approached Ahlquist with the demand that the details of a proposed rematch be agreed upon and embodied in a writing. Defendant, on the other hand, introduced testimony to show that Flaherty's first demand for a rematch was made in Sweden on September 12th, two days before the fight. It is Flaherty's position that as plaintiff's agent he had reached an agreement, prior to his departure for Sweden, that there would definitely be a rematch in the event of a defeat of the plaintiff at the hands of the defendant; that only details remained to be worked out and that this was what he was attempting to do in his pursuit of Ahlquist during the days immediately preceding the September 14th match. Ahlquist, of course, denies that there was an agreement for a rematch and insists that it had been specifically rejected in his June 1958 letter. He insists that the conduct of Flaherty on the eve of the Swedish bout constituted coercion and duress; that Flaherty threatened that if a rematch provision was not promptly reduced to writing and the terms finalized, he and his fighter would leave Sweden at once and not fight Johansson. It is conceded by Flaherty that he told Ahlquist on September 12th that there might be no fight unless a rematch agreement were signed. This, Ahlquist insists, had catastrophic implications for him since he had invested over a $100,000 as promoter. If the fight were cancelled it would have meant financial ruin for Ahlquist and the end of his reputation as a promoter. In any event, on September 13, 1958, a document prepared by Flaherty was signed by Ahlquist in the room of Sidney Flaherty at the Park Avenue Hotel in Gothenburg, Sweden. The document was witnessed by Olof Ahlsted, a Swedish lawyer, who represented Mr. Ahlquist, and Sven Holmberg.

On September 14, 1958, the fight was held between plaintiff and the defendant, resulting in the surprise knock-out of the plaintiff by the defendant in the first round. As a result of his dramatic victory over Machen, Johansson was immediately thrust into a position of prominence in the boxing world. The November 1958 issue of Ring Magazine stated that, as of September 16, 1958, Johansson was the number one ranked contender, and Machen number five. The National Boxing Association ratings listed Johansson as second and Machen as fifth. On January 29, 1959, after months of negotiations between Johansson, Ahlquist, promoter Rosensohn and Cus D'Amato, manager for Floyd Patterson, an agreement was signed for a match between Patterson and Johansson. These negotiations began the day after Johansson's victory.

Defendant has refused to honor the alleged agreement for a rematch and to recognize the document of September 13th on several grounds: (1) He contends that Ahlquist was never his agent, actual or apparent, and was never given authority to sign this agreement in his behalf, and that Flaherty had 'been specifically informed that defendant would not agree to a rematch; (2) that the agreement was obtained by coercion and duress; (3) that the agreement for a rematch is void and unenforceable for lack of consideration and is further invalid because its terms are indefinite and uncertain. Other grounds are urged, such as the inability of the International Boxing Club, named in the document of September 13th as the promoter of the rematch, to perform because of its dissolution pursuant to a decree of Judge Ryan in an anti-trust suit brought against it. United States v. International Boxing Club, D.C., 150 F. Supp. 397; 171 F. Supp. 841; 358 U.S. 242, 79 S. Ct. 245, 3 L.Ed.2d 270.

As I have already stated, plaintiff seeks drastic relief by his prayer for an injunction restraining the defendant from engaging in the boxing match with Floyd Patterson now scheduled for June 25th and for a continuance of this injunction until Johansson shall have engaged with the plaintiff in a rematch. I am convinced that the applicable law prevents me, in the light of the facts in this case, from granting the equitable relief sought by the plaintiff. Furthermore, even if such relief could be granted, I would deny the injunction in the exercise of my discretion. I, therefore, find it unnecessary to determine whether Ahlquist had actual or apparent authority to enter into the September writing on behalf of Johansson or to agree to any provisions for a rematch in his behalf. Likewise it becomes unnecessary to decide whether the document of September 13th was extracted by duress or coercion or whether it was based on adequate consideration.

By reason of this disposition it follows also that any alleged violation of Judge Ryan's decree or assertion of a conspiracy to violate the Sherman Act, 15 U.S.C.A. §§ 1–7, 15 note, need not be dealt with. In short, I make no findings or conclusions concerning the validity of the writing of September 13, 1958, or the enforceability of any part of that writing except the negative covenant contained in paragraph 5 thereof.

Meaning of the Negative Covenant

Even were I to assume that the writing of September 13, 1958, constitutes a valid agreement between Machen and Johansson for a return fight in the event of Machen's defeat in the September 14, 1958, fight, I would be compelled to hold that Machen is not entitled to the injunction he seeks.

It is black letter law that although a contract may be valid it may not necessarily provide the basis for equitable relief. This is not to say that the aggrieved party is left without any remedy. The usual form of redress in cases of breach of contract is money damages. Only in the most unusual case will a court of equity act upon the person of the defendant to restrain him from doing some act which the plaintiff claims may cause him irreparable injury. This is particularly true where, as in this case, the plaintiff seeks to restrain the defendant from freely practicing his trade. His right to this relief must be clear, reasonable and well defined.

In order to determine what rights and obligations may flow from the writing of September 13, 1958, I must first determine what the parties intended to achieve by that writing. My task in this case is to examine the words employed by the parties against the background of all of the circumstances under which the contract was drawn. It is only by interpreting the words of others that we may give meaning to their expressions. In the words of Professor Corbin:

> In reading each other's words, men certainly see through a glass darkly; . . . the best that a judge can do is to put himself so far as possible in the position of that person or persons [whose meaning and intention are in issue], knowing their history and experience . . . and then to determine what his own meaning and intention would have been. Corbin, Contracts 13, 23 (1951).

So viewing the contract, it is clear on its face

that the parties intended to ensure Machen an opportunity to fight Johansson in a return match in the event that Machen lost to Johansson in Sweden. The return bout was to be held in Chicago under the auspices of the International Boxing Club specifically during the last week of January or the first two weeks of February, 1959. No provision was made in the agreement for a postponement or for any alternative time within which the fight was to be held. It, therefore, appears that it was the intent of the parties that Johansson was to have performed the affirmative aspect of the contract by the end of the second week of February 1959 and that if he failed to do so he would have breached his obligation. As I have already stated, there was included in the writing of September 13, 1958, a negative covenant providing that Johansson "will not box anyone in the United States and will not box Floyd Patterson under any conditions any place in the world until the above agreements have been fulfilled." If plaintiff is entitled to the injunction he seeks, that right flows from this negative covenant. However, while the covenant clearly exhibits an intention to place some restrictions on Johansson's activities as a fighter, it provides me with no clue as to the period of time during which those restrictions were intended to run. The only temporal limitation to be found in the negative covenant is contained in the words "until the above agreements have been fulfilled." The "above agreements" must have reference to the provision relating to the return fight. Thus, the contract is subject to two possible interpretations:

(1) that the negative covenant would run until the time when the return match was scheduled to be held, i.e., no later than February 14, 1959;

(2) that it would run until such time as the return fight was actually held, or until a tender of performance by Johansson was refused by Machen, even if that time ran indefinitely beyond the dates specified in the agreement.

I am compelled to conclude that the parties never intended that the negative covenant run beyond February 14, 1959, the last date for performance of the return bout provision. It may be conjectured that Flaherty was fearful that Johansson, should he defeat Machen and thereby gain a reputation which would be readily saleable in the United States, would not be able to resist the temptation to exploit that reputation in the months between the original Machen-Johansson fight and the return. Had Johansson engaged in an interim bout and lost, it would have seriously impaired his reputation and thus have detracted from the value of the return bout agreement. This is the eventuality against which Flaherty sought to protect his fighter.

However, plaintiff would have me adopt a different interpretation of the covenant. He now urges that, in contracting to fight Johansson, Machen gave to Johansson "the opportunity to make an important improvement in his competitive position in the boxing world." The instant covenant, plaintiff argues, was intended to prevent Johansson from utilizing his advanced position in competition with Machen until Machen shall have an opportunity to engage him in a return fight. However, a consideration and evaluation of all of the evidence in the case leads me to the conclusion that the interpretation advanced by plaintiff is the less probable of the two possible alternatives.

Under plaintiff's theory, the negative covenant could run on without restriction for an indefinite length of time. This might conceivably be for the remainder of Johansson's life should he never agree to a return match with Machen. Plaintiff concedes that the possible advancement in Johansson's position as a fighter was one of the primary inducements on Johansson's part in entering into the contract for the September 14, 1958, fight with Machen. It is difficult to believe that Ahlquist, if he was acting in Johansson's behalf, or Johansson himself, would ever agree to a contract term which might forever bar Johansson from the beneficial enjoyment of that advanced position.

I find that plaintiff has failed to establish that at the time the parties entered into the alleged agreement of September 13, 1958, they intended the negative covenant to run beyond February 14, 1959, the last date upon which the return fight was to be held.

The Injunctive Relief Sought

However, even were I to conclude that the parties intended to restrict Johansson's right to fight indefinitely and until such time as he would agree to engage Machen in a return fight, I would not enforce such a covenant by injunction.

Plaintiff urges upon me that the instant covenant is similar to that category of restrictive covenants ancillary to contracts of employment, where the employee, having gained a professional advantage through the employment, may properly be restrained from using that advantage in such a way as to do serious injury to his employer after the employment has terminated. Plaintiff argues that, by engaging Johansson in the initial fight, he advanced Johansson's professional standing, and that it was, therefore, reasonable for him to restrain Johansson from using that advanced standing to harm Machen.

Defendant, on the other hand, answers that restrictive covenants based upon a promise to refrain from competition are not valid unless they are ancillary either to a contract for the transfer of good will or other property, or to an existing employment or contract of employment. Restatement of Contracts, § 515. Defendant asserts that he was never an employee of Machen's nor was he ever engaged in a transfer of good will.

I need not pass upon the correctness of this proposition of law. I find that the instant covenant even as interpreted by plaintiff is not enforceable by injunction for two reasons:

(1) It is not reasonable in its terms;
(2) The granting of an injunction would inflict serious injury on the defendant, while not providing the plaintiff with the protection he seeks.

(a) *Reasonableness of the terms of the covenant.*

Injunctive relief is an extraordinary remedy to be granted sparingly. Worthington Pump & Machinery Corp. v. Douds, D.C.S.D.N.Y. 1951, 97 F. Supp. 656, 661. Where restrictive covenants have been enforced they have usually been sharply defined as to time and area. See 9 A.L.R. 1468 et seq. and cases cited therein. While it is true that there are cases in which restrictive covenants, running for the life of the one restrained, have been enforced, in such cases the restriction extended to a very limited area only. See Fitch v. Dewes, 2 A.C. 158 (Eng. 1921). The instant covenant is extremely broad geographically. It prevents Johansson from fighting anyone

in the United States and from fighting Floyd Patterson anywhere in the world. If such a restriction is imposed upon Johansson for an indefinite period of time it would be tantamount to denying him the right to advance himself within his trade or to fight in the United States which, it was testified to, offers the most fertile field for fights. I find that this would constitute an unreasonable restraint.

(b) *The ineffectiveness of the remedy sought.*

Finally there is no way that an injunction could be framed to secure for plaintiff the results he seeks without at the same time placing Johansson under an intolerable restriction. "Equity not infrequently withholds relief which it is accustomed to give where it would be burdensome to the defendant and of little advantage to the plaintiff." Di Giovanni v. Camden Fire Ins. Ass'n, 1935, 296 U.S. 64, 71–72, 56 S.Ct. 1, 5, 80 L.Ed. 47.

A restriction running for only a limited period would be ineffective. Let us explore this further. Were I to restrain Johansson from fighting Patterson or fighting anyone in the United States for, let us say, one year, he might well return to Sweden, engage in several contests in Europe during the year, and then, upon the expiration of the injunction, again contract to meet Patterson. This would neither safeguard Machen's reputation nor secure for him a return match.

Nor would a longer term injunction be satisfactory. Were I to restrain Johansson from fighting for two or three years the damage to him would be very great. He would be unable to advance his position by fighting in the United States during a period that might well represent a relatively large portion of his effective ring career. Yet the benefit to plaintiff from such a restriction would be small. Machen would undoubtedly engage in bouts with other fighters during the period when Johansson was under the restriction. Indeed, he has already engaged in one such fight since his defeat by Johansson on September 14, 1958. Each time Machen fought, the outcome would have an impact, for good or ill, upon his standing as a fighter. These subsequent fights, and not any activity upon Johansson's part, would form the basis of the sports world's evaluation of Machen's abilities. Thus, while it may be argued that at this moment Johansson in effect carries Machen's reputation into the ring with him, this is a situation which will be of but short duration.

In summary, I find that plaintiff has failed on a number of grounds to demonstrate his right to the extraordinary relief he seeks:

(1) There is nothing to indicate that the parties intended that the negative covenant was to run beyond February 14, 1959 and in fact it is apparent that the parties intended the restriction to run only until that date.

(2) If the covenant was intended to run indefinitely beyond February 13, 1959, it is unenforceable because it would place an unreasonable restriction upon defendant.

(3) No injunction could be framed which would provide plaintiff with the results he asks without placing defendant under an intolerable and unreasonable burden.

Any one of these grounds would be sufficient in itself to deny plaintiff the relief sought. . . .

Vanguard Recording Society, Inc. v. Kweskin, 276 F. Supp. 563 (S.D.N.Y. 1967)

BONSAL, DISTRICT JUDGE

Plaintiff, Vanguard Recording Society, Inc. (Vanguard), instituted this action in Supreme Court, New York County, based on a contract between it and the defendant Jim Kweskin (Kweskin) dated April 17, 1963. Thereafter, on August 17, 1967, defendants Warner Bros. Records, Inc. (Warner Bros.) and Kweskin removed the action to this court on the ground of diversity of citizenship.

Vanguard moves pursuant to Rule 65, F.R.Civ.P., for a preliminary injunction enjoining:

(a) defendants Kweskin and Warner Bros. from performing any agreements between them for the recording and sale of phonograph records embodying the performances of Kweskin;

(b) defendant Warner Bros. from entering agreements with third persons for the production or distribution of phonograph records embodying the performances of Kweskin, from advertising or using the name and likeness of Kweskin with regard to phonograph records, and from interfering with the exclusive recording agreement that Vanguard claims exists between it and Kweskin;

(c) defendant Warner Bros., its licensees and agents from manufacturing, selling or distributing any phonograph records embodying the performances of Kweskin, and ordering Warner Bros. to destroy any master tape recordings or other material embodying the performances of Kweskin.

Plaintiff's motion for a preliminary injunction is denied.

Kweskin is the leader of a musical group called "Jim Kweskin and The Jug Band," or "Jim Kweskin Jug Band" (hereinafter referred to as the Jug Band). The Jug Band entered into a recording contract with Vanguard dated April 1, 1963 (the Jug Band contract), that provided for an initial term until April 30, 1964 and provided for two options, each permitting Vanguard to extend the contract for one year by giving the Jug Band written notice at least 30 days prior to the expiration of the existing term of the contract. Thereafter, Kweskin entered into the recording contract with Vanguard dated April 17, 1963 (the solo contract), that also provided for an initial term until April 30, 1964 and for two options on the same terms as those in the Jug Band contract. In other respects, the provisions in the Jug Band contract are the same as those in the solo contract. Both contracts provide in part as follows:

1—We [Vanguard] hereby agree to employ your personal services as a recording artist for the purpose of making phonograph records and you [the Jug Band and Kweskin respectively] hereby agree to record solely and exclusively for us according to the terms and provisions of this agreement.

2—. . . A minimum of sixteen 45 or 78 rpm record sides shall be recorded during the initial term of this agreement, and additional recordings shall be made at our election. The musical compositions to be recorded shall be mutually agreed upon between you and us, and each recording shall be subject to our approval as satisfactory for manufacture and sale. We shall have the right to call upon you to repeat any work until a satisfactory master recording has been made. . . .

6—During the term of this agreement you will not perform for the purpose of making phonograph records for any person other than us, . . . and you acknowledge that your services are unique and extraordinary. . . .

11—If, by reason of illness, injury, accident or refusal to work, you fail to perform for us in accordance with the provisions of paragraph 2 of this agreement, . . . without limiting our rights in any such event, we shall have the option without liability to suspend operation of paragraph 2 of this agreement for the duration of any such contingency by giving you written notice thereof; and, at our election, a period of time equal to the duration of such suspension shall be added to the end of the then current period of the term hereof, and then such period and the term of this agreement shall be accordingly extended.

On February 23, 1967, Warner Bros. entered into a recording contract with the Jug Band (the Warner Bros. contract), and since that date, an LP album with recordings of the Jug Band has been made and 11,000 to 12,000 of the albums have been distributed at a cost of some $21,000. According to the affidavit of its Vice-President, Warner Bros. is a financially solvent corporation with cash on hand in excess of $10 million and a gross annual business of some $24 million.

Vanguard contends that, for the reasons hereinafter stated, the solo contract, which had an initial term of one year running until April 30, 1964, is still in effect, and that it is entitled to a preliminary injunction. (Vanguard also claims that the Jug Band contract is still in effect, but in its motion it is relying only on the solo contract.) At oral argument, all parties agreed that determination of the motion for a preliminary injunction did not require an evidentiary hearing.

It is Vanguard's position that Kweskin refused to perform from March 3, 1964 to April 21, 1965 (a period of 1 year, 1 month and 18 days), justifying Vanguard in suspending the solo contract under paragraph 11 and in adding this period to the then current term of the contract, thereby extending it until April 21, 1966. Since the suspension continued after the expiration of the original term of the contract, viz., April 30, 1964, Vanguard argues that for purposes of paragraph 11, the original term did not end on April 30, 1964, but ended when Vanguard lifted the suspension on April 21, 1965, and that it was entitled to add the period of suspension to the new date, April 21, 1965. Vanguard then renewed the solo contract until April 21, 1967 under the first option and until April 21, 1968 under the second option. On January 12, 1967 Vanguard again sus-

pended the solo contract under paragraph 11 and claims that the contract is now in its second year with more than a year remaining before it expires. Vanguard contends that Kweskin ratified its interpretation of the contract by performing under the solo contract on July 11, 19 and 20, 1966 and on August 18 and 22, 1966.

Kweskin, on the other hand, denies that his performances make Vanguard's interpretation of the contract binding on him, and contends that even if the solo contract was still in effect in July and August 1966, two letters from Vanguard to him dated July 27, 1966 and August 22, 1966 released him from any obligations he had thereunder. Vanguard denies that these letters constituted a release, claiming that they were an offer that Vanguard withdrew by letter to Kweskin and the Jug Band dated November 29, 1966.

Vanguard's motion for a preliminary injunction must be denied since the affidavits, exhibits and pleadings before the court evidence issues of fact which can only be resolved at trial. . . .

These issues of fact include, but are not limited to, the following:

(1) If, as appears from the papers before the court, the Warner Bros. contract is with the Jug Band and not with Kweskin individually, does the solo contract give Vanguard the right to enjoin performances by the Jug Band? The solo contract appears to relate only to performances by Kweskin as an individual and not to performances by him as a member of the Jug Band.

(2) Did Kweskin refuse to perform under the solo contract?

(3) If Kweskin did refuse to perform, which he denies, did such refusal end by June 12, 1964 as Kweskin contends or did it continue until April 21, 1965 as Vanguard contends?

(4) Did Kweskin ratify Vanguard's interpretation of the solo contract by performing for Vanguard on July 11, 19 and 20, 1966 and on August 18 and 22, 1966?

(5) If the solo contract was in effect in July and August 1966, did Vanguard, by reason of the letters from Vanguard to Kweskin dated July 27, 1966 and August 22, 1966, release Kweskin from his obligations?

(6) Assuming that Kweskin is still bound by

the solo contract, are his services so unique and extraordinary as to warrant the issuance of an injunction? . . .

Vanguard has not shown that it is reasonably certain to prevail at trial or that it will suffer irreparable injury outweighing the harm that a preliminary injunction is likely to cause to Kweskin and other members of the Jug Band. . . .

There is serious doubt that Vanguard is correct in interpreting paragraph 11 of the solo contract so as to give it the right to extend the contract until April 21, 1966. Under paragraph 11 Vanguard could add a period of time equal to the duration of any suspension to the end of the then current term of the contract. Since the initial term was to expire on April 30, 1964, the period of suspension could only extend the contract until sometime in June 1965 rather than until April 21, 1966. Vanguard so interpreted paragraph 11 in the Jug Band contract (letter of July 8, 1966 from Vanguard to Kweskin and the Jug Band), and this appears more reasonable than the construction here urged. If the suspension extended the solo contract only until June 1965, then on April 21, 1965 the contract would have approximately two months more to run and Vanguard would receive the same period of performance as it would have received had there been no suspension. On the other hand, if the suspension extended the contract until April 21, 1966, then Vanguard would receive a period of performance that was 10 months longer than the period of performance it would have otherwise received.

If Vanguard was entitled to extend the solo contract only until June 1965, then Vanguard did not validly exercise the first and second options to renew and the contract would not presently be in effect.

According to Vanguard's interpretation of the solo contract, it is entitled to turn a one-year contract with two one-year renewal options into a contract that will run for more than five years. If Vanguard's interpretation of the contract is correct, it would appear that the contract was harsh and unreasonable and on equitable grounds the court would decline to issue a preliminary injunction. . . .

Vanguard has not shown that it is reasonably certain to prove at trial that Kweskin ratified its interpretation of the contract . . . or that the letters of July and August 1966 did not release Kweskin.

Even if Vanguard had made a stronger showing of probable success at trial, Vanguard's motion would be denied in the exercise of the court's discretion because Vanguard has not shown that if a preliminary injunction is denied it will suffer irreparable injury outweighing the harm that a preliminary injunction is likely to cause to the defendants and other members of the Jug Band. . . . It appears that Warner Bros. will be able to respond in full to any damages Vanguard proves at trial it is entitled to recover. On the other hand, a preliminary injunction is likely to restrain performances by the other members of the Jug Band as well as Kweskin since they and Kweskin perform as a group. Moreover, it appears that Warner Bros. has already begun the distribution of its album with the recordings of the Jug Band, has entered into contracts for the distribution of the album, and has incurred substantial advertising expenses.

The foregoing constitutes the court's findings of fact and conclusions of law. Rule 52(a), F.R.Civ.P.

Vanguard's motion for a preliminary injunction is denied.

It is so ordered.

American Broadcasting Companies, Inc. v. Wolf, 430 N.Y.S.2d 275 (App.Div. 1980)

SULLIVAN, JUSTICE

At issue is whether, at the instigation of CBS, Warner Wolf, a sportscaster, breached the good faith negotiation and first refusal provisions of his contract with ABC and, if so, whether ABC is entitled to equitable relief. Contrary to Trial Term's finding, we hold that Wolf did indeed breach his contract, although we also conclude that the grant of equitable relief is not warranted.

Wolf had been employed by ABC since 1976 as a sportscaster, and for the past three years he had been the regular sportscaster on WABC–TV, its New York affiliate. In February 1978, he and ABC negotiated an employment agreement which, by virtue of ABC's subsequent exercise of a renewal option, had a termination date of March 5, 1980. The agreement contained what is commonly referred to in the broadcasting industry as a "first negotiation/first refusal" clause. It provided:

> You agree, if we so elect, during the last ninety (90) days prior to the expiration of the extended term of this agreement, to enter into good faith negotiations with us for the extension of this agreement on mutually agreeable terms. You further agree that for the first forty-five (45) days of this negotiation period, you will not negotiate for your services with any other person or company other than WABC–TV or ABC. In the event we are unable to reach an agreement for an extension by the expiration of the extended term hereof, you agree that you will not accept, in any market for a period of three (3) months following expiration of the extended terms of this agreement, any offer of employment as a sportscaster, sports news reporter, commentator, program host, or analyst in broadcasting (including television, cable television, pay television and radio) without first giving us, in writing, an opportunity to employ you on substantially similar terms and you agree to enter into an agreement with us on such terms. We shall have five (5) business days following receipt in which to accept such offer as it is made or make changes that are not, in the aggregate, material; and we shall be required to match the character of employment only in substance and not in every particular. Any such written notice from you to us of an offer received shall specify compensation; term of employment, options to terminate, character of employment, and other principal terms and conditions. . . .

At his request Wolf met with WABC executives in September of 1979 (almost two months before they were required to do so under the contract) to discuss a renewal contract. At that meeting Wolf, who was receiving an annual compensation of $150,000 in the last year of the 1978 agreement, requested a two-year contract at an annual compensation of $400,000 for the first year and $450,000 for the second year. He also wanted the opportunity to do sixteen half-hour football specials. ABC countered with a three-year offer at an annual graduated salary of $325,000, $367,500 and $400,000. ABC would not agree to Wolf's request to do football specials, however, and asked for additional time until October 15th. Wolf, who was anxious to have the matter resolved, agreed.

Unknown to ABC, Wolf met with representatives of CBS on October 4, 1979, and expressed interest in joining CBS, requesting a two-year contract on the same terms he had requested of ABC. At that meeting Wolf discussed the good faith negotiation and first refusal provisions of his ABC contract and, in fact, gave a copy of the first page of his ABC contract containing those provisions to CBS' representatives. On that copy, received in evidence at trial, the following was underscored:

> . . . you agree that you will not accept in any market for a period of three (3) months following expiration . . . any offer of employment as a sportscaster.

Wolf and ABC's representatives met again on October 12th, with Wolf expressing willingness to reduce his salary demands if ABC would commit itself to the sixteen football specials. ABC increased its salary offer, but still refused to agree to the other terms and promised "to get back" to Wolf in ten days. Four days later, on October 16th, unknown to ABC, Wolf again met with CBS' representatives. Wolf's contractual demands were again discussed, as were the terms of the good faith negotiation and first refusal provisions.

Despite the promise ABC did not contact Wolf again until January 2, 1980. At this time Wolf refused to "budge" from his original salary demand of $400,000/$450,000. A subsequent meeting took place on January 17th, and the next day Wolf was given a written proposal which provided for a three year contract at an annual compensation of $400,000/$450,000/$500,000, with a commitment for the sixteen half-hour football specials subject, however, to approval by ABC's board of directors. Wolf advised that he would not accept the offer because of ABC's delay in getting back to him and the imminent expiration of the forty-five day exclusive negotiation period. He also told ABC that his lawyer had advised him to "see what the other options are." Wolf agreed to get back to ABC within a week.

On February 1st, Wolf again met with CBS' representatives and advised them that he wanted to work at CBS at the earliest possible date. By the close of their meeting CBS and Wolf had agreed on the terms of Wolf's employment as the WCBS sportscaster, and the parties shook hands on the deal. No discussion took place about any producer's contract, or of splitting Wolf's employment into two separate contracts, or of Wolf's freedom to accept an off-air position prior to June 4th, the termination date of ABC's right of first refusal. Wolf acknowledges that at the February 1st meeting "the oral understanding was $400,000 for my sportscasting services."

That weekend (February 2–3), a CBS executive called Wolf and advised him that CBS had prepared two different contracts, one a producer's agreement for immediate execution, and the other the sportscaster's agreement. According to Wolf, CBS' executive told him "We're going to divide up the money, one in an on-the-air sportscaster's contract, another in an off-the-air sports producer's contract. We'll divide the $400,000 in equal parts of 200, 200. Second year 225, 225," to which Wolf replied "Fine, it makes no difference to me."

On Monday, February 4, Wolf was presented with two contracts, one an 18-page sportscaster's agreement signed by CBS, annexed to which was a one-page letter, also signed by CBS, providing that in return for $100 paid by Wolf "WCBS–TV agrees to hold open its offer of employment, under the terms and conditions set forth in the attached draft agreement, until June 4, 1980, and WCBS–TV shall not withdraw such offer prior to that date."

The second contract, the producer's agreement, related to Wolf's services as an off-air producer of sports specials, primarily the sixteen half-hour football specials, and was to take effect March 6, 1980, for an initial pay period of thirteen weeks followed by a two-year term. This agreement contained the following "exclusivity" clause:

> Artist's services shall be completely exclusive to CBS during the term of this Agreement, and during such term Artist will not perform services of any nature for, or permit the use of Artist's name, likeness, voice or endorsement by, *any person, firm or corporation, or on* Artist's own account, without Station's prior approval, which approval shall not be unreasonably withheld.

That same day, February 4th, after discussing the exclusivity provision, Wolf signed the producer's agreement, and gave CBS a $100 check for the irrevocable option on the sportscaster's agreement. A salary of $400,000 for the first year, $450,000 for the second year, was divided equally between the two agreements.

The next day, February 5th, Wolf submitted to ABC a letter of resignation, which concluded:

> Since the expiration date does occur in midweek, I would be more than happy to complete the week & work Thursday & Friday, March 6 and 7—providing of course, it is clearly understood, for all concerned, *all legal obligations of the binding contract terminate upon conclusion of the late night news, March 5, 1980.* (Emphasis added.)

At this juncture Wolf had not told ABC about his written contractual arrangements with CBS.

On February 6th, Wolf met again with ABC's representatives and expressed his grievances against WABC and ABC sports. These included ABC's delay in negotiating with him and downgrading of his worth. In his words, he felt he had no future with ABC network sports. ABC responded with various offers and promises, including network exposure. Wolf answered that it was too late; he had made a "gentlemen's agreement," a "moral commitment," and would leave ABC on March 5th, "unless they wanted me to finish the week." In neither this discussion nor a similar one the next day did Wolf mention his February 4th contractual arrangement with CBS, nor did he inform ABC that he was contractually barred by reason of the exclusivity provision in the producer's agreement with CBS from offering his sportscaster's services in any possible renewal of his employment contract with ABC. On February 6th and 7th, thirty days remained under the 90-day good faith negotiation period of Wolf's contract with ABC.

On February 11th, Wolf called Richard O'Leary, an ABC executive, and asked if ABC would compromise on its three-month first refusal right, and allow him to work a portion of that period. On February 19th, after contacting ABC's legal department, O'Leary advised Wolf that ABC wanted him to work during this 90-day period but that it "was unwilling to waive any of its contractual rights."

On February 19, Wolf, at his attorney's suggestion, sent ABC a handwritten letter "embodying the terms of the contract I [want]" for the 90-day first refusal period, stating: "Number two, it is also clear, that *effective March 6, 1980, or there-*

after, I am free to *accept* an offer to work elsewhere, upon the expiration of the 90 day period, which is June 4, 1980." . . . (Emphasis added.)

Thereafter, after consultation with Wolf's attorney, a letter agreement covering Wolf's employment for the 90-day first refusal period was drafted by an ABC lawyer. It provided in pertinent part:

> The term shall be for the period from March 6, 1980 through May 28, 1980 at 12:00 midnight. It is understood and agreed that *on or after June 4, 1980,* you may accept an offer of employment with anyone of your choosing and immediately begin performing on-air services. It is further understood and agreed that this agreement shall in no way affect our mutual rights and obligations pursuant to the agreement between us dated February 1, 1978. (Emphasis added.)

Wolf signed the letter agreement on February 22nd on the advice of his attorney. The second sentence of the agreement was a concession to Wolf's attorney, who wanted it understood that Wolf was free to go elsewhere, with no strings attached, at the end of the 90-day period. In his pre-trial deposition, used at trial, Wolf testified that before signing the letter agreement he asked what was meant by the sentence "[i]t is further understood and agreed that this agreement shall in no way affect our mutual rights and obligations pursuant to the agreement between us dated February 1, 1978," and that he was told "all it means is that you cannot sign an agreement, on the air agreement, during these ninety days." Wolf replied, "Fine that's no problem. Let's sign it."

Both parties thereafter performed their respective obligations under the February 22nd letter-agreement. Although suspicious that Wolf might have made a deal in violation of its right of first refusal, ABC did not commence this action until May 6th, by which time Wolf's anticipated switch to CBS was a matter of public knowledge.

In its complaint ABC sought injunctive relief only, seeking to bar Wolf from working at WCBS–TV and specific performance of its 1976 contract by a direction that Wolf submit CBS' offer of employment to ABC to be matched. In fact, at trial, both in its opening statement and to a lesser extent in its summation, ABC abjured any claim for damages. The essence of ABC's complaint is that Wolf and CBS negotiated a contract for Wolf's services as a sportscaster on WCBS–TV, the principal competitor of WABC–TV, in violation of ABC's contract with Wolf, and that CBS, with actual knowledge of the ABC contract and its terms, induced Wolf to make the deal and breach the good faith negotiation and first refusal clauses of that contract.

A preliminary injunction was issued enjoining CBS from employing Wolf as a sportscaster on WCBS–TV and preliminarily enjoining Wolf from so entering CBS' employ, with a direction for an immediate trial which was concluded on June 3rd after this court refused to intervene. In a decision filed June 9, 1980, Trial Term dismissed the complaint but continued the preliminary injunction for 48 hours. A Justice of this court refused to continue the preliminary injunction pending appeal but granted ABC's application for an expedited appeal, with the merits of which we are now confronted.

We take judicial notice that after the close of this record and expiration of the preliminary injunction Wolf commenced performing sportscaster's services for WCBS, and continues to do so, while WABC carries on with a replacement for Wolf, whose services, we are told, are unique.

In our opinion, the evidence adduced at trial amply supports the conclusion that, at CBS' instigation, Wolf breached the first refusal provision of the ABC contract. Pursuant to that provision, Wolf could not, prior to June 4, 1980, accept any offer of employment as a sportscaster "without first giving [ABC] in writing, an opportunity to employ [him] on substantially similar terms and [Wolf] agree[d] to enter into an agreement with [ABC] on such terms."

In varying forms, the right of first refusal is used throughout the radio and television industry as a device in aid of the broadcaster-employer's retention of the services of major talent in whom the broadcaster has made a significant investment. The contractual right of first refusal, also known as a "right to match," is a valuable right which has enjoyed the protection of the courts. . . .

Even though a grantee's right of first refusal may never ripen into a right absolute, the grantor of such right owes the grantee "the obligation of dealing in good faith." . . .

Analysis of the evidence discloses that on February 1, 1980 Wolf and CBS had orally agreed that CBS would engage Wolf as a sportscaster for two years, at an annual compensation of $400,000 for the first year of the contract and $450,000 for the second year. The subject of a separate producer's role or producer's contract or splitting the $400,000/450,000 compensation between two separate roles, sportscaster and producer, was never discussed. The agreement provided that Wolf would be paid for his sportscasting services. It was not until later, sometime over the February 23 weekend, that CBS, whose executives had obtained a copy of ABC's first refusal provision from Wolf in October 1979, advised Wolf that the agreement would be covered by two contracts.

On February 4, 1980 when Wolf signed the producer's agreement, he did so with full knowledge of its exclusivity provision which precluded him from rendering services of any nature for anyone or appearing on television in any capacity for the two-year term of his contract, which was to become effective on March 6, 1980, the first day of the three-month first refusal period of his contract with ABC. That same day Wolf, apparently fully satisfied with all of the terms and conditions in the 18-page sportscaster's agreement, obtained a signed letter from CBS giving him an irrevocable option until June 4th to sign that agreement, thus securing the sportscaster's position at CBS immediately upon the expiration of ABC's right of first refusal.

This record makes apparent that the producer's agreement was, in fact, one-half of a contrived bifurcation of the sportscaster's agreement, already orally reached on February 1st, and that its all-inclusive exclusivity provision was the mechanism utilized by CBS to obtain, prior to the expiration of ABC's right of first refusal and in avoidance of it, Wolf's commitment to become the CBS sportscaster on June 4, 1980. Thus, CBS accomplished its goal of securing Wolf's sportscasting services on February 4th without the necessity of having Wolf actually sign a sportscaster's agreement until ABC's right of first refusal had expired. By so arranging the February 4, 1980 agreements, with knowledge of ABC's right of first refusal, CBS induced Wolf's breach of his 1978 contract with ABC. . . .

In concluding that the execution of the producer's agreement and the simultaneous grant of an irrevocable option to Wolf to enter into a sportscaster's contract on June 4, 1980 did not violate ABC's rights under the first refusal clause because Wolf had not, on February 4th, formally accepted CBS' offer of employment as a sportscaster, Trial Term lauded form over substance and ignored compelling evidence that Wolf and CBS had structured the February 4th agreements so as to circumvent ABC's right of first refusal. Wolf's own testimony made clear that he never considered the possibility of working for CBS only as a producer, and not as an on-air sportscaster. . . .

Moreover, at the time the February 4th agreements were executed, 30 days remained in the 90-day good faith negotiation period provided in the 1978 ABC contract. By virtue of the all-inclusive exclusivity provision contained in the CBS producer's contract, Wolf was contractually precluded from accepting any ABC offer, no matter how attractive. Thus, by entering into the producer's contract, Wolf had deprived ABC of its right under the 1978 contract to his good faith negotiations for the extension of that contract. . . .

Contrary to defendants' contentions, we do not find that the February 22nd letter agreement between Wolf and ABC covering the extended 90-day work period extinguished ABC's right of first refusal. Although this agreement was concededly beneficial to both parties—ABC had the use of Wolf's services during the "May sweeps," an important rating period in the television industry, and Wolf, on the other hand, would not be forced to remain "on the beach" for three months—it was Wolf, not ABC, who initiated the proposal that he work beyond the March 5th expiration of his contract.

Wolf conceded that when ABC's O'Leary accepted his offer to work for the additional 90 days he told Wolf that ABC was unwilling to waive any of its contractual rights. Wolf further admitted that he understood this to mean he could not accept a sportscaster's offer before June 4th. The documentary evidence is consistent with this position. In his handwritten letter of February 19th to CBS, Wolf wanted it made clear that "effective March 6, 1980, or thereafter, I am free to accept an offer to work elsewhere, upon the expiration of the 90 day period." His letter concluded with the provision "If this summarizes your understanding of our 90 day agreement, please show your acceptance by signing below." Needless to say, Wolf never obtained ABC's consent to this proposed agreement. Instead, he signed the February 22nd letter agreement which explicitly provided that "this agreement shall in no way affect our mutual rights and obligations pursuant to the agreement between us dated February 1, 1978." Thus, in language which is unmistakably clear and not in conflict with the preceding sentence that "on or after June 4, 1980, you may accept an offer of employment with anyone of your choosing and immediately begin on-air services"—a right which Wolf had under the 1978 contract—the parties were merely maintaining the status quo. The sentence allowing Wolf to accept an offer after June 4th was, no doubt, felt by Wolf to be essential to preclude the claim that the three-month period of first refusal would run anew by virtue of his agreement to work until June 4th.

Having established that Wolf breached the good faith negotiation/first refusal provisions of the ABC contract by accepting the February 4, 1980 CBS offer, the issue remaining is whether ABC is entitled to equitable relief. . . .

Among the equitable remedies which ABC suggests is specific performance, that is, affording ABC the right to match the CBS offer. Precedent exists. It has been held that once a grantor is willing to accept a particular offer, he must afford his grantee the opportunity to accept the terms of the offer before contracting with anyone else, and if the grantor violates this obligation, the grantee will be awarded specific performance if it matches the third party's offer. . . .

In the alternative ABC asks for injunctive relief. It seeks to restrain Wolf, for no longer than the two year term of his February 4, 1980 agreement with CBS, from working for CBS as a sportscaster unless and until he gives ABC a written opportunity to employ him on substantially similar terms as those provided in the February 4, 1980 CBS agreement. ABC's acceptance of such offer within five days thereafter and Wolf's execution of an agreement with ABC on those terms would terminate the injunction. Conversely, Wolf's failure either to make the offer or enter into the agreement would continue the injunction restraining him from working for CBS for up to two years.

Against CBS, assertedly its principal rival, ABC seeks an injunction, *inter alia*, restraining it from employing Wolf as a sportscaster until he complies with the terms of the injunction issued against him and from enforcing any rights under the February 4, 1980 agreement and its progeny. The rationale underlying such relief, if granted, may be simply stated: "No one shall be permitted to profit by his own fraud, or to take advantage of his own wrong. . . ." (*Riggs v. Palmer*, 115 N.Y. 506, 511–512, 22 N.E. 188, 190.)

Of course, insofar as these remedies are applied in the factual setting presented, no distinction exists between an injunction and order of specific performance. An order to perform is no more than an injunction in mandatory form directed to the person of the defendant. But, irrespective of whatever remedies are available, this is not, in our view, a case where equitable relief is either warranted or appropriate.

It has long been a principle of equity that the performance of contracts for personal services depends upon the skill, volition and fidelity of the person who has engaged to perform such services and that it is impracticable, if not impossible, for a court to supervise or secure the proper and faithful performance of such contracts. . . . Thus, as a general rule equity will not enforce performance of contracts for personal services. . . .

While equity has fashioned injunctive relief in other right of first refusal cases . . . we are unable to find any instance where personal services were involved. Aside from equity's disdain for the specific enforcement of contracts for personal services, specific enforcement of ABC's right to match CBS' offer under the first refusal clause and ultimate award of the contract to ABC is all the more impractical as a remedy here in light of Wolf's stated reluctance to continue working for ABC. As Trial Term noted, this lawsuit has only exacerbated an already strained relationship, and Wolf is now apparently adamant. No cogent reason is shown to break with precedent and to order an unwilling party to perform services of a personal nature, especially since we remain unconvinced that ABC does not have an adequate remedy at law for any damages suffered as a result of Wolf's breach.

In arguing inadequacy of the remedy at law, ABC stresses that Wolf's services are unique, that it introduced him to the New York market, and that it expended considerable sums in advertising him to the public, secure in the knowledge that the right to match provision of its agreement with Wolf would afford it a fair opportunity to retain his services under a new contract. Of course, if the services to be rendered are of an unusual or unique nature, then the situation is more clearly one in which an adequate remedy at law does not exist. In such cases a rule, generally traced to the English case of *Lumley v. Wagner* (1 DeG., M. & G. 604, 42 Eng.Rep. 687), decided in 1852, has developed. Where a contract for such unique services contains a negative covenant by the one who is to render the services that he will not render like services for anyone else during the contract term, equity will enjoin the breach of this negative covenant, if no adequate remedy at law is available and the contract is fair and reasonable. . . .

Injunctive relief is especially appropriate where the breach of the negative covenant entails a damage by itself apart from the breach of the affirmative covenant. (See Pound, Progress of the Law—Equity, 33 Harv.L.Rev., 420, 440 [1920].) Thus, in recognition of the harm that a unique performer can cause an employer by working for a rival in breach of his contract, our courts have restrained newspaper columnists, athletes, actors, singers and other performers from working for the new employer for periods ranging from one to three years or seasons. . . .

But even where an employer seeks to enjoin the performance of a unique service by an ex-employee for a competitor, an injunction will be granted only where the covenant sought to be enforced is reasonable. . . .

With this principle as a guide we conclude that the imposition of any restraint on Wolf performing sportscasting services for CBS would be inappropriate. The restrictive covenant in the 1978 contract is an integral part of the first refusal provision and is limited to a term of three months following expiration of the contract, during which period ABC had the right to match any other offer received by Wolf and to employ him on terms substantially similar to those offered by a third party. Thus, even were restraint appropriate,

three months, and not the term of the CBS contract, would be the measure of the length of any restrictions against Wolf working for a competitor.

Moreover, the first refusal clause was not a restrictive covenant in the true sense. Rather, it was a three-month moratorium on Wolf's employment as a sportscaster *"in any market"* (emphasis added), and, coupled with ABC's right to match during the same period, was obviously intended as the bargaining tool by which to force Wolf into extending his contract with ABC. If Wolf did not renew he would have to remain "on the beach" for the three months following the expiration of his contract, an absence which, given the ever changing tastes of the viewing public, might prove fatal to the career of a less imposing media personality. Arguably, of course, Wolf's absence would serve another purpose. His successor at ABC would have three months, free of the competition of Wolf at CBS, in which to cultivate the viewing public's taste. In any event, with formal notice that Wolf would not renew, ABC opted to utilize his talents during the May ratings sweeps, and waived its right to place him in television limbo for the same period of time.

In such circumstances, the grant of equitable relief, the effect of which is to force Wolf to continue a strained relationship with ABC, would be highly inappropriate. Although, in light of our holding, we need not reach the issue of whether ABC comes to us with unclean hands and laches, we note that we do not find factual support in the record for Trial Term's finding that ABC was barred from equitable relief on these grounds.

ABC has also argued that if we cannot grant some form of appropriate equitable relief, we should remit this matter to Trial Term for a hearing on damages. As already noted, ABC failed to submit any proof on this issue. While a court of equity may award money damages, even though none were sought, when it is unable to grant the specific relief demanded . . . a remand to take proof on damages is not warranted. This action was commenced before Wolf had ever performed a single sportscast for CBS, and even before the expiration of the three-month first refusal period, during which ABC would have been without his services had he elected to remain "on the beach." It was the function of this lawsuit to secure the continued services of a valued performer, and it seems fairly obvious that no thought was given to damages, if indeed any have been or will ever be sustained as a result of Wolf's departure. ABC may, of course, if it be so advised, commence a new action at law. We note, in passing, that the acts of which ABC complains are of recent occurrence, so that the statute of limitations is not a consideration.

Accordingly, the judgment, Supreme Court, New York County, entered June 9, 1980, dismissing the complaint, should be affirmed, without costs or disbursements.

Judgment, Supreme Court, New York County, entered on June 9, 1980, affirmed without costs and without disbursements.

All concur except Kupferman, J., who concurs in the result and Murphy, P.J., who dissents in separate Opinions.

KUPFERMAN, JUSTICE (CONCURRING IN THE RESULT)

The majority opinion fairly sets forth the facts. However, as to the law, I can agree only with the conclusion. An injunction and adherence to the terms of the employment agreement would be warranted were it not for the letter agreement of February 22, 1980 drafted by the plaintiff, which I am satisfied released the defendant Wolf (and therefore the defendant CBS) "on and after June 4th, 1980."

MURPHY, PRESIDING JUSTICE (DISSENTING)

I agree with the majority's finding that defendant Wolf breached the 1978 contract with ABC. However, I disagree with its conclusion that ABC is without remedy even though Wolf is in breach of that 1978 contract. This Court should exercise its equitable powers to grant ABC injunctive relief.

In the exercise of discretion, which is exercised with caution and reluctance, a court of equity will, in a proper case, enforce a negative covenant against the performance of services elsewhere, if the services of a defendant under a contract are so peculiar, special, unique, extraordinary and irreplaceable that a breach of the contract will result in irreparable injury to the plaintiff, and there is no adequate remedy at law. It should be stressed that a negative covenant need not be expressly set forth in a contract; it may be implicitly found in a contract. . . .

In view of the substantial salary that CBS has agreed to pay defendant Wolf under the producer's and sportscaster's agreements, CBS can not seriously contest the fact that Wolf's services are unique. Moreover, paragraph 6(a) of the producer's agreement confirms the unique character of Wolf's services in the following language:

> 6. (a) Artist acknowledges that his services and the rights and privileges granted to CBS hereunder are unique; and CBS shall be entitled to injunctive and other equitable relief to prevent any breach of this Agreement by Artist.

In determining whether injunctive relief is appropriate, the next question presented is whether ABC has an adequate remedy at law. As the majority observes, ABC did not prove monetary damages at trial. This failure on ABC's part is not an indication that it has not been damaged; rather it is a sign that ABC's damages are very difficult to prove.

At this early juncture, ABC can only speculate as to how its ratings might be adversely affected by the loss of Wolf's services. Even at a much later date, ABC will have a formidable task in establishing that its ratings suffered as a direct result of Wolf's defection. Television ratings are influenced and ultimately set by countless variables. The loss of Wolf's services is but one variable that is not easily measured.

The 1978 contract between Wolf and ABC does not contain a negative covenant prohibiting him from working for other television stations if he does not honor the "matching" provision in that contract. Nonetheless, a negative covenant must be read into that contract if ABC's rights thereunder are to be effectively protected. . . . Under the terms of that 1978 contract, ABC has a right to match, in substance, any offer made to Wolf in the three month period after its expiration. As the majority found, Wolf not only received an offer, he accepted an offer prior to the expiration of the 1978 contract. This Court, in the exercise of its equitable powers, should give ABC the benefit of the contract and permit it to match, in substance, the terms of Wolf's agreements with CBS. For purposes of the "matching" provision, ABC must be required to make an offer that is substantially similar to the combined terms of the sportscaster's and producer's agreements.

Therefore, ABC should be given five business

days to match the combined offer made by CBS to Wolf. If ABC makes an appropriate offer within that five day period, Wolf has the choice of either accepting or rejecting it. If he chooses to reject the offer, he should be enjoined from competing against ABC in the New York City area for the two year period of that contractual offer. . . .

NOTE _____

1. Negative covenants in entertainment agreements may extend for a stated period after the termination of the personal services contract. Recording agreements typically provide that the artist will not re-record material recorded for the record label for a certain period of time, generally a number of years succeeding both the recording of the material and the termination of the recording agreement.

While not as common today, recording agreements in the past provided that the artist would not record *any* material for any company for a period of time following the completion of the initial contract. In *Okeh Phonograph Corp. v. Armstrong,* 63 F.2d 636 (9th Cir. 1933), the exclusivity provision of the record contract between the label and Louis Armstrong prevented Armstrong from recording for any other record label for the term of the agreement, plus three months. The contract terminated on May 7, 1933, and on May 8, 1933, the legendary trumpet player entered a new agreement with RCA Records.

An injunction was denied the plaintiff on the grounds that the duration and exclusivity provisions of the contract were too ambiguous and uncertain to enforce. The court did not address the issue of undue restraint under California statute (see Section 1.54). The applicable clause deemed overly ambiguous was as follows:

> The period of engagement is defined in the contract as "The time and any extensions thereof embraced by the date hereof (April 22, 1928) and the number of years hereinabove stated subsequent to the first acceptance of a master record (which the parties agree occurred on May 7, 1927), the duration of the prolongations aforesaid and any extensions thereof, and any periods of time during which the Artist renders service to OKEH under any agreements made subsequent hereto." So far as material, the paragraph which grants plaintiff the renewal option, is as follows: "OKEH shall have the option to prolong the time and any extensions thereof embraced by the date hereof and the number of years hereinabove stated subsequent. The duration of such prolongation shall be measured by the date of the termination of the aforesaid time or any extensions thereof and like number of years as hereinabove stated subsequent. OKEH shall have the option for four (4) successive years to prolong for one (1) additional year the time last named and any extensions thereof in like manner, measure and effect as herein specified."

1.54 California Injunction Statutes

In reviewing the various statutory provisions of applicable states, most particularly California, the company's ability to enforce a personal services contract must be considered when the contract is initially entered into. Under certain statutes, an artist may have a right to terminate the contract for cause, which would obviously relieve the artist of the duty to perform under that contract. This remedy is to be distinguished from an artist's ability to cease performing and remain free from an injunction on other statutory grounds.

The collective California statutes may represent to the artist the only realistic opportunity to terminate the personal services contract prematurely and, likewise, may create an enormous number of pitfalls that the company may be subject to that ultimately may restrict or prevent enforcement of the agreement.

Two sections of the California statutes, California Code of Civil Procedure § 526 and California Civil Code § 3423, are collectively referred to as the "$6,000 per year statute." The rule basically states that in order to provide the basis for injunctive relief, a contract must be in writing, provide for services that are unique and extraordinary, and provide for a minimum compensation at the rate of not less than $6,000 per year.

It is obvious that, without injunctive relief, the validity, importance, and position of the exclusive personal services contract in the entertainment industry are significantly undermined. While the motion picture studio, record company, music publishing company, or television studio may still seek damages against the breaching artist, a negative injunction may be the only effective remedy in ultimately enforcing the personal services contract.

It is important to note that the $6,000 per year rule is not a mandatory condition placed on all employers but, ultimately, inclusion of that clause in all entertainment service contracts would have a significant economic effect on the entertainment industry and its member personnel.

We consider first two important sections of the California Civil Code. Then we turn to cases that have applied the $6,000 per year statutes.

§ 3390. *Obligations not specifically enforceable*

The following obligations cannot be specifically enforced:

1. An obligation to render personal service;
2. An obligation to employ another in personal service;
3. An agreement to perform an act which the party has no power lawfully to perform when required to do so;
4. An agreement to procure the act or consent of the wife of the contracting party, or of any other third person; or,
5. An agreement, the terms of which are not sufficiently certain to make the precise act which is to be done clearly ascertainable.

§ 3423. *Injunction; circumstances requiring denial*

An injunction cannot be granted: . . .

Fifth—To prevent the breach of a contract, other than a contract in writing for the rendition or furnishing of personal services from one to another where the minimum compensation for such service is at the rate of not less than six thousand dollars per annum and where the promised service is of a special, unique, unusual, extraordinary or intellectual character, which gives it peculiar value the loss of which cannot be reasonably or adequately compensated in damages in an action at law, the performance of which would not be specifically enforced; *provided, however,* than an injunction may be granted to prevent the breach of a contract entered into between any nonprofit cooperative corporation or association and a member or stockholder thereof in respect to any provision regarding the sale or delivery to the corporation or association of the products produced or acquired by such member or stockholder. . . .

Foxx v. Williams, 244 Cal. App. 2d 223, 52 Cal. Rptr. 896 (1966)

FILES, P. J.

Plaintiff Redd Foxx, an entertainer in nightclubs and on phonograph records, brought this action against Walter D. Williams, Jr., Dootone Record Manufacturing, Inc., and others, for a declaration of rights, accounting, and other relief under a written contract called "Artist Recording Royalty Agreement." Dootone cross-complained against Foxx to recover moneys paid by mistake, for damages, and for an injunction to prohibit breaches of the contract. After a court trial, judgment was entered declaring the rights of the parties, awarding a money judgment in favor of cross-complainant for overpayments, and enjoining Foxx. We have here Foxx' appeal from the judgment.

In the latter part of 1955, while Foxx was performing at the Club Ossis in Los Angeles, defendant Williams suggested that he be allowed to record Foxx' comedy routine there and find out if phonograph records made therefrom would be salable. Foxx had been a performer for many years but had never made a successful phonograph record. His one previous attempt had sold about 40 copies. Williams was established in the record manufacturing and distributing business, being the president and sole stockholder of defendant Dootone Record Manufacturing, Inc.

The market tests were encouraging, and on January 6, 1956, Foxx and Dootone entered into a written agreement, which will be referred to as the first contract. It stated "we [Dootone] hereby employ you [Foxx] for the purpose of making phonograph records," and provided for a royalty to Foxx of 2 percent of the distributor price. As a minimum, four sides were to be recorded, and additional recordings were to be made at Dootone's election. The term of the contract was one year from the date of execution, with the option in Dootone to renew for an additional two years.

The option in the first contract was not exercised. On January 28, 1957, the parties executed another writing similar in form to the first, but calling for a royalty of 3 percent of the distributor price. This contract also expired at the end of one year, the option not having been exercised.

On April 4, 1958, the parties entered into the third contract, this time for a term of five years, with the option to extend for two years more. This contract provided that "a minimum of 12 78 RPM record sides, or the equivalent thereof shall be recorded, and additional recordings shall be made at our [Dootone's] election." The royalty was 3 percent of the list price (as distinguished from 3 percent of the distributor price provided for in the second contract). The distributor price is approximately one-half of the list price.

To place in context the problems of interpretation which are involved here, the authorship of those writings should be mentioned. The first and second contracts were on a mimeographed form, with the royalty rate and minimum number of record sides typed in. Williams testified that he obtained this form from another manufacturer and changed only the name of the company. Williams further testified:

"Q. Now with respect to Contract 3, who made that one?

"A. I did, after research and inquiry in the industry.

"Q. Did you consult an attorney?

"A. No.

"Q. Used somebody else's form again?

"A. No, I consulted a number of contracts that were in use at the time and consolidated the items that I thought—

"Q. Took what you thought would be the best from each one?

"A. Yes, that is right."

Between April 4, 1958, and April 6, 1961, Foxx recorded for Dootone under the third contract 16 longplaying records, 26 extended play records and 5 single records. This was many times over the minimum specified in the agreement. It has been stipulated that Dootone has given the notice required to extend the stated term of this contract for its sixth and seventh years.

Commencing in 1956, Dootone submitted to Foxx semiannual statements purporting to show the number of copies sold of each record and the royalty due. Each statement was accompanied by a check for the balance due as shown by the statement. Foxx made no effort to verify the accuracy of any of these statements except that on one occasion in 1957 an accountant employed by him for tax purposes examined some of Dootone's books.

In early 1961, on a trip east, Foxx talked to some distributors who told him how well his records were selling and who, as he testified, "just sort of aroused my curiosity as to whether I was getting a fair shake and that's how I got started in the thing." Foxx consulted an attorney, and this action was filed April 6, 1961. . . .

The trial court found that Foxx had entered into an agreement with another manufacturer to make recordings as soon as he was legally free to do so, and concluded that, unless restrained, Foxx would make records for a manufacturer other than Dootone. The findings of fact also contain this statement:

That Cross Complainant has suffered damage and injury by reason of Cross Defendant's refusal to make or produce recordings since April 6, 1961, but that such damages are exceedingly difficult to compute and that it would be more equitable and to the best interests of both parties to extend the term of the contract of April 4, 1958, by a term equal to that period during which Cross Defendant has refused to perform rather than to impose damages for such failure. That the total period during which Cross Defendant has refused to perform is two years, five months and ten days. That the contract of April 4, 1958, provided, *inter alia*, that should Plaintiff Redd Foxx fail to make recordings at times designated by Defendant Dootone Record Manufacturing, Inc. the then current recording year might be extended for such period of time as shall elapse until the Plaintiff Redd Foxx renders the required services.

The judgment, which was entered October 9, 1963, includes an injunction in the following language:

It is Further Considered, Ordered and Adjudged that Plaintiff and Cross Defendant Redd Foxx be, and he is hereby restrained and enjoined during the term of the contract of April 4, 1958, as extended to and including September 14, 1967, from making sound recordings for any other person, firm or corporation, or from making, distributing, selling or authorizing any other person, firm or corporation, to make, distribute or sell any phonograph records, or from recording for himself or any other person, firm or corporation any sound recordings or from using his name, likeness or any other identification in connection with any sound recordings except those made and produced by Defendant Dootone Record Manufacturing, Inc. That such injunction shall remain in full force and effect only so long as royalties earned by Plaintiff under the contract of April 4, 1958, equal or exceed the sum of $3,000 for any royalty period beginning with the royalties due on December 31, 1963, and that if on that date or thereafter royalties fall below the sum of $3,000 for any six-month royalty period as that term is defined in said contract then such injunction shall be dissolved and shall be of no further force or effect but the dissolution of said injunction, in the event it occurs, shall be without prejudice to any other remedies available to Defendant Dootone Record Manufacturing, Inc. as provided by operation of law or under the terms of the contract of April 4, 1958.

After Foxx had perfected his appeal in this court he filed a petition for writ of supersedeas on August 13, 1965, to stay the enforcement of that injunction. On August 20, 1965, this court made its order staying the enforcement of the injunction until further order of this court. . . .

The Injunction

Civil Code Section 3423 provides in part:

> An injunction cannot be granted: . . .
> Fifth—To prevent the breach of a contract, other than a contract in writing for the rendition or furnishing of personal services from one to another where the minimum compensation for such service is at the rate of not less than six thousand dollars per annum and where the promised service is of a special, unique, unusual, extraordinary or intellectual character, which gives it peculiar value the loss of which cannot be reasonably or adequately compensated in damages in an action at law, the performance of which would not be specifically enforced; . . .

Similar language appears in Code of Civil Procedure section 526.

It is a familiar rule that a contract to render personal services cannot be specifically enforced. (Civ. Code, § 3390; *Lyon v. Goss*, 19 Cal. 2d 659, 674 [123 P. 2d 11]; *Poultry Producers etc. Inc. v. Barlow*, 189 Cal. 278, 288 [208 P. 93]; see 5A Corbin on Contracts, § 1204, p. 398.) It follows that the breach of such a contract may not be enjoined except in cases falling within the exception provided for in the quoted statute. The 1958

contract recites that the artist's performances "are of a special, unique, unusual, extraordinary and intellectual character which gives them a peculiar value," and at pretrial the parties agreed that such characterization was correct. There remains the question whether this is a contract "where the minimum compensation for such service is at the rate of not less than six thousand dollars per annum."

At the trial the parties stipulated to the amounts which Foxx had received as royalties each year from 1956 through 1962, but these figures were not broken down to show what portion was paid for recordings made under the 1958 contract. The royalty statement for the six months ending June 30, 1963, which was the accounting period immediately preceding the trial, showed total royalties for the period as $2,682.27, less advances and charges of $156.

We do not place our decision upon the absence of proof of the amount of royalties earned under the 1958 contract. In our opinion this royalty contract does not meet the requirements of the injunction statute even though it should ultimately appear that the royalties earned, over any given period, should exceed the rate of $6,000 per year.

An injunction which forbids an artist to accept new employment may be a harsh and powerful remedy. The monetary limitation in the statute is intended to serve as a counterweight in balancing the equities. The Legislature has concluded that an artist who is not entitled to receive a minimum of $6,000 per year by performing his contract should not be subjected to this kind of economic coercion. Under the statutory scheme, an artist who is enjoined from accepting new employment will at least have the alternative of earning $6,000 or more per year by performing his old contract.

The trial court's solution to the problem was to grant the injunction for only so long as the royalties for each half year equaled $3,000. This means that the artist is enjoined for 7½ months at a time (6 months plus the 45 days thereafter which the contract allows for the preparation of the royalty statement) without any assurance of earning anything. This is not what the statute calls for.

The portion of the judgment which enjoins Foxx must be deleted.

The elimination of the injunction does not

require a remand of the case to the trial court for consideration of a new remedy for the breach of contract. Although the trial court made a finding that Dootone had suffered damage, there was no evidence to support it. Under the circumstances the most that Dootone would be entitled to for Foxx' breach would be nominal damages. A judgment should not be reversed simply to permit such a recovery. . . .

Extension of the Contract

Based upon the stipulated fact that Foxx had "failed and refused to make any recordings . . . from and after April 6, 1961," the trial court computed the period of his refusal, to the date the trial ended, as two years, five months and ten days, and added it to the term of the 1958 contract. The judgment declares that the contract of April 4, 1958, is in effect to and including September 14, 1967.

This portion of the judgment is erroneous for two independent reasons, which will be discussed separately.

The first is that there is nothing in the 1958 contract or elsewhere in the evidence which would justify extending the term during which Foxx is required to record for Dootone and abstain from recording for anyone else. Paragraph 12 of the agreement provides that "during the term" the artist will not record for anyone other than Dootone, but this negative covenant contains no language calling for an extension of the term or of the period of exclusivity.

The duty of Foxx to make recordings during the term of the 1958 contract is set forth in the following language:

> These creative sound productions, recordings or masters, are to be made during the term of this contract and a minimum of 12 78 RPM record sides, or the equivalent thereof, shall be recorded, and additional recordings shall be made at our [Dootone's] election.

It is undisputed that recordings exceeding the minimum had been made prior to the commencement of the action, and there is no evidence of any "election" by Dootone to make recordings other than those which were made.

The trial court's remarks indicate it relied upon paragraph 15 of the 1958 contract which reads as follows:

15. Should Artist, for any reason whatever, be unavailable for the making of recordings at the times designated by the Company as herein provided, or fail to make recordings at such times, the then current "recording year" hereof may be extended by the Company for such period of time as shall elapse until Artist renders the required services for the Company. The Company shall have at least thirty (30) days' notice before the Company is required to arrange for the making by Artist of the recordings for which Artist was unavailable or which Artist failed to make as aforesaid.

Preliminarily it is noted that the words "the then current 'recording year' " are not defined in the contract, nor are they used elsewhere, except in paragraph 17, the force majeure clause, which will be discussed later. This incongruity of language is explained by Williams' testimony that he consulted a number of contracts used by others and "consolidated the items" that he thought were the best in each. To make paragraph 15 applicable it is necessary to interpret "the then current 'recording year' " to mean the term of the contract.

The form of paragraph 15 suggests that it was lifted from a contract in which the artist was obligated to make a determinable number of recordings within a "recording year," but at times designated by the company. The paragraph provides that if the artist fails to make recordings "at such times," the "recording year" may be extended "for such period of time as shall elapse until Artist renders the required services. . . ."

Such extension is not necessarily for a period equal to the time during which the artist was in default. Rather it is for the period which shall elapse until the artist "renders the required services." The distinction is a substantial one.

It is obvious, from the nature of the business, that the parties did not contemplate that Foxx would be engaged continuously in making records for the entire seven-year term of the contract. The evidence shows that each recording session was about three hours in length, and Foxx testified that he needed eight to ten days to prepare his material for each recording session. The parties must have recognized that they had time to produce a great many more recordings than the market could absorb. The actual number which could be made and sold profitably was not a matter that could be determined when the contract was written. Hence the parties left it to Dootone to call for more recordings as its business judgment dictated. Foxx' obligation under the contract was not to render a given number of days, weeks or years of service, but to make as many records during the seven-year period as Dootone elected to finance, produce and market.

The language of paragraph 15 may be contrasted with the force majeure clause, which is paragraph 17. The latter provides that in the event of fire, strikes, et cetera, the company may suspend its obligations and "A number of days equal to the total of all such days of suspension shall be added to the then current 'recording year.'"

The extension under paragraph 17, unlike paragraph 15, is for a period measured by the period of nonperformance.

Since an extension under paragraph 15 is only for the period which shall elapse "until Artist renders the required services," it is necessary to inquire what are the required services. Since Foxx had made more than the minimum, he was not obligated to make any more unless Dootone so elected, of which there is no evidence. Foxx' refusal to perform after April 6, 1961, constituted an anticipatory breach of the contract, which justified Dootone's suing him immediately on the contract. . . . But without proof that Dootone had elected to make any more recordings, the extension provided for in paragraph 15 was not applicable at all. . . .

The judgment is reversed and the action remanded to the superior court with directions to determine the balance then due as between plaintiff and Dootone, under the three contracts, using, so far as applicable, the findings of fact heretofore made, and to enter a judgment consistent with this opinion.

MCA Records, Inc. v. Newton-John, 90 Cal.App.3d 18, 153 Cal.Rptr. 153 (1979)

FLEMING, J.

Defendant Olivia Newton-John, a singer, appeals a preliminary injunction restraining her from recording for anyone other than plaintiff MCA Records while MCA's action is pending "or until April 1, 1982, if that date shall occur during the pendency of this action." . . .

On April 1, 1975, the parties entered the following agreement: Defendant Newton-John would record and deliver to plaintiff master recordings for two albums per year for an initial period of two years, and, at plaintiff's option, further similar recordings for three additional periods of one year each. If defendant failed to deliver a recording when due, plaintiff would become entitled to extend the term of the agreement. In return, plaintiff would pay defendant royalties and a nonreturnable advance of $250,000 for each recording received during the initial two years, and an advance of $100,000 for each recording received during the option years. The cost of producing the recordings would be borne by defendant.

The first three recordings were delivered on schedule; the fourth was delivered late. Plaintiff exercised its first option to renew, but never received another recording. Under the terms of the contract plaintiff paid defendant approximately $2,500,000 in royalties and nonreturnable advances.

On May 31, 1978, the parties filed breach-of-contract actions against one another. Both parties sought damages and injunctive relief, and defendant additionally sought declaratory relief. Plaintiff obtained a preliminary injunction, and defendant has appealed.

I.

Defendant asserts the preliminary injunction was improperly granted because: (1) the agreement failed to guarantee payment of minimum compensation of $6,000 a year; (2) she had already been suspended by the plaintiff and could not be further restrained from engaging in her occupation; and (3) there was no showing or finding that irreparable injury would be imminent if the injunction were not granted.

A. A party to a personal service contract may not be enjoined from rendering personal services to others unless, under the terms of the contract, she is guaranteed minimum annual compensation of $6,000 (Civ. Code, § 3423, subd. Fifth; Code Civ. Proc., § 526, subd. 5). Defendant argues that the agreement at bench fails to meet the statutory minimum because the cost of producing two recordings a year exceeds $194,000, and when this expense is deducted from the guaranteed $200,000 annual advance, her net compensation becomes less than $6,000 annually.

The trial court found: (1) the "minimum compensation" referred to in the statutes does not mean "net profits"; (2) even if it did, suitable recordings could be made at costs that would net the defendant minimum compensation of $6,000 a year. It is decisive here that under the terms of the agreement exclusive control of production costs remained in defendant's hands at all times. Defendant was free to record in as tight-fisted or as open-handed a manner, costwise, as she chose. Defendant's interpretation of the minimum compensation statutes would allow her to nullify her contract at any time merely by increasing her production expenses, which at all times remained under her exclusive control. We do not believe the Legislature intended to sanction such a one-sided bargain, and we agree with the trial court's ruling in both its aspects.

The cause of *Foxx v. Williams* (1966) 244 Cal.App.2d 223 [52 Cal.Rptr. 896], cited by defendant, is clearly distinguishable. In that cause, comedian Redd Foxx agreed to record comedy routines for Williams, a record manufacturer and distributor. In return, Foxx was to receive royalties from the sale of the records. Foxx sued Williams and Williams' recording company for an accounting, and the company cross-complained for damages and injunctive relief. The lower court enjoined Foxx from recording for anyone other than cross-complainant, but the appellate court reversed for the reason that Foxx' royalty contract did not guarantee him annual compensation of $6,000. Unlike the defendant at bench, who is guaranteed minimum annual compensation of $200,000 in the form of nonreturnable advances in addition to any royalties she may receive, Foxx' sole compensation was in the form of royalties contingent upon prospective sales which could amount to nothing.

B. Defendant next contends she cannot be suspended by plaintiff and at the same time enjoined from rendering personal services for others. . . . But defendant has not been suspended. She is still free to record for plaintiff, and, in the event she chooses to record, nothing in the agreement relieves plaintiff from its obligation to compensate her.

C. Defendant maintains the grant of the pre-liminary injunction was improper because plaintiff failed to show, and the trial court failed to explicitly find, that such relief was necessary to prevent irreparable injury. The grant of a preliminary injunction lies within the discretion of the trial court . . . and an explicit finding of irreparable harm is not required to sustain the trial court's exercise of that discretion. . . . In requesting injunctive relief plaintiff alleged that if defendant were permitted to record for a competitor, it would suffer irreparable injury, both in loss of profits and loss of goodwill. This allegation was supported by substantial evidence that defendant's services are unique. Absent any indication to the contrary, we can presume from the trial court's order granting the preliminary injunction that the court did in fact find that irreparable injury would be imminent unless the injunction were granted. . . .

II.

Defendant contends that even if the court did not err in granting a preliminary injunction, it erred in authorizing the preliminary injunction to extend beyond the five-year term of the agreement. Plaintiff responds, in effect, that so long as defendant fails to perform her obligations under the contract, the term of the agreement, and thus of the preliminary injunction, may be extended until the seven-year statutory maximum has elapsed. (Lab. Code, § 2855.)

Because a period of five years has not yet passed since defendant began her employment on April 1, 1975, the issue of the availability to plaintiff of injunctive relief after April 1, 1980, is technically premature. Nevertheless, we consider the language in the preliminary injunction extending its possible duration to April 1, 1982, inappropriate for two reasons:

First, if defendant had performed under the contract, plaintiff would not be entitled to prevent her from recording for competitors at the end of the five-year term of the agreement. We have grave doubts that defendant's failure to perform her obligations under the contract can extend the term of the contract beyond its specified five-year maximum. . . .

Second, the injunction appealed here is merely a preliminary injunction, whose sole function is to preserve the status quo pending a final judgment in the action. . . . Plaintiff's general duty to exercise due diligence in the prosecution of its action and to bring it to conclusion within a reasonable time (Code Civ. Proc., §§ 581a, 583) is particularly strong when, as here, the cause involves injunctive and declaratory relief (see Code Civ. Proc., §§ 527 and 1062a, which give priority to such actions). To the extent the phrase "until April 1, 1982" suggests that plaintiff, without taking further action, may prevent defendant from recording for competitors until 1982, the phrase is misleading.

The order for preliminary injunction is modified by deleting the phrase, "or until April 1, 1982, if that date shall occur during the pendency of this action," and as so modified, the order is affirmed.

Motown Record Corporation v. Brockert, 160 Cal.App.3d 123, 207 Cal.Rptr. 574 (1984)

[In 1976, Brockert (known as "Teena Marie") signed exclusive recording and songwriting agreements with Motown and its music publishing affiliate, Jobete. An unknown, Brockert's previous experience consisted of singing with local bands at weddings, parties, and local shopping centers and roles in school musicals. Each contract provided for a fixed, one-year term, and the company had six, one-year renewal options. Each contract reserved to the company the further option to guarantee Brockert compensation at the rate of $6,000 per annum for the balance of the term.

Between 1979 and 1980, Teena Marie recorded four successful albums, the last of which, "It Must Be Magic," went "gold."

In May 1982, Teena Marie notified Motown and Jobete that she would perform no further. In August, the companies sought injunctive relief. In September, the companies exercised their options to guarantee Brockert $6,000 per year. The lower court enjoined Brockert from recording or writing for third parties until the expiration of the seventh year of her agreements. Although the case was settled and the seventh year had expired, the Second District nonetheless proceeded to consider the appeal and to reverse the grant of the preliminary injunction.]

JOHNSON, ACTING P.J.

. . . The companies argue by exercising their option to pay Teena Marie $6,000 a year, a new contract came into existence which did guarantee her the statutory sum and it was this new contract guaranteeing $6,000 a year—not the old contract giving them an option to pay $6,000 a year—that they were seeking to enforce by injunction. We note this lawsuit was filed in August, but the option clauses were not exercised until September. It is a novel litigation strategy to sue for injunctive relief to enforce a contract not yet in existence. At least the plaintiffs cannot be accused of laches.

The contracts between the companies and Teena Marie are not option contracts with respect to the exclusivity clause. In the contracts, Teena Marie does not give the companies the option to enjoy her services exclusively on condition they pay her $6,000 a year. Rather, the promise to perform exclusively for the companies is one of the terms to which Teena Marie agrees from the outset of the contracts.

Alternatively, the companies argue the letters they sent Teena Marie advising her they had elected to "revise" her contract and guarantee her no less than $6,000 per year constituted new contracts modifying the former ones. (*See* California Civil Code § 1698(a).) Section 1698(a) provides, "A contract in writing may be modified by a contract in writing." The California Supreme Court has interpreted the language of § 1698(a) literally, holding that an executory written modification must meet the requirements of a valid contract. . . . Specifically, the Court has held the modification must be supported by new consideration. . . . Accordingly, an executory agreement to pay more for the same performance is unenforceable. . . . In this case Teena Marie was required by the original contracts to perform exclusively for the companies. Consequently, there was no consideration for the purported modification of the contracts. Were we to interpret defendants' letters as attempts to create new contracts, the new contracts would be unenforceable by Teena Marie and thus would not guarantee her compensation at the rate of $6,000 a year.

Even if exercising the option clauses created "new" contracts, we question whether the provisions of the contracts regarding compensation meet the requirement of § 3423. In order to obtain an injunction to prevent the breach of a personal services contract, the compensation for services under that contract must be at the rate of not less than $6,000. The fact the performer was being paid at least $6,000 under some other contract with the same employer would not satisfy the statute. For example, if the performer had two personal services contracts with the same employer, one to record songs and the other to write songs, the fact the performer was guaranteed $6,000 a year under the recording contract would not support injunctive relief to prevent breach of the songwriting contract. Nor would a $6,000 guarantee under the songwriting contract support injunctive relief to enforce the record-making contract.

The contracts in the case at bench appear to attempt such a set-off of compensation. The recording contract with Motown provides, "Any amounts paid under [the $6,000 compensation clause] may be credited against monies thereafter payable to you pursuant to this or any other agreement between [Motown] and you, or between [Motown's] associated, affiliated, or subsidiary corporations and you." The songwriting contract with Jobete contains virtually identical language. There is no dispute that Motown and Jobete are associated or affiliated corporations. If Teena Marie received $6,000 in 1982, from Jobete for songwriting, she would be guaranteed nothing from Motown for recording. Moreover, there is evidence suggesting Teena Marie performed other services for Motown and possibly Jobete as a producer, technician and the like. Presumably she received compensation for these efforts unrelated to her singing, songwriting and recording work. If she was already receiving $6,000 a year as a sound technician, for example, then she would be guaranteed nothing under the contracts before us.

Accordingly, these cagily drafted option clauses might not guarantee a cent in additional compensation for Teena Marie's songwriting and recording services or, at best, she would be guaranteed a single $6,000 a year payment for her services under both contracts.

Still, because we hold a contract giving the employer the discretion to pay the performer $6,000 a year if and when it chooses does not

meet the requirements of § 3423, we need not decide whether the provisions for setting off compensation in the contracts before us would, independently, require refusal of injunctive relief. . . .

We believe the option clause is analogous to the contingent payment rejected in *Foxx*. It is nothing more than a new arrangement of an old song. . . .

As the Court in [*Lumley v. Wagner*] candidly admitted, it had no power to compel Madame Wagner to sing at Lumley's theatre, but the injunction prohibiting her from performing elsewhere might well accomplish the same result. (42 Eng. Rep. at page 693.) Thus there is a danger that an artist prohibited from performing elsewhere may feel compelled to perform under the contract and, under the stress of the situation, turn in an unsatisfactory performance. This would lead to further litigation between the parties on the adequacy of the artist's performance; the very thing the Courts traditionally sought to avoid. (*See*, e.g., *Bethlehem Engineering Export Co. v. Christie*, 105 F.2d 933, 935 (2d Cir. 1929) (HAND, J.).) There is less likelihood of this conundrum arising if the performer is of great renown. Such a performer may well choose not to perform rather than risk her reputation by delivering a sub-par performance.

In 1919, the sum of $6,000 a year was more than five times the average national wage of $1,142. (Historical Statistics of the United States (1976) at page 164, Table: Average Annual Earnings of Employees: 1900 to 1970.) This is equivalent to setting the minimum compensation figure at $100,000 today. (Based on the 1982 median income level of $20,171. See *Statistical Abstract of the United States* (1984) at page 459, Table 754.) By selecting such a large sum, the Legislature indicated an intent that injunctive relief not be available against a performer, however capable, who had not yet achieved distinction. The fact that the bill was further amended to provide that the services must be special is a further indication that the Legislature intended the statute to apply only to persons who had attained "star quality," no matter how special their services might be.

Without doubt, the passage of time has diluted the effect of this legislative intent, but the option clauses before us would totally wash it away. It would allow a record company to bind the entire student body of "Rydell High" to personal services contracts (and pay them nothing) on the off-chance one of them turns out to be Olivia Newton-John.

It is no answer to say that by the time Motown and Jobete sought injunctive relief to enforce the exclusivity clauses, Teena Marie had become a star. By their own admission, they contracted with a "virtual unknown." Nothing in § 3423 prevents the companies from seeking damages from Teena Marie for breach of the exclusivity clause. That section merely says for reasons of public policy that the exclusivity clause of a contract can only be enforced by injunction when the contract is with a performer of requisite distinction as measured by the compensation the employer is willing to pay.

The monetary limitation in the statute is intended to serve as a counterweight in balancing the equities. The Legislature has concluded that "an artist who is not entitled to receive a minimum of $6,000 per year by performing his contract should not be subjected to this kind of economic coercion." . . .

If we were to hold that the option clause satisfied § 3423, we would nullify the $6,000 compensation requirement as a counterweight on the employer. Whereas the $6,000 compensation requirement was intended to balance the equities, the $6,000 option clause is intended to allow record companies to avoid payment of minimum compensation while retaining the power of economic coercion over the artist. . . . This is accomplished in two ways. First, the option clause gives the company the coercive power of a credible threat of injunctive relief without it having to guarantee or pay the artist anything. The threat of a prohibitory injunction may be just as effective as the injunction itself in discouraging the artist from seeking more lucrative employment. . . . Second, in practice, the company will exercise its option to pay minimum compensation only when it is certain the artist intends to breach the exclusivity clause by performing for another and, even then, only when exercising the option is necessary to enable the company to assert in court the contract does indeed provide for the statutory minimum compensation. Of course, by

then, the company's agreement to pay the artist a minimum of $6,000 a year is meaningless. If the artist was not already earning far in excess of that amount from royalties, the artist's worth to the company would not justify the expense of litigating the case. The record company is in fact merely "electing" to pay that which it would have to pay anyway as a result of royalties from sales.

Based on the foregoing we conclude the option clauses in the Motown and Jobete contracts do not support equitable relief in the form of an injunction restraining Teena Marie from performing for other employers.

NOTES _____

1. As a consequence of *Motown Record Corporation v. Brockert*, record labels have searched for various ways to counter the interpretations placed on California law by that decision. One device is to guarantee the minimum $6,000 but require the artists to give notice of any amounts by which royalties and advances fail to total $6,000 in any year of the contract. In addition, the compensation is "back-end" loaded, whereby the $6,000 guaranteed compensation is paid at the end of each year, with such sums to be an advance against royalties on sales that hopefully would have accrued during that calendar year period. An example of a clause providing such terms is as follows:

> We each hereby acknowledge and agree that Company has guaranteed payment to Joseph Perry and Steven Tallarico p/k/a Steve Tyler of Six Thousand Dollars ($6,000.00) per annum for each of their exclusive recording services as set forth in paragraph 3(e) of the Agreement. If during any twelve (12) month period during the term of this Agreement (with the first such period commencing as of the date hereof and ending one (1) year after such date) the aggregate of royalties, advances and aforementioned individuals by Company or Producer has not equalled or exceeded Six Thousand Dollars ($6,000.00), the applicable individual shall give Company written notice thereof as set forth in paragraph 3(e) of the Agreement. All amounts paid by Company to any such individual pursuant to this paragraph 3 shall be advances against any and all royalties and other monies payable to any such individual hereunder or under the Agreement. In the event that Company shall make any payment directly to any of us in accordance with the provisions of this paragraph 3, Company shall not thereby gain any rights which Company would not otherwise have had hereunder or under the Agreement.

2. After the *Motown* decision, many smaller record labels have contemplated circumvention of the California statute by inclusion of specific choice of law and forum provisions outside the state of California. For

example, a current recording agreement used by Arista Records in signing artists contains the following provisions:

This Agreement shall be construed pursuant to the laws of the State of New York applicable to contracts to be performed wholly therein. All claims, disputes or disagreements which may arise out of the interpretation, performance, or breach of this Agreement shall be submitted exclusively to the jurisdiction of the state courts of the State of New York or the Federal District courts located in New York City. I hereby submit to the jurisdiction of the aforesaid courts.

3. Another device aimed at blunting the full effects of Motown is to guarantee $6,000 only to key and leading members of a group. Arguably, this keeps the essential people legally bound and makes it unlikely that lesser members of a group will invoke the $6,000 rule.

4. For further discussion of the California injunction statutes, see Schlesinger, "$6000 Per Year," *Beverly Hills Bar Association Journal*, December 1968; and Light, "The California Injunction Statutes and the Music Industry: What Price Injunctive Relief?" 7 *Columbia Journal of Art in the Law* 141 (1982).

1.60 Wrongful Discharge and Damages

The prior section considered actions taken against the breaching performer. The principal remedy discussed was the negative injunction, which restrains the performer from working elsewhere. In certain situations, the performer who has been wrongfully discharged may also obtain a negative injunction against the employer. The performer may seek to restrain the employer from hiring a replacement. However, such an action often creates great hardship, since this may cause a production company that employs many individuals to cease operation. Thus, the negative injunction is often denied. In addition, the performer may have difficulty in proving that the remedy at law is inadequate. A court's normal response is that the damages incurred when the performer is wrongfully discharged are the lost expected earnings under the contract. This is finite, and therefore a court may find this grounds to deny injunctive intervention.

The performer, on the other hand, often believes this remedy is inadequate, because being compensated for lost earnings in the engagement in question does not take into consideration the loss of earning potential that would have been realized had the current contract remained in force. Accordingly, performers wrongfully discharged will seek, in addition to lost expected earnings, damages to reputation, lost opportunities to enhance one's career and, perhaps, mental distress arising from circumstances surrounding the breach. As the following cases illustrate, these claimed damages have received cool receptions by U.S. courts. Even where the window is opened, as it was in *Redgrave v. Boston Symphony Orchestra*, it has been later shut through the court's novel co-joining of tort and contract theories.

Even so, performers rightfully worry about their reputations. For most, the peak earning years are few. A lost opportunity can be a great setback. Since an order that the producer specifically perform by rehiring the performer will almost never be granted (see *Redgrave* below), and since even a negative injunction is often unavailable, there is legitimate impetus for the performer to seek not just lost earnings but consequential damages as well. Thus, the following cases should be analyzed carefully for insights into ways a performer's damage theories can be broadened.

NOTE ――――――――――――――――――――

1. For analysis of the possibilities of expanding the discharged employee's right to damages, see "The Loss of Publicity as an Element of Damages for Breach of Contract to Employ an Entertainer," 27 *University of Miami Law Review* 465 (1973).

―――――――――――――――――――――――――

Quinn v. Straus Broadcasting Group, Inc., 309 F. Supp. 1208 (S.D.N.Y. 1970)

[Quinn was the host of a "talk show" on radio station WMCA in New York City. After Quinn had been on the air for slightly more than three months, WMCA notified him that he was to be taken off the schedule and that his services would no longer be required. WMCA apparently offered Quinn the balance of the $50,000 compensation provided for in Quinn's contract. Instead, Quinn sued WMCA, seeking $500,000 damages for wrongful discharge, an additional $500,000 for damage to Quinn's professional reputation as a result of the cancellation because of "the unique nature of Quinn's services and his need to appear before the public to advance his professional reputation," and a final $500,000 for holding Quinn up to "public ridicule [causing] his reputation as a performer to be seriously and permanently impaired."

Quinn's contract referred to him as a "staff announcer," and ran for one year, from April 1, 1969, at a $50,000 salary, with two one-year renewal options at $57,000 and $65,000, respectively.]

BONSAL, D.J., granted WMCA's motion to dismiss, holding [at page 1209]

. . . The New York rule is that damages for breach of an employment contract are limited to the unpaid salary to which the employee would be entitled under the contract less the amount by which he should have mitigated his damages. . . . This rule was recently applied with respect to the conductor of the orchestra of the Metropolitan Opera in *Amaducci v. Metropolitan Opera Association*, 33 A.D.2d 542, 304 N.Y.S.2d 322 (1st Dept. 1969), where plaintiff sought damages for mental anguish and defamation resulting from his discharge, the Court stating:

> It is well settled that the optimum measure of damages for wrongful discharge under a contract of employment is the salary fixed by the contract for the unexpired period of employment, and that damages to the good name, character and reputation of the plaintiff are not recoverable in an action for wrongful discharge. 33 A.D.2d 542, 304 N.Y.S.2d at 323.

While *Amaducci* does not directly answer plaintiff's contention that he is entitled to damages for the loss of opportunity to practice his profession before the public, there is no reason to believe that the State Courts would adopt a different rule in this contest. Moreover, it is clear that by signing a $30,000 contract with radio station WCAU in Philadelphia in September 1969, plaintiff has not lost his opportunity to practice his profession. Plaintiff relies on a 1930 House of Lords case (*Clayton & Waller, Limited v. Oliver*, [1930] A.C. 209) and a 1965 California Court of Appeals case (*Colvig v. RKO General, Inc.*, 232 Cal.App.2d 56, 42 Cal.Rptr. 474 (1st Dist. 1965)) for the proposition that the New York courts would make an exception to the New York rule in this case. *Colvig* is clearly distinguishable as it involved the enforcement of an arbitration award. *Clayton* was decided 40 years ago, and no New York cases have been cited to indicate that New York would follow *Clayton*. Taken together, these two cases cannot be said to be a precursor of an exception to the New York rule, and therefore this court is bound to follow the rule as stated in *Cornell* and *Amaducci*. . . .

Since, under the New York rule, plaintiff's damages are limited to a maximum of $50,000, his ad damnum clause of $500,000 in the first cause of action is clearly excessive and will be stricken.

The second and third causes of action are not recognized in the New York rule as laid down in *Cornell* and *Amaducci*. The second alleges that plaintiff's services were unique and that by reason of the breach of contract plaintiff was deprived of an opportunity to perform before large audiences; and the third alleges that his reputation as a performer had been impaired. No authority has been suggested for the proposition that loss of opportunity to perform entitles the employee to a separate cause of action. *Amaducci* holds that no separate cause of action can be stated for loss of reputation. Divested of these allegations, the second and third causes of action merely repeat the first cause of action. Accordingly, they will be stricken.

Colvig v. RKO General, Inc., 232 Cal.App.2d 56, 42 Cal.Rptr. 473 (1965)

[The Court affirmed the award of an arbitrator (appointed under a collective bargaining agreement) who held that Colvig, although a staff announcer, was a "highly paid professional man" who was entitled to air time on radio station KRFC, not merely to the stated compensation under his contract. The arbitrator therefore ordered KRFC to keep Colvig on the air until the end of the term of his contract. According to the appellate court (per Molinari, J.), which reversed the lower court's grant of KRFC's demurrer to the complaint:]

As a general rule an employer does not have the duty to provide work for his employee, but may utilize his employee's services when and how he chooses so long as he pays the employee the agreed-upon salary. An exception to this rule exists where the employee's reputation will suffer if he is not allowed to practice his profession. The rationale of this exception is that the parties are deemed to have contracted on the assumption that the employee was to be given opportunities for the exercise of his abilities during a reasonable portion of the period covered by the contract. (35 Am.Jur., § 115, page 542.) In the Restatement (Second) of Agency, § 433, we find this statement:

> If the agent's compensation is not dependent upon the amount of work done, as where he is to receive a fixed salary, a promise by the principal to furnish him with work is inferred from a promise to employ only if it is found that the anticipated benefit to the agent from doing the work is a material part of the advantage to be received by him from the employment. This anticipated benefit may be the acquisition of subsidiary pecuniary advantages as in the case of the employment of public performers whose reputation will be enhanced by their appearance or diminished by their failure to appear. . . . (Page 313)

From the facts pleaded, although somewhat ineptly, it can be gleaned that under his contract of employment, plaintiff, as a highly paid professional man, was to be given the opportunity to exercise his abilities, an anticipated benefit of which was the acquisition of a reputation in the public eye which would be enhanced by his appearance through the media of the radio waves and diminished by his failure to make such appearance. To hold otherwise would be tantamount to saying that as a matter of law plaintiff cannot fit into the category of employees coming within the exception of the general rule. Such a conclusion cannot be reached herein upon the facts pleaded.

The complaint in the instant case suffices as a basis for all damages that will compensate plaintiff for the detriment proximately caused by the alleged breach or which in the ordinary course of things is likely to result therefrom. We do not think that such general damages are, as claimed

by defendant, necessarily restricted to plaintiff's salary. It may well be that under the evidence plaintiff may be able to show other damages which are the normal and natural result of the breach complained of.

Redgrave v. Boston Symphony Orchestra, 557 F. Supp. 230 (D.Mass. 1983)

KEETON, DISTRICT JUDGE

Following cancellation by the Boston Symphony Orchestra ("BSO") of a series of concerts that she was to narrate, Vanessa Redgrave and Vanessa Redgrave Enterprises, Ltd. filed this suit. Plaintiffs allege that the concerts were cancelled because of opposition to Ms. Redgrave's publicly stated political views, in particular her views on Israel and the Palestine Liberation Organization. The complaint contains ten claims, six against the BSO and four against defendants whose identity is not yet known and who are alleged to have put pressure on the BSO to cancel the concerts. The claims against the BSO are the following: breach of contract claim requesting monetary damages (first claim); breach of contract claim requesting specific performance (second claim); tortious repudiation of contract claim requesting monetary damages (third claim); tortious repudiation of contract claim requesting specific performance (fourth claim); claim under 42 U.S.C. § 1986 (seventh claim); and claim under the Massachusetts Civil Rights Act (eighth claim). . . .

Plaintiff's claims against the BSO will be reviewed separately below. . . .

Defendant BSO concedes that the complaint states a breach of contract claim, but argues that, as a matter of law, plaintiffs may "recover nothing more than the alleged $31,000 contractual fee." Defendant's Memorandum at 4. Because the BSO has offered to pay plaintiffs' $31,000 contractual fee, BSO argues that the claim must be dismissed.

BSO's argument, in effect, is that there is no set of facts plaintiffs could prove that would entitle them to incidental or consequential damages. The argument relies heavily on *Quinn v. Straus Broadcasting Group, Inc.*, 309 F. Supp. 1208, 1209 (S.D.N.Y. 1970), where the court stated that "[t]he New York rule is that damages for breach of an employment contract are limited to the unpaid salary to which the employee would be entitled under the contract less the amount by which he should have mitigated his damages. . . ." Even assuming that the instant case is properly characterized as a breach of employment case, a point which plaintiffs apparently concede, and assuming further that the case would not be taken outside the "New York rule" by the specific allegation that the employment termination caused others to refrain from employing plaintiff, defendant has not demonstrated that the "New York rule" relied on by *Quinn* is also the Massachusetts rule. The general Massachusetts rule of contract damages was stated in the often-quoted case of *John Hetherington & Sons, Ltd. v. William Firth Co.*, 210 Mass. 8, 21, 95 N.E. 961, 964 (1911):

> The fundamental principle of law . . . for breach of contract . . . is that the injured party shall be placed in the same position he would have been in, if the contract had been performed, so far as loss can be ascertained to have followed as a natural consequence and to have been within the contemplation of the parties as reasonable men as a probable result of the breach, and so far as compensation therefor in money can be computed by rational methods upon a firm basis of facts.

In light of the fact that defendant has not demonstrated that the New York rule as stated in *Quinn, supra*, controls the case, I cannot say that, in terms of the *Hetherington* formulation, there is no state of facts plaintiffs could prove that would entitle them to consequential or incidental damages. For instance, if plaintiffs proved other employers refused to hire Redgrave after termination of the BSO contract because of that termination (that loss of the other employment "followed as a natural consequence" from the termination of the contract), that this loss of other employment would reasonably have been foreseen by the parties at the time of contracting and at the time of termination, and that damages are rationally calculable, then plaintiffs may be entitled to damages that include monies for loss of the other employment. Although plaintiffs certainly have a heavy burden to carry here, it cannot be said with certainty at this time that they will not be able to meet this burden. . . .

In their first claim, discussed directly above, plaintiffs allege breach of contract; in their third claim, they allege that the BSO committed a tort when it broke the contract "solely because of Ms. Redgrave's exercise of her fundamental statutory and constitutional rights of freedom of expression. . . ." In claims two and four, plaintiffs allege that they have no adequate remedy at law for the breach of contract and "tortious repudiation of . . . contract" respectively, and request an order directing the BSO to reschedule the performances called for under the contract.

Defendant argues that the specific performance prayed for here is barred by the United States Constitution and by common law. Because I agree that this court may not, under the common law, order specific performance in this case, it is unnecessary to reach the constitutional issue.

As the court noted in *Loeb v. Textron, Inc.*, 600 F.2d 1003, 1023 n. 34 (1st Cir. 1979), "[u]nder traditional principles of contract law, courts normally do not enforce employment contracts with orders for specific performance." The policy is reflected in 34 M.G.L. ch. 214 § 1A, which excludes contracts for personal services from those that may be specifically enforced:

> The fact that the plaintiff has a remedy in damages shall not bar an action for specific performance of a contract, *other than one for purely personal services*, if the court finds that no other existing remedy, or the damages recoverable thereby is in fact the equivalent of the performance promised by the contract relied on by the plaintiff, and the court may order specific performance if it finds such remedy to be practicable. (Emphasis added.)

Plaintiffs argue correctly that the cases do not establish that specific performance is never to be granted in an employment contract case. However, it is clearly true that specific performance in personal service cases is the exception, and plaintiffs offer no facts or argument, beyond the flat and unsupported assertion in their complaint that "plaintiffs have no adequate remedy at law," as to why specific performance is necessary or appropriate in this case. *Cf. Dewey v. University of New Hampshire*, 694 F.2d 1 at 5 (1st Cir. 1982) (on specificity required in pleadings). Nor do plaintiffs cite any cases in which specific performance has been ordered in a situation even remotely similar to the situation here, where an artistic organization would be forced to schedule a series of concerts in two cities involving literally hundreds of performing personnel, not to mention support personnel, in addition to Ms. Redgrave. Such a result would inevitably constitute the kind of "undue hardship upon one party" that itself may be reason to deny specific performance. . . .

Plaintiff's third claim alleges that the BSO broke the contract because of Ms. Redgrave's speaking out on Israel and the Palestine Liberation Organization, and that this conduct "constitutes a tort under common law." Although the complaint does not identify exactly what tort this is, plaintiffs' supporting memorandum advances two theories—that it is the tort of intentional infliction of emotional distress as described in *Agis v. Howard Johnson Co.*, 371 Mass. 140, 355 N.E.2d 315 (1976). . . .

As to intentional infliction of emotional distress, I note, first, that nowhere in the complaint, as distinguished from the supporting memorandum, are the elements of this tort pleaded or even alluded to. In order for a plaintiff to prevail on a claim of intentional infliction of emotional distress, it must be shown: (1) that the actor intended to inflict emotional distress or that he knew or should have known that emotional distress was the likely result of his conduct; (2) that the conduct was "extreme and outrageous," was "beyond all possible bounds of decency," and was "utterly intolerable in a civilized community"; (3) that the actions of the defendant were the cause of the plaintiff's distress; and (4) that the emotional distress sustained by the plaintiff was "severe" and of a nature "that no reasonable man could be expected to endure it." . . . Plaintiffs have not pleaded these elements of the tort.

The flaw in plaintiffs' claim, however, is not merely one of deficient pleading; were that the case, the court would be inclined to allow plaintiffs to amend the complaint in order to plead the elements of the tort properly. But an amendment would be of little help here. It is the responsibility of the court in the first place to determine whether the conduct alleged may reasonably be viewed as extreme, outrageous and beyond all possible bounds of decency. Taking as true the factual allegations of the complaint—including the allegation that the BSO repudiated the contract because of Ms. Redgrave's exercise of her First Amendment rights—there is simply no way that the BSO's conduct can reasonably be seen as

"extreme and outrageous" and "beyond all bounds of human decency" as those phrases are defined by precedents bearing on this theory of action. The BSO's alleged behavior does not, for instance, rise to the level found sufficient to survive a motion to dismiss in *Armano v. Federal Reserve Bank of Boston*, 468 F. Supp. 674 (D.Mass. 1979), where the plaintiff alleged that his employer systematically harassed him by, *inter alia*, circulating rumors that he was suspected of stealing money and directing supervisory personnel to assign him to the lowest and most menial tasks. . . . The BSO's alleged conduct is neither the kind of systematic harassment nor the single but dramatically cruel incident that the courts have found to be sufficiently "outrageous" to sustain a claim of infliction of emotional distress. Contracts are frequently broken, and even willful breach is not unusual. But it is unusual, perhaps unprecedented, for such a breach to constitute the tort of infliction of emotional distress. The facts of the present case will not sustain finding the tort and therefore, if count three is seen as alleging the tort of infliction of emotional distress, it must be dismissed. . . .

Actions for breach of contract protect interests in having promises performed, and tort actions protect interests in freedom from harms incident to intrusions upon legally protected interests. See, *e.g.*, W. Prosser, *Torts* 613, § 92 (4th ed. 1971). The duties of conduct enforced in tort actions may or may not be based in part upon manifested promises, and the interests protected may or may not arise from relationships that involve contracts. *Id*. A contract for services may create a relationship between parties by reason of which the law recognizes a duty of reasonable care in performance that will support a tort action as well as an action for breach of contract. Massachusetts precedents establish the availability of a tort remedy in such circumstances.

> When a party binds himself by contract to do a work or to perform a service, he agrees by implication to do a workmanlike job and to use reasonable and appropriate care and skill in doing it. . . . The count in tort states a cause of action as well as the count in contract. Although the duty arises out of the contract and is measured by its terms, negligence in the manner of performing that duty as distinguished from mere failure to perform it, causing damage, is a tort . . . (citations omitted).

Neither in these precedents nor elsewhere, however, is there support for the contention that repudiation of a contract is as well a tort.

Absent some identifiable tort theory, no reason appears for enlarging remedies for the breach of contract alleged in this case beyond those, supported by precedents, protecting the interest in having promises performed. Thus, I need not determine whether in some special circumstances conduct amounting to repudiation of a contract may also support an action in tort. Plaintiffs in this case have called attention neither to special circumstances of fact nor to precedents that would support such an action in tort. . . .

NOTES _____

1. The court also discussed Redgrave's civil rights claims under the First and Fourteenth Amendments, under 42 U.S.C.A. §§ 1985, 1986, and under the Massachusetts Civil Rights Act. Although acknowledging that Redgrave's claims were stated in vague and conclusory terms, the court refused to dismiss these claims and set them down for trial.

2. After Judge Keeton's preliminary rulings in *Redgrave v. Boston Symphony Orchestra*, the dispute proceeded to trial on the legal theories deemed actionable by the judge. On November 9, 1984, the jury rendered a verdict against Ms. Redgrave on her civil rights claims but in her favor on contract breach, awarding her $100,000 in damages for both direct and consequential damages. Motions were made by each side for Judge Keeton to vacate the verdict. His subsequent rulings are discussed in the following report.

_____

Redgrave v. Boston Symphony Orchestra, 602 F. Supp. 1189 (D.Mass. 1985)

KEETON, DISTRICT JUDGE

[The judge first denied Ms. Redgrave's motion to vacate the jury's finding against her on her claim under the Massachusetts Civil Rights Act. The judge then considered the BSO's motions on the contract's issues.]

. . . Protection of freedom is a prime objective of our legal system. Freedom of speech, freedom of artistic expression, freedom of contract, and freedom of choice on political and moral issues are among the protected activities. Implicit in the protection of freedom in these and other contexts is a conception of society in which pluralism may flourish. Individuals are free to be very different in their political and moral convictions, in their religious faiths, and in their artistic, social, and personal interests and activities. Individuals are free to come together in private organizations that express their personal interests, and the organizations that they create may be quite diverse. Individuals may, for example, come together for political expression, for the practice of religion or the profession of faith, to foster recreational interests, or to promote their common interests in music, drama, or some other form of art. They are free to create a private entity that promotes one special interest and seeks to remain pluralistic in other respects, bringing together individuals who share one special interest even though they differ sharply about other matters—political, moral, religious, or artistic.

The law does not forbid an entity organized to promote a form of art—or those who function as its managerial agents—from taking account of recognized differences among its members and patrons regarding controversial political issues. For example, it is not illegal for a private entity to make a choice not to contract with an artist for a performance if its agents believe that the artist's appearance under their sponsorship would be interpreted by others as in some degree a political statement. Thus, BSO was entirely free not to make a contract with Redgrave for such reasons even though its agents considered her a superb actress and exceptionally qualified to perform as narrator in Oedipus Rex.

Once BSO contracted for Redgrave to appear in the production of Oedipus Rex, BSO gave up part of its freedom. By contracting with a party, however, an entity does not entirely surrender all of its freedom to act. BSO retained to a certain extent its interests in freedom of expression and freedom of choice at least regarding conditions that in good faith it considered essential to an artistic production or to protection against physical risks. The freedom that BSO retained may even include freedom to break the contract (subjecting itself of course to liability for damages under the law) for any reason other than one specially forbidden by the law (for example, discrimination on grounds of sex or race). The suggested freedom to break a contract and suffer liability only for the legally recognized damages is within the scope of the idea often referred to as Holmes' bad man theory of contract law—that one who is willing to pay the penalty of such damages as the law assesses is free to break the contract and pay. See O.W. Holmes, *The Path of the Law*, 10 Harv.L.Rev. 457, 461–62 (1897). As to contracts not specifically enforceable in equity, the law provides no other remedy. Even if it is inappropriate to say that one has a legal "right" to break the contract and pay the assessed damages, legal redress is limited to those damages. Of course, if this point of view is accepted, one must determine the critical question as to the measure of damages under the law. The measure of damages clearly includes the performance fee less any expenses that would have been incurred to perform the contract. Does it also include compensation for harm to Redgrave's professional career in the circumstances of this case? This perspective does suggest, however, that unless plaintiffs can demonstrate that the consequential damages they seek are within the scope of legal redress for breach of contract, or can show that BSO's reason for cancellation is one forbidden by the law in a sense beyond merely being a breach of contract, BSO is free to break the contract without incurring liability beyond the performance fee.

As noted above, even though individuals and entities are free in various contexts to make choices for whatever reasons they find sufficient, the law does impose constraints against actions based upon reasons that are classified as invidious (illustrated by discrimination on the basis of race or sex). Plaintiffs, of course, assert in this case that BSO cancelled for an invidious reason—retaliation against plaintiff because of her exercise of her right to speak freely on controversial political issues of worldwide concern. That contention was rejected by the jury in the answers to interrogatories 1 and 2A. As noted above, these findings are supported by the evidence. Thus, I need not consider whether an affirmative answer to one or both of these questions would have affected the measure of damages for breach of contract. . . .

As noted above, the law does not require that a producer enter into a contract without regard to the artist's political activities. Having entered into the contract, however, the producer may not break it without incurring liability for damages according to the law of contracts. Under the contract, plaintiffs were to receive a performance fee of $31,000, but were responsible for paying all travel expenses incidental to the engagement. The parties have stipulated that the net amount after expenses would have been $27,500. The jury's answer to interrogatory 3 establishes that plaintiffs are entitled to judgment for this amount, at least, as actual damages for breach of contract. . . .

Plaintiffs argue that in addition to the performance fee they are entitled to consequential damages for Redgrave's loss of future professional opportunities caused by the breach of contract. Plaintiffs assert that the publicity of BSO's cancellation caused producers and theatre operators, who otherwise would have engaged Redgrave, not to do so. Under Massachusetts law, damages may be awarded for consequential harm if such harm was within the contemplation of the parties and was caused "directly" by the breach or "indirectly" by the combined effect of the breach and foreseeable intervening causes. . . .

Under the court's instructions, the jury could find that harm to Redgrave's professional career, of which BSO's cancellation was a cause, was "within the contemplation of the parties" at the time of making the contract if, on the basis of what BSO did know at that time about her public expressions and anything more that it then should have known in the exercise of reasonable care, BSO did foresee or should have foreseen that harm to her career from the cancellation was sufficiently likely that it would have been taken into account by an ordinarily prudent person in assessing the costs and benefits of entering into the contract at the time of making the decision to contract. . . . The jury found that consequential harm was foreseeable in this sense and that $100,000 would fairly and adequately compensate Redgrave for such harm. . . .

BSO presents several arguments to support its motion for judgment notwithstanding the verdict on the consequential damages. The first two arguments attack the findings on the basis of insufficiency of the evidence presented by the plaintiffs. The remaining contentions assert that, even if the jury's verdict is supported by the evidence, this court must as a matter of law treat the finding of $100,000 in damages for harm to Redgrave's professional career as irrelevant to the judgment to be entered. . . .

First, BSO contends that the evidence was insufficient to support the jury's finding that harm to Redgrave's professional career was within the contemplation of the parties. I conclude that this contention is without merit.

Under Massachusetts law the legal standard as to what is within the contemplation of the parties includes consequences that were foreseeable to a person of reasonable prudence in the position of the party charged with the breach (BSO) at the time the contract was made. . . . The evidence in this case was sufficient to support a finding that a reasonable person, having the knowledge of Redgrave's public expressions of political views that BSO had or should have had in the exercise of reasonable care at the time of contracting, would have foreseen harm to her professional career as a consequence of a cancellation by BSO.

Second, BSO contends that the evidence presented during trial was insufficient to support a finding as to any particular amount that is fair and reasonable compensation for harm to Redgrave's professional career—in other words, the plaintiffs have failed to prove with adequate certainty the damages caused by BSO's cancellation. This issue involves the need to separate the effect of the harm caused by Redgrave's political expressions from any added harm caused by BSO's cancellation. BSO points to the general principle that plaintiffs have the burden of showing not merely a reduction of professional opportunities after BSO's breach as compared to those opportunities that would have been expected for one with Redgrave's qualifications as an actress; they must demonstrate the difference between the professional opportunities she had after the breach and the opportunities she would have had but for the breach. Thus, she must offer proof from which the jury could reasonably find, by a preponderance of the evidence, that her expressions on political issues would not have affected her professional opportunities but for the breach, or that the effect would have been more limited. BSO contends that the proof offered is too speculative to determine a reasonable award.

One response to these arguments points to instructive analogies in the precedents relating to tort actions for physical injuries to persons who have special susceptibilities to harm. Plaintiffs thus may invoke the rule that a wrongdoer takes the victim as is and therefore is liable for all of the harm resulting from aggravation of a pre-existing susceptibility to harm. *See generally Restatement (Second) of Torts* § 461 (1965). Nevertheless, the liability does not extend to harm that would have resulted from the pre-existing condition even if the tort had not occurred.

Although the issue presented as to the sufficiency of the evidence in this case is a close and debatable one, I conclude that the evidence is sufficient to support a finding that the BSO cancellation was a but-for cause of substantial harm to Redgrave's professional career and that $100,000 in damages is reasonable compensation for that harm. Plaintiffs' inability to prove the measure of the harm precisely does not defeat the claim under Massachusetts contract law. . . .

BSO contends that plaintiffs' claim for consequential harm to Redgrave's professional career implicates, first, constraints imposed by the First and Fourteenth Amendments to protect against intrusive state action, including judicially created state law rules that allow damages awards based upon communicative conduct, and, second, state law constraints aimed at protecting freedom of expression. These contentions require closer examination.

In the circumstances of this case, in order to establish that BSO's breach of contract caused loss of future opportunities for professional engagements, plaintiffs must prove that in some way information about BSO's action was communicated to others, that they thereafter acted differently because of the communicated message, and that BSO is legally responsible for harm caused by that communication and its consequences. These requirements are not independent elements of a cause of action for breach of contract. Instead, they emanate, by necessary implication, from a requirement of proof of causal connection between breach and harm; that is, in the context of this case, causal connection cannot be proved in any other way. Nonetheless, these corollaries of requiring proof of cause in the circumstances of the present case are closely analogous to recognized elements of the law of defamation—treated in that context as elements independent of theories of legal cause.

Judicial opinions resolving disputed claims in the law of defamation have exposed a clash among sets of interests that are all valued highly in the legal system. The clash of these highly valued interests remains, whatever the rubric of theory may be—whether, for example, it is "contemplation of the parties" or "proximate cause" rather than "privilege" incident to constitutional and other legal protections for freedom of expression.

As already noted, BSO invokes the First and Fourteenth Amendments on the factual premise that the evidence in this case would not support a finding that BSO's cancellation caused harm to Redgrave's career by any means other than some form of communication by BSO to others. In other words, the only possible mechanism of harm to Redgrave's professional career, revealed by the evidence, is the alleged influence of some statement made by BSO on later decisions of others—a statement of fact or opinion implied in BSO's cancellation, or express or implied in BSO's press release.

I conclude that BSO is correct in asserting that this factual premise is an inescapable element of the claimed causal connection between BSO's cancellation and consequential harm to Redgrave's professional career. The evidence does support the jury's finding, in answer to interrogatories 4A, 4B, and 5, that BSO's cancellation was a cause, along with other causes, of harm to her professional career for which $100,000 is reasonable compensation. But it does so only because a factfinder may reasonably infer that others, upon receiving the news of BSO's cancellation, interpreted the cancellation as conveying a message about Redgrave. No evidence was presented as to any means by which BSO's cancellation could cause others to deny her performance opportunities unless they first learned about the cancellation and derived some message from it.

The testimony regarding the one loss of an opportunity that was specifically identified at trial illustrates the point. The witness Theodore Mann testified that he decided against offering Redgrave a role in "Heartbreak House," playing at the Circle in the Square Theater in New York, because of BSO's cancellation. His explanation was, in essence, that if BSO couldn't take the risk, neither could he. The necessary implication is that he interpreted BSO's cancellation as saying

BSO had decided it could not take the risk of presenting Redgrave in a live performance for one or more of the reasons to which he alluded, including concerns about fundraising, ticket sales, and physical disturbance of the performances. . . .

All factual hypotheses advanced had one characteristic in common. Expressly or impliedly, they depended on the decision of another person, who otherwise would have offered Redgrave a performance opportunity, not to do so because that other person was influenced by some message he or she derived from the BSO cancellation and the press coverage that followed. With understandable zeal of advocacy, plaintiffs' counsel phrased their hypotheses in ways that did not explicitly identify any communicative step in the sequence of causation. Yet, close analysis revealed its presence in every hypothesis advanced. The imagery of a chain of causation is apt here. Though the stated hypotheses did not express the communicative link in the chain of causation, there is in every hypothesis advanced a missing link unless the communication of some message from BSO to others can be found. The presence of this communicative link invokes the analogy to the law of defamation.

Under the law of defamation, at least as applied to media defendants, a public figure plaintiff may not recover damages unless he or she can establish clearly and convincingly that the defendant had knowledge of the falsity or acted in reckless disregard of the truth of the defamatory matter published. *See, e.g., Gertz v. Robert Welch, Inc.,* 418 U.S. 323, 342, 94 S.Ct. 2997, 3008, 41 L.Ed.2d 789 (1974). The Supreme Court has not yet determined whether these protections are also available to non-media defendants. *See Greenmoss Builders, Inc. v. Dun & Bradstreet, Inc.,* 143 Vt. 66, 461 A.2d 414, *cert. granted,——U.S.——,* 104 S.Ct. 389, 78 L.Ed.2d 334 (1983) (argued Mar. 21, 1984, reargued Oct. 3, 1984). Even if they are not, however, state law protects against liability for harm caused by truthful statements of fact about a person. *See, e.g., Restatement (Second) of Torts* § 581A (1977).

The suggested analogy to defamation cases adds substantial weight to the defense position that the judgment in this case should not include damages for consequential harm. If a judgment for such damages were entered, pursuant to this court's enforcement of state law, that application of state law would constitute state action to which Fourteenth Amendment constraints (and First Amendment constraints through Fourteenth Amendment incorporation) would apply. *Cf. New York Times Co. v. Sullivan,* 376 U.S. 254, 256, 276–78, 84 S.Ct. 710, 713, 723–24, 11 L.Ed.2d 686 (1964). The debatable issues as to whether federal constitutional constraints and state constitutional and decisional constraints against state law defamation awards would be extended to state law awards for consequential harm as to which a communicative link is essential to the causal chain are issues of first impression. But the analogy is compelling.

Plaintiffs contend that the analogy to defamation cases should be rejected. They argue that the interests they assert here, in contrast with those asserted by a plaintiff in a defamation case, are of the type that ranks highest in the First Amendment hierarchy—Redgrave's interests in freedom of expression and freedom from retaliation against her because of her openly expressed political views. Extending the notion of retaliation to harm to Redgrave's professional career caused by publicity generated by BSO's cancellation, plaintiffs have explicitly referred to the interests they assert here as "First Amendment" rights. In fact, the alleged intrusions upon plaintiffs' interests in freedom of expression are not intrusions against which the First Amendment (or the Fourteenth by incorporation of the First) affords protection. The First and Fourteenth Amendments protect only against governmental intrusions. . . . The intrusion alleged in this case is an intrusion by a private entity—BSO. Nonetheless, the interests in freedom of expression that plaintiffs assert are highly valued in our legal system. First and Fourteenth Amendment protections against governmental intrusion are only part of the total array of legal protections of freedom of expression.

Even though incorrectly characterized by plaintiffs as invoking First Amendment rights, their argument as to the high value the law places on Redgrave's interests in freedom of expression is cogent. Their argument shows at least that the issue presented in this case is not directly controlled by precedent—that it is truly one of first impression. The defense argument, fairly appraised, shows not that logic requires the denial of consequential damages but that the analogy to defamation suggests it.

It is debatable whether interests in free expression generally would be more effectively protected and promoted if the legal system awarded damages in the circumstances presented here, to vindicate compelling interests in free expression (represented by the plaintiffs in this instance), even though doing so would to some extent impair interests in free expression, or interests in freedom of action with communicative implications (represented by defendant in this instance). If the issue is framed in terms of which outcome is more likely to serve and promote freedom of expression in the long run, the answer is unclear. Certainly a rule of law allowing consequential damages would deter breach. But it would deter contract as well. It is a question open to debate whether in the long run artists who openly express their political views would be offered more performance opportunities if such a rule were clearly established as applicable law. I conclude that the issue concerning the law applicable to claims of consequential harm such as this one, when squarely presented to the courts of last resort—state and federal—will be resolved on other grounds and not by answering this debatable question about the net impact of different rules of law on freedom of expression by performing artists.

A more compelling ground for resolving the issue is that legal constraints protecting freedom of expression are primarily designed as a shield, not a sword. They may be invoked generally in defense of freedom and only rarely to sustain an action for damages. The legal system stands ready to shield freedom against unlawful governmental intrusion, but reluctant to use the sword of damages to vindicate one claim of freedom by striking down another. . . .

In a system of equal justice, a conception of freedom that depends upon repressing equal freedom of others is self-contradictory. In relation specifically to freedom of expression—whether political or nonpolitical, artistic or banal, vital or frivolous—invoking the compulsion of law to compensate for the impact of one exercise of freedom upon another would be in the long run self-defeating. Inevitably it would draw the legal system into making judgments about the content of expression—the very kind of governmental action that is most threatening to individual freedom.

I conclude that the analogy to defamation cases is compelling. Predicting the resolution of issues in courts of last resort, as I must do in order to determine the judgment to be entered in this case, I conclude that both state and federal constraints against damages awards will be imposed by the courts of last resort when these issues are presented for decision, and that these constraints bar the plaintiffs' claim for consequential damages in the circumstances of the present case.

I conclude further, that one of these legal constraints upon awards of damages is that a plaintiff who seeks an award for harm connected with the wrongful act of the defendant through a communicative link must show at least that the communicative link involved some unprivileged statement. Absent such a showing, the causal connection between wrong and harm is broken because an essential link of the chain is itself legally protected expression. Thus, a plaintiff who seeks to use a communicative link as a part of the chain of causation must disentangle actionable expression from protected expression in that communicative link. . . .

The communicative link may, of course, be either a statement of fact or a statement of opinion. Each statement of fact or opinion may be express or it may be implied. If a statement of fact, it may be true or it may be false. If a statement of opinion, it may be an opinion that BSO's managerial agents did in fact hold, or it may be one they did not hold. Will any of the communicative links that now remain as factual possibilities, after taking account of the jury's answers to interrogatories, sustain liability for consequential harm to Redgrave's professional career?

Accepting the analogy to the law of defamation, I conclude, first, that plaintiffs are not entitled to harm caused by any message conveyed by BSO's cancellation if in substance that message was no more than a statement of fact about Redgrave that is not shown to be false or a statement of opinion that was in fact held. Second, even if some element of the message was a false statement of fact about Redgrave or a statement of opinion not in

fact held, additional barriers to liability must be overcome before an actionable claim for harm to Redgrave's professional career is established. Plaintiffs must prove that the harm was caused by some impermissible element or elements of the message rather than by legally privileged expressions of fact or opinion. As stated above, disentangling privileged from actionable expressions is a burden that plaintiffs must meet to establish liability for harm to Redgrave's professional career.

Viewed in the perspective of the defamation analogy, this claim is brought by and on behalf of a person who is a "public figure" both because of her acknowledged recognition as an actress and because of her having voluntarily expressed her views openly on political issues of worldwide interest and concern. Consultations between the court and counsel, during preparation of the charge to jury, disclosed that on this point there is no dispute. Thus, in whatever way the communicative content of BSO's actions may be described, as a formulation of the contention that BSO's cancellation foreseeably caused Redgrave to lose professional opportunities that would otherwise have been available to her, the legal argument for allowing damages for the resulting harm must overcome BSO's claim of freedom to act as it did, in order to serve the artistic and security interests that it alleges as a basis for its actions, even though its action implicitly had communicative consequences of harm to Redgrave's professional career. Because the analogy to the law of defamation is apt, it is a likely prediction that the higher courts where this unsettled issue must ultimately be resolved will hold that plaintiff can succeed in this burden only by showing that BSO has impliedly communicated to others some material statement of fact (and not merely opinion) about Redgrave that it knew to be false, or that BSO acted with reckless disregard for the truth or falsity of a material statement of fact it impliedly communicated. . . .

In the present case, harm to Redgrave's career resulting from any implied statement about her—including any statement about the extent of her public expression on political issues—plainly would not be actionable if the statement was true. Plaintiffs were invited to call to the court's attention any factual hypothesis, supported by evidence, involving a false statement of fact about

Redgrave that was allegedly implied in BSO's cancellation and press release. The best efforts of plaintiffs' counsel to respond to this invitation were incorporated in five formulations they submitted to the court near the close of extended consultations on this subject. These were proposed as statements that might be placed before the jury as a basis for interrogatories asking the jury to determine whether or not any such statement was impliedly communicated by BSO's cancellation and press release and, if so, whether the statement was false and whether BSO knew it to be false or acted with reckless disregard for its truth or falsity. The five formulations were as follows:

> 1. Because Vanessa Redgrave was engaged to narrate the "Oedipus Rex" centenary concerts, those concerts were irreparably wrecked and had to be cancelled.
>
> 2. Vanessa Redgrave's politics created such turmoil, disturbance and opposition that the Boston Symphony Orchestra's centenary "Oedipus Rex" concerts were irreparably wrecked and had to be cancelled.
>
> 3. Vanessa Redgrave's engagement to play the role of narrator in the Boston Symphony Orchestra's "Oedipus Rex" centenary concerts caused the concerts to be cancelled because the Boston Symphony Orchestra received threats both to disrupt the performance and to withhold significant financial support if she appeared, many performers refused to perform if she appeared and the artistic integrity of the performance would have been compromised if she appeared.
>
> 4. Vanessa Redgrave could not be permitted to appear in the role of narrator of the "Oedipus Rex" centenary concerts because to permit her to appear in those concerts would pose unacceptable risks to the audience, to the musicians and to Symphony Hall.
>
> 5. Vanessa Redgrave cannot be hired to perform without wrecking a production and no measures can be taken to protect against such damage.

Plaintiffs' Proposed Inserts for Special Interrogatories, Docket No. 268 (Nov. 6, 1984).

Close analysis reveals that each of these formulations of some message allegedly conveyed by the BSO cancellation includes one or more opinions. None of these formulations disentangles from opinion a statement of fact about Redgrave that with support in evidence, the jury could find to be false and to have been made with knowledge of falsity or with reckless disregard for its truth or falsity. . . .

Thus, plaintiffs failed entirely to meet their burden of identifying any way of disentangling protected expression from a form of expression that even arguably might be actionable.

I turn, finally, to possible hypotheses about expressions of opinion as part of the communicative link between BSO's cancellation and harm to Redgrave's career.

The Supreme Court has declared that opinion statements are constitutionally protected. "Under the First Amendment there is no such thing as a false idea." *Gertz*, 418 U.S. at 339, 94 S.Ct. at 3007.

Relevant sections of the *Restatement (Second) of Torts*, drafted after *Gertz* and with painstaking attention to the implications of *Gertz*, call attention to the possibility that a statement in opinion form may impliedly state facts. *See Restatement (Second) of Torts* §§ 566, 581A comment c (1977). In this case, however, as noted above, plaintiffs have wholly failed to identify any statement of fact that can be disentangled and treated as a basis for a claim. . . .

In summary . . . plaintiffs' claim for consequential harm to Redgrave's professional career must be denied. . . .

Judgment will be entered for plaintiffs, on the breach of contract claim, in the amount of $27,500, and for defendant as to all other claims.

On November 16, 1982, defendant made a Rule 68 offer of judgment in the amount of $31,000. *See* Fed.R.Civ.P. 68. Judgment finally obtained by plaintiff being "not more favorable than the offer," costs will be assessed in conformity with Rule 68. . . .

1.70   Bankruptcy and Personal Services Contracts

Chapter 1 has considered in depth the legal underpinnings of the entertainment personal services contract. This final section discusses an arena that no one wishes to enter—the bankruptcy court. However, entertainment ventures too often proceed on miscalculation and overextension. Entertainment executives and performers alike often go broke when going for broke.

The nature of a personal services contract is examined in the cases that follow. The basic inquiry is to what extent the personal services contract (or at least some of the rights and duties contained therein) survives the bankruptcy of a principal party to a contract. In the two central cases examined, the bankrupt party is the performer. As seen in contrasting the *Waldschmidt* and *Noonan* decisions, there is no single answer to the extent to which a contract survives a declaration of bankruptcy. For some purposes, the contract still lives; for others, it is terminated, and the bankrupt party is free to begin anew. Beyond the question of bankruptcy, both cases probe the nature of the personal services contract.

Waldschmidt v. CBS, Inc., 14 B.R. 309 (U.S.Dist.Ct. M.D.Tenn. 1981)

WISEMAN, DISTRICT JUDGE

This action involves a dispute between the bankruptcy trustee for the estate of musician George Jones and the defendant CBS, Inc., concerning who is entitled to the royalties from the sale of certain records made by Mr. Jones pursuant to his recording contract with CBS. Because the recordings were made by Mr. Jones prior to the date of his voluntary bankruptcy petition, the trustee argues that any royalties derived from their sale are the property of Mr. Jones' estate and therefore should pass to the trustee. CBS, on the other hand, argues that because the royalties actually stem from services rendered under a personal services contract—the recording contract between Mr. Jones and CBS—they are not the property of Mr. Jones' estate and do not pass to the trustee. CBS's argument is important be-

cause it also alleges that under the contract it is entitled to recoup from these royalties certain advances it made to Mr. Jones prior to his bankruptcy. CBS's fear is that if the royalties are deemed the property of the estate, its right of recoupment would dissipate and it would be forced to proceed as an ordinary creditor of Mr. Jones to recover the money it advanced to him. The advances far exceed the royalties collected to date, and if treated like any other creditor, CBS would be unable to recover the full amount of the advances.

Each party in this action has moved for summary judgment pursuant to Rule 56, F.R.Civ.P. Because no genuine issue regarding any material fact exists, this cause is ripe for summary judgment. Having reviewed the pertinent facts and law, this Court now makes the following determinations: (1) that the royalties are the property of Mr. Jones' estate; (2) that although the royalties are the property of the estate, CBS is entitled to recoup the full amount of the advances from these royalties; and (3) that the trustee is entitled to an accounting of the royalties and of the amounts recouped by CBS. . . .

The threshold issue in this case is whether the royalties constitute "property" within the meaning of section 70(a)(5) of the old Bankruptcy Act. That section provides in relevant part:

> (a) The trustee of the estate of a bankrupt . . . shall . . . be vested by operation of law with the title of the bankrupt as of the date of the filing of the petition initiating a proceeding under this title, except insofar as it is to property which is held to be exempt, to all of the following kinds of property wherever located. . . . (5) property, including rights of action, which prior to the filing of the petition he could by any means have transferred. . . .

CBS bases its argument that the royalties are not property within the scope of section 70(a)(5) on two grounds. First, CBS argues that because the recording contract between Mr. Jones and CBS was one for personal services, both the contract itself and any rights growing out of it—such as the right to royalties—were nontransferable and nonseverable as of the date of the bankruptcy petition, December 13, 1978. Second, CBS argues that even if Mr. Jones had transferable rights in the royalties in December 1978, royalty rights are not the type of property intended to be covered by section 70(a)(5). The trustee counters CBS's contentions by arguing that Mr. Jones had unquestionable rights in any royalties collected by CBS from sales of his records, that these rights were clearly alienable by Mr. Jones, and that "property" as meant by section 70(a)(5) includes the rights to the royalties here in dispute.

In regard to the first point of contention, this Court finds that nothing in the nature of the recording contract itself prevents the rights to the royalties from passing to the trustee. As CBS argues, it is generally true that a contract for personal services is "nonassignable." What this rule means, however, is simply that the performance of the particular personalized service itself is nondelegable, not that the right to payment for any such service may not be assigned once performance has occurred. *See* Corbin, Corbin on Contracts 805 (1952). . . .

. . . CBS argues that Mr. Jones was still obligated under the contract to certain promotional activities, as well as live performances, before he was entitled to receive the royalties.

While it is true that Mr. Jones did have certain obligations outstanding under the overall contract with CBS, this Court cannot agree that Mr. Jones' right to the royalties was expressly conditioned on such additional activity. Mr. Jones completed performance of the basic contractual duties upon which the receipt of royalties was conditioned by making the master recordings from which the records were ultimately pressed. Mr. Jones did have other obligations under the contract, but these obligations did not affect his right to royalties from the record sales. If anything, Mr. Jones' further obligations seemed designed to boost record sales, and it is only in that respect that they affected the royalties. This Court rejects CBS's argument, then, and accepts the contention of the trustee that any contingency that did exist in Mr. Jones' contract regarding the royalties would at most affect the marketability of Mr. Jones' interest, but not its assignability. *See In re Malloy*, 2 B.R. 674 (Bkrtcy.M.D. Fla. 1980).

Having concluded that the personal services nature of the recording contract does not preclude passage to the trustee of Mr. Jones' rights to the royalties, this Court must now decide whether these rights are in fact the sort of "property" intended to pass to the trustee under section 70(a)(5). Although the definition of property under section 70(a)(5) has been considered by the courts on numerous occasions, no case appears to have addressed this particular question directly. Despite the absence of a specific precedent, the voluminous case law that has evolved under section 70(a)(5) does provide guidelines for this Court's inquiry. Taking the existing interpretations into consideration, this Court concludes, in this case of apparent first impression, that the royalty rights here are property under section 70(a)(5) of the Bankruptcy Act.

It is well established that the term "property" as employed in section 70(a)(5) is to be given a broad interpretation. . . . The simple fact that Mr. Jones could not actually collect the royalties until some time after the date of his bankruptcy petition, then, does not prevent his rights to those royalties—which effectively accrued before his bankruptcy—from being considered property under section 70(a)(5). . . .

While "property" under section 70(a)(5) is thus broadly defined, its scope is not unlimited. As the Supreme Court noted in *Segal*, "[L]imitations on the term do grow out of other purposes of the Act; one purpose . . . is to leave the bankrupt free after the date of his petition to accumulate new wealth in the future." 382 U.S. at 379, 86 S.Ct. at 514, 15 L.Ed.2d at 432. Elaborating on this restriction, the Court in *Lines v. Frederick*, 400 U.S. 18, 19, 91 S.Ct. 113, 114, 27 L.Ed.2d 124, 127 (1970), stated,

> The most important consideration limiting the breadth of the definition of "property" lies in the basic purpose of the Bankruptcy Act to give the debtor a "new opportunity in life and a clear field for future effort, unhampered by the pressure and discouragement of preexisting debt. The various provisions of the bankruptcy act were adopted in the light of that view and are to be construed when reasonably possible in harmony with it so as to effectuate the general purpose and policy of the act."

(citing *Local Loan Co. v. Hunt*, 292 U.S. 234,

244–45, 54 S.Ct. 695, 699, 78 L.Ed. 1230, 1235 (1984)). The test for determining whether the inclusion of certain items in the estate is consistent with the purpose and policy of the Bankruptcy Act is whether the bankrupt's claim to the asset is "sufficiently rooted in the prebankruptcy past and so little entangled with the bankrupt's ability to make an unencumbered fresh start that it should be regarded as 'property' under § 70a(5)." *Segal v. Rochelle*, 882 U.S. 375, 380, 86 S.Ct. 511, 515, 15 L.Ed2d 428, 432 (1966). This Court believes that Mr. Jones' interest in the royalties meets this test and should be considered the property of his estate under section 70(a)(5). . . .

In characterizing assets for the purposes of section 70(a)(5), the courts have developed no clear mode of classification. Indeed, the Supreme Court itself has stated that "property" as meant by section 70(a)(5) "has never been given a precise or universal definition." Moreover, "it is impossible to give any categorical definition to the word . . ., nor can we attach to it in certain relations the limitations which would be attached to it in others." *Kokoszka v. Belford*, 417 U.S. 642, 645, 94 S.Ct. 2431, 2433, 41 L.Ed.2d 374, 378–79 (1974). Rather than erecting hard and fast categories, then, the courts have taken a case-by-case approach and analyzed each asset on an individualized basis. Essentially, the courts have applied a balancing test to each specific situation, employing the *Segal* formula and weighing the degree of relation between the asset and the "prebankruptcy past" against the potential effect that placing the asset in the estate would have on the bankrupt's ability to make an "unencumbered fresh start" after bankruptcy.

Applying this balancing test to the facts of this case, this Court finds that Mr. Jones' rights to the royalty payments are indeed sufficiently rooted in the prebankruptcy past to warrant inclusion of the royalties within Mr. Jones' estate. The recordings involved here, from which the royalties derive, were completed prior to the filing of the bankruptcy petition. Moreover, while Mr. Jones did have certain outstanding obligations under his contract with CBS, his right to payment was not so conditioned on his performance of these

additional duties that the royalties should not be deemed property under section 70(a)(5). Moreover, including the royalties within the estate would not unduly handicap Mr. Jones' efforts to make an unencumbered fresh start because the royalties are in fact derived from recordings made prior to Mr. Jones' bankruptcy. As this Court is aware from other proceedings involving Mr. Jones, he has already devised a plan to repay his creditors and is presently once again engaged in recording and public appearances. . . .

Although the royalty payments owed to Mr. Jones were not due *in toto* on any one specific date, the arrangement between Mr. Jones and CBS did require a regularized system of accounting and payment to Mr. Jones at six-month intervals. Moreover, nothing in the fact of Mr. Jones' bankruptcy has (or had) any effect at all upon CBS's obligation to pay the royalties. That obligation matured upon the completion of the recordings by Mr. Jones, and nothing has since occurred to alter it. While the example of wages is not a perfect analogy—for there is no perfect analogy to this case—the reasoning of the Sixth Circuit in this respect is persuasive. Coupled with this Court's previous conclusion that any impediment to Mr. Jones' ability to start anew is far outweighed by the prebankruptcy nature of the royalties' roots, *Aveni* provides ample basis for including the royalties within the estate.

This Court thus rules that the royalties owed by CBS, Inc., to George Jones because of recordings made by Mr. Jones prior to the date of his bankruptcy petition are property within the scope of section 70(a)(5) of the Bankruptcy Act and pass to the trustee for the benefit of the estate. The argument of CBS is accordingly rejected. . . .

Although this Court has ruled that the royalties are the property of the estate under section 70(a)(5), this Court also holds that CBS is entitled to recoup the full amount of its advances to Mr. Jones from these royalties.

The trustee attempts to argue that CBS must proceed with its claim under the restrictive set-off provisions of section 68 of the Bankruptcy Act, instead of possessing a general right of recoupment. The trustee apparently seeks to argue not only that recoupment is covered by section 68 but also that the set-off and recoupment processes are equivalent. The trustee is sorely mistaken on both points.

In the first place, no authority exists to support the trustee's assertion that recoupment is within the ambit of section 68. Indeed, there is ample authority to the contrary. . . .

Additionally, the recoupment process is different from the requirements for set-off. While set-off under section 68 is limited to instances involving mutuality of obligation, recoupment is subject to no such limitation. . . . The only real requirement regarding recoupment is that a sum can be reduced only by matters or claims arising out of the same transaction as the original sum. . . . Despite the trustee's contention, the advances and royalties involved in this case unquestionably arise from the same transaction. Both grow out of the recording contract between Mr. Jones and CBS. In fact, no dispute over the royalties would exist but for the express provision in the contract calling for advances and their recoupment from royalties. Additionally, no question exists regarding the enforceability of such a contract provision against the bankruptcy trustee. . . . In view of these considerations, CBS is clearly entitled to recoup its advances from the royalties at issue in this case. . . .

As a final point, this Court rules that the trustee is entitled to an accounting of all royalties received by CBS from the sale of recordings made by George Jones prior to the date of his bankruptcy. The trustee is also entitled to an accounting of all advances to date recouped by CBS from these royalties. Because this Court has held that the royalties are the property of the estate, but subject to CBS's right of recoupment, the trustee must have all information regarding the royalties and advances. The trustee now stands in the place of the bankrupt with regard to these royalties. Should CBS recoup its advances and there be undepleted royalties, these would pass to the trustee for the benefit of the estate. The trustee must know if that event is a possibility, and if so, at what point in time it might occur. An accounting is thus necessary so that the trustee may be fully informed. Accordingly, this Court hereby orders CBS, Inc., to provide the trustee with an accounting of the royalties received and any advances recouped therefrom.

NOTE

1. In *In re Sherman,* 627 F.2d 594 (2d Cir. 1980), an insurance company was permitted to recoup a bankrupt agent's advance commissions from commissions actually earned subsequent to filing of the petition. These were advances, not loans. No "security interest" was involved, and therefore the company was not required to perfect its interest under U.C.C. § 9.302.

In the Matter of Noonan, 17 B.R. 793 (U.S.Dist.Ct. S.D.N.Y. 1982)

BABITT, BANKRUPTCY JUDGE

On its motion to convert the debtor's voluntary chapter 7 case to an involuntary chapter 11 case, the moving creditor invites this court to come up with a square holding in its favor on nice, round, undisputed facts. The court must decline the invitation and rule for the debtor as a round hole cannot accept the square peg which sets this case apart from others fitting more snugly into the statutory scheme. That uniqueness is based on who the debtor is, who the creditor is, what it wants from the debtor, and how it can go about getting it!

The controlling facts are not in dispute: Robert A. Noonan (Noonan or debtor) known professionally as Willie Nile, is a songwriter who performs and records his and the popular music of others. On June 24, 1981, Noonan filed a voluntary petition for the relief afforded by chapter 11 of the 1978 Bankruptcy Reform Act, 11 U.S.C. § 1101 *et seq.* (Supp. IV 1980), Pub.L. 95–598, 92 Stat. 2549 *et seq.* The sworn schedules filed with Noonan's petition reveal there are virtually no free assets from which dividends might be paid to his creditors. His artistic endeavors generate Noonan's sole source of income, and as to these, he is subject to an exclusive recording contract (Arista contract) with Arista Records, Inc. (Arista), the moving party in this dispute. And, as the debtor's endeavors to terminate his relationship with Arista are at the crux of their differences, some key points of the Arista contract should be noted. Noonan entered into it on November 14, 1978 and by its terms he was obligated to record exclusively for Arista for an initial period of eighteen months. Noonan was obligated to record at least two albums during this period and Arista was given an option to extend this eighteen month period for three consecutive periods of like duration.

Noonan did record two albums pursuant to this Arista contract for which Arista advanced approximately $300,000. Noonan is not personally obligated to repay this money; Arista is entitled, on the other hand, to recoup these advances from future royalties. Although these albums received acclaim from critics, sales were modest and royalties fell far below the amount Arista is entitled to recoup.

Nonetheless, Arista has decided to exercise its option to hold Noonan to a second 18-month term, during which time he would be obligated to record two additional albums. There is nothing invidious in this action, as it is clear Arista hopes to recoup its losses from future recordings. Noonan, however, sees things otherwise for he now finds himself in a position where the sales for a third album would have to exceed one million units to reach the $500,000 recoupment Arista would be entitled to after advancing production costs for this new album.

Dissatisfied with this arrangement, and with his eyes and mind focused on a more favorable artistic and monetary environment, Noonan, as debtor in possession, 11 U.S.C. § 1101(1), moved for an order rejecting the Arista contract as executory, a right given by 11 U.S.C. § 365 to trustees and to chapter 11 debtors in possession by the force of 11 U.S.C. § 1107. The right given to reject executory contracts as a matter of a debtor's business judgment, is part of the warp and woof of the fabric of bankruptcy. It was in the 1898 Act, and kept in later revisions in Sections 70(b) and in the debtor relief chapters, Section 77(b) (Reorganization of Railroads), Section 82(b)(1) (Adjustment of Debts of Political Subdivisions, etc.), Section 116(1) (Chapter X), Section 313(1) (Chapter XI), Section 413(1) (Chapter XII) and Section 613(1) (Chapter XIII). Indeed, plans offered creditors by these debtor relief supplicants under earlier statutes could provide for the rejection of executory contracts. By thus seeking rejection of the Arista contract, Noonan swiftly and surely let Arista know that he would no longer record for that company.

Arista vehemently opposed Noonan's motion and began to prepare for all out war. Perceiving the effusion of time, energy and money he would need to battle Arista on the contract, Noonan exercised his absolute right to convert his chapter 11 case to a chapter 7 case. 11 U.S.C. § 1112(a). Noonan's application acknowledged that the impulse for converting to a chapter 7 case was to take advantage of the automatic rejection of executory contracts given by 11 U.S.C. § 365(d)(1). Noonan quite properly sensed that his bankruptcy trustee could not assume the Arista contract, for while he might force Noonan to the recording studio, he could not make him sing or play. Noonan also understood that the Arista contract is not the kind of contract capable of assignment by the trustee after assumption. As there could be no assumption or assignment, the trustee would either reject or the Arista contract would be deemed rejected. 11 U.S.C. § 365(d)(1) is clear as to this synergism. Thus, the court entered an order achieving the conversion to chapter 7. The United States Trustee appointed an interim trustee who later qualified as trustee. 11 U.S.C. § 15701.

Understandably shaken by the direction Noonan's life may take following the unfolding of the chapter 7 process and the exclusion of Arista from Noonan's future, the former moved under 11 U.S.C. § 706(b) to put the debtor back into chapter 11 nullifying his chapter 7 choice. Arista also moved the court to shorten Noonan's time to file his chapter 11 plan and to permit Arista to file its plan, a course permitted by 11 U.S.C. § 1121's scheme.

Arista's position is that it will fund a plan which will give the debtor's creditors, Arista included, more than they could hope to garner from a liquidation of his non-exempt property. Moreover, Arista says that its plan will give Noonan a $10,000 advance to be recouped later.

But all of this generosity to Noonan's other creditors is not engendered by eleemosynary motives. Any such plan offered by Arista is dependent upon a condition precedent, *i.e.*, the assumption and the affirmance by Noonan of the Arista contract.

Arista claims to find support for all this in the authority in the 1978 Code for an involuntary chapter 11 case, the impulse for which was Congress' feeling that a debtor's creditors should be able to realize on his assets through reorganization just as in a liquidation. H.R.Rep.No. 95-595, 95th Cong., 1st Sess. 322 (1977) U.S.Code Cong. & Admin.News 1978, p. 5787. In furtherance of this, Arista says that reconversion to chapter 11, assumption of its contract with Noonan and confirmation of its plan will work and everyone will be happy.

Everyone except Noonan, that is. He says nothing can compel him to assume or reaffirm his contract with Arista and that this court, even if it could force him, should not as a matter of equity, for to do so would interfere with his fresh start and place him in involuntary servitude.

Therefore, Noonan argues that for the court to decree reconversion would be a futile act preordained to result in his return to chapter 7 as Arista's chapter 11 dreams can never be realized. So, he says, Arista's motion should be denied, a view with which the court agrees.

The court has carefully considered these factors for all are clearly relevant, since the decision to convert under Section 706(b) is left to the sound discretion of the court, an exercise which should include consideration of the best interests of both the creditors and the debtor. See House Report, *supra*, at 880; S.Rep.No.95 989, 95th Cong., 2d Sess. 94 (1978). But, of equal importance is "what is fair and equitable under the *peculiar circumstances of the particular case, guided by the spirit and purpose of the law.*" *Manekas v. Allied Discount Co.*, 6 Misc.2d 1079, 166 N.Y.S.2d 366 (N.Y.Sup.Ct. 1957).

Wisely, Congress did not give creditors the unfettered right to insist on conversion of a debtor's case for, by leaving this decision to the court's discretion, the court is free to explore "what is below the surface of the statute and yet fairly part of it." Frankfurter, *Some Reflections on the Reading of Statutes*, 47 Colum.L.Rev. 527, 533 (1947).

Arista says that in exercising its discretion the court should not consider the Noonan contract now. And so, the court now addresses what it considers relevant to Arista's contention.

The purpose of the usual chapter 11 case is a business reorganization. It is premised upon the theory that the assets of a business in use are more valuable than those same assets sold in a liquidation sale for the benefit only of their purchaser. Efforts are made to preserve and conserve the value of assets. House Report, *supra*, at 22. And by permitting involuntary reorganization, Congress reasoned that creditors should be able to realize on these assets through reorganization, as well as liquidation. But these typical factors are foreign to this case, as it simply refuses to be typical and application of customary chapter 11 principles on the facts here cannot work. This debtor is an individual; an artist. He has no tangible assets available for distribution. He earns his living by his creativity, by his voice, and by the combination of the two. The Arista contract is merely the instrumentality for the exploitation of the debtor's talents.

The Arista contract is clearly an executory contract. 11 U.S.C. § 541 vests the debtor's estate with all the debtor's property as of the commencement of the case. A seeming exception to the sweep of this rule continues for executory contracts, for the Code continues prior law by postponing vesting of the debtor's rights and duties until assumption. 2 *Collier on Bankruptcy* (15th ed.) ¶ 365.01.

But a personal service contract was never the kind of contract treated by Section 70(b) of the 1898 Act; it never was and could not be property of the estate for the purposes of the section. The law under the 1898 Act was clear and there is nothing in the 1978 Code indicating any change. Where an executory contract between the debtor and another is of such a nature as to be based upon the debtor's personal skill, the trustee does not take title to the debtor's rights and cannot deal with the contract. . . . The Arista contract is simply not the kind of an asset to which the creditors can look by insisting that the debtor assume it.

Since a personal service contract does not vest in the debtor's trustee, services performed under it would appear not to be "for the benefit of the estate, but rather for the personal benefit of the bankrupt. . . ." *Ford, Bacon & Davis, Inc. v. Holahan*, 311 F.2d 901, 904 (5th Cir. 1962). For policy, practical and constitutional reasons, these contracts are *sui generis*. Clearly, the answer to Arista is that its contract is not an asset that can be used for its benefit nor in the debtor's plan absent his consent. And, as it appears to be Noonan's only potential asset of value, the underpinning for Arista's conversion motion has been removed.

To be sure, Arista's frustration is understandable. However, it must have known it was dealing in an area which historically fashioned its own rules. It is a longstanding rule that courts of equity will not order specific performance of personal service contracts. . . .

In *ABC v. Wolf.*, 52 N.Y.2d 394, 438 N.Y.S.2d 482, 420 N.E.2d 363 (1981), the plaintiff, ABC, and the defendant, Wolf, a prominent New York City sportscaster, had entered into an employment contract containing a good faith negotiation and right of first refusal clause. This provision operated to bind Wolf to negotiate with ABC for 90 days, following which Wolf was required to afford ABC a right of first refusal before he accepted another offer of employment. In its action, ABC alleged that Wolf had breached this provision and sought specific performance as well as an injunction to bar Wolf's employment at CBS. The Court of Appeals refused to grant this relief after its review of the principles of specific performance applicable to personal service contracts. . . .

These considerations are the indices of a mature, democratic society. And hand in hand with their reaffirmation is recognition that where problems have arisen in a contractual relationship calling for the performance of purely personal services, the termination of that relationship terminates the problems, to paraphrase Mr. Justice Frankfurter in *Peres v. Brownell*, 356 U.S. 44, 60, 78 S.Ct. 568, 2 L.Ed.2d 603 (1958). It follows from all these generalities not only that Noonan cannot be compelled to abide by his contract with Arista but that it must be rejected for it cannot be assumed unless Noonan wants it so. It therefore must also follow that Arista's attempt to restore Noonan to chapter 11 status has to be denied for its rationale is rejected by Noonan on the facts and by this court on the law.

And that result is consistent with Congress' views found elsewhere. Congress was not unaware that the prohibition against involuntary servitude loomed large in bankruptcy, and Congress therefore magnified its concern on the area of involuntary chapter 13 cases. 11 U.S.C. §§ 1301 *et seq*. Here Congress acted to dispel even the remotest possibility of involuntary servitude by prohibiting involuntary chapter 13 cases. 11 U.S.C. § 303(a); 11 U.S.C. § 706(c).

Arista would have the court ignore this expression of a general Congressional mood by insisting that Congress' concerns in the chapter 13 case are irrelevant to the motion to convert Noonan to a chapter 11 debtor pursuant to 11 U.S.C. § 706(b), for Arista says that it is a party in interest and that Noonan, at least facially, is an eligible chapter 11 debtor. 11 U.S.C. §§ 109(a),(d). So, Arista concludes, the statute is satisfied and it must prevail. But this syllogism ignores the reality. Courts are often faced with situations not envisioned by the most gifted legislative imagination.

The fact is that Congress perceived the usual 13 case as emanating from a non-business debtor and determined to make the relief of that chapter voluntary in order to avoid the spectre of involuntary peonage for a hapless debtor laboring for his creditors on their petition and their plan which could strip the debtor and his family of all that made their lives otherwise worth living.

It is also the fact that Congress perceived chapter 11 of the 1978 Code, an amalgam of many of the features of chapters X, XI and XII of the 1898 Act, as a reorganization device, mainly for non-individually operated businesses, and occasionally for the small sole proprietor ineligible for chapter 13 relief. . . . From that vantage point, it was Congress' view that the chapter 11 petition could emanate from the debtor's creditors, thereby bringing the debtor involuntarily into the bankruptcy process.

The possibility, therefore, that the rare and unique kind of fact pattern present here in which there lurks the real possibility of the involuntary servitude with which Congress was concerned in chapter 13 never occurred to it when it perceived chapter 11.

But this is not to say that this court should ignore Congress' concerns on facts it did not foresee because comment was made about concerns on facts it did foresee. The policy against forcing an individual to work against his will is applicable, if the facts present themselves, in chapter 11 as well as in chapter 13. Congress' concerns are so strongly expressed in connection with chapter 13 that this court would be remiss were it to apply them only there. . . .

It is thus clear from the strong policy considerations of Congress which, on the facts here, touch on Constitutionally protected areas, that Arista's motion, addressed to this court's discretion, must fail. This is so because the relief it seeks, *i.e.*, reinstatement of Noonan's chapter 11 case, is itself destined to fail for the reasons already described.

Finally, it is clear that Arista's proposed plan would defeat a primary purpose of the Code "to allow the individual debtor to obtain a fresh start, free from creditor harassment and free from the worries and pressures of too much debt." House Report, *supra*, at 125. See *Perez v. Campbell*, 402 U.S. 637, 91 S.Ct. 1704, 29 L.Ed.2d 233 (1971). If the debtor could be compelled to assume the Arista contract, he would leave this bankruptcy court subject to at least $300,000 of indebtedness, which Arista could recoup from his future earnings. Moreover, as Arista concedes, a confirmed plan reaffirming the contract would subject Noonan to the very real likelihood of protracted litigation. Clearly, the full potential reach of Arista's "scheme" would deprive Noonan of the full scope of his discharge.

As the full measure of a debtor's fresh start flowing from the bankruptcy process is vital to Congress' mission in enacting the Code, *cf.*, *Powell v. U.S. Cartridge Co.*, 339 U.S. 497, 516, 70 S.Ct. 755, 765, 94 L.Ed. 1017 (1950), anything which would frustrate the mission must be scrutinized carefully. Arista's attempts to manipulate the bankruptcy process for its own ends is found seriously wanting. . . .

Chapter 2

LITERARY PUBLISHING

2.00 Publishing as Entertainment

To begin our analysis of the various entertainment industries with literary publishing may seem strange until one realizes that in terms of longevity literary publishing by far predates movies, TV, records, and the like. It is a business that entertainment consumers enjoyed long before advancing technology began to capture images on film and sounds on metal. Writers such as Agatha Christie, Georges Simenon, P. G. Wodehouse, and Barbara Cartland have written hundreds of books, with aggregate sales in the hundreds of millions. In addition, literary works are often the source for many creative by-products that allow other entertainment media to prosper. Consider the degree to which the novels of such authors as Harold Robbins, Judith Krantz, and Jacquelinn Susann have become the stuff of movie and TV fare, not to mention such old-line writers as Ernest Hemingway, William Faulkner, and F. Scott Fitzgerald.

Newspapers, magazines, and books proliferated through the second half of the nineteenth century and into the twentieth century. What had started as individual enterprises became a booming industry. As technology advanced, printing became faster and more economical and ever-greater markets were reached. By the mid-1800s, the American reading public was the largest ever. A staple for those who could afford leisure time was the printed word, now expanded beyond religious and philosophical tracts to novels, short stories, biographies, histories, and informational texts designed to please and entertain. The writer not only was recognized for his or her craft, but was now aided by others in producing and promoting the writer's works. Whereas early American writers such as Washington Irving and John Fennimore Cooper had to pay to publish their own works, later authors found others eager to publish and distribute. This was a boon, but it brought the inevitable problems that occur when people with different skills, backgrounds, and motives have to work together. Separate roles had to be defined, and individual businesses—now part of a fledgling industry—had to establish patterns for doing business. With variations, these nuances have persisted, and later entertainment industries have taken these patterns and developed their own.

Our initial focus, therefore, will be on the trends that have developed in literary publishing. Although the later entertainment industries devised their own permutations, much can be traced to the problems first faced in the area of the printed word.

2.01   The Business of Literary Publishing

Publishing houses began as family businesses. Ownership passed from generation to generation, and an intimate relationship was the norm between the company ownership and its group of authors. While today numerous specialty houses and small publishers continue to service their authors on a close, personal basis, they are no longer prevalent. The larger publishing houses have gone the way of the corporate America that emphasizes acquisitions and mergers. The publishing company is often part of a national or multinational conglomerate, and close ties between an author and the publishing ownership are generally nonexistent. Strong relationships may still exist between an author and an editor at a particular company, but this relationship is always subject to the vagaries of the economic bottom line.

The prevalence of mergers and acquisitions has led to interesting combinations of companies in the past few years. Three patterns have developed. The first trend is the acquisition of a publishing house by another publisher. The second pattern occurs when a company in the larger information or communications field adds print publishing to its interests. Third is the trend for an outside company to add publishing as a means of diversity among its holdings. All three types of acquisitions or mergers have caused concern in the publishing industry, but the third type especially raises concerns about the future of publishing if those with nonpublishing backgrounds begin to dictate what is or is not published.

The combinations resulting from these recent trends raise intriguing scenarios. For example, consider Time, Inc., the long-time publisher of such magazines as *Time, Life, Sports Illustrated, People, Fortune, Money* and *Discover*. Time, Inc., is also in book publishing, with its direct-mail *Time-Life Books and Records*. It also owns Book-of-the-Month Club and the Boston publishing firm, Little, Brown & Co. In 1986, it added yet another book publisher, Scott, Foresman & Company, to its holdings. Time, Inc. also has taken a foothold in the emerging video fields with its ownership of Home Box Office (HBO), which has for several years controlled a substantial percentage of the U.S. pay-TV market. Time, Inc. has also introduced less successful video ventures such as TV-Cable Week. One can get some sense of Time, Inc.'s history by comparing its changing revenue base, as the following figures for 1975 and 1982 indicate:

Percent of Total Revenues (Time, Inc.)

Holdings	1975 (Total: $910.7 million)	1982 (Total: $3.56 billion)
Magazines	35%	26%
Books	23	14
Video	4	24
Forest products	28	32
Other	10%	4%

Doubleday, the leading publisher of trade books (books aimed at a general readership), also owns Dell (a leading publisher of paperbacks), Delacorte, the Literary Guild, and, through its glorious 1986 season, the New York Mets. In late 1986, however, the Mets were sold to the publishing company's principal owner, Nelson Doubleday. Doubleday the publishing house, and its holdings, were bought by Bertelsmann A.B., a giant West German company with numerous communications holdings in Europe.

CBS, Inc., the giant broadcasting company, also owns a publishing house—its CBS Publishing Group. Until recently, this division included Holt, Rinehart & Winston, one of the nation's leading publishers of textbooks for the college, high school, and elementary markets; W. B. Saunders, the world's largest medical publisher; CBS International Publishing; and Neisa/Inter-Americana, a Latin American and Spanish publishing company. The first three companies, including Holt, Rinehart, were recently sold to Harcourt Brace Jovanovich, Inc., another leading textbook publisher, for $500 million. Neisa/InterAmericana was sold to other interests. Even with these sales, CBS did not move entirely out of the publishing business. It still retains several publishing operations that have, over the past few years, contributed about $700 million, or 15 percent, to CBS's total revenues of just under $5 billion per year.

The acquisition of the CBS companies by Harcourt Brace Jovanovich was more significant for the buyer than the seller. The move immediately catapulted Harcourt Brace ahead of SFN Companies and Simon & Schuster as the projected leader in the textbook markets. SFN had $289.4 million high school and elementary textbook revenues in 1985, Simon & Schuster had $278 million, and Harcourt Brace Jovanovich had $221.4. Adding the $81.8 million of the CBS Publishing Group vaulted Harcourt Brace over the $200 million mark for 1986, and put it in a new position of power.

The revenues stated above for Simon & Schuster are only partial reports of its income. Simon & Schuster is owned by Gulf & Western, which owns such diverse holdings as insurance companies, Paramount Pictures, candy manufacturers, Madison Square Garden (which in turn owns the New York Knicks and Rangers), and other wide-ranging enterprises. Simon & Schuster's entry into the textbook market is fairly recent, aided by Gulf & Western's acquisition in February 1984 of Esquire, Inc. (no relationship to the magazine), which had a large education publishing group that included Allyn & Bacon, the Globe Book Company, Modern Curriculum Press, and the Cambridge Company. Simon & Schuster had long had a substantial presence in general trade publishing; now, with the Esquire companies, Simon & Schuster moved with great influence into the textbook market. Gulf & Western was not yet finished. In late 1984, it acquired Prentice-Hall, Inc. for approximately $700 million. Prentice-Hall is the nation's leading publisher of college textbooks, and thus joined with Simon & Schuster's newly developed presence in elementary and high school textbook publishing. A final example of an interesting combination is the mammoth Newhouse newspaper chain, which owns Random House (along with the Modern Library imprint), prestigious Alfred A. Knopf, Pantheon, and the major paperback house, Ballantine Books.

These examples are of the big growing even bigger, with constant changes in the actual ownership of the well-known publishing houses. In total, the 50 largest publishing houses account for approximately 75 percent of total U.S. sales. Since estimates are that there are over 10,000 publishing companies, that leaves about 9,950 others to scramble for the remaining 25 percent. Despite this seemingly disparate picture, many small publishing houses do manage to survive and even prosper. In all, though, the picture is bleak. Estimates are that some 100 publishing companies open for business each year, and in one form or another two-thirds do not survive more than a few years. Either they collapse entirely or are bought by larger concerns.

Book publishing in the United States is a multibillion dollar business. In 1985, more than $7 billion was spent on recreational books alone, with a projected rise by 1989 to just under $11 billion. When magazines and newspapers are added, the total more than doubles. In 1985, almost $13.5 billion was spent in the United States on magazines and newspapers, up from $10.4 billion in 1980. In the entertainment fields, only television is larger in terms of total revenues, and it gained that edge over print publishing as recently as the early 1980s.

The potentials for large revenues are felt throughout the vertical ladder of the publishing business, causing new methods of doing business in manufacturing, distributing, and retailing. For example, booksellers have changed over the past few years. The small bookstore has faced the unwelcome challenge of chains, most notably B. Dalton, Waldenbooks, Barnes & Noble, and Crown. Waldenbooks has over 1,000 stores, and B. Dalton over 700. Those two chains alone account for $1 billion in yearly sales. Waldenbooks is a subsidiary of department-store conglomerate K. Mart and accounts for a substantial share of that company's overall profits. When the bookstore chains began expanding rapidly in the late 1970s, book sale revenues increased an average of 9.4 percent per year from 1978 to 1982, and the total number of books sold increased 2.3 percent each year, according to the trade publication *Book Industry Trends.*

The appearance of bookstore chains has created legal problems. Independent booksellers have charged that many publishing companies and distributors are giving the chains special discounts that unfairly and illegally discriminate against the independents. Numerous antitrust suits have been filed, charging price discrimination in violation of the Robinson Patman Act. Early victories have gone to the independents, although it will likely be years before these suits reach final settlement. (See Bishop,

"The Battle of the Booksellers," *New York Times*, March 17, 1987, p. DA, col. 3.)

Another sector of print publishing that has been able to escape several aspects of antitrust scrutiny through federal government intervention is the newspaper industry. The Newspaper Preservation Act of 1970, passed in response to a 1969 U.S. Supreme Court decision that found certain combinations by newspapers to be antitrust violations, allows competing newspapers in a city, under certain circumstances, to share manufacturing plants and commercial operations and to engage in such otherwise unlawful practices as setting joint advertising rates and circulation prices. The legal standard that allows operations to be joined is a showing that one of the newspapers faces bankruptcy.

Clearly, newspapers have struggled to survive in the twentieth century, as other forms of communications have developed. In 1909, 609 cities had competing daily newspapers. In 1968, that number had shrunk dramatically to 45, and in 1986 it was only 27. Even so, there are questions over whether certain newspapers that joined forces really needed to do so. In 1986, for example, the *Detroit News* and *Detroit Free Press* announced they were joining forces, despite both having shown substantial 1985 profits. However, a questionable action such as the Detroit example should not cloud the overall effectiveness of the act. Estimates are that newspapers in 21 cities have avoided bankruptcy by joining with a more affluent competitor. (See Randolph and Behr, "Newspaper Preservation Law Produces Windfall," *Washington Post*, July 13, 1986, p. 1, col. 1.)

2.02   Contracts in Publishing

The basic literary work may be only the beginning of the process by which a "story" is created and sold through numerous media. A book may be turned into a movie, the movie into a TV series, the book into a sequel, the sequel into a movie, and on and on. The first contract between the publisher and author is crucial in determining who has control over the process. Several other contracts are likely to be entered into before the creative work reaches its ultimate saturation of all available markets. In addition to the contract between the publisher and author, there are likely to be contracts for paperback, foreign, and merchandise licensing and for motion picture, television, and video/audio cassette options. There might also be a contract between the author and a literary agent.

2.02–1 Publisher-Author Contract

As noted above, this contract is the table-setter that may greatly determine what can or cannot be included in later agreements. This contract is discussed in detail in Section 2.03.

2.02–2 Paperback Licensing

If the prospective book has possibilities for both hard-cover and paperback markets, provisions for such exploitation will be detailed in the original publisher-author contract. In fact, for well-known authors, it is not unusual to arrange for the paperback publishing at the same time the hard-cover contract is signed. In the usual scenario, the publisher-author contract allows the original publisher to license the paperback edition with another company. One issue is whether there will be restrictions in the original publisher-author contract limiting the companies with which the original publisher can deal. The subsequent licensing agreement between the hard-cover and paperback publisher must then set forth the marketing promises made by the paperback publisher, the licensing fee arrangements, the quality of the product, the timetable for publication

of the paperback edition, and restrictions on the assignment of the license.

2.02–3 Foreign Licensing

A foreign license may involve translating the work into another language. A question to be resolved is to what extent the original publisher (or the author) has an opportunity to review the quality and faithfulness of the translation. A restriction on the territory for distribution of the foreign work should be included. The precise purposes for which the license is granted must be defined. The ability to receive a proper accounting for sales is also important.

2.02–4 Merchandise Licensing

Literary works at times attain such popularity that items in clothing, toys, posters, and other merchandise may have substantial commercial possibilities. The first case in this chapter, *Geisel v. Poynter Products*, emphasizes what happens when the ownership of a creative product is not properly protected. The facts of the case also illustrate the marketing possibilities for characters in a literary work, sometimes several years after the original work featuring the characters first appears. The merchandise licensing agreement must define precisely for what purposes the license is granted in terms of what product can be produced, what degree of quality control exists, and how long the license runs. Restrictions on areas and types of marketing should also be negotiated.

2.02–5 Motion Picture/Television Option Contract

A film producer may spot a literary work that has possibilities for transformation to the theater or television screen. Often the first step is to obtain an option on the work, pending a decision as to whether the work is transmittable to film and whether the appropriate financing and talent can be obtained. The option agreement should define not only the length and cost of the option but also the terms of the ultimate agreement should the option be exercised. The ability to grant the option, whether it be publisher or author, will depend on the original contract between the two, as will the division of payments received for granting the option and ultimately licensing the film. The option contract, including the ultimate license granted, must define the creative control retained by publisher or author, the time limits on the license, the precise purposes of the license, and, of course, the royalty or fee arrangements. These types of agreements typically provide for a set fee for the option, but the actual payment if the option is exercised may be either a fee or percentage of the proceeds. A determination of the proceeds will be based on whether the film is made originally for theatrical release or is made strictly for television.

2.02–6　Other Media Licensing

As technologies advance, print publishers may find it advantageous to put their works directly into other media forms, such as audio or video cassettes. The basic publisher-author agreement should cover this possibility (see Section 2.03); the publisher may then find itself licensing the rights for an audio or video cassette to another company if the publisher itself does not have such capacity. Restrictions must be included in the license as to the marketing of such cassettes, the quality control over their production, advertising rights (which may include the right to use the name and image of the original author), and fee payments, whether it be a set amount or a percentage of revenues.

2.02–7　Author-Literary Agent

Authors who write for the mass market usually require a literary agent to represent them. The agent in this role assumes somewhat different responsibilities than agents or managers in other entertainment fields, but there are also similarities. The general legal requirements of agents, including those of a fiduciary relationship to the client, are discussed at length in Chapter 9. As to the literary agent, the contract should specify how long the contract is to run, the different types of income on which the agent's fees will be based, the representations by the agent as to what can be done for the author, and the ability of the agent to act on the author's behalf. In general, the agent promises good-faith efforts to market the author. The reality is that a young author's big opportunity may lie in obtaining the services of a reputable and well-placed literary agent.

2.03　Publisher-Author Contract

Because of the vast variety of books published for today's markets, no single form could ever be appropriate for all publisher-author contracts. A law school casebook, for example, has little potential for later adaptation to the silver screen. A grant of rights to the publisher as to motion picture rights, therefore, is not an item likely to consume a great deal of negotiating time. When the prospective book is a novel by a well-known author, however, the ability to license the work for motion pictures and television may be a central issue. Thus, the following comments may or may not apply to any particular publisher-author contract. The points discussed are those that must be considered when approaching such contracts, with an initial decision to be made as to their applicability.

2.03–1 Rights Granted and Assigned

The rights granted by the publisher and assigned to the author run the gamut and must be carefully negotiated. The publisher is likely to ask for the sole and exclusive rights in a work, including those for trade and quality paperback, book clubs, reprint licensing, mass market paperback reprints, selections for anthologies, textbooks, abridgements and condensations, periodical and broadcast selection, digests, transcriptions, special editions for the handicapped, the theatre, motion pictures and television, radio, educational pictures, merchandising, foreign language, export, and "all others." The author will want to limit such grants or at least retain royalty rights in all such possible uses of the work. An author should not assume that such grants are normally accorded the publisher; rather, the author should consider each item separately negotiable.

2.03–2 Manuscript

The manuscript provisions define who has ultimate creative control over the work, the delivery date for the manuscript (and the consequences for late delivery), the rights/duties of the publisher to edit and comment, and some type of "satisfactory manuscript clause." The failure of publisher-author contracts to provide these important details has been the basis for substantial litigation, which is discussed further in Section 2.20. The Authors Guild has addressed one of these problems by drafting the following model "Satisfactory Manuscript Clause":

(a) Author shall deliver a manuscript which, in style and content, is professionally competent and fit for publication. A manuscript shall be deemed professionally competent and fit for publication if it substantially follows Author's prior works and/or Author's style at the time the contract between Author and Publisher is signed.

(b) Publisher shall be deemed to have agreed that the manuscript complies with the conditions of (a) above unless, within 60 days of the manuscript's receipt, Publisher sends the author a written statement of the respects in which Publisher maintains the manuscript is not, in style and content, professionally competent and fit for publication. Author may, within 60 days after receipt of that statement, submit changes in the manuscript.

(c) If the manuscript (with any changes by the author) is not, in style and content, professionally competent and fit for publication, and Publisher has given the statement required by (b) above, Publisher may terminate this contract by written notice to Author given within 60 days after receipt of the changes pursuant to (b) above, or if no changes are submitted, within 90 days after Publisher sent the statement pursuant to (b) above.

(d) If the contract is terminated pursuant to (c) above:

(i) Author shall be entitled to retain __ percent of the total advance and shall receive any portion of that amount not yet paid, and

(ii) if Author has received more than __ percent of the total advance, Author shall repay to Publisher any portion that exceeds __ percent of the total advance, but only from those proceeds, if any, received by Author under a subsequent contract for publication of the work by another publisher.

2.03–3 Noncompetition

The publisher's form agreement often contains provisions that the author will not publish a future book that is based on the material of the book under contract or that interferes or competes with that book. The provisions are generally sweeping and are potentially applicable to a wide range of works that the author might want to undertake. One can sympathize with a publisher's not wanting an author to come out immediately with a competing work that will under-cut the sales of the book in question. However, rarely is the publisher willing to give the same guarantees; indeed, the publisher may have several competing books in the same field. This suggests that the author should grant no more than a very limited, specific noncompete provision.

The Authors Guild has made these comments about noncompete clauses:

> These clauses can cause an author considerable harm. A publisher might claim that the characters in a novel or children's story could not be used in sequels: that the author of a textbook could not write other works on the same subject; or that one cookbook or other specialized work is all that an author could write, without the publisher's release from the non-compete clause. We do not think these claims are valid. These clauses, absolute restrictive covenants, are probably unenforceable; and they may violate the antitrust laws.

> Non-compete clauses should be deleted. If the publisher refuses, the clause should be tightened. There should be a reasonably short time period, after which it expires. The types of books to which it applies should be stated, specifically. Authors of textbooks should be particularly careful that they limit the effect of the clause, so that the contract for one book on a subject does not prevent them from writing other texts on the subject for other age groups, or for different types of classes or schools.

2.03–4   Publication

Several provisions in the publisher-author contract generally detail publication rights and duties. The publisher is likely accorded the exclusive right to publish. An order of publication vis-à-vis hard cover and paper-back may be established. Specification of duties to advertise and market the book should be negotiated. The publisher arguably has an implied duty to promote a work, but certain details, such as an advertising budget and schedule, may be desirable.

2.03–5   Copyright

The publisher will probably request that the copyright be assigned by the author. The author may want to resist. In any event, the ownership of the copyright is a question that is distinct from the granting of rights under Section 2.03–1 above. The contract should be precise both as to copyright ownership and the rights to license that flow therefrom.

2.03–6   Royalties and Other Payments

These very important provisions in the publisher-author contract require close scrutiny. Beyond the issue of the percentage actually named for the royalty, of equal and perhaps even greater importance is the definition of what that percentage is based on. A 10 percent royalty of "net receipts" will vary greatly depending on what the publisher is entitled to deduct before a calculation of "net receipts" is reached. The author should be wary of a publisher definition that allows exclusion of revenues to compensate the publisher for items that should generally be assumed by the publisher.

Advances often are included in publisher-author agreements. The advance may be paid on the signing of the contract, or it may be paid in stages, as parts of the manuscript are submitted. Advances vary greatly according to the likely commercial success of the book. In recent years, advances for novels have reached new heights. For example, in 1985 Bantam Books reportedly paid an advance in excess of $1 million to an English author, Sally Beauman, for her first novel. This advance exceeded an $850,000 advance paid a few years earlier by New American Library for another first novel by Anne Tolstoi Wallach. While the amounts of these advances are unusual, to say the least, they do indicate that substantial advances are available for certain types of literary works.

Expenses incurred by the author in preparing or later helping market the book should be reimbursed by the publisher. The author's duty to exploit and the publisher's duty to reimburse are items to include in the original publisher-author agreement.

Time of payment of royalties and duty by the publisher to account are provisions that authors should not automatically accept as "givens." The time of payment can be adjusted to an author's needs. In addition, the right to an outside audit might be included (even if never exercised), and provisions for legal rates of interest to accrue if the publisher is late in payment should be considered.

2.03–7 Warranties and Indemnities

The provisions for warranties and indemnities attempt to shift the burden to the author if suit is brought by a third party claiming copyright violations, libel, invasions of privacy, or other actionable claims against the author's work. These provisions are typically quite broad and extend not only to breach but also to alleged breach. The publisher may include a right to withhold royalties pending disposition of the matter. Obviously, this could tie up the author's income for years and subject the author to substantial liability. Before acceding to these types of provisions, an author should attempt to narrow the coverage. For example, the Authors Guild suggests that an author be held responsible only for situations in which he or she knew of the violation. In any event, substantial time should be spent scrutinizing the warranty and indemnity provisions to calculate the variety of situations that might be called into play.

2.03–8 Revisions of an Existing Work

Most books have only a limited life, although certain types have continued vitality if revised and updated. The rights/duties of the author to participate in the revisions should be carefully negotiated, including provisions for when the author is unable or unwilling to participate.

2.03–9 Option for Next Work

Some publisher-author contracts attempt to bind an author to a future contract by giving the publisher an option on the next work. The Authors Guild deplores this restriction and urges authors to watch for and then refuse such clauses. In general, there is little reason to bind an author to a one-way option. At most, a publisher might be given a right of first refusal so that the author can negotiate the best deal possible with another publisher. This sets some market value on the author's present worth but still gives the original publisher the first opportunity to publish the new work.

2.03–10 Other Provisions

Numerous other provisions are included in most publisher-author contracts. Typically, the contract is not assignable by the author but is by the publisher. The author may want restrictions placed on the publisher's ability to assign. Provisions for discontinuance of publication should be negotiated, including the disposal of the books on hand and possible return of the copyright if such has been assigned by the author. Breach by the publisher and an opportunity to cure are standard provisions that may nevertheless be tailored to specific situations. The publisher's right to publicize the book by using the author's name and likeness is also standard, but at times the language is overly broad and should be narrowed so that other publicity rights of the author are not impaired.

When there is more than one author, care must be exercised in defining the authors' joint and several liabilities, not only to the publisher but also to each other. Finally, there are often provisions as to proofreading duties, responsibility for an index, payment to others for use of copyrighted materials, governing law, ability to modify the agreement, an integration clause, notice procedures, number of copies of the work to the author, bankruptcy of the publisher, and procedures for adjudication of disputes. All should be carefully examined.

NOTES ————————————————

Numerous sources discuss the publishing industry's economics, business background, and legal problems, including the following:

1. S. Metcalf, *Rights and Liabilities of Publishers, Broadcasters and Reporters* (Colorado Springs, Colo.: Shepard's/McGraw-Hill, 1982).

2. K. Henderson (ed.), *Trends in American Publishing* (Champaign: University of Illinois, 1968).

3. L. Coser, C. Kadushin, and W. Powell, *Books: The Culture and Commerce of Publishing* (New York: Basic Books, 1982).

4. J. Tebbel, *A History of Book Publishing in the United States*, four volumes (New York: R. R. Bowker, 1981)—note particularly vol. IV, *The Great Change, 1940–1980*.

5. L. Duboff, *Book Publishers' Legal Guide* (Seattle: Butterworth, 1984).

6. *Literary Publishing and the Law* (Chicago: American Bar Association, 1986)—collected materials, distributed through ABA.

7. V. Kovner and E. Perle (co-chair), *Book Publishing 1984* (New York: Practicing Law Institute, 1984)—collected forms and materials.

2.10   Basic Interests in a Literary Work

Authors are often so anxious to publish that they pay little attention to the small print of contract provisions. Despite a heightened consciousness of the pitfalls of indiscriminate contract signing, many authors still sign whatever is thrust before them. Later, whether it be next month, next year, or several years later, many authors live to regret their hasty actions.

The time of contracting, of course, is the time to plan for the future. The following statements from *Geisel v. Poynter Products, Inc.* are particularly revealing. The lengthy opinion covers several important legal issues. The court's decision is ample warning that one must anticipate any number of future contingencies, even those that occur 20 or 30 years down the road.

Burnett v. Warner Brothers Pictures contains a similar warning. If a broad assignment-of-rights clause is included in a written agreement, the court states that it is for the assigning party to *reserve* any rights not assigned. In other words, the presumption is in favor of the assignment of a particular right when there is a broad assignment clause.

————————————————

Geisel v. Poynter Products, Inc., 295 F. Supp. 331 (S.D.N.Y. 1968)

HERLANDS, DISTRICT JUDGE

Can an artist who sells his signed cartoon to a magazine validly object to the magazine's making and selling a doll which is truthfully advertised as based upon the cartoon? This, capsulated, poses the critical issue herein. . . .

Plaintiff, Theodor Seuss Geisel, is the world-famous artist and author, whose nom de plume is "Dr. Seuss." In a complaint against the four defendants, filed March 8, 1968, plaintiff charged that the defendants manufactured and were advertising and selling dolls "derived from" . . . certain material which plaintiff "prepared for publication" . . . for the now defunct *Liberty Magazine* in 1932 and which was published in that magazine from June to December 1932; that, although plaintiff had nothing to do with the design or manufacture of the dolls, they were being advertised and sold as "Dr. Seuss" creations; and that the dolls are "tasteless, unattractive and of an inferior quality". . . .

On the basis of these and other allegations, plaintiff requested compensatory and punitive damages as well as an injunction enjoining defendants from using the name "Dr. Seuss" in any manner without plaintiff's consent, or in connection with any product not designed or approved by plaintiff.

In support of this prayer for relief, plaintiff pleaded five causes of action: (1) violation of Section 43(a) of the Lanham Act, 15 U.S.C. §1125(a) (1964); (2) unfair competition, including violation of Section 368–d of the New York General Business Law, McKinney's Consol. Laws, c. 20; (3) violation of plaintiff's right of privacy as provided by the New York Civil Rights Law, McKinney's Consol. Laws, c. §§ 50, 51; (4) defamation; and (5) conspiracy with intent to injure plaintiff (prima facie tort).

The Preliminary Injunction

An order to show cause for a preliminary injunction was signed on March 8, 1968. On March 12, this Court heard argument on that motion, issued a temporary restraining order (which, in substance, restrained defendants from using the name "Dr. Seuss" in any manner in connection with any doll, toy or other product), and granted the parties leave to conduct discovery and to submit further papers.

On April 9, 1968, this Court concluded that there was a reasonable probability of plaintiff's success upon the trial of the Lanham Act (first) cause of action and issued a preliminary injunction restraining defendants as follows:

> The defendants, their officers, agents, servants, employees and all persons acting under their control and each of them are hereby enjoined and restrained pendente lite from committing any of the following acts in connection with the manufacturing, displaying, advertising, distributing, selling or offering for sale of any doll, toy or other similar product:
>
> A. Representing that defendants' doll, toy or other similar product has been created, designed, produced, approved or authorized by plaintiff;
>
> B. Describing defendants' doll, toy or other similar product as having been created, designed, produced, approved or authorized by plaintiff; or
>
> C. Representing, describing or designating plaintiff as the originator, creator, designer, or producer of defendants' doll, toy or other similar products. . . .

It would be useful to summarize defendants' basic contentions, as formulated in the pre-trial order. Defendants claim that they have the right

to manufacture and sell the dolls in question for the reason that either (1) defendant Liberty Library Corporation—as successor-assignee of *Liberty Magazine*—owns complete rights, including copyright, in the cartoons published in 1932, and "the owner of copyright in cartoons has the exclusive right to make three-dimensional figures therefrom," or (2) the cartoons are in the public domain and, therefore, "anyone may use such cartoons as the basis for the three-dimensional figures." . . .

In addition, defendants argue that they have the right to state truthfully the relationship between plaintiff-cartoonist and the dolls, including the circumstance that the dolls were "based on, adapted from or inspired by" the plaintiff's *Liberty Magazine* cartoons. Finally, defendants have urged a variety of other defenses to the causes of action set forth in the complaint. . . .

At the trial, a substantial amount of the evidence concerned the nature of the 1932 agreement between plaintiff and Liberty Publishing Corporation (hereafter *Liberty Magazine*). Plaintiff contends that the evidence proves that plaintiff assigned to *Liberty Magazine* the title to the cartoons with their accompanying text "with the understanding that Liberty would copyright this work as part of the entire issue of the magazines in which they appeared. It was understood, however, that while Liberty had the complete rights to publish these works in one issue of *Liberty Magazine*, Liberty held all other rights to this work (including the right to renew the copyright and the right to make other uses of the work) in trust of plaintiff." (P.T.O.) Plaintiff presents this contention as an additional reason why he is entitled to the relief prayed for in the complaint.

On the other hand, defendants contend that the 1932 agreement provided for the transfer to *Liberty Magazine* of all or complete rights in the cartoons and accompanying text without reservation of any rights in plaintiff.

Certain facts relating to the 1932 transaction have been stipulated as not in dispute. The parties agree that, in 1932, plaintiff ". . . prepared and sold to *Liberty Magazine* material which was published in weekly issues of *Liberty Magazine* during the months of June through December 1932" (P.T.O. Stip.); that the material consisted of a series of twenty-three "cartoon essays" and that "each work [consisted of a page which] contained at least three cartoons and each cartoon contained several animal creations" (P.T.O. Stip.); that the material appeared in *Liberty Magazine* under the following titles: "Goofy Olympics," "Some Recent Developments in Zoology," "A Few Notes on Birds," "A Few Notes on the Coming Elections," "A New Idea in Taxation," "The Summer Problems and How to Solve Them," "A Few Notes on Torture," "Some Recent Inventions in the Offspring Field," "Educational Projects," "A Few Bright Spots on the Business Horizon," "Three Glorious Movements in the Clothing Field," "A Few Notes on Games," "The Rough Road to International Harmony," "House Cleaning the English Language," "A Few Hints on Hypnotism," "Some New Aids to Better Living," "A Few Notes on Origins," "A Few Notes on Fires," "A Few Hints on Navigation," "Is the Bird in Hand Really Worth Two in the Bush, Part I," "Is the Bird in Hand Really Worth Two in the Bush, Part II," "A Few Notes on Facial Foliage," "A Few Notes on Sleep" (P.T.O. Stip); and that plaintiff received $300 for each work (P.T.O. Stip.). . . .

There is also no dispute that the issues of *Liberty Magazine* in which the cartoons appeared were copyrighted by *Liberty Magazine* as entire issues (P.T.O. Stip.). Each issue contained the required notice of copyright; and Certificates of Copyright Registration were secured by *Liberty Magazine* (P.T.O. Stip.; Deft. Ex.). It is also agreed that "[n]o separate copyright was obtained . . ." by the plaintiff upon the cartoons (P.T.O. Stip.).

The only evidence describing the negotiations and consummation of the agreement between plaintiff and *Liberty Magazine* in 1932 was the testimony of plaintiff himself and of Leland Hayward. Hayward, presently a theatrical producer, was a literary agent from about 1929 to 1943. . . . According to plaintiff's and Hayward's testimony, one Ben Wasson approached plaintiff and asked whether he could represent him in seeking to place his work in magazines. Plaintiff agreed. . . . Prior to this conversation, in the 1920s and early 1930s plaintiff had sold other drawings to a num-

ber of magazines, including *Judge*, *Vanity Fair*, and the *Saturday Evening Post*. . . . During this period, plaintiff also drew cartoons for the Standard Oil Company of New Jersey to advertise a product known as "Flit." The "Quick, Henry the Flit" series appeared in magazines . . ., including *Liberty Magazine*. . . .

Ben Wasson, who did not appear as a witness, represented plaintiff in the negotiations with *Liberty Magazine*. . . . In so doing, Wasson acted as an employee of the Leland Hayward Agency. . . . Although Hayward did not personally handle the transaction, he recalls that he had one conversation with Fulton Oursler, then editor-in-chief of *Liberty Magazine*. Oursler stated that plaintiff was "popular" and that his work was "very suitable" for *Liberty Magazine*. . . . Hayward could not remember anything else said at that or any other time relating to the negotiations. . . . To the best of his recollection, there was no formal written contract executed in connection with this transaction. . . .

Plaintiff's only contact in 1932 with *Liberty Magazine* was a meeting of about fifteen minutes' duration with Fulton Oursler. . . . However, all that plaintiff recalls of the occasion is that Oursler said ". . . 'Glad to have you aboard,' or something like that." . . . Prior to that meeting, Wasson had told plaintiff of a "firm commitment" for plaintiff ". . . to do a number of pages, a small number of pages, because everything was sort of on a try-out basis . . . to see if they worked. I don't know how many pages they said they would buy, but they were $300 a piece." . . . From this and other evidence . . . the Court infers that the works which plaintiff sold to *Liberty Magazine* were not in existence at the time the contract was entered into; instead, they were created at *Liberty Magazine*'s request. . . .

Nothing was expressly said by either side during the negotiations regarding the scope of rights that *Liberty Magazine* obtained by the purchase of the material. . . . Plaintiff denies that the words "all rights" or "complete rights" were used by either side during the negotiations. . . .

This evidence demonstrates that plaintiff agreed to prepare cartoons for publication in *Liberty Magazine*; that the cartoons were published; that plaintiff received $300 a page; that the only copyright upon this material was in the name of Liberty Publishing Company; and that plaintiff did not *expressly* reserve any rights in the cartoons.

There is evidence, and the Court so finds, that, with certain exceptions which do not apply in this case, the custom and usage in 1932 in the magazine trade were that an agreement for the sale of a work between authors or their agents and magazines was oral and not a formal written contract. . . . The agreement was usually reached after *only* monetary terms were discussed. . . . This contrasts with the custom in the book publishing field in which similar contracts were written. . . .

If, arguendo, all rights in the cartoons were not assigned to *Liberty Magazine* in 1932, *Liberty's* copyright upon the entire issues of the magazine does not cover the cartoons. It would then follow that the cartoons would be in the public domain because admittedly they were *published* in 1932 without a separate copyright. . . . This result would transpire for the reason that a work can be copyrighted only by its "author or proprietor" (17 U.S.C. § 9); the "proprietor" can be the assignee but not the licensee of the right to use the work; and to be the assignee of the work, one must have been assigned all rights in the work.

Consequently, if the cartoons are not to be deemed in the public domain, it must be shown that all rights in the cartoons were assigned to *Liberty Magazine* in 1932. To escape from this logical dilemma plaintiff argues that, although legal title to the copyright was in *Liberty Magazine's* name as assignee-"proprietor," the copyright was held in trust for the cartoon's true or equitable owner, plaintiff. . . .

Whether this trust relationship exists is primarily a question of fact dependent upon the circumstances of the case.

In this case, there was no *express* agreement that *Liberty Magazine* would hold the copyright in trust for plaintiff or that plaintiff reserved any rights in the cartoons. However, much evidence was offered by both sides with respect to the issue whether there was any settled and established custom and usage in the magazine publishing trade in 1932 by which any terms or conditions

were implied in fact or understood to be part of a contract between an author or his agent and a weekly magazine; and if so, what were those implied-in-fact terms.

Evidence was also offered with respect to the issue whether there was any settled and established custom and usage concerning what the magazine was impliedly agreeing to in fact with respect to the extent of the magazine's use of the purchased material; and concerning the alleged practice of a magazine to hold its copyright in trust for the author and to reassign its copyright upon the request of the author.

Section 209 of the Copyright Law, 17 U.S.C. § 209 (1964), provides in relevant part that the certificate of copyright registration ". . . shall be admitted in any court as prima facie evidence of the facts stated therein."

Plaintiff offered the testimony of three witnesses with respect to the above mentioned customs and usages in 1932 in the magazine publishing trade: Bennett Cerf, Leland Hayward and plaintiff himself.

Mr. Cerf has been a *book* publisher since 1925 and has himself written books as well as articles for periodicals. . . . Plaintiff's books are published by the firm of which Cerf is chairman of the board . . .; and, in fact, plaintiff is the president of a division of that firm. . . . Mr. Cerf is an eminent personality in the field of *book* publishing. However, his testimony with respect to customs and usages in the *magazine* trade is found by the Court to be tenuous and unpersuasive. He repeatedly admitted his unfamiliarity with magazine customs . . . and with contracts between magazines and authors or their agents. . . . Furthermore, some of his testimony presents internal inconsistencies and self-contradictions. . . .

Three witnesses called by defendants testified about the relevant customs and usages: Meyer Dworkin, Alfred Wasserstrom and Alden Norton. . . .

On the basis of the great weight of the credible evidence, the Court finds that during the relevant period it was the custom and usage in the magazine trade for the magazine to obtain a copyright upon the entire contents of the magazine. . . . However, the author or artist *could* also obtain a separate copyright upon his particular work, as plaintiff did with respect to a "Quick, Henry the Flit" cartoon-advertisement which appeared in *Liberty Magazine* in 1931. . . .

Virtually all the testimony was in agreement on the proposition, which the Court finds established, that there was a settled custom and usage in the magazine publishing trade in the early 1930s by which a term or condition defining the scope of rights was implied in fact or understood to be part of the agreement between the author or his agent and the magazine. . . . What that term or condition provided is a subject, however, about which the testimony is sharply conflicting.

Mr. Cerf testified that, if nothing was said with respect to scope of rights purchased, the term "always" implied in the agreement provided for the sale of "one-shot publication"—publication in one issue of the magazine—and return of the copyright thereafter upon the request of the author. . . . He stated that the term "all rights" meant this understanding. . . .

Mr. Cerf indicated that the basis of his knowledge of this custom or understanding was the "minimal" amount paid to plaintiff for the cartoons. . . . He also testified that, if an author-artist received anything less than $1,000 a page in 1932 for his work, it meant that only one-time magazine rights were sold. . . .

Although the price paid may be a circumstance probative of the scope of rights purchased by *Liberty Magazine* in 1932. . . . the clear preponderance of the credible evidence demonstrates that the price of $300 per page in 1932 was a "reasonable price for that particular year" in view of the near "panic" caused by the depression. . . .

Mr. Hayward testified that the "standard practice" or usage in the magazine trade in 1932 "was [for the material] to appear in one issue of the magazine or, in the case of a serialization, in several issues. . . . The magazine was limited in its use of the material to single or serial publication . . . and those rights are called 'complete rights'—or were." . . . He, and other witnesses, stated that the expressions "all rights" and "complete rights" had the same meaning. . . . But, Mr. Hayward repeatedly stated that "all rights" did

not mean "all" and that "complete rights" did not mean "complete" . . . rather, that these terms had a limited meaning. . . . According to Mr. Hayward, "complete rights" in the magazine trade meant ". . . the complete right to publish that particular piece of material in a single issue or, in the case of serial rights, to publish parts of the material in several or more issues." . . . Mr. Hayward also testified that, although the term "all rights" was not expressly used in negotiations, it was *"implicit" in the agreement.* . . .

Mr. Hayward further asserted that after publication, the custom provided that the magazine ". . . would *always* assign the copyright to anyone the author requested" (emphasis added). The magazine was thus the "custodian of the copyright." . . . He added that he had *never* heard of a magazine sharing the revenues gained on the material after the assignment back. . . .

Plaintiff also testified that, in 1932 custom or usage implied in fact in the agreement a condition that the magazine would use the purchased material only in a single insertion in the United States and Canada. . . .

If believed in its entirety, the evidence adduced in behalf of plaintiff would prove that in 1932 custom or usage in the magazine trade implied in fact in the Geisel-*Liberty Magazine* agreement that (a) each cartoon could be used only in a single insertion in the magazine; that (b) thereafter the copyright was held in trust for plaintiff and would be reassigned to him at his request; and that (c) the term "all rights" or "complete rights," which was understood to mean (a) and/or (b), was "implicit" in the agreement.

Meyer Dworkin, called as a witness for defendants, testified that he did not recall, and, in fact, there "categorically" never was, any custom or understanding in 1932 whereby an author ". . . would reserve impliedly all rights except the right to have the magazine publish in that issue the particular work of art". . . . On the contrary, the custom was that "where the author said nothing and sold the manuscript to the company, the company would receive all rights. . . ." He stated that this custom was understood by *Liberty Magazine*, Mcfadden Publications *and by the authors* who dealt with them. . . . Mr. Dworkin defined "complete rights" and "all rights, full rights" . . . with no residual rights in anyone else. . . .

Although Mr. Dworkin admitted that *Liberty Magazine* (or Mcfadden Publications) occasionally would reassign its rights to an author without charge, he stated that at other times the reassignment would be for a fee or for a share of the author's profits after the assignment back. Whether reassignment would be made and whether it would be made without payment depended upon who the author was and the purpose for which the assignment back was sought. . . . Mr. Dworkin explained that sometimes reassignment would be made to retain the author's friendship and goodwill. . . .

Alden Norton convincingly testified that, although every story purchased by a magazine was individually bargained for, ". . . if you sold me a story and you didn't ask for anything, you sold me all rights and it would say so on the check". . . . He also testified that, if there were no written or oral agreement and no legend on the check and the author or artist simply delivered the work to a magazine and was paid $300 a page, the custom and usage in 1932 provided that "[u]nless otherwise specified, [the author granted] all rights". . . . Mr. Norton rejected the assertion that, if nothing was said, only first publication rights were acquired by the magazine. . . . He testified that, if all rights were not acquired, there were specific negotiations—i.e., something *was said* . . .—and a lower price would be paid for the material. . . .

Alfred Wasserstrom also testified persuasively that he knew of no custom or usage which gave the words "all rights" a specialized meaning in the magazine trade in 1935. . . . He agreed that the words "all rights" had a plain, colloquial English meaning [1372–1374, 1375]. Likewise, he testified that he knew of no custom or usage giving the words "complete rights" ". . . any meaning different from their ordinary, accepted English meaning." . . .

On the basis of the clear preponderance of the credible evidence, the Court finds that the custom and usage in 1932 in the magazine trade implied in fact in the Geisel-*Liberty*

Magazine agreement a provision whereby all rights or complete rights were assigned to *Liberty Magazine*. . . .

In ordinary acceptance, the expressions "all rights" or "complete rights" have a nontechnical and literal meaning. Plaintiff has failed to sustain the burden of proof which is upon him when he seeks to impart to these words a connotation that is diametrically opposite to their plain, colloquial sense. The Court finds the testimonial assertions of plaintiff's witnesses, in this respect, to be incredible and factitious. The terms "all rights" and "complete rights," when understood according to their plain meaning, signify a totality of rights, including the right of reproduction or common law copyright and the right to secure statutory copyright without qualification. . . .

Having decided that *Liberty Magazine* acquired *all* rights to the cartoons published in 1932, the Court now considers and determines what rights defendants have to make the dolls . . . and to what extent, if any, defendants may use the name "Dr. Seuss" in connection therewith.

Plaintiff's basic contentions are that defendants ". . . may not use plaintiff's name in any way in connection with the toy dolls because the toy dolls do not bear a sufficient relationship to the original work and differ in material respects from it"; and that "the toy dolls destroy the artistic integrity of plaintiff's original work and are so inferior in quality that the use of plaintiff's name in connection with them is disparaging and damaging to him." . . .

Additional details of the factual background of this litigation must be mobilized in order to consider the respective rights of the parties in proper context.

On September 1, 1949, Lorraine Lester entered into an option agreement with Liberty Magazine, Inc. . . . which, as amended on March 13, 1950 . . . , permitted her, upon certain conditions, to exploit short story material which had appeared in *Liberty Magazine* during the period 1924 to 1949 for use in connection with radio, television and motion pictures. . . . The exclusive license agreement provided in part: "2. We shall make available for your inspection all short stories which have been published by *Lib-*

erty. With respect to any stories selected by you of which we own all rights, your use thereof may commence immediately. As to any other stories selected by you, we will endeavor at your request to obtain all rights which may be required, but in no event will you be licensed to sue them hereunder until we have authorized such use."

On September 20, 1949, Miss Lester signed an agreement assigning the option agreement . . . to Lester-Fields Productions, Inc. . . . , a company in which she was a principal. . . .

In 1950, Miss Lester learned from Osborne B. Bond, the publisher of *Liberty Magazine*, that *Liberty* planned to cease publication. . . . She thereupon entered into negotiations on behalf of Lester-Fields Productions, Inc. to acquire the magazine's "copyright library". . . . On August 10, 1950, Miss Lester received a letter from *Liberty* . . . accepting her prior oral offer to purchase the "rights to all material contained in the Library of Liberty Magazine, Inc. from May 10, 1924 to July, 1950, inclusive. . . ."

Thereafter, on September 8, 1950 Lester-Fields and Liberty Magazine, Inc. entered into an agreement . . . terminating the 1949 option agreement with Miss Lester and providing in part as follows: "3. Liberty hereby sells, assigns and transfers to Lester any and all right, title or interest it may have in or to any and all of the stories and articles which have been published in *Liberty Magazine* from May 1924 to July 1950 inclusive, provided, however, that Liberty makes no representation as to the extent of its right, title or interest in and to such stories and articles." The material referred to in that agreement included short stories, articles, cartoons and crossword puzzles which had appeared weekly in *Liberty Magazine* over a period of 26 years. . . . Approximately 17,000 literary properties were included. . . . Lester-Fields also bought *Liberty Magazine*'s permanent purchase record cards and checks covering the period of 1943 to 1950. . . .

On October 5, 1950, Lester-Fields assigned this agreement . . . to George Lessner, Lorraine Lester, Robert Fields and Samuel H. Evans. . . . Fields subsequently assigned his interest to the others. . . . Thereafter, on November 10, 1964, this agreement . . . was assigned to Liberty

Library Corporation. . . . Thus, defendant Liberty Library Corporation is successor to all the literary assets of Liberty Publishing Corporation, publisher of *Liberty Magazine* in 1932. . . .

In August 1964 Mr. Robert Whiteman called on Miss Lester in connection with film production. In the course of their conversation, he saw the 90 bound volumes of *Liberty Magazine* on her shelves; and, after discussion, suggested that he could help her make money by exploiting the literary properties contained in this magazine. . . . Thereafter, Whiteman entered into an agreement with Liberty Library, whereby Whiteman represented Liberty "on an exclusive basis" in exploiting the material from defendant *Liberty Magazine*. . . .

Commencing in 1964, defendant Liberty embarked on a program of actively exploiting the material which had appeared in *Liberty Magazine* from 1924 to 1950. In the course of selecting material for sale or licensing, Whiteman came upon plaintiff's cartoons in the 1932 issues of *Liberty Magazine*. . . . Whiteman checked the Liberty record cards and secured a copyright search on that material. . . . After receiving expressions of interest in the cartoons, "as a matter of courtesy," Whiteman contacted Random House which referred him to plaintiff's agent, Mrs. Phyllis Jackson of Ashley Famous Agency. Whiteman showed her copies of the cartoons and of the copyright search and offered plaintiff the opportunity either to join with Liberty in exploiting the material or to repurchase the rights in the works. . . . Whiteman agreed to keep her informed regarding any offers which he received with respect to the material. . . . Subsequently, Whiteman informed her by letter of December 15, 1964, that he had received an offer for reprint rights to the material. . . .

Prior to the letter of December 15th, Mrs. Jackson contacted plaintiff who rejected defendant Liberty's offer. . . .

Finally, in 1967, Whiteman undertook to sell merchandising rights to the cartoons. . . . Whiteman, who was experienced in licensing and merchandising items, including toys . . . , decided to grant a license to manufacture dolls based on the cartoons. . . . Whiteman licensed defendant

Poynter Products, Inc. because he had had successful dealings with Donald B. Poynter in the past and he considered Poynter to be ". . . a man of tremendous capabilities in the field of molding, sculpture, art, taste. . . ." . . . The licensing agreement . . . was executed (on September 8, 1967), after Poynter had been shown the cartoons and informed of plaintiff's objection to the publication of the paperback book. . . .

Donald B. Poynter was and is an experienced designer and manufacturer of toys, novelties and gift items, including items made for children. . . . He had previously designed a variety of items based upon works of well known artists. . . . He had also produced puppets . . .; "premiums," such as T-shirts and tags, given away by sponsors of children's radio and television shows; theatrical sets . . . and advertising artistic layouts for a large toy manufacturer. . . .

In view of the protest telegram from plaintiff's attorney in 1964, Whiteman decided to submit everything done with respect to the dolls to Mr. Abelman. In fact, all meetings between Whiteman and Poynter took place in Mr. Abelman's office. . . . In November 1967, Whiteman and Poynter came to Mr. Abelman's office to discuss design of the dolls. . . . Poynter brought with him a hand sculptured styrofoam and papier-mâché model . . . of one of the cartoon "characters" . . . which he had prepared from "rough" sketches. . . . Mr. Abelman found the prototype doll to be "reasonably acceptable and a faithful reproduction" . . . and Whiteman agreed. . . .

At the meeting in November, 1967, Mr. Abelman also advised Poynter ". . . that under no circumstances should he consult any book written by Dr. Seuss, watch any television program by Dr. Seuss or use any material of Dr. Seuss outside the Liberty drawings in preparing the drawings for his dolls, and I told him that when he watched those drawings he should look at them very carefully, reproduce them as close as he possibly could, taking into account the fact that you are moving from a two-dimensional medium of paper and publishing into the three-dimensional medium of dolls." . . . In fact, the Court finds that Poynter used the cartoons *only* as they appeared in *Liberty Magazine* or in the paper-

back book . . . in the preparation and design of the dolls. . . .

At a meeting in February 1968, Abelman, Whiteman and Poynter carefully examined each doll and compared it with the cartoons. Abelman expressed the opinion that Poynter . . . had done a very fine job of faithfully reproducing the cartoons in the doll medium, the three-dimensional medium." . . . Previously, Poynter had submitted to Abelman, by letter of December 30, 1967, prototypes of the "hang tag" . . . which was originally used with the dolls. . . . Abelman approved the tag and suggested that a copyright notice also be permanently imprinted in the base of each doll. . . . By letter dated February 16, 1968, Whiteman approved the dolls and the advertising material which he had viewed at the meeting. . . .

Prior to March 12, 1968 (when the Court entered a temporary restraining order in this matter), defendants offered and sold the dolls using the name "Dr. Seuss" in the following ways:

1. It was engraved in very small letters on the vinyl bottom of each doll . . . with the statement: "From Original Illustrations of Dr. Seuss ® 1932 Liberty Library Corporation Copyright Renewed ® 1966 Poynter Products Inc., Cincinnati, Ohio Made in Japan." This was done pursuant to the suggestion of defendants' counsel. . . .

2. A round hang tag [Pltf. Ex. 26] tied around the neck of each doll stated, on one side: "From the Wonderful World of Dr. Seuss—an original Merry Menagerie"; and, on the other side: "This is my _____ (you name it) from Dr. Seuss' Merry Menagerie." Mr. Abelman approved this tag. . . .

The following [see page 116] are reproductions of both sides of this hang tag:

It is to be noted that the format of the name "Dr. Seuss" copies exactly the characteristic style of plaintiff's nom de plume as it appears in all his works.

As will be pointed out shortly, defendants discontinued the above wording and format after March 12, 1968.

straining order was entered in this action, until April 9, 1968, when a preliminary injunction was entered, defendants did not ship any of the dolls for sale. . . . After the preliminary injunction was entered, defendants again began to offer the dolls for sale accompanied by revised labels and sales materials using the name "Dr. Seuss" in the following manner:

a. The hang tag tied around the neck of each doll . . . stated, on one side: "Wacky Merry Menagerie Everybody loves 'em"; and, on the other side: "Toys Created, Designed & Produced Exclusively by Don Poynter MERRY MENAGERIE Based on Liberty Magazine Illustrations by Dr. Seuss";

The following are reproductions of both sides of this revised hang tag:

3. The dolls were sold in a display carton. . . . On the base of this carton was the statement: "Dr. Seuss' Merry Menagerie" and the words "Lovable . . . Huggable"; on the backboard attached to the base of the carton was the statement: "From the Wonderful World of Dr. Seuss . . . Everybody Loves 'em . . . From Original Illustrations by Dr. Seuss." This carton, as well as the hang tag, also contained Liberty Library and Poynter Products copyright notices. The carton contained a statement that defendant Abelman is the exclusive U.S.A. distributor. Although Abelman did not recall whether he approved the display box, he did approve the title "From the Wonderful World of Dr. Seuss" and the remainder of the text used. . . .

From March 12, 1968, when a temporary re-

It is to be noted that, subsequent to April 9, 1968, defendants discontinued using plaintiff's characteristic style of printing "Dr. Seuss."

b. The backboard of the display carton . . .:

MERRY MENAGERIE

Toys Created, Designed	Based On Liberty
& Produced Exclusively	Magazine Illustrations
By Don Poynter	By Dr. Seuss

The name "Dr. Seuss" and the name "Don Poynter" were in the same size and style of type. The base section of the carton . . . contained no mention of Dr. Seuss.

c. The revised handbill . . . read: "MERRY MENAGERIE. Toys Designed, Created & Produced Exclusively by Don Poynter Based on Liberty Magazine Illustrations by Dr. Seuss."

The name "Don Poynter" and the name "Dr. Seuss" were in the same size and style of type. In regular-size type in the handbill appeared the following copy: "These lovable, huggable little creatures are from original illustrations by the celebrated author-illustrator Dr. Seuss. These early drawings were featured in the famous Liberty Magazine. Now, from these drawings Don Poynter, the inventor of 'The Thing,' has created, designed and produced the newest, cutest, most charming 'merry menagerie' to 'hit' the market in many years." . . .

As the owner of a copyright on the two-dimensional cartoons, defendant Liberty Library has the right to make three-dimensional figures or dolls therefrom or to license another (e.g., defendant Poynter Products) to do so. See *King Features Syndicate v. Fleischer*, 299 F. 533, 535 (2nd Cir. 1924) (owner of copyright upon cartoon sued manufacturer of toy horse ". . . fashioned after, labelled, and sold as . . ." "Sparky," the cartoon character; *held*: there is a claim for copyright infringement because a three-dimensional toy figure can be a copy of a two-dimensional cartoon). As the Court of Appeals for this Circuit stated in *King Features Syndicate*: "Copying is not confined to a literary repetition, but includes various modes in which the matter of any publication may be adopted, imitated, or transferred with more or less colorable alteration" (299 F. at 535).

A copyright upon a work in one medium may be asserted affirmatively by the copyright owner to obtain protection against infringement accomplished in a different medium. . . .

A corollary of the rule just stated is that a copyright upon a work in one medium empowers the copyright owner to transform or copy the work into a different medium. More specifically, in this case the owner of the copyrighted two-dimensional cartoons has the right to make three-dimensional figures from the cartoons.

The manifest logic of the foregoing conclusion is demonstrated by assuming *arguendo* that the cartoons are in the public domain. In that suppositious situation, clearly defendants could copy the cartoons at will. In the present case, defendants, as owners of the copyrighted cartoons, cannot be in a less advantageous position.

Based upon a variety of legal theories set forth in the complaint, plaintiff's primary argument is that defendants' use of plaintiff's trade and pen name "Dr. Seuss" is wrongful. . . .

Plaintiff charges that defendants have violated Section 43(a) of the Lanham Act, 15 U.S.C. § 1125(a), and are guilty of unfair competition and of violating Section 368–d of the New York General Business Law. The counterargument advanced by defendants is that a series of federal cases involving trademark infringement and unfair competition establishes the defendants' indisputable right to use the name "Dr. Seuss" to describe truthfully the nature and origin of their product, the dolls.

In this area of federal trademark law, the governing principle was expounded by the Court of Appeals for this Circuit when it declared in *Societe Comptoir De L'Industrie Cotonniere Etablissements Boussac v. Alexander's Department Stores, Inc.*, 299 F.2d 33, 36 (2nd Cir. 1962), aff'g, 190 F. Supp. 594 (S.D.N.Y. 1961), that registration of a mark

> . . . bestows upon the owner of the mark the limited right to protect his goodwill from possible harm by those uses of another as may engender a *belief in the mind of the public that the product identified by the infringing mark is made or sponsored by the owner of the mark. Champion Spark Plug Co. v. Sanders*, 331 U.S. 125, 67 S.Ct. 1136, 91 L.Ed. 1386 (1947) citing with approval, *Prestonettes, Inc.*

v. Coty, 264 U.S. 359, 44 S.Ct. 350, 68 L.Ed. 731 (1924). The Lanham Act does not prohibit a commercial rival's truthfully denominating his goods a copy of a design in the public domain, though he uses the name of the designer to do so. Indeed it is difficult to see any other means that might be employed to inform the consuming public of the true origin of the design.

Those cases involving sponsorship, whether trademark infringement or unfair competition, protecting the owner of the mark, are based upon a finding that *the defendant's goods are likely to be thought to have originated with, or to have been sponsored by, the true owner of the mark*. [Emphasis added.]

In *Prestonettes*, Coty, the owner of a registered trademark, sought to enjoin another from selling Coty's genuine products in smaller bottles and packages with Coty's name on it. The District Court issued a limited injunction which allowed the defendant to affix a label truthfully describing the relationship between defendant's product and Coty's product. The Court of Appeals issued a broad, absolute injunction restraining defendant from using Coty's marks *in any way* (as plaintiff requests in the case at bar). The Supreme Court reversed, holding that defendant could state the nature of the component parts of its product and the source from which it was derived. . . .

In *Champion Spark Plug*, defendant repaired and reconditioned Champion's used sparkplugs and sold them using the name "Champion." The Supreme Court, noting that, in fact, the plugs *were* plaintiff's, stated: "Inferiority is immaterial so long as the article is clearly and distinctly sold as repaired or reconditioned rather than as new. The result is, of course, that the second-hand dealer gets some advantage from the trademark. . . ."

The doctrine of *Prestonettes* and *Champion Spark Plug*—that a trade name may be used by another as long as there is full and meticulously truthful disclosure communicating the actual character of the product—has been followed in a long line of decisions. . . .

Another case that illuminates the problem before the Court is *Chamberlain v. Columbia Pictures Corp.*, 186 F.2d 923 (9th Cir. 1951). There the Court affirmed the dismissal of a complaint by the heirs of Samuel Clemens against the defen-

dant which had released a motion picture advertised as "A Story Only Mark Twain Could Tell," "Mark Twain's Tale of a Gamble in Hearts," and "Mark Twain's Favorite Story" and, therefore, assertedly conveyed the impression that Clemens had authored the picture. In fact, alleged plaintiff, the picture was of inferior quality; had only slight resemblance to Clemens' story; and was merely a "corny love story." The Court held that, because Clemens' story and, therefore, his name, were in the public domain, plaintiff had no monopoly in it and there could be no violation of plaintiff's rights; and that nothing in the advertisements could lead anyone to believe that the movie was plaintiff's business or that plaintiff was in any way connected with it (186 F.2d at 925). In the case at bar, plaintiff likewise has, to the extent that defendant Liberty Library owns all rights in the cartoons which appeared with the name "Dr. Seuss," no absolute monopoly in the name "Dr. Seuss."

With these guidelines as to the scope of the permissible use of the trade name "Dr. Seuss" in mind, the Court reaffirms, on the merits, that defendants violated Section 43(a) of the Lanham Act by their "use" of the name "Dr. Seuss" "in connection with" the advertising and sale of the dolls *prior to March 12, 1968* (when this Court issued a temporary restraining order). See *Geisel v. Poynter Products, Inc.*, 283 F. Supp. 261 (S.D.N.Y. 1968) (opinion on preliminary injunction). In the exercise of the Court's discretion the Court will make permanent that preliminary injunction. . . .

The critical question for decision is whether defendants' "use" of the name "Dr. Seuss" *after April 9, 1968* (when this Court issued a preliminary injunction) violates Section 43(a) of the Lanham Act. The Court holds that defendants' activities *after April 9th* do *not* constitute "a false designation of origin, or any false description or representation" within the meaning of Section 43(a).

While defendants' prior activities created a false impression that the dolls were designed, manufactured or authorized by plaintiff, no such impression was intended to be, is, or can be, created by defendants' "use" of the name "Dr. Seuss" *after* April 9th.

No actual deception or confusion of, or tendency to deceive, the public is possible. Defendants have, in fact, satisfied the criteria of full and meticulously truthful disclosure. The phrase "based on" or the word "based," as used by defendants after April 9th, like the phrases "derived from," "suggested by," or "inspired by," accurately characterizes the genetic link between the cartoons and the dolls. Differences between the two are readily discerned. The dolls are not exact reproductions or replicas of the cartoons. But these morphological differences are within the accepted limits in the licensed toy trade. . . .

The Court does not adopt plaintiff's view that "based on" is a misrepresentation because it allegedly implies that plaintiff approved the dolls. . . . Section 43(a) of the Lanham Act cannot be read as permitting such an inference as to defendants' actions *after* April 9th without deleting the word "false" from that statute. No such application of Section 43(a) is justified.

As to the claims of unfair competition, plaintiff cannot recover for the "appropriation" of the cartoons themselves because defendant Liberty Library owns the copyright and plaintiff has no rights in them. . . .

Plaintiff also seeks relief pursuant to article 5 of the New York Civil Rights Law, §§ 50, 51, which creates a "right of privacy."

Plaintiff consented neither to the manufacture and sale of the dolls nor to the use of the name "Dr. Seuss" therewith. . . . In addition, it cannot be doubted that the name "Dr. Seuss" was ". . . used . . . for advertising purposes or for the purposes of trade . . ." within the meaning of Section 51. *Neyland v. Home Pattern Co., Inc.*, 65 F.2d 363, 364 (2nd Cir.), cert. denied sub nom. *Curtis Publishing Co. v. Neyland*, 290 U.S. 661, 54 S.Ct. 76, 78 L.Ed. 572 (1933).

However, plaintiff cannot succeed under the right of privacy statute because that statute does not protect an assumed or trade name. *Jaggard v. R. H. Macy & Co.*, 176 Misc. 88, 26 N.Y.S. 2d 829, 830 (Sup. Ct. 1941), aff'd sub nom. *Jaggard v. R. H. Macy & Co.*, App. Div. 15, 37 N.Y.S.2d 570, 571 (1942).

In *Jaggard*, the plaintiff's actual name was "Ginette Jaggard" but she designed dresses under the assumed name of "Ginette de Paris." The court held that ". . . a name assumed for business purposes only . . ." is not within the protection of the statute. . . .

In the case at bar, plaintiff's actual name is "Theodor Seuss Geisel." He began using the name "Seuss" in 1925 and added the "Dr." to create the name "Dr. Seuss" in 1927. . . . In fact, plaintiff stipulated that " 'Dr. Seuss' has been plaintiff's pen name and trade name since 1927 or 1928" [P.T.O. Stip.]. The Court holds that the name "Dr. Seuss" is an assumed name or pseudonym rather than a surname and is, therefore, not a protectible "name" within the meaning of Section 51 of the New York Civil Rights Law. . . .

Plaintiff argues that the dolls are "tasteless, unattractive and of an inferior quality" . . . and, therefore, sale of them with his trade or pen name holds him up to ridicule and contempt in his profession as a distinguished artist and author.

That plaintiff is a distinguished artist and author is not disputed [P.T.O. Stip]. The Court, however, rejects as unpersuasive and contrary to the preponderance of the credible evidence the testimony adduced in behalf of plaintiff that the dolls are "repellant" and of "inferior quality." . . . The Court finds that the execution of defendants' dolls was done with great care, skill and judgment by a qualified designer and manufacturer. . . .

This claim must also fail because defendants' activities *after April 9th do* not imply that plaintiff created, designed or approved of the dolls. . . .

Plaintiff alleges for his fifth and final cause of action essentially that defendants have conspired to commit all the other acts alleged with an intent to injure plaintiff. This claim has not been established.

The Court finds, on the basis of the great preponderance of the credible evidence, that with respect to the exploitation of plaintiff's cartoons by Liberty Library, Liberty's dealings with plaintiff's agent, Mrs. Jackson, reflect the good faith of defendant Liberty; and that all of the actions of defendant Liberty and of its licensee Poynter Products were under bona fide advice of experienced and competent counsel who had been specifically requested to remain in the role of advising defendants by plaintiff's agent. . . . The Court reiterates that the designs and manufacture of the dolls were executed with great care and skill by persons with extensive experience.

Far from there being an intention to injure, the Court finds that defendants, at all stages of exploiting the *Liberty Magazine* cartoons, conducted themselves carefully and conservatively. There was no malice or intention to inflict injury on plaintiff. . . .

Burnett v. Warner Bros. Pictures, 493 N.Y.S.2d App. Div., 1st Dept. 1985

. . . In 1941 plaintiffs wrote a play entitled "Everyone Comes to Rick's." On January 12, 1942, plaintiffs assigned their rights to the unproduced play to defendant Warner Brothers, Inc., in exchange for $20,000. The agreement entitled "Assignment of All Rights" states that plaintiffs

> . . . give, grant, bargain, sell, assign, transfer and set over all now or hereafter existing rights of every kind and character whatsoever pertaining to said work, whether or not such rights are now known, recognized or contemplated and the complete and unconditional and unencumbered title in and to said work for all purposes whatsoever.
>
> 2. I further give . . . the absolute and unqualified right to use said work in whole or in part, in whatever manner said purchaser may desire, including (but not limited to) the right to make, and/or cause to be made, literary, dramatic, speaking stage, motion picture, photo play, television, radio, and/or other adaptations of every kind and character, of said work, or any part thereof; and for the purpose of making or causing to be made such adaptations or any of them the purchaser may adapt, arrange, change, novelize . . . add to and subtract from said work, and/or title. . . .

In 1942 Warner Brothers released the motion picture "Casablanca" which was based on plaintiffs' play. Later, in 1955, Warner Brothers produced a television series entitled "Casablanca" which was essentially a sequel to the movie and set in the 1950s. Plaintiff Burnett, although aware that the television series had been produced, made no protest to Warner Brothers of infringement of character or sequel rights. Warner Brothers then obtained a copyright registration for another adaptation of plaintiffs' play, which was produced for television in 1983. This production was a "pre-quel" story set in 1940, one year prior

to the action of both plaintiffs' play and the movie "Casablanca." The weekly series was broadcasted from April 10 to May 7, 1983.

Plaintiff learned that the new "Casablanca" television series was being planned but raised no objection until June 21, 1983, after the series had been aired. Plaintiffs' attorney complained to the National Broadcasting Company, Inc. (NBC), which broadcasted the series, that the television series, based on the characters plaintiffs had created, violated their rights to those characters. Plaintiffs followed this complaint by commencing the instant action in July 1983, seeking a declaratory judgment that the defendants had no rights under the contract to use the characters of his play except for the use in the movie "Casablanca." Plaintiffs sought $10,000,000 in compensatory and $50,000,000 in punitive damages. Defendants Warner Brothers and NBC answered, asserting five affirmative defenses, including failure to state a cause of action and lack of jurisdiction over the subject matter due to federal preemption under 17 U.S.C. § 301, the federal copyright law.

Justice Bradley granted defendants' motion to dismiss the complaint on the ground that the court did lack subject matter jurisdiction to determine the controversy because of federal preemption. The court, therefore, dismissed the complaint, but without prejudice, to enable plaintiffs to bring an action in federal court.

Plaintiffs argue on appeal that the court erred in finding that their causes of action concerning their rights to their characters were preempted by the federal copyright law. Defendants argue, *inter alia*, on their cross-appeal, that plaintiffs' complaint should have been dismissed with prejudice because plaintiffs contracted away any and all rights they had in their play.

We need not determine whether plaintiffs' causes of action are preempted by the federal copyright law, for it is beyond question that plaintiffs failed to retain any rights, copyrightable or otherwise, which defendants could infringe, and have consequently failed to state a cause of action, thus requiring dismissal with prejudice.

The very words of the agreement between plaintiffs and Warner Brothers unequivocally demonstrate plaintiffs' intent to assign all their rights "of every kind and character whatsoever pertaining to said work, whether or not such rights are now known, recognized or contemplated . . . for all purposes whatsoever." Moreover, plaintiffs granted Warner Brothers the absolute right to use the work in any manner or medium they desired and to add to or subtract from the work. The assignment of rights agreement contains no clauses specifically enumerating any rights retained by plaintiffs or enumerating any rights excluded to Warner Brothers. Rather, it contains only general clauses assigning all imaginable rights to defendant Warner Brothers. The explicit wording of the clause belies plaintiffs' allegation that the assignment "contains no grant with respect to characters, continuation or sequel rights." The assignment was very obviously designed to grant the assignee the broadest of rights with respect to plaintiffs' play. In instances where the assignment clauses were drafted in the broadest of terms, courts have concluded that had the plaintiff intended to retain certain rights, specific clauses to that effect should have been included in the agreement. . . .

Since plaintiff retained no rights in his play which could be infringed, the complaint below fails to state a cause of action and is dismissed with prejudice.

NOTE _____

1. In April 1986, on appeal to the New York Court of Appeals, the decision of the Appellate Division was summarily affirmed.

2.20 Satisfactory Manuscripts and "Unearned Advances"

Authors seem among the most susceptible to failing to deliver what they promise. Between the idea for a literary work and the finished manuscript lie many stumbling (and writers') blocks. Even when a manuscript is at length produced, the publisher may cringe at the quality of the submitted work. If the author has received an advance, the likelihood of conflict increases.

Several cases in recent years have raised new questions about author and publisher responsibilities. The first issue is whether a publisher must critique a defective manuscript or provide editorial assistance before rejecting it. A second issue concerns conditions attached to an advance, such as the requirement that the advance be returned if a satisfactory manuscript is not delivered by a certain date or if no manuscript is delivered at all. A third consideration is the author's possible liability to the publisher for additional damages, such as lost anticipated profits.

A publisher's responsibility to review a manuscript and offer suggestions before rejecting it seems to be increasing. But, as the following cases will show, the exact extent of such responsibility is still ill-defined. If the manuscript is rejected for valid reasons or if no manuscript is delivered, there is often an implied obligation to return any advances made, although the precise language of the publisher-author contract may be controlling.

In *Stein and Day v. Morgan*, the court emphasizes that express contract language prevails over trade custom and usage, however clear and persuasive the latter may be. *Random House, Inc. v. Gold* explores the additional problems attending a contract that provides for the writing and publication of a series of books, particularly if the contract form used was obviously drafted for a single publication. The court has to separate author advances for works published and for those that were not.

Doubleday & Company v. Curtis and *Harcourt Brace v. Goldwater* both involve so-called celebrity authors, and a central question is whether certain types of authors require special assistance by the publisher's editors. The two cases hold that duties to comment and edit may be implied in publisher-author contracts. Left open is further exploration of the extent to which courts will imply higher or lesser duties on the part of the publisher in relation to the background and qualifications of the author. In this respect, note should also be taken of the Authors Guild "Satisfactory Manuscript Clause," set forth earlier in Section 2.03–2.

Stein and Day v. Morgan, 5 Med. L. Rptr. 1831 (N.Y.S.C. 1979)

STICHER, J.

This is an action tried without a jury. After I make the following findings:

On Sept. 6, 1972, the parties entered into a written agreement pursuant to which the defendant Morgan would write, and the plaintiff Stein and Day Incorporated would publish, two books: one was to be entitled *Anchor Woman* and the other *NBC, A Biography of the Corporation*. By its terms [Para. 8] the author agreed

> to deliver to the Publisher on or before [see Cl. 19(B)] a copy of the manuscript complete and satisfactory to the Publisher, and ready for press. . . . If the Author fails to deliver the manuscript in a form acceptable to the Publisher within the specified time, unless extended in writing by the Publisher, the Publisher may decline to publish the Work and recover any and all amounts that may have been advanced to the Author, and terminate this agreement subject to the Publisher's right to recover any and all amounts that may have been advanced to the Author.
>
> 19(B). Delivery Date—*Anchor Woman*, Sept. 15, 1973.
>
> *NBC, A Biography of the Corporation*, Sept. 15, 1971.

An advance of $35,000 was given to Mr. Morgan in four quarterly installments beginning Dec. 15, 1972 conditioned upon the scheduled delivery of portions of *Anchor Woman*.

Anchor Woman was timely delivered, published and has earned royalties for the defendant of $20,424.51. None of the royalties have been paid to the defendant but have been applied, in accordance with the terms of the contract, against the advance.

The *NBC* book was never delivered. At some time in 1974, Morgan, who had been with NBC in a variety of capacities for some twenty years and had by this time left NBC's employ, discussed with Mr. Stein, president of the plaintiff, his reluctance to write the *NBC* book. In his words, he was in a "no win" situation—he didn't wish to write a critical book for it would be rejected as "sour grapes" and he did not wish to write a laudatory book. Morgan and Stein agreed that, in lieu of the NBC book, the defendant would deliver a novel entitled *First Lady*. Sometime in June or July 1975, Stein received about 130 pages of *First Lady*. This portion of the draft and Stein's criticism were delivered to Morgan's agent, Mrs. Pryor, under cover of Stein's letter of July 13, 1975 and, thereafter, by letter dated July 23, 1975. Morgan wrote to Stein agreeing in substance with the criticism.

Between July and October what purported to be a complete *First Lady* novel was delivered to the plaintiff. By letter of Oct. 15, 1975, Stein sent to Morgan's agent a criticism of the novel written by one of Stein's senior editors whose conclusion it was that the draft was not worth editing. Stein requested that the book be rewritten. A week later, Mrs. Pryor requested the return of the manuscript concluding that there was no point to resubmission.

Upon the return of the manuscript, Mrs. Pryor attempted to sell it to at least four other well known publishers and each of them rejected the manuscript. She had and has no plans for submitting it anew to any publishers.

The plaintiff pursuant to the provisions of the agreement set forth above seeks to recoup that portion of the advance which was not covered by the royalties earned by *Anchor Woman*. No portion of the advance was allocated to either book, it being the intention of the parties that the entire advance be covered by both books and that the royalties from both books, together, be charged against the entire $35,000 advance. No claim is made by the plaintiff concerning the timeliness of delivery of the manuscript; the claim involves solely the question of acceptability to the publisher.

The defendant contends presumably that objectively the manuscript was "acceptable" and argues with greater emphasis that the custom of the publishing industry bars a refund of any portion of the advance.

There can be no doubt that the publisher was motivated in refusing this manuscript by "an honest dissatisfaction" with *First Lady* [see *Baker v. Chock Full o'Nuts Corp.*, 30 A.D. 2d, 329, 332] and that the rejection was made in good faith.

The defendant offered testimony that the custom of the publishing industry with respect to an unsatisfactory manuscript required that all sums advanced to the time of submission of the manuscript be retained by the author; that no further installments of the advance need be paid; that if the manuscript is thereafter sold to another publisher, it is the author's obligation, from the new consideration, to reimburse the first publisher to the extent of the advance; and that in the absence of sale to a new publisher, the publisher making the advance absorbs the loss represented by the advance. The testimony as to custom was uncontradicted.

A custom of an industry cannot overcome the express language of a written agreement. If custom and language are consistent both shall be enforced; but where, as here, they are in conflict, the express language shall prevail [UCC1-205 subd 4]. The parties expressly agreed that if the manuscript was not acceptable to the publisher, the publisher was entitled to recoup his advance. In this case, it was the intention of the parties that the advance be recouped less those sums of money attributable to royalties earned. It would thus appear that the plaintiff was entitled to judgment for the amount of the advance which exceeded royalties. In accordance with the stipulation of the parties, however, there shall be deducted from the amount to which the plaintiff is entitled a reserve held by the publisher against another book as set forth in Exhibit (I) for identification dated June 30, 1978 in the sum of $1,194.82.

Accordingly, the plaintiff is entitled to judgment in the net amount of $13,380.67 with interest from Oct. 14, 1977, the date of the plaintiff's demand for reimbursement and judgment may be entered accordingly.

Random House, Inc. v. Gold, 464 F. Supp. 1306 (S.D.N.Y. 1979)

POLLACK, DISTRICT JUDGE

This is an action to recover sums paid to the defendant as advances under a contract for the publication of up to four books to be written by defendant. Defendant has counter-claimed, alleging a breach of the contract in bad faith. . . .

In 1970, Random House and Gold entered into an agreement dated September 17, 1970, which called for the publication of four literary works to be written by Gold with an option to cancel the fourth book. The contract was drawn on a printed form customarily used for arrangements pertaining to a single book. The form was adapted by Random House to cover the proposed books involved herein.

Prior to the execution of the 1970 agreement, Random House had published several other works by Gold, including two books published pursuant to a 1965 contract. The latter two books were quite successful, and Gold received advances and royalties from them in excess of $100,000.

The 1970 agreement provided for the payment of advances of $150,000, payable to Gold in ten equal annual installments. The advances were against and on account of all moneys accruing to Gold under the agreement. The contract required Gold to submit manuscripts for the works "in content and form satisfactory to the publisher" and in accordance with a delivery schedule set forth therein.

The 1970 contract also provided that Gold had the right to terminate the agreement with respect to a fourth work if he had earned $150,000 or more from the publication of works #1, 2 and 3. Gold also gave Random House an option to publish any other books he wrote during the term of the contract as well as the first book thereafter.

Gold wrote and delivered the first two works and Random House accepted and published them. In January 1973, Random House paid Gold the fourth installment of the agreed advances, making a total of $60,000 thereon to that date. As of December 1973, Gold's royalties on the two published works totaled $9,304.71.

On July 30, 1973, James Brown, Gold's literary agent, delivered the manuscript of the third work, a novel entitled *Swiftie the Magician*. James Silberman, the editor-in-chief at Random House, read the manuscript and also asked another fiction editor, Joe Fox, to read it. Silberman also asked his staff to check on the financial results of the Gold contract. His secretary reported to him that Random House had paid a total of $60,000 and that the two published books had earned a total of $11,579.35, as of March 31, 1973.

Fox reported to Silberman on August 23, 1973. He admitted he was not a fan of Gold's work, and criticized the manuscript as shallow and badly designed. In considering whether Random House should agree to publish the book, Fox asked whether Random House was behind financially on the contract with Gold.

On September 11, 1973, Silberman sent some of Fox's comments to Gold, with a covering letter stating that he was "uneasy" about the manuscript. Gold went to work on a revision of the manuscript.

On December 20, 1973, just ten days before another installment of the agreed advances would have fallen due and after being assured by Random House's attorneys that in their opinion Gold would have to repay about $50,000 if the contract were terminated, Silberman wrote to Brown, stating that the manuscript was unsatisfactory in form and content and that Random House was terminating the agreement pursuant to Paragraph 2 thereof. Silberman testified that he decided to reject the book after reading a second, revised manuscript. He did not give the second manuscript to Fox or to anyone else to read. He could not remember exactly why he thought that the work was not a good book, and he did not keep a written memorandum of his criticisms, but said that they were the same as those in the Fox memo. Silberman admitted that he was conscious of the financial circumstances of the Gold contract at the time he decided to reject the book.

On January 2, 1974, Silberman and Brown spoke over the telephone about the third work by Gold. Silberman offered to renegotiate the terms of the Gold contract, and told Brown that the manuscript for the third work would be acceptable to Random House on different terms.

After the rejection by Random House, Brown offered the Gold manuscript for *Swiftie the Magician* to McGraw-Hill, which accepted the work for publication and paid Gold an advance of $10,000. . . .

Random House now seeks to recover from Gold the amount of all the advances paid to Gold in excess of the royalties accrued with respect to the two published works, or approximately $50,000. It contends that the sum represents an "unearned" advance which Gold agreed to repay in the event the contract was terminated.

Gold denies that he is obligated to repay all the advances he had received, viz., the $60,000 (less accrued royalties) and maintains that he is entitled to the $90,000 balance of the agreed advances because Random House breached the agreement in bad faith. Gold argues that he is at least entitled to an additional $15,000 for that part of the agreed advances attributable to the two works accepted and published by Random House. . . .

Gold contends that Random House acted in bad faith when it rejected the *Swiftie* manuscript because it gave undue and improper weight to financial considerations in the making of that decision and to escaping from the remaining financial obligations if it rejected the third work. Gold points to the plaintiff's offer to accept and publish the third work on different terms. Gold has offered no authority, however, for the proposition that a publisher's financial circumstances and the likelihood of a book's commercial success must be excluded from the range of factors that may be weighed in the decision to accept or reject a manuscript offered for publication, and this Court declines to endorse such a view. The requirement that a manuscript be satisfactory to the publisher gives it the right to reject a work if it acts in good faith; the publisher is not bound to incur the significant costs of publication if it declines to accept the risk of financial loss. There has been no other suggestion that Random House's view of the manuscript as unsatisfactory from its viewpoint was not held honestly and in good faith, and Gold's claim of a breach of contract in bad faith has not been established by a preponderance of the credible evidence. . . .

Random House seeks to recover the entire amount of the advances paid to Gold, less the sum of royalties accrued on the published works. Random House's claim for repayment, however, lacks any support in the express language of the agreement of the parties.

Paragraph "2" of the contract states that, "*as to any undelivered works,*" (emphasis added):

> . . . the Author agrees to repay forthwith all unearned amounts which may have been advanced hereunder, and Publisher will not be liable for any further advance installments.

Similarly, with respect to repayment of moneys advanced on published works, paragraph "9" of the contract states in harmony with the foregoing quotation from paragraph "2" that:

> Any such advance shall not be repayable, provided that the Author has delivered the manuscript in conformity with Paragraph 2 and is not otherwise in default under this agreement.

The quoted sentence from paragraph "9" refers to "*the* manuscript" rather than to *all four* manuscripts, and in the face of the express limitation on recovery of advances to "any undelivered works," the manuscript referred to in the proviso of paragraph "9" must be interpreted to distinguish delivered from undelivered works. This is cogent evidence that paragraphs "9" and "2" must be interpreted as applying independently to each of the four contemplated manuscripts. Thus, since Gold delivered the first two manuscripts in conformity with paragraph "2," advances attributable to those manuscripts are not repayable.

The evidence as a whole makes clear that, in effect, the parties made four separable arrangements in the adapted printed form, one for each work.

The notion of the plaintiff that the contract which it drew (adapted) is to be read as providing for a forfeiture by the defendant of all the advances it had received over a four year period because the plaintiff decided not to publish the third work, does violence to the contract, common sense and industry practice. Plaintiff's vice-president and editor-in-chief, Mr. Silberman testified that where separate works have been contracted for, an allocation is to be made of advances to each of the several works involved and that such an arrangement is common in the publishing industry. Moreover, when used in such a contract "all moneys earned" applies to each of the several works separately. . . .

The defendant Gold received $60,000 advanced against the possibility of four works. He failed to deliver the third manuscript in satisfactory form and the contract was terminated as to the third and fourth works. As to those "undelivered works," Gold must repay the portion of his advance attributable to them, or $30,000, which was not earned by the timely delivery of a satisfactory manuscript. Gold's promise to repay advances did not extend to delivered, accepted and published works, however, and Gold may retain the $30,000 attributable to the two published books. . . .

Random House contends that it was not obligated to continue to pay any part of the advances due in the years 1974 through 1979. This contention, however, is also without support in the terms of the contract.

The *only* circumstance in which Random House was permitted to suspend all advance payments, notwithstanding its acceptance and publication of one or more of the four works was the disability of the author. Paragraph "9" states in part:

> If the Author becomes physically or mentally incapacitated prior to delivery of *all the Works*, Publisher may discontinue payments of installments and will have no further obligation to make such payments for the duration of the disability. (Emphasis added.)

In this provision of paragraph "9," the rights and obligations of the publisher are clearly expressed: it may suspend all advance payments even where, for example, a disability delays delivery of a fourth manuscript after three works have been delivered and published. In contrast, there is no similar provision in the contract allowing Random House to suspend *all* payments when the contract is terminated *in part* as to undelivered works.

Paragraph "2," on which Random House relies, grants the publisher only partial relief from the continuing obligation to make advance payments. It provides:

> If the Author fails to deliver any manuscript . . ., as to any undelivered works, . . . Publisher will not be liable for any further advance installments.

Conversely, as to delivered and published works, Random House remains liable for further advance installments after a partial termination of the contract.

Therefore, with respect to the six advances due for the years 1974 through 1979, Random House is not liable for those attributable to the two "undelivered works," but Random House is liable for the portion of those installments attributable to the delivered and published books, or $45,000. . . .

Accordingly, the further findings and conclusions of this Court are as follows:

(1) Random House rejected the manuscript for *Swiftie the Magician*, the 3rd work, as unsatisfactory in form and content in good faith, and was privileged to terminate the 1970 agreement as to the third and fourth works, the undelivered works.

(2) Random House is entitled to recover from Gold the advances paid as to the undelivered works, or $30,000.

(3) Random House is *not* entitled to recover from Gold the advances paid as to the two published books.

(4) Gold is *not* entitled to recover from Random House the unpaid advances attributable to the undelivered works.

(5) Gold is entitled to recover from Random House the unpaid advances attributable to the two published books, or $45,000.

(6) Therefore, Gold is entitled to recover from Random House the net amount of $15,000, plus interest and costs, and the Clerk is directed to enter judgment accordingly. . . .

Doubleday & Company, Inc. v. Curtis, 763 F.2d 495 (1985)

KAUFMAN, CIRCUIT JUDGE

Mindful of the limited function of the judiciary in the private contractual realm, and aware of the dangers arising from judicial interference with the editorial process, we are today required to interpret an agreement entered into by an author and his publisher.

This dispute arose when, pursuant to the terms of a standard publishing agreement, Doubleday & Co. rejected as unsatisfactory a manuscript submitted by Tony Curtis. Each party then sued for breach of contract; Doubleday brought an action for recovery of the advance it remitted Curtis, and Curtis counterclaimed for anticipated earnings.

After a nonjury trial, the district court dismissed both actions. Judge Sweet rejected Curtis's claim, finding that Doubleday's unfavorable evaluation of the manuscript had been made in good faith and, assuming the publisher had a duty under the contract to provide editorial assistance to Curtis, this obligation had been fulfilled. Doubleday's complaint was dismissed on the basis that the company had waived its right to demand return of its advance. For the reasons set forth below, we affirm the dismissal of Curtis's counterclaims, but reverse the dismissal of Doubleday's claim. . . .

In the early 1970s, Tony Curtis, a respected dramatic and comedic actor, sought to enrich his career by becoming a novelist. He prepared a manuscript—later titled *Kid Andrew Cody and Julie Sparrow* ("Kid Cody")—and enlisted the aid of Irving Paul ("Swifty") Lazar, a well-known literary agent. Doubleday & Co., the venerable New York publishing house, foresaw within Curtis the potential for great commercial success and entered into a two-book contract with him in the winter of 1976.

As part of their arrangement, Doubleday promised to pay Curtis royalties on hardcover sales, and a share of the proceeds from the sale of subsidiary rights (e.g., paperback rights), provided Curtis could deliver—within a specified period of time—final manuscripts, "satisfactory to Publisher in content and form." The agreement was a standard industry form, and did not elaborate on the meaning of the penultimate condition—"satisfactory to Publisher in content and form."

Amid much fanfare, *Kid Cody* was accepted for publication. The final draft was generally acknowledged to have been a joint effort of Curtis and Larry Jordan, a Doubleday editor. Through a series of face-to-face meetings in New York, the experienced Jordan was able to assist the novice Curtis in the successful completion of his first novel.

Inspired by Curtis's literary debut and somewhat intrigued by an eight-page outline for his next novel, Doubleday agreed to renegotiate the contract governing publication of the second book. On September 7, 1977, the parties executed the document that spawned this litigation. Curtis was to receive one hundred thousand dollars as an advance to be charged against future royalties. One-half of the advance was paid upon the signing of the contract, with the balance due on "acceptance of complete satisfactory manuscript." In addition, Curtis was to receive fifty percent of any proceeds Doubleday might earn from the sale of reprint rights. Doubleday's performance was again contingent upon Curtis's ability to produce a "satisfactory" manuscript by a date no later than October 1, 1978. This deadline, as well as the conditions relating to acceptable "form" and "content," were expressly stated to be "of the essence of the Agreement." The document further stated that failure to comply with the satisfaction clause granted the publisher the right to terminate the contract, and require Curtis to return any sums advanced. As with the *Kid Cody* contract, this agreement did not speak to the methods and standards by which the publisher would determine whether a manuscript was "satisfactory." Indeed the contract omitted any reference to the plot, subject, title, length or tone of the proposed novel.

If Doubleday's arrangement with Curtis appeared to favor the publishing house, the company's subsequent reprint agreement with New American Library ("NAL") epitomized the firm's bargaining acumen. NAL promised to pay Doubleday $200,000 merely for the right to publish Curtis's second novel in paperback, in the event it was accepted for publication by Doubleday. NAL's position was thus wholly dependent upon Doubleday's opinion of the manuscript. Indeed, no matter how inferior or unsaleable the novel might prove to be, if Doubleday published the work before December 31, 1980, NAL was bound by the terms of the contract and Doubleday was ensured a handsome profit.

The great expectations that surrounded the project never materialized. It was not until April 1980 that Curtis delivered even a partial first draft of his would-be second novel, *Starstruck*, a rags-to-riches story of a lascivious Hollywood starlet. Doubleday appeared unperturbed, however, and blithely ignored the October 1978 deadline. Equally generous was NAL, which willingly extended its own deadline one year to December 31, 1981.

Those portions of *Starstruck* that Curtis had forwarded to Doubleday were routed from one editor's desk to another, finally coming to rest in August 1980 with Adrian Zackheim, then a stranger to Curtis. Zackheim's review of the first half of *Starstruck* was slow but painstakingly thorough. After four months of intermittent reading—totaling perhaps fifty hours—he sent Curtis a seven-page letter. In it, Zackheim criticized the numerous inconsistencies and inherent contradictions that pervaded the manuscript and exhorted Curtis to tighten the plot. Yet, sprinkled among this criticism was praise for the author's story-telling ability. To this end, Zackheim emphasized he was generally "charmed" with the "wonderful possibilities" of *Starstruck* and was not expecting substantial changes in "the basic outlines of the novel."

The following months, however, did not prove conducive to *Starstruck*'s completion. The few telephonic and face-to-face conversations between Curtis and Zackheim contrasted dramatically with the considerable contact Curtis had maintained with Larry Jordan. To a large extent, the dearth of communication was a product of circumstance rather than neglect. Curtis was preoccupied with complex divorce proceedings, and his visits to New York became more and more infrequent. Zackheim, for his part, was willing to review changes and additions piecemeal, but Curtis eschewed this alternative.

The spring of 1981 elapsed without any significant progress being made on the manuscript. As a result, Doubleday executives became increasingly anxious that they would be unable to accept

Starstruck for publication before the December 31, 1981 deadline with NAL. The prevailing sentiment at Doubleday was that it would prove fruitless to appeal to NAL for a further extension.

In early August, Curtis finally forwarded to Zackheim what he represented to be a completed draft of the book. Zackheim was appalled at the product, and reluctantly concluded that *Starstruck* was unpublishable. Not only had Curtis ignored suggestions involving the story's first half, but he had composed such an unexpectedly poor conclusion that *Starstruck* was transformed from a potential success into an almost certain debacle.

Without apprising Curtis of his impressions, Zackheim asked his supervisor at Doubleday, Elizabeth Drew, to read the revised manuscript. Drew's response, in the form of an intrafirm memorandum, clearly demonstrates the dilemma then confronting Doubleday. She acknowledged that rejecting *Starstruck* would require forfeiture of the lucrative reprint arrangement with NAL, but nonetheless recommended that Doubleday abandon the book. In her opinion, *Starstruck* was "junk, pure and simple," and could not be "edited into shape or even rewritten into shape." To accept the manuscript for publication solely because of the NAL contract was, in Drew's words, "not a way to sleep nights, at least not if one's concerned with ethics."

As a final means of salvaging the book and the NAL deal, Zackheim approached Lazar and suggested that Curtis submit the manuscript to a "novel doctor" in an attempt to put the shine back on the fallen *Starstruck*. When Lazar demurred, Doubleday finally admitted defeat. It cancelled the reprint deal with NAL, formally terminated the September 1977 agreement with Curtis and demanded repayment of the original $50,000 advance. When Curtis refused, Doubleday commenced this litigation. . . .

Characterizing the litigation as a "dispute about creativity and the respective responsibilities of an author and his publisher," the district court dismissed Doubleday's complaint and Curtis's litany of counterclaims. 599 F.Supp. 779 (S.D.N.Y. 1984). In considering whether to infer a duty to edit from a clause requiring delivery of a manuscript "satisfactory to the publisher," the

court acknowledged that New York's appellate courts had yet to resolve this issue. Without deciding the issue, Judge Sweet concluded that, "[e]ven if a duty to provide editorial services is accepted as required under New York law, here, Doubleday performed it." *Id.* at 784.

Turning to the question of bad faith, the trial judge deemed the testimony of Doubleday's witnesses credible, and held that the decision to reject Curtis's manuscript had been animated by a genuine belief that *Starstruck* was unpublishable. Curtis's remaining counterclaims were summarily dismissed as contrary to the relevant provisions of the 1976 and 1977 contracts.

Finally, the court dismissed Doubleday's claim seeking recovery of the $50,000 advance. Judge Sweet held that Doubleday had waived the "time of the essence" clause by accepting Curtis's manuscript nearly eighteen months after the original deadline had passed. Moreover, the court found that because Doubleday had led Curtis to believe that *Starstruck* would eventually be published, it had also waived its right to a return of the advance even if it found the manuscript unsatisfactory. . . .

We note at the outset that Curtis has never defended his August 1981 manuscript as a work of publishable quality. Rather, Curtis maintains that but for Doubleday's inability and unwillingness to provide adequate editorial assistance, *Starstruck* would have met the "satisfactory to publisher" condition. Curtis concedes that his proposed interpretation is not supported by a literal reading of the 1977 agreement. On its face, the document is completely silent regarding any obligation on Doubleday's part to ensure that Curtis's rough drafts are transformed, through the company's affirmative efforts, into a polished novel.

Our task, then, is to delineate the extent to which New York law requires us to infer such an obligation from the agreement. Because New York's appellate courts have not yet addressed this question, we must attempt to divine the likely response of our state brethren.

The 1977 agreement expressly granted Doubleday the right to terminate the contract if it deemed Curtis's manuscript to be unsatisfactory. In similar circumstances—where the satisfactory performance of one party is to be judged by another party—New York courts have required the party terminating the contract to act in good faith. . . .

This principle—that a contract containing a "satisfaction clause" may be terminated only as a result of honest dissatisfaction—would seem especially appropriate in construing publishing agreements. To shield from scrutiny the already chimerical process of evaluating literary value would render the "satisfaction" clause an illusory promise, and place authors at the unbridled mercy of their editors.

A corollary of this duty to appraise a writing honestly is an obligation on the part of the publisher not to mislead an author deliberately regarding the work required for a given project. A willful failure to respond to a request for editorial comments on a preliminary draft may, in many instances, work no less a hardship than would an unjustifiable rejection of a final manuscript. A publisher's duty to exercise good faith in its dealings toward an author exists at all stages of the creative process.

Although we hold that publishers must perform honestly, we decline to extend that requirement to include a duty to perform skillfully. The possibility that a publisher or an editor—either through inferior editing or inadvertence—may prejudice an author's efforts is a risk attendant to the selection of a publishing house by a writer, and is properly borne by that party. To imply a duty to perform adequate editorial services in the absence of express contractual language would, in our view, represent an unwarranted intrusion into the editorial process. Moreover, we are hesitant to require triers of fact to explore the manifold intricacies of an editorial relationship. Such inquiries are appropriate only where contracts specifically allocate certain creative responsibilities to the publisher.

Accordingly, we hold that a publisher may, in its discretion, terminate a standard publishing contract, provided that the termination is made in good faith, and that the failure of an author to submit a satisfactory manuscript was not caused by the publisher's bad faith. . . .

Evaluating the Doubleday-Curtis relationship in light of these principles, we are convinced that *Starstruck*'s failure was not attributable to any

dishonesty, willful neglect or any other manifestations of bad faith on the part of Doubleday. The factual landscape illustrates the complete frustration experienced by Doubleday's editors, who were forced to harmonize an inferior manuscript, a lucrative reprint agreement and a recalcitrant author. Zackheim sincerely endeavored to assist Curtis in the completion of his manuscript. Although Zackheim's suggested revisions may have been offered somewhat belatedly, the evidence indicates that he extended numerous offers to discuss the novel with Curtis, as well as to review portions of the second draft. Indeed, it was Curtis who refused these renderings of assistance. That Zackheim's editing was perhaps inadequate is beside the point, as is any comparison with Larry Jordan. Curtis neither alleged, nor does the record support a finding that Doubleday deliberately or even recklessly assigned *Starstruck* to an editor unfit or unsuited for the project.

Admittedly, the selection of an editor is a matter of paramount importance to a writer, but we note once again that the power to control this decision—like all aspects of the publication process—could have been reserved to Curtis in his contract.

Turning our attention to the actual termination of the contract, we believe the district court's finding that Doubleday rejected *Starstruck* in good faith is amply supported by the record before us. Zackheim and Drew were in complete agreement that no amount of in-house editing could save the project. Moreover, the suggestion that Curtis consult a "novel doctor"—though perhaps somewhat humiliating—appears to have been made sincerely, rather than as a stratagem for avoiding the responsibilities attendant to a difficult editing job.

Curtis argues with some force that Doubleday terminated his contract in November 1981 primarily because of the impending NAL deadline. Although we agree the two events were not unconnected, we choose to characterize the relationship between them quite differently. Were it not for the extremely lucrative arrangement with NAL, it is likely that Doubleday would have abandoned *Starstruck* without hesitation, and perhaps at a much earlier date. Only the prospect of a commercially profitable reprint deal prevented Zackheim from rejecting the August 1981 manuscript immediately. Doubleday's decision to sacrifice financial reward for "ethics," as Zackheim's superior Drew framed the choice, can hardly be said to constitute an act of bad faith.

In light of all the circumstances, we agree with the district court's finding that Doubleday exercised good faith in its dealings with Curtis, and thus affirm the dismissal of Curtis's counterclaim. . . .

In dismissing Doubleday's complaint, which sought recovery of the $50,000 advance paid to Curtis, the district court found that Doubleday had waived its right to demand return of the advance. Because the issue was not properly before the court, we conclude dismissal on that basis was improper.

Among the cardinal principles of our Anglo-American system of justice is the notion that the legal parameters of a given dispute are framed by the positions advanced by the adversaries, and may not be expanded *sua sponte* by the trial judge. The dismissal of Doubleday's claim based on an issue never pleaded by Curtis—or even implicitly raised at trial—is inconsistent with the due process concerns of adequate notice and an opportunity to be heard. Moreover, such a result runs counter to the spirit of fairness embodied in the Federal Rules of Civil Procedure. . . .

Harcourt Brace v. Goldwater, 8 Med. L. Rptr. 1217 (S.D.N.Y. 1982)

GRIESA, JUDGE

. . . In early 1977 a proposal was submitted to Harcourt Brace Jovanovich, which I will refer to hereafter as HBJ, for the publication of the memoirs of Barry Goldwater.

The proposal was to have Stephen Shadegg act as the actual writer, working closely with Goldwater who was to provide the material and work and comment on the substance of what was presented.

Shadegg had previously had a long relationship with a literary agent by the name of Oscar Collier and he relied on Collier to market this proposal. Oscar Collier was associated as a literary agent with his daughter, Lisa Collier.

The Collier firm submitted the proposal to certain publishers, including HBJ, in early 1977. An editor at HBJ by the name of Carol Hill received the proposal. She talked about it to her editor-in-chief, Daniel Okrent. There was a meeting involving Hill, Okrent and the Colliers. The HBJ people were very enthusiastic and quickly agreed to publish the Goldwater memoirs on the basis of the proposal which had been submitted.

There is testimony demonstrating that although the HBJ people were enthusiastic about having the Goldwater memoirs, they had reservations about the writer Shadegg. There is a dispute as to whether they communicated these reservations to the Colliers. Whether they did or did not communicate the reservations is unimportant. But it is important to note that the HBJ people did have reservations and would have preferred another writer.

However, it is also to be noted that the Colliers furnished the HBJ people with four books previously written by Shadegg, a writer of long experience, who had engaged in journalistic writing as well as having written books, political biographies and so forth. The HBJ people were fully on notice as to exactly the degree of talent possessed by Shadegg.

There was a meeting in Washington, D.C., the main purpose of which was to meet Senator Goldwater. The contract was then signed January 26, 1977. It names Stephen Shadegg and Barry Goldwater as the authors and HBJ as the publisher.

The contract contains the normal provisions about royalties and many other detailed provisions not relevant here. It contains certain paragraphs referring to the concept of the manuscript being "satisfactory to the publisher in form and content," particularly paragraph 2 which states as follows: "The author will deliver to the publisher on or before October 1, 1973, one copy of the manuscript of the work as finally revised by the author and satisfactory to the publisher in form and content."

The agreement provided for an advance totaling $200,000, a remarkably high advance. $65,000 was to be paid at the time of contract signing. Another $75,000 was due on delivery and acceptance of the completed manuscript. The balance of $60,000 was due on publication.

There was an exchange of letters in February 1977 between Hill and Goldwater in which Hill in effect offered to do a vigorous job of editing and Goldwater made it clear that he welcomed such editing. He stated in his letter of February 15, 1977 that Hill should not hesitate to criticize or make suggestions, even though he might be a little bullheaded here and there.

The project began between Shadegg and Goldwater. One of the things which was a feature of these memoirs was that Goldwater had over the years collected what he called the Alpha File. It consisted of memos and notes of conversations he had with other political and governmental leaders in the United States and he had dictated these notes and memos and prepared them at the time of various meetings and events.

These items had been collected in the Alpha File and one of the ideas of the memoirs was to publish materials of substance, anecdotes and so forth, from the Alpha File, to the extent they did not involve purely personal information or the normal kind of information which sometimes is held back until the death of certain living people in order not to hurt them.

In any event, materials from the Alpha File were turned over to Shadegg and other materials were given to Shadegg. Goldwater commenced consulting with Shadegg and Shadegg set to work writing.

This process continued over the period of time involved in the lawsuit. Shadegg would write a section and submit it to Goldwater; Goldwater would comment, offer criticisms, provide additional material, and so forth.

On June 22, 1977, Shadegg wrote a letter to Hill enclosing a draft of seven chapters, approximately 30,000 words. At the same time Shadegg sent Oscar Collier the same draft material. The letter to Hill concluded with the following paragraph: "We would be most interested in having your comments and your suggestions. One of the problems we face is how much to put in and how much to leave out. The available material is almost overwhelming. Your objective viewpoint will be extremely helpful."

Hill did not communicate with either Shadegg or Goldwater in response to the receipt of this draft material. This caused understandable puzzlement on the part of Shadegg and Goldwater. They were eager to have her reaction and they did not have it.

Goldwater has made it clear in his testimony in the case that he expects and needs editorial work on the part of a publisher. He has published a number of books and feels the need of editorial work. He expected it here and he was particularly puzzled that none was forthcoming.

Goldwater relied on Shadegg for the principal communications with either the publisher or the agent and, pursuant to this, Shadegg made inquiries of Oscar Collier as to what was going on. Shadegg has testified that he placed one telephone call to Hill at about this time which was not returned. He candidly admitted at trial that he did not act more persistently in going to Hill directly because he was angry and hurt at the lack of what he considered a normal response.

In any event, in September of 1977, there was a discussion between Hill and Oscar Collier. Hill gave a general unfavorable comment about the seven-chapter draft, criticizing the tone, the lack of drama and what she considered flat writing. . . .

Even Hill's comments to Collier did not involve normal, detailed editorial work. They did not convey specific comments as to what should be cut or what should be added or what was unclear or any of the other things that one would expect in editorial work.

Consequently, in connection with the first seven chapters, it is clear that Hill did not perform any editorial work, either directly with the authors or indirectly through Collier.

The evidence indicates strongly that Hill was considering, and to some degree pursuing, the idea of replacing Shadegg with another writer.

In late September 1977, an item appeared in the Washington Post indicating that Goldwater was looking for a ghost writer. Goldwater and Shadegg heard about this. They inquired and were told by Hill that there was nothing to it. Hill wrote them a letter of reassurance which indicated that she was in fact enthusiastic about the book and expected that it would be an important one.

Thus, in her only direct contact with the authors at this juncture, Hill was not only withholding her negative views of the draft, she was indicating support and enthusiasm.

Behind the scenes, there were certain maneuvers going on about the possibility of getting a new writer. Apparently there was talk at HBJ on this subject, and the desire for a possible new writer was known. This resulted in some communications with a literary agent about a possible writer by the name of Clay Blair. Hill went so far as to write the agent to try to see if Clay Blair would be available. Hill did not expressly mention the Goldwater project. She spoke in veiled terms, at least to the outsiders. But the point is that a new writer for the Goldwater book was definitely on her mind. . . .

As I have already described, Oscar Collier had received from Hill some general negative comments, which he conveyed to Shadegg and which were in turn conveyed to Goldwater.

There is a letter dated November 14, 1977 to Hill from Lisa Collier indicating that comments had been passed on and that work was going forward.

The intention of Shadegg and Goldwater and their agents was to keep going ahead with the writing in the hopes that whatever problems there were would work out with the further production of manuscript. Obviously, the authors had an obligation under the contract to write and they continued to fulfill that obligation.

In the absence of any editorial work forthcoming from Hill, Shadegg solicited comments from Oscar Collier, who made detailed suggestions on draft material. These comments were not the substitute of editorial work from the publisher. They tended to deal with rather trivial points about precise phrasing and so forth. But at least Shadegg was soliciting what assistance he could from the agent.

On July 13, 1978, 24 chapters were sent to Hill. These were sent by Goldwater. The idea had been adopted that if Goldwater himself submitted the material there might be a better chance of getting some editorial work from Hill. Also it was hoped that the production of a substantial part of the book would encourage some progress with the publisher.

The Goldwater letter of July 13, 1978 concludes with the following:

> If you have any suggestions or would like to make some we could arrange to meet in Arizona at your convenience, in Washington or even New York. Let me know your honest opinion of what has been done so far and let me have any suggestions as soon as possible that might be incorporated in further writing.

The letter was not responded to. Hill made no attempt to communicate with Shadegg or Goldwater in order to offer the kind of opinions, suggestions, or comments which had been solicited in the Goldwater letter.

Hill has testified that she felt that the materials submitted in the 24-chapter package were poor and she was very concerned about whether the book could be successfully marketed. She asked two other editors at HBJ to read the materials. The other two editors were also negative about the contents of the 24-chapter package.

However, as I have said, there was no attempt to communicate with the authors and go over the matter in detail and see what, if anything, could be done to remedy the perceived difficulties.

Hill's communications again were with the agents, particularly with Oscar Collier. She conveyed her negative impression of the 24 chapters in a general way and, at this time, expressly suggested that another writer be brought in. This suggestion was rejected by Oscar Collier.

At this time Hill indicated to Oscar Collier that HBJ would probably not publish the book and would probably reject the manuscript.

Oscar Collier and Hill discussed seeking another publisher. It was indicated to Collier that he was free to do this and Collier, in order to cover the contingency he was faced with, and in order to ensure publication of the book, commenced inquiries about the possibility of another publisher.

However, Shadegg and Goldwater kept on working on the book to finish it and the intention still was to submit the final manuscript to HBJ pursuant to the existing contract.

It should be noted that on August 31, 1978, Hill sent a memo to the head of the firm, Mr. Jovanovich, which stated, among other things, "that the original idea was to have Taylor Branch rewrite the manuscript when it was delivered." Taylor Branch was a writer who had been favored by the HBJ people for this project if they could have chosen the writer.

The memo has significance, in indicating that there was an intention to refrain from doing editorial work with Shadegg in the hopes that another writer could come in and do the job.

On September 29, 1978, the full manuscript was submitted to HBJ. It contained revisions of materials earlier submitted and certain additional chapters. The full manuscript was submitted with a letter from Oscar Collier which attempted to explain what Collier felt were the merits of the manuscript.

There was further review by Hill and certain of her colleagues at HBJ, and submission to a free-lance manuscript reader. All took a very negative view of the manuscript. However, one suggestion by an associate editor was that the manuscript be reworked and that the authors be bargained down to a lower advance.

On August 31, 1978, HBJ wrote Oscar Collier returning the manuscript, stating that it was un-acceptable, and demanding the return of the $65,000 advance.

Prior to this time neither Hill nor any other editor at HBJ had communicated directly with Shadegg or Goldwater regarding the manuscript material. No one at that firm attempted to do so. There was never any detailed comment about what should be added, what should be deleted, what was unclear, or about any other specific matters in the manuscript. There was no such comment made either directly to Shadegg or Goldwater, or indirectly through the agent, Collier.

Following the rejection of the manuscript by HBJ, there were discussions by Collier with a few other publishers. The result was that the book was bought by William Morrow & Company who agreed to pay an advance of $80,000. The same manuscript which had been rejected by HBJ was the one submitted to Morrow.

An experienced editor at Morrow by the name of Howard Cady has testified that he found the manuscript fascinating. He saw problems with it but felt that it could yield a best-selling book.

Prior to entering into any agreement with Shadegg and Goldwater, Cady went to see Shadegg in Phoenix, Arizona, where Shadegg lived to see whether he could work with Shadegg. This was in January 1979.

Cady found Shadegg thoroughly professional and cooperative. Cady had certain comments that were discussed with Shadegg at that time, and the two developed an immediate working relationship.

Over the next few weeks, after Morrow had bought the rights to the book, Cady sent off to Shadegg in Phoenix communications with detailed comments about items to cut, questions to be answered and so forth. In other words, Cady was engaging in the normal editorial activity. . . .

The book was ready for galley proofs in a relatively short time. It was published in the fall of 1979 by Morrow under the title "With No Apologies" and it became a best-seller.

Cady has testified that the process he went through with Shadegg was a normal editorial process. There were substantial cuts of superfluous material, which he has testified is not unusual in work on a manuscript of a book being prepared under contract. The cuts were made leaving what Cady felt was valuable narrative and commentary material.

As far as additions to the manuscript which had been submitted to Cady, he said that there was less than 1 percent of the material in the present book which was added pursuant to his requests and questions. Again Cady said this involved normal editorial effort.

We come to the conclusions of law to be drawn. It is true that under the contract which was in force here between HBJ and the authors, the publisher has a very considerable discretion as to whether to refuse a manuscript on the ground that it is unsatisfactory to the publisher in form and content.

It cannot be, however, that the publisher has absolutely unfettered license to act or not to act in any way it wishes and to accept or reject a book for any reason whatever. If this were the case, the publisher could simply make a contract and arbitrarily change its mind and that would be an illusory contract. It is no small thing for an author to enter into a contract with a publisher and be locked in with that publisher and prevented from marketing the book elsewhere.

It is clear, both as a matter of law and from the testimony in this case, that there is an implied obligation in a contract of this kind for the publisher to engage in appropriate editorial work with the author of a book. Both plaintiff's and defendants' witnesses testified to this effect, based on the custom of the trade.

It is clear that an author who is commissioned to do a work under a contract such as this generally needs editing to produce a successful book. There has been testimony by Goldwater, as I have mentioned, to the effect that he feels the need of editing work and expected it here. The letters from both Shadegg and Goldwater to the publisher indicated their desire for editorial work on the part of the publisher.

In a general way, it is clear that the editorial work which is required must consist of some reasonable degree of communication with the authors, an interchange with the authors about the specifics of what the publisher desires; about what specific faults are found; what items should be omitted or eliminated; what items should be added; what organizational defects exist, and so forth. If faults are found in the writing style, it seems elementary that there should be discussion and illustrations of what those defects of style are. All of this is necessary in order to allow the author the reasonable opportunity to perform to the satisfaction of the publisher.

If this editorial work is not done by the publisher, the result is that the author is misled and, in fact, is virtually prevented from performing under the contract.

There is no occasion in this decision to determine the full extent or the full definition of the editorial work which is required of a publisher under the contract. Here there was no editorial work. I emphasize, no editorial work. There was nothing approaching any sensible editorial activity on the part of the publisher. There were no comments of a detailed nature designed to give the authors an opportunity to remedy defects, even though such comments were specifically invited and requested. . . .

As far as any qualms about having Shadegg as writer, it should be emphasized that the contract was with Shadegg as well as with Goldwater. The contract was not with Goldwater alone. And, as I have already indicated, the publisher entered into this contract with a full opportunity to determine the exact abilities and talents of Shadegg.

In a given situation it could be that after a contract is entered into of the kind we have here, and after draft material is submitted, the material is so hopeless that editorial work might be fruitless. It is difficult to imagine such a situation occurring but I suppose it is conceivable. But this was far from the case here.

I note that the publisher claims that there were no revelations of fact, no "revelatory material" as the term has been used. It is difficult to even comprehend that claim. The book as it was published is full of facts. It is full of conversations with illustrious personages. It is full of comments and judgments in detail about presidents and other public figures, presidential administrations and so forth. It is simply not true that the book had no factual material in it of a valuable nature.

It is quite clear that the bulk of the manuscript which was submitted to HBJ must have contained valuable and interesting factual material. This is not the case of a manuscript of no merit which ended up unpublished or was published in a book of clearly low-grade quality.

A distinguished editor, Howard Cady, found the manuscript fascinating. He edited the manuscript in the normal way and produced a successful book.

Consequently, I conclude that HBJ breached its contract with Shadegg and Goldwater by wilfully failing to engage in any rudimentary editorial work or effort. Consequently, HBJ cannot rely on the concept that the manuscript was unsatisfactory in form and content and can be rejected. HBJ had no right under its contract to reject that manuscript.

I have examined the legal authorities cited by the parties. No case directly in point has been referred to. I would note particularly that the case most heavily relied upon by HBJ, *Random House, Inc. v. Gold*, 464 F. Supp. 1306 (S.D.N.Y.), aff'd mem., 607 F.2d 998 (2d cir. 1979), holds that the type of contract involved in the present case requires the publisher to act in good faith, and notes the obvious point that, allowing unfettered license to publishers to reject a manuscript submitted under contract would permit "overreaching by publishers attempting to extricate themselves from bad deals." 464 F. Supp. at 1308 n.1. In the present case, for the reasons already stated, it must be concluded that HBJ did not act in good faith.

This concludes my findings on the issues I have set out to deal with.

NOTES ─────────────────────────

1. In *Dell Publishing Co. v. Whedon*, 577 F. Supp. 1459 (S.D.N.Y. 1984), the publisher reviewed the author's outline for the book before contracting with the author; an advance was paid on the basis of the outline. Under these circumstances, the court held there was an implied duty for the publisher in good faith to offer suggestions to the author as to what needed to be revised to make the manuscript satisfactory. Editorial assistance had to be offered, and a manuscript could not be rejected without this degree of assistance. The publisher's failure to comply with these procedures prevented the publisher from recovering the advances made to the author.

2. In *William Morrow & Co. v. Davis*, 583 F. Supp. 578 (S.D.N.Y. 1984), a three-sided dispute erupted between the publisher (William Morrow & Co.), a celebrity (Bette Davis) who was to have her autobiography written, and an author (Mickey Herskowitz) who was to assist the celebrity in the writing. The court denied the publisher's motion for summary judgment, holding that triable issues of fact existed as to what is meant by contract language that requires the authors to deliver a manuscript satisfactory to plaintiff publisher in form and content.

The court held that each of the three principals in the case had set forth reasonable interpretations as to what was satisfactory in the context of the dealings among the three. Only a trial on the matter could determine what would constitute a satisfactory manuscript.

3. In *J. B. Lippincott Co. v. Lasher*, 430 F. Supp. 993 (S.D.N.Y. 1977), the author (Lasher) contracted with plaintiff publisher to write *The Last Jew in Berlin*. Lasher received advances totaling $18,000, but failed to deliver the manuscript. Plaintiff sought return of these advances, plus compensation for lost anticipated profits. The court denied the claim for lost profits, holding the claim to be without merit: "It is almost impossible to compute what profit would have been made by the publisher if the defendant had, in fact, completed the work and the publisher had properly promoted and published the book. This claim is by far too speculative to be ruled upon, and it is entirely rejected." 430 F. Supp. at p. 995.

As to the advances, the author urged a contract interpretation that would require advances to be returned only if the author sold the rights in the same book to a third party, since that was the only explicit provision in the contract specifically calling for advances to be returned. While the court termed this an "intriguing interpretation," it nevertheless held for plaintiff publisher, saying it was implied that advances should be returned if a manuscript was not delivered.

4. Several other significant cases explore the ramifications of satisfactory manuscript clauses, including the following:

(a) *Crawford v. Mail & Express Publishing Co.*, 163 N.Y. 404 (1900)—A contract for writing a newspaper column provided that "services shall be satisfactory to the publisher." The court held this clause involved subjective factors of "taste, fancy and judgment," not objective criteria; thus, actual dissatisfaction for any reason, even absent reasonable grounds, was sufficient basis for termination by the publisher.
(b) *Frederick A. Praeger, Inc. v. Montagu*, 35 C. O. Bull. 562 (N.Y. 1965)—A good faith rejection of a manuscript as "not satisfactory in content" entitled the publisher to recover the advance.
(c) *Goodyear Publishing Co. v. Mundell*, 427 N.Y.S.2d 242 (1980)—A publisher was granted a summary judgment for return of an advance when the author failed to deliver an acceptable, complete manuscript.
(d) *G. P. Putnam's Sons v. Owens*, 51 A.D.2d 527 (N.Y. 1976)—A publisher's rights to return of an advance accrues on the date in the contract calling for delivery of the manuscript, and not when the publisher gives notice of termination of the contract.
(e) *Prentice-Hall, Inc. v. Bregman*, Civil Ct., N.Y. Co., No. 57741-82 (1985)—A publisher was granted summary judgment in its suit to recover an advance. The author's unsupported allegations that the publisher must provide suggestions and guidance after reading the author's first draft were merely conclusory. No triable issue of fact was presented, absent further factual allegations.

5. In an unreported arbitration award, *Safire v. William Morrow & Co.*, the arbitrator held that a publisher's decision to reject a manuscript as unacceptable was solely at the publisher's discretion. This obviated any need for the arbitrator to read the manuscript or hear expert testimony on the work's literary value. However, while the remaining portion of the advance need not be paid, the publisher was not entitled to any

return of advances paid because of author's diligence, good faith, and delivery of a lengthy manuscript. Also, despite common practice wherein author would repay advances if the author later received royalties from the book being published elsewhere, the arbitrator held that such repayment need not be made in this case. For more on this arbitration, see *New York Times*, January 10, 1975, p. 35; and *Publishers Weekly*, January 20, 1975, p. 21.

6. For further discussion of the evolving rights and duties of parties to a literary publishing contract, see Simensky, "Redefining the Rights and Obligations of Publishers and Authors," 5 *Loyola Entertainment Law Journal* 111 (1985).

2.30   Failure to Publish or Promote

In the prior section we reviewed the developing doctrines of a publisher's responsibility to review, critique, and perhaps attempt to edit a manuscript before rejecting it. We now turn to related issues on the publisher's duties to publish and promote.

The first case, *Freund v. Washington Square Press*, discusses possible remedies for failure to publish and seems to limit damages perhaps more than is necessary or desirable. *Zilg v. Prentice-Hall* deals with situations that are more likely to occur; from the author's perspective in this case, however, the result is hardly more satisfactory than that in *Freund*. Even so, the analyses in both cases are important and instructive.

Freund v. Washington Square Press, Inc., 34 N.Y.2d 379, 357 N.Y.S.2d 857 (1974)

SAMUEL RABIN, JUDGE

In this action for breach of a publishing contract, we must decide what damages are recoverable for defendant's failure to publish plaintiff's manuscript. In 1965, plaintiff, an author and a college teacher, and defendant, Washington Square Press, Inc., entered into a written agreement which, in relevant part, provided as follows. Plaintiff ("author") granted defendant ("publisher") exclusive rights to publish and sell in

book form plaintiff's work on modern drama. Upon plaintiff's delivery of the manuscript, defendant agreed to complete payment of a nonreturnable $2,000 "advance." Thereafter, if defendant deemed the manuscript not "suitable for publication," it had the right to terminate the agreement by written notice within 60 days of delivery. Unless so terminated, defendant agreed to publish the work in hardbound edition within 18 months and afterwards in paperbound edition. The contract further provided that defendant would pay royalties to plaintiff, based upon specified percentages of sales. (For example, plaintiff was to receive 10% of the retail price of the first 10,000 copies sold in the continental United States.) If defendant failed to publish within 18 months, the contract provided that "this agreement shall terminate and the rights herein granted to the Publisher shall revert to the Author. In such event all payments theretofore made to the Author shall belong to the Author without prejudice to any other remedies which the Author may have." The contract also provided that controversies were to be determined pursuant to the New York simplified procedure for court determination of disputes (CPLR 3031–3037, Consol. Laws, c. 8).

Plaintiff performed by delivering his manuscript to defendant and was paid his $2,000 advance. Defendant thereafter merged with another publisher and ceased publishing in hardbound. Although defendant did not exercise its 60-day right to terminate, it has refused to publish the manuscript in any form.

Plaintiff commenced the instant action pursuant to the simplified procedure practice and initially sought specific performance of the contract. The Trial Term Justice denied specific performance but, finding a valid contract and a breach by defendant, set the matter down for trial on the issue of monetary damages, if any, sustained by the plaintiff. At trial, plaintiff sought to prove: (1) delay of his academic promotion; (2) loss of royalties which would have been earned; and (3) the cost of publication if plaintiff had made his own arrangements to publish. The trial court found that plaintiff had been promoted despite defendant's failure to publish, and that there was no evidence that the breach had caused any delay. Recovery of lost royalties was denied without discussion. The court found, however, that the cost of hardcover publication to plaintiff was the natural and probable consequence of the breach and, based upon expert testimony, awarded $10,000 to cover this cost. It denied recovery of the expenses of paperbound publication on the ground that plaintiff's proof was conjectural.

The Appellate Division (3 to 2) affirmed, finding that the cost of publication was the proper measure of damages. In support of its conclusion, the majority analogized to the construction contract situation where the cost of completion may be the proper measure of damages for a builder's failure to complete a house or for use of wrong materials. The dissent concluded that the cost of publication is not an appropriate measure of damages and consequently, that plaintiff may recover nominal damages only. We agree with the dissent. In so concluding, we look to the basic purpose of damage recovery and the nature and effect of the parties' contract.

It is axiomatic that, except where punitive damages are allowable, the law awards damages for breach of contract to compensate for injury caused by the breach—injury which was foreseeable, i.e., reasonably within the contemplation of the parties, at the time the contract was entered into. . . .

In other words, so far as possible, the law attempts to secure to the injured party the benefit of his bargain, subject to the limitations that the injury—whether it be losses suffered or gains prevented—was foreseeable, and that the amount of damages claimed be measurable with a reasonable degree of certainty and, of course, adequately proven. . . . But it is equally fundamental that the injured party should not recover more from the breach than he would have gained had the contract been fully performed. . . .

Measurement of damages in this case according to the cost of publication to the plaintiff would confer greater advantage than performance of the contract would have entailed to plaintiff and would place him in a far better position than he would have occupied had the defendant fully performed. Such measurement bears no relation

to compensation for plaintiff's actual loss or anticipated profit. Far beyond compensating plaintiff for the interests he had in the defendant's performance of the contract—whether restitution, reliance or expectation (see Fuller & Perdue, "Reliance Interest in Contract Damages," 46 *Yale L.J.* 52, 53–56)—an award of the cost of publication would enrich plaintiff at defendant's expense.

Pursuant to the contract, plaintiff delivered his manuscript to the defendant. In doing so, he conferred a value on the defendant which, upon defendant's breach, was required to be restored to him. Special Term, in addition to ordering a trial on the issue of damages, ordered defendant to return the manuscript to plaintiff and plaintiff's restitution interest in the contract was thereby protected. . . .

At the trial on the issue of damages, plaintiff alleged no reliance losses suffered in performing the contract or in making necessary preparations to perform. Had such losses, if foreseeable and ascertainable, been incurred, plaintiff would have been entitled to compensation for them. . . .

As for plaintiff's expectation interest in the contract, it was basically two-fold—the "advance" and the royalties. (To be sure, plaintiff may have expected to enjoy whatever notoriety, prestige or other benefits that might have attended publication, but even if these expectations were compensable, plaintiff did not attempt at trial to place a monetary value on them.) There is no dispute that plaintiff's expectancy in the "advance" was fulfilled—he has received his $2,000. His expectancy interest in the royalties—the profit he stood to gain from sale of the published book—while theoretically compensable, was speculative. Although this work is not plaintiff's first, at trial he provided no stable foundation for a reasonable estimate of royalties he would have earned had defendant not breached its promise to publish. In these circumstances, his claim for royalties fails for uncertainty. . . .

Since the damages which would have compensated plaintiff for anticipated royalties were not proved with the required certainty, we agree with the dissent in the Appellate Division that nominal damages alone are recoverable. . . . Though these are damages in name only and not at all compensatory, they are nevertheless awarded as a formal vindication of plaintiff's legal right to compensation which has not been given a sufficiently certain monetary valuation. . . .

In our view, the analogy by the majority in the Appellate Division to the construction contract situation was inapposite. In the typical construction contract, the owner agrees to pay money or other consideration to a builder and expects, under the contract, to receive a completed building in return. The value of the promised performance to the owner is the properly constructed building. In this case, unlike the typical construction contract, the value to plaintiff of the promised performance—publication—was a percentage of sales of the books published and not the books themselves. Had the plaintiff contracted for the printing, binding and delivery of a number of hardbound copies of his manuscript, to be sold or disposed of as he wished, then perhaps the construction analogy, and measurement of damages by the cost of replacement or completion, would have some application.

Here, however, the specific value to plaintiff of the promised publication was the royalties he stood to receive from defendant's sales of the published book. Essentially, publication represented what it would have cost the defendant to confer that value upon the plaintiff, and, by its breach, defendant saved that cost. The error by the courts below was in measuring damages not by the value to plaintiff of the promised performance but by the cost of that performance to defendant. Damages are not measured, however, by what the defaulting party saved by the breach, but by the natural and probable consequences of the breach to the *plaintiff*. In this case, the consequence to plaintiff of defendant's failure to publish is that he is prevented from realizing the gains promised by the contract—the royalties. But, as we have stated, the amount of royalties plaintiff would have realized was not ascertained with adequate certainty and, as a consequence, plaintiff may recover nominal damages only.

Accordingly, the order of the Appellate Division should be modified to the extent of reducing the damage award of $10,000 for the cost of publication to six cents, but with costs and disbursements to the plaintiff.

Zilg v. Prentice-Hall, Inc., 717 F.2d 671 (2d Cir. 1983)

WINTER, CIRCUIT JUDGE

. . . Gerard Colby Zilg is the author of *DuPont: Behind the Nylon Curtain*, an historical account of the role of the DuPont family in American social, political and economic affairs. Early in 1972, after one partially successful and several unsuccessful efforts to find a publisher for his proposed book, Zilg's agent introduced him to Bram Cavin, a senior editor in P–H's Trade Book Division. Cavin expressed interest in the book, and he and Zilg submitted a formal proposal to John Kirk, P–H's Editor-in-Chief at that time. Kirk approved the proposal, which described the future book

> as a thoroughly documented study of the major role the DuPont family has played in the development of modern America and its corporate and social institutions. After skimming lightly over the family's origins in France and its development of its gunpowder business up to and through the Civil War, the book will concentrate on the period after that conflict right down to the present day. The story—essentially one of money and power—is going to be told in human terms and in the lives of the members of the family and their actions. The family will be looked upon as a unit in its relations to the outside world. But it will also be shown to be, as many families frequently are, one torn by feuds and struggles over the money and the power. . . .

Zilg submitted the first half of his completed manuscript to Cavin in November 1972, and the remainder a year later. Cavin authorized acceptance of the work on behalf of P–H, apparently without the participation of Peter Grenquist, who had become president of P–H's Trade Book Division sometime after execution of the contract but before submission of the manuscript. P–H's legal division scrutinized the manuscript for libelous content and concluded that, if a libel action were brought, P–H "would ultimately prevail" because the subject matter of the work was constitutionally privileged and the plaintiffs would have to prove actual malice. The division's opinion noted, however, that litigation against the DuPonts would be very costly.

A decision was made to accept the manuscript, which was distributed to selected wholesalers, reviewers, and booksellers. Copies were also sent to the editorial director of the Book of the Month Club ("BOMC"). Although BOMC decided not to offer the book as a selection of its main club, a subsidiary, the Fortune Book Club, which appealed to a readership composed largely of business executives, did choose it as a selection.

A committee of various P–H department representatives, including the book's editor, met on March 28, 1974 to discuss production plans. The sales estimates of committee members varied from 12 to 15 thousand copies for the first year although by May two members were predicting sales of only 10 thousand. Estimates of from 15 to 20 thousand sales over a five year period were also made. Cavin, an ardent supporter of the book, made estimates of 20 to 25 thousand in the first year and 25 to 35 thousand over five years. The committee decided on a first printing of 15,000 copies at a retail price of $12.95 per copy. At a later meeting, the committee decided to devote roughly $15,000 to advertising.

Although the literary or scholarly merits of the book are not our concern, its nature, tone and marketability among various audiences are key facts in this litigation, for they bear upon the book's prospects for commercial success and illuminate the negative reactions which later set in at P–H. The book is a harshly critical portrait of the DuPont family and their role in American social, political and economic history. Indeed, it is a harshly critical portrait of that history itself. The reactions of readers and reviewers in the record indicate that the book is polarizing, the difference in viewpoint depending in no small measure upon the politics of the beholder. A significant number of readers regard the book as a strident caricature, drawing every conceivable inference against the DuPont family and firms with which members of the family were or are associated. One judge at BOMC, for example, described it as "300,000 words of pure spite." On the other hand, the book has a loyal band of admirers. It received a favorable review in many newspapers, including the *New York Times* Book Review section. Its comprehensiveness and the extensive research on which it was based were frequently noted. The book also has some appeal to another audience, namely readers with a taste for gossip about the rich and powerful, particularly readers

in Delaware. Indeed, it was once first in non-fiction sales in that state.

In the American market, the book's appeal is somewhat limited by the fact that it is not a work critical of business on grounds that reform of capitalism is necessary in order to save it, a viewpoint with mainstream appeal. Rather, it presents a Marxist view of history. Also weighing against its overall marketability were its size (586 pages of text, 2 inches thick, three and one-half pounds), complexity (almost 200 family members with the surname DuPont and 170 years of American history) and price ($12.95 in 1974 dollars).

Prior to June 1974, Grenquist appears not to have been aware of the nature and tone of the book, of the intensity of negative feeling it might arouse in some readers or of evidence of serious inaccuracies. He may have been reassured partly by Cavin's enthusiasm and partly by the book's selection by the Fortune Book Club. That selection itself remains something of a mystery since the Club's inside reader concluded it was "a bad book, politically crude and cheaply journalistic." However, instead of accepting his recommendation that it "be fed back to the author page by page," BOMC contracted with P–H to have it adopted by the Fortune Book Club.

In June 1974, a chain of events was set in motion which apprised Grenquist of the negative aspects of Zilg's work. A member of the DuPont family obtained an advance copy of the manuscript from a bookseller and, predictably outraged, turned it over to the Public Affairs Department of the DuPont Company. Members of that department sought to locate individuals in P–H's management whom they knew personally in order to speak privately about the book, but to no avail. They advised the family member to do nothing before the book was published.

In July, the DuPont Company learned that the book had been accepted as a Fortune Book Club selection and decided to act before publication anyway. Harold Brown of DuPont ("DuPont-Brown") telephoned Vilma Bergane, a manager of Fortune Book Club, having received her name from the managing editor of *Fortune Magazine*. He told her that the book had been read by several persons, some of whom were attorneys, and that the book was "scurrilous" and "actionable." Bergane passed on a version of DuPont-Brown's remarks to F. Harry Brown, Editor-in-Chief of BOMC ("BOMC-Brown"). DuPont-Brown then told BOMC-Brown that DuPont family attorneys found the book abusive and that he was to try to locate someone at P–H with whom to discuss the book. He also told BOMC-Brown that the DuPont Company did not intend to throw its weight around. BOMC-Brown referred DuPont-Brown to Peter Grenquist at P–H.

Some days later, apparently in an effort to quash rumors or inaccurate messages to the contrary, DuPont-Brown phoned Grenquist to assure him that DuPont was not attempting to block publication of the book, initiate litigation, or even approach P–H in any kind of adversarial posture. One such rumor, allegedly passed on to Cavin by an editor at BOMC who does not remember the conversation, was that DuPont had gone to *Fortune Magazine* and threatened to pull all its advertising. *Fortune*, owned by Time, Inc., had no connection with the Fortune Book Club at this time.

Meanwhile, BOMC-Brown decided to look into the matter personally. Over the July 27–28 weekend, he "spent a horrible two days reading" the book and decided it was an unsuitable selection for the Fortune Book Club. He later stated he felt no pressure from the DuPont Company in reaching this decision. In view of the nature of the book and the Club's audience of business executives, his decision seems an inevitable result of his reading the book. BOMC immediately notified P–H of its decision not to distribute the book. The reason given was BOMC's belief that the book was malicious and had an objectionable tone.

P–H's own detailed examination of the manuscript may also have introduced or heightened skepticism on Grenquist's part. A toning down was found to be necessary even after the book was in page proof. Mistakes of fact, such as a statement that Irving S. Shapiro (DuPont's Chief Executive Officer) had served as an Assistant District Attorney in Queens County, New York, were discovered. More serious matters also came to light. The original manuscript attacked Judge Harold R. Medina for matters irrelevant to the

DuPonts and in a fashion which the district court characterized as libelous. Zilg admitted at trial that there was no factual foundation for this attack. Some eyebrows at P–H may well have been raised when this passage was discovered and deleted, since it was not only unfounded but also irrelevant.

P–H continued to correct and tone down the book, hoping to reverse BOMC's decision not to offer it through the Fortune Book Club. A certain defensiveness also began to creep into P–H's attitude toward the book. On August 2, Grenquist circulated a memorandum which noted that questions had arisen regarding both the tone of the book and Zilg's approach and recommended that the adjective "polemical" henceforth be used because "[t]he book is a polemical argument and no pretense is made that it is anything else." More importantly, he also cut the first printing from 15,000 copies to 10,000, stating that 5,000 copies were no longer needed for BOMC. The proposed advertising budget was also slashed from $15,000 to $5,500.

Judge Brieant held that the DuPont Company had a constitutionally protected interest in bringing the "scurrilous" nature of the book and its unsuitability as a Fortune Book Club selection to the attention of senior officials at BOMC and P–H. He expressly found that the Company did not engage in coercive tactics but limited its actions to the expression of its good faith opinion.

As to P–H, Judge Brieant found that the publishing contract required the publisher to "exercise its discretion in good faith in planning its promotion of the Book, and in revising its plans." This obligation required that Prentice-Hall use "its best efforts . . . to promote the Book fully and fairly." He held that P–H breached this obligation because it had no "sound" or "valid" business reason for reducing the first printing by 5,000 volumes and the advertising budget by $9,500, which allowed the book to go briefly out of stock (although wholesalers had ample copies) just as it gained sales momentum. He expressly found that since BOMC did its own printing of club selections, the first printing cut could not be attributed to the cancellation of the BOMC order. He also found that the book would have sold 25,000 copies had P–H not taken these actions.

Having concluded that P–H had no sound or valid business reason for reducing the first printing and advertising budget, Judge Brieant held that P–H "privished" Zilg's book on the basis of the testimony of plaintiff's expert, William Decker. Decker testified that publishers often mount a wholly inadequate merchandising effort after concluding that a book does not meet prior expectations in either quality or marketability. Such "privishing" is intended to fulfill the technical requirements of the contract to publish but to avoid adding to one's losses by throwing "good money after bad." . . .

We agree with Judge Brieant that DuPont did not tortiously interfere with Zilg's beneficial commercial relationships. We disagree, however, with his conclusion that P–H breached its contract with Zilg and reverse that judgment.

1. Tortious Interference by DuPont

Judge Brieant held that DuPont's approach to BOMC and subsequent communications with P–H were protected by the First Amendment. We affirm, but on the narrower grounds that these activities are not tortious under New York law.

The parties agree that New York law applies and that New York courts would follow the Restatement (Second) of Torts (1977). . . . The Restatement visits tort liability upon an actor who "intentionally and improperly" interferes with contractual relations between others by causing a party to those relations not to perform. Restatement (Second) of Torts § 766 (1977). We will assume that DuPont's actions were a cause in fact of BOMC's decision not to offer the book as a Fortune Book Club selection and of P–H's alleged breach of contract. We now turn to the propriety of DuPont's conduct.

Section 767 of the Restatement catalogues the factors considered in evaluating the propriety of interference with contractual relations. The section reads:

> In determining whether an actor's conduct in intentionally interfering with a contract or a prospective contractual relation of another is improper or not, consideration is given to the following factors:
> (a) the nature of the actor's conduct,
> (b) the actor's motive,

(c) the interests of the other with which the actor's conduct interferes,
(d) the interests sought to be advanced by the actor,
(e) the social interests in protecting the freedom of action of the actor and the contractual interests of the other,
(f) the proximity or remoteness of the actor's conduct to the interference and
(g) the relations between the parties.

As to section 767(a), the nature of the DuPont Company's conduct, Judge Brieant found that it did not entail threats of economic coercion or baseless litigation but was limited to a good faith expression of views about the merits, objectivity and accuracy of the book. We agree. The length and breadth of the evidence of economic coercion is a conversation between two parties without firsthand knowledge, which only one recalls. Moreover, it involved Time, Inc., which had nothing to do with publication or distribution of the book. As to threats of litigation, DuPont did convey to BOMC its view that the work was "actionable." Since BOMC was completely indemnified under its contract with P–H, it is unlikely that the remark, made only to BOMC, was coercive to BOMC. In any event representatives of the DuPont Company quickly informed both BOMC and P–H that it had no intention of suing.

As to section 767(b), the DuPont Company's motive, the record amply demonstrates that it desired to bring to the attention of BOMC and, later P–H, what it in good faith believed were plainly negative aspects of the book. It wanted to expose those negative aspects in the hope of causing BOMC to abandon its plans and of inducing P–H to reconsider publication without substantial revision.

Zilg just as clearly had an interest, section 767(c) in the Restatement, in avoiding these very consequences since publication under his contract with P–H and selection by the Fortune Book Club (assuming, without deciding, that relationship to be contractual) would enhance the dissemination of his views, enrich him, and might also launch him on a career as a well known author.

Conversely, the DuPont Company had a substantial interest, section 767(d), in communicating its views to BOMC and to P–H. While much of the book's accusatorial material related to specific family members, the company itself could reasonably believe that it might suffer damage to its public image and good will if the book was given widespread credence. For most of the period covered by the book the company was controlled and operated by various members of the family who are the subjects of Zilg's attacks. The title itself, *DuPont: Behind the Nylon Curtain*, seems more a reference to the company than to the family. . . . We regard Zilg's argument that only family members had a cognizable interest in commenting on the book as ignoring the reality of the circumstances and the character of the book itself. . . .

Such communications seem to me socially beneficial because they promote the free flow of ideas. Zilg argues that such communications should be privileged only when made to the public at large. I see no basis for such a limitation. There is no self-evident harm in book clubs and publishing houses learning what the targets of a harsh "polemical argument" believe about the merits of that argument. Such firms surely have, or ought to have, an interest in avoiding unjustified attacks as well as factual error, and such information aids in achieving those goals. . . .

As to BOMC and Fortune Book Club, there can be no doubt of their interest in receiving the communication from the DuPont Company since the book was an utterly inappropriate selection for the Club. Book clubs have a strong interest in avoiding the wrath of their members and such communications further this interest.

Society benefits from such communications because they increase the information available to publishers and book clubs and thus aid those firms in meeting the desires of potential purchasers. . . .

After weighing the factors comprising section 767, we hold that the DuPont Company's conduct in communicating its views on Zilg's book was not tortious. Authors have no exclusive right to the ear of those who disseminate their works, for intelligent decisions by publishers and others distributing books are enhanced by the free flow of information. So long as the expression of views is done in good faith and in a non-coercive way, it is not tortious. . . .

2. P–H's Breach of Contract

We believe Judge Brieant's discussion of P–H's obligations under its contract with Zilg, and his finding of a breach of those obligations, is more troubling than his dismissal of the case against the DuPont Company. Judge Brieant read the contract in question to oblige P–H "to use its best efforts . . . to promote the Book fully. . . ." and found that the decision to cut the first printing and original advertising budget resulted in a loss of sales momentum when the book was briefly out of stock. These actions by P–H, he held, breached its agreement with Zilg because they lacked a sound or valid business reason.

Putting aside for the moment P–H's motive in slashing the first printing and advertising budget, we note that Zilg neither bargained for nor acquired an explicit "best efforts" or "promote fully" promise, much less an agreement to make certain specific promotional efforts. . . .

While P–H obligated itself to "publish" the book once it had accepted it, the contract expressly leaves to P–H's discretion printing and advertising decisions. Working as we must in the context of a surprising absence of caselaw on the meaning of this not uncommon agreement, we believe that the contract in question establishes a relationship between the publisher and author which implies an obligation upon the former to make certain efforts in publishing a book it has accepted notwithstanding the clause which leaves the number of volumes to be printed and the advertising budget to the publisher's discretion. This obligation is derived both from the common expectations of parties to such agreements and from the relationship of those parties as structured by the contract. . . .

Zilg, like most authors, sought to take advantage of a division of labor in which firms specialize in publishing works written by authors who are not employees of the firm. Under contracts such as the one before us, publishing firms print, advertise and distribute books at their own expense. In return for performing these tasks and for bearing the risk of a book's failure to sell, the author gives a publisher exclusive rights to the book with certain reservations not important here. Such contracts provide for royalties on sales to the author, often on an escalating basis, *i.e.*, higher royalties at higher levels of sales.

While publishers and authors have generally similar goals, differences in perspective and resulting perceptions are inevitable. An author usually has a bigger stake in the success or failure of a book than a publisher who may regard it as one among many publications, some of which may lose money. The author, whose eggs are in one basket, thus has a calculus of risk quite different from the publisher so far as costly promotional expenditures are concerned. The publisher, of course, views the author's willingness to take large risks as a function of the fact that it is the publisher's money at peril. Moreover, the publisher will inevitably regard his or her judgment as to marketing conditions as greatly superior to that of a particular author.

One means of reconciling these differing viewpoints is "up-front" money—$6,500 in Zilg's case—which provides a token of the publisher's seriousness about the book. Were such sums not bargained for, acquisition of publishing rights would be virtually costless and firms would acquire those rights without regard to whether or not they had truly decided to publish the work.

However, up-front money alone cannot fully reconcile the conflicting interests of the parties. Uncertainty surrounds the publication of most books and publishers must be cautious about the size of up-front payments since they increase the already considerable economic risks they take by printing and promoting books at their own expense. Negotiating such matters as the number of volumes to be printed and the level of advertising efforts might be possible but such bargaining in the case of each author and each book would be enormously costly. There is never a guarantee of ultimate agreement, and if a set of negotiations fails over these issues, the bargaining must begin again with another publisher. Moreover, publishers must also be wary of undertaking obligations to print a certain number of volumes or to spend fixed sums on promotion. They will strongly prefer to have flexibility in reacting to actual marketing conditions according to their own experience. . . .

Once P–H had accepted the book, it obtained the exclusive right to publish it. Were the clause empowering the publisher to determine promotional expenses read literally, the contract would allow a publisher to refuse to print or distribute any copies of a book while having exclusive rights to it. In effect, authors would be guaranteed nothing but whatever up-front money had been negotiated, and the promise to publish would be meaningless. We think the promise to publish must be given some content and that it implies a good faith effort to promote the book including a first printing and advertising budget adequate to give the book a reasonable chance of achieving market success in light of the subject matter and likely audience. . . .

However, the clause empowering the publisher to decide in its discretion upon the number of volumes printed and the level of promotional expenditures must also be given some content. If a trier of fact is free to determine whether such decisions are sound or valid, the publisher's ability to rely upon its own experience and judgment in marketing books will be seriously hampered. We believe that once the obligation to undertake reasonable initial promotional activities has been fulfilled, the contractual language dictates that a business decision by the publisher to limit the size of a printing or advertising budget is not subject to second guessing by a trier of fact as to whether it is sound or valid. . . .

Given the line we draw, a breach of contract might be proven by Zilg in two ways. First, he might demonstrate that the initial printing and promotional efforts were so inadequate as not to give the book a reasonable chance to catch on with the reading public. Second, he might show that even greater printing and promotional efforts were not undertaken for reasons other than a good faith business judgment. Because he has shown neither, we reverse the judgment in his favor.

As to P–H's initial obligation, Zilg has not shown that P–H's efforts on behalf of his book did not give it a reasonable chance to catch on with the reading public. It printed or reprinted 13,000 volumes (3,000 over the volume of sales at which the highest royalty was triggered), authorized an advertising budget of $5,500 (1974 purchasing power), distributed over 600 copies to reviewers, purchased ads in papers such as the *New York*

Times and *Wall Street Journal*, and made reasonable efforts to sell the paperback rights. The documentary record shows that Grenquist took a continued interest in marketing the book, made suggestions as to promoting it effectively and ordered that "rave reviews" be sent to BOMC as late as January 1975.

The fact that initial decisions as to promotional efforts were trimmed is of no relevance absent evidence that the actual efforts made were so inadequate that the book did not have a reasonable chance to catch on with the reading public. The record is barren of such evidence. . . .

The district court read the contract as imposing on P–H a continuing obligation to use "its best efforts . . . to promote the Book fully and fairly" and as empowering a trier of fact to second guess a publisher's judgments as to the soundness of the decisions made. We disagree. So long as the initial promotional efforts are adequate under the test we outline above, a publisher's printing and advertising decisions do not breach a contract such as that before us unless the plaintiff proves that the motivation underlying those decisions was not a good faith business judgment. Zilg failed to produce such evidence. His case was based on the theory that economic coercion by the DuPont Company caused P–H to reduce its promotional efforts. Judge Brieant found against him on this issue and, for reasons stated above, we affirm this determination. . . .

. . . [T]he contract between P–H and Zilg left the decisions in question to the business judgment of the publisher, the author's protection being in the publisher's experience, judgment and quest for profits. P–H's promotional efforts were, in Decker's words, "adequate," notwithstanding the reduction of the first printing and the initial advertising budget. Indeed, those reductions, coming on the heels of BOMC's decision not to distribute the book, appear to be a rational reaction to that news. Decker himself testified that the Fortune Book Club selection was an important barometer of marketability since it was an independent judgment that the book had an audience. Zilg's contract with P–H did not compel the publisher to ignore the implications of BOMC's change of heart.

Affirmed in part, reversed in part. . . .

PIERCE, CIRCUIT JUDGE (CONCURRING)

I am in agreement with the result reached in Judge Winter's able opinion. Thus, I respectfully concur, but I reach the same conclusions on narrower grounds.

My concurrence is directed to that portion of the opinion addressing Zilg's claim of tortious interference by DuPont. Recognizing that applicable law requires a showing of "intentional and improper" interference with a contract before tort liability may be visited upon a defendant, Restatement (Second) of Torts § 766 (1977), I consider the pivotal facts in this case to be the district court's findings—fully supported by the record evidence—that, in effect, DuPont's communications to BOMC concerning alleged inaccuracies in the book were made in good faith and were non-coercive. . . .

Because DuPont's conduct in this case was found to be undertaken in good faith and was non-coercive, I conclude that DuPont committed no tort by communicating to BOMC its concerns about the accuracy of the book. Moreover, the determination of no contractual breach *alone* would suggest DuPont's non-liability for tort, since under New York law, breach of the contract allegedly interfered with is an essential element of the tort claimed herein. . . .

NOTES ─────────────────────────

1. In *Van Valkenburgh, Nooger & Neville, Inc. v. Hayden Publishing Co., Inc.*, 330 N.Y.S.2d 329, 287 N.E.2d 142 (1972), the New York Court of Appeals found that the publisher had breached the implied covenant of fair dealing and the explicit contractual obligation to use its best efforts to promote the author's work when it produced and marketed a series of books that were extremely similar to the plaintiff author's series and whose royalty agreements were more advantageous to the publisher.

Although the court recognized a publisher's right to produce competing works which may lessen an author's royalties, ". . . [t]here may be a point where such activity is so manifestly harmful to the author, and must have been seen by the publisher so to be harmful, as to justify a court in saying there was breach of covenant to promote the author's works."

2. In *Demaris v. G. P. Putnam's Sons*, 379 F. Supp. 294 (C.D. Ca. 1973), the court allowed expert testimony as to author's lost profits (royalties) on two books.

The court calculated the damages by taking the midpoint between author's experts' estimates ($56,000) and publisher's experts' estimates ($10,000) and awarded $33,000 in damages. But the court then subtracted certain obligations owed by the author to the publisher. The final amount awarded to the author was $18,000.

As to other claims by author, the court rejected as a matter of law any damages for loss from sale of foreign rights or for loss of sale to radio, motion pictures, or television. The court concluded these alleged damages were too speculative and uncertain.

On yet another issue involving one manuscript, the court held a manuscript could be deemed not satisfactory when the publisher's outside legal counsel opined it might well subject the publisher to lawsuits for invasion of privacy and common-law copyright infringement.

3. In *Hewlitt v. Caplin*, 88 N.Y.S.2d 428 (App. Div., 1st Dept. 1949), the plaintiff could not collect damages for his share of royalties from the prospective sale of a book, when both the price of the book and the amounts of prospective sales were uncertain. However, the plaintiff should have been allowed to submit evidence showing the reasonable value of plaintiff's services, plus expenses incurred in connection with plaintiff's contract with defendant.

2.40 Authorship Attribution

Credit is of paramount importance to the creative talent, whether that person is an author, performer, director, or artist. The creator wants proper credit for the work. At times, just as importantly, he or she does not want false attribution for what is actually the work of another. The problems of proper credit are pursued in several chapters of this book through various forms of creative endeavors. Our principal case at this point has well-known author Ken Follett seeking to restrain what he believes is unjust exploitation of his name.

Follett v. Arbor House Publ Co., 497 F. Supp. 304 (S.D.N.Y. 1980)

SWEET, DISTRICT JUDGE

This action presents questions arising out of the intended publication by Arbor House this fall of a book, *The Gentlemen of 16 July*, which Arbor House intends to attribute to Follett as principal author, "with Rene Louis Maurice," a pseudonym for three French authors. Follett has written *Key to Rebecca*, which will also be published by New American this fall, and seeks to restrain Arbor House from publishing *The Gentlemen of 16 July* and from using the currently proposed authorship attribution. Arbor House seeks to restrain Follett, Morrow, and New American from disparaging *The Gentlemen of 16 July* and its authorship attribution. The principal statute involved is section 43 of the Lanham Act, 15 U.S.C. § 1125, and in varying degrees counsel agree that there is no directly relevant precedent.

The issue for decision is both unique and fascinating, requiring the court to consider the practices in the publishing industry with respect to authorship attributions, the meteoric rise of Follett as a novelist, the distinction between creating and editing a literary work, and ultimately, the effect of all of this on the public. Based upon the evidence that has been presented by highly skilled counsel, at least one of whom has authored as well as litigated, an injunction must issue requiring Arbor House to indicate that *The Gentlemen of 16 July* is a work of nonfiction written by Rene Louis Maurice with Ken Follett, with attribution to be equal and in chronological order—that is, with Rene Louis Maurice first. The following constitutes the court's findings of fact and conclusions of law.

Despite the difficulty in reaching the ultimate conclusions relating to creativity and publishing integrity, the facts revealed by the testimony and the exhibits are largely undisputed.

On July 16, 1976, Albert Spaggiari and his confederates began tunnelling under the streets of Nice, France. By July 19, 1976, they had reached their goal, a bank vault, and had removed some 60 million francs of property in various forms. Subsequently, certain of the confederates were apprehended, as was Spaggiari. On March 10, 1977, by a dramatic leap from a courthouse window, Spaggiari escaped. These events were, of course, chronicled in the press at the time.

Shortly after the theft, three French journalists collaborated on a book-length account of these events. This account was published in France as "Cinq Milliards au Bout de l'Egout" under the attribution Rene Louis Maurice, the pseudonym of the three reporters. Jean Claude Simoen certified in May 1977 that he was the author of this work. Be that as it may, Clemens von Bezard, the director and principal owner of the Star Agency Establishment ("Star"), a Liechtenstein company engaged in publishing, acquiring and licensing literary rights, entered into negotiations with Simoen. As a consequence of those negotiations, Bezard testified that he acquired the right to publish the account outside France. Bezard translated the account into German and had it translated into English by Jeffrey Robinson.

In the summer of 1977, Bezard communicated with his agent in England, Burnett Rigg, to arrange for publication of the account by a British publisher. As a consequence of Rigg's efforts, William Collins Sons & Company Ltd. ("Collins") purchased the account for publication by Fontana Paperbacks, a division of Collins.

At the same time, Follett became involved, also through Rigg who acted as his agent. Follett had started his literary career by working as a reporter. By 1977 he had written ten books, including one children's novel and two thrillers, seven of which had been published under a by-line other than Ken Follett. To further his knowledge of his profession, he had sought and obtained employment as an editor and had progressed to a position as deputy managing director of a publishing house.

Rigg suggested to Collins and Star that Follett be given the translation to review and, according to the final agreement between Star and Collins, to edit the work and prepare it for publication. On July 12, Follett wrote to Rigg suggesting that considerable work was required, including restructuring the story, bringing style to the writing, exploiting the drama, developing the characters and filling in gaps. On August 5, 1977, Simon King, on behalf of Collins, agreed to pay Follett 850 pounds "for refashioning the typescript" as Follett had suggested, on condition that Follett visit Nice to obtain background material. Thereafter Follett went to work to revise the manuscript which was subsequently published under the title *The Heist of the Century*.

Follett is an efficient, careful and diligent ex-reporter and editor. Fortunately for this writer, his work is carefully detailed and explicit. First, he prepared his "schema" for rewrite, a six-page document posing certain questions to which Follett sought answers. He sent this to Bezard, and it was followed up by a trip to Nice in September 1977.

In Nice, Follett was met by Bezard. They visited certain of the locations referred to in the account and were joined by Carolyn Atkinson, then a part-time employee of Bezard. The next day, Saturday, was spent without progress on the assignment, but on Sunday, Bezard, Follett and Atkinson met with Rene Cenni, one of the journalists who had written the French account. Atkinson translated and Follett meticulously recorded Cenni's answers to the questions posed in the "schema." During this working luncheon, Follett requested by-line credit from Bezard, a request casually and quickly granted in order not to raise the issue in Cenni's presence.

On his return Follett worked daily for twelve days using the Robinson translation, a second translation of the French account, newspaper clippings, his own notes and the "schema." The work when completed contained between 42,000 and 43,000 words on 160 printed pages. It was submitted to Rigg on September 26, 1977. King's response in late November characterized the work as a "rewrite," "splendid," and "terrific."

Notwithstanding this reaction, the question of copyright and attribution was not so satisfactorily resolved. King refused Follett's requested copyright, citing Rigg, but agreed to credit Follett on the title page. Follett insisted on a copyright for his "rewrite," claimed a further financial interest in the book, and implied that legal action would be taken to enforce his position. Letters were exchanged and then on May 22, 1978, David Grossman, Follett's London agent, assured King that no copyright claim would be made by Follett, and that the attribution of "Rene Louis Maurice with Ken Follett" on the title page would be satisfactory to Follett.

The Heist of the Century was published in England in the fashion just described, namely "Rene Louis Maurice with Ken Follett" on the title page, and the pseudonym alone on the cover. It was thereafter offered to at least seven publishing houses in the United States by Zuckerman in May 1978. No publication ensued, and New American declined the book again in the fall of 1979.

Also in the fall of 1977, Follett contracted for the publication in the United States of his book *Storm Island,* which had already come out in England. It was retitled *Eye of the Needle,* and Arbor House, the publisher, embarked upon a campaign to promote the book. The book was a great success, achieving best seller status, and possessed what Donald Fine, the president and chief executive officer of Arbor House, described as "narrative drive." It was in the view of this reviewer an exciting spy story, laid in England during World War II with a challenging plot animated, as Follett explained, not only by external events but also by the characters of the protagonists. This was particularly so with respect to its dramatic denouement.

Arbor House obtained an option for Follett's next book, ultimately titled *Triple,* a tale involving espionage relating to the establishment of nuclear capacity by Israel. Follett had also conceived of a plot relating to Marshal Rommel's desert campaign and the espionage and counterespionage which was involved. Fine liked the World War II plot better than *Triple* and urged Follett to let Arbor House publish it. However, Follett decided to proceed with *Triple* partly, according to Fine, to avoid being typed as an author writing only about the World War II period. *Triple* was submitted to Arbor House in outline form late in 1978, and the manuscript was delivered early in 1979. A dispute over editing ensued, Follett threatened litigation to bar certain changes in the manuscript, the matter was resolved, and *Triple* was published successfully, completing Follett's obligation to Arbor House.

Follett then contracted with New American for future works and received an advance against royalties of $3,000,000 for his next three books. He delivered the first of these, *Key to Rebecca,* the desert campaign book, early this year and its publication this fall was announced to the trade in the spring. *Key to Rebecca* will be a volume of 384 pages to be sold for $12.95.

In May 1980, Star, still claiming possession of

the rights to *The Heist of the Century,* retained Meredith to represent its interests in the United States. On May 13, Star sent Fine the book to review for publication. Shortly after reading it, Fine determined to publish the book as *The Gentlemen of 16 July* and entered into a contract with Star which provided for a $25,000 advance royalty payment. Fine knew of New American's plans for the publication of *Key to Rebecca* in the fall.

Arbor House has prepared a jacket for *The Gentlemen of 16 July* that has the following authorship attribution:

by the author TRIPLE and EYE OF THE NEEDLE
KEN FOLLETT
with Rene Louis Maurice

Only Follett's name is listed on the spine portion of the jacket. *The Gentlemen of 16 July* is expected to constitute 208 printed pages and to sell for $9.95.

No cases have been brought to the attention of the court relating to the question of attribution, and the testimony established contrasting practices in the publishing industry. Different attributions which frequently are used include "as told to," "by," "with," and co-authorship. One witness testified that there is no difference between "by" and "with" with respect to attribution. There are instances of publication of books under the name of one author actually written by another, without attribution, or written entirely by one author with principal attribution to another. These attributions are arrived at by negotiations with the authors and at the direction of the publisher. There was testimony that if the publisher possesses all the rights, the attribution is at his discretion.

Both Arbor House and Morrow plan to promote their respective Follett books vigorously, have announced their intentions to the trade, and have invested substantial sums in the promotion and publication of their respective books. Both books are scheduled for release this fall. All parties agree that the critical and public success of each book will substantially affect sales of the other. No testimony concerning public opinion was presented, and it is difficult, if not impossible, to conceive how such evidence could be obtained as events now stand.

Much of the evidence, naturally, centered on an analysis of Follett's work which resulted in the *The Heist of the Century*, retitled for United States publication as *The Gentlemen of 16 July*, including a line-by-line comparison of Follett's product and its principal predecessor, the Robinson version. What is without challenge is that Follett added to the previous versions a prologue, an epilogue, chapter headings, about half a page of analysis of Spaggiari's psychology obtained conveniently from a next door neighbor of Follett's who was a psychologist, and details obtained from Cenni. It is also conceded that Follett eliminated the frequent use of flashback in favor of a chronological march of events, and made alterations to Anglicize the references. In addition, the work was rewritten, and characterizations were sharpened. . . .

While there are a number of instances of rewriting of this kind, which enhance the personalities of the characters for the reader, the characterizations themselves remain essentially the same as depicted by the French authors. The incidents reported are unchanged though the sequence is altered so that each follows chronologically. There can be no doubt that to the reader of the English language, *The Heist of the Century* is a more compelling version of the historical events surrounding the Nice bank robbery than the Robinson translation. . . .

Although hired to edit according to the Star/Collins agreement, Follett did more. Fine, a concerned and capable editor who is justly proud of his ability to discern works of quality and even to improve them, drew the line between editing and authorship on a practical level. He noted that authors do not permit editors to obtain authorship credit, as a practical matter, even if the revisions are substantial. Here, Follett in fact rewrote the work. The language and presentation of the work were substantially improved and altered. Follett sought and obtained some authorship credit, though less than he felt he had earned at the time. . . .

Although the parties have attempted to frame the issues in this case in different, and in some

respects contradictory fashion, the controlling question is whether the attribution to Ken Follett as the principal author of *The Gentlemen of 16 July* constitutes a false representation and false designation of origin. . . .

In *Gieseking v. Urania Records, Inc.*, 17 Misc.2d 1034, 155 N.Y.S.2d 171 (N.Y. Co. Sup. Ct. 1956), the court suggested that an author has a right under the New York Civil Rights law to ensure that any attribution to him accurately reflects his contribution to a manuscript. The court stated, "A performer has a property right in his performance that it shall not be used for a purpose not intended, and particularly in a manner which does not fairly represent his services." By analogy, it may well be that Follett is entitled to an accurate description of his role in preparing *The Gentlemen of 16 July*. Any rights which he may hold in this regard are co-extensive with his right under the Lanham Act, discussed below.

Arbor House and Meredith contend that the Lanham Act issues in this case are controlled by a determination as to whether Follett's version of *The Heist of the Century* was copyrightable under the Copyright Act, 17 U.S.C. §§ 101 *et seq.* They urge that Follett's version could have been copyrighted, since in a non-fiction work such as *The Heist of the Century*, the right to obtain a copyright derives from the form of words in which events are recounted, and not from the interpretation of the events themselves. See *Hoehling v. Universal City Studios, Inc.*, 618 F.2d 972 (2d Cir. 1980). Arbor House and Meredith point out that the form of the script after Follett's editing differs substantially from that which he received as to the words used, the order of events, the development of characters and the depiction of events, so that Follett's edited version was copyrightable. . . .

However, the analysis of whether an editing or rewriting of an existing manuscript is copyrightable should not control the Lanham Act issue presented here. . . . Although an edited version would apparently be copyrightable so long as the editor's alterations were more than "merely trivial," it could still be misleading to designate that editor as the principal author of the work. Thus the fact that Follett sought and might have been entitled to obtain a copyright interest in his edited version is not dispositive of the issue before the court.

The parties have submitted conflicting evidence as to trade practices in the publishing industry. Meredith and Arbor House contend that if an individual makes a contribution to a literary work which bears certain indicia of authorship, that person can be described as an author and the form of attribution rests within the discretion of the publisher. Follett, New American and Morrow have presented evidence that even the substantial revisions performed by Follett amount to no more than what is customarily performed by freelance editors. They contend that such alterations rarely, if ever, result in the editor's receiving authorship credit.

These industry practices are largely irrelevant to the issues in this case. Even if an attribution of authorship were consistent with industry practices, it would nevertheless be illegal under the Lanham Act if it misrepresented the contribution of the person designated as author.

The key issue, then, is whether the designation of authorship which Arbor House proposes to utilize on the cover of *The Gentlemen of 16 July* constitutes a violation of section 43(a) of the Lanham Act, 15 U.S.C. § 1125(a). . . . Section 43(a) is designed to provide a statutory cause of action for false description or advertisement of goods by any person likely to be injured by such description or advertising. . . . In order to determine whether a description or representation is false, a court should first assess the meaning of particular representations and then determine whether the claims made are false. . . . Where a description concerning goods is unambiguous, the court can grant relief based on its own findings of falsity without resort to evidence of the reaction of consumers of the goods. . . . Moreover, in order to obtain injunctive relief under the Lanham Act, a plaintiff need only establish a "likelihood of confusion or a tendency to mislead." . . .

The attribution of authorship of *The Gentlemen of 16 July* as designated on the cover and title page of the book and in Arbor House's advertisements, contains an unambiguous representation that Follett is the principal author of the book. The name Ken Follett is printed in bold typeface approximately 15 mm. high. The subtitle, "with Rene Louis Maurice," is printed in much smaller type and is only 6 mm. in height. Above Ken Follett's name, the notation "by the author of TRIPLE and EYE OF THE NEEDLE" appears in type 4 mm. high. The name Ken Follett appears on the spine of the book unaccompanied by any reference to "Rene Louis Maurice." This attribution clearly indicates that Ken Follett is the principal author of the book.

The concept of authorship is elusive and inexact. Although I do not presuppose to offer a definitive analysis of qualities which give rise to authorship, some such definition is essential to a resolution of the issue before the court. The parties have cited no cases in which the concept of authorship has been carefully dissected, and this court has discovered none.

Arbor House and Meredith contend that Follett is the principal author of *The Gentlemen of 16 July* because of his substantial contribution to the form of the book. The actual words used in the final draft were supplied in large measure by Follett. Follett altered the method of telling the story by shifting the chronology and removing flashbacks. The characters are more vividly portrayed in Follett's edited version than in the draft he received. Follett has modulated the unfolding of events carefully in order to achieve what Fine described as "narrative drive" and to enhance the dramatic effect of the plot. Follett's contribution bears certain indicia of authorship. His alterations were substantial, and the finished product bears the mark of his style and craftsmanship.

Yet, these refinements are not sufficient to render Follett the principal author of the book. Authorship connotes something more than style, form and narrative approach. It includes a special element of creativity, of the definition of scope and content. In this case, Follett received a fixed plot, a cast of characters and a set of themes and reworked these elements to make them more palatable and comprehensible to the intended audience. He neither conceived the framework or format of the book, nor played a substantial role in selecting the material to be included.

Almost every significant occurrence, personality and theme can be traced directly to the materials from which Follett worked.

As a result, although Follett's revisions may have been more substantial than those which an editor would ordinarily perform in correcting, polishing and revising, it is misleading to depict him as the principal author of *The Gentlemen of 16 July.* His contributions display none of the special creative attributes which are associated with authorship. Thus, the representation that Follett is the principal author of the book is literally false. . . .

The Lanham Act . . . is designed not only to vindicate "the author's personal right to prevent the presentation of his work to the public in a distorted form," . . . but also to protect the public and the artist from misrepresentations of the artist's contribution to a finished work.

Based on the facts found and legal conclusions reached, judgment will be granted in favor of Follett, Morrow and New American. Although the court must proceed cautiously in dictating the form of presentation of *The Gentlemen of 16 July,* some accommodation is essential to assure that the public will not be misled by the attribution of authorship, yet protect Arbor House's legitimate commercial interests in publication of the work. Arbor House will be required to give equal attribution to Rene Louis Maurice and Ken Follett, in that order, and to indicate on the cover and jacket that the work is non-fiction. . . .

NOTE _____

1. In *Vargas v. Esquire, Inc.,* 164 F.2d 522 (7th Cir. 1947), an artist sued to enjoin a publisher's use of pictures made and delivered by the artist. In the contract between artist and publisher, the artist completely divested himself of all property rights in the pictures, including the right to possession, control, and use. After the contract was terminated and the publisher sought to use remaining pictures without crediting the artist, the artist could not enjoin the publisher's use of the pictures without credit on the grounds of implied contractual provisions or "moral rights" theory.

The artist's principal contention that publication of the pictures without his name violated an implied agreement between artist and publisher was rejected because the concept is applicable only when an author or artist enters into a contract which grants limited rights to a publisher and reserves other rights to the author. Implied agreements cannot be found in a contract where the artist in clear, unambiguous language completely divests himself of all possible rights in the artistic work.

The artist's contention that "moral rights" protect the integrity of an artwork and preempt any assignable economic rights was also rejected by the courts, which noted that although the "moral rights" of artists are recognized in civil law countries, the concept is unsupported by American authority.

2.50   Alteration

The author and artist are as concerned over the handling of their work as they are with receiving proper credit for the work's creation. Our principal cases, *Chesler v. Avon Book Division* and *Bobbs-Merrill Co. v. New American Library,* focus on the artist's creative control, including limitations on others' rights to edit the original work. The issues in these cases are similar to the problems that arise in other entertainment settings (see, for example, the *Gilliam* and *Preminger* cases in Section 7.30).

Often the problem is not between the creative person and the original publisher or producer. Troubles occur when the work is sublicensed or subcontracted. Books are transformed from hard-cover to paperback to, perhaps, movies. Movies move from the screen to television. Network television programs are later syndicated. Editing, or worse, occurs, and the original author or director cries foul.

The *Chesler* case points to the limitations that restrict authors' rights, *unless* there is adequate protection in the original contract. While protections have been forged to deal with the more drastic situations (see, for example, *Gilliam,* § 7.30), the overall picture is still not encouraging for the artist seeking to protect the integrity of his or her work.

Chesler v. Avon Book Division, 76 Misc. 2d 1048, 352
N.Y.S.2d 552 (Sup. Ct. N.Y. Co. 1973)

FEIN, JUSTICE

Plaintiff, a prominent feminist psychologist, author and lecturer, is the author of a book entitled *Women and Madness*, published in 1972 in hard cover by Doubleday, Inc. (Doubleday). The work has received widespread recognition and varying critical comment. . . .

Following publication of the hard-cover edition, Doubleday entered into a written contract with Avon, dated December 27, 1972, granting Avon the right to publish plaintiff's work in paperback form. This motion is addressed to Avon's paperback edition. . . .

Plaintiff alleges that Avon's paperback edition is not a faithful reproduction of her original work as published by Doubleday. She asserts that relevant portions of the text, as well as various illustrations and footnotes, are either omitted, altered or rearranged in the Avon publication. Plaintiff charges that these changes are so extensive as to amount to "mutilation" of her work, making it so confusing and incomprehensible as to modify substantially and dilute seriously its meaning and intent.

Plaintiff asserts that Avon's paperback version, in its present form, will subject her to negative criticism, damage her reputation and invalidate her book for use as an authoritative work by potential students and other serious readers.

Shortly after argument on the motion was heard by the court, plaintiff served a complaint pleading nine causes of action. The complaint requests a permanent injunction and damages on the grounds of breach of contract, copyright infringement, tortious conduct, including the unfaithful and negligent reproduction of her work, libel and a violation of civil rights. Although named in the complaint as a defendant, Doubleday was not named in the summons, nor, as far as appears, was it served with the summons or other papers in this action or on this motion for a temporary injunction.

The agreement between plaintiff and Doubleday does not reserve to plaintiff any rights to edit, change or otherwise pass upon the final manuscript of the hard cover edition. . . . Despite the fact that the agreements do not give plaintiff the right to pass upon the format or text of the paperback edition, plaintiff, as an author, is not powerless to prevent slipshod or truncated use of her work.

Although the authorities are sparse, it is clear that even after a transfer or assignment of an author's work, the author has a property right that it shall not be used for a purpose not intended or in a manner which does not fairly represent the creation of the author. . . .

Plaintiff relies in part on the doctrine of an author's "moral right" which she asks the court to enforce so as to protect the integrity of her work. The authorities she cites do not establish that such right is recognized in New York. . . .

However, the plaintiff's right to relief need not be bottomed upon the application of a theory of law which has not been afforded full recognition in this state. The court should not withhold appropriate relief by applying a rigid construction to causes of action or claims asserted by a plaintiff, if a right entitled to protection is shown.

An author or artist is entitled to judicial protection where there is a sufficient demonstration of "mutilation" or other serious alteration of the creator's work. . . .

The court has compared the relevant portions of the hard cover book, and the paperback edition. It cannot be seriously disputed that defendant did omit the illustrations and a number of reference sources from the paperback edition and did not follow the text of the hard cover book with respect to chapter introductions and column juxtaposition.

The court cannot pretend to be either a literary critic or a well-versed scholar in the field of the plaintiff's work. The book is obviously an original, careful and perhaps revolutionary study filled with many new and provocative insights. It is neither easy to read nor to live with.

These essential qualities inhere in both the hard cover and paperback editions. Even granting the variations in the paperback, they do not justify plaintiff's claim that Avon did not attempt to publish a faithful reproduction of her work or that the paperback edition materially alters the intent of her work.

Unfortunately for plaintiff, the agreement between plaintiff and Doubleday did not forbid alterations or omissions in her work without her consent. . . .

Nonetheless appropriate action must be taken by Avon in connection with the distribution of further paperbacks and advertising to indicate to the public and prospective purchasers of the paperback version that changes have been made involving chapter introductions, omission of illustrations and footnotes and column juxtaposition. To this extent, there has been a condensation or abridgement. Although the right to do so exists under the contracts, there is an obligation to make known to readers that the right has been exercised. This is simply telling the truth.

The motion is granted only to the foregoing extent.

Bobbs-Merrill Co., Inc. v. New American Library, Copyright. Rep. (CCH), ¶25,752 (S.D.N.Y. 1985)

BRODERICK, J.

Plaintiff's application for a preliminary injunction is granted and the defendants will be enjoined from proceeding with the publication of the four works which have been derived from the *Joy of Cooking*.

The defendants will further be enjoined from any further infringement of plaintiff's copyright in the *Joy of Cooking*.

Plaintiff owns the copyright in the work. Plaintiff by agreement with the representatives of the author's estate had the right to license the preparation of and the publication of condensation of that work. In its contract with New American Library plaintiff granted to New American Library an exclusive license to print, publish and sell soft cover reprint editions in multiple, single or condensed volumes and any revisions thereof.

The contract between plaintiff and defendant specifically provided that the defendant "shall have the right to publish condensations of the book." Those condensations were subject to approval by plaintiff under the terms of the contract and that approval could not, under the contract or otherwise, be unreasonably withheld. . . .

The initial question presented is a contract question whether the four volumes which the defendant proposes to publish and sell are encompassed within the terms of the contract between the plaintiff and defendant.

I find, certainly for purposes of this application for a preliminary injunction, that they are not. They are in no sense a condensation of the copyrighted work. Each of them constitutes a selection from the copyrighted work and taken together they cannot possibly be construed as a condensation because they leave out the major portion of the copyrighted work.

It is certainly clear under the contract that the defendant has the right, subject to approval which is not to be unreasonably withheld, of publishing a condensed version of the copyrighted work in multiple volumes.

It is also the right of the defendant, under the contract, to determine whether those multiple volumes are to be published simultaneously or otherwise. The import of those provisions is that the condensation which is authorized under the contract is a condensation of the copyrighted work and not a condensation of some selected portions of that copyrighted work.

During the colloquy we had some reference to paragraph 3 of the contract between the parties, dated December 22, 1982. Paragraph 3 spells out commitments on the part of the plaintiff to the defendant. In that paragraph the plaintiff undertakes that it will not during the term of its agreement with the defendant publish or permit to be published by anyone other than the defendant in "soft cover book form an abridgment or condensation, or adaptation or selection" of the copyrighted work.

A similar commitment was made by the plaintiff to the defendant in the 1973 version of its contract with the defendant, except that the word "selection" was excised.

Thus, in drawing up the 1982 contract and its predecessor contract plaintiff and defendant had clearly in mind the possibilities that selections might be made from the copyrighted work, that adaptations might be made of the copyrighted work, that abridgments might be made of the copyrighted work and that condensations might be made of the copyrighted work. Under the

1982 contract, and its predecessor, the defendant was authorized only to make condensations. . . .

Counsel for both sides have drawn my attention to various conversations which took place in connection with the negotiation of the original 1973 agreement between plaintiff and defendant and the 1982 agreement. Since I find that the language of those agreements is clear, and that they are integrated documents, I see no reason to consult or take into consideration the parol evidence of their negotiation.

The four works which defendant proposes to publish are, as I have noted, selected and do not in any wise constitute a condensation. They are not authorized by any provision of the contract between the parties. They would constitute, therefore, if published, violations of plaintiff's copyright in the work. . . .

The publications which defendant proposes to make are not only selective but they are highly selective. The recipes which would be included in the four works would constitute a bare fraction of the recipes contained in the copyrighted work. They would omit much of the textual material in the copyrighted work. They would embody, moreover, a selection not by the authors of the copyrighted work or by persons in privity with those authors but by persons who had nothing to do with the preparation of the copyrighted work.

If these four works were sold at a price of $2.50 this would mean that members of the public who bought all of them would have purchased a small fraction of the materials contained in the copyrighted work for a price that was probably more than the price that would be paid for a soft cover edition of the copyrighted work.

It is certainly probable that at least some part of this purchasing public would feel shortchanged and that the impact of this perception would have deleterious effects on reputation of the copyrighted work and on future sales of the copyrighted work either in hard cover or soft cover editions.

It is also probable that if this injunction were not granted and the defendants proceeded with their project to publish the four volumes of selections the plaintiff would run into serious difficulties with the authors' representatives since I find nothing in any documents between authors' representatives and plaintiff which authorize the publication of selections.

Beyond all this, the proposed publication by defendant will not be within the framework of any contractual relationship between plaintiff and defendant and will constitute a direct copyright infringement. In such a situation irreparable harm is to be presumed.

With respect to probability of success, in my judgment the plaintiff will probably succeed in this action. Even if that were not so there is certainly presented a litigatable issue and the balance of hardships lean substantially towards the plaintiff.

The papers indicate that the out of pocket investment by defendant thus far has been some $11,000 which was paid to the author of the proposed four volumes. I have no doubt that there have been further expenses in-house that have been incurred by the defendant in the way of planning for ultimate publication, in the way of reediting the work done by a retained author, et cetera. It will not amount to a substantial sum.

The possible risks so far as the plaintiff is concerned are considerable. These four publications would be issued using the name the *Joy of Cooking* with no input from the authors and no input from the plaintiff and the possible ultimate financial impact on the plaintiff is immeasurable but could very possibly be quite drastic. . . .

NOTE _____

1. In *Seroff v. Simon & Schuster, Inc.*, 162 N.Y.S.2d 770 (Sup. Ct. N.Y. Co. 1957), the author of the biography *Rachmaninoff* brought a libel suit against his publisher for damage to his reputation resulting from a mistranslated French version of the book. Although the court recognized what has been called the "moral right" of an author or artist to protection from deformation or alteration of his or her work, it also found that these rights can be transferred or surrendered through contract.

The parties entered into a standard publishing contract in which the author granted additional rights of translation and foreign publication. With respect to these translation rights, the relationship between author and publisher became one of joint venture because the proceeds of the sale were to be shared equally between author and publisher. The only duty assumed by the publisher was to take reasonable care in the sale of the foreign translation rights, and this duty was discharged when Simon & Schuster sold the French rights to a publisher of fine repute. The French firm acted as an independent contractor, and the author could not hold Simon & Schuster responsible for its mistranslation.

2.60 Breach of Contract

Earlier considerations of breach of contract and the remedies for breach were explored in Chapter 1 (see, for example, Sections 1.40 to 1.60). We also confronted damages issues earlier in our analysis of literary publishing disputes (see, for example, *Freund v. Washington Square Press*, Section 2.30).

These earlier discussions lead here to an examination of recurring problems in publishing. *Pinnacle Books v. Harlequin Enterprises* considers the question of duty to renegotiate and whether an alleged failure to bargain in good faith is a contract breach. In *Frankel v. Stein and Day*, the publisher and author exchange charges as to the other being at fault for a book's not being published. The court considers carefully the competing contract and copyright claims and devises remedies, including injunctive relief, that respond to each party's interests and rights.

Pinnacle Books, Inc. v. Harlequin Enterprises Ltd., 519 F. Supp. 118 (S.D.N.Y. 1981)

DUFFY, DISTRICT JUDGE

This is an action for a permanent injunction and damages resulting from the allegedly unlawful interference of defendant Harlequin Enterprises Limited ["Harlequin"] with the contractual relationship between plaintiff Pinnacle Books, Inc. ["Pinnacle"] and its most successful author, Don Pendleton ["Pendleton"]. Pinnacle claims that Harlequin induced Pendleton to breach his contract with Pinnacle and to enter into an agreement with Harlequin pursuant to which it will publish new books in or relating to a series of paperback men's action/adventure books entitled "The Executioner" [sometimes referred to herein

as the "Series"]. Pinnacle now moves for summary judgment. . . .

Pinnacle is a publisher of mass-market and trade paperback books. The company has offices in New York City and Los Angeles. It has been publishing "The Executioner" series since the inception of the series in 1969. Pinnacle has published thirty-eight different titles in "The Executioner" series and sold approximately twenty million copies. Pendleton, the author of the Series, is the copyright owner of the Series.

In 1976, Pinnacle and Pendleton entered into an agreement whereby Pinnacle agreed to publish books 29 through 38 in "The Executioner" series. The 1976 Agreement provided, *inter alia*, that Pendleton would not offer rights in "The Executioner" series to any other publisher until, after extending their best efforts, Pinnacle and Pendleton were unable to agree on the terms of a new contract for the Series. In the event that the parties were unable to consummate a new contract, Pendleton was free to offer the Series to other publishers so long as any new publication did not occur for three months following the first publication of book 38 by Pinnacle. The pertinent provision provides:

> VII. The Author grants the Publisher the option to renew this contract for the books in THE EXECUTIONER series following the ten books covered hereby on terms to be agreed, and, if, after extending their best efforts, the parties are unable to reach an agreement thereon, then Author shall be free to offer rights in such other books in THE EXECUTIONER series to any other publisher, provided the publication thereof does not occur until the expiration of 3 months following the first publication of the tenth book hereunder.

The manuscript for the last book under the 1976 Agreement was delivered to Pinnacle on December 14, 1979. By that time, Andrew Ettinger, the Editorial Director of Pinnacle, had begun negotiations with Pendleton for an extension of the 1976 Agreement. These discussions between Ettinger and Pendleton occurred as early as September 8, 1978 and continued until November 1979, at which time Ettinger left Pinnacle and joined Harlequin. According to Ettinger, he was unable to consummate a renewal of the 1976 Agreement before he left Pinnacle because an outstanding dispute between Pendleton and Pinnacle regarding foreign royalty rights had not been resolved. By late 1979, however, an acceptable resolution of the dispute had been reached and Pendleton was ready and willing to discuss an extension of the 1976 Agreement.

Negotiations between Pinnacle and Pendleton continued until about February 10, 1980. According to Pinnacle, the discussions had been congenial and the conditions established by Pendleton had either been satisfied in full or could have been met if the parties had proceeded with the negotiations in good faith and using their best efforts.

Meanwhile, Harlequin, a Canadian publisher and distributor of paperback books throughout the world, also had developed an interest in Pendleton. Having achieved spectacular success in the romance novel market, Harlequin was exploring the feasibility of entering the action/adventure line of book publishing. Ettinger, who was now affiliated with Harlequin, began meeting with Pendleton in early January 1980 to discuss the possibility of Harlequin becoming Pendleton's publisher. On about February 10, 1980, Pendleton advised Pinnacle that, at Harlequin's invitation, he was planning to visit its Toronto headquarters where he expected Harlequin to discuss the possibility of licensing to it rights in "The Executioner" series. Pendleton also indicated that he wished to halt discussions on the Pinnacle offer until he heard from Harlequin. At the conclusion of his discussion with Harlequin, Pendleton signed a preliminary agreement to license the Series and its characters to Harlequin. On May 15, 1980, Pendleton signed the formal agreement with Harlequin pursuant to which twelve books in "The Executioner" series and four to six spin-offs from that Series would be published annually by Harlequin.

Pinnacle instituted this action in September 1980 against Harlequin seeking injunctive and compensatory relief. Pinnacle alleges that Harlequin, although fully aware of Pendleton's contractual obligations to Pinnacle and that Pinnacle was still negotiating with Pendleton, induced Pendleton to break off negotiations with Pinnacle just as final agreement on new contract terms was near. Pinnacle now moves for summary judgment. Harlequin argues against the motion for summary

judgment on the grounds that the option clause on which Pinnacle bases its case is unenforceable. . . .

To succeed in an action for interference with contractual relations, the plaintiff must establish first and foremost the existence of a valid contract. . . .

In the instant case, Pinnacle accuses Harlequin of interfering with the option clause in the 1976 Agreement. As noted above, that clause provides that, after Pendleton has fulfilled his obligation to deliver books 29 through 38 of "The Executioner" Series, the parties would use their "best efforts" to negotiate a new contract "on terms to be agreed" for delivery of an unspecified number of new Executioner books. Clause VII of the 1976 Agreement. Harlequin contends that this clause is unenforceable because either (i) it is nothing more than an unenforceable "agreement to agree"; or (ii) the material terms of the "best efforts" clause are too vague.

Harlequin's first contention that the "best efforts" clause is an unenforceable "agreement to agree" is inappropriate in this case. Clause VII of the 1976 Agreement does not require that any agreement actually be achieved but only that the parties work to reach an agreement actively and in good faith. . . .

Harlequin is correct, however, in arguing that the "best efforts" clause is unenforceable because its terms are too vague. "Best efforts" or similar clauses, like any other contractual agreement, must set forth in definite and certain terms every material element of the contemplated bargain. It is hornbook law that courts cannot and will not supply the material terms of a contract.

Essential to the enforcement of a "best efforts" clause is a clear set of guidelines against which the parties' "best efforts" may be measured. . . . The performance required of the parties by a "best efforts" clause may be expressly provided by the contract itself or implied from the circumstances of the case. . . . In the case at bar, there simply are no objective criteria against which either Pinnacle or Pendleton's efforts can be measured.

Pinnacle's argument that the parties' obligations under the "best efforts" clause are clear from the circumstances of the case is without merit. While it is possible to infer from the circumstances the standard of performance required by a "best efforts" clause where the parties have agreed to work toward a specific goal, see, e.g., *Bloor, supra; Perma Research & Development, supra*, it is not so here where the parties have agreed only to negotiate. The performance required by a contract to negotiate with best efforts, unlike the performance required by a distribution contract or a patent assignment, simply cannot be ascertained from the circumstances. Unless the parties delineate in the contract objective standards by which their efforts are to be measured, the very nature of contract negotiations renders it impossible to determine whether the parties have used their "best" efforts to reach a new agreement. Certainly, no party to a negotiation, no matter what the circumstances, is required to make a particular offer nor to accept particular terms. What each party offers or demands in the course of any negotiation is a matter left strictly to the business judgment of that party. Thus, absent express standards, a court cannot decide that one party's offer does not constitute its best efforts; nor can it say that the other party's refusal to accept certain terms does not constitute its best efforts.

In the instant case, therefore, where the parties agreed only to negotiate and failed to state the standards by which their negotiation efforts were to be measured, it is impossible to determine whether Pinnacle or Pendleton used their "best efforts" to negotiate a new agreement. For instance, there simply is no objective standard by which the court can determine whether Pinnacle's offer constituted its best efforts; nor can it decide whether Pendleton's participation in negotiations with Pinnacle for over a year were his best efforts. In short, the option clause is unenforceable due to the indefiniteness of its terms. Accordingly, Pinnacle's motion for summary judgment is denied. . . .

On Motion for Reargument

By my opinion and order of May 13, 1981, the complaint herein was dismissed. The plaintiff now moves in effect for reargument and/or temporary injunctive relief pending the appeal of the May 13, 1981 order of this court. . . .

The injunctive relief sought by the plaintiff is based solely upon the 1976 Agreement between plaintiff and Pendleton. As it appeared that the 1979 Agreement had never been executed or accepted by Pendleton, I was under the impression that the plaintiff had abandoned its claim under that alleged contract. Accordingly, upon determining that the renewal clause in 1976 contract is unenforceable, I dismissed the entire complaint.

It now appears, however, that the plaintiff believes that even if the renewal clause of the 1976 Agreement is unenforceable, they still have certain rights under the claimed 1979 Agreement. Plaintiff requests that my order of May 13 be modified so as to dismiss only those portions of the amended complaint which seek relief under the 1976 Agreement between the parties. While it appears, at this juncture, that plaintiff may have great difficulty in proving the claimed 1979 Agreement, I had no intention of depriving them of the right to litigate this matter. Accordingly, the opinion and order of May 13 is amended to restrict the relief therein to a dismissal of those portions of plaintiff's amended complaint which seek relief under the 1976 Agreement.

Plaintiff also seeks an order of this court affirmatively enjoining the defendant from publishing any of the books bearing the generic title "The Executioner" or from publicizing any such books pending the appeal of this case. It is the plaintiff's position that the appeal from my order will be in good faith and, indeed, I have no doubt that it will be so prosecuted. . . .

It is suggested that should an order not be entered, the egg will be scrambled to such a point that should an appellant court disagree with my interpretation of the contract the parties could never be restored to the position they were in prior to the May 13, 1981 order of this court.

On the other hand, the contract whereby Harlequin obtained rights to books in "The Executioner" series from Don Pendleton was entered into many, many months ago and that the plaintiff had knowledge of that fact at or about the time that the contract was executed. Since then, Harlequin has expended large sums in order to prepare for this new venture in its business. The damage to Harlequin, should a stay be entered at this point, cannot be said to be insubstantial. It seems clear to me that the equities do not tip decidedly in favor of the plaintiff. . . . Accordingly, the requested affirmative injunction pending appeal is denied. . . .

NOTE _____

1. In *Thompson v. Liquichimica of America, Inc.*, 481 F. Supp. 365 (S.D.N.Y. 1979), a "best efforts" clause was distinguished from an agreement to agree and was held enforceable. The court found it to constitute a "closed proposition discrete and actionable." The foregoing *Pinnacle* court disagreed with the reasoning in *Thompson*. In addition, *Pinnacle* distinguished the *Thompson* situation, asserting the terms of the agreement in *Thompson* were more specific and provided sufficient criteria against which the parties' efforts could be measured. See 519 F. Supp. at 122. Even so, despite the *Pinnacle* court's attempted distinguishing of *Thompson*, the two cases stand in contrast with each other.

_____

Frankel v. Stein and Day, Inc., 470 F. Supp. 209 (S.D.N.Y. 1979)

LASKER, DISTRICT JUDGE

This suit results from a falling out between Sandor Frankel and Webster Mews (a pseudonym), authors of *The Aleph Solution*, and their publisher, Stein and Day, Inc. The authors seek damages and injunctive and declaratory relief against Stein and Day as a result of the latter's alleged infringement of their copyright and violation of a publishing agreement. Stein and Day counterclaims that the authors have breached the agreement and seeks damages. Both parties have moved for summary judgment.

On June 1, 1978, the authors entered into a written agreement with Stein and Day setting forth the terms under which *The Aleph Solution* was to be published. The agreement required the publisher: (1) to apply for a copyright to be held in the authors' names (¶2), (2) to take out a total of three advertisements publicizing the book (¶19), and (3) to pay the authors two-thirds of any signature payment for the paperback rights to the book (¶4). A rider to this last clause specified that:

Time of payment of royalties and of rendering of accountings by publisher to Author is of the essence

of this agreement. If any such payment is not timely made or if any such accounting is not timely rendered and if any such default shall continue for a period of 30 days following written notification by Agent to Publisher of such default, *then at the option of Author all rights granted to Publisher under this agreement shall automatically revert to Author.* [emphasis added]

The authors, in turn, were required to deliver two copies of their manuscript "complete and satisfactory to the Publisher" on or before June 20, 1978, time being deemed "of the essence." (¶8) The contract also contained the following provision:

This agreement constitutes the whole agreement between the parties and may not be modified, altered, waived, amended, or changed except by an instrument in writing signed by both parties. This agreement shall be interpreted according to the laws of the State of New York.

The complaint alleges that on or about September 18, 1978, Stein and Day entered into an agreement granting Jove Publications the paperback rights to *The Aleph Solution* and received in return a signature payment of $27,500. Although the authors have made written demand for the part of the payment to which they are entitled under their agreement with the publisher, they have not been paid. Accordingly, Frankel and Mews assert that all rights granted Stein and Day under the agreement have, pursuant to the terms of the rider to clause 4, reverted automatically to them but that the publisher is nevertheless continuing to sell, distribute and collect monies with respect to *The Aleph Solution* and "to otherwise infringe upon the copyright." Moreover, they allege that Stein and Day has breached an oral agreement to spend a minimum of $30,000 on advertisements for the book. The complaint seeks a mandatory injunction barring Stein and Day from holding itself out as having any interest in the book or "from otherwise infringing" the authors' copyright; a declaratory judgment that all rights in the book have reverted to the authors; and damages for infringement, for breach of the signature payment agreement, for breach of the oral advertising agreement, and for negligent promotion of the book.

Stein and Day does not dispute the facts set out above; however, it contends that they represent only half the story. The essential provision in the agreement, the publisher asserts, was that a satisfactory manuscript be submitted by June 20th to ensure that the book would be in the stores in time for the important Christmas market. Sol Stein, President of Stein and Day, states that the June 20th deadline was made a "mockery" by Frankel and Mews and that a manuscript was not submitted until August, destroying the publication schedule and substantially impairing Stein and Day's ability to recoup its investment. (Affirmation of Sol Stein, February 8, 1979, ¶10) Defendant also submits affirmations of other employees which assert, most forcefully, that the authors' unreasonable behavior further delayed publication. (Affirmations of Wallace Exman and Marilee Talman) According to Stein, the publisher has lost more than $25,000 on *The Aleph Solution* and the paperback agreement merely salvaged some of the loss. (Affirmation, ¶12) Accordingly, Stein and Day counterclaims for damages resulting from the authors' alleged breach and argues that it would be inequitable, in light of plaintiffs' conduct, to require it to turn over a substantial amount of the signature payment. . . .

Stein and Day moves for summary judgment dismissing the complaint under Rules 12, 19 and 56, Fed.R.Civ.P., on the grounds that . . . the court lacks subject matter jurisdiction over the lawsuit. . . .

The complaint specifies that this action arises under the federal copyright laws and that the court therefore has jurisdiction under 28 U.S.C. § 1338. However, Stein and Day argues that the lawsuit is in reality an action to enforce a contract since, in its view, the infringement claim is dependent on an interpretation of the publishing agreement to determine whether there has been a forfeiture or reversion of the licensed rights. It argues that when a plaintiff must secure a judicial determination of its rights before it is entitled to relief under the copyright laws, no federal jurisdiction exists in the absence of diversity between the parties. . . .

However, Stein and Day is incorrect in characterizing the plaintiffs' infringement claim as being dependent on an interpretation of the publishing agreement. As the authors point out, under clause 2 of the agreement, the copyright has always been in the authors' name. Moreover, under the rider to clause 4, all rights in the book licensed to the publisher reverted automatically to the authors following Stein and Day's failure to advance the signature payment. Accordingly, this is not a case, such as those relied on by defendant, in which a "preliminary question arises unrelated to the copyright laws." . . .

Instead here the authors are entitled to seek immediate relief for infringement and, indeed, their complaint sets out as the very first form of relief requested an injunction to enjoin such infringement. Under these circumstances, copyright jurisdiction exists. . . .

Stein and Day also asserts that plaintiffs are not entitled to "rescission" of the publishing agreement because the publisher's failure to pay two-thirds of the signature payment from Jove was not a material breach of the agreement. It relies on *Nolan v. Sam Fox Publishing Co., Inc.*, 499 F.2d 1394 (2d Cir. 1974). . . .

Nolan held that rescission is permitted when a breach is " 'material and willful, or, if not willful, so substantial and fundamental as to strongly tend to defeat the object of the parties in making the contract.' " 499 F.2d at 1397. Whereas in *Nolan*, the court found that Fox's failure to pay royalties was the result of " '[o]versight, negligence and less than meticulous bookkeeping . . . ,' " *id.* at 1399, it is undisputed here that defendant's failure to pay the money in question was willful. Moreover, the contract in this case specifies that all rights revert automatically to the authors in the event the publisher fails to pay them their share of the signature payment. This unambiguous language is strong, if not conclusive, evidence that the parties considered that such a breach would be material and thus, that to deny rescission on this ground, would " 'tend to defeat the object of the parties in making the contract.' " Indeed, since the plain language of the contract specifies that reversion "shall automatically" result upon the publisher's failure to perform the obligation in question here, we believe that the contract must be complied with literally and that notions of materiality are irrelevant. . . .

Stein and Day also moves to dismiss the author's claim for damages for breach of the alleged oral advertising agreement on the ground that evidence as to it is barred by the parol evidence rule. We agree that this claim must be dismissed. At a conference in chambers, one of the authors, an experienced attorney who helped prepare the publishing agreement, stated that the oral agreement was made prior to signing the written agreement between the parties. However, the written agreement, which deals specifically with the topic of advertising, makes no mention of a $30,000 budget. Moreoover, the contract provides that it "constitutes the whole agreement between the parties and may not be modified, altered, waived, amended, or changed except by an instrument in writing signed by both parties." In the face of such clear evidence that the contract was intended to incorporate the entire understanding between the parties, evidence of a prior oral agreement, which would substantially increase the publisher's financial obligation, is barred. . . .

Two written trade releases, referring to a $30,000 budget, which were circulated by Stein and Day do not compel a contrary conclusion. The authors provide no authority for the proposition that such releases to third persons are contractually binding as between the parties here. . . .

The sixth cause of action alleges that Stein and Day was grossly negligent "in failing to attempt to develop, exploit, publicize, or promote *The Aleph Solution*" in accordance with customary professional standards. Stein and Day moves to dismiss this claim, arguing that it is "clearly hyperbolical and has no demonstrable basis in the face of defendant's completed performance." Whether or not Stein and Day was grossly negligent is a question of fact which cannot be decided on the papers before us. The motion to dismiss this claim is therefore denied pending a hearing on the underlying factual matters which it raises. . . .

Plaintiffs move for summary judgment under Rule 56, Fed.R.Civ.P., on all but the negligence claim. Since the damage claim for violation of the oral advertising agreement has been dismissed above, there remain for decision claims for a mandatory injunction barring infringement of the authors' copyright, damages for infringement and breach of the paperback provision of the publishing agreement, and for a declaratory judgment that all rights under the publishing agreement have reverted to the authors. . . .

The authors have established that Stein and Day is liable on account of its failure to comply with the paperback signature payment provision and, pursuant to that provision, all rights in the agreement have reverted to the authors. Therefore, Frankel and Mews are entitled to a declaratory judgment that the rights have reverted, and we hereby declare that all rights licensed to Stein and Day under the publishing agreement of June 1, 1978, have reverted to the authors. The authors are also entitled to damages for infringement and for breach of the paperback payment provision.

However, as stated above, Stein and Day has counterclaimed that the authors breached the publishing agreement by failing to submit a timely manuscript, with the result that the marketability of the book was impaired and the publisher was substantially damaged. This counterclaim goes to the heart of the authors' entitlement to injunctive relief since it suggests that Frankel and Mews destroyed the publisher's ability to recoup its investment in the book. Therefore, before the court exercises its equitable power on behalf of the authors, it is entitled to determine whether they themselves have lived up to their end of the bargain with Stein and Day. Similarly, the decision whether to award the affirmative remedies sought pursuant to the declaratory judgment—which are so sweeping as to partake of an equitable nature—should be deferred pending determination of the authors' conduct in regard to the contract.

Accordingly, the motion for summary judgment is granted as to the damages claims in the second and fourth causes of action and as to the claim for a declaratory judgment. A hearing, to be combined with trial pursuant to the provisions of Rule 65(a), Fed.R.Civ.P., will be held promptly to resolve outstanding factual questions affecting the remainder of the relief sought by plaintiffs as well as the merits of Stein and Day's counterclaim. . . .

Frankel and Mews also move for a preliminary injunction enjoining Stein and Day and its agents from "holding themselves out as having any interest whatsoever in the book *The Aleph Solution.*" Under the familiar standard of this circuit, a preliminary injunction may be granted "only upon a clear showing of either (1) probable success on the merits *and* possible irreparable injury, *or* (2) sufficiently serious questions going to the merits to make them a fair ground for litigation *and* a balance of hardships tipping decidedly toward the party requesting the preliminary relief," *Sonesta Int'l Hotels Corp. v. Wellington Associates*, 433 F.2d 247, 250 (2d Cir. 1973) (emphasis in original).

The same unresolved factual questions which compel denial of plaintiffs' motion for summary judgment render it impossible to determine the likelihood of their succeeding on the merits. . . .

NOTE ───────────────────────

1. An attempt at self-help as a remedy was taken by the aggrieved party in *Dodd, Mead & Co., Inc. v. Lilienthal*, 514 F. Supp. 105 (S.D.N.Y. 1981).

Dodd had "the exclusive right of printing, publishing and selling in book form" Lilienthal's *The Zionist Connection*, under contract in which Lilienthal agreed that he would not publish the work or any book of similar or competing character without Dodd's consent. Dodd distributed 14,500 copies of the book in a 10-month period, spending $66,000 to manufacture and promote it. Dissatisfied when he found that many stores were out of the book and that Dodd did not intend to reprint it, Lilienthal issued his own edition, claiming that since his contract with Dodd provided that he had the right to buy copies from Dodd and resell, and Dodd had refused to fill his orders, he had the right to "cover" pursuant to UCC Section 2-712 by making his own copies. However, said the Court, "Lilienthal's major grievance is that Dodd, Mead was not printing enough books to keep up with the public's demand. . . . However, Dodd Mead's alleged failure to meet the public demand [while it might be a breach of contract on the part of Dodd, Mead] did not permit Lilienthal to publish his own copies in contravention of the contract between the parties." If aggrieved, Lilienthal, among other remedies, had recourse to the provision of his contract, which allowed him to recapture his work (and the "plates" therefor) if it became out of print for six months and Dodd, Mead did not reissue it within six months after notice. Lilienthal was enjoined from further distribution of his edition of the book.

2.70   Protections Against Tortious Conduct

An author may feel aggrieved by actions taken by parties completely removed from any contractual relationship with the author. These instances are to be distinguished from the sublicensing and subcontracting problems discussed in Section 2.50. Our discussion here concentrates on issues more consonant with the general rights of creative persons explored in Chapter 10.

In the case discussed below (*Blatty v. New York Times*), an author asserts that his book was not given proper credit for its success by the *New York Times* best seller list. It is alleged that this failure has caused a loss of additional sales and other damages. Several tort theories are examined to determine whether the author has an actionable claim.

───────────────────────

Blatty v. New York Times Co., 175 Cal.App.3d 571 (Cal.App. 1985)

LILLIE, P. J.
William Blatty sued the New York Times Company for damages on several theories, all of which were based on defendant's failure to include in its best seller list a book written by plaintiff. The trial court sustained defendant's general demurrer to the first amended complaint without leave to amend. Plaintiff appeals from the ensuing judgment of dismissal. . . .

The original complaint contained four causes of action. The first cause of action (negligent interference with prospective business advantage) included the following allegations: Defendant owns, publishes and distributes the newspaper *New York Times* and publishes weekly therein a list entitled "Best Sellers" purporting to rank best selling books, fiction and nonfiction, based on actual sales. Authors whose works appear on the list have a significant and valuable prospective business advantage in promoting and maximizing the sales of such books in both hardback and paperback editions, and the sale of movie rights to such books. Although the list purports to rank books on the basis of sales and expresses no opinion on their merits, the reputation of the *New York Times* and its perceived expertise in literary matters are such that many book sellers promote, and many persons purchase, current works of fiction primarily because they are included in the list. Defendant knew or should have known that the list has such influence on the sale and promotion of books. Plaintiff authored, and Simon and Schuster published, a new work of fiction entitled *Legion* which sold more than sufficient copies to warrant inclusion in the list and otherwise met all criteria for such inclusion. Defendant negligently failed to include *Legion* in the list, thereby depriving plaintiff of the prospective advantage which he otherwise would have obtained.

The second cause of action (intentional interference with prospective business advantage) alleged: Acting on plaintiff's behalf, Simon and Schuster provided defendant's management employees with information that *Legion* had sold more than sufficient copies to warrant inclusion in the list, and requested that *Legion* be included; despite such information defendant, intentionally or recklessly and without cause, refused to include *Legion* in the list; as a result plaintiff suffered damage by loss of the advantage he otherwise would have obtained.

The remaining causes of action (negligence and trade libel) incorporated most of the foregoing allegations of the first and second causes of action.

Less than two months after filing the complaint plaintiff noticed the taking of depositions and the production of documents. Thereafter defendant filed a general demurrer to the complaint. Plaintiff moved for an order compelling the taking of the depositions and the production of documents previously noticed, asserting his right to discovery despite the pendency of the demurrer. In support of the motion plaintiff submitted his declaration which incorporated by reference an attached newspaper article presumably intended to show the relevancy of the proposed discovery. The newspaper article caused the trial court to question the allegation that defendant refused to include *Legion* in the best seller list despite the information furnished to it by Simon and Schus-

ter. The court stated that it could not rule on the demurrer until it was sure that such allegation was supported by admissible evidence. Accordingly, on the court's insistence and over plaintiff's objection, the parties took depositions of an employee of Simon and Schuster and an employee of defendant limited to the issue of the nature of information about sales of *Legion* allegedly supplied by Simon and Schuster to defendant.

The court took judicial notice of the depositions and concluded they contained no evidence that Simon and Schuster supplied defendant with any figures of sales of *Legion*. The demurrer to the second cause of action was sustained with leave to amend to allege facts showing that (1) defendant "violated its public duty or trust to sell or distribute its newspaper to the public containing a fair and honest report of all news without bias or prejudice"; and (2) defendant had in its possession reports of the actual sales of *Legion* which would qualify the book for inclusion in the best seller list and nevertheless deliberately refused to list it. The demurrer to the remaining causes of action was sustained without leave to amend on the ground that defendant had no duty to include a book in the list except as indicated above, and those causes of action did not allege facts showing such a duty. . . .

In the amended complaint plaintiff again attempted to state a cause of action for intentional interference with prospective advantage, and set forth three additional theories of liability.

The first and second cause of action (both labeled intentional interference with prospective advantage) repeated in essence the allegations of the original complaint regarding defendant's publication of the best seller list and the prospective advantage accruing to authors whose books appear on the list. They further alleged: Defendant expressly and impliedly advertised and represented to authors, book sellers and the general public that the list was an objective, unbiased and accurate compilation of actual sales of books each week by 2,000 book stores in every region of the United States. Defendant knew such representation was false because, among other things, defendant did not use actual sales in compiling the list but rather used an undisclosed method of "weighting" certain sales more than others. In July or August 1983 Simon and Schuster, acting on plaintiff's behalf, contacted management employees of defendant and told them it had sales figures showing that *Legion* qualified for the list. Defendant intentionally, or recklessly and without cause, refused to review such figures and to include *Legion* in the list for many weeks thereafter. In September 1983 defendant included *Legion* in the list for one week only, and then in last position. As a result of defendant's acts plaintiff was deprived of the prospective advantage which he otherwise would have obtained; he thereby sustained damages in excess of $3 million through lost sales of and higher promotional expenses for *Legion*, lost value in paperback editions and lost value in movie rights. Defendant acted maliciously and with intent to deprive plaintiff of his rights and property by refusing to include *Legion* in the list for many weeks during which it qualified for inclusion. Accordingly, plaintiff is entitled to punitive damages of not less than $3 million.

Each of the subsequent causes of action incorporated most of the foregoing allegations. The third and fourth causes of action (unfair competition, and false and misleading advertising, respectively) alleged that defendant's representations concerning the list constituted fraudulent business practices, false and misleading statements, and untrue and misleading advertising which deceived consumers as to the popularity of books available for sale, all in violation of Business and Professions Code section 17200 et seq. and section 17500 et seq. As a result many book sellers and consumers who otherwise would have purchased *Legion* did not do so and instead purchased other books in competition with *Legion*. Plaintiff thereby sustained damages in excess of $3 million. The fifth cause of action, apparently based on the court's comments in sustaining the demurrer to the complaint, alleged that defendant had a public duty or trust to sell and distribute newspapers containing a fair and honest report of all news without bias or prejudice; defendant's conduct and representations concerning the list constituted a breach of such duty which caused plaintiff to sustain damages of more than $3 million.

Defendant demurred generally to the amended complaint on grounds that each cause of action is barred by the First Amendment to the United States Constitution and article I, section 2 of the California Constitution, and the facts pleaded do not state a cause of action on any of the theories set forth. The demurrer was sustained without leave to amend on the grounds stated. Judgment was entered dismissing the action. . . .

Plaintiff contends the original complaint as well as the amended complaint stated valid causes of action. While an appellate court ordinarily will not consider the allegations of a superseded complaint . . . that rule is inapplicable where the trial court denied plaintiff leave to include those allegations in an amended complaint. . . .

A legal duty to use due care is a necessary element of a negligence action. . . . In *J'Aire Corp. v. Gregory* (1979), 24 Cal.3d 799, 804 [157 Cal. Rptr. 407, 598 P.2d 60], the Supreme Court set forth six criteria for determining whether a duty of care is owed: (1) the extent to which the transaction was intended to affect the plaintiff; (2) the foreseeability of harm to the plaintiff; (3) the degree of certainty that the plaintiff suffered injury; (4) the closeness of the connection between the defendant's conduct and the injury suffered; (5) the moral blame attached to the defendant's conduct; and (6) the policy of preventing future harm. In connection with the last factor, countervailing public policies which may preclude recovery must also be considered. . . .

Assuming a sufficiently close connection between defendant's conduct and plaintiff's injury and that the harm to plaintiff was foreseeable, the other factors compel the conclusion that defendant owed no duty to plaintiff to include his book in its best seller list. The complaint did not specifically allege that the omission of the book from the list was intended to affect plaintiff, and no facts are alleged which show such an intent on defendant's part. Further, no facts are pleaded from which it may be inferred that defendant's conduct was morally blameworthy. The complaint alleges that defendant failed to include plaintiff's book in its best seller list despite knowledge that it "sold more than sufficient copies to warrant inclusion and otherwise met all criteria for inclusion." The complaint fails to allege how it was determined that enough copies of the book were sold to warrant its inclusion, or what other criteria were met and by whom they were established. For all that appears defendant, for reasons of its own and employing criteria different from those which plaintiff considered to be conclusive, deemed the book unqualified for inclusion in the list. Public policy factors also weigh against imposition of such a duty. The list is a means of informing the public of the relative popularity of current works of fiction and nonfiction. If defendant were held to owe a duty to plaintiff to include his book in its list, other authors could assert a like duty owed to them. Faced with such a situation defendant might well cease compilation and publication of the list, thereby depriving the public of a valuable service. For all of these reasons we conclude as a matter of law that defendant owed plaintiff no duty to include his book in its best seller list. It follows that the complaint does not state causes of action for either negligent interference with prospective advantage or negligence.

Trade libel is defined as "an intentional disparagement of the quality of property, which results in pecuniary damage to plaintiff." (*Erlich v. Etner* (1964), 224 Cal.App.2d 69, 73 [36 Cal.Rptr. 256].) "The distinction between libel and trade libel is that the former concerns the person or reputation of plaintiff and the latter relates to his goods." (*Shores v. Chip Steak Co.* (1955), 130 Cal.App.2d 627, 630 [279 P.2d 595].) The complaint fails to state a cause of action for trade libel. Such libel allegedly consisted of defendant's intentional and false omission of *Legion* from its best seller list. Silence is not libel. . . . "[T]he law does not recognize libel by omission as a tort. Libel, by definition, consists of the publication of a false and unprivileged fact. Thus, liability may be imposed in a libel case only for an assertion or implication of fact that is false and unprivileged, and not for mere omission of a relevant fact." (*Janklow v. Newsweek, Inc.* (8th Cir. 1985) 759 F.2d 644, 648; fn. omitted.) Of particular significance in the present case is the *Janklow* court's further conclusion that refusal to impose liability for omission of facts "has strong underpinnings in Amendment." (759 F.2d at p. 648.). . . .

We turn now to the amended complaint. Defendant argues no cause of action is stated under the unfair competition and false advertising laws (Bus. & Prof. Code, § 17200 et seq., § 17500 et seq.) because the remedy for violation of such laws does not include damages for private individuals, but is limited to injunctive relief (*id.*, §§ 17203, 17535) and imposition of civil penalties (*id.*, §§ 17206, 17207, 17535.5, 17536). In *United Farm Workers of America v. Superior Court* (1975), 47 Cal.App.3d 334, 343–345 [120 Cal.Rptr. 904], it was held that damages are recoverable by an individual plaintiff for violation of the unfair competition law. The court there reasoned: "[T]he breach of a duty imposed by statute gives rise to a cause of action for damages if damages can be shown. The fact that the statutes sound in equity and by their terms do not specify that damages may be awarded does not bar the recovery of damages in a proper case even though the action be one in equity rather than law." (*United Farm Workers, supra*, 47 Cal.App.3d at p. 344.) However, in *Chern v. Bank of America* (1976), 15 Cal.3d 866 [127 Cal.Rptr. 110, 544 P.2d 1310], the Supreme Court stated: "Plaintiff's cause of action to recover damages for false or misleading statements (Bus. & Prof. Code, § 17500) was likewise properly dismissed. The applicable statutes do not authorize recovery of damages by private individuals. Private relief is limited to filing of actions for an injunction (*id.*, § 17535); and civil penalties are recoverable only by specified *public* officers (*id.*, §§ 17535.5, 17536)." (P. 875; original italics.). . . .

Inasmuch as *Chern* is a decision of the Supreme Court, we are bound to follow it. . . . We therefore conclude that the amended complaint does not state causes of action for damages sustained by plaintiff as a private individual based on defendant's alleged violation of the unfair competition and false advertising laws.

As previously noted, it appears that the cause of action labeled "breach of public duty and trust to report the news fairly and honestly without bias or prejudice" was included in the amended complaint in response to the trial court's comments in sustaining the demurrer to the complaint. That the First Amendment prohibits imposition of such a duty is made clear by the United States Supreme Court. "For better or worse, editing is what editors are for; and editing is selection and choice of material. That editors—newspaper or broadcast—can and do abuse this power is beyond doubt. . . . Calculated risks of abuse are taken in order to preserve higher values. The presence of these risks is nothing new; the authors of the Bill of Rights accepted the reality that these risks were evils for which there was no acceptable remedy other than a spirit of moderation and a sense of responsibility—and civility—on the part of those who exercise the guaranteed freedoms of expression." (*Columbia Broadcasting v. Democratic Comm.* (1973), 412 U.S. 94, 124–125 [36 L.Ed.3d 772, 796, 93 S.Ct. 2080].) The principle was stated even more forcefully in *Miami Herald Publishing Co. v. Tornillo* (1974), 418 U.S. 241, 258 [41 L.Ed.2d 730, 741, 94 S.Ct. 2831]: "The choice of material to go into a newspaper, and the decisions made as to limitations on the size and content of the paper, and treatment of public issues and public officials—*whether fair or unfair*—constitute the exercise of editorial control and judgment. It has yet to be demonstrated how governmental regulation of this crucial process can be exercised consistent with First Amendment guarantees of a free press as they have evolved to this time." (Italics added.)

The elements of a cause of action for intentional interference with prospective economic advantage are: (1) an economic relationship between the plaintiff and some third person containing the probability of future economic benefit to the plaintiff; (2) knowledge by the defendant of the existence of the relationship; (3) intentional acts on the part of the defendant designed to disrupt the relationship; (4) actual disruption thereof; and (5) damages to plaintiff proximately caused by the act of the defendant. . . .

The complaint sets forth each of these elements. It alleges that plaintiff, as author of the novel *Legion*, owns valuable rights in the book and in revenues from its sale. Many persons purchase current novels, and many book sellers promote current novels, primarily because such novels are included in defendant's best seller list; many book stores discount books appearing in the list and display such books more prominently than those not on the list. Thus, books included in the list sell substantially more copies than those not appearing therein. Defendant knew the list had and has such influence. Because of this influence, authors whose books appear on the list have a "significant and valuable prospective business advantage" in promoting and maximizing sales of their books. Defendant expressly and impliedly represented to authors, book sellers and the general public that the list was an objective, unbiased and accurate compilation of actual sales of books each week by 2,000 book stores in every region of the United States. At the time it made such representations defendant knew they were untrue. With knowledge that the list had substantial influence on book sellers and the general public and that plaintiff would be deprived of the prospective advantage by omission of his book from the list, defendant "intentionally or recklessly and without cause" refused to include the book in the list. Defendant acted with the intent and purpose of depriving plaintiff of his rights and property. As a direct and proximate result of defendant's acts, plaintiff suffered damages.

Defendant argues that the foregoing allegations do not include the first and second elements of a cause of action for intentional interference with prospective economic advantage because there is no showing that plaintiff had an existing economic relationship with any specific third person, but only a showing of possible future relationship with potential purchasers of his book; the allegation that defendant knew of the list's influence on such purchasers is not tantamount to an allegation that defendant knew of an existing relationship subject to intentional interference. The contention lacks merit. The tort of interference with prospective advantage lies for interference with relations which are merely prospective or potential. . . . Liberally construed with a view to substantive justice between the parties . . . the amended complaint alleges the requisite relationship and defendant's knowledge of the existence of that relationship. . . .

Defendant further argues that inasmuch as the list was compiled in the exercise of its editorial judgment and represented its opinion of which books were best sellers, the First Amendment shields defendant from liability for interference with plaintiff's prospective advantage by refusing to include his book in the list. . . . This contention ignores the amended complaint's allegation that defendant falsely represented, with knowledge of falsity, that the list was an accurate and objective compilation of actual sales of books each week in 2,000 book stores throughout the United States. The list thus was not held out as the product of defendant's editorial judgment or an expression of its opinion, but was falsely represented to be in fact a compilation of best sellers based on objective criteria. Under these circumstances the First Amendment does not foreclose plaintiff's cause of action. "[T]here is no constitutional value in false statements of fact. Neither the intentional lie nor the careless error materially advances society's interest in 'uninhibited, robust, wide-open' debate on public issues. [Citation.] They belong to that category of utterances which 'are no essential part of any exposition of ideas, and are of such slight social value as a step to truth that any benefit that may be derived from them is clearly outweighed by the social interest in order and morality.' [Citation.]" (*Gertz v. Robert Welch, Inc.*, *supra*, 418 U.S. at p. 340 [41 L.Ed.2d at p. 805].)

We conclude that the judgment of dismissal must be reversed as to the causes of action for intentional interference with prospective economic advantage. . . .

NOTE

1. The *Blatty* decision was reversed by the California Supreme Court on December 29, 1986 (Case No.'s B008737 and B010053). A four-member majority (two of whom, Chief Justice Bird and Justice Reynoso, had been recalled in the 1986 general election) held that Blatty would have had to make the same "of and concerning" showing in this instance as would have been required in a defamation case, and that he failed to do so. The three concurring justices (one of whom, Justice Grodin, was also recalled) disagreed with the majority as to the "of and concerning" requirement, but felt that Blatty had failed to show that the Times had knowingly published false information in order to injure him.

Chapter 3

MUSIC PUBLISHING

3.00 Background on Music Publishing

Prior to the explosive growth of the record business beginning in the 1950s, marked by the advent of the LP, stereo, and rock-and-roll, the role of the music publisher was quite different from what it has been since that time.

In the early years of this century, music publishers made most of their money from the sale of printed music. They hired "song pluggers" (such as the young Irving Berlin and George Gershwin) to play their numbers on pianos set up in music stores to encourage the purchase of printed music. The "song pluggers" also auditioned numbers for theatrical, vaudeville, and cabaret performers in the hope of achieving exposure for the catalogs of their employers.

With the organization of the American Society of Authors and Composers (ASCAP), a second major source of income—from so-called "small performing rights"—emerged. Fees were collected from live performances and later from radio (and still later from TV) by ASCAP and by its competitor, Broadcast Music, Inc. (BMI), which arrived on the scene in the 1940s.

The record business grew slowly. As was the case with vaudeville and cabaret performers, early recording artists rarely wrote their own material and were receptive to the offerings of the "song pluggers," a situation that continued to prevail until the emergence of the self-contained rock-and-roll and "folk performers," who tended to write their own material. Artists such as Bing Crosby, Frank Sinatra, and Doris Day rarely, if ever, wrote their own material nor, for the most part, did the great big-band names such as Tommy Dorsey, Harry James, Benny Goodman, and Artie Shaw.

As the primary revenue sources for music publishers shifted from printed music and live performances to "mechanical royalties" from phonograph records and fees from radio and then TV "airplay," so too did the role of the music publisher. The "song plugger" was gradually replaced by the "professional manager," who bears some relationship to the "A&R" (artists and repertoire) man/woman in the record business. "Professional managers" attempt to convince recording artists and producers to record their companies' catalogs, but they are perhaps more oriented toward talent scouting—that is, finding young writers or, preferably, writer/performers with recording potential in whom the music publisher will invest. There are still "staff writers," especially in the country music field, in which recording artists remain quite receptive to outside songs. There is no question, however, that today's music publisher is most interested in writer-performers who can record their own material (hopefully with success).

The music publishing business is far less concentrated than the record industry. However, as is the case with book publishing, most major music publishers in the United States are affiliated with large conglomerates. For example, Thorn/EMI, an English conglomerate, owns Screen Gems/EMI Music. Warner Bros. Music is owned by Warner Communications, Inc. Chappel Music, formerly an affiliate of PolyGram, which, in turn, was owned by the behemoth Dutch conglomerate, Philips N.V., was recently acquired by a consortium headed by the principals of Carlin Music, a prominent English publisher. There are a number of other significant independent music publishers such as Almo/Irving (subsidiary of A&M Records, the largest privately owned U.S. record company); Tree Music and Peer-Southern, which function primarily in the country music area; and aggressive U.K. publishers such as Island, Virgin, and Zomba.

3.01   Sources of Revenue

In decreasing order of importance, music publishing revenues are derived from the following sources:

- Royalties paid for the use of musical compositions on phonograph records and tapes ("mechanical royalties," so named because the earliest royalties were derived from perforated paper player-piano music rolls).
- Fees from so-called "small performing

rights" (payment for the playing of music on radio and TV, in concert halls and arenas, stadiums, bars, and other venues).
- Fees from "synchronization" of music in TV and film soundtracks (the recording of music in the soundtrack of the production and, in a growing number of cases, the inclusion of the soundtrack in home video devices), as well as commercials and political advertisements.
- Royalties from printed editions (actually a rather small market, selling mostly to amateur vocalists and musicians and the smaller number of professionals).

There are other types of income: so-called "grand rights" uses, either on the living stage or by way of TV or film dramatization of a song or the use of its title (for example: "The Ballad of Billy Joe," a dramatization, and "Breaking Up Is Hard to Do," a TV movie-of-the-week using the title of a popular song but not based on that song); merchandising use of song titles and/or lyrics on greeting cards, T-shirts, and so forth; lyric magazines; royalties from "concert videos"; and other miscellaneous uses yielding minor amounts of income.

For many years now, revenues essentially have been divided 50 percent to the publisher and 50 percent to the songwriter, a practice followed throughout most of the world. Thus, 50 cents of every dollar collected by the publisher will be paid to the songwriter, and 50 cents will be retained by the publisher. Theoretically.

There are two great exceptions to this statement. These involve so-called small performance fees and co-publishing situations.

3.01–1   Small Performance Fees

Small-performance fees are collected by performing rights "societies" (ASCAP and BMI in the United States, the Canadian Association of Composers, Authors and Publishers and the Performing Rights Organization in Canada, SACEM in France, GEMA in Germany, JASRAC in Japan, and so on), which, after deduction of their own administration fee, pay half directly to the songwriter and half directly to the publisher. Generally speaking, the songwriter's half is inviolate. The society will never pay it to the publisher (except in a limited number of instances in the United States in which major advances by the publisher to the songwriter are involved, and then only to the extent necessary to recoup; that is, the publisher cannot commission the fees so collected).

3.01–2   "Co-publishing" Situations

Songwriters with even modest bargaining power can negotiate the retention of a portion (sometimes 100 percent) of the copyright in their songs—that is, they will be entitled to part of the publisher's 50 percent as well as their own 50 percent. In some instances, the publisher retains the copyright in its entirety but pays the songwriter (in addition to the songwriter's 50 percent share) a portion of the publisher's 50 percent. (While arrangements of both kinds are often referred to interchangeably as "participation agreements," this term is more appropriately limited to the latter type of arrangement.) When a music publisher talks about "50/50 co-publishing" or "50-50 participation," this means that the songwriter/co-publisher or songwriter/participant will receive an aggregate of 75 percent of the total income (50 percent as a songwriter and 25 percent as a co-publisher or participant).

3.02   Principal Types of Agreements

While many different types of agreements are used in the music publishing industry, the following are the most common.

3.02–1   Songwriter Agreement

Whether for a single song, a number of specified songs, all songs written during an exclusive term, or some songs written during a specified term (for example, songs written and recorded by the writer as a recording artist), the songwriter agreement stipulates that the writer receive royalties of 50 percent of the income (with or without an advance against royalties).

3.02–2   Co-publishing or Participation Agreement

As already discussed, with a co-publishing or participation agreement, the songwriter retains part of the copyright and/or a share of the publisher's 50 percent of income. As is the case with the songwriter agreement, the publisher customarily retains its rights for the life of copyright (subject to the statutory right of recapture available to the songwriter, generally after forty years). And, as is the case in the songwriter agreement, the publisher will undertake to administer (establish a file, register copyright, issue licenses, collect funds, protect the copyright against infringement, and defend infringement suits against the song) and account to and pay the songwriter.

3.02–3   Administration Agreement

Under the administration agreement, the songwriter retains 100 percent of the copyright, the publisher undertakes the same functions as under the co-publishing or participation agreement, and the publisher receives an "administration fee" (usually 15 to 25 percent of gross income, depending on the songwriter's bargaining strength and the amount of advances the administrating publisher is called on to make). In contrast to the co-publishing/participation type of agreement, the administrator's rights usually expire after a stated period—perhaps three years, or three years following the delivery of the final songs under the agreement, or until advances have been recouped or reimbursed. In the latter case, an outside termination date of a year or two following the term will be specified.

3.02–4 Collection Agreement

As in the administration agreement, the publisher acquires no ownership rights under a collection agreement, merely rights for a term of years (typically, three years). Under this type of agreement, the publisher generally does not undertake any affirmative obligation to exploit the songs, but merely to handle the paperwork of registration, licensing, and collection. The collection fee under such an agreement will generally range from 5 to 15 percent of gross receipts, settling most often at around 10 percent. These percentages may vary if advances are involved. Many publishers believe that a collection agreement at less than 10 percent is uneconomical unless a catalog is very successful and its paperwork is well organized.

3.02–5 Foreign Subpublishing Agreements

Since well over half of music publishing income derives from records and TV and radio performances, and since the United Kingdom, Germany, Japan, France, Italy, Scandinavia, and Australia/New Zealand yield hundreds of millions of dollars of publishing income, U.S. publishers enter into deals with subpublishers in these and other territories which are quite similar to U.S. administration agreements. These agreements will typically include provisions imposing additional artistic and economic controls on the subpublisher. For example, a typical subpublishing agreement may provide that the subpublisher will not license a so-called "lo-

cal cover recording" (a recording of a song produced and recorded in the local territory by an artist other than the artist who originally recorded that song) unless the translated or adapted lyrics have been approved by the original publisher. There may be a prohibition against licensing songs for films and/or TV. Clauses frequently provide that timely payment of advances and royalties is "of the essence." These agreements tend to be for short terms—three years is typical.

3.03 "At the Source"

In publishing parlance, a deal can be either a "receipts" deal or a "source" deal. Under a receipts deal, the division of income between publisher and writer (or publisher and co-publisher/participant) is based on what is collected by the original publisher from subpublishers and other licensees, not necessarily on all the income generated by specific uses.

Most music publishing income, whether generated within or outside of the United States, is initially handled by mechanical and performing rights societies. We have already mentioned performing rights societies. There are *mechanical* rights licensing societies as well. In the United States, the Harry Fox Agency, Inc. (not really a society but rather a subsidiary of the National Music Publishers Association) represents more than nine thousand publishers for this purpose, while STEMRA (The Netherlands), SDRM (France), NCB (Scandinavia), and other national societies perform the same function elsewhere around the world. Foreign income is processed and paid over to local subpublishers, who deduct their administration fees and remit the balance to the originating publisher in the United States. Under a *receipts* deal, the U.S. publisher would in turn deduct its publisher/administration/collection percentage (whichever is applicable) and pay over the remainder to the songwriter (or co-publisher or participant). Under a *source* deal, the fee of the foreign subpublisher is absorbed by the originating U.S. publisher out of the U.S. publisher's percentage of income.

Clearly, the income resulting to the songwriter/co-publisher/participant can be reduced considerably under a receipts deal. Indeed, in the hands of an unscrupulous publisher, application of the receipts concept can have an effect that is little short of catastrophic. For example, under a receipts deal providing for the publisher to keep 25 percent of its receipts and pay over 75 percent to the writer/co-publisher, if the original publisher subpublishes to a foreign affiliate under an agreement allowing that foreign affiliate to keep 25 percent of gross receipts, and that foreign affiliate in turn subpublishes to affiliates in other foreign countries under agreements allowing *them* to retain 25 percent of gross receipts, the following is the result:

$1.00	collected by ultimate sub-publisher.
.75	remitted to intermediate sub-publisher.
.5625	remitted to original publisher.
.4218	paid to songwriter/co-publisher/participant.

Such a multitiered arrangement is, of course, open to attack as overreaching and a breach of fiduciary obligation, but it is simple to avoid the necessity for such an attack by stipulating that the division of income must be "at the source." At a very minimum, if the client's bargaining strength is such that the publisher is able to insist on a receipts deal, the agreement should specify the maximum percentage that may be retained by the publisher's foreign subpublishers for the purpose of calculating the ultimate division of income.

3.04   Typical Requirements and Controls

Music publishers do not have a free hand; they occupy a quasi-fiduciary status with respect to songwriters and co-publishers/participants. However, it is always a good idea to spell out in some detail the obligations and restrictions under which the publisher (or subpublisher) is to operate. We have already discussed a typical restriction vis-à-vis "local cover records." Here are some others:

1. No change to the English-language title and/or lyric to a composition, and no change to the melody or rhythmic structure except to the extent necessary to accommodate the syllabic requirements of foreign languages.

2. No license of grand rights and/or title uses for films, TV, or stage without prior consent.

3. No synchronization licenses for X-rated films or equivalent TV programs, for commercials, or for political advertisements (indeed, some powerful writers impose a total prohibition on such licensing without prior consent, although the vast majority agree to routine background [nonvisual, usually instrumental] licenses for episodic TV, as being minor uses for little money).

4. In subpublishing situations, no issuance of a mechanical license for a cover record for a stated period after the release of the artist-songwriter's own record of a song (in rare cases, an artist-songwriter may prohibit a publisher from issuing a negotiated U.S. mechanical license for a stated period after such release, in which case any prospective record manufacturer is remitted to the compulsory license procedure under Section 115 of the Copyright Act).

5. Prior approval of uses of the writer's likeness and/or biographical material

(although the publisher will generally insist that any likeness and/or material approved for use by a songwriter-artist's record company is to be deemed approved for use by the publisher [subject to the record company's consent if the materials are the property of, or subject to the control of, the record company]).

6. A requirement that the publisher issue licenses in accordance with the so-called "controlled compositions" clause in any recording contract to which an artist/songwriter may be or become a party. Record companies commonly insist on licenses at three-fourths of the minimum U.S. statutory mechanical copyright royalty rate (in 1986, 5 cents for the first five minutes of playing time) on songs written by their recording artists, with no payment on so-called "free goods" (records shipped for resale but not billed to the customer; for example, 100 LPs are shipped to a customer but the customer will be billed for only 85) and no payment for use of songs in promotional videos (and, sometimes, no payment if such videos are licensed for a profit and/or included in home video cassettes). (In return, the publisher may seek to establish minimum standards, with the right to reimburse itself from the artist-songwriter's royalties to the extent that collections fall short of the publisher's contractual expectations.)

While no music publisher will guarantee a particular level of exploitation and/or success with respect to any specific song, publishers will sometimes agree to relinquish rights with respect to unexploited songs. Thus, in the songwriter agreement or a co-publishing agreement, the publisher might agree that any song not embodied on a recording re-leased commercially in the United States during the term or within two years thereafter will revert to the songwriter/co-publisher/participant. In some instances, reversion may be deferred until all advances have been recouped, if later than the two-year date. Such clauses are quite typical in U.K. agreements, as a result of *Schroeder v. Macaulay* (see Section 3.21).

NOTES _____

For additional readings and resources, the following should be consulted:

1. D. Biederman, Chairman, *Legal and Business Problems of the Music Industry* (New York: Practicing Law Institute, 1980). This collection of articles and forms on records, music publishing, music in films and video, and tax considerations is somewhat dated; however, it contains several articles not readily available elsewhere.

2. S. Shemel and M. Krasilovsky, *This Business of Music*, 5th ed. (New York: Billboard Publications, Inc., 1985). This classic, now in its fifth edition, is generally considered the best all-around introduction to the worldwide music business. It contains concise discussions of such arcana as performing rights societies and international music publishing as well as overviews of more mainstream topics.

3.10   Performing Rights

After mechanical income, radio and television performances are the second greatest source of income to music publishers. For almost 40 years, there has been a steady drumfire of litigation between broadcasters and music publishers, which culminated in the *Buffalo Broadcasting* case.

Buffalo Broadcasting v. ASCAP, 744 F.2d 917 (2d Cir. 1984)

NEWMAN, CIRCUIT JUDGE

Once again we consider the lawfulness under section 1 of the Sherman Antitrust Act of the blanket license offered by the American Society of Composers, Authors and Publishers (ASCAP) and Broadcast Music, Inc. (BMI). The license permits the licensee to perform publicly any musical composition in the repertory of the licensor. In this litigation the blanket license is challenged by a class of licensees comprising all owners of "local" television stations in the United States, *i.e.*, stations not owned by any of the three major television networks, ABC, CBS, and NBC. After a bench trial in the District Court for the Southern District of New York (Lee P. Gagliardi, Judge), the blanket license was held to be an unreasonable restraint of trade. *Buffalo Broadcasting Co. v. ASCAP*, 546 F. Supp. 274 (S.D.N.Y. 1982). ASCAP and BMI were enjoined from licensing to local television stations non-dramatic music performing rights for any "syndicated" program. For reasons that follow, we conclude that the evidence was insufficient as a matter of law to show that the blanket license is an unlawful restraint of trade in the legal and factual context in which it currently exists. We therefore reverse the judgment of the District Court. . . .

The five named plaintiffs own and operate one or more local television stations. They represent a class of all owners of local television stations in the United States who obtain music performing rights pursuant to license agreements with ASCAP and/or BMI. The class does not include the three major television networks, ABC, CBS, and NBC, each of which owns five television stations. The class includes approximately 450 owners who, because of multiple holdings, own approximately 750 local television stations. Only one owner has opted out of the class. The class includes some relatively small corporations that own a single station with relatively modest revenue and some major corporations with significant television revenue and profits, such as Metromedia, Inc., which owns seven stations including those in the major markets of New York City (WNEW-TV) and Los Angeles (WTTV). [These stations have since been sold to 20th Century-Fox—Ed.] Since 1949 most stations have been represented in negotiations with ASCAP and BMI by the All-Industry Television Station Music License Committee ("the All-Industry Committee").

Defendant ASCAP is an unincorporated membership association of composers, authors, and publishers of music, formed in 1914. It has approximately 21,000 writer and 8,000 publisher members. It holds non-exclusive licenses for the non-dramatic performing rights to more than three million musical compositions. BMI is a non-profit corporation organized in 1939 by radio broadcasters. It has approximately 38,000 writer and 22,000 publisher affiliates. Its repertory, for which it holds non-exclusive licenses for non-dramatic performing rights, includes more than one million compositions. The eleven individual defendants represent two classes of defendants that include all persons from whom ASCAP and BMI have obtained the non-exclusive right to license non-dramatic music performing rights to others. . . .

The subject matter of this litigation is music transmitted by television stations to their viewer-listeners. Television music is classified as either theme, background, or feature. Theme music is played at the start or conclusion of a program and serves to enhance the identification of the program. Background music accompanies portions of the program to heighten interest, underscore the mood, change the pace, or otherwise contribute to the overall effect of the program. Feature music is a principal focus of audience attention, such as a popular song sung on a variety show.

More particularly, we are concerned with the licensing of non-dramatic performing rights to copyrighted music, that is, the right to "perform" the music publicly by transmitting it, whether live or on film or tape, to television audiences. This performance right is created by the Copyright Act as one of the exclusive rights enjoyed by the copyright owner. 17 U.S.C. § 106(4) (1982). Also pertinent to this litigation is the so-called synchronization right, or "synch" right, that is, the right to reproduce the music onto the soundtrack of a film or a videotape in synchronization with the action. The "synch" right is a form of the reproduction right also created by statute as one of the exclusive rights enjoyed by the copyright owner. *Id.* § 106(1). The Act specifically accords the copyright owner the right to authorize others to use the various rights recognized by the Act, including the performing right and the reproduction right, *id.* § 106, and to convey these rights separately, *id.* § 201(d)(2).

The Act recognizes that conveyance of the various rights protected by copyright may be accomplished by either an exclusive or a non-exclusive license. *Id.* § 101.

Music performed by local television stations is selected in one of three ways. It may be selected by the station itself, or by the producer of a program that is sold to the station, or by a performer spontaneously. The stations select music for the relatively small portion of the program day devoted to locally produced programs. The vast majority of music aired by television stations is selected by the producers of programs supplied to the stations. In some instances these producers are the major television networks, but this litigation is not concerned with performing rights to music on programs supplied to the local stations by the major networks because the networks have blanket licenses from ASCAP and BMI and convey performing rights to local stations when they supply network programs. Apart from network-produced programs, the producers of programs for local stations are "syndicators" supplying the stations with "syndicated" programs. Most syndicated programs are feature length movies or one-hour or half-hour films or videotapes produced especially for television viewing by motion picture studios, their television production affiliates, or independent television program producers. However, the definition of "syndicated program" that was stipulated to by the parties also includes live, non-network television programs offered for sale or license to local stations. These syndicated programs are the central focus of this litigation. The third category of selected music, songs chosen spontaneously by a performer, accounts for a very small percentage of the music aired by the stations. These spontaneous selections of music can occur on programs produced either locally or by the networks or by syndicators.

Syndicators wishing to include music in their programs may either select pre-existing music (sometimes called "outside" music) or hire a composer to compose original music (sometimes called "inside" music). Most music on syndicated programs, up to 90% by plaintiffs' estimate, is inside music commissioned through the use of composer-for-hire agreements between the producer and either the composer alone or the com-

poser and a corporation entitled to contract for a loan of the composer's services. Composer-for-hire agreements are normally standard form contracts. The salary paid to the composer, sometimes called "up front money," varies considerably from a few hundred dollars to several thousand dollars. The producer for whom a "work made for hire" was composed is considered by the Act to be the author and, unless the producer and composer have otherwise agreed, owns "all of the rights comprised in the copyright." . . . However, composer-for-hire agreements for syndicated television programs typically provide that the producer assigns to the composer and to a music publishing company the performing right to the music composed pursuant to the agreement.

When the producer wishes to use outside music in a film or videotape program, it must obtain from the copyright proprietor the "synch" right in order to record the music on the soundtrack of the film or tape. "Synch" rights vary in price, usually within a range of $150 to $500. When the producer wishes to use inside music, as is normally the case, it need not obtain the "synch" right because it already owns this right by virtue of the "work made for hire" provision of the Act.

Whether the producer decides to use outside or inside music, it need not acquire the television performing right since neither the making of the program nor the selling of the program to a television station is a "performance" of the music that would require a performing right. The producer is therefore free either to sell the program without the performing right and leave it to the station to obtain that right, or to obtain the performing right from the copyright proprietor, usually the composer and a publishing company, and convey that music performing right to the station along with the performing rights to all other copyrighted components of the program. If the producer obtains the music performing right from the copyright proprietor and conveys it to the station, the transaction is known as "source licensing" or "clearance at the source." If the station obtains the music performing right directly from the copyright proprietor, the transaction is known as "direct licensing."

The typical arrangement whereby local television stations acquire music performing rights in syndicated and all other programs is neither source licensing nor direct licensing. Instead, the stations obtain from ASCAP and BMI a blanket license permitting television performance of all of the music in the repertories of these organizations. The license is conveyed for a fee normally set as a percentage of the station's revenue. That fee, after deduction of administrative expenses, is distributed to the copyright proprietors on a basis that roughly reflects the extent of use of the music and the size of the audience for which the station "performed" the music. The royalty distribution is normally divided equally between the composer and the music publishing company.

In addition to offering stations a blanket license, ASCAP and BMI also offer a modified form of the blanket license known as a "program" or "per program" license. The program license conveys to the station the music performing rights to all of the music in the ASCAP or BMI repertory for use on the particular program for which the license is issued. The fee for a program license is a percent of the revenue derived by the station from the particular program, *i.e.*, the advertising dollars paid to sponsor the program.

The blanket license contains a "carve-out" provision exempting from the base on which the license fee is computed the revenue derived by the station from any program presented by motion picture or transcription for which music performing rights have been licensed at the source by the licensor, *i.e.*, ASCAP or BMI. The program license contains a more generous version of this provision, extending the exemption to music performing rights licensed at the source *either* by ASCAP/BMI *or* by the composer and publisher. Thus, for film and videotaped syndicated programs, a station can either obtain a blanket license for all of its music performing rights and reduce its fee for those programs licensed at the source by ASCAP/BMI, or obtain program licenses for each of its programs that use copyrighted music and avoid the fee for those programs licensed at the source by either ASCAP/BMI or by the composers and publishers. . . .

The merits of the current lawsuit cannot properly be assessed without consideration of the extensive history of litigation concerning the li-

censing of music performing rights. In 1941 an antitrust suit brought by the United States against ASCAP and BMI was settled by entry of consent decrees, imposing some limitations on the operations of ASCAP and BMI. Those decrees, however, permitted ASCAP and BMI to obtain exclusive licenses for music performing rights from their members and affiliates. The exclusive nature of these licenses prevented those requiring performing rights from negotiating directly with composers for rights to individual compositions. That limitation precipitated suit by operators of movie theaters, who successfully challenged the blanket license they were obliged to take from ASCAP in order to exhibit films with music from the ASCAP repertory. *Alden-Rochelle, Inc. v. ASCAP*, 80 F. Supp. 888 (S.D.N.Y. 1948). *See also M. Witmark & Sons v. Jensen*, 80 F. Supp. 843 (D.Minn. 1948), *appeal dismissed*, 177 F.2d 515 (8th Cir. 1949).

The restraining nature of the ASCAP blanket license, as applied to movie theater operators, prompted the Government to reopen the 1941 ASCAP consent decree and secure in 1950 a significant amendment. The amended decree, known as the "Amended Final Judgment," prohibits ASCAP from acquiring exclusive music performing rights, limiting it solely to nonexclusive rights. ASCAP is also prohibited from limiting, restricting, or interfering with the right of any member to issue to any user a non-exclusive license for music performing rights.

The Amended Final Judgment requires ASCAP to grant a blanket license to anyone requesting it. The decree also requires ASCAP to offer to any television or radio broadcaster a program license. ASCAP is also required "to use its best efforts to avoid any discrimination among the respective fees fixed for the various types of licenses which would deprive the licensees or prospective licensees of a genuine choice from among such various types of licenses." Amended Final Judgment, ¶ VIII, 546 F. Supp. at 278 n. 6. Finally, in the event license applicants believe they are being overcharged, the decree permits any applicant for a blanket or program license to apply to the District Court for the determination of a "reasonable" fee, and in such a proceeding, "the burden of proof shall be on ASCAP to establish the reasonableness of the fee requested by it." *Id*. ¶ IX(A), 546 F. Supp. at 278–79 n. 6.

In 1951 local television stations instituted suit pursuant to the Amended Final Judgment to determine reasonable license fees and terms. *United States v. ASCAP (Application of Voice of Alabama, Inc.)*, Civ. No. 13–95 (S.D.N.Y. 1951). In 1954 the parties reached agreement to set the per program license rate at 9% of the revenue of programs using ASCAP music and to reduce the blanket license rate to 2.05% of total station revenue, less certain deductions. In light of this agreement the *Voice of Alabama* proceeding was discontinued.

In 1961 local television stations requested from ASCAP a modified blanket license that excluded syndicated programs. When ASCAP refused, the stations sued in the consent decree court to require ASCAP to issue such a license. The District Court declined to require such a license, *United States v. ASCAP (Application of Shenandoah Valley Broadcasting, Inc.)*, 208 F. Supp. 896 (S.D.N.Y. 1962), *aff'd*, 331 F.2d 117 (2d Cir.), *cert. denied*, 377 U.S. 997, 84 S.Ct. 1917, 12 L.Ed.2d 1048 (1964). In affirming, this Court observed that if the blanket license was serving to restrain trade unreasonably in violation of the antitrust laws, the stations' remedy was to urge the Department of Justice to seek modification of the consent decree or to initiate a private suit. 331 F.2d at 124.

Rather than press an antitrust challenge, the stations initiated another round of fee determination pursuant to the consent decree. That litigation, known as the *Shenandoah* proceeding, was settled upon the parties' agreement that the form of blanket and program licenses then in use "may be entered into lawfully by each party to this proceeding" and that the rate for the blanket license was reduced to 2% of 1964–65 revenue plus 1% of incremental revenue above that base. *United States v. ASCAP (Application of Shenandoah Valley Broadcasting, Inc.)*, Civ. No. 13–95 (S.D.N.Y. July 28, 1969) (final order). The All-Industry Committee reported to the stations that this rate reduction would save them approximately $53 million through 1977, an estimate that was exceeded because of the rapid growth of station revenue.

Thereafter, while the local television stations took blanket licenses from ASCAP and BMI, the legality of the license was challenged by a network licensee, CBS. Its suit, filed in 1969, was dismissed by Judge Lasker after an eight-week trial. *CBS, Inc. v. ASCAP*, 400 F. Supp. 737 (S.D.N.Y. 1975). Judge Lasker ruled that the evidence failed to show that the blanket license restrained CBS from obtaining music performing rights to individual compositions if it chose to seek and pay for them. On appeal, this Court reversed, ruling that the blanket license was an unlawful price-fixing device, a *per se* violation of section 1. *CBS, Inc. v. ASCAP*, 562 F.2d 130 (2d Cir. 1977). That decision was reversed by the Supreme Court, which ruled that the blanket license was not a *per se* violation of section 1. *BMI, Inc. v. CBS, Inc.*, 441 U.S. 1, 99 S.Ct. 1551, 60 L.Ed.2d 1 (1979). Upon remand from the Supreme Court, we affirmed Judge Lasker's decision, agreeing that the blanket license had not been proven to be a restraint of trade. *CBS, Inc. v. ASCAP*, 620 F.2d 930 (2d Cir. 1980) ("*CBS-remand*"), *cert. denied*, 450 U.S. 970, 101 S.Ct. 1491, 67 L.Ed.2d 621 (1981).

Perhaps encouraged by our 1977 ruling in favor of CBS, the local stations began this litigation in 1978. A four-week bench trial occurred in 1981 before Judge Gagliardi, resulting in the decision now on appeal. That decision holds that the blanket licensing of music performing rights to local television stations unreasonably restrains trade in violation of section 1 and enjoins ASCAP and BMI from granting to local television stations music performing rights in any syndicated programs. With respect to syndicated programs, the injunction thus bars ASCAP and BMI from offering either blanket or program licenses and also prohibits them from conveying performing rights with respect to such programs on any basis at all. . . .

Is There a Restraint?

We think the initial and, as it turns out, dispositive issue on the merits is whether the blanket licensing of performing rights to the local television stations has been proven to be a restraint of trade. *See CBS-remand, supra*, 620 F.2d at 934–

35. Arguably the answer is *a fortiori* after the Supreme Court's decision and our decision on remand in the CBS litigation. The Supreme Court noted that "the necessity for and advantages of a blanket license for (television and radio networks) may be far less obvious than is the case when the potential users are individual television or radio stations. . . ." 441 U.S. at 21, 99 S.Ct. at 1563. And on remand we upheld the blanket license against the claim of a network. However, for several reasons, it does not follow that the local stations lose simply because the CBS network lost. First, the Supreme Court's observation concerned the relative pro-competitive effects of the blanket license for a network compared to local stations. Even though the pro-competitive effects may be greater when the licensees are local stations, those pro-competitive effects do not necessarily outweigh the anti-competitive effects. Second, the Supreme Court's comparative statement does not determine the threshold issue of whether the blanket licensing of performing rights to local television stations is a restraint at all. The fact that CBS did not prove that blanket licensing of networks restrained competition does not necessarily mean that blanket licensing of local stations may not be shown to be a restraint. Finally, in *CBS-remand* we reviewed a District Judge's ruling that no restraint had been proved; here, we review a ruling that the local stations proved the existence of a restraint.

In reaching his conclusions as to the existence of a restraint, Judge Gagliardi endeavored to apply the mode of analysis we had used in *CBS-remand*. We there noted that trade is restrained, sometimes unreasonably, when rights to use individual copyrights or patents may be obtained only by payment for a pool of such rights, but that the opportunity to acquire a pool of rights does not restrain trade if an alternative opportunity to acquire individual rights is realistically available. 620 F.2d at 935–36. We recognized, as CBS had urged, that a plaintiff will not be held to have an alternative "available" simply because some imaginable possibility exists. We agreed that CBS's "alternative" of hiring composers to fill its need for music was not the sort of realistic alternative that prevented the blanket license from

being a restraint. "An antitrust plaintiff is not obliged to pursue any imaginable alternative, regardless of cost or efficiency, before it can complain that a practice has restrained competition." *Id.* at 936. What we examined in *CBS-remand*, as Judge Lasker had done in the District Court, was whether the plaintiff had proved that it lacked a realistic opportunity to obtain performance rights from individual copyright holders.

We continue to believe that this is the appropriate inquiry, especially in light of the Supreme Court's recent decision concerning the NCAA's attempt to regulate the televising of college football games. *NCAA v. Board of Regents of the University of Oklahoma*,—U.S.—, 104 S.Ct. 2948, 82 L.Ed.2d 70 (1984). Two aspects of that ruling are especially pertinent. First, the Court was there concerned, as we are here, with an agreement whereby a pool of rights was conveyed. In determining that the agreement constituted a restraint, the Court stated, "[S]ince as a *practical* matter all member institutions need NCAA approval, members have no *real* choice but to adhere to the NCAA's television controls." *Id.* at 2963 (emphasis added) (footnote omitted). Thus, the restraining effect of the challenged agreement arose not by virtue of its terms alone, but because as a "practical" matter no "real" alternative existed whereby individual negotiations could occur between member schools and television broadcasters. Second, the Court had occasion to characterize the blanket license for music performing rights that it had sustained against a *per se* challenge in *CBS* and stated that under the blanket license "each individual remained free to sell his own music *without restraint*." *Id.* at 2968 (emphasis added). *NCAA* thus reinforces our view that the first issue is whether the local television stations have proven that they lack, as a "practical" matter, a "real" alternative to the blanket license for obtaining music performing rights.

In reaching the conclusion that plaintiffs had proven the lack of realistically available alternatives to the blanket license, Judge Gagliardi gave separate consideration to three possibilities: the program license, direct licensing, and source licensing. We consider each in turn.

[1] *Program License*. Judge Gagliardi based his conclusion that a program license is not realistically available to the plaintiffs essentially on two circumstances: the cost of a program license and the reporting requirements that such a license imposes on a licensee. "The court therefore concludes that the per program license is too costly and burdensome to be a realistic alternative to the blanket license." 546 F. Supp. at 289 (footnote omitted). Without rejecting any subsidiary factual finding concerning the availability of a program license, we reject the legal conclusion that it is not a realistic alternative to the blanket license.

The only fact found in support of the conclusion that the program license is "too costly" is that the rates for such licenses are seven times higher than the rates for blanket licenses. *Id*. The program license rate is 9%; the blanket license rate is between 1% and 2%. This difference in rates does not support the District Court's conclusion for several reasons. First, the rates are charged against different bases. The blanket license rate is applied to a station's total revenue; the program license rate is applied only to revenue from a particular program. Since the base for the blanket license fee includes revenue from network programs, for which the networks have already acquired performing rights by virtue of their blanket licenses, as well as some local programs that use no music, it is inevitable that the rate for a local station's blanket license will be less than the rate for a program license taken solely to permit use of music on a particular program.

Second, the degree of difference between the two rates is largely attributable to the stations themselves. In negotiating a revision of license rates in the *Shenandoah* proceeding in 1969, the All-Industry Committee elected not to press for reduction of the program license rate and instead concentrated on securing a reduction of the blanket license rate, believing, as it informed the broadcasters it represented, that "the critical matter at this time was to get the best possible blanket license." Having preferred to win a lower price for only the blanket license, the stations are in no position to point to the widened differential between rates to show that program licenses are not realistically available.

Third, the only valid test of whether the program license is "too costly" to be a realistic alternative is whether the price for such a license, in an objective sense, is higher than the value of the rights obtained. But plaintiffs presented no evidence that the price of the program license is "high" in terms of value received. Instead, they rely, as did the District Court, on a comparison between the program license rate and the blanket license rate. That comparison, defendants contend, leads to the anomalous result that the more the blanket license is a bargain, the more it is likely to be a restraint. The anomaly is more apparent than real. Within reasonable price ranges, the program license is not an unrealistic alternative to the blanket license simply because the rate for the latter is less. The differential in rates may reflect the inherent difference in the bundle of rights being conveyed. Even if the blanket license is objectively the "better buy" for most users, the program license would be a realistic alternative so long as it was fairly priced for those who might find it preferable for reasons other than price. But if the program license were available only at a price beyond any objectively reasonable range, the "bargain" nature of the blanket license would not immunize it from characterization as a restraint. Sellers of alternatives may not set absurdly high prices at which they have no real intention of making sales and then point to the cheaper price of the package under attack to argue that it is not a restraint but the object of customer preference.

Thus, while the relative cheapness of the blanket rate does not necessarily mean that it is not a restraint, the absence of evidence that the program license has been artificially priced higher than is reasonable for value received bars any conclusion that the program license is "too costly" to be a realistic alternative. . . .

Fourth, even if there were evidence that showed the program license rate to be too "high," that price is always subject to downward revision by Judge Conner, who currently supervises the administration of the Amended Final Judgment. Two aspects of that judgment are especially pertinent to any claim that the price of the program license is too "high." In a proceeding to redetermine rates, the burden is on ASCAP to prove the reasonableness of the rates charged, and the judgment expressly requires ASCAP "to use its best efforts to avoid any discrimination among the respective fees fixed for the various types of licenses which would deprive the licensees or prospective licensees of a *genuine choice* from among such various types of licenses," Amended Final Judgment, ¶ VIII, 546 F. Supp. at 278 n. 6 (emphasis added). The availability of a judicially enforceable requirement of a "reasonable" fee precludes any claim that the program license rate is too high, especially in the context of television stations regularly represented by a vigorous committee with the demonstrated resources, skill, and willingness to invoke the rate-adjustment process.

In addition to cost, Judge Gagliardi considered the program license not realistically available because of the burdens of required record-keeping that accompany its use. This conclusion is similarly flawed by the lack of evidence that the record-keeping requirements have been unnecessarily imposed. . . .

The lack of evidence that the program license is not realistically available has a two-fold significance in determining whether the blanket license has been shown to be a restraint. First, the program license itself remains as an alternative to the blanket license for the local stations to acquire performing rights to the music on all of their syndicated programs. That consequence is not necessarily determinative since the program license is in reality a limited form of the blanket license and, like the blanket license, is subject to the objection that its use by stations would continue the present practice whereby no price competition occurs among individual songs with respect to licensing of performing rights. However, the availability of the program license has a second and more significant consequence: The program license provides local stations with a fallback position in the event that they forgo the blanket license and then encounter difficulty in obtaining performing rights to music on some syndicated programs either by direct licensing or by source licensing. Whether those alternatives were proven to be unavailable as realistic alternatives is our next inquiry.

[2] *Direct Licensing.* The District Court concluded that direct licensing is not a realistic alternative to the blanket license without any evidence that any local station ever offered any composer a sum of money in exchange for the performing rights to his music. That evidentiary gap exists despite the 21-year interval between entry of the Amended Final Judgment and the trial of this case, during which the local stations had ample opportunity to determine whether performing rights could be directly licensed.

The District Court declined to attach any significance to the absence of purchase offers from stations directly to copyright proprietors for two related reasons. Judge Gagliardi concluded, first, that direct licensing could not occur without the intervention of some agency to broker the numerous transactions that would be involved and, second, that the television stations lack the market power to induce anyone to come forward and perform that brokering function. 546 F. Supp. at 290. We have no quarrel with the first proposition. Some intermediary would seem essential to negotiate performing rights licenses between thousands of copyright proprietors and hundreds of local stations, in the same manner that the Harry Fox Agency for years has brokered licenses for "synch" rights between copyright proprietors and program producers.

However, we see no evidentiary support for the District Court's second proposition—that no one would undertake the brokering function for direct licensing of performing rights. Judge Gagliardi was led to this conclusion, not on the basis of any evidence of an expressed reluctance on anyone's part to broker direct licensing, but because of his view of the difference between the market power of CBS and that of the local television stations. In *CBS* Judge Lasker had found, 400 F. Supp. at 779, and we had emphasized, 620 F.2d at 938, that if CBS were to seek direct licensing, "copyright proprietors would wait at CBS' door." In this case, Judge Gagliardi found that "local television stations acting individually and severally would possess no such awesome power over copyright owners." 546 F. Supp. at 290. From this finding he concluded, "Since no lines would form at the doors of local television stations, no centralized machinery would arise to facilitate direct licensing." *Id.*

This reasoning escalates a characterization of the evidence in *CBS* into a minimum requirement for future cases. The plaintiffs in this case do not discharge their burden of proving that local stations cannot realistically obtain direct licenses by showing that they have less market power than CBS, "the giant of the world in the use of music rights," *CBS v. ASCAP, supra*, 400 F. Supp. at 771 (quoting testimony of a former CBS vice-president). The issue is whether the local stations have been shown to lack power sufficient to give them a realistic opportunity to secure direct licenses. To conclude that they do not simply because no one of them is as powerful as CBS disregards the functioning of a market. Sellers are induced to sell by a perception of aggregate demand, existing or capable of stimulation. . . . Thus, it avails plaintiffs nothing to cite the testimony of Salvatore Chiantia, president of the National Music Publishers Association, that as a publisher he would not line up at the door of KID–TV in Idaho Falls to license performing rights. . . . What is pertinent is Chiantia's point that while it would be difficult for him to have a staff that would wait at the doors of 700 television stations, "if [direct licensing] was the way I was going to get my music performed, I would have to devise a system which would make it possible for me to license." The plaintiffs have not presented evidence to show that a brokering mechanism would not handle direct licensing transactions if the stations offered to pay royalties directly to copyright proprietors. . . .

[3] *Source Licensing.* As Judge Gagliardi noted, the "current availability and comparative efficiency of source licensing have been the focus of this lawsuit." *Id.* at 291. The availability of source licensing is significant to the inquiry as to whether the blanket license is a restraint because so much of the stations' programming consists of syndicated programs for which the producer could, if so inclined, convey music performing rights. Most of these syndicated programs use composer-for-hire music. As to such music, the producer starts out with the rights of the copyright, including the performing right, by operation of law, 17 U.S.C. § 201(b), unless the hiring agreement otherwise provides. Thus it becomes important to determine whether the stations can obtain from the producer the music performing right, along with all of the other rights in a syndicated program that are conveyed to the stations when the program is licensed. As to "inside" music, source licensing would mean that the producer would either retain the performing right and convey it to the stations, instead of following the current practice of assigning it to the composer and a publishing company, or reacquire the performing right from the composer and publisher for conveyance to the stations. As to "outside" music, source licensing would mean that the producer would have to acquire from the copyright proprietor the performing right, in addition to the "synch" right now acquired.

Plaintiffs sought to prove that source licensing was not a realistic alternative by presenting two types of evidence: "offers" from stations and analysis of the market. Prior to bringing this lawsuit, the stations had not sought to obtain performing rights via source licensing. Perhaps prompted by the evidentiary gap emphasized in our decision in *CBS-remand* or by the taunting of defendants in this litigation, plaintiffs began in mid-1980, a year and one-half after the suit was filed, to create a paper record designed to show the unavailability of source licensing.

Various techniques were used. Initially, some stations simply inserted into the standard form of licensing agreement for syndicated programs a new clause specifying that the producer has obtained music performing rights and that the station need not do so. No offer of additional compensation for the purchase of the additional rights was made. Not surprisingly most producers declined to agree to the proposed clause. . . .

Another approach, evidenced by King Broadcasting Co.'s letter to MCA, attached a music performing rights rider to the standard syndication licensing agreement and added, "If [*sic*] an additional fee is in order, we would certainly consider favorably any such reasonable fee." . . . Metromedia, Inc., owner of several stations, went further and asked Twentieth Century-Fox Television ("Fox"), "Since you are the 'seller,' what is the price you would affix to the altered product [the syndication license including music performing rights]?" In reply Fox made the entirely valid point that since syndication licensing without music performing rights had been the industry practice for years, it was Metromedia's "responsibility to advise us in what manner you would like" to change the current arrangements. Notably absent from all of the correspondence tendered by the plaintiffs is the customary indicator of a buyer's seriousness in attempting to make a purchase—an offer of a sum of money.

Judge Gagliardi properly declined to give any probative weight to the plaintiffs' transparent effort to assemble in the midst of litigation evidence that they had seriously tried to obtain source licensing. He found "plaintiffs' source licensing foray so darkened by the shadow of the approaching trial that its results may not be relied upon to support either side." 546 F. Supp. at 292. Nevertheless the District Court concluded that source licensing was not a realistic alternative because the syndicators "have no impetus to depart from their standard practices and request and pay for television performing rights merely in order to pass them along to local stations." *Id*. This conclusion does not follow from some of the Court's factual findings and rests on a view of the syndication market that is contradicted by other findings.

The District Court viewed the syndication market as one in which the balance of power rests with the syndicators and the stations have no power to "compel" a reluctant syndicator to change to source licensing. *Id*. Yet the Court found that there are eight major syndicators, *id*. at 280 & n. 13, and that they distribute only 52% of all syndicated programs, *id*. at 281, hardly typical of a non-competitive market. Moreover, the Court characterized production of syndicated programs as a "risky business," *id*. at 282, a finding fully supported by the evidence. It may be that the syndicator of a highly successful program has the upper hand in negotiating for the syndication of that program and would not engage in source licensing for music in that program simply to please any one station, but it does not follow that the market for the wide range of syndicated programs would be unresponsive to aggregate demand from stations willing to pay a reasonable price for source licensing of music performing rights. . . .

Defendants vigorously assert that whatever reluctance producers may have to undertake source licensing reflects their view of the efficiency of the blanket license. They contend that the blanket license may not properly be found to be a restraint simply because producers of syndicated programs regard it as efficient. We need not determine whether defendants have correctly analyzed the motivation of those syndicators who have expressed reluctance to undertake source licensing. Our task, in determining whether plaintiffs have presented evidence sufficient to support a conclusion that the blanket license is a restraint of trade, is not to psychoanalyze the sellers but to search the record for evidence that the blanket license is functioning to restrain willing buyers and sellers from negotiating for the licensing of performing rights to individual compositions at reasonable prices. Plaintiffs have simply failed to produce such evidence.

Instead they suggest that source licensing is not a realistic alternative because the agreements producers have made with composers and publishers are a "contractual labyrinth," Brief for Appellants at 53 n. 73, and because the composers have precluded price competition among songs by "splitting" performing rights from "synch" rights, *id*. at 2. But plaintiffs have made no legal challenge to the "composer-for-hire" contracts by which "inside" music is customarily obtained for syndicated programs, with provisions for producers to assign performing rights to composers and publishers. And composers have not "split" performing rights from "synch" rights; they have separately licensed distinct rights that were created by Congress. Moreover, the composers' grant of a performing rights license to ASCAP/BMI is on a non-exclusive basis. That circumstance significantly distinguishes this case from *Alden-Rochelle*, where ASCAP's acquisition of *exclusive* licenses for performing rights was held to restrain unlawfully the ability of motion picture exhibitors to obtain music performing rights directly from ASCAP's members.

[4] *The Claimed Lack of Necessity.* Plaintiffs earnestly advance the argument that the blanket license, as applied to syndicated programming, should be declared unlawful for the basic reason that it is unnecessary. In their view, the blanket license is suspect because, where it is used, no

price competition occurs among songs when those who need performing rights decide which songs to perform. The resulting absence of price competition, plaintiffs urge, is justifiable only in some contexts such as night clubs, live and locally produced programming of television stations, and radio stations, which make more spontaneous choices of music than do television stations.

There are two fundamental flaws in this argument. First, it has not been shown on this record that the blanket license, even as applied to syndicated television programs, is not necessary. If all the plaintiffs mean is that a judicial ban on blanket licensing for syndicated television programs would not halt performance of copyrighted music on such programs and that some arrangement for the purchase of performing rights would replace the blanket license, we can readily agree. Most likely source licensing would become prevalent, just as it did in the context of motion pictures in the aftermath of *Alden-Rochelle*. But a licensing system may be "necessary" in the practical sense that it is far superior to other alternatives in efficiency and thereby achieves substantial saving of resources to the likely benefit of ultimate consumers, who usually end up paying whenever efficient practices are replaced with inefficient ones.

Moreover, the evidence does not establish that barring the blanket license as to syndicated programs would add any significant price competition among songs that the blanket license allegedly prevents. When syndicators today decide what music to select for their programs, they do so in the vast majority of instances, by deciding which composer to hire to compose new music for their programs. As to that "inside" music, which plaintiffs estimate accounts for 90% of music on syndicated programs, there is ample price competition: Prices paid as "up front" money in order to hire composers vary significantly. Even when syndicators consider use of pre-existing music (for which copyright protection has not expired), there is some price competition affecting the choice of that "outside" music because prices for "synch" rights vary. . . .

The second flaw in the argument is more fundamental. Even if the evidence showed that most of the efficiencies of the blanket license could be achieved under source licensing, it would not follow that the blanket license thereby becomes unlawful. The blanket license is not even amenable to scrutiny under section 1 unless it is a restraint of trade. The fact that it may be in some sense "unnecessary" does not make it a restraint. This is simply a recognition of the basic proposition that the antitrust laws do not permit courts to ban all practices that some economists consider undesirable. Since the blanket license restrains no one from bargaining over the purchase and sale of music performance rights, it is not a restraint unless it were proven that there are no realistically available alternatives. As we have discussed, the plaintiffs did not present evidence to establish the absence of realistic alternatives. It is therefore irrelevant whether, as plaintiffs contend, the blanket license is not as useful or "necessary" in the context of syndicated programming on local television stations as it is in other contexts. Not having been proven to be a restraint, it cannot be a violation of section 1.

The blanket license has been challenged in a variety of contexts. It has been upheld for use by nightclubs and bars, *BMI v. Moor-Law, Inc.*, 527 F. Supp. 758 (D. Del. 1981), *aff'd mem.*, 691 F.2d 490 (3d Cir. 1982), by radio stations, *K-91, Inc. v. Gershwin Publishing Corp.*, 372 F.2d 1 (9th Cir. 1967), *cert. denied*, 389 U.S. 1045, 88 S.Ct. 761, 19 L.Ed.2d 838 (1968), and by a television network, *CBS-remand, supra*. Without doubting that the context in which the blanket license is challenged can have a significant bearing on the outcome, we hold that the local television stations have not presented evidence in this case permitting a conclusion that the blanket license is a restraint of trade in violation of section 1.

The judgment of the District Court is therefore reversed.

WINTER, CIRCUIT JUDGE (CONCURRING)
I disagree with little stated in Judge Newman's thoughtful and comprehensive opinion. I write separately because I believe that it demonstrates that the blanket license as presently used cannot have an anti-competitive effect and hope that his analysis, used out of context, will not lead to future needless litigation over blanket licenses in the music industry. . . .

NOTES _____

1. The controversy about public performance licensing continues unabated. Following the denial of certiorari by the Supreme Court in the *Buffalo Broadcasting* case, the broadcasters persuaded Representatives Hyde of Illinois and Boucher of Virginia to introduce H.R. 3521 (the counterpart of which, S. 1980, was introduced in the Senate by Senator Thurmond of South Carolina). There were over 100 co-sponsors in the House, and a large number in the Senate as well. These bills would mandate the licensing by music publishers to program producers of performance rights for use in local television at the same time as synchronization rights are licensed for such programs. In other words, these bills would prohibit either direct licensing to local TV stations or blanket licensing through ASCAP or BMI.

In addition, both the NBC Television Network and the NBC Radio Network notified advertising agencies that they would no longer air commercials in respect of which performance rights had not been licensed directly to the advertiser or the agency.

While hearings were held in both the House and Senate on H.R. 3521/S. 1980 during March and April of 1986, no definitive action had been taken by either house at the time of this writing. Additionally, although a groundswell of protests from advertisers and advertising agencies had been directed at NBC as of this writing, there was no indication that NBC would retreat from its new policy. Further, CBS TV was customarily including in programming agreements clauses requiring producers to obtain the agreement of music licensors to negotiate with CBS as to performance licenses and, if negotiations proved inconclusive, to arbitrate.

2. The trial record in *Buffalo Broadcasting* revealed a sharp disparity among economists as to whether blanket licensing of music performing rights was economically beneficial or harmful. The appellate court noted one authority who argued that the blanket license was economically sound, citing Sobel, "The Music Business and the Sherman Act: An Analysis of the 'Economic Realities' of Blanket Licensing," 3 *Loyola Entertainment Law Journal* 1 (1983).

3. In *Buffalo Broadcasting*, frequent mention is made of the lengthy litigation brought by CBS against ASCAP and BMI. These performing rights societies have had their actions frequently challenged over the years, including antitrust inquiries initiated by the United States government, resulting in different consent decrees. See, *United States v. ASCAP*, 1940–43 Trade Cas. (CCH) ¶ 56,104 (S.D.N.Y. 1941); *United States v. BMI*, 1940–43 Trade Cas. (CCH) ¶ 56,098

(S.D.N.Y. 1941); *United States v. ASCAP*, 1950–51 Trade Cas. (CCH) ¶62,595 (S.D.N.Y. 1950); and *United States v. BMI*, 1966 Trade Cas. (CCH) ¶ 71,941 (S.D.N.Y. 1966).

4. The court in its *Buffalo Broadcasting* decision discussed at several points a nondramatic performing right. In a footnote, the court explained this right as follows:

> A non-dramatic performing right is the right to perform a musical composition other than in a dramatic performance, which the ASCAP blanket license defines as "a performance of a musical composition on a television program in which there is a definite plot depicted by action and where the performance of the musical composition is woven into and carries forward the plot and its accompanying action." *See* 3 *Nimmer on Copyright* § 10.10[E] (1984).

5. The court in *Buffalo Broadcasting* noted limitations on the program license as follows:

> The program license is not an alternative means of obtaining performing rights to individual compositions since it permits the licensee to use all compositions in the repertory of the licensor for an individual program. Its use would not afford a station a choice among competitive prices of performing rights for individual compositions. Nevertheless, to whatever extent it is available, it is an alternative means of obtaining performing rights needed to broadcast one program. Moreover, the program license, if available, may facilitate the stations' efforts to pursue direct licensing and source licensing, as we discuss later in the text. In any event, the parties joined issue as to whether it is a realistically available alternative, the District Court ruled on the issue, and we review that ruling.

3.20 The Publisher's Obligations

A songwriter desires two basic services from a music publisher: that the song be successfully exploited in all available markets and that the publisher provide a full and accurate accounting of revenues and resulting royalties. Both services are more easily described in the abstract than defined in strict, enforceable language. The following sections explore the elusive obligations of the music publisher, in terms of duties both express and implied arising from the publisher-songwriter agreement.

3.21 The Obligation to Exploit

As with many different types of agreements in the entertainment industry, music publishing contracts usually contain clauses embodying variations on the theme that earnings from compositions are inherently speculative, that the publisher does not guarantee any particular level of success, and, incidentally, that the publisher is not really obligated to do *anything* except the customary housekeeping details (registration of copyright, setting up of song files, and so on), and accounting and payment for royalties if compositions *are* exploited. In this regard, the contract in the *Schroeder* case, which follows, is fairly typical of U.S. contracts as well as English contracts such as that in *Schroeder*. The *Witmark* case demonstrates that a similar attitude prevailed among American publishers as well, and long before the *Schroeder* agreement.

Subsequent to the *Schroeder* decision, many English publishers adopted the custom of providing in their agreements that songs not exploited by two years following the end of the term would revert to the songwriter, especially in cases where advances and other commitments were less than robust. Such provisions are not uncommon in American agreements but are not routinely agreed to by publishers.

A. Schroeder Music Publishing Co. v. Macaulay, (1974) 3 All ER 616 (HL)

[In 1966, Schroeder signed Macaulay (then a 21-year-old unknown) to an exclusive songwriter's agreement essentially in Schroeder's "standard form," a form in large part typical of those then in use in the music publishing industry in England. Macaulay received a signing advance of 50 pounds, and was to receive a further advance of 50 pounds whenever a previous advance was recouped. If Macaulay had received an aggregate of 5,000 pounds by the end of the initial five-year period of the term, the term would automatically be extended for a second five-year period. However, Schroeder had the right to terminate the term at any time upon one month's notice.

While Macaulay engaged himself exclusively to Schroeder for the term, undertook to obey all lawful orders and directions from Schroeder, and agreed to use his best efforts to promote Schroeder's interests, the only affirmative obligation undertaken by Schroeder (apart from the advances referred to above) was to pay royalties in the event any were earned. In addition, the agreement was freely assignable by Schroeder, but Macaulay was prohibited from assigning his rights under the agreement without Schroeder's consent.

Although this fact does not appear in the House of Lords report, it is worth noting that the lower court opinions indicate that since this agreement did not require that royalty calculations be "at the source," *i.e.*, without reduction by reason of income shares deducted and retained by subpublishers before remitting foreign income to the original publisher, Schroeder entered into foreign subpublishing agreements with its own subsidiaries which, in turn, entered into sub-subpublishing agreements with other Schroeder subsidiaries. Each level of subsidiaries deducted its own fees before remitting royalties up the chain, so that Macaulay, who thought he would receive 50% of the income, actually received only a small fraction thereof.

In 1970, Macaulay brought suit seeking a declaration that the agreement was in restraint of trade, against public policy, and void.]

LORD REID

. . . It is not disputed that the validity of the agreement must be determined as at the date when it was signed and it is therefore unnecessary to deal with the reasons why the respondent now wishes to be freed from it. . . . I think that in a case like the present case two questions must be considered. Are the terms of the agreement so restrictive that either they cannot be justified at all or that they must be justified by the party seeking to enforce the agreement? Then, if there is room for justification, has that party proved justification—normally by showing that the restrictions were no more than what was reasonably required to protect his legitimate interests. . . . [The agreement] must of course be read as a whole and we must consider the cumulative effect of the restrictions contained therein.

. . . Five thousand pounds in five years appears to represent a very modest success, and so if [Macaulay's] work became well known and popular he would be tied by the agreement for ten years. The duration of an agreement in restraint of trade is a factor of great importance in determining whether the restrictions in the agreement can be justified but there was no evidence as to why so long a period was necessary to protect [Schroeder's] interests.

. . . There may sometimes be room for an argument that although on a strict literal construction restrictions could be enforced oppressively, one is entitled to have regard to the fact that a large organization could not afford to act oppressively without damaging the goodwill of its business. But the power to assign leaves no room for that argument. We cannot assume that an assignee would always act reasonably.

The public interest requires in the interests both of the public and of the individual that everyone should be free so far as practicable to earn a livelihood and to give to the public the fruits of his particular abilities. The main question to be considered is whether and how far the operation of the terms of this agreement is likely to conflict with this objective. [Macaulay] is bound to assign to [Schroeder] during a long period the fruits of his musical talent. But what are the [Schroeders] required to do with those fruits? Under the contract nothing. If they do use the songs which [Macaulay] composes they must pay in terms of the contract. But they need not do so. . . . [T]hey may put them in a drawer and leave them there. No doubt the expectation was that if the songs were of value they would be published to the advantage of both parties. But if for any reason [Schroeder] chose not to publish them [Macaulay] would get no remuneration and he could not do anything. Inevitably [Macaulay] must take the risk of misjudgment of the merits of his work by the [Schroeders]. But that is not the only reason which might cause the [Schroeders] not to publish. There is no evidence about this so we must do the best we can with common knowledge. It does not seem fanciful and it was not argued that it is fanciful to suppose that purely commercial consideration might cause a publisher to refrain from publishing and promoting promising material. He might think it likely to be more profitable to promote work by other composers with whom he had agreements and unwise or too expensive to try to publish and popularize [Macaulay's] work in addition. And there is always the possibility that less legitimate reasons might influence a decision not to publish [Macaulay's] work.

It was argued that there must be read into this agreement an obligation on the publisher to act in good faith. I take that to mean that he would be in breach of contract if by reason of some oblique or malicious motive he refrained from publishing work which he would otherwise have published. I very much doubt this but even if it were so it would make little difference. Such a case would seldom occur and then would be difficult to prove.

I agree with the [Schroeders'] argument to this extent. I do not think that a publisher could reasonably be expected to enter into any positive commitment to publish future work by an unknown composer. Possibly there might be some general undertaking to use his best endeavors to promote the composer's work. But that would probably have to be in such general terms as to be of little use to the composer.

But if no satisfactory positive undertaking by the publisher can be devised, it appears to me to be an unreasonable restraint to tie the composer for this period of years so that his work will be sterilized and he can earn nothing from his abilities as a composer if the publisher chooses not to publish. If there had been . . . any provision entitling the composer to terminate the agreement in such an event the case might have had a very different appearance. But as the agreement stands not only is the composer tied but he cannot recover the copyright of the work which the publisher refuses to publish.

It was strenuously argued that the agreement is in standard form, that it has stood the test of time, and that there is no indication that it ever causes injustice. [Lord Reid then discussed cases according great weight to commercial practices and accepted standard forms.]

But those passages refer to contracts "made freely by parties bargaining on equal terms" or "molded under the pressures of negotiation, competition and public opinion." I do not find from any evidence in this case, nor does it seem probable, that this form of contract made between a publisher and an unknown composer has been molded by any pressure of negotiation. Indeed, it appears that established composers who can bargain on equal terms can and do make their own contracts.

Any contract by which a person engages to give his exclusive services to another for a period necessarily involves extensive restriction during that period of the common law right to exercise any lawful activity he chooses in such manner as he thinks best. Normally the doctrine of restraint of trade has no application to such restrictions: they require no justification. But if contractual restrictions appear to be unnecessary or to be reasonably capable of enforcement in an oppressive manner, then they must be justified before they can be enforced.

. . . I need not consider whether in any circumstances it would be possible to justify such a one-sided agreement. It is sufficient to say that such evidence as there is falls far short of justification. It must therefore follow that the agreement so far as unperformed is unenforceable.

I would dismiss this appeal.

[Viscount Dilhorne, Lord Simon of Glaisdale, Lord Brandon and Lord Diplock concurred.]

M. Witmark & Sons v. Peters, 149 N.Y.S. 642 (1914)

DOWLING, J.

Plaintiff, a publisher of music, entered into a written agreement with the defendant Peters, who was a composer, on or about December 8, 1911, under the terms of which Peters was to deliver to the plaintiff for publication during a period of five years all the music which he alone or in conjunction with others should either write or compose or acquire control of, and by which the composer agreed that all musical compositions which he might write or compose during said period, including the titles, words, and music thereof, should, immediately upon the same being written or composed, or control thereof secured, become and be the absolute property of the plaintiff, and Peters granted and conveyed to plaintiff the copyright or copyrights thereof, with all renewals. Peters also agreed not to write for, compose, or deliver to any person other than the plaintiff any musical composition at any time during the period of five years, or the titles, words, or music of any such composition, or any part thereof, and that he would not permit any publisher, person, firm, or corporation other than the plaintiff to use the same. Peters further agreed under his contract to submit all the new or original compositions written and composed by him alone, or in conjunction with others, or controlled by him, to the extent of not less than six compositions in each year, and plaintiff agreed to publish not less than three compositions acquired from Peters during each year of the term of the agreement. Complete works, such as comic operas, musical comedies, or groups of numbers or cycles, were to be considered as single compositions. In return for all this plaintiff agreed to pay to the party of the second part, upon each and every copy sold by it of any operatic, standard, or high-class composition which the party of the second part shall have written, composed, or acquired control of, four cents when he furnished both words and music, and two cents when he furnished either the words or music only; also certain other sums upon the various other kinds of compositions supplied by Peters under his contract. It was also agreed that, should plaintiff sell any of the so-called "popular" compositions at less than regular rates, the party of the second part should accept as royalty 1½ cents per copy if he supplied both words and music, and ¾ of a cent per copy if he supplied either the words or music only, upon all copies sold at a reduced rate down to 10 cents. Upon all copies sold at less than 10 cents he was to accept a still further reduction in his royalties. Peters by the agreement also transferred to plaintiff all mechanical rights in any composition theretofore written or composed by him, either alone or jointly with others, or in which he had, either alone or with others, acquired such rights, as well as on all of his future compositions during the life of the agreement. Plaintiff was to collect the royalties under such rights and deliver one-half thereof to Peters. Semiannual statements were to be rendered and payments made for any balances due within 30 days thereafter.

During the first year of the life of this agreement, Peters submitted three compositions to plaintiff, none of which it published. During the second year five additional numbers were delivered by Peters, all of which were published by plaintiff during that year, the last on June 9, 1913. On June 5, 1913, Peters made a contract with the other defendant herein, Harms & Francis, Day & Hunter, a corporation, having knowledge of the agreement between plaintiff and Peters. Peters thereafter delivered to his codefendant the music of the musical comedy "Iole," three numbers of which were thereafter published by the defendant company. Plaintiff seeks to enforce specific performance of the affirmative covenant contained in the contract between it and Peters, by compelling the defendants to assign to it the music of the comedy "Iole," and also to enforce the negative covenant of said agreement by which Peters was not to compose or deliver to any person other than plaintiff any musical composition during the life of his agreement with plaintiff. From the judgment granting the relief demanded, these defendants appeal.

There is no substantial dispute as to the facts. The question for determination is whether the contract between the plaintiff and Peters was one which will be enforced in a court of equity. The contract contains no express provision by which the plaintiff binds itself to sell any of the compositions published by it and composed by Peters, nor does it undertake to issue any fixed or definite minimum number of copies thereof. But, even if the agreement to publish carries with it by inference an agreement to offer the copies so published for sale, then the contract seems to be so inequitable that a court of equity would not be justified in enforcing its provisions by injunctive or mandatory relief, either as to the affirmative or negative covenants thereof. Peters for a period of five years is required to turn over every musical composition which he either originates or controls, no matter what the aggregate number may be, and they at once become the absolute property of the plaintiff, which, while agreeing to publish any three which it may select in each year, does not bind itself to publish them in the year that they are submitted, but may do so at any time during the life of the agreement, as it may see fit. It could literally comply with the terms of the agreement by publishing five· or ten copies of each of the three compositions which it finally selected in each year, and thus make itself absolute master of the entire productive capacity of Peters for five years, preventing him from finding a market for his efforts elsewhere, and at the same time paying him a royalty ridiculously small and entirely inadequate for the services which he was required to perform for them. Where a contract is as inequitable as the one now under examination, and where the benefits accruing to the plaintiff are so palpably disproportioned to the services required to be performed by Peters, a court of equity will not interfere to enforce such an inequitable and improvident agreement, but will relegate the plaintiff to its cause of action at law, particularly where, as in this case, there is no allegation whatever that the defendants are financially irresponsible or unable to respond to the plaintiff for such damages as it may establish in an action at law.

The judgment appealed from will therefore be reversed, and the complaint dismissed, with costs to the appellants. All concur.

3.22   The Obligation to Account and Pay

The payment to writers, monitored by proper accounting procedures, is a primary responsibility of any music publisher. As the *Nolan* case illustrates, a publisher may not, absent express contractual provisions so permitting, sell its rights in a manner that diminishes the writer's contractual expectancy.

By the same token, the writer is more than a mere creditor; as the *Waterson* case illustrates, a purchaser of a bankrupt catalog must continue to account to and pay the writers, who have an equitable lien on the copyrights.

Nolan v. Williamson Music Inc., 300 F. Supp. 1311 (S.D.N.Y. 1969)

[Nolan, a member of the famed singing group "The Sons of the Pioneers" (which, during its early years, included a young singer who went on to fame as cowboy star Roy Rogers), wrote an extremely popular country/western song, "Tumbling Tumbleweeds," which he sold to Sam Fox Publishing Company in return for Fox's promise to pay stated composer royalties. In most instances, these were a percentage of royalties received by the "Publisher" (defined in the contract as Fox, "its successors and assigns forever").

After publishing the song for 12 years, Fox conveyed it to Williamson, which, in turn, agreed to pay Fox between 50% and 66⅔% of Williamson's receipts, and paid Fox an advance of $17,500. As between Fox and Williamson, Fox continued to have the duty to account to and to pay Nolan his share of royalties (essentially, 33⅓% of "Publisher's" receipts).

In 1960, when he became entitled to renew the copyright on "Tumbling Tumbleweeds," Nolan (as required pursuant to his original contract with Fox) assigned the renewal to Fox, which, in turn, executed a further assignment to Williamson.

While Fox never notified Nolan of the assignments to Williamson, Williamson had taken out an ad in *Variety* at the time of the original assignment, announcing that it had acquired "the sensational Western song, 'Tumbling Tumbleweeds' by Bob Nolan." In addition, Williamson had registered the assignment in the Copyright Office. Further, Gray, who was Nolan's business manager for some 19 years, learned of the assignment in the course of representation of a different client.

Throughout the period following the assignment to Williamson, Fox essentially paid Nolan 33⅓% of what Williamson paid Fox, not 33⅓% of what Williamson collected. In addition, Fox failed to pay Nolan 74% of the royalties due Nolan for a six-year period (including a total failure to pay him any foreign royalties for that period).

Nolan sued seeking to rescind the contract and recover his copyright, by reason of fraud. In addition, Nolan sought royalties and damages for copyright infringement.]

EDELSTEIN, DISTRICT JUDGE

The basic claim which plaintiff has urged in this suit is that he had the legal right to, and, in fact, did rescind his agreements with Fox by the May 29, 1963 notice. Plaintiff argues that rescission is justified in this case because over the years Fox has allegedly committed the following breaches: (1) non-payment of all royalties earned by foreign sources (this is conceded by Fox); (2) non-payment of the royalties due from domestic performing income; (3) non-payment of all of the royalties due on octavo editions of the song, electrical transcriptions, synchronizations, and on lyric uses of the song; (4) assignment of the copyright and its renewal term to Williamson; (5) payment of royalties by Fox based only on Fox's receipts from Williamson; [etc.]. . . .

The court finds that it was not a breach of contract for Sam Fox to assign the copyright to Williamson. The 1934 transfer from plaintiff to Sam Fox of "all rights of every kind, nature and description" which plaintiff had in the copyright was clearly absolute on its face. Furthermore, the agreement specifically provided that the conveyance was to "Publisher, its successors and assigns." Whether a contract is assignable or not is, of course, a matter of contractual intent, and one must look to the language used by the parties to discern that intent. Clearly the language just quoted contemplated that the agreement was to be assignable. Williston on Contracts sec. 423 (3rd ed. 1962).

The plaintiff . . . seems to be saying, however, that this contract involved such personal elements of trust and confidence that it was not assignable without the consent of the parties despite the clear language to the contrary. This argument, though, is not premised upon any reliable evidence adduced at the trial which would demonstrate that Nolan entered into his agreement with Fox because of any personal trust and confidence which he placed in Fox. Further, rescission of copyright exploitation agreements much like the one in issue in the case at bar was also sought in the case of *In re Waterson, Berlin & Snyder Co.* when the original assignee of the copyrights at issue there attempted to assign them to other publishers. The District Court, 36 F.2d 94 (S.D.N.Y. 1929), granted rescission in that case on the ground that the agreements were not assignable because of the degree of personal trust involved in them. The Court of Appeals, *In re Waterson, Berlin & Snyder Co. v. Irving Trust Co.*, 48.2d 704 (2d Cir. 1931), however, reversed that decision and held that the copyrights could be assigned further.

Plaintiff's assertions of fraud are based in part upon the allegation that Fox concealed from plaintiff its relationship with Williamson by never giving plaintiff actual notice of the assignment. The evidence, however, does not support a finding of fraud in this regard. . . . [T]he court has already held that the contract was assignable without Fox's first having to obtain the plaintiff's consent. Further, far from demonstrating an intent to conceal the assignment, the evidence shows that the defendants openly announced the fact of their arrangement in . . . *Variety* [and] the assignment was registered in the Copyright Office and the Fox-Williamson relationship was noted on the copies of sheet music which were distributed.

In this regard it is also important to note that . . . [Gray] had, at the least, notice that Williamson was publishing the song, and since Gray was plaintiff's authorized business agent in general and specifically acted as such with regard to "Tumbling Tumbleweeds," this notice is imputable to plaintiff. See, e.g., *Farr v. Newman*, 14 N.Y.2d 183, 250 N.Y.S.2d 272, 199 N.E.2d 369, 4 A.L.R.3d 215 (1964).

The other part of plaintiff's claim of fraud is predicated upon the failure of Fox to render clearer and more detailed accountings to plaintiff and to pay him all of the royalties which were due him. Again, however, the reliable evidence fails to demonstrate fraud. Essentially what plaintiff is really complaining of here is mere breaches of contract by Fox; fraud consists of something more

than the mere breach of a contract. . . . [R]escission can be permitted only when the complaining party has suffered breaches of so material and substantial a nature that they affect the very essence of the contract and serve to defeat the object of the parties.

Cases which have considered the problem of rescission in situations analogous to the one presented by the case at bar have granted rescission only after finding the equivalent of a total failure in the performance of the contract. In *Raftery v. World Film Corp.* [180 App.Div. 475, 167 N.Y.S 1027 (1st Dept. 1917)], the plaintiff temporarily turned over to the defendant prints from which movies were to be made and then distributed. The contract provided that the defendant was to render weekly accounts of the earnings on the movies and to pay the plaintiff fifty percent thereof. The prints were to be returned at the expiration of the contract term. The court found that the defendant never paid plaintiff the full amount due, deliberately maintained a set of fictitious records, deliberately rendered false accountings, refused to permit inspection of the records as was required by the contract, and failed to return the prints to the plaintiff. Based on all of these factors rescission was granted. . . . [A]nd finally in *DeMille Co. v. Casey*, 115 Misc. 646, 189 N.Y.S. 275 (Sup.Ct. 1921), a contract permitting the defendant to produce motion pictures based on plaintiff's plays was rescinded when royalty payments ceased and the defendant, because of various sublicensing agreements over which he had lost effective control, was no longer in a position to comply with the contract and to protect the plaintiff's future interest. . . .

Although defendant has been guilty of diverse breaches, these breaches involve a failure to comply fully with the contractual provisions for payment of royalties in various categories, and as to these breaches, it is clear to the court that plaintiff may be rendered whole by an award of monetary damages. Moreover, there seems little danger that Nolan will be deprived of his royalties in the future. This is not a case where the defendant has repudiated his obligation to pay royalties, nor is this a case in which plaintiff's song has not been exploited fully in the past or threatened with not being fully exploited in the future. . . .

[Turning to the issue of the basis upon which Nolan is to be paid:] Plaintiff maintains that he is entitled to royalties based on all earnings of "Tumbling Tumbleweeds" and not just those which are based on Williamson's payments to Fox (i.e., Fox's receipts). Fox insists that the 1934 contract envisioned payments to Nolan based exclusively on receipts of Fox. Again, defendant's objection must fail.

Ab initio the contract refers to "[T]he Publisher [paying] the Composers," and it is undisputed that Williamson is the de facto publisher of the composition. Although in the preamble to the 1934 contract the "Publisher" is referred to as the Sam Fox Publishing Company, the third paragraph of the document speaks of the "Publisher, its successor and assigns." That this is the intended definition of the word "Publisher" is clear when it is considered that the original publisher, Sam Fox Publishing Company, dissolved subsequent to the execution of the 1934 contract and the Sam Fox Publishing Co., Inc., then was organized as the successor to the partnership. Taking defendant's argument to its extreme, it would argue that only the Sam Fox Publishing Company was liable for the payment of royalties to Nolan and that the corporate entity was absolved because it was not the "Publisher" as that word was used in the preamble. To avoid this impossible situation—which even the defendant does not urge—it is necessary to define "Publisher" with reference to Par. 3, i.e., as Sam Fox Publishing Company, Sam Fox Publishing Company, Incorporated (a successor) and Williamson Music, Inc. (an assign). As a result Williamson is the publisher insofar as that term is used to decide the basis on which royalties are to be determined. The court therefore finds that it was a breach of the 1934 Nolan-Fox agreement for Fox, when accounting to Nolan for the royalties due to him, to have excluded the share of the earnings on "Tumbling Tumbleweeds" retained by Williamson. If the court were to conclude otherwise, plaintiff's interest could be endlessly diluted by successive assignments.

Nolan also demands a share of the $17,500.00 which Fox received as an "advance against royalties" from Williamson for the assignment. . . . To the extent that the $17,500.00 was applied against

the royalties which Williamson paid to Fox, then to that extent, and only to that extent, is Nolan entitled to royalties based on the $17,500.

The statute of limitations defense, however, has merit. The New York statute of limitations for an action based on breach of contract or mistake is six years from the breach. C.P.L.R. sec. 213. Although the plaintiff attempts to bring his case within the limitation provision for action based on fraud (six years from date of discovery), he has failed to prove fraud. Oversight, negligence, and less than meticulous bookkeeping do not amount to fraud, and a mere allegation of fraud is insufficient to bring the fraud provision of sec. 213 into play. *Braunwarth v. Wellington*, 48 N.Y.S.2d 159 (Sup.Ct. 1943), aff'd 269 A.D. 747, 55 N.Y.S.2d 116 (1st Dept. 1945), aff'd 272 A.D. 878, 72 N.Y.S.2d 406 1st Dept. 1947). . . .

It is the judgment of this court that plaintiff's agreements with Fox are not rescinded. Plaintiff is entitled to the payment of royalties due him under his 1934 and 1960 agreements with Fox and the court directs an accounting limited to the period commencing six years prior to the commencement of this action, except that this six-year limitation does not apply to the money due plaintiff for royalties derived from foreign mechanical income [which, Fox conceded, had never been paid at all, and as to which Fox waived the application of the statute of limitations]. . . .

[After findings by a Special Master, the Court found for Nolan in the amount of $94,148, including interest and costs. Both sides appealed.]

Nolan v. Sam Fox Publishing Company, Inc., 499 F.2d 1394 (2d Cir. 1974)

WATERMAN, CIRCUIT JUDGE

. . . [The *Variety* ad] is, of course, patently inconsistent with the theory that Fox and Williamson were intent on concealing their relationship. Moreover, Williamson's name was displayed on all the sheet music copies of the song published by it. Nolan argues, however, that nowhere in the *Variety* announcement or on the sheet music was Williamson identified as the "publisher." This omission, in and of itself, surely would not demonstrate fraud. In addition, it is significant that the assignment from Fox to Williamson was recorded at the Copyright Office. Inasmuch as that assignment was recorded, we need not even reach the question of whether Nolan can be charged with knowledge of the assignment because of the recording, for it suffices to say here that this recordation further illustrates that Williamson and Fox had no intention whatever of concealing their relationship from Nolan or from anyone else. . . . [In addition, it] is unimportant what Gray actually did or did not tell Nolan about the knowledge Gray obtained. Whatever knowledge Gray had is imputed to Nolan. . . .

Although the existence of fraud is a sufficient ground for permitting rescission it is not a necessary one. Rescission has also been allowed, despite the absence of any showing of fraud, in cases in which a publisher has made none of the royalty payments. The rationale of these decisions is, of course, that an essential objective of a contract between a composer and publisher is the payment of royalties, and a complete failure to pay means this objective has not been achieved. Here, however, Fox did pay 26% of the royalties due to Nolan for the applicable six-year period, and this partial payment of royalties due distinguishes this case from cases where there was total failure to pay the required royalties. . . .

Nolan argues that the statute of limitations pertaining to actions in contract should not apply here, for the relationship of a writer or composer to his publisher is one of trust, that there has been not only a breach of contractual relationship but a breach of fiduciary duty, as well, and therefore we should hold that Nolan's cause of action for any of the royalty payments allegedly withheld by Fox at any time accrued only upon Nolan's discovery of all the facts which he claims Fox had concealed from him until shortly before his declaration of rescission. It is true that several New York courts have mentioned the trust elements that are part of the relationship between a writer and a publisher. See *Nelson v. Mills Music, Inc.*, 278 App. Div. 311, 104 N.Y.S.2d 605 (1st Dept. 1951); *Schisgall v. Fairchild Publications, Inc.*, 207 Misc. 224, 137 N.Y.S.2d 312 (Sup.Ct. 1955). . . . None of these cases, however, are concerned with the statute of limitations

question. Rather, these cases involve only the question of what effect the relationship between the composer or writer and publisher has on the publisher's acknowledged obligation to exploit the copyright. . . . [E]xploitation of the copyright not being at issue here, the cases cited by Nolan are inapposite. . . .

In re Waterson, Berlin & Snyder Co., 48 F.2d 704 (2d Cir. 1931)

HAND, CIRCUIT JUDGE

The bankrupt was a music publisher. Prior to bankruptcy it had purchased from the petitioner Fain, and others, musical compositions, including words and music, under agreements all of which were identical except as to royalty rates and advance royalties. There were agreements made with twenty-two such composers.

The provisions of the royalty contracts important for consideration are illustrated by the following taken from the contract with one of the composers:

For the Consideration of the sum of One dollar, in hand paid to Jimmie Monaco, party of the first part, by Waterson, Berlin & Snyder Co., party of the second part, the receipt whereof is hereby acknowledged, the said party of the first part does hereby sell, set over and transfer unto the said party of the second part, its successors and assigns, a certain song or musical composition, including the words and music thereof, bearing the title "You Went Away Too Far and Stayed Away Too Long" or any other title, name or style the said party of the second part may at any time give to said composition, together with the right to take out a copyright for or upon the same, and each and every part thereof, including the words and music, to the full extent in all respects as the party of the first part could or might be able to do if these presents had not been executed.

And The Said Party of the second part hereby covenants and agrees in the event of the publication by it of the said song or musical composition, to pay to the party of the first part 1¢ cents upon each and every ordinary printed pianoforte copy sold and paid for of the said song or musical composition hereafter sold by the party of the second part in the United States, except as hereinafter mentioned or specified, such payment to be made only upon a full and complete compliance with all and singular the terms and conditions herein contained on the part of the party of the first part. And it is hereby expressly agreed that out of the first royalties to which the party of the first part may be entitled by or under the terms of this agreement the sum of $500.00 dollars, paid as advance Royalty, shall be deducted. . . .

And The Party of the first part hereby covenants and represents to Waterson, Berlin & Snyder Co., for the purpose of inducing it to accept an assignment of said song and musical composition, and to enter into and execute this agreement and make the payment above mentioned, that he has not heretofore sold, mortgaged, hypothecated, or otherwise disposed of or incumbered any right, title or interest in or to said song or musical composition or any part thereof, and has not made or entered into an agreement with any person, firm or corporation in any wise affecting the said song, words or musical composition, and that he is the author and composer and absolute owner thereof, and has the full right, power and authority to make this assignment and agreement.

We agree to pay 33⅓% jointly of all revenue received from Mechanical reproductions less any expense incurred.

Settlement On This Agreement shall be made semi-annually within thirty (30) days after the first days of January and July, respectively, during the whole term in existence of the copyright of said song and musical composition, according to such correct and proper statements of account as may be available on such days. Any such payment when made and accepted shall operate as a release to the said party of the second part, his successors or assigns, from any further claim or liability for any royalty up to the date thereof.

On September 20, 1929, and after the adjudication in bankruptcy which occurred late in August or early in September, 1929, the Irving Trust Company, which had been appointed receiver of Waterson, Berlin & Snyder Company, sent a circular to various persons in the music trade inviting bids before October 1, 1929, for all of the right, title, and interest of the bankrupt estate in the copyrights for the songs free from royalty claims. The circular stated that on October 1, 1929, the receiver proposed to submit the bids for individual songs, including rights to mechanical royalties, to the court for acceptance.

Thereupon Fain and the other composers filed a petition in the District Court alleging that in entering into their contracts they had relied on the reputation and organization of Waterson, Berlin & Snyder Company as leading musical publishers to popularize their publications and to increase sales of the songs, that the bankruptcy of the publishers had disabled them from further performance of the contracts to publish, and that, if the receiver was permitted to sell the compositions and copyrights free from royalty claims, purchasers would publish them without obligation to pay further royalties to the composers, who would thus be deprived of all revenue from their productions. The petitioners prayed for an order directing the receiver or trustee in bankruptcy to reassign the copyrights to them, or, in the alternative, not to sell without provision for the payment of future royalties to the composers, and for other and further relief.

The District Judge, though finding that each agreement involves "a transfer, absolute on its face, in exchange for a covenant by the publisher for the payment of certain agreed royalties," held that the "royalty contracts . . . involve such personal elements of trust and confidence that they are not assignable without the consent of the parties," and that they may "be rescinded by the composers when the publisher, as here, is unable or definitely refuses to fulfill his obligations thereunder." He therefore granted the petition and ordered that the royalty contracts be rescinded and that the trustee in bankruptcy should reassign each copyright to the composer upon the return to the bankrupt estate of any unearned advance royalties paid thereon to such composer.

The trustee has taken this appeal, which raises the questions (1) whether the trustee has a right to sell the copyrights at all; (2) whether, if he has a right to sell them at all, he may sell them free and clear of royalties.

The questions involved are interesting, and few precedents can be found in the American courts that throw direct light on the problems involved. We find difficulty in taking the view adopted by the District Judge, in spite of his interesting and informing opinion, because it disregards the unqualified grant to the publisher, and because it appears to give no weight to the labor, skill, and capital which a publisher expends in putting a song on the market. The expense of maintaining an organization, of building up a business and making it available to the composers of songs, as well as the more direct cost of making plates, advertising, and distributing the songs so as to give them popularity, largely go for nought if a rescission of the contracts be ordered on the sole condition that the composers return unearned advance royalties. Such a disposition seems specially inequitable where in the case of some, if not many, of the songs there are no unearned advances whatever.

In attempting to allow the composers any relief, we are confronted by certain decisions holding that an agreement to pay royalties in exchange for a transfer of title is nothing but an executory contract to pay, enforceable only at law. Bigham, J., in *Re Grant Richards*, [1907] 2 Q. B. 33, held that the trustee in bankruptcy of a publisher, who had purchased the copyright of a book and agreed to pay royalties to the author upon sales, could sell the copyright and was not even liable for royalties upon sales of the publication made by him as trustee. In other words, the relation was held to be that of debtor and creditor and the author was allowed no more than the right to prove his claim against the bankrupt estate. The foregoing decision of Bigham, J., is referred to with approval by Scrutton, L. J., in the Court of Appeal in *Barker v. Stickney*, [1919] K. B. 121, where an author who had sold his copyright under an agreement with the purchaser to pay royalties was held to have no lien upon the copyright in the hands of a subvendee who took title with notice of the original agreement. It was said (page 132) that "a person acquiring a chose in action is not bound by mere notice of a personal covenant by his predecessor in title."

The foregoing decisions would indicate that the assignor of a copyright has only the right to recover at law for the breach of an agreement to pay royalties, and would have no control over the use of the copyright by his vendee or a subvendee. This rigorous doctrine, attributed to the English courts, is certainly far less satisfactory than that adopted by the court below, for, in case of bankruptcy or insolvency of the purchaser of the copyright, it deprives the author of any substantial remedy, though the consideration he was to receive for parting with his compositions was to depend on royalties accruing from a business

during a long period of years. Under such a doctrine rescission could not be had even in the event of a complete failure to publish the songs.

But *In re Grant Richards* and *Barker v. Stickney* do not represent the sole current of English authority regarding the rights of a person in the position of the trustee in the present case.

In *Werderman v. Society Generale d'Electricite*, 19 Ch. D. 246, a patentee had assigned letters patent to A and B, who covenanted with him that they and their assigns would use their best endeavors to introduce the invention by granting licenses or working the patent or by selling it, and that the patentee should be entitled to 5 per cent of all net profits received by A and B, their executors or assigns, whether arising from royalties, sales, or otherwise, and that an account of profits should be rendered yearly to the patentee and his share of the profits paid to him by A and B and their executors or assigns, with a proviso that, after a sale had been made of the patent, the interest of the patentee in the profits should cease and a final account be come to. A and B had taken the assignment with a view to forming a company to work the patent. The company was formed and the patent made over to them. The patentee sued the company for an account of profits. The company demurred on the ground that there was no privity between it and the plaintiff and that the plaintiff's right, if any, was against A and B only. The Court of Appeal held that the plaintiff could sue the company for an account of profits because the stipulations of the assignment to A and B amounted to a covenant that the owners of the patent for the time being should account for and pay to the plaintiff a share of profits unless a sale within the meaning of the deed was effected, and that no person taking the patent with notice of this contract could refuse to give effect to it. . . .

But most of the decisions do not regard an agreement to pay a royalty based upon a certain percentage of the profits as creating an equitable ownership in a patent or copyright. . . .

In the case at bar there was an agreement to pay "33⅓% . . . of all revenue received from Mechanical reproductions less any expenses incurred," as well as to pay one cent upon each copy of the songs sold. Such a provision involved an implied covenant to work the copyright so far as was reasonable under all the circumstances. Under the doctrine of the Werderman Case, any purchaser of the copyrights who took with notice of such a covenant would take them subject to it, and, we believe, also subject to payment of royalties, without which the obligation to work the copyright would be futile. . . .

Courts in the United States have enforced rights resembling an equitable servitude binding on a third party who has acquired personal property from one who is under a contract to use it for a particular purpose or in a particular way. . . .

In both countries, where there has been a conveyance upon an agreement to pay the grantor sums of money based upon the earnings of property transferred, the courts have implied a covenant to render the subject-matter of the contract productive—if the property was a mine, a covenant to mine, quarry, or drill; if it consisted of a patent or copyright, a covenant to work the patent or copyright. . . .

The difference between the English and American decisions lies in the fact that our courts have allowed rescission where there has been a failure on the part of the grantee or assignee to act in accordance with his obligation to render the property conveyed productive, while the English courts have refused to allow it except for fraud. . . .

To allow rescission, the default must be such that it "destroys the essential objects of the contract," *Rosenwasser v. Blyn Shoes, Inc.*, 246 N.Y. at page 346, 159 N. E. 84, 85, or it "must be so fundamental and pervasive as to result in substantial frustration." *Buffalo Builders' Supply Co. v. Reeb*, 247 N. Y. at page 175, 159 N. E. 899, 901.

In our opinion a rescission could only be decreed in the case at bar if there had been a gross failure to work the copyrights, which has nowhere been indicated. Moreover, such a drastic remedy as rescission has often been withheld, and an equitable lien upon the subject-matter involved has been substituted even where rescission might have been allowed. This is illustrated in various cases where conveyances of land have been made in consideration of maintenance and support. Rescission has sometimes been granted because of a fundamental breach of the contract

on the part of the grantee. . . . But in other cases the relief afforded has been through the imposition of an equitable lien upon the property conveyed, enforceable at the suit of the grantor. . . .

In the case at bar, within a month after August 1, 1929, which was the date when royalty payments became due under the contract, and only about three weeks after the adjudication, the receiver called for bids and attempted to sell the copyrights. Any default in working the copyrights had not been long enough in itself to justify a rescission and the proposed sale cannot be said to have been an act that would "result in substantial frustration" of the composer's rights upon the record before us. We can see no justification for decreeing rescission unless the transfer of title to the bankrupt, "its successors and assigns," though absolute in form, be held as naught.

It may be that the songs, or some of them, are worth much more than when they were copyrighted, and it is not unlikely that a large part of their value is due to the labor and expense laid out upon them by the bankrupt as entrepreneur. The trustee in bankruptcy ought to be able to retain for the creditors these contributions to the copyrighted songs, as well as any fortuitous increment, if the right of the composers to receive royalties from working the copyrights can be reasonably safeguarded.

Whether or not the copyrights may have become burdened with equities in favor of the composers, their title is in the bankrupt estate. The assignments were absolute, and Waterson, Berlin & Snyder Company would have had no right to take out the copyrights had it not been the "proprietor" within the meaning of the Copyright Act. . . .

In our opinion there is a middle course between the extreme doctrine of *In re Grant Richards* and *Barker v. Stickney*, supra, and the cases which have allowed rescission for failure to work a patent, which we should take in the circumstances here. In view of the absolute terms of the transfer, the presence of the word "assigns" in the instrument of conveyance, and the statutory requirement that one who takes out a copyright must be the "proprietor," we see no reason to imply a covenant that Waterson, Berlin & Snyder Company must itself publish the songs. The composers cannot object if the trustee sells the copyrights. . . .

But it is a different matter to say that the sale of the copyrights should be free from all equities on behalf of the composers. In ordinary circumstances, and between the original parties, it may be that the only remedy of the composers would be an action at law for breach of the promise to pay royalties. Even between the original parties, rescission would be granted at the suit of the composers, if the publisher failed to work the copyrights in good faith, so that they might so far as possible yield royalties and thus afford the measure of compensation agreed upon. But, even where the publisher failed to work the copyrights, it could not be said that there would be actually no remedy at law, for the courts allow actions at law because of failure to observe such implied covenants. . . . The damages for the breach of such a covenant, however, would necessarily be determined by estimates that at best could be no more than speculative substitutes for the definite royalties prescribed by the contracts. Accordingly a court of equity would decree a rescission where the breach was so fundamental as to amount to frustration, because the remedy at law would be inadequate. . . . A restrictive covenant affecting the use is imposed in such cases, and rescission is granted for failure to observe it.

It is true that the royalties on the songs are definitely provided to be paid only "in the event of the publication" by Waterson, Berlin & Snyder Company, but, where the words of assignment of the musical compositions are absolute, it is unreasonable to suppose that there may be no exploitation of the songs, except by Waterson, Berlin & Snyder Company. It seems to us equally unreasonable to suppose that the trustee may sell them free from all rights of the composers and thus deprive the latter of the only means of fixing the royalties which they have been promised. In our opinion, while the copyrights may be sold by the trustee, they should be sold subject to the right of the composers to have them worked in their behalf and to be paid royalties according to the terms of the contracts. . . .

We can discover no justification for decreeing a rescission . . . because the facts here do not warrant a remedy so extreme and so disastrous to the bankrupt estate. If the purchaser at the trustee's sale should fail to work any copyright that he purchased, when it was reasonably practicable to do so, rescission doubtless might be granted at the instance of the composer in some future suit. If the trustee shall be unable within a reasonable time to obtain a purchaser who will take title subject to the terms mentioned, the District Court should direct a reassignment of any copyright thus affected upon repayment of any unearned advance royalties upon such copyright. Rescission ought to be allowed only where there is manifestly no purpose to render the copyright productive to the composer. . . .

If a right to rescind the contract may be granted because of a fundamental breach of the implied obligation to work the copyrights, surely a lien may be imposed for royalties accruing through the use of the copyright by a subvendee, for in no other way can the right of a composer to receive royalties be preserved in a case where the publisher has parted with title. . . .

The order of the District Court is reversed, and the proceeding is remanded, with directions to enter an order in accordance with the views expressed in this opinion.

NOTE _____

1. In *Harris v. Emus*, 734 F.2d 1329 (9th Cir. 1984), a distinction was drawn with the foregoing case to the extent that it was held that a mere license would not be transferable in bankruptcy.

3.30 Breach of Contract Versus Copyright Infringement

The copyright licensor may on occasion have to resort to powerful copyright infringement sanctions rather than the traditional remedies for breach of contract. However, as the *Marks* case makes clear, not every breach may be transmogrified into an infringement. Yet, as we see in the *Kamakazi* case, an erroneous interpretation as to the expiration of a licensee's rights can, on occasion, lead to extremely negative consequences.

As an interesting sidelight to the *Kamakazi* case, in *Motola v. EMI Records*, No. 82–6308–PAR, the U.S. District Court for the Central District of California held that the Stray Cats' recording of "Jeanie, Jeanie, Jeanie" by the plaintiff, with "changed and vulgarized lyrics," so mutilated the original song as to constitute copyright infringement, notwithstanding the fact that a consensual mechanical license had been obtained for the recording. Although such a license would carry with it a limited right to adapt or arrange the song, the changes actually made in this case went far beyond such limited right. Unhappily for Motola, the court subsequently vacated its partial summary judgment in his favor because he had apparently assigned his copyright prior to the date of issuance of the subject license. And not every unsatisfactory arrangement will support a claim of copyright infringement; a plaintiff's claim that a particular recording of a composition was inferior and should have been made under plaintiff's supervision was rejected in *Harms, Inc. v. Tops Music Enterprises, Inc.*, 160 F. Supp. 77 (C.D. Ca. 1958).

Edward B. Marks Music Corp. v. Foullon, 171 F.2d 905 (2d Cir. 1949)

HAND, CIRCUIT JUDGE
This is an appeal from a judgment, dismissing a complaint in two counts: the first, for infringing the copyright of a Spanish dance song, entitled "Malaguena," by an unauthorized "arrangement"; the second, for making phonograph records of the "arrangement" and selling them without filing the notice which § 25(e) of the Copyright Act, 17 U.S.C.A. § 25(e), requires of those who would avail themselves of the compulsory license given by § 1(e), 17 U.S.C.A. § 1(e). The facts, which were all undisputed, were as follows. The plaintiff's assignor became the owner of a copyright of the words and music of the song, used it to make phonograph records, and in 1931 filed the notice required by § 1(e) of an owner who so uses the

composition. The defendant, Foullon, had organized the defendant, United Masters, and was its president and one of its shareholders; and at some time before May 8, 1946 that company had made an "arrangement" of the plaintiff's song for a well-known group of performers. It is the making of this "arrangement" which is the infringement charged in the first count. On May 8 United Masters wrote to the plaintiff, declaring that it planned to make—"press"—phonograph records of the group's performance—naming them—and wished to get "copyright clearance" upon "Malaguena" and another song. The plaintiff agreed as to "Malaguena," and enclosed and executed what it called its "Mechanical License agreement," which United Masters in its turn also executed. This "License" gave to United Masters the right "to use the said musical composition . . . in the manufacture of its sound records in any form whatsoever," and in return United Masters agreed to pay two cents for each record, and to make "statements of account" and payment of the royalties as § 1(e) of the Copyright Act required. The "License" ended with the stipulation that the song should "not be used in connection with a musical medley for band or orchestra, or any other medley." United Masters had already made an acetate record of a performance by the group of its "arrangement"; and, either before or after, it coated this record with copper to form a matrix, and from the matrix made two "stampers," which after May 9 it sent to the Bard Record Company to "press": i.e., to produce those shellac records, which it delivered to United Masters. It is the manufacture of these records which is the infringement charged in the second count. United Masters never paid the agreed royalty, or filed any statements of account as it had agreed; and it is now insolvent. The judge dismissed the first count against United Masters without costs, but awarded against it on the second count a royalty of six cents a record, together with costs and attorneys' fees under § 1(e). He dismissed the complaint against Foullon without costs or allowance; and against the Bard Compny without costs but with an allowance of $500 for attorneys' fees. Only the plaintiff has appealed.

The plaintiff's position is that the "Mechanical License agreement" must be taken, not as a contract or consensual license substituted for the compulsory license of § 1(e), but only as a recognition—a mere acknowledgment, as it were—that § 1(e) and § 25(e) did in fact govern the parties' rights and obligations. Turning to these sections, the plaintiff then argues that, although they gave United Masters a compulsory license, which allowed it to make records, those were only records of the copyrighted composition as it was, and did not authorize any "arrangement." The "arrangement" for the group of performers was therefore itself an infringement under § 1(e), and the manufacture of the records was a second infringement. In both aspects United Masters exposed itself to the remedies provided in § 25 as a tort feasor. Foullon and the Bard Company were equally liable as contributors to both torts, and, since United Masters had not paid the prescribed royalties, it was also liable for triple damages under § 1(e).

Section 1(e) gives only a limited protection to musical compositions against reproduction by phonographic records; and evinces that unfriendliness towards extending the copyright of musical compositions to mechanical reproduction. . . . Thus, it still remains true that any owner, who himself so uses his composition, or who even consents to such use by others, gives a license to all at a royalty of two cents. Any one, who takes advantage of the license, must, however, make monthly statements of his sales, if the owner demands it, and monthly payments of his royalties before the twentieth day of the month after they are made. Moreover, § 1(e) allows the judge to triple the royalties against him if he defaults in his payments; and § 25(e) does the same if he does not serve upon the owner notice of his intention in advance. These are the measure of the rights and liabilities under the compulsory license. On the other hand, it needs no argument to prove that the parties may substitute for them any other rights and obligations on which they can agree; and § 25(e) so recognizes in declaring "that whenever any person, *in the absence of a license agreement*, intends to use a copyrighted musical composition" by means of records, he shall file the notice we have just mentioned. The question at bar is whether the agreement of May 9, 1946 was "a license agreement."

Clearly it was. The plaintiff had filed the necessary notice on its part, it is true; and United Masters might have made records of the song as it stood at a royalty of two cents, merely by filing its corresponding notice, if in the language of § 25(e) it had been "relying" upon the compulsory license provision of § 1(e). But it did not wish to rely upon that provision, conceivably because it thought that it needed express consent for the "arrangement" already made, and for the manufacture of the records which it "planned." It had to choose between becoming a bare infringer and thereby exposing itself to the attendant remedies and seeking "a license agreement." By its letter of May 8, it chose the second course, and it got such an agreement, when both parties executed the "Mechanical License agreement." So far as the parties chose to incorporate into this any of the terms of § 1(e), these of course became the measure of their relations like its other terms; but that was only by virtue of the incorporation. Ex proprio vigore the statute fixed nothing between them.

So viewed, the question becomes whether the "License" released United Masters from the consequences of any existing infringement in composing the "arrangement" of "Malaguena" already made, and consented to its future use in manufacturing records. Even from within the four corners of the "License" it is plain that it did both. When the licensor excepted from the licensee's rights any "use" without its consent of the song in a "medley," the only reasonable implication was that other "arrangements" did not need its consent, for a medley is an "arrangement." It is not necessary to depend upon the earlier phrase: "in any form whatsoever," which for argument we may suppose to refer only to the means of mechanical reproduction. This conclusion becomes irresistible when we consider the correspondence which went before. . . . For, when United Masters declared that it planned to "press" records for the group of performers, it was at once evident that it must have an "arrangement" of the song. When, therefore, both parties agreed to the "use" of the song in records, they could have meant only that particular "use."

Hence United Masters not only got a release for composing the "arrangement," and for any steps already taken in the manufacture of the records; but it got a consent to complete that manufacture and to sell the records. That consent also covered the Bard Company's share in the manufacture and its delivery of the finished product to United Masters for sale. The only liability at any time, or of any one, was that of United Masters, and that was contractual. Its failure to fulfill its obligations made it liable to triple damages because of the incorporation of § 1(e) in the "License"; and would have authorized the plaintiff to repudiate the "License." Had the plaintiff done so, any later use of the "arrangement" would have been an infringement; but that would not have made an infringement out of anything done while the "License" was in force.

Obviously the Bard Company is not liable for the royalties which United Masters agreed to pay, for it was not a party to the "License." If it is to be held at all, it must be because the "License" was limited to records wholly made by United Masters; and that would be quite absurd, for the plaintiff had neither information as to who was to make them, or any interest in it. . . .

Judgment affirmed.

Kamakazi Music Corp. v. Robbins Music Corp., 522 F. Supp. 125 (S.D.N.Y. 1981)

SWEET, DISTRICT JUDGE
This is an action in which injunctive relief and damages were sought for copyright infringement, interference with contractual rights and related violations of state law. The plaintiff Kamakazi Music Corp. ("Kamakazi") has moved pursuant to 9 U.S.C. § 9 (1970) to confirm certain awards of an arbitrator, and defendant Robbins Music Corp. ("Robbins") has cross-moved to vacate those awards. . . .

This arduous litigation arises out of Robbins' printing and selling of the compositions of plaintiff Barry Manilow ("Manilow"), a well-known songwriter and recording artist, in so-called personality folios and other formats allegedly in violation of copyrights owned by Kamakazi and in violation of the interests of Manilow and Warner. The fervor of the litigants is understandable in view of the large profits at stake in the high-

volume commerce of popular music and of these copyrights in particular. Manilow is the sole stockholder in Kamakazi. Kamakazi, a New York corporation, apparently is the duly registered owner of the copyrights in musical compositions written in whole or in part by Manilow, who receives percentage royalties from Kamakazi based on sales or license fees. In November, 1976 Kamakazi and Robbins entered into a written license agreement (the "Agreement") with respect to the publication of certain Manilow compositions by Robbins, which provided that Robbins would have the exclusive right to publish and sell those compositions in various forms, including personality folios—printed publications which feature musical compositions by a particular artist, in this case, Manilow. After the alleged expiration of the Agreement, plaintiff Warner was secured by Kamakazi to produce and sell its Manilow compositions and this dispute arose.

Plaintiffs alleged that by the terms of the Agreement, Robbins' right to print and manufacture copies of the compositions in the form of Manilow personality folios would "immediately cease" on December 31, 1979, and, given appropriate notice by Robbins, the right to sell off these folios would continue until July 31, 1980. Robbins alleged that pursuant to paragraph 6 of the Agreement, it had the right to print and manufacture the personality folios until December 31, 1980, and to sell off these folios thereafter. . . . [However, certain internal Robbins memoranda produced during discovery indicated an awareness of the correctness of Kamakazi's position.]

The complaint was filed on May 19, 1980. Three days later Kamakazi first sought the intercession of the court, seeking a preliminary injunction to bar Robbins from manufacturing and selling copies of the personality folios during the pendency of the action. Robbins cross-moved for dismissal for lack of jurisdiction or alternatively, pursuant to 9 U.S.C. § 3, for a stay of all further proceedings pending arbitration, as provided for in the Agreement. A hearing was held and by opinion dated June 5, 1980, the court concluded that the action arose under the copyright laws, and so denied Robbins' motion to dismiss for lack of jurisdiction, but granted Robbins' alternative motion to stay proceedings pending arbitration. . . .

Upon a record compiled over some eight months of litigation before the American Arbitration Association ("AAA"), appearing in over 2,000 pages of transcript, the arbitrator rendered a decision on March 6, 1981 (the "March Award"). . . . In essence, the arbitrator vindicated Kamakazi's interpretation of the Agreement and the rights of Robbins upon its termination, concluding that Robbins' printing and sale of Manilow personality folios as well as individual sheet music and individual editions after December 31, 1979 was without license and therefore constituted copyright infringements. Robbins' activities were found to have infringed twenty-five separate copyrights of Kamakazi's comprising twelve individual works of Manilow and thirteen so-called compilations or derivative works. Robbins' printing and sale of mixed folios was found to be under license. Acting upon Kamakazi's election of statutory "in lieu" damages under the Copyright Act, 17 U.S.C. § 504(c), the arbitrator found that the Robbins infringements were "willful," and concluded that a "just" recovery for Kamakazi would be $10,000 for all of the multiple infringements of each copyright, for a total of $250,000, plus costs and reasonable attorney's fees pursuant to 17 U.S.C. § 505. Kamakazi was awarded $250,000 damages in accordance with the foregoing findings, as well as appropriate permanent injunctive relief. Robbins was taxed costs and fees. Robbins' counterclaim, alleging damages to its exclusive sell-off rights under the Agreement, was dismissed. The award of attorney's fees was postponed pending receipt of an affidavit of legal services. On April 7, 1981, in a supplemental award of the arbitrator (the "April Award"). . . . Robbins was assessed $50,127.72 in legal fees, to be divided between present and previous counsel for Kamakazi.

The instant motions, respectively to confirm and to vacate the awards, and Robbins' motion to dismiss the interference with contract cause of Kamakazi and Warner, followed. . . . It is Robbins' broadside assault on the March and April Awards (collectively the "Awards"), pursuant to 9 U.S.C. § 10, which has required this opinion.

Capsulized, Robbins' position is that pursuant to this court's opinion of June 5, 1980 and the arbitration clause of the Agreement, the arbitrator was given, and accepted, jurisdiction to determine whether or not Robbins' publication and sale of the Manilow compositions in various forms was under license—a matter of interpretation of the Agreement between it and Kamakazi. This, it is submitted, simply involves the application of principles of contract law and, if need be, consideration of evidence as to damages—all under the law of New York. In springing from his interpretation (essentially favorable to Kamakazi) of the Agreement, to the application of the federal copyright laws to find willful infringements (after presuming the validity of the allegedly infringed copyrights) and to the award of statutory damages and attorney's fees, Robbins asserts, the arbitrator exceeded his jurisdiction, violated public policy, and manifestly disregarded the law. Thus, it is argued, pursuant to 9 U.S.C. § 10(d) and the case law, the awards must be vacated. . . .

Kamakazi, in turn, asserts that the arbitrator acted properly under the circumstances and the law to resolve the entire dispute between it and Robbins which was before him. In this regard Kamakazi presses that it was Robbins which successfully urged, over Kamakazi's objection, that the dispute be relegated to arbitration; that, contrary to Robbins' professed view, the nature and scope of the arbitration proceedings was made clear from the outset, when Kamakazi, in its demand for arbitration, characterized the dispute being submitted as "violations by Robbins Music Corporation of copyrights owned by Kamakazi Music Corp." and constantly thereafter; and that it was Robbins, again over Kamakazi's objection, which prevailed in its insistence that the issue of damages—which ultimately occupied a major part of the proceedings—be heard by the arbitrator. . . . It is suggested by Kamakazi that Robbins got everything it sought before and during arbitration except for a favorable result.

On the entire record before the court, which includes only small segments of the arbitration transcript attached as exhibits to the parties' instant motion papers, Kamakazi's review of events appears to have merit. I conclude as well that Kamakazi's position is basically supported by the law. . . .

The two overriding principles which are posed in this action apparently conflict. First, there is a strong federal policy in favor of the settlement of private disputes by consensual arbitration. This is expressed in several ways, including the mandatory language of 9 U.S.C. § 3 providing for stay of federal court proceedings and referral to arbitration of issues or actions covered by arbitration agreement, the reluctance of federal courts to question the alleged errors of fact or law if the findings and conclusions of the arbitrator are "barely colorable," . . . and the extremely narrow reading given to the Arbitration Act's authorization to vacate awards where the arbitrator exceeded his powers. . . .

On the other hand, actions arising under certain federal statutes which provide for exclusive federal court jurisdiction, including antitrust, securities and patent, even if between private parties, are considered to be of public concern, and thus, as a matter of public policy, generally have been held to be not justiciable in state court, or referable to arbitration notwithstanding an agreement between the parties to arbitrate. . . .

At least as far as patent and copyright law are concerned, often, as here, it is not clear whether an action—typically involving a license agreement and possible infringement or royalties due—"arises under" the relevant statute or is essentially a contract dispute which "involves" a patent or copyright. Both the formal allegations and the substance of the complaint are considered. . . . In this court's opinion of June 5, 1980, it was determined that this action arises under the copyright law, in that the complaint is directed against an offending use, and refers to the license agreement only by way of anticipatory replication. . . . Such a determination establishes the court's jurisdiction over the subject matter under 28 U.S.C. § 1338, as it did in this case, defeating Robbins' motion to dismiss, and also, traditionally, precludes arbitration of the dispute, since the subject matter of the dispute has been thus cast as belonging to the exclusive competence of the federal courts. . . .

However, notwithstanding the public policy concerns, arbitration clauses commonly are enforced in trademark, patent and copyright infringement cases, as was the arbitration claim in the Agreement in this case. Various issues arising in a dispute involving a trademark, patent or copyright may be arbitrated with the exclusion, perhaps, of the validity of the federally protected interest itself. . . . Here, of course, the court previously has determined that this action arises under the Copyright Act. However, there appears to be no reason why the arbitrator, having been presented with the dispute over the Agreement, which was basic to this action, lacked the power, once he had interpreted the Agreement and concluded that certain of Robbins' activities with respect to Manilow compositions were without license, to find the infringements had occurred, and to assess damages and attorney's fees with reference to the Copyright Act. This is not a case in which the question of infringement must be decided as a prerequisite to the determination of the meaning of a contract. . . . Indeed, the opposite is true here, and no authority has been presented which, as a jurisdictional matter, would preclude the arbitrator from making the findings he did with reference to the Copyright Act, as an extension of his primary task in this case. . . .

While an arbitrator, even in this context, is commonly thought to lack jurisdiction to determine the validity of a copyright, . . . here the arbitrator did not make the determination of validity. Indeed, the one of Robbins' objections to the conduct of the arbitration proceedings which is well taken is that the arbitrator apparently accepted into evidence certain certificates of registration as prima facie evidence of validity of the copyrights, a prerequisite to the establishment of infringement . . . and then refused to hear rebuttal evidence on the issue of validity. . . .

Nevertheless, Robbins claims, in effect, that the matter of interpreting the Agreement alone was presented to arbitration . . . and that it was surprised to its prejudice by the awards which included determinations under the Copyright Act. I conclude that the arbitration clause is broad enough to include the infringement claims made by Kamakazi. . . . Furthermore, I conclude that Robbins is estopped from this challenge to the awards. . . . Although Robbins did not prevail on its motion to dismiss, it was Robbins which, aware of the nature of Kamakazi's chief claim, argued successfully for a stay in favor of arbitration pursuant to the Agreement. On the record before the court, there is no basis for a conclusion that the arbitrator's invocation of the copyright law was contrary to the reasonable expectations of the parties. . . .

In any event, the facts at bar support the conclusion that, beyond having been party to the Agreement containing the arbitration clause pertaining to all future disputes, Robbins agreed, by virtue of the position it took before this court last year, to arbitrate this *existing* dispute, with its known copyright infringement element. Thus any public policy concern about arbitrating such matters is vitiated. . . .

There is no apparent reason why Robbins could have precluded the court from consideration of statutory damages in this case had the arbitrator assigned contract damages, for regardless of how the action is labeled, infringement unmistakably was the injury to be addressed upon an interpretation of the Agreement favorable to Kamakazi. . . . There was nothing surprising or improper about the arbitrator's so doing in these circumstances, upon Kamakazi's election of remedies. Indeed, there is nothing in the record before the court by way of response to Kamakazi's election or anything else, to indicate that at any time during the lengthy proceedings preceding the March Award Robbins raised an objection to the clearly expressed potential scope of the proceedings as far as infringement and the assessment of damages are concerned, which apparently differed substantially from its own view of the limitation of the proceeding. . . .

Thus, assuming for the moment the validity which Kamakazi asserts, the infringements are, in effect, established since the only issue with respect to copying was whether or not Robbins' activities were under license. Robbins' weak challenge in that regard has run up against the very strict standard for vacating such findings of an arbitrator, and failed. Similarly, given the arbitrator's findings that Robbins "was aware of the time limitation [with regard to personality folios, contained in the agreement], and [Kamakazi's] intention to rely thereon, that Robbins did not comply with the requirements for gaining further sell-off

rights, and that [Robbins] did sell [Kamakazi's] copyrighted works after December 31, 1979 without license," there is adequate basis for the finding of willfulness. . . . Robbins has suggested no reason why, given this foundation and all of the evidence in the arbitration record, an award of statutory in-lieu damages would be inappropriate . . . or why the award of $10,000 per infringement is unreasonable, no less subject to vacation. Indeed, Robbins has raised no such challenge.

Beyond the arguments addressed to the arbitrator's lack of power and his disregard of the intentions of the parties as to the scope of arbitration, Robbins raises a number of challenges to the findings and conclusions which can be disposed of summarily. . . .

As recounted above, whether or not he had the power to do so under these circumstances, the arbitrator made no finding concerning the validity of the copyrights, a prerequisite to a finding of infringement. It thus remains for this court to pass on copyright validity before confirmation of the awards can be considered. I deem Kamakazi's submissions in this regard, including copies of copyright certificates of registration submitted as Exhibit 7 to its reply affidavit, a motion for summary judgment on the issue of validity. Although the challenge to validity thus far does not raise a genuine issue of material fact, since Robbins was cut off before the arbitrator on this issue, such a motion cannot be granted on the present record. . . .

Other than on issue of the validity of the twenty-five copyrights comprising, according to the arbitrator, "twelve individual works and thirteen compilations or derivative works," which were found to have been infringed, there is no basis upon which to upset or tamper with the awards.

The awards of the arbitrator are thus held in abeyance pending this court's determination of the issue of the validity of twenty-five copyrights found to have been infringed. . . .

NOTES ⎯⎯⎯⎯⎯⎯⎯⎯⎯⎯⎯⎯

1. The foregoing district court opinion was affirmed by the Second Circuit. See 648 F.2d 228 (2d Cir.

1982). The court of appeals based its holding primarily on the arbitration issues discussed in the district court's opinion.

2. For a discussion of this case, see Biederman, "Breach of Contract or Copyright Infringement: Walking the Line," 1 *Journal of Copyright, Entertainment and Sports Law* 136 (1982).

3. The arbitration clause at issue in the *Kamakazi* case provided as follows: "[A]ny controversy or claim arising out of, or relating to this agreement or the subject matter thereof, or the breach hereof shall be settled by arbitration in the City of New York in accordance with the rules then obtaining of the American Arbitration Association, and judgment upon the award rendered may be entered in any Court having jurisdiction thereof."

Chapter 4

SOUND RECORDINGS

4.00   Development of the Industry

Thomas Edison could never have foreseen the magnitude and complexity of the record business as it has developed in this century. Not only has the content of the records changed—from classical and vaudeville to heavy metal and new age music—but technology has changed the "discs" from the piano roll, to the 78 rpm record, to the 45 rpm, to the 33⅓ rpm, to the compact disc. Changes in music and technology have created challenges and new issues to the legal and business side of the record industry, especially in the past 30 years.

At the turn of the century, the record industry, dominated by two companies, the Victor Talking Machine Company (later to become RCA) and the Columbia Graphophone Company, found an enormous market for spoken words and classical and vaudeville show tunes. Although the growth of the record industry was later tempered by the advent of radio in the 1920s and television in the late 1940s, by 1950, U.S. record sales were approximately $189 million. In 1985, U.S. record sales totaled $4.4 billion based on sales of 653 million units sold domesti-

cally. The industry realized unprecedented growth in the 1950s through 1978. Suddenly, the record business suffered an unprecedented decline in sales and profits, partially attributable to new competition for entertainment dollars from video games, videocassettes, and cable. That recession lasted approximately six years. Beginning in 1984, the record business enjoyed increased sales and profits, largely from sales of its "superstar" vocalists such as Michael Jackson, Bruce Springsteen, and Prince.

In the late 1940s, magnetic recording tape and modern tape recorders were introduced. The improved sound reproduction that resulted made it easier for independent record companies and producers to record "hit" records. The high-fidelity long-playing phonograph record was introduced by Columbia in 1948, which changed the format of records from 78 revolutions per minute to 33⅓ rpm.

Thus began what was known as the "battle of the speeds" between the two record giants of the time, RCA and Columbia. RCA released the 45 rpm record to compete with Columbia's LP. These vinyl formats remained the dominant configuration formats for the record industry until the 1970s and then the 1980s, when two additional formats emerged to compete and possibly replace vinyl recordings: cassettes and compact discs (CDs).

The record sales figures released in 1985 by the Recording Industry Association of America (RIAA) indicate the present state of the industry. The statistics clearly point to the continued decline of LP sales, which dropped 18 percent between 1984 and 1985, from 204 million to 167 million. In 1985, cassette tape sales continued to lead the record industry, selling over 339 million units in 1985, as compared with 332 million units in 1984. Compact discs registered sales of 22,600,000 units in 1985, up substantially from 5,800,000 units in 1984. A survey of records sold in 44 countries currently shows sales in excess of $12 billion, based on worldwide sales of 800 million singles, 850 million LPs, and 660 million tapes.

With the advent of rock-and-roll in the mid-1950s, the record industry enjoyed double-digit growth and a proliferation of small independent record labels that were able to record and market both rhythm-and-blues music and rock-and-roll music. Such successful independent labels included Sam Phillips's Sun Records; Chess Records, which recorded Muddy Waters, Howlin' Wolf, and Chuck Berry; and Atlantic Records in New York, which was a primary force in the recording of rhythm and blues in the 1950s. Two additional developments affected the business side of music: (1) Beginning with the Columbia Record Club in 1955, major record labels began alternate distribution of their records through mail order, and (2) in 1957 the first stereo record was released.

The modern-day record business may have been launched with the coming of the Beatles to America in 1962. For the next 15 years the record industry experienced a great growth period.

One trend between 1962 and 1986 was a significant consolidation of the record business. Fewer companies controlled a larger portion of the record business, both domestically and internationally. In arguing against the proposed merger of Warner Communications and Polygram Records on antitrust grounds, the Federal Trade Commission noted that the top four U.S. record distributors owned 67 percent of the market (*FTC v. Warner Communications*, 742 F.2d 1156 [9th Cir. 1984]).

Increasingly, corporate giants in the record business control the majority of the market through releases on their own labels and affiliate labels and through use of their distribution systems. Four major companies—CBS, Warner Communications (consisting of Warner Bros. Records, Elektra/Asylum Records, and Atlantic Records), PolyGram, and BMG (the Bertelsmann Music Group, formerly RCA Records)—control approximately 70 percent of records distributed in the United States. Other major record companies include Capitol-EMI, MCA, A&M, Motown, and Arista. Small independent record labels continue to exist, especially in the United Kingdom and in segments of music that have not been developed by the major labels, such as new-age music and electronic music.

As in the motion picture industry, the major motivating factor in consolidation of the industry is distribution. Into the 1970s the record industry relied on a series of independent record distributors that acted as intermediaries between record manufacturers and retailers. In the 1960s the major record labels began their own branch distribution systems, which were increasingly utilized by smaller independent labels that either merged with or entered into exclusive long-term distribution agreements with the major record label distributors. Such was the case when the "independent" labels in Arista, Motown, and A&M left independent distribution and agreed to be distributed by a major record label. The consolidation trend has continued in recent years—for example, the "new age" label, Windham Hill Records, entered into a distribution agreement with A&M Records, and the heavy metal label, Enigma, entered into distribution with Capitol.

Music and movies have always enjoyed a certain amount of collaborative success, from the early recordings of vaudeville shows to the phenomenal success of such soundtrack records as "My Fair Lady" and "The Sound of Music." The 1980s brought these two industries together on an unprecedented level, as filmmakers found use of diverse popular music in soundtracks could result in success of both the movie and the soundtrack record. The success of "Saturday Night Fever" began this trend of popular music soundtracks. In May 1986, the Billboard Top 200 Top Pop Albums chart listed ten soundtrack records.

Another development in the record business has been the growth of the music video, particularly as a promotion tool for the sale of records through MTV, VH-1, and other video outlets. In addition, extended-length videos, concert videos, and video compilations have established new sources of revenue and deals for the record industry through videocassettes, video discs, and pay and cable television licensing.

4.01 How the Business Works

The "break-even" point on records is high and reflects the high-risk nature of the industry. According to figures released by the RIAA, in the 1980s less than one record out of five released sells enough copies to recoup its recording costs. For a major record company, the break-even point for record sales for an album is approximately 250,000 copies. As in other segments of the entertainment industry, the record company relies on

one hit album, such as Michael Jackson's "Thriller," to pay for the majority of unsuccessful albums.

Records, cassettes, and compact discs are relatively inexpensive to manufacture. An LP or cassette, when reproduced in quantity, can be made for less than $1 per copy, with the wholesale price between $4 and $5 and a retail price usually between $7 and $9 (as of 1986). A compact disc can be manufactured for less than $5, wholesaled for approximately $10, and sold at retail for $15 (again, as of 1986). The production costs, rather than manufacturing costs, therefore, account for the great costs and risks. In addition, the perceived need to produce a video for new songs has greatly increased overall costs.

As technology has increased the sophistication of recording techniques to multitrack recording and digital recording, the costs of making a technically satisfactory record and CD today can be significant. It is not uncommon for a group to spend between $50,000 and $200,000 recording an LP. When the promotional advertising and manufacturing costs are added to these expenses, a record label can easily have invested $500,000 in a record before selling any copies.

Once recorded, the recording can be released in three basic formats: conventional records (45, EP [extended play] or LP), cassette, and compact disc. The 45, the initial medium of rock-and-roll in the 1950s and 1960s, is no longer the popular or profitable format it once was and is generally released only as a promotional tool for the record labels. Likewise, the phonograph record is decreasing in sales and popularity, while sales of cassettes and compact discs are increasing.

A unique element of the record industry is the distinction between a "distributed" record and a "sold" record. Usually, the arrangement between record retailers and wholesalers allows return of some or, in many cases, all of the unsold records delivered to the retailer. The potential "returned" record causes great concern in contracts both between retailer and record wholesaler, and between record company and artist.

One of the most challenging and difficult aspects of the record industry is the promotion of records. Traditionally, records were promoted through radio airplay; however, "tightening" of radio play lists beginning in the 1970s made such promotion efforts extremely difficult. Charges of "payola" have been periodically leveled against the record labels and radio stations, initially in congressional investigations in 1959 and 1960 (including the subsequent indictment of Allen Freed, the "father of rock-and-roll") and most recently in a congressional investigation and grand jury investigation into the hiring of independent record promoters and their role with radio stations and radio airplay.

As radio airplay has become increasingly difficult to obtain, record companies and artists have sought alternative means of promoting and ultimately selling records. Live performance tours have been a consistent means of promoting records. Beginning in the early 1980s, the advent of MTV and music videos brought an entirely new avenue of record promotions to the industry. As MTV broke new talent and promoted records, virtually all major record artists and labels began to produce music videotapes, primarily for promotion purposes, with ultimate sights on an audiovideo combination as a new medium in a videocassette or laser disc.

The legal and business considerations for music videos have raised several issues. For example, who pays the costs of the video production (in many cases, $100,000 or more)? If the record company advances these costs, are they recoupable from subsequent sales? Who owns the video? Who has artistic control over the video? How are profits divided if the video is sold in a cassette or disc format?

Just as technology has given the record industry significant advances which have helped sales (the advent of stereo, high fidelity, video, and compact discs), it has also been the cause of significant problems and loss of revenue. Record counterfeiting has been a constant problem. Efforts by the RIAA to combat counterfeiting have resulted in civil and criminal lawsuits. Estimates are that in 1982 the music industry lost $350 million from commercial counterfeiting, piracy, and bootlegging.

A more costly problem has been home taping of music on blank cassettes, a practice that, according to the labels, has been the cause of billions of dollars in lost sales. To date, the record industry has been unable to achieve passage of legislation to combat home taping, primarily through a proposed levy on tape and/or the hardware (tape machines). The record industry was successful in changing the first sale doctrine of section 109 (a) of the Copyright Act in 1984 by a record rental amendment which basically makes it unlawful to rent records. The record industry estimates that it loses $1 billion a year to home taping. Studies commissioned by the RIAA conclude that 84 percent of all blank tapes purchased in the United States are used to record copyrighted music and that the equivalent of 564 million albums are taped in the United States each year.

4.02   Principal Types of Agreements

The process by which music gets put on a record often involves several transactions. The rights and interests of the songwriters, performers, record companies, producers, distributors, and, at times, third parties must all be accommodated. The most common agreements in use in the record industry are the artist agreement, the producer agreement, the mechanical license agreement, the synchronization agreement, the master purchase agreement, the master license agreement, the custom label agreement, the pressing and distribution agreement, and the special products agreement.

4.02–1 Artist Recording Agreement

The most common agreement is the artist recording agreement between the recording artist(s) and the record company for the recording and distribution of records. The increasing sophistication of the business in recent years and the increasing potential income from the sale of recordings have caused the agreement to become significantly more complex. In the 1920s singer Bessie Smith signed a recording contract that was less than one page. Today, a first draft of an artist recording agreement for a major label may be in excess of 70 single-spaced pages.

Typically, a record label will want to sign the artist to an exclusive recording agreement that has a short initial term with a series of options exercisable by the label to extend the term of the agreement with the delivery of additional masters. This initial term-plus-options arrangement was traditionally based on a standard one-year agreement plus four one-year options available to the record company. Now, more typically, it is the initial period plus option periods that are based on the completion of delivery of certain master recordings under the contract.

From the perspective of the record labels the option arrangement gives the label the maximum amount of flexibility, with minimum risks, as the label will exercise the option to renew only in the event the artist succeeds during the initial period. The artist typically will seek a longer fixed period during the initial term and fewer option periods.

Modern recording agreements are almost always "exclusive" to the extent that the artists agree to render their exclusive recording services during the term of the agreement for the label. Exceptions, which may be reflected in the agreement, include recording work as a "sideman" on another artist's recording session and performances on soundtrack records. An additional exclusive provision is what is known as the "rerecording restriction," which restricts, usually for a period of three to five years, the rerecording of compositions recorded during the term of the agreement after the contract has expired and the artist has moved on to another record company.

Payment to the artist is usually in the form of advances against royalties. Advances may be paid directly to the artist for living expenses or be paid as incentives to sign the agreement, for recording costs to make the records under the contract, for video production costs, or for tour support. In most recording agreements, these various advances to the artist are then recouped against the artist's royalties, which are usually based on the percentage of the total wholesale or retail revenues of the artist's records sold.
records sold.

The artist's royalties (typically beginning at the rate of 10 percent of the suggested retail price or 20 percent of the wholesale price) are reduced by subsequent language in the record contract, including reductions for the record packaging and free records given away by the record label; lower royalties for foreign records, singles, PX and record club sales, mid-priced or "cutout" records; and reserves for returns of records to the label. Royalties for "superstar" artists are in the range of 14 to 18 percent of the retail price. In virtually all modern contracts, record royalties escalate both on a sales threshold and on subsequent records of the artist. The royalty may be "all-in," which means that the artist has to pay the producer the producer's royalty.

From the artist's perspective, an essential element of the contract is the label's commitment to record and to release the record. Record labels will generally agree to record a minimum number of sides during each contract period; however, they are reluctant to guarantee the release of a record. Additionally, the artist will wish to retain some creative control over the record, including selection of material, choice of producer and studio, album artwork, advertising materials, and test pressings. In recent years, record labels have been increasingly hesitant to grant such creative control to clients and instead have required artists to deliver "commercially and technically" satisfactory master recordings. This provision gives the label the greatest amount of flexibility in controlling the finished product.

An additional consideration requiring negotiation in recording agreements is the territory. Record labels will normally request the world (or universe). An artist with significant bargaining leverage may wish to restrict the territory to one or more countries, allowing that artist to enter into foreign record agreements without the consent or participation of the original record company. In addition, the modern recording agreement will usually include some provision for video. This includes provisions for promotional videoclips (including grants of rights and determination of ownership and payment) and also provisions for distribution of compilation promotional videoclips or full-length videos of the artist, thus synchronizing the recording made under the agreement.

Unlike many other segments of the entertainment industry, the record company often signs an agreement with several individuals doing business as a group. This factor creates unique problems due to the reality that many groups disband, fire members, and hire new members. In addition, individuals within the group may pursue simultaneous solo careers. Accordingly, the recording contract will contain "leaving member" clauses, which will usually give the label options to renew the agreement if members leave the group. This clause is discussed in *Forrest R.B. Enterprises, Inc. v. Capricorn Records, Inc.* (see Section 4.40).

The recording agreement will also attempt to limit the amount of mechanical royalties to be paid by the record label through what is known as a controlled composition clause. This clause reduces the mechanical royalties required to be paid by the record label to the music publisher for compositions appearing on the artist's album, and "controlled" by the artist, to a rate less than the statutory rate set by the Copyright Royalty Tribunal under copyright law.

Needless to say, a significant amount of negotiation between the artist's attorney and the record label executive (usually the in-house counsel or vice-president of legal business affairs) precedes the signing of a record label contract. In turn, significant modifications of the record label's initial contract draft may be negotiated, but such negotiation is largely dependent on the bargaining leverage of the artist.

NOTE

1. For a more detailed discussion and analysis of the negotiation of recording agreements, review the following articles:

(a) Cooper, "Recording Contract Negotiation: A Perspective," 1 *Loyola Entertainment Law Journal* 43 (1981).

(b) Phillips and Graham, "New Developments in Recording Contract Negotiations: Reflections of a Changing Economic Profile," *Entertainment and Sports Lawyer* 1 (Winter 1984).

(c) Sobel, "Record Artist Royalty Calculation: Why Gold Records Don't Always Yield Fortunes," *Entertainment Law Reporter*, vol. 6, no. 12, May 1985.

4.02–2 Producer Agreement

The agreement between either the record label or artist and the record producer usually provides for the producer's commitment to complete production on an album project, with the possible option for a subsequent LP. The producer is paid advances against royalties (usually 2 to 5 percent of retail).

4.02–3 Mechanical License Agreement

A short agreement between the record label and music publisher grants the label a license to use the musical composition in record or tape format on payment of an agreed-upon royalty.

4.02–4 Synchronization License

A synchronization license is an agreement between a motion picture producer and the record label for synchronization rights of master recordings for use in a motion picture (as distinct from a soundtrack album agreement between the film studio and the label).

4.02–5 Master Purchase Agreement

An agreement to sell master recordings usually includes warranties by the seller upon payment of a flat fee and/or payment or royalties on subsequent sales.

4.02–6 Master License Agreement

In a master license agreement, the owner of master recordings grants to a third party a license for a specified term, territory, and use. There is usually a provision for an advance against royalties.

4.02–7 Custom Label Agreement; Pressing and Distribution Agreement

Two of the common agreements between a small independent record company and a major record label are the custom label agreement and the pressing and distribution (P&D) agreement. The P&D agreement provides for the pressing and distribution of records by the major label. In the case of a custom record label (as has often been created for "superstar" talent), the major label will produce, release, and promote several recordings of the custom label, generally with payment of royalties to the custom label.

4.02–8 Special Products Agreements

Special products agreements generally cover special uses of masters, including mail order complications, such as those marketed through mail order by K-Tel and record club sales.

NOTE _____

1. For additional readings and resources, see:

(a) S. Chapple and R. Garofalo, *Rock n' Roll Is Here to Pay* (Chicago: Nelson-Hall, 1977). A comprehensive though dated overview of the history from an antilabel perspective.

(b) D. Biederman, Chairman, *Legal and Business Problems of the Music Industry* (New York: Practicing Law Institute, 1980). A collection of articles and forms on records, music publishing, music in films and video, and tax considerations. Somewhat dated; however, it contains several articles not readily available elsewhere.

(c) G. Burton, *A Musician's Guide to the Road* (New York: Billboard, 1981). A practical guide to training and organizing a successful music tour written by a professional musician.

(d) C. Davis and J. Willwerth, *Clive: Inside the Record Business* (New York: Wm. Morrow & Co., 1975). The autobiography of one of the most successful and controversial record executives from the mid-1960s on. A good "inside" look at how a record company operates.

(e) B. Monaco and J. Riorean, *A Platinum Rainbow* (Sherman Oaks, Calif.: Swordsman Press, 1980). A realistic and informative commentary on how to succeed in the music business.

(f) E. Pierson, Chairman, *Legal and Business As-*

pects of the Music Industry (Chicago: American Bar Association, Yearly Publications). Materials from yearly programs on the music industry, focusing on the negotiation of recording contracts, entertainment servicemarks, copyright, music producer agreements, and other related topics.

(g) S. Shemel and M. Krasilovsky, *This Business of Music*, 5th ed. (New York: Billboard Publications, 1985). Generally considered the best all-around introduction to the worldwide music business. Concise discussions of such arcana as performing rights societies and international music publishing, as well as an overview of more mainstream topics.

(h) M. Silfen, Chairman, *Counselling Clients in the Entertainment Industry* (New York: Practicing Law Institute, Yearly Publications). An excellent source of material, specifically current contracts used in the record industry and recording agreements. The material is revised yearly.

(i) G. Stokes, *Star-Making Machinery: The Odyssey of an Album* (New York: The Bobbs-Merrill Co., 1975). How the "hype" works. A sort of "Pilgrim's Progress" of the rock business, tracing the progress of an album by "Commander Cody and His Lost Planet Airmen."

4.10   Initial Contract Considerations: "We'll Worry About That Down the Line"

Parties deal casually with each other in music situations as well as most other commercial ventures. The presumption is that things will work out and that an agreement can easily be forged when the time comes. Events do not always transpire as forecast, however, and the parties can later fall into dispute. Whether a contract was in fact formed by free and loose dealing is the question. In *Sound Doctor Recording Studio v. Conn*, the parties recorded music through joint efforts but never agreed as to the precise rights each party was to have. The casual method of doing business proved fatal to the studio's efforts to exact payment for its efforts. In *Long v. Decca Records*, the plaintiffs entered a contract they later regretted. Their claims that the defendants misrepresented what was to be done with the recordings received no sympathy from the court. If

limitations as to production quality or later use are to be imposed, such should be stipulated in the original agreement.

Sound Doctor Recording Studio, Inc. v. Conn, 391 So.2d 520 (La. 1980)

DOMENGEAUX, JUDGE

. . . In early to mid-1977, Conn and others were asked by Vernon to record musical work at Sound Doctor Recording Studio. Conn (and presumably the others) acceded to this request. Shortly before recording was to begin, Conn asked Vernon "What's in this for you?" or words to that effect, to which Vernon replied "We'll worry about that down the line." After this brief and inconclusive rapport, Conn recorded approximately twelve tunes at the recording studio. These tunes were recorded on a "master tape." At no time did Conn and Vernon engage in any verbal or written agreement regarding any recompense to Vernon or Sound Doctor for recording time given to Conn.

Subsequent to the recording session, Conn participated in a "musical showcase"—an exhibition of local musical talent arranged by Vernon— which was designed to appeal to Mr. Judd Phillips, a representative of Mercury-Phonograph [sic], a recording company, for whose benefit the exhibition was staged.

Later, in June or July of 1977, Vernon and Conn traveled to New York City for the purpose of discussing with Ms. Helena Bruno of Chapel [sic] Music, a large publishing company, the possibility of publishing some of Conn's music. Shortly thereafter, while still in New York, Conn inexplicably severed his business relationship with Vernon and Sound Doctor Recording Studio.

Sound Doctor has retained possession of the "master tape" on which are recorded Conn's tunes but it has never been able to secure Conn's oral or written permission to market, sell, or distribute the tunes recorded on this tape.

Nothing has ever been paid to Sound Doctor by Conn for its efforts to record and promote Conn's music. For this reason, Sound Doctor instituted suit on open account hoping to recover for 66 hours of uncompensated studio time with an alleged value of $30.00 per hour (or $1,980.00), $1,000.00 expended on the fruitless trip to New York, and $85.00 which represented the cost of the tape.

The trial court correctly held that Sound Doctor was not entitled to recover on open account. Neither party has appealed from that determination. We believe, however, that the lower court incorrectly held that Sound Doctor was entitled under La.C.C.P. Art. 862, to market, sell, and distribute the musical tunes of Steve Conn. . . .

The trial court was of the opinion that the relief accorded plaintiff was justified under the relevant facts that were properly proven at the trial. We are left wondering, by the court's brief reasons for judgment, which relevant facts were properly proven and which were not. We are also left wondering which law, or which theory of recovery entitles plaintiff to market, sell, and distribute the songs of another, and to recoup an unspecified amount of expenses as well as other unknown benefits "to which it might be entitled." . . .

The record establishes that neither party is entitled to relief. La.C.C. Art. 1779 lists four requisites which are necessary to the validity of every contract: (1) parties legally capable of contracting; (2) their consent legally given; (3) a certain object which forms the matter of agreement; and (4) a lawful purpose. Sound Doctor is not entitled to recover under the theory of implied contract because two essential elements are lacking. From the facts surrounding the relationship between Sound Doctor and Steve Conn, we conclude: (1) there was no express or implied consent to contract, and (2) there was no certain object which formed the matter of agreement.

The most that can be said of the relationship existing between Sound Doctor and Steve Conn is that Conn recorded songs at Sound Doctor Recording Studio at the continued insistence of Robert Vernon; that Conn participated in a "musical showcase" arranged by Vernon; and that Conn traveled to New York, at Vernon's expense, to meet with a representative of a publishing company. We do not think these facts, especially when considered in the light of other facts duly established by testimony (discussed hereinafter), are sufficient to support a finding of an implied contract.

Those other facts demonstrate a complete lack of mutuality, or meeting of the minds. Although both parties may have assumed that Conn's songs might eventually be sold as a result of the efforts of Conn and Vernon, this common goal or desire was never discussed. Even if this goal had been commonly agreed upon, when might an implied contract have been confected and the parties bound thereto? There was no contract when the songs were being recorded because the studio time was being provided free of charge. Conn's testimony to this effect was corroborated by that of J. D. Milliner, a fellow musician who recorded with Conn at Vernon's studio. Although this testimony clashes with that of Vernon who testified he was "fronting" time to the musicians, the musicians' understanding that the time was provided free is reasonable in the light of other circumstances. For instance, at that time, Vernon was a relative newcomer to the recording business, having opened his studio approximately six months before. Conn felt that Vernon was seeking to gain "prestige through association" by having Conn and other musicians record at his studio. Vernon admitted that he solicited Conn's services and also admitted that he considered Conn to be one of the area's best musicians. Under this set of circumstances, Conn's belief that the studio time was being provided free of charge was a reasonable one.

In contrast, Vernon testified he was fronting time to the musicians. "Fronting" was essentially a credit arrangement whereby a musician would record his work at a studio but would not pay for the time used until the recordings were successfully marketed. Vernon claims that Conn was aware that theirs was such an arrangement. Conn denied that he agreed to or was aware of a fronting arrangement. We conclude that if Vernon *had* told Conn of the fronting arrangement, there would have been no need for Conn to ask the question: "What's in this for you?" because he demonstrated from his testimony that he (Conn) was very familiar with the term fronting. In any event, Vernon had an excellent opportunity in the early stage of their relationship to explain what he expected of that relationship when he was questioned by Conn. Instead of answering forthrightly, however, Vernon's answer "We'll worry about that down the line" was vague and uncertain.

To further refute the contention that Vernon was fronting him time, Conn testified that at the time the recording took place in 1977, he had a recording studio in his backyard upon which he could make demonstration tapes for distribution. According to Conn, although Vernon's recording studio was more sophisticated, he, Conn, considered the tape produced there nothing more than a demonstration tape (although of a higher quality than what could be produced in his backyard studio), rather than a "master tape" which Vernon claimed it was. A "master tape" is of such quality that record albums meant for retail sales can be produced from the sound contained on the tape without further need of the musician's talents. Conn testified that this tape is not a "master tape" because more studio work is required of the musicians to perfect and polish the sound already recorded thereon. Again, J. D. Milliner corroborated Conn's testimony that the tape recorded at Sound Doctor Recording Studio was only a rough demonstration.

Did the parties, by their actions, implicitly contract with one another subsequent to the recording session? Again we think not. Sound Doctor argues that Conn's participation in the musical showcase and his acceptance of Sound Doctor's offer to go to New York were evidence of an implied contract. We disagree with this contention. We note that Sound Doctor made no claim for expenses incurred in producing the musical showcase. Obviously, he did not (and does not) expect any compensation from defendant for expenses incurred in arranging the showcase, especially since no agreements or commitments resulted therefrom. Of course, if something would have developed as a result of Vernon's efforts, Sound Doctor's argument that a contract was created at that time might have more merit.

As for the trip to New York, if Conn and Ms. Bruno had reached an agreement as a result of Vernon's efforts, then Sound Doctor would have been entitled to some type of compensation. Vernon needed Conn to accompany him on the

trip to New York, because he (Vernon) recognized that he did not have a contract with Mr. Conn and that he did not have the right to contractually bind Conn. We note in this regard that Vernon's testimony indicates that he had other business to tend to in New York—he was not there solely to promote the music and talents of Steve Conn.

Finally, we think it is worthy of mention that both Conn and Vernon testified that some form of payment to Sound Doctor was anticipated but *only if* the tape made at the recording studio or Conn's musical talents were sold or successfully marketed as a result of Sound Doctor's (and Vernon's) efforts. In that event, both Sound Doctor (Vernon) and Conn would have reaped the benefits. The record is devoid of any understanding, though, that their business relationship was intended to endure *until* Sound Doctor's (Vernon's) efforts bore fruit. For these reasons, we do not think any enforceable contract was ever created.

Sound Doctor argues alternatively that it is entitled to an award based on the equitable doctrine of quantum meruit. . . .

Sound Doctor claims the value of the labor and materials furnished by it was $3,065.00. We note that $1,980.00 of that claim is for studio time. We believe the record supports a determination that this time was given to Conn free of charge (see discussion, supra) and cannot properly form part of an award based on quantum meruit.

With respect to the expense allegedly incurred on the trip to New York, Sound Doctor claimed $1,000.00 worth of expenses in its petition. However, this amount was later adjusted downward to $900.00 by Vernon during his testimony. Further, as we commented previously, Vernon had other business to tend to in New York besides the promoting of Conn's talents. Yet he seems to have claimed all of his New York expenses in his suit against Conn. Vernon produced no evidence to substantiate his claim for expenses on the New York trip. We think he has completely failed to prove the amount of his expenses.

Finally, the last item of expenses claimed is $85.00 for the tape. Sound Doctor is clearly not entitled to recover this amount. The tape itself is locked safely away in the recording studio. Steven Conn has made no claim to ownership of the tape. His only claim is to ownership of the songs recorded thereon. Sound Doctor need only erase Conn's songs from the tape to restore the tape to its original condition. We thus conclude that Sound Doctor Recording Studio has simply failed to prove that it is entitled to any amount based on the equitable doctrine of quantum meruit. . . .

For the above and foregoing reasons the judgment of the District Court in favor of Sound Doctor Recording Studio, Inc. on its original demand against defendant Steve Conn is reversed. The judgment of the District Court rejecting the demands of the plaintiff in reconvention, Steve Conn, is affirmed.

It is hereby Ordered, Adjudged, and Decreed that all demands be dismissed and that the costs be equally divided between Sound Doctor Recording Studio, Inc. and Steve Conn.

Affirmed in part, reversed in part and dismissed.

Long v. Decca Records, Inc., 76 N.Y.S.2d 133 (1947)

COHALAN, JUSTICE

Plaintiffs are actors and vocalists. The defendant Reisman is a band leader. The defendant Decca makes phonograph records. On February 11, 1942, a contract was signed by Decca and Reisman under which the services of an organization known as "Leo Reisman and his Orchestra" were to be given to Decca in return for certain payments. On March 13, 1942 and April 10, 1942, the plaintiffs appeared with Reisman and his instrumentalists at the Decca Studios and sang to dance music played by the orchestra. Six records were made from the operetta "Porgy & Bess." At that time the plaintiffs were principals in that operetta. They sang the songs they rendered in the play and other songs rendered in the play by other principals. The plaintiffs appeared as a result of negotiations they had with Reisman in January 1942. They had no negotiations of any kind on that date or later with Decca until May 1942 (infra).

These records were sold commercially for the first time in April and May 1942. On May 14, 1942, a Decca contract was made with each of the individual plaintiffs looking to further services by

them. These documents were substantially the same as the Reisman contract (supra). In each (paragraph 4, subdivision a) Decca is given the right to manufacture, advertise, etc., records to be recorded thereunder and in subdivision b "the right to use and publish . . . the artist's name and photograph . . . for advertising and trade purposes in connection with the exploitation and sale of Decca products." Plaintiffs did render services under this contract of May 14, 1942, for which they were paid.

Under these circumstances plaintiffs bring four causes of action which their counsel characterize as (1) the wrongful use of plaintiffs' commonlaw right of property; (2) in fraud because of alleged false representations made by Reisman; (3) that their rights under the Civil Rights Law have been violated; (4) that the records made on the two dates are inferior and are consequently unfair competition to possibly other and better records of theirs. They ask judgment for (1) a permanent injunction; (2) an accounting; (3) damages; (4) destruction of the records, mold, etc.

As all four claimed causes of action stem from the original interviews with Reisman, the second cause of action (fraud) is the one first considered.

I find as a fact that each plaintiff willingly agreed that they would sing the records in question and that they were not to receive any money for their services. I find further that no false representations were made to them by Reisman, to the effect that the records were not to be used commercially, but that, on the contrary, their services were rendered to Reisman and through him to Decca in the hope on their part that the professional and commercial exploitation of the records might redound to their credit in their profession and might be of assistance to their being engaged professionally by the Rainbow Room in which Reisman had a contract to appear with his orchestra made in the preceding year. It is an unquestioned fact that Reisman and his orchestra did appear in the Rainbow Room beginning April 1, 1943. The court having found that the plaintiffs are not the victims of any false representations on the part of Reisman but that on the contrary the plaintiffs well knew what they were doing, the complaint in the second cause of action is dismissed as to both defendants.

This court also finds that the plaintiffs by their agreement with Reisman and by their appearance and the rendition of services at the Decca studios knew or should have known that the records were made for commercial purposes and holds that they have not proven any cause of action as alleged in the claimed first cause of action and that is dismissed as to each defendant.

As to the fourth alleged cause of action: The uncontradicted testimony is that certain songs which were part of the production of "Porgy & Bess" and were not performed on the stage in "Dance Time" were made on these records by these vocalists as part of dance records. The singers were consequently required to render the selections with the regularity of "Dance Time" and they did not have the interpretive range that would be present were the songs to be rendered as originally written, or as rendered from the stage in the operetta. Consequently, there is no basis of comparison between these dance records and any interpretive record they subsequently made. This cause of action is likewise dismissed.

In deciding the third cause of action—the alleged violation of civil rights—the court has in mind that no such claim has been made or can be made against the defendant Reisman, and this cause of action is dismissed as to him. It is likewise held that a like result shall obtain for other reasons as to the defendant Decca. Section 51 of the Civil Rights Law has a proviso reading in part as follows: ". . . nothing contained in this act shall be so construed as to prevent any person, firm or corporation . . . *from using the name, portrait or picture of any author, composer or artist in connection with his literary, musical or artistic productions which he has sold or disposed of with such name, portrait or picture used in connection therewith.*"

I find that the records which plaintiffs made were musical productions; that they were disposed of under the plaintiffs' agreement with Reisman; that in this industry it was quite usual for singers to appear as part of an orchestra and that no claim that the plaintiffs were acting otherwise was brought home to Decca; that the plaintiffs had the right of disposing of their services to Reisman and Decca without receiving actual money therefor, but could receive as payment what to them were other and perhaps better considerations than the small amount of money that would have been paid (a total of $75 each) had they contracted as singers to perform the services. The Civil Rights Law was passed primarily to protect individuals whose rights of privacy in these respects were taken from them without any action on their part. It does not forbid advertising of the facts in a case and the facts here were that the plaintiffs voluntarily rendered services. . . . Any claimed violation under this cause of action would only be for the short period between the sale of the original record in April or May 1942, and the right given to Decca in Subdivision 4, paragraph B, of the contracts of May 14, 1942, of the individual plaintiffs with Decca. No damages under the Civil Rights Law during that time have been proven nor have any such damages been proven as to any other time.

In general, the court is satisfied that the plaintiffs knew what they were doing in dealing with Reisman; that the plaintiffs had no direct dealings with the defendant Decca; that Reisman was not in any wise authorized by Decca to deal with the individual plaintiffs as an agent for Decca, but that on the contrary and in the trade or business, the word "orchestra" is broad enough to include singers where singers are necessary.

I find nothing in the record to charge Decca with any violation of business ethics in its dealings with the plaintiffs.

4.20 Remedies for Record Label Breach

When the record company fails to perform and breach occurs, the nonbreaching party often faces a difficult task in proving damages. However, most courts approach the problem in a manner similar to *Phillips v. Playboy Music*. There need not be a perfect measure of damages, only credible evidence tending to show a discernible measure. In addition, the duty of the nonbreaching party to mitigate damages by seeking other contracts must take into account the factual limitations under which that party operates. Thus, in reality, a duty to mitigate does not exist in a substantial percentage of breach-of-contract situations in the music industry.

Phillips v. Playboy Music, Inc., 424 F. Supp. 1148 (N.D. Miss. 1976)

[Sam Phillips gained fame during the early years of rock-and-roll by discovering and recording such noteworthy talents as Elvis Presley, Conway Twitty, and Johnny Cash. His partner, Harris, was also well known as a talent finder as well as a recording producer/engineer.

In 1972 Phillips and Harris secured an agreement with Playboy to produce and deliver eight LPs a year for two years. Playboy reserved the right, however, to reject any or all of the recordings. The deal called for the Phillips/Harris company to receive a $40,000 advance on signing, as well as advances of $5,000 per month during the first year, $4,166.66 per month during the second year, and $5,000 each time an LP was delivered.

Phillips/Harris proceeded to sign five recording artists and to deliver 50 master recordings (enough for five LPs) all but two of which were immediately accepted by Playboy; the other two were accepted after being rerecorded.

As is frequently the case in the entertainment industry, the executive who had made the deal left the employ of Playboy. A successor executive then called Harris and told him that the deal was being terminated because Playboy had decided to emphasize 45 rpm "singles" rather than LPs. Playboy ignored verbal and written requests for written confirmation of the message.]

SMITH, DISTRICT JUDGE

. . . The court finds that Playboy willfully and intentionally breached the contract with plaintiffs by refusing to continue the advance of funds in accordance with the contract provisions. . . .

In breaching the contract, Playboy refused to pay plaintiffs two monthly payments during the first year of the term aggregating the sum of $10,000 and the $50,000 which was due in equal monthly installments for the second year of the term. . . .

[The court then observed that the contract chose California law and proceeded to review

California precedents concerning election of remedies and measure of damages.]

The plaintiffs did not elect to bring an action to enforce performance of the contract. They contend that the refusal of Playboy to serve a written notice of termination of payments effectively prevented them from seeking a new contract for the production of records. Playboy contends that by virtue of [plaintiffs' counsel's] letter [requesting written confirmation of termination] plaintiffs elected to treat the contract as having been breached and to seek damages therefor.

The Supreme Court of California in *McConnell v. Corona City Water Co.*, 149 Cal. 60, 85 P. 929, 931 (1906) quoting from 1 *Sutherland on Damages* 113, said:

> A party to a contract is entitled to recover, against the other party who violated it, damages for the profits he would have made out of it had it been performed. It is no objection to their recovery that they cannot be directly and absolutely proved. In the nature of things, the defendant having prevented such profits, direct and absolute proof is impossible.

Again, quoting from *Schumann v. Karrer*, 184 Cal. 50, 192 P. 849, 853 (1920), in *Steelduct Co. v. Henger-Seltzer Co.*, 26 Cal.2d 634, 160 P.2d 804, 814 (1945), the court held that under California law a party "who wilfully breaches his contract cannot wholly escape on account of the difficulty which his own wrong has produced of devising a perfect measure of, or method of proving, damages."

The California rule is that "a plaintiff must mitigate damages so far as he can without loss to himself." *Bomberger v. McKelvey*, 35 Cal.2d 607, 220 P.2d 729, 733 (1950). [And a plaintiff who does not do "everything reasonably possible to minimize his own loss . . . cannot recover damages for detriment which he could have avoided by reasonable effort and without undue expense." *Sackett v. Spindler*, 248 Cal.App.2d 220, 56 Cal.Rptr. 435, 447 (1967)]

. . . Defendant argues that plaintiffs cannot recover in the action sub judice because plaintiffs did not make an effort to secure a substitute contract for the balance of the term thereby minimizing or eliminating the loss occasioned thereby.

The law is clear, as above-indicated, in California and elsewhere, [that] a plaintiff is only required to exercise a reasonable diligence in this regard. The nature, term, and other pertinent aspects of the contract, must be considered in light of the circumstances surrounding the undertakings of the contracting parties.

Here, the contract relates to a rather restricted, limited and sensitive area of personal services to be performed by plaintiffs. The agreement does not constitute a contractual agreement which can be readily or easily negotiated in the average or usual marketplace. In fact, the evidence shows that [Playboy's] familiarity with the successful performances of Phillips and Harris prompted [Playboy] to seek their services in the production of masters for Playboy. The parties were engaged in negotiating the contract over a substantial period of time before the agreement was finally consummated.

The evidence also creates the inference that a contract in the recording industry providing for the payment of nonreturnable advances is difficult to obtain. This is especially true when the producer has been under a contract of this nature and is seeking a new contract to take the place of one which has been cancelled by the manufacturer or distributor of the records.

The circumstances surrounding the breach developed in the evidence did not afford plaintiffs a reasonable opportunity to seek a contract with another manufacturer or distributor and reduce or minimize their loss. . . .

[The court thereupon proceeded to award damages of $60,000 less studio and payroll costs saved by the shutdown of the Harris/Phillips operation and the obtaining of alternative employment by Harris. However, the court *declined* to award $250,000 sought as "special damages for the injury to the reputations" of Phillips and Harris as finders and developers of new talents, and of Harris as a producer/engineer.]

. . . While there is some evidence to support plaintiffs' contention [in this regard], the court finds that plaintiffs have not offered evidence which justifies the court in awarding damages for an injury to the reputation of either Harris or Phillips or for the loss or damage to the goodwill of the partnership. The court does not find that the reputation of either Harris or Phillips has been materially damaged by Playboy in the termination of their contract. . . .

4.30   Contract Term: The Label Option

One of the constant sore points in entertainment contracts is the option running in favor of the entertainment company. Record labels are no different from other companies in seeking to ensure a recording artist's services for as long a period as possible. The label wants to bind the artist, but at the same time the label does not want to commit to keeping the artist if the artist's albums start to bomb. The label option is the answer.

In recording contracts, options may be for one or several years or for a succession of years (one year at a time). The more prevalent option today is one enabling the label to bind the artist one additional album or single at a time. Whatever the device, artists often chafe under such options in which conditions change and the original contract seems disadvantageous to the artist in his or her present circumstances.

In *Polygram Records, Inc. v. Buddy Buie Productions*, the court holds the record company to a strict interpretation of the company's rights to exercise its option. The company's failure to exercise in a timely fashion proves fatal to its claims. Under the contract, the right to exercise was circumscribed by the happening of an event and not dependent on a set date. This provided the plaintiff maneuverability, but it was not enough.

Polygram Records, Inc. v. Buddy Buie Productions, Inc., 520 F. Supp. 248 (S.D.N.Y. 1981)

WEINFELD, DISTRICT JUDGE
Plaintiff, Polygram Records, Inc. ("Polygram") is in the business of exploiting, marketing and selling phonograph records. Buddy Buie Productions, Inc. ("BBP") is a production company

which produces and furnishes the recording services of the five individual defendants, a rock and roll music band, professionally known as The Atlanta Rhythm Section ("ARS"). Perry C. Buie, "Buddy" Buie ("Buie"), has been the President of BBP since its formulation. BBP, under an agreement with the individual defendants, is entitled to their exclusive services in the recording of phonograph records. Polygram, BBP and the individual defendants had a contractual relationship commencing in 1973 under which Polygram became the exclusive recording company for all ARS records.

The 1973 agreement was superseded by another on October 1, 1977 (the "1977 agreement") under which the defendants again granted plaintiff Polygram the exclusive right to all ARS recordings during the existence of the agreement. Under its terms BBP was obligated to produce and deliver four albums of ARS master recordings to plaintiff for its exclusive exploitation, manufacture and distribution.

Plaintiff commenced this action upon a claim that the defendants breached their exclusive service agreement by entering into an agreement in May 1981 with CBS Records Inc., a competing record company. Plaintiff seeks to enjoin the defendants from producing or recording any records for CBS or any other recording company, and money damages. Plaintiff can prevail only if the 1977 agreement was in effect at the time of the alleged breach. The parties are in agreement that the resolution of this issue depends upon whether plaintiff timely and properly exercised an option to extend the agreement for a further period so that it was in effect when defendants entered into their agreement to record for CBS.

The initial period of the 1977 agreement was for a term beginning October 1, 1977 and ending 180 days subsequent to the delivery by BBP to Polygram of master recordings for the fourth and final ARS album. Polygram had an option to extend the agreement for a further term covering four additional albums by sending a written notice to BBP at least 30 days prior to the date that the contract otherwise would expire. Since the agreement by its terms expired 180 days after the delivery of the fourth album, the date of delivery is crucial on the issue of whether the option was

timely exercised so that plaintiff was entitled to ARS' exclusive services at the time of the alleged breach.

Delivery under the agreement required BBP to "deliver completed, edited and fully mixed master tapes in accordance with the Company's reasonable instructions comprising "a two-track stereo and a discrete quadraphonic master tape for each Master recorded hereunder together with a 'reference lacquer' therefor, which tape shall be fully edited, mixed and leadered prior to delivery to Company [Polygram] so that they are in proper form for the production of parts necessary for the manufacture of commercial Phonograph Records."

The defendants contend that they made delivery of the last and fourth album in accordance with the foregoing contract provisions by delivery on June 11, 1980 of a reference lacquer to plaintiff at its offices where it was played in the presence of various Polygram executives who approved and accepted it and on that day mailed a check for $150,000 to BBP as the final payment.

The plaintiff, contrariwise, contends that the reference disc played and delivered on June 11, 1980 was an "unapproved" disc and that the final approved reference disc was not delivered and accepted by it until June 17, 1980. Accordingly, plaintiff claims that its notice of exercise of the option mailed on November 14, 1980, was sent on the 150th day after delivery, within the required time for the exercise of the option and hence the contract was renewed for a further term and was in effect in May 1981, the date of the alleged breach by the defendants. The defendants not only dispute that June 17, 1980 was the date of delivery but they challenge that in fact the notice was mailed on November 14, 1980. The envelope in which the exercise of option letter was mailed bears a November 16 postmark and was received by BBP on November 18. Two days later, on November 20, defendants' counsel notified Polygram orally and in writing that plaintiff had not timely exercised its option and that the defendants deemed the agreement terminated. Plaintiff made no response to defendants' disavowal until two months later when, on January 19, 1981, it notified all recording companies that a contract existed between plaintiff and the defendants. Thus a threshold question is on what day, June 11 or June 17, 1980, delivery was made by BBP to plaintiff of a completed master tape and reference lacquer as required by the provisions of the contract.

Masterdisk Corporation is a disc-cutting studio where the final artistic changes are made in a recording. The artist's product is originally recorded on many different tracks and subsequently "mixed down"—that is, reduced to a two-track tape which is then taken to a mastering facility, such as Masterdisk, where final sound adjustments are made. A reference disc and a master disc are produced. The reference disc is used so that it may be heard by those interested in the product either for approval or suggested changes or modifications. The master disc is retained by the studio and upon approval is sent to a plating plant where it is used to manufacture the record that is sold to the public. Masterdisk was the studio used for the mastering of the ARS recordings. The parties' practice with respect to the first three albums was that the final two-track tape, after mastering, was left at Masterdisk and, upon final approval, Polygram would contact Masterdisk and order "the parts" necessary for the production of the album. This was the procedure followed with respect to the fourth album, the subject matter of this action.

Plaintiff, to support its claim that June 17, 1980 is the effective delivery date, relies in the main upon the testimony of two witnesses, Stuart Fine, then its East Coast Director of Artists and Repertoire, and James Del Balzo, then its Assistant National Album Promotion Manager. Fine testified in substance that on June 11, 1980, Buddy Buie, who mastered the recordings of the artists, came to his office together with Ronnie Hammond, lead singer of the ARS artists, and their respective wives, and played, in his presence and at times in the presence of other executives, a reference disc which Buie said he had been working on the previous two days; that before other Polygram people joined the meeting Buie told him that there were still some changes to be made; that he had "to roll off the bottom end"; that he would be working with Bob Ludwig, Masterdisk's chief engineer, later that day at Masterdisk to effect the changes, and that

what they would be listening to was an unapproved reference disc. Fine acknowledged that everybody who heard the record liked it. Finally, he testified that after Buie and Hammond left the office, he wrote upon the cover of the reference record "not approved." However, he did not inform any superior or anybody else that it was not approved.

Fine also testified that later that day Arnold Geller, co-manager of ARS, telephoned and advised him that Buie and Ludwig would make the final changes and Polygram was not to place the order for final parts until it received from Buie another reference disc or Fine heard from defendants. Fine stated that he did nothing further until Geller called him on June 17 and gave BBP's approval, whereupon Fine voluntarily waived further Polygram approval and sent the "reference" approval form to the production department so they would "order parts" and commence commercial production of the album.

Del Balzo testified that on June 11 he was present when Buie played the reference record and asked Buie for cassettes of the record, to which Buie responded, "no, it was not an approved record." Finally, in addition to the reference approval form, plaintiff offered other internal documents to support its claim that Polygram regarded June 17, 1980 as the delivery date. Based in large part upon the foregoing testimony and related events, plaintiff contends that the date of delivery was June 17.

Defendants' evidence is in sharp contradiction to that of plaintiff. Buie testified that on June 9 and 10 he and Bob Ludwig, the engineer at Masterdisk, worked there in producing a reference lacquer and two-track tape which were completed and in final and satisfactory form on June 10; that on June 11, accompanied by Hammond and their respective wives, he went to the Polygram offices for the purpose of delivering the reference lacquer to Polygram, to share his excitement about the record with company officials, and to obtain final payment of $150,000. He delivered the record to Fine in his office, where it was played for Fine and other Polygram executives, including Freddie Haayan, its President; that all who heard it were enthusiastic and ecstatic about the record; they, as well as he, approved the record, and Haayan was so enthusiastic that he asked for a cassette that Buie had in his hand. Buie categorically denied the testimony of Fine and Del Balzo that he said the reference disc was "unapproved" or that he had to "roll off some bass." Buie testified that nothing further was to be done on the record and that he did not return to Masterdisk at any time thereafter for the purpose of making any changes. He expected to receive payment of $150,000 of the balance due under the contract, then and there, but Ms. Barbara Patralites, contract administrator, said there had been a foul up and she would express mail the check to Atlanta. The next day, June 12, he received plaintiff's check for $150,000 accompanied by a letter dated June 11, which reads:

> Pursuant to paragraph 9(a)(ii) of the above-cited Agreement enclosed please find Polydor's check No. 219756 in the amount of $150,000.00 representing the balance due upon delivery of the 4th LP entitled "The Boys From Doraville."

The letter was signed by Ms. Patralites, who testified the check was drawn by her pursuant to instructions from Dr. Ekke Schnable, Senior Vice President, Legal & Business Affairs. The check stub contains the legend "Advance due upon delivery of the 4th LP by the Atlanta Rhythm Section pursuant to paragraph 9(a)(ii) of the October 1, 1977 agreement." In sum, Buie testified that the reference lacquer left with Fine and the master two-track tape left at Masterdisk were fully edited, mixed and leadered and were in proper form for the production of the parts necessary to make commercial phonograph records and that there was no further work to be done.

Hammond also testified and denied that he heard any discussion on June 11 as to the reference lacquer being either unapproved or unsatisfactory; that all those who listened to the album were "very excited" about it. He acknowledged he did not hear any conversation Buie may have had with Fine or Del Balzo.

Arnold Geller, co-manager of ARS, also testified and flatly denied that he told Fine that further work was required on the reference disc or that he called him to give BBP approval on June 17, 1980. Geller stated that he had acknowledgment from several senior officers of Polydor;

that they had received the album, loved the album and accepted it.

The General Manager and Vice President of Masterdisk, Douglas Levine, whose duties included overseeing all work performed there, testified, based on company records and his own knowledge, that no work was done by Masterdisk on the records between June 11 and June 17, 1980 except on June 12 when, in response to Buie's request, a duplicate reference disc was made to replace the one Buie had lost on a plane trip on his way home to Atlanta, Georgia on June 11th. According to the company records, all work was completed on the records on June 10 and there was no further work to be done on them.

The plaintiff has the burden of proof to establish by a fair preponderance of the credible evidence the existence of the contract under which it claims to be entitled to injunctive relief and damages. Based upon an appraisal of the demeanor of the witnesses, notes made during the trial, a word-by-word re-reading of the trial transcript, analysis of the exhibits and consideration of all surrounding circumstances, the Court concludes that at best the credible evidence is in balance, in which circumstance, as juries are instructed, the party who has the burden of proof on an issue has failed to sustain it. But the Court further finds that the credible evidence preponderates in favor of the defendants and against the plaintiff—a finding buttressed by circumstances that are not in dispute.

First, the reference record left with Fine on June 11 and retained by him was exactly similar to the master two-track disc produced by Masterdisk and used for the commercial production of the record upon plaintiff's order. In sum, no changes were made in the record as produced for distribution, a circumstance that in some measure challenges the testimony that the reference delivered to plaintiff on June 11 was "unapproved." Further, contrary to Fine's testimony that Buie said further work was to be done on the record and that he planned to return to Masterdisk for that purpose, the evidence establishes that Buie never returned there for that purpose.

Second, the mailing on June 11, after delivery of the reference disc to plaintiff, of the balance of $150,000 accompanied by a letter specifically stating it represented "the balance due upon delivery of the 4th LP" and a similar legend on the check stub. Although Fine knew that the final payment was to be made upon delivery, he did not inform anyone that the reference disc was "not approved" and did nothing to hold up the check.

Third, the plaintiff's failure to call as a witness at the trial Dr. Ekke Schnabel, to testify as to the circumstances attendant upon his direction for the issuance of the final payment check or to offer any explanation for his failure to testify at the trial.

Fourth, the plaintiff's failure to call as a witness Freddie Haayan, plaintiff's President, who, it was testified, was one of those who expressed approval of the record on June 11th, or to offer any explanation for his nonappearance as a witness.

Fifth, the failure over a period of almost two months to respond to defendants' letter of November 20, 1980 which rejected plaintiff's option notice of November 14 on the ground that plaintiff had "not timely exercised its option to extend the term of the agreement" and that defendants regarded the agreement as terminated. Significantly, this letter was addressed to the attention of David Braun, plaintiff's President at that time, a lawyer, with a copy to Eileen Garrish, also a lawyer and who, at the time, was Director of Legal and Business Affairs of Polygram and had drafted the option notice. Surely the significance of the defendants' denial that the contract had been extended could not have been lost upon Braun and Garrish. Common experience suggests that these plaintiff's executives, also lawyers, would have responded immediately and on the record rejected defendants' claim and would affirmatively have asserted plaintiff's position that the option notice had been timely and by reason thereof that the contract had been extended for another term. David Braun was not called as a witness nor any explanation offered for his nonappearance. Eileen Garrish did testify principally with respect to the mailing of the notice on November 14. However, with respect to defendants' November 20 letter, when asked why no response was made thereto she testified that she had been instructed by her superiors "not to do anything." It is rather singular that when defen-

dants denied the effectiveness of the option notice and the renewal of the contract, two lawyers who were directly involved in the matter on behalf of plaintiff failed to assert plaintiff's basic position over a two-month period.

Upon the totality of all the credible evidence, the Court finds that the defendants made delivery to plaintiff on June 11, 1980 of the fourth and final album in accordance with the terms of the 1977 agreement and that plaintiff accepted such delivery on that day. The complaint is dismissed upon the merits and judgment may be entered accordingly.

The foregoing constitutes the Court's Findings of Fact and Conclusions of Law.

NOTES ———————————————

1. While notice is generally ineffectual if not given by the specified date, late notice may still be valid in New York if delay is excusable and in good faith and there has been no change of position by the artist. See *Sy Jack Realty Co. v. Pergament Syosset Corp.*, 27 N.Y.2d 449 (1971).

The result appears to be different in California. Time is of the essence when a contract specifies the time for exercise, *Rosenaur v. Pacelli*, 345 P.2d 102 (Cal. App. 1959). If the contract is silent as to time, an option may be exercised until the end of the current term, *Cicinelli v. Iwasaki*, 338 P.2d 1005 (Cal. Ap. 1959). But see *Bell v. Minor*, 199 P.2d 718 (Cal. App. 1948) (one day's lateness excused).

2. The delivery provisions of a recording contract often contain specific restrictions on finished masters which may be delivered to a record company, including a standard clause that they be "technically" satisfactory or a more stringent clause stating that they shall be "technically and commercially satisfactory" in the record label's discretion.

3. In *Arista Records, Inc. and Careers Music, Inc. v. Woolf Songs, Ltd., Allan Parsons, et al.*, the delivery of masters was the source of dispute between the record label and artist, in this case the Allan Parsons Project. The recording contract provided that all masters be delivered "subject to [Arista's] approval as satisfactory for the manufacture and sale of phonograph records." The artists delivered masters for a record entitled "The Sicilian Defense." The record label and its president, Clive Davis, contended these were unmarketable. See United States District Court for the Southern District of New York, Action No. 81 CIV 2620.

4.40 Signing Multiple Group Members to the Recording Contract

Record companies frequently deal with groups rather than individual artists. The company wants to have all members of a group under contract, but the company must cope with the reality that membership in a band undergoes frequent change. The contract must deal with the possibility that one or more members of the group may depart and that others will take their places. Not only must the contract keep continuity with the group as presently constituted, but it must also attempt to determine whether departing members are still committed to some kind of contract with the label.

As illustrated in the following case, *Forrest R.B. Enterprises v. Capricorn Records*, the consequences of changing group membership are not always properly anticipated. Language is used in a contract that creates ambiguities. Only a full trial can resolve the issues. The imprecise drafting of the pertinent contract provisions causes delay, expense, and uncertainty.

Forrest R.B. Enterprises, Inc. v. Capricorn Records, Inc., 430 F. Supp. 847 (S.D.N.Y. 1977)

DUFFY, DISTRICT JUDGE

Plaintiff, the corporate employer of Forrest Richard Betts (Betts), a singer and guitarist formerly associated with the "rock group" known as the Allman Brothers Band (the "Band"), has moved for summary judgment and dismissal of the counterclaims in this action for a declaratory judgment freeing Betts as a solo recording artist from any contractual obligation to defendant Capricorn Records, Inc. (Capricorn), for whom, it is undisputed, the Band was exclusively obligated to record. The counterclaims sought to be dismissed allege, as against plaintiff and one Steven Massarsky, Betts' business manager, tortious interference with the contract in question, and, as against plaintiff, Betts and Massarsky, tortious interference with the execution of, and refusal by Betts to

so execute, a new management agreement with Phil Walden and Associates, who purportedly had been acting as Betts' personal manager since July 1969.

It is uncontroverted that in November 1972, the Band and its members entered into a recording contract with defendant, and that in June 1976 the Band ceased to function as a group. Thereafter, Betts notified defendant that since he was no longer a member of the Band, he desired to perform as a solo recording artist for another company of his choice. The instant suit followed.

The sole question presented by this motion is whether, under the terms of the recording agreement, Betts is obligated individually to perform exclusive recording services for defendant as a solo artist, despite the Band's dissolution as a recording group. The pertinent contractual provisions provide:

> AGREEMENT made this 1st day of November 1972 by and between CAPRICORN RECORDS, INC. and/or its associates, subsidiaries, nominees, successors and assigns (hereinafter called "Company") and GREGORY LENOIR ALLMAN, CLAUDE HUDSON TRUCKS, JR., RAYOND BERRY OAKLEY III, JOHNNY LEE JOHNSON, FORREST RICHARD BETTS, professionally known as the ALLMAN BROTHERS BAND (hereinafter referred to as "Artist").
>
> /jointly and severally*
>
> 1. The Artist hereby grants and Company engages the Artist's exclusive personal services in connection with the production of phonographic records. If this agreement is with more than one individual, this agreement shall be binding upon

---

*This phrase was typewritten into the contract, unlike the second reference to "jointly and severally" which appeared in printed "boilerplate" type, a fact to which defendant attributes great weight in construing the meaning of the phrase. It is unclear to me, however, whether this typewritten phrase (uninitialled by the parties, in contrast to other changes in the "boilerplate" language of the contract as a whole) refers to the preamble, so as to read "(hereinafter referred to jointly and severally as 'Artist')," or to paragraph 1, so as to read "The Artist jointly and severally hereby grants . . .". Both parties appear to have accepted the phrase as properly part of paragraph 1 and it shall be so treated for the purposes of this motion.

each individual who is a signatory hereto as an Artist, jointly and severally.

Rider

. . .

3. If any member of the group shall leave the group or ceases to perform as a member of the group, the Artist and the Company may mutually designate a new member who shall be deemed substituted in this agreement in place of such leaving member and shall be automatically bound by all the terms and conditions of this agreement. The artist shall execute such documents as the company may require in connection therewith. Any such leaving member shall continue to be bound individually by the applicable provisions of this agreement, and shall continue to record for the Company under each and all terms and conditions contained in this agreement except that any such leaving artist shall receive A.F. of M. scale as his sole advance or payment for recording hereunder and shall receive a basic royalty of ____%.

Additionally, paragraph 14 provides in part: "This agreement may not be modified, except in writing signed by both parties. This agreement shall be subject to the laws of the State of Georgia applicable to agreements to be wholly performed therein. . . ."

Plaintiff contends that Rider paragraph 3 is the sole governing provision of the instant controversy, and since it is conceded that the space provided for the applicable royalty rate was never filled in nor made the subject of any subsequent written agreement, that the provision is unenforceable for lack of a material term. Defendant disputes the applicability of such clause in the present absence of the Band's existence as a performing entity. Relying instead on the "joint and several" language of paragraph 1, defendant contends that Betts is exclusively obligated as a solo performer, and that this obligation survives the existence of the group. Alternatively, defendant argues that if Rider paragraph 3 is found to control, then a triable issue of fact is presented as to the parties' intention regarding the applicable royalty rate.

I find it unnecessary to address this alternative contention, since I have resolved the threshold question of whether the Rider paragraph 3 controls in the negative. This determination, essentially one of construction of an unambiguous provision, is clearly one for the court. . . .

Initially, I note that defendant, who essentially seeks to bind Betts under the contract, strenuously contends that this provision does not do so. Strangely, it is rather plaintiff who, in its efforts to free Betts, attempts to show the applicability of this clause in the first instance. With these positions in mind, I turn to an analysis of the language of the clause itself.

Although the provision addresses both a "leaving member" and one who "cease[s] to perform as a member of a group," it further recites that "the artist and the company may mutually designate a new member who shall be deemed substituted in place of such leaving member. . . ." In so providing, it indicates a primary concern with protecting the integrity of the Band as a performing entity; that is, by allowing for the replacement of a member, the continued existence of the Band is contemplated. In the absence of an existing group, however, applicability of this clause would mean permitting the creation of an entirely new group, totally unrelated to the original Band. Such a situation could not possibly have been intended as encompassed within the four corners of this agreement.

The ultimate question, then, is whether the "joint and several" language of paragraph 1 merely describes the nature of Betts' liability in case of breach, as urged by plaintiff, or represents a separate recording obligation on the part of Betts as a solo artist despite the Band's nonexistence, as posited by defendant. Supporting plaintiff's position is the absence of any other reference in the agreement to individual services rights or responsibilities. However, militating against that construction is the fact that the contract was executed by the members of the Band, both individually and in their group capacity. There is no indication within paragraph 1 or otherwise in the agreement whether the parties intended their joint and several obligations to survive the life of the group. Although it is doubtful that the agreement would have been intended to create six separate recording contracts—with the Band and each member thereof—not only during the life of the group but also thereafter, the intention revealed by the language of paragraph 1 is sufficiently ambiguous to require some further showing. Since neither party has submitted any type of proof on this issue, and since, in any event, resolution of this issue will not obviate the need for a trial on the unrelated counterclaim asserted against plaintiff, Betts and Massarsky, unaddressed by the parties on this motion, summary judgment is denied at this time. . . .

4.50 Interference with Contract and Inducement to Breach

Entrepreneurs in the recording industry are constantly looking for angles and advantages, and if it means luring someone away from another contract, that may be how the entrepreneur will proceed. In assessing the remedies that can be invoked against the defecting performer in the form of a negative injunction, we mentioned in Chapter 1 the possibility of a suit in tort for interference with a contractual relationship (see Section 1.50).

In *Roulette Records v. Princess Production Corp.*, the court interprets narrowly those circumstances under which an interference can occur, requiring actual knowledge of the existence of the contract allegedly interfered with. The dissent in the case would imply knowledge in circumstances such as those before the court. The *Bonner* and *Westbound* cases, which are presented in Section 4.51, have the court first considering the validity of the contract (*Bonner*) before establishing potential liability for interference with the contract (*Westbound*).

Roulette Records, Inc. v. Princess Production Corp., 224 N.Y.S.2d 204 (App. Div. 1st Dept. 1962)

[After entering into an exclusive recording agreement with Roulette (on execution of which a $25,000 advance was paid), Sarah Vaughan performed two songs in the soundtrack of the film *Murder, Inc.* The producer licensed a third-party record company to distribute records embodying Vaughan's soundtrack performances.

The producer did not have actual knowledge of the Roulette contract at the time the producer signed Ms. Vaughan. However, trade publications had carried announcements of the Roulette signing some eight months earlier. Roulette was aware of the Princess signing the next day but did not contact Princess for more than three months, and only after some 7,500 records had been distributed.]

McNally, Justice

. . . On this record the sole basis for recovery . . . is . . . intentional interference with the contractual rights of the plaintiff. . . . Plaintiff was required to establish actual knowledge of the underlying agreement on the part of [Princess] in order to support a recovery for intentional interference therewith. . . .

The trial court did not find and on this record the evidence is insufficient to sustain a finding of actual knowledge on the part of [Princess] of [Roulette's prior] contract with Sarah Vaughan. . . . Although proof of actual knowledge may be predicated upon circumstantial evidence, this record does not demonstrate it.

We are also of the option that the basis for damages relied on by the plaintiff is too speculative. Plaintiff claimed it was entitled to damages equal to such profits as it would have made if it had sold the quantity of sound track records sold by defendants. Plaintiff was required to prove by a preponderance of the evidence that profits resulted from the phonograph recordings . . . and was also required to advance a reasonable basis for estimating the amount. (Restatement, Torts, sec. 912, comment d, p. 581 et seq.)

The trial court found that there were 7,667 of said records of which 1,273 were distributed for promotional purposes. Although the evidence is that the balance of 6,394 was distributed largely on a consignment basis, the award of damages is based upon final sales thereof. The award does not reflect a deduction for payment of $4,800 made by or for [Princess] to the musicians' union for the privilege of reproducing the sound track of the [supporting] instrumentalists . . . nor does the award take into consideration that the phonograph records here involved include the recordings of other artists. Moreover, the testimony of plaintiff's witness is that the sale of 7,500 records does not normally serve to return the production costs. The sale of 6,394 records here involved would not appear to serve to recoup the expenses incident to their production. . . .

Judgment [enjoining further distribution of the records and awarding damages to Roulette] reversed on the law and on the facts, and a new trial ordered, with costs to abide the final judgment in the action.

All concur except Stevens and Steuer, J.J., who dissent in dissenting opinion by Steuer, J.

STEUER, JUSTICE (DISSENTING)

. . . The relief of an injunction and damages has been attacked on several grounds. The first might be styled mechanical. The record was made not by Miss Vaughan but by a sound track of her voice. The contract provided for "phonograph records or reproductions of any kind of the performances by any method now or hereafter known." A second contention, that the recording was made for purposes of exploiting the picture rather than for commercial sales of the record, both legally and factually barely survived announcement of the contention.

There are, however, two contentions that cannot be disposed of so abruptly. The trial court found that before making the record defendants knew, or ought to have known, of the contract between Miss Vaughan and plaintiff. It is claimed that nothing short of actual knowledge will suffice. This is not a precise statement of the law. Let us assume the accuracy of the text writers that there is no liability for negligent interference with contract (Harper and Jones, *The Law of Torts*, vol. 1, 509; Prosser, *Handbook of the Law of Torts*, 2d ed., p. 732, et seq.). There is quite a distinction between a negligent failure to know and a deliberate intent to stay in ignorance of what one suspects. . . . [I]t was proved that news of the contract was published in two trade papers, attesting to the general interest of such an occurrence in the milieu in which these people operated. It was also established through the testimony of defendants' own expert that the practice was to inquire of the performer, before using him

to make a record, whether the performer had existing contractual commitments. . . . [I]t was certainly a reasonable conclusion for the trier of the fact to draw that the failure of the defendants to inquire was due to a desire not to be told. If this is not the equivalent of knowledge, it would seem to be an extremely technical exception in the law, as well as one without any basis in policy. . . .

[Justice Steuer additionally disagreed with the majority's conclusion that no damages had been proved.]

The judgment should be affirmed.

NOTES

1. Every few years, there is a flurry of label-change moves by artists from one record company to another. Since artists and producers tend to share the basic insecurities afflicting the general population, there is rarely a hiatus between contracts. If the artist is in the final stages of an existing contract, he or she will sign a "futures' deal,"—that is, a contract to come into effect immediately upon the expiration of the artist's existing deal. If the artist, rightly or wrongly, feels aggrieved with the current label, a deal may be cut with a new label immediately after a notice of a breach is served on the current label. (Caution must be employed in the matter of timing; see *Westbound Records, Inc. v. Phonogram, Inc., infra*.) To avoid such surprises and to afford themselves a period within which to remedy defaults and to improve artist relations, record companies routinely insert into their form agreements clauses providing for cure periods, usually 30 to 60 days.

2. Suits claiming inducement to breach, interference with contractual relations, or interference with prospective advantage are encountered frequently. See, generally, *Handling the Business Tort Case* (Cal. Continuing Education of the Bar, 1978).

Among the elements considered by the court are the following:

(a) A valid agreement must first be shown as a condition precedent to recovery. See, for example, *Israel v. Wood Dolson Co.*, 1 N.Y.2d 116, 134 N.E.2d 99 (1956); and *Hornstein v. Podwitz*, 254 N.Y. 443, 73 N.E. 674 (1930).

(b) There can be no action for breach or inducement to breach a contract that is void or against public policy. See, for example, *Farbman & Sons v. Continental Casualty Co.*, 308 N.Y.S.2d 493 (1970), *aff'd* 319 N.Y.S.2d 775 (1971); *Paramount Pad Co. v. Baumrind*, 4 N.Y.2d 393, 175 N.Y.S. 809 (1958).

(c) It must additionally be shown that the performer (who was allegedly interfered with) would have performed but for the defendant's interference. If the performer has previously repudiated the agreement, the defendant cannot be liable for dealing with the performer thereafter. See, for example, *Warner Bros. Pictures, Inc. v. Simon*, 251 N.Y.S.2d 70 (1st Dept. 1964), *aff'd*, 15 N.Y.2d 836, 205 N.E.2d 869 (1965); and *Dryden v. Tri-Valley Growers*, 65 Cal. App.3d 990, 135 Cal. Rpts. 720 (1977).

(d) The defendant must be shown to have actively and intentionally interfered with an agreement to which the performer was then adhering; and the defendant must be the proximate cause of the ensuing breach by the performer. See, for example, *Israel v. Wood Dolson, Co., supra.*

(e) Defendant's knowledge of the prior agreement and of the plaintiff's claim is insufficient for liability to be found without active, intentional interference. See, for example, *P.P.X. Enterprise, Inc. v. Catala*, 232 N.Y.S.2d 959 (1st Dept. 1962).

(f) However, circumstantial evidence may be sufficient for a finding of active, intentional interference. *Westbound Records, Inc. v. Phonogram, Inc.*, 394 N.E.2d 1315 (Ill. App. 1979). (Summary judgment for defendant was *reversed*, in companion case to *Bonner v. Westbound Records, Inc.*, where the second record company was accused of negotiating a complete deal with a group before the group even put the first record company on notice of claimed breach; "steering" group to favored attorney, and so forth. For discussion of *Bonner* and *Westbound*, see the case that follows.)

(g) Jurisdictions differ as to agreements terminable at will. If intentional interference is shown, the California courts deem it immaterial that the agreement is terminable at will by the performer. See, for example, *Freed v. Manchester Service Inc.*, 165 Cal.App.2d 186 (2d Dist. 1958).

(h) While interference may be justified, justification is an affirmative defense; competition and economic gain, while matters of foundation, are not sufficient justification in and of themselves. See, for example, *Freed v. Manchester Service Inc., supra;* and *Augustine v. Trucco*, 124 Cal.App.2d 299, 268 P.2d 780 (2d Dist. 1954).

(i) However, where a party enters into a contract in good faith reliance on the representation that the other contracting party is free to do so, it is not necessary to delve into the facts surrounding disputes over the prior contracts of such other party to ascertain that such other party is free.

(j) There is no requirement that a party become a "trier of fact" to avoid a claim of interference. See,

for example, *Wooden Nickel Records, Inc. v. A&M Records, Inc.*, Superior Court (Los Angeles) #104271, 11/7/75 per Caldecott, J.

(k) New York apparently places more of the burden on the plaintiff than California. To sustain an action for inducement to breach in an agreement which was terminable at will by the breaching party, it must be shown that defendant intended solely to injure plaintiff without any expectation of social or economic advantage, or that defendant used unlawful, dishonest or improper means to bring about the termination. See, for example, *Goldfarb v. Strauss*, 212 N.Y.S.2d 579 (1961); and *Noah v. L. Daitch & Co.*, 192 N.Y.S.2d 380 (1959).

(l) An active, intentional interferer is not permitted to avail himself of a contractual indemnity granted to him by the performer. See, for example, *Reiner v. North American Newspaper Alliance*, 259 N.Y. 250 (1932).

(m) Those dealing with country artists must be particularly careful. Under Sec. 47–15–113, Tenn. Code Anno., a successful plaintiff in an inducing-breach case is entitled to treble damages. However, as illustrated by *Lichter v. Fulcher*, 125 S.W.2d 501 (Tenn.App. 1938), there must be a "clear showing" of inducement in order to make this remedy available; if the standard is met, a treble damage award is mandatory and mitigation is *not* an issue. See *Howard v. Haven*, 198 Tenn. 572, 281 S.W.2d 480 (Tenn. 1955).

(n) Even when no contract exists, action may be available for interference with prospective advantage, a broader tort than inducement to breach of interference with contractual relations. See, for example, *Buckaloo v. Johnson*, 14 Cal.3rd 815, 573 P.2d 865 (1975) (free competition is justifiable as long as a deal is merely contemplated or potential but may become wrongful once a relationship is established).

(o) An artist's present company will often send notices to other companies in the event of a dispute with the artist, advising them of the existence of a contract and threatening suit in the event of interference. While normally privileged, this can be hazardous if done without caution. See Rudell, "The Discreet Lawsuit," 179 *New York Law Journal*, p. 1, March 13, 1978.

(p) Courts are reluctant to grant injunctions that might prevent a performer from earning a living as a performer, especially when there appear to be no viable alternatives available to the performer. See *Machen v. Johanssen* (Section 1.53); *Vanguard Recording Society v. Kweskin* (Section 1.53). However, in the case of a highly compensated star performer, the degree of vigilance exercised by the court may be somewhat more relaxed. Injunctive relief, against both the star and the interfering third party, is a distinct possibility.

4.51 Existence of Contract and Interference: The *Bonner* and *Westbound* Cases

Recording artists frequently move from small to large labels. At times, the smaller labels are little more than "farm clubs" for the "majors." This movement was particularly prevalent in the 1960s to the mid 1970s.

At times, it was simply a case of an artist moving on at the end of a contract term; in other situations, the move was attempted in mid-term and accompanied by a claim that the smaller label was in material breach of its agreement with the artist, justifying termination on the part of the artist. At times, the artist was the prime mover; in other cases, the impetus came from the prospective new label.

The Ohio Players (a previously unsuccessful recording group) entered into exclusive five-year recording and music publishing agreements with Westbound and Bridgeport, its music publishing affiliate. The companies were headquartered in the Detroit area; the contracts were made with reference to Michigan law. The recording agreement provided, in part: "[Westbound] is not obligated to make or sell records manufactured from the master recordings made hereunder or to license such master recordings or to have [the Ohio Players] record the minimum [number] of record sides [specified in the agreement]."

The publishing agreement provided in part that "the extent of exploitation" of compositions written by The Ohio Players was to be "entirely within the discretion" of Bridgeport.

During the first 21 months of the term, Westbound advanced $59,380 in recording costs, artwork, travel expenses, and recording session wages to the members of the group. In addition, although not contractually required to do so, Westbound advanced the members of the group an aggregate of $22,509 to enable them to pay income taxes and settle litigation against them. There was a signing advance of $4,000.

During the first 21 months of the contract, four singles and two LPs by the group were released. One achieved "gold status" (i.e., $1,000,000 in sales under the then-current industry standard).

In the fall of 1973, The Ohio Players began looking around for a new deal. There was a dispute in the evidence as to whether The Ohio Players approached Phonogram first, or vice versa. In any event, Phonogram officials became aware of the desire of The Ohio Players to obtain a new recording agreement and referred the matter to the president of Mercury Records (a Phonogram label), who authorized his A&R ("artists and repertoire"—talent scout/talent coordination) representative to pursue the matter, but only if the group were free to contract. According to Mercury Records, upon becoming aware of the fact that the terms of the Westbound agreements had not yet expired, the president abruptly terminated the talks. The group, however, persisted and were told that negotiations could resume when the group was free. The group's spokespersons represented that Westbound and Bridgeport were in breach and that the agreements could be terminated, whereupon Mercury Records responded with a draft agreement setting forth the offer which would be made if and when the group became free. The royalties provided in the draft agreement were to be the highest Mercury had ever paid. The group retained an attorney well known to Mercury and its president, but previously unknown to the group or its representatives (and to whom the group may or may not have been "steered" by Mercury). This attorney, together with Mercury's own attorney, worked together to find a means whereby the group could escape from its agreement with Westbound and Bridgeport. The final terms of the Mercury agreement were worked out verbally.

At this point, The Ohio Players acting through their new attorney repudiated the Westbound and Bridgeport agreements, and signed with Phonogram, Inc. and its music publishing affiliate. The Players received a $50,000 advance, $40,000 of which was to be held in escrow until Mercury was "of the opinion that there [was] no likelihood of litigation with Westbound," and brought an action for declaratory judgment on the grounds that the recording and publishing agreements were invalid and unenforceable. At the same time, Mercury signed the manager who had served as the go-between in the negotiations with the group to a one-year contract as "National Promotion Director, Rhythm & Blues," but, according to the opinion, the manager had "only vague and unspecified duties."

The lower court granted summary judgment to The Ohio Players on the grounds that the agreements lacked mutuality. The court then granted summary judgment to Phonogram, who had been joined as a third-party defendant, on the grounds that Phonogram could not be liable for interference with a contractual relationship where there was no enforceable contract.

The Illinois Court of Appeals reversed both judgments. Portions of Justice Simon's opinions in these cases follow.

Bonner v. Westbound Records, 394 N.E.2d 1303 (Ill.App. 1979)

. . . Proceeding to the merits, the plaintiffs contend that the recording agreement is unenforceable because no consideration passed from Westbound to The Ohio Players for their agreement to record exclusively for Westbound. Plain-tiffs emphasize especially that the recording agreement lacked mutuality because even though The Ohio Players were obligated to make a minimum number of recordings, Westbound was not required to make even a single recording using The Ohio Players. . . .

Contrary to the conclusion reached by the circuit court judge, it is our view that consideration passed to The Ohio Players when they accepted $4,000 to enter into the agreements. The fact that this payment was made by Westbound and Bridgeport by a check containing the notation that it was "an advance against royalties" does not disqualify the payment from being regarded as consideration. If sufficient royalties were not earned to repay Westbound the $4,000, The Ohio Players would not have been obligated to return it. By making the $4,000 advance, Westbound suffered a legal detriment and The Ohio Players received a legal advantage. . . . It is not the function of either the circuit court or this court to review the amount of the consideration which passed to decide whether either party made a bad bargain . . . unless the amount is so grossly inadequate as to shock the conscience of the court. . . . The advance The Ohio Players received, taken together with their expectation of what Westbound would accomplish in their behalf, does not shock our conscience. On the contrary, to a performing group which had never been successful in making records, Westbound offered an attractive proposal. The adequacy of consideration must be determined as of the time a contract is agreed upon, not from the hindsight of how the parties fare under it. . . .

Although the $4,000 payment to plaintiffs was not recited in either of the agreements, parol evidence was properly admitted to establish that the payment was made in consideration of the agreements. Where a contract is silent as to consideration, its existence may be established through parol evidence. . . . The agreements are valid and enforceable even if they lack mutuality because they are supported by the executed consideration of $4,000 passing from the defendants to The Ohio Players. . . .

Even had the defendants not made the $4,000 advance, the plaintiffs could not prevail. The circuit court judge erred in finding that "there was no obligation on the part of the defendants to do anything under their respective agreements" with The Ohio Players. During the first 21 months after the date of the recording agreement, Westbound expended in excess of $80,000 to promote The Ohio Players and to pay their taxes and compromise litigation against them, and during this period the performers recorded four single records and two albums. The consistent pattern of good faith best efforts exerted by the parties during the first third of the term of the agreements demonstrates that they intended to be bound and to bind each other. Even contracts which are defective due to a lack of mutuality at inception may be cured by performance in conformance therewith. *Adkisson v. Ozment* (1977), 55 Ill.App.So. 108, 110, 12 Ill.Dec. 790, 370 N.E.2d 594.

Disregarding the performance under the agreements, the conclusion that the parties intended to be and were mutually obligated is also compelled by the rule that the law implies mutual promises to use good faith in interpreting an agreement and good faith and fair dealing in carrying out its purposes. (*Mueller v. Bethesda Mineral Spring Co.* (1891), 88 Mich. 390, 50 N.W. 319; *Michigan Stone & Supply Co. v. Harris* (6th Cir. 1897), 81 F. 928; *Martindell v. Lake Shore National Bank* (1958), 15 Ill.2d 272, 286, 154 N.E.2d 683; *Wood v. Lucy, Lady Duff-Gordon* (1917), 222 N.Y. 88, 118 N.E. 214.) In *Wood v. Lucy,* an often cited decision, the plaintiff, a dress manufacturer, obtained exclusive rights to market dresses designed by the defendant, a prominent designer, in return for the plaintiff's agreement to pay the designer one-half of its profits. The designer endorsed fabrics and dresses of plaintiff's competitors, and defended the plaintiff's suit for damages by contending, as the plaintiffs in this case argue, that the contract lacked mutuality because it did not require the plaintiff to do anything. Mr. Justice Cardozo speaking for the New York Court of Appeals rejected this argument, saying:

> [The defendant insists] that the plaintiff does not bind himself to anything. It is true that he does not promise in so many words that he will use reasonable efforts to place the defendant's indorsements

and market her designs. We think, however, that such a promise is fairly to be implied. . . .

The doctrine announced in *Wood v. Lucy* is the law of Illinois. (*Martindell v. Lake Shore National Bank* (1958), 15 Ill.2d 272, 154 N.E.2d 683; *Cook-Master, Inc. v. Nicro Steel Products, Inc.* (1950), 339 Ill.App. 519, 90 N.E.2d 657.) It also appears to have been the law in Michigan even prior to *Wood v. Lucy* (*Mueller v. Bethesda Mineral Spring Co.* (1891), 88 Mich. 390, 50 N.W. 319, relied on in *Lucy; Michigan Stone & Supply Co. v. Harris* (6th Cir. 1897), 81 F. 928), and has been adopted by many other states. . . .

The plaintiffs attempt to distinguish *Wood v. Lucy* in three ways. First, they contend that the agreements in this case resulted in the transfer of their total creative efforts, while the designer in *Wood v. Lucy* transferred only limited rights. The reverse is true. The designer transferred not only endorsement rights, but the exclusive right to sell her designs and to license others to sell them. In other words, she transferred the identity of her creative efforts and her major source of livelihood as a dress designer. In this case, The Ohio Players retained the right to perform in nightclubs and in concerts. This is significant, for at the time these agreements were signed, the major portion of The Ohio Players' income was from their live performances rather than their recording or songwriting efforts.

Next, the plaintiffs contend that the recording agreement is assignable and that an assignable contract is not subject to an implied promise of good faith. This distinction is not persuasive for the manufacturer in *Wood v. Lucy* had the exclusive right to sell or to license others to sell the designer's creations (222 N.Y., at 90, 118 N.E., at 214), which in effect meant that his contract rights were assignable.

Finally, plaintiffs, relying upon provisions of the recording agreement and the publishing agreement, argue that those agreements expressly negated any implied promise by defendants to perform in good faith, and *Wood v. Lucy* is, therefore, not applicable. . . .

Plaintiffs' argument is inconsistent with the meaning of the agreements, taken in their entirety; and also is at odds with the interpretation placed upon the agreements by the parties. Neither of the above quoted provisions states that Westbound and Bridgeport may sit idly by for 5 years, and they did not. Neither agreement states that Westbound and Bridgeport may act in bad faith. Neither provision quoted above contradicts the implied promises of good faith which we attribute to the agreements.

As we interpret the provision of the recording agreement quoted above, it states only that Westbound is not obligated to record the full minimum number of records set forth in another provision of the contract which The Ohio Players were obligated to record, or after going to the expense of making master recordings, to license them or make or sell records from the master recordings in the event the master recordings proved not to be suitable for that purpose. It does not mean, as plaintiffs urge, that Westbound is not required to make even one recording with The Ohio Players. And, the Bridgeport provision merely left to the discretion of the publisher the amount of advertising and publicity that would be given to any musical composition written by The Ohio Players. These provisions reserve to Westbound and Bridgeport discretion to control the content of recordings and the timing and number of releases. Flexibility of this type was essential in order to achieve the greatest success for The Ohio Players as well as Westbound and Bridgeport. Nothing in either the recording agreement or the publishing agreement or in the conduct of the parties demonstrates that Westbound or Bridgeport could or did use this discretion arbitrarily or in bad faith.

This interpretation of the recording agreement finds support in a seemingly unrelated provision of that agreement. The agreement was to run for an initial term of 5 years, but Westbound had the option to extend it for 2 years. If, as the plaintiffs contend, Westbound had absolutely no obligations under the contract, that extension would be practically automatic, for Westbound would have nothing to lose by exercising its option, and perhaps something to gain. The agreement would be essentially for one 7-year term, and the "option" phrasing a meaningless complication. Under our interpretation of the contract, however,

the option provision makes perfect sense: Westbound could extend its right to the plaintiffs' services, but only at the cost of renewing its own obligation to use reasonable efforts on their behalf. The law prefers an interpretation that makes sense of the entire contract to one that leaves a provision with no sense or reason for being a part of a contract. . . .

The circuit court also erred in failing to give effect to the doctrine of promissory estoppel as a substitute for consideration. Decisions in Illinois as well as Michigan state that promissory estoppel may be relied upon to uphold a contract otherwise lacking in consideration or mutuality at the time of its execution, where injustice can be avoided only by enforcement of the promise. . . .

Westbound, in reliance upon the execution of the recording agreement by The Ohio Players, undertook a substantial business risk, incurring more than $80,000 in expenses which it could recoup only if the recordings were successful. The recording agreement provided for royalty payments to The Ohio Players at percentage rates ordinarily found in the record industry in contracts providing for exclusive services of performers over a period of time. Assuming Westbound and Bridgeport were not obligated to do anything, the expenses and liabilities they incurred in reasonable reliance upon enjoying the exclusive services of The Ohio Players for a 5-year period obligated The Ohio Players to perform as they promised to do.

Plaintiffs assert that promissory estoppel is not an appropriate doctrine in this case because it applies only when there is unjust enrichment. No Michigan authority is cited. However, because the agreements are supported by consideration, the defendants need not rest on the doctrine of promissory estoppel as a substitute for consideration. Our purpose in considering the promissory estoppel issue is primarily to illuminate the fundamental unfairness of the plaintiffs' claim, and so we shall, for the sake of argument, accept the plaintiffs' legal doctrine that unjust enrichment is required.

The plaintiffs' theory is that there is no unjust enrichment once Westbound recoups its advances from the royalties The Ohio Players have earned, and thereby suffers no actual loss. This, however, is possible only because of the success The Ohio Players enjoyed in recording for Westbound. If we adopt the plaintiffs' view and refuse to enforce the agreement, the outlook at the time promissory estoppel arises, when Westbound, relying on plaintiffs' promises, works and advances money on their behalf, but before those efforts succeed or fail, is this: if the venture fails, Westbound's money will vanish, but if The Ohio Players become a hit, they will allow Westbound to break even. Conversely, The Ohio Players can do no worse than break even, having nothing invested, and they may perhaps enjoy a great profit, largely due to Westbound's work and backing. It is obvious that no one would ever voluntarily take Westbound's end of this deal. The Ohio Players should not be able to impose it on Westbound by backing out of their agreement. For The Ohio Players to obtain for themselves the possibility of a bonanza, while imposing the risk of loss on Westbound, by breaking their promises after Westbound's reliance on those promises for a period of almost 2 years, would unfairly enrich The Ohio Players at Westbound's expense.

The Ohio Players had nothing to offer Westbound but an interest in their future, the chance to make a great deal of money by making them famous. The Ohio Players had nothing to lose; Westbound was to take all the risks. Having induced Westbound to perform as fully and faithfully as anyone could desire by signing these agreements, The Ohio Players now seek to deny Westbound the sole reward of its success. Their aim is to keep for themselves the fame and money which, judging by their past experience, they could not have acquired without Westbound's aid, by asserting that Westbound did not originally *promise* to do what it has already actually done. This the plaintiffs are estopped to do; even if the agreements were not originally supported by consideration, they became enforceable when Westbound performed in reliance on the promises of The Ohio Players, and indeed advanced additional monies not called for by the contract, to protect its investment.

The plaintiffs refer us to two recent English decisions involving exclusive service contracts for an extended period of time between song-

writers and music publishers. The cases are: *A. Schroeder Music Publishing Co. v. Macaulay*, [1974] 3 All E.R. 616 (H.L.); *Clifford Davis Mgt. Ltd. v. WEA Records Ltd.*, [1975] 1 All E.R. 237 (C.A.). These decisions are distinguishable. They void contracts not for lack of consideration but as unconscionable restraints of trade. Both of these cases emphasize that the exclusive service agreements were oppressively one-sided, and that the songwriters in both cases were not represented by attorneys or advisers and lacked equality of bargaining power with the publishers. This is not the case here. The Ohio Players were represented by an attorney and advisers who conducted a portion of the negotiations with Westbound, and prior to signing their agreement with Westbound, The Ohio Players received competing offers from at least one other company engaged in the music recording business. Also, in contrast with the efforts expended and advances made by Westbound to promote and publicize The Ohio Players, there was no indication in either of the English decisions that there had been substantial activity by the music publisher which resulted in the distribution and sale of successful artistic creations produced by the songwriters.

For the above reasons, we conclude that the recording agreement and the publishing agreement were supported by consideration consisting of the cash advances and the mutual promises of the parties, and that the agreements may also be upheld by the doctrine of promissory estoppel. . . .

An additional portion of the circuit court's order which requires scrutiny is its termination of the recording agreement and the publishing agreement as of January 8, 1974, based on the finding that the agreements were severable and divisible into units of performance by the parties. We do not construe the agreements in that way. Partial performance by The Ohio Players was not the consideration Westbound and Bridgeport bargained for. Neither the recording agreement nor the publishing agreement specified that, by performing a specific portion of the agreement, The Ohio Players could be relieved from further performance. Nothing contained in the agreements indicates any intention of the parties that any single record, recording session or composition of The Ohio Players would serve as consideration for a specific unit of performances by Westbound or Bridgeport. Westbound and Bridgeport agreed to pay the royalty rates called for by the agreements because The Ohio Players promised to make a minimum number of recordings and to give Westbound and Bridgeport their exclusive services for 5 years.

A contract is not severable where the parties assented to all promises as a single whole. . . . A contract is non-severable if the striking of any promise or set of promises would destroy the basis of the entire bargain. . . . These agreements gave The Ohio Players benefits early, and were to reward Westbound only later, if at all. To treat them as severable would allow The Ohio Players to take Westbound's services as long as they desired, and then abandon Westbound as soon as Westbound commenced to benefit from the arrangement. Westbound could only lose. We find nothing in either agreement to warrant plaintiffs in accepting and rendering part performance and then repudiating the remainder of the contracts on the ground that their performance was severable. . . .

Because the agreements which this action involves were valid and enforceable and not susceptible of division and apportionment, the circuit court erred in granting summary judgment in favor of the plaintiffs on the various counts of the complaint seeking a declaratory judgment. The court also erred in denying summary judgment in favor of Westbound and Bridgeport on those counts raising only the issue of the validity and enforceability of the agreements.

Westbound Records, Inc. v. Phonogram, Inc., 394 N.E.2d 1315 (Ill. App. 1979)

. . . The foundation for the circuit court's summary judgment in favor of Mercury Records is shattered by our decision in *Bonner v. Westbound Records, Inc*. Therefore, the summary judgment in this case must be reversed and remanded for further proceedings unless no issue of fact appears with respect to whether Mercury Records may have tortiously interfered with the contractual or business relationships between The Ohio Players and Westbound or induced the Satchell group to breach those agreements. . . .

Whether Mercury Records offered the Satchell group $50,000 and the service of attorneys to desert their contractual obligation or whether Mercury Records innocently negotiated with and signed a performing group which it in good faith believed had no commitment to Westbound is a disputed question of fact.

Mercury Records explains that its initial contact with The Ohio Players was when its officials thought that the agreement between Westbound and The Ohio Players had already expired. However, Mercury Records concedes that after obtaining copies of the Westbound agreements which showed Mercury Records that the contracts had 3 years to run, it persevered in its efforts to persuade The Ohio Players to terminate their relationship with Westbound. Whether Mercury Records' pursuit of the Satchell group from September 1973 until January 1974 and the inducements offered the Satchell group to leave Westbound constitute proper or improper interference also presents an issue for the trier of fact. . . .

Westbound's allegations cannot be disposed of without the resolution of many disputed factual issues and without considering facts from which many inconsistent inferences could be drawn by a trier of fact. For these reasons the circuit court erred in granting summary judgment in favor of Mercury Records and this cause must be reversed and remanded for trial.

Westbound presents several theories to justify recovery against Mercury Records even if it had no valid contract with The Ohio Players; but, we need not discuss them. There was a valid contract, and none of the other theories advanced by Westbound offers it any advantage over its claim for interfering with or inducing a breach of a valid contract.

Reversed and remanded.

4.60 Creative Control

The creative talent wants to ensure the continuing integrity of the artistic work. This need applies whether we are discussing books, movies, television shows, or music. The key is to have protections in the original contract. But that is not always done; and even if attempted, it is not always effective. While our considerations here parallel other discussions of creative control, they focus particularly on problems in music.

In *Granz v. Harris*, a jazz promoter sold master discs of a concert he had produced and recorded. The defendant buyer deleted several minutes of the music when he manufactured records from the discs. The court considers the issues from a contractual perspective, reading into the contract an implied duty by the defendant not to distort the product by presenting, in effect, a false representation as to its origin. Judge Frank's concurrence explores the possibility of imposing a "moral rights" standard, something used in many European countries to protect artists' rights. However, he rejects that standard as unnecessary in this case.

Granz v. Harris, 198 F.2d 585 (2d Cir. 1952)

SWAN, CHIEF JUDGE

This is an appeal by the plaintiff from a judgment dismissing his complaint on the merits after trial to the court without a jury. The complaint sought rescission of a contract of sale of master phonographic recordings of portions of a jazz concert presented by the plaintiff, damages for breach of the contract, an accounting of profits, a permanent injunction, and attorney's fees in the amount of $3,000. Federal jurisdiction rests on diversity of citizenship. The district judge rendered an opinion, reported in 98 F. Supp. 906, and made detailed findings of fact and conclusions of law in conformity with his opinion. Only two of the findings of fact are attacked by the appellant. They will be discussed hereinafter.

Norman Granz is a well-known promoter and producer of jazz concerts under the designation "Jazz At The Philharmonic." One such concert he caused to be recorded in its entirety on a sixteen-

inch master disc from which he re-recorded on six twelve-inch master discs that part of the concert constituting the rendition of two musical compositions entitled "How High the Moon" and "Lady Be Good." These master discs, three for each composition, revolved at 78 revolutions per minute, and were usable in manufacturing commercial phonograph records of the same size and playable at the same speed as the master discs. Granz sold the master discs to the defendant pursuant to a contract dated August 15, 1945. The contract required that in the sale of phonograph records manufactured from the purchased masters the defendant should use the credit-line "Presented by Norman Granz" and explanatory notes which Granz had prepared. Some time in 1948 the defendant re-recorded the musical content of the purchased masters on ten-inch 78 rpm masters from which he manufactured phonograph records of the same size and speed. Such records he sold both in an album and separately. Concededly, at first the album cover did not conform to the contract in that, although it bore the designation "Jazz At The Philharmonic" it did not contain the credit-line or the explanatory notes, but the court found that the cover was later corrected upon the plaintiff's demand. He found also that there was no deletion of music in the ten-inch 78 rpm records. In 1950 the defendant re-recorded the entire contents of the purchased masters on a ten-inch 33⅓ rpm master and from this manufactured records of the same size and speed for retail sale.

The questions presented by the appeal are whether any right of the plaintiff was violated by the defendant: (1) by manufacturing and selling ten-inch 33⅓ records; or (2) by manufacturing and selling ten-inch 78 rpm records; or (3) by selling records singly instead of as part of an album containing both "How High the Moon" and "Lady Be Good."

On the authority of *RCA Mfg. Co. v. Whiteman*, 2 Cir., 113 F.2d 86, certiorari denied 311 U.S. 712, 61 S.Ct. 393, 85 L.Ed. 463, and a finding that the contract was one of sale rather than license, the district court answered the first question in the negative, 98 F. Supp. 906, 910. We agree with this conclusion and see no need to add to his opinion.

He also gave a negative answer to the third question, 98 F. Supp. 910–911. We adopt his reasoning and conclusion on this point also.

Determination of the second question turns upon findings of fact. Obviously a ten-inch record revolving at 78 revolutions a minute has a shorter playing time and a smaller content than a twelve-inch record revolving at the same speed. Findings 25 and 26 state that all that was deleted in the smaller record was audience reaction consisting of whistles, cheers and screams; that there was no deletion of music, and the plaintiff's contribution to the original musical production was not changed or affected in any way; and, "Accordingly, when the defendant, at the plaintiff's insistence, corrected the album covers of the ten-inch 78 rpm records to conform to the agreement, he was not, as claimed, attributing to the plaintiff the work of some one else." The court based his finding that there was no deletion of music on his own listening to the records (exhibits 4 and 14 played in the court room) and on the testimony of Mr. Hammond, a musical expert called by the plaintiff. A perusal of this expert's testimony discloses statements patently at odds with the judge's finding. Nor can we understand, after ourselves listening to the records, the judge's finding that nothing but audience reaction was omitted from the ten-inch records. Fully eight minutes of music appear to us to have been omitted, including saxophone, guitar, piano and trumpet solos. In our opinion the trial judge's finding that there was no substantial musical deletions is erroneous.

We are therefore faced with the question whether the manufacture and sale by the defendant of the abbreviated ten-inch records violated any right of the plaintiff. Disregarding for the moment the terms of the contract, we think that the purchaser of the master discs could lawfully use them to produce the abbreviated record and could lawfully sell the same provided he did not describe it as a recording of music presented by the plaintiff. If he did so describe it, he would commit the tort of unfair competition. But the contract required the defendant to use the legend "Presented by Norman Granz," that is, to attribute to him the musical content of the records offered for sale. This contractual duty carries by implication, without the necessity of an express prohibition, the duty not to sell records which make the required legend a false representation. In our opinion, therefore, sale of the ten-inch abbreviated records was a breach of the contract. No specific damages were shown to have resulted. As such damages are difficult to prove and the harm to the plaintiff's reputation as an expert in the presentation of jazz concerts is irreparable, injunctive relief is appropriate. Hence we think the plaintiff was entitled to an injunction against having the abbreviated ten-inch records attributed to him unless he waived his right. . . .

Dismissal of the complaint is affirmed with respect to sales of the ten-inch 33⅓ rpm records and with respect to selling records singly. With respect to the sale of ten-inch 78 rpm records and the claim of attorney's fees the cause is remanded for further proceedings in conformity with the opinion. One-half costs of appeal are awarded the appellant.

FRANK, CIRCUIT JUDGE (CONCURRING)

1. I agree, of course, that, whether by way of contract or tort, plaintiff (absent his consent to the contrary) is entitled to prevention of the publication, as his, of a garbled version of his uncopyrighted product. This is not novel doctrine: Byron obtained an injunction from an English court restraining the publication of a book purporting to contain his poems only, but which included some not of his authorship. American courts, too, have enforced such a right. Those courts have also enjoined the use by another of the characteristics of an author of repute in such manner as to deceive buyers into erroneously believing that they were buying a work of that author. Those courts, moreover, have granted injunctive relief in these circumstances: An artist sells one of his works to the defendant who substantially changes it and then represents the altered matter to the public as that artist's product. Whether the work is copyrighted or not, the established rule is that, even if the contract with the artist expressly authorizes reasonable modifications (e.g., where a novel or stage play is sold for adaptation as a movie), it is an actionable wrong to hold out the artist as author of a version which substantially departs from the original.

Under the authorities, the defendant's conduct here, as my colleagues say, may also be considered a kind of "unfair competition" or "passing off." The irreparable harm, justifying an injunction, becomes apparent when one thinks what would be the result if the collected speeches of Stalin were published under the name of Senator Robert Taft, or the poems of Ella Wheeler Wilcox as those of T. S. Eliot.

2. If, on the remand, the evidence should favor the plaintiff, I think we should grant him further relief, i.e., an injunction against publication by the defendant of any truncated version of his work, even if it does not bear plaintiff's name. I would rest the grant of that relief on an interpretation of the contract.

Plaintiff, in asking for such relief, relied in part not on the contract but on the doctrine of artists' "moral right," a compendious label of a "bundle of rights" enforced in many "civil law" countries. Able legal thinkers, pointing out that American courts have already recognized a considerable number of the rights in that "bundle," have urged that our courts use the "moral right" symbol. Those thinkers note that the label "right of privacy" served to bring to the attention of our courts a common center of perspectives previously separated in the decisions, and that the use of that label induced further novel and valuable judicial perspectives.

To this suggestion there are these objections: (a) "Moral right" seems to indicate to some persons something not legal, something meta-legal. (b) The "moral right" doctrine, as applied in some countries, includes very extensive rights which courts in some American jurisdictions are not yet prepared to acknowledge; as a result, the phrase "moral right" seems to have frightened some of those courts to such an extent that they have unduly narrowed artists' rights. (c) Finally, it is not always an unmitigated boon to devise and employ such a common name. As we have said elsewhere: "A new name, a novel label expressive of a new generalization, can have immense consequences. Emerson said, 'Generalization is always a new influx of the divinity into the mind. Hence the thrill that attends it.' Confronted with disturbing variety, we often feel a tension from which a generalization, an abstraction, relieves us. It serves as a de-problemizer, aiding us to pass from an unstable, problematical, situation to a more stable one. It satisfies a craving, meets what Emerson called 'the insatiable demand of harmony in man,' a demand which translates itself into the so-called 'law' of 'the least effort.' But the solution of a problem through the invention of a new generalization is no final solution: The new generalization breeds new problems. Stressing a newly perceived likeness between many particular happenings which had theretofore seemed unlike, it may blind us to continuing unlikenesses. Hypnotized by a label which emphasizes identities, we may be led to ignore differences. . . . For, with its stress on uniformity, an abstraction or generalization tends to become totalitarian in its attitude towards uniqueness."

Without rejecting the doctrine of "moral right," I think that, in the light of the foregoing, we should not rest decision on that doctrine where, as here, it is not necessary to do so.

4.70   Ownership and Protection of Performers' Names

Various legal theories protecting the individual and his or her name, image, and work product are considered in Chapter 10. In the following article by Jay L. Cooper we explore special aspects of this protection concerning musicians. This article, titled "The Ownership and Protection of Performers' Names," first appeared in the *Entertainment and Sports Lawyer*, vol. 1, no. 2, p. 1, Fall 1982. It is reprinted by permission of the American Bar Association Forum Committee on the Entertainment and Sports Industries and by permission of Jay L. Cooper.

THE OWNERSHIP AND PROTECTION OF PERFORMERS' NAMES

by Jay L. Cooper

A name is probably the most important individual asset that a performer or group will ever own. Most of us are familiar with names like the "Rolling Stones," the "Commodores," "Journey," "Foreigner," "Queen" and "Pink Floyd," but usually, we are not as familiar with the names of any of the individuals comprising those groups. Some groups, for example the "Byrds," the "Fifth Dimension," the "Supremes," and the "Platters," have changed most, if not all, of their members at one time or another, sometimes frequently; yet the drawing power of the group has normally remained. It is easy to see, therefore, that a name can be extremely valuable, that it can, in fact, sell records, products of all sorts and draw audiences into concert halls and movie theatres.

Ownership of the Name

More often than not, members of a group fail to execute a contract among themselves, particularly during the early stages of their career. Consequently, in absence of any agreement, the ownership of the group's name must be determined by examining the facts and the applicable law.

The California Business and Professions Code, Section 14400, has adopted the common law provision which states that a name is owned by the person who first adopts and uses that name. However, a name is not recognized as a property right until it acquires a "secondary meaning." "Secondary meaning" is acquired through association; that is, when the public associates the name with the particular service being given, then under the law, that name will have acquired "secondary meaning." It is then elevated to the status of a property right and can then be protected by injunction.

Whether a name has acquired a secondary meaning is a question of fact. It is established by showing, among other things, duration of use, extent of advertising, drawing power, continuity of use, and identification of the market (that is, whether the group works in California or California, Arizona, and New Mexico or throughout the country).

In an action claiming an infringement of a name, after establishing the existence of sec-ondary meaning in the name, it must be shown that use of the name by the alleged infringer creates a likelihood of confusion. If, for example, somebody were to open a health club called "Blood, Sweat & Tears," the musical group of that name probably could not enjoin the club from the use of the name, because the two users would not be competing in the same marketplace and therefore there would be little likelihood of the public's being confused by the two uses of the same name.

Since ownership of the name will vary with the particular circumstances, it would be appropriate to examine a few different situations as to the likely result.

A. Assume that a clarinet player, an accordion player and a drummer are performing together under the name "Atomic Bomb." After bombing for ten years they add a lead singer who takes control of the group and substitutes a trumpet for the clarinet, an organ for the accordion, has the drummer add bongos, and adds a bass player. The new group is then composed of the three original and two additional musicians. The group finds a great record producer and becomes an overnight success performing under the same name. Subsequently, disputes arise within the group. In absence of any agreement who owns the name?

According to California statutory law, the person who first adopts and uses the name is its owner. But are the owners the original three musicians who first used the name, or all five who made a success with the use of the name?

The case law suggests it is all five. In *Peterson v. Lightfoot*, 47 Cal.App. 646, 191 Pac. 48 (1920), the court stated that even though one or more persons first adopted the use of the name, those that are members of the partnership or group when it acquires its secondary meaning are the owners of the name.

In the instance where the name has a secondary meaning as to only some of the members of the band, those members will have a protectable interest whereas the others will not. See *Boogie Kings v. Guillory*, 188 So.2d 445 (1966).

B. Assume now an existing group breaks up, and some of the individuals start competing groups with each group using the original name. In absence of an agreement could either group enjoin the other from using the name? Probably not. A court would probably invoke the "unclean hands" doctrine and find that the members who have adopted the name, to the exclusion of other members, cannot complain against others who have done the same. Therefore, it is likely that neither group could recover.

C. Suppose the group fires one of its members without cause, and that person subsequently forms another group with the same name. The group probably could not enjoin the ex-member from establishing the new group. Reason: unclean hands. The court could say "you excluded this person and appropriated the name; therefore, you have no right to come in and complain." The ex-member could, however, sue the group for damages, based on the theory that partners who exclude another partner and appropriate the name are guilty of conversion of a property right (the name) and are subject to claims for damages. (See *Driskill v. Thompson*, 141 Cal.App.2d 479; 296 Pac.2d 834 (1956).)

D. In a situation where two competing groups are using the same name, but neither of the groups have ever been associated together, several results are possible.

Take, for example, a West Coast group which first adopts a name but their career remains fairly stagnant with their only work being local club dates in California. Two years later, in New York, another group under contract to a major record company, without prior knowledge of the first group, becomes widely known throughout the country performing under the same name. Can the second group enjoin the first group from continuing to work under that name?

Assuming the second group first acquired secondary meaning, there appear to be conflicting cases on the subject. In the "Palladin case," concerning the television show "Have Gun, Will Travel," the court held that the second user, who acquired the secondary meaning first, would have a right to use the name, but in all likelihood, could not stop the earlier user from continuing to use the name. See *Columbia Broadcasting v. DeCosta*, 377 F.2d 315 (1967). A second case, which concerned the television show "I Spy," held that the latter user who acquired the "secondary meaning" first could stop the prior user. See *Cinepix v. Triple F Productions*, 150 USPQ 134 (NY 1966). However, in a third case wherein the question of knowledge by a second user was central, the court held that a second user could be guilty of infringement when the infringer's use of the first user's mark results in confusion as to the origin of the first user's product, so-called "reverse confusion."

In this latter case Big O Tire Company began selling their tires under the trademark "Big Foot." Big O did not register the mark nor did they establish secondary meaning. The second user, Goodyear, with knowledge of Big O's use of the mark "Big Foot" commenced a major television advertising campaign across the 50 states of a Goodyear tire they called "Big Foot."

The court held that the mark "Big Foot" as used by Big O was not merely descriptive, was indeed a distinctive mark entitled to common law trademark protection as well as protection under the Lanham Act. The court further stated that the intent of the law is not to limit recovery to "passing off"; otherwise anyone with adequate size and resources could adopt any existing trademark and develop new meaning for that trademark as identification of the second user's products. The court held that the activities of Goodyear were unquestionably unfair competition. See *Big O Tire Dealers, Inc. v. The Goodyear Tire & Rubber Co.*, 561 F.2d 1365 (1977).

These cases point up the fact that great care should be used in the selection of a performing name so that it is not confusingly similar to an already existing name particularly in the same professional field. An infringement suit brought by a prior user could result in the loss of substantial monies, not only in the payment of potential damages to the prior user, but in material created using the name, such as albums, advertising materials for records, concerts, etc., merchandising items and credits on television shows and in motion pictures.

It therefore would be good practice to check all available name sources, for example, the records in the patent and trademark office, state trademark registrations, the various industry publications and the listings maintained by certain unions or guilds. While these sources are not absolutely conclusive as to the availability of a name, such an examination would certainly reduce the artists' chances of adopting a confusingly similar name.

E. Assume a group sells five (5) million records and then breaks up. Subsequently, some new eager young musicians form a group and decide to use the same name. Do they have the right to do so? The cases indicate that the answer depends upon whether or not the name that had acquired secondary meaning was abandoned. Abandonment requires that there be a specific intent to terminate use of the mark, not merely a hiatus in its use. If it was abandoned, which is a question of fact, a second group may come along and use the name. See *Hair v. McGuire*, 10 Cal.Rptr. 414, 188 Cal.App.2d 348 (1961).

Although a band has broken up they may still have a protectable interest in their name. In determining if this is true, the following factors may be considered: continued sales of their past works, continued association in the public's mind between the band and the name, a demonstrated intent to retain an interest in that name as evidenced by timely objections to the use of the name by others, and the likelihood of public confusion. See *Giammarese v. Delfino* (Bockinghams), 197 USPQ 162 (1977), District Court N.D. Ill. E.Div.

It is possible, however, for a band/performer to assign its interests in a name to another. Nevertheless, such an assignment in gross of a name dependent on the personal skill and professional qualifications of the persons using it probably cannot be made or transferred independently, without the goodwill of the business. *Bailly v. Betti*, 241 N.Y. 22, 148 N.E. 776 (1925); *Ward-Chandler*

Building Co. v. Caldwell, 8 Cal.App.2d 375, 47 P.2d 758 (1935); Cal. Bus. Prof. Code §14260. The assignee will have a protectable interest. See *Marshak v. Green* (the Drifters), 505 F. Supp. 1054 (1981) U.S. District Court S.D.N.Y.

F. Some management contracts require that the artist assign to the manager his or her interest in the group name, pursuant to a provision similar to the following one. "Artist hereby gives, grants and sets over to Manager any and all of Artist's right, title and interest in and to any trade name or other designation (herein called 'The Name') used by any entertainment unit of which Artist is or may become a part during the term hereof. Notwithstanding the generality of the foregoing, any such entertainment unit may continue to use the name during the term hereof so long as Artist is not in breach of any provision of this agreement."

However, since it is generally held that the persons who are identified with the name when it acquires secondary meaning own the name, because the public normally associates the name with the group and not the manager, the group probably would own the name, despite the assignment. (See *Peterson v. Lightfoot*, 47 Cal.App. 646, 191 Pac. 48 [1920].)

If the name was used by the artist before engaging the manager, there is no reason to make such a grant. Even if the manager creates the name, the artist should resist such a provision because that artist's future ability to work may be substantially dependent on his or her right to that name. Such a provision may only be reasonable for an artist to grant when he or she is a new artist joining an existing group as an employee, and then only to grant such to the group itself.

G. Almost all record contracts contain clauses concerning the group name. One type of clause provides that the group assigns the name to the record company for all purposes, that the group has no right to use the name other than as specified by the company, that the company licenses the use of the name back to the group for nonrecord purposes. This clause presents a similar problem to the manager's claim to ownership of the group name, and the same rules are probably equally applicable to a record company. If this clause was in the contract before the name acquired secondary meaning, it becomes a difficult issue to determine to whom the secondary meaning attaches. While it is a question of fact, it is my opinion that the group would in all probability own the name, that is, the individual members that were associated with the performance of the group at the time of acquiring the secondary meaning.

There are instances, though, in which a record company uses a name for a "house group" in which studio musicians are used, sometimes changed frequently, and to which their individual names are not associated. Normally there are no personal appearances, but if there are, no regular set of musicians are used. In this situation, it might be proved that the public associates the name with the record company, as distinguished from the group, and that the record company acquired the secondary meaning and the resulting ownership.

Organization Structure

The organizational structure through which performers operate will generally have a meaningful impact on their rights in a name.

A. *Corporations:* Some musical performers have decided to conduct business as a corporation and to make the group name a corporate asset through one or more agreements between the performers and the corporation. In such a case, the agreements normally provide that the individual members will have no rights to the name outside of their ownership interest in the corporation, which interest also may be shared by persons other than members of the band.

Pursuant to the typical agreement, when a shareholder leaves the band he or she relinquishes any interest in the name. By contrast, a party might leave the band and retain his or her interest in the corporation. In such a case, that party will still retain an interest in the name but only to the extent of his or her percentage of interest in the corporation. Some bands also employ musicians that are not

shareholders, and in such instances it would be prudent to have such employee execute an agreement in which the employee acknowledges that he or she has no ownership interest in the name, and that upon termination of his or her services, for whatever reason, he or she foregoes all right to the use of the name.

Although the name may be a corporate asset, the Lanham Act provides standing to sue for anyone likely to be injured by the wrongful use of a name. Hence, a corporate member or a non-corporate band member may have standing to sue on their own behalves. See *Rare Earth, Inc. v. Hoorelbeke et al.*, 401 F. Supp. 26 (1975), *The Five Platters v. Purdie*, 419 F. Supp. 372 (1976).

B. *Partnership:* Some musical performers operate as a partnership. Such partnership agreements usually provide that the name is an asset of the partnership, and each member's interest in the name is limited to that of a partner. In addition, when an individual leaves the partnership, he will be held to have relinquished his interests in the name. Finally, the goodwill will normally belong to the partnership rather than to the individuals. See *Giammarese v. Delfino*, 197 USPQ 162 (1977) District Court M.D. Ill.

C. *Unincorporated Association:* Many musical groups have neither entered into a formal partnership agreement, nor proceeded with their endeavors in a corporate form. In such situations, the band may be called an unincorporated association. Courts treat the legal status of such groups in the same manner as the group treats itself, without regard to the expressed declarations of the individuals. The existence of an implied partnership or joint venture is determined by the conduct of the parties. If the individuals are sharing profits and losses, a court could reasonably assume that the group is a partnership. As an unincorporated association or partnership, the group may appropriate a name, by mutual agreement, and the name will belong to the association, not to the individual members. Thus, for purposes of interests in a name, the association is similar to a partnership. Where the association has demonstrated a clear right to their name (after establishment of secondary meaning), they will have been deemed to have a protectable interest in that name. See *Boogie Kings v. Guillory*, 188 So.2d 445 (1966), for a discussion regarding the interests an unincorporated association may have in a name.

D. *Individual Performer:* An individual, of course, has a protectable interest in his actual name. Where a performer uses a fictitious name (e.g., Herman of "Herman's Hermits"), he or she must be able to demonstrate that the name has achieved secondary meaning with respect to him or her in order to be protected. In either case, where a protectable interest has been established, he or she will have the exclusive right to exploit that name. See *Winterland Concessions Co. v. Creative Screen Design, Ltd.*, 210 USPQ 6 (1981) U.S. District Court M.D.Ill. E.Div., and *Noone v. Banner*, 398 F. Supp. 260 (1975), with respect to individuals and their rights to their names.

Protection of the Name

There are several sources of protection an individual or group may turn to in an effort to prevent another from infringing the rights in the artist's performing name. Depending on the facts, one or more of the following may be used.

A. *A Claim under the Lanham Act*, Section 43(a) (15 USC 1125a) states as follows:

Any person who shall affix, apply, or annex, or use in connection with any goods or services, or any container or containers for goods, a false designation of origin, or any false description or representation, including words or other symbols tending falsely to describe or represent the same, and shall cause such goods or services to enter into commerce, and any person who shall with knowledge of the falsity of such designation of origin or description or representation cause or procure the same to be transported or used in commerce or deliver the same to any carrier to be transported or used, shall be liable to a civil action by any person doing business in the locality falsely indicated as that of origin or in the region in which said locality is situated, or by any person who believes that he is or is likely to be damaged by the use of any such false description or representation.

The policy reasons for the Lanham Act are of course to protect the public from being misguided as to the source of services and to protect the sources from having their efforts exploited. The factors involved are:

1. *Likelihood of confusion* in the public's mind as evidenced by one or more of the following: actual confusion; similarity between parties' names, considering visual, aural and meaning similarities; similarity between the types of performers and channels of trade; geographical issues; the degree of care the consumers are likely to use in determining the source of the products and finally the intent of the subsequent user to capitalize on the original user. A trademark is infringed when a second person (later user) uses it in a manner which is likely to cause confusion among ordinary prudent purchasers or prospective purchasers as to source of the services. The test is not one of actual confusion, it is the likelihood of confusion. *Big C Tire Dealers v. Goodyear*, *supra*.

2. *"Secondary meaning"* established in the name, imaginativeness of the name, the more arbitrary, fanciful or fictitious, the broader the protection as there is an increased likelihood of finding secondary meaning. If the name is of generic nature, or has been used in a similar form by others, there is a decreased likelihood of establishing the existence of secondary meaning and thus less protection available.

See *The Boogie Kings v. Guillory* ("The Boogie Kings"), La., 188 So.2d 445, 7-28-66; *Rare Earth, Inc. v. Hoorelbeke* ("Rare Earth"), 401 F. Supp. 26, 7-15-75; *Noone v. Banner Talent Associates, Inc.* ("Herman's Hermits"), 398 F. Supp. 260, 8-1-75; *The Five Platters, Inc. v. Purdie* ("The Platters"), 419 F. Supp. 372, 7-9-76; *Marshak v. Green*, ("The Drifters"), 505 F. Supp. 1054, 1-26-81; *Winterland Concession Co. v. Creative Screen Design, Ltd.*, 210 USPQ 6, 10-20-81.

3. *Other* matters to be considered are as follows:

a. Foreigners may be protected under the Lanham Act, and may be sued under it if they infringe in this country.

b. A performer's name is registrable under the Lanham Act as a service mark. A "service mark" is defined under Section 45 of the Lanham Act as "a mark used in the sale or advertising of services to identify the services of one person and distinguish them from the services of others." It is highly recommended that one registers such service mark, as registration becomes constructive notice of the use of the name and destroys the argument of innocence by the defendant. Of course, actual use of the name is required before one can register and obtain a service mark.

Cases interpreting the Lanham Act have held that while registration is prima facie evidence of the validity of a band's right to its name, it is not a prerequisite to bringing a suit under the Lanham Act. Further, anyone likely to be injured due to the wrongful use of a name may have standing to sue.

c. Anyone, by way of challenge, can file a petition to cancel a registration of a mark within five years from registration. After five years the registration becomes "conclusive" as to its ownership except that it still may be challenged at any time on a number of grounds, such as abandonment, fraud, misrepresentation, or the fact that the name has become descriptive of the article. Section 14 (16 USC 1064).

d. The courts interpreting the Lanham Act have held that *anyone* who knowingly participates in the use of a name which violates the rights of another under said act may be brought before the court as a defendant. Thus, where a subsequent band performs under a name in which another band has a protectable interest, the booking agent, and other active participants in promoting the subsequent band may be found liable in addition to the subsequent band.

e. A recent case interpreting the Lanham Act has held that a film distributor's removal of an actor's name from both the film credits and advertising materials by substituting another's name amounted to express reverse passing off.

The court further held that the plaintiff did not have to prove competition, that it was sufficient for plaintiff to prove fraud or deception; that the use of another's services, misbranded to appear as that of a competitor (i.e., reverse passing off) is a false designation of origin actionable under Section 43(a). See *Smith v. Montoro*, 648 Fed. 2d 602 (1981) (U.S. Court of Appeals, 9th Circuit).

f. The court may grant various forms of relief under the Lanham Act. Injunctive relief may be granted where there is a possibility of continuing infringement by the defendant and if it can be shown there is a likelihood of confusion. An injunction may include the prohibition of any future infringing activities and the surrendering of any infringing materials in the defendant's possession. Monetary relief may also be granted under Section 35, including any combination of the following: defendant's profits for unjust enrichment, plaintiffs' damages, treble damages (generally where defendant willfully infringed plaintiffs' rights), and attorneys' fees in extraordinary cases (generally where the infringement can be characterized as "willful, malicious, deliberate, and fraudulent").

g. The use of a logo protects the "artistic impression," i.e., the appearance of the logo, as well as the name used "in" the logo. The term "trademark" includes any word, name, symbol, or device or any combination thereof adopted by the owner of the services, and the same rules set forth herein for the protecting of the name are equally applicable to protection of the logo. A "tradename," however, which is the name of the business entity, such as a corporation, is not registrable under the Lanham Act as such, and is distinguishable from a trademark, service mark and logo, all of which are registrable.

B. *Right of Publicity*

The courts have recognized that an individual's name can be a valuable monetary asset. This commercial value stems from the right to control the exclusive use of the name, which right has come to be known as the right of publicity.

The right of publicity is a property right,

although there is substantial question as to its descendibility like property.

The rationale for this right is based on the desire of the court to prevent unjust enrichment by the theft of a performer's goodwill or name. A defendant should not get for free some aspect of a plaintiff which has a market value and for which he or she would normally have to pay. In other words, an entertainer has the sole right, subject to an assignment or other transfer, to commercially exploit his or her name.

The fact that a person is well known increases the value of the right. Additionally, the First Amendment's freedom of the press is not a defense to the commercial exploitation of a performer's name, subject of course to the distinction between news and commercial exploitation.

A performer may assign all or part of the publicity rights to his name to another party. In such an instance, the assignee will have a protectable interest in the assigned rights and standing to sue. This is subject, of course, to the question of the descendibility of such right, which appears to have been rejected by California and Tennessee. Note, however, that California has not specifically dealt with the issue of descendibility in a factual situation wherein the publicity rights were assigned and/or exploited during the lifetime of the performer.

C. *State and Local Laws*

The following California statutes are representative of similar statutes available in other states:

1. *California Civil Code Section 3369* prohibits unfairly competitive activities of various and varied types.

2. *California Business & Professions Code Sections 17500 and 17535* prohibit acts of false and misleading advertising and related unfair activities. The types of unfair trade practices barred are virtually unlimited.

3. *California Business & Professions Code Section 14330* prevents dilution of common law or registered trademarks, service marks, or trade names, and injury to another's business reputation. Section 14330 protects established marks and tradenames and business reputations, even if no competition between the parties exists, and even if no confusion exists as to the source.

4. *California Civil Code Section 3344* prohibits use, without permission, of anyone's name, photograph or likeness in any manner for commercial purposes. This section grants broad protection to celebrities in their professional images.

5. *California Business & Professions Code Sections 14400 and 14415* protect trade names and create a rebuttable presumption of ownership with respect to confusingly similar trade names.

D. *Unfair Competition*

Under common law, where services are known to the public by a name which has acquired secondary meaning, any imitation which has the effect of deceiving consumers as to the origin of the services may be enjoined as unfair competition. There is no need to prove an intent to defraud or to prove actual deception. It is only necessary to show that ordinary members of the public are likely to be deceived.

Cases have varied as to whether the plaintiff must also prove actual competition and/or passing off (misrepresentation).

E. *Breach of Contract*

As discussed in the section regarding organizational structure, the rights to a name may, to some extent, be affected by contractual arrangements. Thus a band or performer may seek to protect his rights in a name through an action on contract where the infringement is based on a breach of contract. However, as previously discussed, the issues of secondary meaning and public confusion may make certain contractual provisions unenforceable.

Conclusion

The name under which one performs can have a value far exceeding everything else the performer may own, thereby requiring a careful determination of its availability in the first instance and the exercise of great care in the protection of all its rights in and to that name, in the second instance.

4.80   Record Re-issues: Sound-Alikes and Truth in Marketing

Stylistic imitations are not copyright infringements (17 USCA section 114[b]). However, the public and the imitated artist *may* have cause for complaint if an attempt is made to pass off the imitation as the genuine article. Further, even when the recording is genuine, its age and the style in which it was recorded may not be representative of the current style and musical genre of the artist. Nor may the significance of the artist's contribution to a particular recording be overemphasized.

There is a healthy market for so-called "nostalgia packages," records marketed through mail order and television to an older audience not likely to visit record stores. During the late 1960s and early 1970s, this submarket experienced a boom. One company that sought to tap into this audience was Time-Life Records. Determining that the technical quality of most of the old 78 rpm recordings was inferior, Time-Life re-created hit arrangements of the Big Band era, utilizing studio musicians and the latest recording techniques. The company released and massively promoted some 450 different recordings in the styles of such bands as Tommy Dorsey, Glenn Miller, Duke Ellington, and Artie Shaw. Time-Life did not represent the recordings as originals but rather as in the style of the originals—for example, the "Artie Shaw sound," or "Artie Shaw versions." Meanwhile, Shaw's former record label, RCA, arranged for the release of a four-album set of Shaw's own recordings (electronically rechanneled to simulate stereo), with Reader's Digest Record Album Service, a competitor of Time-Life that aggressively promoted the Shaw recordings.

Shaw received royalties from RCA but not from Time-Life.

Shaw brought suit, claiming, inter alia, (1) violation of sections 50 and 51 of the New York Civil Rights Law and (2) unfair competition. In *Shaw v. Time-Life Records*, 379 N.Y.S.2d 390 (Ct.App. 1975), the New York Court of Appeals affirmed the grant of summary judgment in favor of Time-Life on the civil rights violations but remanded the unfair competition claim for jury trial.

Shaw (per Jasen, J.) had not copyrighted the arrangements his band had played and hence did not have any property interest in the "Artie Shaw sound." Since he had "disposed of" his arrangements and had performed them with his name "used in connection therewith," the Civil Rights Law was inapplicable. However, it would not be permissible for Time-Life to palm its recordings off as those of Shaw, and the issue was whether "defendant assembled a product which bears so striking a resemblance to plaintiff's product that the public be confused as to the identity of the products. . . . The test is whether persons exercising 'reasonable intelligence—and discrimination' would be taken in by the similarity." The court observed that the use of the term "versions" might well be misleading.

Nostalgia boomers principally rely on re-issues of previously released recordings. However, there was also a demand in more traditional markets for newly discovered recordings or recordings previously considered unworthy of release but which suddenly acquired value due to the subsequent successful efforts of the artists who recorded them. For example, after Jimi Hendrix achieved prominence, Capitol Records released an album entitled "Get That Feeling: Jimi Hendrix plays and Curtis Knight sings," with Hendrix's name set out above, larger, and with more prominence than Knight's. Additionally, the words "plays" and "sings" were in much smaller type and were omitted in ads for the album.

In *Yameta Co., Ltd. v. Capitol Records, Inc.*, 279 F. Supp. 582 (U.S.D.C. 1968), relief under sections 50 and 51 of the Civil Rights Law was *denied*, on the authority of *Long v. Decca Records, Inc.*, because Hendrix had knowingly participated in the recording sessions. However, section 43(a) of the Lanham Act *was* available because of the false impression created by the album cover and the advertising that Hendrix was the principal performer, his performance being in fact "limited to providing conventional guitar accompaniment to the singing of Curtis Knight and perhaps providing additional guitar 'overdubbing' after the original taping."

After a long career as a performer and songwriter, Charlie Rich first achieved stardom with his recording of "Behind Closed Doors" for CBS in the early 1970s. Because he wore his grey hair in a modish long style with large sideburns, he was dubbed "The Silver Fox" and he adopted that as his sobriquet. Gusto Records, a small Nashville label, acquired a number of recordings made by Rich some 10 to 15 years earlier, in a different singing style and under older studio techniques, and released them (without disclosing these facts) in an album bearing a recent picture of Rich and entitled "Charlie Rich—The Silver Fox," which was held to be violative of Section 43(a). *CBS, Inc. v. Gusto Records, Inc.*, 403 F. Supp. 447 (M.D. Tenn. 1974). The court, however, declined to order recall of the offending albums (apparently concerned that the devastating impact of such action might drive the defendant out of business) but instead prescribed the affixation of large, bright orange decals containing explanatory information, and observed that a prompt trial was available.

RCA Records then released its own Charlie Rich compilation, entitled "Charlie Rich—She Called Me Baby," consisting of recordings 10 to 14 years old (four of which had not been previously released) and bearing a current likeness of the artist. Asterisks were placed next to the previously released selections, and, in small type at the bottom of the back of the jacket appeared a statement that the asterisked recordings had been released previously. There was no indication of the age of the recordings. In this instance, a preliminary injunction *was* granted under Section 43(a). *Rich v. RCA Corporation*, 390 F. Supp. 530 (U.S.D.C. 1975).

In Chapter 10 we consider the commercial value of artists' names and likenesses for merchandising purposes. However, what about the value of the name in connection with the artist's own performances?

Stuart, a "little known performer," sued "Bootsy" Collins and Collins's label, Warner Bros. Records, for infringement of his federally registered service mark in the group name "The Rubberband." The group, which was not very profitable, did make recordings on minor labels, but these were essentially used for promotional purposes, and, when Stuart testified, he did not know whether any albums were sold. Collins, on the other hand, performing with a group known as "Bootsy's Rubber Band," became a hit act. About three months after Warner released the first Bootsy album, Stuart became aware of it and his attorney sent Warner a cease-and-desist letter. Unsuccessful settlement talks ensued. Warner released a second Bootsy album the following year, after which Stuart sued. During the pendency of the action, Warner released a third and then a fourth album.

Stuart's suit claimed that Bootsy and Warner had created a likelihood of confusion as to the source of the parties' musical services, and that Warner's successful promotion had caused an appropriation of Stuart's group name, which no longer had any value to Stuart. Warner and Collins asserted that Stuart had abandoned the mark earlier (and that he had then misrepresented himself by filing a false "continuing-use" affidavit with the Patent Office) and that he had misused his mark through indiscriminate substitution of musicians and by failing to exercise quality control.

The jury (with whom the trial judge agreed) found for Stuart on the issue of likelihood of confusion and held that Collins and Warner had infringed Stuart's mark. The jury, absolving Collins of willful infringement (the name had been suggested by his producer) but finding that Warner had willfully infringed, awarded $50,000 for Stuart's loss (trebled to $150,000) and attributed $350,000 of Warner's $992,587 profits to the infringement. The court (per Leval, J.) basically sustained these verdicts, stating:

> In my view, the profits attributable to the infringing name were not large. In addition, however, plaintiff was entitled to receive all the profits earned by willful infringement, even though the profit was not attributable to the infringement. Where infringement is done knowingly and with callous disregard of the rights of a mark holder, all the profits of such activity are awardable although the use of the infringing name may not have contributed causally to the sales or profits. See *W. E. Bassett Co. v. Revlon, Inc.,* 435 F.2d 656, 664 (2d Cir. 1970).

> The jury found that Warner infringed in knowing, willful disregard of plaintiff's rights. I concur. There was no question Warner was fully aware of plaintiff's rights from an early date following his lawyer's letter in June of 1976. The evidence of the settlement negotiations rather suggested that Warner had strung the plaintiff along, giving no real recognition to his legal rights, but confident that he would not sue. The testimony of the Warner executive Krasnow, furthermore, bluntly proclaimed a callous policy on such matters. On the questions of concern for the possibility of service mark violations, he explained, "We at

Warner Bros. are not policemen; we are in the music business." His further testimony appeared to say that promotional decisions at Warner paid little heed to possible adverse trademark rights, but were based only on commercial factors. His testimony to the effect that Warner intended at present time to market the recordings of a new musical group under the name "Billy Karloff and the Supremes," in spite of the fact that a famous group had used the name "The Supremes," may have impressed the jury as either false or callous. Finally, Krasnow, in his determination to convey that it is not the name but what is "in the grooves" that sells a record, expressed the opinion that a recording by a well-known group would sell neither better nor worse under the group's famous name than if the group concealed its identity under an unknown name. The jury may well have found in this testimony (as did the court) a callous disregard for the oath, suggesting the possibility of an equally callous disregard for adverse rights.

> Although awareness of an adverse claim would not necessarily make infringement willful, especially where the defendant believed in good faith that its name did not infringe, the evidence in this case rather showed that Warner gave short shrift to plaintiff's claim out of arrogance and confidence that he would not mount any significant legal attack. By reason of Warner's willful violation from an early date, I would find, like the jury, that $350,000 of Warner's profits from Bootsy recordings (which amounted in total to $992,587) were earned during willful infringement and were therefore awardable.

However, Judge Leval reduced the award to $250,000 and refused to enjoin further use of the name by Collins and Warner, stating that these damages were sufficient, since

> . . . [t]his was far from being the most reprehensible kind of willful infringement. It was not a case in which the defendant chose its name in an attempt to trade on plaintiff's goodwill or in a bad faith effort to harm the plaintiff. Indeed there was no suggestion that either

defendant was even aware of plaintiff at the times the name was selected and first promoted. Warner did not become aware of plaintiff's claim until it had already launched the first Bootsy's Rubber Band album and had expended considerable sums in publicizing the name. While Warner could have dealt with the plaintiff in a manner more sensitive to his legitimate rights, it could not have ceased using the Rubber Band name on receipt of plaintiff's notice without incurring large expenses, sacrificing extensive promotion already undertaken, and risking to scuttle the successful launching of a new artist. Without undermining, or suggesting disagreement with the jury's finding that Warner proceeded callously thereafter, this was nonetheless a far cry from the most pernicious infringements that statute was designed for. In view of these considerations, an award of $350,000 profits seems excessively punitive to Warner (not to mention its possible impact on Collins if Warner succeeds in imposing on him the contractual indemnity which it claims).

From plaintiff's point of view also, the award seems excessive. Plaintiff acknowledges he has never had earnings significantly in excess of his expenses. The happenstance of defendants' infringement and the jury's award would suddenly raise his earnings by his musical endeavors to half a million dollars, substantially more than Bootsy Collins' considerable success has yet netted him (even after allowing for plaintiff's counsel's share). *Stuart v. Collins*, 489 F. Supp. 827 (S.D.N.Y. 1980).

The issue in *Kingsmen v. K-Tel International Ltd.*, 557 F. Supp. 178 (S.D.N.Y. 1983), involved the question of whether the former lead singer of a popular group could later rerecord a group hit and bill the performance as that of the group. While the five original group members were still in high school in 1962, they recorded "Louie, Louie," with Ely as lead singer. Ely then left the group. The song rose to number 2 on the "charts," and record albums, concert tours, and television appearances followed—all

without Ely. The group disbanded in 1967, and no member used the name professionally for the next nine years. A company specializing in nostalgia packages entered into separate agreements with Ely to rerecord the song. Although the company's separate contract with another group member referred to him as "Lynn Easton, a/k/a Kingsmen," neither man had expressly represented that he had the right to refer to himself as "The Kingsmen," and the Court found that Ely had not made even an arguable representation to this effect nor had he attempted to grant any right to use the name. The album cover listed "Louie, Louie . . . The Kingsmen" and stated "These selections are re-recordings by the original artists."

Although the group name had not been registered, recourse could be had by the five members to the Lanham Act, Section 43(a). The five members had continued to receive royalties on their old recordings, and therefore had not abandoned the group name. Noted the court:

> Moreover, . . . [w]e stress the ensemble nature of The Kingsmen's music. Although the listener can discern the lead singer from the background vocals and music on a number of Kingsmen songs, the group's "sound" is clearly a collective one. No one member of the group can be singled out as representing the essence of The Kingsmen's performing style. Given the evidence referred to above and the nature of The Kingsmen's recordings to which we have listened, we find as a fact for purposes of this preliminary proceeding that the five plaintiffs herein constitute the band known to the public as The Kingsmen and therefore have standing to sue under the Lanham Act.

Plaintiffs have also made the necessary showing of the likelihood of irreparable harm. Plaintiffs have submitted a number of record albums that are collections of popular dance music of the 1960s. These albums appear to compete directly with the "60's Dance Party" album produced by the defendants. . . . It is clear from these facts that the defendants' record directly competes with original recordings by The Kingsmen for which plaintiffs continue to receive royalties and that preliminary injunctive relief is therefore appropriate. . . .

It is the misleading labelling of defendants' album that is the gist of this action. For example, we would see no objection to defendants' marketing of this particular recording of "Louie, Louie" under the name of Jack Ely with the caption, "formerly of the Kingsmen" or "Jack Ely, lead singer on the original Kingsmen recording of Louie, Louie." It is the representation that the rendition of "Louie, Louie" appearing on defendants' album was rerecorded by the individuals collectively known as The Kingsmen that we find likely to confuse and therefore objectionable under the Lanham Act.

NOTES _____

1. For a more detailed discussion of record reissues, review the following cases:

(a) *Fugua v. Watson*, 107 U.S.P.Q. 251 (N.Y. 1955), aff'd 182 N.Y.S.2d 336 (1959). Mark: "The Ink Spots." Former members of the group "The Ink Spots" failed to enjoin use of the name despite prior written agreement. "Fraud on the public" theory was used because membership of the new group differed from that of the original group.

(b) *The Boogie Kings v. Guillory*, 188 S.2d 445 (La. 1966). Mark: "The Boogie Kings." The first to adopt a group name acquires proprietary rights, and a former member of the group has no rights in the name and cannot transfer rights to another party. The court considered the band's popularity and value of the group name.

(c) *Anderson v. Capitol Records, Inc.*, 178 U.S.P.Q. 238 (Ca. 1973). Mark: "Flash." The first user of the mark was protected despite the second user's earlier registration. The court also considered the likelihood of confusion and secondary meaning.

(d) *Ford v. Howard*, 229 N.W.2d 841 (Mich. 1975). Mark: "The Dramatics." "The Dramatics" had not been disposed of and was therefore the property of all the partners in common. The partners had the right to use it *in common*, but not to the exclusion of the other partners.

2. Additional discussion of these issues may be found in the following articles:

(a) Borchard, "Trademark and the Arts," 7 *Art and the Law* 1 (1982).

(b) Gottlieb, "The Right of an Individual to Register His Own Name for Services He Personally Performs," 68 *Trade-Mark Rep.* 596 (1978).

(c) Heneghan and Wamsley, "The Service Mark Alternative to the Right of Publicity: Estate of Presley v. Russen," 2 *Loyola Entertainment Law Journal* 113 (1982).

(d) Rudell, "Protecting Group Names," 187 *New York Law Journal* 102 (1982).

(e) Spiegel, "Rights in Group Names," 1 *Performing Arts Review* 417 (1970).

Chapter 5

THEATRE

5.00   Business of the Theatre

For generations, Broadway has been "dying"; the "Fabulous Invalid" is always on the verge of extinction. Yet somehow it survives. In one year, fresh new plays blossom. In others, a paucity of new talent causes Broadway producers to look to British imports such as *Cats*, revivals such as *42nd Street*, and lavish musicals like *La Cage Aux Folles*. By scratching and scraping, Broadway trundles along—big, bold, and often brassy.

Theatre economics are formidable. A major musical, for example, costs from $4 million to $5 million just to mount—a doubling of costs in the past five years. Although straight drama and comedies have preopening costs only in the $1.5 million range, these amounts are still double the costs of the early 1980s. With opening night closings all too common, investors risk a great deal; often they lose their entire investment. Most musicals and plays depend heavily on instant success and immediate critical acclaim. A few, such as *Pippin*, overcome early indifference by such devices as heavy advertising on the 11 P.M. news, but these success stories are few. Financial failures are far more common than successes on Broadway.

Even when a play survives opening night, the odds are still against a lengthy run. Operating costs kill many marginal productions. To stay open, a play must present reasonable prospects that its gate will meet running costs and will eventually pay back the investors. For most productions, this means that in the first few months the house must operate at near full capacity. If attendance slips to 70 or 80 percent capacity, the show is generally doomed. Even if the prospects for eventual success are positive, a Broadway show generally requires a year or more to recoup its investment. One great hit, *Dreamgirls*, opened in 1981 with $2.9 million production costs—high for that time. Operating at full capacity, *Dreamgirls* grossed $375,000 a week, with running costs of $292,000. Thus, *Dreamgirls* showed a profit of $83,000 per week and could pay off production costs in 36 weeks. This almost record pace was accomplished with high ticket prices, full capacity for months, and, not insignificantly, advance sales of $3 million. *Dreamgirls* went on to smash several Broadway records and gave Michael Bennett another great and profitable hit. His earlier big money-maker was *Chorus Line*, which earned over $22 million in profits—not bad for a production that cost $1 million to $1.5 million to mount. The allure of a smash hit keeps the investors coming back for more, but the odds are against them.

Broadway accommodates some 200,000 theatre goers per week. Over the course of a year, Broadway ticket sales gross in the neighborhood of $500 million, a small total compared to the other entertainment industries we consider, but not insignificant in terms of helping sustain a creative lifeblood in the performing arts in this country. The number of Broadway openings in the past 50 years has declined significantly, from about 100 in the 1930s to around 50 today. Economics is again a cause, aided also by the emergence of Off-Broadway and even Off-Off-Broadway theatres. Several shows that years ago would have originated on Broadway now are first produced elsewhere. An Off-Broadway production costs less than half of one on Broadway. As we will see in Section 5.02, other alternatives to a Broadway production exist as well.

Increasingly, producers are reluctant to attempt an immediate plunge into Broadway, with its huge production and running costs. Even so, finding a Broadway house in which to open a new play during the peak months of September to December is no easy task. With just under 40 Broadway theatres, some productions have to wait until another play closes—an expensive proposition if the cast and other personnel are under contract.

The number of Broadway theatres has remained basically constant for the past 30 years. In the early 1980s, the Morosco and Helen Hayes theatres were torn down in connection with the 42nd Street–Portman Hotel Redevelopment Project, which later produced a new theatre at the Marriott Hotel on Times Square. In net, all this meant was one less Broadway house.

The definition of what constitutes a Broadway theatre is somewhat disputed. There is agreement that the Broadway geographic area is bounded by 53rd Street (north), 41st Street (south), 6th Avenue (east), and 9th Avenue (west), but not all theatres within that area are necessarily accorded full Broadway status. Five with seating capacities under 500 are often described as Middle Houses, even though two (the Little and the Edison) both have a seating capacity of 499. In all, 28 houses have seating capacities above 1,000, 5 are in the 500 to 999 range, and the 5 Middle Houses are below 500.

Most preopening costs are for sets, lighting, costumes, and other staging expenses. Operating expenses cover the range of performer and artistic salaries, stagehands, and other technical salaries; royalties and fees; and administrative and advertising costs. One study sponsored by the League of American Theaters and Producers (see W. Baumol, E. Wolff, and H. Baumol, "Ticket Prices in the Broadway Theatre: Perspective on Their Rates of Increase," January 1986) presented the following operating costs breakdowns for plays and musicals, comparing the percentage for 1965–1967 with 1980–1981.

	1965-1967		1980-1981	
	Plays	*Musicals*	*Plays*	*Musicals*
Performers and other artistic salaries	45.9%	42.6%	33.8%	36.9%
Stagehands and other technical salaries and expenses	9.9	9.4	17.0	26.5
Royalties and fees	17.1	30.3	18.8	15.6
Administrative, advertising, and other expenses	27.1	17.7	30.3	21.0

From these figures, one can readily see that the largest increases in terms of percentages have been in the salaries of stagehands and other technical salaries and expenses. At the same time, royalties and fees have dropped, at least for musicals, from 30.3 to 15.6 percent. In particular, composers, lyricists, and other writers have had to compromise in order to get their works on the stage.

Concurrent with the concern over rising costs is the big concern over the rising price of tickets on Broadway. Figures from the Baumol, Wolff, and Baumol study (cited above) show the rise over a ten-year period:

Average Top Ticket Prices

	Plays	*Musicals*
1976–1977	$13.80	$15.95
1980–1981	24.25	29.00
1984–1985	35.29	45.26

Although these rises soften somewhat when a GNP price deflator is applied, there has still been a consistent, constant dollar increase each year from 1976 to 1985. The Baumol study argues that Broadway ticket prices did not keep pace with inflation for many years in the 1950s and 1960s and are just catching up; but the fact remains that the steady increases over the past decade have caused consternation to theatre goers and legitimate concern to other theatre interests.

Television has had its effects on Broadway. As mentioned earlier in the case of *Pippin*, television is perceived as an effective advertising medium, both in New York City and elsewhere. Thus, a show's advertising budget may devote 40 to 50 percent to TV spots, which means as much as $40,000 a week for a Broadway musical. In addition, a full-page ad in the Sunday *N.Y. Times* costs $34,000, and the daily so-called "ABC" listings about $3,500 a week. Total advertising costs are high and continue to rise.

Television is seen as having substantial benefits for the theatre. It promotes the stage by televising such events as the Tony Awards, given each year for Broadway's best productions. An estimated 35 million people nationwide watch the awards; some undoubtedly note what plays they want to see when they are next in New York or when a touring company comes through their area. Also, television, particularly cable, has embraced Broadway plays with ever-greater fervor, as more and more productions are needed for straight telecasting or for adaption. The subsidiary rights that flow to Broadway producers and investors are great lures, as television has reached out and embraced (at least to a limited extent) the live stage.

Broadway is part of a larger live theatre and entertainment industry in this country. Its $500 million gross per year is approximately one-sixth of the estimated $3 billion expended each year on live entertainment. Live entertainment, overall, is a growing business. As the following figures illustrate, dollar grosses have been escalating at a much higher rate than those for spectator sports since 1975.

Dollar Grosses for Live Entertainment and Spectator Sports (in $ millions)

	1975	*1980*	*1985*
Live theatre & entertainment	787	1786	2977
Spectator sports	1333	2033	2840

Live theatre is not a beneficiary of advancing technologies to the extent that films, television, and music have profited. No technological cost-saving devices enhance Broadway theatres and other stages. The theatre is still a labor-intensive operation, requiring the same hours of devotion as was true 50 years ago. New technologies may produce more dazzling lights and intricate stagings, but these improvements add to costs rather than reduce them. Predictably, the theatre will struggle with economics in the future, as it does at present and has in the past. Before examining the broader range of legal questions, therefore, some further comments need to be made about the theatre business as it relates to producers, investors, and theatre owners (Section 5.01); alternatives to Broadway (Section 5.02); and the impacts of unions and guilds, and their contracts (Section 5.03).

NOTE

1. For general background and an irreverent account of a year's observations on the creative and business aspects of the New York theatre, see W. Goldman, *The Season* (New York: Limelight Editions, 1984). The author wrote the screenplays for *Butch Cassidy and the Sundance Kid*, *Marathon Man*, and other successful movies. He also wrote a couple of Broadway flops.

5.01   Broadway Producers, Investors, and Theatre Owners

Three groups (Shubert, Nederlander, and Jujamcyn) control the New York theatre and most of the "first class" theatres around the country. These groups house the shows and frequently finance them. At a recent American Bar Association seminar, one speaker characterized the three theatre groups as "the only true producers" in today's Broadway theatre.

The Shubert Organization, the oldest, has been producing, booking, and housing theatrical attractions since the early 1900s. By the 1940s, Shubert owned more than half of all Broadway theatres and controlled approximately 40 theatres in out-of-town "touring" and "try-out" cities. In the 1950s, Shubert's dominance caused the federal government to charge the organization with multiple antitrust violations. In a landmark case, *U.S. v. Shubert*, 348 U.S. 222 (1955), the U.S. Supreme Court held that Shubert's theatrical attractions on a multi-state basis were both interstate and commerce. The Court relied heavily on *Hart v. Keith Vaudeville Exchange*, 262 U.S. 271 (1923), a case that had early recognized the interstate dimensions of much of the entertainment business. While holding the Shubert Organization subject to the federal antitrust laws, the Court nevertheless remanded to determine if in fact there were violations.

Before trial, the Shubert Organization entered into a consent decree with the government. The decree required Shubert to divest itself of 12 theatres in 6 cities outside New York and restrained Shubert from acquiring any additional theatres in or outside of New York without prior federal court approval. At the time of the decree, Shubert controlled 7 of 9 theatres in Chicago; all 6 in Boston; all 4 in Philadelphia; 2 of 2 in Washington D.C.; 2 of 3 in Detroit; the single theatrical houses in Los Angeles, Baltimore, and Pittsburgh; and several houses in smaller cities. By 1981, in contrast, Shubert controlled only 6 theatres in the major cities, and the Shubert Organization influence outside New York had dwindled significantly.

In New York, although Shubert could not purchase additional Broadway theatres, it could and did hold on to most that it had, and it used these properties to great advantage. Thus, in 1981, Shubert owned outright 16 of 39 theatres in the Broadway area and had a half interest in one other. When Shubert returned to the federal court in 1981 to have the 1956 consent decree modified, its influence on the Broadway stage was evident. Indeed, when Shubert appeared before the court asking for an eventual end to the decree, Shubert had successful dramas and musicals playing in 13 of its 17 Broadway theatres, including such hits as *Ain't Misbehavin'*, *The Elephant Man*, *42nd Street*, *Evita*, *Amadeus*, *Children of a Lesser God*, *A Chorus Line*, *Deathtrap*, and *Dancin'*.

The federal district court in 1981 allowed

the Shubert Organization to acquire theatres outside New York City without prior court approval. The court also held that Shubert after 1985 could acquire interests in Broadway theatres without having to demonstrate to the court that such purchases would not unduly restrain competition. The Shubert Organization's ability to convince the court (and also the government lawyers) that it could act in the best interests of the Broadway area was undoubtedly predicated in part on its projected involvement in the 42nd Street–Portman Hotel Redevelopment Project. But whatever the eventual winning arguments, Shubert was allowed to reenter the competitive acquisition market, despite the protests of many, including the Nederlanders.

Theatre owners and producers such as Shubert and Nederlander often seek additional backers for shows to supplement their own financing. Outside investors, however, have changed in character over the years. Largely gone are the individuals who invest large amounts in a show. Occasionally this occurs, as in a recent incident involving David Susskind while he was attending a pre-Broadway tryout of *La Cage Aux Folles* at the Colonial Theatre in Boston. After Act I, Susskind saw James Nederlander, the producer, and asked Nederlander how much he could invest in *La Cage*. Susskind himself evidently pressed for it to be $500,000; Nederlander held out for $250,000, provided Susskind also put $500,000 into *Chaplin*, a forthcoming musical starring Anthony Newley. Mr. Susskind hesitated only a few moments, said it was a deal, shook hands with Nederlander, and recorded the transaction on a napkin before returning to his seat for Act II of *La Cage*. In the following months, Nederlander and Susskind disagreed as to what happened during intermission. Susskind stuck to his story on the division between *La Cage* and *Chaplin*, which later flopped; Nederlander claimed all $750,000 was to go into *Chaplin*. Had *Chaplin* succeeded, of course, the stories might have been reversed. (For a full account, see Freedman, "Why 'Chaplin' Is Not Opening on Broadway," *N.Y. Times*, November 10, 1983, p. 1, ed. 1.)

The Susskind-Nederlander story recalls images of the way Broadway financing was traditionally packaged. Indeed, extant records about old plays suggest a casual way of doing business, involving several backers coming in on a whim or out of self-interest. *Arsenic & Old Lace* enjoyed a recent revival, the new production coming in at a now modest $700,000. The original production, which opened January 10, 1941, cost $37,000 and required 23 backers to finance its opening, including the producer Russel Crouse ($500), the director Howard Lindsey ($2,500), the press agent ($500), the journalist ($500), and one of the principal stars, Boris Karloff ($5,000). Other notable investors included Clare Boothe Luce, Nedda Logan, and Katherine B. Day, whose family had inspired the earlier Lindsey and Crouse hit, *Life with Father*.

The trend today is away from individual backers. The more likely scenario involves institutional investors. For *Dreamgirls* (discussed in Section 5.00), four institutional investors put up the entire $2.9 million, including the Shuberts, Metromedia, and ABC Broadcasting at $600 thousand each, and Geffen Records at $1 million. Of course, beyond recouping their investments and showing a profit therefrom, many institutional investors have other interests as well. Geffen, for its investment in *Dreamgirls*, also obtained the right to record the original cast album and release it in both albums and singles. (One of the featured players in the original *Dreamgirls* cast, Jennifer Holliday, also signed a recording deal with Geffen.) For other shows, frequent institutional investors outside the immediate legitimate theatre group include Warner Communications, Columbia Pictures, various record companies, and cable television interests.

An alternative to the institutional investor and the well-heeled backer are the multitude of small investors who might like to own a part of a Broadway show. This idea has been pursued several times in recent years, but with less than hoped for success. A substantial problem is that a public solicitation of investments means compliance with both federal and state securities laws. For example, New York has its own complicated statutory provisions in its Arts and Cultural Affairs Act, which is set forth in detail in Section 5.20.

NOTE ─────────────────────────

1. For further reading about the Shubert Organization's antitrust battles during the 1950's and the resulting consent decrees, see "The Curtain Rises on Consent Decree Modification in the Theatre Industry: United States v. Shubert," 2 *Cardozo Arts & Entertainment Law Journal* 91 (1983).

5.02 Alternatives to Broadway

With Broadway production costs continually escalating, more and more authors and producers are looking elsewhere for initial production efforts. The London stage, Off-Broadway, Off-Off-Broadway, the New York workshop, and nonprofit residential theatres are all important vehicles for original productions.

Musicals can be mounted in London at much less cost than Broadway. As a consequence, most musicals the past three or four years have in fact debuted in London and then been imported to New York only after proving to be a success. *Les Miserables* and *Me and My Girl* are two examples of this recent trend. Discussed in Section 5.30 is *Gennaro v. Rosenfield*, which deals with the musical *Singin' in the Rain*, a thoroughly

American epic that nevertheless was first produced in London and later opened on Broadway.

Off-Broadway and Off-Off-Broadway are other "proving grounds." Not all plays that appear on those stages aspire to Broadway, but more than a few do. The same is true of workshops, although these have not produced a great number of plays that later successfully transferred to Broadway. Under an Actor's Equity Association workshop contract, producers use a nonprofit theatre to stage performances that may not exceed six weeks, must be performed before only an invited (not a paying) audience, likely use only minimal sets and costumes, and offer actors wages that are well below Broadway and even Off-Broadway minimums. But even a workshop musical production may cost $400,000, and the lack of a successful track record has led many producers to seek other alternatives.

The most successful Off-Broadway productions have been nonprofit resident theatres, including the so-called regional theatres. In the last 20 years, a number of regional theatres have emerged—the Arena Stage in Washington D.C., the Tyrone Guthrie in Minneapolis, and the Mark Taper Forum in Los Angeles are prime examples. To an extent, they have excelled in developing their own plays and musicals. For example, the Mark Taper Forum's production of *Children of a Lesser God* moved to an award-winning run on Broadway and has since been made into a motion picture that was nominated for Best Picture of the Year. Regional theatres often book tryout productions in conjunction with Broadway producers. This arrangement provides a lower-risk look at the production than if the show went directly to a full-scale Broadway production that proceeded through the usual "out of town" tryout route.

Regional theatres have their own life and vitality. Companies such as San Francisco's

ACT, Los Angeles' L.A. Stage, and Cambridge's ART are innovative and important to the cultural activities of their home cities. Although touring companies of successful shows still provide a solid basis for professional theatre in the United States outside New York, the "action" is increasingly regional. Significantly, the number of national tours has declined markedly in recent years. Unless a show features major stars or comes off a smash Broadway run, it is unlikely to succeed "on the road."

Original works mounted in regional theatres have the advantage of a full run without regard to critics' reviews. Typically, a regional theatre production has a month's rehearsal and a playing time of four to six weeks. If the play is well received, it may run much longer. Many regional theatres are part of the League of Resident Theatres (LORT), which is a trade association representing the theatres in collective bargaining. Actors in regional theatres receive well below Broadway standards and are often paid based on a royalty derived from revenues. Actors may also be able to obtain assurances that they will be able to be in the play if it later moves to another regional theatre, Off-Broadway, or to Broadway itself. If this is not possible, actors may secure a buy-out if the play is later produced elsewhere.

Authors benefit from the regional theatres, with substantially increased opportunities for their work to be staged. Although the price is lower royalties and less artistic control, generally the advantages outweigh the drawbacks. The regional theatres in turn may retain an interest in the play if it moves elsewhere. These ongoing rights may be a percentage of the later box office, a percentage of net profits of the production, a percentage of the author's share, or even an option to stage the production. For example, in March 1987, *Fences* opened on Broadway to substantial acclaim. It was a Yale Repertory Theater production that finally reached New York after appearances in numerous regional theatres.

In total, it is significant that every play that has received the Pulitzer Prize in the last ten years originated in a nonprofit resident theatre.

NOTE

1. For additional discussion of regional and other non-Broadway theatre, see: Deutsch, "Non-Profit Resident Theatres Producing Hits," *Entertainment Law & Finance*, vol. 2, no. 12, March 1987, p. 1.

5.03 Unions and Guilds and Their Contracts

Labor unions and other associations play dominant roles in the legitimate theatre. Numerous basic contracts flow from union negotiations with the League of New York Theatres and Producers. A similar situation exists in the regional theatre with LORT and the Off-Off-Broadway Association (OOBA). Producers and theatre owners must deal with the following unions or guilds and their contracts:

- Actors' Equity Association. Represents actors and stage managers.
- The Society of Stage Directors and Choreographers. Represents directors and choreographers.
- The United Scenic Artists. Represents set designers, costume designers, and lighting designers.
- Theatrical Wardrobe Attendants Union. Represents wardrobe supervisors and dressers.
- The Dramatists Guild. Is not a union but nevertheless represents authors, composers, lyricists, and bookwriters (see Section 5.10).
- Association of Theatrical Press Agents and Managers. Represents press agents, company managers, and house managers.

- American Federation of Musicians. Represents any musicians in a production.
- Theatrical Protective Union, IATSE. Represents the house crew, including carpenters, electricians, those handling the properties, and curtain and sound personnel.
- Legitimate Theatre Employees Union. Represents ushers, doormen, ticket takers, and the backstage doormen.
- Treasurers and Ticket Sellers Union. Represents treasurers and other box office personnel.
- Theatre, Amusement and Cultural Building Service Employees. Represents porters, elevator operators, and cleaners.
- International Union of Operating Engineers. Represents those involved with the operation and maintenance of the physical plant, including the heating and air conditioning systems.

As discussed earlier, the bulk of a theatre production's start-up costs relate to sets, costumes, lights, and other staging expenses. Many of these costs are dictated by the minimum union contracts. At the same time, since it may take over a year of full houses to repay the backers' investment, inevitable pressure has grown for the creative participants to look more to net profits than to box office gross for compensation. Particular pressures have been applied to authors, composers, lyricists, and bookwriters associated with the Dramatists Guild. Their resistance to the perceived lowering of royalties resulted in the filing of an antitrust suit by the producers against the guild. A motion to dismiss was denied in *Barr v. Dramatists Guild*, 573 F. Supp. 555 (S.D.N.Y. 1983). The matter was resolved by negotiations between the two groups, which resulted in the adoption of the Approved Production Contract (APC) in the spring of 1985. (The im-

portance of the APC has caused us to reprint in Section 5.10 Alvin Deutsch's article comparing the APC with the old MBPC.)

Under the union contracts, arbitration, not litigation, is the prevailing method of settling disputes in the theatre industry. Because arbitration decisions in this area are not public, reported decisions concerning the theatre are scarce. However, important court cases occasionally emerge, and these are discussed later in the chapter.

NOTE

1. For further information on legitimate theatre contracts, see D. Farber, *Producing Theatre* (New York: Drama Book Publishers, 1981).

5.10 The APC and the Old MBPC

The following article originally appeared in the *Entertainment and Sports Lawyer,* vol. 3, no. 4, Spring 1985. It is reprinted with the permission of the Forum Committee on the Entertainment and Sports Industries of the American Bar Association and Alvin Deutsch.

MBPC: REQUIESCAT IN PACE—APC: QUO VADIS?

by Alvin Deutsch*

In July 1982, Richard Barr, a member and president of the League of New York theatres and Producers, Inc.† (the League) com-

---

*Alvin Deutsch, a senior partner in the New York law firm of Linden and Deutsch, is the immediate past chairman of the Legitimate Theatre Division, and currently serves on the Governing Committee, of the Forum Committee on the Entertainment and Sports Industries. Mr. Deutsch represents authors and producers and annually lectures on theater contracts for the Practising Law Institute in New York and Los Angeles.

†Effective as of April 17, 1985, changed to The League of American Theatres and Producers, Inc.

menced an antitrust suit against The Dramatists Guild, Inc. (the Guild) and its officers alleging that the Guild's enforcement of its Minimum Basic Production Contract (MBPC) violated the antitrust laws. In an effort to settle the action, representatives of the League and the Guild met over the past eighteen months (in some seventy sessions) for the purpose of working out the terms and conditions of a new agreement. On February 27, 1985, the Guild, acting through its president, Peter Stone, and the League, acting through Norman Kean, chairman of the League's Production Committee, announced that these meetings had resulted in a new contract to be promulgated by the Guild known as the Approved Production Contracts (APCs)* covering plays and musical plays.

On March 28 and 29, Norman Kean, who chaired the League's negotiating team, together with its counsel, held two sessions sponsored by the League in New York. These two sessions were attended by approximately 400 persons, including League members, attorneys, and accountants, for the purpose of reviewing the salient features of the APC. The new agreements were negotiated over the past year by the Guild negotiating team comprised of Peter Stone, the president of the Guild, David LeVine, the Guild's executive director, and the Guild's counsel, Cahill Gordon & Reindel. The negotiating team for the producers was comprised of Norman Kean, the chairman of the League's Production Committee, together with the League's counsel, Proskauer Rose Goetz & Mendelsohn. (At the time of this writing, the actual contract was *not* available. Accordingly, the information that is now being supplied is based upon this writer's attending the March 29 meeting and subsequent conversations with Norman Kean.)

It can be fairly stated that the old MBPC has been laid to rest. While certain of its terms

---

*Former members of the U.S. armed forces will recognize the APC (the "all purpose capsule") as a medicinal pill issued to servicemen for all maladies—just short of those requiring surgery. Any similarity between the Guild's new contract and the military cure is most assuredly unintentional.

and conditions are incorporated into the APC, it is clear that the latter is a far cry from its predecessor.

The following highlights the major clauses of the new APC and, where possible, indicates how they differ from the former MBPC.

I. PRODUCTION RIGHTS

Under the APC, the producer receives not only first-class production rights, in the United States and Canada, but (a) additional second-class rights, (b) the right to initially present the play as a developmental production (i.e., Equity Code Workshop); and (c) the right to present the play off-Broadway in New York after the "vesting" of the producer's rights. (See subhead IX, *infra*.)

The APC, like its predecessor, includes the producer's option to present a first-class production in the United Kingdom and expands that territory to include New Zealand and Australia. (Note the APC can be made to apply to revivals of previously produced plays or musicals and will be considered a "special circumstance" within the Certification Procedure.)

II. OPTIONS AND ADVANCES

MBPC

One of the most evident changes brought about by the APC is the revision of the former option payments and royalty formula. Under the old MBPC, the aggregate option payment to all authors of a play or musical was a minimum of $2,000 for a twelve-month option and a royalty of 10 percent of the gross weekly box office receipts for a play and 6 percent for a musical.

APC

The payment to the author to option a play under the APC is $5,000 for six months, renewable for six months for an additional $2,500. If a producer wishes a second twelve-month option he or she is required to pay $5,500 (in stages) subject to the producer having raised 50 percent of the estimated production cost, plus having secured one of the following: a signed contract with a theater, star, director, or for a developmental theater production. The aforesaid option can be further extended (to a maximum of eight weeks plus sixty days) to cover the duration of any tryout or a developmental-type production.

For a musical the payment is $18,000 for a twelve-month option, renewable for an additional twelve months for a $9,000 option payment, and for a third year at $900 per month. There are no other conditions attached to this right of extension.

Neither the $7,500 nor the $18,000 option payments, for a twelve-month option period, is payable until delivery of a play's script of 110 pages, and in the case of a musical, eighty script pages plus twelve songs.

Option payments are recoupable from 50 percent of the royalty payments due the authors *after* the producer has recouped his production cost.

In addition to the aforesaid option payments, authors will receive advances when the play or musical is capitalized. With respect to a play the author will receive, on the first day of rehearsals, an advance of (a) 3 percent of the capitalization up to a maximum of $35,000 and (b) for a musical, 2 percent of the capitalization up to a maximum of $60,000. However, the producer is entitled to deduct from the 3 percent advance any option payments made to an author of a play during the second year; and on a musical the producer can deduct from the 2 percent advance any option payments made to the authors during the second and third years. In determining the capitalization of a play or musical, certain enumerated items are excluded from the computation (e.g., 10 percent of overcalls; up to 20 percent of loans, bonds and other recoverables; payments due any regional or like theater that has previously presented the play). The advance payable on capitalization is thereafter recoupable by the producer from 50 percent of the authors' weekly royalty *after* recoupment of the producer's production costs.

III. ROYALTIES AND GUARANTEES

While total option and advance payments to authors have markedly increased, royalties have substantially diminished, and in other respects, certain weekly minimim payments have been guaranteed.

Guarantees
The author of a play will always receive a weekly guarantee of $1,000. The authors of a musical (bookwriter, composer, and lyricist) will receive a weekly guarantee of $3,000 in the aggregate. These payments are not subject to diminution for any reason and cannot be invaded by the recoupment of any option payments or advances.

In an attempt to crystalize the structure of guarantee payments and royalties to authors, one should first separate all performances up to and including the New York press opening from all subsequent performances. Thus:

Out-of-Town Performances, Previews and Press Opening
(i) Play: The author receives 5 percent of the gross (no "royalty adjustment") including $1,000 per week guarantee.
(ii) Musical: The authors receive, collectively, $4,500 per week (divided among them as they elect) during out-of-town performances and previews in New York, to a maximum of twelve weeks.

Performances Following Press Opening
(iii) Play: First three playing weeks (i.e., twenty-four performances) a weekly guarantee of $1,000.
(iv) Musical: First three playing weeks (i.e., twenty-four performances) 4.5 percent of the gross (subject to "royalty adjustment") but no less than $3,000 per week.

It is my understanding that no guarantee payment can be waived by an author, regardless of the financial status of the play. While the MBPC did not, by its terms, deal with "cuts," "waivers," or "royalty adjustments," during losing weeks custom and usage caused authors to accept such practice if other royalty recipients did likewise. The APC's intent, in making weekly guarantees to each author, is to put a floor under such formulae.

Royalties—As a Percentage of Gross Weekly Box Office Receipts

Play. Royalties to the "author" of a play, commencing out-of-town through previews, including the press opening, are 5 percent of the gross until recoupment of production costs and thereafter 10 percent. The word "author" includes any underlying rights owners (e.g., a novelist, owner of a motion picture screenplay) from whom rights to adapt have been acquired (excluding translators). However, the *adaptor* must receive at least one-third of the total royalty. (This is comparable to the definition of an "author" in the MBPC.)

Musical. In a musical the royalty to the "authors" prior to recoupment is 4.5 percent of the gross increasing to 6 percent on recoupment. The term "authors" *excludes* any underlying rights owners.

IV. ROYALTY ADJUSTMENT FORMULA

Another major issue that has been addressed in the APC is the balancing of equities between the authors' contractual right, under the old MBPC, to receive full royalties, regardless of whether the producer was "breaking even" and the producer's inability to attract investors unless the authors were willing to convert royalty payments to a percentage of "net weekly operating profits" that the producer felt necessary to attract investors. To resolve this, the APC creates a "royalty adjustment formula." This formula operates in the "gray area," which occurs when a "play" producer's gross is 110 percent or less of his "break even," pre-recoupment. The formula similarly applies post-recoupment except that the gray area is increased to 120 percent. In a musical the gray area is 110 percent pre-recoupment and 115 percent post-recoupment.

I will elaborate on the specifics of the royalty adjustment formula and the gray area. Its governing principle is a recognition that when a play or musical is faltering, the APC automatically gives the producer economic relief, with-

out the necessity of negotiating a royalty adjustment with the authors. The royalty adjustment formula operates as follows for all performances of a play commencing with the fourth week following the press opening. The royalty adjustment formula is triggered to the point at which the producer of the play "breaks even" (i.e., where "gross weekly box office receipts" equal the "weekly operating costs") as determined by the accountants for the play. Any gross in excess of "break even" is deemed "profit." (N.B.: Regardless of whether the play is operating at a weekly loss or making a small weekly profit, the play's author is always guaranteed $1,000 per seek and the musical authors $3,000.)

Play—Pre-Recoupment

When the producer earns a profit which is not greater than 110 percent of break even (e.g., if break even requires a gross of $100,000 and the play actually grossed $110,000, then the gross is *not greater* than 110 percent of break even), the author receives the $1,000 guarantee plus 25 percent of the profit earned by the producer in that week in lieu of his royalty (i.e., for a play: 5 percent of the gross until recoupment of production costs). In no event can the aforesaid payments exceed the maximum royalty to which the author is then entitled.

If, however, the gross exceeds 110 percent of break even (e.g., using the above example, the gross is $110,001) then the author receives his or her regular royalty (inclusive of the $1,000 guarantee) which pre-recoupment is 5 percent of $110,001.

Play—Post-Recoupment

In the post-recoupment period the royalty adjustment changes to 120 percent of the break even, in which event the author continues to receive the $1,000 guarantee and the author's participation increases to 35 percent of the profit under 120 percent of weekly break even. (Using the same hypothesis, if gross is $120,000, then the author receives the $1,000 guarantee and 35 percent of $20,000.) If the gross is more than 120 percent of break even, then the author receives full post-recoupment royalties (i.e., 10 percent of gross).

Musical—Pre-Recoupment

In respect to a musical the same royalty adjustment formula applies pre-recoupment (i.e., a weekly guarantee of $3,000 in the aggregate to bookwriter, composer, lyricist, plus 25 percent of that portion of the gross which is not greater than 110 percent of break even, and full royalties—4.5 percent—above 110 percent).

Musical—Post-Recoupment

Post-recoupment, the royalty adjustment occurs if gross does not exceed 115 percent of break even.

While royalties payable on a straight play may never exceed 10 percent on recoupment, the authors of a musical may elect to waive the advance payable on capitalization (i.e., 2 percent of the capitalization, not to exceed $60,000) in exchange for a royalty after recoupment exceeding 6 percent. If the parties agree to this, the gray area will be 120 percent in lieu of 115 percent post-recoupment.

Royalty Adjustment: During
Christmas Season

The above formulae are subject to further adjustment covering a period between December and January in which the producer is entitled, by written notice to the authors, to elect a four-week period in which to adjust the authors' royalties. The foregoing gives recognition to a historical truism in the theater that the weeks preceding Christmas have invariably been loss weeks for most plays and musicals, whereas during the week between Christmas and New Year many plays can sell out, hopefully overcoming the pre-Christmas loss.

V. OUT-OF-TOWN THEATERS

Fixed Fees/Gross

One of the vexing problems under the MBPC was determining the authors' royalties on those theaters which, outside New York, paid producers a guarantee either in lieu of or in addition to a participation in the gross.

Play. Under the APC if the play is presented in a first-class out-of-town theater where, subsequent to January 1, 1977, the authors of plays have "customarily" been paid a percentage of the gross (i.e., royalties) above a guarantee, the author of a play will now receive (a) 10 percent of the guarantee, plus (b) 25 percent of (a) payable from up to 50 percent of producer's weekly "profits" plus (c) 10 percent of the balance of producer's "profit."*

If, however, the out-of-town theater in which the play is being presented was not in the foregoing category, then the author will receive (a) 10 percent of the guarantee plus (b) 10 percent of the producer's "profit," if any.†

Musical. For a musical the formula is identical except that the authors receive 6 percent of the guarantee and profit in lieu of 10 percent.

VI. UNITED KINGDOM, AUSTRALIA, AND NEW ZEALAND

Once the producer's rights have "vested" (see subhead IX, *infra*) then he is entitled to present the play as a first-class production in the United Kingdom, and in Australia and New Zealand. If the producer elects to "license" his rights in Australia and New Zealand, the authors are entitled to match the terms which the producer is willing to accept from his licensee.

To exercise rights in Australia or New Zealand, the producer must present the play in that territory within the following periods:

---

*Thus if the producer's contract with a theater, which grosses $300,000, guarantees the producer $100,000 and 60 percent over $200,000, then at capacity the producer would earn $100,000 plus $60,000. The author would receive (a) 10 percent of the guarantee ($10,000), plus (b) 25 percent of (a) ($2,500); and (c) 10 percent of the producer's guarantee and profit after deducting (a) and (b) ($5,750) for a total royalty of $18,250.

†The profit is the amount the producer receives from the local presentor in excess of the guarantee. Thus, using the figures in the preceding note, the producer's profit is 60 percent over $200,000 or $60,000 (of which the author receives 10 percent).

(a) play—six months after the producer's rights vest in the United States and (b) musical—six months after the close of the New York production. In both cases, the producer has the right to extend his or her opening date for an additional twelve months by making certain option payments to the authors.

The royalties covering a United Kingdom production are the same as the United States touring and fixed fee royalties (see subhead V, *supra*) but the guarantees to the authors (i.e., $1,000 for a play and $3,000 for a musical) are reduced to one-third.

If the producer elects not to present the play in any of these territories, then provided his rights have "vested," the producer will receive from any such productions licensed by the authors in the United Kingdom: 25 percent of the amount received by the authors, including subsidiary rights, for contracts executed seven years from the date the producer's rights have vested; and for revivals 10 percent for a period of forty years from vesting.

In Australia and New Zealand it is 35 percent of the authors' compensation covering contracts entered into six years following vesting (but no revival rights).

VII. REOPENING RIGHTS

The producer's reopening rights in the United States require notification to the author, within four months after the producer's last first-class performance, of his intention to reopen the play, which reopening must occur within twelve months from its last performance. During the first four months the producer has a free option; thereafter, he must pay the authors $500 per month for four months and $1,000 per month for the last four months. These latter payments are required if the producer fails to reopen the play within the initial or subsequent four-month period.

VIII. SUBSIDIARY RIGHTS

The APC retains and expands on the producer's right under the MBPC to participate in the so-called subsidiary rights, i.e., radio, television, and motion picture; stock perfor-

mances; amateur and like performances; and revivals and commercial uses. The subsidiary rights previously defined in Article Seventh of the MBPC have been retained except that they now include revivals in all theaters in New York (including Lincoln Center productions), regardless of the type of contract governing the performance, and off-Broadway productions. (In the case of revivals presented in New York City theaters the original producer will receive 20 percent of the authors' royalties for a period of forty years after the producer's first-class rights have expired. There are separate provisions governing first- and second-class revivals in the United States outside New York.)

Under the MBPC, the producer received 40 percent of the authors' net receipts from dispositions of subsidiary rights made within ten years after the producer's last first-class production, which diminished every two years thereafter. Now the producer is obliged to elect on the first day of rehearsals (except Alternative III of the musical, which must be elected on execution of the APC) one of the participation alternatives (called the Producer's Alternative) listed in the chart appearing on pages 260 and 261, which indicates the nature of the election for both plays and musicals.

IX. VESTING

Under the MBPC the producer's rights "vested" (i.e., the point at which the producer was entitled to share in subsidiary rights proceeds) if the play or musical was presented for twenty-one consecutive performances in New York (including the press opening), of which ten performances prior to the official opening could be paid previews; or sixty-four first-class performances whether outside or in New York City in an eighty-day period; or one performance in New York, provided certain defined payments had been made to the authors.

Now the vesting period requires ten paid previews plus a press opening in New York City; or five paid previews plus a press opening, and five regular performances following the press opening; or five out-of-town per-

PRODUCER'S ALTERNATIVES

PLAYS

Under "Producer's Alternative"	If any of the following Subsidiary Rights are disposed of:	*Author will promptly pay Producer, based on the following percentages of Author's compensation directly or indirectly earned (after deduction of agent's commissions, if any), from such dispositions pursuant to each contract entered into on or after the Effective Date of this Contract but prior to the expiration of the specified periods of time after the last performance of the Play hereunder (regardless of when such compensation is paid):*
I	Media Productions	50% in perpetuity
	Stock Performances	50% for the first 5 years, then 25% for the next 3 years
	Amateur and Ancillary Performances	0%
	Revival Performances	20% for 40 years
	Commercial Use Products	See SECTION 11.05 of the APC
II	Media Productions	50% in perpetuity
	Stock and Ancillary Performances	0%
	Amateur Performances	50% for the first 5 years, then 25% for the next 3 years
	Revival Performances	20% for 40 years
	Commercial Use Products	See SECTION 11.05 of the APC
III	Media Productions	50% in perpetuity
	Stock, Amateur and Ancillary Performances	10% for the first 5 years, then 25% for the next 5 years
	Revival Performances	20% for 40 years
	Commercial Use Products	See SECTION 11.05 of the APC
IV	Media Productions	30% in perpetuity
	Stock, Amateur and Ancillary Performances	30% for the first 20 years, then 25% for the next 10 years, and 20% for the next 10 years (total of 40 years)
	Revival Performances	20% for 40 years
	Commercial Use Products	See SECTION 11.05 of the APC

(*Provided, however,* that if this Alternative IV is chosen, Producer hereby assigns to Author the first $100,000 otherwise payable to Producer pursuant to this Alternative.)

MUSICALS

Author will promptly pay Producer, based on the following percentages of Author's compensation directly or indirectly earned (after deduction of agent's commissions, if any), from such dispositions pursuant to each contract entered into on or after the Effective Date of this Contract but prior to the expiration of the specified periods of time after the last performance of the Play hereunder (regardless of when such compensation is paid):

Under "Producer's Alternative"	If any of the following Subsidiary Rights are disposed of:	
I	Media Productions	50% in perpetuity
	Stock and Ancillary Performances	50% for the first 5 years, then 25% for the next 5 years
	Amateur Performances	25% for 5 years
	Revival Performances	20% for 40 years
	Commercial Use Products	See SECTION 11.05 of the APC
II	Media Productions	50% in perpetuity
	Stock and Ancillary Performances	30% for 36 years
	Amateur Performances	0%
	Revival Performances	20% for 40 years
	Commercial Use Products	See SECTION 11.05 of the APC
III	Media Productions	30% in perpetuity
	Stock, Amateur and Ancillary Performances	30% for the first 20 years, then 25% for the next 10 years, and 20% for the next 10 years (total of 40 years)
	Revival Performances	20% for 40 years
	Commercial Use Products	See SECTION 11.05 of the APC

formances, five paid previews, and a press opening in New York.

If the play is presented out of town for sixty-four performances in an eighty-day period, then the vesting will occur on the sixty-fourth first-class performance (which can include performances in arenas and auditoriums).

X. SPECIAL CIRCUMSTANCES

To cover those situations in which the APC either fails to come to grips with certain issues or where special circumstances arise, such as the producer's inability to acquire the full panoply of rights (i.e., audiovisual rights are unavailable) or he or she is unable to finance the production, because of a particular problem with the play or musical, the APC has established a Theatrical Conciliation Council. The council is a joint board consisting of seven producer and seven author members that will appoint a Joint Review Board comprising one member from each group to rule on permitted variations in the APC, where the Guild has refused to "certify" the contract because it falls outside accepted parameters. In effect the Joint Review Board is an appeals body from the Guild's determination.

XI. ARTICLE XXII

Article XXII replaces former paragraph Tenth of the old MBPC, with one major difference. Article XXII is limited, under the APC, to the types of clauses that can be inserted. However, none of its clauses can modify or conflict with other terms of the APC. Examples of permissible clauses are: right to present developmental productions; revised definition of a "completed" play; billing; travel expenses; house seats, and clauses to counterbalance "special circumstances," as defined in the APC.

XII. CONCLUSION

The APC recognizes that authors should not be writing plays or musicals virtually "on spec" nor should they alone be receiving remuneration from a successful Broadway run that has a large weekly operating cost. Similarly, producers, whose estimated production costs range from $300,000 (plays) to $5 million (musicals) should be able to attract investors by demonstrating that royalties, as a percentage of gross, will always reflect their ability to break even and that in producing a successful play or musical their subsidiary remuneration will be expanded to new and meaningful areas and for a possibly greater duration.

The intent of the parties is salutary: It lowers the weekly operating costs (particularly when the play or musical is at or near break even) by eliminating full royalty payments and substitutes certain guarantees in their stead. Once a play is operating successfully the authors will receive their full royalty, which is lower than under the former MBPC. (Under the 1955 MBPC a 6 percent royalty for musical authors was based on grosses of $80,000, or less, as distinguished from today's grosses which can easily exceed $350,000.) Furthermore, and with rare exceptions, few producers are now paying percentages of the gross on musicals. They have converted to "pooling" formulae containing weekly guarantees to all royalty participants who also receive a percentage of the net weekly operating profits (anywhere from 30 percent to 50 percent), with investors receiving another 30 or 40 percent and the theatre owner 10 to 20 percent. The major benefit of the pooling formula was that all royalty recipients (i.e., authors, pro-

ducers, designers, underlying rights owners, and the director-choreographer, subject to the rules of the Society of Stage Directors and Choreographers) were included in the pool, thus reducing the producer's fixed weekly operating costs.

The question confronting authors and producers is whether unions such as the Society of Stage Directors and Choreographers will join in this effort to reduce royalties. Similarly, when one acquired adaptation rights to an underlying work (such as a motion picture, book, or short story) each of those parties will have to recognize that whatever royalty they might have freely negotiated prior to the APC must be reduced if the structure and intent of the APC is to be honored by them.

5.20 Business Structures of Theatrical Ventures

The overwhelming majority of Broadway shows are presented through the efforts of limited partnerships. A general partner proposes the scheme, raises the money necessary to float the venture by obtaining limited partners, and makes the business decisions, including when to fold the operation. The limited partners are just that—limited. To retain the protections of a limited partner, mainly liability limited to the amount of one's investment, the business decisions must remain solely with the general partner. In turn, the limited partner is protected somewhat by requirements imposed on theatrical organizers by federal and state laws. Notable are the stringent requirements of the United States Securities Act of 1933 and the various state Blue Sky laws. One who deals in theatrical ventures and seeks to obtain investments from others must consult these regulations carefully.

A high degree of expertise is involved in structuring limited partnerships in order to comply with all federal and state requirements. For example, a number of federal exemptions under SEC Regulation D set limits on the amount that may be raised and the time within which it may be raised. The regulations also prescribe "sophisticated investor" characteristics that are designed to make it less likely that people will invest without sufficient knowledge or expertise. Counterpart state enactments, such as section 25101 et seq. of the California Corporations Code, reiterate such regulations.

Being the site of primary theatrical activity in this country, the state of New York has a special enactment dealing exclusively with investments in legitimate theatrical offerings. Because of its importance to the theatre and also as insight to the various business problems involved in financing theatrical ventures, substantial portions of the New York Arts and Cultural Affairs Law, sections 23.01 to 23.23, are here set forth.

NOTE

1. For further discussions of federal and New York law regarding theatrical offerings, see the following articles:
(a) Brown, "Federal Law Governing Theatrical Offerings," *Entertainment Law & Finance*, vol. 1, no. 9 (December 1985), p. 1.
(b) Pottash, "N.Y. Rules Governing Investment Offerings," *Entertainment Law & Finance*, vol. 1, no. 2 (May, 1985), p. 1.

§ 23.01 *Legislative findings and declaration of policy*

The legislature hereby finds and declares that:
1. The maintenance and well-being of the legitimate theatre in this state is essential to the cultural, moral and artistic well-being of the people of the state.
2. It is hereby determined and declared that the promotion and financing of theatrical productions, as defined in this article, are matters affected with a public interest and subject to the supervision of the state for the purpose of safeguarding investors and other members of the public against fraud, fraudulent accountings, financial misconduct, exorbitant rates and similar abuses.

§ 23.03 *Definitions*

1. The following terms, whenever used or referred to in this article, shall have the following meanings, unless the context clearly requires otherwise:
(a) A "theatrical production" shall mean those live-staged dramatic plays and dramatic-musical productions which hereafter are shown to the public for profit and which are financed wholly or in part by the offering or sale in or from this state, directly, or through agents or distributors, of investment agreements, evidences of interest, limited partnerships, producer shares, equity or debt securities, pre-organization subscriptions or any other syndication participation, when any persons are offered, solicited to purchase or sell, directly or indirectly, such syndication interests for moneys or services within or from the state of New York.
(b) "Fraud," "deceit," and "defraud," as such terms are used in this article, are not limited to common-law deceit.
(c) "Syndication" shall mean all forms, methods and devices for pooling of investment funds for the chief purpose of participating in a theatrical production, as defined herein.
(d) A "principal" shall mean and include every person or firm directly or indirectly controlling the business affairs or operations of a theatrical production, as defined herein.
(e) A "person" shall mean an individual, firm, company, partnership, corporation, trust or association.
2. Accurate books and records of account shall be maintained by each theatrical production. Every producer of a theatrical production shall at least once for each twelve month fiscal period beginning with the initial expenditure of investors' funds (other than those of any principal), within four months after the end of such period or the last public performance of the original production in New York state, whichever is sooner, furnish to all investors and to the department of law a written balance

sheet and statement of profit and loss which shall be prepared by an independent public accountant and contain an express opinion by such accountant that such statements fairly present the financial position and results of operations of the production company, hereinafter referred to as "certified statement." Notwithstanding the aforesaid, in no event shall a producer be required by this subdivision to submit certified statements to investors for any period less than twelve months following the period covered by a prior certified statement. Irrespective of the aforesaid, and in addition thereto, every such producer shall also furnish each investor and the department of law with an accurate and truthful itemized statement of income and expenditure for every six month period not covered by a previously issued certified statement or a certified statement required to be issued hereunder for a period ending at such time, which additional statement shall be subscribed to by the producer as accurate, and may be submitted within three months after the close of such six month period. Following the last public performance in New York state of the original production, the producer shall accurately report to the investors and the department of law, at least once within four months after the end of each year thereafter, with respect to any subsequent earnings or expenditures by the production, which shall be truthful and accurate and which shall be subscribed to by the producer as accurate. The attorney general may adopt, promulgate, amend and rescind rules and regulations setting forth other accounting requirements than set forth above, which may be selected by a producer in lieu of the accounting requirements set forth above. Such rules and regulations may further provide for the issuance of an exemption from the requirements herein for offerings of less than two hundred fifty thousand dollars or made to less than thirty-six persons in or from this state upon conditions set forth by the attorney general.

This subdivision shall not apply to any production whose first performance in New York state preceded June first, nineteen hundred sixty-four.

3. Except as otherwise provided herein, no offering of syndication interests in a theatrical production, as defined herein, shall be made within or from this state without the use of a prospectus or offering circular making full and fair disclosure of material facts pertaining to the particular venture. The attorney general may also issue rules and regulations requiring the submission to prospective investors in such offerings an offering circular and amendments thereto containing a concise and accurate description of the nature of the offering, profits to promoters and others, the background of the producers, a description of subsidiary rights and other pertinent information as will afford potential investors or purchasers and participants an adequate basis upon which to found their judgment, but the attorney general shall accept offering literature filed with the Securities and Exchange Commission and authorized for use by such agency as complying therewith as of the date of receipt of a true copy by the department of law of such literature and proof of authorization by the Securities and Exchange Commission by affidavit or otherwise. The attorney general may also provide for the method of filing of offering literature other than that filed with the Securities and Exchange Commission, as well as underlying documents, with the department of law at its office in the city of New York, prior to the offering of the syndication interest involved; however, any such regulation also shall provide that all funds derived from the sale of such theatrical syndication interests shall be held in trust in a special bank account until the attorney general has issued to the issuer or other offeror a letter stating that the offering has been permitted to be filed; but in that event such regulation promulgated by the attorney general shall also provide that the attorney general, not later than fifteen days after such submission, shall issue such a letter or, in the alternative, a notification in writing indicating deficiencies therein. The provisions of this subdivision shall not apply to offerings to less

than thirty-six persons where express waivers in writing to the filing and offering circular requirements of this subdivision are filed with the department of law by or on behalf of all investors.

4. A limited partnership that is a syndication for a theatrical production is exempt from the requirement for publishing its certificate or notice under section ninety-one of the partnership law so long as the words "limited partnership" appear in its name.

5. It shall be unlawful for any person, in connection with the offer, sale, or purchase of any syndication interest in any theatrical production, as defined herein, directly or indirectly:

(a) To employ any device, scheme, or artifice to defraud;

(b) To willfully make any untrue statement of a material fact or to omit to state a material fact necessary in order to make such statement made, not misleading; or

(c) To engage in any act, practice, or course of business which he knows or reasonably should have known operates or would operate as a fraud or deceit upon any person.

6. Any person, partnership, corporation, company, trust or association or any agent or employee thereof, who (or which), having engaged in any act or practice constituting a violation of subdivision five of this section, commits additional acts under such circumstances as to constitute a felony, the crime of conspiracy, petit larceny, or more than one of the aforesaid, shall be punishable therefor, as well as for the violation of subdivision five of this section, and may be prosecuted for each crime, separately or in the same information or indictment, notwithstanding any other provision of law.

§ 23.05 *Investigations*

1. Whenever it shall appear to the attorney general either upon complaint or otherwise that any person has violated or is about to violate any provision of this article, or that he believes it necessary to aid in the enforcement of this article or in the prescribing of rules or regulations hereunder, the attorney general:

(a) May make such public or private investigations within or outside of this state as he deems necessary to determine whether any person has violated or is about to violate any provision of this article or any rule or regulation hereunder, or to aid in the enforcement of this article or in the prescribing of rules and forms hereunder; and

(b) May require or permit any person to file a statement in writing, under oath or otherwise as the attorney general determines, as to all the facts and circumstances concerning the matter to be investigated.

2. The attorney general, or any officer designated by him, is empowered to subpoena witnesses, compel their attendance, examine them under oath before him or a court of record or a judge or justice thereof, and require the production of any books or papers which he deems relevant or material to the inquiry. Such power of subpoena and examination shall not abate or terminate by reason of any action or proceeding brought by the attorney general under this article.

3. No person shall be excused from attending such inquiry in pursuance to the mandate of a subpoena, or from producing a paper or book, or from being examined or required to answer a question on the ground of failure of tender or payment of a witness fee and/or mileage, unless at the time of such appearance or production, as the case may be, such witness makes demand for such payment as a condition precedent to the offering of testimony or production required by the subpoena and unless such payment is not thereupon made. The provision for payment of witness fee and/or mileage shall not apply to any officer, director or person in the employ of any person, partnership, corporation, company, trust or association whose conduct or practices are being investigated.

4. If a person subpoenaed to attend such inquiry fails to obey the command of a subpoena without reasonable cause, or if a person in attendance upon such inquiry shall without

reasonable cause refuse to be sworn or to be examined or to answer a question or to produce and permit reasonable examination of a book or paper when ordered so to do by the officer conducting such inquiry, or if a person, partnership, corporation, company, trust or association fails to perform any act required hereunder to be performed, he shall be guilty of a misdemeanor.

5. It shall be the duty of all public officers, their deputies, assistants, subordinates, clerks or employees and all other persons to render and furnish to the attorney general or other designated officer when requested all information and assistance in their possession or within their power with respect to all matters being investigated by the attorney general under this article. Any officer participating in such inquiry and any person examined as a witness upon such inquiry who shall disclose to any person other than his attorney or the attorney general the name of any witness examined or any other information obtained upon such inquiry except as directed by the attorney general shall be guilty of a misdemeanor.

§ 23.07 *Records; bank accounts*

All moneys raised from the offer and sale of syndication interests in theatrical productions, as defined herein, shall be held in a special bank account in trust until actually employed for pre-production or production purposes of the particular theatrical production or returned to the investor or investors thereof. All the records of such bank account and bank transactions shall be preserved for at least two years. It shall be clearly set forth in writing in an investment agreement and any prospectus or circular distributed to each investor in a theatrical production, as defined herein, that all moneys raised from the offer and sale of syndication interests in theatrical productions, as defined herein, shall be held in a special bank account in trust until actually employed for pre-production or production purposes of the particular theatrical production or returned to the investor or investors thereof.

Any provision of any contract or agreement or understanding, whether oral or in writing, whereby a person who so purchases an interest in any theatrical production syndication, as defined herein, waives any provision of this section is absolutely void.

§ 23.11 *Injunctions; modification or dissolution*

1. Whenever the attorney general shall believe from evidence satisfactory to him that any person has engaged or is about to engage in any act or practice constituting a violation of any provision of this article or any rule or regulation hereunder, he may in his discretion bring an action in the supreme court of the state of New York to enjoin the acts or practices and to enforce compliance with this article or any rule or regulation hereunder. Upon a proper showing a permanent or temporary injunction or restraining order shall be granted, which may include the appointment of a temporary or permanent receiver of all of the assets and affairs of a theatrical production, as defined herein, for the purpose of transacting the affairs or liquidating such production, upon conditions set by the court, whenever such relief is deemed by such court in the interest of the investor and the public generally. Upon a showing by the attorney general that a violation of this article or any rule or regulation thereunder has occurred, he may include in an action under this article an application to direct restitution of any moneys or property obtained directly or indirectly by such violation.

2. Any person against whom an injunction has been granted under the provisions of this article may apply to the supreme court at any time after five years from the date such permanent injunction became effective, upon at least sixty days' notice to the attorney general, for an order dissolving such injunction or modifying the same upon such terms and conditions as the court deems necessary or desirable. Such application for dissolution or modification of such injunction shall contain a recitation of the facts and circumstances which

caused the granting of the injunction; the occupation and employment of the person making the application and his financial remuneration therefrom since the time the injunction was granted; his net worth at the time of the application and the sources thereof, together with any other facts bearing upon the reasonableness of the application and the character of the applicant, as may enable the court to issue an order that will properly dispose of such application in the interests of justice. A copy of such application, together with copies of any other papers in support thereof, shall be served upon the attorney general at least sixty days prior to the return date thereof. In addition thereto the applicant shall file with the court a good and sufficient surety bond in the sum of one thousand dollars guaranteeing that he will pay all costs and expenses of an investigation by the attorney general of such applicant and the statements and claims alleged in the application together with any further investigation which the attorney general may deem necessary or desirable to determine whether he should consent to the application, oppose the same or make such other recommendations to the court as in his opinion are desirable to be included in any modification of such injunction. Should it appear in the course of such investigation by the attorney general that said sum is not sufficient, the attorney general may apply to the court by usual notice of motion or order to show cause for an increase in the amount of security or further surety bond necessary to fully pay all of the costs of the investigation and the court may require such further bond as the situation requires to fully pay such costs and expenses. Upon the completion of such investigation, the attorney general may file an answer to such application setting forth such facts as are pertinent to the determination by the court of the matter before it and whether said injunction should be dissolved, modified or continued in whole or in part and what conditions, if any, shall be attached to any dissolution or modification of said injunction. After a hearing upon such application and after any further investigation, proof or testimony which the court may order, it may make a final order dissolving the permanent injunction or modifying the same upon such terms and conditions as in its opinion are just and desirable, or in its discretion, may deny the application. Such order shall contain a direction that the applicant pay to the attorney general the costs and expenses of the investigation in connection with the proceeding, and any judgment entered thereon may be enforced directly against the surety on the bond. The court shall grant no temporary or other relief from the injunction in force pending a final determination of such application. No application under this subdivision shall be entertained: (a) where the injunction was granted as an incident to a crime of which the applicant has been convicted, nor (b) in any case where the applicant has been convicted of a felony or a crime that would be a felony if committed in the state of New York since the issuance of the injunction, nor (c) convicted at any time of any crime involving stocks, bonds, investments, securities, or like instruments, nor (d) convicted at any time of any crime involving theatrical syndication interests, which are the subject matter of this article. Nor shall anything contained in this subdivision be construed to deny to or interfere with the power of the attorney general to bring any other action or proceeding, civil or criminal, against the applicant at any time.

§ 23.13 *Application of the provisions of civil practice law and rules*

The provisions of the civil practice law and rules shall apply to all actions and proceedings brought under this article except as herein otherwise provided.

§ 23.17 *Enforcement by attorney general*

The attorney general may prosecute every person charged with a criminal offense in violation of this article and regulations issued thereunder, or any violation of any other law of this state applicable to or in respect to fraudulent practices in connection with the offer, sale, negotiation or advertising of syndication interests in theatrical productions, as defined herein. In all such proceedings, the attorney general may appear in person or by his deputy before any court of record or any grand jury and exercise all the powers and perform all the duties in respect of such actions or proceedings which the district attorney would otherwise be authorized or required to exercise or perform; or the attorney general may in his discretion transmit evidence, proof and information as to such offense to the district attorney of the county or counties in which the alleged violation has occurred, and every district attorney to whom such evidence, proof and information is so transmitted may proceed to investigate and prosecute any corporation, company, association, or officer, manager or agent thereof, or any firm or person charged with such violation. In any such proceeding, wherein the attorney general has appeared either in person or by deputy, the district attorney shall only exercise such powers and perform such duties as are required of him by the attorney general or the deputy attorney general so appearing.

§ 23.19 Unlawful retention of payments

Any producer, promoter, principal, employee, general manager, company manager or agent of a theatrical production, as defined herein, who knowingly receives, directly or indirectly, from any supplier, advertising agency, publication, theatre owner, theatre treasurer, ticket agent, ticket broker, or other firm or person having dealings with, or applicable to, the theatrical production, or from any employees or agents thereof, any cash, checks, rebates, commissions, gifts, gratuities or other payments or consideration for reason of the business operations, management, bidding, negotiation or other operation of such theatrical production or arising out of the business of such theatrical production, and who does not pay such amounts or consideration into such theatrical production within a period of seventy-two hours thereafter, except where such retention is expressly permitted by the production company and where a written investor agreement signed by all investors represented

that such retention would be permitted by the production company, shall be guilty of a misdemeanor, punishable by a fine of not more than five hundred dollars or imprisonment for not more than one year, or both.

§ 23.21 Violations and penalties

Any person, partnership, corporation, company, trust or association willfully violating any of the provisions of this article or any rule or regulation issued thereunder shall be guilty of a misdemeanor punishable by a fine of not more than five hundred dollars, or imprisonment for not more than one year, or both.

§ 23.23 Prohibited activities of theatre and sporting event personnel

1. The term "theatre and sporting event personnel," as used in this section, shall mean all owners, operators or operating lessees who control the operation of a theatre, stadium, garden, or other place where theatre or sporting events are held, including the allocation or distribution of tickets to a theatrical production or sporting event, and all controlling partners, and controlling stockholders and controlling officers of the aforesaid; and all agents, representatives, employees and licensees of any of the aforementioned, including without limitation theatre or sporting event box office treasurers and assistant treasurers, who for any period of time have control of the allocation or distribution by designation or authority of the aforementioned, of theatre or sporting event tickets in connection with the showing of theatrical productions or sporting events, as defined herein but shall not include subordinate personnel performing non-discretionary or ministerial functions in connection with the allocation or distribution of theatre or sporting event tickets.

2. A "theatrical production" as used in this section shall mean those live-staged dramatic plays and dramatic-musical productions which hereafter are shown to the public in a theatre run for profit.

3. A "sporting event" as used in this section shall mean those contests, games, or other

events involving athletic or physical skills which are shown to the public in a stadium, garden, or any other place of amusement run for profit and whose participants are paid for the exhibition of their athletic or physical skills, but not exhibitions under the jurisdiction of the state racing or state harness racing commissions.

4. It shall be illegal and prohibited for any owner, lessee or operator or manager or treasurer or assistant treasurer or any other theatre and sporting event personnel of a theatre showing theatrical productions, as defined in this article, or any stadium, garden or other place of amusement showing sporting events, as defined in this article, to sell tickets in this state directly or indirectly, through agents, employees or otherwise, unless and until there is filed with the department of law of the state of New York by the owner or operator or lessee or any other person, directly or indirectly, controlling the distribution of tickets a registration known as a "ticket distributor registration" on which shall be contained the names, addresses and connection with the distribution of tickets of all theatre and sporting event personnel, as defined herein, on forms issued by the attorney general of the state of New York, as applicable to such registration and amendments thereto. It shall be illegal for any theatre and sporting event personnel to sell tickets, or control the sale thereof, unless named on such registration. The attorney general may issue an order cancelling or suspending the name of a particular individual or individuals from such registration or issue an order barring such person from selling any theatre or sporting event tickets as aforesaid whether or not the person's name appears on any particular registration after a hearing, conducted by him or a designated officer, when, based upon substantial evidence on the entire record, it is determined that: such theatre or sporting event personnel subsequent to October first, nineteen hundred sixty-five, directly or indirectly, has willfully aided, abetted or participated in exacting, demanding, accepting or receiving, directly or indirectly, any premium or price in excess of the regular or established price or charge, plus lawful taxes, as printed upon the face of each ticket or other evidence of the right of entry thereto, for theatre and sporting event tickets from members of the public or ticket brokers or agents, whether designated as price, gratuity or otherwise; or whenever such theatre and sporting event personnel has been convicted of any crime relating to the sale of tickets to theatrical productions or sporting events, or violations of this article; or whenever such theatre and sporting event personnel shall have engaged in any practice in connection with the sale of tickets to theatrical productions or sporting events which operates as a fraud upon the public or amounts to financial misconduct, or the exacting of exorbitant rates or other similar abuses; or whenever any theatre and sporting event personnel has willfully violated any provision of this article or any rule or regulation issued thereunder. The attorney general may also issue rules and regulations relating to the maintenance of theatre and sporting event box office records and with respect to the filing and content of ticket distributor registrations.

5. All theatre and sporting event ticket personnel as defined in this section shall keep or cause to be kept books, records, memoranda or correspondence containing the following information in connection with the sale or distribution of tickets:

(a) The number of tickets sold, allocated or distributed to ticket brokers licensed pursuant to article twenty-five of this chapter or other known brokers, specifying the price and location of each ticket sold, allocated or distributed to each broker and the date and time of performance of each such ticket.

(b) The number of tickets among those allocated and distributed to brokers by theatre and sporting event ticket personnel, returned by each broker to theatre and sporting event ticket personnel specifying the price of each such returned ticket and the date and time of performance of each such ticket.

(c) The number of tickets sold or distributed as house seats with recipients thereof; or to duly licensed theatre party agents representing charitable or eleemosynary organizations, specifying the price and location of each ticket sold, allocated or distributed and the date and time of performance of each such ticket.

(d) All mail order correspondence, including disposition thereof.

All records required to be kept pursuant to this section shall be preserved for a period of not less than one year subsequent to the date of performance to which such record relates.

6. Any person aggrieved by an order of the attorney general hereunder may obtain a review of such order in the appellate division of the supreme court pursuant to article seventy-eight of the civil practice law and rules by filing in such court within ten days after the entry of such order, a notice of petition, petition and suitable affidavits as provided in subdivision (c) of section seven thousand eight hundred four of the civil practice law and rules, praying that the order of the attorney general be modified or set aside in whole or in part upon any of the grounds set forth in section seven thousand eight hundred three of the civil practice law and rules.

7. If any provision of this section is in conflict with any provision of any law of the state of New York or any municipality or subdivision thereof or any rule or regulation thereof in force on October first, nineteen hundred sixty-five, the provisions of this section shall prevail.

5.30 Individual Contract Dealings in the Theatre

Disputes in the legitimate theatre produce few reported cases. Most disputes are submitted to arbitration, pursuant to individual contract provisions or under union collective bargaining agreements. The written decisions in these cases are not made public. Occasionally, however, a case reaches the courts that illustrates themes running throughout the entertainment industries. Such is the following discussion in *Gennaro v. Rosenfield*, which not only deals with matters of injunctive relief previously considered (see Section 1.50 to 1.54) but lends insight into the complexities and sensitivities of the business and artistic aspects of theatre.

Gennaro v. Rosenfield, 600 F. Supp. 485 (S.D.N.Y. 1984)

GOETTEL, DISTRICT JUDGE

In the eyes of many, Hollywood's heyday was the era of the musical, often based on the Broadway show. One of the preeminent films of that era, "Singin' in the Rain," starred Gene Kelly, Debbie Reynolds, and Donald O'Connor. This litigation concerns an apparently new phenomenon—the proposed stage adaptation of that now legendary film.

The plaintiffs, Peter Gennaro and his company, Geannie Productions, Inc., allege that Mr. Gennaro has contracted to choreograph the proposed Broadway production of "Singin' in the Rain" for the defendant, Maurice Rosenfield. The plaintiffs claim that the defendant has breached this contract and, therefore, seek damages for breach of contract and defamation. Presently before the Court is the plaintiffs' motion for a preliminary injunction which, in essence, would prevent the defendant from engaging any other choreographer pending the outcome of the litigation. The Court must deny this motion for the reasons stated below. . . .

The individual plaintiff, Peter Gennaro, is a choreographer and dancer. He has choreographed a number of well-known Broadway musicals, including "Fiorello," "The Unsinkable Molly Brown," and "Annie" (for which he won a Tony Award). Mr. Gennaro is also the president of the corporate plaintiff, Geannie Productions, Inc. The defendants, Maurice and Lois Rosenfield, are husband and wife. Mr. Rosenfield is a Broadway producer. Among his credits are the 1980 Broadway musical "Barnum" and the 1983 revival of Tennessee Williams's "The Glass Menagerie." In 1980, Mr. Rosenfield acquired the right to adapt "Singin' in the Rain" for stage presentation from Metro-Goldwyn-Mayer and Robbins Music Company. Rosenfield subsequently granted a license to Harold Fielding for the London production of "Singin' in the Rain."

The events giving rise to the instant controversy commenced in November 1980, when Ian

Bevan, a British theatrical agent and manager, contacted Mr. Gennaro's agent and attorney, Robert M. Cavallo. According to Mr. Cavallo, Mr. Bevan said that Mr. Fielding wanted Peter Gennaro to choreograph the London production. Mr. Cavallo relayed this offer to Mr. Gennaro, who allegedly said that he would agree to choreograph the London production only on the condition that he also receive the option to choreograph any first-class stage production of "Singin' in the Rain" in the United States, including any Broadway production. Mr. Gennaro alleges that Mr. Bevan proceeded to negotiate with Mr. Cavallo for Mr. Gennaro's services and with Mr. Rosenfield to obtain the desired option. The plaintiff further alleges that an agreement was reached on both counts and that the option agreement was embodied in a January 20, 1983, letter signed by both Bevan and Rosenfield. . . .

On February 2, 1983, Mr. Fielding forwarded a copy of the January 20 letter to Mr. Gennaro along with his own letter confirming an agreement between himself and Mr. Gennaro. According to this letter, Mr. Bevan had "negotiated conditions for [Mr. Gennaro to choreograph] the American and other first-class productions of "Singin' in the Rain" which [would] be separately confirmed to [Mr. Gennaro] by the American producer, Mr. Maurice Rosenfield." . . . On April 5, 1983, Ronald Taft, Mr. Rosenfield's attorney, forwarded a draft contract to Mr. Cavallo and requested Mr. Cavallo's comments. According to Mr. Rosenfield, this contract concerned both the London and American productions. Mr. Gennaro maintains that the April 5 draft only concerned the London production. For unknown reasons, Mr. Cavallo informed Mr. Taft that he would not comment on the draft. At the same time, Mr. Cavallo was negotiating with Mr. Fielding. On April 14, 1984, Harold Fielding, Ltd. and Geannie Productions, Inc. entered into a written agreement with regard to Mr. Gennaro's role in the London production. Mr. Gennaro alleges that this agreement formalized the January 20 letter with respect to the American production. . . .

In early June, Mr. Rosenfield visited Mr. Cavallo in his New York office. Precisely what transpired at that meeting is unclear. Soon thereafter, Mr. Cavallo sent Mr. Taft a letter commenting on the April 5 draft. There were no further discussions about that document.

The London production opened on June 30, 1983, and is still running. Mr. Gennaro has met twice with Mr. and Mrs. Rosenfield since the opening, once in June 1983, and again in December 1983. Precisely what was said at those meetings is also in dispute.

During the summer of 1984, Mr. Cavallo heard that the American production of "Singin' in the Rain" was being planned and that the plans did not involve Peter Gennaro. On September 17, 1984, Mr. Cavallo sent a mailgram to Mr. Rosenfield advising him that Mr. Gennaro had elected to exercise the option to choreograph the American production. On September 20, 1984, Mr. Taft responded for Mr. Rosenfield in a letter that stated, "Mr. Rosenfield has not asked Mr. Gennaro whether he would like to choreograph the production of 'Singin' in the Rain' which Mr. Rosenfield plans to produce in New York." . . . The plaintiffs then brought the instant action by order to show cause seeking, *inter alia*, a preliminary negative injunction enjoining the defendants and their agents from

(a) producing any American first-class stage production of the musical "Singin' in the Rain" (the "American production") with choreography by any choreographer other than Peter Gennaro;

(b) entering into any contract for choreography of the American production with any choreographer other than Peter Gennaro;

(c) advertising, promoting or otherwise publicizing the American production, in print or any other media, whereby the actual or prospective choreography is represented as by any choreographer other than Peter Gennaro. . . .

A court will grant preliminary injunctive relief if a plaintiff can show (a) irreparable harm and (b) either (1) likelihood of success on the merits or (2) sufficiently serious questions going to the merits to make them a fair ground for litigation and a balance of hardships tipping decidedly toward the party requesting the preliminary relief. . . . Even if the plaintiffs have established irreparable harm, they have shown neither a likelihood of success on the merits, nor a balance of hardships tipping decidedly in their favor. . . .

An inadequate remedy at law is a necessary prerequisite to a showing of irreparable harm. . . . Mr. Gennaro argues that he will continue to suffer two wrongs for which money damages will not compensate: harm to his reputation and erosion of his professional skills. While it may be that the harm to the plaintiff's reputation constitutes irreparable harm, we do not believe that erosion of his skills constitutes such harm. . . .

Although courts recognize that atrophy of professional skills could constitute irreparable harm, . . . we are aware of only one case finding that, under the facts established, such atrophy constitutes irreparable harm. In that case, *Neeld v. American Hockey League*, 439 F. Supp. 459 (W.D.N.Y. 1977), the court found that a young hockey player would suffer irreparable harm were he denied the right to play professional hockey during the pendency of his lawsuit challenging certain league restrictions that would have prevented him from playing. The district court noted that

> [t]he denial to plaintiff of an opportunity to play professional hockey in the AHL will result in the possibility of irreparable harm to plaintiff's professional hockey career. A young athlete's skills diminish and sometimes are irretrievably lost unless he is given an opportunity to practice and refine such skills at a certain level of proficiency. Therefore, plaintiff has shown the possibility of irreparable harm if an injunction *pendente lite* is not granted.

Id at 461. Mr. Gennaro argues that the alleged breach of contract will limit his opportunities for work, thereby denying him the chance to develop and refine his skills. The plaintiff's situation, however, differs markedly from the young hockey player's in *Neeld*. The plaintiff, an established choreographer with a first class reputation, will not be denied the opportunity to embark on a promising artistic career. Nor are his skills likely to diminish or atrophy. Since he has already choreographed the London production, the Broadway production represents less than a unique opportunity to develop his skills. In addition, as a top flight choreographer, he is likely to gain other work during the time he would be choreographing "Singin' in the Rain." Thus, we

decline to follow *Neeld*. The plaintiff has not established that his skills will diminish so as to cause him irreparable harm.

Mr. Gennaro also asserts that his reputation has been irreparably harmed. In his words,

> The world of theatre is small, and its every event is illuminated by the bright spotlight of public curiosity. Reputations which have been built up over many years can be torn apart overnight when it appears that other artists are more desirable. Colleagues have been asking me why I was "replaced" as choreographer for the American production. The situation is painfully embarrassing to me and is severely damaging the first-class reputation and professional credibility I have worked so hard to establish over so many years. I have no traditional monetary remedy, since no amount of money can fully compensate me for this injury; indeed, its subtle effects can never be fully known. . . .

Several cases from this circuit establish that damage to reputation often constitutes irreparable injury and justifies injunctive relief. For example, in *Madison Square Garden Boxing, Inc. v. Shavers*, 434 F. Supp. 449 (S.D.N.Y. 1977), the court found that a promoter of major boxing matches would be irreparably injured were its credibility destroyed by virtue of a boxer breaching his contract with the promoter. . . . Similarly, Peter Gennaro has worked for many years to establish a reputation as a first class choreographer. His reputation is of great commercial value to him. The apparent replacement of the plaintiff could damage his reputation in the theatre community. Those who had thought Mr. Gennaro would choreograph the production may now hold him in lower esteem. As the plaintiffs correctly point out, such damage to reputation is difficult if not impossible to measure in money terms.

On the other hand, show business arrangements often take into account considerations other than artistic merit. One bad review cannot tarnish the image of an established artist such as Peter Gennaro. Theatre people may well find fault with Mr. Rosenfield in this situation—particularly in light of the success of the London production. This situation resembles that where a baseball manager replaces the starting pitcher in the late innings despite the fact that he is pitching a shut out and has a comfortable lead. If the relief pitcher fails, the manager looks terrible. . . .

Setting aside the question of irreparable harm, we next consider whether the plaintiffs have demonstrated a likelihood of success on the merits. We conclude that they have not.

The nub of this case is a dispute over whether Mr. Rosenfield ever contracted with Mr. Gennaro. . . .

Mr. Gennaro asserts that the January 20 letter from Ian Bevan to Maurice Rosenfield, countersigned by Mr. Rosenfield, standing alone, constitutes a binding contract. That letter states, in part:

> I write to record the heads of agreement I have reached on your behalf in negotiations with Mr. Robert M. Cavallo . . . for the services of Mr. Peter Gennaro as choreographer for the above production [("Singin' in the Rain")].
>
> His services have been engaged by Harold Fielding Ltd. for the London production. . . . Subject to that production running not less than 100 consecutive performances, you undertake to offer Mr. Gennaro a contract to choreograph the first American and/or Broadway production.
>
> . . . This letter is to record in "heads of agreement" style the basic terms agreed between you and Mr. Gennaro, which terms will now be converted into a formal document or documents in such form as shall be to the approval of your respective legal advisers. By our respective signatures to this letter we confirm to each other and to Mr. Gennaro that the basic terms to be incorporated into the formal documentation are those outlined in this letter. . . .

The letter further specified Gennaro's fee and his share of the royalties. No other terms were detailed.

Acknowledging that this letter contemplated more formal documentation, the plaintiffs nevertheless contend that it constitutes a binding agreement. They rely on authority to the effect that a letter containing the essential terms of a contract may create a binding obligation although the parties may have contemplated executing a more formal agreement at a later date. . . . The plaintiffs argue that the evidence conclusively establishes that the parties intended the January 20 letter to be a contract. The plaintiffs point out that the letter contained the material financial terms of the deal and that Mr. Gennaro's agent made it known to Mr. Fielding that Mr. Gennaro

would not choreograph the London production unless he had an option to choreograph the Broadway production. To buttress this position, Mr. Cavallo and Mr. Gennaro also offer their recollection of several conversations with Mr. Rosenfield allegedly confirming the agreement. The plaintiffs also submit a letter from Mr. Bevan that purports to support their position. Standing alone, their evidence might establish the likelihood of success on the merits.

However, the defendants make a number of points in rebuttal. They thus make clear that whether the January 20 letter is a contract is, at most, a serious question going to the merits and a fair ground for litigation.

The defendants first argue that the behavior of the parties subsequent to January 20, 1983, indicated their intention *not* to be bound by the January 20 letter. They also take issue with the plaintiffs' characterization of the January 20 letter. According to the defendants, "[t]he January 20 letter is not a contract because it expressly provides that it is to be followed by a detailed agreement to be crafted and approved by counsel and to contain additional terms." Defendants' Reply Memorandum at 15. "[Such a]n agreement . . . does not bind the parties until such documentation and approval are accomplished." *Id.* at 17. They cite *C.H. Rugg & Co. v. Street*, [1962] 1 Lloyd's List L.P. 364, 369 (Q.B.); *Reprosystem B.V. v. SCM Corp.*, 727 F.2d 257 (2d Cir.), *cert. denied*,—U.S.—, 105 S.Ct. 110, 83 L.Ed.2d 54 (1984); and *Read v. Henzel*, 67 A.D.2d 186, 415 N.Y.S.2d 520, 523 (1979), to support this proposition. However, these cases turned not on the law, or on any hard and fast rule of contract interpretation, but rather on the particular intentions of the parties to the alleged contract. Similarly, the dispute about the January 20 letter turns not on the law but on the facts. Whether the parties intended to contract is a serious question for the factfinder.

The defendants also claim that the January 20 letter is not sufficiently definite to constitute a binding agreement. Under the general principles of contract law, there can be no contract if the parties fail to agree on all the essential terms. . . . The January 20, 1983, letter specifies only the fee and royalty terms. Mr. Cavallo asserts that this accords with industry practice, an assertion that the defendants vigorously dispute. We are not sure who has the better of this dispute, but we are certain that the plaintiffs have not demonstrated that they are likely to prevail.

The plaintiffs also argue that, even if the January 20 letter is too indefinite to constitute a contract, the April 14 long form agreement between Geannie Productions, Inc. and Harold Fielding Ltd. is sufficiently definite. This detailed agreement contains the essential terms necessary for a binding contract. However, the defendants argue that Fielding lacked actual or apparent authority to bind Rosenfield. In rebuttal, the plaintiffs argue that, even if Fielding lacked actual authority, he had apparent authority. The Restatement (Second) of the Law of Agency § 8 defines apparent authority as "the power to affect the legal relations of another person by transactions with third persons, professedly as agent for the other, arising from and in accordance with the other's manifestations to such third persons." *Restatement (Second) of the Law of Agency* § 8. According to Mr. Gennaro, Mr. Rosenfield manifested Mr. Fielding's authority in his January 20 letter. The defendants, of course, reject this contention. They claim that the plaintiffs have alleged no act by Mr. Rosenfield whereby he conferred authority upon Mr. Fielding to act as his agent or whereby he communicated that authority to Mr. Gennaro or Mr. Cavallo. Again, the facts are so vague that to draw any conclusion with regard to the likelihood of either side prevailing on the authority issue is impossible.

Finally, the defendants argue that, even assuming *arguendo* that the January 20th letter constitutes a valid agreement, Mr. Gennaro breached that agreement when his agent, Mr. Cavallo, refused to comment on the April 5 draft contract. However, the plaintiffs' response undercuts the defendants' position. As noted above, Mr. Gennaro maintains that the January 20 letter in and of itself constituted a contract. Therefore, he had no duty to negotiate with Mr. Rosenfield and did not breach his contract when he refused to comment on the April 5 draft. In addition, Mr. Gennaro offers another credible explanation for his refusal to comment. The April 5 draft concerned, at least in part, Mr. Gennaro's obligations with respect to the British production. The plaintiffs argue that, since Mr. Cavallo was already negotiating with Mr. Fielding about that production, the April 5 draft contract was duplicative and unnecessary. However, this argument is undercut by the plaintiffs' failure to explain Mr. Cavallo's June 15 letter to Mr. Taft reviewing the April 5 contract. Whether Mr. Cavallo's refusal to comment constituted a breach is thus as unclear as the other matters in dispute.

The foregoing discussion leaves no doubt that the plaintiffs have not established the likelihood of success on the merits. There exist too many unresolved factual questions to justify any such conclusion. . . .

Given our conclusion regarding the likelihood of success on the merits, we may grant the requested relief only if the plaintiff can "show that the harm which he would suffer from the denial of his motion is 'decidedly' greater than the harm which [the defendants] would suffer if the motion was granted." *Buffalo Forge Co. v. Ampco-Pittsburgh Corp.*, 638 F.2d 568, 569 (2d Cir. 1981). In this case, the balance of hardships does not tip decidedly in favor of the plaintiffs. We therefore decline to grant the requested relief.

If the motion is denied, the plaintiffs may suffer some additional irreparable harm. However, even if we accept Mr. Gennaro's assertion of irreparable harm, most of the damage to his reputation has already been done. No doubt, if we grant the requested relief, a group of individuals who would otherwise learn of Mr. Gennaro's alleged dismissal will remain uninformed (assuming the defendants choose to go ahead with the production). A denial of injunctive relief will harm the plaintiff's reputation among this group. However, the plaintiff's primary concern is his reputation among those in the theatre industry. That group is well informed, and has by now learned of this controversy. Thus, the denial of injunctive relief will do little to mitigate the total harm the plaintiff will suffer as a result of his alleged replacement.

On the other hand, should we grant the requested relief, the defendants will have two choices. They may hire Mr. Gennaro, or abandon the production. Abandonment, while not unrealistic—given the assertions to this effect in Mr. Rosenfield's papers—would constitute self-inflicted harm. We do not believe such harm is cognizable or relevant to our determination. Assuming Mr. Rosenfield opts to have Mr. Gennaro choreograph his production, Mr. Rosenfield would find himself in the uncomfortable position of working closely with someone whom he allegedly had replaced, had litigated against, and had no desire to work with. In addition, Mr. Rosenfield would be forced to abandon any discussions or contract into which he might have already entered with another choreographer. He would then suffer the obvious consequences of such an action. In our view, the defendants will suffer at least as much if not more harm from a grant of injunctive relief than the plaintiffs will suffer from a denial.

Although our judgment about the relative harms each party would suffer is subjective, we think it clear that the plaintiff has failed to show that the balance of hardships tips decidedly in his favor. . . . Therefore, we decline to grant the requested prohibitive injunctive relief. . . .

5.40 Protection of Various Theatrical Media of Expression

The field of entertainment law deals with creative and constantly changing media of expression. Law and business practices must likewise be creative in order to accommodate the constant changes. Hopefully, the law will adjust to the realities of the entertainment world. In the following case, the court itself admits it is dealing with a "novel question"—that of copyright of the choreography in a ballet. The court has the copyright revisions of 1976 to rely on—up to a point. From the facts, though, the court clearly must venture into uncharted waters.

The *Horgan* case concerns a defendant who published a book containing still photographs of a Balanchine ballet. What basic protections exist for a choreographer? And do these extend to still photos of an "action" sequence? Some hint of the court's predisposition can be found in the court's citation of a law review comment that described the plight of Agnes De Mille, choreographer of the musical *Oklahoma!* Noted the comment, and later the court:

> Since copyright protection was not available for her work, she initially received $15,000 but no royalties for her work. Yet in various adaptations and stills using her choreography, *Oklahoma!* is estimated to have earned over $60 million during a period of fifteen years. In contrast to Ms. De Mille's small remuneration, Rodgers and Hammerstein, who collaborated on the musical score, still receive royalties every time a tune from the musical is played on radio, television, or for a live and paying audience. ["Comment, Moving to a New Beat: Copyright Protection for Choreographic Works," 24 *UCLA Law Review* 1287, n. 4 (1977)]

The facts of the *Horgan* case, although resolved in the plaintiff's favor in this instance, point out the many varieties of expression that can utilize basic themes and ideas created by one person and sought to be exploited by others. These problems are repeated in numerous settings in later chapters of this book. The considerations in *Horgan* extend well beyond what is or is not protected under the copyright of a choreographic work.

Horgan v. Macmillan, Inc., 789 F.2d 157 (2d Cir. 1986)

FEINBERG, CHIEF JUDGE

George Balanchine, who died on April 30, 1983, was director, ballet master and chief choreographer of the New York City Ballet, a company he co-founded in 1948 with Lincoln Kirstein, its present Artistic Director. It is undisputed that Balanchine was a recognized master in his field. In 1954, Balanchine choreographed his own version of the ballet *The Nutcracker*, set to music by Tchaikovsky. The ballet is an adaptation of a 19th century folk tale by E.T.A. Hoffman, "The Nut-cracker and the Mouse King," and of a previous choreographic version of that fable by the Russian choreographer Ivanov. The parties disagree on the extent to which the "Balanchine Nutcracker," as it is commonly known, incorporates pre-existing material by Hoffman and Ivanov. The Balanchine *Nutcracker* has been performed by the New York City Ballet Company each Christmas season for the last thirty years and has become a classic. Each year, all seats for all performances are sold out. *The Nutcracker*, we are told, is the nation's most commercially successful ballet. The Company paid Balanchine, and then his estate, a royalty each time *The Nutcracker* or any other Balanchine ballet was performed. Balanchine, and then his estate, also licensed other ballet companies to perform his ballets, and other media to reproduce them, for which he received either royalties or other consideration.

In December 1981, Balanchine registered his claim to copyright in the choreography of *The Nutcracker* with the United States Copyright Office. As part of his claim, he deposited with the Copyright Office a videotape of a New York City Ballet Company dress rehearsal of the ballet. Under Balanchine's will, which is presently in administration, all media, performance and other rights in *The Nutcracker* were left to certain named legatees, including Ms. Horgan, who was his personal assistant at the New York City Ballet for 20 years.

In early April 1985, appellant Horgan learned for the first time that Macmillan was planning to publish, under its Atheneum imprint, a book about the New York City Ballet/Balanchine version of *The Nutcracker*. Atheneum had sent galleys of a text and photocopies of photographs to Lincoln Kirstein, who gave the material to appellant. (Ms. Horgan continues to be employed by the New York City Ballet Company as Director of Special Projects.) According to appellees, the galleys and photocopies forwarded at that time were "virtually identical" to the final version of the book, published some six months later in October 1985.

The book is designed primarily for an audience of young people. The title page displays three black and white photographs of George Balan-

chine directing a rehearsal of the ballet. The book begins with a 15-page text by defendant Switzer regarding the origins of *The Nutcracker* as a story and as a ballet. The remainder of the book is introduced by a second title page, as follows:

THE
BALANCHINE
BALLET
As Performed by the Dancers
of the New York City Ballet Company

The principal section of the book consists of 60 color photographs by Caras and Costas of scenes from the New York City Ballet Company production of *The Nutcracker*, following the sequence of the ballet's story and dances. The photographs are interspersed with Switzer's narration of the story, including those portions not portrayed visually. The final section of the book contains interviews with ten of the dancers, with black and white photographs of them out of costume. Defendants Switzer, Carras and Costas obtained this material through their access to company rehearsals and performances. Switzer is a free lance journalist who was apparently given such access by the press liaison for the Company. Carras and Costas are considered "official photographers" of the New York City Ballet. According to appellant, this means that Balanchine authorized them to take photographs of the Company, some of which might be purchased by the Company for publicity and related purposes.

On the day that Horgan received the galleys, she contacted the attorney for the estate, who immediately wrote to Atheneum. The letter, dated that same date—April 3—questioned Atheneum's right to "create such a derivative work" and suggested that "in light of the Estate's ownership of the work in question," Atheneum suspend any further production expenses until "appropriate licenses" were in place. In a second letter, dated April 15, 1985, the attorney for the estate advised Macmillan's publishing counsel that Horgan was not willing to grant the necessary licenses for the book. After an exchange of correspondence, Macmillan's counsel advised the attorney for the estate, in a letter dated May 10, 1985, that Atheneum intended to proceed without Horgan's authorization. The letter stated that after considerable thought and analysis, we have concluded that it is unnecessary for us to obtain any authorization from the Ballanchine [sic] Estate in connection with our proposed work since, as a legal matter, we are completely satisfied that the work in no way violates or infringes upon any proprietary rights of Mr. Balanchine or his successors-in-interest.

The attorney for the estate responded some three weeks later, warning Macmillan that publication would constitute a "willful violation of the rights of the Estate" and demanding immediate assurance that the book would not be published without the estate's permission. There apparently were no further significant written communications between the parties until October 8, 1985, when lawyers for the estate received from Macmillan a copy of the book in final form.

On October 11, 1985, Horgan brought suit on behalf of the estate, seeking declaratory relief and both a preliminary and permanent injunction against publication of the book. At the same time, Horgan applied for a temporary restraining order. The district court denied the application in a memorandum endorsement dated October 17, 1985. Some five weeks later, after receiving additional papers and hearing argument, the judge denied Horgan's motion for a preliminary injunction. The judge stated, in an opinion and order substantially similar to his earlier memorandum, that the book did not infringe the copyright on Balanchine's choreography because

> choreography has to do with the flow of the steps in a ballet. The still photographs in the Nutcracker book, numerous though they are, catch dancers in various attitudes at specific instants of time; they do not, nor do they intend to, take or use the underlying choreography. The staged performance could not be recreated from them.*

621 F. Supp. at 1170 & n. 1. As a separate ground for denying preliminary injunctive relief, Judge Owen found that on May 10, 1985, Macmillan had "unequivocally notified" Horgan that it was going to proceed with the book despite her objections. Since Horgan took no action until Macmil-

---

*Just as a Beethoven symphony could not be recreated from a document containing only every twenty-fifth chord of the symphony.

lan had already changed its position by printing the book, the scales were tipped in Macmillan's favor. This appeal followed. . . .

The principal question on appeal, whether still photographs of a ballet can infringe the copyright on the choreography for the ballet, is a matter of first impression. Explicit federal copyright protection for choreography is a fairly recent development, and the scope of that protection is an uncharted area of the law. The 1976 Copyright Act (the Act), 17 U.S.C. § 101 et seq., was the first federal copyright statute expressly to include "choreographic works" as a subject of protection. Choreography was not mentioned in the prior law, the 1909 Copyright Act, 61 Stat. 652, and could only be registered, pursuant to regulations issued under that law, as a species of "dramatic composition." Dance was protectible only if it told a story, developed or characterized an emotion, or otherwise conveyed a dramatic concept or idea. . . . The rights of a choreographer in his work were not clearly defined, in part because the means for reducing choreography to tangible form had become readily available only comparatively recently, . . . and in part because of resistance to the acceptance of abstract, non-literary dance as a worthy form of artistic expression. . . .

There were numerous proposals over the years to amend the copyright law to include coverage for abstract choreographic works, but none were successful. . . . In a comprehensive report on revision of the copyright laws, the Copyright Office recommended to Congress in 1961 that the law be amended to insure protection for "abstract" as well as traditional dramatic ballet. Report of the Register of Copyrights, supra at 17. Choreography had long held an important position in the entertainment and artistic worlds, yet the "economic remuneration of choreographers" had not kept pace "with their creative achievements." . . . By including choreographic works as a separate copyrightable form of expression, the 1976 Act broadened the scope of its protection considerably.

The Act does not define choreography, and the legislative reports on the bill indicate only that "social dance steps and simple routines" are not included. See, e.g., H.R. Rep. No. 1476, 94th

Cong., 2d Sess. 53-54, reprinted in 1976 U.S. Code Cong. & Ad. News 5659, 5666-67. The Compendium of Copyright Office Practices, Compendium II (1984), which is issued by that office, defines choreographic works as follows:

> Choreography is the composition and arrangement of dance movements and patterns, and is usually intended to be accompanied by music. Dance is static and kinetic successions of bodily movement in certain rhythmic and spatial relationships. Choreographic works need not tell a story in order to be protected by copyright.

Section 450.01. Under "Characteristics of choreographic works," Compendium II states that "choreography represents a related series of dance movements and patterns organized into a coherent whole." Section 450.03(a). "Choreographic content" is described as follows:

> Social dance steps and simple routines are not copyrightable. . . . Thus, for example, the basic waltz step, the hustle step, and the second position of classical ballet are not copyrightable. However, this is not a restriction against the incorporation of social dance steps and simple routines, as such, in an otherwise registrable choreographic work. Social dance steps, folk dance steps, and individual ballet steps alike may be utilized as the choreographer's basic material in much the same way that words are the writer's basic material.

Section 450.06. The Act grants the owner of a copyrighted original work that is "fixed in any tangible medium of expression," 17 U.S.C. § 102(a), the exclusive right "to reproduce the copyrighted work in copies . . . ," "to prepare derivative works based upon the copyrighted work" and, "in the case of . . . choreographic works, . . . to display the copyrighted work publicly." 17 U.S.C. § 106(1), (2) & (5). Appellant claims that the Switzer book is a "copy" of Balanchine's copyrighted work because it portrays the essence of the Balanchine *Nutcracker*, or, in the alternative, that the book is an infringing "derivative work." The test for infringement, appellant asserts, is not whether the original work may be reproduced from the copy—as the district judge held—but whether the alleged copy is substantially similar to the original. . . .

In response, appellees assert that the photographs in the Switzer book do not capture the flow of movement, which is the essence of dance, and thus cannot possibly be substantially similar to the choreographic component of the production of the ballet. Appellees rely on the various definitions of choreography in Compendium II, quoted above, to support their position that the central characteristic of choreography is "movement." According to appellees, since each photograph in the book captures only a fraction of an instant, even the combined effect of 60 color photographs does not reproduce the choreography itself, nor provide sufficient details of movement to enable a choreographic work to be reproduced from the photographs.

Appellees also argue that little, if anything, of Balanchine's original choreographic contribution to the New York City Ballet production of *The Nutcracker* is shown in the photographs. That production, they contend (and appellant does not disagree entirely here), is based on extensive preexisting material by Hoffman and Ivanov that is in the public domain and not subject to copyright. According to appellees, the Switzer book is composed primarily of a combination of material in the public domain and the special non-choreographic aspects of the New York City Ballet production—the costumes by Karinska and the sets by Rouben Ter-Artunian, both produced under licensing agreements between those artists and the Company. Appellant makes no claim to those components of the production, and appellees assert that the choreography—even if it were conveyed by the photographs—is visually indistinguishable from the integrated whole of the production. Appellees thus argue that the book does not infringe any copyrighted or copyrightable choreographic material. . . .

The question whether the photographs in the Switzer book infringe the copyright on Balanchine's choreography is not a simple one, but we agree with appellant that in resolving that issue the district court applied an incorrect test. The district judge found no infringement because the photographs catch only "dancers in various attitudes at specific instants of time," rather than "the flow of the steps in a ballet," and thus "[t]he staged performance could not be recreated" from the photographs. 621 F. Supp. at 1170. However, the standard for determining copyright infringement is not whether the original could be recreated from the allegedly infringing copy, but whether the latter is "substantially similar" to the former. . . .

When the allegedly infringing material is in a different medium, as it is here, recreation of the original from the infringing material is unlikely if not impossible, but that is not a defense to infringement. See, e.g., *King Features Syndicate v. Fleischer*, 299 F. 533, 535 (2d Cir. 1924) (cartoon character infringed by toy doll); *Filmvideo Releasing Corp. v. Hastings*, 509 F. Supp. 60, 63-65, aff'd in part, rev'd in part, 668 F.2d 91 (2d Cir. 1981) (books infringed by movies). It surely would not be a defense to an infringement claim against the movie version of *Gone with the Wind* that a viewer of the movie could not create the book. Even a small amount of the original, if it is qualitatively significant, may be sufficient to be an infringement, although the full original could not be recreated from the excerpt. . . .

Moreover, the district judge took a far too limited view of the extent to which choreographic material may be conveyed in the medium of still photography. A snapshot of a single moment in a dance sequence may communicate a great deal. It may, for example, capture a gesture, the composition of dancers' bodies or the placement of dancers on the stage. Such freezing of a choreographic moment is shown in a number of the photographs in the Switzer book. . . . A photograph may also convey to the viewer's imagination the moments before and after the split second recorded. On pages 76–77 of the Switzer book, for example, there is a two-page photograph of the "Sugar Canes," one of the troupes that perform in *The Nutcracker*. In this photograph, the Sugar Canes are a foot or more off the ground, holding large hoops above their heads. One member of the ensemble is jumping through a hoop, which is held extended in front of the dancer. The dancer's legs are thrust forward, parallel to the stage and several feet off the ground. The viewer understands instinctively, based simply on the laws of gravity, that the Sugar Canes jumped up from the floor only a moment earlier, and came down shortly after the photographed moment. An ordinary observer, who had only recently seen a performance of *The Nutcracker*, could probably perceive even more from this photograph. The single instant thus communicates far more than a single chord of a Beethoven symphony—the analogy suggested by the district judge.

It may be that all of the photographs mentioned above are of insufficient quantity or sequencing to constitute infringement; it may also be that they do copy but also are protected as fair use. But that is not what the district judge said in denying a preliminary injunction. The judge erroneously held that still photographs cannot infringe choreography. Since the judge applied the wrong test in evaluating appellant's likelihood of success on the preliminary injunction, we believe that a remand is appropriate. But since further proceedings in the district court will be necessary, we strongly suggest that the parties proceed promptly toward a final judgment on the merits upon an adequate record. The validity of Balanchine's copyright, the amount of original Balanchine choreography (rather than Ivanov's) in the New York City Ballet production of *The Nutcracker* and in the photographs, and the degree to which the choreography would be distinguishable in the photographs without the costumes and sets (in which appellant claims no right) are all matters still to be determined, preferably on a fuller record including expert testimony, which we assume would be of considerable assistance. The same is true with respect to appellees' claim that the New York City Ballet Company, as either sole or joint owner with the estate of the choreography, authorized the publication of the Switzer book and the use of the photographs. Appellants respond that Balanchine alone, and now his estate, have the exclusive right to license the use of his works, as evidenced by the royalties paid him by the Company over the years. The district court did not rule on this issue, and, on the record before us, there is considerable confusion about the overlapping proprietary rights of Balanchine's estate, the New York City Ballet Company and the "official photographers," including defendants Caras and Costas.

Finally, appellees contend that appellant's delay in suing should bar injunctive relief, as the district court held. Appellant argues that "[p]arties should not be encouraged to sue before a practical need to do so has been clearly demonstrated," *Playboy Enterprises, Inc. v. Chuckleberry Publishing, Inc.*, 486 F. Supp. 414, 435 (S.D.N.Y. 1980). . . . In response, appellees claim that when a copyright holder has definitive advance knowledge of a planned infringement, yet fails to take legal action, and the defendant changes its position to its detriment, preliminary injunctive relief may be denied. . . . There is a factual dispute here over whether "a practical need" to sue had been *clearly* demonstrated prior to October 1985, and we are not certain whether the district court examined the question closely enough. The judge's opinion states that appellant was aware of Macmillan's "general intentions" as early as April 3, but knowledge of a general nature is not sufficient basis for judicial intervention. Appellees claim that the materials they sent Kirstein at that time were "virtually identical" to the book as published, but appellant asserts she expected the proposed book to be modified in response to her warning. She also indicates that she tried to get an advance copy of the book, but this was "not so easy" to do. In any event, in view of our holding that the district judge applied the wrong standard of law on infringement and our strong view that this case should proceed to a final disposition on the merits rather than to merely a reconsideration of the motion for a preliminary injunction, the issue of plaintiff's allegedly undue delay becomes less significant. As we pointed out in *Citibank,* "a particular period of delay" may be sufficient to justify denial of a preliminary injunction but still "not rise to the level of laches and thereby bar a permanent injunction," Id. at 756 F.2d 276. Accordingly, we do not believe it fruitful to address the issue further at this time.

We reverse and remand for further proceedings consistent with this opinion.

NOTES ───────────────────────

1. The statutory provision relied on by the *Horgan* court is 17 U.S.C. § 102(a)(4):

> (a) Copyright protection subsists, in accordance with this title, in original works of authorship fixed in any tangible medium of expression, now known or later developed, from which they can be perceived, reproduced, or otherwise communicated, either directly or with the aid of a machine or device. Works of authorship include the following categories: . . . (4) pantomimes and choreographic works . . .

2. The *Horgan* court also had to deal with the statutory definition of a derivative work, which is found in 17 U.S.C. § 101 and is defined as a work "based upon one or more preexisting works, such as a translation, musical arrangement, dramatization, fictionalization, motion picture version, sound recording, art reproduction, abridgment, condensation, or any other form in which a work may be recast, transformed, or adapted."

3. Earlier cases not dealing with choreographic works, which tend to support the *Horgan* court's decision, include the following:

(a) *Roy Export Co. Establishment v. Columbia Broadcasting System, Inc.*, 503 F. Supp. 1137 (SDNY 1980), *aff'd*, 672 F.2d 1095 (2d Cir.), *cert. denied*, 459 U.S. 826 (1982). Short film clips used in a memorial to Charlie Chaplin infringed Chaplin's full-length films.

(b) *Elsmere Music, Inc. v. National Broadcasting Co.*, 482 F. Supp. 741 (S.D.N.Y.), *aff'd*, 623 F.2d 252 (2d Cir. 1980). The use of four notes from a musical composition containing one hundred measures could nevertheless be an infringement of the copyrighted original work. (However, the court ultimately ruled the use was a parody and thus constituted a fair use.)

4. In addition to the "Comment . . .", cited in the introduction to this section, see also Mirell, "Legal Protection for Choreography," 27 *NYU Law Review* 792 (1952).

Chapter 6

FILMS

6.00 The Motion Picture Industry

Author John Gregory Dunne once commented that Hollywood motion picture deals are now more interesting than the actual films themselves. The perplexity and variety of legal and business problems confronted in the film industry today are unparalleled. These complexities are partly attributable to the current costs of making motion pictures, with the average cost skyrocketing in recent years to between $10 million and $15 million. The most expensive motion pictures now approach $50 million or more.

These numbers are startling in light of the fact that, in 1985 net profits were generated from major studio pictures on only one or two out of every 20 films produced. The "break-even" point for major motion pictures had traditionally been 2.5 to 3 times the "negative costs"—that is, the cost of production. On low-budget films, the break-even can often times be 6 to 8 times the costs of production, due largely to significant distribution expenses and fees, including advertising and print costs. The business is not for the timid or faint-hearted.

6.01 Background of the Motion Picture Industry

In the United States, the film industry today is dominated by seven major film studios that engage in the financing, production, and distribution of films: Universal Pictures (a division of MCA, Inc.), Paramount Pictures Corporation (owned by Gulf and Western, Inc.), MGM/UA, Twentieth Century-Fox Pictures (a division of Twentieth Century Fox Film Corporation), Columbia (a subsidiary of Coca-Cola), Warner Bros. (a subsidiary of Warner Communications), and Disney. There are also several film companies known as "mini-majors"; these are smaller distributors, such as New World Pictures and the Cannon Group. Generally, majors and mini-majors are distinguished by the fact that majors have real estate and mini-majors do not.

As in the other entertainment industries, the motion picture business has been both a victim and a beneficiary of technology. The enormous growth of cable television and the videocassette market has provided significant new markets and sources of licensing and income for the film studios. On the other hand, the problem of home taping of copyrighted films has been a major concern to the studios and was the principal motivation for the lawsuit in *Universal City Studios v. Sony Corp. of America,* the 1984 decision in which the Supreme Court ruled that home taping was "fair use" under copyright law and not an infringement of copyright. (See Section 8.30.)

Historically, the major studios owned enormous production facilities in the Los Angeles area. Beginning in the 1920s, there developed what was known as the "studio system," in which the studio employed and housed all the required talent, actors and actresses, directors, writers, and other artists under long-term exclusive personal service agreements. (Several such contracts are discussed in Chapter 1.)

After World War II, motion picture attendance began to decline. The growth of television was one cause. There were also legal complications, such as antitrust litigation, that forced the major studios to sell their theatres. (See Section 6.10.) The result was that motion picture studios began to hire talent on a film-by-film basis rather than on an exclusive employment arrangement. This has been the pattern since then, although in the 1980s, the studios did begin to enter into exclusive long-term contracts with "superstar" talent such as Richard Pryor (Columbia), Eddie Murphy (Paramount), and Michael Keaton (Twentieth Century-Fox).

6.02   Financing Motion Pictures

In recent years, one of the most complex aspects of the motion picture business has been finance, raising the millions of dollars necessary to make and distribute a major motion picture. In a speech in 1986 before an association of film exhibitors, Jack Valenti, president of the Motion Picture Association of America, noted some startling statistics regarding the motion picture industry. While the costs of filmmaking have increased, the revenues have been declining. Of 150 major pictures released in 1985, only 12 yielded income from rentals of $20 million or more. In 1984, the number of films that yielded more than $20 million was 14; in 1983 that figure was 18.

Compounding these numbers are Valenti's assertions that the average "negative" cost of a feature made by a major studio, including acquisitions from third parties, was $16 million in 1985. Adding the costs of printing and advertising, Valenti computed that the average film has to gross $24 million before a studio will recoup its investment. Valenti also discussed the explosion of VCR purchases. By the end of this decade, Valenti estimated 24 million homes will have VCRs, a 1,000 percent increase over the VCR market in 1980.

Traditionally, motion pictures were financed by a major studio, which paid for the development, production, and ultimate distribution of its films. The studio generally hired a producer who received a fee, plus a percentage of the profits. The studio was entitled to recoup all its costs in both the production and distribution of the film, plus interest and overhead, prior to disbursement of profits to the producer and other participants.

Both major and mini-major studios are still involved in some of the financing of motion pictures which they ultimately distribute. However, the number of films financed by studios has decreased over the years, as the costs of making a movie have skyrocketed. In the 1980s, Wall Street financing of motion pictures through public or private offerings or partnerships has grown. The prototype of this type of financing has been Silver Screen Partners, which funded a series of films through a single offering.

The financing of motion pictures through limited partnerships may become more difficult with the tax reform bill of 1986, which will eliminate the investment tax credit traditionally available for films. Many of the prior tax shelters and advantages that had been available to the film industry were already eliminated by the Tax Reform Act of 1976.

NOTE _____

1. For a more detailed analysis of the financing of films, see Sobel, "Financing the Production of Theatrical Motion Pictures," *Entertainment Law Reporter*, vol. 5, no. 12 (May 1984).

6.03 Producing the Film: The Agreements

6.03–1 Acquisition of Underlying Rights

Once the financing of a film has been secured, either through traditional studio financing, public offerings, or presales of rights to selected markets (video, network television, pay TV, or foreign markets), the next step is the acquisition of the underlying rights to either a screenplay or finished work, be it a novel, theatrical play, film treatment, or nonfictional story or book. In many instances, when financing has not been guaranteed, the producer of a proposed film project may "option" the rights to the underlying work for a fee, giving the producer a certain period of time in which to raise the capital to pay the sales price for the rights. Agreements for acquisition of underlying rights and screenplays generally provide for a grant of rights in the material to the studio upon cash payment, followed by a percentage of net profits derived from the film. Essential terms that must be negotiated include subsidiary rights, remake and sequel rights, television rights, merchandising rights, screen credit, and warranties.

The sales price for motion picture rights to existing works may be as low as $50,000 and as high as $10 million, depending on the marketing leverage of the parties. Motion picture rights for *All The President's Men* sold for $450,000; for *The Sound of Music*, it was $1.25 million against 10 percent of the gross profit; and for the play *Annie*, it was $9.5 million. (Copies of the underlying property agreement acquiring rights to the original magazine article entitled "Tribal Rites of the New Saturday Night," which became the basis for the movie *Saturday Night Fever*, are contained in *Counselling Clients in the Entertainment Industry 1986*, pp. 455–524, Martin E. Silfen, Chairman, Practising Law Institute, New York. The underlying screenplay agreement for that film is also set forth.)

6.03–2 Producer-Actor Agreements

As previously discussed, agreements for talent are usually on a film-by-film basis as opposed to an exclusive employment agreement with a particular studio. On a one-film agreement, an actor or actress may be paid a flat fee in accordance with guidelines of the Screen Actors Guild or, in the case of major talent, there may be a fee (potentially millions of dollars for a Sylvester Stallone) against a percentage of the net or gross profits from the film. In some cases, the producer or studio will attempt to secure an option for the actor or actress to perform in a sequel to the original motion picture.

6.03–3 Other Agreements

An additional agreement that needs to be negotiated is between the studio/producer and the director, generally on a one-film basis (with a possible option exercise by the studio/producer). Primary concerns in the director's agreement include artistic control (who has rights to the "final cut"), credits, compensation, and contingent compensation. Minimum contracts and disputes between the director and the studio are generally controlled by the Directors' Guild of America, its collective bargaining agreements and arbitration tribunal.

Producer agreements are negotiated between the producer of the film, who oversees the entire production of the picture, and the company owning the film. The producer is charged with seeing that the film is completed and delivered to the studio. These agreements contain provisions setting forth the producer's compensation, both up-front fees and the producer's profits in the film, provisions for over-budget expenditures, and provisions for credit.

On completion of a motion picture, the major agreement that has been or will be negotiated is the film distribution agreement. This agreement is among the most complex of all entertainment industry agreements. While there is no typical or standard distribution agreement, a distribution agreement between an independent film producer and a major studio may include the following, with the percentages generally being taken from the gross profits from the film from all sources, including theatrical release, video licensing, television sales, and merchandising·

- A distribution fee for a domestic, theatrical, and nontheatrical exploitation of 30 to 35 percent.
- Home video distribution fee: 30 percent.
- Television syndication fee: 35 percent.
- Merchandising distribution fee: 40 to 60 percent.
- Recoupment of release costs, which include laboratory costs and prints and advertising materials, usually totaling several million dollars, at a minimum, for a major release.
- Deductions for gross profit participants in the film.

In most cases, interest of 125 percent of prime is paid back to the studio for its costs in producing the film, which includes such expenses as the "negative costs," studio overhead, facility, and equipment rental.

The remaining monies constitute 100 percent of the net profits, which are then distributed among the producer, writer, director, actors/actresses, and investors according to their contractual arrangements.

NOTE _____

1. Additional readings and resources on motion pictures include the following:

(a) S. Berkowitz and D. Lees, *The Movie Business: A Primer* (New York: Vintage Books [Random House], 1981). Another viewpoint on the filmmaking process, less technical and more anecdotal than Squire, *The Movie Business Book*.

(b) J. Dunne, *The Studio* (New York: Touchstone Books [Simon & Schuster], 1969). A memoir of the author's year at Twentieth Century-Fox in the late 1960s.

(c) J. Squire, ed., *The Movie Business Book* (Englewood Cliffs, N.J.: Prentice-Hall, Inc., 1983). A collection of articles by industry professionals detailing the filmmaking process from the beginning of the creative process through theatrical distribution and beyond.

(d) S. Van Petten, ed., *Producing for Motion Pictures and Television: A Practical Guide to Legal Issues* (Los Angeles: Los Angeles County Bar Association, 1983). Articles on rights clearance, use of foreign talent, labor matters, production insurance and completion guarantees, production accounting, and other matters.

(e) E. Yeldell, *The Motion Picture and Television Business: Contracts and Practices* (Beverly Hills, Calif.: Entertainment Business Publications Co., 1985). The best reference and resource book regarding contracts and practices in the motion picture industry today.

(f) J. Fell, *A History of Films* (New York: Holt, Rinehart & Winston, 1979). Fell describes many important developments in the motion picture industry that involve both business and legal considerations. His accounts of the 1910s and 1920s are particularly interesting.

(g) D. Cook, *A History of Narrative Film* (New York: W. W. Norton & Co., 1981).

6.10 Motion Pictures and Antitrust

The history of the motion picture industry can almost be chronicled through the host of antitrust litigation that has surrounded the industry's progress. In a sense, the Sherman and Clayton Antitrust Acts and the motion picture industry grew up together. At a time when the antitrust statutes were being thoroughly tested and concepts accordingly expanded, the motion picture business entered its boom period. Antitrust and motion pictures collided at an early date, with film industry practices challenged in a case going all the way to the U.S. Supreme Court in 1923 (see *Binderup v. Pathe Exchange*, 263 U.S. 291 [1923]). Although the Supreme Court had held a year earlier that baseball was neither interstate in nature nor commerce in the constitutional sense (see *Federal Baseball Club of Baltimore, Inc. v. National League of Professional Baseball Clubs*, 259 U.S. 200 [1922]), the motion picture studios, distributors, and exhibitors were not so fortunate. Federal antitrust laws were held to be fully applicable to the industry. The *Binderup* case was only the first of a long series of movie cases through the 1920s, '30s, and into the '40s, culminating in the famous *U.S. v. Paramount* which follows.

To read the movie antitrust decisions is to delve into the development of business practices in the industry. Two cases (*Paramount* and *Loews*) are particularly instructive, both for historical purposes and for insights into more current practices. For that reason, these are set forth in detail. The antitrust applications are instructive, but equally important are the discussions of business practices, some of which were curtailed by the two decisions but not totally abandoned. Since they vitally affect business in motion pictures, such practices as clearances and runs, blind-bidding, block-booking, franchising, and other methods must be understood

for later considerations in this chapter to make sense.

In recent years, antitrust litigation involving motion pictures has continued unabated, but with a significant shift. The early cases all were initiated by the U.S. government against various parts of the industry. Today, one segment of the industry suing another constitutes the focus of action. The government rarely gets involved, especially in the last few years under the Reagan administration. Even so, the private parties are just as intense in fighting the antitrust wars as the government ever was. Distributors rail against exhibitors and their "split arrangements," when the available product is split among the exhibitors by prior agreement to avoid costly and destructive competitive bidding. Small exhibitors feel frozen out of the most timely and highest quality films and allege a conspiracy between more powerful exhibitors and certain distributors to give preference to the better-financed and more influential exhibitors. Exhibitors seek legal redress against booking without having a chance to view a film first. To understand how these practices came to be, it is necessary to go back to *Paramount* and *Loews* for introductions to the industry.

United States v. Paramount Pictures, Inc., 334 U.S. 131 (1948)

MR. JUSTICE DOUGLAS DELIVERED THE OPINION OF THE COURT

. . . The suit was instituted by the United States under § 4 of the Sherman Act to prevent and restrain violations of it. The defendants fall into three groups: (1) Paramount Pictures, Inc., Loew's, Incorporated, Radio-Keith-Orpheum Corporation, Warner Bros. Pictures, Inc., Twentieth Century-Fox Film Corporation, which produce motion pictures, and their respective subsidiaries or affiliates which distribute and exhibit films. These are known as the five major defendants or exhibitor-defendants. (2) Columbia Pictures Corporation and Universal Corporation, which produce motion pictures, and their subsidiaries which distribute films. (3) United Artists Corporation, which is engaged only in the distribution of motion pictures. The five majors, through their subsidiaries or affiliates, own or control theatres; the other defendants do not.

The complaint charged that the producer defendants had attempted to monopolize and had monopolized the production of motion pictures. The District Court found to the contrary and that finding is not challenged here. The complaint charged that all the defendants, as distributors, had conspired to restrain and monopolize and had restrained and monopolized interstate trade in the distribution and exhibition of films by specific practices which we will shortly relate. It also charged that the five major defendants had engaged in a conspiracy to restrain and monopolize, and had restrained and monopolized, interstate trade in the exhibition of motion pictures in most of the larger cities of the country. It charged that the vertical combination of producing, distributing, and exhibiting motion pictures by each of the five major defendants violated § 1 and § 2 of the Act. It charged that each distributor-defendant had entered into various contracts with exhibitors which unreasonably restrained trade. Issue was joined; and a trial was had.

First—Restraint of Trade—(1) Price Fixing

No film is sold to an exhibitor in the distribution of motion pictures. The right to exhibit under copyright is licensed. The District Court found that the defendants in the licenses they issued fixed minimum admission prices which the exhibitors agreed to charge, whether the rental of the film was a flat amount or a percentage of the receipts. It found that substantially uniform minimum prices had been established in the licenses of all defendants. Minimum prices were established in master agreements or franchises which were made between various defendants as distributors and various defendants as exhibitors and in joint operating agreements made by the five majors with each other and with independent theatre owners covering the operation of certain theatres. By these later contracts minimum ad-

mission prices were often fixed for dozens of theatres owned by a particular defendant in a given area of the United States. Minimum prices were fixed in licenses of each of the five major defendants. The other three defendants made the same requirement in licenses granted to the exhibitor-defendants. . . .

The District Court found that two price-fixing conspiracies existed—a horizontal one between all the defendants; a vertical one between each distributor-defendant and its licensees. The latter was based on express agreements and was plainly established. The former was inferred from the pattern of price-fixing disclosed in the record. We think there was adequate foundation for it too. It is not necessary to find an express agreement in order to find a conspiracy. It is enough that a concert of action is contemplated and that the defendants conformed to the arrangement. . . .

On this phase of the case the main attack is on the decree which enjoins the defendants and their affiliates from granting any license, except to their own theatres, in which minimum prices for admission to a theatre are fixed in any manner or by any means. The argument runs as follows: *United States v. General Electric Co.*, 272 U.S. 476, held that an owner of a patent could, without violating the Sherman Act, grant a license to manufacture and vend, and could fix the price at which the licensee could sell the patented article. It is pointed out that defendants do not sell the films to exhibitors, but only license them and that the Copyright Act (35 Stat. 1075, 1088, 17 U.S.C. § 1), like the patent statutes, grants the owner exclusive rights. And it is argued that if the patentee can fix the price at which his licensee may sell the patented article, the owner of the copyright should be allowed the same privilege. It is maintained that such a privilege is essential to protect the value of the copyrighted films.

We start, of course, from the premise that so far as the Sherman Act is concerned, a price-fixing combination is illegal *per se*. . . . We recently held in *United States v. Gypsum Co.*, 333 U.S. 364, 400, that even patentees could not regiment an entire industry by licenses containing price-fixing agreements. What was said there is adequate to bar defendants, through their horizontal conspiracy, from fixing prices for the exhibition of films in the movie industry. Certainly the rights of the copyright owner are no greater than those of the patentee.

Nor can the result be different when we come to the vertical conspiracy between each distributor-defendant and his licensees. The District Court stated in its findings:

> In agreeing to maintain a stipulated minimum admission price, each exhibitor thereby consents to the minimum price level at which it will compete against other licensees of the same distributor whether they exhibit on the same run or not. The total effect is that through the separate contracts between the distributor and its licensees a price structure is erected which regulates the licensees' ability to compete against one another in admission prices.

That consequence seems to us to be incontestable. We stated in *United States v. Gypsum Co.*, . . . that "The rewards which flow to the patentee and his licensees from the suppression of competition through the regulation of an industry are not reasonably and normally adapted to secure pecuniary reward for the patentee's monopoly." The same is true of the rewards of the copyright owners and their licensees in the present case. For here too the licenses are but a part of the general plan to suppress competition. . . .

(2) Clearances and Runs

Clearances are designed to protect a particular run of a film against a subsequent run. The District Court found that all of the distributor-defendants used clearance provisions and that they were stated in several different ways or in combinations: in terms of a given period between designated runs; in terms of admission prices charged by competing theatres; in terms of a given period of clearance over specifically named theatres; in terms of so many days' clearance over specified areas or towns; or in terms of clearances as fixed by other distributors.

The Department of Justice maintained below that clearances are unlawful *per se* under the Sherman Act. But that is a question we need not consider, for the District Court ruled otherwise and that conclusion is not challenged here. In its view their justification was found in the assurance they give the exhibitor that the distributor will not license a competitor to show the film either at the same time or so soon thereafter that the exhibitor's expected income from the run will be greatly diminished. A clearance when used to protect that interest of the exhibitor was reasonable, in the view of the court, when not unduly extended as to area or duration. Thus the court concluded that although clearances might indirectly affect admission prices, they do not fix them and that they may be reasonable restraints of trade under the Sherman Act.

The District Court held that in determining whether a clearance is unreasonable, the following factors are relevant:

(1) The admission prices of the theatres involved, as set by the exhibitors;

(2) The character and location of the theatres involved, including size, type of entertainment, appointments, transit facilities, etc.;

(3) The policy of operation of the theatres involved, such as the showing of double features, gift nights, give-aways, premiums, cut-rate tickets, lotteries, etc.;

(4) The rental terms and license fees paid by the theatres involved and the revenues derived by the distributor-defendant from such theatres;

(5) The extent to which the theatres involved compete with each other for patronage;

(6) The fact that a theatre involved is affiliated with a defendant-distributor or with an independent circuit of theatres should be disregarded; and

(7) There should be no clearance between theatres not in substantial competition.

It reviewed the evidence in light of these standards and concluded that many of the clearances granted by the defendants were unreasonable. We do not stop to retrace those steps. The evidence is ample to show, as the District Court plainly demonstrated, see 66 F. Supp. pp. 343–346, that many clearances had no relation to the competitive factors which alone could justify them. The clearances which were in vogue had, indeed, acquired a fixed and uniform character and were made applicable to situations without regard to the special circumstances which are necessary to sustain them as reasonable restraints of trade. The evidence is ample to support the finding of the District Court that the defendants either participated in evolving this uniform system of clearances or acquiesced in it and so furthered its existence. That evidence, like the evidence on the price-fixing phase of the case, is therefore adequate to support the finding of a conspiracy to restrain trade by imposing unreasonable clearances.

The District Court enjoined defendants and their affiliates from agreeing with each other or with any exhibitors or distributors to maintain a system of clearances, or from granting any clearance between theatres not in substantial competition, or from granting or enforcing any clearance against theatres in substantial competition with the theatre receiving the license for exhibition in excess of what is reasonably necessary to protect the licensee in the run granted. In view of the findings this relief was plainly warranted.

Some of the defendants ask that this provision be construed (or, if necessary, modified) to allow licensors in granting clearances to take into consideration what is reasonably necessary for a fair return to the licensor. We reject that suggestion. If that were allowed, then the exhibitor-defendants would have an easy method of keeping alive at least some of the consequences of the effective conspiracy which they launched. For they could then justify clearances granted by other distributors in favor of their theatres in terms of the competitive requirements of those theatres, and at the same time justify the restrictions they impose upon independents in terms of the necessity of protecting their film rental as licensor. That is too potent a weapon to leave in the hands of those whose proclivity to unlawful conduct has been so marked. It plainly should not be allowed so long as the exhibitor-defendants own theatres. . . .

Objection is made to a further provision of this part of the decree stating that "Whenever any clearance provision is attacked as not legal under the provisions of this decree, the burden shall be upon the distributor to sustain the legality thereof." We think that provision was justified. Clearances have been used along with price fixing to suppress competition with the theatres of the exhibitor-defendants and with other favored exhibitors. The District Court could therefore have eliminated clearances completely for a substantial period of time, even though, as it thought, they were not illegal *per se.* . . . The court certainly then could take the lesser step of making them *prima facie* invalid. But we do not rest on that alone. As we have said, the only justification for clearances in the setting of this case is in terms of the special needs of the licensee for the competitive advantages they afford. To place on the distributor the burden of showing their reasonableness is to place it on the one party in the best position to evaluate their competitive effects. . . .

(3) *Pooling Agreements; Joint Ownership*

The District Court found the exhibitor-defendants had agreements with each other and their affiliates by which theatres of two or more of them, normally competitive, were operated as a unit, or managed by a joint committee or by one of the exhibitors, the profits being shared according to prearranged percentages. Some of these agreements provided that the parties might not acquire other competitive theatres without first offering them for inclusion in the pool. The court concluded that the result of these agreements was to eliminate competition *pro tanto* both in exhibition and in distribution of features, since the parties would naturally direct the films to the theatres in whose earnings they were interested.

The District Court also found that the exhibitor-defendants had like agreements with certain independent exhibitors. Those alliances had, in its view, the effect of nullifying competition between the allied theatres and of making more effective the competition of the group against theatres not members of the pool. The court found that in some cases the operating agreements were achieved through leases of theatres, the rentals being measured by a percentage of profits earned by the theatres in the pool. The District Court required the dissolution of existing pooling agreements and enjoined any future arrangement of that character.

These provisions of the decree will stand. The practices were bald efforts to substitute monopoly for competition and to strengthen the hold of the exhibitor-defendants on the industry by alignment of competitors on their side. Clearer restraints of trade are difficult to imagine.

There was another type of business arrangement that the District Court found to have the same effect as the pooling agreements just mentioned. Many theatres are owned jointly by two or more exhibitor-defendants or by an exhibitor-defendant and an independent.* The result is, according to the District Court, that the theatres are operated "collectively, rather than competitively." And where the joint owners are an exhibitor-defendant and an independent the effect is, according to the District Court, the elimination by the exhibitor-defendant of "putative competition between itself and the other joint owner, who otherwise would be in a position to operate theatres independently." The District Court found these joint ownerships of theatres to be unreasonable restraints of trade within the meaning of the Sherman Act.

The District Court ordered the exhibitor-defendants to disaffiliate by terminating their joint ownership of theatres; and it enjoined future acquisitions of such interests. One is authorized to buy out the other if it shows to the satisfaction

---

Theatres jointly owned with independents:

Paramount	993
Warner	20
Fox	66
RKO	187
Loew's	21
Total	1287

Theatres jointly owned by two defendants:

Paramount-Fox	6
Paramount-Loew's	14
Paramount-Warner	25
Paramount-RKO	150
Loew's-RKO	3
Loew's-Warner	5
Fox-RKO	1
Warner-RKO	10
Total	214

Of the 1287 jointly owned with independents, 209 would not be affected by the decree since one of the ownership interests is less than 5 percent, an amount which the District Court treated as *de minimis*.

of the District Court and that court first finds that such acquisition "will not unduly restrain competition in the exhibition of feature motion pictures." This dissolution and prohibition of joint ownership as between exhibitor-defendants was plainly warranted. To the extent that they have joint interests in the outlets for their films each in practical effect grants the other a priority for the exhibition of its films. For in this situation, as in the case where theatres are jointly managed, the natural gravitation of films is to the theatres in whose earnings the distributors have an interest. Joint ownership between exhibitor-defendants then becomes a device for strengthening their competitive position as exhibitors by forming an alliance as distributors. An express agreement to grant each other the preference would be a most effective weapon to stifle competition. A working arrangement or business device that has that necessary consequence gathers no immunity because of its subtlety. Each is a restraint of trade condemned by the Sherman Act.

The District Court also ordered disaffiliation in those instances where theatres were jointly owned by an exhibitor-defendant and an independent, and where the interest of the exhibitor-defendant was "greater then 5 percent unless such interest shall be 95 percent or more," an independent being defined for this part of the decree as "any former, present or putative motion picture theatre operator which is not owned or controlled by the defendant holding the interest in question." The exhibitor-defendants are authorized to acquire existing interests of the independents in these theatres if they establish, and if the District Court first finds, that the acquisition "will not unduly restrain competition in the exhibition of feature motion pictures." All other acquisitions of such joint interests were enjoined.

This phase of the decree is strenuously attacked. We are asked to eliminate it for lack of findings to support it. The argument is that the findings show no more than the existence of joint ownership of theatres by exhibitor-defendants and independents. The statement by the District Court that the joint ownership eliminates "putative competition" is said to be a mere conclusion without evidentiary support. For it is said that the facts of the record show that many of the instances of joint ownership with an independent interest are cases wholly devoid of any history of or relationship to restraints of trade or monopolistic practices. Some are said to be rather fortuitous results of bankruptcies; others are said to be the results of investments by outside interests who have no desire or capacity to operate theatres, and so on.

It is conceded that the District Court made no inquiry into the circumstances under which a particular interest had been acquired. It treated all relationships alike, insofar as the disaffiliation provision of the decree is concerned. In this we think it erred.

We have gone into the record far enough to be confident that at least some of these acquisitions by the exhibitor-defendants were the products of the unlawful practices which the defendants have inflicted on the industry. To the extent that these acquisitions were the fruits of monopolistic practices or restraints of trade, they should be divested. And no permission to buy out the other owner should be given a defendant. . . . Moreover, even if lawfully acquired, they may have been utilized as part of the conspiracy to eliminate or suppress competition in furtherance of the ends of the conspiracy. In that event divestiture would likewise be justified. . . . In that situation permission to acquire the interest of the independent would have the unlawful effect of permitting the defendants to complete their plan to eliminate him.

Furthermore, if the joint ownership is an alliance with one who is or would be an operator but for the joint ownership, divorce should be decreed even though the affiliation was innocently acquired. For that joint ownership would afford opportunity to perpetuate the effects of the restraints of trade which the exhibitor-defendants have inflicted on the industry.

It seems, however, that some of the cases of joint ownership do not fall into any of the categories we have listed. Some apparently involve no more than innocent investments by those who are not actual or potential operators. If in such cases the acquisition was not improperly used in furtherance of the conspiracy, its retention by defendants would be justified absent a finding that no monopoly resulted. . . .

(4) Formula Deals, Master Agreements, and Franchises

A formula deal is a licensing agreement with a circuit of theatres in which the license fee of a given feature is measured, for the theatres covered by the agreement, by a specified percentage of the feature's national gross. The District Court found that Paramount and RKO had made formula deals with independent and affiliated circuits. The circuit was allowed to allocate playing time and film rentals among the various theatres as it saw fit. The inclusion of theatres of a circuit into a single agreement gives no opportunity for other theatre owners to bid for the feature in their respective areas and, in the view of the District Court, is therefore an unreasonable restraint of trade. The District Court found some master agreements open to the same objection. Those are the master agreements that cover exhibition in two or more theatres in a particular circuit and allow the exhibitor to allocate the film rental paid among the theatres as it sees fit and to exhibit the features upon such playing time as it deems best, and leaves other terms to the discretion of the circuit. The District Court enjoined the making or further performance of any formula deal of the type described above. It also enjoined the making or further performance of any master agreement covering the exhibition of features in a number of theatres.

The findings of the District Court in these respects are supported by facts, its conclusion that the formula deals and master agreements constitute restraint of trade is valid, and the relief is proper. The formula deals and master agreements are unlawful restraints of trade in two respects. In the first place, they eliminate the possibility of bidding for films theatre by theatre. In that way they eliminate the opportunity for the small competitor to obtain the choice first runs, and put a premium on the size of the circuit. They are, therefore, devices for stifling competition and diverting the cream of the business to the large operators. In the second place, the pooling of the purchasing power of an entire circuit in bidding for films is a misuse of monopoly power insofar as it combines the theatres in closed towns with competitive situations. . . .

The District Court also enjoined the making or further performance of any franchise. A franchise is a contract with an exhibitor which extends over a period of more than a motion picture season and covers the exhibition of features released by the distributor during the period of the agreement. The District Court held that a franchise constituted a restraint of trade because a period of more than one season was too long and the inclusion of all features was disadvantageous to competitors. At least that is the way we read its findings.

Universal and United Artists object to the outlawry of franchise agreements. Universal points out that the charge of illegality of franchises in these cases was restricted to franchises with theatres owned by the major defendants and to franchises with circuits or theatres in a circuit, a circuit being defined in the complaint as a group of more than five theatres controlled by the same person or a group of more than five theatres which combine through a common agent in licensing films. It seems, therefore, that the legality of franchises to other exhibitors (except as to block-booking, a practice to which we will later advert) was not in issue in the litigation. . . .

We can see how if franchises were allowed to be used between the exhibitor-defendants each might be able to strengthen its strategic position in the exhibition field and continue the ill effects of the conspiracy which the decree is designed to dissipate. Franchise agreements may have been employed as devices to discriminate against some independents in favor of others. We know from the record that franchise agreements often contained discriminatory clauses operating in favor not only of theatres owned by the defendants but also of the large circuits. But we cannot say on this record that franchises are illegal *per se* when extended to any theatre or circuit no matter how small. . . .

We do not take that course in the case of formula deals and master agreements, for the findings in these instances seem to stand on their own bottom. . . .

(5) *Block-Booking*

Block-booking is the practice of licensing, or offering for license, one feature or group of features on condition that the exhibitor will also license another feature or group of features released by the distributors during a given period. The films are licensed in blocks before they are actually produced. All the defendants, except United Artists, have engaged in the practice. Block-booking prevents competitors from bidding for single features on their individual merits. The District Court held it illegal for that reason and for the reason that it "adds to the monopoly of a single copyrighted picture that of another copyrighted picture which must be taken and exhibited in order to secure the first." . . . The court enjoined defendants from performing or entering into any license in which the right to exhibit one feature is conditioned upon the licensee's taking one or more other features.

We approve that restriction. The copyright law, like the patent statutes, makes reward to the owner a secondary consideration. . . . It is said that reward to the author or artist serves to induce release to the public of the products of his creative genius. But the reward does not serve its public purpose if it is not related to the quality of the copyright. Where a high quality film greatly desired is licensed only if an inferior one is taken, the latter borrows quality from the former and strengthens its monopoly by drawing on the other. The practice tends to equalize rather than differentiate the reward for the individual copyrights. Even where all the films included in the package are of equal quality, the requirement that all be taken if one is desired increases the market for some. Each stands not on its own footing but in whole or in part on the appeal which another film may have. As the District Court said, the result is to add to the monopoly of the copyright in violation of the principle of the patent cases involving tying clauses.

Columbia Pictures makes an earnest argument that enforcement of the restriction as to block-booking will be very disadvantageous to it and will greatly impair its ability to operate profitably. But the policy of the anti-trust laws is not qualified or conditioned by the convenience of those whose conduct is regulated. Nor can a vested interest in a practice which contravenes the policy of the anti-trust laws receive judicial sanction.

We do not suggest that films may not be sold in blocks or groups, when there is no requirement, express or implied, for the purchase of more than one film. All we hold to be illegal is a refusal to license one or more copyrights unless another copyright is accepted.

(6) Discrimination

The District Court found that defendants had discriminated against small independent exhibitors and in favor of large affiliated and unaffiliated circuits through various kinds of contract provisions. These included suspension of the terms of a contract if a circuit theatre remained closed for more than eight weeks with reinstatement without liability on reopening; allowing large privileges in the selection and elimination of films; allowing deductions in film rentals if double bills are played; granting moveovers and extended runs; granting road show privileges; allowing overage and underage; granting unlimited playing time; excluding foreign pictures and those of independent producers; and granting rights to question the classification of features for rental purposes. The District Court found that the competitive advantages of these provisions were so great that their inclusion in contracts with the larger circuits and their exclusion from contracts with the small independents constituted an unreasonable discrimination against the latter. Each discriminatory contract constituted a conspiracy between licensor and licensee. Hence the District Court deemed it unnecessary to decide whether the defendants had conspired among themselves to make these discriminations. No provision of the decree specifically enjoins these discriminatory practices because they were thought to be impossible under the system of competitive bidding adopted by the District Court. These findings are amply supported by the evidence. We concur in the conclusion that these discriminatory practices are included among the restraints of trade which the Sherman Act condemns. . . .

There is some suggestion on this as well as on other phases of the cases that large exhibitors with whom defendants dealt fathered the illegal practices and forced them onto the defendants. But as the District Court observed, that circumstance if true does not help the defendants. For acquiescence in an illegal scheme is as much a violation of the Sherman Act as the creation and promotion of one.

Second—Competitive Bidding

The District Court concluded that the only way competition could be introduced into the existing system of fixed prices, clearances and runs was to require that films be licensed on a competitive bidding basis. Films are to be offered to all exhibitors in each competitive area. The license for the desired run is to be granted to the highest responsible bidder, unless the distributor rejects all offers. The licenses are to be offered and taken theatre by theatre and picture by picture. Licenses to show films in theatres in which the licensor owns directly or indirectly an interest of ninety-five percent or more are excluded from the requirement for competitive bidding. . . .

At first blush there is much to commend the system of competitive bidding. The trade victims of this conspiracy have in large measure been the small independent operators. They are the ones that have felt most keenly the discriminatory practices and predatory activities in which defendants have freely indulged. They have been the victims of the massed purchasing power of the larger units in the industry. It is largely out of the ruins of the small operators that the large empires of exhibitors have been built. Thus it would appear to be a great boon to them to substitute open bidding for the private deals and favors on which the large operators have thrived. But after reflection we have concluded that competitive bidding involves the judiciary so deeply in the daily operation of this nation-wide business and promises such dubious benefits that it should not be undertaken.

Each film is to be licensed on a particular run to "the highest responsible bidder, having a theatre of a size, location and equipment adequate to yield a reasonable return to the licensor." The bid "shall state what run such exhibitor desires and what he is willing to pay for such feature, which statement may specify a flat rental, or a percentage of gross receipts, or both, or any other form of rental, and shall also specify what clearance such exhibitor is willing to accept, the time and days when such exhibitor desires to exhibit it, and any other offers which such exhibitor may care to make." We do not doubt that if a competitive bidding system is adopted all these provisions are necessary. For the licensing of films at auction is quite obviously a more complicated matter than the like sales for cash of tobacco, wheat, or other produce. Columbia puts these pertinent queries: "No two exhibitors are likely to make the same bid as to dates, clearance, method of fixing rental, etc. May bids containing such diverse factors be readily compared? May a flat rental bid be compared with a percentage bid? May the value of any percentage bid be determined unless the admission price is fixed by the license?"

The question as to who is the highest bidder involves the use of standards incapable of precise definition because the bids being compared contain different ingredients. Determining who is the most responsible bidder likewise cannot be reduced to a formula. The distributor's judgment of the character and integrity of a particular exhibitor might result in acceptance of a lower bid than others offered. Yet to prove that favoritism was shown would be well-nigh impossible, unless perhaps all the exhibitors in the country were given classifications of responsibility. If, indeed, the choice between bidders is not to be entrusted to the uncontrolled discretion of the distributors, some effort to standardize the factors involved in determining "a reasonable return to the licensor" would seem necessary.

We mention these matters merely to indicate the character of the job of supervising such a competitive bidding system. It would involve the judiciary in the administration of intricate and detailed rules governing priority, period of clearance, length of run, competitive areas, reasonable return, and the like. . . . The judiciary is unsuited to affairs of business management; and control through the power of contempt is crude and clumsy and lacking in the flexibility necessary to make continuous and detailed supervision

effective. Yet delegation of the management of the system to the discretion of those who had the genius to conceive the present conspiracy and to execute it with the subtlety which this record reveals, could be done only with the greatest reluctance. At least such choices should not be faced unless the need for the system is great and its benefits plain.

The system uproots business arrangements and established relationships with no apparent overall benefit to the small independent exhibitor. If each feature must go to the highest responsible bidder, those with the greatest purchasing power would seem to be in a favored position. Those with the longest purse—the exhibitor-defendants and the large circuits—would seem to stand in a preferred position. If in fact they were enabled through the competitive bidding system to take the cream of the business, eliminate the smaller independents, and thus increase their own strategic hold on the industry, they would have the cloak of the court's decree around them for protection. Hence the natural advantage which the larger and financially stronger exhibitors would seem to have in the bidding gives us pause. . . .

Our doubts concerning the competitive bidding system are increased by the fact that defendants who own theatres are allowed to pre-empt their own features. They thus start with an inventory which all other exhibitors lack. The latter have no prospect of assured runs except what they get by competitive bidding. The proposed system does not offset in any way the advantages which the exhibitor-defendants have by way of theatre ownership. It would seem in fact to increase them. For the independents are deprived of the stability which flows from established business relationships. Under the proposed system they can get features only if they are the highest responsible bidders. They can no longer depend on their private sources of supply which their ingenuity has created. Those sources, built perhaps on private relationships and representing important items of good will, are banned, even though they are free of any taint of illegality.

The system was designed, as some of the defendants put it, to remedy the difficulty of any theatre to break into or change the existing system of runs and clearances. But we do not see how, in practical operation, the proposed system of competitive bidding is likely to open up to competition the markets which defendants' unlawful restraints have dominated. Rather real danger seems to us to lie in the opportunities the system affords the exhibitor-defendants and the other large operators to strengthen their hold in the industry. We are reluctant to alter decrees in these cases where there is agreement with the District Court on the nature of the violations. . . . But the provisions for competitive bidding in these cases promise little in the way of relief against the real evils of the conspiracy. They implicate the judiciary heavily in the details of business management if supervision is to be effective. They vest powerful control in the exhibitor-defendants over their competitors if close supervision by the court is not undertaken. In light of these considerations we conclude that the competitive bidding provisions of the decree should be eliminated so that a more effective decree may be fashioned. . . .

Third. Monopoly, Expansion of Theatre Holdings, Divestiture

There is a suggestion that the hold the defendants have on the industry is so great that a problem under the First Amendment is raised. . . . We have no doubt that moving pictures, like newspapers and radio, are included in the press whose freedom is guaranteed by the First Amendment. That issue would be focused here if we had any question concerning monopoly in the production of moving pictures. But monopoly in production was eliminated as an issue in these cases, as we have noted. The chief argument at the bar is phrased in terms of monopoly of exhibition, restraints on exhibition, and the like. Actually, the issue is even narrower than that. The main contest is over the cream of the exhibition business— that of the first-run theatres. By defining the issue so narrowly we do not intend to belittle its importance. It shows, however, that the question here is not *what* the public will see or *if* the public will be permitted to see certain features. It is clear that under the existing system the public will be denied access to none. If the public cannot see the features on the first-run, it may do

so on the second, third, fourth, or later run. The central problem presented by these cases is which exhibitors get the highly profitable first-run business. That problem has important aspects under the Sherman Act. But it bears only remotely, if at all, on any question of freedom of the press, save only as timeliness of release may be a factor of importance in specific situations.

The controversy over monopoly relates to monopoly in exhibition and more particularly monopoly in the first-run phase of the exhibition business.

The five majors in 1945 had interests in somewhat over 17 percent of the theatres in the United States—3,137 out of 18,076. Those theatres paid 45 percent of the total domestic film rental received by all eight defendants.

In the 92 cities of the country with populations over 100,000 at least 70 percent of all the first-run theatres are affiliated with one or more of the five majors. In 4 of those cities the five majors have no theatres. In 38 of those cities there are no independent first-run theatres. In none of the remaining 50 cities did less than three of the distributor-defendants license their product on first run to theatres of the five majors. In 19 of the 50 cities less than three of the distributor-defendants licensed their product on first run to independent theatres. In a majority of the 50 cities the greater share of all of the features of defendants were licensed for first-run exhibition in the theatres of the five majors.

In about 60 percent of the 92 cities having populations of over 100,000, independent theatres compete with those of the five majors in first-run exhibition. In about 91 percent of the 92 cities there is competition between independent theatres and the theatres of the five majors or between theatres of the five majors themselves for first-run exhibition. In all of the 92 cities there is always competition in some run even where there is no competition in first runs.

In cities between 25,000 and 100,000 populations the five majors have interests in 577 of a total of 978 first-run theatres or about 60 percent. In about 300 additional towns, mostly under 25,000, an operator affiliated with one of the five majors has all of the theatres in the town.

The District Court held that the five majors

could not be treated collectively so as to establish claims of general monopolization in exhibition. It found that none of them was organized or had been maintained "for the purpose of achieving a national monopoly" in exhibition. It found that the five majors by their present theatre holdings "alone" (which aggregate a little more than one-sixth of all the theatres in the United States), "do not and cannot collectively or individually, have a monopoly of exhibition." The District Court also found that where a single defendant owns all of the first-run theatres in a town, there is no sufficient proof that the acquisition was for the purpose of creating a monopoly. It found rather that such consequence resulted from the inertness of competitors, their lack of financial ability to build theatres comparable to those of the five majors, or the preference of the public for the best-equipped theatres. And the percentage of features on the market which any of the five majors could play in its own theatres was found to be relatively small and in nowise to approximate a monopoly of film exhibition.

Even in respect of the theatres jointly owned or jointly operated by the defendants with each other or with independents, the District Court found no monopoly or attempt to monopolize. Those joint agreements or ownership were found only to be unreasonable restraints of trade. . . .

The District Court did, however, enjoin the five majors from expanding their present theatre holdings in any manner. It refused to grant the request of the Department of Justice for total divestiture by the five majors of their theatre holdings. It found that total divestiture would be injurious to the five majors and damaging to the public. Its thought on the latter score was that the new set of theatre owners who would take the place of the five majors would be unlikely for some years to give the public as good service as those they supplanted "in view of the latter's demonstrated experience and skill in operating what must be regarded as in general the largest and best equipped theatres." Divestiture was, it thought, too harsh a remedy where there was available the alternative of competitive bidding. It accordingly concluded that divestiture was unnecessary "at least until the efficiency of that system has been tried and found wanting."

It is clear, so far as the five majors are concerned, that the aim of the conspiracy was exclusionary, *i.e.*, it was designed to strengthen their hold on the exhibition field. In other words, the conspiracy had monopoly in exhibition for one of its goals, as the District Court held. Price, clearance, and run are interdependent. The clearance and run provisions of the licenses fixed the relative playing positions of all theatres in a certain area; the minimum price provisions were based on playing position—the first-run theatres being required to charge the highest prices, the second-run theatres the next highest, and so on. As the District Court found, "In effect, the distributor, by the fixing of minimum admission prices, attempts to give the prior-run exhibitors as near a monopoly of the patronage as possible."

It is, therefore, not enough in determining the need for divestiture to conclude with the District Court that none of the defendants was organized or has been maintained for the purpose of achieving a "national monopoly," nor that the five majors through their present theatre holdings "alone" do not and cannot collectively or individually have a monopoly of exhibition. For when the starting point is a conspiracy to effect a monopoly through restraints of trade, it is relevant to determine what the results of the conspiracy were even if they fell short of monopoly. . . .

The District Court in its findings speaks of the absence of a "purpose" on the part of any of the five majors to achieve a "national monopoly" in the exhibition of motion pictures. First, there is no finding as to the presence or absence of monopoly on the part of the five majors in the *first-run* field for the entire country, in the *first-run* field in the 92 largest cities of the country, or in the *first-run* field in separate localities. Yet the *first-run* field, which constitutes the cream of the exhibition business, is the core of the present cases. Section 1 of the Sherman Act outlaws unreasonable restraints irrespective of the amount of trade or commerce involved . . . and § 2 condemns monopoly of "any part" of trade or commerce. "Any part" is construed to mean an appreciable part of interstate or foreign trade or commerce. . . . Second, we pointed out in *United States v. Griffith,* . . . that "specific intent" is not necessary to establish a "purpose or intent" to create a monopoly but that the requisite "purpose or intent" is present if monopoly results as a necessary consequence of what was done. The findings of the District Court on this phase of the cases are not clear, though we take them to mean by the absence of "purpose" the absence of a specific intent. So construed they are inconclusive. In any event they are ambiguous and must be recast on remand of the cases. Third, monopoly power, whether lawfully or unlawfully acquired, may violate § 2 of the Sherman Act though it remains unexercised, for the existence of power "to exclude competition when it is desired to do so" is itself a violation of § 2, provided it is coupled with the purpose or intent to exercise that power. The District Court, being primarily concerned with the number and extent of the theatre holdings of defendants, did not address itself to this phase of the monopoly problem. Here also, parity of treatment as between independents and the five majors as theatre owners, who were tied into the same general conspiracy, necessitates consideration of this question.

Exploration of these phases of the cases would not be necessary if, as the Department of Justice argues, vertical integration of producing, distributing and exhibiting motion pictures is illegal *per se*. But the majority of the Court does not take that view. In the opinion of the majority the legality of vertical integration under the Sherman Act turns on (1) the purpose or intent with which it was conceived, or (2) the power it creates and the attendant purpose or intent. First, it runs afoul of the Sherman Act if it was a calculated scheme to gain control over an appreciable segment of the market and to restrain or suppress competition, rather than an expansion to meet legitimate business needs. . . . Second, a vertically integrated enterprise, like other aggregations of business units . . . will constitute monopoly which, though unexercised, violates the Sherman Act provided a power to exclude competition is coupled with a purpose or intent to do so. As we pointed out in *United States v. Griffith*, . . . size is itself an earmark of monopoly power. For size carries with it an opportunity for abuse. And the fact that the power created by size was utilized in the past to crush or prevent competi-

tion is potent evidence that the requisite purpose or intent attends the presence of monopoly power. . . . Likewise bearing on the question whether monopoly power is created by the vertical integration, is the nature of the market to be served . . . and the leverage on the market which the particular vertical integration creates or makes possible.

These matters were not considered by the District Court. For that reason, as well as the others we have mentioned, the findings on monopoly and divestiture which we have discussed in this part of the opinion will be set aside. There is an independent reason for doing that. As we have seen, the District Court considered competitive bidding as an alternative to divestiture in the sense that it concluded that further consideration of divestiture should not be had until competitive bidding had been tried and found wanting. Since we eliminate from the decree the provisions for competitive bidding, it is necessary to set aside the findings on divestiture so that a new start on this phase of the cases may be made on their remand.

It follows that the provision of the decree barring the five majors from further theatre expansion should likewise be eliminated. For it too is related to the monopoly question; and the District Court should be allowed to make an entirely fresh start on the whole of the problem. . . .

NOTES

1. May 3, 1948, was an important date in motion picture antitrust history. In addition to announcing its decision in *U.S. v. Paramount*, the U.S. Supreme Court also rendered its opinions in two other important film cases. See *U.S. v. Griffith*, 334 U.S. 100 (1948), and *Schine Chain Theatres v. U.S.*, 334 U.S. 110 (1948).

2. For an early article discussing the implications of the many antitrust cases leading to the *Paramount* decision, see Reich, "The Entertainment Industry and the Federal Antitrust Laws," 20 *Southern California Law Review* 1 (1946).

3. The significance of the *Paramount* decision is evident by such recent discussions of its current implications as:

(a) Phillips, "The Recent Acquisition of Theatre Circuits by Major Distributors and the *Paramount*

Case," *Entertainment and Sports Lawyer*, vol. 5, no. 3 (Winter 1987), p. 1.

(b) Phillips, "Block Booking Perhaps Forgotten, Perhaps Not Understood, But Still Illegal." Paper presented by Gerald Phillips to the Intellectual Property and Unfair Competition Section, Los Angeles County Bar Association, March 21, 1987.

United States v. Loews, Inc., 371 U.S. 38 (1962)

MR. JUSTICE GOLDBERG DELIVERED THE OPINION OF THE COURT

These consolidated appeals present as a key question the validity under § 1 of the Sherman Act of block booking of copyrighted feature motion pictures for television exhibition. We hold that the tying agreements here are illegal and in violation of the Act.

The United States brought separate civil antitrust actions in the Southern District of New York in 1957 against six major distributors of pre-1948 copyrighted motion picture feature films for television exhibition, alleging that each defendant had engaged in block booking in violation of § 1 of the Sherman Act. The complaints asserted that the defendants had, in selling to television stations, conditioned the license or sale of one or more feature films upon the acceptance by the station of a package or block containing one or more unwanted or inferior films. No combination or conspiracy among the distributors was alleged; nor was any monopolization or attempt to monopolize under § 2 of the Sherman Act averred. The sole claim of illegality rested on the manner in which each defendant had marketed its product. The successful pressure applied to television station customers to accept inferior films along with desirable pictures was the gravamen of the complaint.

After a lengthy consolidated trial, the district judge filed exhaustive findings of fact, conclusions of law, and a carefully reasoned opinion, 189 F. Supp. 373, in which he found that the actions of the defendants constituted violations of § 1 of the Sherman Act. . . .

The judge recognized that there was keen competition between the defendant distributors, and therefore rested his conclusion solely on the individual behavior of each in engaging in block booking. In reaching his decision he carefully considered the evidence relating to each of the 68 licensing agreements that the Government had contended involved block booking. He concluded that only 25 of the contracts were illegally entered into. Nine of these belonged to defendant C & C Super Corp., which had an admitted policy of insisting on block booking that it sought to justify on special grounds.

Of the others, defendant Loew's, Incorporated, had in two negotiations that resulted in licensing agreements declined to furnish stations KWTV of Oklahoma City and WBRE of Wilkes-Barre with individual film prices and had refused their requests for permission to select among the films in the groups. Loew's exacted from KWTV a contract for the entire Loew's library of 723 films, involving payments of $314,725.20. The WBRE agreement was for a block of 100 films, payments to total $15,000.

Defendant Screen Gems, Inc., was also found to have block booked two contracts, both with WTOP of Washington, D.C., one calling for a package of 26 films and payments of $20,800 and the other for 52 films and payments of $40,000. The judge accepted the testimony of station officials that they had requested the right to select films and that their requests were refused.

Associated Artists Productions, Inc., negotiated four contracts that were found to be block booked. Station WTOP was to pay $118,800 for the license of 99 pictures, which were divided into three groups of 33 films, based on differences in quality. To get "Treasure of the Sierra Madre," "Casablanca," "Johnny Belinda," "Sergeant York," and "The Man Who Came to Dinner," among others, WTOP also had to take such films as "Nancy Drew Troubleshooter," "Tugboat Annie Sails Again," "Kid Nightingale," "Gorilla Man," and "Tear Gas Squad." A similar contract for 100 pictures, involving a license fee of $140,000, was entered into by WMAR of Baltimore. Triangle Publications, owner and operator of five stations, was refused the right to select among Associated's packages, and ultimately purchased the entire library of 754 films for a price of $2,262,000 plus 10% of gross receipts. Station WJAR of Providence, which licensed a package of 58 features for a fee of $25,230, had asked first if certain films it considered undesirable could be dropped from the offered packages and was told that the packages could not be split.

Defendant National Telefilm Associates was found to have entered into five block booked contracts. Station WMAR wanted only 10 Selznick films, but was told that it could not have them unless it also bought 24 inferior films from the "TNT" package and 12 unwanted "Fabulous 40's." It bought all of these, for a total of $62,240. Station WBRE, before buying the "Fox 52" package in its entirety for $7,358.50, requested and was refused the right to eliminate undesirable features. Station WWLP of Springfield, Massachusetts, inquired about the possibility of splitting two of the packages, was told this was not possible, and then bought a total of 59 films in two packages for $8,850. A full package contract for National's "Rocket 86" group of 86 films was entered into by KPIX of San Francisco, payments to total $232,200, after KPIX requested and was denied permission to eliminate undesirable films from the package. Station WJAR wanted to drop 10 or 12 British films from this defendant's "Champagne 58" package, was told that none could be deleted, and then bought the block for $31,000.

The judge found that defendant United Artists Corporation had in three consummated negotiations conditioned the sale of films on the purchase of an entire package. The "Top 39" were licensed by WAAM of Baltimore for $40,000 only after receipt of a refusal to sell 13 of the 39 films in the package. Station WHTN of Huntington, West Virginia, purchased "Award 52" for $16,900 after United Artists refused to deal on any basis other than purchase of the entire 52 films. Thirty-nine films were purchased by WWLP for $5,850 after an initial inquiry about selection of titles was refused. . . .

This case raises the recurring question of whether specific tying arrangements violate § 1 of the Sherman Act. This Court has recognized that "[t]ying agreements serve hardly any purpose beyond the suppression of competition," *Standard Oil Co. of California v. United States*, 337 U.S. 293, 305–306. They are an object of antitrust concern for two reasons—they may force buyers into giving up the purchase of substitutes for the tied product, see *Times-Picayune Pub. Co. v. United States*, 345 U.S. 594, 605, and they may destroy the free access of competing suppliers of the tied product to the consuming market, see *International Salt Co. v. United States*, 332 U.S. 392, 396. A tie-in contract may have one or both of these undesirable effects when the seller, by virtue of his position in the market for the tying product, has economic leverage sufficient to induce his customers to take the tied product along with the tying item. The standard of illegality is that the seller must have "sufficient economic power with respect to the tying product to appreciably restrain free competition in the market for the tied product. . . ." *Northern Pacific R. Co. v. United States*, 356 U.S. 1, 6. Market dominance—some power to control price and to exclude competition—is by no means the only test of whether the seller has the requisite economic power. Even absent a showing of market dominance, the crucial economic power may be inferred from the tying product's desirability to consumers or from uniqueness in its attributes.

The requisite economic power is presumed when the tying product is patented or copyrighted. . . . This principle grew out of a long line of patent cases which had eventuated in the doctrine that a patentee who utilized tying arrangements would be denied all relief against infringements of his patent. . . . These cases reflect a hostility to use of the statutorily granted patent monopoly to extend the patentee's economic control to unpatented products. The patentee is protected as to his invention, but may not use his patent rights to exact tribute for other articles.

Since one of the objectives of the patent laws is to reward uniqueness, the principle of these cases was carried over into antitrust law on the theory that the existence of a valid patent on the tying product, without more, establishes a distinctiveness sufficient to conclude that any tying arrangement involving the patented product would have anticompetitive consequences. . . .

A copyrighted feature film does not lose its legal or economic uniqueness because it is shown on a television rather than a movie screen.

The district judge found that each copyrighted

film block booked by appellants for television use "was in itself a unique product"; that feature films "varied in theme, in artistic performance, in stars, in audience appeal, etc." and were not fungible; and that since each defendant by reason of its copyright had a "monopolistic" position as to each tying product, "sufficient economic power" to impose an appreciable restraint on free competition in the tied product was present, as demanded by the *Northern Pacific* decision. 189 F. Supp., at 381. We agree. These findings of the district judge, supported by the record, confirm the presumption of uniqueness resulting from the existence of the copyright itself.

Moreover, there can be no question in this case of the adverse effects on free competition resulting from appellants' illegal block booking contracts. Television stations forced by appellants to take unwanted films were denied access to films marketed by other distributors who, in turn, were foreclosed from selling to the stations. Nor can there be any question as to the substantiality of the commerce involved. The 25 contracts found to have been illegally block booked involved payments to appellants ranging from $60,800 in the case of Screen Gems to over $2,500,000 in the case of Associated Artists. A substantial portion of the licensing fees represented the cost of the inferior films which the stations were required to accept. These anticompetitive consequences are an apt illustration of the reasons underlying our recognition that the mere presence of competing substitutes for the tying product, here taking the form of other programming material as well as other feature films, is insufficient to destroy the legal, and indeed the economic, distinctiveness of the copyrighted product. . . . By the same token, the distinctiveness of the copyrighted tied product is not inconsistent with the fact of competition, in the form of other programming material and other films, which is suppressed by the tying arrangements.

It is therefore clear that the tying arrangements here both by their "inherent nature" and by their "effect" injuriously restrained trade. . . .

Appellant C & C in its separate appeal raises certain arguments which amount to an attempted business justification for its admitted block booking policy. C & C purchased the telecasting rights in some 742 films known as the "RKO Library." It did so with a bank loan for the total purchase price, and to get the bank loan it needed a guarantor, which it found in the International Latex Corporation. Latex, however, demanded and secured an agreement from C & C that films would not be sold without obtaining in return a commitment from television stations to show a minimum number of Latex spot advertisements in conjunction with the films. Thus, since stations could not feasibly telecast the minimum number of spots without buying a large number of films to spread them over, C & C by requiring the minimum number of advertisements effectively forced block booking on those stations which purchased its films. C & C contends the block booking was merely the by-product of two legitimate business motives—Latex' desire for a saturation advertising campaign, and C & C's wish to buy a large film library. However, the obvious answer to this contention is that the thrust of the antitrust laws cannot be avoided merely by claiming that the otherwise illegal conduct is compelled by contractual obligations. Were it otherwise, the antitrust laws could be nullified. . . .

The United States contends that the relief afforded by the final judgments is inadequate and that to be adequate it must also: (1) require the defendants to price the films individually and offer them on a picture-by-picture basis; (2) prohibit noncost-justified differentials in price between a film when sold individually and when sold as part of a package; (3) proscribe "temporary" refusals by a distributor to deal on less than a block basis while he is negotiating with a competing television station for a package sale. . . .

Under the final judgments entered by the court, a distributor would be free to offer films in a package initially, without stating individual prices. If, however, he delayed at all in producing individual prices upon request, he would subject himself to a possible contempt sanction. The Government's first request would prevent this "first bite" possibility, forcing the offer of the films on an individual basis at the outset (but, as we view it, not precluding a simultaneous package offer . . .).

This is a necessary addition to the decrees, in

view of the evidence appearing in the record. Television stations which asked for the individual prices of some of the better pictures "couldn't get any sort of a firm kind of an answer," according to one station official. He stated that they received a "certain form of equivocation, like the price for the better pictures that we wanted was so high that it wouldn't be worth our while to discuss the matter, . . . the implication being that it wouldn't happen." A Screen Gems intracompany memorandum about a Baton Rouge station's price request stated that "I told him that I would be happy to talk to him about it, figuring we could start the old round robin that worked so well in Houston & San Antonio." Without the proposed amendment to the decree, distributors might surreptitiously violate it by allowing or directing their salesmen to be reluctant to produce the individual price list on request. This subtler form of sales pressure, though not accompanied by any observable delay over time, might well result in some television stations buying the block rather than trying to talk the seller into negotiating on an individual basis. Requiring the production of the individual list on first approach will obviate this danger. . . .

The final judgments as entered only prohibit a price differential between a film offered individually and as part of a package which "has the effect of conditioning the sale or license of such film upon the sale or license of one or more other films." The Government contends that this provision appearing by itself is too vague and will lead to unnecessary litigation. Differentials unjustified by cost savings may already be prohibited under the decree as it now appears. Nevertheless, the addition of a specific provision to prevent such differentials will prevent uncertainty in the operation of the decree. To ensure that litigation over the scope and application of the decrees is not left until a contempt proceeding is brought, the second requested modification should be added. The Government, however, seeks to make distribution costs the only saving which can legitimately be the basis of a discount. We would not so limit the relevant cost justifications. To prevent definitional arguments, and to ensure that all proper bases of quantity discount may be used, the modification should be worded in terms of allowing all legitimate cost justifications. . . .

The Government's third request is, like the first, designed to prevent distributors from subjecting prospective purchasers to a "run-around" on the purchase of individual films. No doubt temporary refusal to sell in broken lots to one customer while negotiating to sell the entire block to another is a proper business practice, viewed *in vacuo*, but we think that if permitted here it may tend to force some stations into buying pre-set packages to forestall a competitor's getting the entire group. In recognition of this the Government seeks a blanket prohibition against all temporary refusals to deal. We agree in the main, except that the modification proposed by the Government fails to give full recognition to that part of this Court's holding in *Paramount Pictures* which said,

> We do not suggest that films may not be sold in blocks or groups, when there is no requirement, express or implied, for the purchase of more than one film. All we hold to be illegal is a refusal to license one or more copyrights unless another copyright is accepted. 334 U.S., at 159.

We therefore grant the Government's request, but modify it only to the limited degree necessary to permit a seller briefly to defer licensing or selling to a customer pending the expeditious conclusion of bona fide negotiations already being conducted with a competing station on a proposal wherein the distributor has simultaneously offered to license or sell films either individually or in a package.

The modifications we have specified will bring about a greater precision in the operation of the decrees. We have concluded that they will properly protect the interest of the Government in guarding against violations and the interest of the defendants in seeking in good faith to comply. . . .

NOTES

1. Several books explore the antitrust problems in motion pictures. As examples, see:

(a) R. Cassady, Jr., *Monopoly in Motion Picture Production and Distribution: 1908–1915* (Los Angeles: Bureau of Business & Economic Research. University of California, 1959).

(b) R. Cassady, Jr., and R. Cassady III, *The Private Antitrust Suit in American Business Competition: A Motion Picture Industry Case Analysis* (Los Angeles: Bureau of Business & Economic Research, University of California, 1964).

(c) M. Conant, *Antitrust in the Motion Picture Industry* (New York: Arno Press, 1978).

(d) M. Huettig, *Economic Control of the Motion Picture Industry: A Study in Industrial Organization* (Philadelphia: University of Pennsylvania Press, 1944).

2. Articles concerning movie antitrust problems include the following:

(a) R. Cassady, Jr., "Impact of the Paramount Decision on Motion Picture Distribution and Price Making," 31 *Southern California Law Review* 150 (1958).

(b) R. Cassady, Jr., "Monopoly in Motion Picture Production and Distribution: 1908–1915," 32 *Southern California Law Review* 325 (1959).

(c) J. Cirace, "Five Conflicts over Income Distribution in the Motion Picture-Television Industry," 25 *Villanova Law Review* 417 (1980).

(d) M. Conant, "The Paramount Decrees Reconsidered," 44 *Law and Contemporary Problems* 79 (1981).

(e) J. Lieberman, "A Motion Picture Producer's Standing to Recover Treble Damages from a Movie Distributor for Block Booking," 14 *Journal of the Beverly Hills Bar Association* 185 (1980).

(f) "Motion Picture Split Agreements: An Antitrust Analysis," 52 *Fordham Law Review* 159 (1983).

(g) M. Price and M. Nadel, "Antitrust Issues in the New Video Media," 3 *Cardozo Arts & Entertainment Law Journal* 27 (1984).

6.20 Protection of Ideas and Stories

The motion picture business exists on the ability of creative talent to transform ideas into stories and hence into films. Writers, and would-be writers, see motion pictures (and, today, television) as vehicles to realize their greatest dreams—fame and fortune. For the unproved talent, however, the path to recognition and reward is treacherous. Ideas can easily be stolen; and the redress for such theft is uncertain at best. Absent a fully written story, properly copyrighted, the protections are few. Ideas by themselves are not copyrightable and may be "borrowed" at will. But ideas can be contracted for and have value as contract property. It is unusual, though, for a fully written contract to be executed with an unknown talent for that person's undeveloped ideas. So a central inquiry is just what it takes to constitute a contract for the sale of an idea. This is the inquiry examined in the first three cases in this section, *Desny v. Wilder, Mann v. Columbia Pictures*, and *Blaustein v. Burton*.

Even when there is a contract, the terms may be capable of more than one interpretation. The final case in this section, *Mel Hardman Productions Inc. v. Robinson*, analyzes what is meant by the term "photoplay." This suggests that, even though we have come far in resolving legal problems in the motion picture industry, all is not settled. Lawyers constantly must return to their contract drafting boards to clear away confusing contractual provisions.

Desny v. Wilder, 299 P.2d 257 (Ca. 1956)

SCHAUER, JUSTICE

Plaintiff appeals from a summary judgment rendered against him in this action to recover the reasonable value of a literary composition, or of an idea for a photoplay, a synopsis of which composition, embodying the idea, he asserts he submitted to defendants for sale, and which synopsis and idea, plaintiff alleges, were accepted and used by defendants in producing a photoplay. . . .

[I]t appears from the present record that defendant Wilder at the times here involved was employed by defendant Paramount Pictures Corporation (sometimes hereinafter referred to as Paramount) either as a writer, producer or director, or a combination of the three. In November 1949, plaintiff telephoned Wilder's office. Wilder's secretary, who was also employed by Paramount, answered, and plaintiff stated that he wished to see Wilder. At the secretary's insistence that plaintiff explain his purpose, plaintiff "told her about this fantastic unusual story. . . . I described to her the story in a few words. . . . I told her that it was the life story of Floyd Collins who was trapped and made sensational news for two weeks . . . and I told her the plot. . . . I described to her the entrapment and the death, in ten minutes, probably. She seemed very much interested and she liked it. . . . The main emphasis was the central idea, which was the entrapment, this boy who was trapped in a cave eighty-some feet deep. I also told her the picture had never been made with a cave background before." Plaintiff sought to send Wilder a copy of the story but when the secretary learned of its length of some 65 pages she stated that Wilder would not read it, that he wanted stories in synopsis form, that the story would first be sent to the script department, and "in case they think it is fantastic and wonderful, they will abbreviate it and condense it in about three or four pages, and the producers and directors get to see it." Plaintiff protested that he preferred to do the abbreviating of the story himself, and the secretary suggested that he do so. Two days later plaintiff, after preparing a three or four page outline of the story, telephoned Wilder's office a second time and told the secretary the synopsis was ready. The secretary requested plaintiff to read the synopsis to her over the telephone so that she could take it down in shorthand, and plaintiff did so. During the conversation the secretary told plaintiff that the story seemed interesting and that she liked it. "She said that she would talk it over with Billy Wilder and she would let me know." Plaintiff on his part told the secretary that defendants could use the story only if they paid him "the reasonable value of it. . . . I made it clear to her that I wrote the story and that I wanted to sell it. . . . I naturally mentioned again that this story was my story which has taken me so much effort and research and time, and therefore if anybody used it they will have to pay for it. . . . She said that if Billy Wilder of Paramount uses the story, 'naturally we will pay you for it.' " Plaintiff did not remember whether in his first telephone conversation with the secretary anything was said concerning his purpose of selling the story to defendants. He did not at any time speak with defendant Wilder. It seems clear, however, that one of the authorized functions of the secretary was to receive and deliver messages to Wilder and hence, as is developed infra, that on this record her knowledge would be his knowledge. Plaintiff's only subsequent contact with the secretary was a telephone call to her in July 1950, to protest the alleged use of his composition and idea in a photoplay produced and exhibited by defendants. The photoplay, as hereinafter shown in some detail, closely parallels both plaintiff's synopsis and the historical material concerning the life and death of Floyd Collins. It also includes a fictional incident which appears in plaintiff's synopsis and which he claims is his creation, presumably in the sense of being both original and novel in its combination with the facts from the public commons or public domain.

. . . In his opening brief plaintiff states "It is conceded *for purposes of argument* [italics added] that the synopsis submitted by plaintiff to defendants was not sufficiently unique or original to be the basis for recovery under the law of plagiarism or infringement. It is conceded that the plaintiff first obtained the central idea or theme of his story, which involves the entrapment of a man in an underground cave and the national interest promoted by the attempt to rescue him, from the Floyd Collins incident which occurred in the 1920's.

"It is appellant's [plaintiff's] contention, however, that in spite of this, the lower court committed reversible error in granting a summary judgment in this case for the reason that the summary judgment had the effect of denying the plaintiff the right to prove that his idea or synopsis was the subject of a contract wherein the defendants promised to pay him for it if they used it. It is clear that 'ideas,' as such, may still be the subject of a contract in California and may be protected, as such, even though not protectible under the laws of plagiarism."

Plaintiff also asserts that he "is not suing defendants for plagiarizing his idea but is suing defendants because they agreed to pay him the reasonable value of the use of his idea and story synopsis if they used it" and that "defendants so used plaintiff's idea and synopsis but refused to pay him as they agreed." But the complaint, as already shown, alleges that "Plaintiff conceived, originated and completed [and offered for sale to and defendants accepted submission of and thereafter used] a certain untitled literary and dramatic composition (hereinafter called 'Plaintiff's Property') based upon the life of Floyd Collins."

If plaintiff is seeking to recover for a mere abstract, unprotectible idea, he must meet certain rules; if he seeks recovery for a literary composition in which he conceivably had a property right, the rules are quite different, as will subsequently be shown. . . .

Defendants concede, as they must, that "the act of disclosing an unprotectible idea, if that act is in fact the bargained-for exchange for a promise, may be consideration to support the promise." They then add, "But once the idea is disclosed without the protection of a contract, the law says that anyone is free to use it. Therefore, subsequent use of the idea cannot constitute consideration so as to support a promise to pay for such use." And as to the effect of the evidence defendants argue that plaintiff "disclosed his material before . . . [defendants] did or could do anything to indicate their willingness or unwillingness to pay for the disclosure. The act of using the idea, from which appellant attempts to imply a promise to pay, came long after the disclosure. . . . Accordingly, even if a promise to pay could be found . . . it came after the disclosure had been made and is therefore unenforceable." The conclusion of law asserted in the last sentence, insofar as it might be applicable to an express (whether proved by direct or by circumstantial evidence) promise to pay for the service (the conveyance of the idea) previously rendered from which a profit has been derived, for reasons which hereinafter appear (infra, 299 P.2d 269), is not tenable. . . .

From what has been indicated above it appears necessary for us in the proper disposition of this case, having in mind the problems which apparently will confront the trial court at a trial on the merits and the duty imposed on us by section 53 of the Code of Civil Procedure, to consider not only (1) the rules for recovery pertaining to the conveyance of ideas, as such, but also (2) the question whether the synopsis of plaintiff's untitled composition could on any view of the evidence be deemed entitled to the status of a

literary property, and (3) the rules defining rights of recovery, so far as pertinent on this record, if plaintiff has a literary property in his composition.

The Law Pertaining to Ideas. Generally speaking, ideas are as free as the air and as speech and the senses, and as potent or weak, interesting or drab, as the experiences, philosophies, vocabularies, and other variables of speaker and listener may combine to produce, to portray, or to comprehend. But there can be circumstances when neither air nor ideas may be acquired without cost. The diver who goes deep in the sea, even as the pilot who ascends high in the troposphere, knows full well that for life itself he, or someone on his behalf, must arrange for air (or its respiration-essential element, oxygen) to be specially provided at the time and place of need. The theatrical producer likewise may be dependent for his business life on the procurement of ideas from other persons as well as the dressing up and portrayal of his self-conceptions; he may not find his own sufficient for survival. As counsel for the Writers Guild aptly say, ideas "are not freely usable by the entertainment media until the latter are made aware of them." The producer may think up the idea himself, dress it and portray it; or he may purchase either the conveyance of the idea alone or a manuscript embodying the idea in the author's concept of a literary vehicle giving it form, adaptation and expression. It cannot be doubted that some ideas are of value to a producer.

An idea is usually not regarded as property, because all sentient beings may conceive and evolve ideas throughout the gamut of their powers of cerebration and because our concept of property implies something which may be owned and possessed to the exclusion of all other persons. . . .

The principles above stated do not, however, lead to the conclusion that ideas cannot be a subject of contract. As Mr. Justice Traynor stated in his dissenting opinion in *Stanley v. Columbia Broadcasting System* (1950), . . . 35 Cal.2d 653, 674, 221 P.2d 73: "The policy that precludes protection of an abstract idea by copyright does not prevent its protection by contract. Even though an idea is not property subject to exclusive ownership, its disclosure may be of substantial benefit to the person to whom it is disclosed. That disclosure may therefore be consideration for a promise to pay . . . Even though the idea disclosed may be 'widely known and generally understood' [citation], it may be protected by an express contract providing that it will be paid for regardless of its lack of novelty." . . .

In other words the recovery may be based on contract either express or implied. The person who can and does convey a valuable idea to a producer who commercially solicits the service or who voluntarily accepts it knowing that it is tendered for a price should likewise be entitled to recover. In so holding we do not fail to recognize that free-lance writers are not necessarily members of a learned profession and as such bound to the exalted standards to which doctors and lawyers are dedicated. So too we are not oblivious of the hazards with which producers of the class represented here by defendants and their related amici are confronted through the unsolicited submission of numerous scripts on public domain materials in which public materials the producers through their own initiative may well find nuclei for legitimately developing the "stupendous and colossal." The law, however, is dedicated to the proposition that for every wrong there is a remedy (Civ. Code, § 3523) and for the sake of protecting one party it must not close the forum to the other. It will hear both and seek to judge the cause by standards fair to both. To that end the law of implied contracts assumes particular importance in literary idea and property controversies.

The Law Pertaining to Contracts, Express, Implied-in-Fact and Implied by Law, and Quasi Contractual Obligations, as Related to Ideas and Literary Property. . . .

We agree that whether a contract be properly identified as express or as implied-in-fact or inferred from circumstances; or whether the bargain meets the subjective test of a meeting of minds or is held to reside in the objective evidence of words and acts with or without a meeting of minds; or whether the obligation be recognized as implied by law from acts having consensual aspects (and therefore often termed implied-in-fact); or whether the obligation be imposed by law because of acts and intents which, although tortious rather than consensual, should in justice give rise to an obligation resembling that created by contract and, hence, should be termed quasi-contractual, is important here to the extent that we recognize the situations and discriminate appropriately in the governing rules. . . .

If it were not for precedent we should hesitate to speak of an implied-in-fact contract. In truth, contracts are either made in fact or the obligation is implied in law. If made in fact, contracts may be established by direct evidence or they may be inferred from circumstantial evidence. The only difference is in the method of proof. In either case they would appear to be express contracts. Otherwise, it would seem that they, or the presumed contractual obligation, must be implied at law. A so-called "implied-in-fact" contract, however, as the term is used by some writers, may be found although there has been no meeting of the minds. Even an express contract may be found where there has been no meeting of minds. The classic example of this situation is set up by the parol evidence rule. The law accepts the objective evidence of the written contract as constituting the contract and, subject, of course, to certain exceptions, precludes oral evidence to show that the minds of the parties did not meet in the writing. Professor Williston recognizes in effect, if not specifically, that the law implies (or construes) contractual obligations in many cases where there is no true contract in the historically conventional sense and that such implied obligations are of the nature of, and governed by the rules applicable to, contracts termed implied-in-fact by many writers. In a paper published in 14 *Illinois Law Review* 85, 90, Mr. Williston says: "The parties may be bound by the terms of an offer even though the offeree expressly indicated dissent, provided his action could only lawfully mean assent. A buyer who goes into a shop and asks and is given [told] the price of an article, cannot take it and say 'I decline to pay the price you ask, but will take it at its fair value.' He will be liable, if the seller elects to hold him so liable, not simply as a converter for the fair value of the property, but as a buyer for the stated price." . . .

Whether the resulting "contract" . . . is classified as express (as may be fictionized by the law's objective test) or as implied-in-fact (as also may be fictionized by the law) or whether in the same or slightly differing circumstances an obligation shall be "implied" and denominated "quasi contractual" because it is strong-armed by the law from non-consensual acts and intents, is probably important in California—and for the purposes of resolving the problems now before us—principally as an aid to understanding the significance of rulings and discussions in authorities from other jurisdictions. Here, our terminology and the situations for application of the pertinent rules are simplified by codification.

Our Civil Code declares that (§ 1619) "A contract is either express or implied"; (§ 1620) "An express contract is one, the terms of which are stated in words" and (§ 1621) "An implied contract is one, the existence and terms of which are manifested by conduct." The same code further provides that (§ 1584) "[T]he acceptance of the consideration offered with a proposal, is an acceptance of the proposal"; (§ 1589) "A voluntary acceptance of the benefit of a transaction is equivalent to a consent to all the obligations arising from it, so far as the facts are known, or ought to be known, to the persons accepting"; (§ 1605) "Any benefit conferred . . . upon the promisor, by any other person, to which the promisor is not lawfully entitled . . . is a good consideration for a promise"; and (§ 1606) "[A] moral obligation originating in some benefit conferred upon the promisor . . . is also a good consideration for a promise, to an extent corresponding with the extent of the obligation, but no further or otherwise." . . .

From what has been shown respecting the law of ideas and of contracts we conclude that conveyance of an idea can constitute valuable consideration and can be bargained for before it is disclosed to the proposed purchaser, but once it is conveyed, i.e., disclosed to him and he has grasped it, it is henceforth his own and he may work with it and use it as he sees fit. In the field of entertainment the producer may properly and validly agree that he will pay for the service of conveying to him ideas which are valuable and which he can put to profitable use. Furthermore, where an idea has been conveyed with the expectation by the purveyor that compensation will be paid if the idea is used, there is no reason why the producer who has been the beneficiary of the conveyance of such an idea, and who finds it valuable and is profiting by it, may not then for the first time, although he is not at that time under any legal obligation so to do, promise to pay a reasonable compensation for that idea—that is, for the past service of furnishing it to him— and thus create a valid obligation. . . . But, assuming legality of consideration, the idea purveyor cannot prevail in an action to recover compensation for an abstract idea unless (a) before or after disclosure he has obtained an express promise to pay, or (b) the circumstances preceding and attending disclosure, together with the conduct of the offeree acting with knowledge of the circumstances, show a promise of the type usually referred to as "implied" or "implied-in-fact." . . .

Such inferred or implied promise, if it is to be found at all, must be based on circumstances which were known to the producer at and preceding the time of disclosure of the idea to him and he must voluntarily accept the disclosure, knowing the conditions on which it is tendered. Section 1584 of the Civil Code ("[T]he acceptance of the consideration offered with a proposal, is an acceptance of the proposal") can have no application unless the offeree has an opportunity to reject the consideration—the proffered conveyance of the idea—before it is conveyed. Unless the offeree has opportunity to reject he cannot be said to accept. . . . The idea man who blurts out his idea without having first made his bargain has no one but himself to blame for the loss of his bargaining power. The law will not in any event, from demands stated subsequent to the unconditioned disclosure of an abstract idea, imply a promise to pay for the idea, for its use, or for its previous disclosure. The law will not imply a promise to pay for an idea from the mere facts that the idea has been conveyed, is valuable, and has been used for profit; this is true even though the conveyance has been made with the hope or expectation that some obligation will ensue. So, if the plaintiff here is claiming only for the conveyance of the idea of making a dramatic production out of the life of Floyd Collins he must fail unless in conformity with the above stated rules he can establish a contract to pay.

From plaintiff's testimony, as epitomized above (299 P.2d 261), it does not appear that a contract to pay for conveyance of the abstract photoplay idea had been made, or that the basis for inferring such a contract from subsequent related acts of the defendants had been established, at the time plaintiff disclosed his basic idea to the secretary. Defendants, consequently, were at that time and from then on free to use the abstract idea if they saw fit to engage in the necessary research and develop it to the point of a usable script. Whether defendants did that, or whether they actually accepted and used plaintiff's synopsis, is another question. And whether by accepting plaintiff's synopsis and using it, if they did accept and use it, they may be found to have implicitly—by the rules discussed, supra, 299 P.2d 267—agreed to pay for whatever value the synopsis possessed as a composition embodying, adapting and implementing the idea, is also a question which, upon the present summary judgment record, is pertinent for consideration in reaching our ultimate conclusion. That is, if the evidence suggests that defendants accepted plaintiff's synopsis, did they not necessarily accept it upon the terms on which he had offered it? Certainly the mere fact that the idea had been disclosed under the circumstances shown here would not preclude the finding of an implied (inferred in fact) contract to pay for the synopsis embodying, implementing and adapting the idea for photoplay production. . . .

The basic distinction between the rights in and to literary productions as they may exist at common law and as they are granted by statutory copyright is that the common law protects only a property right while the copyright statute grants a limited monopolistic privilege. (34 Am.Jur. 401, § 2.) Plaintiff here has no statutory copyright. His claim as to the synopsis, therefore, necessarily must rest in a common law property right or in contract. He has chosen to rest it in contract. If plaintiff has a literary composition it may be the subject of a property right and its use by defendants, if established, could entitle him to remedies, notwithstanding the concessions he has made, which would be unavailable if he had only an idea to be appropriated or to be the subject of contract.

Literary property which is protectible may be created out of unprotectible material such as historical events. It has been said (and does not appear to have been successfully challenged) that "There are only thirty-six fundamental dramatic situations, various facets of which form the basis of all human drama." (Georges Polti, "The Thirty-Six Dramatic Situations"; see also, Henry Albert Phillips, "The Universal Plot Catalog"; Eric Heath, "Story Plotting Simplified.") It is manifest that authors must work with and from ideas or themes which basically are in the public domain. History both in broadly significant and in very personal aspects has furnished a wealth of material for photoplays. The Crusades, The French Revolution, The War Between the States, the lives, or events from the lives, of rulers, ministers, doctors, lawyers, politicians, and military men, among others, all have contributed. Events from the life of the late General William Mitchell are even now the basic theme of a current showing. Events from the life of Floyd Collins were avowedly the basic theme of plaintiff's story. Certainly, it must be recognized that a literary composition does not depend upon novelty of plot or theme for the status of "property," if it is entitled to that status at all. The terms "originality" and "novelty" have often been confused, or used without differentiation, or with meanings which vary with different authorities. We therefore suggest the sense in which we use them. A literary composition may be original, at least in a subjective sense, without being novel. To be original it must be a creation or construction of the author, not a mere copy of another's work. The author, of course, must almost inevitably work from old materials, from known themes or plots or historical events, because, except as knowledge unfolds and history takes place, there is nothing new with which to work. But "Creation, in its technical sense, is not essential to vest one with ownership of rights in intellectual property. Thus, a compiler who merely gathers and arranges, in some concrete form, materials which are open and accessible to all who have the mind to work with like diligence is as much the owner of the result of his labors as if his work were a creation rather than a construction." . . .

Writing—portraying characters and events and

emotions with words, no less than with brush and oils—may be an art which expresses personality. Accordingly, the language of Mr. Justice Holmes, speaking for the Supreme Court in a copyright case relating to circus posters is apropos: "Others are free to copy the original. They are not free to copy the copy. . . . The copy is the personal reaction of an individual upon nature. Personality always contains something unique. It expresses singularity even in handwriting, and a very modest grade of art has in it something irreducible, which is one man's alone. That something he may copyright unless there is a restriction in the words of the act." (*Bleistein v. Donaldson Lithographing Co.* (1903), 188 U.S. 239, 249–250, 23 S.Ct. 298, 47 L.Ed. 460.) As indicated, the theme of a writer must almost inevitably be neither novel nor original. The finished work probably will not be novel because it deals only with the public domain or public commons facts. But the completed composition may well be the original product of the researcher who compiles or constructs it. He gives it genesis, and genesis in this sense requires only origin of the composition, not of the theme. The composition will be the property of the author. Whether it possesses substantial value, and to what extent, if any, it may be entitled to copyright protectibility, may be quite another matter.

The time of the author; his resourcefulness in, opportunity for and extent of, research; his penetration in perception and interpretation of source materials; the acumen of his axiological appraisals of the dramatic; and his skill and style of composition, including the art of so portraying accurate narration of events long passed as to arouse vivid emotions of the present, are all elements which may contribute to the value of his product. Some of those elements in varying quanta and proportions must exist in any literary composition; thereby the composition reflects the personality of the author. And any literary composition, conceivably, may possess value in someone's estimation and be the subject of contract, or, conversely, it may be considered totally devoid of artistic, historic, scientific or any practical value. Obviously the defendants here used someone's script in preparing and producing their photoplay. That script must have had value to them. As

will be hereinafter shown, it closely resembles plaintiff's synopsis. Ergo, plaintiff's synopsis appears to be a valuable literary composition. Defendants had an unassailable right to have their own employees conduct the research into the Floyd Collins tragedy—an historical event in the public domain—and prepare a story based on those facts and to translate it into a script for the play. But equally unassailable (assuming the verity of the facts which plaintiff asserts) is plaintiff's position that defendants had no right—except by purchase on the terms he offered—to acquire and use the synopsis prepared by him. . . . We are satisfied that, for the purposes of this appeal, plaintiff's dictation to defendant Wilder's secretary of the synopsis of his composition, embodying the core of his idea and his concept of a desirable entertainment media adaptation of it, is equivalent to submission of the synopsis in typed form.

Under the principles of law which have been stated it appears that for plaintiff to prevail on this appeal the record must indicate either that the evidence favors plaintiff, or that there is a triable issue of fact, in respect to the following questions: Did plaintiff prepare a literary composition on the Floyd Collins tragedy? Did he submit the composition to the defendants for sale? Did the defendants, knowing that it was offered to them for sale, accept and use that composition or any part thereof? If so, what was the reasonable value of the composition?

It is not essential to recovery that plaintiff's story or synopsis possess the elements of copyright protectibility if the fact of consensual contract be found. . . .

The Law Applied to the Facts. Here, as conceded by defendants for purposes of their summary judgment motion, plaintiff, in accordance with his testimony, submitted his synopsis to them through defendant Wilder's secretary and such submission included a declaration by both plaintiff and the secretary that defendants were to pay for his story if they used it. The mere fact that at the time of plaintiff's first telephone call to Wilder's office he described the central idea of the story to the secretary in response to her insistence that he explain the purpose of his call would not as a matter of law deprive plaintiff of the right to payment for the story as discussed by him and the secretary when he again spoke with her two days later and at her request read his synopsis to her, for her to take down in shorthand for defendants' consideration; the two conversations appear to have been parts of a single transaction and must be construed as such. The affidavits submitted on behalf of defendants by Wilder and by an officer of Paramount to the effect that neither Wilder nor Wilder's secretary had authority to negotiate contracts for the purchase of scripts do not compel the conclusion as a matter of law that an implied (inferred) contract binding defendants to pay for plaintiff's story was not created if (as is hereinafter shown) the record discloses any substantial evidence indicating that defendants did accept and make use of plaintiff's composition. . . .

With respect to whether defendants used plaintiff's composition, it may be first noted that defendants presented no affidavits in any way denying such use, but merely exhibited their photoplay to the court for purposes of comparison between plaintiff's synopsis and defendants' production. Defendants also produced extracts from a magazine and newspaper to which plaintiff had already freely testified in his deposition that he had referred in preparing his story. A script of the photoplay was, however, attached to plaintiff's complaint as an exhibit, and plaintiff has provided an outline comparing his synopsis with defendants' scenario. Defendants in their brief have likewise outlined the story of their photoplay.

In defendants' motion picture script the trapped man expresses a fear of the curse of dead Indians, as did Collins in the fictional portion of plaintiff's synopsis. Other similarities between plaintiff's story and the scenario of defendants' picture are these:

Defendants' Scenario

Cave where Minosa trapped was on property owned by him and father. Minosa operated Indian Curio Shop. Minosa cave open to tourist trade. Minosa's difficulty in extricating himself from cave was due to large flat slab wedged against wall of his cell, which slanted across him, pinning him down.

Minosa's father calls sheriff.

Tatum is first reporter to arrive; tells Minosa not to worry, as "they'll get you out."

Tatum suggests setting up a drill on top of the mountain and going straight down; this is done.

Local miners object that drilling is unnecessary.

Tatum comments that the news story is "Big. As big as they come, I think. Maybe bigger than Floyd Collins," and refers to fact that reporter on Collins story received a Pulitzer Prize.

Carnival trucks are described, and persons operating concessions are shown; excursion train is referred to; rescue equipment assembled and public address system used.

Minosa's father protests.

Doctor diagnoses pneumonia.

Tatum is only reporter who saw Minosa.

Other reporters are suspicious of the "whole set-up and criticized and complained about Tatum's control of the situation"; one threatened to "take this all the way to Santa Fe. To the Governor."

Minosa dies.

Plaintiff's Story

Cave where Collins trapped was underneath father's farm.

Collins sold Indian relics to tourists.

Crystal Cave open to tourist trade.

Rock wedge fell across Collins' left ankle and pinioned both legs, holding him prisoner.

Collins' father spread alarm.

Miller is first reported to reach Collins, and tells him, "The world is coming, old man."

Lt. Burdon says, "There is only one way to save Collins without maiming him, and that is to sink a shaft to him."

Opposition develops between the natives and the rescue crew.

Collins story carried on front page of Louisville newspaper every day; Miller was later awarded Pulitzer Prize.

Cave City took on appearance of Klondike gold rush town; special reporters came; special trains stopped to unload travelers and equipment; occasion regarded as picnic by many.

Collins' father resented the behavior.

Doc Hazlett fears pneumonia.

Miller is only reporter who saw Collins.

Some reporters make accusations expressing strong suspicions with respect to lack of good faith in rescue of Collins; governor summons Board of Military Inquiry; two reporters considered whole thing a giant publicity scheme and hoax. Collins dies.

For the purposes of appellate review of this summary judgment proceeding it is apparent from the comparisons above tabulated, and from the outlines which are set out in the margin, that a factual issue, rather than one of law, is presented as to whether defendants used plaintiff's synopsis or developed their production independently thereof. . . . Particularly does this appear true in view of the fact that plaintiff submitted his synopsis to defendants in November 1949, and that as early as July 1950, the latter were producing their photoplay which, despite their assertion that it "does not purport to be a biography of the life of Floyd Collins. . . . Its characters, plot and development are wholly imaginative," obviously does bear a remarkable similarity to plaintiff's story both in respect to the historical data and the fictional material originated by plaintiff.

It has been suggested that this court view the photoplay (which defendants in their brief offer to make available) in order to determine whether a triable issue of fact exists. The scope of the implications in that suggestion is persuasive to us that the issues here are not for summary disposition. In the light of the conclusions we have reached on the evidence already discussed it appears that viewing the photoplay would relate merely to the weight of the evidence. . . . We therefore find it unnecessary to view the film.

At the trial the trier of fact should proceed with nicety of discrimination in applying the evidence to resolve the issues. Inasmuch as plaintiff's story is taken from the public domain, and as both his story and that of defendants are in principal substance historically accurate, it must be borne in mind that the mere facts that plaintiff submitted and offered to sell to defendants a synopsis containing public domain material and that thereafter defendants used the same public domain material, will not support an inference that defendants promised to pay for either the synopsis or for the idea of using the public domain material. The plaintiff can have no property right in the public domain facts concerning Floyd Collins or in the abstract idea of making a photoplay dramatizing those facts. On the other hand, the fact that plaintiff used the public domain material in constructing his story and synopsis would afford no justification whatsoever for defendants to appropriate plaintiff's composition and use it or any part of it in the production of a photoplay—

and this, of course, includes the writing of a scenario for it—without compensating plaintiff for the value of his story. And the further fact, if it be a fact, that the basic idea for the photoplay had been conveyed to defendants before they saw plaintiff's synopsis, would not preclude the finding of an implied (inferred-in-fact) contract to pay for the manuscript, including its implemented idea, if they used such manuscript. . . .

Mann v. Columbia Pictures, Inc., 180 Cal. Rptr. 422 (Cal. App. 1982)

[Bernice Mann, a former beauty salon employee, wrote *Women Plus*, a brief description of six characters in a beauty salon setting, together with a short narration of a number of scenes. She registered this work with the Writers' Guild of America in 1969 (a procedure not limited to members of the Guild nor, indeed, to professional writers). Mann's friend's neighbor (Florence Klase) knew Caplan, who was described to Mann as "an important man at Columbia." As a favor to Mann, Klase convinced Caplan to agree to have *Women Plus* (and a second "treatment," for a story entitled *Two Weeks*) reviewed by a Columbia reader.

In May 1971, Mann placed the two works in separate manila folders in a large envelope and gave them to Klase, who turned the envelope over to Caplan. Although Mann never met with or spoke to Caplan, and never discussed the question with Klase, Mann expected to be paid if her work was used. Caplan later testified that he knew Mann expected to be paid.

At the time, Caplan was employed by Filmmakers (an independent production company) as "production manager" on a film entitled *Happy Birthday Wanda June*. Filmmakers occupied a former Columbia storage facility, located on Columbia property just outside the main gate. Caplan's salary was paid by Columbia pictures. Caplan's job was to calculate production costs (*e.g.*, transportation, wardrobe, set construction, set operation). He had nothing to do with the creative aspects of films or with the compensation to be paid to creative personnel such as writers. Caplan passed the unopened envelope to Crutcher, a Filmmakers story editor, who agreed to evaluate the contents and send Mann a written opinion of her work. While Caplan and Crutcher both ultimately ended up working for Columbia, neither had any connection with Columbia at the time.

Crutcher's practice was to synopsize recommended submissions and pass them along to his superiors, and to return unacceptable submissions to their authors with rejection letters. He kept a file of his rejection letters. While he had a copy of a rejection letter for *Two Weeks*, his files had no entry to either the submission of *Women Plus* or its recommendation or rejection, and he had no copy of a rejection letter. (No record of the material or its disposition was ever found in Columbia's records either.)

About four years later (two years after Crutcher and Caplan went to work for Columbia), Columbia released *Shampoo*, written by Robert Towne (who also wrote *Chinatown* and wrote and directed *Personal Best*) in collaboration with Warren Beatty and starring Beatty. Mann and her husband saw *Shampoo*, recognized several similarities between *Shampoo* and *Women Plus*, and brought suit.

The trial court granted summary judgment to the defendants on Mann's causes of action for plagiarism, breach of confidential relationship, and constructive trust. On Mann's claim of an implied-in-fact contract, the jury disregarded the lack of direct evidence to connect the submitted material to Columbia and, believing that the material *had* made its way to Columbia and been utilized by Towne, despite contrary testimony from personnel in charge of Columbia's story department, awarded her $185,000. However, the court then determined that Towne's 1970 script was an independent effort and granted judgment n.o.v. to the defendants.

Mann appealed.]

STEPHENS, ACTING P.J.

. . . Whether Mann has a protectible property interest in *Women Plus* depends upon the originality of its form and manner of expression, the development of characters and sequence of events. (*Weitzenkorn v. Lesser* [1953] 40 Cal.2d 778, 789 [256 P.2d 947].) If defendants used the ideas contained in *Women Plus*, as alleged, this use does not imply that plaintiff's 29-page outline was protectible literary property or that there was any copying as to form or manner of expression. (*Minniear v. Tors* [1968] 266 Cal.App.2d 495, 504-505 [72 Cal.Rptr. 287]; *Donahue v. Ziv Television Programs, Inc.* [1966] 245 Cal.App.2d 593, 601 [54 Cal. Rptr. 130].) The outline of various characters and scenes was no more than a collection of ideas which was never developed in the form of a script or a story. (*Minniear, supra,* at p. 505.)

Defendants could use the theme, plot, and ideas contained in *Women Plus*. Mann's abstract ideas are not literary property. (*Desny v. Wilder* [1956] 46 Cal.2d 715, 732-733 [299 P.2d 257].) "The idea alone, the bare, undeveloped story situation or theme, is not protectible. [Citations.]" (*Weitzenkorn v. Lesser, supra,* 40 Cal.2d 778, 789.) In order for Mann's complaint to state a cause of action for plagiarism, there must be some substantial similarity between defendants' *Shampoo* and protectible portions of plaintiff's *Women Plus*. (*Kurlan v. Columbia Broadcasting System* [1953] 40 Cal.2d 799, 809 [256 P.2d 962].) But abstract ideas are not entitled to protection by a tort action for plagiarism. (3 Witkin, Summary of Cal. Law [8th ed. 1973] Personal Property, § 35, p. 1647.)

The material allegedly used by defendants must also constitute protectible property if Mann is to recover in quasi-contract. (*Weitzenkorn v. Lesser, supra,* 40 Cal.2d 778, 795.) "Therefore, the proof necessary to recover upon the theory of a contract implied in law is the same as that required by the tort action for plagiarism." (*Ibid.*) The lower court correctly determined that "there is no substantial similarity" between *Shampoo* and plaintiff's outline as to form and manner of expression, the portion which may be protectible property. Because defendants have used no property belonging to Mann, she cannot recover upon a quasi-contractual theory for the alleged use of her ideas. (*Ibid.;* 1 Witkin, Summary of Cal. Law [8th ed. 1973] Contracts, § 4, pp. 31-32.)

Summary adjudication of the cause of action for plagiarism was properly rendered for defendants. In light of this determination, the trial court's dismissal of the count for quasi-contract is necessarily affirmed. Plaintiff's complaint was narrowed to the count for implied-in-fact contract. Mann's action rests entirely on defendants' alleged use of her ideas and the finding of an implied promise to pay the reasonable value of her material. (*Donahue v. Ziv Television Programs, Inc., supra,* 245 Cal.App.2d 593, 599, 601.) . . .

Plaintiff's alleged chain of submission to Columbia has several missing links. . . . Towne's testimony that he "could have" obtained comments from Columbia's story department on material he read does not support the access argument. Uncontradicted testimony shows that neither Towne nor Beatty had any contact with either Caplan or Crutcher prior to this litigation. Aside from their alleged access to Columbia's story department, Mann offers no evidence demonstrating how Towne or Beatty could possibly have read her treatment. . . .

The access of Towne and Beatty to *Women Plus* may only be inferred from the similarities between plaintiff's treatment and the motion picture *Shampoo*. Apart from these similarities, Mann's evidence is insufficient to infer defendants' access to *Women Plus*, as plaintiff offers only speculation and the mere possibility that Caplan or Crutcher submitted the missing treatment to Columbia's story department.

At trial, defendants presented extensive evidence on Towne's "prior creation" of the 1970 *Shampoo* screenplay. The trial judge cited Towne's "independent effort" in granting judgment notwithstanding the verdict as to all defendants, and this court will review the screen writer's endeavor.

Towne testified that the idea for a screenplay involving a hairdresser first occurred to him in 1965. The screenwriter also met defendant Beatty that same year, and they discussed an effort to write a hairdresser script. Towne identified a personal journal in which he recorded notes for his eventual screenplay as early as 1965. In addition to script ideas, the journal entries included the screenwriter's thoughts on structure, dialogue, and his initial meeting with Beatty.

Towne and Beatty further developed ideas for a hairdresser script in 1966. Towne wrote a screenplay which exceeded 200 pages in 1967. This manuscript was not completed, but it contained scenes ultimately incorporated in the motion picture *Shampoo*. In 1968 Towne sat in beauty shops and observed their operation. The screenwriter and Beatty discussed development of the script through the year. Towne wrote another script with an incomplete narrative in 1969. This script also included scenes which appeared in the motion picture *Shampoo*.

Defendant Towne wrote the first complete screenplay on the hairdresser subject from January 1 to January 20, 1970. Initially titled *Up or Down*, Towne changed the title to *Shampoo* and submitted a copy of the screenplay to Jerry Ayres. Ayres was a producer who worked at Columbia. He gave Towne's manuscript to Robert Lovenheim, who was an executive in the creative affairs department at Columbia.

Lovenheim testified that he read the *Shampoo* screenplay in 1970 and submitted it to Columbia's story department. Phillip Ansalone later testified that he was the Columbia "reader" who summarized Towne's screenplay in New York on August 7, 1970. Ansalone's summary of *Shampoo* was received into evidence. Bosley Crowther, a retired motion picture critic and Columbia consultant, indicated at trial that he read the *Shampoo* screenplay, and prepared a memorandum covering the manuscript for Columbia's president on October 6, 1970. Defendants stress that the submission of Towne's *Shampoo* screenplay and subsequent sequence of events all occurred long before the alleged submission of plaintiff's *Women Plus* in 1971. . . .

The analytical framework for the case at bar is shaped by the answers to two questions. . . . First, did Mann submit *Women Plus* to defendants for sale? The trial record shows no evidence, nor does plaintiff even allege, that her treatment was ever submitted to either defendant Beatty or defendant Towne. Mann alleges, however, that *Women Plus* was submitted to defendant Columbia through either Caplan or Crutcher. The alleged access of Towne and Beatty to the treatment is contingent upon its purported presence in Columbia's story files. Therefore, the asserted contractual obligation exists, if at all, only between Mann and Columbia. . . .

The existence of that contractual obligation is also dependent upon the answer to the second question. Did Columbia, knowing that *Women Plus* was offered to it for sale, accept and use that treatment, or any part thereof, in the motion picture *Shampoo?* Since there was no express agreement in this case, Mann must show Columbia's implied promise to pay for the alleged use of her ideas. . . .

For this court to find that Mann and Columbia entered an implied-in-fact contract, plaintiff must demonstrate that she clearly conditioned her offer of *Women Plus* upon an obligation to pay for it, or its ideas, if used by Columbia; and Columbia, knowing the condition before it knew the ideas, voluntarily accepted their disclosure (necessarily on the specified basis) and found them valuable and used them. (*Desny, supra*, 46 Cal.2d at p. 739.) Columbia's implied promise, if it is to be found, must be based on circumstances which were known to the studio at and preceding the time the ideas were allegedly disclosed to it. Columbia must have voluntarily accepted *Women Plus* with knowledge of the conditions of tender. (*Ibid.*; *Faris v. Enberg* [1979] 97 Cal.App.3d 309, 318 [158 Cal.Rptr. 704].)

In this case, Mann must prove Columbia's conduct from which defendant's promise may be implied. (*Weitzenkorn v. Lesser, supra*, 40 Cal.2d 778, 794.) The trial court properly instructed the jurors on Mann's burden, and the preceding prerequisites for finding an implied-in-fact contract.

The submission of *Women Plus* to Columbia is not only a requirement for the contractual obligation alleged herein, but it is also the basis for plaintiff's argument that defendants Beatty and Towne had access to her treatment. For purposes of this discussion, the court assumes that *Women Plus* remained enclosed in the envelope transferred from plaintiff to Florence Klase, Evelyn Light, and Harry Caplan. Caplan was a Filmmakers production manager when he received plaintiff's envelope from Light. Mann concedes that the submission of the envelope was not condi-

tioned on its delivery to Columbia. Caplan transferred the envelope to a colleague, Gary Crutcher, who was a story editor at Filmmakers. There is no substantial evidence in the trial record that either Caplan or Crutcher acted for Columbia in accepting Mann's submission. . . .

Mann stresses that the jury viewed the motion picture *Shampoo*. The jurors also examined plaintiff's chart comparison of several similarities between *Women Plus* and *Shampoo*. Mann also emphasizes the script changes made while filming *Shampoo*, and Columbia's willingness to review something Towne had read and offer comments before filming the motion picture. Plaintiff concludes that the foregoing is substantial evidence for the jury's determination that *Women Plus* was submitted to Columbia. Mann also asserts that the jury reasonably inferred the access of Towne and Beatty to her treatment, and their use of her ideas in filming *Shampoo*.

Similarity, access, and use present questions of fact for the jury. (*Kurlan v. Columbia Broadcasting System, supra*, 40 Cal.2d 799, 810.) One of the jury's functions in this action was to determine whether such similarity existed between *Shampoo* and *Women Plus* as to suggest defendants' use of ideas originating with plaintiff. (*Stanley v. Columbia Broadcasting System* [1950] 35 Cal.2d 653, 660 [221 P.2d 73, 23 A.L.R.2d 216].) . . .

The jury's determination of similarity between *Women Plus* and *Shampoo* was substantially supported by the jurors' examination of plaintiff's chart comparison and view of the motion picture. But any similarities between the two works in this case are without legal significance. The jury may have inferred defendants' access and use of *Women Plus* from its comparison with *Shampoo*. This inference, however, was rebutted by clear, positive and uncontradicted evidence. . . .

This court is not restricted to a consideration of Towne's 1970 screenplay as a representation of the motion picture *Shampoo*. (*Barbaria v. Independent Elevator Co.* [1956] 139 Cal.App.2d 474, 482 [285 P.2d 91].) Mann alleges that Towne and Beatty had access to *Women Plus* in Columbia's story department before they made changes in the "shooting script" for *Shampoo*. If the two defendants did not use her ideas in the "shooting script," the fact that the motion picture may strongly resemble *Women Plus* does not afford plaintiff a cause of action against Columbia for breach of an implied contract. . . .

The "independent effort" of Towne and Beatty in developing the *Shampoo* script provides Columbia with a complete defense against the contractual obligation alleged herein. . . . The defense is established in this case because the inference of access and use was rebutted. Since there was neither a submission of *Women Plus* to Columbia, nor any contact between the screenplay authors and the people alleged to have possessed plaintiff's treatment, there is no substantial evidence to support the jury verdict.

The action of the trial court in granting judgment notwithstanding the verdict was correct. . . .

For access, "[t]here must be a reasonable possibility of viewing plaintiff's work—not a bare possibility." (3 Nimmer on Copyright [1981] § 13.02 [A], p. 13-12.) We have already detailed the rebuttal of the access inference. And the foregoing possibilities of submission to Columbia are conjectural. Since plaintiff alleges this basis for the access of Towne and Beatty, the bare possibility of their viewing *Women Plus* is premised on mere speculation. This is insufficient proof of an essential element. *(Ibid.)*

Finally, "if the word 'substantial' means anything at all, it clearly implies that such evidence must be of ponderable legal significance. Obviously the word cannot be deemed synonymous with 'any' evidence. It must be reasonable in nature, credible, and of solid value; it must actually be 'substantial' proof of the essentials which the law requires in a particular case." . . . With the "ponderable legal significance" of the similarities between plaintiff's treatment and *Shampoo* removed from this case, rumination over *Women Plus* is but speculation on possibilities.

We have resolved the conflicting evidence in favor of Mann. Defendants rebutted the legitimate inference to which her evidence was entitled. Viewed in its most favorable light, plaintiff's evidence is legally insufficient to support a recovery. . . .

Blaustein v. Burton, 88 Cal. Rptr. 319 (Cal. App. 1970)

Appellant, in his deposition, testified that he had been in the motion picture business since 1935. After serving as a reader, a story editor, the head of a story department, and an editorial supervisor, he became a producer of motion picture films in 1949. The films he has produced include *Broken Arrow; Mr. 880; Half Angel; Just One More Chance; Take Care of My Little Girl; The Day the Earth Stood Still; The Outcasts of Poker Flat; Don't Bother to Knock; Desiree; The Racers; Storm Center; Cowboy; Bell, Book and Candle; The Wreck of the Mary Deare; Two Loves; The Four Horsemen of the Apocalypse;* and *Khartoum.* The functions of a producer of a motion picture are to (1) generate the enthusiasm of the various creative elements as well as to bring them together; (2) search out viable locations which would be proper for the artistic side of the production and would be proper from the logistic physical production side; (3) create a budget that would be acceptable from the physical point of view as well as satisfactory from the point of view of implementing the requirements of the script; (4) make arrangements with foreign government where the photography would take place; (5) supervise the execution of the script, the implementation of it onto film; (6) supervise the editing of all the production work down through the dubbing process and the release printing process, at least through the answer print process with Technicolor in this case; (7) the obligation of consulting with the United Artists people on advertising and publicity; (8) arrange casting; (9) engage the interests of the kind of star or stars that they (the United Artists' people) would find sufficiently attractive to justify an investment, and (10) develop the interest of a proper director.

During 1964, appellant conceived an idea consisting of a number of constituent elements including the following: (a) the idea of producing a motion picture based upon William Shakespeare's play *The Taming of the Shrew;* (b) the idea of casting respondents Richard Burton and Elizabeth Taylor Burton as the stars of this motion picture; (c) the idea of using as the director of the motion picture Franco Zeffirelli, a stage director, who at that time had never directed a motion picture and who was relatively unknown in the United States; (d) the idea of eliminating from the film version of the play the so-called "frame" (i.e., the play within a play device which Shakespeare employed), and beginning the film with the main body of the story; (e) the idea of including in the film version the two key scenes (i.e., the wedding scene and the wedding night scene) which in Shakespeare's play occur offstage and are merely described by a character on stage; (f) the idea of filming the picture in Italy, in the actual Italian settings described by Shakespeare.

On April 6, 1964, appellant met with Hugh French, an established motion picture agent who was then, and was at the time of the taking of the deposition (March 20, 1968), the agent for respondent Richard Burton. Prior to such meeting, appellant knew that Mr. French was Mr. Burton's agent and Mr. French knew that appellant was a motion picture producer, as appellant and Mr. French had been involved in business dealings together in the past. At such meeting, appellant first asked Mr. French "if he could tell me anything about the availability of Mr. and Mrs. Burton." Mr. French replied: "Well, they have many commitments; but, as you know, they are always interested in good ideas or good scripts or good projects." Appellant then replied: "Well, I have a thought about a picture for the Burtons, but it makes no sense to discuss it unless you would be interested in it or unless you tell me that they would be available to consider a production beyond their current commitments." Mr. French responded: "No, indeed, I would like to hear what you have in mind." Appellant then said that he thought there would be something uniquely attractive at that time to do a film based on Shakespeare's "Taming of the Shrew" with respondents as the stars of the picture. Mr. French's reaction was "instantaneous and affirmative." Appellant then asked Mr. French if the idea had ever been previously discussed, and Mr. French replied no, that to his knowledge it had not been. Mr. French further stated that he would discuss appellant's idea with Mr. Burton, and would try to arrange a meeting in New York between appellant and the Burtons.

Thereafter, at Mr. French's suggestion and with tickets arranged for by Mr. French, appellant attended the opening of Mr. Burton's stage production of *Hamlet* in New York City on April 9, 1964. At that time, Mr. French introduced appellant to Mr. Burton as "the man who had been talking about *Taming of the Shrew*." Because of Mr. Burton's preoccupation with his stage production, it was not possible at that time for appellant to have a private meeting with the Burtons, so appellant proceeded on to London, where he was engaged in production work on another motion picture.

Upon arriving in London, appellant decided to explore the possibility of using the services of Franco Zeffirelli as the director of *The Taming of the Shrew* motion picture. Accordingly, on May 11, 1964, appellant met with John Van Eyssen, Mr. Zeffirelli's agent, in London. Appellant related his idea to Mr. Van Eyssen, and his disclosure thereof to Mr. French. To appellant's inquiry as to the possible availability of Mr. Zeffirelli, Mr. Van Eyssen replied "that he thought it was just a splendid idea, that he was absolutely certain that his client would agree with his reaction, but that he would telephone him in France and discuss it with him as quickly as he could reach him. . . ." Thereafter, appellant, together with Mr. Van Eyssen, met with Mr. Zeffirelli in Paris on May 22, 1964. Appellant there related his idea in some detail to Mr. Zeffirelli, and Mr. Zeffirelli's response was: "I can't tell you how much I would like to do it, but why would the Burtons accept me?" Appellant replied ". . . that is my job, to generate their enthusiasm for you . . . [and] I think there is a very good chance of my persuading them to accept you."

On May 25, 1964, appellant, while still in London, telephoned to Mr. French in Los Angeles, suggested the idea of Mr. Zeffirelli acting as director of the proposed motion picture, told of the meeting with Zeffirelli, and suggested that this information be communicated to Mr. and Mrs. Burton. . . .

Upon his return to Los Angeles, appellant met with Martin Gang on June 25, 1964. Mr. Gang at that time was appellant's lawyer. Mr. Gang's firm was also the attorneys for respondents Richard Burton and Elizabeth Taylor Burton. Aaron

Frosch, a New York lawyer, acted as general counsel for Mr. and Mrs. Burton. At the meeting between appellant and Mr. Gang, appellant disclosed his above described idea, and related his dealings up to that point with Mr. French. Appellant told Mr. Gang that "Mr. French has so far been unable to arrange a meeting" with Mr. and Mrs. Burton. Mr. Gang offered to attempt to arrange such a meeting. Mr. Gang thereupon phoned Aaron Frosch and informed him of appellant's desire to meet with Mr. and Mrs. Burton and of the reasons for such a meeting. Mr. Frosch stated that he believed that he could arrange such a meeting, suggesting that appellant phone him upon appellant's arrival in New York.

Upon his arrival in New York, appellant phoned Mr. Frosch's secretary on June 29, 1964, and was told to contact Richard Hanley, appointments secretary for Mr. and Mrs. Burton. Appellant did phone Mr. Hanley, who recognized him and stated "It looks fine. Richard and Elizabeth know you are here and we will get it set up as quickly as we can." On the afternoon of June 30, 1964, Mr. Hanley phoned appellant and said: "Can you come up to see them?" Appellant proceeded to Mr. and Mrs. Burton's hotel suite, was introduced to Mr. Burton by Mr. Hanley, and then met for a period alone with Mr. Burton. Later, Mrs. Burton joined them. At the beginning of the conversation between appellant and Mr. Burton regarding *The Taming of the Shrew*, Mr. Burton commented upon what a good idea it was for Mrs. Burton and him to make such a motion picture, adding, "I don't know how come we hadn't thought of it."

After Mrs. Burton joined them, appellant explained in full his ideas regarding the proposed project. This included the use of Mr. Zeffirelli as the director. Mr. Burton said of Zeffirelli "I think he is a marvelous idea. The idea of who directs this picture is naturally very important, and I just think you have made a very good choice. And you have met with him?", to which appellant replied in the affirmative. They then discussed the cost of the film, and of appellant's prior discussion with Mr. Zeffirelli relative to the cost area. Mr. Burton stated "Well, certainly with you as an experienced producer, you can contribute that part of it to him."

There then was a discussion of possible conflicting commitments, and Mr. Burton stated with reference to another project, "Well, look, we are not actually committed to that, and I do believe that could be pushed back anyway. This idea is such a good one and this picture is so important that we do it that I think we should plan on doing it. And we can try to juggle our other productions to fit this." Toward the end of the meeting, Mr. Burton stated, "Well, let's plan to go ahead now. Elizabeth and I would like to do this. We think Zeffirelli is a good idea. We will accept him. You tell me you have worked out a potential deal with him." Appellant had discussed Mr. Zeffirelli's connection with the proposal with Mr. Van Eyssen. Mr. Burton instructed appellant to work out appropriate arrangements with Aaron Frosch. The meeting ended with a mutual expression of looking forward to working together.

After the above meeting, and before appellant left the United States, he called Martin Gang in California from New York City. In this telephone conversation, he told Mr. Gang "Look, you do whatever you think is right about structuring a deal with Aaron Frosch, and you know I am not going to be difficult about my end of this because this is a very important picture to me and I don't want you to feel that we have got to fight with anybody, whatever might come up, about any fees and my participation and so forth. It's a picture I want very badly to do, and please keep me in touch." Mr. Gang replied, "Congratulations. I will get onto it right away and keep you informed."

Upon appellant's return to London, where he was working on another motion picture, he met with Mr. Van Eyssen and proceeded further with the negotiation of a deal for the services of Mr. Zeffirelli as director. Appellant reported progress made in these negotiations in a letter dated July 7, 1964, which he sent to Martin Gang.

On August 11, 1964, appellant received a phone call in London from Mickey Rudin, who was then a partner in Mr. Gang's law firm. Mr. Rudin worked in close contact with Mr. Frosch in connection with *The Taming of the Shrew*. Mr. Rudin represented Mr. and Mrs. Burton in connection with *The Taming of the Shrew*, and as far as Mr. Gang knows, has continued to do so even after Mr. Rudin disassociated from the Gang firm. In the phone call of August 11, 1964, appellant asked Mr. Rudin what percentage share of the gross receipts from the motion picture *The Taming of the Shrew* appellant would receive if he were paid no guaranteed fee; what percentage share he would receive if he were paid a guaranteed fee of $50,000, and what percentage share he would receive if he were paid a guaranteed fee of $100,000. Mr. Rudin replied that he would think about it and let appellant know.

About November 27, 1964, appellant "felt that there was nothing to do but wait until the Burtons are in a position to and have an inclination to make a commitment."

On December 30, 1964, appellant met with Mr. Gang and Mr. Rudin in Mr. Gang's office in Los Angeles. At this meeting appellant learned that his position in the project was in jeopardy. At this time both Mr. Rudin and Mr. Gang advised appellant that he had no legal rights in the project, and appellant "simply accepted that."

In March 1965, a meeting was held in Dublin, Ireland, where Mr. Burton was filming another motion picture, attended by Mickey Rudin, among others. The meeting concerned *The Taming of the Shrew* project, including appellant's participation in connection therewith. Following this meeting, Mr. Rudin stopped off in London, en route back to Los Angeles, and on March 18, 1965, phoned appellant. In that phone conversation, Mr. Rudin stated to appellant that "[he] might not be the producer if the picture is ever made." Mr. Rudin further stated, "under any conditions, however, there would be a reward for your contribution to the project." On March 20, 1965, appellant addressed a letter to Messrs. Rudin and Gang in which he said in part: "There's no point rehashing the various elements involved; nor is there any point attempting to 'try the case,' particularly with my own attorney. I realize I must simply accept whatever Aaron Frosch and you agree is proper 'reward' for my contribution. But it's important to me, Mickey, that you understand I can never consider any such payment to be a satisfactory substitute for the function that has been denied me on a project I initiated." In conversations with Mr. Van Eyssen (face to face) and with Mr. Zeffirelli (via

telephone) on March 25, 1965, appellant was advised that the suggestion that appellant not be the producer of the film had come from "the other side" and from "the Burton lawyer." Appellant understood this reference to be directed toward Mr. Aaron Frosch and so advised both Mr. Zeffirelli and Messrs. Gang and Rudin.

Upon Mr. Rudin's return to Los Angeles, he reported events at the Dublin meeting to his then partner, Martin Gang. Mr. Gang wrote to appellant on April 27, 1965, stating that Mr. Rudin had reported to him that "there is no question in anybody's mind that this was your idea, of *Taming of the Shrew* and bringing Zeffirelli in was your idea, and this is so recognized by all the principals, including Mr. Burton and Mr. Zeffirelli."

In December 1965, appellant heard rumors of a "deal" being made for the production of *The Taming of the Shrew* involving the respondents and was informed by Mr. Gang that discussions to this effect were then taking place with Columbia Pictures Corporation. In a letter to Mr. Gang dated January 3, 1965, but, in fact, written and sent on January 3, 1966, appellant suggested the possibility of informing Columbia of his participation in the project, noting that "Burton has acknowledged the obligation involved," and stating, "I should imagine Columbia wouldn't hesitate to acknowledge Burton's (and Zeffirelli's) obligation to me as an obligation of the production—provided it's discussed at the proper time, which is during the negotiations of the entire deal." Mr. Gang's response to this suggestion was to advise appellant against contacting Columbia since by doing so "he might upset the possibility of any deal being made because Columbia wouldn't want to get involved in litigation, and that if he wanted to get any rewards out of it for any reason, without giving any legal opinions, that it would be best not to upset that apple cart." Appellant did not communicate with Columbia.

Thereafter, a motion picture based upon William Shakespeare's play *The Taming of the Shrew* was produced and exhibited commencing in or about March 1967. The motion picture stars respondents Richard Burton and Elizabeth Taylor Burton, and is directed by Franco Zeffirelli. The motion picture was financed and distributed by

Columbia Pictures Corporation, although at the time of taking Mr. Gang's deposition (March 26, 1968), the formal contract between Columbia and the respondents remained to be completed. Mr. Rudin has represented Mr. and Mrs. Burton in the negotiations with Columbia. The motion picture as completed utilizes the following ideas disclosed by appellant to respondents: (1) It is based upon the Shakespearean play *The Taming of the Shrew;* (2) it stars Elizabeth Taylor Burton and Richard Burton in the roles of Katherine and Petruchio, respectively; (3) the director is Franco Zeffirelli; (4) it eliminates the "frame," i.e., the play within a play device found in the original Shakespearean play, and begins with the main body of the story; and (5) it includes an enactment of the two key scenes previously referred to by appellant which in Shakespeare's play occur off-stage.

In addition, the film was photographed in Italy, although not in the actual locales in Italy described by Shakespeare.

Respondents have paid no monies to appellant, nor have they accorded him any screen or advertising credit.

Respondents, while not challenging the foregoing statement of facts, except to say that they do not acquiese in the claimed "characterizations" and "conclusions" contained therein, urge that critical facts have been omitted therefrom. These critical facts, according to respondents, as revealed by the record, are as follows: In connection with appellant's meeting on April 6, 1964, with Hugh French, motion picture agent for respondent Richard Burton, appellant, was, according to his own testimony, familiar with the function of an agent for an established star in the motion picture industry. Appellant was aware of the role usually played by an agent for an established star, which was to screen projects submitted to the star, in turn submitting them to the star for a determination of interest. If there is interest, the agent usually pursues it further on the star's behalf.

Appellant was aware that an agent for a major star cannot commit the star without the star's approval. This is the practice in very close to 100 percent of the cases and in that sense differs from other agencies. The "few cases" in which the star permits his agent to make commitments on his behalf "are very rare."

Appellant testified in his deposition that there is nothing unique about doing Shakespeare on the screen. It has been done many times. It has been done by leading stars of the calibre of Laurence Olivier. Respondent Richard Burton has himself previously appeared in a motion picture made of Shakespeare's *Hamlet*. Shakespearean productions in motion picture form have been made in the United States, with leading stars, and also in England, the Soviet Union and other countries of the World.

Appellant testified that there is nothing unique about the idea of making a motion picture entitled *The Taming of the Shrew*, based on Shakespeare's play of that title. Such has been done in the United States before the making of the film here in issue, and the earlier film featured in its leading roles (Petruchio and Katherine) stars who were then married to each other and who were perhaps the leading idols of the screen at the time, Mary Pickford and Douglas Fairbanks. The Pickford-Fairbanks film *The Taming of the Shrew* was done in the 1930's. The declaration of Norman B. Rudman filed in support of the motion disclosed that the earlier version of the film also (1) eliminated the "frame" (the play within a play device utilized by Shakespeare), and (2) depicted on screen the wedding night scenes which in the Shakespearean original occurs off-stage and are merely described by narration.

Appellant testified in his deposition that there was nothing unique or unusual about doing *The Taming of the Shrew* with two of the leading actors of the time, in the sense that it had been done once before, but "there was something unusual about the particular notion of doing it under other circumstances." There is nothing unique about a stage director of good repute coming directly from the stage to motion pictures and directing a major motion picture. Such has been done often in the past by such directors as Ruben Mamoulian, Josh Logan, Danny Mann, Orson Welles, Elia Kazan, and by Mike Nichols, who directed the film *Who's Afraid of Virginia Woolf,* which starred the respondents in its leading roles, as his first film production.

Appellant testified further in his deposition

that there is nothing unique about a non-American director directing English speaking actors in a film. Zeffirelli speaks quite good English, was distinguished for his directorial work in the field of opera and had done many stage productions in different languages in Italy, France and England. Zeffirelli was well known and distinguished as a director of at least one Shakespearean production, *Romeo and Juliet,* prior to his direction of the respondents in *The Taming of the Shrew.*

Appellant testified further, by way of deposition, that he asked Mr. French to communicate with the Burtons to ascertain whether or not they would be interested in doing *The Taming of the Shrew.* Appellant was interested in this from a business point of view so that he might have an interest in the film as a producer. One of appellant's objects was to negotiate a co-production or joint venture agreement with respondents under which he would be engaged as producer of the film under specific terms and conditions, and respondents would be committed to star in the film, their services to begin on a given start date. Appellant's company and respondents or their company would be co-venturers and co-owners of the film. The negotiations did not result in a co-production or joint venture agreement.

Appellant testified further, by way of deposition, that his interest in the possibility of using the services of Franco Zeffirelli as director of the motion picture was based upon Zeffirelli's potential in contributing to the commercial success of the picture to such extent that appellant could point out its commercial potential to a possible distributor whose prime interest would be commercialism. The key elements of the picture, so far as appellant was concerned, besides the play itself, were Mr. and Mrs. Burton to play the leads. In appellant's letter of July 11, 1964, addressed to Mr. Martin Gang, his attorney, he stated that if Mr. Zeffirelli were not available as director of the film, respondent Burton might himself direct the film; the only requirement was that there be a top-flight director.

In appellant's first meeting with John Van Eyssen, Zeffirelli's agent, which occurred in London on May 11, 1964, he told Van Eyssen that interest in the project had been expressed by the Burtons' agent, and by the Burtons through their agent,

but that nothing had been done beyond that and that appellant had not yet met with the Burtons personally to discuss the subject. Appellant urged Mr. Van Eyssen to discuss the matter with Zeffirelli, but did not enjoin the former from discussing it with others as such an injunction is implicit in any discussion with an agent. Before meeting the Burtons, appellant had possibly discussed the matter of the picture informally with one David Chasman of United Artists.

When Mr. Gang, at appellant's request, telephoned Aaron Frosch on June 25, 1964, to assist appellant in obtaining an audience with the Burtons, Mr. Frosch had already known about the proposal of the Burtons doing a film *The Taming of the Shrew* because of appellant's approach to Mr. Zeffirelli, who was also a client of Mr. Frosch's office.

Appellant, since the meeting with respondents of June 30, 1964, has not seen them personally nor had any conversations with them. He has no written contract in connection with the proposed project signed by respondents, or either of them, or any agent of the respondents wherein he was promised the position of producer of the film *The Taming of the Shrew. . . .*

The rights of an idea discloser to recover damages from an idea recipient under an express or implied contract to pay for the idea in event the idea recipient uses such idea after disclosure is discussed in *Desny v. Wilder*, 46 Cal.2d 715, 731-739 [299 P.2d 257]. . . .

It is held that ". . . if a producer obligates himself to pay for the disclosure of an idea, whether it is for protectible or unprotectible material, in return for a disclosure thereof he should be compelled to hold to his promise. There is nothing unreasonable in the assumption that a producer would obligate himself to pay for the disclosure of an idea which he would otherwise be legally free to use, but which in fact, he would be unable to use but for the disclosure.

"The producer and the writer should be free to make any contract they desire to make with reference to the buying of the ideas of the writer; the fact that the producer may later determine, with a little thinking, that he could have had the same ideas and could thereby have saved considerable money for himself, is no defense against the claim of the writer. This is so even though the material to be purchased is abstract and unprotected material." (*Chandler v. Roach*, 156 Cal.App.2d 435, 441-442 [319 P.2d 776].)

An idea which can be the subject matter of a contract need not be novel or concrete. (*Donahue v. Ziv Television Programs, Inc.*, 245 Cal.App.2d 593, 600 [54 Cal.Rptr. 130]; *Minniear v. Tors*, 266 Cal.App.2d 495, 502 [72 Cal.Rptr. 287].)

It may be noted here that the law of the State of New York no longer requires that an idea be "novel" in order to be the subject of contract protection. As stated in *Frederick Chusid & Co. v. Marshall Leeman & Co.* (S.D.N.Y. 1968) 279 F. Supp. 913. 917: "Under New York law the parties have the right by contract to prevent disclosure of such materials, even though they are not secret or confidential and may indeed be a matter of public knowledge." The court in *Krisel v. Duran* (S.D.N.Y. 1966) 258 F. Supp. 845, 860 stated: "Under New York law, an idea, if valuable, even though it does not contain novel, secret or confidential material, may be protected by such an agreement. This doctrine applies even when the subject matter of the idea is common or open to public knowledge."

We are of the opinion that appellant's idea of the filming of Shakespeare's play *The Taming of the Shrew* is one which may be protected by contract.

Express or implied contracts both are based upon the intention of the parties and are distinguishable only in the manifestation of assent. . . .

The making of an agreement may be inferred by proof of conduct as well as by proof of the use of words. . . . Whether or not the appellant and respondents here, by their oral declarations and conduct, as shown by the depositions and affidavits, entered into a contract whereby respondents agreed to compensate appellant in the event respondents used appellant's idea, is a question of fact which may not be properly resolved in a summary judgment proceeding, but must be resolved upon a trial of the issue. . . .

Statute of Frauds. Respondents urge that the agreement is barred by the statute of frauds, section 1624 subdivision 1 of the Civil Code.

The application of section 1624 subdivision 1 of the Civil Code to the transaction here under consideration rests upon a triable issue of fact. The trier of fact might conclude that from the negotiations and conduct of the parties and their agents there was an implied contract. That is, the respondents may be found to have made an implied promise of payment, conditioned upon subsequent use, in return for appellant's act of disclosing his idea—not in return for his promise to disclose such idea. This being a unilateral contract (a promise for an act—see Rest., Contracts, § § 12 and 55), it does not fall within the section of the statute of frauds dealing with contracts not to be performed within one year. (Rest., Contracts, § 198, com. a.) If the trial court should find that appellant disclosed his idea to respondents on the condition that respondents would not use the idea unless they compensated appellant for such use, and respondents accepted the disclosure on that condition, then the compensation would, at respondents' option, take one of two forms: they would engage appellant as producer of the film or pay him the monetary equivalent. Since it appears from the record that appellant has made his disclosure and respondents have elected not to engage him as producer of the film, all that remains to be done is payment by respondents. Where a contract has been fully performed by one party and nothing remains to be done except the payment of money by the other party, the statute of frauds is inapplicable. . . . Furthermore, to fall under the bar of subdivision 1 of section 1624 of the Civil Code, the contract must, by its terms, be impossible of performance within a year. If it is unlikely that it will be so performed, or the period of performance is indefinite, the statute does not apply. . . .

Confidential Relationship. Respondents urge that the record is devoid of any evidence tending to establish the fact that they breached a duty of confidence owed to appellant.

Appellant, in his affidavit, stated: "Because I knew Mr. French to be a highly reputable agent, had had prior dealings with him, had the same firm of attorneys as the Burtons and had been the recipient of an invitation, constantly renewed, to disclose my ideas and render services on the project, I reposed trust and confidence in the Burtons and their representatives and expected that my ideas would be kept in confidence by them. I did not expect or intend that defendants would go forward with production of *Shrew* and make use of my ideas without my participation."

Under the rules governing the granting of a summary judgment, the foregoing declaration on the part of appellant, made in opposition to the motion for summary judgment, is sufficient to raise a triable issue of fact as to whether the disclosure of his idea to respondents was made in confidence, and was accepted by respondents upon the understanding that they would not use it without the consent of appellant. . . .

The judgment is reversed.

Mel Hardman Productions, Inc. v. Robinson, 604 P.2d 913 9 (Utah 1979)

CROCKETT, CHIEF JUSTICE

. . . On July 24, 1973, Robinson and Productions entered into a Production Agreement whereby Robinson was to produce a "photoplay" sufficient to produce a feature-length motion picture about one "Grizzly Adams," a historical character who was known for his friendliness and association with wild animals. Under the agreement, Robinson was to produce a photoplay "to the sole satisfaction" of Productions "sufficient to produce a motion picture of not less than ninety (90) minutes in duration, filmed on location in the wilds, tentatively entitled *Grizzly Adams* based on and pursuant to a final story and script to be submitted" by Robinson, and with him playing the main character.

As payment therefor, Robinson was to receive $150,000 in four installments, plus a percentage of Productions' gross receipts from the sale, distribution, or other disposition of the photoplay or Productions' rights therein. The amount he was to receive was subject to deductions provided for in a distribution agreement between Productions and Pictures, and any costs incurred in the distribution, sale, or other disposition of the photoplay not otherwise to be deducted under that agreement.

Robinson began filming in mid-August 1973 and delivered about 20 hours of film to Productions by October 31, 1973. One month later, after it had paid Robinson the $150,000, Productions hired one John Mahon to assemble a preliminary

film from the footage that had been submitted by Robinson. After Productions reviewed the film, they allegedly notified Robinson that the result was not satisfactory; and advanced him another $35,000 to complete the motion picture. The position of plaintiffs is that defendant still failed to deliver a satisfactory motion picture; and in April 1974, this action was initiated for the money it had paid him and for claimed loss of profits because of his alleged breach of the agreement.

On June 10, 1974, Productions employed one Charles Sellier "to salvage the Grizzly Adams project." He reviewed the film that Robinson had submitted and he states that it was his opinion that, due to the deficiencies in the film and Robinson's lack of cooperation, it could not be used; and that he proceeded to produce a different motion picture entitled *The Life and Times of Grizzly Adams*, which contained none of the actual film which had been produced by Robinson. This Sellier version of the story was released in November 1974, and is conceded to be a financial success. It was subsequently distributed to theaters throughout the United States and foreign countries, and shown on television. It was also the basis for a weekly television series which ran for over two years. In July of 1975, Robinson filed his counterclaim for percentages of the proceeds plaintiffs had realized from the distribution of that film. Following extensive discovery procedures and after numerous pre-trial motions and conferences, the case came to trial on January 8, 1979.

The position essayed by Productions and Pictures, both in the trial court and on appeal, is that the intent of the term "photoplay," as used in the agreement, was restricted to the specific motion picture on film (with sound and voice recording) actually produced by Robinson, and to the satisfaction of Productions. Whereas the position taken by the defendant is that the meaning intended was more general, including the aggregate of the name, the general concept of the story, and the literary and work product, which he fashioned into the Grizzly Adams story, all of which he delivered to the plaintiffs and which they made use of.

We note our agreement with the thought that it is simply not consistent with principles of justice and fair dealing for one party to impose upon another a requirement that something be done to his satisfaction and then arbitrarily withhold his approval. Equity and good conscience require that he act in good faith, and prevent him from stubbornly refusing to acknowledge satisfaction without some reasonable justification for doing so.

In the course of the trial, the jury heard and saw all of the evidence relating to those issues. This included the viewing of the Sellier version, which was distributed, and a three-hour edited version of the film which Robinson had produced and delivered to the plaintiffs.

The jury was given proper instructions as to the issues involved and the case was submitted to them on special interrogatories. Instruction No. 18 was:

> This case will be submitted to you in the form of a *set of questions* to answer *which will resolve the factual issues in this case*. After you have resolved the factual questions, the court will determine how your factual determinations apply to the legal issues involved here.

As has been stated above, the jury answered the interrogatories generally favorable to the defendant, and this included this pivotal question: "Did productions or its agent distribute Robinson's photoplay as that term is used in the contract?" to which the jury answered "Yes."

After the jury had returned its answers to the interrogatories, the trial court gave further consideration to the plaintiff's motion for directed verdict and decided to grant it. In doing so, he stated:

> . . . In order for the court to determine whether or not the finding as to the distribution of the "photoplay" can stand the court has to ascertain whether or not the Agreement . . . clearly defines the term. Robinson is only entitled to deferred compensation *if his photoplay was distributed* and box office receipts obtained therefrom. . . .
> Paragraph 6 of the Agreement is the only one that attempts to define "photoplay" and it says that it "shall be *deemed to include,* [emphasis added by the trial court] but not limited to, a motion picture production consisting of 16mm Ektrachrome professional color reversal stock film complete to the post-production stage produced and/or exhibited with or accompanied by sound and voice recording.

. . ." This court concludes and holds that *since neither Productions nor Pictures ever distributed any of the film produced by Robinson,* he is not entitled to any residuals nor deferred compensation.

No matter what other parts of the agreement may include items that may be included in the term "photoplay" this definition requires that *part of it must be the celluloid motion picture.* . . . In so holding this court is fully aware of the rule that this court should accept the jury verdict if there is any evidence to support it. [Citing cases.]

It will be seen that, in so ruling, the trial court decided to disregard the findings of the jury and to rule in favor of the plaintiff on the issues in dispute as a matter of law. It is our opinion that the court erred in concluding that defendant Robinson could not recover merely because plaintiffs did not use any of the actual film produced by him.

The agreement provides that the term photoplay "shall be deemed to include, *but not limited to,* a motion picture production consisting of . . ." film complete to the post-production stage. . . ." The definition of "photoplay" contained in the contract is an illustrative, but not an all-inclusive one. From a consideration of the circumstances surrounding this contract, and the conduct of the parties with respect thereto, it would not be unreasonable to conclude that the term "photoplay" is not necessarily limited to the actual film produced by Robinson.

The question as to what was intended by the term "photoplay" and whether Productions or Pictures distributed Robinson's photoplay as that term was intended to mean in the contract, was a question which the trial court had originally considered as a question of fact, and submitted to the jury for determination. In that regard, this Court has heretofore stated:

> It is to be conceded that ordinarily the interpretation of the terms of a document is a question of law for the court, but this is not necessarily true in all situations. Where, as here, it is made to appear that the terms may have a particularized application or meaning and there is room for uncertainty or disagreement . . . it was proper for the trial court to regard this dispute as an issue of fact.

There are numerous parts of the record which are consistent with and support the court's initial treatment of the issue as being one of fact. In a minute entry dated July 1, 1977, in denying Production's motion for summary judgment against Robinson on his counterclaim, the trial court stated:

> The court finds that *there is ambiguity in the term "Photoplay"* in that the definition states it includes, "but is not limited to" the 16mm film. *This dispute permeates the whole transaction and leaves large issues of fact to be resolved.* . . .

As we have numerous times indicated, the right of trial by jury is one which should be carefully safeguarded by the courts, and when a party had demanded such a trial, he is entitled to have the benefit of the jury's findings on issues of fact; and it is not the trial court's prerogative to disregard or nullify them by making findings of his own. Therefore, in ruling on motions which take issues of fact from the jury (this includes both motions for directed verdict and for judgment notwithstanding the verdict), the trial court is obliged to look at the evidence and all reasonable inferences that fairly may be drawn therefrom in the light favorable to the party moved against; and the granting of such a motion is justified only if, in so viewing the evidence, there is no substantial basis therein which would support a verdict in his favor. On appeal, in considering the trial court's granting of such motions, we look at the evidence in the same manner.

In further accord with what has been said above, and the conclusion we have reached, is the statement the trial court made to counsel after the jury had been discharged: that he thought the jury had examined the case very carefully. Moreover, in his judgment on the special verdict, the court recited that the jury "was most cooperative during the course of the trial and by reason of the questions submitted and requests made of the court during deliberations was one of the most conscientious juries this court has observed."

On the basis of our discussion herein, it is our conclusion that the trial court was correct in his previously expressed views as to the disputed issues; and also that the evidence justified submitting those disputed issues to the jury. Accordingly, the findings of the jury entitling the defendant to recover on his counterclaim should be reinstated.

In view of our conclusion just stated, the question as to damages to be assessed becomes pertinent. On that subject we make these observations: the parties submitted different calculations as to the amounts of damages. When the matter of damages is in dispute, it is an issue upon which the parties are entitled to a jury trial, the same as on other disputed issues of fact. Consistent with what has been said herein, the case is remanded for a determination as to the damages to be awarded on the defendant's counterclaim. Costs to defendant (appellant).

6.30   Breach of the Producer-Artist Contract

In various contexts, we have discussed the consequences of breach, whether it be the company seeking to enjoin the defecting performer (see, for example, Sections 1.50 to 1.54) or the wrongfully discharged performer seeking both lost earnings and consequential damages from the breaching company (see Section 1.60). Our considerations here go one step further. A film company decides to pull the plug on a film after it has contracted with a well-known movie actress to star in the film. The actress seeks only lost earnings, but these are considerable. The company responds that she must act in another movie of its choosing and cannot simply take a vacation while collecting her promised salary.

The central legal issues revolve around the traditional contract concepts of mitigation of damages, now explored in a motion picture setting. In mitigation, there are two general inquiries: (1) if the nonbreaching party does in fact accept alternative employment, whether amounts earned under the other contract are taken in mitigation of the damages owed that party; and (2) assuming the nonbreaching party did not in fact accept alternative employment, whether he or she will have damages reduced to the extent that other employment was available and should have been accepted.

Beyond the question of mitigation of damages, the majority and dissenting opinions in *Parker v. Twentieth Century-Fox Film Corporation* present differing views on the essence of the actor's art. The majority assumes that all pictures are different and that an actor cannot be required to transfer one's talents from one role to another; the dissent has much greater doubts about this and feels that it is at least a triable issue.

Parker v. Twentieth Century-Fox Film Corporation, 3 Cal.3d 176, 474 P.2d 689 (1970)

BURKE, J.

Defendant Twentieth Century-Fox Film Corporation appeals from a summary judgment granting to plaintiff the recovery of agreed compensation under a written contract for her services as an actress in a motion picture. As will appear, we have concluded that the trial court correctly ruled in plaintiff's favor and that the judgment should be affirmed.

Plaintiff is well known as an actress, and in the contract between plaintiff and defendant is sometimes referred to as the "Artist." Under the contract, dated August 6, 1965, plaintiff was to play the female lead in defendant's contemplated production of a motion picture entitled *Bloomer Girl*. The contract provided that defendant would pay plaintiff a minimum "guaranteed compensation" of $53,571.42 per week for 14 weeks commencing May 23, 1966, for a total of $750,000. Prior to May 1966 defendant decided not to produce the picture and by a letter dated April 4, 1966, it notified plaintiff of that decision and that it would not "comply with our obligations to you under" the written contract.

By the same letter and with the professed purpose "to avoid any damage to you," defendant instead offered to employ plaintiff as the leading actress in another film tentatively entitled *Big Country, Big Man* (hereinafter, *Big Country*). The compensation offered was identical, as were 31 of the 34 numbered provisions or articles of the original contract. Unlike *Bloomer Girl*, however, which was to have been a musical production, *Big Country* was a dramatic "western type" movie. *Bloomer Girl* was to have been filmed in California; *Big Country* was to be produced in Australia. Also, certain terms in the proffered contract varied from those of the original. Plaintiff was given one week within which to accept; she did not and the offer lapsed. Plaintiff then commenced this action seeking recovery of the agreed guaranteed compensation.

The complaint sets forth two causes of action. The first is for money due under the contract; the second, based upon the same allegations as the first, is for damages resulting from defendant's breach of contract. . . .

The general rule is that the measure of recovery by a wrongfully discharged employee is the amount of salary agreed upon for the period of service, less the amount which the employer affirmatively proves the employee has earned or with reasonable effort might have earned from other employment. . . . However, before projected earnings from other employment opportunities not sought or accepted by the discharged employee can be applied in mitigation, the employer must show that the other employment was comparable, or substantially similar, to that of which the employee has been deprived; the employee's rejection of or failure to seek other available employment of a different or inferior kind may not be resorted to in order to mitigate damages. . . .

In the present case defendant has raised no issue of *reasonableness of efforts* by plaintiff to obtain other employment; the sole issue is whether plaintiff's refusal of defendant's substitute offer of *Big Country* may be used in mitigation. Nor, if the *Big Country* offer was of employment different or inferior when compared with the original *Bloomer Girl* employment, is there an issue as to whether or not plaintiff acted reasonably in refusing the substitute offer. Despite defendant's arguments to the contrary, no case cited or which our research has discovered holds or suggests that reasonableness is an element of a wrongfully discharged employee's option to reject, or fail to seek, different or inferior employment lest the possible earnings therefrom be charged against him in mitigation of damages.

Applying the foregoing rules to the record in the present case, with all intendments in favor of the party opposing the summary judgment motion—here, defendant—it is clear that the trial court correctly ruled that plaintiff's failure to accept defendant's tendered substitute employment could not be applied in mitigation of damages because the offer of the *Big Country* lead was of employment both different and inferior, and that no factual dispute was presented on that issue. The mere circumstance that *Bloomer Girl* was to be a musical review calling upon plaintiff's talents as a dancer as well as an actress, and was to be produced in the City of Los Angeles, whereas *Big Country* was a straight dramatic role in a "Western Type" story taking place in an opal mine in Australia, demonstrates the difference in kind between the two employments; the female lead as a dramatic actress in a western style motion picture can by no stretch of imagination be considered the equivalent of or substantially similar to the lead in a song-and-dance production.

Additionally, the substitute *Big Country* offer proposed to eliminate or impair the director and screenplay approvals accorded to plaintiff under the original *Bloomer Girl* contract . . . and thus constituted an offer of inferior employment. No expertise or judicial notice is required in order to hold that the deprivation or infringement of an employee's rights held under an original employment contract converts the available "other employment" relied upon by the employer to mitigate damages, into inferior employment which the employee need not seek or accept. . . .

SULLIVAN, ACTING C.J., DISSENTING
The basic question in this case is whether or not plaintiff acted reasonably in rejecting defendant's offer of alternate employment. The answer depends upon whether that offer (starring in *Big Country, Big Man*) was an offer of work that was substantially similar to her former employment (starring in *Bloomer Girl*) or of work that was of a different or inferior kind. To my mind this is a factual issue which the trial court should not have determined on a motion for summary judgment. The majority have not only repeated this error but have compounded it by applying the rules governing mitigation of damages in the employer-employee context in a misleading fashion. Accordingly, I respectfully dissent. . . .

Over the years the courts have employed various phrases to define the type of employment which the employee, upon his wrongful discharge, is under an obligation to accept. Thus in California alone it has been held that he must accept employment which is "substantially similar." . . .

For reasons which are unexplained, the majority . . . select from among the various judicial formulations which they contain one particular phrase, "Not of a different or inferior kind," with which to analyze this case. I have discovered no historical or theoretical reason to adopt this phrase, which is simply a negative restatement of the affirmative standards set out in the above cases, as the exclusive standard. Indeed, its emergence is an example of the dubious phenomenon of the law responding not to rational judicial choice or changing social conditions, but to unrecognized changes in the language of opinions or legal treatises. However, the phrase is a serviceable one and my concern is not with its use as the standard but rather with what I consider its distortion.

The relevant language excuses acceptance only of employment which is of a *different kind*. . . . It has never been the law that the mere existence of *difference between two jobs in the same field* is sufficient, as a matter of law, to excuse an employee wrongfully discharged from one from accepting the other in order to mitigate damages. Such an approach would effectively eliminate any obligation of an employee to attempt to minimize damage arising from a wrongful discharge. The only alternative job offer an employee would be required to accept would be an offer of his former job by his former employer.

Although the majority appear to hold that there was a difference "in kind" between the employment offered plaintiff in *Bloomer Girl* and that offered in *Big Country* . . ., an examination of the opinion makes crystal clear that the majority merely point out differences between the two *films* (an obvious circumstance) and then apodically assert that these constitute a difference in the *kind of employment*. The entire rationale of the majority boils down to this: that the *"mere circumstances"* that *Bloomer Girl* was to be a musical review while *Big Country* was a straight drama "demonstrates the difference in kind" since a female lead in a western is not "the equivalent of or substantially similar to" a lead in a musical. This is merely attempting to prove the proposition by repeating it. It shows that the vehicles for the display of the star's talents are different but it does not prove that her employment as a star in such vehicles is of necessity different *in kind* and either inferior or superior.

I believe that the approach taken by the majority (a superficial listing of differences with no attempt to assess their significance) may subvert a valuable legal doctrine. The inquiry in cases such as this should not be whether differences between the two jobs exist (there will always be differences) but whether the differences which are present are substantial enough to constitute differences in the *kind* of employment or, alternatively, whether they render the substitute work employment of an *inferior kind*.

It seems to me that *this* inquiry involves, in the instant case at least, factual determinations which are improper on a motion for summary judgment. Resolving whether or not one job is substantially similar to another or whether, on the other hand, it is of a different or inferior kind, will often (as here) require a critical appraisal of the similarities and differences between them in light of the importance of these differences to the employee. This necessitates a weighing of the evidence, and it is precisely this undertaking which is forbidden on summary judgment. . . .

It is not intuitively obvious, to me at least, that the leading female role in a dramatic motion picture is a radically different endeavor from the leading female role in a musical comedy film. Nor is it plain to me that the rather qualified rights of director and screenplay approval contained in the first contract are highly significant matters either in the entertainment industry in general or to this plaintiff in particular. Certainly, none of the declarations introduced by plaintiff in support of her motion shed any light on these issues. Nor do they attempt to explain why she declined the offer of starring in *Big Country, Big Man*. Nevertheless, the trial court granted the motion, declaring that these approval rights were "critical" and that their elimination altered "the essential nature of the employment."

The plaintiff's declarations were of no assistance to the trial court in its effort to justify reaching this conclusion on summary judgment. Instead, it was forced to rely on judicial notice of the definitions of "motion picture," "screenplay" and "director" (Evid. Code, § 451, subd. [e]) and then on judicial notice of practices in the film industry which were purportedly of "common knowledge." (Evid. Code, § 451, subd. [f] or § 452, subd. [g].) This use of judicial notice was error. Evidence Code section 451, subdivision (e) was never intended to authorize resort to the dictionary to solve essentially factual questions which do not turn upon conventional linguistic usage. More important, however, the trial court's notice of "facts commonly known" violated Evidence Code section 455, subdivision (a). Before this section was enacted there were no procedural safeguards affording litigants an opportunity to be heard as to the propriety of taking judicial notice of a matter or as to the tenor of the matter to be noticed. . . .

The majority do not confront the trial court's misuse of judicial notice. They avoid this issue through the expedient of declaring that neither judicial notice nor expert opinion (such as that contained in the declarations in opposition to the motion) is necessary to reach the trial court's conclusion. *Something*, however, clearly *is* needed to support this conclusion. Nevertheless, the majority make no effort to justify the judgment through an examination of the plaintiff's declarations. Ignoring the obvious insufficiency of these declarations, the majority announce that "the deprivation or infringement of an employee's rights held under an original employment contract" changes the alternate employment offered or available into employment of an inferior kind. . . .

I remain convinced that the relevant question

in such cases is whether or not a particular contract provision is so significant that its omission creates employment of an inferior kind. This question is, of course, intimately bound up in what I consider the ultimate issue: whether or not the employee acted reasonably. This will generally involve a factual inquiry to ascertain the importance of the particular contract term and a process of weighing the absence of that term against the countervailing advantages of the alternate employment. In the typical case, this will mean that summary judgment must be withheld. . . .

6.40   Screen Credit and Creative Control

One recurring theme in the motion picture industry is that creative talent strives for full credit and control over the product as finally presented. We discussed the matter of proper credit attribution in *Follett* (see Section 2.30) and control over one's work in *Chesler* (see Section 2.40). Several cases discussed these issues in connection with performing musicians (see, for example, Section 5.40). The issue arises in Chapter 7 on what television editing can do to a work (see *Preminger* and *Gilliam*, Section 7.30). Regardless of the specific type of entertainment business, the problems of credit and control are constantly an issue.

In the motion picture industry, many of the screenplays that make their way into film are written pursuant to the Writers' Guild of America contracts, under which disputes concerning writer credit are decided by arbitration. Even so, many pictures are still made on a nonunion basis. As to these disputes that result in litigation, the cases that follow are instructive on the handling of such disputes.

Whether the dispute is arbitrated or litigated, an injunction restraining the showing of a film because it gives improper credit is rarely granted, as is discussed below in *Poe v. Michael Todd Company*. When a film has cost several million dollars to produce and several million more to print, promote, and advertise, the financial imbalance of investment versus credit becomes manifest. Dispute resolution therefore seeks another solution. In the *Smith* case which follows, the court attempts to measure damages. On occasion, one will also note full-page ads in the *Hollywood Reporter* and *Daily Variety*, the "trades" of the film and television industries, acknowledging the contributions by writers and producers to various films. These are generally the outgrowth of arbitration proceedings or litigation, in which the ad is ordered as a partial remedy. While these may be second-best to actual credit on the film, they are a compromise fashioned to assuage in part the hurt feelings that led to the legal proceedings.

Paramount Pictures, Inc. v. Smith, 91 F.2d 863 (9th Cir. 1937)

HANEY, J.

. . . The complaint alleged that in 1934 appellant completed the production and thereafter exhibited generally throughout the United States a "talking motion picture" under the title of *We're Not Dressing*, which "was based upon, and adapted from, said original story of plaintiff herein, entitled *Cruise to Nowhere* . . ."; that appellant violated the eighth provision of the contract quoted, in that appellant "wholly failed to announce upon said films, or at any of the public exhibitions thereof, that the same was either written by plaintiff, or that it was based upon, or adapted from, a story written by" appellee. Appellant admitted production and exhibition of the picture *We're Not Dressing*, but denied the remainder of these allegations.

At the trial appellee introduced into evidence over appellant's objections a sheet showing production cost prepared by appellant's accounting department. This sheet contained the following:

Production No. 983.
Title *We're Not Dressing*.
From Story *Cruise to Nowhere*.

The objection was "upon the ground that no proper foundation is laid to show that anyone connected with the accounting or auditing department, or that department itself, had anything to do with selecting either the title for a given picture, or determining whether a given picture should be based upon or adapted from a given story or not."

Appellee also offered in evidence an item released by the publicity department of appellant dated September 7, 1933, which contained the following statement: "*We're Not Dressing* is an original story by Walton Hall Smith." Appellee also offered in evidence a similar item dated December 13, 1933, which stated in part:

> Francis Martin . . . today was assigned to write the screen adaptation of *We're Not Dressing* to be produced soon. . . .

> Others working on the story, an original by Walton Hall Smith called *A Cruise to Nowhere*, are . . .

Objection was made to both items on grounds identical with those urged against the admission of the production cost sheet, and counsel also stated: ". . . There is no foundation whereby the corporation may be bound, because, in order for the evidentiary matter to be an admission properly received as such, it must be made by one within the scope of his authority, and it must pertain to authority which he has."

The objections were overruled.

The trial court gave the following instruction to the jury: "Now, gentlemen, upon the evidence that the court has discussed a moment or so ago, upon the testimony as to earnings and the testimony as to failure on the part of the plaintiff to minimize the damages, there is an experience table of mortality that is applicable, and that may be used because in cases of this kind it is necessary to utilize the instruments that are possible or capable of utilization. One of these is that the experience table of mortality may be used if the jury concludes that it is proper to use it in the particular case; and under the American Experience Table of Mortality the expectant age of the defendant, under the stipulation that he is now 37 years of age, is 30.35 years. So that if you reach this question of damages you have the right to consider that together with all of the other elements that have been included in all of the instructions that have been heretofore given or that will be hereafter given in this case."

Upon the issues, the jury found in favor of appellee in the sum of $7,500. Judgment was entered on the verdict, from which judgment this appeal was taken.

Appellant contends that it was incumbent on appellee to prove that the accounting department and the publicity department were authorized to determine whether or not the picture produced was based upon or adapted from appellee's story. Appellant urges that, "in order to be binding upon the principal, admissions must be made by an agent while acting within the scope of his authority and must relate to matters to which that authority extends." . . .

At the time the cost sheet was offered, there was no evidence as to the origin of the sheet, nor its content. There was proof that it was taken from the files of appellant, and produced by it. There was no proof, at the time it was offered, that it was made by or on behalf of any department. So far as the record shows, it might have been made by or on behalf of the board of directors, or by or on behalf of the production department, which appellant admits had authority to make such an admission. In other words, at the time the cost sheet was offered, the proof showed it was made for the corporation. If one agent or officer made it, it would have been made within his authority; if another agent or officer made it, it would not have been made within his authority.

There seems to be good ground for an exception to the rule mentioned. For example, suppose a prospectus is issued by a large corporation, which contains simply the corporate name at the end thereof, and in which an admission is made. If the rule mentioned is extended, then the person offering the prospectus would have to first prove who made the prospectus, before he could prove such person's authority. It is difficult to see how the party could prove such identity, short of questioning each officer, agent, and employee. Many corporations employ thousands of people. Such a rule would be impractical. Logic would compel admission as evidence of the admission so made, and, if the identity of the person who made the admission is thereafter proven, then the authority of the person should be proven, or the admission, on motion, stricken.

However, assuming without deciding, that the rule relied upon by appellant is applicable here, then we believe the error did not affect the substantial rights of appellant. 28 U.S.C.A. § 391.

Appellant also contends that the cost sheet had no evidentiary value because the later evidence showed "that it was the practice of the accounting department to charge a story to a production when it had been bought for it, or for a specified star, whether the story was actually used or not. . . ." In the first place, this contention relates to the weight of the evidence and not to the admissibility thereof. In the second place, when such fact was proven, there was no renewal of the objection or a motion to strike. Therefore, no ruling of the trial court exists for review.

With respect to the publicity items it should be noted that both of them were issued before filming, and before the screen adaptation was written. We believe the error, if any, was cured by the repeated instructions of the trial court that the finished picture must have been based upon or adapted from appellee's story, since it was apparent to the jury that appellant may have changed its program. . . .

With reference to the instruction hereinabove set forth, appellant says that mortality tables are inadmissible as evidence in such a case as this. . . .

We believe the error, if any, did not affect the substantial rights of the parties, but was a technical error. 28 U.S.C.A. § 391. The mortality table was not introduced into evidence. The court, judicially noting the table, simply instructed the jury to consider it with all the other evidence "if the jury concludes that it is proper to use it in the particular case."

Appellant says that the primary question is whether or not the picture was based upon or adapted from appellee's story. That statement is only partially true. Our function is to ascertain whether or not there is any substantial evidence to sustain the verdict. Specifically, the question presented is whether or not there is any substantial evidence to sustain the finding of the jury that

the picture *We're Not Dressing* was based upon or adapted from appellee's story, *Cruise to Nowhere*.

An examination of the record discloses that the evidence was conflicting. Three of appellant's witnesses defined and distinguished between "based upon" and "adapted from." There was evidence showing that the picture produced was not based upon or adapted from appellee's story. We are not interested in such evidence, however, but only in the evidence of the opposite fact.

The cost sheet hereinabove discussed is some evidence of the fact found by the jury. Correspondence between officers of appellant had some months before filming was started indicates that appellant may have used the story. Appellee introduced a manuscript of his story into evidence, and read it to the jury. During the trial, the court and its attendants, the jury, appellee, and counsel for the parties saw a showing of the picture. The jury was able to make a comparison. Afterward, appellee testified, "I saw in the picture much of the plot which I originally had in mind; much of the basic idea." We believe this is sufficient to warrant submission of the issue to the jury, and, since the jury believed it, the verdict is supported thereby.

Finally, appellant urges that there is a lack of evidence to support the award of damages, in that there was no standard by which damages could be gauged. Appellee contends that the true rule on uncertainty of damages is that the prohibition is directed against uncertainty as to cause, rather than uncertainty as to measure or extent.

We do not believe the evidence is subject to the charge of uncertainty. Appellee testified that he and another writer collaborated in writing a story and sold it without screen credit for $10,000, which the two writers divided. Appellee's story was sold for $2,500, but under a contract that required that he be given screen credit. From these figures, the jury might easily compute the advertising value of the screen credit. He also testified that he received screen credit for a play; that prior thereto his salary was $250 per week; and that afterward he received $350 per week at one time, and $500 per week for a period of two weeks, due to the screen credit he had received. That evidence is, if believed, likewise sufficient as a gauge for the measure of the damages.

Finding no error affecting the substantial rights of appellant, the judgment is affirmed.

WILBUR, J., DISSENTING

I dissent. With reference to the question as to whether or not there was substantial evidence that the film play produced by the defendant was based upon a story written by the plaintiff entitled *Cruise to Nowhere* and purchased by the defendant for the purpose of screen production, I am unable to agree with the conclusion of my associates. In the first place, statements contained in the books of the corporation showing that the cost of the story purchased from the plaintiff was charged against the film play produced by the defendant was clearly admissible as a declaration against interest. The same is true with reference to the press release indicating that the defendant produced a screen play based upon plaintiff's story. These admissions might be sufficiently substantial to sustain the verdict were it not for the fact that other evidence supplements and explains these admissions and deprives them of any weight. Beyond question, the defendant purchased the plaintiff's story for film reproduction and went to work to adapt it for screen reproduction. The admissions above referred to were made during the preliminary stages of screen adaptation. But the evidence shows that it was later decided that plaintiff's story was not suitable for the type of production desired at that time, and that several screen writers were employed to write the scenario for reproduction. Later, when the play was produced, they were given credit for this work, and the plaintiff was not given the credit to which he deemed himself entitled under his contract with the defendant. That the story produced was vastly different from that purchased is clear from a comparison of the two stories. It follows that the admissions of the defendant made at the time when it was the intention to use plaintiff's story became valueless in determining whether or not they did in fact use his story. I conclude, therefore, that the admissions of the defendant that the produced story *We're Not Dressing* was based upon plaintiff's story *Cruise to Nowhere* are without proba

tive value in determining whether or not the plaintiff was entitled to screen credit. . . .

If we assume there has been a breach of contract, there is no evidence of loss or damage proximately resulting therefrom. The evidence leaves the damages to be determined by the jury by guess and speculation. The burden is upon the plaintiff to establish, not only the breach of the contract, but the damages, if any, proximately resulting therefrom, and, unless he has shown such damage, he is not entitled to recover. It is clear that the contract for screen credit is in effect a contract to advertise the fact that the plaintiff was the author of the story reproduced on the screen. It seems clear that the damages he seeks in this action and the damages awarded are speculative in the absence of some proof as to special damages resulting from the breach of the contract. . . .

The plaintiff's contention is that, if his reputation had been enhanced by the advertisement that he had produced the story upon which the screen play was based, it would have been an advantage to him in securing other contracts of a similar nature and upon that hypothesis introduced evidence as to a past contract in which he had sold a story for less with screen credit than he had received for another story without screen credit. In the main opinion it is suggested that this evidence is not only pertinent to the inquiry but is a proper basis for determining damage. While it is manifest that favorable publicity of any kind in connection with the production of a screen play would be valuable to one seeking to sell a story or play, it is clear it would be impossible to measure the value of one story by the amount paid for an entirely different story even though the author is the same. There is no basis for comparison, and to permit the jury to determine the value of one play with or without screen credit by evidence of the value of another and entirely dissimilar play would evidently require the jury to enter the domain of speculation. The same thing may be said concerning the evidence referred to in the main opinion concerning the salary received by the plaintiff before and after he had obtained screen credit. There is no evidence that the increase in salary was due to the fact that screen credit had been given on a previous play. I think this evidence was too remote and speculative and should not have been received and that the conclusion of the jury . . . was based upon speculation and guess and not upon evidence. . . .

The defendant also complains of an instruction by which the court informed the jury of the life expectancy of the plaintiff and instructed the jury that if in their judgment this life expectancy was relevant they should consider it in arriving at their verdict. Such an instruction might be considered harmless in some cases because a jury is presumed to know, that is, to take judicial notice of, the life expectancy of an individual, and, it may be assumed, will apply this knowledge to any problem submitted to it where it is deemed by the jury to be germane to the solution. But the life expectancy of the plaintiff had no relation to the problem presented to this jury. They were to award such damages as the plaintiff had suffered up to the time of trial, or reasonably certain to result in the future. The court seemed to be of the impression that the failure to advertise the plaintiff in accordance with the terms of the contract may have permanently decreased his earning power and that such decreased earning power might be considered in arriving at a verdict. This was a direct invitation to the jury to speculate on the future possibilities of the defendant's earning capacity and upon the question of whether or not it would be affected by the defendant's breach of the contract. There was and could be no proof that he was permanently injured. As a matter of fact the evidence shows that the plaintiff abandoned his efforts in the moving picture line and withdrew from the field and devoted his time to writing a novel. Although he testified that he intended at some time to return to Hollywood for the purpose of engaging as an author in the moving picture industry, the testimony as to his change of occupation increases the speculative character of the jury's verdict based upon hypothetical losses due to a failure to secure contracts in the moving picture industry.

Poe v. Michael Todd Company, Inc., 151 F. Supp. 801 (S.D.N.Y. 1957)

[The writer sought to enjoin the exhibition of *Around the World in 80 Days* because only S. J.

Perelman had been accorded screen credit. Poe claimed that the screenplay had been based on his script, and that under industry custom and usage he was entitled to screen credit. Todd admitted that Poe had been engaged to write the screenplay but contended that very little of what he wrote made it to the screen. Poe, on the other hand, claimed that Perelman's work had consisted essentially of revisions to the original screenplay.

There was apparently no affirmative commitment by Todd (the agreement with Poe was oral) for screen credit by Poe, who rested his claim solely on custom and usage. In addition, Todd contended there was no inherent right to screen credit, under industry custom or otherwise. Moreover, although Poe had submitted the matter to the WGA for arbitration (with a resultant award of credit to Poe, Perelman, and John Farrow), Todd was not a WGA signatory and did not participate in the arbitration proceedings.

Given the numerous points of controversy, the court denied Poe's motion, pointing out that an injunction would "alter rather than preserve the status quo and yield to [Poe] the full measure of relief which normally he would be entitled to after a trial on the merits" if he prevailed. The court was also influenced by the fact that Poe had been aware of the situation for three months before he moved for injunctive relief. The court did, however, order a prompt trial, stating that "[n]ot only would money damages be difficult to establish, but at best they would hardly compensate for the real injury done. A writer's reputation, which would be greatly enhanced by public credit for authorship of an outstanding picture, is his stock in trade; it is clear that irreparable injury would follow the failure to give him screen credit if in fact he is entitled to it."]

NOTE ⎯⎯⎯⎯⎯⎯⎯⎯⎯⎯⎯⎯⎯⎯⎯⎯⎯

1. An agreement between a major motion picture studio and a director may provide the following language with respect to ending and the "director's cut":

> Provided that Employee is not in default in the performance and observance of all of his obligations hereunder and, provided further, that Employee shall be entitled to receive credit as Director pursuant to the provisions of the Directors' Guild of America, Inc. (Agreement of 1973), the

Employee shall be entitled to make the first cut, also known as the "Director's Cut," of the Photoplay and to two (2) public previews of the composite print of the Photoplay, subject to the following:

(a) the Photoplay shall have a running time at standard projection speed of 90 feet per minute, of not less than ninety (90) minutes;

(b) Employee shall deliver the Director's Cut of the theatrical version of the Photoplay to Employer on or before eight weeks following completion of principal photography of the Photoplay;

(c) the television version of the Photoplay shall be completed and delivered by Employee to Employer within 30 days following the delivery of the final answer print of the theatrical version of the Photoplay.

The term "television version of the Photoplay," as used herein, means a complete version, not less than 9,000 feet in length nor more than 11,880 feet in length, in which there is contained all or any part of the alternate scenes and/or dialogue and/or eliminations which are required to render the Photoplay acceptable under now existing United States television network continuity standards (the "network standards"). Director shall photograph or cause the photography of the final approved screenplay for the Photoplay in such a manner that any scenes containing total or partial nudity, excessive or undue violence, or any other visual material or language which, in Employer's sole judgment, might render the Photoplay unacceptable under the network standards, will be covered by such alternate scenes and/or dialogue and/or eliminations (herein collectively called the "cover shots") as are necessary to render the television version of the Photoplay acceptable, in Employer's judgment, under the network standards. Director shall fully and scrupulously comply with such instructions as Employer may give to Director regarding the cover shots to be so made.

Subject to Employee's right to make the Director's Cut, Employer shall have the sole and exclusive right to determine the final cut of all versions of the Photoplay, without any restriction whatsoever.

Chapter 7

TELEVISION

7.00 Developments in the Industry

Television has changed radically since 1970. At that time, CBS was the unquestioned king of the hill and had been the ratings and advertising revenue champion for many years, with NBC second and ABC an extremely distant third. Network TV was overwhelmingly predominant; the three networks accounted for about 90 percent of the viewing audience and produced most of their own programs.

Then the FCC adopted the "financial interest and syndication" rules, essentially prohibiting the networks from owning a substantial portion of prime-time entertainment programming and preventing them from engaging in the increasingly lucrative business of licensing to local stations programming that had run its course on the networks. In addition to the major motion picture studios, a host of independent producers sprang up to fill the programming void, such as Spelling-Goldberg (a major factor in the process by which ABC captured the number one spot during the mid- to late-1970s—a position which was in turn occupied by NBC for the first time in the mid-1980s), MTM ("Hill Street Blues," "St. Elsewhere," "Remington

Steele"), and Lorimar (creators of "Dallas," "Falcon Crest," and other hit series, and recently merged with syndication giant Tele-pictures).

The studios and the independents delivered half-hour, hour, and multiple-hour programming to the networks essentially at cost (or less) in the hope of reaping huge returns from the increasingly important syndication market. Each of the three networks has approximately 200 affiliated local stations, and there are about 200 independent local stations (including, in addition to small-town outlets, such important major-city outlets as superstations WTBS-Atlanta, WGN-Chicago, and WOR-TV New York, as well as Los Angeles stations KTLA and KTTV). A Commerce Department statement recently indicated that the combined advertising revenue of these 800 stations was approximately $4.3 billion per annum, and a 1986 survey by McCann-Erickson, a leading advertising agency, predicted 1986 network ad revenues of $8.6 billion.

To achieve maximum success in the syndication market, it is necessary for a producer to accumulate at least 80 to 90 episodes (three to four years' worth) so that local stations can run them five days per week. As a show's network run continues, cast salaries escalate, production values are enhanced to freshen the show's appeal, and the show tends to run an even larger deficit. Unless the show does well in syndication (or, worse, if it fails to run long enough to be attractive in syndication), the producer may face financial ruin.

Until the mid-1970s, however, the system (such as it was) remained relatively stable. Two events changed the situation dramatically: HBO and home video.

Originally laughed at when it was launched on a small scale in Eastern Long Island ("Who's going to pay to see movies when they can see them free on the networks?"), HBO grew enormously for many years. Although growth has slowed, HBO and its sister service Cinemax account for approximately 18 million subscriber homes (about two-thirds of the total, the major competitor being Showtime/The Movie Channel). In addition to draining audiences away from the networks, HBO and its competitors' aggressive bidding for theatrical films has priced some films out of the network market.

Off to a somewhat shaky start in the early years, home video has come on with a rush, to the point that a report in *Variety's* February 26, 1986, issue predicted that 40 percent of the films viewed in 1986 would be viewed on videocassette recorders (indicating a negative impact on movie theatres as well as TV).

Another threat—pay-per-view—fizzled after initial success but now seems to be poised to make a major comeback due to improvements in scrambling devices. Services such as ON-TV and SelecTV sprouted in many cities, only to dwindle (and in some cases disappear), as cable operators with multiple-channel offerings proliferated. For a while, direct broadcast satellite ("DBS")

was touted as the primary carrier of the future, but did not develop into a major activity. Recently, however, Rupert Murdoch's "Sky Channel" has reached a wide audience in Europe, HBO is distributing unscrambling devices to backyard dish owners, and DBS seems to be making a new run. Indeed there are so many owners of backyard satellite dishes that legislation has been introduced in Congress, which, if enacted, would restrict the ability of broadcasters to scramble their signals.

Meanwhile, the networks and Hollywood have been battling in Washington over whether the "financial interest and syndication" rules should be retained. Indeed, there are already chinks in the armor: ABC owns and produces the highly successful "Moonlighting," while NBC, which owned and produced the long-running hit "Little House on the Prairie," is currently the owner-producer of "Punky Brewster" and is expected to continue to produce episodes for "first-run syndication" after its anticipated demise on the network. This issue is an important one for the networks. They are under increasing pressure from the producers to raise network license fees. For example, MCA, parent of Universal pictures, threatened to move production of the smash hit series "Miami Vice" from Miami to Hollywood if NBC did not increase the license fee—approximately $950,000 per episode for two network plays, while production costs were running in the neighborhood of $1,500,000 per episode. MCA also announced that it was re-editing the hour-long "Knight Rider" into half-hour segments because of softness in the syndication market for hour-long programming. (Half-hour is still king in the syndication market: *Variety* recently reported that a syndicator had achieved renewal syndication sales for one popular sitcom of $85 million—on top of the $150 million achieved from the initial syndication of this series. On the other hand, an esteemed hour-long show such as "Lou Grant" has not done well in syndication.) The networks, faced with a long-term shrinkage of audience and the resulting prospect of reduced advertising revenues, are understandably resistant to this pressure.

Another threat faces the networks in so-called "first run syndication." Shows such as "Fame" and "Too Close for Comfort," after being dropped by the networks, have continued to run through direct syndication to local television stations. Other shows, such as all-time local TV ratings champion "Wheel of Fortune," are created specifically for this market. "Operation Prime Time" has put together a number of star-studded mini-series for local stations, and the April 9, 1986, issue of *Variety* announced the formation of "Alternative Network Television," aimed at forming an ad hoc fourth network to obtain theatrical films for local TV before they are shown on cable or network. After acquiring Twentieth Century-Fox, newspaper giant Rupert Murdoch inaugurated a fourth network built around the nucleus of his recently acquired TV stations (six major market stations—in New York, Los Angeles, Chicago, Washington, Dallas, and Houston—covering 22 percent of the nation's TV households, with a proposed seventh station to be added in Boston). The programming is largely to be supplied by the production facilities of Fox Films. In October 1986, the newly reorganized "Fox Broadcasting Company" went on-line, with Joan Rivers hosting a late-night talk show to compete with NBC's "Tonight Show Starring Johnny Carson," and FBC declared its intention to spend more than $100 million to expand the new network among the local independent stations.

The face of TV is ever-changing, and not just in the United States. Despite opposition from state-owned RAI, Italian TV entrepreneur Silvio Berlusconi has succeeded in stitching together a highly successful commercial network in Italy. He also joined with French entrepreneur Jerome Seydoux to form La Cinq, a new French network, which promptly encountered opposition from the French government. Pan-European groups are creating programming for their own use and perhaps for sale to the U.S. and Canada.

The many problems of television, and its ever-changing nature, are examined in both this chapter and in Chapter 8.

7.10 Idea Sources and Submissions

Discussed in Chapter 6 was substantial litigation based on quasi-contractual and implied-in-fact contractual claims that authors' materials are used without compensation in the production of theatrical films. This is equally true in television, as demonstrated by the following cases. *De Costa* is not strictly quasi-contractual, since the plaintiff there claimed an outright misappropriation, but the issues can be considered on quasi-contractual grounds as well. *Faris* and *Whitfield* demonstrate again the analysis required in idea-submission cases.

Columbia Broadcasting System, Inc. v. DeCosta, 377 F.2d 315 (1st Cir. 1967)

COFFIN, J.

This is an appeal by defendants from jury verdicts in the total amount of $150,000 awarded plaintiff on his claim that he created, and the defendants misappropriated, the character of Paladin, the protagonist of the CBS television series entitled "Have Gun Will Travel."

The story of this case—more bizarre than most television serial installments—is one of "coincidence" run riot. The plaintiff, of Portuguese parents, is a Rhode Island mechanic whose formal education ceased after the fourth grade. During the Depression, having tired of factory work, he hopped a freight for the West, lived in hobo jungles, and eventually became a range hand on a Texas ranch. After two years of riding and roping he returned to Rhode Island to work as a mechanic and later received training as a motor machinist in the Coast Guard. But he retained his passion for all things western. In 1947 he began to participate in rodeos, horse shows, horse auctions, and parades.

From the beginning plaintiff indulged a penchant for costume. He was already equipped with a moustache. He soon settled on a black shirt, black pants, and a flat-crowned black hat. He had acquired a St. Mary's medal at a parade and affixed this to his hat. He adopted the name Paladin after an onlooker of Italian descent had hurled an epithet at him containing the word "Paladino." On looking up the word Paladin in a dictionary he found it meant "champion of Knights" and was content that people began so to call him. One day when he had donned his costume in preparation for a horse show, and was about to mount his horse, one of a group waiting for him shouted "Have Gun Will Travel," a cry immediately picked up by the children present.

The finishing touches were a chess knight, bought for fifteen cents at an auction, which plaintiff thought was a good symbol, and which he used on a business card along with the words "Have," "Gun," "Will," "Travel," and "Wire Paladin, N. Court St., Cranston, R.I.," hand-printed with separate rubber stamps; a silver copy of the chess piece on his holster; and an antique derringer strapped under his arm. So accoutered, he would appear in parades, the openings and finales of rodeos, auctions, horse shows, and a pony ring he once operated. From time to time at rodeos he would stage a western gunfight, featuring his quick draw and the timely use of his hidden derringer. He would pass out photographs of himself and cards—printed versions soon replacing the rubber-stamped ones. Hospitals, drug stores, barber shops, sports shops, diners—all were the repositories of his cards, some 250,000 of them. Children clamored for the cards, and clustered about him to the extent that he was likened to the Pied Piper and Gene Autry. This was perhaps one of the purest promotions ever staged, for plaintiff did not seek anything but the entertainment of others. He sold no product, services, or institution, charged no fees, and exploited only himself.

Ten years after he had begun to live his avocational role of Paladin, he and his friends saw the first CBS television production of "Have Gun Will Travel," starring moustachioed Richard Boone, who played the part of an elegant knight errant of the Old West, always on the side of Good—for a fee. The television Paladin also wore a black costume, a flat-crowned black hat bearing an oval silver decoration, and a silver chess knight on his holster, and announced himself with a card featuring a chess piece virtually—if not absolutely—identical with the plaintiff's and the words HAVE GUN WILL TRAVEL, WIRE PALADIN, SAN FRANCISCO." The series was notably successful; it appeared in 225 first-run episodes in the United States, was licensed in foreign countries, and by the time of trial had grossed in excess of fourteen million dollars.

The writers and network executives responsible for the series testified in detail that the television Paladin was a spontaneous creation, developed in total ignorance of the attributes of his Rhode Island predecessor. The writers, Herb Meadow and Sam Rolfe, testified that the germ of the idea was the title, "Have Gun Will Travel," which Meadow had evolved from mulling over a familiar theatrical advertising phrase, "Have tux, will travel." The character was originally conceived as a denizen of contemporary New York, but was changed to a western hero because the network hoped to cast Randolph Scott in the role. The name "Paladin" resulted from a thesaurus search for words meaning "knight" or "hero" or "champion." The chess piece symbol was inspired by Meadow's observation, while teaching his son the game, that the knight's movements were uniquely erratic and unpredictable. In the pilot script for the series, Paladin used a hidden derringer because it was a convenient way to extricate him from the obligatory dangerous situation.

The show's original producer, Julian Claman, testified that after Randolph Scott and other "fairly well known" actors were found to be unavailable he selected Richard Boone to be tested for the role of Paladin. Boone appeared for the test with a moustache, for reasons unknown, and was outfitted in a black suit because it was the only available costume that fitted. The hat, bearing a silver "conche," was selected by Claman because it looked appropriate. The card, which had been described in Meadow and Rolfe's original prospectus, was realized by the CBS art department from a rough sketch by Claman. The "shocking similarity" to DeCosta's cards was pure coincidence. Boone's test was successful, and Claman, reluctant to change any element of a winning combination, decided to keep card, costume, and moustache intact for the pilot film. He also decided to add the silver chess knight to Paladin's holster because it produced a distinct article that would be marketable if the series succeeded.

Meadow, Rolfe, Claman, and the other witnesses for the defendants all testified that they had never seen DeCosta or any of his cards. The jury obviously disbelieved at least this much of their testimony, and we think it clear that they were amply justified. Thus, the plaintiff has had the satisfaction of proving the defendants pirates. But we are drawn to conclude that that proof alone is not enough to entitle him to a share of the plunder. Our Paladin is not the first creator to see the fruits of his creation harvested by another, without effective remedy; and although his case is undeniably hard, to affirm the judgments below would, we think, allow a hard case to make some intolerably bad law.

In the first place, it is by no means clear that such state law of intellectual property as we have found supports relief on these facts. Several cases have been cited around the general proposition that it is an actionable wrong to appropriate and exploit the product of another's creative effort; but all seem to involve distinguishable wrongs of at least equal or even superior significance. Most rest on the tort of "passing off": appropriation not of the creation but of the value attached to it by public association (the so-called "secondary meaning"), by misleading the public into thinking that the defendant's offering is the product of the plaintiff's established skill. E.g., *Lone Ranger, Inc. v. Cox*, 4 Cir., 1942, 124 F.2d 650; *Chaplin v. Amador*, 1928, 93 Cal.App. 358, 269 P. 544. Others add an element of injury to reputation caused by a poor imitation. E.g., *Lahr v. Adell Chem. Co.*, 1 Cir., 1962, 300 F.2d 256. And at least one combined both of these with an element of injury to a valuable contract to assert "the

broader principle that property rights of commercial value are to be and will be protected from any form of unfair invasion or infringement and from any form of commercial immorality. . . ." *Metropolitan Opera Ass'n v. Wagner-Nichols Recorder Corp.*, Sup.Ct. 1950, 199 Misc. 786, 793, 101 N.Y.S.2d 483, 492. . . . The jury was instructed that the plaintiff would be entitled to the verdict if he established:

> First. That he conceived and created said idea and character of "Paladin, Have Gun Will Travel"; and that said idea and character was novel, original, and unique; and that he did not at any time abandon said idea and character by a publication thereof.
>
> Second. That the defendants . . . did copy said idea and character without the permission of the plaintiff and used them in the television series, "Have Gun Will Travel."
>
> And third. That the plaintiff sustained damages as a result of such copying and use of said idea and character. . . .

Thus, the judgment can only be supported on a rule of law that would allow recovery upon proof of creation by the plaintiff and copying by the defendants, and nothing else. We do not find such a rule in the cases cited above.

Moreover, the leading case affording a remedy for mere copying, *International News Serv. v. Associated Press*, 1918, 248 U.S. 215, 39 S.Ct. 68, 63 L.Ed. 211, is no longer authoritative for at least two reasons: it was decided as a matter of general federal law before the decision in *Erie R. R. v. Tompkins*, 1938, 304 U.S. 64, 58 S.Ct. 817, 82 L.Ed. 1188; and, as it prohibited the copying of published written matter that had not been copyrighted (indeed, as news it could not be copyrighted, 248 U.S. at 234, 39 S.Ct. 68, 63 L.Ed. 211), it has clearly been overruled by the Supreme Court's recent decisions in *Sears, Roebuck & Co. v. Stiffel Co.*, 1964, 376 U.S. 225, 84 S.Ct. 784, 11 L.Ed.2d 661, and *Compco Corp. v. Day-Brite Lighting, Inc.*, 1964, 376 U.S. 234, 84 S.Ct. 779, 11 L.Ed.2d 669. While this normally would not prevent the state court from adopting the reasoning of *INS* in fashioning a rule of state law, we think it important to consider the scope of state power in this area in view of *Sears* and *Compco*.

It is true that *Sears* and *Compco* both deal with copying of articles covered by invalid design patents. But the opinions refer throughout to both copyright and patent; and in *Compco* the Court took pains to articulate the broad scope of its decisions:

> Today we have held . . . that when an article is unprotected by a patent or a copyright, state law may not forbid others to copy that article. To forbid copying would interfere with the federal policy, found in Art. I, § 8, cl. 8, of the Constitution and in the implementing federal statutes, of allowing free access to copy whatever the federal patent and copyright laws leave in the public domain. 376 U.S. at 237, 84 S.Ct. at 782.

More fully, that policy is to encourage intellectual creation by offering the creator a monopoly in return for the disclosure and eventual surrender of his creation to the public.

Does the language in *Compco,* "whatever the federal patent and copyright laws leave in the public domain," refer to creations that Congress has deliberately chosen not to protect or more broadly to those it has simply not protected, whether by choice or by chance? In the case of patents the two questions are coterminous, for Congress has deliberately chosen not to protect inventions lacking the element of originality, and an invention is thus either patentable or unprotectible. In the case of "writings" there is no such universal test of qualification. But Congress has established a procedural scheme of protection by notice and registration. The necessary implication of this approach, we conclude, is that, absent compliance with the scheme, the federal policy favoring free dissemination of intellectual creations prevails. Thus, if a "writing" is within the scope of the constitutional clause, and Congress has not protected it, whether deliberately or by unexplained omission, it can be freely copied. . . .

The compelling reasons for this rule are well stated in Judge Learned Hand's prophetic dissent in *Capitol Records, Inc. v. Mercury Records Corp.,* 2 Cir., 1955, 211 F.2d 657, 664–667, where he referred to (1) the anomaly of allowing a creator to acquire a perpetual monopoly of his work under state law when he cannot obtain the limited right of exploitation under federal law, and (2) the impossibility of affording effective

protection against copying except by a uniform national law. . . .

To this plaintiff gives two answers. He argues that a character is not copyrightable—by which we must understand that it is not within the scope of Congress's power under the copyright clause— and that in any event a creation in the form of a public performance is protectible as an unpublished work under 17 U.S.C. § 2. For the first proposition the authority cited is *Warner Bros. Pictures, Inc. v. Columbia Broadcasting Sys.,* 9 Cir., 1954, 216 F.2d 945, which held that the assignee of the copyright of the novel *The Maltese Falcon* could not prevent the author from using the character Sam Spade in a sequel. But that case is inapposite, because it held only (a) that the contract of assignment did not convey the exclusive right to use the characters in the novel, and (b) that the sequel, *The Kandy Tooth,* was not so similar as to infringe the copyright. That is far from saying that characters are inherently uncopyrightable.

A more substantial argument for this first proposition is that the plaintiff's creation is not a "writing" in the sense used in the copyright clause (or, what is the same thing, that it is not an "article" in the sense used in *Sears* and *Compco*). There is no question that the term is to be interpreted more broadly than its common meaning would indicate. . . . But it has been argued that it should be limited to mean some identifiable, durable, material form. Nimmer, Copyright Publication, 56 Colum.L.Rev. 185, 196 n. 98 (1956). And it is argued here that the plaintiff's creation, being a personal characterization, was not reduced and could not be reduced to such a form.

To this argument there are several answers. First, while more precise limitations on "writings" might be convenient in connection with a statutory scheme of registration and notice, we see no reason why Congress's power is so limited. Second, we cannot say that it would be impracticable to incorporate into the copyright system a procedure for registering "characters" by filing pictorial and narrative description in an identifiable, durable, and material form. Finally, however, there comes a point where what is created is so slight a thing as not to warrant protection by any law. All human beings—and a good part of the animal kingdom—create characters every day of their lives. Individuals often go beyond the realm of unconscious creation and devise characterizations for their own and others' amusement. Many a starred performer has so begun, and continued to grow on the borrowings from others. At some point his innate talent and eclectic poaching may enable him to attract a following, and ultimately to secure the law's protection against imitators. At what point short of this there should be additional protection we do not say. But in view of the federal policy of encouraging intellectual creation by granting a limited monopoly at best, we think it sensible to say that the constitutional clause extends to any concrete, describable manifestation of intellectual creation; and to the extent that a creation may be ineffable, we think it ineligible for protection against copying *simpliciter* under either state or federal law.

For the second proposition, that the plaintiff's creation is an unpublished work protected under 17 U.S.C. § 2, the leading authority is *Ferris v. Frohman*, 1912, 223 U.S. 424, 32 S.Ct. 263, 56 L.Ed. 492, which held that the public performance of a play did not constitute publication in the sense of an abandonment to public use. But in that case the Court specifically noted that the play involved had not been "printed and published"; that is, no copies of the script had been distributed publicly.

Here, plaintiff's "performance" consisted of two components: appearing in public and passing out cards and photographs. No other "action" was involved, except an occasional "quick draw" demonstration at a rodeo. So far as his costume and menacing appearance were concerned, it was fully conveyed on the cards bearing his photograph—which also contained the chess piece, the slogan, and the name "Paladin." The cards were passed out in great quantities over the years to all who would have them. So far as any action accompanying his personal appearance is concerned, whether it be simply riding a horse, or staging a quick-draw gun fight, these are hallowed shelf items in the tradition of the early West. In any event, the theme and plots of defendants' television series could not be said to have derived from anything created by plaintiff which was not revealed by his cards.

The cards were unquestionably "writings" within the meaning of the copyright clause, and arguably were copyrightable under the statute. See 17 U.S.C. §§ 1, 5(g), 5(k). . . . The consequence is that the plaintiff's character-creation was published, even under the doctrine of *Ferris*, and that this case falls squarely under the rule of *Sears* and *Compco*. Not having copyrighted the cards, the plaintiff cannot preclude others from copying them. We accordingly reverse.

NOTE _____

1. For later developments in the lengthy *DeCosta* litigation, see *DeCosta v. Columbia Broadcasting System, Inc.*, 520 F.2d 315 (1st Cir. 1975).

_____

Faris v. Enberg, 158 Cal.Rptr. 704 (Cal.App. 1979)

ROTHMAN, J.

The developer of an idea for a television sports quiz show (Edgar C. Faris) sued a television sports announcer (Richard Enberg) and others in two separate actions for appropriating his idea and producing a sports quiz show based upon it. This appeal follows the granting of defendants' motion for summary judgment in the trial court. We affirm the judgment. . . .

Faris conceived a sports quiz show idea in 1964, and prepared and registered a format of the idea. A few days before June 4, 1970, Faris called KTLA studios and told a secretary that he had created a sports television show that would interest Mr. Enberg. He left his name and number. The next day Enberg telephoned Faris, who told Enberg that he ". . . had a sports oriented TV show that I intended to produce and that *I desired to talk to him about participating in the show as the master of ceremonies.*" (Italics added.) Enberg was interested and asked when they could meet, and the next day was agreed upon. They met at KTLA studios. Enberg was late and apologized. Faris told Enberg the format of the show and gave Enberg a copy, which Enberg read through at the meeting, and again expressed interest. Enberg asked for a copy, and Faris said it was his "creation" and "literary property." "I discussed with Mr. Enberg his prospects as to both being an MC for the show or, if he desired, actually participating with me in the production of the show and could participate then as a part owner thereof. At all times I discussed my show and Mr. Enberg's participation as a business proposal or offer to Mr. Enberg and I mentioned to him that, if he came with me, we would both make money on the show." Enberg told Faris he was going to talk the next week with some KTLA producers about a sports show. He asked Faris to leave a copy of the format for further review. Faris made these additional statements in his declaration (although the declaration does not say that he told Enberg any of them); that he did not authorize Enberg to discuss the format with anyone or to give it to anyone else; that had Enberg told Faris he planned to show the format to anyone else or discuss the format with anyone else, Faris would not have left a copy with Enberg, and that had Enberg told Faris of his commitment with another sports quiz show, Faris would not have discussed the show with him or let Enberg read or have the format, and would not have "proposed a contractual relationship with him involving either his participation as an owner or acting as MC for my Sports Panel Quiz. . . ."

Also attached to the response to the motion for summary judgment were portions of Enberg's deposition wherein he testified that he may have revealed to the people that ultimately produced the "Sports Challenge" quiz show, that he had been contacted by someone about a sports quiz show.

From defendants' motion for summary judgment, these facts were excerpted from Faris' deposition. In December of 1969 Faris saw Enberg on television. Faris was thinking about his quiz show idea and thought: "It was just a question of getting the right person to do the show. Enberg impressed me. He was articulate, he was very, I thought, fine announcer, and this brought to mind—I said, that man, in my mind, suited the role of the MC for this show, . . . [¶] [S]o my idea was to go to Mr. Enberg with this format in an attempt to go with me on it." He had considered

many other sports personalities for master of ceremonies, and decided on Enberg. He told Enberg at the meeting that "if you will come with me and do the show, you can have a piece of the show. You can own it. You won't have to work for a salary for somebody else."

At some time following this meeting, the "Sports Challenge" show appeared on television with Enberg as master of ceremonies, and produced by defendant Gross. There were certain differences and similarities between the show and plaintiff's idea. Although Gross claimed the production of the show was well under way before Faris met Enberg, we cannot in this appeal assume such to be true, nor do we consider any facts in conflict with plaintiff's version of events. . . .

Since the claims of plagiarism and implied-in-law contract were decided against plaintiff by the Court of Appeal in *Faris I*, plaintiff was left with the causes of action on implied-in-fact contract and breach of confidence. The Court of Appeal ruled that plaintiff's idea concerning a sports quiz show was not novel and concrete and thus not subject to copyright protection. Accordingly, the court sustained dismissal of the plaintiff's first cause of action for infringement. Further, the Court of Appeal held as to the second cause of action that plaintiff could only recover on a theory of an implied-in-fact contract, and not on a theory of a contract implied-in-law. This latter holding was based upon the rule that an implied-in-law contract required virtually the same proof as a suit for plagiarism (that the property must be protectable, i.e., novel and concrete). The Court of Appeal pointed out that the existence and the terms of an implied-in-fact contract are manifest by conduct, and there need be no showing of literary protectability. Thus, no matter how slight or commonplace is the material or idea which is revealed, the courts will not question the adequacy of the consideration.

Turning, then, to consideration of the question of whether there was an implied-in-fact contract, two notable Supreme Court cases have thoroughly dealt with the subject in the area of literary works or ideas. In *Weitzenkorn v. Lesser*, 40 Cal.2d 778 [256 P.2d 947], plaintiff wrote a story about Tarzan and the fountain of youth, and submitted it to producer Sol Lesser. The plaintiff sued on a theory of express contract, defendant's demurrer was granted in the trial court, and reversed by the Supreme Court. The Supreme Court held that regardless of a work's lack of originality, it could be valuable and the subject of contract: " 'While the idea disclosed may be common or even open to public knowledge, yet such disclosure if protected by contract, is sufficient consideration for the promise to pay. [Citations.]' " Even if the plaintiff's story and the movie Sol Lesser produced were grossly dissimilar, the court found that plaintiff was entitled to try to prove that defendant agreed to pay for the use of this commonplace idea. (40 Cal.2d at p. 792.) . . .

Accordingly, for an implied-in-fact contract one must show: that he or she prepared the work; that he or she disclosed the work to the offeree for sale; under all circumstances attending disclosure it can be concluded that the offeree voluntarily accepted the disclosure knowing the conditions on which it was tendered (i.e., the offeree must have the opportunity to reject the attempted disclosure if the conditions were unacceptable); and the reasonable value of the work. . . .

Applying these elements to the instant case, we find that the trial court correctly determined that there was no triable issue of fact on a cause of action for an implied-in-fact contract. The trial judge correctly concluded that "Enberg . . . is entitled to summary judgment, since there is no evidence to support an implied-in-fact contract for the services of revealing plaintiff's format to him. All the evidence is to the contrary. Both participants to the conversation agreed that the format was submitted to Enberg in connection with an inquiry as to whether Enberg would act as master of ceremonies for plaintiff's television show. . . . There is absolutely no evidence that plaintiff expected, or indicated his expectation of receiving compensation for the service of revealing the format to Enberg. To the contrary, the sole evidence is that plaintiff voluntarily submitted it to Enberg for the sole purpose of enabling Enberg to make a determination of his willingness to enter into a future business relationship with plaintiff."

So far as the record before us reveals, plaintiff never thought of selling his sports quiz show idea to anyone—including Enberg. He appears at all times to have intended to produce it himself, and sought out Enberg, as a master of ceremonies. He obviously hoped to make his idea more marketable by hiring a gifted sports announcer as his master of ceremonies. Not only did Faris seek to induce Enberg to join him by showing him the product, but also sought to entice him by promises of a "piece" of the enterprise for his involvement. Plaintiff never intended to submit the property for sale and did not tell Enberg that he was submitting it for sale. There is no reason to think that Enberg, or anyone else with whom Enberg spoke, would have believed that Faris' submission was an offer to sell something, which if used would oblige the user to pay.

Based on the clear holding of *Desny* an obligation to pay could not be inferred from the mere fact of submission on a theory that everyone knows that the idea man expects to be paid. Nor could it be inferred from the comment by Faris that the format was his "creation" and "literary property." In *Desny* the court held that the mere submission of an idea by a writer could not create the obligation. So, necessarily, the converse must also be the case: that knowledge on the part of the recipient that the submitter is a writer possessing his or her unprotected literary creation could not create an obligation to pay. Plaintiff's statements that he would not have revealed the format or idea to Enberg had he known that Enberg was going to show it to anyone else were not germane since he never told this to Enberg.

Plaintiff attempted to impose a contract on the facts of this case by asserting that Enberg solicited the submission, returned plaintiff's phone call and asked to keep a copy of the format. We do not agree. Faris solicited Enberg's involvement. It would be entirely inconsistent with *Desny* to hold that an implied-in-fact contract could be created because a telephone call was returned or because a request was made for an opportunity to read the work that was unconditionally submitted. . . .

In plaintiff's third cause of action in case . . . he alleged a breach of fiduciary obligation: that he "submitted in confidence to the defendants, both orally and in writing," the sports quiz show idea;

that "Defendants accepted the submission of such idea in confidence, and on the understanding that they would not use the idea without the consent of the plaintiff"; and that defendants did use the idea without plaintiff's consent. . . .

It is defendants' major contention that a literary work has to be protectable under copyright law in order to be the basis of a breach of confidence action. They argue that since *Faris I* held that the sports quiz show format was not protectable, plaintiff should have no access to a cause of action for breach of confidence. . . .

Nimmer on Copyright, section 16.06, states that protection of the disclosure takes place "only if the confidential nature of the disclosure is made clear prior to the exhibition." Nimmer explains that "Probably proof that the plaintiff offered the idea upon condition of confidence and a clear understanding that payment would be made upon use would suffice in some instances" to establish a confidential relationship.

We conclude that copyright protectability of a literary work is not a necessary element of proof in a cause of action for breach of confidence. An actionable breach of confidence will arise when an idea, whether or not protectable, is offered to another in confidence, and is voluntarily received by the offeree in confidence with the understanding that it is not to be disclosed to others, and is not to be used by the offeree for purposes beyond the limits of the confidence without the offeror's permission. In order to prevent the unwarranted creation or extension of a monopoly and restraint on progress in art, a confidential relationship will not be created from the mere submission of an idea to another. There must exist evidence of the communication of the confidentiality of the submission or evidence from which a confidential relationship can be inferred. Among the factors from which such an inference can be drawn are: proof of the existence of an implied-in-fact contract (*Davies v. Krasna*, 245 Cal. App. 2d 535 [54 Cal. Rptr. 37]); proof that the material submitted was protected by reason of sufficient novelty and elaboration (*Fink v. Goodson-Todman Enterprises, Ltd.*, 9 Cal. App. 3d 996 [88 Cal. Rptr. 649]); or proof of a particular relationship such as partners, joint adventurers, principal and agent or buyer and seller under certain circumstances.

(*Blaustein v. Burton*, 9 Cal. App. 3d 161, 187 [88 Cal. Rptr. 319]; *Thompson v. California Brewing Co.*, 150 Cal. App. 2d 469, 475 [310 P. 2d 436].)

With these rules as a base, we consider plaintiff's contention that the trial court erred in granting defendants' motion for summary judgment on the cause of action for breach of confidence.

Among the facts mentioned and not mentioned in plaintiff's declaration were these: he told defendant that the sports quiz show format was his "creation" and "literary property"; he told Enberg that he wished to hire Enberg to be the master of ceremonies for the show; he said that he would never have told Enberg about the idea if he knew Enberg would disclose it to others, although he apparently never advised Enberg of this thought; and he did not, so far as we can tell from his declaration, tell Enberg that the material was given in confidence. . . . We do not believe that the unsolicited submission of an idea to a potential employee or potential business partner, even if that person then passes the disclosed information to a competitor, presents a triable issue of fact for confidentiality. Here, no rational receiver of the communications from Faris could be bound to an understanding that a secret was being imparted. One could not infer from anything Enberg did or said that he was given the chance to reject disclosure in advance or that he voluntarily received the disclosure with an understanding that it was not to be given to others. To allow the disclosure which took place in this case to result in a confidential relationship, without something more, would greatly expand the creation of monopolies and bear the concomitant danger to the free communication of ideas. Our conclusion that evidence of knowledge of confidence or from which a confidential relationship can be implied is a minimum prerequisite to the protection of freedom in the arts. In the instant case, there was no direct evidence that either party believed that the disclosure was being made in confidence. Only in plaintiff's response to summary judgment is there reference to his own thoughts from which one might infer that he felt there was a confidence. But he never, so far as we can tell, communicated these thoughts to Enberg, and nothing of an understanding of confidence can be inferred from Enberg's conduct. No other special facts exist from which the relationship can be inferred: there was no implied-in-fact contract; the material was not protectable; and they were not yet partners or joint adventurers, and there was no buyer/seller or principal/agent relationship. Plaintiff might argue that he and Enberg were joint adventurers, but such was only Faris' unfulfilled hope. There was no evidence of more than a conversation which might have developed into a relationship later on. . . .

Whitfield v. Lear, 751 F.2d 90 (2d Cir. 1984)

WINTER, J.

. . . During the years 1975 through 1977, appellee Topper Carew worked on a proposed television series called "The Righteous Apples." On August 29, 1977, he filed a sixteen page registration with the Writers Guild consisting of a brief description of the series, descriptions of the characters, and marketing and production information. The document describes "The Righteous Apples" as a situation comedy involving a multiracial rock band of six junior high school students aged 13 through 15. A seventh student is the group's business manager. A primary theme of the series is the interaction of youths in a multiracial setting.

Carew was president of defendant Rainbow Television Workshop. On February 3, 1978, Rainbow entered into an agreement with the Corporation for Public Broadcasting ("CPB") to determine the feasibility of producing a pilot film based on "The Righteous Apples." On December 19, 1978, CPB agreed to provide funding to produce a pilot, which was filmed but never aired. The shooting script for the pilot, entitled "The Righteous Apple Wrangle," is in the record. That script is a situation comedy involving the characters described *supra*, and the plot essentially traces the resolution of racial tensions between one of the band members and another student. Another pilot script, with similar characteristics, is in the record.

During this period, appellant Whitfield was also working on a format for a television series and eventually he copyrighted a script for a show entitled "Boomerang." This was a dramatic show about an interracial, crime-fighting rock band,

called Boomerang. The band had five members, two white, one Spanish-surnamed, and two black. All five were recent graduates of the same high school where they had formed the band. In the "Boomerang" script, which is also in the record, the band members fight crime using their athletic talents and occasionally a boomerang as a weapon.

Following the copyrighting of "Boomerang," Whitfield added additional scenes to the script and circulated it to television producers. In March 1979, he sent a mailgram to the defendant Norman Lear and his company, Tandem Productions, informing them that a script was forthcoming. Lear forwarded the mailgram to another company he controlled, defendant TAT Communications, and so informed Whitfield. In 1980–1981, a twenty-episode series entitled "The Righteous Apples," produced by Carew, was broadcast under CPB auspices. Whitfield contends that "The Righteous Apples" series differs from the original pilot script and that the series as actually broadcast bears a strong resemblance to "Boomerang," resulting from Carew's access to the latter script through Tandem Productions and his appropriation of the ideas contained therein.

On June 4, 1981, appellant commenced this action alleging federal and state claims and diversity of citizenship. His complaint alleged the following causes of action under California law:

(1) Breach of contract;
(2) Breach of confidential or fiduciary relationship;
(3) Breach of implied covenant of good faith and fair dealing;
(4) Fraud and misrepresentation;
(5) Misappropriation and commercial piracy;
(6) Unfair competition;
(7) False designation of origin and false advertising;
(8) Restitution based on quasi-contract and unjust enrichment.

He also alleged copyright infringement under 17 U.S.C. § 501 and a violation of the Lanham Act, 15 U.S.C. §§ 1051–1127. Appellees moved for summary judgment, and both parties submitted affidavits. Appellees conceded access to Whitfield's script, and, apparently, their group involvement for Carew's series, solely for purposes of the motion. Judge Glasser granted the motion. . . .

Appellant has never alleged that the appellees actually copied from his script, only that they misappropriated ideas contained therein. Such a claim does not implicate the federal copyright laws, and appellant withdrew his copyright and Lanham Act claims in the district court. He thus now relies solely on a variety of causes of action under California law.

Appellant claims an interest in the ideas contained in his script and seeks redress for misappropriation of the ideas, not their literary or artistic expression. This theory narrows the legal ground available for recovery even further. Under California law, the fraud, misappropriation, unfair competition, and quasi-contract claims are actionable only to vindicate legally protected property interests, and an idea is not recognized as a property right. *Weitzenkorn v. Lesser*, 40 Cal.2d 778, 789, 256 P.2d 947, 956 (1953) (en banc). Recovery for the appropriation of an idea, therefore, may be had only on a contractual theory. *See Donahue v. Ziv Television Programs, Inc.*, 245 Cal.App.2d 593, 601, 54 Cal.Rptr. 130, 137 (1966).

While an idea is not property and is not subject to copyright under California law, its disclosure may be valid consideration for a contract. There is no evidence of an express contract between Whitfield and any of the defendants. However, California law will imply a contract from the conduct of the parties in certain circumstances. Thus, if a producer accepts a submitted idea with full knowledge that the offeror expects payment in the event of use, California courts impose liability under a theory of implied-in-fact contract. *Desny v. Wilder*, 46 Cal.2d 715, 299 P.2d 257 (1956) (en banc). . . .

Appellees argue that, even accepting Whitfield's version of the facts surrounding submission of "Boomerang," there is insufficient evidence to support an implied contract. They rely upon the statement in *Wilder* that:

> The law will not imply a promise to pay for an idea from the mere facts that the idea has been conveyed, is valuable, and has been used for profit; this is true even though the conveyance has been made

with the hope or expectation that some obligation will ensue.

46 Cal.2d at 739, 299 P.2d at 270.

In the instant case, Whitfield sent a mailgram to Lear and Tandem Productions informing them that a script was forthcoming and then sent the "Boomerang" script. An assistant to Lear wrote to Whitfield stating that, although Lear was not personally interested in "Boomerang," the mailgram had been forwarded to the Senior Vice President for Creative Affairs at TAT Communications. The parties had no further communications.

Whitfield contends that the custom in the television industry is that a studio or producer not desiring any outside submissions states so explicitly and, when a studio or producer is not interested in reviewing a particular script, the script is returned unopened. If, however, a studio or producer is notified that a script is forthcoming and opens and reviews it when it arrives, that studio or producer has by custom implicitly promised to pay for the ideas if used. *See* M. Nimmer, *Nimmer on Copyright* § 16.05[c] (1984) (if recipient has advance warning of and opportunity to reject disclosure, and knows that person submitting expects payment, California law will infer promise to pay in the event of use).

We conclude that the communications in question and the allegation of custom in the industry are sufficient to withstand a motion for summary judgment on this point. In *Minniear v. Tors*, 266 Cal.App.2d 495, 72 Cal.Rptr. 287 (1968), the plaintiff produced a pilot film and permitted a television director to view it at the latter's request. The parties engaged in no negotiations. The director's company later produced an arguably similar television series. Based on the plaintiff's claim that "it is understood in the industry that when a showing is made, the offeror shall be paid for any ideas or materials used therein," *id.* at 500, 72 Cal.Rptr. at 291, the court held that a jury could infer that the defendant accepted the ideas with the knowledge that plaintiff expected payment.

The facts of the instant case are similar to *Minniear*. The correspondence between the parties, brief as it was, has some of the attributes of bargaining. Whitfield's mailgram described his experience as a radio broadcaster and his knowledge of the entertainment market. These statements were obviously designed to persuade the recipient to open the script and give it careful scrutiny. The letter from Lear's assistant stated that the Vice President for Creative Affairs at TAT Communications would contact him "should we be interested in accepting new material from writers outside of our organization." This is arguably an acknowledgment that Whitfield's ideas were not freely appropriable. If, as appellees argue, they were perfectly free to use Whitfield's ideas without compensation as soon as they received them, there was nothing to "accept," and no further communication with Whitfield was necessary. On the whole, the record raises a material issue of fact as to whether the appellees accepted Whitfield's submission on an understanding common in the industry that he expected payment if the ideas were used.

The appellant has a second hurdle to clear. To support recovery on an implied-in-fact contract, he must show not only access but also that the appellees actually used his ideas by demonstrating "some substantial similarity" between the ideas and themes of the two programs. *Kurlan v. Columbia Broadcasting System*, 40 Cal.2d 799, 809, 256 P.2d 962, 969 (1953). Access having been conceded for purposes of the motion for summary judgment, the district court concluded that "there are *no* similarities between the ideas contained in defendant's production and plaintiff's work." Mem. at 9 (emphasis in original).

We are unable to verify this conclusion. The scripts of the actual episodes of "The Righteous Apples" that appeared on television are not in the record and were not reviewed by the district court. The only "Righteous Apples" scripts in the record are pilots prepared *before* appellant's submission of "Boomerang" to Lear. However, the essence of Whitfield's claim is that "The Righteous Apples" as televised differed significantly from the appellees' original pilots.

Since no scripts of the actually televised series are in the record, the critical comparison can be made only on the basis of other materials submitted by the parties. However, these materials are in utter conflict over the existence of similarities between the televised series and the

"Boomerang" script. Appellees thus describe the first ten televised episodes of "The Righteous Apples" in a manner wholly at odds with Whitfield's description of similarities between those episodes and his "Boomerang" script.

Assuming access by the defendants to the "Boomerang" script and accepting Whitfield's assertions regarding the content of the televised series as true, as we must on a motion for summary judgment, we conclude that the alleged similarities between the "Righteous Apples" series and "Boomerang," viewed in light of the earlier pilot scripts, are sufficient to allow a trier of fact to find that Whitfield's ideas were misappropriated under California law. There is thus dispute over material facts which can be resolved only by comparing the pilot scripts (in the record) prepared before the submission of "Boomerang," the Boomerang script (in the record), with "The Righteous Apples" scripts actually used in the televised series (not in the record). There were, therefore, insufficient grounds to grant summary judgment. . . .

7.20 Adaptation for Television

A great deal of prime-time television is based on material adapted from other media. The recent theatrical film *Gung Ho* is being adapted to a weekly sitcom, as were *Private Benjamin* and *Fast Times at Ridgemont High*. Indeed, some potential producers of mini-series actively discourage submission of original teleplays for consideration, claiming that a mini-series will not sell unless it has some prior notoriety, such as that generated by a best seller.

In the adaptation of a book or movie for television, the ownership of the rights to authorize the adaption is frequently contested. In the typical scenario, the author of the original work has licensed the transformation of the work from a book to a movie. The inquiry is whether the license also gives the motion picture company the right to develop a later TV series based on the book and movie. In *Goodis v. United Artists Tele-*

vision, the court examines the grant of contract rights by which the novel *Dark Passage* first became a movie and then was the basis for the television series *The Fugitive.* The author's estate claimed that the rights to do the TV series were not part of the motion picture contract. A similar situation is explored in *Landon v. Twentieth Century-Fox Film Corporation.* In both cases, the courts closely scrutinize the contract language in light of common understandings and usages within the motion picture and television industries.

Goodis v. United Artists Television, Inc., 425 F.2d 397 (2d Cir. 1970)

LUMBARD, J.

. . . The plaintiffs are the executors of Davis Goodis, author of the novel *Dark Passage,* a work which has proved both popular and adaptable to presentation in many of the entertainment media. When Goodis completed the novel in 1945, he made arrangements for the book to be printed in April 1946. Later, on December 20, 1945, Goodis sold the exclusive motion picture rights in the novel to Warner Brothers for $25,000. The contract was Warner Brothers' standard form for acquiring movie rights, but, as we state below, it contained additional specially negotiated clauses to cover radio and television broadcast rights.

Before the book was published, Goodis also received $12,000 from Curtis Publishing Co. for the right to serialize the novel in *The Saturday Evening Post,* one of Curtis' publications. The book publisher agreed to postpone distribution of the book until October 1946, and *Dark Passage* was first published in eight installments of *The Saturday Evening Post* running from July 20 to September 7, 1946. Each issue contained a single copyright notice in the magazine's name as provided by the Copyright Act. There was no notice in Goodis' own name.

In due course, Warner Brothers produced a motion picture, also titled *Dark Passage,* based on the novel. After the film was exhibited in theaters and shown on television, Warner Brothers in 1956 assigned its contract rights to defendant United Artists. United Artists produced a television film series, "The Fugitive," which was broadcast in weekly installments by defendant American Broadcasting Co. The series enjoyed considerable popularity on television, and early in 1965 Goodis instituted this action claiming $500,000 damages for copyright infringement. The defendants answered that the television series was covered by the contract which had been assigned to them by Warner Brothers. . . .

The district court granted defendants' motion for summary judgment and dismissed the complaint on the grounds . . . that the contract between Goodis and Warner Brothers clearly conveyed the right to produce a film series like "The Fugitive." . . . The critical clause in paragraph 19(c) of the contract conveys ". . . the right to broadcast and transmit *any photoplay produced hereunder* by the process of television . . ." [emphasis added]. Although my brothers discuss "springboards" and "sequels," the only question which the district court had to decide was whether this particular television series could be produced under this particular contract.

This is not a case where the question is the right to broadcast a movie on television. . . . The contract clearly provided for the presentation of the movie *Dark Passage* on television and appellant concedes the propriety of such broadcasts. Appellant claims, however, that "any photoplay produced hereunder" does not encompass "The Fugitive," a film series produced directly for television without any intention to show it in motion picture theaters. I think a fair interpretation of the contract indicates that the grant of motion picture rights was sufficiently broad to include this use.

Under paragraph 17, defendants purchased the "absolute and unlimited right . . . to make such changes, *variations, modifications, alterations, adaptations, arrangements, additions in* and/or eliminations and omissions from *said Writings and/or the characters, plot,* dialogue, *scenes, incidents, situations, action,* language and theme thereof . . ." [emphasis added]. Under paragraph 19(c), Goodis retained "[t]he right to broadcast said Writings by television from the performances given by living actors."

Had Goodis sold specific, limited rights in 1945

and retained for his future use or disposition the general reservoir of broadcast rights, I might be persuaded that a question of fact existed. But Goodis retained only the specific right to "broadcast said Writings by television from performances by living actors," and I find it difficult to imagine a broader transfer of rights than that which these parties drafted. It seems clear to me the district judge properly decided on summary judgment that defendants could produce and televise films in any manner they might choose other than from the performances of live actors.

The majority claims that my construction may affect the interpretation of many similar contracts which do not explicitly mention the right to make "sequels" using the original characters. I do not share this concern.

First, unlike most of the contract, which was Warner Brothers' standard form, the paragraph describing television broadcast rights was specially drafted by the parties. It is unlikely any other contracts drafted circa 1945 will be affected by our determination of these parties' intentions as expressed in these specially negotiated terms.

Second, although the majority shows great concern for the use of "sequels," the question of sequels was not, in my opinion, before the district court. In paragraph 16 of the complaint, Goodis took particular care to show an exact parallel between "Dark Passage" and "The Fugitive." The content of "The Fugitive" was not raised by Goodis as a factual issue in his opposition to the summary judgment motion. For all that appears in the record, the "sequel" argument was raised for the first time on appeal in an effort to overturn the grant of summary judgment.

The majority implies in a footnote that this view reflects a return to "dangerously technical methods of pleading." Apparently they are assuming that a litigant in Goodis' position would have to walk a narrow line between pleading sufficient identity for infringement on the one hand and sufficient difference for a "sequel" claim on the other. Whether or not this might be a real problem in the ordinary infringement action, it is certainly not crucial in a case where a defendant has a contractual right to use a work and the only question is whether he has exceeded his rights. . . .

I would affirm the grant of summary judgment by the district court as the contractual rights of the parties were clearly defined.

Reversed and remanded.

WATERMAN, J., CONCURRING

My brother Kaufman and I concur in that part of Chief Judge Lumbard's opinion which holds that Goodis did not surrender his copyright in *Dark Passage* because of the *Saturday Evening Post* publication. We do not agree with his view that the defendant below is entitled to summary judgment on the issue of whether the contract between Goodis and Warner Brothers conveyed the right to make and broadcast a television series such as "The Fugitive." Accordingly, on this branch of the case our holding is that of the majority.

The party to whom summary judgment is awarded must have shown "that there is no genuine issue as to any material fact and that the moving party is entitled to a judgment as a matter of law." Fed.R.Civ.P. 56(c). The question presented here is whether the contract language demonstrates unambiguously that Goodis meant to convey to Warner Brothers the right to create a television series such as "The Fugitive" or whether a genuine issue of material fact exists as to what the parties intended by the language they used.

The rights which the contract conveyed to Warner Brothers "in said writings" included "the exclusive, complete and entire motion picture rights," and "the right to broadcast and transmit any photoplay produced hereunder by the process of television . . . provided that such broadcasts and transmissions are given from the film of such photoplay and not directly from the performances of living actors." The judge below held that the term "any photoplay produced hereunder" unambiguously included a television series of photoplays such as "The Fugitive." Accordingly, he awarded summary judgment to the defendants.

We disagree. It is our holding that the contract language does not so clearly permit production of "The Fugitive" as to entitle the defendant to the grant of a summary judgment.

The language of the contract clearly conveys to

Warner Brothers the right to make a movie of *Dark Passage* and to show that movie on television. Moreover, Paragraph 17 of the contract conveys the right to vary the plot and characters of *Dark Passage* in making that movie. The question before us, however, is whether the contract unambiguously fails to put any limits on the degree to which Warner Brothers could change or modify the original story while using the story's characters.

In an appeal from summary judgment we must resolve all disputed questions of fact in favor of the appellant. Therefore, we accept appellant's factual representations in the complaint and assume that "The Fugitive" television series took the characters in *Dark Passage* and, using the novel's plot as a springboard, placed the characters the author created in a whole series of new plot situations developed by the motion picture company. It seems to us that the right to make "additions in . . . said writings" and in the characters and plot of *Dark Passage* does not necessarily go so far as to show that there is no genuine issue as to whether the characters of *Dark Passage* may be depicted in photoplay adventures which bear little relationship to the "said writings" of *Dark Passage*. Viewed in the context of the entire contract, the "additions" and "alterations" clauses of Paragraph 17 could be read in a more restrictive manner to permit only those alterations necessary to adapt a written story to the medium of film. Similarly, use of the word "unlimited" with respect to the rights to alter and supplement could have been intended only to prevent Goodis from protesting that his story had been distorted or mutilated.

Among the reasons that have caused us to conclude that this case should not be decided without a full inquiry into the intent of the parties is that our disposition of this appeal may affect the interpretation of other contracts which convey some of the divisible rights in a given story but do not explicitly mention among the conveyed rights the right to make subsequent stories employing the same character, i.e., "sequels" as such stories are called in the publishing industry. Too, a proper decision as to what the parties intended in this case may largely depend upon the general custom and expectations of authors and of members of the publishing, broadcasting, and film vocations. Because this case reaches us after a grant of summary judgment, we have before us no evidence as to these customs and expectations. Many authors have used characters they created in one novel in a whole series of subsequent works; surely it would be rash of us to hold on summary judgment that the sale of rights in one of an author's works ends, without specific mention that it ends, the author's exclusive ownership of the valuable characters he created in that one work, when he may well desire to create sequels of his own using these same characters. . . .

We further note, contrary to our brother Lumbard's view, that the issue of the right of defendants to use the characters from *Dark Passage* in new plot situations was properly raised by appellant before the district court. The court below was not misled into thinking that "The Fugitive" contained no plot material beyond that of *Dark Passage*. Judge Mansfield noted in his opinion that the plaintiff asserted that the contract limited Warner Brothers' rights to a photoplay made from the original story, so it is obvious that the judge understood plaintiff's contention that "The Fugitive" was not identical to *Dark Passage* although it built upon that story's theme and used the author's characters. Moreover, common sense indicates that the material used in a television series which was broadcast for one hour a week for more than one season could not possibly be confined to the limited material found in a single movie or in a short novel. The arguments made to this court were therefore properly raised below. Once plaintiff's assertion was understood below, namely that Goodis had retained certain rights in the characters of *Dark Passage*, and that "The Fugitive" used these characters, it is certainly not crucial whether the complaint used the term of art "sequel" in referring to the television series. . . .

Landon v. Twentieth Century-Fox Film Corp., 384 F. Supp. 452 (S.D.N.Y. 1974)

LASKER, J.

In 1944 Margaret Landon entered into an agreement with Twentieth Century-Fox Film Corporation (Fox) to sell, among other things, "motion picture rights" to her book entitled *Anna and the King of Siam*. In 1972 Fox produced 13 films which were broadcast on the CBS Television network as a weekly serial entitled "Anna and the King."

This suit presents the question whether the 1944 agreement between Landon and Fox authorized Fox to produce and exhibit the 1972 series through defendant CBS. In addition to her assertion that the series infringed her copyright in the literary property *Anna and the King of Siam*, Landon raises the novel claim that the 1944 agreement constituted a tying arrangement in violation of Section 1 of the Sherman Act, 15 U.S.C. § 1, on the grounds that Fox allegedly acquired the original copyright "on condition that" it also acquire the copyright renewal rights. She also argues that the assignment of the renewal copyright is unenforceable for lack of consideration. Landon's final claim is that production and exhibition of the television series constituted tortious misconduct on the part of defendants, that is, defamation, invasion of her right of privacy, misappropriation of literary property and wrongful attribution to Landon of credit for the series, which she claims to have "mutilated" her literary property. . . .

The heart of Landon's contention that the series infringed her copyright is that the granting language of the 1944 agreement gave Fox the right to produce only motion pictures of feature length intended for first exhibition in movie theaters, and not those intended for first exhibition on television. The grant clauses of the agreement provide, in relevant part:

FIRST: The Owner does hereby grant, convey and assign unto the Purchaser, its successors and assigns forever:

(a) The sole and exclusive motion picture rights and motion picture copyright throughout the world in and to said literary property. . . .

(c) The sole and exclusive right to make, produce, adapt, sell, lease, rent, exhibit, perform and generally deal in and with the copyright motion picture versions of said literary property, with or without sound accompaniment and with or without the interpolation of musical numbers therein, and for such purposes to adapt one or more versions of said literary property, to add to and subtract from the literary property, change the sequence thereof, change the title of said literary property, use said title, or any of its components, in connection with works or motion pictures wholly or partially independent of said literary property, change the characters in said literary property, change the descriptions of the said characters, and use all thereof in new versions, adaptations and sequels in any and all languages, and to register and obtain copyright therein, throughout the world. . . .

(f) The sole and exclusive right to broadcast by means of the method generally known and described as television, or any process analogous thereto, any of the motion picture versions of said literary property produced pursuant hereto. The Owner specifically reserves to herself the right to broadcast the literary property by television direct from living actors; provided, however, that the Owner agrees that, for a period from the date hereof until eight (8) years after the date of general release of the first motion picture produced by the Purchaser based upon the literary property, or until ten (10) years after the date hereof, whichever period first expires, she will not exercise or grant the right to broadcast the literary property, or any part thereof, by television, or by any other device now known or hereafter to be devised by which the literary property may be reproduced visually and audibly for an audience not present at a performance thereof and with living actors speaking the roles thereof. The Owner grants to the Purchaser the exclusive option to license, lease and/or purchase said reserve rights to broadcast the literary property by television from living actors, or otherwise, at the same price and upon such bona fide terms as may be offered to the Owner by any responsible prospective buyer and which shall be acceptable to the Owner.

(g) The right to broadcast by means of radio processes, portions of said literary property, or the motion picture version or versions thereof, in conjunction with or exploitation of or as an advertising medium or tie-up with the production, exhibition and/or distribution of any motion picture based on said literary property, provided that, in exercising said radio broadcasting rights, Purchaser shall not broadcast serially an entire photoplay produced hereunder. Except as herein stated, the Owner agrees that she will not permit the said literary property or any part thereof to be broadcast by any method or means until two years after the general distribution date of the first motion picture made by the Purchaser based upon the said literary property, or four years after the date hereof, whichever period first expires. This restriction on broadcasting, however, shall not in any way affect or restrict the rights on television herein granted.

(h) The right to publish, copyright or cause to be published and copyrighted in any and all languages, in any and all countries of the world, in any form or media (including, but not limited to, press books, press notices, trade journals, periodicals, newspapers, heralds, fan magazines and/or small separate booklets) synopses revised and/or abridged versions of said literary property, not exceeding 7,500 words each, adapted from the said literary property or from any motion picture and/or television version thereof, with or without sound accompaniment, produced, performed, released or exhibited pursuant hereto.

It is evident that the grant clauses are broadly drafted and do not contain or suggest the purported distinction between motion pictures made for first exhibition on television and those made for theater presentation. Clause (c) expressly grants to Fox the sole right to "make" and "generally deal in" an apparently unlimited number of "motion picture versions" of the property. It confers the right to use and modify the plot, characters and title in "new versions, adaptations, and sequels," again without apparent limit on the number of such versions. Clause (f) cedes the "exclusive" right to broadcast on television "any of the motion picture versions" of the property produced pursuant to the agreement.

The broad construction of the phrase "motion picture versions" to include the 1972 series is confirmed by related provisions of the agreement. These indicate that when the parties sought to reserve to Landon certain rights, they did so carefully and specifically. Such reservations are themselves strong evidence that if Landon had intended to reserve the right to make and exhibit filmed television versions of the property, she and her noted and experienced literary agents, the William Morris Agency, knew how to do so. For example, Clause (g) gives Fox the right to broadcast by radio portions of the property for advertising or promotional purposes, but by express language states that Fox "shall not broadcast serially an entire photoplay. . . ." Significantly the provision states that "[t]his restriction on broadcasting . . . shall not in any way affect or restrict the rights on television herein granted." Clause (f), the television clause, specifically reserves to Landon the right to "broadcast the literary property by television direct from living actors," but contains a covenant providing that she shall not exercise even that limited right for a period of years. In view of this covenant obviously drafted to protect Fox from Landon's competition with Fox's own films, it is far-fetched to believe that the parties so carefully restricted Landon's right to exhibit live television performances only to leave her completely free to show an unlimited number of filmed television versions of the property. . . .

We conclude that the only reasonable construction of the 1944 agreement is that Fox was granted the right to make an unlimited number of motion picture versions of the property, without limitation as to length, or place of first exhibition. This conclusion is consistent with the law in this Circuit as to the interpretation of copyright grants. *Bartsch v. Metro-Goldwyn-Mayer, Inc.*, 391 F.2d 150 (2d Cir.) cert. denied, 393 U.S. 826, 89 S.Ct. 86, 21 L.Ed.2d 96 (1968) is precisely in point. There the copyright owners of a musical play assigned to Bartsch in 1930 the "motion picture rights" in the play together with the right to "copyright, vend, license and exhibit" motion picture photoplays throughout the world. There was no television clause in the assignment. Later in 1930, Bartsch assigned his rights to Warner Brothers, which in turn transferred its rights to MGM. MGM produced and distributed a feature-length motion picture based on the musical play in 1935. In 1958 MGM licensed the picture for exhibition on television and Bartsch's widow, to whom his copyright interest had devolved, sued to enjoin the broadcast. The issue was comparable to ours: whether, under the terms of original grant by the copyright authors to Bartsch in 1930 (and then from Bartsch to Warner), the right to "copyright, vend, license and exhibit . . . motion picture photoplays" included the right to license a broadcaster to exhibit the picture on television without a further express grant by the copyright owner (Bartsch). In deciding that the grant did include such a right, Judge Friendly emphasized that Bartsch's assignment to Warner was "well designed to give [Warner] the broadest rights" with respect to the right to produce motion pictures, and noted that " '[e]xhibit' means to 'display' or to 'show' *by any method,* and nothing in the rest of the grant sufficiently reveals a contrary intention." 391 F.2d at 154 (emphasis added). The court stated the rule which controls the present case:

> As between an approach that "a license of rights in a given medium (e.g., 'motion picture rights') includes only such uses as fall within the unambiguous core meaning of the term (e.g., exhibition of motion picture film in motion picture theaters) and exclude any uses which lie within the ambiguous penumbra (e.g., exhibition of motion picture film on television)" and another whereby "the licensee may properly pursue any uses which may reasonably be said to fall within the medium as described in the license," [Professor Nimmer] prefers the latter. So do we. . . . If the words are broad enough to cover the new use, it seems fair that the burden of framing and negotiating an exception should fall on the grantor; if Bartsch or his assignors had desired to limit "exhibition" of the motion picture to the conventional method where light is carried from a projector to a screen directly beheld by the viewer they could have said so. 391 F.2d at 155.

There was no question in *Bartsch* that the parties were aware of the possibilities of television even in 1930. In the present case, involving a 1944 agreement, there is, of course, no question on that score either: the Landon contract is sprinkled with references to television and one does not have to roam far into the penumbral meanings of "motion picture versions" to conclude that the term was intended by the parties to embrace rather than exclude the right to produce a television series. Indeed, Clause (h) of the agreement, (to which, curiously, the parties pay only passing attention) expressly refers to "any motion picture and/or television version . . . produced, performed, released or *exhibited pursuant hereto*." (emphasis supplied)

Goodis v. United Artists Television, Inc., 425 F.2d 397 (2d Cir. 1970) also supports our conclusion that the 1944 agreement authorized the 1972 television series. . . .

Significantly, the right to make "sequels," critically absent in *Goodis*, is explicitly expressed in the language before us. Clause (c) of the agreement recites the usual "additions" and "alterations" provisions in regard to adapting the property to the film medium and then grants the "sole

and exclusive right" to use the property in "new versions, adaptions and sequels . . . and to register and obtain copyright therein, throughout the world." Such broad language, particularly when read in combination with the grant in Clause (f) of the "sole and exclusive right" to broadcast on television "any of the motion picture versions" which the contract gives Fox the "sole and exclusive" right to make (Clause (c)), leads inescapably to the conclusion that Fox is entitled to summary judgment on the infringement claim.

We have carefully considered Landon's argument that, at the least, the presence of genuine issues as to material facts precludes the grant of summary judgment to Fox. Apart from the fact that such an assertion is undercut by her own motion for similar relief, the argument is without merit. Landon contends first that Fox's contracting practices as reflected in a number of other agreements drafted during the 1940's demonstrate that Fox often and explicitly contracted for the right to produce "television versions," and that its failure to do so here is probative of its intent as to the 1944 agreement. The contention is effectively rebutted by the undisputed facts that (1) Fox maintained both East coast and West coast legal departments, each with its own drafting style, and (2) Landon's contract was drafted in the office which, as a matter of consistent practice, did not use the magic words "television versions" to acquire the rights in issue here, relying instead on general language to achieve the same result. In any event, contracts made between Fox and other copyright owners have little probative value as to what Fox and Landon intended in their particular agreement. . . .

Landon also contends that "motion picture versions" is a term of art whose meaning can be established only by extrinsic "technical evidence." It is, of course, a familiar principle that where the terms of a contract are ambiguous, such evidence may be introduced, not to vary the meaning of a contract but to establish the intent of the parties. But in the context here, the terms of the contract are not ambiguous and do not raise a triable issue of fact. . . .

Plaintiff also argues that it was not her intention to grant to Fox the right to make television versions of the property. She takes the position that her intentions in 1944 present an issue of disputed fact requiring a trial on the merits. The argument is wide of the mark for two reasons. First, it is axiomatic that evidence of plaintiff's intent is admissible only insofar as it was expressed to Fox. Her affidavit is silent on the question whether she ever expressed to Fox in 1944 the construction of the agreement she presses on the present motions, and it is undisputed that she had very little, if any direct contact with Fox at all. Albert B. Taylor, an executive with William Morris Agency (plaintiff's literary agents) with some familiarity with the negotiation of the 1944 agreement, does not state that he, or any other employee of the Agency communicated Landon's understanding of the agreement to Fox. More to the point, the opposing affidavit of Helen Strauss, who was personally responsible for plaintiff's account and for negotiation on Landon's behalf of the Fox agreement, states that in 1944 Strauss understood the agreement to convey to Fox all film rights, including television rights, while reserving to Landon "dramatic rights," including the right to televise a "live" dramatic rendition of the property.

In sum, there is no genuine issue as to any material fact and defendants are entitled to summary judgment as to the infringement claim. . . .

The second count of the complaint alleges as an unlawful tying arrangement Fox's requirement that it acquire the renewal copyright as a condition to its purchase of the original copyright. As plaintiff concedes, there is no reported case recognizing such a cause of action. Assuming, without deciding, that such an arrangement may violate the anti-trust laws, the particular claim asserted here is fatally deficient. As the Second Circuit has recently stated, the exercise of actual coercion by the defendant (as distinguished from the mere presence of market power) is a necessary element of an unlawful tying arrangement. See *Capital Temporaries, Inc. of Hartford v. The Olsten Corporation*, 506 F.2d 658 (2d Cir. 1974). . . . As we read *Capital Temporaries*, to state a valid claim plaintiff would have to allege that (1) she wished to sell only the original copyright at the time she signed the 1944 agreement, (2) expressed that fact to Fox, and (3) that sale of the renewal copyrights was forced upon her by virtue

of the superior economic strength or market dominance of Fox. However, neither the complaint nor any supporting affidavit suggest the presence of these elements. Indeed, the contrary appears: Landon testified at her deposition (at p. 266) in connection with the question of copyright renewals that she did not have any discussion "at all" on that subject at the time the agreement was negotiated. Neither her own affidavit on the present motion nor those of her literary agents refer to any such discussions or any proposed modification of the draft agreement in connection with renewals.

As to Fox's market dominance, the record indicates that Landon's agents offered the literary property to various theater companies and film companies but that Fox was the "only film company to make an offer, despite efforts on my part to secure offers from other film companies." (Opposing Affidavit of Helen Strauss, at Paragraph 5.) Although Fox, as the only interested buyer may have been in a position to drive a hard bargain with Landon, the exercise of such power is not the kind of conduct proscribed by the antitrust laws, and indeed there is no evidence that Fox exercised it all. Indeed the Strauss affidavit (Paragraph 5) states that *Anna and the King of Siam* was, as a factual work rather than a novel, not an easily saleable property but that Fox paid "a good purchase price" for it.

Moreover, even if plaintiff's claim of an unlawful tying arrangement were otherwise sufficient, it would be barred by the four-year Statute of Limitations in 15 U.S.C. § 16(b). . . .

In the present case, however, the alleged violation arises from a single act—the 1944 agreement—by a single defendant. As a general rule, claims based on anti-competitive agreements to which the plaintiff is a party accrue at the time of their execution. . . .

Landon's final claim charges that certain episodes in the 1972 television series "fail to retain and give appropriate expression to the theme, thought and main action of plaintiff's work," resulting in damage to her privacy and reputation and the literary property itself. (Complaint, Paragraph 24) As fleshed out by the material in support of her motion, the basis of this allegation is that her book was a serious literary work concerned with the struggle for human rights, whereas the television series was light in tone, and punctuated with bursts of dubbed laughter from the audience.

It is undisputed that the television credits stated that the scripts were "based on" plaintiff's literary property, with screenwriting credit given to the actual authors of the series in the same titles as Landon's name appears.

For several reasons, the claim is insufficient as a matter of law. Even without permission from an author or the existence of a written agreement with him, any person may truthfully state that a work is "based on" or "suggested by" the work of that author. I Nimmer, Copyright, § 110.41 at p. 447; *Geisel v. Poynter Products, Inc.*, 295 F. Supp. 331, 353 (S.D.N.Y. 1968). Although plaintiff would have a valid claim against defendants if they had falsely attributed the authorship of the series to her, see *Granz v. Harris*, 198 F.2d 585, 589 (2d Cir. 1952), her claim must fail where, as here, she contracted to (1) *require* Fox to give her appropriate credit "for her contribution to the literary material upon which such motion pictures shall have been based" (1944 Agreement, Article X); and (2) grant Fox the right to:

> reproduce . . . spoken words taken from and/or *based on* the text or theme, of said literary property . . . in . . . motion pictures, using for that purpose all *or a part of the theme*, text and/or dialogue contained in said literary property. . . . [and] adapt one or more versions of said literary property, to add to and subtract from the literary property, change the sequence thereof, change the title . . . in connection with works or motion pictures *wholly or partially independent of said* literary property . . . *change the characters* . . . change the *descriptions of the said characters*, and use all thereof in new versions, adaptations and sequels. . . . (Agreement, Article I, paragraphs (b), (c)). (emphasis added)

These provisions clearly grant Fox the right to alter the literary property substantially and to attribute to plaintiff credit appropriate to her contribution. Accordingly, we find that Fox did not violate the agreement or engage in tortious conduct when it truthfully stated that the series was "based on" the property. . . .

7.30 Editing for Television

Television editing of works is a frequent battleground between directors on the one hand and studios and TV networks on the other. Films are constantly edited to provide for commercial material and to delete material deemed unsuitable for the home viewing audience. Warren Beatty recently won an arbitration preventing the editing of his *Reds* for broadcast by ABC-TV. The result is that ABC did not show the film, and Paramount Pictures returned a reported $6 million fee to ABC. The Directors' Guild subsequently announced that control over editing for television would be a principal issue in its next negotiations with the film producers.

The *Preminger* case below warns that a director such as Otto Preminger, who retained final theatrical editing rights in his film *Anatomy of a Murder*, did not protect himself by contract language that also accorded him final say over editing for television. The *Preminger* court suggests there can be legal redress if the editing is too severe, but holds this did not occur in this instance. In *Gilliam*, however, the court is sympathetic to Monty Python's complaints about excessive cutting done on its sketches when they were edited for United States television.

Preminger v. Columbia Pictures Corp., 267 N.Y.S.2d 594 (Sup.Ct. 1966)

KLEIN, J.

The interesting question presented for decision is the right of a producer, in the absence of specific contractual provision, to prevent, by injunction, minor cuts in his motion picture when shown on television and the usual breaks for commercials.

The litigation involves the production of the motion picture *Anatomy of a Murder*.

The complaint alleges that plaintiff Preminger is a producer and director of motion pictures, including the motion picture involved; and plaintiff Carlyle Productions, Inc., a California corporation, was the owner of all rights to the picture, and Carlyle Productions, a limited New York partnership, its assignee; that Carlyle Productions, Inc. entered into a series of agreements with Columbia Pictures Corporation between 1956 and 1959, which are collectively referred to as the contract, copies of which are annexed to the complaint.

Defendant Columbia and defendant Screen Gems, Inc., its subsidiary, the complaint continues, have licensed over 100 television stations to exhibit the motion picture on television, and those license agreements purport to give the licensees the right to cut, to eliminate portions of the picture, and to interrupt the remainder of the picture for commercials and other extraneous matter.

Unless enjoined, the complaint asserts, defendants will

a) detract from the artistic merit of *Anatomy of a Murder*;
b) damage Preminger's reputation;
c) cheapen and tend to destroy *Anatomy's* commercial value;
d) injure plaintiffs in the conduct of their business;
e) falsely represent to the public that the film shown is Preminger's film.

It is then alleged, and not denied, that *Anatomy* is one of a very few motion pictures with a rating of AA-1; that it has been licensed in blocks of 60–300 pictures; and that the others are artistically and commercially inferior to *Anatomy*.

Finally it is alleged that defendants have allocated an unfairly and unreasonably low share of license fees to *Anatomy*. This allegation is denied.

All these acts are described as willful and wanton breaches of the contract with Carlyle as owner and Preminger as producer.

Injunctive relief and accounting, for plaintiffs' damages, are prayed for.

Specifically, it is demanded that judgment be granted:

a) enjoining defendants from performing their obligations under the licensing agreements;

b) enjoining defendant from entering into further agreements violative of plaintiffs' rights;
c) enjoining defendants to withdraw all prints previously distributed;
d) directing defendants to account to plaintiffs, for what are presumably plaintiffs' damages; profits are not requested;
e) other and further relief. . . .

The plaintiffs plant themselves upon Article VIII of the contract, which provides:

> You [Carlyle] shall have the right to make the final cutting and editing of the Picture, but you shall in good faith consider recommendations and suggestions with respect thereto made by us [Columbia]; nevertheless, you shall have final approval thereof, provided however that notwithstanding the foregoing, in the event that cutting or re-editing is required in order to meet censorship requirements and you shall fail or refuse to comply therewith, then we shall have the right to cut and edit the Picture in order to meet censorship requirements without obligation on our part to challenge the validity of any rule, order, regulation or requirement of any national, state or local censorship authority.

The import of the paragraph is that plaintiffs have the right to make the final "cutting and editing" of the picture; giving the defendants the right to make suggestions, only.

This article must be read, however, in juxtaposition with Article X of the contract, which provides as follows:

> The rights herein granted, without limiting the generality of the foregoing, shall include and embrace all so-called "theatrical" as well as "nontheatrical" rights in the Picture (as those terms are commonly understood in the motion picture industry); and shall include the right to use film of any and all gauges. You hereby give and grant to us throughout the entire world the exclusive and irrevocable right during the term herein specified to project, exhibit, reproduce, transmit and perform, and authorize and license others to project, exhibit, reproduce, transmit and perform, the picture and prints thereof by television, and in any other manner, and by any other means, method or device whatsoever, whether mechanical, electrical or otherwise, and whether now known or hereafter conceived or created.

This Article, it will be noted, which contains the specific grant of television rights, makes no reference to "cutting and editing."

In these circumstances the Court is inclined to the view that the right to the "final" cutting and editing, reserved to the plaintiffs, is limited to the original or theatrical production of the picture and not to showings on television; and that as to such showings, in the absence of specific contractual provision, the parties will be deemed to have adopted the custom prevailing in the trade or industry. . . .

We begin with the proposition that the law is not so rigid, even in the absence of contract, as to leave a party without protection against publication of a garbled version of his work. . . .

In the case at bar, however, the contract must serve as a guide to the intention of the parties. . . .

Thus, where the parties have particularized the terms of a contract, an apparently inconsistent general statement to a different effect must yield. . . . Therefore, the clause in this contract, general in its terms, giving plaintiffs the right to "finally" cut and edit as to the original production of the motion picture, must yield to the specific clause with respect to television showing, which contained no such right. . . .

At the trial, extensive testimony was presented by both sides with respect to the normal customs prevailing in the television and motion picture industries as to the significance of the right to "final cut."

A review of the testimony demonstrates that, at least for the past fifteen years, the right to interrupt the exhibition of a motion picture on television for commercial announcements and to make minor deletions to accommodate time segment requirements or to excise those portions which might be deemed, for various reasons, objectionable, has consistently been considered a normal and essential part of the exhibition of motion pictures on television.

Implicit in the grant of television rights is the privilege to cut and edit. *Autry v. Republic Productions,* 213 F.2d 667, 669 (9 Cir. 1954). . . .

No proof has been adduced that this cutting and editing would be done in such a manner as to interfere with the picture's story line.

The licensing agreements provide:

Licensee shall telecast each print, as delivered by Distributor, in its entirety. However, Licensee may make such minor cuts or elimination as are necessary to conform to time segment requirements or to the orders of any duly authorized public censorship authority and may add commercial material at the places and of the lengths indicated by Distributor, but under no circumstances shall Licensee delete the copyright notice or the credits incorporated in the pictures as delivered by the Distributor, provided, however, in no event may the insertion of any commercial material adversely affect the artistic or pictorial quality of the picture or materially interfere with its continuity. . . .

Defendants' witnesses, Lacey of WCBS, Howard of WNBC and Gilbert of WABC, testified with respect to the practices customarily prevailing throughout the television industry. Plaintiffs' witnesses did not controvert the testimony concerning the customary practices in the trade with regard to interruptions for commercials, and minor cuts. As a matter of fact, Sherwin, one of plaintiffs' witnesses, the program director of KHJ, Los Angeles, testified, as had defendants' witnesses, that his station had never purchased any motion picture without the right to make interruptions as well as minor cuts. Whether or not, in an isolated instance, a picture was exhibited with less than the customary number of commercials is not determinative of the issue. We are concerned not with what might have happened in some rare instance but instead with what was the common practice and custom at the time the parties herein signed their contract.

Thus, Villante, a vice president of the Batten, Barton, Durstine & Osborn advertising agency, described a program known as the "Schaefer Award Theatre" which is handled by his advertising agency. This is a late show program in which feature films are shown without cuts, and with only four interruptions for commercial announcements. Villante acknowledged repeatedly that the Schaefer program was unique. In one instance, he stated, a picture called *The Nun Story* was shown on this same program without any interruptions for commercials whatsoever. He further testified that the purpose of deviating from usual industry practice in the case of this one program was not out of any concern for the rights of the producer, but rather as a public relations device to contribute to the public image of the Schaefer Company, and pursuant to agreement with said sponsor.

With respect to the expression "final cut," sufficient testimony was adduced to indicate that this phrase, as used in Article VIII of the contract, relates only to a phase in the production of the picture for theatrical showing and has no relation to the interruptions and minor cuts here under discussion. Even plaintiffs' own witnesses identified the "final cutting and editing" of a picture as the last stage in its production *for theatrical exhibition*. (emphasis supplied) . . .

Although plaintiffs consistently refer to the practice of interrupting and making minor cuts as "mutilation," their own witnesses have conceded that the minor cuts customarily made in a television exhibition of a picture have such a minimal impact upon its overall effect that these are rarely even noticed.

Undisputed is the fact that not a single television station has ever failed to insist upon the right to interrupt for commercials. Similarly unrefuted is defendants' proof to the effect that no station ever purchased a motion picture without reserving to itself the right to interrupt for commercials and to make minor cuts. . . .

Plaintiff Preminger admitted that when he signed the agreement for *Anatomy of a Murder*, he was aware that the practice of the television industry was to interrupt motion pictures for commercials and to make minor cuts. Aware of this practice, plaintiffs at the time the instant contract was signed nevertheless did not specifically provide for conditions other than those known to them to be prevalent in the industry.

Two contracts between Preminger and United Artists Corporation were received in evidence. These were contracts pertaining to *Man With a Golden Arm* and *The Moon Is Blue*, the last two pictures produced by Preminger prior to *Anatomy of a Murder*, which he made for Columbia. In both the contract for *The Moon Is Blue* and the contract for *Man With a Golden Arm*, clauses appeared which demonstrate that Preminger was aware of the prevailing practice in the television industry with respect to interrupting motion pictures for commercials and making minor cuts therein for normal television purposes. These contracts further show that when Preminger desired to prevent television distribution in the normal manner, he so provided.

In the contract between the Carlyle corporation and United Artists Corporation, dated December 20, 1954, for *Man With a Golden Arm*, it was expressly provided that United Artists' right "to make such changes, additions, alterations, cuts, interpolations and eliminations as may be required for the distribution of the picture in television" should be subject to the approval of Producer.

In similar fashion, the contract with United Artists Corporation with respect to *The Moon Is Blue*, dated April 28, 1952, provided that United Artists' right "to make such changes, additions, alterations, cuts, interpolations, and eliminations as may be required for the distribution of the picture in television" should be "subject to the approval of Producer or its sales representative."

Both Preminger and United Artists were aware that granting the producer this right of approval was tantamount to giving him a veto power over ultimate television distribution of the film, for in other provisions of both of the above contracts it was expressly recognized that television distribution was not to take place without the producer's prior approval.

Plaintiffs' entry into the instant contract which failed to contain such a clause may be considered by the Court as evidence of the parties' intention. . . .

Should a viewer resent the fact that the film is interrupted too often for commercials, and assuredly many do, this resentment would be directed at the station or the sponsor of the program. It is difficult to conceive how such resentment would be directed at the film's producer or director.

So standardized has the practice of interrupting films for commercials become, that guidelines have been established in the television industry as to the maximum number of commercials regarded as acceptable in a given time period. . . .

It is of no import that some viewers may not approve of the advertising practices prevalent in the industry—that is, the number and types of commercials. However, the parties to this distribution agreement signed it knowing of the existence of such practices. The plaintiffs, as well as any independent producer or director, could have obviated this problem by specifically prohibiting such cuts or interruptions by contract. This, of course, might have had an adverse effect on the extent of television distribution—an eventuality which most producers would not welcome. Accordingly, in the absence of any contractual provision to the contrary, they must be deemed to have contemplated that what was permissible, under the existing practice, would continue in effect. . . .

The criterion for the determination of what the defendants were likely to do with respect to interrupting and cutting the subject film, in the absence of a specific contractual arrangement, was not what plaintiffs might disapprove of or dislike but, rather, what was the normal custom and practice in the industry.

The issues in the case, in the Court's view, are therefore issues of law: i.e. (1) whether plaintiffs may thwart the making of minor cuts or interpolations in the absence of specific contractual provision; the Court finds the answer to this question to be in the negative; and (2) whether, under this contract, in the light of the custom in the trade, plaintiffs left to the stationmasters the right to use their judgment and exercise their discretion, instead of plaintiffs', as to which minor cuts, eliminations, and interpolations are appropriate. In view of the variety of stations, localities, audiences, and commercials, the Court answers this question in the affirmative.

The running time of the full motion picture is 161 minutes. The brochure for WABC-TV advertised the picture to potential sponsors as a 100-minute feature. The stationmaster, however, testified, and the Court credits his testimony, that this was a mistake; that it was never intended to permit any such extensive cutting. This applies as well to the asserted cutting of the picture to 53 minutes. Obviously such cuts would not be minor and indeed could well be described as mutilation. Should such "mutilation" occur in the future, plaintiffs may make application to this Court for

injunctive or other relief against such violation as they may be advised. . . .

Gilliam v. American Broadcasting Companies, 538 F.2d 14 (2d Cir. 1976)

[The Monty Python comedy group was extremely popular in England on the basis of its BBC television series. In 1973, BBC licensed Time-Life Films to distribute the series in the United States. ABC, which had previously attempted unsuccessfully to obtain from the group the right to broadcast excerpts from the Python shows, secured a license from Time-Life to broadcast two 90-minute specials, each consisting of three 30-minute Python programs not previously aired in the United States.

Although BBC had assured the group that the programs would be shown in their entirety, in fact each segment was edited by Time-Life to allow for the insertion of commercials (BBC did not show commercials). As aired, the first special included only 66 of the original 90 minutes, having been edited further by ABC to remove material ABC considered offensive or obscene. Although the BBC/Time-Life license permitted editing "for insertion of commercials, applicable censorship or governmental . . . rules and regulations," the underlying Python-BBC agreement contained no such broad grant. The BBC could only make "minor alterations" and "such other alterations as in its opinion are necessary in order to avoid involving the BBC in legal action or bringing the BBC into disrepute." Changes of the latter type could only be made by BBC through a procedure requiring an approach to the group, and only after the group unreasonably refused to do so.

Dismayed at the first program, the group tried to negotiate with ABC over editing of the second special. When these negotiations failed, Monty Python sought a preliminary injunction against the showing of the special. U.S. District Court Judge Lasker denied the motion. Although he held that Monty Python had established irreparable damage by reason of an impairment of the integrity of the group's work, which caused the program to lose its iconoclastic verve, Judge

Lasker felt it was unclear whether BBC or the group was the copyright proprietor of the programs, that it was unclear whether Time-Life and BBC were indispensable parties, that ABC would suffer significant financial loss if the broadcast was enjoined a week prior to air date, and that Monty Python had displayed a "somewhat disturbing casualness" in pursuing the matter. He did, however, require ABC to broadcast a disclaimer during the special indicating that Monty Python disassociated itself from the program because of the editing.

The Second Circuit reversed.]

LUMBARD, J.

. . . There is nothing clearly erroneous in Judge Lasker's conclusion that any injury suffered by appellants as a result of the broadcast of edited versions of their programs was irreparable by its nature. ABC presented the appellants with their first opportunity for broadcast to a nationwide network audience in this country. If ABC adversely misrepresented the quality of Monty Python's work, it is likely that many members of the audience, many of whom, by defendant's admission, were previously unfamiliar with appellants, would not become loyal followers of Monty Python productions. The subsequent injury to appellants' theatrical reputation would imperil their ability to attract the large audience necessary to the success of their venture. Such an injury to professional reputation cannot be measured in monetary terms or recompensed by other relief. . . .

In contrast to the harm that Monty Python would suffer by a denial of the preliminary injunction, Judge Lasker found that ABC's relationship with its affiliates would be impaired by a grant of an injunction within a week of the scheduled December 26 broadcast. The court also found that ABC and its affiliates had advertised the program and had included it in listings of forthcoming television programs that were distributed to the public. Thus a last minute cancellation of the December 26 program, Judge Lasker concluded, would injure defendant financially and in its reputation with the public and its advertisers.

However valid these considerations may have

been when the issue before the court was whether a preliminary injunction should immediately precede the broadcast, any injury to ABC is presently more speculative. No rebroadcast of the edited specials has been scheduled and no advertising costs have been incurred for the immediate future. Thus there is no danger that defendant's relations with affiliates or the public will suffer irreparably if subsequent broadcasts of the programs are enjoined pending a disposition of the issues. . . .

In concluding that there is a likelihood of infringement here, we rely especially on the fact that the editing was substantial, i.e., approximately 27 percent of the original program was omitted, and the editing contravened contractual provisions that limited the right to edit Monty Python material. . . . Judge Lasker denied the preliminary injunction in part because he was unsure of the ownership of the copyright in the recorded program. Appellants first contend that the question of ownership is irrelevant because the recorded program was merely a derivative work taken from the script in which they hold the uncontested copyright. Thus, even if BBC owned the copyright in the recorded program, its use of that work would be limited by the license granted to BBC by Monty Python for use of the underlying script. We agree. . . .

Since the copyright in the underlying script survives intact despite the incorporation of that work into a derivative work, one who uses the script, even with the permission of the proprietor of the derivative work, may infringe the underlying copyright. . . .

One who obtains permission to use a copyrighted script in the production of a derivative work, . . . may not exceed the specific purpose for which permission was granted. . . .

The rationale for finding infringement when a licensee exceeds time or media restrictions on his license—the need to allow the proprietor of the underlying copyright to control the method in which his work is presented to the public—applies equally to the situation in which a licensee makes an unauthorized use of the underlying work by publishing it in a truncated version. Whether intended to allow greater economic exploitation of the work, as in the media and time cases, or to ensure that the copyright proprietor retains a veto power over revisions desired for the derivative work, the ability of the copyright holder to control his work remains paramount in our copyright law. We find, therefore, that unauthorized editing of the underlying work, if proven, would constitute an infringement of the copyright in that work similar to any other use of a work that exceeded the license granted by the proprietor of the copyright.

If the broadcast of an edited version of the Monty Python program infringed the group's copyright in the script, ABC may obtain no solace from the fact that editing was permitted in the agreements between BBC and Time-Life or Time-Life and ABC. BBC was not entitled to make unilateral changes in the script and was not specifically empowered to alter the recordings once made; Monty Python, moreover, had reserved to itself any rights not granted to BBC. Since a grantor may not convey greater rights than it owns, BBC's permission to allow Time-Life, and hence ABC, to edit appears to have been a nullity. . . .

Although a holder of a derivative copyright may obtain rights in the underlying work through ratification, the conduct necessary to that conclusion has yet to be demonstrated in this case. It is undisputed that appellants did not have actual notice of the cuts in the October 3 broadcast until late November. Even if they are chargeable with the knowledge of their British representative, it is not clear that she had prior notice of the cuts or ratified the omissions, nor did Judge Lasker make any finding on the question. While [Monty Python's representative], on September 5, did question how ABC was to broadcast the entire program if it was going to interpose 24 minutes of commercials, she received assurances from BBC that the programs would not be "segmented." . . .

On the present record, it cannot be said that there was any ratification of BBC's grant of editing rights. ABC, of course, is entitled to attempt to prove otherwise during the trial on the merits.

Aside from the question of who owns the relevant copyrights, ABC asserts that the contracts between appellants and BBC permit editing of the programs for commercial television in the United States. ABC argues that the scriptwriters'

agreement allows appellants the right to participate in revisions of the script only *prior* to the recording of the programs, and thus infers that BBC had unrestricted authority to revise after that point. This argument, however, proves too much. A reading of the contract seems to indicate that Monty Python obtained control over editing the script only to ensure control over the program recorded from that script. Since the scriptwriters' agreement explicitly retains for the group all rights not granted by the contract, omission of any terms concerning alterations in the program after recording must be read as reserving to appellants exclusive authority for such revisions. . . .

Finally, ABC contends that appellants must have expected that deletions would be made in the recordings to conform them for use on commercial television in the United States. ABC argues that licensing in the United States implicitly grants a license to insert commercials in a program and to remove offensive or obscene material prior to broadcast. According to the network, appellants should have anticipated that most of the excised material contained scatological references inappropriate for American television and that these scenes would be replaced with commercials, which presumably are more palatable to the American public.

The proof adduced up to this point, however, provides no basis for finding any implied consent to edit. Prior to the ABC broadcasts, Monty Python programs had been broadcast on a regular basis by both commercial and public television stations in this country without interruption or deletion. Indeed, there is no evidence of any prior broadcast of edited Monty Python material in the United States. These facts, combined with the persistent requests for assurances by the group and its representatives that the programs would be shown intact belie the argument that the group knew or should have known that deletions and commercial interruptions were inevitable.

Several of the deletions made for ABC, such as elimination of the words "hell" and "damn," seem inexplicable given today's standard television fare. If, however, ABC honestly determined that the programs were obscene in substantial part, it could have decided not to broadcast the specials at all, or it could have attempted to reconcile its differences with appellants. The network could not, however, free from a claim of infringement, broadcast in a substantially altered form a program incorporating the script over which the group had retained control.

It also seems likely that appellants will succeed on the theory that, regardless of the right ABC had to broadcast an edited program, the cuts made constituted an actionable mutilation of Monty Python's work. This cause of action, which seeks redress for deformation of an artist's work, finds its roots in the continental concept of droit moral, or moral right, which may generally be summarized as including the right of the artist to have his work attributed to him in the form in which he created it. . . .

American copyright law, as presently written, does not recognize moral rights or provide a cause of action for their violation, since the law seeks to vindicate the economic, rather than the personal, rights of authors. Nevertheless, the economic incentive for artistic and intellectual creation that serves as the foundation for American copyright law . . . cannot be reconciled with the inability of artists to obtain relief for mutilation or misrepresentation of their work to the public on which the artists are financially dependent. Thus courts have long granted relief for misrepresentation of an artist's work by relying on theories outside the statutory law of copyright, such as contract law, *Granz v. Harris*, 198 F.2d 585 (2d Cir. 1952) (substantial cutting of original work constitutes misrepresentation), or the tort of unfair competition, *Prouty v. National Broadcasting Co.*, 26 F. Supp. 265 (D. Mass. 1939). See Strauss, "The Moral Right of the Author," 128–138, in *Studies on Copyright* (1963). Although such decisions are clothed in terms of proprietary right in one's creation, they also properly vindicate the author's personal right to prevent the presentation of his work to the public in a distorted form.

Here, the appellants claim that the editing done for ABC mutilated the original work and that consequently the broadcast of those programs as the creation of Monty Python violated the Lanham Act Sec. 43(a), 15 U.S.C. Sec. 1125(a). This statute, the federal counterpart to state unfair competition laws, has been invoked to prevent misrepresentations that may injure plaintiff's business or personal reputation, even where no registered trademark is concerned. . . . It is sufficient to violate the Act that a representation of a product, although technically true, creates a false impression of the product's origin.

We find that the truncated version at times omitted the climax of the skits to which appellants' rare brand of humor was leading and at other times deleted essential elements in the schematic development of a story line. We therefore agree with Judge Lasker's conclusion that the edited version broadcast by ABC impaired the integrity of appellants' work and represented to the public as the product of appellants what was actually a mere caricature of their talents. We believe that a valid cause of action for such distortion exists and that therefore a preliminary injunction may issue to prevent repetition of the broadcast prior to final determination of the issues.

GURFEIN, J., CONCURRING

I concur in my brother Lumbard's scholarly opinion, but I wish to comment on the application of Section 43(a) of the Lanham Act, 15 U.S.C. Sec. 1125(a).

I believe that this is the first case in which a federal appellate court has held that there may be a violation of Section 43(a) of the Lanham Act with respect to a common-law copyright. The Lanham Act is a trademark statute, not a copyright statute. Nevertheless, we must recognize that the language of Section 43(a) is broad. It speaks of the affixation or use of false designations of origin or false descriptions or representations, but proscribes such use "in connection with any goods or services." It is easy enough to incorporate trade names as well as trademarks into Section 43(a) and the statute specifically applies to common law trademarks, as well as registered trademarks. Lanham Act Sec. 45, 15 U.S.C. Sec. 1127.

In the present case, we are holding that the deletion of portions of the recorded tape constitutes a breach of contract, as well as an infringement of a common-law copyright of the original work. There is literally no need to discuss whether plaintiffs also have a claim for relief under the Lanham Act or for unfair competition under New York law. . . .

The Copyright Act provides no recognition of the so-called *droit moral* or moral right of authors. Nor are such rights recognized in the field of copyright law in the United States. . . . An obligation to mention the name of the author carries the implied duty, however, as a matter of contract, not to make such changes in the work as would render the credit line a false attribution of authorship.

So far as the Lanham Act is concerned, it is not a substitute for *droit moral* which authors in Europe enjoy. If the licensee may, by contract, distort the recorded word, the Lanham Act does not come into play. If the licensee has no such right by contract, there will be a violation in breach of contract. The Lanham Act can hardly apply literally when the credit line correctly states the work to be that of the plaintiffs which, indeed it is, so far as it goes. The vice complained of is that the truncated version is not what the plaintiffs wrote. But the Lanham Act does not deal with artistic integrity. It only goes to misdescription of origin and the like. . . . The misdescription of origin can be dealt with, as Judge Lasker did below, by devising an appropriate legend to indicate that the plaintiffs had not approved the editing of the ABC version. With such a legend, there is no conceivable violation of the Lanham Act.

7.40   Development and Production Agreements

The following article traces how material, however acquired and/or adapted, moves from idea to distribution. The *Merrick* case supplements the article in its discussion of the consequences of a producer's failure to produce as required under the contract. This article first appeared in the *Los Angeles Lawyer,* January 1985. It is reprinted here with the permission of the authors. (Footnotes have been omitted.)

TV DEVELOPMENT AND PRODUCTION AGREEMENTS

by Henry I. Bushkin and Beth Maloney Jelin

In recent years, the television industry has been shaken to its foundation by a revolution in the business. Through cable television, major new areas have been created to exhibit programming and the appetite for programs is ravenous. Nonetheless, network television remains the most important force in the medium and competition among the networks is more rivalrous than ever before in television history. Today, television programs are on the air an average of 18 hours a day and are broadcast on more than 1,000 over-the-air channels and hundreds of cable channels. Notwithstanding the tremendous increase in the volume of television production, the basic contractual prerequisites which a producer must follow to make a new television show remain the same.

This article focuses on various agreements which the individual producer must have in order to produce a television show for exhibition on one of the three major networks (hereinafter "network" is used to refer to any of the three). The focus is the individual producer (the "producer"), because he is most likely to be the private practitioner's client.

The Basic Agreement

The producer must deal with two basic entities: the network and the production company. A common scenario is as follows: a producer approaches a network with a project. The network likes the project and would like to go forward. However, it does not feel that the producer has the resources to actually deliver the show. The network therefore will require the producer to enter into a production agreement with a production company. This article tracks the elements of these two related deals: 1) the producer and the network, and 2) the producer and the production company.

At the threshold, there is the "development deal," an agreement between the network and the producer to develop a particular show. It is documented in a "deal memo," a short letter or memorandum of agreement which sets forth the material terms of the agreement. The network negotiates for the rights to the producer's property, the right to order the script and the right to order the movie, the special, the pilot, or the series. The producer agrees to deliver a script. If the script is acceptable, then the network negotiates license fees and exercises its option rights for production and delivery of the show. Neither the producer nor the network is interested in investing the time or effort required at this point to reach a comprehensive "long form" agreement, since it is uncertain whether the particular show will progress beyond the development stage. Moreover, if the producer needs to ally himself with a major production company, he must be cautious not to lock himself into terms which may prove objectionable to the production company. Nevertheless, the deal memo is prepared whenever a network negotiates a program order.

The producer has several options to consider in securing a development deal. The most obvious is to approach the network directly and present the idea. This entails a meeting with the network's creative affairs executive who is responsible for the particular area into which the concept falls. If the creative affairs executive likes the idea, it will be passed through the appropriate decision-making levels until the network decides whether to make a development deal.

One of the network's concerns will be the identity of the producer and what the network perceives as his ability to deliver an acceptable staff for the show. Under certain circumstances, the network may insist that the producer enter into a production agreement with a "major," "mini-major," or otherwise acceptable independent production company to actually produce the show. If the producer is relatively inexperienced, lacks a strong financial backing, or is unable to obtain a letter of credit or post a completion bond, the network will probably make a production agreement a condition of the development deal.

As an alternative, the producer should consider whether to approach a production company prior to approaching the network, especially if there is good reason to believe that the network will insist upon the involvement of a production company. The advantage to this approach is that the production company will have access to network executives who have greater decision-making power than the executive with whom the producer would otherwise meet.

There are other advantages to starting with a production company. For example, a production company may be in a better position to evaluate which network would be most interested in the producer's show. Furthermore, especially in the case of a novice producer, a production company will lend him credibility, experience and the ability to staff the show to the network's approval. In any event, if the producer is unable to make an agreement with a production company, he still has the opportunity to approach a network directly.

Obviously, if the producer succeeds in obtaining a development deal directly from a network, he has more than just an idea to sell when he contacts the production company. Although he still may have to give up some or all of the ownership rights in the show to the production company, he will be in a far better position to bargain for a strong compensation package with profit participation.

A more recent twist is the network's desire that the show be produced through the network's own television production company. The network's production unit is normally used when the idea for a particular show is generated internally at the network. Some networks are more aggressive than others in this regard. If the network wants to use its own television production company, this naturally places the producer in a difficult bargaining position with respect to compensation, ownership, control and credit. On the other hand, when two shows are being considered for the same time slot, the one made by the network's production unit will have an advantage. In addition, if the producer participates in the show's profits, he may receive significant benefits since network profit definitions sometimes are more liberal than those of studios, without nearly the typical studio overhead factors.

The foregoing considerations affect the negotiations of various types of development and production agreements.

For the producer, the most sought after program is an episodic series, with the half-hour situation comedy being the most desired. Ordinarily, a series is the result of a "step deal" whereby the network has sequential options to place orders: first, for the script; next, for the pilot; and then, for the series.

At any point, the network may decline to take the next step, or two steps may be taken at the same time. For example, the network may agree to develop the project, contingent upon finding an acceptable writer. If the producer's initial presentation includes a committed, acceptable writer, the network will proceed directly to order the script. On occasion, the network may commit itself to order a pilot based on a yet-to-be delivered script.

In the exceptional circumstance, the producer might obtain an immediate order for a series and by-pass the traditional step deal. This exception occurs in the rare instance when the series evolves from a movie-of-the-week (MOW) or special that has aired already, or a producer packages an approved concept, writers, production staff and one or more star performers.

The producer may present his concept in a variety of forms: original idea, synopsis, short treatment, short story, novel, article, or true-to-life incident depending upon the circumstances. He may outline the overall framework of the show supplemented by a brief synopsis of the basic plot, themes and principal characters. He also may present the network with a list of possible ideas or story lines for the first few episodes of the show. Alternatively, the producer may present the network with a "package" that includes writers, story editors and performers committed to the project. Obtaining commitments for talented and reputable personnel can help sell the project to the network. As a result, the producer will strive to make them a part of his initial presentation.

An early decision will be which network to

approach. The practitioner's knowledge can be of great assistance in this selection process. Each network has its own research department that conducts on-going studies of product need and continually evaluates the strengths and weaknesses in its overall program schedule. The producer wants to find a network with a programming gap which his show will fill. This requires both an objective evaluation of a network's particular type of television programming and a subjective appraisal of the network's internal judgment.

Since the most successful network will renew the greatest number of existing shows for the upcoming season, the producer may have a greater chance for success by approaching a network with low Nielsen ratings. The producer also should consider which time slots are achieving high ratings within a given network's overall program schedule. In addition, it is important to consider that shows, for the most part, are designed for given time periods. For example, family-oriented shows generally air within the 8 PM to 9 PM time slot, children's programs on Saturday morning, soap operas in the early afternoon and game shows in the late morning or early evening.

The Script Order

After the producer and network agree upon a suitable writer, the network places the script order, which typically provides for the reimbursement to the producer for his development costs, including the writer's salary and any payments made by the producer to option any underlying property. Generally, reimbursement payments for the writer's salary are tied to the delivery dates for different stages of the script—first draft, revisions, polish—and coincide with the dates when the producer owes payments to the writer.

If the producer also functions as the writer, the deal memo provides for compensation to the producer for such writing services. The producer who also writes may commission the script to an outside writer, while locking himself into the project in the capacity of script supervisor, but rarely will be separately compensated for such supervisory services. If the producer has a significant reputation or has written previously successful shows, the network may insist that the producer supervise the project.

Among the deal memo terms that pertain to the script order, the network will be granted certain creative controls, such as the right to review the script in various development stages. Although the network's creative input may be viewed by the producer as a loss of creative control, the producer must assume that the network is developing the script along the lines of a show that it will want to broadcast. Of course, it is always possible that the network will decide not to pursue the project further than the script stage and no pilot will be ordered.

To deal with this possibility, it is important for the deal memo to delineate clearly the producer's rights and responsibilities in that regard. If there is no pilot order within the negotiated time period, which will be a minimum of 60 days after delivery of the final script, then the producer should have the right to "turnaround" and sell the project to another network. However, the original network will condition the producer's turnaround rights on its right to recoup all of its development costs if the producer is successful in making a deal elsewhere.

It is not until a pilot or series is ordered that the network and producer begin to negotiate the license fee that the network will pay the producer for the right to broadcast the show. The deal memo usually will provide only two things with respect to the license fee: that it will be negotiated in good faith at the time of the pilot or series order and that all development costs reimbursed to the producer by the network will apply against and reduce the license fee. The deal memo also should set forth the producer's turnaround rights in the event that the producer and the network fail to reach an agreement on the license fee.

The Pilot Order

Assuming the final script is approved, the next step will be for the network to order a pilot.

The deal memo generally specifies the period of time within which the pilot order must be placed, such as 60 to 180 days after delivery of the script. The pilot order should specify the fees the producer will be paid for producing the pilot; the time period in which the network may broadcast the pilot (for example, not later than two broadcast seasons following delivery of the pilot); and the license fee.

The network will retain control over creative elements, such as the title and the format, and over key creative personnel such as producers, directors, writers and talent or replacement of any of the foregoing elements. The pilot order may be conditioned on the involvement of certain persons, such as a particular star. It also may be conditioned on the involvement of an acceptable production company. Since the producer wants maximum flexibility with respect to this decision, he should attempt to obtain a "guarantee clause" permitting him to take the project to any production company.

The network, however, prefers a blanket provision preserving absolute approval over selection of a production company. If it obtains such control, it will be able to force the producer to align himself with a specific production company. Such forced alignment may be detrimental to the producer since he will be precluded from shopping his network commitment among various production companies.

The license fees for the pilot may be negotiated before the show is completely packaged. Fees for the services of most of the professionals associated with the show tend to be standard or can be reasonably estimated. The cast will be subject to "breakage fees" (described below in discussion of the series order). The fee for the pilot generally is negotiated on a cost-up-to basis, which usually fails to cover the full cost of production. In the unlikely event that the pilot is produced under budget, the cost-up-to arrangement means that the network gains the benefit of any efficiency.

However, in the more likely event that the pilot runs over budget, the producer must make up the deficit from his own funds. Nevertheless, as a practical matter, the producer readily will incur deficit financing because a pilot is a promotional vehicle. If the pilot is well received, the network will order the series. A producer, therefore, will be willing to spend substantial sums to enhance the pilot's production value, even at the risk of incurring deficits.

Typically, the fee for the pilot is paid in three installments, the first due upon commencement of principal photography, the next upon completion of the production and the last upon delivery of the pilot (after post production). However, the producer with a fair measure of bargaining power or lack of cash flow may insist that as much as two-thirds of the pilot fee be paid upon commencement of principal photography.

The pilot fee generally entitles the network to broadcast an hour or half-hour pilot twice within two broadcast years after delivery. If the pilot is a two-hour show and no series is ordered or picked up, the network will be able to broadcast it twice within four years. If the network decides to pick up the show and places a series order, this period automatically will be extended to authorize repeat broadcasts of the pilot during the period when the network broadcasts the series.

After delivery of the pilot, the network has a given period of time to decide whether or not to order the production of a program series. The initial network television series order includes 22 or more episodes, which may be ordered in two option periods. The first option permits the network to order 12 episodes (13 including the pilot). The second option permits the network to order nine additional episodes. The date on which the network must exercise the second option is timed to enable the network to obtain an adequate rating sampling while permitting the production company to maintain an uninterrupted program production schedule.

If the network declines to order nine additional episodes, its option to order programs for subsequent years is lost. Production orders for all years after the first are on a 22-episode basis.

The producer should amortize his costs on the assumption that both options will be exercised and 22 episodes will be produced. However, the deal memo should contain a "short-rate" payment which is due to the producer if the network does not exercise its second option. The short-rate payment reimburses the producer for costs incurred during production of the first 13 episodes, which were amortized on a 22-episode basis. It specifically does not cover production overages.

In negotiating the license fee, certain additional factors must be considered. Since a successful series will continue for years, the license fee should be subject to built-in inflationary increases. In addition, the producer should attempt to obtain a specific and well-defined breakage clause which will require the network to pay for costs in excess of the license fee, if certain "special" creative elements in excess of budgeted amounts are added to the production at the network's request or with its approval. For example, a breakage provision might estimate an amount to be added to the license fee if the producer obtains a certain caliber of performer to star in an episode or in the series.

In certain situations, the breakage figure may be applicable to additional desirable creative elements such as extraordinary special effects, set designs or costumes required for a special period piece episode. In addition, it is important to obtain a breakage fee to cover special production difficulties anticipated in relation to the particular context of a series. As with the pilot fee negotiation, breakage fees are granted by the network on a cost-up-to basis, which places the risk of overages on the producer or production company while providing the benefit of any economic or organizational efficiencies to the network. The more specific and carefully delineated the breakage provision, the more the producer will be protected should the license fee fail to cover production costs. As additional protection, the producer may negotiate for reimbursement of location costs and set construction. Such reimbursements are unusual, but if the network consents, those expenses will be repaid on a cost-up-to basis.

A producer with certain talents can assure himself of receiving continued revenues after the series is ordered. If he is experienced and on the network's list of preapproved "line producers," he may want to serve as line producer for the series, rendering services on an exclusive basis with responsibility for daily production activities. A line producer will be given screen credit as producer and may be able to obtain this position on a pay-or-play basis for the first order of episodes, so that he must be paid the agreed fee for his services regardless of whether he is actually used.

Alternatively, the producer may seek the position of "executive producer" of the series. In contrast to a line producer, the executive producer renders services on a non-exclusive basis and generally is responsible for overseeing the entire production schedule as well as the various line producers engaged throughout the season. An executive producer may be able to obtain his position on a pay-or-play basis (although this is difficult to achieve because of the difference in the nature of the position), and will be accorded credit as executive producer.

An executive producer may want to provide line-producing services at the beginning of the series, and then later serve as executive producer. This enables him to establish the quality and continuity of the show before he delegates important creative and decision-making tasks to others. Once the series has been established, he then acts as executive producer in order to be free to develop other projects while maintaining his involvement with the series.

A producer of lesser stature may attempt to persuade the network that he should render line-producing services on the series, but this is rarely granted if the producer has no prior credits in that capacity. In any event, the producer's ability to obtain such a position is subject to the agreements, if any, between the producer and a production company.

The producer with relatively little experience may reasonably hope to obtain a co-production credit from the production company, depending upon the production company's enthusiasm for the show. Alternatively, the producer should be able to receive consultation fees, which may be negotiated on either a per-episode or one-time-only basis, but this will not necessarily entitle the producer to receive screen credit.

The producer who also writes the show may be able to negotiate a royalty payment for creating the series. This royalty is not contingent upon the producer's performance of any particular services in the event the series is produced, but rather is paid in addition to any other series-related compensation. The series royalty is generally negotiated in the form of a fixed sum and is typically payable to the producer on a per-episode basis, contingent upon the producer receiving sole "created by" credit in accordance with standards set by the Writers Guild of America. In the event that created-by credit must be shared, the series royalty is generally reducible to not less than a floor of approximately one-half the negotiated sum.

Production Agreements

The producer with a network development agreement for a particular show has to get his show made in a form acceptable to the network. The producer has three principal types of arrangements available to him: an employment or co-production agreement, a joint venture or a straight distribution agreement.

The novice producer most likely will enter into an agreement with a production company in which the producer will be an employee and/or co-producer of the particular show. A producer with some producing experience may be in a position to enter into a partnership arrangement with a production company. Finally, the veteran producer, who has the financial backing and expertise to produce the show himself, usually will seek an agreement directly with the network to produce the show and, at some later point, enter into a distribution arrangement for that show with a distributor.

Employment Co-production Agreement

When a producer associates with a production company, he invariably gives up certain controls as a result of their agreement. The production company will either employ him or coproduce the project with him. As an employee, the producer usually relinquishes all ownership rights to the underlying property so that the project belongs to the production company.

All dealings with the network are conducted through the production company, with the producer coordinating the effort to convince the network to proceed to each subsequent step of the step deal. After execution of this agreement, the producer, practically speaking, will be an employee of the production company. Consequently, the agreement should enumerate all of the producer's rights in the event of the success or failure of the project. The initial contract typically will be a form agreement originating with the production company which, on its face, will be most favorable to the production company.

If the producer goes to the production company before going to the network, he will give the production company a specific length of time in which to obtain a network commitment for his show. If the production company does not obtain a network production commitment, the producer receives turnaround rights to reacquire from the production company all of the right, title and interest in the project by reimbursing the production company for its costs.

This is an important consideration for the novice producer. The producer should not put himself in the position where, as an employee, he has no rights to the project and thus cannot force the production company to proceed further with the development of the project. With a turnaround right, the producer is in a position to develop the property on his own or in association with another studio or production company.

As part of his arrangement with the production company, the producer may be employed to supervise the writing of a pilot script or, if he is a writer, to write the script himself. Either way, the producer will receive a fee and credit appropriate for the services he performs. The producer should be paid for such services on a pay-or-play basis so that he will receive his production fee even if the production company decides to replace him.

The producer may provide services to the production company on an exclusive or non-exclusive basis. If the producer works on a non-exclusive basis, he can pursue other opportunities and projects while under contract to the production company. When the producer works as a line producer of the show, he has no choice but to be exclusive; however, any other position will enable the producer to work on a non-exclusive basis.

The employment agreement between the producer and the production company must include terms regarding the producer's services after a production commitment has been obtained. For example, the producer should be employed as a producer or executive producer (preferably at the producer's election) for the first and each succeeding production year throughout the term of the network series deal. While the production company may agree to this arrangement, the network will make the final decision on the show's actual producer.

For each production year of the series for which the producer renders his services, he should be compensated on a per episode basis, measured in part by the length of each episode and the producer's role in the show. Because the series may run for several seasons, cumulative or noncumulative increases in compensation for successive seasons should be included in the agreement.

The producer's credit and various royalty payments will depend upon the nature of his services and whether or not he is the sole creator of the underlying idea for the show. In most cases, production credit will be listed as executive producer or supervising producer. Writing credit, although subject to final Writers' Guild determination, probably will be "created by" or "written by." If the producer receives sole or shared created-by credit, he will be entitled to series royalties, which are payable as a production royalty for each episode produced and as a repeat royalty for each rebroadcast of an episode. While the repeat royalty is equal in amount to the production royalty, it is generally payable in 20 percent installments over the second through sixth repeats of each episode.

Regarding credits, the practitioner can negotiate regarding the actual onscreen presentation of the credit. The producer will want his credit to be on a "separate card," so that his credit will not appear at the same time as that of another producer or artist. In addition, if the producer is rendering services through his "loan out" company, he probably will want his corporation to receive a separate credit.

In terms of contingent compensation, the novice producer lacks bargaining power to negotiate with a production company for a large percentage of the show's profits. Notwithstanding some rare exceptions, unless the producer has entered into a true co-production agreement, he will not share the profits equally with the production company. More likely, the producer who is an employee will receive between 10 and 25 percent of the series' net profits.

Two factors are particularly important regarding profit participations. First, the profit definition of the production company must be analyzed with precision, since the method followed to determine profits will make a significant difference in the amount of money the producer actually receives. Second, it is important to note whether third-party participations will be paid solely by the producer, solely by the production company, or shared equally by each. The producer's consent should be required prior to the grant of any net profit participation which will reduce his share.

The producer who is an employee most likely will be required to share the creative, business, financial and legal decisions with the production company to a greater extent than the experienced producer. It may be anticipated that the production company will have final approval over such elements, though at the very least, the producer should seek the right to have the production company consult with him in good faith on these matters.

As an employee, the producer is unlikely to obtain any benefits from the investment tax credit available to the producers of a television show. Although there are exceptions, and this is subject to negotiation, the investment tax credit usually is taken by the production company.

In a joint venture arrangement, the producer with some successful television experience joins forces with a production company, perhaps for financial reasons or for enhanced negotiating position with a network, to produce a particular show. Since the bargaining position of the producer and production company tend to be more balanced in this situation, the terms tend to be more equal than those obtainable by the producer-employee. The benefit to the producer from this arrangement is that he has many of the same advantages he would have if he produced the show himself, without the attendant financial exposure.

All property and assets of the joint venture, including all of the tangible and intangible rights, such as copyrights, relating to the show will be held in the joint venture's name. Ordinarily, the joint venture will exist for the longer of 1) the duration of all copyrights relating to the show which are owned by the joint venture or 2) the term of all agreements relating to the show.

Many items included in the joint venture agreement are the same points of negotiation discussed above regarding services, credits, fees and royalties. For example, in the joint venture, the best situation for the producer is to receive production or presentation credit "in association with" the production company and/or the joint venture. If possible, the producer's services should be non-exclusive and he should not be required to present any projects to the joint venture (except the one that is the subject of the joint venture agreement), thereby ensuring his freedom to develop projects outside the joint venture.

One important item unique to joint venture

agreements is capital contributions, which represent each party's contribution of a specified percentage of the joint venture's required capital (and additional capital, if the initial contributions are not sufficient). Each party's capital contribution probably will, although not necessarily, determine the amount of income, depreciation, profits, losses and investment tax credit which will be allocated to the producer and the production company. Thus, if the producer contributes 25 percent of the joint venture's capital, he may be allocated 25 percent of its profits and losses.

The responsibility for management and control of the joint venture will be specified in the joint venture agreement. Management and control usually are divided into the creative, business, financial and legal areas. Final authority for decisions with respect to each area may be delegated separately and may vary depending upon the stage of the production. Thus, there may be joint creative approval prior to principal photography of the pilot, while during principal photography the production company has final approval.

Final approval will be a key area of negotiation for the producer, since he will be interested in obtaining maximum creative control. If the producer does not have final authority for a particular area, he should at least obtain consultation rights. Ultimately, however, creative decisions will be subject to approval by the network with which the joint venture makes its development deal.

Finally, in the joint venture structure, the producer may be able to negotiate for additional fees and advances. He can seek development and consultation fees and should have a strong argument for them, especially if he relinquishes his approval rights. If the producer is entitled to a share of the joint venture's profits, he may ask for advances against his entitlement. He may be able to receive a specified sum for each episode of the series which the network licenses for broadcast. This can take different forms such as advances against foreign sales or advances against domestic distribution of the show. It should be remembered, however, that advances also are available in the other types of production agreements discussed in this article.

Straight Distribution Agreement

The experienced producer who has a firm development deal in place with the network, and has the financial capacity to produce network programming, is in the enviable position of having to look only for ways to maximize the return on the investment in his shows. Since a producer usually realizes little or no profit—and most likely suffers a loss—on the network production (particularly if he has not covered his deficit and overhead costs from network revenues), he will look to subsequent distribution of his show in order to recoup and profit from his investment.

This distribution takes the form of syndication which occurs after the show's initial network run, and when the show is aired on domestic non-network stations and in the foreign market.

Since the license agreement with the network grants it exclusive television broadcast rights in the domestic market, syndication broadcasts are prohibited during the series or license term. The producer may obtain some additional income on his investment from network reruns, and from network "stripping," that is, running the show either early in the morning or late at night on a five-times-per-week basis; however, the network normally will pay only out-of-pocket scale residual costs for network reruns and little more than the producer's costs for network stripping because of the limited audience for these shows. Therefore, it is unlikely that the network will be a source of significant additional income. Thus, the area of the non-network distribution agreement offers the best income opportunities for the producer.

Notwithstanding the network's exclusivity rights, the financially strong producer who has a network deal can make a distribution agreement in which he will be able to pre-negotiate substantial non-returnable advances or guarantees against his share of the distributor's profits from foreign and domestic non-network exploitation of his show.

Furthermore, since the network license agreement does not have any restrictions on foreign television distribution (other than the telecast overlaps with Mexico in the San Diego market and Canada in the Detroit market), the foreign television market offers the producer and his distributor an immediate, though not the most profitable, source of income. Therefore, the producer's advances against foreign distribution profits should be negotiated separately from advances against domestic distribution profits.

Ideally, advances against foreign distribution should be payable in installments for a minimum of the first 13 episodes of any series (although they are sometimes paid for all episodes produced). Payments should commence upon the distributor's receipt of a copy of the network's written order for the episodes, with the last payment due no later than one year later.

Of the various income sources, the most profitable for the producer will be the domestic syndication market, so that advances against domestic distribution profits will be significantly higher than foreign advances. Domestic syndication usually requires completion of four production years, with a minimum of 88 episodes, to realize the maximum financial potential for successful domestic syndication.

While the network generally broadcasts one episode of the series per week, the series will be broadcast five times per week when it is exhibited in domestic syndication, so that a series of 88 episodes will be repeated once in its entirety every 16 weeks.

Because audience dilution is the major concern for successful syndication, the greater the number of episodes, the greater the chance for success. However, this does not mean that the producer must wait until he has 88 episodes produced before he can receive domestic advances. Domestic advances should be triggered upon completion of three years of production (with a minimum of 66 episodes), plus there should be an escalation clause to increase the amount of the advances upon completion of four years of production (with a minimum of 88 episodes). The distributor will want to condition payment of the domestic advances upon the availability of the episodes for domestic syndication and their having been broadcast on the network in prime time.

Advances for domestic distribution can range to more than $200,000 per episode, with the dramatic one-hour series episodes commanding the highest sum. The range of such advances varies depending upon whether they are for foreign or domestic markets, whether the series is successful in the network market, whether the series is perceived to be likely to be successful in the foreign or domestic markets, and whether episodes are a half-hour or an hour long. In addition, the producer may be able to obtain non-returnable advances or guarantees for foreign and domestic syndication of pilots which do not become a part of a series.

Although the producer may not be able to pre-negotiate advances in areas of distribution other than free television, he should be careful to protect his rights to receive residuals from the distributor's exploitation in such other areas.

Where the distributor has agreed to pay an advance to the producer, it will usually want to recoup its costs, including the amount of the advance, prior to the producer's participation in profits. This is commonly accomplished by applying the advance against what otherwise would have been the producer's share of the gross profits. Although the gross profits division between the producer and distributor may vary, depending upon the distributor's target fee for its distribution efforts in each market of exploitation, a distributor normally takes a 35 to 40 percent fee for foreign and domestic syndication, and a 20 percent fee for network stripping of a series.

In a gross participation deal, the producer usually pays all residual costs and any third-party profit participations granted by the producer from his share of the gross profits, while the distributor pays for all other distribution costs from its share. In negotiating an overall distribution agreement with the distributor for more than one type of show or series, there should be no cross-collateralization for purposes of recouping advances, but rather each show or series should be treated as an entirely separate unit. It should be noted that while the distributor will differentiate between foreign and domestic advances for a series, the producer may be able to pre-negotiate one advance which would cover both foreign and domestic distribution for MOWs.

In contrast to other types of production agreements, with a distribution agreement, items such as property rights, copyrights and investment tax credit benefits with respect to the shows are retained solely by the producer, subject only to the distribution rights granted to the distributor. The producer retains control over all creative, business and legal matters as well as credits, in connection with the production of the shows.

The producer described in this section will be able to negotiate some form of gross participation deal. If for any reason the producer must enter into a traditional net profits or joint venture arrangement, the practitioner must carefully scrutinize each and every element of the proposed agreement, since traditionally, it favors the production company. While a comprehensive discussion of this type of arrangement is beyond the scope of this article, it should be noted that the net profits definition is a critical consideration.

A distributor involved in a net profits arrangement normally charges varying distribution sales fees (except with respect to the network sale which is normally the producer's province) and production and distribution expenses, which normally include a percentage of overhead and interest. After three to four years of production, these expenses reach a level where it becomes difficult to achieve net profits, unless the term has been defined very favorably to the producer.

Conclusion

The producer with a proven track record and independent financial backing can obtain highly favorable terms in negotiating development agreements with the networks, and pro-

duction or distribution agreements with production companies. In many cases, he is in a position to deal directly with the networks to make a production deal rather than having to resort to a production company for assistance—both financial and in negotiations with the networks.

At the other extreme, the inexperienced producer should anticipate that he will have to work his way up, probably starting in an employment arrangement with a production company. Between these extremes are various arrangements, the terms of which depend far more upon the diverse needs and capabilities of the parties than upon the nature of the particular project.

In representing a party entering (or seeking to enter) into negotiations for a development or production agreement, the practitioner must be familiar not only with the types of terms generally present in these agreements but also with the needs and capabilities of the parties. It is only through the effective combination of these elements that a viable agreement can be reached which will meet the ultimate objective: completion of production and delivery of the finished product to the network for broadcast.

[Note: The investment tax credit to which the authors refer was repealed in 1986.]

CBS, Inc. v. Merrick, 716 F.2d 1292 (9th Cir. 1983)

[Merrick, a leading Broadway and film producer, acquired the film and TV rights to the best-selling novel, *Blood and Money*. He then entered into a two-part contract with CBS to produce a mini-series based on the property. Under the agreement CBS was to pay $1,250,000 for the right to do the series ($833,333.34 on execution and the balance in installments at various stages of production) and $250,000 for Merrick's production services. If principal photography did not commence within two years, the contract would terminate, CBS would pay Merrick in full, and all rights would revert to Merrick. All contractual modifications were required to be in writing.

An operating budget was to be prepared upon delivery of the final screenplay, and CBS was to have 90 days within which to decide whether or not to proceed with the project.

On CBS' behalf, Merrick hired a director and a screenwriter (at respective fees of $500,000 and $250,000), who were then engaged (to Merrick's knowledge) on another project. He did not disclose the deadline to either of them, and he ignored suggestions to engage a second writer.

The screenplay was not delivered until two months prior to the deadline. Even before delivery, it became apparent that the deadline could not be met because pre-production required at least six months, and Merrick verbally agreed to an extension (although he never signed the extension agreements submitted to him by CBS). Some six weeks later, Merrick's attorney telexed CBS that Merrick would not agree to any changes in the original agreement. Merrick, however, dismissed the telex as "lawyer stuff" and continued to act as though the deadline would be extended. Five days prior to the deadline, CBS notified Merrick that it would go ahead, and Merrick met with CBS to plan the project several times after the deadline.

The following month, Merrick notified CBS that the deadline had passed, the project was off, and he was entitled to be paid.]

SOLOMON, J.

. . . The district court found Merrick's conduct and words inconsistent with the August 1, 1979, deadline. Merrick had hired a writer and director, both of whom were unable to work on *Blood and Money* until they had finished another project. He did not tell either of them about the deadline, and he ignored suggestions to hire a second writer. He orally agreed to waive the deadline, and he met with CBS and encouraged the development of the project both before and after the deadline had passed. These discussions amply support the district court's finding that Merrick waived his right to enforce the deadline and that CBS relied on that waiver to its detriment.

There is no merit in Merrick's contention that any amendment to the agreements must be in writing. The contract so provides, but a clause in a contract that requires amendments to be in writing may itself be waived. *Beatty v. Guggenheim Exploration Co.*, 225 N.Y. 380, 387–88, 122 N.E. 378, 381 (1919) (Cardozo, J.). By his words and conduct, Merrick waived the provision. CBS's detrimental reliance on the oral modification also prevents Merrick from invoking the clause to prevent proof of the modification. *Rose v. Spa Realty Assoc.*, 42 N.Y.2d 338, 344, 366 N.E.2d 1279, 1283, 397 N.U.S.2d 922, 927 (1977). . . .

In its findings on damages, the district held that "Merrick must return to CBS the amounts which it paid him under the contract." The court also found that CBS is entitled to rescission "both because Merrick expressly repudiated the modified contract and because he breached the original contract," and it therefore awarded CBS $916,666.67, the amount it paid both to Merrick and his agent, the William Morris Agency.

This award of restitution damages is proper under either rescission or breach of contract. When a breach occurs after the execution of the contract, the injured party in a contract action is entitled to both restitution and reliance damages.

Here, the district court found substantial breaches of contract. Nevertheless, the court limited recovery to restitution, the only recovery available when the contract is illegal or void from its inception. The court refused to allow reliance damages even though it found breach of the contract.

This was an error. This action must therefore be remanded to the district court to determine what part, if any, of the $750,000 paid to the director and screenwriter are legitimate reliance damages. In connection with this determination, the court should consider questions like reasonable reliance on the agreement, attempts to mitigate damages, the value of the screenplay delivered to CBS, and the foreseeability of the loss.

The district court's finding that Merrick is liable to CBS for breach of contract is AFFIRMED. The award to CBS of $916,666.67 it paid to Merrick and his agent is also AFFIRMED. The denial of amounts paid to Friedkin, the director, and Green, the screenwriter, by CBS in reliance on its contract with Merrick is REVERSED and

REMANDED for proceedings consistent with this opinion.

NELSON, J., CONCURRING

I concur with the majority's conclusion that a New York court would permit recovery of restitution plus additional measures of contract damages in this case. I also concur with the necessity of a remand. In rejecting CBS's claim for full contract damages and relying instead on purely restitutionary measure, the district court failed to pass on several issues necessary to measure breach of contract damages. Both parties address these issues in their briefs on appeal, but these are topics best left to the trier of fact.

7.50 Problems with Credits

As discussed at several points in earlier chapters, the "billing" accorded the creative talent is fought over bitterly. This is as true in television as in books, music, and films. An actor's credits can substantially influence career progress and thus eventual income.

An important consideration in the *Smithers* case, which follows, is the court's observation that Smithers was willing to work for a lower-than-normal fee in order to achieve the desired billing.

Smithers v. Metro-Goldwyn-Mayer Studios, 139 Cal.App.3d 643 (1983)

NELSON, J.

Metro-Goldwyn-Mayer Studios, Inc. (MGM), Harris Katleman (Katleman), and Bernard Weitzman (Weitzman) appeal from the judgment (as well as from the denial of a motion for judgment notwithstanding the verdict) in this action by William Smithers (Smithers). A cross-appeal from the trial court's remittitur of punitive damages was filed by Smithers.

Smithers sued MGM, Katleman and Weitzman for breach of contract, tortious breach of contract

(covenant of good faith and fair dealing), and fraud. The jury returned its verdict as follows:

1. For Smithers against MGM, damages in the sum of $500,000, for breach of contract (count I);
2. For Smithers against MGM, for tortious breach of contract (covenant of good faith and fair dealing), damages in the sum of $300,000 (count II);
3. For Smithers against MGM, Katleman and Weitzman for fraud damages of $200,000 (count III);
4. For Smithers against MGM, punitive damages of $2 million (count IV).

The trial judge denied the motions of MGM, Katleman and Weitzman for judgment notwithstanding the verdict, and for new trial on Smithers' acceptance of reduction of damage for fraud (count III) from $200,000 to $1, and punitive damages from $2 million to $1 million. MGM, Katleman, and Weitzman appeal. Smithers cross-appeals.

Beginning in January 1976, MGM produced a television series entitled "Executive Suite." Harris Katleman was president of MGM television and Bernard Weitzman was vice president of MGM in charge of business affairs. MGM hired an independent casting agency, the Melnick/Holstra Agency, to hire actors for the "Executive Suite" series. Through the Melnick/Holstra Agency, MGM negotiated with Smithers' agent, the William Morris Agency, to cast Smithers in the role of Anderson Galt in the series.

William Smithers is a professional actor of more than 30 years' experience. He has appeared in motion pictures, theater, and radio productions, and has been a regular or cast member in several television series. For approximately 11 years he has been billed as a "guest star," usually with his name and possibly his picture appearing alone on the screen. Appellants concede, as was established by numerous witnesses, that Smithers is a highly regarded actor.

In the course of negotiations between Smithers' agent and the casting agency, the casting director offered a provision known as a "Most-Favored-Nations" billing arrangement. This provision ultimately read as follows: "Except for the parts of DON WALLING, HELEN WALLING, and HOWARD RUTLEDGE, this deal is on a Most Favored Nations basis, i.e., if any other performer receives greater compensation than Artist, Artist shall receive that compensation.

"Additionally, no other performer shall receive more prominent billing or a better billing provision than Artist (except with respect to where his name is placed alphabetically on the crawl)." This Most-Favored-Nations provision was offered by the casting director for MGM since Smithers was being offered a lower than usual compensation rate. Further, MGM by this provision could "get some good people to work for reasonably low money and to not have to take up a great deal of space in the main titles." Because of the provision, and in hopes of an improved role, Smithers accepted the role. An interim agreement, called the outline deal memo, was signed by the casting director for MGM and Smithers' agent setting forth the above, being binding pending the execution of a long form contract. Smithers' understanding was that he would get billing at the end of the show, name alphabetically, but that only three other actors would be given more prominent billing at the front of the show.

At a screening of the pilot film, Smithers saw that there were *four* actors with "up-front" billing, instead of the agreed upon three actors. The casting agency had employed another actor for the series during the filming of the pilot film, and had given him "star billing." Smithers saw that his billing remained the same, but preferred to wait until he was in a better bargaining position to complain. Ultimately, 10 or 11 actors were given "up-front" billing, while Smithers' end-of-show-name-only billing remained the same.

When the series "Executive Suite" was sold to the CBS network, Smithers' contract provided that he would perform in at least seven of the thirteen episodes. He actually performed in 10 of the episodes. Beginning in September 1976, the program was broadcast over the CBS television network. Owing to poor ratings, MGM decided to make several changes, including the "story line" and the billing of the actors. After being informed of these changes, Smithers complained

that his billing was not in conformity with the most-favored-nations provision. Upon perusal by Smithers and his agency, it was discovered that the provision had been changed in the long-form contract (which was then—November 1976—still unsigned). The change would allow any number of actors to be billed more prominently than Smithers. MGM's attorney in charge of drafting the contracts testified concerning the change: "There were only two plausible explanations. Either I made a mistake or someone told me to do it," and "Generally somebody who had more authority than I told me to change it."

In mid-December Smithers was told that his role was to be written out of the series. In late December of 1976, Smithers' agent was told that the most-favored-nations provision had been a mistake, and that Smithers should waive the provision. Upon Smithers' refusal to agree to the change, Katleman told Smithers' agent, ". . . if he didn't, that he (Katleman) would be hard pressed to use Mr. Smithers again on any shows that he (Katleman) was involved with, and that if he (Katleman) were to tell this to Bud Grant, who was then the head of CBS for programing, if he (Katleman) were to tell him (Grant) this, that he (Katleman) was certain he (Grant) would go along as well with not using Mr. Smithers." This threat was reported to go along with the change. MGM then went ahead and changed Smithers to an end-of-show billing, however, on a separate card from the rest of the end-of-show billing.

The testimony was considerable on the importance of billing to an actor. Several witnesses testified that billing reflects the actor's stature in the industry, and affects his negotiations for roles, since it reflects what his status and compensation has been in the past. Billing reflects recognition by the producer and the public of the actor's importance or "star quality," and in turn affects the actor's compensation in present and future roles.

Issues on MGM's Appeal

MGM contends that Smithers was not entitled to proceed on a theory of a tortious breach of an implied covenant of good faith and fair dealing (tortious breach of contract); that damages for breach of contract were not shown, but if shown, were speculative, uncertain, and excessive; that there was no evidence of fraud, but if there were, damages should not have been allowed for emotional distress on that theory, so that no basis exists for punitive damages, which were also excessive; and that the trial court erred in refusing to give certain instructions. Our approach is, as always, to determine whether substantial evidence supports the judgment in the trial court, viewing that evidence in the light most favorable to respondent.

A. *Tortious Breach of Duty of Good Faith and Fair Dealing.*

The jury found that Katleman issued what amounted to a threat to blacklist Smithers and to encourage others to blacklist him also unless he would forgo his contractual rights. The question is whether the act gave rise to an action in tort. Prior to trial, Judge Cole ruled that such conduct, if proved, fit "to a T" the definition enunciated in *Sawyer v. Bank of America* (1978) 83 Cal.App.3d 135, 139 [145 Cal.Rptr. 623]: "[T]he tort of breaching an implied covenant of good faith and fair dealing consists in bad faith action, extraneous to the contract, with the motive intentionally to frustrate the obligee's enjoyment of contract rights." This developing, and confusing, area of the law has had much discussion. . . .

MGM takes the position that the rule is clearly established; however, it has an applicability limited to insurance cases or contracts of adhesion. . . . Smithers refers us to dictum in *Tameny v. Atlantic Richfield Co.* (1980) 27 Cal.3d 167, 179, fn. 12 [164 Cal.Rptr. 839, 610 P.2d 1330, 9 A.L.R.4th 314] and the holding in *Cleary v. American Airlines* (1980) 111 Cal.App.3d 443 [168 Cal.Rptr. 722], both wrongful discharge cases. *Cleary* noted that the doctrine was first formulated in insurance cases, but applies to all contracts.

The trial judge, on the motion for judgment notwithstanding the verdict, found the evidence on the issue sufficient, and we agree. Further, it is clear that . . . the threat was extraneous to the contract, not only intending to bludgeon Smithers into foregoing his contractual rights but also threatening action directly affecting the practice of his art and damaging to his future earning power. (cf. *Ericson v. Playgirl, Inc.* [1973] 73 Cal. App. 3d 850 [140 Cal. Rptr. 921, 96 A.L.R. 3d 427].) We agree with Judge Cole that such bad faith conduct fits the *Sawyer* definition. The jury's verdict is supported by substantial evidence.

B. *Breach of Contract.*

MGM concedes that its contract with Smithers was breached, but takes the position that damages arising from such breach were speculative and incapable of ascertainment. Damages for breach of contract must, of course, be clearly ascertainable as to their nature and origin. (Civ. Code, § 3301.) However, it is clear that one who wilfully breaches the contract bears the risk as to the uncertainty or the difficulty of computing the amount of damages. . . . A number of witnesses established the relationship between billing and the actor's future negotiations for compensation. The jury could reasonably conclude from the evidence that Smithers suffered an economic loss by reason of MGM's failure to live up to its agreement. Although witnesses were unable to estimate with precision how much Smithers had lost or how much he would earn in future years, the jury was provided a reasonable basis upon which to calculate damages. That fulfills the requirement of Civil Code section 3301. . . .

C. *Fraud.*

The evidence, viewed most favorably for Smithers, adequately showed that MGM, based upon later actions of its agents, had no intention of living up to its most-favored-nations provision, which was offered to induce Smithers to accept a lower than usual compensation rate. The evidence is further sufficient to sustain the jury's determination that Smithers relied upon the promise when he entered the contract. MGM's main point here is that damages were improperly allowed for emotional distress based upon a fraud theory. . . . Here the jury, based upon substantial evidence, determined that actual damage had been suffered by Smithers as a result of MGM's fraud and deceit. Following precedent, as we must, that determination will be upheld. . . .

We therefore affirm the judgment. . . .

NOTE ─────────────────────────────

1. In *Tamarind Lithography Workshop, Inc. v. Sanders*, 83 Daily Journal D.A.R. (Cal.App. 1983), the writer-producer-director of an award-winning industrial film was granted specific performance that ordered all future uses of the film to carry the contractually agreed credit, "A Film by Terry Sanders." The appellate court ordered this, even though the plaintiff had received a damage award in a previous trial. The court reasoned that the damages were only for the previous denial of credit and that "pecuniary compensation for Sanders' future harm is not a fully adequate remedy."

7.60   Contract and Antitrust Issues in Distribution

Once a television program is produced, it must be distributed. Generally, the distributor (whether it be a network, a syndicator, or a satellite "superstation") will try to obtain as great an exclusive over distribution rights as possible. By the same token, a local outlet will also try to achieve the greatest possible degree of exclusivity. The distributor will want assurance that an entire series will run on the same station, so that viewers will not have to dial-hop to find their favorite programs. Obviously, the conflicting interests create legal problems, both contract and antitrust.

The cases discussed below are instructive not only on the legal issues but on business trends. They also serve as a useful introduction to new dimensions in entertainment analyzed in Chapter 8. For example, the first *Viacom* case (*Viacom International v. Tandem Productions*) deals with the frequent buy-outs, mergers, resulting assignments of contracts, and other changing business circumstances that companies in the television and cable industries must constantly face. Both contract and antitrust issues are raised. In the second *Viacom* case (*Viacom International v. Lorimar Productions*), contract interpretation is the central issue that determines which party has distribution rights to *Sybil* and *Helter Skelter*.

In *Ralph C. Wilson Industries v. American Broadcasting Companies*, the complaint is a familiar one in both the motion picture and television industries. The plaintiff complains about defendants' restrictive business practices that allegedly deprive plaintiff of badly needed programming. The issues in *Metromedia Broadcasting* are also familiar. The plaintiff complains that the defendant requires unwanted products to be bought if the plaintiff is to obtain new and desired programs. The issue of illegal tie-ins, discussed in Chapter 6 in the *Loews* decision, is once again a central focus.

─────────────────────────────

Viacom International, Inc. v. Tandem Productions, Inc., 526 F.2d 593 (2d Cir. 1975)

[Between May and July 1970, Tandem and CBS reached oral agreement on 15 essential points of a deal under which Tandem was to produce the series "All in the Family." The parties did not discuss assignability of rights.

On September 25, 1970, CBS circulated a "Memorandum of Agreement" dated "As of July 10, 1970." Paragraph 20 provided that

CBS may assign its rights hereunder in full or in part to any person, firm or corporation provided, however, that no such assignment shall relieve CBS of its obligations hereunder.

By October 1970, Tandem had moved into CBS offices and was utilizing CBS personnel in production of the series.

The FCC's financial interest and syndication rules, which had been promulgated early in 1970, did not become effective until July 23, 1971.

In the interim, CBS distributed and syndicated "All in the Family" through its subsidiary CBS Enterprises, Inc. In June 1971, with FCC approval, CBS merged the subsidiary into Viacom via a spin-off, and assigned its distribution and syndication rights in the series to the new entity.

Sometime following these events, CBS presented Tandem with a formal agreement dated "As of July 10, 1970" embodying the 15 agreed points and the assignment clause. After fruitless objections to the assignment clause, Tandem signed the agreement and then entered into a foreign distribution agreement with a Canadian distributor. The Second Circuit affirmed the District Court's declaration that Viacom was the assignee of an exclusive distributorship.]

LUMBARD, J.

. . . As Judge Gurfein stated, the behavior of CBS and Tandem in producing the show immediately after July 1970 constitutes strong evidence that they considered themselves bound by a contract at that time. . . . Tandem argues that this behavior could not create an effective oral agreement because there was not meeting of the minds on the question of program control, a material element of that contract. Judge Gurfein found that the question of program control was not left open but was settled by both parties agreeing that "All in the Family" would ridicule the entire political spectrum. While the written agreement more explicitly delineated certain areas of control, we cannot say that Judge Gurfein's determination of previous agreement on the general subject of control was clearly erroneous. . . . [A]n oral agreement will not be denied legal effect because it does not reflect all the terms to be included in the subsequent writing with complete certainty. . . .

Tandem next argues that even if a binding oral agreement did exist after July 1970, the written agreement constituted a novation and discharge of the prior contract. Tandem thus suggests that two separate agreements existed, that Viacom obtained its rights only through the inclusion of the assignment clause in the written contract, and that those rights are void because the written agreement violated the financial interest rule, which became effective before the written agreement was fully executed. In order to constitute a novation, however, a contract must discharge a previous contractual duty, create a new contractual duty, and add a party who neither owed nor was entitled to its performance. Restatement, Contracts § 424. These criteria are not present here. The written contract merely continued and memorialized the parties' rights and obligations as already agreed upon. The addition of an assignment clause would not suffice to create a novation.

Since CBS received the distribution and syndication rights to "All in the Family" as part of a contractual arrangement in force as of July 1970, the district court was correct in holding that the FCC regulation, effective July 23, 1971, did not affect the legality of CBS's proprietary interest.

Tandem next claims that even if that interest is not vitiated by the FCC regulation, CBS' assignment of the distribution and syndication license transcends the power of assignment granted by the written agreement. Tandem reads the clause, which speaks of the assignment of "rights" and forbids CBS to relinquish its "obligations," as limiting assignment to the "right" to receive the distribution or syndication fees called for by the contract. Tandem contends that CBS was not empowered to delegate its duty actually to distribute or syndicate.

The district court properly explored the parties' intended meaning of the term "assignment" and determined that Tandem signed the written agreement with full knowledge that CBS intended to assign the distribution and syndication rights to Viacom. We find no error in the district court's eminently sensible determination that all parties knew that the assignment of distributorship rights would include the concurrent delegation of distributorship duties. . . .

The district court's rejection of Tandem's attempt to invalidate the distribution and syndication agreement as violative of the antitrust laws presents greater difficulty. Tandem has claimed that CBS conditioned its agreement to broadcast "All in the Family" on a grant of the disputed distribution and syndication rights to CBS. Tandem asserts that the tie-in of distribution and syndication rights to broadcast rights coerced it into relinquishing what it would have preferred to retain. If Tandem could prove these allegations in addition to demonstrating that CBS possessed sufficient economic power with respect to the exhibition of television programs appreciably to restrain free competition for distribution of those programs by tying the services to each other, then the contract would violate section 1 of the Sherman Act, 15 U.S.C. § 1. . . . The district court allowed Tandem to submit an offer of proof of its claim and assumed that Tandem could prove the allegations of an illegal tying arrangement. Nevertheless, the district court refused to entertain the antitrust defense, relying heavily on *Kelly v. Kosuga*, 358 U.S. 516, 79 S.Ct. 429, 3 L.Ed.2d 475 (1958), in which the Supreme Court refused to entertain an antitrust defense in a breach of contract action.

The *Kelly* decision followed a series of opinions in which the Supreme Court had expressed antipathy towards the interposition of antitrust defenses in contract actions. Through various rationales, such as deeming the contracts to be "collateral" to the antitrust violation, the Court has carved out an exception to the general rule against judicial enforcement of contracts that foster illegal ends. . . .

The parties have urged us to analyze the claims before us in terms of the standards that have been articulated in the above cases. Thus Viacom argues that any tying arrangement is not "inherently illegal" and that the distribution and syndication agreement constitutes an "intelligible economic transaction." Conversely, Tandem contends that enforcing the contract would aid and abet the "precise conduct made unlawful" by the Sherman Act.

These standards, by themselves, may be too imprecise to be useful in this case. Whether a court classifies a sale as an "intelligible economic transaction in itself" or as "part of . . . any general plan or scheme that the law condemned"; 212 U.S. at 260, 29 S.Ct. at 291, may well depend on how much of the circumstances surrounding the sale the court is willing to consider. Similarly, a determination of whether a contract to purchase a tied product is "inherently invalid" may depend on the court's perception of the contract as a separate or "collateral" entity or as an integral part of an attempt to stifle competition, enforcement of which would effectuate "the precise conduct made unlawful." . . .

Application of these standards is facilitated by considering the Supreme Court's apparent belief that other policies may override the need to prevent antitrust violations by not enforcing contracts where, as here, the antitrust laws may be vindicated in a separate action. That procedure may be particularly appropriate where, as here,

the alleged wrongdoer under the antitrust laws is not a party to the contract in dispute. Rather, Viacom is an independent assignee for value of the rights obtained by CBS. No claim has been made that Viacom either has or has attempted to wield the power necessary to create an illegal tying arrangement.

It seems apparent that the overriding consideration which has persuaded the Supreme Court is its concern that the successful interposition of antitrust defenses is too likely to enrich parties who reap the benefits of a contract and then seek to avoid the corresponding burdens. . . .

Tandem claims that its arrangement with Viacom presents no possibility of unjust enrichment because no distribution or syndication of "All in the Family" has yet occurred and Tandem has received no payments for these services. Thus, Tandem argues, the reasoning of *Kelly* does not mandate exclusion of the antitrust defense in this case. Some support for this claim may be found in Judge Gurfein's determination that the consideration in the contract for broadcast rights was separate from the consideration for distribution and syndication rights. 368 F. Supp. at 1277. Viacom, however, does point to some evidence in the record suggesting that while payments for distribution and syndication were to be made separately from those for broadcast rights, the level of the payments for broadcast reflected the fact that CBS was receiving distribution and syndication rights. Tandem has also received large sums of money from CBS for clearing foreign distribution areas. Whether interposition of an antitrust defense would allow Tandem to obtain unjust enrichment by continuing to receive higher fees for broadcast rights without surrendering distribution and syndication rights, therefore, is by no means a clear-cut issue.

In any event, there are additional reasons which convince us that we must relegate Tandem to its antitrust remedies in a separate action. As the First Circuit has noted "such defenses would tend to prolong and complicate contract disputes" and thus convert a facially simple litigation into one involving the complexities of antitrust law. . . .

An easy toleration of antitrust defenses to contract actions would threaten to involve parties claiming under the contract in litigation so protracted and expensive that they might be coerced into unsatisfactory settlements or be compelled to forego any prosecution of their claims. It is well known that the litigation of antitrust issues is more likely to involve lengthy and expensive proceedings, both before trial and at trial, than any other kind of federal court litigation. The scope of the additional details that would have to be litigated in this case is suggested by a listing of the proof necessary to demonstrate an illegal tying arrangement: (1) two separate and distinct products, a tying product and a tied product; (2) sufficient economic power in the tying market to coerce purchase of the tied product; (3) actual exercise of economic power to force purchase of the tied product; (4) anti-competitive effects in the tied market; and (5) involvement of a "not insubstantial" amount of interstate commerce in the tied market. . . .

In this case, plaintiff, who would suffer most by the prolonged determination of the defense, was not even a party to the alleged illegality. Under these circumstances, it seems proper to limit Tandem to any cause of action it might have against CBS rather than to force Viacom to meet the vagaries of an antitrust defense action.

For all the above reasons, we agree that Judge Gurfein's refusal to consider Tandem's proffered antitrust defense was well advised and supported by guiding precedents.

Affirmed.

Viacom International, Inc. v. Lorimar Productions, Inc., 486 F. Supp. 95 (S.D.N.Y. 1980)

WEINFELD, J.

. . . Plaintiff commenced this action against the defendant for a declaratory judgment that it is entitled to the worldwide distribution rights to two 2-hour programs ("Sybil" and "Helter Skelter") and enjoining the defendant from claiming ownership of or purporting to distribute anywhere in the world the television rights in the form they appeared on United States television networks, in the form they appeared in movie theaters, or in any other form.

The issues arise under a contract entered into between the parties and the basic dispute there-

under is whether the programs "Sybil" and "Helter Skelter" are "television movies," as plaintiff contends, in which event, it acquired worldwide distribution rights thereto under paragraph 4 of the agreement, or are "mini-series" as defendant contends, in which event, under paragraph 5(E) there was to be a first negotiation and first refusal with respect to the worldwide distribution rights to such mini-series.

The contract was the subject of extended negotiation between the plaintiff's and defendant's representatives and finally was agreed upon and became effective as of January 1, 1974. The contract provides:

1. Viacom shall have exclusive, perpetual television distribution rights . . . to all series and programs (including made-for-television movies) that are initially broadcast during the three-year period commencing as of the date hereof.
2. The territory for which we [Viacom] acquire these rights is the world with respect to made for television movies and with respect to series the territory shall be the world excluding the U.S. network territory.
3. We [Viacom] are acquiring these rights in perpetuity.

Under the agreement Viacom received distribution rights to all Lorimar television programs initially broadcast during the three-year period beginning January 1, 1974. Payment for the rights acquired and, in some instances, the extent of the rights secured varied according to the type of program. The evidence establishes there were three categories of programs. The first category was made-for-television movies (television movies)—programs on film consisting of either one or two segments of at least 90 minutes in length. Paragraph 4 of the contract headed "Television movies" is the governing provision. . . . Viacom guaranteed "that [Lorimar's] share shall equal at least $90,000 with respect to each 90-minute movie and at least $100,000 with respect to each movie two hours or greater in length." The guarantee payments were to be made at prefixed times.

The second category was a television series—a

program containing no less than 13 original 30- or 60-minute episodes. In this instance, Viacom received foreign distribution rights and exclusive first negotiation rights with respect to domestic distribution following network cancellation of any series. With respect to foreign distribution guarantees were provided for according to a schedule.

The third category was a mini-series defined in paragraph 5(E) "as a fictionalized film series (as opposed to an Eleanor and Franklin) carrying an annual network commitment of less than 13 original episodes." Here it was further provided that "in lieu of distributing individual episodes" Lorimar had the option to provide Viacom "with up to two movies of each mini-series, either 90 minutes or two hours (or longer) in length which are representative of the series" in which event "such movies shall be deemed television movies and the terms set forth in paragraph 4 [television movies] shall govern the distribution of same."

"Helter Skelter" and "Sybil" were produced by Lorimar and were initially broadcast within the contract period. "Helter Skelter" was first broadcast over CBS television on April 1 and 2, 1976 and "Sybil" was first broadcast over the NBC television network on November 14 and 15, 1976. Each was in the form of two 2-hour telecasts. Prior to their initial United States broadcasts, Lorimar delivered to Viacom the "pre-print elements" necessary to make the movies "Helter Skelter" and "Sybil" in that form for distribution. Those deliveries by Lorimar were pursuant to paragraph 4(E) which concerns only "television movies." Viacom has been distributing "Sybil" and "Helter Skelter" for more than three years. It has made sales of the movies in 17 countries (on five continents), Puerto Rico and Hong Kong. Viacom has paid during 1977, 1978 and 1979 up to the commencement of this action over $228,000 to Lorimar as its share of the distribution proceeds based on domestic and international sales of the two programs by Viacom.

The parties were in harmonious relationship over an extended period during which they treated the programs as television movies and Lorimar recognized Viacom's exclusive distribution rights to "Sybil" and "Helter Skelter." That relationship and understanding was abruptly terminated in and about August 1979 and this litigation fomented by an attorney engaged at Lorimar, as its Vice President and General Counsel, almost 5 years after the contract had been entered into between the parties and was in effective operation, who was of the view that the programs were mini-series. However, I reject his testimony as a purported expert in the industry. Also, the clear language of paragraph 5(E) itself and the parties' conduct in carrying out the agreement thereunder requires rejection of his testimony. The defendant, as was its option under paragraph 5(E), elected to provide plaintiff with "two movies of each mini-series, either 90 minutes or two hours (or longer) in length which are representative of the series." They were, therefore, to "be deemed television movies and the terms set forth in paragraph 4 [governed] the distribution of same." By its action with respect to "Sybil" and "Helter Skelter," Lorimar made paragraph 4 the operative provision.

The substantial and overwhelming weight of the evidence, including the conduct of the parties from the effective date of the agreement, January 1, 1974, and from the time defendant provided Viacom with the two 2-hour programs of "Sybil" and "Helter Skelter," supports plaintiff's claim that they are television movies governed by paragraph 4 of the agreement and that plaintiff is entitled to the exclusive distribution rights provided for therein. Significantly, the plaintiff paid and the defendant accepted the guarantees provided for in the agreement for a television movie—a guarantee far in excess of any payment required if in fact the programs are mini-series.

Apart from the contract provision and the practical construction by the parties as indicated by their course of dealings thereunder, the evidence supports a further finding that under the custom and usage of the industry the two 2-hour films, "Sybil" and "Helter Skelter," are television movies. Moreover, defendant itself, in public advertisements, so categorized them. The record is replete with numerous instances, oral and written, wherein defendant recognized that paragraph 4, which applies to television movies, is the governing provision. Defendant's present position not only flies in the face of overwhelming proof that defendant delivered the programs as television movies and received added financial benefits by reason thereof, but suggests a brazen attempt to avoid a firm commitment which it accepted for more than five years.

The house counsel responsible for this litigation was not a party to the negotiations leading to the contract, had no knowledge of the practical interpretation of its provisions by the parties themselves during the three-year period when they deemed the programs television movies, and during which defendant received the guarantee for that category. It is rather significant that no officer or employee who either played a role in the negotiations leading to the contract or who were participants during the period that "Sybil" and "Helter Skelter" were produced and made available to plaintiff or who had knowledge of the basis on which payments therefor were received by the defendant, were called as witnesses by defendant to challenge plaintiff's version nor was any explanation made for their lack of testimony on this subject, whether upon trial or by way of deposition. . . .

Ralph C. Wilson Industries, Inc. v. American Broadcasting Companies, Inc., 598 F. Supp. 694 (N.D.Ca. 1984)

CONTI, J.

. . . Plaintiff is the owner of a television station, KICU Channel 36 (jointly referred to as "plaintiff" herein). Defendants Chronicle Broadcasting Co. (KRON Channel 4), Miami Valley Broadcasting Co. (KTVU Channel 2) and Field Communications Corp. (KBHK Channel 44) are television stations located in the San Francisco Bay Area. These three defendants will be referred to as the "station defendants." Defendants Viacom International, Inc., P.I.T.S. Films, Twentieth Century-Fox Film Corp., Paramount Television Domestic Distribution Inc., Warner Bros. Television Distribution, Inc., M.C.A. Television Ltd., Metro-Goldwyn-Mayer, Inc., and United Artists Television, Inc., are suppliers or distributors of television programs. These defendants will be referred to as the "supplier defendants."

Plaintiff filed this action on December 29, 1980. Plaintiff's complaint alleges that defendants have violated the antitrust laws because of various practices they follow concerning the licensing of programs and conspiracies to boycott plaintiff. Plaintiff is pursuing three claims against defendants based upon these alleged practices. First, plaintiff claims that all defendants have violated the Sherman Act by unreasonably restraining trade. Plaintiff contends that defendants unreasonably restrain trade by licensing programs on an exclusive basis as against plaintiff, by making the licenses unreasonably long and by incorporating, implicitly or explicitly, rights of first refusal into those licenses. Secondly, plaintiff claims that the station defendants have committed a *per se* violation of the Sherman Act by a horizontal conspiracy to boycott plaintiff. Plaintiff alleges that these three defendants have conspired, through direct communication, to exercise exclusivity of programming against plaintiff. Thirdly, plaintiff claims that defendant Miami Valley Broadcasting Co. has committed a *per se* violation of the Sherman Act by conspiring with the Independent Television News Association (ITNA) to exclude plaintiff from membership in that organization. These three claims will be developed in more detail below. . . .

Generally, summary judgment is appropriate only when the moving party meets his burden of showing that there is no genuine issue of material fact and that he is entitled to judgment as a matter of law. Fed.R.Civ.P. 56. . . .

A. *Rule of Reason Claim*

Plaintiff's primary claim against the defendants is that they have unreasonably restrained trade through a vertical contract by their combined practices of licensing television programs on an exclusive basis, making the licenses unreasonably long, and by implicitly or explicitly incorporating rights of first refusal into those licenses. The factual basis for these contentions, referred to herein as plaintiff's "rule of reason" claim, is set forth below. First, however, is a brief summary of the statutory basis of plaintiff's claim.

Section 4 of the Clayton Act, 15 U.S.C. § 15, confers a private right of action for treble damages upon "any person who shall be injured in his business or property by reason of anything forbidden in the antitrust laws." "Antitrust laws" is defined to include the Sherman Act, 15 U.S.C. §§ 1–7. 15 U.S.C. § 12(a). Section 1 of the

Sherman Act, 15 U.S.C. § 1, prohibits "[e]very contract, combination in the form of trust or otherwise, or conspiracy, in restraint of trade or commerce among the several States. . . ." This blanket proscription, however, has been interpreted to prohibit only "unreasonable" restraints of trade. *See, e.g., Standard Oil v. United States*, 221 U.S. 1, 31 S.Ct. 502, 55 L.Ed. 619 (1911). These sections, therefore, form the statutory basis for plaintiff's claim against defendants for their allegedly unreasonable restraint of trade.

The unreasonable restraint of trade complained of is as follows. The supplier defendants herein are in the business of licensing television programs to television stations. The undisputed practice of these suppliers is to license programs to the stations on an exclusive basis after a competitive bidding process among interested stations. Thus, for example, a supplier would sell an exclusive license for M*A*S*H to defendant KTVU, who would then be the only station in that area permitted to air "M*A*S*H" (or specified episodes of "M*A*S*H") for the duration of the license.

It is undisputed that the station defendants herein enforce this exclusivity against all television stations, including plaintiff, which they consider to be located in the "San Francisco" market area. This area includes San Francisco, Oakland and San Jose, as well as most of the area around these cities. The area includes all station defendants and plaintiff, as well as several non-party stations. The scope of this exclusive licensing area is determined on the basis of the A.C. Nielson Co. and Arbitron Co. ratings services' categorization of geographic area into market groups, both of which ratings services include San Francisco and San Jose in the same market group.

Plaintiff does not contend that the practice of licensing television programs on an exclusive basis automatically violates the Sherman Act's prohibition of restraints of trade. In fact, plaintiff itself licenses programs on an exclusive basis. All parties agree that exclusive licenses, as such, may further competition by providing an incentive to the station to invest in promotion and development of the program product and do not constitute a *per se* violation of Section 1.

Rather than argue that exclusive licenses automatically violate Section 1 of the Sherman Act, plaintiff contends that they constitute an unreasonable restraint of trade when enforced by the station defendants against plaintiff. Plaintiff argues that the station defendants are entitled to license programs on an exclusive basis, but that that exclusivity should not apply to plaintiff because it is not in the same "relevant market" as the station defendants. Plaintiff submits that the station defendants are licensed to and operate in the San Francisco-Oakland Bay Area market. Plaintiff argues that it, on the other hand, is located in and operates in the "South Bay." (Plaintiff does not define the area included within the "South Bay," but it apparently covers San Jose and other areas in and around Santa Clara County.) Accordingly, plaintiff contends that it should be placed in a different geographic market than the station defendants for exclusivity purposes. To illustrate, plaintiff's argument is that defendant KTVU should be permitted to obtain a license for "M*A*S*H" which is exclusive against the other station defendants and other stations in the San Francisco area, but not those in the "South Bay" area, which includes plaintiff. Consequently, plaintiff could also bid for and obtain an exclusive license to show "M*A*S*H," which would be exclusive only against other South Bay stations. Thus, plaintiff argues that the exclusive licenses violate the antitrust laws because they are overbroad in geographic scope, are unreasonably long in duration and incorporate unreasonable rights of first refusal.

The economic motivation for this suit is to enable plaintiff to license quality programming at a price below that paid by the station defendants, such as KTVU, for their exclusive licenses to such programs. It is uncontested that the level of prices for exclusive licenses for quality programming is primarily determined by the broadcast market of the prospective licensees. Presently, all the station defendants and plaintiff are placed in the same market for purposes of bidding for the supplier defendants' quality programming. Thus, if defendant KTVU bids $150,000 for an exclusive license for "M*A*S*H," plaintiff must better that bid to obtain the license. Plaintiff has made no argument and there is no evidence showing that plaintiff has been excluded from bidding for quality programming at these price levels. In fact, the evidence shows that if plaintiff wished to bid at this "San Francisco" market price, it could obtain quality programming.

Plaintiff contends that, as a small UHF station, it is not commercially feasible for it to bid at the same price levels as the station defendants to obtain quality programming. What plaintiff seeks is to be placed in some market other than that containing the station defendants for purposes of bidding for quality program licenses. If, for example, plaintiff were placed in the Salinas-Monterey market, in which non-party channel 11 is placed, it could bid for quality programming at a much lower price than that paid by the station defendants. The outcome would be, for example, that defendant KTVU would obtain a license for "M*A*S*H," exclusive against the other San Francisco stations, but not plaintiff, for $100,000, while plaintiff could also license "M*A*S*H," exclusive against other South Bay stations, for, say, $15,000. That is the result plaintiff seeks to achieve by means of this antitrust suit. This, then, is the factual basis for plaintiff's rule of reason antitrust claim.

The court will briefly summarize the legal standards to be applied to plaintiff's rule of reason claim. First, plaintiff must show that the defendants' challenged practices injure, or decrease, competition in the relevant market. If plaintiff fails to prove that competition has been injured, it cannot prevail. . . . Secondly, if plaintiff has shown an injury to competition, it must then show that the challenged restraint is "unreasonable." . . . To show that the restraint is unreasonable, plaintiff must, in this case, prove one of two things. First, plaintiff may show that the restraint is unreasonable because it applies to television stations which are not in "substantial competition" with each other. . . . If plaintiff cannot show that it is not in substantial competition with the station defendants, it may nevertheless prevail if it can show that the challenged practices of exclusivity, length of license and rights of first refusal, are "unreasonable" under the circumstances of this case. . . . For the reasons set forth below, the

court holds that plaintiff has not, as a matter of law, met its burden of offering evidence sufficient to support a finding that defendants' exclusivity practices unreasonably restrain trade.

1. *Injury to Competition.*

As noted above, the first inquiry must be whether plaintiff has presented genuine issues of material fact which would support a finding that defendants' exclusivity practices injure competition. In order to meet this first test, plaintiff may pursue one of three avenues. First, it may offer evidence to show that the defendants have conspired to restrain competition. Plaintiff does not make this argument and offers no evidence which could justify a finding that the defendants conspired. Secondly, plaintiff could offer evidence showing that the defendants' exclusivity practices actually injure competition. This is the argument plaintiff primarily relies upon. As shown below, however, plaintiff fails to offer evidence of injury to competition which would withstand a directed verdict for defendants. Thirdly, plaintiff could, as an alternative, seek to show that a defendant has "market power," tending to make any action of that defendant have a substantial effect on competition. Plaintiff offers some argument on this point but, as addressed below, it is unpersuasive. Accordingly, as set forth below, the court holds that plaintiff has failed to offer evidence which would support a finding that defendants' exclusivity practices injure competition.

The first inquiry is whether plaintiff has offered evidence which could support a finding that the exclusive license contracts injure competition. In order to address this inquiry, the court must first determine what is the "relevant market" in which competition has allegedly been restrained. *See, Gough v. Rossmoor*, 585 F.2d at 385–89. This "relevant market" is generally determined by reference to both the relevant product market and the relevant geographic market. *See, e.g., Harris & Jorde, Antitrust Market Definition: An Integrated Approach*, 72 Cal.L.Rev. 1, 46–52 (1984). In this case, the parties agree, and the court accepts, that the relevant product market is quality television programming. The relevant geographic market, however, is more complex.

Plaintiff contends that the relevant geographic market is the "South Bay." Although they contested this definition in their earlier motion for summary judgment, defendants now accept, for purposes of this motion, plaintiff's definition. The court, however, is not persuaded by this definition.

The relevant market is not defined by the parties. . . . Rather, the court must consider the commercial realities of the situation to arrive at the definition of the relevant market. . . . In this case, the commercial realities are so clear that the court holds that the relevant geographic market is the entire San Francisco-Oakland-San Jose Bay Area, as currently defined.

These commercial realities are as follow. First, the Federal Communications Commission (FCC) considers San Jose and San Francisco to be in the same market. *See*, 47 C.F.R. § 76.51; Memorandum Opinion, 37 R.R.2d 695, 698 (1976); 40 R.R.2d 473, 477–78 (1977). Secondly, the two recognized national ratings services, A.C. Nielson Co. and Arbitron Co., consider San Jose and San Francisco to be in the same market. . . . Thirdly, there is a large overlap in the signal coverage of plaintiff's and the station defendants' signals. . . . Finally, plaintiff and the station defendants share a substantial overlap of viewers. . . .

These facts are so clear that a reasonable jury would have to find that the relevant geographic market is the entire San Francisco Bay Area, including San Jose. Accordingly, the court holds that the relevant market in this case is the San Francisco Bay Area quality television programming market. Even were the court to accept the parties' definition of the relevant market as the "South Bay" quality programming market, however, the outcome would be the same. For the reasons set forth below, it is clear that plaintiff cannot prove that defendants' exclusivity practices unreasonably restrain trade in either market. . . .

[I]t is not sufficient for plaintiff to establish an injury to itself or its own competitive position. . . . This is all plaintiff has done. Plaintiff offers no evidence tending to show that it cannot obtain quality programming, that prices are fixed, that program offerings are detrimentally affected, or that program output has in any way been re-stricted. Some showing of this type is necessary to establish injury to competition. . . .

Despite the fact that plaintiff has produced no evidence to show that defendants' exclusivity practices actually injured competition, a jury might find injury to competition if plaintiff proved that any one defendant has market power. If a defendant has market power, it is much more likely that its actions can injure competition. Thus, if plaintiff submitted evidence tending to show that a defendant has market power, the court might permit the issue to go to the jury. The court finds, however, that plaintiff has not offered evidence from which a jury could find that any defendant has market power.

Plaintiff has offered no evidence showing that any one defendant has market power. The evidence shows that the ten or more Bay Area stations all compete vigorously in both the South Bay and the Bay Area as a whole. The evidence also shows that the supplier defendants actively compete in both areas. . . . There is no evidence showing that any one defendant has the power to significantly affect prices, available programming, or any other important market component. Consequently, plaintiff has not offered evidence sufficient to go to the jury on the issue whether a defendant has market power.

To summarize the above, the court holds that the plaintiff has not met its burden of producing evidence which would support a finding that the challenged practices restrain competition. Plaintiff has not shown that the exclusivity practices actually injure competition or that any defendant has market power. Accordingly, the court holds that plaintiff cannot prevail on its rule of reason claim. Defendants are consequently entitled to summary judgment.

The court might end its inquiry at this point. In deference to the enormous record before the court and in the interests of caution, however, the court will proceed to address the parties' other arguments.

Assuming, contrary to this court's ruling, that plaintiff had offered sufficient evidence of an injury to competition, plaintiff must then show that the exclusivity practices are "unreasonable." The first way plaintiff may establish this is by offering sufficient evidence to show that plaintiff and defendants are not in "substantial competition." If plaintiff is not in substantial competition with defendants, the exclusivity practices are presumptively unreasonable. *See, United States v. Paramount Pictures, Inc.*, 334 U.S. at 144–48, 68 S.Ct. at 922–24. If the parties are in substantial competition, plaintiff must then offer evidence showing that the challenged exclusivity practices are unreasonable given the particular circumstances of this case. . . .

As noted above, plaintiff argues that it is not in substantial competition with the station defendants because it is a "local" station attracting "local" advertisers. The evidence shows, however, that the station defendants actively compete with plaintiff for viewers, quality programming and advertising in both the San Francisco Bay Area and the South Bay markets. . . .

Given that plaintiff and the station defendants are in substantial competition with each other, plaintiff must now offer evidence sufficient to find the exclusivity practices "unreasonable" under the particular circumstances of this case. If plaintiff cannot submit evidence sufficient to support a finding that the exclusivity practices are unreasonable, it cannot prevail on its rule of reason claim. After careful review of the evidence in the record, the court finds that plaintiff has failed to offer evidence to support a finding that the exclusivity practices herein, consisting of the geographic breadth of the exclusivity, the length of the licenses and the alleged rights of first refusal, are unreasonable under the circumstances of this case.

The court holds that no reasonable jury could find that the practices complained of herein are unreasonable. The parties agree that exclusivity, in itself, is a reasonable practice in the television programming industry. Such exclusivity gives the licensee the incentive to promote and develop the licensed program. Without exclusivity, it is likely that no one licensee would expend the resources necessary to fully develop the program. . . . Plaintiff itself utilizes exclusive licenses similar to those attacked herein. The exclusive licenses used herein promote competition by maximizing the number of available programs and preventing audience fragmentation for a program. . . .

This exclusivity also promotes competition by maximizing the program's value and avoiding overexposure, which can shorten the program's useful life. . . . Exclusivity permits each station to plan programming to compete with another station's programming, with the knowledge that no other station will dilute the value of this competitive programming by airing the same program at the same time. . . . Exclusive licenses promote competition among suppliers by providing an incentive to maximize the number of programs offered and by maximizing the supplier's revenues from the licenses.

B. *Conspiracy Claim Against Station Defendants.*

Plaintiff's second antitrust claim is directed against the station defendants. Plaintiff contends that the station defendants have violated Section 1 of the Sherman Act by a *per se* horizontal conspiracy to enforce exclusivity against plaintiff. . . .

Plaintiff's first argument is that the defendants' parallel conduct permits an inference of conspiracy. Even if plaintiff could show that the defendants' conduct with respect to exclusivity is parallel, which defendants dispute, such evidence could not, by itself, support plaintiff's conspiracy claim. . . .

Similarly, plaintiff's offered proof of an opportunity to conspire, even if accepted by a fact finder, cannot, even when combined with proof of parallel conduct, support a finding of conspiracy. . . .

In order to go to the jury on its conspiracy claim, plaintiff must submit some sort of proof that the defendants actually conspired—some "conscious commitment to a common scheme"— or other special facts permitting a finding of conspiracy. . . .

Despite extensive discovery, plaintiff offers only one item of evidence to substantiate its claim that the station defendants conspired to enforce exclusivity against it. This one item is telephone calls by KTVU's Mr. Breen to other stations in the area, in which they discussed exclusivity practices. Defendants do not dispute that these telephone calls occurred. Rather, defendants present convincing and undisputed evidence showing that these calls were made *after* the alleged conspiracy began, on advice of counsel after plaintiff threatened litigation concerning exclusivity, and were undertaken to *discover* the exclusivity practices of other stations in the area. . . . Such overwhelming and uncontested evidence shows that plaintiff's only item of evidence cannot, as a matter of law, substantiate its conspiracy claim. . . .

In addition to their evidence rebutting plaintiff's meager evidence of conspiracy, the defendants have submitted overwhelming evidence that their exclusivity practices were undertaken in the exercise of their independent and sound business judgment. . . . This showing, which makes it more likely than not that defendants' exclusivity practices were the result of independent business judgment, is sufficient to compel summary judgment on plaintiff's conspiracy claim. . . .

The court is confronted with a situation where the plaintiff has offered no evidence from which a jury could find that the station defendants conspired to practice exclusivity against plaintiff. Despite extensive discovery, plaintiff has found no probative evidence showing a conspiracy. On the other hand, the defendants have submitted extensive, convincing evidence that they did not conspire but, rather, made independent decisions concerning exclusivity in the exercise of sound business judgment. Under the circumstances of this case, the court holds that summary judgment for the station defendants is appropriate on plaintiff's conspiracy claim. . . . Accordingly, the court hereby grants defendants' motion for summary judgment on plaintiff's second claim of a horizontal conspiracy.

C. *Conspiracy by Miami Valley and ITNA.*

Plaintiff's third and last antitrust claim is that defendant Miami Valley illegally conspired with the Independent Television News Association (ITNA) to exclude plaintiff from membership in that organization. The facts underlying this claim are as follow.

The ITNA is a cooperative association which provides non-exclusive news feeds to its members. . . . The price charged for membership in the association is based upon the broadcasting market of the prospective station member. It is undisputed that, in 1980, plaintiff applied for membership in ITNA. Mr. Novitz, managing director of ITNA, originally indicated that ITNA would charge plaintiff a membership price based upon the size of the San Jose market. . . . Shortly thereafter, however, Novitz told plaintiff that its membership rate would be set at the San Francisco price, approximately four times the price originally discussed.

Plaintiff claims that Novitz' action in refusing to give plaintiff membership at a San Jose price was the result of a conspiracy with defendant Miami Valley (KTVU) to exclude plaintiff from the organization. Plaintiff's claim is thus not that it was excluded from membership in ITNA completely, but that it was excluded at anything but the San Francisco membership price.

Plaintiff offers no evidence from which a jury could find that KTVU conspired with ITNA to exclude plaintiff from membership. Plaintiff's only allegation is that KTVU, a board member of ITNA, voted to refuse to permit plaintiff membership at less than the San Francisco market rate. The board, however, consists of seven directors who jointly voted to extend plaintiff membership only at the established San Francisco market rate. . . . This evidence without more is legally insufficient to support a finding of conspiracy where, as here, plaintiff offers no proof of improper motive or any illegal concerted action. . . .

Defendants, on the other hand, offer convincing evidence that there was no conspiracy and that ITNA's decision to permit plaintiff membership only at the "San Francisco" price was an independent business decision based upon its established practices. First, ITNA's membership rates are determined by the prospective member's market as defined by Arbitron's ADI book. PX 578. As noted above, that ratings book puts plaintiff in the same San Francisco market as all the station defendants. Evidence from plaintiff's own employee, Buckmaster, who negotiated with ITNA's Novitz, shows that Novitz did not, at the time of the original negotiations, know that plaintiff was listed in the San Francisco Arbitron market. Buckmaster Deposition 102–04, 120. In addition, KTVU's director Alan Bell's uncontradicted testimony is that KTVU did not conspire to exclude plaintiff from membership, but was perfectly willing to permit plaintiff to join ITNA at the same San Francisco price which KTVU paid for membership. Bell Deposition 133, 141.

The court finds that plaintiff cannot, as a matter of law, prevail on its ITNA conspiracy claim. First, plaintiff offers no proof of conspiracy. Secondly, ITNA's decision to abide by its normal pricing structure rather than give plaintiff preferential treatment cannot support such a claim. . . . In addition, plaintiff has offered no evidence whatsoever to prove an injury to competition, as opposed to injury to itself as a competitor, or proof that ITNA has market power, to support its conspiracy claim. . . . For these reasons, plaintiff cannot prevail on its ITNA conspiracy claim and defendant Miami Valley is entitled to summary judgment on that claim.

In summary, the court holds that plaintiff cannot prevail on any of its three antitrust claims. There is no evidence in the record to show that the defendants conspired to exclude plaintiff from quality programming or to enforce exclusivity against plaintiff. Nothing in the record shows that defendants acted anything but reasonably in obtaining and enforcing exclusive licenses, or in any other challenged practice. Rather, the record shows that plaintiff is unwilling to pay the going market price for programs or news feeds, and is seeking redress from this grievance by means of an antitrust suit. This is not the purpose of antitrust laws. Antitrust laws were designed to protect free market competition, not the financial success of any particular competitor. Nothing in the record shows that defendants' challenged actions in any way have decreased or injured competition.

In accordance with the foregoing, the court hereby grants defendants' motion for summary judgment on the entire action.

Metromedia Broadcasting Corp. v. MGM/UA Entertainment Co., 1985 Copyright Law Decisions ¶ 25,786 (C.D.Ca. 1985)

[After "Fame," a weekly series depicting the adventures of students at a New York high school for the performing arts, was dropped by the network, MGM/UA continued to produce episodes for so-called "first-run syndication," licensing them directly to independent local stations. MGM/UA offered a package of 136 episodes, 88 of which were already in existence, and 48 of which were yet to be produced. Metromedia was willing to license the new episodes, but balked at taking the "in-the-can" material, and brought suit, claiming (1) that MGM/UA had refused to negotiate exclusively and in good faith with Metromedia as to the new episodes, (2) that in requiring that Metromedia accept the older material in order to show the new material, MGM/UA was engaging in an illegal "tie-in" in violation of sections 1 and 2 of the Sherman Act and section 3 of the Clayton Act.]

RYMER, J.

. . . Each episode of "Fame" is copyrighted. "Fame" is (by definition) unique; and there appear to be few network-quality syndicated first run dramatic works on the market (examples would be "Too Close for Comfort" and "Paper Chase"), although numerous syndicated first run programs of other sorts are available (such as sporting events and game shows). MGM/UA linked the future licensing of first runs with reruns. . . .

Metromedia argues that first run episodes are a separate product from strip syndicated reruns, because each attracts a different level of advertising revenue and viewership, and is traditionally purchased separately . . . [that] MGM/UA has sufficient market power in the tying product ["Fame" first runs] on account of its holding copyrights on "Fame" and defendants' conduct is virtually identical to the block-booking found *per se* illegal in *United States v. Loew's, Inc.* [1962 Trade Cases par. 70,537], 371 U.S. 38 (1962); conditioning the purchase of first runs on reruns reflects an attempt by MGM/UA to gain a competitive advantage in the market for reruns. . . .

MGM/UA contends, on the other hand, that there is no unlawful tie-in because the bundle of rights subsumed under the "Fame" copyright are a single product which distinguishes the packaging of "Fame" first runs and "Fame" reruns from the block-booking condemned in *Loew's*; . . . no relevant market has been monopolized because there is no such market as the "strip syndicated rerun" market and monopoly power can't exist simply because "Fame" (like all dramatic works) is unique; there has been no attempt to monopolize any relevant market because defendants' conduct does not clearly threaten competition nor is it clearly exclusionary. . . .

Unlike the block-booking in *Loew's* . . . MGM/UA did not condition the license of, or use leverage from, one copyrighted property (like *Star Wars*) to license another, unrelated (and unwanted) property (like *Planet of the Apes*). It did offer two rights, the right to telecast first runs (which Metromedia wants) with the right to telecast reruns (which Metromedia does not want but Tribune [another station group] took). However, both these rights inhere in the copyright. 17 U.S.C. sec. 106. Therefore a substantial question exists about plaintiff's ability to show that the scope of the monopoly is enlarged by the granting of one license only, cf. *Paramount* . . . or that competition is suppressed beyond that which is permitted by the copyright laws.

In its recent decision in *Jefferson Parish Hosp. Dist. No. 2 v. Hyde* [1984-1 Trade Cases par. 65,908],—U.S.—. 104 S.Ct. 1551, 80 L.Ed. 2d 2 (1984), the Supreme Court defined the test for separate products to be whether the arrangement "link[s] two distinct markets for products . . . distinguishable in the eyes of buyers." 104 S.Ct. 1562. This, in turn, depends not on the functional relation between the two items, but on the character of the demand for them. *Id*. at 1562. The test is intended to prohibit only those arrangements which create the possibility of "foreclos[ing] competition on the merits in a product market distinct from the market for the tying item." *Id*. at 1563.

In *Hyde* the Court found that two distinguishable services were provided in a single transaction in part because anesthesiological services could efficiently be offered separately from hospital services and were billed separately, so that consumers differentiated between anesthesiological services and the other hospital services provided by the defendant. In this case, plaintiff is likely to show that syndicated reruns generally are offered separately from first runs; but neither side has adduced evidence of how syndicated reruns are marketed vis-a-vis *syndicated* first runs. That there may be a difference is suggested by the original programming package in this case, which included first runs and reruns. There is no track record with respect to whether "Fame" reruns and first runs could be separately *sold;* however, there is evidence that they could not be simultaneously *shown* without confusing the viewer and diluting the value of both. Although first runs and reruns generally appear to be independently priced, and first run rights to "Fame" are essentially barter [*i.e.*, furnished to the local station free of charge under an arrangement whereby the syndicator usually gets half the advertising minutes, which it then turns around and sells for its own account] while reruns are essentially cash, those "Fame" reruns that were part of the original programming package were priced together with first run episodes on a barter basis. Thus the normal distinction may be blurred in this case. Finally, although not directly relevant since the competition impacted is among producers trying to syndicate reruns or television stations that are rerun consumers, the public would appear to perceive reruns differently from first runs in that ratings (and in turn advertising revenues) are less for reruns tha[n] for their corresponding first runs. . . . However, there is nothing in the record to suggest that some reruns are not perceived more favorably than first runs (or other reruns) against which they may be competing in any given time slot or any given market.

Plaintiff faces a further difficulty because of how it posits power in the tying market. For that purpose, Metromedia defines the tying product as "Fame" 's copyright and uniqueness. In other words, all of "Fame" that inheres in the copyright is the product from which market power derives. However, the "tied" product has the same copyright and uniqueness. Accordingly the copyright and/or uniqueness that constitutes the tying product is not distinguished from the product to which it is tied.

On balance, while a serious question may be raised about whether the demand for first runs is separate from that for reruns under *Hyde*, that may not be material when the licensing of a single intellectual property is at issue. *Cardinal Films; Waldbaum*. In such a case competition on the merits of unrelated properties, whether in strip syndication or first run, is unlikely to be implicated for any reason other than quality. Thus, to carve up the "Fame" copyright would not appear to serve the competitive purposes of the rule against tying.

2. *Market power*.

The tie of one product to another is *per se* illegal only if the seller possesses sufficient market power in the tying product ["Fame" first runs] appreciably to restrain trade in the tied product ["Fame" reruns]. Forcing must be probable. *Hyde*, 104 S.Ct. at 1560. Assuming a threshold showing of a substantial potential for impact on competition (as, for example, when a tie affects more than a single purchaser or a substantial volume of commerce is foreclosed), *Hyde* reaffirms the proposition that a seller, in this case MGM/UA, may be presumed to have the power in the tying product ["Fame" first runs] when it holds a copyright or has an otherwise unique item. But see *Hyde*, 80 L.Ed. 2d at 25 (O'Connor, J., concurring opinion). In so doing the Court relied on the rationale of *Loew's*, as follows: "Any effort to *enlarge the scope* of the patent monopoly by using the market power it confers to restrain competition in the market for a *second* product will undermine competition on the merits in that second market. Thus, the sale or lease of a patented item on condition that the buyer make all his purchases of a separate tied product from the patentee is unlawful. . . . In each of these cases *per se* illegality was premised on misuse of the copyright or patent or unique commodity to foreclose competition on an item bearing an *unrelated* copyright or patent or attribute. . . . Because the scope of the defendants' monopoly has not been enlarged so as to impact sales of anything other than a right included within the copyright on "Fame," I doubt the applicability of the *per se* rule.

Neither side makes any particularly extensive analysis of the markets in which first runs and/or reruns are sold, *Hyde*, 104 S.Ct. at 1561. There is insufficient evidence in the record from which to conclude whether the relevant market would be all television shows, or all first runs, or all syndications, or syndicated first runs, or some combination of these—or nationwide, or territory by territory, or independent network by independent network; or whether the relevant competitors would be all producers of first run episodes, or only of syndicated first run episodes, or only of first run episodes which have been (prematurely) cancelled for network play. Nor is there any substantial indication of what MGM/UA's share of any of these markets would be. The contract at issue has an effect on six Tribune stations plus one independent in St. Petersburg; or seven Metromedia stations. Thus, I cannot say that plaintiff is likely to show that defendants' share of any relevant market is more than the shares held insufficient in *Hyde* and *Times-Picayune*.

There likewise is no way to determine whether there are close substitutes in any meaningful market. Plaintiff raises a potentially serious question with respect to power in the market for syndicated first runs, since there evidently are but a handful of dramatic works now in production. However I cannot conclude that there is any reasonable likelihood of such a restricted market's being defined. Finally, there is nothing to suggest that television stations are not price conscious or are without ample information about the quality of competing properties.

3. *Restraint or effect on rerun market*.

Plaintiff raises an issue (based on hearsay evidence), which may be serious, about a glut on the rerun market in general that may give MGM/UA the ability to foreclose competition in the syndication market because of leverage which comes from its relatively unique position as producer of syndicated first runs. However there is no evidence that quality or supply or television station choice or demand, is affected, or likely to be affected, by the tying arrangement at issue (except inferentially to the extent that money otherwise being paid for "Fame" would be spent on different reruns—for which there is no support in the record). Since MGM/UA could exert the market power directly in the tying product which it legitimately has through ownership of the "Fame" property by affixing any price it wishes to the first run license, it may be irrelevant that it does so indirectly by "forcing" a station to buy the rerun rights. This may particularly be the case when to do so is the only means by which to reverse negative cash flow, recoup costs of production, and continue to create new episodes.

4. *Damages*.

In order for plaintiff to prevail on the merits it must also show injury causally related to defendants' antitrust violation. . . . *Hyde* recognizes that it is not unlawful for one with market power simply to increase the price of the tying product so long as competition on the merits in the market for the tied product is not impaired in order to insulate an inferior product from competitive pressures. Simply to show that a noncompetitive price has been paid for the product which is tied is not enough. . . . Accordingly, "to demonstrate the injury necessary to establish defendant's liability, plaintiff must prove that the payment for both the tied and tying product exceeded their combined fair market value." *Casey*, 59 F. Supp. at 1571. There is no indication that this is the case. . . .

C. *Irreparable Injury*.

Metromedia argues that "Fame" is the centerpiece of its new programming image for which there is no substitute, that it has been a door-opener to an important viewing audience of urban youth, and that "Fame" has become identified with Metromedia through a substantial advertising campaign. Because of this it claims irreparable injury from loss of image, momentum and goodwill as well as revenue from spot sales and barter. MGM/UA contends that Metromedia's interest is only economic and that loss of viewers and injury to reputation are compensable in money damages.

I do not believe that irreparable injury has been shown. First, Metromedia's existence is not threatened in any respect. Whatever its loss of revenue on account of an antitrust violation, or MGM/UA's failure to negotiate, is compensable in damages. *Cass Communications*. Second, the difference between advertising revenue generated on "Fame" and a replacement is measurable. Metromedia has both a track record on "Fame" (as well as adjacent time periods), along with audience surveys and ratings, as a basis for comparison and calculation of loss. An even more direct basis for comparison will exist in the two markets in which there is overlap with Tribune. . . . Third, while "Fame" (like all works of art) is unique and its loss may affect Metromedia's mo-

mentum, it also may not; taste, like "Fame," is fleeting and there is nothing to show that a substitute may not catch on even more. To this extent the injury claimed is theoretical and not properly the basis for preliminary relief. *A.L.K. Corporation v. Columbia Pictures Industries, Inc.*, 440 F.2d 761 (3rd Cir. 1971); but see *Courier Times, Inc. v. United Feature Syndicate, Inc.*, 445 A.2d 1288 (Pa. Super. Ct. 1982) (irreparable injury on account of loss of unique product, "Peanuts," came from premier position assigned to "Peanuts" by the Inquirer in its effort to attract former Bulletin readers). Nor does it appear that loss of good will should be differently treated. In effect Metromedia has already placed a value on all of "Fame" (first runs and reruns) by the offer it made to MGM/UA. Finally, it has always been possible for Metromedia to lose "Fame." At the end of either last season or this, MGM/UA could itself have decided not to produce new episodes. That being the case, Metromedia must have considered the risk worth taking, or put another way, not irreparable.

By the same token MGM/UA stands also to suffer, if the relief requested were granted. The Tribune sale would be lost and possibly also the property. Without support from syndicated reruns it may be unable to continue first run production. Some additional deference to possible harm to MGM/UA is indicated because Metromedia delayed seeking relief until the time for commitments for the 1985–86 season is imminent, despite the fact that the package to which objection is made was proposed in October, four months ago. *Capital Cities*, Slip Op. at 9–10.

Conclusion

Given the extraordinary nature of relief that is sought, the likely unenforceability of a right of first negotiation, the lack of a convincing showing that each of the constituent elements of an unlawful tying arrangement exists, the probable compensability of whatever injury is proved, and the potential for harm to MGM/UA as well, I cannot conclude that irreparable injury will occur or that the balance of hardships tips so sharply in Metromedia's favor that the requisite showing is made. Accordingly, plaintiff's motion for a preliminary injunction is denied. . . .

Chapter 8

ADVANCING TECHNOLOGIES

8.00 The Changing Scene

The basic pleasures we enjoy have not changed that much. There are good books to read, music to appreciate, theatre and other live entertainment to attend, and movies, sports, and other programming to view in the venue or on television. What has changed—and changed dramatically—are the methods of delivery of entertainment, particularly the methods of delivery into the home. The same basic fare is offered, but in greater abundance and perhaps with better technological quality. The end result is that we are more and more immersed in entertainment, and we spend more dollars for this entertainment than we thought imaginable a few years ago.

Woody Allen's movie *Radio Days* reminds us that at one time we were "glued" to our radios much in the fashion we later became "glued" to our televisions. Radio and the phonograph were the first invaders of the household, forever changing much of our entertainment. The quiet book and the gathering around the piano for a few songs gave grudging but inevitable ground first to sounds and then, with television, to sights of others performing. Increasingly, we became

listeners and viewers. Stories came alive as described on radio and depicted on television. Music danced in our ears. Those who deliver entertainment saw that, even though part of the populace might wish to venture out for entertainment, a substantial segment enjoyed the pleasures of their home. The trick was to deliver those pleasures in increased variety and abundance.

Chapter 7 dealt with television from a fairly traditional viewpoint. The legal problems discussed were largely with issues that also exist in literary works, music, the theatre, and motion pictures. These issues dealt with protection of ideas for a script, adaptation of works from other media to television, and editing a work for television. The final section of Chapter 7, however, began to explore new ventures as television moved into expanded methods of delivery. This chapter carries forward the exploration of the continuum of delivery, from radio and television to the developing technologies—cable, satellite transmissions, multipoint distribution systems, scramblers and decoders, direct broadcast to individual earth dishes, and home recording and viewing devises such as videocassettes and videodiscs.

The following sections (8.01 to 8.06) detail business developments in these various technologies. Sections 8.10 to 8.13 examine the legal contexts in which the businesses operate, particularly the laws of copyright, communications, and antitrust. The succeeding sections examine current important issues such as interception of over-the-air signals (8.20), home taping of programming (8.30), and visual copying of film and videogame imagery (8.40).

8.01 Conventional Radio and Television

The Federal Communications Commission (FCC) licenses radio and television stations and exercises other forms of control, which are more fully explored in Section 8.12. In the past few years, the FCC has granted additional licenses each year, with net gains in the number of both commercial and educational radio and television stations. Figures for 1984 and 1985 illustrate a single year's expansion.

	Number of Stations	
	1984	*1985*
Radio		
Commercial AM	4,754	4,805
Commercial FM	3,658	3,846
Educational FM	1,165	1,220
	9,577	9,871
Television		
Commercial VHF	535	541
Commercial UHF	358	381
Educational VHF	114	113
Educational UHF	173	185
	1,180	1,220

Of the 922 commercial VHF and UHF television stations listed for 1985, 632 were network-owned or affiliates, and 290 were independents.

In addition, the FCC in the early 1980s authorized the licensing of low-power television stations (LPTV). These are "drop-ins" with very limited signal range (often no more than 10 to 15 miles) that do not interfere with stronger signals authorized for the same frequency band. Both VHF and UHF low-power stations have been licensed. The following figures, again for 1984 and 1985, illustrate that the licensing of LPTV stations is much more accelerated than for the more powerful stations.

	Number of Stations	
	1984	*1985*
VHF LPTV	202	408
UHF LPTV	102	210
	304	618

The growing number of stations, particularly when combined with wider varieties of programming, provide additional channels for cable systems to intercept and retransmit. But it is largely the cable system's choice to make. The FCC used to have "must carry" rules, ensuring conventional station access to cable systems' offerings within the same geographic region, but these rules were successfully challenged on free speech grounds. The FCC has been trying to establish modified "must carry" rules that will pass legal muster, but the future is unclear as to just what a cable system must carry and what lies in its business judgment to make. At the other end of the spectrum, some stations have found themselves turned into so-called "superstations," beamed to a satellite involuntarily and offered by satellite companies to cable systems all over the country. Attempts to resist becoming a superstation have been unsuccessful.

Currently, 98 percent of U.S. households have television sets; 57 percent have more than one set. Some 80 million households now have color sets, accounting for approximately 90 percent of the total TV households. Estimates are that the average house-hold has a television set on for 47 to 48 hours per week. Viewing time is, of course, divided among various household members, with females age 18 and over leading the parade with an average viewing time of 32 hours a week. Homes that actually have the television on during prime time were estimated at 59.5 percent in 1980, and that number is expected to rise to 64 percent by 1990. Indicative of the inroads of cable (particularly pay cable channels) is the estimate that back in 1980 84 percent of those sets were tuned into network programming. The total network share of prime-time viewers is expected to drop to 64 percent by 1990. Overall, while combined network ratings were 50 percent in 1980, they will be only 40 percent on average by 1990.

The diminution of network dominance in viewer ratings has led to substantial speculation about the future economic health of the networks and, as fall-out, of conventional television stations as well. The big fear is that advertising revenues will decline as network viewer audiences seek other fare. Advertisers no longer assume that television is necessarily the best medium to push their products. Network advertising rates are high, and advertisers are looking increasingly to cable, to sponsorship of live events, and to other media. More competition means more advertising slots, which translate into problems for conventional television. In 1985, for example, network advertising revenues declined for the first time since 1971, when cigarette advertising was banned from television. Although the 1985 slippage was only 2.8 percent, down to $8.313 billion from 1984's $8.555 billion, some analysts predicted this as an ongoing trend. When advertising revenues rallied in early 1986, the pessimists were still warning of long-term adverse effects.

A recent phenomenon in television and radio is the high rate of ownership turnover of stations. In 1985, records were easily set for total dollar volume involved in station sales and in the number of radio and television stations that changed hands. In 1985, according to FCC data, 99 TV stations, 1,558 radio stations, and 218 combined TV/radio stations were sold. The total transactions were valued at $5.668 billion, almost double the previous high of $2.854 billion in 1983. Network affiliate stations in major metropolitan areas were sold for as much as $400 million.

Several reasons contribute to the high sales volume, the most obvious being that large companies are moving aggressively, adding to their holdings. Takeovers are consolidating the conventional television and radio industries and allowing the largest companies to use these stations as bases for moves into other media enterprises. The FCC has indirectly encouraged this movement by changing its rules to allow the three major networks to own 12 television stations, rather than the 5 to which they had been restricted. The 12-station largesse is modified by a further FCC ruling that a network cannot own stations that, in total, reach more than 25 percent of the national television audience.

8.02   Basic Cable (CATV)

Community Antenna Television (CATV) developed in the late 1940s to serve remote communities that could not receive conventional television signals because of the distance between the community and the nearest TV stations or because of mountainous terrain that interfered with the reception. The first effort was in the small town of Oregon, Pennsylvania, where the community erected a large antenna on a hilltop outside the town and strung cable down to the community's homes. Shortly thereafter, private companies entered the business, but the early precedent was set that a community and its local government could control access because terrestrial cable had to be laid under or strung over a city's streets in order to service the locality's inhabitants. By 1950, cable systems were operating in 70 communities but servicing only 14,000 subscribers.

CATV remained a relatively small industry for several years. The technology was developed only to the point of picking up nearby signals. The service was viewed as a convenience to those who could not otherwise receive the signals, and little concern was expressed by television station owners about their signals being misappropriated. If anything, the cable systems increased the stations' viewer base, always an important concern to an industry that depends on increased viewership to justify higher sponsor fees.

Beginning in the 1960s and continuing to the present, television station owners began to express different attitudes. Because advancing technology, particularly satellite transmissions, has allowed for ever-greater access to distant signals, cable system offerings have increased from 6 or 7 channels to 40, 50, and more. In addition, the 70 communities served in 1950 swelled to over 7,300 communities with operating systems by 1986, meaning 48 percent of all TV households are now wired to cable. The magical 50 percent of TV households subscribing to cable will be reached sometimes during 1987, and the figure should approach 60 percent by the early 1990s.

Basic cable refers to the minimum package offered by a cable system to its viewers. Typically, for a set fee (which in 1987 averaged just over $10 a month across all systems), subscribers get access to high-quality reception of all local stations, several additional stations in the surrounding region, one or two distant stations (generally the so-called superstations), and several specialty "networks." The specialty networks may be exclusively news, weather, stock market quotations, sports, movies, or programming for restricted audiences, such as children, minorities, or foreign languages. The specialty networks, such as Entertainment Sports Program Network (ESPN) and Cable News Network (CNN), accept advertising and also charge a cable system a monthly fee, ranging from 3 to 25 cents per subscriber.

8.03   Pay Cable

Cable television is not free. To designate some cable as "basic" and other as "pay" is therefore misleading. Since this is industry terminology, we use it to prevent confusion. The distinction between "basic" and "pay" is that a subscriber pays a set monthly fee for a "basic" package (see Section 8.02), which then entitles the subscriber to choose (or not) a tier of "pay" channels, consisting of various combinations of channels which can be purchased at additional prices. At times, a network such as ESPN is part of the basic package in one cable system and is an add-on pay channel, or in a cluster of pay channels, in another.

Pay cable that is tiered on top of basic cable has been accepted by a majority of basic cable subscribers. In its infancy in 1976, only 4 percent of basic cable subscribers paid for pay cable as well. As new networks emerged and improved, pay cable subscribers grew rapidly. In 1980, 35 percent of basic subscribers were pay subscribers as well; in 1984, 60 percent had both. Despite this growth, a leveling occurred. In the early 1980s, pay cable's subscribers were increasing by as much as 50 percent a year. By 1987, the growth rate slowed to around 2 percent. A saturation of the market, the increasing popularity of videocassette recorders, and consumer dissatisfaction over too-frequent repetition of pay cable programming all undoubtedly contributed to the decline. In addition, while industry analysts had hoped that the average household would subscribe to at least two special pay networks, the actual average to date is only 1.3 per household. Thus, while pay cable's potentials are still positive, there are clearly problems.

Movie channels are a staple of pay cable. Many cable systems offer viewers choices among several movie channels, a trend that has caused head-to-head competition among these companies. Home Box Office (HBO) is the unquestioned leader, with over 40 percent of the market share (based on number of subscribers) among pay television services. Even so, HBO is feeling the effects of increased competition. Reports as to precise market shares vary, but one report had HBO's share slipping from 49 percent in 1983 to 43 percent in 1985. According to this report, trailing HBO in 1985 was Showtime (16 percent), Cinemax (12 percent), The Movie Channel (10 percent), Disney Channel (7 percent), and Playboy (2 percent).

The pay networks are engaged in constant competition for product as well as subscribers. A service such as the Disney Channel has the luxury of looking to its own library for 50 percent of its product and thus can obtain the remaining 50 percent from outside acquisitions (20 percent) and through original productions (30 percent). The other pay systems do not have extensive libraries and must license both established and new products. In the early 1980s, HBO spent hundreds of millions to get exclusives on about one-fourth of the total U.S. movie output. HBO also helped form a new movie studio, Tri-Star. In the meantime, Showtime (the second-largest pay network) paid more than $400 million to gain exclusives from Paramount.

The competition for product has inevitably led to legal confrontations. Most notable was the proposed venture by Getty Oil, Columbia Pictures, and other movie studios to involve themselves in a united effort to produce and distribute movies for pay television. HBO protested loud and long at what it perceived to be a venture that would corner a good deal of the movie output market. This led to *U.S. v. Columbia Pictures,* which is discussed in Section 8.13.

Pay cable also refers to individual offerings that operate completely outside a normal cable system. Instead of a multiplicity of channels, these special services feed more limited offerings via wire or microwave. The leading services of this type are Subscription Television (STV) and Multipoint Distribution Service (MDS). A third service, Direct Broadcast Satellite (DBS), is discussed in Section 8.04.

STV is pay television broadcast by a local station on a subscriber basis. Typically, a UHF station converts during prime time to a pay channel by sending out scrambled signals. A subscriber who pays a monthly fee for that one channel has a decoder in the home to unscramble the signals. At one time, the future of STV was promising, but its decline has closely tracked the increase of communities wired to a cable system. A one-channel offering has not been able to compete effectively with a system offering 20 or more channels. Other problems have undermined STV. Customers have not paid bills, parties have pirated the signals through purchase of nonauthorized decoders, and UHF station owners, seeing a shrinking subscriber base, have deemed their property too valuable to devote to STV and have turned to higher profit offerings.

MDS, on the other hand, may have a better future, particularly with FCC authorization of multichannel systems known as MMDS. Total subscribers to MDS services numbered 750,000 in 1982 and declined to 500,000 in 1984. However, with the authorization for multichannel as opposed to single-channel services, 16,000 applications for MMDS licenses were filed in 1984. Although these were for 4-channel services, current hopes are for MMDS systems that will offer 10 or more channels.

MMDS and MDS use low-power over-the-air microwave signals. A tall antenna (such as on top of the Empire State Building) sends the signals for a limited range, generally no more than 25 miles. The future of MMDS and MDS is undoubtedly tied into cable. Since an MMDS system's start-up costs are small compared to wiring a community for cable, the existence of a successful MMDS operation may discourage cable systems from invading that territory. In addition, economics may dictate that conventional cable is simply not appropriate for certain areas, leaving the door open for MMDS. Estimates are that by 1990, 21 million homes in the U.S. will still not be serviced by cable.

Pay-per-view (PPV), where available, permits cable subscribers to pay on a per-program basis for the privilege of viewing a special event, usually a sports contest, a movie not available on TV or regular cable, or a concert. The subscriber phones in the order, and the cable system's computer activates a box on the subscriber's set that unscrambles the signal for the subscriber on the system's special pay-per-view channel. As of 1985, 5 million homes, through their cable systems, were equipped with the technology for pay-per-view.

The PPV performance record has been spotty. Many failures have offset a few notable successes. It is clear the event on PPV must indeed be special. Thus, the Hagler-Leonard fight grossed millions, while an earlier Hearns-Duran bout attracted only 70,000 viewers. Movies have not attracted large PPV audiences, and rock concerts on PPV have had more failures than successes. Even so, some forecasts predict eventual triumphs for PPV. An Arthur D. Little study predicted that a $78 million PPV gross in 1987 would climb to $1.1 billion in 1990. Such forecasts seem high, but promoters and other entrepreneurs are certainly assessing PPV as an alternative.

Estimates for basic cable's 1987 subscriber revenues are just over $6 billion; pay cable's gross is estimated at $3.6 billion; and other cable system revenues should reach almost another $3 billion. Overall, cable in 1987 was a $12 billion to $13 billion industry. These revenues are spread among the 7,300 operating cable systems, though in fact the 20 largest multiple system companies service 70 percent of the nation's cable subscribers. As with conventional TV and radio stations, ownership of cable systems is constantly changing. The trend is toward mergers and acquisitions by the large companies, with the television networks and other media interests doing more than their share of acquiring.

8.04　Direct Broadcast Satellite (DBS)

DBS systems were approved by the FCC in 1983. These systems beam signals directly from satellites to home-receiving devices called "earth dishes." By 1985, 15,000 homes had their own dishes, but these were generally used to intercept signals from special pay networks intended for cable systems. Actual DBS delivery systems are still in the development stage and may have trouble getting started.

In the meantime, the pay channel owners moved to prevent home dish owners from getting their product for nothing. In 1986, most pay networks began scrambling their signals and equipping their cable system contractors with decoders. Individual decoders were also offered to dish owners, but most owners balked at paying substantial monthly fees for each network's decoder. These fees, when added to the several hundred dollars paid for the receiving dish, suddenly made the cost of television very high. Perhaps future DBS systems can reach an accommodation that makes direct broadcasting to individual dishes both efficient and economical, but those days have not yet arrived. Even so, predictions are that by 1990 some 9 percent of U.S. households will subscribe either to DBS, MMDS, or STV.

8.05 Videocassette Recorders

The penetration of videocassette recorders (VCRs) into the home entertainment market has been rapid and influential. In 1982, 6 percent of the nation's TV households had VCRs; this figure rose to 11 percent in 1983, 20 percent in 1984, 33 percent in 1985, over 40 percent in 1986, and an estimate upward of 50 percent by the end of 1987. In raw numbers, 11 to 12 million cassette recorders are sold each year, with well over 40 million sets now in homes around the country.

Not all ventures into home viewing devices have been successful. RCA's videodisc was a significant disappointment. In contrast to the millions of VCRs sold each year, the videodisc accumulated only a million sales over a six-year period (1980–1985). Undoubtedly, the fact that the disc could only show prerecorded programming and could not record off-air TV contributed to its commercial failure.

Motion picture studios have been cranking out prerecorded cassettes in ever-increasing numbers. In 1984, 22 million cassettes were produced. In 1985, the number more than doubled to 52 million; in 1986, it was over 60 million. Prerecorded cassettes have found their largest market through rental outlets, a circumstance that at one time caught the

motion picture industry by surprise. As a partial response, several new releases are now priced to sell, not rent. The 1986 hit *Top Gun* was immediately marketed at under $30 and enjoyed unprecedented success.

VCRs compete directly with pay cable networks. The HBOs and Showtimes still go after new movies, but at times the movies can be obtained in cassette form through video outlets up to six months before they are aired on pay cable. Viewing the movie through the VCR also has the obvious advantage that such can be done when the viewer wishes to watch.

The convenience of time scheduling also applies to recording off-the-air programming. Home taping of televised programs has been one of the great business and legal controversies of the 1980s. The well-known "Betamax" case is examined at length in Section 8.30.

Attempts have been made to use the VCR as a marketing tool for pay cable, capitalizing on the time-shifting potentials of the VCR. ABC Video Enterprises underwrote a venture called TeleFirst that used the ABC Chicago affiliate station (WLS-TV) to convert to a scrambled signal in the early morning hours. The pitch to potential subscribers was that they could tune in their VCRs to an attractive movie offering and record the movie while they were sleeping. The subscriber could then watch the movie whenever he or she desired. The pitch did not work. The service never attracted more than 3,000 subscribers. ABC lost $15 million, and TeleFirst collapsed after six months of operation.

8.06 Video Games

Video games for the home and coin-operated models for shopping malls and other public gathering areas burst on the scene in the early 1980s with spectacular effects. But within a couple of years, the video game market plummeted, disintegrating almost as spectacularly as the sight of the asteroids shot down on numerous game screens. Sales of consoles and cartridges dropped markedly. Grosses from coin-operated machines likewise fell. The numbers tell a graphic story.

The sales of electronic games, including consoles and cartridges, totaled $70 million in 1977. By 1980, sales were six times the 1977 figure—some $455 million. In 1981, this doubled to $1 billion, and doubled again in 1982 to $2.14 billion. Thereafter, the signs of recession appeared. The 1983 sales were basically the same as 1982, but then a steady decline sent sales to pre-1980 levels.

The same was true for the coin-operated enterprises. In 1982, gross revenues from coin-ops were a startling $8.9 billion, more than twice the gross of the U.S. motion picture industry. Then, in a single year, grosses fell to $6.4 billion, and the next year (1984) to $4.5 billion. Thus, in a two-year span, the industry's revenues were cut in half. Further evidence of the decline was seen in the average weekly take per coin-operated machine. In 1982, the figure was $109 weekly, in 1983 it dropped to $70, and in 1984 the take was only $53.

The inevitable consequence of this sharp decline was that profits for companies heavily committed to video games quickly turned to staggering losses. Thus, in 1983, Activision reported a $11.3 million loss; Bally was in the red over $35 million, as was Coleco at $22 million and Milton Bradley at $30 million. The most lethal losses, though, were Mattel's $361 million and Atari's $539 million. Several of these companies did not survive the reversals and had to liquidate in one form or another.

A legacy of the video game phenomenon was legal fights over the depictions of games on TV and other screens. Unquestionably,

game manufacturers rushed to emulate the most successful games. But was emulation actually an illegal copying? The copyrightability of game depictions is explored with other problems of visual imagery in Sections 8.40 to 8.42.

8.10   Legal Confrontations: Copyright, Communications, and Antitrust

As methods of delivering entertainment to the public develop, inevitable legal problems ensue. We have discussed in the prior sections the growth of cable, videocassette recorders, and video games. All of these forms of entertainment present copyright problems. Some areas are also directly affected by federal communications laws and regulations. And the methods of doing business may raise antitrust complications. The backgrounds on these legal areas, as they may apply to advancing technologies, are discussed in Sections 8.11 to 8.13.

8.11   Copyright

At issue are provisions of the federal copyright statutes pertinent to broadcasts. As cable systems developed into businesses with the capacity to bring in distant signals, thus at times showing duplicate programming to that on local channels, immediate challenges were raised by conventional broadcasters against the fledgling cable industry. The question was whether the interception and retransmission of a television station's signals was a "performance" of a copyrighted work and thus violative of the copyright laws. Two important U.S. Supreme Court cases held that no copyright infringements were involved.

In *Fortnightly Corporation v. United Artists*, 392 U.S. 390 (1968), United Artists (UA) claimed that Fortnightly, a CATV system, was illegally retransmitting signals of movies copyrighted by UA. The U.S. Court of Appeals had held that under a quantitative standard there was a complete copying and thus a violation. However, the U.S. Supreme Court disagreed. The Court held instead that the correct standard was to assess the function that CATV played in the total process of television broadcasting and reception.

In the Court's analysis, the copyright statutes enumerate certain rights that are exclusive to the copyright owner, including the right to perform. United Artists claimed that the broadcasting of its movies over the Fortnightly system was a "performance" within the meaning of the act. The Supreme Court, however, thought that CATV systems, if they did not alter the programs they retransmitted, were more like viewers than performers. Without any editing of or changing the program's presentation, CATV was simply an extension of the viewer. The retransmission of television signals sent out to the public was therefore not a copyright infringement.

In *Teleprompter Corporation v. CBS*, 415 U.S. 394 (1974), the issue of copyright infringement was raised. CBS contended that the manner of Teleprompter's operations was significantly different than in *Fortnightly*. CBS claimed the current CATV operations were different in three ways: Cable systems now sold advertising, they originated some of their own programming, and there were interconnections among many CATV systems. In addition, most CATV systems now intercepted and imported distant television signals and did not simply retransmit those in the immediate geographical area.

The U.S. Supreme Court again held for cable systems' abilities to capture over-the-air signals. The Court said that the differences emphasized by CBS were inconsequential because they related to noncopyrighted portions of the CATV programming. While cable systems might be able to compete more effectively for the television

market by using these new business techniques, these factors were nonetheless extraneous to the copyrighted material. The Court also dismissed the claim of a distinction between nondistant and distant signal retransmission. A cable system's importation of signals that could not normally be received with ordinary consumer antennas did not alter the basic function of CATV. The Court said that anyone who had the capacity to intercept and retransmit signals had the legal privilege to do so.

Twice defeated in the courts, conventional television interests then pressed Congress for action. They requested that Congress revise the copyright laws to declare the retransmission of signals a copyright violation. These efforts were only partially successful. In its general revisions of the copyright statutes in 1976, Congress passed what is now 17 U.S.C. § 111. This important section creates a compulsory licensing system that allows cable systems to convey secondary transmissions of primary transmissions, including those of copyrighted works. For this license, cable systems must pay a copyright fee to the Copyright Tribunal. There must be compliance with certain formalities, such as notice.

Under this compulsory license, secondary transmission is allowed if simultaneous with the primary transmission and if the programming and advertising are not altered by the cable system. In other words, if there is compliance with the formalities of the section, passive carriage of signals by a carrier is not copyright infringement. As noted in 17 U.S.C. § 111(a)(3), there is no copyright liability when there is "a secondary transmission . . . by any carrier who has not direct or indirect control over the content or selection of the secondary transmission, and whose activities with respect to the secondary transmission consist solely of providing . . . communications channels for the use of others."

The provisions of § 111 are lengthy and complex and have led to substantial litigation regarding the question of whether a cable system's carriage of signals is in fact passive. Some of these cases are considered in Section 8.20. Another aspect of the passage of § 111 was that it required the Copyright Tribunal not only to collect the compulsory license fees but also to determine how those should be allocated among various interests vying for a cut of the copyright royalty pie. When the tribunal announced its overall formulas for such division, the National Association of Broadcasters and others immediately protested and filed suit.

In *National Ass'n of Broadcasters v. Copyright Royalty Tribunal*, 675 F.2d 367 (D.C. Cir. 1982), the U.S. Court of Appeals noted that the revised act invested the Copyright Tribunal, in its decisions as to the distribution of royalty fees collected from cable operators, with broad discretion in apportioning the fees among the copyright owners. Specific awards were reversible only if the agency's decision was not supported by "substantial evidence" or was "arbitrary, capricious, an abuse of discretion or otherwise not in accordance with law."

The consolidated cases considered by the court arose out of the first royalty distribution for the 1978 calendar year. The tribunal proposed that the $15 million fund be distributed as follows:

Program syndicators and movie producers	75.00%
Sports leagues	12.00
Television broadcasters	3.25
Public television	5.25
Music claimants	4.50

After hearing arguments and examining data advanced by the parties, the tribunal had determined that the following criteria would guide its allocation of the shares:

1. The harm caused to copyright owners by secondary transmissions of copyrighted works by cable systems;
2. The benefit derived by cable systems from the secondary transmissions of certain copyrighted works.
3. The marketplace value of the works transmitted. Among the secondary factors determined by the tribunal were the quality of the copyrighted program material and time-related considerations.

The U.S. Court of Appeals upheld the tribunal's decisions in all but one instance; it reversed the tribunal's decision to award $50,000 to National Public Radio (NPR). The court was troubled by apparent procedural flaws in its reconsideration and decision to rescind the award to NPR and remanded only that portion. As to all other claimants—the National Association of Broadcasters; the Joint Sports Claimants, a group including professional baseball, basketball, hockey, and soccer leagues; ASCAP, a membership association of music publishers and composers; and the Canadian Broadcasting Corporation—the court was satisfied that the tribunal's resolution was reasonable and comported with congressional intent. The court recognized that it was impossible to satisfy all the claimants, whose combined requests totaled roughly three times more than the finite amount of the fund. However, the administrative record provided rational support for the distribution of the royalty shares, and the tribunal's allocations were upheld.

Since the original allocation of $15 million in 1978, the yearly sums to be divided have multiplied many times over the original figure, but the same basic percentile allocations remain. The Copyright Tribunal was also challenged as to its allocations within each of the major categories detailed above, but again its basic formulas were upheld.

8.12 Communications

The Communications Act of 1934 created the Federal Communications Commission (FCC) and invested it with the power both to license and regulate all television and radio stations. While the FCC does not directly license television networks, it does exercise significant influence over them through its licensing of individual stations and its regulations which directly affect network operations. The FCC allocates space in the radio frequency spectrum, determines how many stations can be located in particular geographic areas, and issues rules and procedures concerning a wide variety of practices ranging from cross-ownership of different types of communications enterprises to selection of broadcasters for sports events.

Television and radio stations are licensed to serve the public and are required to have their licenses renewed either every five years (television) or seven years (radio). A station's license renewal application can be challenged, and valuable properties have been forfeited through FCC action. The FCC can also reprimand, fine, and impose other short-term measures.

FCC power to regulate the cable industry was established in *United States v. Southwestern Cable Co.*, 392 U.S. 157 (1968). In that instance, the FCC had restricted the expansion of Southwestern Cable into the television area covered by Midwest Video Corporation's San Diego station. The FCC acted at the behest of Midwest, and its order against Southwestern was challenged by Southwestern in the federal courts. The U.S. Court of Appeals for the Ninth Circuit held that the FCC lacked authority under the Communications Act to impose the restriction on Southwestern. The U.S. Supreme Court reversed.

The Court first determined that the FCC has the authority to regulate cable systems. The Court noted that nothing in the Communications Act restricted the FCC from such regulation, and no interpretation of the act based on its history or purpose could reasonably infer that the FCC lacked such authority. The Court stated that flexibility in the FCC's authority was essential because of the changing nature and technology of broadcasting. The Court held, however, that the FCC's authority was ". . . restricted to that reasonably ancillary to the effective performance of the Commission's various responsibilities for the regulation of television broadcasting." In this particular instance, the Court concluded the commission's order was proper until a full hearing could be conducted to determine the merits of Midwest's claim against Southwestern.

Again, in *United States v. Midwest Video Corp.*, 406 U.S. 649 (1972), the Court focused on the FCC's authority under the Communications Act to regulate the cable industry. Citing with approval its holding in *Southwestern*, the Court upheld an FCC rule that prohibited cable system broadcasts unless the system had significant originating programs in addition to retransmitting other television programming. (The rule only affected systems with 3,500 or more subscribers.) The Court determined this requirement would promote the public interest, even though the cost to the subscriber might increase. The FCC had proceeded only after substantial hearing on the matter. The Court declared it would not second-guess the commission's perceptions of the public good.

In subsequent decisions, courts have generally upheld FCC regulations. (See examples of these in further discussions below in *WWHT v. FCC, Malrite TV of New York v.*

FCC, and *National Ass'n of Theatre Owners v. FCC*.) In an important ruling, the U.S. Supreme Court upheld FCC regulations forbidding the future formation or transfer in ownership of co-located newspaper-broadcast combinations. In *FCC v. National Citizen's Committee for Broadcasting*, 436 U.S. 775 (1978), the Court deferred to the FCC's judgment that the ownership restrictions would advance a policy of promoting diversity of viewpoints in broadcasting. The Court did not require a showing that diversification would in fact occur, but only that the FCC had proceeded with deliberation before issuing its regulations.

In selected areas, successful court challenges to FCC regulations have been registered. In *HBO v. FCC*, set forth below, pay cable interests successfully overturned FCC regulations designed to impede the transfer of movies and sports events from conventional to pay TV. In *FCC v. Midwest Video Corp.*, 440 U.S. 689 (1979), the U.S. Supreme Court invalidated FCC requirements that cable systems have a 20-channel capacity by 1985. Also overturned were requirements that cable systems make access channels available to segments of the public and that equipment for access purposes be provided.

FCC regulations are often complex and at times confusing. In part, their importance to both the television and cable industries makes complexity inevitable and mandates detailed provisions that attempt to respond to a wide variety of situations. One important area is protection for a TV station against program duplication by the importation of distant signals. Although certain program duplication regulations have been modified, regulations under 47 C.F.R., §§ 76.92 to 76.95, still provide protections. Extensive portions of these sections are set forth below.

In recent years, many FCC regulations have been modified or completely excised. The requirement that radio stations ascertain their communities' needs for specific programming has been eliminated. Also removed are requirements that radio and TV stations air a certain amount of nonentertainment programming. Limits on the number of commercial minutes per broadcast hour are gone. In total, it is estimated that 90 percent of all FCC regulations have been reviewed, modified, or eliminated since 1981.

Finally, special note must be made of 47 U.S.C. § 605, which is set forth below. This provision, amended extensively in 1984, proscribes the interception of broadcast signals intended for private use. The 1984 amendments address directly the problems of satellite transmissions. Several cases dealing with the interception and retransmission of signals are analyzed in Section 8.20. Since these cases pre-date the 1984 amendments, they should be read in connection with § 605 as it currently reads.

8.12–1   WWHT, Inc. v. FCC

In 1968, the FCC established a nationwide over-the-air subscription television broadcasting service and adopted rules designed to ensure the integration of the new STV service into the total television broadcasting service. No further action, however, was taken with respect to the 1968 rule-making proceeding until September 21, 1978, when the commission terminated the proceeding without adopting the proposed amendments. The following day, Blonder-Tongue Laboratories petitioned the commission to institute rule-making proceedings to amend its mandatory cable carriage rules to include the carriage of STV signals. Comments in favor of the petition were also submitted by the Motion Picture Association of America and the NBA, jointly with the NHL.

After reviewing the comments, the commission denied the request for rule making, setting forth reasons justifying the denial and concluding that it was "appropriate that STV operators and cable television operators be left free to bargain in their own best interests for cable carriage." The commission also denied Suburban Broadcasting Corporation's request for a declaratory ruling on the scope of the existing cable carriage rules. Suburban had argued that the commission's rules already required mandatory STV carriage. The FCC in reply declared that it had "publicly, clearly, and consistently" over the preceding 12 years neither intended nor enforced its rules to require STV carriage.

The court's review of the record (*WWHT, Inc. v. FCC*, 656 F.2d 807 [D.C. Cir. 1981]) indicated that no procedural infirmity marred the actions of the FCC, and the court had before it a challenge to the factual and policy determinations of the FCC. The court held that under 5 U.S.C. § 706(2)(A) it had the jurisdiction to review actions committed to agency discretion, but the scope of review should be extremely narrow. The court found that the explanations given by the FCC were adequate to explain the facts and policy concerns it had relied on, and there was nothing to indicate that the opinions of the commission were unlawful, arbitrary, capricious, or wholly irrational. The interest sought to be protected by petitioners was primarily economic and did not present unusual or compelling circumstances to justify overturning the FCC's decision. Moreover, the policy determinations as to the relative merits of mandatory cable carriage of STV signals were not suitable for determination by the court and thus were well within the discretion of the agency.

8.12–2 National Ass'n of Theatre Owners v. FCC

On the basis of its 17-year inquiry into the feasibility of over-the-air subscription television (STV), the FCC issued its Fourth Report and Order concluding that STV would provide a beneficial supplement to free broadcasts. In its report, the commission imposed a number of restrictions governing technical specifications and modus operandi of the operations but rejected the suggestion that direct regulation of the rates was necessary to prevent "gouging" of the public.

The petitioners advanced arguments in support of their contention that the commission exceeded the proper bounds of its power and also raised equal protection and First Amendment issues. After examining the language and history of the Communications Act of 1934, the court (*National Ass'n of Theater Owners v. FCC*, 420 F.2d 194 [D.C. Cir. 1969]) found that the act was a broad grant of general licensing authority that had been affirmed by subsequent court challenges. The act also did not preclude the commission from approving a system of direct charges to the public as a means of financing broadcasting services; rather it was designed to foster diversity in the financial organization of broadcasting stations. Therefore, the commission did not exceed its authority in concluding that STV was consistent with its goals.

As to the petitioners' argument that the FCC's decision not to employ rate-making measures was arbitrary and capricious, the court found that in its 144-page Fourth Report, the commission had adequately determined that a substantial amount of economic competition would exist between STV and other forms of entertainment, making regulation unnecessary. The court noted that it was very reluctant to declare that free market forces must be supplanted by rate regulation when neither Congress nor the FCC had deemed it essential.

The court also found no merit to the petitioners' constitutional claims. The authorization of nationwide STV would not result in unconstitutional discrimination against people in low-income groups. The public's access to the broadcast media had never been wholly free, since it is necessary to procure and maintain the necessary apparatus. Moreover, under the regulations, any deprivation of access would be slight; at most, one out of five stations serving a community would be devoted to STV, and that station would be required to carry at least 28 hours of free programming per week. Finally, when the net effect of the program restrictions was considered, it was likely that the public in STV areas would receive more rather than less diversity of expression in television programming, thus refuting petitioners' contention that STV would be a prior restraint on free speech in violation of the First Amendment.

In fashioning the remedy in equity, the court granted a permanent injunction against defendant's actions. Furthermore, because the defendant realized proceeds of $1,432.50 through the conversion and disposition to its own use of the property rights of the plaintiff, the amount was deemed to be held in constructive trust for the plaintiff, and plaintiff was held entitled to that sum.

8.12–3　Malrite TV of N.Y. v. FCC

The case of *Malrite TV of N.Y. v. FCC*, 652 F.2d 1140 (2d Cir. 1981), was an attempt to set aside the FCC's order to deregulate the cable television industry by rescinding rules relating to syndicated program exclusivity and distant signal coverage that restricted cable systems in their use of copyrighted works. The FCC's actions were in response to the 1976 Copyright Act, which provided a system of partial copyright liability for cable television with a compulsory licensing scheme. This scheme eliminated the need of cable operators to obtain the consent of or to negotiate licenses with copyright owners by

requiring the payment to the owners of a prescribed royalty fee. Upon inquiry, the FCC found that its copyright protections, the distant signal and syndicated exclusivity, should be eliminated since Congress had resolved the copyright issue. Furthermore, the impact on broadcast stations from the FCC's deregulation would be negligible, and consumers would in fact benefit from increased viewing options.

The petitioners, among them the professional sports leagues, argued that the FCC's action misconstrued the mandate of the 1976 Copyright Act and was arbitrary and capricious. The court rejected the contention that the act was premised on maintenance of the regulatory framework or that a retransmission consent requirement should be adopted. First, in establishing the Copyright Royalty Tribunal, responsible for collecting and distributing the royalty fees, Congress had clearly provided that that entity could readjust the royalty rate if the FCC altered its cable restrictions. Second, the adoption of a retransmission consent rule would undermine Congress' compulsory licensing scheme since it would function no differently from full copyright liability.

The court also did not believe that the FCC overlooked any of the contentions by pertinent segments of the industry that the FCC's actions were arbitrary and capricious. For example, the professional sports leagues contended that cable television, by making available more broadcasts of games from distant cities, would decrease game receipts, threaten the league by hurting the weaker franchises, and ultimately lead to less sports programming. The leagues, however, did not produce any evidence that the number of sports broadcasts by home clubs was reduced in existing areas of high cable penetration. The court held it was not arbitrary for the FCC to conclude that sports programming required no special protection after the repeal of the distant signal rules, especially in light of the fact that the primary means of sports protection, the home broadcast blackout rules (47 C.F.R. § 76.67 [1980]), would continue to exist.

The court concluded that the widespread participation of all industry segments and the comprehensive evaluation of data reflected the "rational weighing of competing policies" that Congress intended to be exercised by the FCC, and upheld the rescission of the rules deregulating the cable industry.

8.12–4   HBO v. FCC

The following report of *Home Box Office, Inc. v. FCC*, 567 F.2d 9 (D.C. Cir. 1977), is a summary of the federal court's findings and was written by the court itself. This syllabus appears at the beginning of the court's decision and can be found at 567 F.2d 9, 13–15.

These 15 consolidated cases challenge four orders of the Federal Communications Commission which, taken together, regulate and limit the program fare cablecasters and subscription broadcast television stations may offer to the public for a fee set on a per-program or per-channel basis. Acting under its rulemaking authority, the Commission in 1975 issued rules which prohibited pay exhibition of: (1) feature films more than three, but less than 10, years old; (2) specific sports events (*e.g.*, the World Series) shown on broadcast television within the previous five years; (3) more than the minimum number of non-specific (*i.e.*, regular season) sports events which had not been broadcast in any of the five preceding years, and in some cases only half that number; and (4) all series programs (*i.e.*, programs with interconnected plot or substantially the same cast of principal characters). In addition, the Commission prohibited commercial advertising in conjunction with pay exhibition of programming and limited the overall number of hours of pay operation which could be devoted to sports and feature films to 90% of total pay operations. *See* 47 C.F.R. §§

73.643, 76.225 (1975). By subsequent orders in the same rulemaking, the series programming restriction was removed and recordkeeping requirements were imposed on feature film programming. The stated purpose of these rules was to prevent competitive bidding away of popular program material from the free television service to a service in which the audience would have to pay a fee to see the same material. Such competitive bidding, or "siphoning," is said to be possible because the money received from pay viewers is significantly more for some programs than money received from advertisers to attach their messages to the same material. For this reason, even a relatively small number of pay viewers could cause a program to be siphoned regardless of the wishes of a majority of its free viewers.

Held:

1. Review of the rulemaking record indicates that the pay cable television regulations must be considered separately from those regulating subscription broadcast television. Because the Commission has exceeded its authority over cable television in promulgating the pay cable rules and because there is no evidence to support the need for regulation of pay cable television, these rules must be vacated. Pp. 29–67.

a. The Communications Act of 1934, 47 U.S.C. § 151 *et. seq.*, contains no provision expressly authorizing the Commission to regulate cable television. The Supreme Court has nonetheless sanctioned regulation of cable television under § 2(a) of the Act, 47 U.S.C. § 152(a), but only where the ends to be achieved were "long established" in the field of broadcast television or were "congressionally approved." *See United States v. Midwest Video Corp.*, 406 U.S. 649, 667–668 (1972); *United States v. Southwestern Cable Co.*, 392 U.S. 157, 173–176 (1968). These cases and considerations of administrative consistency further indicate that in most instances the proper test for Commission jurisdiction over pay cable television is whether the ends proposed to be achieved by Commission regulations are also well understood and consistently held ends for which broadcast television could be regulated. *See United States v. Midwest Video Corp.*, *supra*, 406 U.S. at 667–668; *cf. Greater Boston Television Corp. v. FCC*, 143 U.S. App. D.C. 383, 394, 444 F.2d 841, 852 (1970), *cert. denied*, 403 U.S. 923 (1971). *See also Hampton v. Mow Sun Wong*, 426 U.S. 88, 116 (1976). Pp. 30–34.

b. Under the standard set out above, the Commission has exceeded its jurisdiction and its rules must be vacated as unauthorized by law insofar as they regulate cable television. Pp. 34–48.

c. Even if the Commission had jurisdiction to promulgate its anti-siphoning rules, there is no evidence in the record supporting the need for regulation. Consequently, the rules must be vacated since a "regulation perfectly reasonable and appropriate in the face of a given problem [is] highly capricious if that problem does not exist." *City of Chicago v. FCC*, 147 U.S. App. D.C. 312, 323, 458 F.2d 731, 742 (1971), *cert. denied*, 405 U.S. 1074 (1972). Pp. 48–60.

d. Moreover, although the Commission properly recognized the need to balance the benefits of regulation against the detriment to unfettered competition, it proceeded incorrectly. Contrary to the Commission's position, *United States v. Southwestern Cable Co.*, *supra*, does not sanction regulation of cable television to prevent "unfair competition," but even if it did, the "unfairness" recognized in *Southwestern Cable* is not present here. Moreover, the balance between regulation and competition is not to be resolved on the basis of legal precedent, but by a considered decision upon the record in each rulemaking. Pp. 60–67.

2. The cable television rules are inconsistent with the First Amendment. Even though substantially similar rules which applied to broadcast television were upheld by this court in *National Ass'n of Theatre Owners (NATO) v. FCC*, 136 U.S. App. D.C. 352, 420 F.2d 194 (1969), *cert. denied*, 397 U.S. 922 (1970), that case is not controlling since "differences in the characteristics of news media justify differ-

ences in the First Amendment standards applied to them." *Red Lion Broadcasting Co. v. FCC*, 395 U.S. 367, 386 (1969). Pp. 67–83.

a. The constitutional question in *NATO* was straightforward: whether a grant of a broadcast license could be conditioned on terms which made reference to the kind and content of programs being offered to the public. Phrased this way, the question was identical to that resolved in the affirmative over 25 years before *NATO* in *National Broadcasting Co. v. United States*, 319 U.S. 190, 212–217, 226–227 (1943). Although *NATO* did not itself cite *National Broadcasting Co.*, there was no need for it to break new First Amendment ground and a reading of *NATO* shows that it did not do so. The conflict among speakers using the electromagnetic spectrum which justified Commission regulation in *NATO* and *National Broadcasting Co.* is absent from cable television, however. For this reason, the conventional justification for Commission regulation of broadcast speakers cannot be applied to regulation of cable television. Pp. 67–72.

b. The absence in cable television of the physical limitations of the electromagnetic spectrum does not automatically lead to the conclusion that no regulation of cable television is valid under the First Amendment. Because "the right of free speech . . . does not embrace a right to snuff out the free speech of others," *Red Lion Broadcasting Co. v. FCC*, *supra*, 395 U.S. at 387, government may adopt reasonable regulations separating broadcasters competing and interfering with each other for the same audience. In determining whether such regulations comport with the First Amendment, the proper test is that set out in *United States v. O'Brien*, 391 U.S. 367, 377 (1968). Pp. 73–77.

c. Analysis of the Commission's stated reasons for promulgating the anti-siphoning rules indicates that the rules are intended to remove a conflict between those with and those without access to pay cable television. This purpose is unrelated to the suppression of free expression as required by *O'Brien*. Nonetheless, the rules are invalid because the record here will not support the conclusion that there is in fact conflict between these groups. Moreover, the restraints imposed by the rules are greater than necessary to further any legitimate government interest, and this overbreadth is not cured by the waiver provisions associated with the rules since the procedures established for obtaining a waiver are fundamentally at odds with the standards set out in *Freedman v. Maryland,* 380 U.S. 51 (1965). Pp. 77–83. . . .

4. Rules substantially similar to the subscription broadcast television rules were affirmed by this court over six years ago in *NATO v. FCC, supra.* At that time the commission acted on an elaborate rulemaking record containing data generated in trial operations of a subscription broadcast station at Hartford, Connecticut. It appears that few, if any, subscription stations have begun operation in the interim. Accordingly, the best information available with respect to subscription broadcast television is that reviewed in *NATO,* which has not been called into question in the instant rulemaking. For this reason, *NATO* requires affirmance of the rules promulgated in the dockets here under review to the extent that such rules apply to subscription broadcast television, subject, however, to further review upon completion of additional hearings regarding *ex parte* contacts as ordered herein. Pp. 101–104. *Remanded.*

8.12–5 Federal Communications Commission Regulations

The following FCC regulations (47 C.F.R. §§ 76.92, 76.94, and 76.95) protect TV stations against program duplication by the importation of distant signals.

§ 76.92 Stations entitled to network program nonduplication protection
(a) Any community unit which operates in a community located in whole or in part within the 35-mile specified zone of any commercial television broadcast station or within the secondary zone which extends 20 miles beyond the specified zone of a smaller market television broadcast station (55 miles altogether), and which carries the signal of such station shall, except as provided in paragraphs (e) and (f) of this section, delete, upon request of the station licensee or permittee, the duplicating network programming of lower priority signals in the manner and to the extent specified in §§ 76.94 and 76.95.

(b) For purposes of this section, the order of nonduplication priority of television signals carried by a community unit is as follows:

(1) First, all television broadcast stations within whose specified zone the community of the community unit is located, in whole or in part;

(2) Second, all smaller market television broadcast stations within whose secondary zone the community of the community unit is located, in whole or in part. . . .

(e) Any community unit which operates in a community located in whole or in part within the specified zone of any television broadcast station or within the secondary zone of a smaller market television broadcast station is not required to delete the duplicating network programming of any 100-watt or higher power television translator station which is licensed to the community of the community unit.

(f) Any community unit which operates in a community located in whole or in part within the secondary zone of a smaller market television broadcast station is not required to delete the duplicating network programming of any major market television broadcast station whose reference point (See § 76.53) is also within 55 miles of the community of the community unit. . . .

§ 76.94 Notification requirements and extent of protection
(a) Where the network programming of a television station is entitled to nonduplication protection, a community unit shall, upon request of the station licensee or permittee, refrain from simultaneously duplicating any network program broadcast by such station only if the community unit has received the information

required in paragraphs (a)(1) and (2) of this section:

(1) Notification of the date and time of the programming to be protected and date and time of the programming to be deleted must, at a minimum, be received on a monthly basis. If the station licensee or permittee elects to provide such notification on a monthly basis, it must be submitted no later than six (6) days preceding the calendar month during which nonduplication is requested. If the station licensee or permittee elects to provide such notification on a weekly basis, notice shall be given no later than the Monday preceding the calendar week (Sunday–Saturday) during which nonduplication protection is sought.

(2) Changes in the monthly notification request required by paragraph (a)(1) must be submitted six (6) days preceding the broadcast of the programming to be protected: *Provided, however,* that the licensee or permittee of the television station otherwise entitled to nonduplication protection must notify the affected community unit as soon as possible. . . .

(b) Where a community unit is required to provide same-day network program nonduplication protection, either pursuant to specific Commission order or pending Commission action on a broadcast station petition for special relief filed pursuant to the procedures described in paragraph 25 of the *Second Report and Order in Docket 19995,* FCC 75–820, 54 FCC 2d 229 (1975), the following provisions shall be applicable:

(1) A community unit need not delete reception of a network program if, in so doing, it would leave available for reception by subscribers, at any time, less than the programs of two networks (including those broadcast by any stations whose signals are being carried and whose programming is being protected pursuant to the requirements of this section);

(2) A community unit need not delete reception of a network program which is scheduled by the network between the hours of 6 and 11 p.m., eastern time, but is broadcast by the station requesting deletion, in whole or in part, outside of the period which would nor-

mally be considered prime time for network programming in the time zone involved.

§ 76.95 *Exceptions*

(a) Notwithstanding the requirements of §§ 76.92 and 76.94, a community unit need not delete reception of any program which would be carried on the community unit in color but will be broadcast in black and white by the station requesting deletion.

(b) The provisions of §§ 76.92 and 76.94 shall not apply to a community unit having fewer than 1,000 subscribers. Within 60 days following the provision of service to 1,000 subscribers, each such community unit shall file a notice to that effect with the Commission and shall send a copy thereof to all television broadcast and translator stations carried by the community unit.

(c) Network nonduplication protection need not be extended to a higher priority station for one hour following the scheduled time of completion of the broadcast of a live sports event by that station or by a lower priority station against which a cable community unit would otherwise be required to provide nonduplication protection following the scheduled time of completion.

(d) The Commission will give full effect to private agreements between operators of community units and local television stations which provide for a type or degree of network program nonduplication protection which differs from the requirements of §§ 76.92 and 76.94. . . .

The following FCC regulation (47 U.S.C. § 605) proscribes the interception of broadcast signals intended for private use.

§ 605 *Unauthorized publication or use of communications*

(a) Practices prohibited

Except as authorized by chapter 119, Title 18, no person receiving, assisting in receiving, transmitting, or assisting in transmitting, any interstate or foreign communication by wire or radio shall divulge or publish the existence, contents, substance, purport, effect, or meaning thereof, except through authorized channels of transmission or reception, (1) to any person other than the addressee, his agent, or attorney, (2) to a person employed or authorized to forward such communication to its destination, (3) to proper accounting or distributing officers of the various communicating centers over which the communication may be passed, (4) to the master of a ship under whom he is serving, (5) in response to a subpoena issued by a court of competent jurisdiction, or (6) on demand of other lawful authority. No person not being authorized by the sender shall intercept any radio communication and divulge or publish the existence, contents, substance, purport, effect, or meaning of such intercepted communication to any person. No person not being entitled thereto shall receive or assist in receiving any interstate or foreign communication by radio and use such communication (or any information therein contained) for his own benefit or for the benefit of another not entitled thereto. No person having received any intercepted radio communication or having become acquainted with the contents, substance, purport, effect, or meaning of such communication (or any part thereof) knowing that such communication was intercepted, shall divulge or publish the existence, contents, substance, purport, effect, or meaning of such communication (or any part thereof) or use such communication (or any information therein contained) for his own benefit or for the benefit of another not entitled thereto. This section shall not apply to the receiving, divulging, publishing, or utilizing the contents of any radio communication . . . transmitted by any station for the use of the general public, which relates to ships, aircraft, vehicles, or persons in distress, or which is transmitted by an amateur radio station operator or by a citizens band radio operator.

(b) Exceptions

The provisions of subsection (a) of this section shall not apply to the interception or receipt by any individual, or the assisting (including the manufacture or sale) of such interception or receipt, of any satellite cable programming for private viewing if—

(1) the programming involved is not encrypted; and

(2)(A) a marketing system is not established under which—

(i) an agent or agents have been lawfully designated for the purpose of authorizing private viewing by individuals, and

(ii) such authorization is available to the individual involved from the appropriate agent or agents; or

(B) a marketing system described in subparagraph (A) is established and the individual receiving such programming has obtained authorization for private viewing under that system.

(c) Definitions

For purposes of this section—

(1) the term "satellite cable programming" means video programming which is transmitted via satellite and which is primarily intended for the direct receipt by cable operators for their retransmission to cable subscribers;

(2) the term "agent," with respect to any person, includes an employee of such person;

(3) the term "encrypt," when used with respect to satellite cable programming, means to transmit such programming in a form whereby the aural and visual characteristics (or both) are modified or altered for the purpose of preventing the unauthorized receipt of such programming by persons without authorized equipment which is designed to eliminate the effects of such modification or alteration;

(4) the term "private viewing" means the viewing for private use in an individual's dwelling unit by means of equipment, owned or operated by such individual, capable of receiving satellite cable programming directly from a satellite; and

(5) the term "private financial gain" shall not include the gain resulting to any indi-

vidual for the private use in such individual's dwelling unit of any programming for which the individual has not obtained authorization for that use.

(d) Penalties; civil actions; remedies; attorney's fees and costs; computation of damages; regulation by State and local authorities

(1) Any person who willfully violates subsection (a) of this section shall be fined not more than $1,000 or imprisoned for not more than 6 months, or both.

(2) Any person who violates subsection (a) of this section willfully and for purposes of direct or indirect commercial advantage or private financial gain shall be fined not more than $25,000 or imprisoned for not more than 1 year, or both, for the first such conviction and shall be fined not more than $50,000 or imprisoned for not more than 2 years, or both, for any subsequent conviction.

(3)(A) Any person aggrieved by any violation of subsection (a) of this section may bring a civil action in a United States district court or in any other court of competent jurisdiction.

(B) The court may—

(i) grant temporary and final injunctions on such terms as it may deem reasonable to prevent or restrain violations of subsection (a) of this section;

(ii) award damages as described in subparagraph (C); and

(iii) direct the recovery of full costs, including awarding reasonable attorneys' fees to an aggrieved party who prevails.

(C)(i) Damages awarded by any court under this section shall be computed, at the election of the aggrieved party, in accordance with either of the following subclauses;

(I) the party aggrieved may recover the actual damages suffered by him as a result of the violation and any profits of the violator that are attributable to the violation which are not taken into account in computing the actual damages; in determining the violator's profits, the party aggrieved shall be required to prove only the violator's gross revenue, and the violator shall be required to prove his deductible expenses and the elements of profit attributable to factors other than the violation; or

(II) the party aggrieved may recover an award of statutory damages for each violation involved in the action in a sum of not less than $250 or more than $10,000, as the court considers just.

(ii) In any case in which the court finds that the violation was committed willfully and for purposes of direct or indirect commercial advantage or private financial gain, the court in its discretion may increase the award of damages, whether actual or statutory, by an amount of not more than $50,000.

(iii) In any case where the court finds that the violator was not aware and had no reason to believe that his acts constituted a violation of this section, the court in its discretion may reduce the award of damages to a sum of not less than $100.

(4) The importation, manufacture, sale, or distribution of equipment by any person with the intent of its use to assist in any activity prohibited by subsection (a) of this section shall be subject to penalties and remedies under this subsection to the same extent and in the same manner as a person who has engaged in such prohibited activity.

(5) The penalties under this subsection shall be in addition to those prescribed under any other provision of this subchapter.

(6) Nothing in this subsection shall prevent any State, or political subdivision thereof, from enacting or enforcing any laws with respect to the importation, sale, manufacture, or distribution of equipment by any person with the intent of its use to assist in the interception or receipt of radio communications prohibited by subsection (a) of this section.

(e) Rights, obligations and liabilities under other laws unaffected

Nothing in this section shall affect any right, obligation, or liability under Title 17, any rule, regulation, or order thereunder, or any other applicable Federal, State or local law.

8.13 Antitrust

The growth of cable systems and their need for product are alluring invitations for companies to pool resources in new ventures. Although antitrust activity has diminished in the 1980s, it is still possible that attempts to capture too much of a market will violate sections 1 and 2 of the Sherman Act. The two cases in this section advise caution.

In *U.S. v. Columbia Pictures*, the court granted a preliminary injunction to restrain the proposed joint venture between four motion picture companies and Getty Oil. The projected venture would have had the defendants exclusively licensing their movies to "Premiere," a pay cable service owned by the defendants. The court concluded this was an overreaching attempt to control a large segment of the pay cable market and restrained free and open bidding for pay TV movies.

In *Midwest Communications v. Minnesota Twins*, two sports clubs entered a joint venture to market their games jointly for broadcast purposes. This reduced the possibility that a TV station seeking to broadcast professional sports in that market would be successful in its efforts to obtain a contract with a team. The market was reduced substantially by the joint venture, since there are so few professional sports teams in any market area. The *Midwest* case ultimately turned on the question of a TV station's standing to sue, but its antitrust implications on the merits nevertheless emit warning signals.

8.13–1 United States v. Columbia Pictures Industries

Pay TV was an outgrowth of cable TV, enhanced by satellite transmission. At the time the case, *United States v. Columbia Pictures Industries*, 507 F. Supp. 412 (S.D.N.Y. 1980), arose, 31 million of the 77 million U.S. TV households had access to cable service, 17.2 million were subscribers to "basic cable" (*i.e.*, essentially no more than a better antenna), and 8.3 million were subscribers to "pay cable" (*i.e.*, additional channels not otherwise available). (All these numbers, of course, have since increased, the latter two proportionately more than the former two.) It was estimated that by 1985, 30 percent or more of all subscribers would take more than one pay television service.

HBO, Showtime, The Movie Channel, and Cinemax emerged as the primary "pay cable" vehicles. At the beginning, they did not produce much of their own programming (although HBO/Cinemax and the subsequently merged Showtime/The Movie Channel subsequently *did* go into programming in a big way, especially HBO). The vast majority of their offerings were theatrical feature films, virtually all of which were produced by the major studios, and prominent independents.

Typically, a feature film would have a theatrical "shelf life" of perhaps a year, after which it would be exhibited on pay television for another year, and, finally, it would be shown on commercial television (network and/or syndication). Most films would be licensed to the pay television services following their theatrical releases, with the amount of the fee varying in fairly direct proportion with the preceding theatrical success of a specific film. Other films (especially those made independently of the studios) would be the subject of "pre-buys" (*i.e.*, advance sales prior to release or, in some cases, prior to the making of the film).

The motion picture industry became alarmed at the thought that pay television would siphon off customers who would otherwise go to theaters to see their films. They were even *more* alarmed at what they perceived to be unduly low fees offered by HBO.

In 1979, most of the major studios considered the possible formation of a joint venture to start their own pay television network. Warner Bros., which was in the process of organizing The Movie Channel, declined to participate, as did United Artists, MGM, and Disney. Columbia, Universal, Paramount, and 20th Century-Fox, together with Getty Oil Company (the founders of ESPN, subsequently sold to ABC), formed a joint venture named "Premiere," to establish a satellite-fed pay television feature film service. Revenues would be allocated in accordance with a complicated formula keyed largely to the theatrical performance of specific films. Essentially, revenues from subscribers would be divided at between $250,000 and $4,000,000 per film, by multiplying the joint venture's pay television receipts from all films in the package by a fraction, the numerator of which was the theatrical receipts of the specific film and the denominator of which was the aggregate theatrical receipts of all films in the package.

Premiere was to have a nine-month period of exclusivity as to all films of the four studios, after which the films could be licensed to other television services. (In addition, Premiere was to acquire nonexclusive rights in the films of other producers and distributors.) The pay television services, however, were unwilling to license the films of the joint venturers subject to the nine-month "window" of exclusivity.

The Justice Department commenced suit, claiming that Premiere constituted price-fixing and a group boycott, amounting to a *per se* violation of section 1 of the Sherman Act, 15 U.S.C. sec. 1. The Premiere venturers' principal contentions were (1) that HBO was so dominant as to exert both monopsony (*i.e.*, the ability of a purchaser to dictate the purchase price) and monopoly power, (2) that the nine-month "window" was reasonable because essential in order to differentiate the Premiere venturers' films from the vastly duplicative offerings which characterized the pay television industry, and (3) that Premiere was offering a totally new product in the form of some 50 films per year which had never before been shown on pay TV.

The court (per Goettel, D.J.) found:

1. The allocation formula did not free the venture from the vice of price-fixing, even though the allocation formula fixed prices as between the venturers rather than between the venturers and outside parties.
2. The nine-month "window" constituted a group boycott, exclusionary and coercive in nature. It would inevitably result in the reduced attractiveness of the services whose access to the venturers' films was prevented.
3. Because these restraints were the very reason for Premiere's existence, they were not ancillary to the joint venture but at the very heart of it, and, therefore, subject to the *per se* rule rather than the rule of reason contended for by the venturers (who had characterized Premiere as merely a reasonable response to HBO's market power).
4. Even under the "rule of reason" test as enunciated by the Supreme Court in *Chicago Board of Trade v. United States*, 246 U.S. 231, 238 ("whether the restraint imposed is such as merely regulates and perhaps thereby promotes competition or whether it is such as may suppress or even destroy competition"), the court found the Premiere pricing mechanism "anticompetitive and thus unreasonable. The defendants have, in effect, substituted a profit sharing formula for the compet-

itive negotiations over the value of individual films in the pay television market, in which the movie company venturers used to engage. The price to be charged by Premiere to the cable operators has no fixed cost base and thus can be manipulated to control the market. Since the movie company venturers in recent years have received approximately one-half of the motion picture licensing fees paid by the network programming services, they seem likely to have sufficient economic power in the future to control the market by setting the price and conditions of sale of motion pictures licensed to pay television. . . .

"The allocation formula could serve another anticompetitive function. Even without the nine-month window, the defendants could release their pictures to Premiere and stall negotiations with its competitors, claiming that the prices being offered were inadequate. Since there is no established price to be paid by Premiere, the existing satellite-fed networks would have difficulty in demonstrating that they were victims of the defendants' refusal to deal with them. . . ."

Judge Goettel granted the preliminary injunction, seeing the public interest in unrestrained access to feature films as outweighing the venturers' $10,000,000 in start-up costs. The court observed that Premiere had not actually gone into operation, and would not be able to for many months even if the injunction did not issue.

8.13–2 Midwest Communications, Inc. v. Minnesota Twins

The baseball Minnesota Twins and the hockey Minnesota North Stars formed a third company (TwinStar) to market as a package the television rights to both the Twins and North Stars games. One of the losers in bidding for the package was Midwest Communications, Inc. (WCCO), which then instituted an antitrust action against the clubs, their TwinStar company, and the cable system that successfully bid for the television rights. At trial before a jury, the defendants prevailed on certain theories, but lost on a jury finding that the actions undertaken constituted an illegal tying arrangement. The excerpts from the U.S. District Court's post-trial memorandum and order in *Midwest Communications, Inc. v. Minnesota Twins, Inc. et al.*, 1983—2 CCH Trade Cases § 65719 (D.C. Minn. 1983) are set forth below and discuss defendants' motions to overturn the illegal tie findings.

1. *Two Products in One Market.* Defendants push three arguments founded upon the structure of the local pay sports programming market, any one of which, if accepted, would strangle the finding of an illegal tie. Intertwined, their contentions construct one product standing alone in one market.

Defendants first renew their claim that TwinStar's offer of the Twins and North Star's telecast rights as a year-round package constitutes the sale of a single product. Both teams' broadcasts, defendants claim, are integral to the success of the programming. Business demands, in other words, compelled the creation of a new product.

All agree that two products must be sold in order to create a tying arrangement. *E.g., Times Picayune Publishing Co. v. United States*, 345 U.S. 594, 614 (1953); *Rosebrough Monument Co. v. Memorial Park Cemetery Ass'n.*, 666 F. 2d 1130, 1140 (8th Cir. 1981). The jury was so instructed. . . . Fatal to defendants' claim, therefore, is the jury's finding that the Twins' and North Stars' telecasts formed two distinct products.

The jury's findings depended on two determinations: (1) defining the products and (2) deciding whether the two products are distinct. It had before it conflicting testimony as to the nature of TwinStar's pay sports offering. The evidence provided ample room to refuse to treat the two products as inevitably intermingled and to conclude that TwinStar packaged two products which could be sold separately. TVQ, for instance, wanted only North Stars' telecast rights. Defendants' expert on pay sports, moreover, conceded that a number of existing and planned pay sports channels have seasonal rather than year-round programming. Mr. Guth, plaintiff's expert, added that the "tying" violation caused serious economic dislocation by preventing the sale of the teams' telecast rights on their own merits.

WCCO offered its most convincing evidence in support of its two-product theory, however, when it attacked defendants' defense of business justification. As defendants, in their post-trial briefs, concede, the task of product definition spawned a subsidiary inquiry into whether the TwinStar enterprise could survive if each team's telecasts stood on its own. Although extended an opportunity to adopt this perspective on the local pay sports programming industry, . . . the jury believed WCCO's evidence to the contrary. It rejected again the notion that business success required joint sales or one synergistic product.

Defendants' last two structural arguments contesting the illegality of the tie hinge upon the jury's answer to special verdict question no. 1 where it found that the two clubs' broadcasts stood alone in the same relevant market. They deny that tying could be found when TwinStar marketed two products in the same relevant market. They also argue that since the teams' telecasts co-exist in one market *and* possess monopoly power in that market, there can be no anticompetitive effect from the tie. The court rejects both arguments.

Although courts traditionally refer to tying and tied products, an illegal tie does not demand that the two goods fall into separate relevant markets. As long as the products are distinct, they need not also come from markets which do not compete with one another. That is, two separate products which normally compete may comprise an illegally tied package. For instance, in *United States v. Loew's*, 371 U.S. 38 (1962), and *United States v. Paramount Pictures, Inc.*, 334 U.S. 131 (1948), the

Supreme Court proscribed the blocked book sale of feature films to exhibitors despite the competition amongst the films for the same dollar. Although found within the same market, the films could not be sold together; each had to stand on its own economic footing.

The confusion stems from ambiguity surrounding product versus market definition. The task of defining both products and markets admittedly often devolves into a normative inquiry with product lines blurring with market boundaries. Nevertheless, an illegal tie requires two products, not two markets. The confusion typically manifests itself when two distinct components from different markets are aggregated and sold as a unit by one company. The inquiry into whether separate markets exist involves whether the two components comprise but a single product. In other words, courts speak of distinct markets but their ultimate concern is product differentiation. . . .

Defendants next argue that the package sale of the two clubs' broadcasts cannot be illegal since the two products are the only products in the market. Where the market is already monopolized, they insist, a tie can have no anticompetitive effect.

Monopoly power, however, will not save TwinStar's otherwise illegal tie. A joint venture cannot immunize a tie-in from the antitrust laws simply by having all competing sellers participate in the scheme. This is true even where there would be no adverse effect on any existing competitors. WCCO, however, presented the jury with sufficient evidence to warrant the conclusion that TwinStar's tie required the purchaser to accept terms that could not be exacted in a completely competitive market. . . . Purchasers could not individually bid for each team's telecast rights. In short, the tie-in raised barriers to entry into the pay sports market for purchasers and for other potential sports entities wishing to tap into this emerging broadcast market.

In focusing on the lack of injury to individual competitors, defendants overlook the purposes of the tying laws, including protection of purchasers, potential competitors, and overall competition. These manifest themselves particularly as to the single-product issue, the business justification defense, the economic power issue and the concern with foreclosure. Each, in other words, tests the competitive effect, and thus the legality, of the practice. . . .

Despite the absence of existing competitors in the TwinStar market, therefore, the jury had considerable evidence to allow it to conclude that the TwinStar tying arrangement is anticompetitive. WCCO's evidence shows that the tie could be seen as requiring purchasers to accede to burdensome terms, foreclosing emerging competitors from launching into this pioneer market, and endangering long-run efficiency in this new field. . . .

TwinStar's market power cannot be cast as an unexpected savior against these anticompetitive evils. In *Driskell v. Dallas Cowboys Club, Inc.*, 498 F.2d 321 (5th Cir. 1974), the Ninth Circuit did reject a tying claim by a Cowboys season ticket holder who alleged he was compelled to purchase preseason tickets if he wanted to obtain regular season tickets. The tie in the restricted market for stadium seating simply infringed on consumer choice. Here, however, the jury examined a tie in an emerging market where the two products could have been in keen competition with each other and with other potential entrants. The impact could portend a stagnation of the pay sports market, a market whose long-run characteristics could easily be found by a factfinder to differ substantially from Dallas Cowboys season ticket sales.

2. *Coercion*. Defendants next assert that the court erred in failing to give defendants proposed coercion and unbundling instructions, crucial here, they argue, because their evidence shows that WCCO wanted both teams' telecast rights. But despite defendants' protestations to the contrary, the court finds the instructions to be complete, particularly in light of TwinStar's market power, the jury's rejection of claims of business justification and defense counsel's own arguments to the jury. . . .

This court declines to upset the jury's conclusions. Defense counsel emphasized throughout the trial, including closing arguments, that WCCO wanted both teams. The instructions did not undercut those claims. To the contrary, the court included the essential elements of the defense request in its instructions and left it to counsel to elaborate. With so many issues before the jury, the court did not then, nor does it now, consider defendants' requested instructions appropriate.

Finally, the court notes that neither the Supreme Court nor the Eighth Circuit have focused on the necessity of showing actual coercion in a tie-in case, stating only that tie-ins are coercive. . . .

Here, the court's instructions as to the required proof of "coercion," and the manner in which counsel cast the evidence for the jurors, support a finding that WCCO did not want to bargain for a dual package. Nevertheless, proof of coercion may well have been unnecessary in light of TwinStar's market power over potential entrants and purchaser's bid for a two-product package, and the economic analysis allowing the jury to determine if this tie made economic sense. . . .

3. *Standing*. Defendants also argue that WCCO's tying claim should be dismissed for lack of standing due to failure to incur antitrust injury. To maintain an action for treble damages under section 4 of the Clayton Act, WCCO must be "injured in [its] business or property by reason of anything forbidden in the antitrust laws." Antitrust standing requires not only injury to WCCO's business but that WCCO's actual injury be attributable to something the antitrust laws were designed to prevent. *J. Truett Payne Co. v. Chrysler Motors Corp.*, 451 U.S. 557, 562 (1981).

The determination of whether WCCO is a proper party to bring suit, therefore, hinges upon "an evaluation of the plaintiff's harm, the alleged wrongdoing by the defendants, and the relationship between them." . . .

In discussing the impact of the tie-in on the pay sports cable market, defendants consistently confine those to be protected to actual purchasers and existing competitors. Traditionally, it is true that tying laws provide a remedy for purchasers who must buy the dual package at inflated prices or competing suppliers denied free access to the market. See, e.g., *Kypta v. McDonald's Corp.*, 671 F. 2d 1282, 1285 (11th Cir. 1983); *Heatransfer Corp. v. Volkswagenwerk*, 553 F. 2d 964 (5th Cir. 1977). However, in this case, where we have a novel venture in an emerging market, the scope defendants recommend for tying protections is too narrow. To insure proper regulation of this infant industry, the court must also protect TwinStar's potential competitors from entry barriers constructed by the tie.

WCCO, however, has not suffered this antitrust injury. Giving WCCO the benefit of all inferences reasonably to be drawn in its favor, the harm it incurred is the lost business opportunity to potentially purchase the Twins and/or North Stars' broadcast rights. A potential purchaser, however, can hardly be said to have standing to challenge the TwinStar tie.

Although the evidence allowed the jury to conclude that the tie prevented WCCO from purchasing property it wanted to purchase, more than a violation in the market and harm to WCCO must be shown. . . .

The injury here occurred because another bidder in the market, Spectrum, obtained the available property, albeit at a price which arguably differs from that earned through individual sale. WCCO had both the desire and the capability to enter the pay sports market. Absent the tie, in other words, WCCO may have found itself in Spectrum's place. This result, however, is not the type which Congress sought to rectify. TwinStar's claimed market restraint directly injured only potential competition. Its indirect impact upon WCCO's business at another level of the market structure is too remote to allow it to recover threefold damages or to invoke this court's injunctive power.

It becomes clear that antitrust standing cannot be given to frustrated potential purchasers when one contemplates the difficulties in fashioning a remedy in damages. If WCCO has standing, so also would all potential distributors of sports programming in the Twin Cities, or at least those who spoke to the teams about pay TV. The result would be duplicative recoveries, a traditional tying concern. . . .

The denial of standing is all the more prudent here since the damages to be awarded WCCO would, of necessity, be speculative. Even if WCCO were prepared to purchase telecast rights if sold individually, a chance to participate in a process subjected to the "competitive stresses of the open market" would not guarantee a successful bid. If such rights would have been obtained, moreover, WCCO would yet have to prove it could survive in the cable market and project profits. Such an amount could be but conjecture.

To avoid such ruinous recoveries, standing must be limited to actual or potential competitors foreclosed from the market and to buyers who actually enter the tying arrangement and are damaged by an increased price. . . .

8.20   Interception and Retransmission of Signals

The cases discussed in this section relate to alleged illegal reception and retransmission of a broadcasting company's signals. The methods of delivery of the signals vary, and the circumstances surrounding the alleged infringements also differ. At times, the complainant and alleged infringer have dealt with each other; in other instances, the parties have no history of dealing. The actions of defendants are not always challenged on the same legal grounds. In some cases, § 605 of the communications act is critical (see earlier discussion in Section 8.12); in other cases, § 111 of the copyright statute is a key consideration (see Section 8.11); in still others, the applicability of both sections is explored. Even so, all cases have the common thread of the interception and retransmission of signals.

The first case, *KMLA Broadcasting v. Twentieth Century Vendors*, introduces background on the retransmission of signals intended for private use and the response under § 605 of the communications act. The two HBO cases, *HBO v. Pay TV of Greater New York* and *Orth-O-Vision v. HBO,* discuss violations where a party at one time had the contractual right to retransmit the signals but does no longer. The court in *Pay TV* sticks to § 605, while the *Orth-O-Vision* court investigates both communications and copyright infringements.

The final two cases involve the retransmission of a television station's signals by microwave *(Eastern Microwave v. Doubleday Sports)* and by beaming to a satellite *(WGN Continental Broadcasting v. United Video).* *Eastern Microwave* is of interest since a party other than a TV station is complaining. The owner of the New York Mets contends its product cannot be retransmitted without its consent. The *WGN* decision should be carefully noted for its meticulous examination of the passive carriage provisions of § 111 of the copyright statute.

KMLA Broadcasting Corp. v. Twentieth Century Cigarette Vendors Corp., 264 F. Supp. 36 (C.D. Cal. 1967)

WHELAN, J.
Plaintiffs sued defendants for judgment to enjoin defendants from manufacturing, distributing, selling or using equipment which picks up multiplex radio transmissions by plaintiff KMLA Broadcasting Corporation [hereafter "KMLA"] without plaintiffs' consent, and for damages to plaintiffs arising out of the violation by defendants of Section 605 of the Communications Act of 1934, Title 47, United States Code, Section 605, in intercepting and publishing such transmissions as well as damages for unfair competition and exemplary damages arising out of such interception and publishing.

Plaintiffs and defendants Twentieth Century Cigarette Vendors Corporation [hereafter "Twentieth Century"] and International Industries, Inc., dba International House of Pancakes [hereafter "International"], which two defendants are the only remaining defendants in the action, have

respectively filed motions for summary judgment on the question of liability alone. Plaintiffs on their motion seek declaratory judgment that the transmissions of background music [entitled multiplex transmissions] by KMLA on its subcarrier frequency are non-public radio communications protected by said Section 605 from the activities of defendants and that such activities are in violation of said Act; and that plaintiffs have a private right of action against defendants arising out of the conduct of defendants in violation of said Section 605 and the regulatory pattern thereunder, and unfair competition by defendants by virtue of the same conduct. Defendants on the other hand seek summary judgment that the involved transmissions of plaintiffs are broadcasts not protected by said Section 605 and that defendants are not liable to plaintiffs on a private right of action. . . .

KMLA, a wholly owned subsidiary of plaintiff Musicast, Inc. [hereafter "Musicast"], owns and operates, and has owned and operated at all pertinent times, an FM radio station in the City of Los Angeles, California, under a license from the Federal Communications Commission [hereafter "the Commission"], granting KMLA authority to broadcast. In addition, KMLA has been and is licensed under a Subsidiary Communications Authorization [SCA] to transmit on a separate, subcarrier frequency, a background music program to subscribers. This subcarrier frequency is entitled the multiplex channel; and an FM station broadcasting over its main frequency and at the same time transmitting a background music program to subscribers over its multiplex channel is said to be "multiplexing."

Musicast has been and is, under a license from KMLA, providing background music to industrial and commercial establishments [Musicast's subscribers] in Los Angeles County, California, for a monthly fee. Musicast installed on the premises of each such subscriber a special multiplex receiver fixed to and capable of receiving KMLA's multiplex channel, as well as speakers, amplifiers, volume controls and related equipment. Ownership of the multiplex receiver is always retained by Musicast and the other equipment is either sold or leased to Musicast's subscribers. Musicast services the equipment and provides background music, free of commercials, twenty-four hours of every day, to its subscribers.

There are about six major background music companies, each with between 300 and 800 subscribers, and more than ten smaller background music companies, in Los Angeles County. In the same area there are eight FM radio stations multiplexing background music. There are about 450 FM stations [one-third of all FM stations] in the United States licensed to engage in multiplexing, with related or licensed background music companies.

Neither an FM radio station on its main channel nor an AM radio station [which has only one channel] can broadcast a 100% background music program because rules and regulations of the Commission require all stations to broadcast to the general public a varied program content, some of which has to be the spoken word. FM stations, in operating their main channel, like AM stations, are obligated by the Commission to serve the public interest, provide periodic station identifications, broadcast public service announcements, etc. Background music by radio can thus be obtained only over a subcarrier frequency, separate and apart from, and in addition to, an FM station main channel broadcast.

The main channel broadcasts of FM stations are intended for the public and may be heard without charge by anyone having a radio. On the other hand the background music program of plaintiffs, like those of other FM stations, as transmitted over the multiplex channel, is not intended for the public but is intended solely for paying subscribers; the background music program can't be heard by the public. No radio manufactured or sold in the United States can receive such multiplex transmissions. Only two or three companies in the United States make the special multiplex receivers which can receive them, and these are now made so that each receiver is capable of picking up the multiplex transmission of only a single FM station. Such multiplex receivers are sold only to, or with the express consent of, the FM station to whose subcarrier frequency the receiver is fixed.

Prior to October 1, 1960, plaintiffs supplied background music to subscribers by the following method, termed "simplexing": their subscribers' receiving radio sets were built with a special circuit which, when actuated by the transmission by KMLA of an electronic signal, a "beep," eliminated from reception by the subscribers' radio sets all spoken words of the KMLA broadcast [there was then no separate subcarrier frequency but only the channel for broadcast to the general public]. Thus the subscribers for background music could have the music transmission, as they wanted it, free of any spoken words while the public received both the music and the spoken material as required by the Commission.

The Commission has prohibited the transmission of background music on a simplex basis and now requires all FM stations who desire to engage in a subscription background music program to do so on a multiplex basis under a special license termed Subsidiary Communications Authorization. In making its rule requiring multiplexing the Commission concluded that the public interest will be served by divorcing subscription services from main channel FM broadcasting.

The aggregate cost to plaintiffs in converting from simplexing to multiplexing was approximately $100,000. This amount covered the cost to KMLA in the installation of multiplex transmission equipment at its radio station and the cost to Musicast of the multiplex receivers installed at the premises of its subscribers, and the cost of removing the old simplex receivers, installing the new multiplex receivers, multiplex aerials, etc.

Since 1959 Musicast has had between 750 and 800 subscribers, each paying an average of $22.60 per month for background music, plus additional charges for the leasing and servicing of equipment. Musicast has a staff of approximately ten electronic and radio technicians for installation and servicing of equipment at its subscribers' premises, ten office employees, a full-time program director; and has spent approximately $3500 per month since 1959 for the promotion, advertising and selling of its music service.

Neither plaintiff owns any copyright in any of the musical selections making up the background music program. Musicast constantly acquires a great number of musical recordings, and selects, edits and arranges the selections in a particular order. The type of music transmitted varies at different hours of the day and even during different days of the week. . . .

In 1961 Twentieth Century began to offer a background music service for little or no charge to those commercial establishments which would allow it to place its cigarette vending machines on the premises of such establishments. [Under such arrangement the establishment received a certain percentage of the sale price of cigarettes sold through such machines.] During 1961 and 1962 Twentieth Century purchased twelve multiplex receivers of Japanese origin which were fixed to KMLA's multiplex subchannel frequency and installed them and necessary related equipment on the various premises where Twentieth Century's vending machines were located. Thereafter this equipment received and played the background music transmitted by KMLA on its multiplex channel on each of the premises where Twentieth Century's equipment had been installed, all without the permission of or license from either of plaintiffs.

Commencing in 1962 Twentieth Century supplanted the above-mentioned multiplex receivers with multiplex tuners capable of receiving the background music of all FM stations which were multiplexing. Twentieth Century has installed these variable multiplex tuners to the number of 121 at various commercial establishments which maintained Twentieth Century's vending machines on their premises; and Twentieth Century demonstrated to each of such establishments the capability of the tuner and demonstrated how the tuner could be tuned to pick up the multiplex background music programs of KMLA as well as that of other Los Angeles FM stations providing such type of music over their own multiplex frequencies.

International, which, like Twentieth Century and Musicast, is a California corporation, during the period from 1962 to date had either a fixed multiplex receiver fixed to KMLA's subcarrier frequency or a variable multiplex tuner capable of receiving the background music of KMLA in 24 of its restaurants in the metropolitan area of Los Angeles. All of such receivers and tuners were supplied and serviced by Twentieth Century; and during the period from 1962 to date International received and used in those restaurants the background music transmitted by KMLA over its multiplex subchannel frequency although International has never been a Musicast subscriber and has never sought or obtained any permission or license from either of plaintiffs to do so.

At no time has Twentieth Century or any of its accounts sought or obtained the consent of or license from either of plaintiffs to receive or use the background music program of KMLA. . . .

Section 605 of the Communications Act of 1934, Title 47, U.S.C. § 605, provides a mantle of privacy for all communications, except radio and television broadcasts intended for the public, and those relating to ships in distress, and in pertinent part provides:

> . . . no person not being entitled thereto shall receive or assist in receiving any interstate or foreign communication by wire or radio and use the same or any information therein contained for his own benefit or for the benefit of another not entitled thereto . . . Provided, That this section shall not apply to the receiving, divulging, publishing, or utilizing the contents of any radio communication broadcast, or transmitted by amateurs or others for the use of the general public, or relating to ships in distress.

As to what constitutes "broadcasting," 47 U.S.C. § 153(o) states:

> 'Broadcasting' means the dissemination of radio communications intended to be received by the public, directly or by the intermediary of relay stations. . . .

Rules and regulations of the Commission, published in Volume 47 of Code of Federal Regulations, with regard to background music are in pertinent part as follows:

> § 73.276 Permissible Transmissions.
>
> (a) No FM broadcast licensee or permittee shall enter into any . . . arrangement . . . whereby it undertakes to supply, or receives consideration for supplying, on its main channel . . . background music . . . for reception in the place or places of business of any subscriber.
>
> (b) The transmission (or interruption) of radio energy in the FM broadcast band is permissible only pursuant to a station license, program test

authorization, Subsidiary Communications Authorization [SCA] or other specific authority therefor.

§ 73.293 Subsidiary Communications Authorizations.

(a) An FM broadcast licensee or permittee may apply for a Subsidiary Communications Authorization [SCA] to provide limited types of subsidiary services on a multiplex basis. Permissible uses must fall within one or both of the following categories:

(1) Transmission of programs which are of a broadcast nature, but which are of interest primarily to limited segments of the public wishing to subscribe thereto. Illustrative services include: background music. . . .

(c) SCA operations may be conducted without restriction as to time so long as the main channel is programmed simultaneously. . . .

The background music program of KMLA conforms to the aforesaid rules and regulations and is a permitted type of subsidiary service on a multiplex basis.

The question of whether KMLA's multiplex transmissions over its subcarrier frequency constitute "broadcasting" so as to make the protections of Section 605 inapplicable because of the *proviso,* supra, hinges on whether KMLA intended a dissemination of its multiplex radio communications to the general public.

Here the parties have agreed that neither of plaintiffs had or has intent to transmit their background music program to the general public. It has been held that Section 605 prohibits the interception and divulging by an unauthorized person of a radio communication not intended for the use of the general public or not relating to ships in distress. . . .

The Commission over a long period of time has interpreted the statutory term "broadcasting" not to include transmission such as here involved, and has in fact held that a radio station engaged in broadcasting material of interest only to a particular person or persons [here the transmission of background music is not intended for the general public] is not broadcasting.

Such broadcasting to specific listeners has been ruled by the Commission to be point-to-point communication not authorized by a broadcast license. . . .

The ruling of the Commission that multiplex transmissions as here involved, pursuant to the Commission's rules on subsidiary communications authorizations, do not have the essential attributes of broadcasting within the meaning of 47 U.S.C. § 153(o), and that consequently "Section 605 of the Communications Act is contravened by the unauthorized reception of FM multiplex programs intended solely for reception by industrial, mercantile and other subscribers" is a reasonable determination. When faced with a problem of statutory construction, the courts have unanimously shown great deference to the interpretation given the statute by the officers or agency charged with its administration; particularly is this respect due when the administrative practice at stake involves a contemporaneous construction of a statute by the men charged with the responsibility of setting its machinery in motion, of making the parts work efficiently and smoothly while they are yet untried and new. . . .

The nature of FM multiplex transmissions negates any intention that they be received by the public. Multiplex transmissions cannot be received on conventional FM sets, since they are disseminated not over the main broadcast channel but over a subcarrier frequency that can be received only with special equipment not part of the ordinary radio receiving set. Multiplex operations are specifically geared to the special requirements of commercial institutions, industrial plants, retail shops, and other subscribers equipped with this special FM receiving apparatus. Fundamentally, then, multiplexing is a point-to-point communication service, directed to subscribers at specified locations.

The facts establish that FM multiplex transmissions of background music do not constitute broadcasting as that term is defined in the Communications Act, 47 U.S.C. § 153(o), and that the unauthorized reception and use of such multiplex transmissions by one other than an authorized subscriber is in violation of Section 605 of the Communications Act, 47 U.S.C. § 605.

The facts establish that International has intercepted plaintiffs' multiplex transmissions and has simultaneously divulged or published the same to the customers of International, all without the consent or license of plaintiffs or either of them. The facts establish that Twentieth Century provided to International the means for so intercepting and divulging the multiplex transmissions with the intent that International should so intercept and divulge or publish.

The Court concludes as a matter of law that the activities of the defendants are in violation of Section 605 of the Communications Act and that such multiplex transmissions are protected from intercepting and divulging. The Court holds that defendant International has itself intercepted and divulged or published the transmissions in violation of the Act and that the acts of defendant Twentieth Century in effect conspiring with defendant International to intercept and divulge or publish the transmissions or in causing the intercepting and divulging or publishing by International constitute a violation by Twentieth Century of Section 605, under elementary principles of law in the field of conspiracy and torts not here requiring any citation of authority. . . .

Where, as here, plaintiffs have been aggrieved by the activities of defendants in their violation of Section 605 of the Communications Act of 1934, plaintiffs are entitled to recover damages from defendants in an amount to be hereinafter determined by the Court. . . .

The Commission has determined that it is in the federal interest that FM stations be given a multiplex channel for the transmission of background music to subscribers only. Thus plaintiffs, it would seem, have a private, federal right of action because of the federal interest as determined by the Commission, against defendants arising out of their interception and divulgement, even if the background music transmission were held to be "broadcasting" within the meaning of the Communications Act; however, the Court does not rest its decision on such ground as it has determined that such transmissions do not constitute such broadcasting.

In *Reitmeister v. Reitmeister* (2nd Cir. 1947) 162 F.2d 691, 694, the Court of Appeals for the Second Circuit, in holding that the District Court had jurisdiction of a civil action for damages for violation of Section 605 of the Communications Act, held that a private civil right was created for any injury done to one by others in intercepting and divulging in violation of the Communications Act. . . .

The Court therefore concludes that there is a private federal cause of action for appropriate relief in favor of plaintiffs and against defendants on the facts herein. . . .

In addition to plaintiffs' federal cause of action hereinbefore announced, it appears from the facts that plaintiffs have a pendant cause of action for unfair competition under California law. Congress has not pre-empted the adjustment of property rights in the communication field by the passage of the Communications Act of 1934. *Cable Vision, Inc. v. KUTV, Inc.*, 335 F.2d 348, 349. This case comes within the rule of *International News Service v. Associated Press*, 248 U.S. 215, 39 S.Ct. 68, 63 L.Ed. 211 (1918), [hereinafter INS]. Under INS unfair competition is found to exist when the acts of a defendant amount to interference and diversion of profit at the point where plaintiff's profit is to be made.

"Unfair competition" is defined by California Civil Code Section 3369, subdivision 3, as "unlawful, unfair or fraudulent business practice." The applicable principles governing California courts are those set forth in INS. . . .

Here plaintiffs have expended large sums of money, and continue to do so, to provide background music programs to subscribers; and here defendants have appropriated those programs for the purpose of merchandising their products at the point where plaintiffs' profit is to be made, in order to divert a material portion of the profit from those who have earned it to those who have not. The situation is clearly analogous to that in INS. . . .

Courts have followed and applied the doctrine of INS in cases where rights in private enterprises or events for which the investor had granted exclusive TV or Radio licenses were involved—where the primary purpose of the investor to charge others for the privilege of watching or hearing a program would be frustrated or defeated through exhibition by others than itself or its exclusive licensee. . . .

Here . . . defendants acted to obtain from plaintiffs for nothing the very thing that plaintiffs were selling.

In summary the Court concludes that plaintiffs are entitled to partial summary judgment adjudging (1) that defendants have violated Section 605 of the Communications Act of 1934, (2) that plaintiffs have a private right of action against defendants arising from their violation of said Act and the regulatory pattern for the radio industry established by the Commission under the Act, and (3) that plaintiffs have a cause of action for unfair competition under California law. . . .

Home Box Office, Inc. v. Pay TV of Greater New York, Inc., 467 F. Supp. 525 (E.D.N.Y. 1979)

NICKERSON, J.
Plaintiff, a wholly owned subsidiary of Time Incorporated, moves for a temporary injunction in this action brought to recover damages and to restrain defendant permanently from "pirating" plaintiff's television program service and from infringing plaintiff's copyrights. Viewing the facts stated in the affidavits in the light most favorable to defendant, the court concludes that a preliminary injunction should issue.

Plaintiff is in the business of licensing a subscription television program service comprised of plaintiff's copyrighted or licensed motion pictures, sporting events and other special programs. Licensed affiliates in various parts of the country in turn deliver the service to subscribers for viewing on their television sets. The license agreements with plaintiff require the affiliates to maintain appropriate equipment and customer services and to engage in certain promotional efforts.

In the New York City area plaintiff's service is transmitted to some affiliates by a so-called multipoint distribution service consisting of an omnidirectional terrestrial microwave signal. This high frequency signal is transmitted from the Empire State Building and received by the affiliates at authorized points where it is converted into a lower frequency suitable for reception by individual television sets. A receiver and modulator is installed at each apartment building serviced by the affiliate. After modulation the program is then retransmitted by cable or wire to each subscriber, generally by a master antenna. The signal emitted from the Empire State Building, although not receivable by the general public, can be intercepted by appropriately placed special receivers within an approximate 35-mile radius.

During 1974 and 1975 plaintiff authorized Mi-

croband National Systems, Inc. ("Microband"), to distribute the service to such locations in the New York City area as plaintiff might approve. Microband in turn entered into subcontracts to make the actual distribution. Defendant became one of the subcontractors, signing an agreement with Microband dated October 21, 1975. That agreement provided that defendant would have certain "non-exclusive" rights in Queens County but no rights elsewhere and that the term would be for "so long" as Microband's contract with plaintiff "shall remain in effect." Defendant claims that at that time both plaintiff and Microband "caused" defendant to believe that it "would eventually be substituted" for Microband as the wholesale distributor.

Defendant says that it soon became dissatisfied with plaintiff's denials of approval for new locations obtained by defendant after considerable expenditure of money and effort. Nevertheless in December 1975, according to defendant, it had discussions with plaintiff looking toward plaintiff's grant of exclusive rights in Kings and Bronx Counties. Evidently Microband had made it known that it would terminate its agreement with plaintiff as of May 1976.

On March 1, 1976 Microband wrote plaintiff confirming earlier statements and terminating the agreement with plaintiff effective May 7, 1976. The letter stated that Microband's motive in entering into the agreement had been to assist plaintiff in getting master antenna operators into the business and that Microband wished to give plaintiff "sufficient time to finalize arrangements between itself and the operators."

On March 8, 1976 plaintiff sent to defendant a so-called "working draft" of an affiliation agreement to provide the program service in Kings and Bronx Counties. The draft provided that the agreement was to be for five years and that defendant would have certain exclusive rights in the two counties, provided that plaintiff could terminate the exclusive rights in either county on sixty days notice if any other person obtained a cable franchise in that county. An agreement was never signed, and at that time defendant continued to retransmit the service without plaintiff's objection.

Negotiations between the parties continued,

and defendant claims that at a meeting on July 19, 1976 defendant's representatives offered to sign an affiliation agreement if it contained the exclusive rights set forth in the March 8, 1976 draft, but that plaintiff then refused to grant those rights. In any event no agreement was reached. Defendant further claims that some time in July of 1976 the parties discussed the possibility of plaintiff's buying out defendant but again came to no agreement.

Sometimes around July 20, 1976 plaintiff learned that defendant had expanded its distribution into locations not earlier approved by plaintiff under defendant's subcontract with Microband. Plaintiff protested this expansion but at that time plaintiff acquiesced in defendant's continued distribution at the previously approved locations. Plaintiff says it did so because it still hoped to conclude an acceptable agreement.

By early 1977 no such agreement had been consummated, and on February 17, 1977 plaintiff demanded in writing that defendant cease transmission of the service. Plaintiff did not commence litigation, assertedly because it thought it might yet negotiate an agreement, and defendant continued as before. In the end no agreement was reached, and on August 18, 1978 plaintiff's counsel wrote to defendant advising that its provision of the service without authorization was illegal and an infringement of plaintiff's rights and that legal proceedings would follow if defendant did not cease. This action was brought on December 14, 1978.

Defendant is continuing to retransmit plaintiff's service to some 8000 customers and has been receiving approximately $75,000 a month in subscription fees, none of which has been paid to plaintiff. Defendant says it will pay plaintiff but only if granted exclusive rights in Kings and Bronx Counties.

Defendant claims that from the first, although plaintiff encouraged defendant to make expenditures for equipment and manpower, plaintiff's true intent was to use defendant merely as an inexpensive way of testing the market until plaintiff could bring a subsidiary into the business, and that plaintiff in violation of the Sherman Act conspired with the counterclaim defendants to that end.

In moving for a temporary injunction plaintiff asserts rights under Section 605 of the Communications Act of 1934, the copyright laws, Section 165.15(4) of the New York Penal Law, and the New York common law of unfair competition.

Section 605, 47 U.S.C. § 605, prohibits any person not entitled to intercept or receive radio communications from doing so and from using "such communication (or any information therein contained) for his own benefit or for the benefit of another not entitled thereto." By its terms the section does not apply to the receiving and using of the contents of any communication which is broadcast "for the use of the general public." "Radio communication" is defined by Section 153(b) to include "the transmission by radio of . . . signals, pictures, and sounds of all kinds."

Defendant does not deny that Section 605 prohibits an unauthorized person from intercepting the signals carrying plaintiff's program service. The wording of the section proscribes the interception and use of such signals not intended for broadcast to "the general public." . . .

Here the multipoint distribution service station operates on microwave radio frequencies of such height that the signal is not receivable by conventional television sets until it is modulated by special equipment. The programs are thus intended to be received not by "the general public" but only by paying subscribers. *Cf. Cable Vision, Inc. v. KUTV, Inc.*, 335 F.2d 348 (9th Cir. 1964).

The Federal Communications Commission has concluded that the unauthorized interception of television signals from such a multipoint distribution service violates Section 605. Public Notice dated January 24, 1979. No court appears heretofore to have had occasion to apply the section to television transmissions. But *KMLA Broadcast Corp. v. Twentieth Century Cig. Vend. Corp.*, 264 F. Supp. 35 (C.D.Cal.1967), relied upon it in enjoining a manufacturer of equipment which intercepted and broadcast multiplex radio transmissions capable of receipt only by special equipment and licensed to a limited audience. There is no reason why the result should be different in the case of television transmissions.

While raising no question as to the applicability of Section 605, defendant contends that plaintiff has consented to defendant's interception of the signal, is guilty of laches in seeking temporary relief, and in any event is sustaining no "irreparable" damage and should therefore be left to a remedy in money damages.

Giving the widest possible latitude to the statements made in defendant's opposing affidavit there is no basis for finding a consent. Defendant admits that the parties conducted negotiations commencing in December 1975 looking toward the execution of a written agreement and that no such agreement was ever concluded. Defendant's consistent negotiating position was that it would sign up only if it got exclusive rights, and plaintiff admittedly refused to accede.

Now defendant claims that it always had the right to use the program service which it unsuccessfully negotiated for so long to obtain. Defendant says that as early as June and September 1975, before it entered into the October 21, 1975 agreement with Microband, plaintiff orally induced defendant to get into the business on the representation that plaintiff would grant defendant exclusive rights in Kings and Bronx Counties. This contention is hardly consistent with defendant's later entry into the written agreement with Microband. That agreement gave defendant no rights in any area other than Queens County, and there the rights were "non-exclusive."

But taking defendant's affidavit at face value it at best makes out a representation, but nowhere shows that plaintiff entered into a license agreement with defendant. Nothing is stated as to the duration of any such agreement or indeed as to any of its terms beyond the exclusivity feature. Whether or not plaintiff acquiesced in defendant's use of the service prior to August 18, 1978, plainly plaintiff has not done so since that date. . . .

If defendant can establish at trial that as a result of plaintiff's asserted false representations defendant changed its position it may perhaps be entitled to money damages. But on the papers presented defendant has failed to show a consent by plaintiff to defendant's continued use of the program service.

Despite the clarity of plaintiff's rights under Section 605 and the avowed intention of defen-

dant to continue as in the past, defendant contends that plaintiff has failed to establish the requisite degree of harm to entitle it to preliminary relief and that damages at the close of the case are an adequate remedy. . . .

But where, as here, a defendant shows no justification for continuing to violate a plaintiff's clear statutory rights, there is no reason to withhold preliminary relief even without a showing of the same quantum of "irreparable" damage as would be required where plaintiff's ultimate success was more doubtful. Defendant has had every opportunity to advance whatever facts would support its contention that plaintiff orally consented to the use of the program service, and those facts must be within the knowledge of defendant. On the papers presented defendant has no right to intercept and use plaintiff's program service. If on all those papers plaintiff had moved for summary judgment for a permanent injunction, the court would have been obliged to grant the motion.

Defendant claims that it will be irreparably damaged by the issuance of a preliminary injunction because it will be put out of business. But in determining whether to grant relief the court may consider only harm to defendant's legal rights. Any damages which the temporary injunction inflicts on defendant is occasioned not by the preliminary nature of the decision but by Section 605 of the Act. The only business of defendant which will be prohibited is the unauthorized use of something to which it has no fair claim.

Even if plaintiff were required to make a showing of irreparable injury in more traditional terms, it has done so. While the amount plaintiff is losing in fees can probably be estimated and awarded as damages, the injury to plaintiff's reputation and the interference with its business are not so readily repaired. Plaintiff plausibly claims that its present lack of control over the locations and customers being served by defendant and defendant's representation of the pirated service as its own are damaging plaintiff's name and jeopardizing its expansion plans. A judgment for damages is hardly adequate to compensate for these. . . .

The court's decision as to plaintiff's rights under Section 605 makes it unnecessary to consider the other grounds for relief advanced by plaintiff.

Conceivably defendant may be able to offer testimony at trial showing facts different from or in addition to those set forth in defendant's affidavit. Of course testimony relating to plaintiff's alleged violations of the Sherman Act would be irrelevant to whether an injunction should issue. . . . The remedies for any such violations are set forth in the antitrust laws and do not include allowing the continued appropriation of plaintiff's program service. . . .

Orth-O-Vision, Inc. v. Home Box Office, Inc., 474 F. Supp. 672 (S.D.N.Y. 1979)

GAGLIARDI, J.

Plaintiff Orth-O-Vision, Inc. ("Orth-O-Vision") has commenced this action against Home Box Office, Inc. ("HBO"), Time, Inc. ("Time"), and Morris Tarshis, Director of Franchises of the City of New York, alleging *inter alia,* violations of the federal antitrust laws and breach of contract. . . .

Defendants Time and HBO have counterclaimed for violations of the Federal Communications Act, the Copyright Act, New York's Penal Law and the common law of unfair competition. . . .

HBO, a subsidiary of Time, transmits a pay television subscription program service from a microwave transmitter atop the Empire State Building. HBO's programming consists both of programs originated and copyrighted by HBO and programs, such as motion pictures and sporting events, the performance rights to which it has acquired through licensing agreements. HBO leases its microwave transmitter from Microband Corporation of America ("Microband"), a common carrier licensed to provide Multipoint Distribution Service ("MDS") by the Federal Communications Commission ("FCC"). HBO has contracted with a number of affiliates to provide its program service to multiple fixed receiver points, generally large residential buildings, for a monthly service fee. The affiliates, in turn, acting as middlemen, sell the program service to individual residents. Each building is equipped with reception equipment, including a microwave parabolic antenna, a frequency down-converter, an address decoder, and a coaxial cable or antenna lead-in wire which feeds the MDS generated

signals to home television receivers. Individual subscribers pay a monthly fee to the affiliates for the program service.

By written agreement dated April 3, 1974, Orth-O-Vision became an HBO affiliate. The agreement required Orth-O-Vision to remit monthly payments to HBO on a "per subscriber" basis. The agreement permitted Orth-O-Vision to market the HBO service in two apartment houses in Queens and expressly denied Orth-O-Vision the exclusive right to market the service in Queens or other areas. A standard "merger clause" read as follows:

> This Agreement supersedes and cancels all prior negotiations and undertakings in the premises between the parties, contains all of the terms, conditions and premises of the parties hereto and shall be binding only when executed by both parties hereto. No officer, employee or representative of HBO has any authority to make any representation or promise not contained in this Agreement, and Affiliate has not executed this agreement on reliance of any such representation or promise.

In addition, the agreement provided that in the event of Orth-O-Vision's breach of any of the terms or provisions, HBO "may, at its option, suspend delivery of the HBO Service until such default is ended or remedied, terminate this Agreement, or may declare this Agreement breached and all unpaid amounts including all Minimum Payments immediately due and payable."

Orth-O-Vision's president, Alfred Simon, contends that in the course of the negotiation of the 1974 agreement, HBO officials represented to him that, notwithstanding the unambiguous contractual provisions to the contrary, Orth-O-Vision would have the unlimited right to expand its operations throughout the Borough of Queens. Simon further contends that HBO reaffirmed these oral understandings after the execution of the 1974 agreement. Defendants deny having made any such oral representations to Simon either before or after the execution of that contract.

From the commencement of their relationship in 1974, Orth-O-Vision's payments to HBO were sporadic and incomplete. In November, 1974, the parties met to discuss both Orth-O-Vision's indebtedness to HBO and its right to expand into other buildings. HBO's officers informed Simon that any further expansion had to be "on a solid financial base," and Orth-O-Vision agreed to make minimum monthly payments to HBO of $4500. Orth-O-Vision failed to meet this new payment schedule and in early 1975, HBO sent a letter to Orth-O-Vision stating that Orth-O-Vision's outstanding indebtedness exceeded $31,000 and threatening to terminate HBO's service within forty-five days. This threat was not carried out. In April 1975, the parties met once again and Orth-O-Vision agreed to pay receivables on a current basis and an additional $27,000 over the following year to cover arrearages. Once again, Orth-O-Vision failed to make the required payments. In October 1975, HBO sent Orth-O-Vision notice of termination of the contract because of its continued inability to pay. The parties again met to resolve their differences in November 1975, and HBO agreed to rescind its termination in exchange for Orth-O-Vision's promise to make minimum monthly payments of $2,000 in liquidation of the total amount then due of $65,000. Orth-O-Vision's payments remained sporadic.

Through 1975, the parties also disagreed as to Orth-O-Vision's right to expand its operations to other apartment buildings in Queens. HBO informed Orth-O-Vision that no further expansion would be permitted as a result of New York's enactment of legislation limiting the expansion of MDS systems within the state. Orth-O-Vision contends, however, that HBO engaged in "selective enforcement" of the statute; while prohibiting Orth-O-Vision from entering new buildings in Queens, HBO allegedly permitted other affiliates to expand into other boroughs.

In March 1976, notwithstanding their earlier disputes, Orth-O-Vision and HBO met to discuss a new affiliation agreement. Simon contends that in the course of these negotiations HBO officials told him that Orth-O-Vision would have to give up its rights to deferral of payments to HBO. In addition, HBO's officials allegedly told Simon that Orth-O-Vision would not be permitted to expand until New York changed its law. Simon contends that he told HBO that he disagreed with its interpretation of New York law. Nevertheless,

in July 1976, Orth-O-Vision and HBO entered into a new affiliate agreement superseding the 1974 agreement. Orth-O-Vision was represented by counsel during the course of these negotiations.

Under the 1976 agreement, Orth-O-Vision agreed to pay to HBO $5.00 per month per subscriber. In a separate letter agreement, Orth-O-Vision agreed to pay back its indebtedness of approximately $118,000 in monthly installments of at least $2500. The new affiliate agreement listed approximately thirty-two apartment complexes to which Orth-O-Vision would be permitted to sell HBO's program service and expressly provided that any further expansion would require HBO's consent. The parties clearly viewed MDS as a precursor to cable television in Queens. HBO was expressly permitted to terminate the agreement on forty-five days' written notice if it entered into an agreement to supply programming to a cable television system franchised to operate in Queens. If HBO terminated the agreement pursuant to this clause, it would be required to "make all reasonable efforts" to encourage the cable television system to agree to purchase Orth-O-Vision's assets and subscribers "for reasonable compensation." In the event of Orth-O-Vision's breach, HBO again retained the right either to suspend delivery until the default were remedied, terminate the agreement, or declare the agreement breached and accelerate Orth-O-Vision's payment obligation. The agreement once again recited that it contained the "full understanding of the parties" and that any modification or waiver of its provisions would have to be in writing.

Since commencing this lawsuit in June 1977, Orth-O-Vision has not made any payments to HBO despite the fact that Orth-O-Vision has continued to market HBO's program service to Queens subscribers. Nor has Orth-O-Vision supplied HBO with the monthly subscriber reports required by the contract. Orth-O-Vision's stated justifications for these actions are: 1. the oral understanding with HBO permits Orth-O-Vision to defer payment until it is sufficiently profitable; and 2. the damages sought by Orth-O-Vision from HBO exceed the amount owed pursuant to the contract. Orth-O-Vision currently owes HBO approximately $750,000 and, over the entire course of its relationship with HBO, Orth-O-Vision has made payments of only $187,951.92. On August 17, 1978, counsel for HBO informed Orth-O-Vision, through its counsel, that the 1976 affiliate agreement was terminated and that Orth-O-Vision should cease the appropriation of HBO's signal. MDS technology did not permit HBO to discontinue its transmissions to Orth-O-Vision, but HBO did cease the shipment of subscriber program guides as required by the affiliate contract. In October 1978, after a hearing, this court denied Orth-O-Vision's motion for a preliminary injunction requiring HBO to deliver the program guides on the grounds that Orth-O-Vision had failed to show irreparable injury and had shown doubtful success on the merits.

Orth-O-Vision has continued to market HBO's program service with program guides that identify the service as Orth-O-Vision's and nowhere mention HBO. On November 2, 1978, counsel for HBO again informed Orth-O-Vision's counsel that HBO considered the contract terminated and that Orth-O-Vision's continued interception and use of the HBO signal violated federal and state law. Some of the programs transmitted by HBO are original works in which HBO owns and has registered the copyrights. From September 1978 through February 1979 twelve of these copyrighted works were transmitted approximately 50 times in the aggregate to all of HBO's New York area affiliates. Each of those transmissions was intercepted by Orth-O-Vision and retransmitted to its subscribers. HBO has sent monthly bills to Orth-O-Vision since the August 1978 termination and has, on occasion, referred potential new customers to Orth-O-Vision.

Orth-O-Vision's complaint alleges a conspiracy among defendants HBO, Time and Tarshis in violation of the federal antitrust laws for the purpose of limiting plaintiff's ability to supply pay-television originated by HBO to customers and potential customers in the New York metropolitan area. Orth-O-Vision alleges that Knickerbocker Communications Corporation ("Knickerbocker"), now a Time subsidiary, has applied for a franchise from New York City and State for the delivery of pay television services to the Borough of Queens, and that the defendants have sought

to destroy plaintiff's business so that Knickerbocker would be able to obtain a franchise and operate without competition from Orth-O-Vision. In 1978, the New York City Board of Estimate granted a cable television franchise to Knickerbocker for the Borough of Queens. Orth-O-Vision views the instant motion as part of the scheme to drive it out of business. Orth-O-Vision contends that if HBO prevails on this motion, Orth-O-Vision will be put out of business and Knickerbocker will acquire its goodwill without reimbursing Orth-O-Vision therefor, as required by the 1976 affiliate agreement. . . .

I. The Propriety of HBO's Termination of the 1976 Affiliate Agreement

Since each of HBO's claims turns upon a finding that Orth-O-Vision lacks the authority to use HBO's signal, the threshold issue on this motion is whether HBO lawfully terminated the 1976 affiliate agreement with Orth-O-Vision. Orth-O-Vision's failure to remit payments to HBO and to submit subscriber reports each month since April 1977 is clearly a material breach of the 1976 affiliate agreement. That agreement expressly grants to HBO the right, upon Orth-O-Vision's breach of any of its terms, to suspend delivery of its service and terminate its affiliate relationship with Orth-O-Vision. Orth-O-Vision contends, however, that its refusal to pay was justified in light of HBO's oral representations made both before and after the signing of the 1974 agreement to the effect that Orth-O-Vision would be permitted to defer payments until it was financially capable to do so and to expand without limitation.

It is not at all clear why HBO's oral representations in 1974 and 1975 are relevant to a determination of the parties' rights with respect to the 1976 affiliate agreement, which expressly provides that it is intended to supersede all previous agreements between the parties. Moreover, the 1976 agreement contains a detailed "merger clause" stating that the written agreement constitutes the entire agreement between the parties and that any modification thereof must be signed by the party to be charged. As a matter of New York law, the existence of such a clause creates a strong presumption, unrebutted by Orth-O-Vision, that the parties intended their agreement to be a complete integration of their mutual promises. . . . Indeed, the 1976 agreement unambiguously defines Orth-O-Vision's monthly obligation to pay and explicitly conditions the right of expansion upon HBO's approval. As such, New York's parol evidence rule bars the admission of the alleged prior or contemporaneous oral representations to vary or contradict these terms of the 1976 affiliate agreement concerning payment and expansion.

Orth-O-Vision next contends that HBO's participation in an unlawful conspiracy to limit Orth-O-Vision's expansion and to monopolize the pay television market in Queens renders HBO's termination of the affiliate agreement unlawful. Notwithstanding HBO's contractual right of termination, if HBO's actions "were part and parcel of unlawful conduct or agreement with others or were conceived in a purpose to unreasonably restrain trade, control a market, or monopolize, then such conduct might well run afoul of the Sherman Law." *Poller v. Columbia Broadcasting System, Inc.*, 368 U.S. 464, 468–69, 82 S.Ct. 486, 489, 7 L.Ed.2d 458 (1962). Even if HBO has violated the antitrust laws, however, this would not relieve Orth-O-Vision of its obligations under the affiliate agreement. . . . HBO's alleged anti-competitive activities do not excuse Orth-O-Vision's appropriation of the HBO signal.

Finally, Orth-O-Vision argues that certain of HBO's actions subsequent to the termination of the contract equitably estop HBO from asserting Orth-O-Vision's breach of the agreement. Specifically, Orth-O-Vision contends that HBO, by billing Orth-O-Vision for use of its signal subsequent to termination and referring potential customers for the program service to Orth-O-Vision, acted in a manner inconsistent with the contract's repudiation and must therefore be estopped from terminating it. New York courts have defined the doctrine of equitable estoppel in terms of six essential elements. The party claiming estoppel must establish: 1. conduct by the estopped party which amounts to concealment of material facts; 2. the estopped party's intention that such conduct shall be acted upon by the other party; 3. the estopped party's knowledge of the real facts;

4. the other party's ignorance of the facts; 5. his reliance upon the conduct of the estopped party; and 6. his change of position to his prejudice as a result. . . . Orth-O-Vision's claim of estoppel founders upon virtually every one of these doctrinal elements. HBO's billing of Orth-O-Vision for its use of the signal and its referral of customers to HBO, when considered in conjunction with HBO's letters demanding that Orth-O-Vision desist from the interception of its signal, HBO's termination of the distribution of its program guides, and HBO's vigorous litigation of the instant motion for injunctive relief, can hardly be interpreted as materially misleading behavior. . . .

II. HBO's Claims for Summary Judgment and Permanent Injunctive Relief

A. The Federal Communications Act Claim

The Federal Communications Act provides a "mantle of privacy" for all communications except radio and television broadcasts intended for the public. . . .

The principal issue raised by this claim is whether HBO's radio communications are "broadcast," *i.e.*, intended to be received by the general public and, therefore, exempted from the protections of § 605.

The leading precedent concerning the statutory definition of "broadcast" is *Functional Music, Inc. v. FCC*, 107 U.S.App.D.C. 34, 274 F.2d 543, *cert. denied*, 361 U.S. 813, 80 S.Ct. 50, 4 L.Ed.2d 81 (1958). *Functional Music* involved a functional background music service which had been "superimposed upon traditional [FM] broadcasting services." 274 F.2d at 544. Subscribers, generally commercial institutions, received the petitioner's regularly scheduled broadcasts but with all advertising matter received by the ordinary listener deleted. For a fee, petitioner transmitted a supersonic signal which activated special equipment installed in subscribers' radio receivers to cut off the advertisements heard over conventional receivers. Reasoning that the service's format was highly specialized and directly adaptable to subscribers' needs, and that the petitioner exacted a fee for its services, the FCC concluded that the petitioner's operations were "point-to-point communications" and not properly transmittable by a station licensed to provide a broadcasting service. . . .

The issue presented in this case is whether the converse of the rule in *Functional Music* is also true: does the transmission of programming which is of interest to the general public constitute "broadcasting" even though one cannot view the programs without paying a fee for special equipment? In *In the Matter of Amendment of Part 73 of the Commission's Rules and Regulations (Radio Broadcast Services) to Provide for Subscription Television Service*, 3 F.C.C.2d 1 (1966), the FCC sought to answer this exact question in deciding whether over-the-air subscription television ("STV") fell within the statutory definition. STV involves the over-the-air transmission of programs intended to be viewed only by those who pay a charge. Those transmitting the signal, generally television broadcast stations, transmit a "scrambled" signal that may be viewed intelligibly only by those with "unscrambling" devices attached to their home television sets. Rejecting the contention that limiting transmission to those individuals willing to pay could not constitute "broadcasting," the FCC stated:

> The evident intention of any station transmitting subscription programs would be to make them available to all members of the public within range of the station. . . . [T]he primary touchstone of a broadcast service is the intent of the broadcaster to provide radio or television service without discrimination to as many members of the general public as can be interested in the particular program as distinguished from a point-to-point message service to specified individuals. . . . "[I]ntent" may be inferred from the circumstances under which material is transmitted, and . . . the number of actual or potential viewers is not especially important.

Id. at 9.

From the factual record before the court on this motion for summary judgment, there is little to distinguish HBO's MDS transmissions from those of STV systems. Both media involve the transmission of radio communications that members of the general public cannot receive without the installation of special equipment for a fee. More significantly, HBO's programming, consisting of recent movies, sports events and variety shows, differs little from conventional broadcast fare and is obviously intended to appeal to a mass audience.

One of the important circumstances from which HBO's "intent" might be inferred is the extent to which MDS facilities are technologically capable of reaching the general public. The technological limitations of MDS may be such as to render the analogy to over-the-air subscription television inapt, but no such showing has been made by HBO. Accordingly, HBO's motion for partial summary judgment on its Federal Communications Act claim must be denied. . . .

C. The Copyright Law Claim

As the copyright owner of twelve audiovisual works which have been retransmitted by Orth-O-Vision to its subscribers without authorization, HBO has standing to sue for infringement and, by registering its copyrights, HBO has fulfilled the procedural prerequisite for commencing an infringement suit. 17 U.S.C. §§ 411(a), 501(b).

The initial issue raised by HBO's copyright claim is whether Orth-O-Vision's unauthorized retransmission constitutes infringement. Use of copyrighted material no matter how extensive and widespread is not infringement unless it conflicts with the statutorily recognized exclusive rights. . . . Under the 1909 Copyright Act and two Supreme Court decisions interpreting it, Orth-O-Vision's retransmission of copyrighted material, though unauthorized, would not have been deemed infringement. In *Fortnightly Corp. v. United Artists Television, Inc.*, 392 U.S. 390 . . . (1968) and again in *Teleprompter Corp. v. Columbia Broadcasting System, Inc.*, 415 U.S. 394 . . . (1974), the Court held that cable television systems do not "perform" copyrighted works when they transmit copyrighted works to subscribers. The Court reasoned that the cable television function of enhancing the subscriber's capacity to receive broadcast signals, irrespective of the distance between the subscriber and the broadcaster or the extent to which the cable operator originated his own programming, was too passive a role to be treated as "performance" and thus did not conflict with the copyright owner's exclusive right to perform his work.

The Copyright Act of 1976, however, has substantially revamped the law of secondary transmissions. Although the 1976 Act does not expressly define secondary transmission as "performance," both the structure of the Act and its legislative history establish clearly that this was the Congressional intent. 2 M. Nimmer, *supra* § 8.18[B], at 8–195 to –198. Since Orth-O-Vision's secondary transmissions do not fall within the scope of any of the exemptions or limitations set forth in 17 U.S.C. § 111, its secondary transmissions of HBO's copyrighted works constitute acts of infringement.

A permanent injunction, the relief requested by HBO, is frequently granted to the prevailing party in an infringement action as a matter of equitable discretion. . . .

Conclusion

HBO's motion for partial summary judgment is granted. The court determines that HBO is entitled to a permanent injunction against Orth-O-Vision's infringement of all of HBO's present and future copyrighted works.

Eastern Microwave, Inc. v. Doubleday Sport, Inc., 691 F.2d 125 (2d Cir. 1982)

MARKEY, J.
Appeal from a judgment of the district court for the Northern District of New York, denying plaintiff's and granting defendant's motion for partial summary judgment, holding that a retransmitter of television signals publicly performed a copyrighted work among those signals and was not an exempt carrier. We reverse. . . .

Plaintiff, Eastern Microwave, Inc. (EMI) is licensed by the Federal Communications Commission (FCC) to provide services as a communications common carrier. EMI's services include the retransmission of the television signals of broadcast stations to markets outside the service areas of the broadcast stations. Retransmission is accomplished by converting broadcast signals into microwave signals and relaying the microwave signals via satellite or a string of line-of-sight terrestrial microwave repeater stations. Retransmitted signals are delivered by EMI to the headends of the customers of its transmitting services, cable television (CATV) systems, which then reconvert the microwave signals to television signals for distribution to and viewing by the CATV system's subscribers.

EMI has been retransmitting the original television signals of WOR–TV of New York City by repeater stations since 1965, and more recently by both repeater stations and satellite. WOR–TV has not objected to that retransmission.

Doubleday Sports, Inc. (Doubleday), owner of The New York Mets baseball team, contracts with WOR–TV to broadcast approximately 100 Mets games per season. It is undisputed that The Mets, i.e., Doubleday, owns the copyright in the audiovisual work represented by the Mets games. Since 1965, EMI has retransmitted the entirety of WOR–TV's signals, without selection among programs and without modification or mutilation in any manner of the signals received and retransmitted. Since 1980, when WOR–TV became a twenty-four hour channel, EMI has retransmitted all twenty-four hours of WOR–TV programming, with no editing or selection among programs. Hence, EMI's retransmission of WOR–TV's television signals includes the Mets games, along with numerous other copyrighted audiovisual works. EMI did not request permission of Doubleday or of any other copyright owner to retransmit the signals of WOR–TV.

In March of 1981, EMI was notified by Doubleday of the latter's view that retransmission of WOR–TV Mets game broadcasts infringed Doubleday's copyright. Thereupon, EMI instituted this action, seeking a declaratory judgment that it was a passive carrier exempt from copyright liability under 17 U.S.C. § 111(a)(3) of the Copyright Act of 1976 (Act). Doubleday moved for partial summary judgment declaring EMI's retransmissions non-exempt, and for dismissal of the complaint. EMI cross-moved for partial summary judgment denying Doubleday's motion and granting judgment for EMI. EMI amended its complaint, adding a contention that its transmissions are not "public performances" and that it does not therefore infringe Doubleday's right to display the copyrighted works publicly as required by 17 U.S.C. § 106(5).

The district court, stating that the parties did not dispute that EMI "performs" the WOR–TV signals, held that EMI's retransmissions were to the public, and that EMI is not exempt because it selected WOR–TV's signals, exercised control over recipients of its retransmissions, and did not limit its activities to providing wires, cables, or other communications channels for the use of others. The district court granted Doubleday's motion and denied EMI's. . . .

This case, one of first impression in this circuit, has its genesis in the burgeoning technological advances of the communications industry. Like others before it, the case requires interpretation and application of statutes enacted before adoption of the involved communications arrangements. Because the issues framed by the cross motions for summary judgment involve application of legal standards under the Act to the relatively undisputed facts concerning the nature of EMI's activities, plenary review of the district court's judgment is appropriate. . . .

EMI's activities, described as those of an intermediate or "resale" transmitter, are a new and mixed breed. Unlike those of broadcasters and CATV systems, they do not include the sending of signals intended for reception as such on television sets. Like those of some CATV systems, they do include the acquisition "off the air" of broadcast signals. Unlike the activities of older, established common carriers, e.g., the telephone company, they include carrying the communications desired by receivers rather than those desired by senders. Also unlike older common carriers, EMI is paid by receivers rather than by senders. Like those of older common carriers, EMI's activities are paid for as services and involve transmittal of the entire signal without change.

A television broadcast station sends out "on-the-air" signals at frequencies within the broadcast band. Television sets positioned to receive those signals convert them into an audible and visible, i.e. "audiovisual," display. In rendering a retransmission service, the first step is reception of the same "off-the-air" television signals of a broadcast station. The next step of the retransmitter, however, is not conversion into an audiovisual display, but conversion to a frequency within the microwave band. The third step is transportation of the microwave signal. As above indicated, EMI's microwave signal is transported in one of

two ways: (1) through a string of line-of-sight terrestrial repeater stations; or (2) directly to a receiver dish at the RCA American Communications, Inc. (RCA) earth station uplink site, where it is converted to another microwave frequency, transmitted to an RCA satellite transponder leased by EMI, and relayed by the transponder back to earth. Whichever transporting method is used, the last retransmission step is delivery of the microwave signals to headends of CATV systems, EMI's customers. Distribution of the signals received at a headend, to subscribers for display on their television sets, is a step performed entirely by the CATV system and forms no part of the activities or services of EMI. The retransmission services provided by EMI are thus an intermediate link in an overall chain of distribution of television broadcast signals. . . .

The present activity of EMI cannot be viewed in historical isolation. In 1968, the FCC suspended the hearing process required by its 1966 rules in favor of proposed rules requiring cable systems in the top 100 markets to obtain consent from distant stations before transmitting their signals. *Notice in Docket No. 18397*, 15 F.C.C.2d 417 (1968). That resulted in denial of virtually all transmission rights, and designation of the action as a "freeze" on cable growth.

At about the same time as the 1968 FCC action, distribution of microwave-relayed television signals by CATV systems to subscribers was held not a "performance" under the Copyright Act of 1909, and CATV systems were therefore not liable for copyright infringement. . . .

Congress over the ensuing years worked out a legislative compromise, one part of which was the provision in the Act of a definition of "to perform or display a work publicly" having a breadth sufficient to encompass the distribution of relayed signals by CATV systems. . . .

Under the congressionally mandated scheme, television broadcast stations like WOR–TV continue to pay license or royalty fees directly to copyright owners like Doubleday, while CATV systems pay license fees under their compulsory licenses to the United States Copyright Office in accord with formulae provided in 17 U.S.C. § 111(d)(2)(B). The fees paid by CATV systems are distributed to copyright owners like Doubleday by the Copyright Royalty Tribunal (Tribunal), as provided for in 17 U.S.C. § 111(d)(5). The Congressional scheme thus provided for compensation from CATV systems to copyright owners measured by the number of cable viewers or potential viewers, and placed the responsibility for payment of that compensation on the CATV systems. . . .

We begin, as we must, with the statute, 17 U.S.C. § 111(a)(3) . . . under which EMI is entitled to the "carrier" exemption if its activities are passive, merely retransmitting exactly what it receives, if it exercises no control over the content or selection of the primary transmission, or over the particular recipients of its transmission, and if its retransmission activities consist solely of providing wires, cables, or other communications channels for the use of others.

The first question presented is thus whether EMI exercised "control over selection of the primary transmission" when it chose to retransmit the WOR–TV signal via satellite. Via its terrestrial microwave repeaters, EMI retransmits the broadcast signals of WOR–TV, WNEW, WPIX, WCBS–TV, WSBK, WSTM, WPHL, WIXT, WUAB, CHCH, CKWS, WQXR–FM, Home Box Office, Prism, and programming of the Pennsylvania Educational Television Network. With respect to its extra-terrestrial activity, only one satellite transponder was made available to EMI, enabling satellite retransmission of only one broadcaster's signals.

With satellite transmission of but one broadcaster's signals available, EMI naturally sought to retransmit those of a marketable station. If EMI's CATV satellite customers had preferred the signals of WNEW, for example, over those of WOR–TV, EMI would presumably have chosen the former over the latter. Based on demand shown by numerous CATV systems surveyed and solicited, the marketable station sought proved to be WOR–TV. In meeting that demand by supplying the WOR–TV signal, EMI does so passively, retransmitting exactly what it receives and the entirety of what it receives. That one-time determination by EMI to retransmit WOR–TV's signals reflects EMI's limitation to one technical facility and the realization that once contracts are entered, EMI cannot retransmit any other signals on that facility.

Technical restrictions which forced EMI to make an initial, one-time determination to retransmit the signals of a particular station, whatever the content of those signals, do not evidence the "control over the content and selection of the primary transmission" intended to be precluded under Section 111(a)(3). In the ordinary common carrier context, the carrier must render its service to all comers, denying it to none on the basis of content, and must not select or choose among those who seek to use its service, on any basis other than a legitimate business reason. When the communication service is technologically limited to one sender, however, a type of "selection" is impelled. That type of forced selection cannot be the type precluded by the statute in the context here presented, for to so hold would be to require that exemption be denied to any carrier that did not retransmit every television broadcast of every television station in the country. Moreover, if station selection were the type of "selection" precluded, a failure to retransmit the signals of one station could be viewed as a control of content forbidden to carriers by the Act. To hold that "selection" means station selection would thus emasculate the exemption provision of the Act with respect to intermediate carriers, in derogation of the duty of upholding statutory provisions not contrary to reason, logic, common sense or the Constitution.

To remain exempt, a carrier-retransmitter must avoid content control by retransmitting exactly what and all of what it receives, as EMI does here. To do otherwise could be perceived as the carrier's making the transmission its own. . . .

The second requirement, an absence of direct or indirect control over the particular recipients of its retransmission, is fully satisfied by EMI. It is undisputed that the "particular recipients" of EMI's retransmissions are the many CATV systems which it serves under contract. That it renders its service to certain CATV systems and not others does not itself constitute, however, any control, direct or indirect, over particular recipients. As above indicated, the so-called "resale carriers" are somewhat new in the common carrier world, in that they serve the receiver rather than the sender of a communication. EMI is subject to FCC regulation and has been granted authority under 47 U.S.C. § 214 to operate as a common carrier. As such, it is bound to furnish its communications services upon reasonable requests. 47 U.S.C. § 201(a). That EMI operates under FCC-approved tariffs which a particular CATV system might not be able to meet does not mean that EMI exercises control over its recipient CATV customers. . . .

EMI also meets the third requirement, that it merely provide wires, cables, or other communications channels for the use of others. As above indicated, the "others" here are the receiving CATV systems which cannot afford their own wires, cables, and channels, rather than the originating senders who use (and cannot afford their own) wires, cables, and channels of more traditional common carriers like a telephone company. EMI provides the wires and cables of its repeater stations for use of its CATV customers in acquiring the signals of WOR–TV and those of many other originators. It provides its single satellite transponder for use of its CATV customers in acquiring the signals of necessarily one originator, i.e., WOR–TV.

Doubleday argues in effect that EMI provides wires, etc., for its own use because it is "selling" the Mets games. EMI is selling, however, only its transmission services, CATV systems paying therefore on the basis of number of subscribers only up to a maximum compensation of $3,000 regardless of the content of the retransmitted signals. When the maximum is reached, the payment remains the same, regardless of the number of subscribers. EMI transmits nothing of its own creation. It transmits only to the headends of its customers who employ its services in lieu of obtaining their own wires, cables, etc. . . .

Interpretation of the Act must occur in the real world of telecommunications, not in a vacuum. The centerpiece of the compromise reflected in the Act is the compulsory licensing scheme. That scheme is predicated on and presupposes a continuing ability of CATV systems to receive signals for distribution to their subscribers. Doubleday is but one of numerous copyright owners whose

works may be broadcast by WOR–TV. EMI serves as a signals conduit between the performance by WOR–TV and the performance by its CATV system customers. Adoption of Doubleday's position would stand all copyright owners athwart that conduit between the original broadcast and the opportunity for subsequent performances by CATV systems. In so doing, it would defeat Congress' intent by imposing on EMI the unworkable separate negotiations with numerous copyright holders from which the Act sought to free CATV systems.

Congress drew a careful balance between the rights of copyright owners and those of CATV systems, providing for payments to the former and a compulsory licensing program to insure that the latter could continue bringing a diversity of broadcasted signals to their subscribers. The public interest thus lies in a continuing supply of varied programming to viewers. Because CATV systems served by intermediate carriers cannot provide their full current programming to their subscribers without the services of those carriers, imposition of individual copyright owner negotiations on intermediate carriers would strangle CATV systems by choking off their life line to their supply of programs, would effectively restore the "freeze" on cable growth described above, and, most importantly, would frustrate the congressional intent reflected in the Act by denying CATV systems the opportunity to participate in the compulsory licensing program. After years of consideration and debate, Congress could not have intended that its work be so easily undone by the interposition of copyright owners to block exercise of the licensing program by cable systems. . . .

EMI is, like all common carriers, compensated for its transmission services as such. In accord with its FCC-approved tariff, and as above indicated, EMI is paid by each CATV system in relation to the number of its subscribers up to a maximum of $3,000. The fee does not increase thereafter, regardless of the number of a CATV system's subscribers. In contrast, the royalty fee paid by each CATV system under the Act is limited to no maximum, but is entirely based on percentages of gross receipts from subscribers to the CATV service in accord with 17 U.S.C. § 111. . . .

It is undisputed that if each CATV system had its own string of microwave repeaters or satellite transponder it would be liable through the Tribunal to a copyright owner for only the one established royalty fee when and if it publicly performed the copyrighted work by making it available to its subscribers; and that such an integrated CATV system would not be liable for a second royalty fee for having itself retransmitted the original broadcast signal to its headend. We are unpersuaded by counsel's urging that a different result should obtain when a separate entity, e.g. EMI, supplies the retransmission service. That EMI is a separate entity supplies no justification for subjecting EMI to copyright liability when those same activities would not result in copyright liability if carried out by the CATV systems served by EMI. . . .

In summary, given the nature of EMI's services here involved, and the role those services play in the overall chain of signals distribution, we conclude that EMI is not in law infringing Doubleday's exclusive right to display its copyrighted work by passively retransmitting the entirety of WOR–TV's broadcast signal to the headends of its customer CATV systems, because those services are such as to fall within the exemption provided for in 17 U.S.C. § 111(a)(3). Reversal of the judgment appealed from is accordingly required.

WGN Continental Broadcasting Co. v. United Video, Inc., 693 F.2d 622 (7th Cir. 1982)

POSNER, J.

This appeal requires us to decide a question of first impression under the Copyright Act of 1976, 17 U.S.C. §§ 101 *et seq.*: to what extent does the copyright on a television program also include program material encoded in the "vertical blanking interval" of the television signal?

Each picture that flashes on a television screen is generated by an electron gun behind the screen that moves rapidly back and forth from the top to the bottom of the screen. When the gun reaches the bottom it shuts off and returns to the top of the screen to begin again. The interval in which the gun is shut off—an interval too brief for the viewer to be aware of—is the vertical blanking interval. It has traditionally been used to carry certain signals that "tell" the television set how to set up the next picture on the screen, but the time required for this function is only a fraction of the interval, and the rest is available, and increasingly is used, to carry other information. Subtitles for deaf people are the most common such use; they appear as an overlay at the bottom of the television picture on sets equipped with a suitable decoder to "unlock" the information carried in the vertical blanking interval and to display it—much as the electron gun generates the regular picture—on the screen. But all sorts of other information can be encoded in the unused portion of the vertical blanking interval—news bulletins, weather reports, ballgame scores, station announcements, the stock ticker, etc. Overlaying the information on the television picture is only one method of display; alternatively, the information can be displayed on a different channel of the television set, or on a different set altogether.

WGN is an "independent" television station in Chicago (that is, it is not affiliated with any of the television networks) and it is also a "superstation," meaning that its programs are carried, outside its local area, by cable television systems. To get those programs to the cable systems requires the services of an intermediate carrier such as United Video, a satellite common carrier that plucks broadcast signals off the air, including signals from WGN, and transmits them to cable systems.

WGN decided to experiment with "teletext" (as the use of the vertical blanking interval to carry material intended for the television viewer is called) by broadcasting at first just a test signal, then news stories and a program schedule, in the vertical blanking intervals of its copyrighted 9:00 p.m. news broadcast. The teletext was intended for subscribers to a WGN-affiliated cable system in Albuquerque who own television sets equipped with a suitable decoder. The cable system planned to run the teletext on a different channel (which the viewer would select, if we understand correctly, by pushing a button on the decoder) from the one on which it runs the nine o'clock news. But the cable system never received the teletext. United Video did not retransmit it along with the nine o'clock news but instead substituted teletext supplied by Dow Jones, containing business news. WGN and its affiliate brought this suit to enjoin, as a copyright infringement, United Video's failure to retransmit WGN's teletext along with the nine o'clock news. See 17 U.S.C. §§ 501(a), (b), 502(b). They appeal from the district court's judgment holding that United Video did not violate the Copyright Act and dismissing the complaint. 523 F. Supp. 403 (N.D.Ill.1981).

It used to be that a cable system that picked up and retransmitted a broadcast signal containing a copyrighted program was not an infringer. See *Fortnightly Corp. v. United Artists Television, Inc.*, 392 U.S. 390, 88 S.Ct. 2084, 20 L.Ed.2d 1176 (1968); *Teleprompter Corp. v. Columbia Broadcasting System, Inc.*, 415 U.S. 394, 94 S.Ct. 1129, 39 L.Ed.2d 415 (1974). But the Copyright Act of 1976 changed this, though it allows a cable system to pick up and retransmit broadcast signals without the copyright owner's permission so long as it pays him royalties as fixed in the statute. See 17 U.S.C. § 111. However, "secondary transmissions" made by "any carrier who has no direct or indirect control over the content or selection of the primary transmission or over the particular recipients of the secondary transmission, and whose activities with respect to the secondary transmission consist solely of providing wires, cables, or other communications channels for the use of others . . . ," are exempt from any copyright liability. 17 U.S.C. § 111(a)(3). A "primary transmission" is the initial broadcast; a "secondary transmission" is the "further transmitting" of a primary transmission. 17 U.S.C. § 111(f). The exemption thus allows carriers such as United Video to act as purely passive intermediaries between broadcasters and the cable systems that carry the broadcast signals into the home, without incurring any copyright liability. The cable system selects the signals it wants to retransmit, pays the copyright owners for the right to retransmit their programs, and pays the intermediate carrier a fee for getting the signal from the broadcast station to the cable system. The intermediate carrier pays the copyright owners nothing, pro-

vided it really is passive in relation to what it transmits, like a telephone company. See S.Rep.No. 473, 94th Cong., 1st Sess. 78 (1975). It may not even delete commercials; an important part of the scheme set up in section 111 is the requirement that any cable system that wants to retransmit a broadcast signal without negotiating with the broadcast station or copyright owner transmit intact any commercials it receives from that station. See 17 U.S.C. § 111(c)(3).

What we have explained so far is common ground between the parties; and another point can be disposed of briefly: although United Video's retransmission of WGN's broadcast signal to the cable systems may be immunized from copyright liability by the exemption in section 111(a)(3) for passive carriers, it cannot be immune just because United Video does not retransmit WGN's signal directly to the public—that is, to the cable subscribers—but instead transmits the signal to cable systems which retransmit it to their subscribers. The passive carrier exemption would be superfluous if intermediate carriers such as United Video could never be infringers anyway because they do not transmit directly to the public. And the scheme in section 111 for compensating copyright owners would be disrupted, or at least made cumbersome. United Video could mutilate to its heart's content the broadcast signal it picked up and the copyright owner would have no recourse against it. His only recourse would be against the cable systems— more than a thousand in the case of WGN—that were retransmitting the mutilated signals: a thousand or more copyright infringement suits instead of one.

We cannot find good textual support for the district court's position. The word "public" does not appear either in the definition of secondary transmission or in the provision making the carrier of a secondary transmission liable unless passive. See 17 U.S.C. §§ 111(a), (f). It is true that WGN can complain only if United Video is interfering with its exclusive right to perform or display the copyrighted work publicly. 17 U.S.C. §§ 106(4), 106(5). But the Copyright Act defines "perform or display . . . publicly" broadly enough to encompass indirect transmission to the ultimate public, who in this case are the subscribers to WGN's cable affiliate in Albuquerque. "To perform or display a work 'publicly' means . . . to transmit or otherwise communicate a performance or display of the work . . . to the public, by means of any device or process, whether the members of the public capable of receiving the performance or display receive it in the same place or in separate places and at the same time or at different times." 17 U.S.C. § 101.

Therefore, no exemption for non-public performance is available in this case. And United Video cannot avail itself of the passive carrier exemption, because it was not passive—it did not retransmit WGN's signal intact. But the fact that United Video cannot claim an exemption from copyright liability does not conclude the case. It needs an exemption only if it would otherwise be an infringer, and it would be that only if WGN's copyright of the nine o'clock news includes the teletext in the vertical blanking intervals. If it does, the deletion of the teletext from United Video's retransmission was an alteration of a copyrighted work and hence an infringement under familiar principles. . . .

Before deciding whether WGN's copyright does cover the teletext at issue, we consider briefly what if anything turns on our answer to this question. WGN could copyright its teletext separately; but it has not done so and does not want to do so, because if the teletext were copyrighted separately United Video would have no obligation to retransmit it. United Video is not required to retransmit WGN's entire broadcast day; it is required only to transmit those programs that cable systems ask United Video to carry to them; and they might or might not want WGN's teletext. But if the teletext is covered by the copyright on the nine o'clock news, then any cable system that wants the nine o'clock news must take the teletext with it.

Now WGN cannot in the long run force cable systems to take more of its output than they want; competition with other "superstations" will prevent that. But WGN must perceive some advantage to putting United Video to an all or nothing choice—a choice between the nine o'clock WGN news plus teletext, or no nine o'clock WGN news at all. Although there is a distinct echo in this of

"tie-in" sales and "block booking," practices that in other contexts have been thought to raise serious antitrust problems, the echo is too faint to guide our interpretation of the Copyright Act.

The WGN nine o'clock news is an "audiovisual work," defined in the statute as a work that consists "of a series of related images which are intrinsically intended to be shown by the use of machines or devices such as projectors, viewers, or electronic equipment, together with accompanying sounds, if any, regardless of the nature of the material objects, such as films or tapes, in which the [work is] embodied." 17 U.S.C. § 101. United Video appears to concede, correctly in our view despite an absence of judicial authority on the point, that if WGN's teletext were intended to be overlaid on the television images of the nine o'clock news, in the manner of captions for deaf people or English subtitles for foreign movies, it would be covered by the copyright for that news. Cf. 1 Nimmer, Nimmer on Copyright § 2.09[A] (1981). It would be part of the performance intended to be seen by the viewer and thus one of the "related images" of which section 101 speaks. And though WGN chooses not to use the vertical blanking interval to overlay additional images on those in the nine o'clock news, it is clear that United Video may not use it for that purpose without WGN's permission, any more than if the publisher of a book leaves the inside covers blank the book seller (or book wholesaler, to make the analogy more precise) may inscribe the Lord's Prayer on them in order to broaden the book's appeal. . . .

But while WGN says that it plans eventually to use the vertical blanking interval for overlays, that is not the intended placement of the teletext involved in this case. This teletext fills up the whole television screen; overlaid on the nine o'clock news it would either obliterate the picture portion of the news or produce an unintelligible collage. It is intended to be viewed either on another television set or, more likely, on another channel of the same set. The typical cable system has an abundance of channels and can devote one of them to WGN's teletext. The question is whether it must do so if it wants to use WGN's copyrighted nine o'clock news. We think so, provided the teletext is intended to be seen by the same viewers as are watching the nine o'clock news, during the same interval of time in which that news is broadcast, and as an integral part of the news program.

There is no paradox in suggesting that teletext is covered by the copyright on a regular television program provided that it is intended to be viewed with and as an integral component of that program, even though we have just said that WGN's teletext is to be shown on a different channel from the nine o'clock news, which means that it cannot be viewed simultaneously, as subtitles are. Each frame in a motion picture is covered by the copyright on the motion picture even though the frames are not intended to be viewed simultaneously; and while they are intended to be seen in a rigid sequence, 17 U.S.C. § 101 speaks not of a sequence of related images but only of related images. The pages of books are also usually read sequentially, but this has never been thought a condition of copyright protection. A dictionary can be copyrighted although its pages, and the entries on each page, are not intended to be read in sequence. And if the publisher of a history book includes a fold-out map as an endpaper for the reader to consult from time to time while reading the text, the copyright on the book includes the map although the map is not intended to be read either simultaneously with the text or in some prescribed sequence with it. See 1 Nimmer, *supra,* at § 2.08[A][2].

WGN's proposed use of teletext is analogous. The teletext channel is to contain an announcement of future programming on WGN. The viewer of the nine o'clock news, a compendium not all parts of which may interest every viewer, is thus invited to switch to the teletext channel when his attention to the news flags, to see what is forthcoming on WGN. The teletext channel is also to carry local news of Chicago that parallels the national news carried on the main program. If the main program was discussing inflation nationwide, the teletext channel might provide data on inflation in Chicago; and the viewer in Albuquerque who was interested in conditions in Chicago (maybe his children live there, or he is planning to move there) might decide to switch to the

teletext channel. In short, WGN wants to make its nine o'clock news a two-channel program, and we cannot see that the difference between a one- and a two-channel program is much more profound than that between a silent movie and a talkie. If television technology were so primitive that it required two channels, broadcasting simultaneously, to carry a sound program—one to carry the picture, the other the sound—and if the vertical blanking interval were used to transmit the sound, we do not think it would be argued that the copyright of the program did not include the sound track because it was on a separate channel. Cf. 1 Nimmer, *supra,* at § 2.09[E][1]. Neither do we think it would be argued that a televised musical performance and its "stereo simulcast" require separate copyrights.

We do not pretend to find in these analogies, any more than in the definition of "audiovisual work" in section 101, conclusive evidence of legislative purpose. The fact is that Congress did not foresee the kind of use that WGN has made of the vertical blanking interval. Nor do we find in the language, structure, or legislative history of the Copyright Act of 1976 some overarching purpose that would enable us to deduce how Congress would have decided the copyright question in this case if it had considered it. There is of course a sense in which the Act is "pro" copyright holder—it gave copyright owners protection against cable systems, which the Supreme Court had held the prior act did not. But by also requiring compulsory licensing it stopped far short of giving them complete protection; and there is no evidence that it wanted the WGNs of this world to get the additional protection sought in this case. Extrinsic policies, such as the antitrust policies mentioned earlier, are too remotely involved to provide guidance.

All other aids to statutory construction failing, we fall back on the broad definition of "audiovisual work" in the statute and on the analogy between WGN's use of the vertical blanking interval and examples drawn from both audiovisual and literary media. The broad definition may not be inadvertent. The comprehensive-overhaul of copyright law by the Copyright Act of 1976 was impelled by recent technological advances, such as xerography and cable television, which the courts interpreting the prior act, the Copyright Act of 1909, had not dealt with to Congress's satisfaction. This background suggests that Congress probably wanted the courts to interpret the definitional provisions of the new act flexibly, so that it would cover new technologies as they appeared, rather than to interpret those provisions narrowly and so force Congress periodically to update the act. . . .

We want to make clear, however, that our holding is not that WGN "owns" the vertical blanking interval in the programs that it has copyrighted. The copyright is in the programming rather than in the method by which it is transmitted. See 17 U.S.C. § 102(a); cf. 1 Nimmer, *supra*, at §§ 2.03[C], 2.18[F]. If WGN devised a teletext that was not intended to be viewed in conjunction with the nine o'clock news—a cartoon show for preschoolers, for example—the fact that it used the vertical blanking intervals in the signal transmitting that news to encode the teletext would not give the teletext copyright protection as part of the nine o'clock news. The images in the teletext could not in that case be regarded as "related images" to those in the news. WGN may not, by exploiting the marvels of modern technology, create two or three or 30 channels of unrelated programming and force it all down the throats of any cable system that wants just the nine o'clock news (not that it would find many takers of that news in those circumstances). But if WGN wants to create multichannel news or entertainment for viewers willing to switch back and forth between channels, we cannot find anything in the Copyright Act to prevent it from copyrighting its video smorgasbord.

A simpler line, of course, would be that between overlay material and nonoverlay (shown on a different channel) material. But it would also be an arbitrary line unless we thought Congress meant "related images" to be limited to images shown on a single channel, and we have already rejected such a limiting interpretation. As there is no question that WGN's teletext was intended to be viewed in conjunction with the nine o'clock news, WGN has proved copyright infringement and is entitled to an injunction.

On Petition for Rehearing with Suggestion for Rehearing En Banc

The members of the original panel have voted to deny the petition for rehearing, and no active judge in regular service has voted to grant rehearing *en banc*, so the petition is denied. But we take this opportunity to deal with a misconception that underlies the arguments made in the petition.

In our original opinion, we used some imprecise language on which United Video has constructed its principal argument for a rehearing. We said that WGN's teletext was intended to be shown on a different "channel" from its nine o'clock news. What we should have said to be precise was that the teletext was intended not to be superimposed on the news but to be viewed separately *as if* on a different channel. To switch to the teletext the viewer pushes a button, which on many television sets is also the method of switching channels. But the teletext is not on a different channel; it is on the same channel as the program in whose vertical blanking intervals it is being transmitted; it merely is invisible to the viewer until he pushes the decoder button.

The difference becomes significant in light of United Video's argument that since many cable television systems transmit only 12 channels of programming (though most are capable of transmitting between 50 and 100 channels), and are obliged by law to carry the signals of the local television stations in the system's community, a requirement that they carry teletext intended to be viewed in conjunction with those signals could swamp the capacity of many systems—a consequence too drastic to impute to Congress without clearer evidence of legislative intent than we found. But this assumes, incorrectly, that each station's teletext occupies a different channel. It does not; it is part of the channel on which the station's regular programming is carried. No displacement of any other programming is threatened by our decision.

The petition for rehearing also takes us to task for having given insufficient weight to the word "*series* of related works" in the statutory definition of audiovisual work. 17 U.S.C. § 101 (emphasis added). But the main program and any teletext intended to be viewed with, and as an integral part of, the main program (our condition for recognizing copyright protection of the teletext as part of the copyright on the main program) are in a series or sequence, and though it is one determined by the viewer himself we do not think the statutory term "series" must be interpreted to mean a rigid, predetermined sequence.

Finally, in view of the suggestion in the petition that we have adopted a loose and spongy "relatedness" test to determine when teletext is covered by the copyright on the main program, we repeat what we said in our opinion: WGN's teletext is covered by the copyright on its nine o'clock news "provided the teletext is intended to be seen by the same viewers as are watching the nine o'clock news, during the same interval of time in which that news is broadcast, and as an integral part of the news program." More than "relatedness" is required, and is present here.

8.30 Home Taping

The U.S. Supreme Court's opinion in *Sony Corporation of America v. Universal City Studios*, reprinted below, details the background of the growing use of home taping devices, both audio and video. (See also Section 8.05.) The discussion in both the majority and minority opinions is instructive on the central issues involved in this dispute.

The case presented formidable problems for the Court. After initial arguments before the Court, substantial delays ensued and no opinion was announced. Amid speculation about a badly divided Court, reargument was ordered. More months passed. The final result was a 5-4 decision, which barely upholds the right to home taping and the right to manufacture home recording devices without incurring copyright liability.

A central issue in the case is whether home taping is permitted under the fair use doctrine of the copyright statute. Note therefore should be made of 17 U.S.C. § 107, which reads as follows:

Notwithstanding the provisions of section 106, the fair use of a copyrighted work, including such use by reproduction in copies or phonorecords or by any other means specified by that section, for purposes such as criticism, comment, news reporting, teaching (including multiple copies for classroom use), scholarship, or research, is not an infringement of copyright. In determining whether the use made of a work in any particular case is a fair use the factors to be considered shall include—

(1) the purpose and character of the use, including whether such use is of a commercial nature or is for nonprofit educational purposes;

(2) the nature of the copyrighted work;

(3) the amount and substantiality of the portion used in relation to the copyrighted work as a whole; and

(4) the effect of the use upon the potential market for or value of the copyrighted work.

Sony Corp. of America v. Universal City Studios, Inc., 464 U.S. 417 (1984)

JUSTICE STEVENS delivered the opinion of the Court.

Petitioners manufacture and sell home video tape recorders. Respondents own the copyrights on some of the television programs that are broadcast on the public airwaves. Some members of the general public use video tape recorders sold by petitioners to record some of these broadcasts, as well as a large number of other broadcasts. The question presented is whether the sale of petitioners' copying equipment to the general public violates any of the rights conferred upon respondents by the Copyright Act.

Respondents commenced this copyright infringement action against petitioners in the United States District Court for the Central District of California in 1976. Respondents alleged that some individuals had used Betamax video tape recorders (VTR's) to record some of respondents' copyrighted works which had been exhibited on commercially sponsored television and contended that these individuals had thereby infringed respondents' copyrights. Respondents further maintained that petitioners were liable for the copyright infringement allegedly committed by Betamax consumers because of petitioners' marketing of the Betamax VTR's. Respondents sought no relief against any Betamax consumer. Instead, they sought money damages and an equitable accounting of profits from petitioners, as well as an injunction against the manufacture and marketing of Betamax VTR's.

After a lengthy trial, the District Court denied respondents all the relief they sought and entered judgment for petitioners. 480 F. Supp. 429 (1979). The United States Court of Appeals for the Ninth Circuit reversed the District Court's judgment on respondents' copyright claim, holding petitioners liable for contributory infringement and ordering the District Court to fashion appropriate relief. 659 F.2d 963 (1981). We granted certiorari, 457 U.S. 1116 (1982); since we had not completed our study of the case last Term, we ordered reargument, 463 U.S. 1226 (1983). We now reverse.

An explanation of our rejection of respondents' unprecedented attempt to impose copyright liability upon the distributors of copying equipment requires a quite detailed recitation of the findings of the District Court. In summary, those findings reveal that the average member of the public uses a VTR principally to record a program he cannot view as it is being televised and then to watch it once at a later time. This practice, known as "time-shifting," enlarges the television viewing audience. For that reason, a significant amount of television programming may be used in this manner without objection from the owners of the copyrights on the programs. For the same reason, even the two respondents in this case, who do assert objections to time-shifting in this litigation, were unable to prove that the practice has impaired the commercial value of their copyrights or has created any likelihood of future harm. Given these findings, there is no basis in the Copyright Act upon which respondents can hold petitioners liable for distributing VTR's to the general public. The Court of Appeals' holding that respondents are entitled to enjoin the distribution of VTR's, to collect royalties on the sale of

such equipment, or to obtain other relief, if affirmed, would enlarge the scope of respondents' statutory monopolies to encompass control over an article of commerce that is not the subject of copyright protection. Such an expansion of the copyright privilege is beyond the limits of the grants authorized by Congress.

I

The two respondents in this action, Universal City Studios, Inc., and Walt Disney Productions, produce and hold the copyrights on a substantial number of motion pictures and other audiovisual works. In the current marketplace, they can exploit their rights in these works in a number of ways: by authorizing theatrical exhibitions, by licensing limited showings on cable and network television, by selling syndication rights for repeated airings on local television stations, and by marketing programs on prerecorded videotapes or videodiscs. Some works are suitable for exploitation through all of these avenues, while the market for other works is more limited.

Petitioner Sony manufactures millions of Betamax video tape recorders and markets these devices through numerous retail establishments, some of which are also petitioners in this action. Sony's Betamax VTR is a mechanism consisting of three basic components: (1) a tuner, which receives electromagnetic signals transmitted over the television band of the public airwaves and separates them into audio and visual signals; (2) a recorder, which records such signals on a magnetic tape; and (3) an adapter, which converts the audio and visual signals on the tape into a composite signal that can be received by a television set.

Several capabilities of the machine are noteworthy. The separate tuner in the Betamax enables it to record a broadcast off one station while the television set is tuned to another channel, permitting the viewer, for example, to watch two simultaneous news broadcasts by watching one "live" and recording the other for later viewing. Tapes may be reused, and programs that have been recorded may be erased either before or after viewing. A timer in the Betamax can be used to activate and deactivate the equipment at predetermined times, enabling an intended viewer to record programs that are transmitted when he or she is not at home. Thus a person may watch a program at home in the evening even though it was broadcast while the viewer was at work during the afternoon. The Betamax is also equipped with a pause button and a fast-forward control. The pause button, when depressed, deactivates the recorder until it is released, thus enabling a viewer to omit a commercial advertisement from the recording, provided, of course, that the viewer is present when the program is recorded. The fast-forward control enables the viewer of a previously recorded program to run the tape rapidly when a segment he or she does not desire to see is being played back on the television screen.

The respondents and Sony both conducted surveys of the way the Betamax machine was used by several hundred owners during a sample period in 1978. Although there were some differences in the surveys, they both showed that the primary use of the machine for most owners was "time-shifting"—the practice of recording a program to view it once at a later time, and thereafter erasing it. Time-shifting enables viewers to see programs they otherwise would miss because they are not at home, are occupied with other tasks, or are viewing a program on another station at the time of a broadcast that they desire to watch. Both surveys also showed, however, that a substantial number of interviewees had accumulated libraries of tapes. Sony's survey indicated that over 80% of the interviewees watched at least as much regular television as they had before owning a Betamax. Respondents offered no evidence of decreased television viewing by Betamax owners.

Sony introduced considerable evidence describing television programs that could be copied without objection from any copyright holder, with special emphasis on sports, religious, and educational programming. For example, their survey indicated that 7.3% of all Betamax use is to record sports events, and representatives of professional baseball, football, basketball, and hockey testified that they had no objection to the recording of their televised events for home use.

Respondents offered opinion evidence concerning the future impact of the unrestricted sale of VTR's on the commercial value of their copyrights. The District Court found, however, that they had failed to prove any likelihood of future harm from the use of VTR's for time-shifting. 480 F. Supp., at 469. . . .

II

. . . From its beginning, the law of copyright has developed in response to significant changes in technology. Indeed, it was the invention of a new form of copying equipment—the printing press— that gave rise to the original need for copyright protection. Repeatedly, as new developments have occurred in this country, it has been the Congress that has fashioned the new rules that new technology made necessary. Thus, long before the enactment of the Copyright Act of 1909, 35 Stat. 1075, it was settled that the protection given to copyrights is wholly statutory. *Wheaton v. Peters*, 8 Pet. 591, 661–662 (1834). The remedies for infringement "are only those prescribed by Congress." *Thompson v. Hubbard*, 131 U.S. 123, 151 (1889).

The judiciary's reluctance to expand the protections afforded by the copyright without explicit legislative guidance is a recurring theme. . . . Sound policy, as well as history, supports our consistent deference to Congress when major technological innovations alter the market for copyrighted materials. Congress has the constitutional authority and the institutional ability to accommodate fully the varied permutations of competing interests that are inevitably implicated by such new technology.

In a case like this, in which Congress has not plainly marked our course, we must be circumspect in construing the scope of rights created by a legislative enactment which never contemplated such a calculus of interests. . . .

Copyright protection "subsists . . . in original works of authorship fixed in any tangible medium of expression." 17 U.S.C. § 102(a) (1982 ed.). This protection has never accorded the copyright owner complete control over all possible uses of his work. Rather, the Copyright Act grants the copyright holder "exclusive" rights to use and to authorize the use of his work in five qualified ways, including reproduction of the copyrighted work in copies. § 106. All reproductions of the work, however, are not within the exclusive domain of the copyright owner; some are in the public domain. Any individual may reproduce a copyrighted work for a "fair use"; the copyright owner does not possess the exclusive right to such a use. . . .

The Copyright Act provides the owner of a copyright with a potent arsenal of remedies against an infringer of his work, including an injunction to restrain the infringer from violating his rights, the impoundment and destruction of all reproductions of his work made in violation of his rights, a recovery of his actual damages and any additional profits realized by the infringer or a recovery of statutory damages, and attorney's fees. . . .

The two respondents in this case do not seek relief against the Betamax users who have allegedly infringed their copyrights. Moreover, this is not a class action on behalf of all copyright owners who license their works for television broadcast, and respondents have no right to invoke whatever rights other copyright holders may have to bring infringement actions based on Betamax copying of their works. As was made clear by their own evidence, the copying of the respondents' programs represents a small portion of the total use of VTR's. It is, however, the taping of respondents' own copyrighted programs that provides them with standing to charge Sony with contributory infringement. To prevail, they have the burden of proving that users of the Betamax have infringed their copyrights and that Sony should be held responsible for that infringement.

III

The Copyright Act does not expressly render anyone liable for infringement committed by another. In contrast, the Patent Act expressly brands anyone who "actively induces infringement of a patent" as an infringer, 35 U.S.C. § 271(b), and further imposes liability on certain individuals labeled "contributory" infringers, § 271(c). The absence of such express language in the copyright statute does not preclude the imposition of liability for copyright infringements on certain parties who have not themselves engaged

in the infringing activity. For vicarious liability is imposed in virtually all areas of the law, and the concept of contributory infringement is merely a species of the broader problem of identifying the circumstances in which it is just to hold one individual accountable for the actions of another.

Such circumstances were plainly present in *Kalem Co. v. Harper Brothers*, 222 U.S. 55 (1911), the copyright decision of this Court on which respondents place their principal reliance. In *Kalem*, the Court held that the producer of an unauthorized film dramatization of the copyrighted book Ben Hur was liable for his sale of the motion picture to jobbers, who in turn arranged for the commercial exhibition of the film. Justice Holmes, writing for the Court, explained:

> The defendant not only expected but invoked by advertisement the use of its films for dramatic reproduction of the story. That was the most conspicuous purpose for which they could be used, and the one for which especially they were made. If the defendant did not contribute to the infringement it is impossible to do so except by taking part in the final act. It is liable on principles recognized in every part of the law. *Id.*, at 62–63.

The use for which the item sold in *Kalem* had been "especially" made was, of course, to display the performance that had already been recorded upon it. The producer had personally appropriated the copyright owner's protected work and, as the owner of the tangible medium of expression upon which the protected work was recorded, authorized that use by his sale of the film to jobbers. But that use of the film was not his to authorize: the copyright owner possessed the exclusive right to authorize public performances of his work. Further, the producer personally advertised the unauthorized public performances, dispelling any possible doubt as to the use of the film which he had authorized.

Respondents argue that *Kalem* stands for the proposition that supplying the "means" to accomplish an infringing activity and encouraging that activity through advertisement are sufficient to establish liability for copyright infringement. This argument rests on a gross generalization that cannot withstand scrutiny. The producer in *Kalem* did not merely provide the "means" to accomplish an infringing activity; the producer supplied the work itself, albeit in a new medium of expression. Sony in the instant case does not supply Betamax consumers with respondents' works; respondents do. Sony supplies a piece of equipment that is generally capable of copying the entire range of programs that may be televised: those that are uncopyrighted, those that are copyrighted but may be copied without objection from the copyright holder, and those that the copyright holder would prefer not to have copied. The Betamax can be used to make authorized or unauthorized uses of copyrighted works, but the range of its potential use is much broader than the particular infringing use of the film Ben Hur involved in *Kalem*. *Kalem* does not support respondents' novel theory of liability.

Justice Holmes stated that the producer had "contributed" to the infringement of the copyright, and the label "contributory infringement" has been applied in a number of lower court copyright cases involving an ongoing relationship between the direct infringer and the contributory infringer at the time the infringing conduct occurred. In such cases, as in other situations in which the imposition of vicarious liability is manifestly just, the "contributory" infringer was in a position to control the use of copyrighted works by others and had authorized the use without permission from the copyright owner. This case, however, plainly does not fall in that category. The only contact between Sony and the users of the Betamax that is disclosed by this record occurred at the moment of sale. . . .

If vicarious liability is to be imposed on Sony in this case, it must rest on the fact that it has sold equipment with constructive knowledge of the fact that its customers may use that equipment to make unauthorized copies of copyrighted material. There is no precedent in the law of copyright for the imposition of vicarious liability on such a theory. . . .

The staple article of commerce doctrine must strike a balance between a copyright holder's legitimate demand for effective—not merely symbolic—protection of the statutory monopoly, and the rights of others freely to engage in substantially unrelated areas of commerce. Accordingly, the sale of copying equipment, like the sale of other articles of commerce, does not constitute contributory infringement if the product is widely used for legitimate, unobjectionable purposes. Indeed, it need merely be capable of substantial noninfringing uses.

IV

The question is thus whether the Betamax is capable of commercially significant noninfringing uses. In order to resolve that question, we need not explore *all* the different potential uses of the machine and determine whether or not they would constitute infringement. Rather, we need only consider whether on the basis of the facts as found by the District Court a significant number of them would be noninfringing. Moreover, in order to resolve this case we need not give precise content to the question of how much use is commercially significant. For one potential use of the Betamax plainly satisfies this standard, however it is understood: private, noncommercial time-shifting in the home. It does so both (A) because respondents have no right to prevent other copyright holders from authorizing it for their programs, and (B) because the District Court's factual findings reveal that even the unauthorized home time-shifting of respondents' programs is legitimate fair use.

[T]he statements constitute a finding that the evidence concerning "sports, religious, educational and other programming" was sufficient to establish a significant quantity of broadcasting whose copying is now authorized, and a significant potential for future authorized copying. That finding is amply supported by the record. . . .

If there are millions of owners of VTR's who make copies of televised sports events, religious broadcasts, and educational programs such as Mister Rogers' Neighborhood, and if the proprietors of those programs welcome the practice, the business of supplying the equipment that makes such copying feasible should not be stifled simply because the equipment is used by some individuals to make unauthorized reproductions of respondents' works. The respondents do not represent a class composed of all copyright holders. Yet a finding of contributory infringement would inevitably frustrate the interests of broadcasters in reaching the portion of their audience that is available only through time-shifting.

Of course, the fact that other copyright holders may welcome the practice of time-shifting does not mean that respondents should be deemed to have granted a license to copy their programs. Third-party conduct would be wholly irrelevant in an action for direct infringement of respondents' copyrights. But in an action for *contributory* infringement against the seller of copying equipment, the copyright holder may not prevail unless the relief that he seeks affects only his programs, or unless he speaks for virtually all copyright holders with an interest in the outcome. In this case, the record makes it perfectly clear that there are many important producers of national and local television programs who find nothing objectionable about the enlargement in the size of the television audience that results from the practice of time-shifting for private home use. The seller of the equipment that expands those producers' audiences cannot be a contributory infringer if, as is true in this case, it has had no direct involvement with any infringing activity.

B. *Unauthorized Time-Shifting*

Even unauthorized uses of a copyrighted work are not necessarily infringing. An unlicensed use of the copyright is not an infringement unless it conflicts with one of the specific exclusive rights conferred by the copyright statute. *Twentieth Century Music Corp. v. Aiken*, 422 U.S., at 154–155. Moreover, the definition of exclusive rights in § 106 of the present Act is prefaced by the words "subject to sections 107 through 118." Those sections describe a variety of uses of copyrighted material that "are not infringements of copyright" "notwithstanding the provisions of section 106." The most pertinent in this case is § 107, the legislative endorsement of the doctrine of "fair use."

That section identifies various factors that enable a court to apply an "equitable rule of reason" analysis to particular claims of infringement. Although not conclusive, the first factor requires that "the commercial or nonprofit character of an activity" be weighed in any fair use decision. If

the Betamax were used to make copies for a commercial or profit-making purpose, such use would presumptively be unfair. The contrary presumption is appropriate here, however, because the District Court's findings plainly establish that time-shifting for private home use must be characterized as a noncommercial, nonprofit activity. Moreover, when one considers the nature of a televised copyrighted audiovisual work, see 17 U.S.C. § 107(2) (1982 ed.), and that time-shifting merely enables a viewer to see such a work which he had been invited to witness in its entirety free of charge, the fact that the entire work is reproduced, see § 107(3), does not have its ordinary effect of militating against a finding of fair use.

This is not, however, the end of the inquiry because Congress has also directed us to consider "the effect of the use upon the potential market for or value of the copyrighted work." § 107(4). The purpose of copyright is to create incentives for creative effort. Even copying for noncommercial purposes may impair the copyright holder's ability to obtain the rewards that Congress intended him to have. But a use that has no demonstrable effect upon the potential market for, or the value of, the copyrighted work need not be prohibited in order to protect the author's incentive to create. The prohibition of such noncommercial uses would merely inhibit access to ideas without any countervailing benefit.

Thus, although every commercial use of copyrighted material is presumptively an unfair exploitation of the monopoly privilege that belongs to the owner of the copyright, noncommercial uses are a different matter. A challenge to a noncommercial use of a copyrighted work requires proof either that the particular use is harmful, or that if it should become widespread, it would adversely affect the potential market for the copyrighted work. Actual present harm need not be shown; such a requirement would leave the copyright holder with no defense against predictable damage. Nor is it necessary to show with certainty that future harm will result. What is necessary is a showing by a preponderance of the evidence that *some* meaningful likelihood of future harm exists. If the intended use is for commercial gain, that likelihood may be presumed.

But if it is for a noncommercial purpose, the likelihood must be demonstrated.

In this case, respondents failed to carry their burden with regard to home time-shifting. . . .

On the question of potential future harm from time-shifting, the District Court offered a more detailed analysis of the evidence. It rejected respondents' "fear that persons 'watching' the original telecast of a program will not be measured in the live audience and the ratings and revenues will decrease," by observing that current measurement technology allows the Betamax audience to be reflected. . . . It rejected respondents' prediction "that live television or movie audiences will decrease as more people watch Betamax tapes as an alternative," with the observation that "[t]here is no factual basis for [the underlying] assumption." . . . It rejected respondents' "fear that time-shifting will reduce audiences for telecast reruns," and concluded instead that "given current market practices, this should aid plaintiffs rather than harm them." . . . And it declared that respondents' suggestion that "theater or film rental exhibition of a program will suffer because of time-shift recording of that program" "lacks merit." . . . .

After completing that review, the District Court restated its overall conclusion several times, in several different ways. "Harm from time-shifting is speculative and, at best, minimal." . . . "The audience benefits from the time-shifting capability have already been discussed. It is not implausible that benefits could also accrue to plaintiffs, broadcasters, and advertisers, as the Betamax makes it possible for more persons to view their broadcasts." . . . "No likelihood of harm was shown at trial, and plaintiffs admitted that there had been no actual harm to date." . . .

The District Court's conclusions are buttressed by the fact that to the extent time-shifting expands public access to freely broadcast television programs, it yields societal benefits. . . .

When these factors are all weighed in the "equitable rule of reason" balance, we must conclude that this record amply supports the District Court's conclusion that home time-shifting is fair use. In light of the findings of the District Court regarding the state of the empirical data, it is clear that the Court of Appeals erred in holding that the statute as presently written bars such conduct.

In summary, the record and findings of the District Court lead us to two conclusions. First, Sony demonstrated a significant likelihood that substantial numbers of copyright holders who license their works for broadcast on free television would not object to having their broadcasts time-shifted by private viewers. And second, respondents failed to demonstrate that time-shifting would cause any likelihood of non-minimal harm to the potential market for, or the value of, their copyrighted works. The Betamax is, therefore, capable of substantial noninfringing uses. Sony's sale of such equipment to the general public does not constitute contributory infringement of respondents' copyrights.

V

. . . One may search the Copyright Act in vain for any sign that the elected representatives of the millions of people who watch television every day have made it unlawful to copy a program for later viewing at home, or have enacted a flat prohibition against the sale of machines that make such copying possible.

It may well be that Congress will take a fresh look at this new technology, just as it so often has examined other innovations in the past. But it is not our job to apply laws that have not yet been written. Applying the copyright statute, as it now reads, to the facts as they have been developed in this case, the judgment of the Court of Appeals must be reversed.

It is so ordered.

JUSTICE BLACKMUN, with whom JUSTICE MARSHALL, JUSTICE POWELL, and JUSTICE REHNQUIST join, dissenting

. . . The District Court in this case . . . concluded that the 1976 Act contained an implied exemption for "home-use recording." 480 F. Supp., at 444–446. The court relied primarily on the legislative history of a 1971 amendment to the 1909 Act, a reliance that this Court today does not duplicate. . . . That amendment, however, was addressed to the specific problem of commercial piracy of sound recordings. Act of Oct. 15, 1971, 85 Stat. 391 (1971 Amendment). The House Report on the 1971 Amendment, in a section entitled "Home Recording," contains the following statement:

> In approving the creation of a limited copyright in sound recordings it is the intention of the Committee that this limited copyright not grant any broader rights than are accorded to other copyright proprietors under the existing title 17. Specifically, it is not the intention of the Committee to restrain the home recording, from broadcasts or from tapes or records, of recorded performances, where the home recording is for private use and with no purpose of reproducing or otherwise capitalizing commercially on it. This practice is common and unrestrained today, and the record producers and performers would be in no different position from that of the owners of copyright in recorded musical compositions over the past 20 years. H.R. Rep. No. 92–487, p. 7 (1971) (1971 House Report).

Similar statements were made during House hearings on the bill and on the House floor, although not in the Senate proceedings. In concluding that these statements created a general exemption for home recording, the District Court, in my view, paid too little heed to the context in which the statements were made, and failed to consider the limited purpose of the 1971 Amendment and the structure of the 1909 Act.

Unlike television broadcasts and other types of motion pictures, sound recordings were not protected by copyright prior to the passage of the 1971 Amendment. Although the underlying musical work could be copyrighted, the 1909 Act provided no protection for a particular performer's rendition of the work. Moreover, copyrighted musical works that had been recorded for public distribution were subject to a "compulsory license": any person was free to record such a work upon payment of a 2-cent royalty to the copyright owner. § 1(e), 35 Stat. 1075–1076. While reproduction without payment of the royalty was an infringement under the 1909 Act, damages were limited to three times the amount of the unpaid royalty. . . . It was observed that the practical effect of these provisions was to legalize record piracy. See S. Rep. No. 92–72, p. 4 (1971); 1971 House Report 2.

In order to suppress this piracy, the 1971 Amendment extended copyright protection beyond the underlying work and to the sound recordings themselves. Congress chose, however, to provide only limited protection: owners of copyright in sound recordings were given the exclusive right "[t]o reproduce [their works] and distribute [them] to the public." 1971 Amendment, § 1(a), 85 Stat. 391 (formerly codified as 17 U.S.C. § (f)). This right was merely the right of commercial distribution. . . .

Against this background, the statements regarding home recording under the 1971 Amendment appear in a very different light. If home recording was "common and unrestrained" under the 1909 Act, see 1971 House Report 7, it was because sound recordings had no copyright protection and the owner of a copyright in the underlying musical work could collect no more than a 2-cent royalty plus 6 cents in damages for each unauthorized use. With so little at stake, it is not at all surprising that the Assistant Register "d[id] not see anybody going into anyone's home and preventing this sort of thing." 1971 House Hearings 23.

But the references to home sound recording in the 1971 Amendment's legislative history demonstrate no congressional intent to create a generalized home-use exemption from copyright protection. Congress, having recognized that the 1909 Act had been unsuccessful in controlling home sound recording, addressed only the specific problem of commercial record piracy. . . .

While the 1971 Amendment narrowed the sound recordings loophole in then existing copyright law, motion pictures and other audiovisual works have been accorded full copyright protection since at least 1912, see Act of Aug. 24, 1912, 37 Stat. 488, and perhaps before. . . . Congress continued this protection in the 1976 Act. Unlike the sound recording rights created by the 1971 Amendment, the reproduction rights associated with motion pictures under § 106(1) are not limited to reproduction for *public* distribution; the copyright owner's right to reproduce the work exists independently, and the "mere duplication of a copy may constitute an infringement even if it is never distributed."

I therefore find in the 1976 Act no implied exemption to cover the home taping of television programs, whether it be for a single copy, for private use, or for home use. Taping a copyrighted television program is infringement unless it is permitted by the fair use exemption contained in § 107 of the 1976 Act. I now turn to that issue. . . .

The doctrine of fair use has been called, with some justification, "the most troublesome in the whole law of copyright." . . . Although courts have constructed lists of factors to be considered in determining whether a particular use is fair, no fixed criteria have emerged by which that determination can be made. This Court thus far has provided no guidance. . . .

Nor did Congress provide definitive rules when it codified the fair use doctrine in the 1976 Act; it simply incorporated a list of factors "to be considered": the "purpose and character of the use," the "nature of the copyrighted work," the "amount and substantiality of the portion used," and, perhaps the most important, the "effect of the use upon the *potential* market for or value of the copyrighted work" (emphasis supplied). § 107. No particular weight, however, was assigned to any of these, and the list was not intended to be exclusive. The House and Senate Reports explain that § 107 does no more than give "statutory recognition" to the fair use doctrine; it was intended "to restate the present judicial doctrine of fair use, not to change, narrow, or enlarge it in any way." . . .

Despite this absence of clear standards, the fair use doctrine plays a crucial role in the law of copyright. The purpose of copyright protection, in the words of the Constitution, is to "promote the Progress of Science and useful Arts." Copyright is based on the belief that by granting authors the exclusive rights to reproduce their works, they are given an incentive to create, and that "encouragement of individual effort by personal gain is the best way to advance public welfare through the talents of authors and inventors in 'Science and the useful Arts.'" *Mazer v. Stein*, 347 U.S. 201, 219 (1954). The monopoly created by copyright thus rewards the individual author in order to benefit the public. . . .

There are situations, nevertheless, in which strict enforcement of this monopoly would inhibit the very "Progress of Science and useful Arts" that copyright is intended to promote. An obvious example is the researcher or scholar whose own work depends on the ability to refer to and to quote the work of prior scholars. Obviously, no author could create a new work if he were first required to repeat the research of every author who had gone before him. The scholar, like the ordinary user, of course could be left to bargain with each copyright owner for permission to quote from or refer to prior works. But there is a crucial difference between the scholar and the ordinary user. When the ordinary user decides that the owner's price is too high, and forgoes use of the work, only the individual is the loser. When the scholar forgoes the use of a prior work, not only does his own work suffer, but the public is deprived of his contribution to knowledge. . . .

A similar subsidy may be appropriate in a range of areas other than pure scholarship. The situations in which fair use is most commonly recognized are listed in § 107 itself; fair use may be found when a work is used "for purposes such as criticism, comment, news reporting, teaching, . . . scholarship, or research." . . . Each of these uses, however, reflects a common theme: each is a *productive* use, resulting in some added benefit to the public beyond that produced by the first author's work. . . .

I do not suggest, of course, that every productive use is a fair use. A finding of fair use still must depend on the facts of the individual case, and on whether, under the circumstances, it is reasonable to expect the user to bargain with the copyright owner for use of the work. The fair use doctrine must strike a balance between the dual risks created by the copyright system: on the one hand, that depriving authors of their monopoly will reduce their incentive to create, and, on the other, that granting authors a complete monopoly will reduce the creative ability of others. The inquiry is necessarily a flexible one, and the endless variety of situations that may arise precludes the formulation of exact rules. But when a user reproduces an entire work and uses it for its original purpose, with no added benefit to the public, the doctrine of fair use usually does not apply. There is then no need whatsoever to provide the ordinary user with a fair use subsidy at the author's expense.

The making of a videotape recording for home viewing is an ordinary rather than a productive use of the Studio's copyrighted works. . . .

It may be tempting, as, in my view, the Court today is tempted, to stretch the doctrine of fair use so as to permit unfettered use of this new technology in order to increase access to television programming. But such an extension risks eroding the very basis of copyright law, by depriving authors of control over their works and consequently of their incentive to create. Even in the context of highly productive educational uses, Congress has avoided this temptation; in passing the 1976 Act, Congress made it clear that off-the-air videotaping was to be permitted only in very limited situations. . . .

I recognize, nevertheless, that there are situations where permitting even an unproductive use would have no effect on the author's incentive to create, that is, where the use would not affect the value of, or the market for, the author's work. Photocopying an old newspaper clipping to send to a friend may be an example; pinning a quotation on one's bulletin board may be another. In each of these cases, the effect on the author is truly *de minimis*. Thus, even though these uses provide no benefit to the public at large, no purpose is served by preserving the author's monopoly, and the use may be regarded as fair.

Courts should move with caution, however, in depriving authors of protection from unproductive "ordinary" uses. As has been noted above, even in the case of a productive use, § 107(4) requires consideration of "the effect of the use upon the *potential* market for or value of the copyrighted work" (emphasis added). "[A] particular use which may seem to have little or no economic impact on the author's rights today can assume tremendous importance in times to come." Register's Supplementary Report 14. Although such a use may seem harmless when viewed in isolation, "[i]solated instances of minor infringements, when multiplied many times, become in the aggregate a major inroad on copyright that must be prevented." 1975 Senate Report 65.

I therefore conclude that, at least when the proposed use is an unproductive one, a copyright owner need prove only a *potential* for harm to the market for or the value of the copyrighted work. . . .

The Studios have identified a number of ways in which VTR recording could damage their copyrights. VTR recording could reduce their ability to market their works in movie theaters and through the rental or sale of prerecorded videotapes or videodiscs; it also could reduce their rerun audience, and consequently the license fees available to them for repeated showings. Moreover, advertisers may be willing to pay for only "live" viewing audiences, if they believe VTR viewers will delete commercials or if rating services are unable to measure VTR use; if this is the case, VTR recording could reduce the license fees the Studios are able to charge even for first-run showings. Library-building may raise the potential for each of the types of harm identified by the Studios, and time-shifting may raise the potential for substantial harm as well.

Although the District Court found no likelihood of harm from VTR use, 480 F. Supp., at 468, I conclude that it applied an incorrect substantive standard and misallocated the burden of proof. . . .

In this case, the Studios and their *amici* demonstrate that the advent of the VTR technology created a potential market for their copyrighted programs. That market consists of those persons who find it impossible or inconvenient to watch the programs at the time they are broadcast, and who wish to watch them at other times. These persons are willing to pay for the privilege of watching copyrighted work at their convenience, as is evidenced by the fact that they are willing to pay for VTR's and tapes; undoubtedly, most also would be willing to pay some kind of royalty to copyright holders. The Studios correctly argue that they have been deprived of the ability to exploit this sizable market.

It is thus apparent from the record and from the findings of the District Court that time-shifting does have a substantial adverse effect upon the "potential market for" the Studios' copyrighted works. Accordingly, even under the formulation of the fair use doctrine advanced by Sony, time-shifting cannot be deemed a fair use. . . .

From the Studios' perspective, the consequences of home VTR recording are the same as if a business had taped the Studios' works off the air, duplicated the tapes, and sold or rented them to members of the public for home viewing. The distinction is that home VTR users do not record for commercial advantage; the commercial benefit accrues to the manufacturer and distributors of the Betamax. I thus must proceed to discuss whether the manufacturer and distributors can be held contributorily liable if the product they sell is used to infringe.

It is well established that liability for copyright infringement can be imposed on persons other than those who actually carry out the infringing activity. . . .

The doctrine of contributory copyright infringement, however, is not well defined. One of the few attempts at definition appears in *Gershwin Publishing Corp. v. Columbia Artists Management, Inc.*, 443 F.2d 1159 (2d Cir. 1971). In that case the Second Circuit stated that "one who, with knowledge of the infringing activity, induces, causes or materially contributes to the infringing conduct of another, may be held liable as a 'contributory' infringer." *Id.*, at 1162 (footnote omitted). While I have no quarrel with this general statement, it does not easily resolve the present case; the District Court and the Court of Appeals, both purporting to apply it, reached diametrically opposite results. . . .

In absolving Sony from liability, the District Court reasoned that Sony had no direct involvement with individual Betamax users, did not participate in any off-the-air copying, and did not know that such copying was an infringement of the Studios' copyright. 480 F. Supp., at 460. I agree with the *Gershwin* court that contributory liability may be imposed even when the defendant has no formal control over the infringer. . . .

I therefore conclude that if a *significant* portion of the product's use is *noninfringing*, the manufacturers and sellers cannot be held contributorily liable for the product's infringing uses. . . . If virtually all of the product's use, however, is to

infringe, contributory liability may be imposed; if no one would buy the product for noninfringing purposes alone, it is clear that the manufacturer is purposely profiting from the infringement, and that liability is appropriately imposed. In such a case, the copyright owner's monopoly would not be extended beyond its proper bounds; the manufacturer of such a product contributes to the infringing activities of others and profits directly thereby, while providing no benefit to the public sufficient to justify the infringement. . . . The key question is not the amount of television programming that is copyrighted, but rather the amount of VTR usage that is infringing. Moreover, the parties and their *amici* have argued vigorously about both the amount of television programming that is covered by copyright and the amount for which permission to copy has been given. The proportion of VTR recording that is infringing is ultimately a question of fact, and the District Court specifically declined to make findings on the "percentage of legal versus illegal home-use recording." 480 F. Supp., at 468. In light of my view of the law, resolution of this factual question is essential. I therefore would remand the case for further consideration of this by the District Court. . . .

The Court has adopted an approach very different from the one I have outlined. It is my view that the Court's approach alters dramatically the doctrines of fair use and contributory infringement as they have been developed by Congress and the courts. Should Congress choose to respond to the Court's decision, the old doctrines can be resurrected. As it stands, however, the decision today erodes much of the coherence that these doctrines have struggled to achieve.

The Court's disposition of the case turns on its conclusion that time-shifting is a fair use. Because both parties agree that time-shifting is the primary use of VTR's, that conclusion, if correct, would settle the issue of Sony's liability under almost any definition of contributory infringement. The Court concludes that time-shifting is fair use for two reasons. Each is seriously flawed.

The Court's first reason for concluding that time-shifting is fair use is its claim that many copyright holders have no objection to time-shifting, and that "respondents have no right to prevent other copyright holders from authorizing it for their programs." . . . The Court explains that a finding of contributory infringement would "inevitably frustrate the interests of broadcasters in reaching the portion of their audience that is available only through time-shifting." . . . Such reasoning, however, simply confuses the question of liability with the difficulty of fashioning an appropriate remedy. It may be that an injunction prohibiting the sale of VTR's would harm the interests of copyright holders who have no objection to others making copies of their programs. But such concerns should and would be taken into account in fashioning an appropriate remedy once liability has been found. Remedies may well be available that would not interfere with authorized time-shifting at all. The Court of Appeals mentioned the possibility of a royalty payment that would allow VTR sales and time-shifting to continue unabated, and the parties may be able to devise other narrowly tailored remedies. Sony may be able, for example, to build a VTR that enables broadcasters to scramble the signal of individual programs and "jam" the unauthorized recording of them. Even were an appropriate remedy not available at this time, the Court should not misconstrue copyright holders' rights in a manner that prevents enforcement of them when, through development of better techniques, an appropriate remedy becomes available.

The Court's second stated reason for finding that Sony is not liable for contributory infringement is its conclusion that even unauthorized time-shifting is fair use. . . . This conclusion is even more troubling. The Court begins by suggesting that the fair use doctrine operates as a general "equitable rule of reason." That interpretation mischaracterizes the doctrine, and simply ignores the language of the statute. Section 107 establishes the fair use doctrine "for purposes such as criticism, comment, news reporting, teaching, . . . scholarship, or research." These are all productive uses. It is true that the legislative history states repeatedly that the doctrine must be applied flexibly on a case-by-case basis, but those references were only in the context of productive uses. Such a limitation on fair use

comports with its purpose, which is to facilitate the creation of new works. There is no indication that the fair use doctrine has any application for purely personal consumption on the scale involved in this case, and the Court's application of it here deprives fair use of the major cohesive force that has guided evolution of the doctrine in the past. . . .

8.40   Visual Copying

When a story line is allegedly stolen, comparisons can be made between the plots, characters, and other incidents in the original and offending works. The allegation that the tone and other stylings of the visual depiction have been copied present greater complications. Courts deal with these latter problems in motion pictures, television programming and advertisements, and video games. Although courts have been slow to grant relief over visual infringements, finding in most cases that visual impressions are ideas not within copyright protection, courts have left open the possibility that the most aggregious borrowings will result in violations. In fact, liability is found in some of the cases discussed below. The analysis concentrates first on cases in motion pictures and television (Section 8.41) and then video games (Section 8.42).

8.41   Films and Television

In *Warner Brothers v. Film Ventures International,* Warner expressly disavows substantial similarity between the story and plot of its movie *The Exorcist* and Film Ventures' *Beyond the Door.* Warner's complaint instead concerns the central characters in the two movies, the visual effects used, and the advertisements for *Beyond the Door.* The court in response pays particular attention to claims concerning the visual effects, although it ultimately denies relief on those grounds.

In contrast, in *Sid & Marty Krofft v. McDonald's,* the court is persuaded that the visual similarities between Krofft's H. R. Pufnstuf series and the defendant's depictions of McDonaldland and Mayor Mc-Cheese are actionable. Particular attention should be paid to the court's articulation of the "extrinsic" and "intrinsic" tests to determine if visual imagery has been illegally copied.

Warner Bros., Inc. v. Film Ventures International, 403 F. Supp. 522 (C.D. Cal. 1975)

WILLIAMS, J.

Plaintiffs have produced a film *The Exorcist* which has met with great public acclaim and has been said to be the most terrifying motion picture ever made. The producers contend that the film was produced at a cost of over $10 million and has grossed over $100 million by exhibiting it to more than 100 million viewers world-wide. In this action, plaintiffs sue the distributors and exhibitors of another film entitled *Beyond the Door* (hereinafter *Beyond*) claiming that it infringes copyrightable subject matter contained in *The Exorcist.*

William Peter Blatty wrote the novel *The Exorcist* and then assigned the film rights to plaintiffs and assisted in producing the photoplay based upon the book. It concerns the demonic possession of the character Regan, a 12-year-old girl, and the performance of the religious ritual of exorcism to rid her of the spell when medical science fails to do so. The underlying theme includes the battle between good and evil and how faith can overcome the possession and bring about triumph over the devil. In developing this, there was considerable use of symbolism.

The motion picture shows the progression of physical and emotional infirmities which slowly overcome Regan until she is eventually transformed into a horrid, foul-mouthed, vomiting monster with super-human strength.

The theme of *The Exorcist* deals with the classic battle of good versus evil. Regan's mother, having sought the aid of medical science to no avail, turns to the Catholic Church, and two Jesuit priests are designated to conduct an exorcism. After a long ordeal and at the cost of their own lives, the priests succeed in casting the demon from the girl who then returns to her childlike composure.

Beyond also portrays demonic possession, but of a mature pregnant woman, Jessica, and to a lesser extent to one of her children. While a religious theme and the element of faith dominate plaintiffs' film, it has no part in the development of *Beyond,* a film centered upon the use of the supernatural or occult powers to rid the possessed person of the forces of evil.

Before the Court is plaintiffs' motion for a preliminary injunction to enjoin the alleged infringement of *The Exorcist;* to prevent future exhibition of *Beyond;* to prevent the use by defendants of advertising material which plaintiffs contend infringes a press book it prepared to exploit *The Exorcist,* and to compel defendants to deliver up its allegedly infringing material.

At the outset it is important to note that Warner Bros. does not claim that there is any similarity of story or plot in the two films, for indeed there is not. Rather, plaintiffs claim that the infringement is of the character of Regan and of the cinematic effects used in *The Exorcist* as a means of story expression. These effects include distinctive sounds, special lighting effects, levitation of Regan's body and the bed she is confined to, the spinning of the girl's head 360° and the rolling back of her eyes with pupils covered.

Both films depict objects such as chairs and tables flying through the air and show dresser drawers opening and shutting as a result of some unseen force. Both also show human bodies being propelled with great force across a room. Both possessed persons undergo voice changes which you are to believe is the devil speaking from within, and both persons spew vomit at those attempting to perform the ritual. In *Beyond,* the character Jessica reacts to the spell by experiencing an abbreviated pregnancy and at one point one of her eyes moves back and forth while the other stares straight ahead. In another scene her head turns approximately 180°, or half the spin effected by Regan. In *The Exorcist* religious techniques based upon faith are used to drive the devil from the possessed girl but no similar religious theme finds its way into *Beyond*.

Blatty first learned of the phenomenon of exorcism when an actual happening of a possession was described to him by a Jesuit priest in college. Neither Blatty nor plaintiffs have the right to claim a monopoly in giving expression to this phenomenon. When one thinks of a possessed person he thinks of a person full of inner turmoil and in a long struggle with an evil spirit. The idea seems to be one of the inner person fighting the devil possessing him. One means of giving expression to this characterization is to show the possessed person writhing, vomiting and contorting in a frenzied manner and undergoing rapid physical transformation. The producers of both *The Exorcist* and *Beyond* have used the commonly accepted physical ways of depicting the struggle of the possessed one, and some of the means used are common to each depiction, but neither means is original or subject to copyright. While *The Exorcist* was expensively produced with the aid of costly special effects and makeup technicians and *Beyond* is an inferior picture with a low production budget, the latter cannot be said to have trampled upon cinematic techniques which were the exclusive property of plaintiffs. . . .

Character Protectibility

Plaintiffs urge that in the character Regan they have a property that is protectible under the copyright laws and which defendant has copied with its character Jessica. Ordinarily, characters in a play are not protectible. . . . Cases that uphold copyright protection of a character are those where the character was distinctively delineated by the author and such delineation was copied. *Nimmer on Copyrights*, § 30. . . .

In *Warner Brothers Pictures, Inc. v. Columbia Broadcasting System, Inc.*, 216 F.2d 945 (9th Cir., 1954) the Court held that the Sam Spade character was not protectible and found that no character is protectible under copyright law unless "the character really constitutes the story being told" and is not merely a "chessman in the game of telling the story."

The Walt Disney Mickey Mouse cartoon character was held protectible under this test in *Walt Disney Productions v. Air Pirates*, 345 F. Supp. 108 (N.D.Cal. 1972) because the "plot of the piece not only centers around the character but is quite subordinated to the character's role (and) . . . the principal appeal of each of the plaintiff's work to the primary audience of children for which they were intended lies with the character and nothing else." P. 113. That Court found that the cartoon character(s) as developed by Disney had achieved a high degree of recognition and identification that was protectible.

I cannot conclude that the story *The Exorcist* was subordinated to the character Regan. Even, arguendo, if this were held to be true, there is substantial difference between the character of Regan, a demure child who turns into a profane monster and whose possession is driven from her by religious means, and Jessica, a mature woman in the early stages of pregnancy whose possession exemplifies itself by a more rapid than normal development of her fetus, and whose possession is not expelled by religious faith. . . .

Since plaintiffs do not contend that *Beyond* copies the plot of *The Exorcist* it contends it is damaged because defendant's picture has appropriated the manifestations, visual and aural presentation and special effects which, acting together, blend to create the essence of the motion picture *The Exorcist*. Plaintiffs assert that it is the cinematic elements such as sound effects, lighting, levitation and makeup design by which the Blatty novel was given expression into another art form by the film maker and that this was copied by defendant's film.

Defendants contend that the use of flickering lights, raucous "haunted-house type" noises, flying bodies and objects about a room, levitation and the changing of human features from placid to gruesome are theatrical tricks which have for many years been used in other films and stage plays. They deny that *Beyond* has attempted to group the use of its special effects in a manner that shows substantial similarity to the grouping used in *The Exorcist*. To view the two pictures is to find substantial merit to this argument. It is also evident that *Beyond* does not make a blatant effort to use a character similar to that used in *The*

Exorcist or to duplicate the phenomenon contrived to rid the character of the evil spirit. In *The Exorcist* religious techniques based upon faith are used to drive the devil from the possessed girl; no similar religious theme finds its way into the *Beyond* story.

Press Book Infringement

Plaintiffs claim violation of its copyrights in certain advertisements used in promotion of *The Exorcist*. One advertisement (Plaintiff's exhibit C) shows a door partially opened with light coming through into a dark room. Defendant's advertisement (Plaintiffs' exhibit E) shows substantially the same door with the same effect of light entering a darkened room. The only difference between the two advertisements is the addition of the possessed woman's face in the defendant's advertisement and the different titles. Otherwise the scenes are identical and obviously infringes plaintiffs' rights if this advertisement was properly copyrighted.

Defendant claims that since the advertisement was first published on February 15, 1974 in the *Los Angeles Times* without a valid copyright mark, defendant's use of the door cannot be said to infringe. Plaintiffs admit that no copyright mark appeared on the February 15th advertisement but that a valid copyright for the Warner Bros. press book containing this advertisement was obtained on February 17th, 1974. They further assert that the copyright which the *Los Angeles Times* has over all of its material protects plaintiffs' advertisement. I agree with this contention and grant an injunction against further use by defendant of the door advertisement. *Nimmer*, § 24.41 at p. 109; 17 U.S.C. § 3.

Plaintiffs bring one further complaint which has merit. Defendants, in advertising the picture *Beyond* use a letter "T" in the second word of the title which is intentionally designed to resemble a crucifix. *The Exorcist* has a basic religious theme where through faith the evil spirit is driven from Regan by priests. A crucifix is used as a part of the ritual. In an earlier scene, Regan, crazed by the possession, abuses herself sexually with a crucifix. Thus a crucifix is given great importance by the producers of plaintiffs' film in the depiction of the girl's agony and in the performance of the reli-

gious rite. The theatre public is aware of this. It is therefore a practice of unfair competition on the part of the exhibitors of *Beyond*, a picture having no religious theme and which at no time portrays a crucifix, to prominently (or at all) display a crucifix in its advertising of the picture. There is thus created a suggestion that *Beyond* is a sequel to *The Exorcist* and possibly that it was produced by the same craftsmen who skillfully produced *The Exorcist*, and that it might be a film of the superior quality of *The Exorcist*, which it is not. The defendants are directed to forthwith withdraw the use in any way or manner the advertisement or any other display of the name *Beyond the Door* using a cross or crucifix or any elongated form of the letter "T" as contained in the advertisement now in use and of the open door advertisement. Such discontinuance of the use of these or any similarly deceptive ads shall remain in full force and effect until the further order of this Court.

The petition to enjoin the continued exhibition of *Beyond* is denied but defendants are enjoined from the continued use of the advertisements mentioned hereinbefore.

Sid & Marty Krofft Television Productions, Inc. v. McDonald's Corp., 562 F.2d 1157 (9th Cir. 1977)

CARTER, J.

This is a copyright infringement action. Plaintiffs Sid and Marty Krofft Television Productions, Inc., and Sid and Marty Krofft Productions, Inc. were awarded $50,000.00 in their action against defendants McDonald's Corporation and Needham, Harper & Steers, Inc. Defendants were found to have infringed plaintiffs' "H. R. Pufnstuf" children's television show by the production of their "McDonaldland" television commercials. . . .

Defendants cross-appeal. They contend that their television commercials did not infringe upon plaintiffs' television series as a matter of law. To find infringement, they suggest, would abridge their first amendment rights. . . .

Facts

In 1968, Sid and Marty Krofft were approached by the NBC television network to create a children's television program for exhibition on Saturday morning. The Kroffts spent the next year creating the "H. R. Pufnstuf" television show, which was introduced on NBC in September 1969. The series included several fanciful costumed characters, as well as a boy named Jimmy, who lived in a fantasyland called "Living Island," which was inhabited by moving trees and talking books. The television series became extremely popular and generated a line of "H. R. Pufnstuf" products and endorsements.

In early 1970, Marty Krofft, the President of both Krofft Television and Krofft Productions and producer of the show, was contacted by an executive from Needham, Harper & Steers, Inc., an advertising agency. He was told that Needham was attempting to get the advertising account of McDonald's hamburger restaurant chain and wanted to base a proposed campaign to McDonald's on the "H. R. Pufnstuf" characters. The executive wanted to know whether the Kroffts would be interested in working with Needham on a project of this type.

Needham and the Kroffts were in contact by telephone six or seven more times. By a letter dated August 31, 1970, Needham stated it was going forward with the idea of a McDonaldland advertising campaign based on the "H. R. Pufnstuf" series. It acknowledged the need to pay the Kroffts a fee for preparing artistic designs and engineering plans. Shortly thereafter, Marty Krofft telephoned Needham only to be told that the advertising campaign had been cancelled.

In fact, Needham had already been awarded McDonald's advertising account and was proceeding with the McDonaldland project. Former employees of the Kroffts were hired to design and construct the costumes and sets for McDonaldland. Needham also hired the same voice expert who supplied all of the voices for the "Pufnstuf" characters to supply some of the voices for the McDonaldland characters. In January 1971, the first of the McDonaldland commercials was broadcast on network television. They continue to be broadcast.

Prior to the advent of the McDonaldland advertising campaign, plaintiffs had licensed the use of the "H. R. Pufnstuf" characters and elements to the manufacturers of toys, games, lunch boxes,

and comic books. In addition, the "H. R. Pufnstuf" characters were featured in Kellogg's cereal commercials and used by the Ice Capades. After the McDonaldland campaign, which included the distribution of toys and games, plaintiffs were unable to obtain new licensing arrangements or extend existing ones. In the case of the Ice Capades, the "H. R. Pufnstuf" characters were actually replaced by the McDonaldland characters. . . .

The three week jury trial began on November 27, 1973. The jurors were shown for their consideration on the question of infringement: (1) two "H. R. Pufnstuf" television episodes; (2) various items of H. R. Pufnstuf merchandise, such as toys, games, and comic books; (3) several 30 and 60 second McDonaldland television commercials; and (4) various items of McDonaldland merchandise distributed by McDonald's, such as toys and puzzles. The jury was instructed that it was not to consider defendants' *profits* in determining damages, but could consider the *value of use* by the defendants of plaintiffs' work.

A verdict in favor of plaintiffs was returned and damages of $50,000.00 assessed. After the verdict, the parties briefed the question of whether plaintiffs were entitled to additional monetary recovery in the form of profits or statutory "in lieu" damages. The district court denied plaintiffs' claim for such relief. The court found that these matters were properly for the jury to consider so that it would not exercise its discretion in hearing further evidence. These appeals followed.

I. Infringement

Proof of Infringement

. . . The real task in a copyright infringement action, then, is to determine whether there has been copying of the expression of an idea rather than just the idea itself. "[N]o one infringes, unless he descends so far into what is concrete [in a work] as to invade . . . [its] expression." *National Comics Publication v. Fawcett Publications*, 191 F.2d 594, 600 (2d Cir. 1951). Only this expression may be protected and only it may be infringed.

The difficulty comes in attempting to distill the

unprotected idea from the protected expression. No court or commentator in making this search has been able to improve upon Judge Learned Hand's famous "abstractions test" articulated in *Nichols v. Universal Pictures Corporation*, 45 F.2d 119 (2d Cir. 1930), *cert. denied*, 282 U.S. 902, 51 S.Ct. 216, 75 L.Ed. 795 (1931):

> Upon any work, and especially upon a play, a great number of patterns of increasing generality will fit equally well, as more and more of the incident is left out. The last may perhaps be no more than the most general statement of what the play is about, and at times might consist of only its title; but there is a point in this series of abstractions where they are no longer protected, since otherwise the playwright could prevent the use of his "ideas," to which, apart from their expression, his property is never extended. 45 F.2d at 121.

The test for infringement therefore has been given a new dimension. There must be ownership of the copyright and access to the copyrighted work. But there also must be substantial similarity not only of the general ideas but of the expressions of those ideas as well. Thus two steps in the analytic process are implied by the requirement of substantial similarity.

The determination of whether there is substantial similarity in ideas may often be a simple one. Returning to the example of the nude statue, the idea there embodied is a simple one—a plaster recreation of a nude human figure. A statue of a horse or a painting of a nude would not embody this idea and therefore could not infringe. The test for similarity of ideas is still a factual one, to be decided by the trier of fact. . . .

We shall call this the "extrinsic test." It is extrinsic because it depends not on the responses of the trier of fact, but on specific criteria which can be listed and analyzed. Such criteria include the type of artwork involved, the materials used, the subject matter, and the setting for the subject. Since it is an extrinsic test, analytic dissection and expert testimony are appropriate. Moreover, this question may often be decided as a matter of law.

The determination of when there is substantial similarity between the forms of expression is necessarily more subtle and complex. As Judge Hand candidly observed, "Obviously, no princi-

ple can be stated as to when an imitator has gone beyond copying the 'idea,' and has borrowed its 'expression.' Decisions must therefore inevitably be ad hoc." *Peter Pan Fabrics, Inc. v. Martin Weiner Corp.*, 274 F.2d 487, 489 (2d Cir. 1960). If there is substantial similarity in ideas, then the trier of fact must decide whether there is substantial similarity in the expressions of the ideas so as to constitute infringement.

The test to be applied in determining whether there is substantial similarity in expressions shall be labeled an intrinsic one—depending on the response of the ordinary reasonable person. . . . It is intrinsic because it does not depend on the type of external criteria and analysis which marks the extrinsic test. As this court stated in *Twentieth Century-Fox Film Corp. v. Stonesifer*, 140 F.2d 579, 582 (9th Cir. 1944):

> The two works involved in this appeal should be considered and tested, not hypercritically or with meticulous scrutiny, but by the observations and impressions of the average reasonable reader and spectator.

Because this is an intrinsic test, analytic dissection and expert testimony are not appropriate.

This same type of bifurcated test was announced in *Arnstein v. Porter*, 154 F.2d 464, 468–69 (2d Cir. 1946), *cert. denied*, 330 U.S. 851, 67 S.Ct. 1096, 91 L.Ed. 1294 (1947). The court there identified two separate elements essential to a plaintiff's suit for infringement: copying and unlawful appropriation. Under the *Arnstein* doctrine, the distinction is significant because of the different tests involved.

> [T]he trier of fact must determine whether the similarities are sufficient to prove copying. On this issue, analysis ("dissection") is relevant, and the testimony of experts may be received to aid the trier of facts. . . . If copying is established, then only does there arise the second issue, that of illicit copying (unlawful appropriation). On that issue . . . the test is the response of the ordinary lay hearer; accordingly, on that issue, "dissection" and expert testimony are irrelevant. 154 F.2d at 468 (footnotes omitted).

We believe that the court in *Arnstein* was alluding to the idea-expression dichotomy which we make explicit today. When the court in *Arnstein* refers to "copying" which is not itself an infringement, it must be suggesting copying merely of the work's idea, which is not protected by the copyright. To constitute an infringement, the copying must reach the point of "unlawful appropriation," or the copying of the protected expression itself. We analyze this distinction in terms both of the elements involved—idea and expression—and of the tests to be used—extrinsic and intrinsic—in an effort to clarify the issues involved.

The Tests Applied

In the context of this case, the distinction between these tests is important. Defendants do not dispute the fact that they copied the idea of plaintiffs' "Pufnstuf" television series—basically a fantasyland filled with diverse and fanciful characters in action. They argue, however, that the expressions of this idea are too dissimilar for there to be an infringement. They come to this conclusion by dissecting the constituent parts of the "Pufnstuf" series—characters, setting, and plot—and pointing out the dissimilarities between these parts and those of the McDonaldland commercials.

This approach ignores the idea-expression dichotomy alluded to in *Arnstein* and analyzed today. Defendants attempt to apply an extrinsic test by the listing of dissimilarities in determining whether the expression they used was substantially similar to the expression used by plaintiffs'. That extrinsic test is inappropriate; an intrinsic test must here be used. . . .

Since the intrinsic test for expression is uniquely suited for determination by the trier of fact, this court must be reluctant to reverse it. . . . As a finding of fact, a conclusion as to the question of copying is subject to the "clearly erroneous" standard. Fed. R. Civ. P. 52(a). But it follows that this court will be less likely to find clear error when the subjective test for copying of expression has been applied.

The present case demands an even more intrinsic determination because both plaintiffs' and defendants' works are directed to an audience of children. This raises the particular factual issue of the impact of the respective works upon the minds and imaginations of young people. . . .

The "H. R. Pufnstuf" series became the most popular children's show on Saturday morning television. This success led several manufacturers of children's goods to use the "Pufnstuf" characters. It is not surprising, then, that McDonald's hoped to duplicate this peculiar appeal to children in its commercials. It was in the recognition of the subjective and unpredictable nature of children's responses that defendants opted to re-create the "H. R. Pufnstuf" format rather than use an original and unproven approach.

Defendants would have this court ignore that intrinsic quality which they recognized to embark on an extrinsic analysis of the two works. For example, in discussing the principal characters—Pufnstuf and Mayor McCheese—defendants point out:

> "Pufnstuf" wears what can only be described as a yellow and green dragon suit with a blue cummerband from which hangs a medal which says "mayor." "McCheese" wears a version of pink formal dress—"tails"—with knicker trousers. He has a typical diplomat's sash on which is written "mayor," the "M" consisting of the McDonald's trademark of an "M" made of golden arches.

So not only do defendants remove the characters from the setting, but dissect further to analyze the clothing, colors, features, and mannerisms of each character. We do not believe that the ordinary reasonable person, let alone a child, viewing these works will even notice that Pufnstuf is wearing a cummerbund while Mayor McCheese is wearing a diplomat's sash. . . .

We have viewed representative samples of both the "H. R. Pufnstuf" show and McDonaldland commercials. It is clear to us that defendants' works are substantially similar to plaintiffs'. They have captured the "total concept and feel" of the "Pufnstuf" show. . . . We would so conclude even if we were sitting as the triers of fact. There is no doubt that the findings of the jury in this case are not clearly erroneous.

Unity of Idea and Expression

Defendants argue that dissection is proper and that duplication or near identity is necessary because the competing works are *things*, rather than dramatic works. They cite numerous cases in which infringement was found because the defendants' works were nearly identical to those of the plaintiffs. . . . Defendants fail to perceive, however, that near identity may be required in some cases not because the works are things, but because the expression of those works and the idea of those works are indistinguishable. . . .

The idea and the expression will coincide when the expression provides nothing new or additional over the idea. Thus, the expression of a jeweled bee pin contains nothing new over the idea of a jeweled bee pin. Returning to our own example, the idea of a plaster statue of a nude will probably coincide with the expression of that idea when an inexpensive manufacturing process is used. There will be no separately distinguishable features in the statue's expression over the idea of a plaster nude statue.

The complexity and artistry of the expression of an idea will separate it from even the most banal idea. Michaelangelo's David is, as an idea, no more than a statue of a nude male. But no one would question the proposition that if a copyrighted work it would deserve protection even against the poorest of imitations. This is because so much more was added in the expression over the idea. . . .

No standard more demanding than that of substantial similarity should be imposed here. This is not a case where the idea is indistinguishable as a matter of law from the expression of that idea. . . . The expression inherent in the "H. R. Pufnstuf" series differs markedly from its relatively simple idea. The characters each have developed personalities and particular ways of interacting with one another and their environment. The physical setting also has several unique features.

Lest we fall prey to defendants' invitation to dissect the works, however, we should remember that it is the *combination* of many different elements which may command copyright protection because of its particular subjective quality. . . .

Copyright and the First Amendment

Defendants argue that the first amendment operates in this case to limit the protection for plaintiff's work. They seem to suggest that a more demanding standard than that of substantial similarity should be imposed, and that the threshold question about copying becomes one of "constitutional fact" to be reviewed de novo on appeal. Defendants attempt to analogize the copyright area to those of obscenity and defamation in suggesting that prior law must be modified to accommodate expanding first amendment rights. . . .

With the law of copyright permitting the free use of ideas, it is not surprising that the few courts addressing the issue have not permitted defendants who copy a work's expression to hide behind the first amendment. . . .

There may be certain rare instances when first amendment considerations will operate to limit copyright protection for graphic expressions of newsworthy events. For example, in *Time, Inc. v. Bernard Geis Associates*, 293 F. Supp. 130 (S.D.N.Y. 1968), Life magazine sued a historian for copying frames of the Zapruder films of the assassination of John F. Kennedy. Although the court did not expressly invoke the first amendment, it did justify the defendant's right to copy frames of the film on the ground of the "public interest in having the fullest information available on the murder of President Kennedy." *Id.* at 146. Plaintiffs' work in this case is neither a graphic expression nor concerning newsworthy events. Therefore, no first amendment considerations operate. . . .

Access

In addition to substantial similarity, a plaintiff must show access in order to prove infringement. . . .

In this case, representatives of Needham actually visited the Kroffts' headquarters in Los Angeles to discuss the engineering and design work necessary to produce the McDonaldland commercials. They did this *after* they had been awarded the contract by McDonald's and apparently with no intention to work with the Kroffts. We believe that this degree of access justifies a lower standard of proof to show substantial similarity. Since the subjective test applies, it is impossible to quantify this standard. But there is no question it is met here. . . .

NOTE ───────────────────

1. The court in *Sid & Marty Krofft Television v. McDonald's Corporation* also considered at length the appropriate measure of damages in copyright claims of the type brought by the Kroffts. Three separate opinions on the damages issues appear in the report. See 562 F.2d at 1172 *et seq.*

8.42 Video Games

The issue of visual copying becomes even more complex when applied to video games. On the surface, the ocular comparisons of two games seems to proceed as one would with movies or television depictions. There are sequences of events and moving characters, making analysis appropriate under 17 U.S.C. § 102 (a) (6) pertaining to "motion pictures and other audiovisual works." Arguably, this section and cases considered thereunder are better consulted than those of 17 U.S.C. § 102(a) (5), which protects "pictorial, graphic and sculptural works." Although game boards have been analyzed under this latter section, video games emphasize movement, sequencing, and change.

Video games are not simply movies, however, and blind adherence to visual imagery problems raised in motion picture cases may not address the similarity comparisons needed for video games. In *Atari v. Amusement World*, the court listed both the similarities and differences between two games: Atari's "Asteroids" and Amusement World's "Meteors." Even when there were substantial similarities, the court noted the inevitability of many of these similarities because they were derived from the idea rather than the expression. The court held there was no infringement.

Conversely, the U.S. Court of Appeals for the Seventh Circuit did find a likelihood of copyright infringement in *Atari v. North American Philips Consumer Electronics.* Atari alleged that North American's "K. C. Munchkin" video game infringed on Atari's "Pac-Man." The court was obviously influenced by the developmental history of the Munchkin game, noting North American's awareness of "Pac-Man." Thus, the court reversed the lower court judge who had found no infringement because of substantial differences between Pac-Man and Munchkin.

A third case, not reproduced below, also involved Atari protecting its "Pac-Man" game, this time against a video game called "Jawbreaker." In *Atari, Inc. v. Williams*, 1981–83 Copyright L. Dec., ¶ 25,412 at 17,383 (E.D. Cal., Dec. 28, 1981), the decision went against Atari, under much the same rationale as in *Atari v. Amusement World*.

From these cases, one can conclude that at some point the visual imagery is copyrightable; but just what the copyright covers is not conclusively established. Courts have a difficult time putting a secure handle on how to deal with visual copying. Even so, the following two *Atari* cases do plunge into the process of analysis necessary for coping with these problems.

───────────────────

Atari, Inc. v. Amusement World, Inc., 547 F. Supp. 222 (D. Md. 1981)

Young, J.

Atari, Inc., holder of a copyright on the electronic video game "Asteroids," seeks to enjoin defendants Amusement World, Inc., and its president Stephen Holniker, from manufacturing or distributing any product in violation of plaintiff's copyright.

In October 1979, plaintiff Atari introduced "Asteroids," a video game in which the player commands a spaceship through a barrage of space rocks and enemy spaceships. Plaintiff has sold 70,000 copyrighted "Asteroids" games for a total of $125,000,000, making "Asteroids" the largest-selling video game ever (not counting sales in Japan).

Defendant Amusement World, Inc., is a small closely-held corporation employing a total of five people. Its business has consisted largely of repair work on coin-operated games, but recently it has attempted to enter the lucrative video business by producing and distributing a video game called "Meteors."

On March 13, 1981, plaintiff first became aware that defendants were selling "Meteors," which plaintiff alleges is substantially similar to "Asteroids." On March 18, 1981, plaintiff sent defendants a cease and desist letter, which defendants have ignored. Plaintiff then filed suit and now seeks injunctive relief.

The Games

Each of the two video games is contained in a cabinet with a display screen and a control panel for the player. The course of the game is controlled by a computer program, which has been chemically implanted in printed circuit boards inside the cabinet. When no one is playing the game, the machine is in the so-called "attract mode," in which there appears on the display screen an explanation of the game and/or a short simulated game sequence, which is intended to attract customers. Placing a coin in the machine causes it to go into "play mode," in which the computer program generates scenes of dangerous situations, to which the player responds by pressing various buttons on the control panel.

The principle of the two games is basically the same. The player commands a spaceship, represented by a small symbol that appears in the center of the screen. During the course of the game, symbols representing various sized rocks drift across the screen, and, at certain intervals, symbols representing enemy spaceships enter and move around the screen and attempt to shoot the player's spaceship. Four control buttons allow the player to rotate his ship clockwise or counterclockwise, to move the ship forward, and to fire a weapon. A variety of appropriate sounds accompany the firing of weapons and the destruction of rocks and spaceships.

Many of the design features of the two games are similar or identical. In both games:

(1) There are three sizes of rocks.

(2) The rocks appear in waves, each wave being composed initially of larger rocks.

(3) Larger rocks move more slowly than smaller ones.

(4) When hit, a large rock splits into two medium rocks, a medium rock splits into two small ones, and a small rock disappears.

(5) When a rock hits the player's spaceship, the ship is destroyed.

(6) There are two sizes of enemy spaceships.

(7) The larger enemy spaceship is an easier target than the smaller one.

(8) The player's ship and enemy ships shoot projectiles.

(9) When a spaceship's projectiles hit a rock or another ship, the latter is destroyed immediately.

(10) The destruction of any rock or spaceship is accompanied by a symbol of an explosion.

(11) When an enemy spaceship is on the screen, the player hears a beeping tone.

(12) There is a two-tone beeping noise in the background throughout the game, and the tempo of this noise increases as the game progresses.

(13) The player gets several spaceships for his quarter. The number of ships remaining is displayed with the player's score.

(14) The score is displayed in the upper left corner for one player and the upper right and left corners for two players.

(15) The control panels are painted in red, white, and blue.

(16) Four control buttons, from left to right, rotate the player's spaceship counterclockwise, rotate it clockwise, move it forward, and fire the weapon.

(17) When a player presses the "thrust" button, his spaceship moves forward and when he releases the button the ship begins to slow down gradually (although it stops more quickly in "Meteors").

(18) The player gets an extra spaceship if he scores 10,000 points.

(19) Points are awarded on an increasing scale for shooting (a) large rock, (b) medium rock, (c) small rock, (d) large alien craft, (e) small alien craft.

(20) When all rocks are destroyed a new wave of large rocks appears.

(21) Each new wave of rocks has progressively more large rocks than the previous wave to increase the challenge of the game.

(22) A general overhead view of the battle field is presented.

There are also a number of differences between the games:

(1) "Meteors" is in color, while "Asteroids" is in black and white.

(2) The symbols for rocks and spaceships in "Meteors" are shaded to appear three-dimensional, unlike the flat, schematic figures in "Asteroids."

(3) The rocks in "Meteors" appear to tumble as they move across the screen.

(4) "Meteors" has a background that looks like distant stars.

(5) At the beginning of "Meteors," the player's spaceship is shown blasting off the earth, whereas "Asteroids" begins with the player's spaceship in outer space.

(6) The player's spaceship in "Meteors" rotates faster.

(7) The player's spaceship in "Meteors" fires faster and can fire continuously, unlike the player's spaceship in "Asteroids," which can fire only bursts of projectiles.

(8) The pace of the "Meteors" game is faster at all stages.

(9) In "Meteors," after the player's spaceship is destroyed, when the new spaceship appears on the screen, the game resumes at the same pace as immediately before the last ship was destroyed; in "Asteroids" the game resumes at a slower pace.

The necessary elements for copyright infringement have been stated succinctly in 3 Nimmer, *The Law of Copyright*, § 13.01:

> Reduced to most fundamental terms, there are only two elements necessary to the plaintiff's case in an infringement action: ownership of the copyright by the plaintiff, and copying by the defendant.

Ownership of the Copyright

. . . Defendants challenge the copyrightability of plaintiff's video game. However, the "Asteroids" game clearly fits the Act's definitions of copyrightable material. The Act includes among the types of works of authorship that may be copyrighted "motion pictures and other audiovisual works." 17 U.S.C. § 102(a)(6). . . .

Defendant contends that plaintiff has not properly copyrighted the "Asteroids" game, arguing that the original work of authorship is the computer program, as embodied in the printed circuit board. Plaintiff filed a videotape of what appeared on the display screen during one of an infinite number of possible game sequences with the copyright office, rather than the printed circuit board. Defendant argues that this registration affords no protection for the underlying computer program/printed circuit board.

Defendants' analysis is faulty, because it fails to distinguish between the work and the medium in which it is fixed. In order to receive a copyright, a work must be both copyrightable (that is, it must fit one of the definitions of a copyrightable work) and fixed in a tangible medium of expression. 17 U.S.C. § 102(a). Plaintiff's "work," the thing that plaintiff has created and desires to protect, is the visual presentation of the "Asteroids" game. That work is copyrightable as an audiovisual work and as a motion picture. 17 U.S.C. § 101. . . . Plaintiff's work also happens to be fixed in the medium of circuitry on a printed circuit board. This follows from the definition in 17 U.S.C. § 102 of a tangible medium of expression as a medium "from which [the work] can be perceived, reproduced, or otherwise communicated, either directly or with the aid of a machine." A video game's printed circuit board is clearly such a medium of expression, since the "work," the audiovisual presentation, can be communicated from the printed circuit board with the aid of the video game's display screen. . . . Thus, plaintiff's work meets both the requirements of copyrightability and fixation and is entitled to copyright protection. The specific medium in which the work is fixed is irrelevant—as long as a copyrightable work is fixed in some tangible medium, the work is entitled to copyright protection. 17 U.S.C. § 101. The owner of a copyrightable work need not, and indeed, cannot copyright the medium in which the work is fixed.

Defendants also argue that plaintiff is attempting to copyright an idea, rather than the expression of an idea. The Copyright Act adopted the longstanding common law doctrine that this is impermissible. 17 U.S.C. § 102(b). Apparently defendants are claiming that plaintiff is attempting to monopolize the use of the idea of a video game in which the player fights his way through asteroids and spaceships. . . . [W]hen plaintiff copyrighted his particular expression of the game, he did not prevent others from using the idea of a game with asteroids. He prevented only the copying of the arbitrary design features that makes plaintiff's expression of this idea unique. These design features consist of the symbols that appear on the display screen, the ways in which those symbols move around the screen, and the sounds emanating from the game cabinet. Defendants are entitled to use the idea of a video game involving asteroids, so long as they adopt a different expression of the idea—*i.e.*, a version of such a game that uses symbols, movements, and sounds that are different from those used in plaintiff's game.

Infringement by Defendants

Since direct evidence of copying is seldom available, plaintiff may prove copying by showing that defendants had access to plaintiff's work and that the two works are substantially similar. . . . Access was shown indirectly by evidence that plaintiff's work had been widely disseminated. . . .

Therefore, the crucial issue is whether defendants' game, "Meteors," is substantially similar to plaintiff's game, "Asteroids." Substantial similarity is determined by a general comparison of the two works:

"Substantial similarity" is to be determined by the "ordinary observer" test. Judge Learned Hand in defining this test stated there is substantial similarity where "the ordinary observer, unless he set out to detect the disparities, would be disposed to

overlook them, and regard their aesthetic appeal as the same." *Peter Pan Fabrics, Inc. v. Martin Weiner Corp.* 274 F.2d 487, 489 (2d Cir. 1960). . . .

However, in applying the "ordinary observer" test, a court must also apply the principles of the law of copyright. One of the most basic of these is the concept that, while one's expression of an idea is copyrightable, the underlying idea one uses is not. . . . A corollary to this principle is that when an idea is such that *any* use of that idea *necessarily* involves certain forms of expression, one may not copyright those forms of expression, because to do so would be in effect to copyright the underlying idea.

This principle must also apply in less extreme cases in which a creator's expression of an idea includes some forms of expression that are essential to the idea (*i.e.*, forms of expression which cannot be varied without altering the idea) and some forms of expression that are not essential to the idea. In such a case, the latter forms of expression are copyrightable, but the former are not, because if the creator could copyright the essential forms of expression, then others would effectively be barred from using the underlying idea.

This doctrine has been recognized by courts in a variety of situations. In *Rehyer v. Children's Television Workshop*, 533 F.2d 87, 91 (2d Cir. 1976), *cert. denied*, 429 U.S. 980, 97 S. Ct. 429, 50 L.Ed.2d 588, the court stated that:

Another helpful analytic concept is that of *scenes a faire*, sequences of events which necessarily follow from a common theme. "[S]imilarity of expression . . . which necessarily results from the fact that the common idea is only capable of expression in more or less stereotyped form will preclude a finding of actionable similarity." 1 *Nimmer* § 143.11 at 626.2; *see* Yankwich, *Originality in the Law of Intellectual Property*, 11 F.R.D. 457, 462 (1951). Copyrights, then, do not protect thematic concepts or scenes which necessarily must follow from certain similar plot situations. . . .

This Court has held that plaintiff is entitled to a copyright on "Asteroids," because the idea of a video game in which the player shoots his way through a barrage of space rocks is an idea that is sufficiently general so as to permit more than one form of expression. However, under the doctrine set forth above, the Court must be careful not to interpret plaintiff's copyright as granting plaintiff a monopoly over those forms of expression that are inextricably associated with the idea of such a video game. Therefore, it is not enough to observe that there are a great number of similarities in expression between the two games. It is necessary to determine whether the similar forms of expression are forms of expression that simply cannot be avoided in any version of the basic idea of a video game involving space rocks.

There are, as noted *supra*, a number of similarities in the design features of the two games. However, the Court finds that most of these similarities are inevitable, given the requirements of the idea of a game involving a spaceship combatting space rocks and given the technical demands of the medium of a video game. There are certain forms of expression that one must necessarily use in designing a video game in which a player fights his way through space rocks and enemy spaceships. The player must be able to rotate and move his craft. All the spaceships must be able to fire weapons which can destroy targets. The game must be easy at first and gradually get harder, so that bad players are not frustrated and good ones are challenged. Therefore, the rocks must move faster as the game progresses. In order for the game to look at all realistic, there must be more than one size of rock. Rocks cannot split into very many pieces, or else the screen would quickly become filled with rocks and the player would lose too quickly. All video games have characteristic sounds and symbols designed to increase the sensation of action. The player must be awarded points for destroying objects, based on the degree of difficulty involved.

All these requirements of a video game in which the player combats space rocks and spaceships combine to dictate certain forms of expression that must appear in any version of such a game. In fact, these requirements account for most of the similarities between "Meteors" and "Asteroids." Similarities so accounted for do not constitute copyright infringement, because they are part of plaintiff's idea and are not protected by plaintiff's copyright.

In light of this conclusion that the similarities in the forms of expression are inevitable, given

the idea and the medium, the large number of dissimilarities becomes particularly significant. Given the unavoidable similarities in expression, the Court finds that the ordinary player would regard the aesthetic appeal of these two games as quite different. The overall "feel" of the way the games play is different. In "Meteors" the symbols are more realistic, the game begins with the player's spaceship blasting off from earth, and the player's spaceship handles differently and fires differently. "Meteors" is faster-paced at all stages and is considerably more difficult than "Asteroids."

It seems clear that defendants based their game on plaintiff's copyrighted game; to put it bluntly, defendants took plaintiff's idea. However, the copyright laws do not prohibit this. Copyright protection is available only for expression of ideas, not for ideas themselves. Defendants used plaintiff's idea and those portions of plaintiff's expression that were inextricably linked to that idea. The remainder of defendants' expression is different from plaintiff's expression. Therefore, the Court finds that defendants' "Meteors" game is not substantially similar to and is not an infringing copy of plaintiff's "Asteroids" game. . . .

Atari, Inc. v. North American Philips Consumer Electronics Corp., 672 F.2d 607 (7th Cir. 1982)

Wood, J.

. . . Atari and Midway own the exclusive United States rights in PAC-MAN under the registered copyright for the "PAC-MAN audiovisual work." Midway sells the popular coin-operated arcade version, and Atari recently began to market the home video version. As part of its Odyssey line of home video games, North American developed a game called "K. C. Munchkin" which Park sells at the retail level. Plaintiffs filed this suit alleging that K. C. Munchkin infringes their copyright in PAC-MAN in violation of 17 U.S.C. §§ 106, 501 (Supp. I 1977), and that North American's conduct in marketing K. C. Munchkin constitutes unfair competition in violation of the Illinois Uniform Deceptive Trade Practices Act, Ill. Rev. Stat. Ch. 121½, §§ 311–17 (1980), and the common law. The district court denied plaintiffs' motion for a preliminary injunction, ruling that plaintiffs failed to show likelihood of success on the merits of either claim.

Because this appeal requires us to make an ocular comparison of the two works, we describe both games in some detail. . . .

The copyrighted version of PAC-MAN is an electronic arcade maze-chase game. Very basically, the game "board," which appears on a television-like screen, consists of a fixed maze, a central character (expressed as a "gobbler"), four pursuit characters (expressed as "ghost monsters"), several hundred evenly spaced pink dots which line the pathways of the maze, four enlarged pink dots ("power capsules") approximately located in each of the maze's four corners, and various colored fruit symbols which appear near the middle of the maze during the play of the game.

Using a "joy stick," the player guides the gobbler through the maze, consuming pink dots along the way. The monsters, which roam independently within the maze, chase the gobbler. Each play ends when a monster catches the gobbler, and after three plays the game is over. If the gobbler consumes a power capsule, the roles reverse temporarily: the gobbler turns into the hunter, and the monsters become vulnerable. The object of the game is to score as many points as possible by gobbling dots, power capsules, fruit symbols, and monsters.

The PAC-MAN maze has a slightly vertical rectangular shape, and its geometric configuration is drawn in bright blue double lines. Centrally located on the left and right sides of the maze is a tunnel opening. To evade capture by a pursuing monster, the player can cause the central character to exit through one opening and re-enter through the other on the opposite side. In video game parlance this concept is called a "wraparound." In the middle is a rectangular box ("corral") which has a small opening on the upper side. A scoring table, located across the top of the maze, displays in white the first player's score on the left, the high score to date in the middle, and the second player's score on the right. If a player successfully consumes all of the dots, the entire maze flashes alternatively blue and white in victory, and a new maze, replenished with dots,

appears on the screen. When the game ends a bright red "game over" sign appears below the corral.

At the start of the game, the gobbler character is located centrally near the bottom of the maze. That figure is expressed as a simple yellow dot, somewhat larger than the power capsules, with a V-shaped aperture which opens and closes in mechanical fashion like a mouth as it travels the maze. Distinctive "gobbling" noises accompany this action. If fate (or a slight miscalculation) causes the gobbler to fall prey to one of the monsters, the action freezes, and the gobbler is deflated, folding back on itself, making a sympathetic whining sound, and disappearing with a star-burst.

The four monster characters are identical except that one is red, one blue, one turquoise, and one orange. They are about equal in size to the gobbler, but are shaped like bell jars. The bottom of each figure is contoured to simulate three short appendages which move as the monster travels about the maze. Their most distinctive feature is their highly animated eyes, which appear as large white circles with blue irises and which "look" in the direction the monster is moving. At the start of each play, the monsters are located side-by-side in the corral, bouncing back and forth until each leaves through the opening. Unlike the gobbler, they do not consume the dots, but move in a prearranged pattern about the maze at a speed approximately equal to that of the gobbler. When the gobbler consumes a power capsule and the roles reverse, the monsters panic: a siren-like alarm sounds, they turn blue, their eyes contract into small pink dots, a wrinkled "mouth" appears, and they immediately reverse direction (moving at a reduced speed). When this period of vulnerability is about to end, the monsters warn the player by flashing alternately blue and white before returning to their original colors. But if a monster is caught during this time, its body disappears, and its original eyes reappear and race back to the corral. Once in the corral, the monster quickly regenerates and reenters the maze to resume its pursuit of the gobbler.

Throughout the play of PAC-MAN, a variety of distinctive musical sounds comprise the audio component of the game. Those sounds coincide with the various character movements and events occurring during the game and add to the excitement of the play. . . .

North American's K. C. Munchkin is also a maze-chase game that employs a player-controlled central character (also expressed as a "gobbler"), pursuit characters (also expressed as "ghost monsters"), dots, and power capsules. The basic play of K. C. Munchkin parallels that of PAC-MAN: the player directs the gobbler through the maze consuming dots and avoiding capture by the monsters; by gobbling a power capsule, the player can reverse the roles; and the ultimate goal is to accumulate the most points by gobbling dots and monsters.

K. C. Munchkin's maze also is rectangular, has two tunnel exits and a centrally located corral, and flashes different colors after the gobbler consumes all of the dots. But the maze, drawn in single, subdued purple lines, is more simple in overall appearance. Because it appears on a home television screen, the maze looks broader than it is tall. Unlike that in PAC-MAN, the maze has one dead-end passageway, which adds an element of risk and strategy. The corral is square rather than rectangular and rotates ninety degrees every two or three seconds, but serves the same purpose as the corral in PAC-MAN. The scoring table is located below the maze and, as in PAC-MAN, has places on the left and right for scores for two players. But instead of simply registering the high score in the middle, the K. C. Munchkin game displays in flashing pink and orange a row of question marks where the high scorer can register his or her name.

The gobbler in K. C. Munchkin initially faces the viewer and appears as a round blue-green figure with horns and eyes. The gobbler normally has an impish smile, but when a monster attacks it, its smile appropriately turns to a frown. As it moves about the maze, the gobbler shows a somewhat diamond-shaped profile with a V-shaped mouth which rapidly opens and closes in a manner similar to PAC-MAN's gobbler. A distinctive "gobbling" noise also accompanies this movement. When the gobbler stops, it turns around to face the viewer with another grin. If captured by a monster, the gobbler also folds back and disappears in a star-burst. At the start of each play, this character is located immediately above the corral. If successful in consuming the last dot, the munchkin turns to the viewer and chuckles.

K. C. Munchkin's three ghost monsters appear similar in shape and movement to their PAC-MAN counterparts. They have round bodies (approximately equal in size to the gobbler) with two short horns or antennae, eyes, and three appendages on the bottom. The eyes are not as detailed as those of the PAC-MAN monsters, but they are uniquely similar in that they also "look" in the direction in which the monster is moving. Although slightly longer, the "legs" also move in a centipede-like manner as the monster roams about the maze. The similarity becomes even more pronounced when the monsters move vertically because their antennae disappear and their bodies assume the more bell jar-like shape of the PAC-MAN monsters. Moreover, the monsters are initially stationed inside the corral (albeit in a piggyback rather than a side-by-side arrangement) and exit into the maze as soon as play commences.

K. C. Munchkin's expression of the role reversal also parallels that in PAC-MAN. When the gobbler consumes one of the power capsules, the vulnerable monsters turn purple and reverse direction, moving at a slightly slower speed. If caught by the gobbler, a monster "vanishes": its body disappears and only white "eyes" and "feet" remain to indicate its presence. Instead of returning directly to the corral to regenerate, the ghost-like figure continues to wander about the maze, but does not affect the play. Only if the rotating corral happens to open up toward the monster as it travels one of the adjacent passageways will the monster re-enter the corral to be regenerated. This delay in regeneration allows the gobbler more time to clear the maze of dots. When the period of vulnerability is about to end, each monster flashes its original color as a warning.

There are only twelve dots in K. C. Munchkin as opposed to over two hundred dots in PAC-MAN. Eight of those dots are white; the other four are power capsules, distinguished by their constantly changing color and the manner in which they are randomly spaced, whereas in PAC-MAN, the dots are uniformly spaced. Furthermore, in K. C. Munchkin, the dots are rectangular and are always moving. As the gobbler munches more dots, the speed of the remaining dots progressively increases, and the last dot moves at the same speed as the gobbler. In the words of the district court, "the last dot . . . cannot be caught by overtaking it; it must be munched by strategy." At least initially, one power capsule is located in each of the maze's four corners, as in PAC-MAN.

Finally, K. C. Munchkin has a set of sounds accompanying it which are distinctive to the whole line of Odyssey home video games. Many of these sounds are dissimilar to the sounds which are played in the arcade form of PAC-MAN. . . .

Ed Averett, an independent contractor, created K. C. Munchkin for North American. He had previously developed approximately twenty-one video games, including other maze-chase games. He and Mr. Staup, who is in charge of North American's home video games development, first viewed PAC-MAN in an airport arcade. Later, after discussing the strengths and weaknesses of the PAC-MAN game and its increasing popularity, they decided to commence development of a modified version to add to North American's Odyssey line of home video games. Mr. Averett also played PAC-MAN at least once before beginning work on K. C. Munchkin.

Mr. Staup and Mr. Averett agreed, however, that the PAC-MAN game, as is, could become popular as a home video game, but only if marketed under the "PAC-MAN" name. Thus, as Mr. Averett worked on K. C. Munchkin, North American sought to obtain from Midway a license under the PAC-MAN copyright and trademark. Mr. Staup later learned that the license was not available and so informed Mr. Averett. At that time, Mr. Averett had not yet completed K. C. Munchkin.

When Mr. Averett finished the project, North American examined the game and concluded that it was "totally different" from PAC-MAN. To avoid any potential claim of confusion, however, Mr. Averett was told to make further changes in the game characters. As a result, the color of the gobbler was changed from yellow to its present bluish color. North American also adopted the dissimilar name "K. C. Munchkin" and issued

internal instructions not to refer to PAC-MAN in promoting K. C. Munchkin.

An independent retailer in the Chicago area nonetheless ran advertisements in the *Chicago Sun-Times* and the *Chicago Tribune*, describing K. C. Munchkin as "a Pac-Man type game" and "as challenging as Pac-Man." Another printed advertisement referred to K. C. Munchkin as "a PAC-MAN game." Plaintiffs also sent investigators to various stores to purchase a K. C. Munchkin game. In response to specific inquiries, sales persons in two stores, one being the aforementioned independent retailer, described the Odyssey game as "like PAC-MAN" and as "Odyssey's PAC-MAN.". . .

Under the circumstances of this case, the determination of copyright infringement (or lack thereof) is predicated upon an ocular comparison of the works themselves and does not involve any material credibility issues. Therefore, this court is in as good position as the district court to decide that question. . . .

To establish infringement a plaintiff must prove ownership of a valid copyright and "copying" by the defendant. *See* 3 M. Nimmer, Nimmer On Copyright § 13.01, at 13–3 (1981) ("Nimmer"). Because direct evidence of copying often is unavailable, copying may be inferred where the defendant had access to the copyrighted work and the accused work is substantially similar to the copyrighted work. . . . The parties stipulated to the validity of plaintiffs' copyright and to access; the district court's ruling turned solely on the question of substantial similarity.

Some courts have expressed the test of substantial similarity in two parts: (1) whether the defendant copied from the plaintiff's work and (2) whether the copying, if proven, went so far as to constitute an improper appropriation. . . . Our analysis focuses on the second part of that test and the response of the "ordinary observer." *See Ideal Toy Corp. v. Fab-Lu Ltd. (Inc.)*, 360 F.2d 1021, 1023 n.2 (2d Cir. 1966). Specifically, the test is whether the accused work is so similar to the plaintiff's work that an ordinary reasonable person would conclude that the defendant unlawfully appropriated the plaintiff's protectible expression by taking material of substance and value. . . . It has been said that this test does not involve "analytic dissection and expert testimony,". . . but depends on whether the accused work has captured the "total concept and feel" of the copyrighted work. . . .

While dissection is generally disfavored, the ordinary observer test, in application, must take into account that the copyright laws preclude appropriation of only those elements of the work that are protected by the copyright. . . . Thus, "if the only similarity between plaintiff's and defendant's works is that of the abstract idea, there is an absence of *substantial* similarity and hence no infringement results." 3 Nimmer § 13.03[A][1], at 13–19 (original emphasis). . . .

It follows that copyright protection does not extend to games as such. . . . As Professor Nimmer notes, however, "some limited copyright protection is nevertheless available in connection with games. . . . [A] relatively minimal artistic expression, if original, would render copyrightable . . . the pattern or design of game boards and playing cards as pictorial or graphic works." 1 Nimmer § 2.18[H][3], at 2–212. Recognizing this principle, the Second Circuit has held copyrightable as an audiovisual work, see 17 U.S.C. § 102(a)(6), the "repetitive sequence of a substantial portion of the sights and sounds" of a video game called "SCRAMBLE." *Stern Electronics, Inc. v. Kaufman*, 669 F.2d 852, 856 (2d Cir. 1982). . . . This appeal requires us to address the related question of the *scope* of copyright protection to be afforded audiovisual games such as PAC-MAN. To do so, we must first attempt to distill the protectible forms of expression in PAC-MAN from the game itself. . . .

There is no litmus paper test by which to apply the idea-expression distinction; the determination is necessarily subjective. As Judge Learned Hand said, "Obviously, no principle can be stated as to when an imitator has gone beyond copying the 'idea,' and has borrowed its 'expression.' Decisions must therefore inevitably be *ad hoc.*" *Peter Pan Fabrics*, 274 F.2d at 489. Courts and commentators nevertheless have developed a few helpful approaches. In *Nichols v. Universal Pictures Corp.*, 45 F.2d 119, 121 (2d Cir. 1930), *cert. denied*, 282 U.S. 902, 51 S.Ct. 216, 75 L.Ed. 795 (1931), Judge Hand articulated what is now known as the "abstractions test":

Upon any work . . . a great number of patterns of increasing generality will fit equally well, as more and more of the incident is left out. . . . [T]here is a point in this series of abstractions where they are no longer protected, since otherwise the playwright could prevent the use of his "ideas," to which, apart from their expression, his property is never extended. Nobody has ever been able to fix that boundary, and nobody ever can. . . . As respects plays, the controversy chiefly centers upon the characters and sequence of incident, these being the substance.

(citations omitted). This "test" has proven useful in analyzing dramatic works, literary works, and motion pictures, where the recurring patterns can readily be abstracted into very general themes.

A related concept is that of idea-expression unity: where idea and expression are indistinguishable, the copyright will protect against only identical copying. *Krofft*, 562 F.2d at 1167–68. *Herbert Rosenthal Jewelry Corp. v. Kalpakian*, 446 F.2d 738 (9th Cir. 1971), presents a good example and discussion of this limitation. Plaintiff charged defendants with copyright infringement of a pin in the shape of a bee encrusted with jewels. The court assumed the validity of plaintiff's copyright, but refused to find substantial similarity:

What is basically at stake is the extent of the copyright owner's monopoly—from how large an area of activity did Congress intend to allow the copyright owner to exclude others? We think the production of jeweled bee pins is a larger private preserve than Congress intended to be set aside in the public market without a patent. A jeweled bee pin is therefore an "idea" that defendants were free to copy. Plaintiff seems to agree, for it disavows any claim that defendants cannot manufacture and sell jeweled bee pins and concedes that only plaintiff's particular design or "expression" of the jeweled bee pin "idea" is protected under its copyright. The difficulty, as we have noted, is that on this record the "idea" and its "expression" appear to be indistinguishable. There is no greater similarity between the pins of plaintiff and defendants than is inevitable from the use of jewel-encrusted bee forms in both.

When the "idea" and its "expression" are thus inseparable, copying the "expression" will not be barred, since protecting the "expression" in such circumstances would confer a monopoly of the "idea" upon the copyright owner free of the conditions and limitations imposed by the patent law.

Id. at 742. . . .

In the context of literary works, some courts have adopted a similar *scenes a faire* approach. *Scenes a faire* refers to "incidents, characters or settings which are as a practical matter indispensable, or at least standard, in the treatment of a given topic. " *Alexander v. Haley*, 460 F. Supp. 40, 45 (S.D.N.Y.1978). . . . Such stock literary devices are not protectible by copyright. . . . Thus, "similarity of expression, whether literal or nonliteral, which necessarily results from the fact that the common idea is only capable of expression in more or less stereotyped form will preclude a finding of actionable similarity." 3 Nimmer § 13.03 [A][1], at 13–28. . . . As *Kalpakian* and other cases show, that a work is copyrighted says very little about the scope of its protection. But the *Kalpakian* case is nonetheless instructive in that it represents one end of a spectrum of protection. As a work embodies more in the way of particularized expression, it moves farther away from the bee pin in *Kalpakian,* and receives broader copyright protection. At the opposite end of the spectrum lie the "strongest" works in which fairly complex or fanciful artistic expressions predominate over relatively simplistic themes and which are almost entirely products of the author's creativity rather than concomitants of those themes. . . .

Plaintiffs' audiovisual work is primarily an unprotectible game, but unlike the bee pin, to at least a limited extent the particular form in which it is expressed (shapes, sizes, colors, sequences, arrangements, and sounds) provides something "new or additional over the idea.". . . . In applying the abstractions test, we find that plaintiffs' game can be described accurately in fairly abstract terms, much in the same way as one would articulate the rules to such a game. . . . PAC-MAN is a maze-chase game in which the player scores points by guiding a central figure through various passageways of a maze and at the same time avoiding collision with certain opponents or pursuit figures which move independently about the maze. Under certain conditions, the central figure may temporarily become empowered to chase and overtake the opponents, thereby scoring bonus points. The audio component and the concrete details of the visual presentation constitute the copyrightable expression of that game "idea."

Certain expressive matter in the PAC-MAN work, however, should be treated as *scenes a faire* and receive protection only from virtually identical copying. The maze and scoring table are standard game devices, and the tunnel exits are nothing more than the commonly used "wraparound" concept adapted to a maze-chase game. Similarly, the use of dots provides a means by which a player's performance can be gauged and rewarded with the appropriate number of points, and by which to inform the player of his or her progress. Given their close connection with the underlying game, K. C. Munchkin's maze design, scoring table, and "dots" are sufficiently different to preclude a finding of infringement on that basis alone.

Rather, it is the substantial appropriation of the PAC-MAN characters that requires reversal of the district court. The expression of the central figures as a "gobbler" and the pursuit figures as "ghost monsters" distinguishes PAC-MAN from conceptually similar video games. Other games, such as "Rally-X" (described in *Dirkschneider*) and North American's own "Take the Money and Run," illustrate different ways in which a basic maze-chase game can be expressed. *See also Durham*, 630 F.2d at 914–15. PAC-MAN's particular artistic interpretation of the game was designed to create a certain impression which would appeal to a nonviolent player personality. The game as such, however, does not dictate the use of a "gobbler" and "ghost monsters." Those characters are wholly fanciful creations, without reference to the real world. . . .

North American not only adopted the same basic characters but also portrayed them in a manner which made K. C. Munchkin appear substantially similar to PAC-MAN. The K. C. Munchkin gobbler has several blatantly similar features, including the relative size and shape of the "body," the V-shaped "mouth," its distinctive gobbling action (with appropriate sounds), and especially the way in which it disappears upon being captured. An examination of the K. C.

Munchkin ghost monsters reveals even more significant visual similarities. In size, shape, and manner of movement, they are virtually identical to their PAC-MAN counterparts. K. C. Munchkin's monsters, for example, exhibit the same peculiar "eye" and "leg" movement. Both games, moreover, express the role reversal and "regeneration" process with such great similarity that an ordinary observer could conclude only that North American copied plaintiffs' PAC-MAN.

Defendants point to a laundry list of specific differences—particularly the concept of moving dots, the variations in mazes, and certain changes in facial features and colors of the characters—which they contend, and the district court apparently agreed, shows lack of substantial similarity. Although numerous differences may influence the impressions of the ordinary observer, "slight differences between a protected work and an accused work will not preclude a finding of infringement" where the works are substantially similar in other respects. . . . Exact reproduction or near identity is not necessary to establish infringement. "[A]n infringement . . . includes also the various modes in which the matter of any work may be adopted, imitated, transferred, or reproduced, with more or less colorable alterations to disguise the piracy." . . . In comparing the two works, the district court focused on certain differences in detail and seemingly ignored (or at least failed to articulate) the more obvious similarities. The *sine qua non* of the ordinary observer test, however, is the overall similarities rather than the minute differences between the two works. . . . The nature of the alterations on which North American relies only tends to emphasize the extent to which it deliberately copied from the plaintiffs' work. . . . When analyzing two works to determine whether they are substantially similar, courts should be careful not to lose sight of the forest for the trees. . . .

To assess the impact of certain differences, one factor to consider is the nature of the protected material and the setting in which it appears. . . . Video games, unlike an artist's painting or even other audiovisual works, appeal to an audience that is fairly undiscriminating insofar as their

concern about more subtle differences in artistic expression. The main attraction of a game such as PAC-MAN lies in the stimulation provided by the intensity of the competition. A person who is entranced by the play of the game "would be disposed to overlook" many of the minor differences in detail and "regard their aesthetic appeal as the same." . . .

The defendants and the district court order stress that K. C. Munchkin *plays* differently because of the moving dots and the variety of maze configurations from which the player can choose. The focus in a copyright infringement action, however, is on the similarities in protectible *expression*. Even to the extent that those differences alter the visual impression of K. C. Munchkin, they are insufficient to preclude a finding of infringement. . . . It is irrelevant that K. C. Munchkin has other game modes which employ various maze configurations. The only mode that concerns this court is the one that uses a display most similar to the one in PAC-MAN. . . .

While not necessarily conclusive, other extrinsic evidence additionally suggests that plaintiffs are likely to succeed on their copyright claim. In promoting K. C. Munchkin, several retailers and sales clerks described that game by referring to PAC-MAN. Comments that K. C. Munchkin is "Odyssey's PAC-MAN" or "a PAC-MAN game" especially reflect that at least some lay observers view the games as similar. . . . Furthermore, North American's direction to Mr. Averett that he make certain superficial changes in the gobbler figure may be viewed as an attempt to disguise an intentional appropriation of PAC-MAN's expression.

Based on an ocular comparison of the two works, we conclude that plaintiffs clearly showed likelihood of success. Although not "virtually identical" to PAC-MAN, K. C. Munchkin captures the "total concept and feel" of and is substantially similar to PAC-MAN. . . .

Irreparable injury may normally be presumed from a showing of copyright infringement. . . . Even without the aid of that presumption, plaintiffs clearly have established irreparable harm. The record reveals that Midway's PAC-MAN has become an immensely popular arcade game, sales of which have exceeded $150 million after only one year. In October 1981, Atari had already committed over $1.5 million to the licensing, development, and promotion of its home video version of PAC-MAN, which it intends to put on the market in March 1982. As of the date of the hearing in the district court, Atari had booked orders for PAC-MAN in excess of one million cartridges with a sales value of over $24 million. By marketing K. C. Munchkin, North American jeopardized the substantial investments of Midway and especially Atari. The short-lived nature of video games further underscores the need for a preliminary injunction. . . . Moreover, the Atari and Odyssey game cartridges are not interchangeable. To play K. C. Munchkin, the purchaser must also buy North American's ODYSSEY game console. The impact of North American's infringement therefore extends even beyond the PAC-MAN game to the whole Atari system.

The balance of hardships and public interest factors do not weigh against the entry of a preliminary injunction. North American's only alleged hardship is the profits it would lose if enjoined from marketing K. C. Munchkin. This argument, however, "merits little equitable consideration." . . . This is also not a case in which the plaintiffs' harm would be *de minimis* in comparison to that of the defendants. Finally, a preliminary injunction is necessary to preserve the integrity of the copyright laws which seek to encourage individual effort and creativity by granting valuable enforceable rights. . . .

The district court's conclusion that the two works are not substantially similar is clearly erroneous, and its refusal to issue a preliminary injunction constitutes an abuse of discretion. Since this is an interlocutory appeal, however, we are mindful that our holding does not constitute a conclusive adjudication of the merits of plaintiffs' claim. . . . The ordinary observer test should not be applied in a judicial vacuum. Further development of the facts at trial may command a different conclusion.

For the foregoing reasons, we reverse the district court's denial of plaintiffs' motion for a preliminary injunction and direct the district court to enter a preliminary injunction against continued infringement of plaintiffs' copyright.

Chapter 9

AGENTS, MANAGERS, ATTORNEYS, AND PROMOTERS

9.00   A Business of Intermediaries

Although many creative talents are also adept at handling the business aspects of their professional lives (*e.g.*, Michael Douglas, not only a leading actor but also a highly successful producer), professional representation is a hallmark of the entertainment industries, in which most of the business dealings are undertaken by intermediaries. An established artist will usually have a "team" of advisers: an agent, a personal manager, a business manager, and an attorney. Their combined fees may aggregate in the neighborhood of 30 to 40 percent of an artist's gross receipts.

This chapter discusses problems which arise between talent and various types of professional representatives. In addition, we explore a number of aspects of the increasingly complex and competitive world of concert promotion.

9.01   Deal Makers in the Industries: "Movers & Shakers"

No one with any familiarity with the entertainment industries can fail to recognize "William Morris" and "ICM," the two largest international talent agencies. However, many others, such as Creative Artists Agency and the Agency for the Performing Arts, represent a broad range of creative talents. There are still other agencies, such as Regency and Howard Rose, specializing in live performances, and Schwartz/Gorfaine and Robert Light, who represent film and television composers.

Then, too, there are the *former* agents—people such as David Begelman and Freddie Fields—who have gone on to become film producers. Former agent Guy McIlwaine served for several years as chairman of Columbia Pictures. Indeed, MCA, parent of Universal Pictures, was originally a talent agency which drifted into film production as an outgrowth of successfully "packaging" its various clients in movie deals (*i.e.*, tying together the property, the writer, the director, and the star players, and presenting them to the studio as a totality). Agents are supposed to find work for their clients. While they *do* become involved in their clients' career choices, this involvement is secondary to the finding of work (and the making of deals therefor).

Sections 9.02 and 9.03 of this chapter discuss special statutes in force in New York and California regarding the licensing of agents, as well as cases interpreting these statutes.

"Personal managers" are a slightly different breed, at least under the applicable statutes. Although they resemble the agents in their intimate involvement with the endless dealmaking which characterizes the entertainment industries, they are (at least theoretically) more directed toward the day-to-day activities of their clients than are the agents. They like to characterize their activities as "career direction," a not-unjustified description as applied to effective personal managers.

The present chairman of the MCA Music Entertainment Group, Irving Azoff, came to prominence as the personal manager of such successful pop music acts as the Eagles, Boz Scaggs, Dan Fogelberg, and the Go-Go's. Larry Thompson of Los Angeles has successfully combined the roles of lawyer, personal manager, and film and television producer. Jerry Weintraub, who has managed such diverse talents as Bob Dylan, Dorothy Hamill, and John Denver, has also produced films as diverse as *Cruising, Oh, God,* and *The Karate Kid,* and recently launched Weintraub Entertainment Group after a brief tenure as chairman of United Artists following its spin-off from MGM/UA.

Because of the tendency on the part of managers toward intimate involvement with career development and the creation of public personae for their clients, managers sometimes assume almost Svengali-like relationships with their clients. An example of this is seen in Section 9.04–1 in which we discuss *O'Sullivan v. MAM,* an English case which has some of the same overtones as *Buchwald v. Katz,* in Section 9.03.

In addition to "*personal* managers," there are "*business* managers," usually (but by no means always) CPAs, who generally restrict themselves to *financial* aspects of their cli-

ents' careers. A fee of 5 percent of the artist's gross receipts is common. The business manager's functions can range from simple accounting services to paying the client's bills, advising on investments, effectively running tours, and other extremely complicated functions. A business manager has strong fiduciary obligations to the client, as is illustrated by *ABKCO Music Inc. v. Harrisongs Ltd.,* in Section 9.04–2.

Agents seem to be the dominant dealmakers in the theatre, book publishing, films, and television, although in many areas the roles overlap. For example, Morton Janklow of New York City, a leading author's agent, is also a prominent attorney. However, attorneys and personal managers have for many years been the predominant dealmakers in the fields of records and music publishing. This may be due to the fact that records did not begin to develop into a truly major area of the entertainment industries until the 1950s, and did not receive a great deal of attention from the agents until the attorney/manager pattern had become established. It may also be due to the fact that each of the various entertainment industries is a "people" business—a relatively small number of participants who know and deal with each other constantly. Then, too, in California and New York, fees are effectively limited to 10 percent of gross receipts (while personal managers customarily receive anywhere from 15 to 25 percent), and the California Labor Commission will not approve an agent's contract which does not require a measurable level of performance: a certain amount of work must be secured on a regular basis, or the artist can terminate the term of the agreement. These considerations may act as something of a deterrent to the involvement of agents in records and music publishing.

Lawyers have gone from the law department to many top executive jobs in various areas of the entertainment industries. (Some examples are Sidney Sheinberg, President of MCA; Walter Yetnikoff, Chairman of CBS Records; and M. Richard Asher, Chairman of PolyGram Records. Another chairman, Elliot Goldman of BMG Music Group, is an attorney who did not hold law department positions but came up through business affairs.)

As will be seen in *Croce v. Kurnit* in Section 9.05, attorneys often find themselves in the midst of very complicated relationships in the music and record industries, and may unwittingly undertake quasi-fiduciary obligations to persons other than those who are formally their clients, with potentially disastrous circumstances.

Concert promoters are an important element in the music business. They operate under form contracts prescribed by the American Federation of Musicians to which the artists often add extensive "riders" prescribing items such as electric wiring, security staffing, and dressing room facilities to such arcane matters as the color of M&Ms to be provided backstage. In recent years, cases in New York and California, discussed in Section 9.06–1, have produced contradictory results concerning the degree to which the American Federation of Musicians (AFM) can resolve disputes between artists and nonmembers under internal AFM procedures. Problems between promoters and venues are discussed in Section 9.06–2, while antitrust suits between promoters are discussed in Section 9.06–3.

9.10   Agents

Agents are defined in the entertainment industries as those who actively seek employment for artists. Supposedly, there is a line between an agent and a personal manager. The personal manager attends to career matters while the agent seeks the actual jobs.

Where one function ends and the other begins, however, is often hard to define.

Both California and New York, the states with the largest concentrations in the entertainment industries, have enacted legislation to control agents. At one time, the California statute seemed to be directed at personal managers as well, but a closer reading reveals that the statute applied only when the personal manager was in fact engaged in seeking employment for the artist. The language of the California statute was amended in the late 1970s to reflect more accurately that agents are the ones being controlled.

Both states require licensing of agents. To be an agent and yet fail to register and be licensed can carry severe consequences, as the statutes set forth in Section 9.11 and 9.12 reveal. Both licensed and unlicensed agents are affected by the legislation in these two jurisdictions.

(Section 9.13) relates to an entertainment labor union's attempts to control agents by requiring certain fee structures and other restrictions. The legal focus is on the unsuccessful antitrust action raised by agents against such union controls. However, the victory is not totally one-sided, and there is language in the court's opinion that should make unions hesitate before attempting regulations that are too sweeping.

9.11   New York Regulations of Agents

New York has adopted an extremely detailed legislative scheme to regulate the activities of "agents." But who is an agent is open to question. For example, in the *Pine* case, which follows, an attorney was found to be an agent, whereas in the *Mandel* case the attorney was found to be a manager. In *Gershunov*, we see examples of agents performing dual functions, with the unlicensed agency function predominating.

The considerations in this section begin

with pertinent parts of Article II of the New York General Business Law, particularly those provisions that relate to theatrical employment agencies. Then follow the *Pine, Mandel,* and *Gershunov* cases.

§ 170. *Application of article*

This article shall apply to all employment agencies in the state.

§ 171. *Definitions*

Whenever used in this article:

1. "Commissioner" means the industrial commissioner of the state of New York, except that in the application of this article to the city of New York the term "commissioner" means the commissioner of licenses of such city.

2. a. "Employment agency" means any person (as hereinafter defined) who, for a fee, procures or attempts to procure:

(1) employment or engagements for persons seeking employment . . .

3. "Fee" means anything of value, including any money or other valuable consideration charged, collected, received, paid or promised for any service, or act rendered or to be rendered by an employment agency, including but not limited to money received by such agency or its emigrant agent which is more than the amount paid by it for transportation, transfer of baggage, or board and lodging on behalf of any applicant for employment. . . .

7. "Person" means any individual, company, society, association, corporation, manager, contractor, subcontractor, partnership, bureau, agency, service, office or the agent or employee of the foregoing.

8. "Theatrical employment agency" means any person . . . who procures or attempts to procure employment or engagements for circus, vaudeville, the variety field, the legitimate theater, motion pictures, radio, television, phonograph recordings, transcriptions, opera, concert, ballet, modeling or other entertainments or exhibitions or performances, but such term does not include the business of managing such entertainments, exhibitions or

performances, or the artists or attractions constituting the same, where such business only incidentally involves the seeking of employment therefor.

9. "Theatrical engagement" means any engagement or employment of a person as an actor, performer or entertainer in employment. . . .

§ 172. *License required*

No person shall open, keep, maintain, own, operate or carry on any employment agency unless such person shall have first procured a license therefore as provided in this article. Such license shall be issued by the industrial commissioner, except that if the employment agency is to be conducted in the city of New York such license shall be issued by the commissioner of consumer affairs of such city. Such license shall be posted in a conspicuous place in said agency.

§ 173. *Application for license*

1. An application for such license shall be made to the industrial commissioner, except that if the employment agency is to be conducted in the city of New York the application for such license shall be made to the commissioner of consumer affairs of such city. If the employment agency is owned by an individual such application shall be made by such individual; if it is owned by a partnership such application shall be made by all partners; if it is owned by an association or society, such application shall be made by the president and treasurer thereof, by whatever title designated; if it is owned by a corporation, such application shall be made by all its officers and, if the stock of the corporation is publicly traded, by all stockholders holding ten percent or more of the stock of such corporation. A conformed or photostatic copy of the minutes showing the election of such officers shall be attached to such application.

If the applicant will conduct business under a trade name or if the applicant is a partnership, the application for a license shall be accompanied by a copy of the trade name or partnership certificate duly certified by the clerk of the county in whose office said certificate is filed. Such trade name shall not be similar or identical to that of any existing licensed agency.

2. a. Such application shall be written and in the form prescribed by the commissioner and shall state truthfully the name and address of the applicant. . . .

b. The application for a license shall be accompanied by samples or accurate facsimiles of each and every form which the applicant for a license will require applicants for employment to execute, and such forms must be approved by the commissioner before a license may be issued. The commissioner shall approve any such forms which fairly and clearly represent contractual terms and conditions between the proposed employment agency and applications for employment, such as are permitted by this article. . . .

§ 174. *Procedure upon application; grant of license*

1. Upon the receipt of an application for a license, the commissioner shall cause the name and address of the applicant, the name under which the employment agency is to be conducted, and the street and number of the place where the agency is to be conducted, to be posted in a conspicuous place in his public office. Such agency shall be used exclusively as an employment agency and for no other purpose, except as hereinafter provided. The commissioner shall investigate or cause to be investigated the character and responsibility of the applicant and agency manager and shall examine or cause to be examined the premises designated in such application as the place in which it is proposed to conduct such agency. The commissioner shall require all applicants for licenses and agency managers to be fingerprinted.

2. Any person may file, within one week after such application is so posted in the said office, a written protest against the issuance of such license. Such protest shall be in writing and signed by the person filing the same or his authorized agent or attorney, and shall state reasons why the said license should not be granted. Upon the filing of such protest the commissioner shall appoint a time and place for the hearing of such application, and shall give at least five days' notice of such time and place to the applicant and the person filing such protest. . . . If it shall appear upon such hearing or from the inspection, examination or investigation made by the commissioner that the applicant or agency manager is not a person of good character or responsibility; or that he or the agency manager has not had at least two years experience as a placement employee, vocational counsellor or in related activities, or other satisfactory business experience which similarly tend to establish the competence of such individual to direct and operate the placement activities of the agency; or that the place where such agency is to be conducted is not a suitable place therefor; or that the applicant has not complied with the provisions of this article; the said application shall be denied and a license shall not be granted. Each application should be granted or refused within thirty days from the date of its filing. . . .

4. . . . No license shall be granted to a person to conduct the business of an employment agency where the name of the employment agency directly or indirectly expresses or connotes any limitation, specification or discrimination as to race, creed, color, age, sex or national origin, and the lack of intent on the part of the applicant for the license to make any such limitation, specification or discrimination shall be immaterial, except that any presently licensed employment agency bearing a name which directly or indirectly expresses or connotes any such limitation, specification or discrimination may continue to use its present name and may have its license renewed using its present name, provided that it display under such name, wherever it appears, a statement to the effect that its services are rendered without limitation, specification or discrimination as to race, creed, color, age, sex or national origin.

§ 176. *Assignment or transfer of license; change of location; additional locations*

A license granted as provided in this article shall not be valid for any person other than the person to whom it is issued or any place other than that designated in the license and shall not be assigned or transferred without the consent of the commissioner. Applications for such consent shall be made in the same manner as an application for a license, and all the provisions of sections one hundred seventy-three and one hundred seventy-four shall apply to applications for such consent. The location of an employment agency shall not be changed without the consent of the commissioner, and such change of location shall be indorsed upon the license. . . .

§ 177. *Bonds and license fees*

1. Every person licensed under the provisions of this article to carry on the business of an employment agency shall pay to the commissioner a license fee in accordance with the following schedule before such license is issued. The minimum fee for said license shall be two hundred dollars, and for an agency operating with more than four placement employees, four hundred dollars. . . . He shall also deposit before such license is issued, with the commissioner, a bond in the penal sum of five thousand dollars with two or more sureties or a duly authorized surety company, to be approved by the commissioner. . . .

2. The bond executed as provided in subdivision one of this section shall be payable to the people of the state of New York or of the city of New York, as the case may be, and shall be conditioned that the person applying for the license will comply with this article, and shall pay all damages occasioned to any person by reason of any misstatement, misrepresentation, fraud or deceit, or any unlawful act or omission of any licensed person, his agents or employees, while acting within the scope of their employment, made, committed or omitted in the business conducted under such

license, or caused by any other violation of this article in carrying on the business for which such license is granted. . . .

§ 178. *Action on bond*

All claims or suits brought in any court against any licensed person may be brought in the name of the person damaged upon the bond deposited by such licensed person as provided in section one hundred seventy-seven and may be transferred and assigned as other claims for damages in civil suits. . . .

§ 185. *Fees*

1. Circumstances permitting fee. An employment agency shall not charge or accept a fee or other consideration unless in accordance with the terms of a written contract with a job applicant, except for class "A" and "A1" employment, and except after such agency has been responsible for referring such job applicant to an employer or such employer to a job applicant and where as a result thereof such job applicant has been employed by such employer. The maximum fees provided for herein for all types of placements or employment may be charged to the job applicant and a similar fee may be charged to the employer. . . .

2. Size of fee; payment schedule. The gross fee charged to the job applicant and the gross fee charged to the employer each shall not exceed the amounts enumerated in the schedules set forth in this section, for any single employment or engagement, except as hereinabove provided; and such fees shall be subject to the provisions of section one hundred eighty-six of this article. . . .

4. Types of employment. For the purpose of placing a ceiling over the fees charged by persons conducting employment agencies, types of employment shall be classified as follows: . . . Class "C"—theatrical engagements; . . .

8. Fee ceiling: For a placement in class "C" employment the gross fee shall not exceed, for a single engagement, ten per cent of the compensation payable to the applicant, except that

for employment or engagements for orchestras and for employment or engagements in the opera and concert fields such fees shall not exceed twenty per cent of the compensation. . . .

§ 186. *Return of fees*

1. Excessive fee: Any employment agency which collects, receives or retains a fee or other payment contrary to or in excess of the provisions of this article, shall return the fee or the excess portion thereof within seven days after receiving a demand therefor.

2. Failure to report: If a job applicant accepts employment and thereafter fails to report for work, the gross fee charged to such applicant shall not exceed twenty-five per cent of the maximum fee allowed by section one hundred eighty-five of this article, provided however, if the applicant remains with his same employer, the fee shall not exceed fifty per cent. If a job applicant accepts employment and fails to report for work, no fee shall be charged to the employer.

3. Termination without employee's fault. If a job applicant accepts employment and reports for work, and thereafter such employment is terminated without fault of the employee, the gross fee charged to such employee and to the employer each shall not exceed ten per cent of the salary or wages received by such employee, and in no event shall such fee exceed the maximum fee allowed by section one hundred eighty-five of this article. However, if such employee is a domestic or household employee recruited from a state outside this state the fee of the employer shall not exceed thirty-three and one-third per cent of the wages or salary actually earned.

4. Termination under all other circumstances: If a job applicant accepts employment and reports for work, and thereafter such employment is terminated under any other circumstances, the gross fee charged to such employee and the employer each shall not exceed fifty per cent of the salary or wages received by such employee, and in no event shall such fee exceed the maximum fee allowed by section one hundred eighty-five of this article.

§ 187. *Additional prohibitions*

An employment agency shall not engage in any of the following activities or conduct:

(1) Induce or attempt to induce any employee to terminate his employment in order to obtain other employment through such agency; . . . or procure or attempt to procure the discharge of any person from his employment.

(2) Publish or cause to be published any false, fraudulent or misleading information, representation, promise, notice or advertisement. . . .

(5) Send or cause to be sent any person to any employer where the employment agency knows, or reasonably should have known, that the prospective employment is or would be in violation of state or federal laws governing minimum wages or child labor, or in violation of article sixty-five of the education law relating to compulsory education or article four of the labor law, or, that a labor dispute is in progress, without notifying the applicant of such fact, and delivering to him a clear written statement that a labor dispute exists at the place of such employment, or make any referral to an employment or occupation prohibited by law.

(6) Send or cause to be sent any person to any place which the employment agency knows or reasonably should have known is maintained for immoral or illicit purposes; nor knowingly permit persons of bad character, prostitutes, gamblers, procurers or intoxicated persons to frequent such agency. . . .

(8) Engage in any business on the premises of the employment agency other than the business of operating an employment agency, except as owner, manager, employee or agent, the business of furnishing services to employers through the employment of temporary employees. . . .

§ 189 *Enforcement of provisions of this article*

1. This article shall be enforced by the commissioner of labor, except that in the city of New York this article and such sections shall be enforced by the commissioner of consumer affairs of such city.

2. To effectuate the purposes of this article, the commissioner or any duly authorized agent or inspector designated by such commissioner, shall have authority to inspect the premises, registers, contract forms, receipt books, application forms, referral forms, reference forms, reference reports and financial records of fees charged and refunds made of each employment agency, which are essential to the operation of such agency, and of each applicant for an employment agency license, as frequently as necessary to insure compliance with this article and such sections; but in no event shall any employment agency be inspected less frequently than once every eighteen months. The commissioner shall also have authority to subpoena records and witnesses or otherwise to conduct investigations of any employer or other person where he has reasonable grounds for believing that such employer or person is violating or has conspired or is conspiring with an employment agency to violate this article or such sections.

3. To effectuate the purposes of this article, the commissioner may make reasonable administrative rules within the standards set in this article. . . .

4. Complaints against any such licensed person shall be made orally or in writing to the commissioner, or be sent in an affidavit form without appearing in person, and may be made by recognized employment agencies, trade associations, or others. The commissioner may hold a hearing on a complaint with the powers provided by section one hundred seventy-four of this article. . . . A daily calendar of all hearings shall be kept by the commissioner and shall be posted in a conspicuous place in his public office for at least one day before the date of such hearings. The commissioner shall render his decision within thirty days from the time the matter is finally submitted to him. The commissioner shall keep a record of all such complaints and hearings.

5. Following such hearing if it has been shown that the licensed person or his agent, employee or anyone acting on his behalf is guilty of violating any provision of this article or is not a person of good character and responsibility, the commissioner may suspend or revoke the license of such licensed person and/or levy a fine against such licensed person for each violation not to exceed $500. Whenever such commissioner shall suspend or revoke the license of any employment agency, or shall levy a fine against such agency, said determination shall be subject to judicial review in proceedings brought pursuant to article seventy-eight of the civil practice law and rules. Whenever such license is revoked, another license or agency manager permit shall not be issued within three years from the date of such revocation to said licensed person or his agency manager or to any person with whom the licensee has been associated in the business of furnishing employment or engagements. . . .

§ 190. *Penalties for violations*

Any person who violates and the officers of a corporation and stockholders holding ten percent or more of the stock of a corporation which is not publicly traded, who knowingly permit the corporation to violate sections one hundred seventy-two, one hundred seventy-three, one hundred seventy-six, one hundred eighty-four, one hundred eighty-four-a, one hundred eighty-five, one hundred eighty-five-a, one hundred eighty-six, or one hundred eighty-seven of this article shall be guilty of a misdemeanor and upon conviction shall be subject to a fine not to exceed one thousand dollars, or imprisonment for not more than one year, or both, by any court of competent jurisdiction. The violation of any other provision of this article shall be punishable by a fine not to exceed one hundred dollars or imprisonment for not more than thirty days. Criminal proceedings based upon violations of these sections shall be instituted by the commissioner and may be instituted by any persons aggrieved by such violations.

Pine v. Laine, 321 N.Y.S.2d 303 (1st Dept. 1971)

PER CURIAM

Order of the Supreme Court, New York County, entered on September 30, 1970, denying defendant's motion for summary judgment, unanimously reversed, on the law, the motion granted, and the complaint dismissed. The Clerk is directed to enter judgment in favor of defendant dismissing the complaint, with costs. Appellant shall recover of respondent $50 costs and disbursements of this appeal.

Plaintiff sues for $35,000 for work, labor and services performed in arranging a recording contract between the defendant and ABC Records. The Court at Special Term determined that there was an issue of fact "as to whether the plaintiff was acting as an employment agency or as the personal manager of the defendant when he performed the alleged services for the defendant. . . ."

Inasmuch as the plaintiff was not licensed as an employment agency pursuant to Article 11 of the General Business Law, unless he comes within the exception of § 171(7) as a personal manager where the seeking of employment is only incidental to the business of managing, he may not recover. See *Mandel v. Liebman*, 303 N.Y. 88, 100 N.E.2d 149 (1951).

It is clear that the defendant had a manager, and that the only service performed by the plaintiff, although he sought to become the manager of the defendant, was this one procurement of a recording contract.

Under the circumstances, plaintiff cannot come within the exception.

NOTES ————————————————

1. The section from the New York Business Law cited in *Pine v. Laine* has been renumbered. The statutory section is now 171(8).

2. Until recently, agencies that arranged for speeches and lectures by authors and other celebrities were required to be licensed under the New York General Business Law. See, for example, *Friedkin v.*

Harry Walker, Inc., 395 N.Y.S.2d 611 (1977). Under recent amendments, speakers' bureaus are now specifically excluded from such requirements.

Gershunov v. Panov, 430 N.Y.S.2d 299 (1st Dept. 1980)

In 1974, the Panovs, well-known Russian ballet artists, emigrated to Israel. Due to the attendant policy, they were a "hot property," and they were sought out and ultimately signed by Gershunov, a well-known impresario/manager. Although all three were Russians, the Panovs spoke only Russian, whereas Gershunov was fluent in English as well. In addition, Gershunov was an experienced businessman in the entertainment field.

The contract described Gershunov as "exclusive" impresario manager and provided for a fee of 20 percent of the Panovs' earnings. If Gershunov acted as a promoter for any engagement, however, the fees would be negotiated between them.

As the Panovs, described by the court as "untaught babes" at the time of their emigration, became more familiar with the entertainment business, they became unhappy with the contract and so advised Gershunov. He responded by suing the Panovs for damages and injunctive relief. They in turn sought an accounting for past receipts, as well as the value of engagements which had been offered to Gershunov but which he had not communicated to the Panovs. In addition, they accused him of general misconduct in his fiduciary capacity.

The lower court held that Gershunov was in a conflict of interest between his managerial status and his status as a concert promoter and had "sought to obtain the benefits accruing to both positions while not being burdened with their risks." The court cited an instance in which Gershunov booked the Panovs to appear in Philadelphia for a fee of $20,000 (on which Gershunov was to receive a $4,000 commission), but did not disclose to them that he had entered into an agreement with the venue for a fee of $25,000 under a contract which was signed by him as their manager. Although nominally the promoter, Gershunov in fact bore little or no risk. "By seeking to obtain both the impresario's profit and the manager's commission [stated the lower court] without full and fair disclosure, [Gershunov] has forfeited both." The lower court continued: ". . . It is unnecessary, for the purpose of this decision, to consider whether [Gershunov's] obligations to the Panovs were greater than normal by reason of their unique status as recent emigrees, their inability to speak and read English, their unfamiliarity with the business and the language of their agreement, their lack of independent legal representation, and plaintiff's contrasting expertise in these areas. Considering only the facts established, and specifically the non-disclosure of [Gershunov's] arrangements for the Philadelphia and Washington engagements, his having been paid in advance [$23,500], a sum greater than that which he would pay the Panovs, plaintiff's failure to abide by the requirements of his own contract in not discussing all fees when he was to act as impresario, his failure to disclose these arrangements even when disclosure was demanded, all evidence clear violation by plaintiff of the most minimal obligations imposed upon an agent who acts for his principal. If one adds to the above the positive acts of his concealment and misrepresentation to which [the Panovs] testified, plaintiff's blatant disregard of all obligations becomes even more egregious. . . .

[However, the lower court found no evil motivation,] apparently [according to the Appellate Division] not conceiving greed to be such, and dismissed a claim for punitive damages, explaining that "it appears that plaintiff's acts were based upon his belief that he was entitled to all he could get. . . ." [The lower court therefore allowed Gershunov to offset his legitimate expenses against the Panovs' damages. After extensive evidence, a referee found for the Panovs in the amount of $255,000. However, since the award exceeded the *ad damnum*, the Panovs were required to move to amend, which the lower court denied. The Appellate Division reversed and did allow the amendment, stating:]

. . . If Plaintiff was prejudiced, it was his own doing, he having created the morass which required deep digging to ascertain the extent of his depredations, the knowledge of which was essential even for a claim to be asserted. The earliest

opportunity defendants had to ask the court for this enlargement was at the motion to confirm the referee's report, and it was availed of. The dollar value was not known until the referee had decided. And, as to being a belated application, it was made before [judgment was rendered]. There was only one trial, and that ruling was where it ended. As a matter of discretion, the motion should have been granted. . . . The net effect of what we have done is to insure substantial justice, i.e., that defendants may be made whole for the damage occasioned by plaintiff's fiduciary breach.

Mandel v. Liebman, 100 N.E.2d 149 (N.Y. 1951)

[Max Liebman began his career staging weekend musical revues at a summer camp in the Poconos. He moved on to produce "Your Show of Shows," 90 minutes live every Saturday night, certainly the preeminent variety show in the early years of TV and, arguably, still the best ever. In 1946, prior to his immense success in TV, Liebman signed a contract with Mandel, a nonpracticing attorney engaged in the business of personal management. The contract provided that Mandel would act as Liebman's "personal representative and manager" for five years for compensation of 10 percent of gross receipts from contracts entered into during the term as well as those extending beyond the term. The agreement also provided that any income which might accrue to Liebman from the entertainment business thereafter "shall be due to the opportunities now procured for him" by Mandel.

Mandell had no express duties under the agreement. While the agreement stated that Liebman "hereby employs" Mandel "to use his ability and experience as such manager and personal representative in the guidance and furtherance" of Liebman's career, and "to advise him in connection with all offers of employment and contracts for services, and conclude for him such contracts," the contract went on to state that Mandel "shall only devote as much time and attention to the activities and affairs" of Liebman as Mandel's "opinion and judgment . . . deems necessary."

Two years later, the parties argued, and Mandel brought an action to recover unpaid commissions. The lower court dismissed his complaint on the grounds that the contract was an attorney's retainer agreement, and that a client has the right to discharge his attorney at any time, with or without cause, subject to payment of quantum merit for services rendered. The appellate division upheld the dismissal on the grounds that the agreement was unconscionable and therefore void as against public policy, because "the plaintiff was not required to render any services to defendant . . . and yet defendant was required to pay plaintiff 'what might be called a tribute in perpetuity.' "

The court of appeals reversed and ordered a new trial.]

CONWAY, J.

It is commonplace, of course, that adult persons, suffering from no disabilities, have complete freedom of contract and that the courts will not inquire into the adequacy of the consideration. . . .

Despite the general rule, courts sometimes look to the adequacy of the consideration in order to determine whether the bargain provided for is so grossly unreasonable in the light of the mores and business practices of the time and place as to be unenforceable according to its literal terms. . . . It has been suggested that an unconscionable contract is one "such as no man in his senses and not under a delusion would make on the one hand, and as no honest or fair man would accept on the other." . . .

There might be some force to the claim of unconscionability in the case at bar if the contract could properly be construed as was done by the majority in the Appellate Division. . . . We do not think that that is a permissible construction under our decisions. See *Wood v. Lucy, Lady Duff-Gordon,* 222 N.Y. 88, 90-91. . . . Even if the contract had merely provided that plaintiff was employed "as personal representative and manager," with no further description of his duties, that would have been sufficient, for it could be shown that to these parties, in a specialized field with its own peculiar customs and usages, that phrase was enough to measure the entire extent of plaintiff's required services. . . .

The further provision . . . that plaintiff "shall only devote so much time and attention to [defendant's] activities and affairs . . . as the opinion and judgment [of plaintiff] deems necessary" must be given a reasonable interpretation consonant with the purpose of the contract. . . . The provision seems merely to constitute an attempt on the part of plaintiff to protect himself from excessive and unreasonable demands upon his time. See *Meyers v. Nolan,* . . . 18 Cal. App. 2d at page 323, 63 p.2d at page 1217, where it was said: "The fact that the contract provided that the managers could devote as much time to defendant's affairs as they deemed necessary does not destroy its mutuality. The very nature of the business of the parties was such that representation of other actors was to be expected. The clause was evidently inserted to avoid any misunderstanding on the subject and to more clearly define the rights and obligations of the managers." Of course, as defendant urges, it is theoretically possible that plaintiff, under this provision, could deem it necessary to devote no time to the activities and affairs of defendant, but in that event, it is clear that plaintiff would not be performing the contract but would be breaching it and foregoing his right to compensation.

Since plaintiff, as we hold, was required to render some service to defendant under the contract, it cannot be said that the contract was unconscionable. . . . It is not for the court to decide whether defendant made a good or bad bargain. We fail to see how the contract can be described as one "such as no man in his senses . . . would make" and "no honest or fair man would accept" . . . or one which would "shock the conscience and confound the judgment of any man of common sense" . . . or even one which is "so extreme as to appear unconscionable according to the mores and business practices of the time and place" (1 *Corbin on Contracts,* sec. 128, p. 400), particularly since, as we are told, without denial the contract of May 8, 1946, is similar in most respects to contracts in current and general use in the entertainment industry. . . .

There is thus no need at this time to discuss the measure of compensation provided in the contract which the Appellate Division characterized as "a tribute in perpetuity." We note only, without passing upon the matter, that a question may be raised as to the validity of enforceability of one provision relating to compensation. Defendant agreed that any future earning of his in the entertainment world "shall be due to the opportunities now procured for him" by plaintiff. This provision would seem to create a conclusive presumption that any employments obtained by defendant during the term of the contract, and any continuance or renewal thereof thereafter, shall be deemed to have been due to the efforts of plaintiff, entitling the latter to the agreed percentage thereon. Somewhat comparable provisions have been held unenforceable. . . . The question, however, is not presented on this record for, while defendant did testify as to the amount of his earnings for the year in question and the different sources thereof, there was no evidence as to which sources were referable to plaintiff's advice, guidance and assistance, and which were not. . . .

Finally, we do not think that the contract of May 8, 1946, at least upon its face, may be held to be a retainer agreement between attorney and client with respect to some matter in controversy under which the client may discharge the attorney at any time. . . . Here, plaintiff was employed as defendant's personal representative and manager, a position which might well have been filled by a nonlawyer. As a lawyer, plaintiff might be called upon to use his legal training in handling defendant's affairs, but that is not sufficient, as a matter of law, to transform an otherwise binding contract of employment into a contract at will on the part of the employer. . . .

Likewise, it cannot be said as a matter of law that the contract was illegal and void for the reason that plaintiff, in violation of section 172 of the General Business Law, Consol. Laws, c. 20, was conducting a theatrical employment agency without a license therefor. By express exemption in subdivision 4 of section 171 of the General Business Law, a person engaged in the business of managing "entertainments, exhibitions or performances, or the artists or attractions constituting the same, where such business only incidentally involves the seeking of employment therefor" is not required to be licensed. . . . It was specifically provided that "this contract does not in any way contemplate that [Mandel] shall act as agent for the purpose of procuring further contracts or work for [Liebman]," that [Mandel] was "not required in any way to procure" such contracts or work, and that in the event [Liebman] "needs additional employment or work then an agent shall be employed by [Liebman] to procure such employment, and the services of said agent shall be separately paid for" by defendant. . . .

9.12   California Regulation of Agents

Like New York, California has an extremely detailed legislative regulatory scheme governing talent agents. Unlike the New York statute, there is no statutory exemption for incidental agency functions undertaken by a personal manager. The California statute was amended in 1986 to provide (1) that the negotiation of a recording contract would not by itself constitute the performance of agency functions, (2) that a manager could assist a licensed talent agent at the agent's request, and (3) that any claim by an artist that a personal manager had functioned as an unlicensed agent would be barred if not brought within one year thereafter.

As was the case in *Pine*, the *Buchwald* decision demonstrates that, although the statute does not expressly grant jurisdiction over unlicensed agents to the regulatory department (in California, the Labor Commission), such jurisdiction is implied from the performance of agency functions. The *Pryor* decision illustrates the drastic consequences which may befall an unlicensed agent. *Raden v. Laurie*, on the other hand, achieves a result parallel to that in *Mandel v. Liebman* in New York.

As with the prior section, the considerations begin with the statutes regulating talent agencies. In this instance, it is the California Labor Code, Chapter 4. The pertinent cases follow.

Article 1: Scope and Definitions

§ 1700. Person—Defined

As used in this chapter, "person" means any individual, company, society, firm, partnership, association, corporation, manager, or their agents or employees.

§ 1700.1. Definitions—Engagements

As used in this chapter:

(a) "Theatrical engagement" means any engagement or employment of a person as an actor, performer, or entertainer in a circus, vaudeville, theatrical, or other entertainment, exhibition, or performance.

(b) "Motion picture engagement" means any engagement or employment of a person as an actor, actress, director, scenario, or continuity writer, camera man, or in any capacity concerned with the making of motion pictures.

(c) "Emergency engagement" means an engagement which has to be performed within 24 hours from the time when the contract for such engagement is made.

§ 1700.2. Fee Defined

(a) As used in this chapter, "fee" means:

(1) Any money or other valuable consideration paid or promised to be paid for services rendered or to be rendered by any person conducting the business of a talent agency under this chapter.

(2) Any money received by any person in excess of that which has been paid out by him for transportation, transfer of baggage, or board and lodging for any applicant for employment.

(3) The difference between the amount of money received by any person who furnished employees, performers, or entertainers for circus, vaudeville, theatrical, or other entertainments, exhibitions, or performances, and the amount paid by him to such employee, performer, or entertainer. . . .

§ 1700.3. License, Licensee—Defined

As used in this chapter:

(a) "License" means a license issued by the Labor Commissioner to carry on the business of a talent agency under this chapter.

(b) "Licensee" means a talent agency which holds a valid, unrevoked, and unforfeited license under this chapter.

§ 1700.4. Talent Agency, Artists—Defined

(a) "Talent agency" means a person or corporation who engages in the occupation of procuring, offering, promising, or attempting to procure employment or engagements for an artist or artists, except that the activities of procuring, offering, or promising to procure recording contracts for an artist or artists shall not of itself subject a person or corporation to regulation and licensing under this chapter. Talent agencies may, in addition, counsel or direct artists in the development of their professional careers.

"Artists" means actors and actresses rendering services on the legitimate stage and in the production of motion pictures, radio artists, musical artists, musical organizations, directors of legitimate stage, motion picture and radio productions, musical directors, writers, cinematographers, composers, lyricists, arrangers, and other artists and persons rendering professional services in motion picture, theatrical, radio, television and other entertainment enterprises.

Article 2: Licenses

§ 1700.5. Talent Agency—Must Obtain License

No person shall engage in or carry on the occupation of a talent agency without first procuring a license therefor from the Labor Commissioner. Such license shall be posted in a conspicuous place in the office of the licensee. . . .

§ 1700.6. License Application—Contents

A written application for a license shall be made to the Labor Commissioner in the form prescribed by him and shall state:

(a) The name and address of the applicant.

(b) The street and number of the building or place where the business of the talent agency is to be conducted.

(c) The business or occupation engaged in by the applicant for at least two years immediately preceding the date of application.

(d) If the applicant is other than a corporation, the names and addresses of all persons, except bona fide employees on stated salaries, financially interested, either as partners, associates or profit sharers, in the operation of the talent agency in question, together with the amount of their respective interests.

If the applicant is a corporation, the corporate name, the names, residential addresses and telephone numbers of all officers of the corporation, the names of all persons exercising managing responsibility in the applicant or licensee's office, and the names and addresses of all persons having a financial interest of 10 percent or more in the business and the percentage of financial interest owned by such persons.

The application must be accompanied by two sets of fingerprints of the applicant and affidavits of at least two reputable residents, who have known, or been associated with, the applicant for two years, of the city or county in which the business of the talent agency is to be conducted that the applicant is a person of good moral character or, in the case of a corporation, has a reputation for fair dealing.

§ 1700.7. *License Applicants—Investigation*

Upon receipt of an application for a license the Labor Commissioner may cause an investigation to be made as to the character and responsibility of the applicant and of the premises designated in such application as the place in which it is proposed to conduct the business of the talent agency.

§ 1700.8. *Refusal to Grant License—Hearing, Notice*

The commissioner upon proper notice and hearing may refuse to grant a license. The proceedings shall be conducted in accordance with Chapter 5 (commencing with Section

11500) of Part 1 of Division 3 of Title 2 of the Government Code and the commissioner shall have all the power granted therein.

§ 1700.9. *Refusal to Grant License—Grounds*

No license shall be granted to conduct the business of a talent agency:

(a) In a place that would endanger the health, safety, or welfare of the artist.

(b) To a person whose license has been revoked within three years from the date of application.

§ 1700.10. *License—Renewal Dates*

The license when first issued shall run to the next birthday of the applicant, and each licensee shall then be renewed within the 30 days preceding the licensee's birthday and shall run from birthday to birthday. In case the applicant is a partnership, such license shall be renewed within 30 days preceding the birthday of the oldest partner. If the applicant is a corporation, such license shall be renewed within the 30 days preceding the anniversary of the date the corporation was lawfully formed. Renewal shall require the filing of an application for renewal, a renewal bond, and the payment of the annual license fee, but the Labor Commissioner may demand that a new application or new bond be submitted. . . .

§ 1700.11. *Renewal Applications—Names of Partners, Associates*

All applications for renewal shall state the names and addresses of all persons, except bona fide employees on stated salaries, financially interested either as partners, associates or profit sharers, in the operation of the business of the talent agency.

§ 1700.12. *Filing, License Fees*

A filing fee of twenty-five dollars ($25) shall be paid to the Labor Commissioner at the time the application for issuance of a talent agency license is filed.

In addition to the filing fee required for application for issuance of a talent agency license, every talent agency shall pay to the Labor Commissioner annually at the time a license is issued or renewed:

(a) A license fee of two hundred twenty-five dollars ($225)

(b) Fifty dollars ($50) for each branch office maintained by the talent agency in this state.

§ 1700.13. Filing Fee—Assignment, Transfer of License

A filing fee of twenty-five dollars ($25) shall be paid to the Labor Commissioner at the time application for consent to the transfer or assignment of a talent agency license is made but no license fee shall be required upon the assignment or transfer of a license.

The location of a talent agency shall not be changed without the written consent of the Labor Commissioner. . . .

§ 1700.15. Surety Bond—Deposit

A talent agency also shall deposit with the Labor Commissioner, prior to the issuance or renewal of a license, a surety bond in the penal sum of ten thousand dollars ($10,000).

§ 1700.16. Surety Bond—Contents

Such surety bonds shall be payable to the people of the State of California, and shall be conditioned that the person applying for the license will comply with this chapter and will pay all sums due any individual or group of individuals when such person or his representative or agent has received such sums, and will pay all damages occasioned to any person by reason of misstatement, misrepresentation, fraud, deceit, or any unlawful acts or omissions of the licensed talent agency, or its agents or employees, while acting within the scope of their employment. . . .

§ 1700.19. License—Contents

Each license shall contain all of the following:

(a) The name of the licensee.

(b) A designation of the city, street and number of the house in which the licensee is authorized to carry on the business of a talent agency.

(c) The number and date of issuance of the license.

§ 1700.20. License—Use, Transfer, Assignment

No license shall protect any other than the person to whom it is issued nor any places other than those designated in the license. No license shall be transferred or assigned to any person unless written consent is obtained from the Labor Commissioner. . . .

§ 1700.21. Revocation, Suspension of License—Grounds

The Labor Commissioner may revoke or suspend any license when it is shown that any of the following occur:

(a) The licensee or his or her agent has violated or failed to comply with any of the provisions of this chapter, or

(b) The licensee has ceased to be of good moral character, or

(c) The conditions under which the license was issued have changed or no longer exist.

(d) the licensee has made any material misrepresentation or false statement in his or her application for a license.

§ 1700.22. Revocation, Suspension of License—Hearing, Procedure

Before revoking or suspending any license, the Labor Commissioner shall afford the holder of such license an opportunity to be heard in person or by counsel. The proceedings shall be conducted in accordance with Chapter 5 (commencing at Section 11500) of Part I of Division 3 of Title 2 of the Government Code, and the commissioner shall have all the powers granted therein.

Article 3: Operation and Management

§ 1700.23. Contract Forms—Approval

Every talent agency shall submit to the Labor Commissioner a form or forms of contract to be utilized by such talent agency in entering into written contracts with artists for the employment of the services of such talent agency by such artists, and secure the approval of the Labor Commissioner thereof. Such approval shall not be withheld as to any proposed form of contract unless such proposed form of contract is unfair, unjust and oppressive to the artist. Each such form of contract, except under the conditions specified in Section 1700.45, shall contain an agreement by the talent agency to refer any controversy between the artist and the talent agency relating to the terms of the contract to the Labor Commissioner for adjustment. There shall be printed on the face of the contract in prominent type the following: "This talent agency is licensed by the Labor Commissioner of the State of California."

§ 1700.24.　*Fee Scheduling—Filing*

Every talent agency shall file with the Labor Commissioner a schedule of fees to be charged and collected in the conduct of such occupation, and shall also keep a copy of such schedule posted in a conspicuous place in the office of the talent agency. Changes in the schedule may be made from time to time, but no change shall become effective until seven days after the date of filing thereof with the Labor Commissioner and until posted for not less than seven days in a conspicuous place in the office of such talent agency.

§ 1700.25.　*License to Deposit Funds on Behalf of Artist in a Trust Fund*

(a) A licensee who receives any payment of funds on behalf of an artist shall immediately deposit that amount in a trust fund maintained by him or her in a bank or other recognized depository. The funds, less the licensee's commission, shall be disbursed to the artist within 15 days after receipt.

(b) A separate record shall be maintained of all funds received on behalf of an artist and the record shall further indicate the disposition of the funds.

§ 1700.26.　*Records Required*

Every talent agency shall keep records in a form approved by the Labor Commissioner, in which shall be entered the following:
(1) The name and address of each artist employing such talent agency;
(2) The amount of fee received from the artist;
(3) The employment secured by the artist during the term of the contract between the artist and the agency, and the amount of compensation received by the artist pursuant thereto;
(4) Other information which the Labor Commissioner requires.

No talent agency, its agent or employees, shall make any false entry in any such records.

§ 1700.27.　*Records—Commissioner Inspection*

All books, records, and other papers kept pursuant to this chapter by any talent agency shall be open at all reasonable hours to the inspection of the Labor Commissioner and his agents. Every talent agency shall furnish to the Labor Commissioner upon request a true copy of such books, records, and papers or any portion thereof, and shall make such reports as the Labor Commissioner prescribes. . . .

§ 1700.29.　*Adoption, Amendment of Rules by Commissioner*

The Labor Commissioner may, in accordance with the provisions of Chapter 4 (commencing at Section 11370), Part 1, Division 3, Title 2 of the Government Code, adopt, amend, and repeal such rules and regulations as are reasonably necessary for the purpose of enforcing and administering this chapter and as are not inconsistent with this chapter. . . .

§ 1700.30.　*Sale, Transfer of Interest—Commissioner Consent Required*

No talent agency shall sell, transfer or give away to any person other than a director, officer, manager, employee or shareholder of the talent agency any interest in or the right to participate in the profits of the talent agency without the written consent of the Labor Commissioner.

§ 1700.31. *Illegal Contracts—Prohibited*

No talent agency shall knowingly issue a contract for employment containing any term or condition which, if complied with, would be in violation of law, or attempt to fill an order for help to be employed in violation of law.

§ 1700.32. *Publication of Information, Advertisements*

No talent agency shall publish or cause to be published any false, fraudulent, or misleading information, representation, notice, or advertisement. All advertisements of a talent agency by means of cards, circulars, or signs, and in newspapers and other publications, and all letterheads, receipts, and blanks shall be printed and contain the licensed name and address of the talent agency and the words "talent agency." No talent agency shall give any false information or make any false promises or representations concerning an engagement or employment to any applicant who applies for an engagement or employment.

§ 1700.33. *Prohibited Employment*

No talent agency shall send or cause to be sent, any artist to any place where the health, safety or welfare of the artist could be adversely affected, the character of which place the talent agency could have ascertained upon reasonable inquiry.

§ 1700.34. *Minors—Sending to Saloons Prohibited*

No talent agency shall send any minor to any saloon or place where intoxicating liquors are sold to be consumed on the premises.

§ 1700.35. *Persons of Bad Character*

No talent agency shall knowingly permit any persons of bad character, prostitutes, gamblers, intoxicated persons, or procurers to frequent, or be employed in, the place of business of the talent agency.

§ 1700.36. *Applications from Children—Prohibited*

No talent agency shall accept any application for employment made by or on behalf of any minor, as defined by subdivision (c) of Section 1286, or shall place or assist in placing any such minor in any employment whatever in violation of Part 4 (commencing with Section 1171).

§ 1700.37. *Contracts with Minors—Disaffirmance*

A minor cannot disaffirm a contract, otherwise valid, entered into during minority, either during the actual minority of the minor entering into such contract or at any time thereafter, with a duly licensed talent agency as defined in Section 1700.4 to secure him engagements to render artistic or creative services in motion pictures, television, the production of phonograph records, the legitimate or living stage, or otherwise in the entertainment field including, but without being limited to, services as an actor, actress, dancer, musician, comedian, singer, or other performer or entertainer, or as a writer, director, producer, production executive, choreographer, composer, conductor or designer, the blank form of which has been approved by the Labor Commissioner pursuant to Section 1700.23, where such contract has been approved by the superior court of the county where such minor resides or is employed.

Such approval may be given by the superior court on the petition of either party to the contract after such reasonable notice to the other party thereto as may be fixed by said court, with opportunity to such other party to appear and be heard.

§ 1700.38. *Employment under Strike Conditions*

No talent agency shall knowingly secure employment for an artist in any place where a strike, lockout, or other labor trouble exists, without notifying the artist of such conditions.

§ 1700.39.   *Fee Division with Employer—Prohibited*

No talent agency shall divide fees with an employer, an agent or other employee of an employer.

§ 1700.40.   *Fees—Repayment*

No talent agency shall collect a registration fee. In the event that a talent agency shall collect from an artist a fee or expenses for obtaining employment for the artist, and the artist shall fail to procure such employment, or the artist shall fail to be paid for such employment, such talent agency shall, upon demand therefor, repay to the artist the fee and expenses so collected. Unless repayment thereof is made within 48 hours after demand therefor, the talent agency shall pay to the artist an additional sum equal to the amount of the fee.

§ 1700.41.   *Traveling Expenses—Reimbursement*

In cases where an artist is sent by a talent agency beyond the limits of the city in which the office of such talent agency is located upon the representation of such talent agency that employment of a particular type will there be available for the artist and the artist does not find such employment available, such talent agency shall reimburse the artist for any actual expenses incurred in going to and returning from the place where the artist has been so sent unless the artist has been otherwise so reimbursed. . . .

§ 1700.4.   *Dispute Determination by Commissioner; Appeal*

(a) In cases of controversy arising under this chapter the parties involved shall refer the matters in dispute to the Labor Commissioner, who shall hear and determine the same, subject to an appeal within 10 days after determination, to the superior court where the same shall be heard de novo. . . .

(b) Notwithstanding any other provision of law to the contrary, failure of any person to obtain a license from the Labor Commissioners pursuant to this chapter shall not be considered a criminal act under any law of this state.

(c) No action or proceeding shall be brought pursuant to this chapter with respect to any violation which is alleged to have occurred more than one year prior to the commencement of the action or proceeding.

(d) It is not unlawful for a person or corporation which is not licensed pursuant to this chapter to act in conjunction with, and at the request of, a licensed talent agency in the negotiation of an employment contract.

§ 1700.45.   *Contractual Arbitration Provisions—Validity*

Notwithstanding Section 1700.44, a provision in a contract providing for the decision by arbitration of any controversy under the contract or as to its existence, validity, construction, performance, nonperformance, breach, operation, continuance, or termination, shall be valid:

(a) If the provision is contained in a contract between a talent agency and a person for whom such talent agency under the contract undertakes to endeavor to secure employment, or

(b) If the provision is inserted in the contract pursuant to any rule, regulation, or contract of a bona fide labor union regulating the relations of its members to a talent agency, and

(c) If the contract provides for reasonable notice to the Labor Commissioner of the time and place of all arbitration hearings, and

(d) If the contract provides that the Labor Commissioner or his authorized representative has the right to attend all arbitration hearings.

Except as otherwise provided in this section, any such arbitration shall be governed by the provisions of Title 9 (commencing with Section 1280) of Part 3 of the Code of Civil Procedure.

If there is such an arbitration provision in such a contract, the contract need not provide that the talent agency agrees to refer any controversy between the applicant and the talent agency regarding the terms of the contract to the Labor Commissioner for adjustment, and Section 1700.44 shall not apply to controversies pertaining to the contract.

A provision in a contract providing for the decision by arbitration of any controversy arising under this chapter which does not meet the requirements of this section is not made valid by Section 1281 of the Code of Civil Procedure.

Buchwald v. Superior Court of San Francisco, 62 Cal. Rptr. 364 (Cal. App. 1967)

ELKINGTON, J.

By their "Petition for Writ of Review (and/or, in the Alternative, a Writ of Prohibition or Mandamus)" petitioners seek review of orders of the superior court in an action commenced by them against Matthew Katz, hereinafter referred to as Katz, who is here the real party in interest. Concerned is the Artists' Managers Act* which we shall hereafter refer to as the Act.

The Act comprises sections 1700–1700.46 of the Labor Code. It is found in division 2, part 6 of that code, relating to "Employment Agencies." It requires licensing, and regulates the business, of artists' managers.

The Act is a remedial statute. Statutes such as the Act are designed to correct abuses that have long been recognized and which have been the subject of both legislative action and judicial decision. . . . Such statutes are enacted for the protection of those seeking employment. . . .

Since the clear object of the Act is to prevent improper persons from becoming artists' managers and to regulate such activity for the protection of the public, a contract between an unlicensed artists' manager and an artist is void. . . . And as to such contracts, artists, being of the class for whose benefit the Act was passed, are not to be ordinarily considered as being *in pari delicto*. . . .

---

*Now known as the Talent Agency Act, old references to "managers" having been changed to references to "agents."—Ed.

Section 1700.44 of the Act, as pertinent here, provides: "In all cases of controversy arising under this chapter the parties involved shall refer the matters in dispute to the Labor Commissioner, who shall hear and determine the same, subject to an appeal within 10 days after determination, to the superior court where the same shall be heard de novo."

Petitioners constitute a professional musical group known as the "Jefferson Airplane." They are "artists" as defined by section 1700.4 of the Act. Each petitioner entered into a separate and identical contract with Katz, who for a percentage of each petitioner's earnings undertook, among other things, to act as "exclusive personal representative, advisor and manager in the entertainment field." The contract contained a provision reading: "It is clearly understood that you [Katz] are not an employment agent or theatrical agent, that you have not offered or attempted to promised to obtain employment or engagements for me, and you are not obligated, authorized or expected to do so." It also provided for arbitration of any dispute thereunder in accordance with the rules of the American Arbitration Association.

A dispute arose between the petitioners and Katz in relation to the subject matter of the contract. Katz thereupon, on September 21, 1966, commenced proceedings with the arbitration association seeking to compel arbitration of the dispute.

On October 18, 1966, petitioners filed with the Labor Commissioner a "Petition to Determine Controversy," alleging among other things: "Complainants complain that in September of 1965, defendant [Matthew Katz] acting as an artists-manager and through false and fraudulent statements and by duress, caused complainants to sign with defendant as an artists-manager; that defendant, prior to the time of signing said contracts, promised the complainants and each of them that he would procure bookings for them; that defendant thereafter procured bookings for them; that defendant thereafter procured bookings for the complainants and insisted that the complainants perform the bookings procured by him; that complainants sought to procure their own bookings, and that defendant refused them the right to procure their own bookings; that at the time that said contracts were negotiated, defendant Matthew Katz was not licensed as an artists-manager pursuant to the provisions of the California Labor Code, Section 1700.5; that the contract presented to each complainant was not submitted to the Labor Commissioner, State of California, as required under Section 1700.23; that Matthew Katz has not performed in accordance with Sections 1700.24, 1700.25, 1700.26, 1700.27, 1700.28, 1700.31, 1700.32, 1700.36 and 1700.40 of the Labor Code and other provisions of the Labor Code; that Matthew Katz never rendered an accounting to the complainants for thousands of dollars received by Mr. Katz for their services; that Matthew Katz has not allowed complainants to inspect the books and records maintained by Matthew Katz with respect to fees earned by the complainants and has cashed checks intended for one or more of the above complainants for his own use and benefit."

Katz appeared and filed his answer to the petition in which he objected to the jurisdiction of the Labor Commissioner. . . .

Admittedly, Katz was not licensed as an artists' manager.

The Act, section 1700.3, defines "licensee" as an "artists' manager which holds a valid, unrevoked, and unforfeited license. . . ." Section 1700.4 defines "artists' manager."

Certain sections, i.e., 1700.17, 1700.19, 1700.21, 1700.42, 1700.43, refer to licensee in such context that the word can reasonably apply only to a licensed artists' manager. Other sections, including those which are the subject of the Petition to Determine Controversy, refer to artists' manager in such manner that they apply reasonably to both licensed and unlicensed artists' managers. The Act thus refers to and covers two classes of persons, "licensees" who are artists' managers with valid licenses, and "artists' managers" who may or may not be so licensed. . . .

Remedial statutes should be liberally construed to effect their objects and suppress the mischief at which they are directed. . . . It would be unreasonable to construe the Act as applying only to licensed artists' managers, thus allowing an artists' manager, by nonsubmission to the licensing provisions of the Act, to exclude himself from its restrictions and regulations enacted in the public interest. "Statutes must be given a reasonable and common sense construction in accordance with the apparent purpose and intention of the lawmakers—one that is practical rather than technical, and that will lead to wise policy rather than to mischief or absurdity." (45 Cal. Jur.2d, Statutes, § 116, pp. 625-626.)

We conclude that artists' managers (as defined by the Act), whether they be licensed or unlicensed, are bound and regulated by the Artists' Managers Act. . . .

The Act gives the Labor Commissioner jurisdiction over those who are artists' managers in fact. The petition filed with the Labor Commissioner alleges facts which if true indicate that the written contracts were but subterfuges and that Katz had agreed to, and did, act as an artists' manager. Clearly the Act may not be circumvented by allowing language of the written contract to control—if Katz had in fact agreed to, and had acted as an artists' manager. The form of the transaction, rather than its substance would control. . . .

The court, or as here, the Labor Commissioner, is free to search out illegality lying behind the form in which a transaction has been cast for the purpose of concealing such illegality. (*Lewis & Queen v. N.M. Ball Sons, supra*, 48 Cal.2d 141, 148.) "The court will look through provisions, valid on their face, and with the aid of patrol evidence, determine that the contract is actually illegal or is part of an illegal transaction." (1 Witkin, Summary of Cal. Law (1960) Contracts, § 157, p. 169.)

In support of his position that as a matter of law he is not an artists' manager Katz cites *Raden v. Laurie*, 120 Cal. App.2d 778 [262 P.2d 61]. That case, decided in 1953, concerned the Private Employment Agencies Act, sections 1550–1650 (also found in part 2, div. 6 relating to "Employment Agencies") which at that time regulated persons doing business as artists' managers. . . .

The inapplicability of *Raden v. Laurie* to the instant controversy is obvious. There, on a motion for summary judgment, no showing, prima facie or otherwise, was made (as regards the contract sued upon or its subject matter) that

Raden had agreed to act, or had acted as an artists' manager (or employment agency). The District Court of Appeal found no evidence which would support a conclusion that the contract was a sham or pretext designed to conceal the true agreement or to evade the law. On the uncontroverted facts the court had jurisdiction over the controversy and the Labor Commissioner did not. In the proceedings before us a prima facia showing was made to the Labor Commissioner as to matters over which he had jurisdiction. . . .

Applying to the [Artists' Manager's] Act the construction given to its sister and parent statutes the following appears: The Act is broad and comprehensive. The Labor Commissioner is empowered to hear and determine disputes under it, *including the validity of the artists' manager-artist contract* and the liability, if any, of the parties thereunder. (See *Garson v. Division of Labor Law Enforcement*, 33 Cal.2d 861, 866 [206 P.2d 368].) He may be compelled to assume this power. (*Bollatin v. Workman Service Co.*, 128 Cal.App.2d 339, 341 [275 P.2d 599].) In the settlement of disputes the jurisdiction of the Labor Commissioner is similar to, but broader, than the power of an arbitrator under Code of Civil Procedure sections 1280–1294.2. . . . The Labor Commissioner's awards are enforceable in the same manner as awards of private arbitrators under Code of Civil Procedure sections 1285-1288.8. . . .

Section 1700.44 of the Act is mandatory. It provides that the parties involved, artists and artists' manager, in any controversy arising under the Act, *shall* refer the matters in dispute to the commissioner. . . .

Since the instant controversy was pending before, and was properly within the jurisdiction of, the Labor Commissioner, the doctrine of "exhaustion of administrative remedies" applies. . . . This well known concept is expressed in *Abelleira v. District Court of Appeal*, 17 Cal.2d 280, 292-293 [109 P.2d 942, 132 A.L.R. 715], as "where an administrative remedy is provided by statute, relief must be sought from the administrative body and this remedy exhausted before the courts will act. . . . It is not a matter of judicial

discretion, but is a fundamental rule of procedure laid down by courts of last resort, followed under the doctrine of *stare decisis*, and binding upon all courts." . . .

We hold as to cases of controversies arising under the Artists' Managers Act that the Labor Commissioner has original jurisdiction to hear and determine the same to the exclusion of the superior court, subject to an appeal within 10 days after determination, to the superior court where the same shall be heard de novo. (See § 1700.44.) . . . [Katz argued that the contractual provision for private arbitration prevented application to the Labor Commissioner.]

This argument overlooks the basic contention of petitioners that their agreement with Katz is wholly invalid because of his noncompliance with the Act. If the agreement is void no rights, including the claimed right to private arbitration, can be derived from it.

Loving & Evans v. Blick, supra, 33 Cal.2d 603, 610, states: "It seems clear that the power of the arbitrator to determine the rights of the parties is dependent upon the existence of a valid contract under which such rights might arise. [Citations.] . . .

We conclude that petitioners are entitled, by way of certiorari, to the relief sought by them. The orders of the superior court dated January 17, 1967 are annulled. . . .

Pryor v. Franklin, Case No. TAC 17 MP114 Labor Commissioner, State of California Division of Labor Standards Enforcement (C.G. Joseph, Special Hearing Officer) (August 18, 1982)

[Franklin managed Richard Pryor from 1975 until 1980. In 1981 Pryor and his "loan-out" corporation filed a Petition to Determine Controversy pursuant to Labor Code § 1700.44. After the hearing the special hearing officer determined that Franklin had acted as an unlicensed talent agency and that the agreement between Franklin and Pryor was void and unenforceable as to Pryor. In addition, the hearing officer ordered Franklin to repay $3,110,918 to Pryor.

Franklin had admittedly negotiated numerous agreements on behalf of Pryor. In addition, testimony established that Franklin had promised to procure employment for Pryor and to negotiate the agreements therefor, in all fields of entertainment. Franklin held himself out to third parties as Pryor's "agent" and resisted attempts by other agents to render agency services to Pryor on the ground that he was already doing so. In addition, promptly after commencing his duties on Pryor's behalf, Franklin terminated Pryor's attorney, accountant, and other professional representatives.

Franklin was extremely active. He procured and attempted to procure employment for Pryor with Universal Studios, Paramount Pictures, 20th Century-Fox, Columbia Pictures, Tandem Productions, Steven Krantz Productions, Rastar Productions, Warner Bros. Records, NBC, and others. He also set up a U.S. live concert tour of some 75 dates. Among the films in which Pryor appeared were *Silver Streak, California Suite, The Wiz, Car Wash,* and *Richard Pryor Live in Concert*. At all times, Franklin served as Pryor's "sole and exclusive negotiator."

In his defense, Franklin asserted that he had not solicited or initiated the contacts which led to Pryor's employment, but had merely reacted to the approaches of third parties. However, said the hearing officer, even if this were true, ". . . the furthering of an offer constitutes a significant aspect of procurement prohibited by law since the process of procurement includes the entire process of reaching an agreement." If it were otherwise, the act would be gutted, particularly as to "the most sought after artists whose services are in the greatest demand."

However, the hearing officer found that Franklin had, in fact, initiated contacts which led to the formation of contracts and that he had "often initiated requests to amend and sometimes significantly change or replace an employment agreement."]

. . . Further, respondent's both conceiving and implementing an "overall strategy" concerning Pryor's employment and career, represents an illustration of Respondent's dual activities in both advising, counseling or directing Pryor in the development or advancement of his professional career, while at the same time Respondent was engaged in procuring and attempting to procure

employment for Pryor in various entertainment fields. . . .

[The hearing officer then characterized as a "blatant subterfuge" Franklin's assertion that he had served as Pryor's attorney. Franklin was not licensed to practice law either in Georgia (he had his office in Atlanta) or in California, where Pryor resided and where Franklin performed many of his services. His contention could therefore "invite both civil and criminal proceedings; . . . any underlying contract for such services would be void and unenforceable." However, because of a failure of evidence on this point, the hearing officer stated:]

. . . we do not need to reach the question as to whether Respondent's conduct would have constituted a violation of the Act if he had been licensed to practice law in the State of California—a professional status which would have rendered him subject to another panoply of regulatory statutes, rules and judicial decisions. . . .

[Franklin did handle some purely business and corporate matters, and as to these business-management functions, no violation was seen. Further, Franklin did not violate the act by referring legal and corporate matters to be handled by attorneys. However, these were incidental activities, not the heart of the relationship between Pryor and Franklin. To decide otherwise, "we would have to elevate form over substance, which would emasculate the Act and permit wide ranging abuses through subterfuge and artifice."

Franklin also used the leverage which accrued to him as Pryor's representative to secure employment for other entertainment clients, as well as employment opportunities and consideration for himself. He was paid (and received credit) as executive producer on some of Pryor's films, although he was not required to perform any services, evidencing "conflict of interest and blatant self-dealing."

There was also evidence that Franklin did not account to Pryor for, or return, some $1,850,000 of Pryor's funds.

Therefore, according to the hearing officer:]

. . . In view of the unconscionable and continuing wrongful conduct by Respondent, including numerous acts of embezzlement, fraud and defalcation while acting in a fiduciary capacity, and in view of Respondent's numerous violations of the Act, we hold that this [sic] an appropriate case for the exercise of the broadest remedy of restitution. . . .

[In an attempt to avoid this result, Franklin argued that Pryor was in *pari delicto*, but the hearing officer rejected this argument and held that Franklin was "solely culpable for the numerous violations of law" and that Pryor shared none of the blame or guilt. In support, the hearing officer cited a 1975 memorandum of law prepared at Franklin's request discussing the act, which showed that the violations were not innocent. Therefore, Franklin was ordered to repay his commission from inception, amounting to $753,217, as well as his executive producer fees (which, the hearing officer reasoned, would have gone to Pryor if not diverted to Franklin), together with interest of $506,000 on the three amounts (including the $1,850,000).

However, the hearing officer determined he had no jurisdiction over Pryor's investment funds which might have been misappropriated by Franklin subsequent to being invested, since these were not "related to the artist's employment or the talent agency's unlawful procurement activities."]

Raden v. Laurie, 262 P.2d. 61 (Cal. 1953)

SHINN, J.

. . . In January 1948, by an undated writing signed by plaintiff, by Rosetta Jacobs and Charlotte Jacobs, plaintiff was employed as a nonexclusive manager of Rosetta Jacobs with the duty of "the securing of engagements for me in the motion picture, theatrical, radio, television and allied fields with and upon the consent of myself and my legal guardian, Mrs. Charlotte Jacobs, and in accordance with our wishes," for a consideration of ten percent of all moneys received from engagements obtained directly or indirectly by plaintiff. No time was specified for duration of the agreement. On July 30, 1948, a second agreement was entered into.

Plaintiff sued on the second agreement alleging that Rosetta Jacobs, who it seems uses the name

of Piper Laurie, had earned a considerable sum of money for professional services and had paid none of it to plaintiff; $3,100 was demanded as plaintiff's share of the earnings. It appeared from the affidavit of Charlotte Jacobs, the mother of Rosetta, that the latter was a minor, born January 22, 1932, and that on October 12, 1949, Rosetta, by means of a communication addressed to plaintiff and signed by one Benj. T. Weinstein, terminated and disaffirmed the agreement of July 30, 1948. The affidavit also asserted that when the January 1948 agreement was executed plaintiff stated to Rosetta and Charlotte that he would obtain employment in the entertainment field for the former, and that the same was the understanding between the parties until the notice of disaffirmance; that during 1948 and 1949, plaintiff attempted unsuccessfully to obtain such employment and several times took Rosetta to places where entertainers might find employment. It was also alleged that plaintiff presented the July writing saying merely that it was "a better form." It was further alleged, and is conceded to be a fact, that plaintiff was not licensed as an employment agent or artists' manager, and that the agreement was not approved by the Labor Commissioner of the State of California. While it was alleged that plaintiff did not handle any money for Rosetta or any records or books for her, it was not alleged that he did not keep and perform his obligations under the July 30th agreement. Plaintiff filed an affidavit setting forth that he counseled and advised both defendants respecting Rosetta's career, and in his affidavit he detailed the services which he rendered in transforming her from a "reticent, bashful, introverted, unassuming personality, without appeal, conversational ability, poise, or any social equilibrium" into a mature, interesting, and attractive personality with poise and aplomb which brought forth her ability and possibilities. The affidavit admitted that plaintiff had taken Rosetta to places where entertainers might have found employment, but denied that it was for the purpose of obtaining employment, and alleged that it was for the general development and education of the young woman. It was denied in the affidavit that plaintiff stated to either of the defendants that he could or would obtain employment for Rosetta. It was alleged that the agreement of January 1948, was merged in and superseded by the agreement of July 30, 1948. It was also alleged that defendant Charlotte contributed a sum of money which affiant used to pay a part of the costs of a short motion picture which plaintiff caused to be written, directed and produced, starring Rosetta, and in which she made her professional debut. These services, it was alleged, continued over a period of more than a year and until Rosetta obtained a contract with Universal International Studio, at which time plaintiff was cast aside.

Plaintiff was not licensed as an artists' manager, theatrical manager or employment agent. It is said by respondent that her motion was granted upon the ground that plaintiff was either an unlicensed artists' manager or employment agent. The definition of artists' manager is contained in § 1650 of the Labor Code. One is not an artists' manager unless he both advises, counsels and directs artists in the development or advancement of their professional careers, and also procures, offers, promises or attempts to procure employment or engagements for an artist "only in connection with and as a part of the duties and obligations of such person under a contract with such artist by which such person contracts to render services of the nature above mentioned to such artist." Such is the clear wording of the statute.

We have experienced some difficulty in understanding defendant's construction of the section. It appears to be contended that one who is employed to advise, counsel and direct an artist, thereby promises to procure or attempt to procure employment for his principal; therefore, despite the language of the agreement, plaintiff was bound to seek employment for Rosetta; his efforts to do so were a part of his duties of counseling and advising and he was therefore an artists' manager.

The July agreement is explicit and unambiguous. It specifically provides that plaintiff has no authority and no duty to seek or obtain employment for Rosetta Jacobs. He is required only to give counsel and advice and to assist generally in her training for a professional career and the selection and employment of agents. Although it was alleged in the affidavit of Charlotte that plaintiff endeavored, unsuccessfully, to obtain employment for Rosetta, there was no showing that he procured, offered, promised or attempted to procure employment or engagements for Rosetta "only in connection with and as a part of the duties and obligations of such person under a contract with such artist." It would seem clear that his duties were intentionally limited to the rendition of services which would not require his being licensed as an artists' manager.

Respondent says: "It is the act of seeking employment, not the contract provision, which brings the legislation into play." This might be true if the contract were a mere sham and pretext designed by plaintiff to misrepresent and conceal the true agreement of the parties and to evade the law. But there was no evidence which would have justified the court in reaching that conclusion. There was no evidence of misrepresentation, fraud or mistake as to the terms of the contract nor as to plaintiff's obligations thereunder, nor evidence that defendants did not understand and willingly accept the limitation of plaintiff's duties. The assertions in defendant's affidavit that in January 1948, plaintiff represented that he could and would obtain employment for Rosetta, while immaterial, were denied in plaintiff's affidavit. By the former agreement plaintiff undertook to seek engagements for Rosetta and to act as her manager, but not so under the July agreement.

In the absence of any evidence that the July 30th agreement was a mere subterfuge or otherwise invalid the court was required to give effect to its clear and positive provisions. It was to be presumed that the parties acted in good faith. If there was a doubt whether the later agreement was entered into in good faith, as a substitute for the earlier one, and that it expressed the real intentions of the parties, it should have been resolved in favor of plaintiff. These were not questions to be decided on a motion for summary judgment. . . .

In plaintiff's affidavit it was also denied that plaintiff had promised, or that he attempted to obtain engagements or employment for Rosetta.

On the motion for summary judgment the

averments of plaintiff's affidavit should have been taken as true. . . . Therefore, plaintiff's denial that he agreed or endeavored to obtain engagements or employment for Rosetta was a sufficient answer to the motion for summary judgment.

Since plaintiff was employed only to counsel and advise Rosetta and to act as her business manager in matters not related to obtaining engagements for her, he was not acting as an "Employment Agency" as defined by § 1551, Labor Code.

The Labor Commissioner has filed an amicus brief in which he contends that the later agreement was a sham and subterfuge designed to conceal the fact that plaintiff was acting as an artists' manager. Upon the evidence that was before the court this contention, of itself, presents an issue for regular trial procedure.

We find no merit in the claim that the disaffirmance of the agreement by the minor operated to terminate the obligation of Charlotte Jacobs who, presumably, was entitled to receive the earnings of her daughter, and was one of plaintiff's employers.

The judgment is reversed.

9.13 Union Regulation of Agents

Entertainment labor unions have also become involved in regulating agents who deal with their members. Concerned about the vulnerability of their members due to high unemployment rates, entertainment unions determined to impose strictures on agents to prevent union members from being disadvantaged in their dealings with agents. Included among these regulations were maximum fees that can be charged, as well as a franchise fee that was imposed for the privilege of doing business with union members. Shortly after Actors' Equity implemented its regulations, legal challenge was initiated, resulting in the following case, which eventually made its way to the U.S. Supreme Court.

H. A. Artists & Associates, Inc. v. Actors' Equity Ass'n, 451 U.S. 704 (1981)

JUSTICE STEWART delivered the opinion of the Court.

The respondent Actors' Equity Association (Equity) is a union representing the vast majority of stage actors and actresses in the United States. It enters into collective-bargaining agreements with theatrical producers that specify minimum wages and other terms and conditions of employment for those whom it represents. The petitioners are independent theatrical agents who place actors and actresses in jobs with producers. The Court of Appeals . . . held that the respondents' system of regulation of theatrical agents is immune from antitrust liability by reason of the statutory labor exemption from the antitrust laws, 622 F.2d 647. We granted certiorari to consider the availability of the exemption. . . .

Equity is a national union that has represented stage actors and actresses since early in this century. Currently representing approximately 23,000 actors and actresses, it has collective-bargaining agreements with virtually all major theatrical producers in New York City, on and off Broadway, and with most other theatrical producers throughout the United States. The terms negotiated with producers are the minimum conditions of employment (called "scale"); an actor or actress is free to negotiate wages or terms more favorable than the collectively bargained minima.

Theatrical agents are independent contractors who negotiate contracts and solicit employment for their clients. The agents do not participate in the negotiation of collective-bargaining agreements between Equity and the theatrical producers. If an agent succeeds in obtaining employment for a client, he receives a commission based on a percentage of the client's earnings. Agents who operate in New York City must be licensed as employment agencies and are regulated by the New York City Department of Consumer Affairs pursuant to New York law, which provides that the maximum commission a theatrical agent may charge his client is 10% of the client's compensation.

In 1928, concerned with the high unemployment rates in the legitimate theater and the vulnerability of actors and actresses to abuses by theatrical agents, including the extraction of high commissions that tended to undermine collectively bargained rates of compensation, Equity unilaterally established a licensing system for the regulation of agents. The regulations permitted Equity members to deal only with those agents who obtained Equity licenses and thereby agreed to meet the conditions of representation prescribed by Equity. Those members who dealt with nonlicensed agents were subject to union discipline.

The system established by the Equity regulations was immediately challenged. In *Edelstein v. Gillmore*, 35 F.2d 723, the Court of Appeals for the Second Circuit concluded that the regulations were a lawful effort to improve the employment conditions of Equity members. In an opinion written by Judge Swan and joined by Judge Augustus N. Hand, the court said:

> The evils of unregulated employment agencies (using this term broadly to include also the personal representative) are set forth in the defendants' affidavits and are corroborated by common knowledge. . . . Hence the requirement that, as a condition to writing new business with Equity's members, old contracts with its members must be made to conform to the new standards, does not seem to us to justify an inference that the primary purpose of the requirement is infliction of injury upon plaintiff, and other personal representatives in a similar situation, rather than the protection of the supposed interests of Equity's members. . . .

The essential elements of Equity's regulation of theatrical agents have remained unchanged since 1928. A member of Equity is prohibited, on pain of union discipline, from using an agent who has not, through the mechanism of obtaining an Equity license (called a "franchise"), agreed to comply with the regulations. The most important of the regulations requires that a licensed agent must renounce any right to take a commission on an employment contract under which an actor or actress receives scale wages. To the extent a contract includes provisions under which an actor or actress will sometimes receive scale pay—for rehearsals or "chorus" employment, for example—and sometimes more, the regulations deny the agent any commission on the scale portions of the contract. Licensed agents are also precluded from taking commissions on out-of-town expense money paid to their clients. Moreover, commissions are limited on wages within 10% of scale pay, and an agent must allow his client to terminate a representation contract if the agent is not successful in procuring employment within a specified period. Finally, agents are required to pay franchise fees to Equity. The fee is $200 for the initial franchise, $60 a year thereafter for each agent, and $40 for any subagent working in the office of another. These fees are deposited by Equity in its general treasury and are not segregated from other union funds.

In 1977, after a dispute between Equity and Theatrical Artists Representatives Associates (TARA)—a trade association representing theatrical agents . . . —a group of agents, including the petitioners, resigned from TARA because of TARA's decision to abide by Equity's regulations. These agents also informed Equity that they would not accept Equity's regulations, or apply for franchises. The petitioners instituted this lawsuit in May 1978, contending that Equity's regulations of theatrical agents violated §§ 1 and 2 of the Sherman Act, 26 Stat. 209, as amended, 15 U.S.C. §§ 1 and 2. . . .

The District Court found, after a bench trial, that Equity's creation and maintenance of the agency franchise system were fully protected by the statutory labor exemptions from the antitrust laws, and accordingly dismissed the petitioners' complaint. 478 F. Supp. 496 (S.D.N.Y.). Among its factual conclusions, the trial court found that in the theatrical industry, agents play a critical role in securing employment for actors and actresses:

> As a matter of general industry practice, producers seek actors and actresses for their productions through agents. Testimony in this case convincingly established that an actor without an agent does not have the same access to producers or the same opportunity to be seriously considered for a part as does an actor who has an agent. Even principal interviews, in which producers are required to interview all actors who want to be considered for principal roles, do not eliminate the need for an agent, who may have a greater chance of gaining an audition for his client. . . . Testimony confirmed

that agents play an integral role in the industry; without an agent, an actor would have significantly lesser chances of gaining employment. *Id.*, at 497, 502.

The court also found "no evidence to suggest the existence of any conspiracy or illegal combination between Actors' Equity and TARA or between Actors' Equity and producers," and concluded that "[t]he Actors Equity franchising system was employed by Actors' Equity for the purpose of protecting the wages and working conditions of its members." *Id.*, at 499.

The Court of Appeals unanimously affirmed the judgment of the District Court. It determined that the threshold issue was, under *United States v. Hutcheson*, 312 U.S. 219, 232, whether Equity's franchising system involved any combination between Equity and any "non-labor groups" or persons who are not "parties to a labor dispute." 622 F.2d, at 648–649. If it did, the court reasoned, the protection of the statutory labor exemptions would not apply.

First, the Court of Appeals held that the District Court had not been clearly erroneous in finding no agreement, explicit or tacit, between Equity and the producers to establish or police the franchising system. *Ibid.* Next, the court turned to the relationship between the union and those agents who had agreed to become franchised, in order to determine whether those agreements would divest Equity's system of agency regulation of the statutory exemption. Relying on *Musicians v. Carroll*, 391 U.S. 99, the court concluded that the agents were themselves a "labor group," because of their substantial "economic interrelationship" with Equity, under which "the union [could] not eliminate wage competition among its members without regulation of the fees of the agents." 622 F.2d, at 650, 651. Accordingly, since the elimination of wage competition is plainly within the area of a union's legitimate self-interest, the court concluded that the exemption was applicable.

After deciding that the central feature of Equity's franchising system—the union's exaction of an agreement by agents not to charge commissions on certain types of work—was immune from antitrust challenge, the Court of Appeals turned to the petitioners' challenge of the franchise fees

exacted from agents. Equity had argued that the fees were necessary to meet its expenses in administering the franchise system, but no evidence was presented at trial to show that the costs justified the fees actually levied. The Court of Appeals suggested that if the exactions exceeded the true-costs, they could not legally be collected, as such exactions would be unconnected with any of the goals of national labor policy that justify the labor antitrust exemption. Despite the lack of any cost evidence at trial, however, the appellate court reasoned that the fees were sufficiently low that a remand to the District Court on this point "would not serve any useful purpose." *Id.*, at 651. . . .

Labor unions are lawful combinations that serve the collective interests of workers, but they also possess the power to control the character of competition in an industry. Accordingly, there is an inherent tension between national antitrust policy, which seeks to maximize competition, and national labor policy, which encourages cooperation among workers to improve the conditions of employment. In the years immediately following passage of the Sherman Act, courts enjoined strikes as unlawful restraints of trade when a union's conduct or objectives were deemed "socially or economically harmful." *Duplex Printing Press Co. v. Deering*, 254 U.S. 443, 485 (Brandeis, J., dissenting). In response to these practices, Congress acted, first in the Clayton Act, 38 Stat. 731, and later in the Norris-LaGuardia Act, 47 Stat. 70, to immunize labor unions and labor disputes from challenge under the Sherman Act.

Section 6 of the Clayton Act, 15 U.S.C. § 17, declares that human labor "is not a commodity or article of commerce," and immunizes from antitrust liability labor organizations and their members "lawfully carrying out" their "legitimate object[ives]." Section 20 of the Act prohibits injunctions against specified employee activities, such as strikes and boycotts, that are undertaken in the employees' self-interest and that occur in the course of disputes "concerning terms or conditions of employment," and states that none of the specified acts can be "held to be [a] violatio[n] of any law of the United States." 29 U.S.C. § 52. This protection is re-emphasized and expanded in the Norris-LaGuardia Act, which prohibits federal-court injunctions against single or organized employees engaged in enumerated activities, and specifically forbids such injunctions notwithstanding the claim of an unlawful combination or conspiracy. While the Norris-LaGuardia Act's bar of federal-court labor injunctions is not explicitly phrased as an exemption from the antitrust laws, it has been interpreted broadly as a statement of congressional policy that the courts must not use the antitrust laws as a vehicle to interfere in labor disputes.

In *United States v. Hutcheson*, 312 U.S. 219, the Court held that labor unions acting in their self-interest and not in combination with nonlabor groups enjoy a statutory exemption from Sherman Act liability. . . . The Court explained that this exemption derives not only from the Clayton Act, but also from the Norris-LaGuardia Act, particularly its definition of a "labor dispute," *supra*, in which Congress "reasserted the original purpose of the Clayton Act by infusing into it the immunized trade union activities as redefined by the later Act." 312 U.S., at 236. Thus under *Hutcheson*, no federal injunction may issue over a "labor dispute," and "§ 20 [of the Clayton Act] removes all such allowable conduct from the taint of being a 'violation of any law of the United States,' including the Sherman [Act]." *Ibid*.

The statutory exemption does not apply when a union combines with a "non-labor group." *Hutcheson, supra*, at 232. Accordingly, antitrust immunity is forfeited when a union combines with one or more employers in an effort to restrain trade. In *Allen Bradley Co. v. Electrical Workers*, 325 U.S. 797, for example, the Court held that a union had violated the Sherman Act when it combined with manufacturers and contractors to erect a sheltered local business market in order "to bar all other business men from [the market], and to charge the public prices above a competitive level." *Id.*, at 809. The Court indicated that the union efforts would, standing alone, be exempt from antitrust liability, *ibid.*, but because the union had not acted unilaterally, the exemption was denied. Congress "intended to outlaw business monopolies. A business monopoly is no less such because a union participates, and such

participation is a violation of the Act." *Id.*, at 811. . . .

The Court of Appeals properly recognized that the threshold issue was to determine whether or not Equity's franchising of agents involved any combination between Equity and any "non-labor groups," or persons who are not "parties to a labor dispute." 622 F.2d, at 649 (quoting *Hutcheson*, 312 U.S., at 232). And the court's conclusion that the trial court had not been clearly erroneous in its finding that there was no combination between Equity and the theatrical producers to create or maintain the franchise system is amply supported by the record.

The more difficult problem is whether the combination between Equity and the agents who agreed to become franchised was a combination with a "nonlabor group." The answer to this question is best understood in light of *Musicians v. Carroll*, 391 U.S. 99. There, four orchestra leaders, members of the American Federation of Musicians, brought an action based on the Sherman Act challenging the union's unilateral system of regulating "club dates," or one-time musical engagements. These regulations, *inter alia*, enforced a closed shop; required orchestra leaders to engage a minimum number of "sidemen," or instrumentalists; prescribed minimum prices for local engagements; prescribed higher minimum prices for traveling orchestras; and permitted leaders to deal only with booking agents licensed by the union.

Without disturbing the finding of the Court of Appeals that the orchestra leaders were employers and independent contractors, the Court concluded that they were nonetheless a "labor group" and parties to a "labor dispute" within the meaning of the Norris-LaGuardia Act, and thus that their involvement in the union regulatory scheme was not an unlawful combination between "labor" and "nonlabor" groups. The Court agreed with the trial court that the applicable test was whether there was "job or wage competition or some other economic interrelationship affecting legitimate union interests between the union members and the independent contractors." *Id.*, at 106.

The Court also upheld the restrictions on booking agents, who were *not* involved in job or wage competition with union members. Accordingly, these restrictions had to meet the "other economic interrelationship" branch of the disjunctive test quoted above. And the test was met because those restrictions were " 'at least as intimately bound up with the subject of wages' . . . as the price floors." *Id.*, at 113 (quoting *Teamsters v. Oliver,* 362 U.S. 605, 606). The Court noted that the booking agent restrictions had been adopted, in part, because agents had "charged exorbitant fees, and booked engagements for musicians at wages . . . below union scale." . . .

The restrictions challenged by the petitioners in this case are very similar to the agent restrictions upheld in the *Carroll* case. The essential features of the regulatory scheme are identical: members are permitted to deal only with agents who have agreed (1) to honor their fiduciary obligations by avoiding conflicts of interest, (2) not to charge excessive commissions, and (3) not to book members for jobs paying less than the union minimum. And as in *Carroll,* Equity's regulation of agents developed in response to abuses by employment agents who occupy a critical role in the relevant labor market. The agent stands directly between union members and jobs, and is in a powerful position to evade the union's negotiated wage structure.

The peculiar structure of the legitimate theater industry, where work is intermittent, where it is customary if not essential for union members to secure employment through agents, and where agents' fees are calculated as a percentage of a member's wage, makes it impossible for the union to defend even the integrity of the minimum wages it has negotiated without regulation of agency fees. The regulations are "brought within the labor exemption [because they are] necessary to assure that scale wages will be paid. . . ." *Carroll,* 391 U.S., at 112. . . .

Agents perform a function—the representation of union members in the sale of their labor—that in most nonentertainment industries is performed exclusively by unions. In effect, Equity's franchise system operates as a substitute for maintaining a hiring hall as the representative of its members seeking employment.

Finally, Equity's regulations are clearly designed to promote the union's legitimate self-interest. *Hutcheson,* 312 U.S., at 232. In a case such as this, where there is no direct wage or job competition between the union and the group it regulates, the *Carroll* formulation to determine the presence of a nonlabor group—whether there is " 'some . . . economic interrelationship affecting legitimate union interests . . . ,' " 391 U.S., at 106 (quoting District Court opinion)—necessarily resolves this issue. . . .

The question remains whether the fees that Equity levies upon the agents who apply for franchises are a permissible component of the exempt regulatory system. We have concluded that Equity's justification for these fees is inadequate. Conceding that *Carroll* did not sanction union extraction of franchise fees from agents, Equity suggests, only in the most general terms, that the fees are somehow related to the basic purposes of its regulations: elimination of wage competition, upholding of the union wage scale, and promotion of fair access to jobs. But even assuming that the fees no more than cover the costs of administering the regulatory system, this is simply another way of saying that without the fees, the union's regulatory efforts would not be subsidized—and that the dues of Equity's members would perhaps have to be increased to offset the loss of a general revenue source. If Equity did not impose these franchise fees upon the agents, there is no reason to believe that any of its legitimate interests would be affected. . . .

For the reasons stated, the judgment of the Court of Appeals is affirmed in part and reversed in part, and the case is remanded for proceedings consistent with this opinion.

It is so ordered.

JUSTICE BRENNAN, with whom The Chief Justice and Justice Marshall join, concurring in part and dissenting in part
I join all but Part II-D of the Court's opinion. That part holds that respondents' exaction of a franchise fee is not a "permissible component of the exempt regulatory system." *Ante,* at 722. Rather, I agree with the Court of Appeals that the approximately $12,000 collected annually in fees

is not "incommensurate with Equity's expenses in maintaining a full-time employee to administer the system," 622 F.2d 647, 651 (2d Cir. 1980), and thus is not "unconnected with any of the goals of national labor policy which justify the antitrust exemption for labor," *ibid*. . . .

I find somewhat incongruous the Court's conclusion that an incident of the overall system constitutes impermissible regulation, but that agents in general may be significantly regulated because they are not a "nonlabor group." This incongruity is highlighted by the similarity between union hiring halls and the franchising system, a similarity which the Court itself acknowledges: "Equity's franchise system operates as a substitute for maintaining a hiring hall as the representative of its members seeking employment." . . . The Court disregards this similarity in concluding that the franchising system does not "directly benefit" the agents who are required to pay the fees. . . . It reaches this conclusion by incorrectly assuming that the only parties who directly benefit from the hiring hall and the franchising system are employers and employees and producers and actors, as the case may be. But surely the agents also benefit from the franchising system, which provides an orderly and protective mechanism for pairing actors who seek jobs with producers who seek actors. The system is thus the means by which the agents ultimately receive their commissions; it is as much the source of their livelihood as it is that of the actors.

Because the fee is an incident of a legitimate scheme of regulation and because it is commensurate in amount with the purpose for which it is sought, I would also affirm this holding of the Court of Appeals.

9.20   Managers

Managers are integral parts of various entertainment industies. But managers differ greatly in what they attempt to do for clients. In the previous sections we examined the difficulty that some so-called managers have in remaining just a manager and not, in fact, becoming an agent as well.

Even if one remains just a manager, certain issues have to be addressed. One is whether the manager will attempt to be both a personal and business manager or whether the functions will be split; to be both is to invite later disputes. On the other hand, many circumstances, particularly at the start of an artist's career, preclude having both a personal and business manager.

A second issue involves client trust in the manager. Clear fiduciary obligations exist, and managers, whether they be personal or business managers, must avoid any appearance of abuse of the trust placed in them. Both the *O'Sullivan* (Section 9.21) and *ABKCO* (Section 9.22) cases signal warnings to a manager and suggest that the manager must follow stringent guidelines in meeting fiduciary responsibilities.

9.21   Personal Managers

The English case which follows represents a fairly common fact pattern in the music and recording industries (see *Buchwald, supra*, and *Croce v. Kurnit*, in this chapter). The same individual (or corporate entity) attempts to function as personal manager, music publisher, and record production company.

As the following *O'Sullivan* case indicates, it is inadvisable for managers to sign agreements with unrepresented clients. The three-way contractual arrangement quite frequently ends in litigation as soon as the artist achieves an appreciable level of success.

A more recent decision, *Elton Hercules John v. Richard Leon James*, involves the same issues as *O'Sullivan*. (See also a similar music publishing situation in *A. Schroeder v. Macaulay* in Chapter 3.) Although the reasoning in *Elton John* follows that in *O'Sullivan*, different facts result in far more lenient treatment for James, the manager/record company/music publisher rolled into one.

**O'Sullivan v. Management Agency and Music, Ltd.,
[1984] 3 W.L.R. (Court of Appeal [UK] August 10,
1984)**

[Raymond O'Sullivan, better known as "Gilbert
O'Sullivan," gained fame by writing and record-
ing such hits as "Alone Again, Naturally,"
"Claire," "Get Down," and others.

In 1970, the then-unknown O'Sullivan signed a
management contract with Gordon Mills, who
also managed the extremely successful Tom Jones
and Engelbert Humperdinck. Mills represented
O'Sullivan's professional activities, under a duplicate agreement to those with Jones and Humperdinck. O'Sullivan was not told to seek legal advice; he was at Mills's office just long enough to
sign the agreement.

The management agreement specified a term
of five years, with the option to Mills to renew it
for two additional years. Mills had absolute discretion to make decisions affecting O'Sullivan's
career. Mills could negotiate and sign contracts
on behalf of his client and appoint agents for him
(at O'Sullivan's expense).

In 1970, O'Sullivan was signed to recording
and music publishing agreements with Mills's
M.A.M. companies. These agreements were extremely restrictive of O'Sullivan but disclaimed
virtually all affirmative obligations on the part of
the M.A.M. companies. (Mills, however, did
agree to serve as O'Sullivan's record producer
without additional fee.) At about the same time,
O'Sullivan moved into a cottage on the grounds of
Mills's estate and began to receive an allowance
of 10 pounds per week. In addition, one or the
other of Mills's companies paid his expenses.

By 1972, O'Sullivan had sold 6.5 million records. He bought a house for 95,000 pounds (of
which 60,000 had to be borrowed by O'Sullivan
despite the enormous record sales) and vacated
the cottage.

Creative differences and dwindling commercial
success gradually caused a rift between O'Sullivan and Mills. They recorded their last LP
together in Los Angeles in 1976. It was never
released.

By 1976, Mills's record company, M.A.M., had
determined that it needed better distribution and

entered into agreements with EMI and CBS for
different parts of the world. O'Sullivan signed an
"inducement letter," agreeing to be bound by
these agreements.]

DUNN, L. J.
By this time, O'Sullivan was unhappy with his
contractual arrangements. He was disillusioned
with Mills and did not trust [Mills's business
affairs adviser] Smith. He was horrified to discover that he was spending more and earning less
than he used to. He consulted solicitors who
eventually, on May 15, 1979, wrote alleging that
all the agreements referred to above were illegal,
and these proceedings were commenced.

[In addition], right from the outset O'Sullivan
had wanted what he called a "joint publishing
company." This is an arrangement whereby a
company is set up in which the composer and the
publisher each has a 50% interest. All the composer's copyrights are assigned to the company
which pays the composer a royalty so that in
addition to the royalty, the composer retains 50%
ownership in his copyrights. This is clearly a very
valuable asset for the composer.

. . . O'Sullivan raised the question of the joint
publishing company on numerous occasions with
both Mills and Smith, but it was never achieved
although he was told he would get it. [In fact, it
was approved by the board of directors of Mills's
publishing company, the minutes of the meeting
indicating that Smith stated that "this new agreement was being made in recognition of what had
always been an obligation of the company to
Gilbert O'Sullivan as expressed by both the
chairman and himself."]

[The lower court declared all the agreements
between O'Sullivan and Mills and the Mills companies void and unenforceable *ab initio*, and
voided the 1976 inducement letters. He further
ordered the reconveyance to O'Sullivan of all his
song copyrights as well as all of the master recordings embodying his performances. Further, he
directed that all Mills's and his companies' profits
be paid to O'Sullivan with compound interest.]

The judge held that the agreements were void
and unenforceable because they were in restraint
of trade on the basis of *Instone v. A. Schroeder
Music Publishing Co., Ltd.*, [1974] 1 W.L.R.

1308, and because they had been obtained by undue influence on the basis of *Lloyds Bank v. Bundy*, [1975] Q.B. 326. O'Sullivan himself said in evidence that no actual pressure had been exerted upon him to sign the agreements, but the judge held that undue influence was to be presumed because of the special relationship between O'Sullivan and the defendants [findings from which the defendants did not appeal, although they felt that only the unperformed portions of the agreements should be voidable]. Nor was it disputed that Mills was in a position of confidentiality vis-à-vis O'Sullivan and that he had failed on the judge's findings, which were not disputed on this issue, to offer O'Sullivan independent advice. Accordingly, it was accepted that Mills was in a fiduciary relationship to O'Sullivan. [The same principle extended to the Mills companies, which functioned interchangeably with Mills.] . . .

In equity the term "fraud" embraces not only actual fraud but certain other conduct which falls below the standards demanded by equity, and is known as constructive fraud, one of the examples of which is a transaction which has been procured by undue influence, or where one party is in breach of a fiduciary duty to another. . . .

[O'Sullivan's counsel] pointed out that none of the agreements obliged the defendants to do any work on behalf of O'Sullivan whether by promoting or exploiting him or his works at all, although he conceded that the defendants had in fact done such work gratuitously. He accepted that the defendants, in accounting for their profits, were entitled to credit in respect of their proper and reasonable expenses for the work done, including work done gratuitously, but that they were not entitled to credit for any profit element in such work. . . .

I do not think that equity requires such a narrow approach. It is true that in this case moral blame does lie upon the defendants as the judge's findings of fact show. On the other hand, it is significant that until O'Sullivan met Mills he had achieved no success, and that after he effectively parted company with Mills in 1976, he achieved no success either. During the years he was working with Mills, his success was phenomenal. Although equity looks at the advantage gained by the wrongdoer rather than the loss to the victim, the cases show that in assessing the advantage gained, the court will look at the whole situation in the round. And it is relevant that if [O'Sullivan's counsel's] approach is applied, O'Sullivan would be much better off than if he had received separate legal advice and signed agreements negotiated at arm's length on reasonable terms current in the trade at the time. . . .

In my judgment the judge was right to set the agreements aside and to order an account of the profits and payment of the sums found due on the taking of the account. But in taking the account, the defendants are entitled to an allowance as proposed by Fox, L. J., whose judgment I have read in draft, for reasonable remuneration including a profit element for all work done in promoting and exploiting O'Sullivan and his compositions, whether such work was done pursuant to a contractual obligation or gratuitously. . . .

[The Court proceeded to reaffirm the lower court's order of reconveyance of the copyrights and master recordings to O'Sullivan. However, the Court did uphold the inducement letters and, thereby, CBS' and EMI's rights to distribute O'Sullivan's records subject to a duty to account to and pay O'Sullivan therefor], credit being given for reasonable remuneration to the defendants for work done on O'Sullivan's behalf. . . .

Finally the question of interest. This is a financially significant matter since we are told that on the basis of the judge's order it is estimated that the amount of principal payable by the defendants is some 2.6 million pounds and the amount of interest is 4.37 million pounds. The judge awarded compound interest. . . . He held that since the defendants were fiduciaries who had used the money for the purposes of their business and had made a profit out of it, he was justified on the authority of *Wallersteiner's* case [1975] Q.B. 373.

[Mills's counsel] conceded that in respect of one particular matter the order for compound interest was justified. . . . [Mills' publishing company] had foreign subsidiaries in Germany and New Zealand. Ninety percent of the amount of the foreign sales was paid by the foreign publisher to the subsidiary in the foreign country. Of that 90%, 50% was sent to the United Kingdom of which half was paid to O'Sullivan. The remaining 40% was sent from Germany to the United Kingdom as a dividend for [Mills' publishing company]. From New Zealand, the remaining 40% was [kept by Mills' U.S. subsidiary]. Under the terms of the publishing agreement, O'Sullivan was entitled to a royalty of 50% from [Mills' company] and had no knowledge of the deductions in respect of foreign sales which reduced his royalty to 25% of 90%. . . . [He] conceded that O'Sullivan's royalty should be calculated at source, that is to say, 50% of the sums received by the foreign subsidiaries without any deduction . . . and compound interest should be charged in accordance with the judge's order on all sums found due.

But in respect of all other sums . . . I agree that simple interest should be ordered.

It is only in cases of breaches of fiduciary duty that compound interest can be awarded. . . . But in equity compound interest can be charged where the profits made in breach of a fiduciary duty have been used in trade. . . . In the present case, accepting that the money was used by the defendants for their business purposes, part of it must have been used for the benefit of O'Sullivan himself. I would vary the order by . . . awarding simple interest . . . save for the calculation of profits from foreign sales under the publishing agreement.

Fox, L. J.
[Defendants conceded] that (a) there was inequality of bargaining powers between the plaintiffs and these defendants; (b) Mr. Mills as Mr. O'Sullivan's manager owed him a duty to advise on the agreement and to obtain independent professional advice thereon having regard to the fact that Mr. Mills was chairman of and a shareholder in [the companies]; (c) that given independent advice [O'Sullivan] might have negotiated better terms than those in the agreements; and (d) that accordingly the agreements were voidable.

In my view the facts go rather beyond these concessions. It is, I think, clear that Mr. O'Sullivan, who was at all material times a young man with no business experience, reposed complete trust in Mr. Mills and executed those agreements

. . . without independent advice and because of his trust in Mr. Mills. . . .

In these circumstances I think that the agreements . . . are to be presumed to have been procured by . . . undue influence. . . .

There was no positive pressure by Mr. Mills upon Mr. O'Sullivan to execute the agreements but that does not matter. The fiduciary relationship existed. The onus was then upon those asserting the validity of the agreements to show that they were the consequence of the free exercise of Mr. O'Sullivan's will in the light of full information regarding the transaction. That has not been done. He had no independent advice about these matters at all. . . .

It seems to me, therefore, that, the agreements having been procured by the undue influence of Mr. Mills, the contracting companies and Mr. Mills are liable to account to Mr. O'Sullivan for any profits that they, respectively, obtained thereby. . . .

It is said on behalf of the plaintiffs that, if the principle of equity is that the fiduciary must account for profits obtained through the abuse of the fiduciary relationship, there is no scope for the operation of anything resembling [restitution]. I think that goes too far and that the law has for long had regard to the justice of the matter. . . .

A hard and fast rule that the beneficiary can demand the whole profit without an allowance for the work without which it could not have been created is unduly severe.

[However, it is not appropriate simply to reconstruct a set of contracts on the terms which plaintiffs' expert witness testified could have been obtained at arm's length at the time when they were concluded.]

In the first place, [the expert's] evidence was really only directed to the question of what might reasonably have been negotiated. The question of what recompense in the circumstances of this case it would be reasonable to allow was not investigated. If, for example, there was any failure by the M.A.M. companies or Mr. Mills to promote Mr. O'Sullivan's interests as vigorously or competently as they might have been expected to do, with the result that Mr. O'Sullivan suffered loss that might affect the position. Secondly, an order which, in effect, would involve substantial division of the profits between the beneficiary on the one hand and the fiduciary . . . on the other, goes far beyond anything hitherto permitted.

Once it is accepted that the court can make an appropriate allowance to a fiduciary for his skill and labour, I do not see why, in principle, it should not be able to give him some part of the profit of the venture if it was thought that justice as between the parties demanded that. . . . I am not satisfied that it would be proper to exclude Mr. Mills and the M.A.M. companies from all reward for their efforts. I find it impossible to believe that they did not make a significant contribution to Mr. O'Sullivan's success. It would be unjust to deny them recompense for that. . . .

It would not take full account of it in that the allowance would not be all as much as the defendants might have obtained if the contracts had been properly negotiated between fully advised parties. But the defendants must suffer that because of the circumstances in which the contracts were procured. . . .

The fact that the agreements were in restraint of trade does not, in my view, render them void. They are unenforceable.

WALLER, L. J.

. . . I agree with the [trial] judge that Smith clearly ought to have given . . . a warning to O'Sullivan [to obtain independent counsel]. . . . [However] the plaintiff, until he had come in contact with Mills and the defendant companies, was an unknown and unsuccessful singer earning his living as a postal worker. As a result of his association with Mills he became a pop star of wide renown. This was the result of joint enterprise in which both parties played an important part. The agreement between the two parties was unfair in that the defendants were taking a bigger share of the profits than the plaintiff appreciated but each party contributed to the joint success. . . . We are concerned to see that the plaintiff gets the profit to which he is entitled and at the same time see that the defendants receive fair remuneration but no more for all the work that they have done in pursuance of this joint project. . . . [T]he defendants here did make some profit with the knowledge and assent of the plaintiff. This the

defendants are entitled to keep and would be reasonable remuneration. On the other hand, it is clear that the profit which the defendants kept was excessive. The excess profit was retained without the knowledge of the plaintiff. The defendants must account for this profit. It would be for the official referee to decide what would be a reasonable remuneration. It must include all expenses and a fair profit. . . .

I have come to the conclusion that restitution requires that the court order should include the transfer of all the plaintiffs' [song] copyrights back to him and, disagreeing on this point with Dunn and Fox, L.J.J., that only the master recording in which the copyright would be in the maker should remain with the maker. . . .

The reason for awarding compound interest was that the interest which had not been paid must be taken to have been used by the defaulting party to make a profit for himself. . . . In this case there is a joint venture and the effect of the joint venture would mean that, in part at any rate, the interest was used to further the joint venture. . . . I am of the opinion, therefore, that, this being a joint venture [with the exception of the foreign subpublishing royalties], I would not award compound interest. In [the latter case] there were secret deductions which were not used in the joint interests of the plaintiff and the companies.

Elton Hercules John v. Richard Leon James, High Court of Justice, Chancery Division, 1982 J. No. 15026, decided November 29, 1985

[Dick James (who died shortly after this case was decided) had become Britain's most prominent music publisher by the mid-60s, in large measure by dint of having been the Beatles' first publisher. The James organization set up a number of foreign subsidiaries and entered into subpublishing agreements in other territories; gradually, unaffiliated foreign subpublishers were replaced with James affiliates (some of which were essentially "shell" corporations with no staff), and in some instances the agreements between the James UK company and its subsidiaries resulted in a lower percentage of income being remitted to London than had formerly been the case, while increasing the overall percentage of income to the James group. The James group also included a record production company, which initially licensed its product to third-party manufacturers, later substituting its own manufacturing/distribution entity.

Elton John and his lyricist, Bernie Taupin, signed songwriter agreements with Dick James Music (DJM) in 1967, and John signed management and recording agreements with James entities in 1968. All these agreements were on standard forms used by the James organization, and on the James organization's standard financial terms. In the case of the songwriter agreements, the writers' shares were to be calculated as a percentage of the receipts of DJM in the U.K., rather than on the basis of a calculation "at the source,"—that is, on the basis of monies collected in each country without reduction by reason of the share of monies collected by the local subpublisher. Neither John nor Taupin was represented by a solicitor or a manager, although their parents executed inducement letters because John and Taupin were minors. Dick James did not suggest to John and Taupin that they seek professional representation, nor did he explain the significance of the various contractual terms. For their part, John and Taupin did not ask questions—they were only too thrilled to be under contract to such a successful publisher.

John and Taupin received 50 Pound advances for signing their songwriter agreements, plus weekly advance of 10 or 15 Pounds each. The royalty split was essentially 50/50 (except for the publisher's share of public performance income, which was retained by DJM 100 percent).

The 1968 John-James recording agreement was likewise on a standard James form and provided very low rates of compensation to John.

From 1968 to 1970, John and Taupin achieved very little success, but, starting in 1970, John quickly became a superstar.

In 1969, Island Records had become interested in John and had suggested that he might have grounds for terminating the James agreement. John was unreceptive to the Island overtures, but he did tell James that he wanted to leave DJM. Later that year, the differences between John and DJM were resolved.

In 1970, the recording agreement was split into two agreements for tax reasons, one agreement covering the U.K. and the other covering the balance of the world.

During 1970, after John had had enormous success in the United States, James suggested a renegotiation of their agreements and recommended John (who already had a chartered accountant working for him) to a firm of solicitors. Initially, John's share of music publishing royalties was increased without a quid pro quo from John. Thereafter, the U.S. record licensing agreement between James and MCA Records was renegotiated, and James in turn amended John's recording agreements to provide for an extension of the term and an increased share of record royalties for John.

During this period, DJM hired John Reid to perform its day-to-day personal management functions, with the understanding that at the expiration of John's management agreement with DJM, Reid would become John's manager. In late 1972, after the trial court decision in *Instone v. A. Schroeder Music Publishing Co. Ltd.*, Reid questioned the low level of John's music publishing royalties, and John's solicitors were of the opinion that while the publishing agreement was not objectionable *per se*, DJM should be required to justify its extremely large share of the proceeds. Reid complained to James, who denied the suggestion that DJM was taking an unfairly large share and invited an audit of DJM's books by John. After considering the solicitors' advice in light of his meeting with James, Reid recommended that John finish out the term of his publishing agreement (then due to expire in October 1973) rather than fight at that time.

Shortly thereafter, John and Reid were advised by John Eastman, a prominent New York entertainment lawyer, that it might well be possible to proceed against DJM under the agreements on the grounds that DJM had failed to account properly and that DJM's system of foreign subpublishers had improperly reduced John's royalties. No action was taken at that time.

The publishing agreements expired in November 1973 and the recording agreements in February 1975. Audits of the DJM record and publishing companies were conducted on behalf of John in 1976, and John's representatives made DJM aware that they were considering the legal implications of the shares of royalties retained by the James foreign subpublishing subsidiaries. Discussions continued, and a further audit began in 1979. By 1980, John's managers and solicitors were considering a claim for recovery of John's copyrights. A barrister was consulted, but he advised against a suit to recover the copyrights, being of the opinion that the only remedy available to John was an action for damages for underpayment of royalties as the result of the excessive shares of publishing monies being retained by the DJM subsidiaries. Since John was fond of James and would only proceed if a massive underpayment were to be unearthed, a third audit was undertaken in 1981.

In 1982, John retained a new firm of solicitors, and suit was commenced in October of that year. John (and Taupin) sought to rescind the publishing and recording agreements for undue influence (and to recover the copyrights and master recordings), and to recover from DJM the difference between the royalties they had actually received and "the best possible royalty rates obtainable in the market," including amounts retained by DJM's foreign subpublishers, which would have been included in the calculation of the writers' shares had the publishing agreements been on an "at source" rather than a "receipts" basis (John and Taupin included, but later abandoned, claims that the agreements were in unreasonable restraint of trade).]

MR. JUSTICE NICHOLLS

The plaintiffs put this claim in two ways. The first is that the excess retained was an unauthorized profit made by DJM in the course of a fiduciary relationship arising from the publishing agreements. Secondly, on the true construction of the publishing agreements the excess is money due to the plaintiffs under those agreements or as damages for breach by DJM of an implied term not to establish or maintain arrangements outside the United Kingdom which unfairly, artificially or unjustifiably diminished [plaintiffs'] royalties. [A similar claim was made with respect to record royalties.] . . .

On a natural, fair reading of the documents one would have expected that the writers' entitlement to sums equal to one half of the royalties "received from persons authorised to publish the musical compositions in foreign territories" . . . carried with it the protection for the writers that, in fixing with the overseas "persons" the amount of the royalties to be remitted, DJM would be negotiating with another person an arm's length deal in which the interests of DJM and of the writers would not be in conflict. . . .

For my part I am in no doubt that under the publishing agreements DJM occupied a fiduciary position in respect of any exploitation which it carried out. In particular, in addition to being under a duty to exploit the assigned copyrights only in a way it honestly considered was for the joint benefit of the parties, DJM was under a duty not to make for itself any profit not brought into account in computing the writers' royalties. . . . [C]ommercially, the arrangement was in the nature of a joint venture, and the writers would need to place trust and confidence in the publisher over the manner in which it discharged its exploitation function. . . .

. . . [T]he evidence did establish that there are some advantages in having a subsidiary company even where it is only a "shell" administered by a local administrator. . . . [T]he subsidiaries were set up by DJM in the 1960s and later in the mid-1970s as the first steps towards an international network of local offices with local staff as in the [DJM company in] the United States of America. . . . [T]he subsidiary subpublishers appointed administrators to run their businesses on terms that gave the subsidiaries a profit additional to that of the parent. Apparently a 50% retention by the subsidiaries was normal in the industry. Whatever may be the rights or wrongs of this as far as other writers with their own contracts with DJM or other companies are concerned, the terms of which may be materially different, I am in no doubt that in this case DJM was in breach of its fiduciary duty to Mr. John [and] Mr. Taupin. . . .

[DJM claimed that John and Taupin were estopped to complain, and] pointed to the long history of the absence of any complaint regarding the sub-publishing arrangements despite the knowledge by the individual plaintiffs or their advisers of the nature and terms of the arrangement. . . . I am unable to accept this estoppel argument [because the "shell" arrangement was not disclosed until after the action commenced]. . . .

The defendants' next line of defence was limitation. They submitted that the plaintiffs' claim is essentially one of breach of contract in failing to pay sums to which the writers were entitled under the publishing agreements, and thus the ordinary six-year limitation period applies. . . . [P]laintiffs' claim that DJM should account for the unauthorised profit made by it in the course of a fiduciary relationship is not a claim to recover "trust property" within section 21(1)(b) [of the Limitations Act of 1980]. Royalties received by a publisher under an agreement such as the publishing agreements in this case are not impressed with a trust in favor of the writers (see *In re Grant Richards ex p. Warwick Deeping* 1907 2 KB. 33), and the amount of an unauthorised profit made by a fiduciary is recoverable by a plaintiff either as money had and received to his use or as an equitable debt (*Reading v. The King* 1949 2 KB. 232, per Asquith LJ at 237): the relationship between the fiduciary and the plaintiff "is that of debtor and creditor; it is not that of trustee and cestui que trust" (per Lindley LJ. in *Lister & Co. v. Stubbs* 1890 45 Ch. 1 at 15).

[The Court rejected plaintiffs' claim that the limitations period should be extended due to fraudulent concealment.] From the earliest days the defendants made no secret of the arrangements existing [with respect to the U.S.] . . . [A]t the material times 50 per cent was not the rate normally paid to independent sub-publishers after arm's-length bargaining [and] was, and is now, excessive. . . . [I]n no case from 1964 to 1981 did DJM agree to terms with an independent sub-publisher whereby that independent sub-publisher retained more than 25 per cent in respect of original recordings. . . . [However,] there was not, in relation to the United States, anything of the nature of a "cover-up." Those acting for the individual plaintiffs, both solicitors and accountants, and Mr. John's manager, Mr. Reid, knew who was doing what in that territory and what was being charged. . . . I do not think that there has been conduct by the defendants

such that it would be against conscience to avail themselves of the lapse of time or that there has been deliberate concealment of a fact relevant to the plaintiffs' cause of action.

The position regarding the other sub-publishing subsidiaries is altogether different. . . . Unlike DJM USA, [the other subsidiaries] had no offices or local staff and their businesses were carried on by administrators, but they retained for themselves a percentage of the mechanical royalties substantially larger than the percentage paid to the administrators. . . . [T]hese matters were not disclosed when royalties were accounted for year after year, nor in March 1971 when Mr. James explained [to John's solicitor] the built-in advantages which he said the writers enjoyed under DJM sub-publishing arrangements. . . . [I]t is straining credulity too far to regard the nondisclosure in these circumstances as inadvertence, due to oversight or office muddle. . . . [It] was deliberate . . . unconscionable conduct . . . a deliberate concealment. . . .

I should add that this is not a case in which by the exercise of reasonable diligence the plaintiffs or their advisers could have discovered the concealment. . . . [T]he professional audits which did take place (and it has not been suggested that they were conducted inadequately) did not result in discovery of the administration agreements.

Accordingly, the limitations defence on sub-publishing succeeds in relation to DJM USA but fails regarding [the other DJM subsidiaries, as to which there should be] no allowance from the mechanical royalties received by those companies . . . beyond the sums paid to the [local] administrators. . . .

[As to TRC, DJM's wholly-owned record production company], TRC was under fiduciary obligation to the artist in respect of any exploitation . . . of the master recordings similar to those I have already stated regarding any exploitation of the copyrights under the publishing agreements . . . [and] would be entitled to deduct its expenses or those of its subsidiary when accounting to the artist. . . .

However, subject to deduction of those expenses, TRC is *prima facie* accountable to the artist for the balance of the money obtained from the sale of the records as the profit arising from such sale. . . . [But TRC] formed and licensed a wholly-owned subsidiary, which entered into a pressing and distribution deal. The purpose of this type of arrangement was to ensure that the artist did not receive more than DJM conceived was his entitlement under the recording agreement: a share of the royalties obtained from licensing the master recordings. The thinking behind this was that if Elton John, for example, was not entitled to a share of the profits made by Philips [the former distributor], why should he be entitled to a share of the profits made by TRC if TRC undertook the business activities formerly undertaken by Philips? . . .

To this day the royalty rate paid by DJM Records to TRC remains unchanged. This is so, even though the rates of commission payable to [the previous distributor] improved in DJM Records' favour as sales increased. . . . The fact that it was advantageous to Mr. John to have access to an in-house record manufacturer did not justify keeping the royalty rate paid by DJM Records below the market rate. . . . [T]here is no evidence that before October 1976 Mr. John or his accountancy legal or other advisers were adequately aware of the arrangements with DJM Records. . . . [H]ave the defendants deliberately concealed any fact relevant to the right of action now in point? In my view the answer . . . is yes . . . [and on this branch of the case] the defence of limitation fails. . . .

I return to the question of whether any additional allowance ought to be permitted to TRC. In my view it should. Mr. John has benefitted from the group's efforts over the records, and I do not think that it would be proper to exclude TRC from all reward from those efforts. The objective of the court is not the punishment of the defendants but the attainment of a result that in practice would be just as between the parties. I consider therefore that over and above expenses as already mentioned, TRC should have a reasonable allowance for the skill and labour of TRC and DJM Records in manufacturing, marketing, distributing and selling the records, that allowance to include a fair profit element. . . .

I turn to the plaintiffs' primary claim, to have the various recording and publishing agreements set aside on the basis that they were procured by undue influence. . . . [T]he substance of the two ingredients required before the Court will set aside a transaction are first, a relationship in which one person has a dominating influence over the other and, secondly, a manifestly disadvantageous transaction resulting from the exercise of that influence. . . . [Under the 1967 publishing agreements] the writers obtained precious little. They obtained a right to royalties. The defendants claimed that the writers also obtained the benefit of an implied obligation that DJM would use reasonable diligence to publish, promote and exploit the compositions accepted, but even if this was so such an obligation was necessarily so loose and imprecise that it would have afforded the writers little protection. . . .

It may be inherent in the nature of this type of publishing agreement that the publisher's strictly legal obligations will be very limited. What Mr. John and Mr. Taupin wanted was a foot in the door, the entree to the popular music publishing world, and in practice they obtained this by the 1967 publishing agreement. . . . The value of this to the two young would-be writers is not to be underestimated. They were fortunate to have found in Mr. James a leading music publisher who was willing to encourage and support them. But the agreement contained no provision for early termination or return of copyrights if, for example, successful publication was not achieved and the writers became aware of another publisher who had more confidence in their songs. Conversely, and more importantly, if, as was no doubt the hope in every case, the writers succeeded enormously, their entire output for six years was bound to DJM effectively for ever, whether published or not, and there was no provision for any increase in royalty rates. . . . I consider that to have tied these two young men to DJM in 1967 for six years on the terms in question represented an unacceptably hard bargain.

Did Mr. Dick James assume a role of dominating influence? I consider that, brief though their acquaintance had been at this stage, he did. . . . Mr. James did not regard himself as obliged to give Mr. John or Mr. Taupin, nor did he give them, a thorough explanation of the terms of the proposed agreement. . . . [H]e told them that the terms were the standard terms within the industry. They were, as must have been obvious to him, trusting and relying on him that the contractual terms were fair and reasonable. The formality of requiring parental signature in the circumstances of these two men and their parents was not an adequate counterbalance to . . . their keenness to be signed by Mr. James [and] also, and importantly, and this is partly why they were so keen, in the trust they reposed in him as a man of stature in the industry [who] would treat them fairly. . . .

[A]t its inception the 1967 publishing agreement was an unfair transaction (I prefer to use this expression rather than "unconscionable," but without intending any different meaning). . . . [T]here is no question of Mr. James having sought consciously to obtain an unfair advantage. At the time he thought his normal terms for a publishing agreement were standard in the trade and therefore fair [and] was acting in good faith. . . . [However,] one can obtain an unfair advantage by the exercise of a dominating influence without intending to act unfairly.

I come next to the 1967 recording agreement, regarding which I make the same finding on Mr. James' good faith. . . . [A]t its inception this agreement was significantly disadvantageous to the artist Mr. John, in one important respect. . . . [Since] on the average a new artist will take three years to become established, a five year tie in this instance may not have been unreasonable . . . [but] where the agreement fell short of striking a reasonable balance was that it made no provision for any improvement in the royalty rate if, as happened here, the artist became a major success. . . .

As with the 1967 publishing agreement, so with this agreement, I think it is clear that . . . Mr. James was exercising a dominating influence over Mr. John regarding his career. Again, no proper explanation was given on the substantial implications of the agreement . . . [which,] with the single fixed low royalty rate, if for no other reason, constituted an unfair transaction.

[The Court then found that DJM had acted as John's manager with respect to the 1970 recording agreement, even though DJM never took a commission from John on his publishing or recording activities and felt that he did not need

management in these areas because his agreements were with James entities, because the agreement expressly recited that DJM was to manage "all the affairs of the Artist relating to his professional career" in any one of six enumerated areas. Noting that John was aware of the fact that the new agreement involved a five-year term, that he approved of the new royalty rates, and that he was pleased with DJM's efforts on his behalf, the Court found that the 1970 recording agreement was not unfair. However, the 1971 renegotiation of the publishing agreements was insufficient to cure the taint attaching to the 1967 agreements, since the 1971 negotiations assumed the validity of the earlier agreements.]

One of the features which strikes me first about the present case is the lapse of time involved. The agreements sought to be set aside go back to 1967. It was almost 15 years thereafter before the defendants were given any notice of a claim to set aside the agreements on any ground. Secondly, it is to be noted that the subject matter of the agreements comprises copyrights and master recordings which DJM and TRC were to spend effort and money in exploiting. In all fairness it behooves a party who wishes to claim the return of such property to act promptly when he becomes dissatisfied with the terms on which the property was transferred to the other party. . . . Thirdly, it should be noted that the plaintiffs have never made any criticism of the DJM organisation's skill or diligence in carrying out its work. . . . Mr. John stated candidly in his evidence that they always gave him "100 per cent support." . . . [T]he DJM group has made a significant contribution to [John's and Taupin's] subsequent success. . . . Fourthly, the joint venture has indeed been outstandingly successful. . . . Excluding performance fees, up to the end of 1982 Mr. John and Mr. Taupin (or their employer companies) had received about £ 1.2 million and £ 1.1 million respectively under the publishing agreements and in the same period Mr. John (or his employer companies) had received about £ 13.4 million under the recording agreements. . . .

In 1969 Mr. John . . . had no qualms whatsoever about staying with the Dick James organisation. He accepted that he made a conscious and deliberate decision to stay although he knew that

. . . his contracts might well be void [although he was skeptical about this advice from Island Records, which was anxious to acquire him as an artist]. [The same was true in the 1971 negotiations, in which John] did not raise with his solicitors the possibility that his contracts might be void . . . because "I was quite happy where I was." [Counsel was consulted in 1972 with respect to the potential impact of the *Schroeder* decision, but no action was taken, John and his advisers making a conscious choice to wait out the running of the terms of the contracts, keeping open the possibility of subsequently making claims.] . . . Looking at the matter from the point of view of the DJM group, for years it has conducted its business, and its relationship with Mr. John and Mr. Taupin, on the footing and in the belief that it was entitled to the copyrights on the terms of the publishing agreements. . . .

This state of affairs is not acceptable as a basis on which plaintiffs should come to the court in 1982 and ask for the publishing agreements to be set aside. . . . The balance of justice is firmly against setting aside the publishing agreements now . . . [and] I do not think that a case for equitable relief now in respect of [the 1970 recording] agreement has been made out. . . . [Even though] DJM's contractual management functions included recording, in my view that agreement (and the successor recording agreements) have, in the even, not worked unfairly to Mr. John.

[The Court proceeded to make the same findings with respect to Taupin.]

. . . [T]hose to whom the royalties are payable ought to be able to have trust and confidence that the publishing and record companies will treat them fairly in the exploitation arrangements made. And I have in mind the critical views I have expressed on [the "layering" of companies, each taking its share before John and Taupin were paid]. But in all the circumstances of this case these matters are not sufficient to tip the balance of justice or injustice in the plaintiffs' favour on the setting aside claim. In particular they do not cause me to revise my view that . . . it would not be just now to set aside the 1967 and subsequent publishing agreements or the 1967 recording agreement . . . [and] compensation is an adequate remedy in respect of the defendant's unauthorised profit-taking. . . .

[As for the claim with respect to the management agreement], even if the claim is expressed as a claim against a fiduciary to recover as an unauthorized profit the difference between the payment rates in the publishing and recording agreements and the best obtainable, the claim is not one to recover "trust property"; it is one to which the normal six-year period of limitation applies. . . . No case of fraudulent concealment was put forward. . . .

[The Court additionally declined to impose personal liability on Dick James, because of the finding that the claim did not involve "trust property." Damages against the DJM companies were left to subsequent calculation.]

9.22　Business Managers

The business manager can act in the simple role of paymaster, taking care of the client's bills, tax returns, and similar matters. Some business managers perform the additional role of investment adviser, handling tax shelters, pension plans, and other matters not directly related to the artist's day-to-day financial functions. Inevitably, the business manager is privy to the most intimate details of the client's economic life. As the following case indicates, a very high level of fiduciary duty attaches to the role of business manager.

ABKCO Music, Inc. v. Harrisongs Music, Ltd., 722 F.2d 990 (2d Cir. 1983)

PIERCE, J.

On February 10, 1971, Bright Tunes Music Corporation (Bright Tunes), then copyright holder of the song "He's So Fine" composed by Ronald Mack, brought this copyright infringement action in the United States District Court for the Southern District of New York against former member of the musical group "The Beatles" George Harrison, and also against related entities (hereinafter referred to collectively as "Harrison Interests"), alleging that the Harrison composition, "My Sweet Lord," (hereinafter referred to alternatively as "MSL") infringed the Ronald Mack composition, "He's So Fine," (hereinafter referred to alternatively as "HSF").

When this action was commenced, the business affairs of The Beatles, including Harrison Interests, were handled by ABKCO Music, Inc. (ABKCO) and Allen B. Klein, its President and "moving spirit." *ABKCO Music, Inc. v. Harrisongs Music, Ltd.*, 508 F. Supp. 798, 799 (S.D.N.Y. 1981). ABKCO was Harrison's business manager during the initial stages of the copyright liability action herein, at which time the litigation was handled for Harrison by ABKCO's General Counsel.

The following events preceded the instant appeal. Shortly after this action was commenced in February 1971, Klein (representing Harrisongs Music, Inc. and George Harrison) met with Seymour Barash (President and major stockholder of Bright Tunes) to discuss possible settlement of this lawsuit. Although Klein, at trial, denied having specific knowledge of the details of this discussion, he testified that he had suggested to Barash, around February of 1971, a purchase of the entire stock of Bright Tunes as a way to dispose of this lawsuit. Thus, in 1971, Klein was acting on behalf of Harrison Interests in an effort to settle this copyright infringement claim brought by Bright Tunes, although no settlement resulted.

Subsequent to the Klein-Barash meeting, Bright Tunes went into "judicial dissolution proceedings." This infringement action was placed on the district court's suspense calendar on March 3, 1972, and was resumed by Bright Tunes (in receivership) in early 1973. Also in early 1973 (March 31), ABKCO's management contract with The Beatles expired. Bitter and protracted litigation ensued between The Beatles and ABKCO over the winding down of management affairs—a dispute that ended in 1977 with The Beatles paying ABKCO $4.2 million in settlement.

There is some disagreement as to whether further settlement negotiations took place between Harrison Interests and Bright Tunes between 1973 and mid-1975. It appears undisputed,

however, that Harrison Interests' attorney at least initiated settlement talks in the late summer of 1975; that in the period October 1975 through February 1976, settlement discussions took place between Bright Tunes' counsel and counsel for Harrison Interests regarding settlement of this infringement action (an offer by Harrison Interests based on United States royalties); and that those discussions were in the 50%/50% or 60%/40% range. These discussions culminated in a $148,000 offer by Harrison Interests in January of 1976 (representing 40% of the United States royalties).

At about the same time (1975), apparently unknown to George Harrison, Klein had been negotiating with Bright Tunes to purchase all of Bright Tunes' stock. That such negotiations were taking place was confirmed as early as October 30, 1975, in a letter from Seymour Barash (Bright Tunes' former President) to Howard Sheldon (Bright Tunes' Receiver), in which Barash reported that there had been an offer from Klein for a substantial sum of money. The same letter observed that "[Klein] would not be interested in purchasing all of the stock of Bright Tunes . . . if there was any doubt as to the outcome of this litigation."

In late November 1975, Klein (on behalf of ABKCO) offered to pay Bright Tunes $100,000 for a call on all Bright Tunes' stock, exercisable for an additional $160,000 upon a judicial determination as to copyright infringement. In connection with this offer, Klein furnished to Bright Tunes three schedules summarizing the following financial information concerning "My Sweet Lord": (1) domestic royalty income of Harrisongs Music, Inc. on MSL; (2) an updated version of that first schedule; and (3) Klein's own estimated value of the copyright, including an estimate of foreign royalties (performance and mechanical) and his assessment of the total worldwide future earnings.

Barash considered the Klein offer only a starting point. He thought that a value of $600,000 was more accurate and recommended a $200,000 call, based on a $600,000 gross sales price. Also in December 1975, Barash noted, in a letter to counsel for the Peter Maurice Co., that Harrison Interests' counsel had never furnished a certified statement of worldwide royalties of MSL, but that from conversations between Stephen Tenenbaum (accountant for several Bright Tunes stockholders) and Klein, Bright Tunes had been given that information by Klein.

Shortly thereafter, on January 19, 1976, Barash informed Howard Sheldon (Bright Tunes' Receiver) of the Klein offer and of the Bright Tunes stockholders' unanimous decision to reject it. Barash noted that "[s]ince Mr. Klein is in a position to know the true earnings of 'My Sweet Lord,' his offer should give all of us an indication of the true value of this copyright and litigation." Sheldon responded in a letter dated January 21, 1976, noting, *inter alia*, that Harrison's attorneys were informed that no settlement would be considered by Bright Tunes until total sales of MSL were determined after appropriate figures were checked.

On January 30, 1976, the eve of the liability trial, a meeting was held by Bright Tunes' attorney for all of Bright Tunes' stockholders (or their counsel) and representatives of Ronald Mack. The purpose of the meeting was to present Bright Tunes with an offer by Harrison Interests of $148,000, representing 40% of the writers' and publishers' royalties earned in the United States (but without relinquishment by Harrison of the MSL copyright). At the time, Bright Tunes' attorney regarded the offer as "a good one." 508 F. Supp. at 802. The Harrison offer was not accepted, however. Bright Tunes raised its demand from 50% of the United States royalties, to 75% worldwide, plus surrender of the MSL copyright. The parties were unable to reach agreement and the matter proceeded to trial.

A three-day bench trial on liability was held before Judge Owen on February 23–25, 1976. On August 31, 1976 (amended September 1, 1976), the district judge rendered a decision for the plaintiff as to liability, based on his finding that "My Sweet Lord" was substantially similar to "He's So Fine" and that Harrison had had access to the latter. *Bright Tunes Music Corp. v. Harrisongs Music, Ltd.*, 420 F. Supp. 177 (S.D.N.Y. 1976). The issue of damages and other relief was scheduled for trial at a later date.

Following the liability trial, Klein, still acting for ABKCO, continued to discuss with Bright Tunes the purchase of the rights to HSF. During 1977, no serious settlement discussions were held between Bright Tunes and Harrison Interests. Indeed, the record indicates that throughout 1977 Bright Tunes did not authorize its attorneys to give Harrison a specific settlement figure. By November 30, 1977, Bright Tunes' counsel noted that Klein had made an offer on behalf of ABKCO that "far exceeds any proposal that has been made by the defendants."

On February 8, 1978, another settlement meeting took place, but no agreement was reached at that meeting. Although it appears that everyone present felt that the case should be settled, it also appears that there were no further settlement discussions between Harrison Interests and Bright Tunes subsequent to that date. The Bright Tunes negotiations with ABKCO, however, culminated on April 13, 1978, in a purchase by ABKCO of the HSF copyright, the United States infringement claim herein, and the worldwide rights to HSF, for $587,000, an amount more than twice the original Klein (ABKCO) offer. This purchase was made known to George Harrison by Klein himself in April or May of 1978. Harrison "was a bit amazed to find out" about the purchase. . . .

On July 17, 1978, ABKCO adopted Bright Tunes' complaint and was substituted as the sole party plaintiff in this action. In May 1979, Harrison Interests obtained leave to assert affirmative defenses and counterclaims against Klein and ABKCO for alleged breaches of fiduciary duty relating to the negotiation for and purchase of the Bright Tunes properties. . . .

The damages decision was filed on February 19, 1981. *ABKCO Music, Inc. v. Harrisongs Music, Ltd.*, 508 F. Supp. 798 (S.D.N.Y. 1981). Having determined that the damages amounted to $1,599,987, the district judge held that ABKCO's conduct over the 1975–78 period limited its recovery, substantially because of the manner in which ABKCO had become a plaintiff in this case. Particularly "troublesome" to the court was "Klein's covert intrusion into the settlement negotiation picture in late 1975 and early 1976 immediately preceding the trial on the merits." *Id.* at 802. He found, *inter alia*, that Klein's status as Harrison's former business manager gave special credence to ABKCO's offers to Bright Tunes and made Bright Tunes less willing to settle with Harrison Interests either before or after the liability trial. Moreover, the court found that in the course of negotiating with Bright Tunes in 1975–76, Klein "covertly furnished" Bright Tunes with certain financial information about MSL which he obtained while in Harrison's employ as business manager. The foregoing conduct, in the court's view, amounted to a breach of ABKCO's fiduciary duty to Harrison. The court held that although it was not clear that "but for" ABKCO's conduct Harrison Interests and Bright Tunes would have settled, he found that good faith negotiations had been in progress between the parties and Klein's intrusion made their success less likely, since ABKCO's offer in January 1976 was viewed by Bright Tunes as an "insider's disclosure of the value of the case." *Id.* at 803. Consequently, the district judge directed that ABKCO hold the "fruits of its acquisition" from Bright Tunes in trust for Harrison Interests, to be transferred to Harrison Interests by ABKCO upon payment by Harrison Interests of $587,000 plus interest from the date of acquisition. . . .

ABKCO . . . argues that ABKCO did not breach its fiduciary duty to Harrison because (a) no confidential information was improperly passed from ABKCO to Bright Tunes during the negotiations to purchase HSF, and (b) there was no causal relationship between ABKCO's actions and Harrison Interests' failure to obtain settlement. . . . [W]e reject appellant's arguments and affirm the decision of the district judge. . . .

There is no doubt but that the relationship between Harrison and ABKCO prior to the termination of the management agreement in 1973 was that of principal and agent, and that the relationship was fiduciary in nature. See *Meese v. Miller*, 79 A.D.2d 237, 241, 436 N.Y.S.2d 496, 499 (4th Dep't 1981). The rule applicable to our present inquiry is that an agent has a duty "not to use confidential knowledge acquired in his employment in competition with his principal." *Byrne v. Barrett*, 268 N.Y. 199, 206, 197 N.E. 217, 218 (1935). This duty "exists as well after the employment is terminated as during its continuance." *Id.; see also Restatement (Second) of Agency* § 396 (1958). On the other hand, use of

information based on general business knowledge or gleaned from general business experience is not covered by the rule, and the former agent is permitted to compete with his former principal in reliance on such general publicly available information. *Byrne v. Barrett*, 268 N.Y. at 206, 197 N.E. at 218; *Restatement (Second) of Agency* § 395 comment b (1958). The principal issue before us in the instant case, then, is whether the district court committed clear error in concluding that Klein (hence, ABKCO) improperly used confidential information, gained as Harrison's former agent, in negotiating for the purchase of Bright Tunes' stock (including HSF) in 1975–76.

One aspect of this inquiry concerns the nature of three documents—schedules of MSL earnings—which Klein furnished to Bright Tunes in connection with the 1975–76 negotiations. Although the district judge did not make a specific finding as to whether each of these schedules was confidential, he determined that Bright Tunes at that time was not entitled to the information. 508 F. Supp. at 803. It appears that the first of the three schedules may have been previously turned over to Bright Tunes by Harrison. The two additional schedules which Klein gave to Bright Tunes (the detailed updating of royalty information and Klein's personal estimate of the value of MSL and future earnings) appear not to have been made available to Bright Tunes by Harrison. Moreover, it appears that at least some of the past royalty information was confidential. The evidence presented herein is not at all convincing that the information imparted to Bright Tunes by Klein was publicly available. *Cf. Franke v. Wiltschek*, 209 F.2d 493, 495 (2d Cir. 1953) (former fiduciary precluded from using confidential information in competition with former principal even if the information is readily available from third parties or by other means). Furthermore, the district judge was in a better position to assess the credibility aspects of evidence bearing on this question than we are.

Another aspect of the breach of duty issue concerns the timing and nature of Klein's entry into the negotiation picture and the manner in which he became a plaintiff in this action. In our view, the record supports the position that Bright Tunes very likely gave special credence to Klein's position as an offeror because of his status as Harrison's former business manager and prior coordinator of the defense of this lawsuit. *See, e.g.*, letter from Barash to Sheldon, dated January 19, 1976 ("Since Mr. Klein is in a position to know the true earnings of My Sweet Lord, his offer should give all of us an indication of the true value of this copyright and litigation."). To a significant extent, that favorable bargaining position necessarily was achieved because Klein, as business manager, had intimate knowledge of the financial affairs of his client. Klein himself acknowledged at trial that his offers to Bright Tunes were based, at least in part, on knowledge he had acquired as Harrison's business manager.

Under the circumstances of this case, where there was sufficient evidence to support the district judge's finding that confidential information passed hands, or, at least, was utilized in a manner inconsistent with the duty of a former fiduciary at a time when this litigation was still pending, we conclude that the district judge did not err in holding that ABKCO had breached its duty to Harrison. . . .

In this case, Klein had commenced a purchase transaction with Bright Tunes in 1971 on behalf of Harrison, which he pursued on his own account after the termination of his fiduciary relationship with Harrison. While the initial attempt to purchase Bright Tunes' catalogue was several years removed from the eventual purchase on ABKCO's own account, we are not of the view that such a fact rendered ABKCO unfettered in the later negotiations. Indeed, Klein pursued the later discussions armed with the intimate knowledge not only of Harrison's business affairs, but of the value of this lawsuit—and at a time when this action was still pending. Taking all of these circumstances together, we agree that appellant's conduct during the period 1975–78 did not meet the standard required of him as a former fiduciary.

In so concluding, we do not purport to establish a general "appearance of impropriety" rule with respect to the artist/manager relationship. That strict standard—reserved principally for the legal profession—would probably not suit the realities of the business world. The facts of this case otherwise permit the conclusion reached

herein. Indeed, as Judge Owen noted in his Memorandum and Order of May 7, 1979 (permitting Harrison Interests to assert counterclaims), "The fact situation presented is novel in the extreme. Restated in simplest form, it amounts to the purchase by a business manager of a known claim against his former client where, the right to the claim having been established, all that remains to be done is to assess the monetary award." We find these facts not only novel, but unique. Indeed, the purchase, which rendered Harrison and ABKCO adversaries, occurred in the context of a lawsuit in which ABKCO had been the prior protector of Harrison's interests. Thus, although not wholly analogous to the side-switching cases involving attorneys and their former clients, this fact situation creates clear questions of impropriety. On the unique facts presented herein, we certainly cannot say that Judge Owen's findings and conclusions were clearly erroneous or not in accord with applicable law.

Appellant ABKCO also contends that even if there was a breach of duty, such breach should not limit ABKCO's recovery for copyright infringement because ABKCO's conduct did not cause the Bright Tunes/Harrison settlement negotiations to fail. *See* 508 F. Supp. at 803 & n. 15. Appellant urges, in essence, that a finding of breach of fiduciary duty by an agent, to be actionable, must be found to have been the proximate cause of injury to the principal. We do not accept appellant's proffered causation standard. An action for breach of fiduciary duty is a prophylactic rule intended to remove all incentive to breach—not simply to compensate for damages in the event of a breach. *See Diamond v. Oreamuno*, 24 N.E.2d 494, 498, 248 N.E.2d 910, 912, 301 N.Y.S.2d 78, 81 (1969) ("[T]he function of [an action founded on breach of fiduciary duty] . . . is not merely to compensate the plaintiff for wrongs committed by the defendant but . . . 'to *prevent* them, by removing from agents and trustees all inducement to attempt dealing for their own benefit in matters which they have undertaken for others, or to which their agency or trust relates.' ") (emphasis in original). Having found that ABKCO's conduct constituted a breach of fiduciary duty, the district judge was not required to find a "but for" relationship between ABKCO's conduct and lack of success of Harrison Interests' settlement efforts.

ABKCO argues further that the offer to sell substantially what had been gained in the purchase from Bright Tunes to Harrison for $700,000, and Harrison's rejection of that offer, *see supra* note 7, bars Harrison Interests from obtaining a constructive trust in this action, *per Turner v. American Metal Co.*, 268 A.D. 239, 50 N.Y.S.2d 800 (1st Dep't 1944) (where former fiduciary offers former employer what he obtained in violation of fiduciary duty at price equivalent to his cost of acquisition and former employer refuses offer, fiduciary not held liable for breach of duty), *appeal dismissed*, 295 N.Y. 822, 66 N.E.2d 591 (1946). We find this argument unpersuasive. First, in *Turner*, unlike the case at bar, there was no finding of breach of fiduciary duty. Moreover, we find somewhat disingenuous ABKCO's claim that a $700,000 offer was a "price equivalent to his cost of acquisition," which had been $587,000. In any event, it is unclear whether that which ABKCO offered Harrison Interests was equivalent to that which ABKCO had bought from Bright Tunes.

Finally, on the facts herein, we agree that a constructive trust on the "fruits" of ABKCO's acquisition was a proper remedy. . . . [However,] since the parties or their agents entered into settlement agreements as to certain foreign infringement claims while the damages issues were *sub judice*, the trust should not include that portion of ABKCO's acquisition constituting a purchase of the foreign rights involved in those settlements. We remand the case to the district court to determine what portion of the $587,000 paid by ABKCO to Bright Tunes is attributable to the foreign rights involved in the April 3, 1980 settlement. That sum should be subtracted from the $587,000 to determine the amount the Harrison Interests must pay to acquire only the rights not affected by the April 3, 1980 settlement. . . .

9.30 Attorneys

Attorneys are the predominant dealmakers in the record and music publishing industries. As the following cases indicate, just whom a particular attorney may be representing in a particular transaction can sometimes be confusing—and costly. In *Croce v. Kurnit*, the lawyer was a principal in a record production company that had Jim Croce under contract. Later, the lawyer handled some of Croce's legal and business affairs, leading to the later charge that the lawyer had fiduciary duties to Croce and had breached these duties. In *McCauley Music v. Solomon*, a lawyer was deemed negligent in failing to advise a client of an impending option exercise date, even though the lawyer had never represented the client with respect to the contract in question.

Because of their roles, attorneys often develop hostile relationships with industry executives in the course of their representation of various clients. The article by Judianne Jaffe, which follows the cases, describes one recent example and discusses pitfalls that should be avoided.

Croce v. Kurnit, 565 F. Supp. 884 (S.D.N.Y. 1982)

SWEET, J.

This diversity action, a portion of which was tried to the court, presented facts which evoked memories of *A Star Is Born*, except that the star in this case, James Croce, died all too soon after his ascendancy. The complaint filed by Ingrid Croce, his widow and heir ("Mrs. Croce"), a California resident, sought to obtain certain damages from the defendants, citizens of states other than California, arising out of an alleged breach of certain contracts as well as recission of the contracts on the ground of fraud, and breach of fiduciary duty. On the findings and conclusions set forth below, judgment will be granted to the defendants dismissing the claims of unconscionability and breach of fiduciary duty against Cashman and West and granting Croce's breach of fiduciary claim against Kurnit. The defendants' motion for judgment notwithstanding the verdict is denied. . . .

James Joseph Croce ("Jim Croce") was born in 1943 and in the course of his schooling attended Villanova University. There he met Ingrid, who subsequently became his wife, and also Tommy West, who became both ·his friend and, as it developed, a business associate. During the college years Jim Croce sang, played guitar and wrote songs, as did West.

After graduation from College, Jim Croce sought to shape a career out of his interest in music, played and sang in coffee houses, and developed both his own style and his own music. He managed to produce a record album entitled "Facets" containing certain of his songs which he performed. He sent the album to Tommy and sought to interest the latter in his work.

West in the meantime also developed a career in music, producing, singing and playing for commercials. He had met Cashman with whom he collaborated as well as Kurnit, an attorney who had been working at ABC Records, Inc. By 1968 all three, West, Cashman and Kurnit, were at CBS, Cashman, West in the music department and Kurnit serving in the legal department. The two musicians together with Eugene Pistilli ("Pistilli") decided to enter the record business on their own and set up CP & W for that purpose. Kurnit was also a participant in the enterprise.

In the summer of 1968, while Kurnit was still at CBS, Jim and Ingrid Croce arrived in New York, stayed with West, and met Kurnit, who was introduced to them as "the lawyer." West and the Croces discussed the possibility of CP & W producing a record by Jim Croce. The outlines of the contractual arrangements were discussed, the Croces returned to Pennsylvania and according to West, proposed contracts were taken to them after their trip to New York and before their return to New York on September 17, 1968. Whether or not that occurred (Mrs. Croce maintains it did not), the Croces did not conduct any meaningful review of the contract until September 17, 1968.

On that date the Croces were in New York again, staying with the Wests. They met Kurnit for the second time. He outlined the contract terms to them in a two to three hour meeting. According to Kurnit, there was no negotiation although a minor change in the proposed contract

was made. The Croces signed three agreements, a recording contract with CP & W, a publishing contract with Blendingwell and a personal management contract also with Blendingwell ("the contracts"). The Croces were unrepresented, and they were not advised to obtain counsel by Kurnit who signed the contracts on behalf of the corporate entities. Kurnit was known to the Croces to be a participant with Cashman, Pistilli and West in their enterprises. The Croces did not enter into any retainer agreement with Kurnit, were never billed by him in connection with the contracts, and aside from the meeting of September 17, received no advice from him concerning the contracts.

The contracts that were executed on September 17, 1968 provided that Croce would perform and record exclusively for CP & W, as well as the terms under which all the Croce's songs would be published and managerial services would be provided for the Croces. The contracts placed no affirmative requirements on the defendants other than to pay each of the Croces approximately $600 a year and to make certain royalty payments in the event that music or records were sold. The duration of the contracts was seven years if options to extend were exercised by the defendants. All rights to the Croces' musical performances and writings were granted to the defendants. The management contract was assignable.

The expert testimony offered by Mrs. Croce focused on the effect of the assignability of the management contract, the lack of any objective threshold to be achieved before the exercise of options, and the interrelationship of the three contracts. In addition other significant provisions were cited as being unfavorable to the Croces which would have been the subject of negotiation had the Croces in September 1968 been represented by the expert retained in 1982. These included the term of the contracts, the royalty rate and its escalation, a revision of the copyrights, a minimum recording sides obligation, and the time for making objections to royalty statements.

However, certain of the provisions which were under attack were also contained in the forms published by various organizations involved in the entertainment industry, and there was no evidence presented in this action, meticulously prepared by able counsel on both sides, which established that the terms of these contracts differed significantly from others prepared by Kurnit on behalf of the defendants. These contracts include many terms of art and are customarily the subject of hard bargaining in the event that the artist and the producer both have established economic power. Here, however, no significant changes were made in the contracts as initially proposed by Kurnit on behalf of the other defendants.

After the contracts were executed, the parties undertook their performance. In the summer of 1969 the recording contract was assigned to Interrobang Productions, Inc. ("Interrobang"), as was the management contract a year later. Cashwest is the successor in interest to Interrobang. The management contract was assigned to Showcase Management, a company in which CP & W had an interest, a demonstration record was prepared (a "demo") and thereafter Capital Records undertook to produce a Croce recording under the direction of Nick Vanet. This recording was published in the spring of 1969 and after its publication, Jim Croce worked hard to promote it. By the winter of 1969–70 it was apparent the album was a failure, and Jim turned to other pursuits.

In the fall of 1968 Kurnit represented the Croces in connection with a lease. In April 1969 Kurnit listed his firm as the party to whom all ASCAP correspondence for Croce should be sent. In January 1970 Kurnit executed a document as attorney in fact for the Croces and also was involved in the dispute between the Croces and their then manager.

Notwithstanding, on March 19, 1970 Jim and Ingrid, unhappy with the management with which they had been provided, sought legal advice with respect to breaking the contracts. They retained Robert Cushman ("Cushman") of Pepper, Hamilton & Schatz in Philadelphia. On June 9, 1970 Croce wrote to Kurnit seeking to terminate the contracts and advising him that "Ingrid and I are getting out of music." In the summer of 1970, Cushman met with Kurnit and discussed the grievances which the Croces had expressed to him, supported at one point by a statement of Pistilli, which, according to Cushman, es-

tablished that the Croces had been defrauded. Some revisions and amendments to the contracts were discussed.

In December 1970 Ingrid became pregnant, and Jim returned to songwriting and performing. Thereafter, he sent material to West who expressed interest and delight. Cushman requested a further retainer to pursue the revision or cancellation of the contracts and never heard again from either of the Croces.

In the early part of 1971 West and Cashman worked with Croce and prepared a demo. With Kurnit's help, they sold the idea of its production to ABC, interested an established management agency in Croce with the result that Interrobang delegated its management contract for Croce to BNB Associates, Ltd. ("BNB") in September 1971. Once the relationship with the defendants resumed in 1971 and the birth of his son in September, Jim's career began to move. His work was well received and in April 1971, ABC records contracted to manufacture, distribute and sell Croce records. Jim was on the road late in 1971 and 1972 promoting and performing. His career skyrocketed and until September 20, 1973 the future appeared halcyon for all concerned. During 1972 Kurnit represented Croce on matters other than the contracts.

On September 20, 1973, after a concert in Louisiana, Croce took off in a private plane. The plane crashed in a thunderstorm, and Croce was killed.

Very shortly thereafter Kurnit visited Mrs. Croce and offered to represent the estate and to take care of the wrongful death action arising from the crash. On September 26, 1973, Kurnit became the attorney for the Estate and Mrs. Croce. In connection with the wrongful death action, Kurnit later stated on the form filed with the Appellate Division on October 4, 1973: "Ingrid Croce, and her deceased husband, James J. Croce, have been my clients since 1968. I have been their personal attorney in a majority of their legal matters."

Kurnit served as counsel to the estate from September 26, 1973 until June 24, 1976. During the spring of 1976 Kurnit, on behalf of the defendants, had consulted Donnenfeld and Brent, a Los Angeles law firm, with respect to a movie proposal. Thereafter, at his request on June 24, 1976 that firm was substituted for him as counsel for the estate.

In 1975, Mrs. Croce remarried and in the company of her husband discussed with Kurnit the use of certain material which had not been the subject of the contracts. These discussions, involving what the parties have termed "the estate sides," were the subject of the contract issues concerning the publication of "The Faces I Have Been" album resolved by the jury's Special Verdict. During these discussions Kurnit represented CP & W and after the initial discussion, Mrs. Croce retained Ivan Hoffman, an attorney, to represent her. Hoffman and Kurnit exchanged correspondence, drafts and telephone calls. There is no evidence that Hoffman was consulted about the contracts or Mrs. Croce's rights which resulted from the contracts. . . .

During the period from 1968 to date the defendants received approximately $6.9 million as a consequence of the performance of the contracts. The recording and entertainment career of Croce is not atypical, representing as it does, initially a famine, and ultimately a feast. No expert who testified claimed the prescience to determine in advance what records the public will buy or in what amount. Though the returns on a successful record are unbelievably high, the risk of initial failure is also high. Judgment, taste, skill and luck far outweigh the time spent or the capital expended on any particular recording.

It is on these facts that Mrs. Croce's claims of unconscionability and breach of fiduciary duty must be resolved, as well as the defendants' affirmative defenses of the statute of limitations and election of remedies. The claim of fraud has not been pressed by Mrs. Croce, and indeed there is no proof of misrepresentation, falsity or reliance except in connection with the fiduciary duty claims.

1. Representation by Kurnit

The claims of breach of fiduciary duty and procedural unconscionability are based on the role and actions of Kurnit at the signing and during the performance of the contracts. Indeed, the nature of Kurnit's relationship with the Croces deter-mines whether this action is barred by the statute of limitations. Therefore, this court will assess the September 17, 1968 transaction before proceeding to the merits of each claim.

Mrs. Croce asserts that after Kurnit had been introduced to the Croces on a prior occasion as "the lawyer," Kurnit acted as the Croces' attorney at the signing of the contracts or in such a manner as to lead the Croces to reasonably believe that they could rely on his advice. The Croces were aware of the fact that Kurnit was an officer, director and shareholder of Blendingwell and Cashwest on whose behalf Kurnit signed the contracts.

In light of the facts set forth above, Kurnit did not act as the Croces' attorney at the signing of the contracts. Even in the absence of an express attorney-client relationship, however, a lawyer may owe a fiduciary obligation to persons with whom he deals. . . . In particular, a fiduciary duty arises when a lawyer deals with persons who, although not strictly his clients, he has or should have reason to believe rely on him. . . . Kurnit's introduction as "the lawyer," his explanation to the Croces of the "legal ramifications" of the contracts which contained a number of legal terms and concepts, his interest as a principal in the transactions, his failure to advise the Croces to obtain outside counsel, and the Croces' lack of independent representation taken together establish both a fiduciary duty on the part of Kurnit and a breach of that duty.

In *Howard v. Murray*, 43 N.Y.2d 417, 372 N.E.2d 568, 401 N.Y.S.2d 781 (1977), an action to rescind a mortgage, bond and option arrangement, an attorney-client relationship had existed between the parties before the attorney became a principal in the transaction. The court concluded that any doubt as to whether an attorney-client relationship existed at the time of the transaction "should readily have been resolved against the defendant, absent proof of a clear and forthright statement to his clients that he was no longer their attorney and that they should obtain outside counsel before continuing any negotiations." *Id.* at 422, 372 N.E.2d at 570, 401 N.Y.S.2d at 784. Although I conclude that Kurnit did not act as counsel to the Croces before September 1968, the events surrounding the execution of the contracts, in particular his failure to advise the Croces to obtain counsel, establish the applicability of *Howard v. Murray* in determining the obligations of Kurnit.

Moreover, the limits of the fiduciary relationship as defined in *Penato v. George*, 52 A.D.2d 939, 383 N.Y.S.2d 900 (2d Dep't 1976) apply. The court there realized that the

> exact limits of such a relationship are impossible of statement (see Bogert, Trusts & Trustees [2d ed.], § 481). Broadly stated, a fiduciary relationship is one founded upon trust or confidence reposed by one person in the integrity and fidelity of another. It is said that the relationship exists in all cases in which influence has been acquired and abused, in which confidence has been reposed and betrayed. The rule embraces both technical fiduciary relations and those informal relations which exist whenever one man trusts in, and relies upon, another.

383 N.Y.S.2d at 904–95. (citations omitted).

This definition of a fiduciary duty applies not only to Kurnit's relationship but also on the facts of this case to West and Cashman, in whom the Croces placed their trust. Before further addressing Mrs. Croce's breach of fiduciary duty allegations, however, the defendants' statute of limitations defense warrants examination. For these purposes, Kurnit's relationship with the Croces controls.

2. Statute of Limitations

The applicable statute of limitations is six years for fraud and breach of fiduciary duty. N.Y. Civ. Prac. § 213(1) & (2) (McKinney). To avoid the time bar, Mrs. Croce asserts that Kurnit's continuous representation of the Croces from September 17, 1968 to June 24, 1976 tolls the statute under the "continuous representation" doctrine set forth in *Greene v. Greene*, 56 N.Y.2d 86, 436 N.E.2d 496, 451 N.Y.S.2d 46 (1982). In that case, the New York Court of Appeals held that for statute of limitations purposes a cause of action against an attorney for acts arising out of the attorney's representation of the plaintiff does not accrue during the period of that representation. . . .

Although this court has determined that Kurnit did not act as the Croces' attorney at the signing of the contracts, he did thereafter serve as their attorney in related and unrelated matters.

Indeed, in the retainer statement dated October 4, 1973, to the Judicial Conference of the State of New York referred to above, Kurnit himself stated that his representation commenced in 1968, after the execution of the contracts on September 18.

A lawyer's "various activities" on [a client's] behalf can be seen as part of a course of continuous representation concerning the same or related problem. . . . Although representing the Croces in a lease dispute is not related to the contracts, the representation of the Croces by Kurnit stems from their relationship arising from the contracts. Moreover, Kurnit's listing on the ASCAP application, his correspondence signed as "attorney-in-fact" regarding the songwriting contract and his assistance in resolving claims with the Croce's then-manager indicate continuous representation concerning the performance of the contracts. Kurnit's representation of the Croces on unrelated matters emphasizes the trust and reliance that the Croces placed in Kurnit as their attorney. Consequently, I conclude that Kurnit's representation to the New York Judicial Conference sets the date for the beginning of the tolling period as September 18, 1968.

Kurnit asserts, however, that Jim Croce's consultation of Cushman on March 19, 1970 ends the toll. The rationale for the continuous treatment doctrine lends credence to this assertion. Because a "relationship between the parties is marked by trust and confidence . . . [because] there is presented an aspect of the relationship not sporadic but developing; . . . [and because] the recipient of the service is necessarily at a disadvantage to question the reason for the tactics employed or the manner in which the tactics are executed," the continuous treatment doctrine was extended to continuous representation. . . . However, Jim Croce's retention of Cushman in 1970 to attempt to terminate the contracts also terminated the continuing representation by Kurnit.

Mrs. Croce argues that any interruption of the toll by the retention of Cushman should end by December of 1970 when Jim Croce decided to work pursuant to the contracts and discontinued any relationship with Cushman. However, once Jim Croce consulted Cushman, he was no longer the disadvantaged client unable to question or to pursue remedies for perceived wrongs. He inquired of his right to terminate the contract and chose not to exercise them. Hence, I conclude that the statute of limitations began to run on March 19, 1970 and continued to run for three and one half years until Kurnit was appointed to represent the Estate of Jim Croce.

Nonetheless, once Jim Croce died, his Estate had the right to pursue whatever causes of action survived his death. By the September 26, 1973 appointment of Kurnit as counsel to the Estate, the relationship between the Estate and Kurnit was marked by confidence and trust, once again placing Kurnit in a fiduciary relationship and making the continuing representation doctrine applicable as to the Estate.

Moreover, in *Pet, Inc. v. Lustig*, 77 A.D.2d 455, 433 N.Y.S.2d 934, 935–36 (4th Dep't 1980), the court held that it "would not permit the statute of limitations to run where the one claiming the benefit of the statute is the one charged in law with the duty of asserting and enforcing the claim before the statute runs" (citations omitted). In the instant case, Kurnit asserts the statute of limitations as a bar to Mrs. Croce's claims. However, once he was appointed counsel for the Estate, he had the duty of asserting claims on behalf of the Estate. Although it is understandable that Kurnit did not investigate or pursue claims against his own interest, he may not now claim the benefit of the statute of limitations.

Therefore I conclude that the statute of limitations was tolled for two years and nine months from September 26, 1973 until June, 1976 when Donnenfeld and Brent were substituted as counsel for the Estate. . . .

The statute of limitations ran for three and one half years from March 1970 to September 1973 and for two years and one month from June 1976 to July 21, 1978, the date on which this action was filed. Hence I conclude that this action is not barred by the statute of limitations.

3. *Unconscionability and Breach of Fiduciary Duty*

Mrs. Croce contends that the contracts were unconscionable. An unconscionable contract "affronts the sense of decency," . . . and usually involves gross onesidedness, lack of meaningful choice and susceptible clientele. J. Calamari & J. Perillo, *Contracts* § 9–40 (2d ed. 1977). A claim of unconscionability "requires some showing of 'an absence of meaningful choice on the part of one of the parties together with contract terms which are unreasonably favorable to the other party.'" . . .

Additionally, Mrs. Croce alleges that defendants breached their fiduciary duty to the Croces. A fiduciary relationship is bound by a standard of fairness, good faith and loyalty. . . . Substantial testimony was adduced on the subject of the inherent conflict presented by the control of the management contract by the publisher. The management contract, of course, served only the interest of the artist, although obviously the interest of the artist and his career were inextricably interwoven with the publication and promotion of his product. For example, BNB, when undertaking the assignment to manage Croce, immediately obtained a royalty rate increase, of course, thus affecting its own compensation.

The significance of management contracts depends on the needs of artists, some of whom are entirely capable of performing all the business and promotion duties while others seek to concentrate solely on their artistic efforts. As the relationship developed, Croce depended on his manager significantly, but the conflict between the artist and the producer does not so completely overbalance the mutuality of their interest as to make management and recording contracts held or controlled by the same interests, as occurred here, in and of itself, determinative of the issues of unfairness and unconscionability. Indeed, it was Kurnit who ultimately arranged for a separate management contract, albeit that the contract with BNB barred the manager from urging the artist to terminate the contracts.

As the facts stated above indicate, the contracts were hard bargains, signed by an artist without bargaining power, and favored the publishers, but as a matter of fact did not contain terms which shock the conscience or differed so grossly from industry norms as to be unconscionable by their terms. The contracts were free from fraud and although complex in nature, the provisions were not formulated so as to obfuscate or confuse the terms. Although Jim Croce might have thought that he retained the right to choose whether to exercise renewal options, this misconception does not establish that the contracts were unfair. Because of the uncertainty involved in the music business and the high risk of failure of new performers, the contracts, though favoring the defendants, were not unfair. . . . Therefore, I conclude that the terms of the contracts were neither unconscionable nor unfair and that Cashman and West did not breach a fiduciary duty.

In considering procedural unconscionability this court notes that the instant situation lacks the elements of haste and high pressure tactics. . . . Indeed, they benefitted the Croces by millions of dollars. Thus Kurnit's actions do not rise to the level of procedural unconscionability. Kurnit, however, as a lawyer and principal, failed to advise the Croces to retain independent counsel and proceeded to give legal advice to the Croces in explaining the contracts to them. These actions, as discussed above, constitute a breach of the fiduciary duty Kurnit owed the Croces. . . .

4. Remedy

Mrs. Croce seeks rescission of the contracts or more specifically termination of the contracts on the date of judgment. Since Mrs. Croce sued for breach of contract in Counts 4, 5 and 6, defendants assert that she is barred from seeking rescission because of the doctrine of election of remedies, which prevents a party who pursued two inconsistent theories from obtaining duplicative relief.

Although the doctrine of election of remedies does not preclude rescission, I find that rescission is inappropriate on the facts of this case. The Second Circuit has recognized that rescission is an extraordinary remedy, *Canfield v. Reynolds*, 631 F.2d 169, 178 (2d Cir. 1980), which is granted only where the breach is found to be "material and willful, or, if not willful, so substantial and fundamental as to strongly tend to defeat the object of the parties in making the contract." . . .

The breach of fiduciary duty by Kurnit is not so fundamental as to defeat the intent or purpose of the contract.

Moreover, the contracts have been performed. In attempting to return to the status quo Mrs. Croce would have the defendants retain the money they received under the contracts as compensation for their services and return the master tapes and copyrights to her. Defendants oppose this remedy as unjust enrichment. Although this court has difficulty perceiving how the status quo ante could ever be determined, achieving this possibility does not make rescission appropriate when, as in the instant case, the breach of fiduciary duty is not a breach going to the root of the contract.

Mrs. Croce is, however, entitled to damages resulting from Kurnit's breach of fiduciary duty in failing to advise the Croces to seek independent counsel. Given the bifurcated nature of this lawsuit, and the fact that, but for Kurnit's breach, the second branch of Mrs. Croce's complaint, claiming fraud, unconscionability, and breach of fiduciary duty, would in all likelihood not have arisen, this court assesses Mrs. Croce's damages to be the costs and attorneys' fees expended in prosecuting those claims, and determines that Kurnit is liable for this amount.

NOTE _____

1. The above decision in *Croce v. Kurnit* was affirmed by the U.S. Court of Appeals, 737 F.2d 229 (1984).

_____

McCauley Music Ltd. v. Solomon, Ontario (Canada) Supreme Court, No. 34849/79

[In an unreported case, a Toronto court imposed liability for negligence upon an entertainment lawyer for failure to advise a client of an impending option exercise date, although the lawyer had never represented the client with respect to the particular contract under which the option arose.

Dan Hill (who was later to achieve great success with the recording of his own composition "Sometimes When We Touch") became friendly with Matthew McCauley while at school. Dr. McCauley, Matthew's father, was a composer, conductor, and teacher, with a number of distinguished music industry credits. The McCauleys became involved with Hill's career, absorbing his expenses and paying $50,000 to create recordings of his performances. Hill became close friends with the McCauley family, and Matthew worked full time to promote Hill's career.

It became clear to the McCauleys that it would be appropriate for Hill to have separate legal representation, and through Fiedler (a manager whom Hill had met), Hill retained Solomon as his attorney. In May 1975, Hill (represented by Solomon) signed recording and music publishing contracts with the McCauleys, who were represented by an attorney named Newman (who represented the McCauleys in general matters).

The agreements provided for fixed terms of one year with four one-year options, each exercisable by written notice at least 15 days prior to the commencement of the next option year.

The McCauleys then decided to enter into a record distribution agreement with GRT, a Canadian manufacturer. Newman represented the McCauleys, Solomon represented GRT (as he had for the previous five years).

During the same month, Hill signed a management agreement with Finkelstein and Fiedler, who were represented by Solomon. Hill was unrepresented, but signed a letter (prepared by Solomon) that he had elected not to seek separate legal representation in connection with the management agreement.

The following month, Finkelstein & Fiedler succeeded in favorably renegotiating Hill's contract with the McCauley company, with Newman acting for the McCauley interests and Solomon for Hill. Later that year, the McCauleys (represented by Newman) negotiated an amendment to the GRT agreement (with GRT represented by Solomon).

At about this time, the McCauleys (according to Judge Carruthers) became "dissatisfied or disturbed with Newman's expertise in handling matters which related to the music business." Thereafter, Newman continued to act for the McCauleys with respect to "corporate affairs" and Solomon acted for them with respect to certain music matters (although it was a matter of dispute as to whether Newman also continued to represent them on some music matters).

The following year, Solomon represented the McCauleys in negotiating a foreign subpublishing agreement (which, of course, would also benefit Hill), which was to have a term of three years. During the second year of the subpublishing agreement, Solomon renegotiated the foreign subpublishing agreement, substituting a new contract with a three-year term (so that the overall subpublishing term would be five years). Under the new subpublishing agreement, the McCauley company received $300,000, of which half went to Hill. That same year, Solomon negotiated a printed music license agreement on behalf of the McCauleys.

At about that time, Matthew asked Solomon to prepare summaries of all of McCauley Music's contracts relating to Hill, but Solomon (after consultation with Finkelstein) refused to do so.

During the summer of 1978, Finkelstein & Fiedler asked Solomon to review Hill's contracts with McCauley Music to determine whether they had lapsed because of McCauley's failure to formally exercise its options. (By this time, the agreements had been in effect for almost four years, and neither side had made an issue out of the fact that no option notices had ever been given.) Thereafter, Queen's Counsel was retained to notify McCauley Music of Hill's position that the agreements had lapsed. (Hill subsequently entered into a lucrative recording contract with a major U.S. record company.)

McCauley Music thereupon sued, claiming (1) that Finkelstein & Fiedler, Hill, and Solomon were estopped by their conduct from asserting lapse on the basis of absence of notice, (2) that Finkelstein & Fiedler had wrongfully induced Solomon to fail to advise McCauley Music to pick up its options (with Hill being vicariously liable for the actions of his managers), and (3) that Solomon was liable for negligence for failure to give such advice.

Hill and Finkelstein & Fiedler settled with McCauley after the first day of trial, and the case thereafter proceeded solely against Solomon. Solomon's defense stressed the fact that McCauley Music and Hill had always ignored the absence of formal notice, and asserted that the McCauleys could have pressed the issue of the continuing vitality of the Hill/McCauley agreements. In addition, the defense asserted that Newman had the responsibility of advising the McCauleys on option dates (since Newman had prepared the agreements for the McCauleys and Solomon had never acted for the McCauleys vis-à-vis Hill), and that Dr. McCauley's experience in the music business was such that he, too, was or should have been aware of them.

On the issue of McCauley's acquiescence in Hill's departure, Judge Carruthers stated "I do not think it lies in Solomon's mouth now to maintain or suggest that Hill may not in law be entitled to have terminated the agreements. It was Solomon who, at the urging of Finkelstein & Fiedler, brought about this situation." Although indicating that "it would have been better" if Newman had specifically directed Dr. McCauley's attention, at the time the contracts were executed, to the need to "diarize" option dates, Judge Carruthers did not consider this negligence on Newman's part so as to make Newman liable for McCauley's damages. The problem, according to Judge Carruthers, lay in the fact that after the McCauleys felt it necessary to go beyond Newman in "music matters,"] "Solomon accepted them as clients on many occasions. From the point of the McCauleys, Solomon thereafter provided the legal assistance they needed in this area of their endeavours. Whether he was to work under a general retainer or not is something I do not think ever entered their mind. When something came up in the music field that required the attention of a lawyer, they turned to Solomon. He never suggested that he could not help them, except once." [The one instance, of course, was the request for the summaries of the Hill contracts.

The Court focused on the two occasions upon which Solomon had negotiated foreign subpublishing agreements for the McCauleys, and stated that "it was incumbent upon Solomon to satisfy himself that the [McCauley/Hill] publishing agreement . . . was and could continue to be in full force and effect for the period provided for therein, before beginning to negotiate for and obtain a 'subpublishing' agreement." The Court mentioned the fact that by his own admission, Solomon had considered the option provisions of the McCauley/Hill agreement to some degree at the time of the negotiations (although Solomon stated that he only did so to satisfy himself that

sufficient album commitments remained under the McCauley/Hill agreement to satisfy the requirements of the subpublishing agreement). He admitted that he overlooked the requirement that Hill be paid $5000 in connection with the option exercises for 1977 and 1978. On cross-examination:]

Q. You just never addressed your mind at all. The question is: Would you now regard it as your duty to give [the McCauleys] advice in that respect having just negotiated a valuable contract for them that depended on their keeping alive the McCauley/Hill agreements?

A. Yes.

Q. All right. And you failed in that duty, didn't you, because you forgot about it?

A. Yes.

[The Court found that even if Solomon had never been involved with Hill or Finkelstein & Fiedler, he would have been under this duty with respect to the McCauleys (a position supported by an expert witness called on behalf of Solomon).

Further, the Court stated:]

. . . I am sure that had he been free to do so, Solomon would have done what was necessary because that would be in keeping with the spirit of the relationship which had existed between the McCauleys and Hill from the outset of their getting together. Unfortunately for the McCauleys, at least, Solomon was beholden to others and in particular Finkelstein & Fiedler. If Solomon ever possessed any thought of correcting the situation, it was wiped from his mind by his telephone conversations with Finkelstein & Fiedler. Their object was obviously to cut McCauley Music out of Hill's career and all that went with it. . . . Rather than disassociate himself with this position, which under the circumstances, in my opinion, he should have done, Solomon helped Finkelstein & Fiedler to gain their object.

[Judge Carruthers went on to note that the McCauleys were at all times aware that Solomon represented Hill, Finkelstein & Fiedler, and GRT, and that Matthew's view was that it was the McCauleys' responsibility to consider conflict-of-interest issues. However, Judge Carruthers stated that "it is not the responsibility of the client to be concerned about conflict of interest or potential conflict of interest. It is the concern of the solicitor. . . ."

The problem, however, did not stem from conflict of interest, according to Judge Carruthers, but, rather from the fact that Solomon "purely and simply did not do that which he was required to do on his admission and for that reason alone he is liable to McCauley Music for whatever damage it has sustained by reason of that failure." For this reason, Judge Carruthers declined to award punitive damages and referred the case to a special master to determine actual damages.]

The *Croce* and *Solomon* cases involved suits against lawyers by clients. Inevitably, a lawyer who represents his or her talent clients vigorously in dealings with entertainment companies will rub some executives the wrong way, leading to retaliation in some instances. The following article, by Judianne Jaffe, discusses this phenomenon and its implications for entertainment lawyers. The article originally appeared in *The Entertainment and Sports Lawyer*, vol. 4, no. 1, Summer 1985. It is reprinted by permission of the American Bar Association Forum Committee on the Entertainment and Sports Industries and by permission of Judianne Jaffe. Footnotes appearing in the original article have been omitted.

LICENSE TO KILL—STRENGTHENING THE ATTORNEY'S PRIVILEGE TO ADVISE CLIENTS NOT TO PERFORM CONTRACTS

by Judianne Jaffee

Lawyers who represent entertainers and athletes are called upon frequently to advise clients about their rights and obligations under contracts, particularly personal service contracts. With alarming frequency, breach of contract suits against entertainers also include a cause of action against the entertainer's lawyer for inducing the alleged breach.

Attorney Donald S. Engel, well known for his representation of major recording artists in contract litigation, recently won summary judgment dismissing him as a co-defendant with his rock group client, Boston. When Boston declined to perform for CBS Records and signed a new record deal with MCA Records, CBS sued Boston for breach of contract, and in the same case alleged tortious interference against Engel. Engel asserted he was privileged to give honest advice, even if the advice induced a breach of contract; U.S. District Judge Vincent L. Broderick of the Southern District of New York concurred. He proclaimed from the bench, "I am so outraged . . . that an attorney can be effectively immobilized from representing a client by naming him as a defendant that I very seriously considered awarding attorney's fees against CBS for making this motion necessary."

As Judge Broderick recognized, the mere existence of a tortious interference action against an attorney may "effectively immobilize" him from zealously representing his client, while he simultaneously attempts to avoid personal liability. Courts have struggled to protect attorneys in this situation, but the law throughout the country is still developing. Sound policy dictates that the clearest and strongest protection be furnished to attorneys whose actions may induce a client's breach of contract. In New York, in the absence of separate and independent tortious conduct toward the client or toward third parties, attorneys are immune from tort liability for interference with contracts. The New York rule should be followed in all states.

In addition, the burden should fall upon the plaintiff to prove the attorney's independent tort, rather than upon the attorney to prove affirmatively that his conduct was *not* wrongful. The definition of the tort of "inducing breach of contract" or "interference with contractual relations" implies that the impropriety of the interference is an element of the plaintiff's case. According to the *Restatement (Second) of Torts*, liability arises from the intentional and improper interference with the performance of a contract between another and a third person by inducing or otherwise causing the third person not to perform the contract. The comments to the *Restatement*, however, indicate it is unclear and unsettled whether the burden is on plaintiff to prove the defendant's actions were unjustified or on defendant to prove justification as an affirmative defense.

Before the issue of justifying the attorney's conduct even arises, the plaintiff must prove that the attorney's conduct proximately caused the breach. Since an attorney's legal advice to his client is ordinarily protected by the attorney-client privilege, it seems unlikely in the usual case that a plaintiff could ever prove proximate causation. The mere fact that the client declined to perform a contract after consulting with his attorney should not alone permit an inference of causation, because it is equally likely that the client had already decided not to perform, and simply sought advice on the legal implications of his intended breach; or that the client requested advice on the implications of performance and of nonperformance and made up his own mind without any recommendation by the attorney; or that the lawyer advised the client not to breach and the client chose to do so anyway. No case has ever dealt with this point. The courts have either assumed *arguendo* that there was causation and gone on to the issue of justification, or the client of the attorney has admitted that the attorney's advice induced the breach.

The burden of proving causation should be a difficult obstacle for the plaintiff to overcome. However, since a defendant-attorney cannot, at the time he answers the complaint, rely to a certainty on obtaining summary judgment or a directed verdict on the causation issue, he must plead the affirmative defense of privilege to avoid a waiver. According to the *Restatement (Second) of Torts,* the available justifications or "privileges" fall into two categories: a fiduciary's privilege and an adviser's privilege.

The fiduciary's privilege is defined in Section 770: "One who, charged with the responsibility for the welfare of a third person, intentionally causes that person not to perform a contract or enter into a prospective contractual relation with another, does not interfere improperly with the other's relation if the actor (a) does not employ wrongful means and (b) acts to protect the welfare of the third person."

Section 772 describes the adviser's privilege: "One who intentionally causes a third person not to perform a contract or not to enter into a prospective contractual relation with another does not interfere improperly with the other's contractual relation by giving the third person (a) truthful information, or (b) honest advice within the scope of a request for advice."

These definitions do not supply adequate guidance to the practitioner interested in avoiding potential liability. For example, what is "honest advice"? In New York, knowingly and intentionally wrong advice is not "honest advice." But honest advice may be "honest" without being "correct." Is correct advice always privileged? In New York, correct advice appears absolutely privileged. California, on the other hand, may not recognize an absolute privilege for correct advice, for in California, correct advice does not excuse an attorney even from malpractice liability to his own client. And, in California, one may be liable for interfering with an unenforceable contract, so an attorney's correct advice that a contract is not valid might still subject him to tort liability if he had the wrong intent.

Although the *Restatement of Torts* purports to summarize the law, the courts have expressed the privilege to induce breach of contract in many different ways, most of which do not correspond to the *Restatement*'s two separate definitions. Interference with contract by an attorney or agent has been held privileged where the attorney or agent:

—acted in good faith within the scope of his authority;
—acted strictly in a professional capacity;
—did not act beyond the scope of his honorable employment nor acted maliciously or fraudulently to tread on the rights of others;
—acted in the course of his agency and advice;
—acted in good faith and for the honest purpose of protecting the interest of the client;

—properly practiced his profession and acted without malice;

—was not officious, self-serving, or presumptuous;

—did not act solely for personal benefit;

—had a proper intent, in light of the nature and importance of the relationship between the parties;

—was motivated in part by a desire to protect the principal and reasonably believed the contract to be harmful to the principal's best interests;

—was not guilty of fraud or collusion or malicious or tortious act; or

—used lawful means to protect an interest that has greater social value than the mere stability of the particular contract in question.

Despite their lack of uniformity in defining the privilege, the courts have uniformly rejected tortious interference claims against attorneys or other fiduciaries in all but the most egregious circumstances. The situations in which the attorney's conduct defeated the privilege can be placed in three general categories: (1) where the client obtained no benefit, while the attorney or agent received a personal benefit; (2) where a separate tort was committed by the attorney toward the client or a third party; or (3) where lawyers leaving a law firm took contingent-fee clients with them and attempted to cut their former firm out of the fee. Thus, plaintiffs have successfully either proved or pleaded the tort of inducing breach against an attorney or agent where:

—The attorney's opinion letter was clearly and knowingly dishonest and was written to facilitate a transaction that fraudulently deprived third parties of valuable partnership interests;

—A corporate agent induced the corporation to breach a real estate broker's commission agreement, so that a different broker received the commission and split the commission with the corporate agent. (The corporation obtained no benefit because it paid the same commission in either case, and the only benefit was to the agent.);

—A corporate agent converted corporate property to his own use, preventing the corpo-

ration from performing a contract to deliver those goods;

—The agents acted as "naked competitors" for their sole benefit;

—An accountant could not prove a benefit to the client from his inducement of her change of lawyers; or

—Former law partners disrupted a law firm's fee agreements with its clients.

The reluctance of courts to permit tort suits of this kind against lawyers is understandable, and Judge Broderick's reaction quoted at the beginning of this article was not unusual. Judges, having once practiced law, tend to balk at permitting a lawyer's effectiveness to be undermined by the ethical dilemmas that arise immediately for the attorney sued by his client's adversary.

The Rules of Professional Conduct prohibit an attorney from representing a client when the representation may be materially limited by the lawyer's own interests. A lawyer named in a lawsuit for inducing breach has an obvious self-interest in absolving himself from liability and would be inclined to try to prove the nature of his advice to show he did not induce the breach. Legal advice to the client is confidential information that the attorney may not disclose without the client's consent. In some cases, disclosure of the advice might adversely affect the client's defense in the breach of contract suit, so the attorney would be ethically precluded from seeking a waiver from the client. Were the attorney to seek consent, the client would need independent counsel to assist in determining whether to permit the attorney to disclose privileged communications. This increases the client's legal fees and may well require the defendant-attorney to withdraw from representing his client in the underlying contract dispute. The law should not readily permit an adversary to bring about these results by naming the lawyer as an additional defendant on a tort claim.

When an attorney sued for interfering with contract pleads the defense of "honest advice," the availability of discovery to the plaintiff also creates ethical problems. Tender of "advice of counsel" as a defense by a client waives the client's attorney-client privilege, but the attorney is not the holder of that privilege and cannot waive it by tendering the issue. However, work product protection belongs to the attorney, and tender of the "honest advice" defense may open up discovery into the attorney's impressions, conclusions, and the nature of his research and investigation, at least to the extent client confidences are not thereby disclosed. By suing the lawyer for inducing breach and attempting discovery into the nature of his "honest" advice, a litigant would be able to learn the theories and strategies to be employed by his adversary's counsel in the defense of the same lawsuit. Allowing such discovery undermines the policy behind the work product doctrine—the prevention of undue advantage to adverse litigants. Ethical considerations therefore may prevent the attorney from even raising the honest advice privilege in his own defense since it may place his client's interests in jeopardy.

In light of these concerns, the privilege of attorneys to interfere with their clients' contracts should be defined in a manner that does not invite inquiry into the attorney-client relationship, and that takes into account the underlying policy of this privilege: "The existence and scope of the privilege to induce breach of contract must be determined by reference to the societal interests which it is designed to protect. . . . The privilege is designed in part to protect the important interests served by the confidential relationship between a fiduciary and his principal."

The privilege for attorneys to "induce breach" should be a strengthened version of the *Restatement*'s fiduciary's privilege; i.e., attorneys should be privileged to induce their clients not to perform contracts unless they also commit a separate, independent, intentionally tortious act toward the client or a third party that forseeably results in damage to the plaintiff by disrupting the plaintiff's contractual relations. In addition, the social interests in protecting the relationship between attorney and client and the dangers of unfair advantage in litigation resulting from tortious interfer-

ence suits against lawyers suggest a rule of law that requires lack of justification as an element of plaintiff's prima facie case.

In conclusion, the protection the law affords to the confidential, fiduciary attorney-client relationship requires a near-absolute privilege for attorneys with respect to their advice concerning their clients' contractual performance. Since a tortious interference suit against an attorney inevitably affects the attorney's objectivity and diverts resources and attention from the client's defense in the underlying contract action, the availability of a concurrent tort action against an attorney should be strictly limited.

9.40   Promoters

Concert promoters are an embattled species. Fewer acts tour successfully than was the case in previous years, and new problems arise constantly. For example, a recent article in *Variety* indicated that concert promoters are having trouble obtaining vandalism coverage subsequent to the destruction of approximately 1,000 seats by spectators at an Ozzy Osbourne concert. The following sections deal with some of the more common problems promoters have faced in recent years.

9.41   AFofM Problems

All important American and Canadian musicians and vocalists belong to the American Federation of Musicians (AFofM) and/or the American Federation of Television and Radio Artists. Promoters presenting concerts by AFofM members do so on blank forms provided by the union, to which are often appended lengthy "riders" specifying requirements ranging from the dimensions of the stage and the type and location of electrical outlets, to the decor of dressing rooms and the food to be served backstage. At the heart of the matter, however, is the one-page union form. Until recently, the form specified that all disputes would be subject to the union's constitution and bylaws, which, in turn, call for arbitration of disputes by the union. As the following cases demonstrate, several jurisdictions now limit the scope of intra-union arbitration.

In *Graham v. Scissor-Tail*, the court noted that "if a party resisting arbitration can show that the rules under which arbitration is to proceed will operate to deprive him of what we in other contexts have termed the common law right of fair procedure, the agreement to arbitrate should not be enforced." The court then carefully examined the facts to see if fair procedures would be denied. In similar fashion, in *Taylor v. Nelson*, the court declared: "When, as here, the contract requiring arbitration is a form contract which smacks of adhesion, the court must scrutinize that contract with particular care in order to ensure that 'certain minimum levels of integrity' are maintained."

Graham v. Scissor-Tail, Inc., 623 P.2d 165 (Cal. 1981)

Plaintiff Bill Graham is an experienced promoter and producer of musical concerts. Defendant C. Russell Bridges, also known as Leon Russell (Russell), is a successful performer and recording artist and the leader of a musical group; he is also a member of the American Federation of Musicians (A.F. of M.). Defendant Scissor-Tail, Inc. (Scissor-Tail) is a California corporation, wholly owned by Russell, which serves as the vehicle by which the services of Russell and his group are marketed. Defendant David Forest Agency, Ltd. (Forest) was, at the time here relevant, acting in the capacity of booking agent for Scissor-Tail.

Early in 1973, Scissor-Tail and Russell decided to formulate and structure a personal appearance tour for the latter and his group. Forest was engaged to assist in this project, and at the suggestion of Dennis Cordell, Russell's personal manager and an officer of Scissor-Tail, contacted plaintiff Graham, who had previously promoted a number of Russell concerts, to request that he provide his services for four of the twelve concerts on the projected tour. A series of four contracts was prepared covering, respectively, concerts at Ontario, Oakland, Long Island, and Philadelphia. Graham signed all four contracts; Scissor-Tail (per Dennis Cordell), for reasons to appear, signed only those relating to the Ontario and Oakland concerts, which were to occur on July 29 and August 5, 1973.

The four contracts in question were all prepared on an identical form known in the industry as an A.F. of M. Form B Contract; in this case each bore the heading of the Forest agency. Aside from matters such as date and time, they differed from one another in only two areas—i.e., the contents of the blanks designed "hours of employment" and "wage agreed upon." The former dealt with matters such as hours of performance and the provision of a guest artist to appear on the program prior to the Russell group. The latter provided that payment was to be "applicable A.F. of M. scale" or a specified percentage (85 percent in the case of Ontario, Oakland, and Philadelphia; 90 percent in the case of Long Island) "of the gross receipts after bona-fide, receipted, sanctioned expenses and taxes, whichever is greater." Also here indicated in each case was the capacity of the concert site, the price of tickets, and the potential gross.

The contracts designated Graham as the "purchaser of music" or "employer," the seven members of the group as "musicians." They did not speak explicitly to the question of who was to bear any eventual net losses. The contract forms also provided: "9. In accordance with the Constitution, By-laws, Rules and Regulations of the Federation, the parties will submit every claim, dispute, controversy or difference involving the musical services arising out of or connected with this contract and the engagement covered thereby for determination by the International Executive Board of the Federation or a similar board of an appropriate local thereof and such determination shall be conclusive, final and binding upon the parties."

As indicated above, all four contracts were signed by plaintiff Graham, his signature appearing below his typed name on a blank designated "signature of employer." Only those contracts relating to the Ontario and Oakland concerts bore a corresponding signature; on those contracts, below the typed name "Scissor-Tail, Inc. by Russell Bridges aka Leon Russell" and on a blank designated "signature of leader," is the signature of Dennis Cordell, who as above indicated was Russell's personal manager and an officer of Scissor-Tail.

On the second page of each contract is a list of seven musicians involved (including Russell), together with an indication of the A.F. of M. local of each.

The Ontario concert took place as scheduled and had gross receipts of $173,000 (out of a potential gross reflected in the contract of "$450,000 plus"), with expenses of $236,000, resulting in a net loss of some $63,000. The Oakland concert also took place, resulting in a net profit of some $98,000. Following this second concert a dispute arose among the parties over who was to bear the loss sustained in the Ontario concert and whether that loss could be offset against the profits of the Oakland concert—Scissor-Tail and Forest taking the position that under the contract Graham was to bear all losses from any concert without offset, Graham urging that under standard industry practice and custom relating to $85/15$ and $90/10$ contracts such losses should accrue without offset to Scissor-Tail, et al. This dispute remaining unresolved, Scissor-Tail declined to execute the contracts for the Long Island and Philadelphia concerts; apparently these concerts took place as scheduled, but some party other than Graham performed the promotional services.

In October 1973, Graham filed an action for breach of contract, declaratory relief, and recission against all defendants. Scissor-Tail responded with a petition to compel arbitration. . . .

By letter dated April 12, 1976, the A.F. of M. was advised of the court's order. By late June, however, no hearing date had been set and counsel for Scissor-Tail wrote to the union requesting that a date be set and suggesting certain dates convenient to him. Rather than comply with this request, however, the union, through its International Executive Board, on July 6 issued its decision awarding the full amount of Scissor-Tail's

claim against Graham, or some $53,000. Counsel for Graham, protesting against this procedure, was informed by the A.F. of M. that it conformed with normal practice, which contemplated the entry of award without hearing. Thereupon counsel for Graham enlisted the assistance of Scissor-Tail's counsel in the matter and, upon securing the latter's consent, was successful in reopening the matter and having it set for hearing.

In the meantime, on August 10, 1976, Graham had been placed on the union's "defaulter's list"—apparently a list of persons with whom union members may not do business.

On September 10, 1976, Scissor-Tail increased the claim by $20,000 to a total of some $73,000, urging that some of the expenses claimed by Graham with respect to the two concerts were improper. Scissor-Tail further requested interest on the award and $15,000 as attorney's fees.

On October 29, 1976, a hearing was held at the union's western (Hollywood) office before a "referee" appointed by the union president. The referee was a former executive officer and a long-time member of the union; he had acted as a hearing officer in many previous union matters. All parties (excluding Russell himself) and counsel were present. Graham sought to have the proceedings transcribed by a court reporter brought by him; the request was denied and the reporter excused. The hearing thereupon proceeded. Graham produced considerable evidence—consisting of his own testimony, the testimony of another promoter, the stipulated testimony of a third promoter, and three sworn statements by others engaged in the popular music concert field—to the effect that under common and widely held custom and practice in the industry, the promoter under a $90/10$ or $85/15$ contract was understood to bear no risk of loss because his share of the profits under such contracts was considerably smaller than under the "normal" contract, under which the promoter takes a larger percentage of the profits but is understood to bear the risk of loss; no contrary evidence was offered by Scissor-Tail. The referee also heard evidence regarding the propriety of certain expenses claimed by Graham and questioned by Scissor-Tail.

On November 5, 1976, in his report to the

union's International Executive Board, the referee recommended that Graham be ordered to pay to Scissor-Tail the amount of its original claim (some $53,000). . . . The balance of the claim—consisting of the items added by Scissor-Tail's September 10 request—was denied, the referee noting that the union had issued no directions to him regarding it.

On February 22, 1977, the union's International Executive Board made its award in conformity with the recommendation of the referee.

Scissor-Tail thereupon filed a petition in the superior court to confirm the award; Graham filed a petition to vacate it. (See Code Civ. Proc., § 1285.) The court granted the former petition and denied the latter; judgment was entered accordingly. (Code Civ. Proc., § 1287.4.)

After entry of judgment Scissor-Tail filed a cost bill which included an item of some $16,000 for attorney's fees. The court granted Graham's motion to tax costs, striking this item on the basis of the arbitrator's (referee's) determination.

Graham appeals from the judgment confirming the arbitrator's award. Scissor-Tail appeals from the order taxing costs. . . .

We first turn our attention to the validity of the order compelling arbitration. . . .

Plaintiff's basic contention in this respect is that the order compelling arbitration was in error because the underlying agreement—at least insofar as it required arbitration of disputes before the A.F. of M.—was an unenforceable contract of adhesion. Two separate questions are thus presented, each of which requires separate consideration: (1) Is this a contract of adhesion? (2) If so, is it unenforceable? . . .

The term "contract of adhesion," now long a part of our legal vocabulary, has been variously defined in the cases and other legal literature. The serviceable general definition first suggested by Justice Tobriner in 1961, however, has well stood the test of time and will bear little improvement: "The term signifies a standardized contract, which, imposed and drafted by the party of superior bargaining strength, relegates to the subscribing party only the opportunity to adhere to the contract or reject it." (*Neal v. State Farm Ins. Cos.* (1961) 188 Cal. App.2d 690, 694, 10 Cal. Rptr. 781.)

Such contracts are, of course, a familiar part of the modern legal landscape, in which the classical model of "free" contracting by parties of equal or near-equal bargaining strength is often found to be unresponsive to the realities brought about by increasing concentrations of economic and other power. They are an inevitable fact of life for all citizens—businessman and consumer alike. While not lacking in social advantages, they bear within them the clear danger of oppression and overreaching. It is in the context of this tension—between social advantage in the light of modern conditions on the one hand, and the danger of oppression on the other—that courts and legislatures have sometimes acted to prevent perceived abuses.

We believe that the contract here in question, in light of all of the circumstances presented, may be fairly described as adhesive. Although defendant and its supporting amicus curiae are strenuous in their insistence that Graham's prominence and success in the promotion of popular music concerts afforded him considerable bargaining strength in the subject negotiations, the record before us fairly establishes that he, for all his asserted stature in the industry, was here reduced to the humble role of "adherent." It appears that all concert artists and groups of any significance or prominence are members of the A.F. of M; that pursuant to express provisions of the A.F. of M.'s constitution and bylaws members are not permitted to sign any form of contract other than that issued by the union; that the A.F. of M. Form B. Contract in use at the time here relevant included the arbitration provisions here in question . . . and that Scissor-Tail insisted upon the use of $85/15$ and $90/10$ contractual arrangements. In these circumstances it must be concluded that Graham, whatever his asserted prominence in the industry, was required by the realities of his business as a concert promoter to sign A.F. of M. form contracts with *any* concert artist with whom he wished to do business—and that in the case before us he, wishing to promote the Russell concerts, was presented with the nonnegotiable option of accepting such contracts on an $85/15$ or $90/10$ basis or not at all.

It is argued, however, that other provisions of the contract—e.g., those relating to the length, time, and date of the concert and the selection of a special guest artist to appear on the program preceding the Russell group—were subject to negotiation and that this consideration operated to mitigate or remove all adhesive characteristics from the contract. We do not agree. Although there may be circumstances in which the parties to a contract, negotiating in the context of certain "nonnegotiable" provisions insisted upon by one of them, may yet achieve an agreement of nonadhesive character through accommodation and bargaining with respect to other significant terms, we do not believe that the instant case involves such a situation. The terms here asserted to be subject to negotiation, assuming that they were in fact so, were of relatively minor significance. . . .

Generally speaking, there are two judicially imposed limitations on the enforcement of adhesion contracts or provisions thereof. The first is that such a contract or provision which does not fall within the reasonable expectations of the weaker or "adhering" party will not be enforced against him. . . . The second—a principle of equity applicable to all contracts generally—is that a contract or provision, even if consistent with the reasonable expectations of the parties, will be denied enforcement if, considered in its context, it is unduly oppressive or "unconscionable." We proceed to examine whether the instant contract, and especially that provision thereof requiring the arbitration of disputes before the A.F. of M., should have been denied enforcement under either of these two principles.

We cannot conclude on the record before us that the contractual provision requiring arbitration of disputes before the A.F. of M. was in any way contrary to the reasonable expectations of plaintiff Graham. By his own declarations and testimony, he had been a party to literally thousands of A.F. of M. contracts containing a similar provision; indeed it appears that during the 3 years preceding the instant contracts he had promoted 15 or more concerts with Scissor-Tail, on each occasion signing a contract containing arbitration provisions similar to those here in question. It also appears that he had been involved in prior proceedings before the A.F. of M. regarding disputes with other musical groups arising

under prior contracts. Finally, the discussions taking place following the Oakland concert, together with his telegram indicating that he himself would file charges with the A.F. of M. if the matter were not settled to his satisfaction . . . all strongly suggest an abiding awareness on his part that all disputes arising under the contracts were to be resolved by arbitration before the A.F. of M. For all of these reasons it must be concluded that the provisions requiring such arbitration . . . were wholly consistent with Graham's reasonable expectations upon entering into the contract.

We are thus brought to the question whether the contract provision requiring the arbitration of disputes *before the A.F. of M.*—because it designates an arbitrator who, by reason of its status and identity, is presumptively biased in favor of one party—is for that reason to be deemed unconscionable and unenforceable. Graham, although couching his arguments in other terminology, essentially maintains that it is—the thrust of his position being that to allow the A.F. of M. to sit in judgment of a dispute arising between one of its members and a contracting nonmember is so inimical to fundamental notions of fairness as to require nonenforcement. We proceed to a consideration of this contention.

We are met at the outset of our inquiry with certain provisions of the California Arbitration Act which, it would seem, contemplate complete contractual autonomy in the choice of an arbitrator. Section 1281.6 of the Code of Civil Procedure provides that "[i]f the arbitration agreement provides a method of appointing an arbitrator, such method shall be followed." Section 1282 of the same code states that "*[u]nless the arbitration agreement otherwise provides*" (italics added) arbitration shall be by a neutral arbitrator either alone or in combination with other neutral and/or nonneutral arbitrators. Subsection (d) of the same section provides: "*If there is no neutral arbitrator*, the powers and duties of a neutral arbitrator may be exercised by a majority of the arbitrators." (Italics added.) . . .

The arbitration act, as we read it, expressly recognizes the right of contractual parties to provide for the resolution of contractual disputes by arbitral machinery of their own design and composition. . . . In so doing we do not believe—and the Arbitration Act does not require—that the parties are or should be strictly precluded from designating as arbitrator a person or entity who, by reason of relationship to a party or some similar factor, can be expected to adopt something other than a "neutral" stance in determining disputes. At the same time we must note that when as here the contract designating such an arbitrator is the product of circumstances suggestive of adhesion, the possibility of overreaching by the dominant party looms large; contracts concluded in such circumstances, then, must be scrutinized with particular care to insure that the party of lesser bargaining power, in agreeing thereto, is not left in a position depriving him of any realistic and fair opportunity to prevail in a dispute under its terms.

As the United States Supreme Court has said in a related context, "Congress has put its blessing on private dispute settlement arrangements . . . , but it was anticipated, we are sure, that the contractual machinery would operate within some minimum levels of integrity." (*Hines v. Anchor Motor Freight* (1976) 424 U.S. 554, 571, 96 S.Ct. 1048, 1059, 47 L.Ed.2d 231.) By the same token it appears that the Legislature has determined that the parties shall have considerable leeway in structuring the dispute settlement arrangements by which they are bound; while recognizing that the leeway may permit the establishment of arrangements which vary to some extent from the dead-center of "neutrality," we at the same time must insist—and most especially in circumstances smacking of adhesion—that certain "mimimum levels of integrity" be achieved if the arrangement in question is to pass judicial muster.

It is for the courts of course to determine—largely on a case by case basis—what these "minimum levels of integrity" shall be. In doing so it must not be lost sight of that the "contractual machinery" of the parties is intended by them to serve as a substitute for—although of course not a duplicate of—formal judicial proceedings. . . . In such cases as this, the agreement to *arbitrate* is essentially illusory. Here, clearly, "minimum levels of integrity" are not achieved, and the "agreement to arbitrate" should be denied enforcement on grounds of unconscionability.

There is we think a second basis, related to that just discussed, for denying enforcement on such grounds. The fact that an entity or body designated by contract to act as arbitrator of contractual disputes is one capable of acting as a *tribunal*—i.e., in the sense of *hearing* a dispute and *deciding* fairly and rationally on the basis of what it has heard—is of little consequence if it proceeds under rules which deny a party the fair opportunity to present his side of the dispute. Thus, if a party resisting arbitration can show that the rules under which arbitration is to proceed will operate to deprive him of what we in other contexts have termed the common law right of fair procedure, the agreement to arbitrate should not be enforced. In this respect it is well to reiterate, adapting it to the present context, what we said in the seminal case on this subject. "The common law requirement of a fair procedure does not compel formal proceedings with all the embellishments of a court trial [citation], nor adherence to a single mode of process. It may be satisfied by any one of a variety of procedures which afford a fair opportunity for [a disputant] to present his position. As such, this court should not attempt to fix a rigid procedure that must invariably be observed." (*Pinsker v. Pacific Coast Society of Orthodontists* (1974) 12 Cal.3d 541, 555, 116 Cal. Rptr. 245.) When it can be demonstrated, however, that the clear effect of the established procedure of the arbitrator will be to deny the resisting party a fair opportunity to present his position, the court should refuse to compel arbitration.

We thus return to the narrow question here before us: Is the contract we here consider, insofar as it requires the arbitration of all disputes arising thereunder before the A.F. of M., to be deemed unconscionable and unenforceable?

The answer to this question, we have concluded, must clearly be yes. Although our review of the record has disclosed nothing which would indicate that A.F. of M. procedures operate to deny any party a fair opportunity to present his position prior to decision, we are of the view that the "minimum levels of integrity" which are requisite to a contractual arrangement for the nonjudicial resolution of disputes are not achieved by an arrangement which designates the union of one of the parties as the arbitrator of disputes arising out of employment—especially when, as here, the arrangement is the product of circumstances indicative of adhesion. . . .

. . . [A] contract which purports to designate one of the parties as the arbitrator of all disputes arising thereunder is to this extent illusory—the reason being that the party so designated will have an interest in the outcome which, in the view of the law, will render fair and reasoned decision, based on the evidence presented, a virtual impossibility. Because, as we have explained, arbitration (as a contractually structured substitute for formal judicial proceedings) contemplates just such a decision, a contractual party may not act in the capacity of arbitrator—and a contractual provision which designates him to serve in that capacity is to be denied enforcement on grounds of unconscionability. We have also indicated that the same result would follow, and for the same reasons, when the designated arbitrator is not the party himself but one whose interests are so allied with those of the party that, for all practical purposes, he is subject to the same disabilities which prevent the party himself from serving. Again, a contractual provision designating such an entity as arbitrator must be denied enforcement on the ground that it would be unconscionable to permit that entity to so serve.

A labor union is an association or combination of workers organized for the purpose of securing through united action the most favorable conditions as regards wages or rates of pay, hours, and conditions of employment for its members; the primary function of such an organization is that of bargaining with employers on behalf of its membership in order to achieve these objectives. . . . By its very nature, therefore, a labor union addresses disputes concerning compensation arrangements between its members and third parties with interests identical to those of the affected members; to suppose that it would do otherwise is to suppose that it would act in a manner inconsistent with its reason for being.

In view of these considerations we think it must be concluded that a contractual provision designating the union of one of the parties to the contract as the arbitrator of all disputes arising thereunder—including those concerning the compensation due under the contract—does not achieve the "minimum levels of integrity" which we must demand of a contractually structured substitute for judicial proceedings. Such a provision, being inimical to the concept of arbitration as we understand it, would be denied enforcement in any circumstances; clearly it cannot stand in a case which, like that before us, requires the careful and searching scrutiny appropriate to a contract with manifestly adhesive characteristics. The trial court's order compelling arbitration in the instant case was therefore in error and must be reversed. . . .

It is urged by Scissor-Tail and amicus curiae supporting it, however, that regardless of the validity of the contractual provision at issue under state law, it must be enforced as a matter of federal labor law. Their argument, as we understand it, is: (1) that the contract we here consider is, or is equivalent to, a collective bargaining agreement between Graham and the A.F. of M., each of which is involved in activities involving interstate commerce; (2) that the instant action is a dispute arising under this agreement and therefore could have been brought in federal court under section 301 of the federal Labor-Management Relations Act (see 29 U.S.C.A. § 185); (3) that such an action, if brought in state court, must nevertheless be governed by federal substantive law. . . . and (4) that applicable federal law, as definitively declared and applied in recent federal cases, requires that the instant provision for arbitration of contractual disputes before the A.F. of M. be applied and enforced according to its terms.

While we have no reason to question the primacy of federal substantive law in areas of paramount federal concern under national labor legislation, we have considerable doubt whether the instant case may be said to be within such an area. Moreover, and assuming that it is, we do not believe that the applicable federal law has been established or elaborated to an extent which would require us to conclude that it is contrary to our significant and uniform rule of state policy applicable to arbitration clauses generally.

Section 301 of the federal Labor-Management Relations Act concerns itself with "[s]uits for violation of contracts between an employer and a labor organization representing employees in an industry affecting commerce. . . ." (29 U.S.C.A. § 185(a).) We have grave doubts whether the contract we here consider may be characterized as one falling within this description. In the first place, although the contract designates Graham as the "employer" of Scissor-Tail, the circumstances under which it was solicited, executed, and carried out would seem to suggest that this designation was one of convenience rather than one describing the facts of the relationship. Secondly, and assuming that the A.F. of M. is "a labor organization representing employees in an industry affecting commerce," the A.F. of M. was not a signatory to the contract—nor did it, as such, participate in any of the negotiations preceding its execution. Indeed, the contract was not even signed by a *member* of the A.F. of M. but rather by Dennis Cordell, an officer in a corporate entity formed by a member (Russell).

It is suggested, however, that general principles of agency, which are expressly made applicable to section 301 contracts (see 29 U.S.C.A. § 185(e)), require that the union be considered a party to the instant contract. In so urging, Scissor-Tail and its supporting amicus curiae place heavy reliance on two federal district court cases, unreported in the Federal Reporter System: *Musicians, Local 336 v. Bonatz* (D.N.J. 1974) 90 L.R.R.M. 2956, and *JOT Corp. v. GCS, Inc.* (E.D.Pa. 1976) 94 L.R.R.M. 2038. These cases, involving the use of the A.F. of M. Form B contract, hold under their facts that the signatory musicians and union members were to be considered agents of the union for the purpose of negotiating and executing the contracts; the resulting agreements, it was held, although not collective bargaining agreements strictly speaking (see *Federation of Musicians v. Carroll* (1968) 391 U.S. 99, 104, 88 S.Ct. 1562, 1566, 20 L.Ed.2d 460), were nevertheless to be considered agreements "between an employer and a labor organization representing employees in an industry affecting commerce . . ." within the meaning of section 301. It is to be noted, however, that the contracts involved in *Bonatz* and *JOT* each bore the caption "Contract Blank, American Federation of Musicians of the United States and Canada," the

courts concluding on this basis among others that the affected "employer" should have known or expected that he was bargaining with the union through its agent-member. Even if it be assumed that *Bonatz* and *JOT* are correct on this point, it by no means follows that the instant contract, captioned with the name of the booking agency and signed by a person unaffiliated with the union, should be viewed in an identical light.

We do not, however, rest our conclusion on this narrow ground. Even if we assume this to be a contract of the type described in section 301— and therefore to be viewed in light of federal substantive law—the question remains whether that law requires enforcement of an arbitration clause such as that we here consider. Scissor-Tail and its supporting amicus, relying primarily on the *Bonatz* and *JOT* cases, urge that the answer to that question must be yes. The insistence on union arbitration of contractual disputes, they argue, is simply one of the "economic weapons" which labor may legitimately wield in its negotiations with management. While the indicated cases must be read to lend some support to this position, we by no means consider them dispositive. In the first place, they fail to consider the illusory aspects of a provision calling for exclusive union arbitration of disputes arising in a labor context. More significantly, this court is in any event under no obligation to follow federal lower court precedents interpreting acts of Congress when we find those precedents unpersuasive. "Any rule which would require the state courts to follow in all cases the decisions of one or more lower federal courts would be undesirable, as it would have the effect of binding the state courts where neither the reasoning nor the number of federal cases is found persuasive. Such a rule would not significantly promote uniformity in federal law, for the interpretation of an act of Congress by a lower federal court does not bind other federal courts except those directly subordinate to it. [Citations.]" . . . In short, we decline, to find on the basis of the *Bonatz* and *JOT* cases that the substantive federal law of collective bargaining agreements requires any result different from that which we have reached. Until that law, in its application to circumstances such as that before us, is further elaborated by the federal courts, we assume that it does not differ significantly from our own. . . . We have held today, as a matter of state law and policy, that arbitration provisions which designate as sole arbitrator either an affected contractual party or one with identical interests in the outcome of the dispute fail to achieve the level of basic integrity which we require of a contractually structured substitute for formal judicial proceedings. The fact that the instant case arises in the context of what may be considered a labor dispute should not, in our view, render this rule any the less applicable. . . .

We have held that the provision of the instant contract requiring arbitration of disputes arising thereunder before the A.F. of M. is unconscionable and unenforceable, and that the order compelling arbitration pursuant to it was in error. In light of the strong public policy of this state in favor of resolving disputes by arbitration, however, we do not believe that the parties herein should for this reason be precluded from availing themselves of nonjudicial means of settling their differences. The parties have indeed agreed to arbitrate, but in so doing they have named as sole and exclusive arbitrator an entity which we cannot permit to serve in that broad capacity. In these circumstances we do not believe that the parties should now be precluded from attempting to agree on an arbitrator who is not subject to the disabilities we have discussed. We therefore conclude that upon remand the trial court should afford the parties a reasonable opportunity to agree on a suitable arbitrator and, failing such agreement, the court should on petition of either party appoint the arbitrator. (See and cf. Code Civ.Proc., § 1281.6.) In the absence of an agreement or petition to appoint, the court should proceed to a judicial determination of the controversy. The judgment is reversed and the cause remanded to the trial court with directions to vacate its order compelling arbitration and undertake further proceedings in conformity with the views expressed in this opinion.

Taylor v. Nelson, 615 F. Supp. 533 (W. D. Va. 1985)

TURK, J.

. . . On September 26, 1980, the plaintiff commenced this breach of contract action against the defendant [Willie] Nelson and others. On December 15, 1980, Nelson moved for a stay of that action pending arbitration pursuant to the contract, which provided:

In accordance with the Constitution, By-Laws, Rules and Regulations of the Federation, the parties will submit every claim, dispute, controversy or difference involving the musical services arising out of or connected with this contract and the engagement covered thereby for determination by the International Executive Board of the Federation or a similar board of an appropriate local thereof and such determination shall be conclusive, final and binding upon the parties. . . .

The arbitration began on March 20, 1984 before the executive board of the AFM, which rendered a decision on September 11, 1984. The decision was in favor of the defendant Nelson.

On September 21, 1984, Nelson petitioned the Supreme Court of the State of New York for a judgment confirming the arbitration award. Taylor opposed the motion and, by way of cross-motion dated November 16, 1984, sought to have the petition dismissed on the grounds that the underlying contract action was pending before this court and that the New York court did not have jurisdiction. Taylor's cross-motion was granted and Nelson's petition was dismissed by an order dated January 28, 1985 and filed February 1, 1985. Judgment was entered on that order on March 8, 1985, and was filed on March 11, 1985.

On February 12, 1985, Taylor moved to have the arbitration award vacated. . . .

The Federal Arbitration Act at 9 U.S.C. § 9 provides:

If the parties in their agreement have agreed that a judgment of the court shall be entered upon the award made pursuant to the arbitration, and shall specify the court, then at any time within one year after the award is made any party to the arbitration may apply to the court so specified for an order confirming the award, and thereupon the court must grant such an order unless the award is vacated, modified, or corrected as prescribed in sections 10 and 11 of this title.

The defendant asserts that this section expressly mandates the confirmation of the arbitration award in this case in that the parties have agreed to the entry of judgment upon the arbitration award, the application to confirm has occurred within one year of the award, and the order has not yet been vacated, modified or corrected. This, however, fails to recognize that the plaintiff's motion presently before this court is for the specific purpose of having the arbitration award vacated as prescribed in Section 10. Nowhere does the Act require this or any court to summarily confirm an arbitration award which is also before the court on a motion to vacate which alleges bias, prejudice and evident partiality. . . .

Nelson . . . argues that the doctrine of the "law of the case" compels this court to find that Taylor's motion to vacate should be denied. . . . Nelson maintains that the fourth circuit in staying proceedings in this court pending arbitration "in accordance with the terms of the arbitration clause in the contract at issue" necessarily ruled on the issues of adhesion and evident partiality. In ordering the stay, however, the fourth circuit restricted itself to a determination that the contract had an arbitration provision in it and that it had not been complied with. This limited review is apparent from the fourth circuit's opinion in the matter, which states:

> this court recently observed that a federal court confronted with a motion to stay its proceedings pending arbitration under such a contract must only be satisfied of '(1) the making of the agreement to arbitrate and (2) the breach of the agreement to arbitrate' to find itself under compulsion of the Act to grant the motion.

The fourth circuit did not address or decide the issues of adhesion or evident partiality. There is no reference or discussion whatsoever of these issues in its opinion. Therefore, the doctrine of the "law of the case" is inapplicable to the motions presently before this court. . . .

Arbitration by agreement of the parties is welcomed and encouraged by Congress and by the courts. As the United States Supreme Court has stated, however, what is encouraged is not merely arbitration, but impartial arbitration. *Commonwealth Coatings Corporation v. Continental Casualty Company*, 393 U.S. 145, 89 S.Ct. 337, 21 L.Ed.2d 301 (1968). Therefore, the United States Arbitration Act, 9 U.S.C. § 10,

provides for vacation of an award "where there was evident partiality or corruption in the arbitrators, or either of them."

Nelson argues, citing *International Produce, Inc. v. A/S Rosshavet*, 638 F.2d 548 (2d Cir. 1981), that federal law does not read "evident partiality" in section 10 to include "appearance of bias." The narrow holding in *Rosshavet*, however, dealt with a situation very different from the one now before this court. *Rosshavet*, a maritime arbitration case, involved what the second circuit referred to as "speculation without substance." This court is not persuaded that *Rosshavet* should be so broadly interpreted or applied as, in effect, to overrule the holding in *Commonwealth Coatings*. In that case, the United States Supreme Court clearly stated:

> . . . any tribunal permitted by law to try cases and controversies not only must be unbiased but also must avoid even the appearance of bias. We cannot believe that it was the purpose of Congress to authorize litigants to submit their cases and controversies to arbitration boards that might reasonably be thought biased against one litigant and favorable to another.

393 U.S. at 150, 89 S.Ct. at 340. It is difficult to imagine an arbitration board which could more "reasonably be thought biased against one litigant and favorable to another" than the Executive Board of one party's union. The argument made here by the defendant, that *actual* impartiality or bias must be shown, was also made by the dissenters in *Commonwealth Coatings* and rejected by the majority. It is also rejected by this court. . . .

The only AFM contract available to Taylor contained no choice regarding the forum for arbitration; the sole forum permitted was an arbitration conducted by the International Executive Board of the AFM. When it became evident that an arbitration would be required, Taylor requested that the AFM allow that arbitration to be before the American Arbitration Association. This request, along with a request that the hearing take place in Roanoke, Virginia, was refused. Such evidence points clearly to the fact that Taylor "was required by the realities of his business as a concert promoter to sign A.F. of M. form contracts with any concert artist with whom he wished to do business." *Graham v. Scissor-Tail, Inc.*, 28 Cal.3d 807, 623 P.2d 165, 171 Cal. Rptr. 604 (En Banc, 1981).

When, as here, the contract requiring arbitration is a form contract which smacks of adhesion, the court must scrutinize that contract with particular care in order to ensure that "certain minimum levels of integrity" are maintained. *Id.*, at 824–825, 623 P.2d at 176, 171 Cal. Rptr. at 615. Two separate state courts have reviewed the identical arbitration procedure at issue here and found it to be unconscionable. In each case the award rendered pursuant thereto was held unenforceable. . . .

The Supreme Court of California in *Graham*, while recognizing that nothing on the record before it indicated that the AFM arbitration procedure denies either party an opportunity to be heard, nevertheless found that:

> a contractual provision designating the union of one of the parties to the contract as the arbitrator of all disputes arising thereunder—including those concerning the compensation due under the contract—does not achieve the 'minimum levels of integrity' which we must demand of a contractually structured substitute for judicial proceedings. Such a provision, being inimical to the concept of arbitration as we understand it, would be denied enforcement in any circumstances; clearly it cannot stand in a case which, like that before us, requires the careful and searching scrutiny appropriate to a contract with manifestly adhesive characteristics.

Graham, 28 Cal.3d at 828, 623 P.2d at 178, 171 Cal. Rptr. at 617.

A New Jersey appellate court also called upon to review the AFM arbitration provision, held that it was void as being contrary to public policy, stating:

> In the circumstances we conclude that the so-called arbitration provision, giving the Board power to decide disputes between its members and defendant, is contrary to public policy. The relationship between the Board and its members is obviously too close to assure the dispassionate and impartial resolution of disputes between AFM members and nonmembers.

Chimes, 480 A.2d at 223.

Although the defendant correctly argues that this court is not bound by the decisions of state courts in New Jersey and California, the contract provision at issue is identical in all three cases, and the reasoning of the state courts applies equally in the case at bar. The partiality which is apparent from the procedure itself is made even more evident by the statistical study prepared by the plaintiff. An analysis of claims initiated by non-members against members reveals that approximately fifty-nine percent (59%) were decided in favor of the AFM member. . . .

The evident partiality alleged under 9 U.S.C. § 10 stems from the pervasive control which the AFM union exerted over the entire arbitration procedure, and is supported by the statistics. The contract provided no option except AFM arbitration. Under the contract, the AFM selects the hearing referee, the hearing date and the hearing site. In this case, requests for alternate arbitrators, dates, and sites were refused. The AFM establishes the format, the rules, and the procedure. The AFM Executive Board even makes the final decision and hears any appeal. The integrity of arbitration as a neutral forum for the resolution of disputes was nowhere to be found in the procedure to which Taylor was subject. . . .

NOTES

1. On appeal, *Taylor v. Nelson* was reversed on other grounds. See F.2d (4th Cir. 1986).

2. The New York courts appear to go the opposite way on this issue. In *Jerry Kravat Entertainment Svcs., Inc. v. Cobbs*, 459 N.Y.S.2d 993 (Sup.Ct. N.Y.Co. 1983), the court refused to invalidate the arbitration clause in a standard AFM contract, stating that:

> While the arbitration provision here appears imperfect as to impartiality, it nevertheless promotes speedy resolution and was agreed to by the parties. Under New York Law, an arbitration agreement will rarely be invalidated for partiality because of the relation between the parties and the arbitrators, as long as the relationship is disclosed prior to the making of the agreement, as here.

Although the Court cited *In Re Cross & Brown Co.*, 167 N.Y.S.2d 573, in which an arbitration clause which referred all employee disputes to the employer's board of directors was held invalid, the court distinguished that case by stating that here the individual musicians were the contracting parties, not the AFM. In response to the argument that the AFM form contract was one of adhesion and compulsion, the court stated that the *Graham* decision, while it had "some appeal," was "not consistent with New York Law and . . . not sufficiently persuasive." Kravat was not at the union's mercy; he could, after all, decline to promote the concert. He could also band together with other promoters to try to force changes in the AFM agreement. The court also noted that "apparently music promoters have not found the arbitration provision so oppressive as to make the business unprofitable. They have functioned under these conditions for many years and continue to do so."

To the same effect is *John B. Stetson Co., Inc. v. Chardon, Inc.*, (No. 14981–1983, Sup.Ct.N.Y.Co., 12/12/83), involving an agreement pursuant to which Alabama was to have performed at Madison Square Garden. Stetson was compelled to arbitrate even though it had not received and reviewed a copy of the AFM bylaws prior to signing the agreement which incorporated them by reference, under the accepted principle that "a party to a written contract is under a duty to read the written instrument and is presumed to have done so prior to signing." However, "the alleged bias of the arbitration panel . . . may be a ground for vacating the award (CPLR 7511[b][1][ii]). . . . There is no reason to believe at this juncture that the arbitration board is going to proceed in an unfair manner."

3. Subsequently, a New Jersey appellate court refused to enforce the AFofM internal-arbitration clause. *Chimes v. Oritani Motor Hotel, Inc.* 480 A.2d 218 (N.J.App. 1984), citing the *Graham* case with approval.

9.42   Promoters' Problems with Venues

Many potential concert locations are owned or controlled by municipalities or public authorities, which, in turn, contract in accordance with legislatively prescribed procedures. The *Genesco* case illustrates that some contract principles, which might apply between a promoter and a private concert venue, may not apply when the promoter deals with a city.

The city of San Antonio ordinance is an illustration of local attempts to regulate what may be seen and heard. Many municipalities are understandably fearful of possible injury and/or damage which may occur at rock concerts. (One needs only recall the concert by The Who some years ago in Cincinnati, at which several would-be spectators were trampled to death when the waiting crowd rushed the doors.) Municipalities are also concerned at what they perceive to be hazards to the health and/or morals of their youthful citizens.

Genesco Entertainment v. Koch, 593 F. Supp. 743 (S.D.N.Y. 1984)

WEINFELD, J.

Plaintiff, a concert promoter, sought to lease Shea Stadium, New York City, for the production of a country and western music concert on August 22, 1981. After extensive negotiations, the relationship between the City negotiators and plaintiff's representatives broke down a few days before August 22 and the concert was cancelled. Thereupon, plaintiff commenced this action seeking damages for the cancellation, asserting various claims against combinations of defendants, including Edward R. Koch, the Mayor of the City of New York ("Mayor"), the City of New York ("City"), the Department of Parks and Recreation of the City of New York ("Department"), and Ticketron, a division of Control Data Corporation ("Ticketron"). . . .

Plaintiff's first cause of action against the City and the Department (collectively "municipal defendants") and the Mayor alleges that the plaintiff entered into an oral contract with the municipal defendants whereby plaintiff would pay the City and the Department $40,000 and the New York National League Baseball Club ("the Mets") $35,000 for the use of Shea Stadium for a one-day concert on August 22, 1981; that this oral contract was amended twice, first on August 18, 1981, when the price was increased to an additional $35,000 for the City and an additional $40,000 for the Mets, and again on August 19, when the municipal defendants stated that the aforesaid $75,000 would not suffice and that $121,000 was required. On August 20 the municipal defendants refused to accept the amended and agreed upon $121,000, demanding instead $131,000 for the City and the Department and an additional $50,000 for the Mets; that by their refusal to accept $121,000 and instead demanding the $131,000 for the City and the Department, the defendants breached an oral agreement for the use of Shea Stadium, causing damages of $10,500,000.

The second cause of action names only the Mayor as a defendant and alleges that the demands for the increased fees referred to in the first cause of action were made with his consent, and that he ratified and approved the acts constituting the alleged breach of the oral agreement.

The third cause of action alleges that the Mayor, the municipal defendants and Ticketron committed deceptive acts and trade practices in violation of the New York General Business Law, section 349.

The fourth claim charges that the Mayor and the municipal defendants, through their conduct and representations, sought to convey to the plaintiff the impression that a contract was in effect for plaintiff's use of Shea Stadium on August 22, 1981; that plaintiff relied on such conduct and representations to its detriment; and that thereby an "estoppel in favor of the plaintiff" was created.

Plaintiff's fifth claim alleges that the municipal defendants acted under color of state law in revoking the contract between plaintiff and the defendants, thereby depriving plaintiff of property without due process of law in violation of 42 U.S.C., section 1983.

Koch, the City and the Department move for summary judgment on each of the causes of action alleged against them. The motion is based upon affidavits of various participants in the negotiations, extensive pre-trial discovery of such persons and a statement by the movants pursuant to Local Rule 3(g). Initially it is noted that the plaintiff has failed to controvert the statements in the defendants' 3(g) notice as required by the Rule. . . .

[T]o defeat a motion for summary judgment, the opposing party may not rest on conclusory allegations or denials, but must set forth, by competent evidence, specific facts showing that there is a genuine issue of material fact. Applying these principles to the present case, the Court is persuaded that the City, the Department and the Mayor have borne their burden with respect to all causes of action and are entitled to summary judgment. . . .

Breach of Contract Claim

The municipal defendants first argue that they are entitled to summary judgment on the breach of contract claim as a matter of law because the alleged oral contract is invalid and unenforceable, since it fails to conform to the statutory prerequisites required of contracts for the lease of Shea Stadium. The movants here emphasize that the alleged contract was not in writing; that it had never been agreed to by the authorized officer of the Department; and that it had never been approved as to form by the City Corporation Counsel. . . .

When acting in its corporate capacity, a municipality is held as accountable for its obligations as are individuals and corporations in the conduct of business. Unlike individuals and private corporations, however, a municipality's power to contract is statutorily restricted for the benefit of the public. Statutory restrictions on a municipal corporation's power to contract protect the public from the corrupt or ill-considered actions of municipal officials. To allow recovery under a contract which contravenes such restrictions gives vitality to an illegal act and grants the municipality power which it does not possess "to waive or disregard requirements which have been properly determined to be in the interest of the whole."

Hence, while a municipal corporation must honor its authorized commitments, it is not bound to contracts entered into by employees outside their authority. . . .

None of the parties with whom plaintiff claims to have negotiated . . . were statutorily authorized to enter into an agreement for the lease of Shea Stadium. Gordon Davis, the Commissioner of the Parks and Recreation Department, is the only city official authorized under the Administrative Code to enter into such a contract. The New York City Charter grants the Commissioner power to enter into contracts for recreational purposes subject to the approval of the Mayor. With respect to the use of Shea Stadium, the Commissioner, alone, may enter into a binding contract. Section 532–15.0(d) of the New York Administrative Code provides for the rental of Shea Stadium. The provision states:

Notwithstanding the foregoing provisions . . . or the provisions of any other law, general, special or local, the *commissioner*, acting in behalf of the city, is hereby authorized and empowered, . . . to enter into contracts, leases or rental agreements . . . upon such terms and conditions and for such consideration as may be agreed upon *by the commissioner* and such person or persons. . . .

While the Commissioner may delegate his authority, that delegation is only valid if a written instrument is filed with the Department.

Plaintiff does not dispute that the Commissioner never negotiated with the plaintiff nor signed a written contract. Plaintiff also does not dispute that Commissioner Davis never delegated, in writing, authority to [his deputy] to contract for the use of Shea Stadium.

Plaintiff claims, however, that it reasonably relied on the representations of Deputy Commissioner Levister, General Counsel Taylor, and Deputy General Counsel Ortiz that a duly executed contract was forthcoming. Construed broadly, this contention includes a claim that the negotiating parties, although without actual authority, possessed apparent authority to enter into a contract for the lease of Shea Stadium. However, the New York courts do not generally follow the doctrine of apparent authority in cases involving municipal defendants. New York law places the burden of determining the scope of a municipal officer's authority upon those who deal with municipal government. Unlike a typical agency relationship, the authority of municipal officers is a matter of record to which the public has ready access. Moreover, placing the public on notice of the limitation of the authority of municipal employees furthers the purpose of the statutory restrictions to protect the public against the irresponsible or corrupt actions of municipal employees.

Plaintiff's allegations also suggest a claim that the Commissioner's signature was but a formality that had been assured by Deputy Commissioner Levister, General Counsel Taylor, and Deputy General Counsel Ortiz. It is true that recovery against a municipality may be had where the failure to comply with statutory restrictions involves a mere irregularity or technical violation. Recovery has been uniformly denied, however,

where "the making of the contract flouted a firm public policy or violated a fundamental statutory restriction upon the powers of the municipality or its officers."

The statutory requirement that the Commissioner of the Department must approve all contracts for the lease of Shea Stadium is not a mere technicality, but rather a fundamental statutory restriction. The power to approve or disapprove a municipal contract entails the power to dispose of public assets. Restrictions as to which city officials may invoke that power are not a mere formality, but are fundamental to "responsible municipal government." Without such restrictions any city official, no matter his position, could dispose of public assets. Public accountability requires that restrictions on the persons authorized to enter into municipal contracts be rigidly enforced. The rule, of long standing, is stringent and rigorously exacting since it is designed to protect the public fisc and the public interest. . . .

For the foregoing reasons, the first cause of action is dismissed.

Claim Against Mayor Koch

Plaintiff's second cause of action alleges that the Mayor approved and ratified the alleged representations made by officers of the Department concerning the lease of Shea Stadium to the plaintiff. Defendants deny that Mayor Koch approved the alleged fee increase upon which plaintiff predicates its cause of action for breach of the oral agreement. Even assuming, as plaintiff alleges, that the Mayor did in fact ratify the representations, its second cause of action on its face does not state a claim against the Mayor on which relief can be granted. He cannot be held personally liable for the breach of a municipal contract which is invalid and unenforceable.

Entirely apart from the fact that the cause of action fails as a matter of law, defendant Koch is entitled to prevail on his motion for summary judgment. He and the other defendants deny that he approved the alleged fee increase which plaintiff alleges constituted the breach of the oral contract. . . . Plaintiff has . . . failed to produce any facts supporting its allegations that the Mayor was aware of and approved the alleged representations of the Department employees. Genesco does not respond to defendants' denial of the Mayor's knowledge or participation in the transaction, nor does it refer to the Mayor's role in the negotiations in their supporting affidavits. Moreover, by virtue of its failure to respond to defendants' statement pursuant to Local Rule 3(g), plaintiff must be deemed to have admitted the material facts set forth in defendants' 3(g) statement. That document states that Mayor Koch never approved of any escalation of the proposed fee for the use of Shea Stadium and that plaintiff never met or talked with Mayor Koch. Because plaintiff has failed to produce any competent evidence showing a genuine issue of material fact, summary judgment is also appropriate as to this cause of action.

The Deceptive Practices Claim

Plaintiff's third cause of action against the municipal defendants (and Ticketron) alleges a violation of New York General Business Law, section 349 which prohibits "deceptive acts or practices in the conduct of any business, trade, or commerce or in the furnishing of any service."

The defendants contend that the section is part of a consumer fraud protection statute that is inapplicable to a complex transaction between a corporate plaintiff, here a concert promoter, and a municipal defendant for the rental of a municipal stadium. Plaintiff, noting that "any person" injured by a violation of the Act is authorized to bring an action to recover damages, claims that a corporation is a "person" within the express language of the statute and that if the Legislature intended to limit the right of action to "consumers," it would have done so expressly. Despite the absence of controlling New York precedent, this Court is persuaded that a New York court, based on the statute's legislative history, would grant defendants' motion for summary judgment.

Section 349 wears its purpose on its face; it is entitled "Consumer Protection From Deceptive Acts and Practices." Prior to 1980, the Attorney General was the sole party who could enforce the prohibitions of section 349. "[R]ecognizing the need for private enforcement," however, the

New York Legislature recently "granted individuals the right to sue for injuries resulting from consumer fraud."

Section 349 is a powerful remedy for consumer fraud. Its broad language was intended to provide a "strong deterrent against deceptive business practices" and to "increase the effectiveness of the consumer protection laws." In keeping with these deterrent purposes, section 349 has been construed to allow recovery even in the absence of a showing of intent to deceive. Allegations of fraud are not required.

No New York court has specifically addressed the question whether this consumer fraud statute applies to commercial transactions of the nature here at issue. The Court is, of course, mindful that it sits in diversity in deciding the summary judgment motion on this claim, and therefore must apply the law of New York. While there is no single controlling New York decision here, the statute's legislative history combined with the New York courts' decisions governing construction of the Act persuade us that a New York court would grant defendants' motion for summary judgment.

Summary judgment is appropriate for two reasons. First, plaintiff has not been "injured by reason of any violation" of section 349 because the City's alleged misrepresentations do not constitute a "deceptive practice" within the meaning of the Act. Second, to extend this remedy to plaintiffs would alter completely the legal duties governing commercial relationships in New York. Absent a clear expression from the New York Legislature that it intended to effect so drastic a change in commercial law, this Court declines to interpret the statute to govern an alleged agreement to lease Shea Stadium. . . .

The nature of the instant transaction clearly places it outside the purview of section 349 when that statute is construed in the light of the Federal Trade Commission Act. The rental of Shea Stadium is not an ordinary or recurring consumer transaction. It is in effect a "single shot transaction" involving complex arrangements, knowledgeable and experienced parties and large sums of money. The nature of alleged deceptive government practices with respect to such a transaction are different in kind and degree from those that confront the average consumer who requires the protection of a statute against fraudulent practices. The only parties truly affected by the alleged misrepresentations in this case are the plaintiff and the defendants. . . .

The Court is convinced that summary judgment is appropriate not only because plaintiff has not been "injured by reason of any violation" of section 349, but also because a contrary interpretation would radically alter commercial relations in the State of New York. . . .

The Estoppel Claim

Plaintiff's fourth cause of action against the municipal defendants and the Mayor alleges that by their acts and conduct they represented or conveyed the impression that a contract existed for Shea Stadium and that the plaintiff, to its detriment, relied upon such representations and conduct and expended various sums of money and incurred other obligations; consequently, that such acts and conduct created an estoppel in favor of the plaintiff. The thrust of plaintiff's argument is that Deputy Commissioner Levister, General Counsel Taylor, and Deputy General Counsel Ortiz represented to plaintiff that the City "would furnish the plaintiff with a duly executed contract," which it never provided. While the New York courts, in cases involving exceptional circumstances, have at times applied an estoppel theory to a municipality, estoppel is not available against a municipal corporation where the alleged representations exceed the municipal employee's authority. The New York courts have uniformly declined to estop municipalities where the representations alleged to give rise to the estoppel were beyond the authority of the municipal employee in question. . . . This doctrine is rigidly adhered to. . . .

If Deputy Commissioner Levister, General Counsel Taylor, or Deputy General Counsel Ortiz did in fact assure plaintiff that the Commissioner would approve and duly execute the contract, such representations were outside the scope of their authority and therefore cannot estop the City from denying the existence of a valid contract. The Court grants the municipal defendants summary judgment on this claim.

Plaintiff also names the Mayor as a defendant in this cause of action. For the reasons given above with respect to plaintiff's breach of contract claim, summary judgment is granted. Plaintiff has failed to produce any facts supporting its allegations in this claim that the Mayor represented or authorized City officers to represent to plaintiff that a duly executed contract would be forthcoming. Conclusory allegations do not provide an adequate defense to a summary judgment motion.

42 U.S.C. section 1983 claim

Plaintiff's final cause of action against the municipal defendants is based on 42 U.S.C., section 1983. Plaintiff seeks compensatory and punitive damages for an alleged deprivation of property without due process of law. Defendants contend that section 1983 does not extend to breach of contract claims and that plaintiff has failed to allege a property right secured by the Constitution or to show that a municipal policy, custom or practice caused it injury. Plaintiff argues that it had a legitimate expectation that an oral contract with the City for the use of Shea Stadium would be approved by the Commissioner.

To recover under section 1983, plaintiff must establish a deprivation of a constitutionally protected right. Property interests are not created by the Constitution but "are defined by existing rules or understandings that stem from an independent source such as state law." State law must provide plaintiff with a legitimate claim of entitlement and not simply a unilateral expectation of receiving the alleged "property."

Plaintiff's alleged entitlement to the delivery of a duly executed contract does not rise to the level of a constitutionally protected property right. The Court's disposition of plaintiff's breach of contract and estoppel claims amply demonstrates that state law did not create a legitimate entitlement even if an oral contract was in fact made. New York law places the burden on plaintiff to ascertain the authority of those municipal officials with whom it deals. . . . Unilateral or subjective expectations are insufficient to establish the constitutionally protected property interest necessary to establish a claim under section 1983. . . . To allow breach of contract claims to be pursued under section 1983 would truly open the flood gates of litigation. Summary judgment on this final claim against the municipal defendants is therefore appropriate. . . .

City of San Antonio, Texas, Ordinance 61,850 (Effective November 14, 1985)

WHEREAS, the City of San Antonio owns and operates certain facilities which have been expressly or by implication and practice dedicated to expressive activities, and which have the status of "public forums" for purposes of application of the First Amendment of the United States Constitution to determinations of the validity of regulations pertaining to access to and use thereof; and,

WHEREAS, in such facilities there are performed from time to time certain musical, dramatic or theatrical works, together with incidental and related expressive activity which are vulgar, profane and repulsive to society generally, and which in certain instances where children are present as observers would appeal primarily to the prurient interest of such children (in particular and without limitation, an interest in sadistic and masochistic sexuality, rape, incest, bestiality, pedophilia, pederasty, necrophilia, and abnormal or violent exhibitionism) in sex, and which taken as a whole, lack any serious artistic or literary or social merit as to such children, and which further violate generally prevailing standards in the adult community as to the suitability of such material or performances for observation by children; and

WHEREAS, the City Council has the right under law, and the duty to its citizens, to balance in a constitutionally permissible manner the right of free expression of the population generally, irrespective of age, as against the interest of society in protecting and providing for the normal maturation and mental development of its children, in order that they may attain a position in status of mentally healthy citizens best able to benefit from a society which recognizes the value of free expression and a largely unlimited market place of ideas and thought; and,

WHEREAS, parents are entitled to obtain the assistance of government in controlling the disci-

pline and activity of children, by laws rationally related to the promotion of family oriented objectives, and providing for the normal maturation and development of mental health of young persons, and limiting the availability to children of materials which are damaging to their development, and contrary to community standards as to the decency and suitability of such performances or material for children; and,

WHEREAS, the City Council has informed itself by individual analysis of the facts and circumstances bearing upon this issue, input and comment by members of the public, and by the use of a qualified consultant in the principles commonly accepted by professionals in the mental health disciplines pertaining to the normal psychological development of children, the effects of exposure to certain types of performances, content, or subject matter which are and have been reasonably determined to be harmful or potentially harmful to children, and having further informed itself by the use of a qualified consultant as to the ages at or before which such materials or experiences are reasonably anticipated to have the most significant detrimental effect, and has determined that, balancing the interests of young persons, children, performers, promoters, and society generally, requires the establishment of regulations based upon age for admission to performances which are obscene as to children; and,

WHEREAS, performances, speech, and related activity which are obscene as to children are not constitutionally protected as to such children, nor as to performers or promoters who would display such material to children; NOW, THEREFORE,

BE IT ORDAINED BY THE CITY COUNCIL OF THE CITY OF SAN ANTONIO:

SECTION 1. Definitions:

A. "Performance obscene as to a child" shall mean a performance which contains:

   1. a description of or explicit reference to:
     (a) anal copulation
     (b) bestial sexual relations
     (c) sadistic, masochistic or violent sexual relationships
     (d) sexual relations with a child

(e) sexual relations with a corpse

(f) exhibition of male or female genitals

(g) rape or incest, or

(h) a vulgar or indecent reference to sexual intercourse, excretory functions of the body, or male or female genitals

and which, taken as a whole (1) appeals to the prurient interest of a child under the age of fourteen (14) years in sex and (2) violates generally prevailing standards in the adult community as to the suitability of such performances for observation of a child under the age of fourteen (14) years, and (3) lacks any serious, artistic, literary, political or scientific merit as to a child under the age of fourteen (14) years.

B. "Control over City-owned facilities" shall mean any person, or employee or such person, authorized by lease to produce, direct, participate in or perform any musical, dramatic or theatrical performance at a City-owned facility. This term shall not include peace officers in performance of their official duties.

C. "Person" shall mean any individual, partnership, corporation or other legal entity of any kind.

D. "Intentionally, knowingly, recklessly" shall have those meanings as defined in the Texas Penal Code.

E. "Leased area" shall mean that area of a City-owned facility identified by lease providing for performance of a musical, dramatic or theatrical production.

F. "Produce" shall mean contractual responsibility for advertising, staging or setting up a musical, dramatic or theatrical production.

G. "Perform" shall mean acting or performing a musical, dramatic or theatrical production.

H. "Direct" shall mean commanding movement of any actor, performer, stage equipment or stage props.

I. "Participate" shall mean placing or moving equipment or props used in a musical, dramatic or theatrical production.

J. "Aid or assist" shall mean intentionally or knowingly concealing, disguising or misrepresenting the age of a child.

K. "Performance" shall mean any musical, dramatic or theatrical production performed by any individual or identifiable group whether or not the production includes more than one individual or identifiable group staged in a City-owned facility.

L. "Explicit reference" shall mean the use of words which have a readily recognizable meaning describing or depicting conduct proscribed hereby, but shall not include words which are merely suggestive or have meanings which are equally consistent with actions not proscribed hereby.

SECTION 2. Admission of children.

No person having control over a City-owned facility shall intentionally, knowingly, or recklessly allow or permit a child under the age of fourteen (14) years to enter or to remain within a leased area in a City-owned facility within one hour before or at any time during a performance is scheduled, if such person (1) knows, or (2) has knowledge of sufficient facts and circumstances from which a reasonable person would know that the performance is or will be a performance obscene as to a child, unless such child is admitted with a parent or legal guardian.

SECTION 3. Producing, performing, directing or participating in a performance.

No person shall intentionally, knowingly, or recklessly produce, perform, direct, or participate in a performance within the leased area if such person:

(1) knows, or

(2) has knowledge of sufficient facts and circumstances from which a reasonable person would know that:

    (a) a child under the age of fourteen (14) years of age is present without a parent or legal guardian, and

    (b) the performance is or will be a performance obscene as to a child.

SECTION 4. Advertising and notification.

Any person who shall produce or direct a performance, and who (1) knows, or (2) has knowledge of such facts and circumstances from which a reasonable person would know that the performance is or will be a performance obscene as to a child shall cause and provide by contract or otherwise for inclusion in any advertising for such performance the following notice: "This performance may contain material not suitable for children without supervision. Parental discretion is advised. No child under the age of fourteen (14) years of age will be admitted without a parent or legal guardian."

No person shall intentionally, knowingly, or recklessly contract for or obtain any advertising for a performance which is obscene as to a child, without providing for the notice required by the foregoing sentence to be included therein.

SECTION 5. Aiding or assisting a child in attendance.

No person shall intentionally or knowingly aid or assist a child under the age of fourteen (14) years not accompanied by a parent or legal guardian in gaining admission to, or in remaining present during a performance which the actor (1) knows, or (2) knows such facts and circumstances from which a reasonable person would know that the performance is or will be a performance obscene as to a child.

SECTION 6. Defenses.

It shall be an affirmative defense to any prosecution under Section 2 above if the person having control over a City-owned facility attempts to ascertain the true age of a child seeking entrance to a performance obscene as to a child by requiring production of a birth certificate, school record, including identification showing the child's age or other school record indicating the child to be enrolled in eighth (8th) grade or higher, and not relying solely on oral allegations or apparent age of the child.

SECTION 7. Penalties.

Each act or failure to act as required herein shall be punishable by a fine of not less than $50.00 nor more than $200.00.

SECTION 8. Severability.

If, for any reason, any one or more sections, sentences, clauses or parts of this ordinance are held legally invalid, such judgment shall not prejudice, affect, impair or invalidate the remaining sections, sentences, clauses of parts of this ordinance.

SECTION 9. The requirements of this ordinance shall apply only to leases providing for performances of musical, theatrical or dramatic productions in City-owned facilities executed after the effective date of this ordinance. . . .

NOTES

1. In *City of Renton v. Playtime Theatre, Inc.,*—U.S.—(1986), the Supreme Court upheld (by a 7 to 2 vote, with Justices Brennan and Marshall dissenting) an ordinance prohibiting adult motion picture theaters from locating within 1,000 feet of any residential zone, church, park, or school. Playtime had claimed that the ordinance violated Playtime's rights under the First and Fourteenth Amendments. The Court stated that the ordinance was content-neutral and dealt only with the time, place, and manner of performance, serving a substantial government interest in preserving the quality of urban life (citing *Young v. American Mini Theatres, Inc.*, 427 U.S. 50 [1976]). Although Renton had not itself undertaken studies of the impact that such theaters would have upon Renton itself, the Court stated that Renton was entitled to refer to the experience of other neighboring cities, as long as that experience was reasonably believed to be relevant to Renton's own situation. Additionally, Renton did not attempt to bar all entertainment of the type offered by Playtime, having left more than 5 percent of the entire area of the city open to such uses.

2. The foregoing San Antonio ordinance and *City of Renton* offer two potentially powerful tools to localities seeking to limit the degree to which their younger citizens may be exposed to music and/or films which their elders consider objectionable. As of this writing, the San Antonio ordinance has not been challenged. However, it is not difficult to envision a scenario under which (given the Supreme Court's reasoning with respect to the absence of studies in *Renton*) such ordinances can effectively leapfrog city-to-city across the country, causing potential problems for promoters, as well as producers and exhibitors of films.

9.43 Antitrust Issues Between Promoters

Some years ago, when the concert business was thriving, it was not uncommon for a city to support several successful concert promoters. By the early 1970s, however, a single promoter generally predominated in each specific area. Fewer acts pulled big crowds, and these acts demanded higher and higher fees. Many successful promoters fell by the wayside. As the following cases indicate, new promoters seeking to tap the existing market have challenged the old-line promoters under the antitrust laws.

In *Out Front Productions v. Magid,* plaintiff contended that the defendants tied up both facilities and performers in Philadelphia by contractually obtaining overreaching exclusives. In *Danny Kresky Enterprises v. Magid,* the plaintiff charged that the same defendants as in *Out Front* used their outside market powers in Philadelphia and Cincinnati to force various concert performers to do business with defendants in Pittsburgh and thus shut out plaintiff from similar business opportunities. Plaintiff's charges in *Danny Kresky* succeeded, while those in *Out Front* were deemed insufficient by the court. The legal distinctions in the two situations should be noted.

Out Front Productions, Inc. v. Magid, 748 F.2d 166 (3rd Cir. 1984)

Sloviter, J.

. . . Plaintiff Out Front Productions, Inc., a former promoter of rock concerts, appeals from the grant of summary judgment against it in its antitrust action against defendant concert promoters, Larry Magid, Joseph Spivak, Herbert Spivak, and Allen Spivak, individually and trading as Electric Factory Concerts and Tower Theatre (hereafter collectively referred to as EFC).

Out Front contends that EFC prevented it from successfully promoting large-scale white-oriented rock concerts in Philadelphia because EFC, which had a contractual exclusive arrangement from January 1, 1972 to December 31, 1976 to promote rock concerts at the Spectrum, the largest indoor facility and apparently the most attractive to rock performers, maintained its exclusivity beyond that date and unreasonably de-

nied it access to that facility. It also contends that from at least 1972 until April 1980 EFC attached to the contracts with the performers it promoted a "Standard Addendum," which gave EFC certain exclusive rights to those performers in the Philadelphia area for a 75 day period, provided a six months' right of first refusal of the performer's services, and imposed certain advertising restrictions. It contends that EFC's use of the Standard Addendum was a predatory practice to maintain and bolster the monopoly power it acquired through its exclusive access to the Spectrum for rock concert promotion. Out Front alleged that EFC unlawfully conspired to eliminate competition and restrain trade in violation of section 1 of the Sherman Act, 15 U.S.C. § 1, and monopolized or attempted to monopolize the promotion of white-oriented rock music concerts in the Philadelphia metropolitan area in violation of section 2 of the Sherman Act, 15 U.S.C. § 2. . . .

Out Front was formed in 1977 by Richard Fuller, its sole shareholder and general manager. Between September and November of that year it produced 12 concerts, ten at the Trenton War Memorial, a medium-size facility, and two in Philadelphia, one at the Civic Center and the other at the Tower Theatre, a smaller facility owned by defendants. Fuller had promoted a number of rock concerts in Trenton in 1974 and 1975, when he did business under the name Hollow Moon. Nearly all of Out Front's concerts were unprofitable. Apart from one successful effort to promote a concert in Trenton in 1979, it appears to have ceased operations soon after its last concert in November 1977.

Out Front raises no claim that defendants interfered with its business in Trenton. Its claim in this suit is based on the theory that it would have become a successful promoter of white-oriented rock concerts in Philadelphia had defendants made the Spectrum available for its concerts.

At the close of discovery, defendants moved for summary judgment, claiming Out Front could not show it had been "prevented from presenting concerts" in the absence of evidence that it sought and was refused access to the Spectrum and that it sought the services of rock performers for such concerts. The district court granted summary judgment, stating that the record was "devoid of evidence suggesting that [Out Front] demanded access to the Spectrum," . . . that Out Front "failed to meet its justifiably rigorous burden of proving that a demand for access to Philadelphia-area concert facilities would have been futile," . . . and that Out Front failed to produce evidence that "the standard addendum was a feature of any contract defendants may have had with any [performer] to whom plaintiff claims to have been denied access." . . . The court later denied Out Front's motion to alter or amend judgment based on further submission, reaffirming its original opinion. . . .

As this court recently set forth in *Weiss v. York Hospital*, 745 F.2d 786 (3d Cir. 1984), a private antitrust plaintiff must demonstrate (1) a violation of the antitrust laws and (2) a right either to the treble damage remedy under section 4 of the Clayton Act or to injunctive relief under section 16 of the Clayton Act. At 804–805. In this case, neither the motion for summary judgment nor the court's opinion granting it were predicated on plaintiff's failure to establish a genuine issue of material fact as to defendants' violation of the antitrust laws. Therefore, for purposes of this appeal we assume that EFC violated sections 1 and 2 of the Sherman Act, as alleged, through an unlawful monopoly of large-scale white-oriented rock concerts in Philadelphia, furthered by predatory and conspiratorial practices including unreasonable exclusive dealing arrangements with the owners of the Spectrum and the use of the Standard Addendum in contracts EFC signed with certain rock performers.

However, plaintiff also bears the burden of showing causation, i.e., that defendants' alleged unlawful conduct was a material cause of injury to its business or property. . . . Although the burden is not a heavy one, since "a plaintiff need not exhaust all possible alternative sources of injury," if plaintiff fails to establish a causal relationship between its financial difficulties and defendants' antitrust violations, its case must fail. . . .

[The court reviewed case law that indicated a formal demand by Out Front for access to the Spectrum was not a prerequisite to an antitrust action.]

On the other hand, a refused demand is often the best evidence of causation, and the absence of a demand in the circumstances of the particular case may, indeed, be fatal to plaintiff's ability to show causation. In the three Supreme Court cases holding demand was not a prerequisite there had been a course of dealing and participation in the market from which the Court permitted the fact finder to infer the causal nexus between the antitrust violation and plaintiff's injury. However, in the absence of such circumstances, a similar inference will ordinarily be unavailable. Thus, a company expanding either into a new geographic territory or product line or beginning business altogether must show not only that it had the background, experience, and financial ability to make a viable entrance, but even more important, that it took affirmative actions to pursue the new line of business. . . . Proof of a demand will generally be the best evidence to show that a plaintiff was poised and ready to enter the market. Otherwise there is unlikely to be any plausible evidence to show that defendants impeded this effort. Certainly, the law will not countenance a dormant plaintiff who springs into action only when it is time to file suit.

To recapitulate, an antitrust plaintiff who sues claiming it was excluded from the market, whether by a conspiracy or monopolistic conduct, must produce sufficient evidence from which the trier of fact can find a causal connection between the violation and the injury. Although summary judgment should be used only sparingly in antitrust cases . . . "there are patently justifiable reasons why a trial court should ascertain, before embarking on a lengthy antitrust trial, whether plaintiff will be able to present some evidence that the injury of which it complains can be attributable to the alleged antitrust violation." *Van Dyk Research*, 631 F.2d at 258 (Sloviter, J., concurring). Thus we turn to examine whether the district court was justified in giving summary judgment against plaintiff on the record before it. . . .

EFC filed its motion for summary judgment supported by specific affidavits and deposition testimony stating that plaintiff never sought to lease the Spectrum and that qualified promoters' demands for concert dates were accepted. It filed the affidavit of Allen B. Flexer, Vice-President of the Spectrum's parent corporation, who had the responsibility of negotiating with persons desiring to lease the Spectrum. Flexer's affidavit stated that before suit was filed, he had never heard of Out Front or Richard Fuller, and averred that "during the period 1977 to date, neither Out Front Productions, Inc. nor Richard Fuller ever contacted me or any other Spectrum official responsible for leasing for the purpose of seeking available dates for presentation at the Spectrum of any music concerts." . . . This was supported by the affidavit of his assistant, Stephen Greenberg. . . . Flexer's affidavit set forth a list of promoters to whom the Spectrum was leased during the relevant period.

In response to the motion for summary judgment, plaintiff presented an affidavit by Richard Fuller, its general manager, which asserts in relevant part:

2. Some time during the last half of 1977 or the first half of 1978, I went to the Spectrum to try to obtain a list of available dates, in order to book musical acts on those dates.

3. At the Spectrum, I was told that Larry Magid had it "tied up," that only he "plays there," and that I should "forget it." . . .

6. My company and I were ready, willing and able to promote and present such groups [listed in ¶ 5] in the Philadelphia-Trenton area. I had money in the bank, houses which were not subject to mortgages and other property which could be used as collateral for financing. There were also people who were able and willing to supply me with financial backing. . . . My company and I promoted 12 concerts in 1977. . . . As a principal of Hollow Moon, a promoter of such concerts, I promoted 7 concerts in 1974 and 11 concerts in 1975 . . . and co-promoted 3 concerts in 1975 with EFC, a defendant herein.

7. Because of defendants' exclusionary practices, my company was forced out of business after its last concert on November 17, 1977.

The portion of the Fuller affidavit dealing with the demand for the Spectrum, the issue on summary judgment, contrasts sharply with the defendants' submissions. It is vague as to the timing and content of the request for access; it does not state that Fuller provided EFC with a definite request or proposal; it fails to state to whom the inquiry was made; and it fails to state *for whom* the inquiry was made. There is no written evidence to back up Fuller's assertion of a frustrated

attempt to lease the Spectrum, and plaintiff makes no assertion that any follow-up effort was made. Fuller's earlier deposition testimony had suggested that the inquiry he made regarding availability of the Spectrum was made by him on behalf of Hollow Moon, an entity unrelated to plaintiff Out Front, and occurred before the beginning of the four-year damage period. . . .

Even if plaintiff could rehabilitate Fuller's own deposition with his subsequent affidavit, an issue we do not reach, that affidavit is insufficient to withstand summary judgment.

Fed. R. Civ. P. 56(e) provides, in part, "When a motion for summary judgment is made and supported as provided in this rule, an adverse party may not rest upon the mere allegations or denials of his pleading, but his response, by affidavits or as otherwise provided in this rule, *must set forth specific facts* showing there is a genuine issue for trial. If he does not so respond, summary judgment, if appropriate, shall be entered against him." (emphasis added).

We have interpreted Rule 56 to signify that "mere formal denials or general allegations which do not show the facts in detail and with precision are insufficient to prevent the award of summary judgment." . . . Under this rule, "a party resisting the motion *cannot expect to rely merely on bare assertions,* conclusory allegations or suspicions." . . . Even accepting Fuller's affidavit assertions as true, they fail to show any serious effort on behalf of Out Front to secure access to the Spectrum during the 1977 to 1981 period.

Nor does the record support Out Front's alternative argument, unsupported by any affidavit, that Fuller, an established promoter in Trenton, knew from his past unsuccessful efforts for Hollow Moon that it would have been futile to negotiate for a concert date for the Spectrum. The record is clear that after EFC's contractual exclusive right to the Spectrum ended in December, 1976 and during the damage period, 1977 to 1981, other promoters were in fact given access to the Spectrum. Plaintiff contends that these other promoters were only granted access on highly unfavorable terms, were required to co-promote with EFC, or did not threaten EFC's alleged monopoly over large-scale white-oriented rock concerts. If true, these facts might support viable claims against EFC by the other promoters, but they do not provide the missing link in this plaintiff's proof. In short, there is no probative, objective evidence that plaintiff's intentions vis-à-vis the Spectrum went beyond a pessimistic belief that it was not worth gearing up to use the facility and to compete with Electric Factory. Fuller's affidavit fails to tie defendants' conduct to Out Front's lack of success on its concert venture. . . .

Plaintiff's additional claim, that it was injured because defendants exercised control over performers and agents through unreasonably restrictive contracts, suffers from a similar defect. A jury may find that coercion or control over performers may injure other firms who are unable to use the performers' services. . . . However, this plaintiff presented no evidence that it ever sought to contract for the services of any performers covered by the Standard Addendum and that such performers refused to perform for it as a result. In the absence of any such evidence, there is no basis on which plaintiff would be entitled to damages arising from EFC's use of the Standard Addendum. . . .

Because plaintiff failed to establish the existence of a genuine issue of fact that EFC's alleged actions caused it damage, the district court's order granting summary judgment for defendants will be affirmed.

Danny Kresky Enterprises Corp. v. Magid, 716 F.2d 206 (3d Cir. 1983)

SLOVITER, J.

. . . Kresky Corp. and Electric Factory are competitors in the concert promotion business. Concert promoters ordinarily submit bids to the booking agent of a musical artist in order to obtain an agreement to promote a concert performance by that artist. Often there are bids by several promoters. The decision to accept or reject the bid is made by the artist or the artist's management. Two or more promoters frequently co-promote concerts, sharing in the profits and losses.

Electric Factory is headquartered in Philadelphia, which is acknowledged to be one of the most lucrative markets in the United States for the performance of popular music concerts. The Spectrum Arena is the largest and most attractive facility for this purpose in Philadelphia and provides the most economical site for concert performers with large drawing power. In 1972, Electric Factory was given exclusive access to the Spectrum for the promotion of concerts. The written agreement terminated in 1977, although it was a disputed factual issue whether that exclusive arrangement continued, as plaintiff alleged, pursuant to an oral understanding.

Kresky Corp., which is headquartered in Pittsburgh, filed this suit in the United States District Court for the Western District of Pennsylvania alleging that Electric Factory conspired with others to unlawfully restrain trade in the Pittsburgh market in violation of sections 1 and 2 of the Sherman Act through blockbooking of concerts and group boycotts. In essence, the complaint alleged that Electric Factory used its exclusive arrangement with the Spectrum and its exclusive license for the promotion of concerts at the Cincinnati Riverfront Coliseum to force various concert performers to perform for Electric Factory in Pittsburgh, and that it threatened artists, artists' agents, and artists' managers that it would not deal with them in any market unless it obtained the artists' services for the Pittsburgh market. Among the co-conspirators listed were Spectrum, Inc., Irv Nahan, Georgie Woods, Jot Corporation, Borgas, Inc., and WDAS (Max H. Leon, Inc.), a radio station in Philadelphia alleged to be "one of the most powerful, in terms of influence, black oriented radio stations in the country." The complaint alleged "[i]t is critical to black oriented artists that their music be played on WDAS." Electric Factory filed a counterclaim alleging that Kresky Corp. and several co-conspirators violated sections 1 and 2 of the Sherman Act.

The case was tried before a jury for nine days from February 29 to March 16, 1981. Among the evidence introduced by plaintiff was the testimony of Danny Kresky, plaintiff's chief operating officer, that he was not permitted by the artists' management to discuss or bid for promotion rights to nine black-oriented concerts at the Civic Arena in Pittsburgh between 1976 and 1979, all nine of which were eventually promoted by Electric Factory. Plaintiff also introduced evidence of, *inter alia*, Electric Factory's exclusive agreement to promote concerts at the Spectrum, its arrangement not to compete with Borgas, Inc., one of the alleged co-conspirators, the admission of one of Electric Factory's partners that the purpose of the arrangement with Borgas "was to try to keep [them] from competing with each other," and "to stop [them] from fiercely competing," and threats by Larry Magid, one of Electric Factory's principals, directed to artists and management to induce their use of Electric Factory's promotion services. Plaintiff limited its claim for damages to the profits it would have received from two of the nine concerts in Pittsburgh, the February 3, 1978 and April 9, 1979 Civic Arena concerts by Parliament Funkadelic. Kresky requested damages of estimated profits of $22,000.

The jury returned a special verdict finding that Electric Factory had conspired to restrain trade in violation of section 1 of the Sherman Act, but had not violated section 2 of the Sherman Act; that plaintiff had suffered damages in the amount of $5,500; and that plaintiff had not violated the antitrust laws. Thereafter, plaintiff filed a motion for permanent injunctive relief. The court, relying on the evidence adduced at trial without a separate evidentiary hearing, entered a judgment which, *inter alia*, permanently enjoined Electric Factory "from entering into a conspiracy with concert artists whereby the artists agree to refrain from entering into promotional agreements with [Kresky Corp.] upon the threat of [Electric Factory] to refuse to promote the artists in the future at the Spectrum Arena in Philadelphia."

Electric Factory filed a motion for judgment n.o.v. which the court characterized as "challenging plaintiff's proof of the amount of the damage done." The district court granted the motion and vacated the damage award to plaintiff but left intact the permanent injunction against Electric Factory. . . .

In this case, the jury, in its answers to special interrogatories, found with respect to the section 1 claim both that "defendants entered into a combination or a conspiracy with others" amounting to an unreasonable restraint of trade, and that this combination or conspiracy "proximately re-

sulted in injury to the plaintiff's business or property." The jury established the amount of damages as $5,500, which the court viewed as representing the profits earned by defendant on the two Parliament Funkadelic concerts.

It is far from clear that Electric Factory has preserved the contention, which it presented at oral argument on appeal, that there was insufficient evidence to show a violation with respect to the two Parliament Funkadelic concerts. In its opinion, the district court stated that for the purposes of the motion for judgment n.o.v.: "[D]efendants concede plaintiff has proved a violation of the antitrust laws, that is the conspiracy between defendants and various black artists to prevent plaintiff from successfully bidding for the artists' services. Defendants further concede plaintiff has proved the conspiracy injured its business." Defendant contends it made no such concession. On the assumption that there was no such concession, we have reviewed the record and we conclude that the evidence was sufficient to support the jury's verdict in both respects.

Unlike many antitrust cases where there is no direct evidence that defendant ever overtly used its power or leverage, in this case a number of witnesses testified at trial or at depositions which were introduced at trial regarding threats or other forms of coercion by Magid to induce them to use Electric Factory's services. Larry Fitzgerald, the manager of the Brothers Johnson, testified as follows on cross-examination by defendant:

> Q Mr. Fitzgerald, did you have any discussions with Mr. Magid concerning the performance of the Brothers Johnson in Pittsburgh under the auspices of Mr. Magid? . . .
> A Mr. Magid, after hearing that Mr. Kresky would like to promote a Brothers Johnson show in Pittsburgh, called me following a telephone conversation with my agents, perhaps several conversations with my agents, wherein he strongly objected due to the fact that—well, I will rephrase. Mr. Magid stated that since he promoted the Brothers Johnson in Pittsburgh the year prior, he felt he was entitled to promote them again in the future and felt very strongly about it. . . .
> Q Mr. Fitzgerald, did Mr. Magid, in the conversation that he had with you concerning the Brothers

Johnson, mention his promoting the Brothers Johnson in Philadelphia?

A Yes.

Q Did he relate that to the performance of the Brothers Johnson date in Pittsburgh? Did he mention it in the same conversation? Could you relate to me, as best you can, what he, Mr. Magid, said to you in connection with the performance of the Brothers Johnson in Philadelphia?

A Mr. Magid said that he felt that he was entitled to the performance in Pittsburgh, and Mr. Magid felt so strongly about it that if for some reason he ended up not promoting the Brothers Johnson in Pittsburgh he would just as soon not promote them in other cities as well. . . .

Charles Barnett, the booking agent for the Average White Band, which his agency had booked into Philadelphia to be promoted by a promoter other than Electric Factory, testified that Magid got angry and said "Tear up my card. I don't want to deal with your agency." . . .

Leo Leichter, agent for Dave Mason, a performer, testified that Magid telephoned him after learning he had booked Mason with another promoter in Philadelphia into the Tower Theater as an alternate to the Spectrum, and that Magid was quite upset because Leichter was dealing "with another promoter in his turf," . . . that Magid said, "No one comes into my turf," Tr. 488, and that in that telephone conversation Magid indicated, "He didn't want to do business with me again if the date were to be consummated with [the other promoter], or he indicated he wouldn't buy the act again." . . .

Derek Sutton, who manages rock and roll bands, testified that when Magid learned he wished his group, Procol Harum, to play in Philadelphia at the Tower Theater, Magid "responded angrily," telling him that since Magid "had played them several times in the past . . . it would not be correct business procedure for the group to play for anyone else." . . . Magid also said he would approach a member of the band in order to discuss "the correctness of whether [it] should go with somebody else." . . .

There was testimony on behalf of defendant, including the testimony of Magid, which contradicted some of the above. Credibility, of course, was for the jury to determine. In fact, in a magazine interview in December 1976 which was admitted into evidence at trial, Magid admitted that, "In competition I may have used my muscle and power to excess. I play acts that other people want and I'm not giving too much room for other people to start. One of my earlier faults was that I was vindictive." . . .

Although defendant argued that evidence of threats which preceded the period in suit was irrelevant, the court overruled that objection. The Supreme Court has held that evidence of a conspiracy relating to events occurring prior to the period for which damages are sought is probative of the question whether an antitrust violation has occurred. . . .

We do not understand defendant to contend that there was insufficient evidence from which the jury could have found Electric Factory violated section 1 of the Sherman Act. The evidence summarized would amply support that finding. Thus we turn to the other two elements of a private antitrust damage action, fact of injury (*i.e.*, causation) and amount of damages. It is not totally clear whether the district court granted the motion for n.o.v. because it found there was insufficient evidence of the fact of injury or of the amount of damages. There is language in the opinion susceptible of either construction.

In any event, when both issues are reviewed under the standard appropriate for a jury verdict (the narrowest review available), we conclude that judgment n.o.v. on either ground cannot be sustained. Turning first to whether plaintiff produced sufficient evidence to show defendant's antitrust violation proximately caused plaintiff's injury, the district court correctly stated in its discussion of plaintiff's "burden of showing the fact of injury" that the standard of causation requires only that plaintiff prove that defendant's illegal conduct was a material cause of its injury. The court continued "[P]laintiff need not prove that but for defendants' illegal conduct, he would have promoted some or all of the black-oriented, arena-size concerts in Pittsburgh during the appropriate period. Rather, the jury may conclude that the fact he was unable to even bid on some of them surely contributed to his failure to promote them." In fact, in awarding the permanent injunction, the district court expressly referred to, thereby apparently adopting, the jury's finding that defendant's antitrust conspiracy "proximately caus[ed]" damage to plaintiff's business and property.

The requisite causation, the link between defendant's activity in violation of the antitrust laws and plaintiff's inability to even bid for the concerts in question, was an inferential leap the jury was permitted to make in light of the evidence before it. "Any fact that the jury could have reasonably inferred from the evidence in favor of the verdict winner will be presumed to have been so inferred when the court reviews the evidence supporting the verdict." *Hahn v. Atlantic Richfield Co.*, 625 F.2d 1095, 1099 (3d Cir. 1980). . . . Some of Magid's conversations to which the witnesses testified occurred less than a year before one of the Parliament Funkadelic concerts at issue. The jury could have inferred either that Parliament Funkadelic had been the recipient of coercion similar to that exerted on other artists or that the knowledge of Magid's practices was sufficiently widespread in the industry that it induced Parliament Funkadelic to use Electric Factory's promotion services for the two concerts in question without giving plaintiff an opportunity to bid.

The plausibility of this inference was strengthened by evidence that the terms on which Electric Factory promoted the two Parliament Funkadelic concerts were considerably less favorable to the performers than usual for groups of that stature. Parliament Funkadelic performed both Pittsburgh concerts for Electric Factory without securing any guarantee, under an arrangement to split the profit on a 50-50 basis with Electric Factory. Kresky testified that only rarely will a group not receive a guarantee, and in that case the group will receive a 90–10 share of the profits. He stated that "99.9 percent of the times" a promoter must guarantee a deposit for the performer before a concert. In his experience, the only time a deposit is not guaranteed is when an artist is "looking to yield the lion's share of the profits—usually 90 percent of it." . . . Although this was a disputed case, for purposes of this appeal we must resolve all factual disputes in favor of Kresky Corp., the recipient of the jury verdict. Viewed in that light, we conclude this

evidence was sufficient to support the jury's express finding that defendant's antitrust violation was the proximate cause of plaintiff's injury. . . .

The evidence that Kresky Corp. would have promoted the two concerts in the absence of defendant's illegal conduct is far from overwhelming. Because Kresky Corp. had not been allowed to submit a bid at all, there was, of course, no evidence as to the terms of the bids for the two concerts. However, Kresky did testify that he had never offered terms as unfavorable as those given by Electric Factory to Parliament Funkadelic. From this the jury could reasonably have inferred that plaintiff's bid would have been at least more favorable than defendant's. Moreover, while there were other concert promoters in the Pittsburgh area, there was also evidence that Kresky Corp. was one of the largest and there was no evidence that any other promoter had attempted to submit a bid for the two concerts.

The absence of more specific evidence is in large part attributable to defendant's wrongful conduct, which resulted in no other bids for the concerts being made. As the Supreme Court has stated in explaining its "traditional rule excusing antitrust plaintiffs from an unduly rigorous standard of proving antitrust injury," "it does not 'come with very good grace' for the wrongdoer to insist upon specific and certain proof of the injury which it has itself inflicted." *J. Truett Payne Co. v. Chrysler Motors Corp.*, 451 U.S. at 566–67. . . . "Any other rule would enable the wrongdoer to profit by his wrongdoing at the expense of his victim. It would be an inducement to make wrongdoing so effective and complete in every case as to preclude any recovery. . . ." *Bigelow v. RKO Radio Pictures, Inc.*, 327 U.S. 251, 264, 66 S.Ct. 574, 579, 90 L.Ed. 652 (1946). . . .

In summary, the jury could have reasonably found a causal nexus between defendant's wrongful conduct and plaintiff's failure to promote at least one of the Parliament Funkadelic concerts at issue. The district court's grant of the motion for judgment n.o.v. on the ground that "it cannot be said with certainty that plaintiff's failure to promote and earn profits on the two concerts . . . was the direct and certain result of defendants' conceded antitrust violation" was inconsistent with the Supreme Court's reminder in *Zenith Radio Corp. v. Hazeltine Research, Inc.*, 395 U.S. 100, 123–24, 89 S.Ct. 1562, 1576–77, 23 L.Ed.2d 129 (1969), that:

> [D]amage issues in these cases are rarely susceptible of the kind of concrete, detailed proof of injury which is available in other contexts. The Court has repeatedly held that in the absence of more precise proof, the factfinder may "conclude as a matter of just and reasonable inference from the proof of defendants' wrongful acts and their tendency to injure plaintiffs' business, and from the evidence of the decline in prices, profits and values, not shown to be attributable to other causes, that defendants' wrongful acts had caused damage to the plaintiffs."

We will, therefore, reverse the order of the district court granting defendant's motion for judgment n.o.v. and remand for reinstatement of the jury verdict on damages.

In its cross-appeal, Electric Factory challenges the district court's entry of a permanent injunction against it. The district court's final judgment of April 14, 1981 permanently enjoined defendants "from entering into a conspiracy with concert artists whereby the artists agree to refrain from entering into promotional agreements with the plaintiff upon the threat of defendants to refuse to promote the artists in the future at the Spectrum Arena in Philadelphia." In its subsequent opinion granting defendant's motion for judgment n.o.v. as to damages, the court left the injunction intact, on the ground that "[t]he fact that plaintiff is not entitled to an award of damages does not, however, deprive him of his judgment against defendants."

Defendant's contention that the district court was obliged to dissolve the injunction because it had overturned the damages verdict on what defendant argued was plaintiff's failure to prove causation must obviously now fail. . . .

Chapter 10

PERSONAL RIGHTS

10.00 Protections for the Celebrity's Name and Image

The celebrity in the public eye has two concerns that go beyond his or her creative efforts. First is to guard against intrusions into what exists of a private life. Second is to protect the value of the celebrity's name, image, and other attributes surrounding the person. This chapter considers the means by which a celebrity can use several legal doctrines to gain protections for his or her personal rights.

A celebrity's name and image in our star-conscious society are valuable commodities. They can be commercially marketed and reap substantial rewards if done with expertise and intelligence. The celebrity's concern is that others, without authorization, will attempt to exploit the name or image. In the cases we consider in this chapter, the celebrity's name, image, and other personal characteristics are used without permission in commercial items ranging from T-shirts to portable toilets, in advertisements, as the basis for a live entertainment tour that evokes the imagery of a deceased star, and as the source of discussion in published works

as disparate as serious biographies and the *National Enquirer*. Obviously, outsiders feel few constraints in attempting to profit from a celebrity's name value.

The considerations in this chapter divide into rights of privacy (Section 10.10), publicity (Section 10.20), special problems involving a news function (Section 10.30), misappropriation and unfair competition (Section 10.40), and falsification and libel (Section 10.50). In reading the cases in the various sections, it is apparent that real-life situations do not divide so neatly into separate classifications. The invasion of a celebrity's *persona* may require a response using not one but several legal theories. Consequently, before examining the factual situations, general background on possible legal theories is provided.

10.01 Right of Privacy Defined

The right of privacy as a legally enforceable right is largely a 20th-century development. As with other modern legal doctrines, privacy's roots are embedded in a variety of common law precedents, but its enunciation as an integrated legal concept is of recent origin. Thomas Cooley in his treatise on torts remarked on a right "to be left alone." Two subsequent works receive major credit for articulating, then giving substance to, a right of privacy.

The first was an article by Samuel Warren and Louis Brandeis, published in volume four of the *Harvard Law Review* in 1890. Titled "The Right to Privacy," the article begins its analysis with the following:

> That the individual shall have full protection in person and in property is a principle as old as the common law; but it has been found necessary from time to time to define anew the exact nature and extent of such protection. Political, social, and economic changes entail the recognition of new rights, and the common law, in its eternal youth, grows to meet the demands of society. Thus, in very early times, the law gave a remedy only for physical interference with life and property, for trespasses *vi et armis*. Then the "right to life" served only to protect the subject from battery in its various forms; liberty meant freedom from actual restraint; and the right to property secured to the individual his lands and his cattle. Later, there came a recognition of man's spiritual nature, of his feelings and his intellect. Gradually the scope of these legal rights broadened; and now the right to life has come to mean the right to enjoy life—the right to be let alone; the right to liberty secures the exercise of extensive civil privileges; and the term "property" has grown to comprise every form of possession—intangible, as well as tangible.

As important as Warren and Brandeis's words were and are, their influence was substantially enhanced by various writings of William Prosser. In one of this later efforts, Dean Prosser enunciated again the four categories he asserted were included within a personal right to privacy. These are:

1. Protection against intrusion into one's private affairs;
2. Avoidance of disclosure of one's embarrassing private facts;
3. Protection against publicity placing one in a false light in the public eye; and
4. Remedies for appropriation, usually for commercial advantage, of one's name or likeness.*

Most jurisdictions today have interwoven one or more of these protections into the case law of their states. A few jurisdictions have granted statutory recognition. But in all, an uncertain process has left incomplete the protection many states afford citizens under a right of privacy.

Under Prosser's four areas of classic privacy violations, the first three protect an individual from emotional injury resulting from the harsh and unwelcome glare of publicity. The concerns of these three differ from the theoretical underpinnings of Prosser's fourth intrusion, since the focus of the fourth is not so much on mental harm but on the proprietary interests of protecting against misappropriation of one's name or likeness for commercial gain.

Since this fourth intrusion is similar to the protections afforded by the right of publicity, courts have had difficulty distinguishing the two rights when a misappropriation of name or likeness occurs. Some courts have refused to recognize any differences at all. Courts which have recognized a common law right of publicity have chosen to distinguish the two rights on the grounds that the state's interest in enforcing them is different. Prosser stated:

> The interest protected "in permitting recovery (for a privacy invasion)" is clearly that of reputation, with the same overtones of mental distress as defamation! . . . By contrast, the State's interest in permitting the proprietary interest of the individuals is closely analogous

---

*(See Prosser, "Privacy," 48 *California Law Review* (1960); and W. Prosser, *The Law of Torts* § 117 (4th ed. 1971).

to the goals of patent and copyright law, focusing on the right of the individual to reap the reward of his endeavors and having little to do with protecting feeling. [Prosser, "Privacy," 48 *California Law Review*, p. 406.]

Thus, the decision by a court to apply privacy versus publicity may depend on quite different considerations.

Since the right of privacy is a personal right, generally only persons who are injured may assert a claim. Consequently, the right is not assignable and usually does not survive the injured party's death. These limitations obviously make a publicity claim more attractive if assignment or descendibility is at issue. In addition, as a practical matter, the right of publicity is predominantly a right for celebrities whose names have commercial value; in contrast, the right of privacy is more applicable to the average individual. These compartments are not airtight, however, and celebrities for good reason at times invoke rights of privacy when unwarranted intrusions occur.

A successful right of privacy claim has three elements: the use of one's name or image in an (1) identifiable manner, (2) without consent, and (3) in situations in which the invasion benefits the defendant. It is irrelevant how many people recognize the individual whose privacy is invaded, but recognition may be a factor in assessing damages.

A fictionalized work may give rise to a cause of action if the use of a name or physical characteristics makes the complainant identifiable. Whether fictionalized or not, an unauthorized depiction of an individual need not be a complete facsimile to warrant a privacy invasion. Some jurisdictions do not even require that the person be identified, but allow pictorial surroundings to constitute identification. (See, for example, *Motschenbacher v. R.J. Reynolds Tobacco* in Section 10.23.) In most jurisdictions, the complainant's actual name need not be used if a nickname or other name permits identification.

As with other personal rights, privacy claims may be curtailed by assertion of rights of free speech and press. This raises the important question of when is there a public interest in the depictions presented? This question is explored in Section 10.30.

10.02 Right of Publicity Defined

The right of publicity is a recent legal development. To state that the contours of the right are still being refined is clearly an understatement. For example, some jurisdictions still subsume publicity under a right of privacy; in others publicity is wholly independent and is regarded as property.

The right of publicity is defined as the right of each individual to control and profit from the commercial value of his or her own identity. The right as recognized protects the unauthorized commercial exploitation of a celebrity's name (actual or legal), image, or likeness, as well as other aspects of identity such as biographical facts and records of performance. As a practical matter, celebrities are the principal parties who have value in their names and image. Only rarely will a right of publicity benefit the average person.

The rationale of the right of publicity is the protection of a celebrity's proprietary interest in the development of a marketable image. The right allows the celebrity to reap the benefits of his or her own work and to protect against exploitation by unauthorized sources. Arguably, publicity rights serve social interests by guarding against unjust enrichment and promote creativity by offering financial incentive to those choosing to cultivate a unique *persona*.

Some jurisdictions require that for a right of publicity to be descendible to heirs the celebrity must have exploited his or her rights during life. This same requirement also appears in recent statutes, although most jurisdictions have no such prerequisites.

As stated previously in Section 10.01, courts have struggled with distinctions between publicity and privacy. In 1953, a breakthrough occurred in *Haelan Laboratories, Inc. v. Topps Chewing Gum*, 202 F.2d 866 (2d Cir. 1953), where the court expressly recognized a right of publicity. The court held that "in addition to and independent of the right of privacy . . . a man has a right in the publicity value of his photography, i.e., the right to grant the exclusive privilege of publishing his picture." The court rejected the contention that the only protectable rights, if any, in the publication of a celebrity's picture after it was validly assigned existed in a right of privacy.

Other courts soon followed *Haelan*, such as *Chaplin v. National Broadcasting Co.*, 15 F.R.D. 134 (S.D.N.Y. 1953). Distinctions between publicity and privacy became widely, if not universally, accepted. This actually began a new cycle of problems in defining how far publicity extends. In several states, legislation provided at least partial answers. These developments are explored at length in Sections 10.20 to 10.23.

10.03   Other Rights in Names and Images

In addition to the rights of privacy and publicity, courts have looked to other legal concepts for the protection of personal rights. Many of these come under the rubric of unfair competition, relating to a false representation concerning the source of goods or services. There is no single definition of unfair competition, since it encompasses both statutory and common law rights. Many of these rights might be supposed to protect mainly goods, but courts have extended these to the protection of personal rights as well.

Under the federal Lanham Act, one particular provision (§ 43 of the Act) has been used in recent years to protect against the invasion of personal rights. The text of this provision and cases applying it are set forth in Section 10.40.

One must also consider the possibilities of asserting trademark, tradename, and service mark protections for individuals and their creative efforts. A brief description of each of these concepts illustrates how these might be used in turning the person into a protected business.

10.03–1   Trademarks

A trademark is a sign, device, or mark by which the goods produced or dealt in by a particular person or business are distinguished from those produced or dealt in by others. The Federal Trade-Mark Act (Lanham Act) defines the term "trademark" to include any word, name, symbol or device, adopted and used to identify goods and distinguish them from others.

A trademark is closely analogous to the goodwill of a business or establishment. It represents the "commercial signature" of the trademark owner placed upon the merchandise or the package in which it is sold.

The purpose of a trademark is twofold. Trademarks function to designate goods as the product of a particular trader, thereby protecting that trader's goodwill, as against the sale of another's products as the trader's own. Trademarks also assure the public that they are procuring the genuine goods they seek. It is therefore imperative that for a name, symbol, or device to constitute a trademark it must point distinctly to the origin or ownership of the article to which it is affixed. The reason for this requirement is that unless the words or devices clearly point out the origin or ownership, the person who claims trademark protection cannot be harmed by any appropriation or imitation of them by others; nor can the public be deceived. Trademarks may be

1. fanciful (coined words which have been invented for the sole purpose of functioning as a trademark);
2. arbitrary (words or symbols in common usage in the language but arbitrarily applied to goods);
3. suggestive (words which suggest but do not primarily describe the goods or their characteristics); and
4. descriptive (marks that describe the qualities, ingredients, or characteristics of a product).

Trademark rights are acquired by affixation of the mark on the goods themselves and use of the mark in interstate commerce. Trademark infringement is determined by the likelihood of confusion among the purchasing public. The similarity of the marks in sound, appearance, and meaning, and the similarities of the channels of trade and the goods are all factors in determining whether one trademark infringes another.

10.03–2   Tradenames

The term "tradename" is most commonly used to indicate a part or all of a business or corporate name and includes individual names, surnames, and abbreviations of firm names. It is typically a name, word, or phrase used by one engaged in business, as a means of identifying his or her products, business, or services, and of establishing goodwill. It has been said that a tradename symbolizes the reputation of a business.

A tradename differs from a trademark in that it relates mainly to a business and its goodwill, while a trademark relates mainly to an item sold. Although the Trade-Mark Act distinguishes between trademarks and tradenames by providing that tradenames are not entitled to registration, the use of trade-names is governed in most respects by the same rules applicable to trademarks.

10.03–3   Service Marks

The term "service mark" under the Trade-Mark Act includes a mark used in the sale or advertising of services to identify the services of one person and distinguish them from the services of others. Titles, character names, and other distinctive features of radio and television programs are registrable as service marks. Moreover, entertainment services provided by individuals are among the "services" sufficient to support service mark registration. Service marks are intended to identify and afford protection to things of an intangible nature, as distinguished from the protection already provided for marks affixed to tangible goods and products. However, it is possible for a given symbol to be used in a way that it functions as both a trademark for goods and a service mark for services, and can be the object of separate registrations.

10.10   Right of Privacy

The basic parameters of a right of privacy, whether under common law principles or by statutory enactment, were discussed in Section 10.01. This section looks at right-of-privacy treatment in one important entertainment jurisdiction — the state of New York. In New York, the right of privacy is derived from statute, sections 50 and 51 of the New York Civil Rights Law. The provisions of these sections are set forth below.

The cases that follow are New York cases that involve a variety of situations in which a claim of privacy was pressed, not always successfully. In *Rosemont Enterprises v. Random House*, Howard Hughes attempted to block an unauthorized biography by claiming he had sold all his rights to his life story to Rosemont, the actual plaintiff in the case. The court makes short work of the claim that one can prevent all publication about oneself when the person is as famous as Howard Hughes.

In *Shields v. Gross*, Brook Shields attempted to disaffirm a contract entered on her behalf by her mother when Ms. Shields was 10 years old. The contract involved the young Brook Shields posing nude. On somewhat different grounds than *Rosemont*, but with the same result, Brook Shields was not able to prevent publication of her early pictures.

Nude photos were also involved in *Cohen v. Herbal Concepts*. A neighbor of the plaintiffs secretly took nude photos of a mother and daughter and sold them. The photos were taken from behind, and the faces of the plaintiffs could not be seen. That the husband and father of the plaintiffs could identify them, however, was deemed sufficient by the court to establish an actionable claim.

NEW YORK CIVIL RIGHTS LAW

§50. Right of privacy

A person, firm or corporation that uses for advertising purposes, or for the purposes of trade, the name, portrait or picture of any living person without having first obtained the written consent of such person, or if a minor of his or her parent or guardian, is guilty of a misdemeanor.

§51. Action for injunction and for damages

Any person whose name, portrait or picture is used within this state for advertising purposes or for the purposes of trade without the written consent first obtained as above provided may maintain an equitable action in the supreme court of this state against the person, firm or corporation so using his name, portrait or picture, to prevent and restrain the use thereof; and may also sue and recover damages for any injuries sustained by reason of such use

and if the defendant shall have knowingly used such person's name, portrait or picture in such manner as is forbidden or declared to be unlawful by the last section, the jury, in its discretion, may award exemplary damages. But nothing contained in this act shall be so construed as to prevent any person, firm or corporation, practicing the profession of photography, from exhibiting in or about his or its establishment specimens of the work of such establishment, unless the same is continued by such person, firm or corporation after written notice objecting thereto has been given by the person portrayed; and nothing contained in this act shall be so construed as to prevent any person, firm or corporation from using the name, portrait or picture of any manufacturer or dealer in connection with the goods, wares and merchandise manufactured, produced or dealt in by him which he has sold or disposed of with such name, portrait or picture used in connection therewith; or from using the name, portrait or picture of any author, composer or artist in connection with his literary, musical or artistic productions which he has sold or disposed of with such name, portrait or picture used in connection therewith.

Rosemont Enterprises, Inc. v. Random House, Inc., 294 N.Y.S. 2d 122 (Sup. Ct. N.Y. Co. 1968)

FRANK, J.

The plaintiff Rosemont Enterprises, Inc., is identified in the complaint as a corporation engaged "in the business of developing and acquiring literary and dramatic properties and rights, biographical material and the right to use such material . . . for purposes of trade, and producing, publishing and otherwise using the same for profit." The basis for the present action is an alleged agreement between Rosemont and Howard Hughes, characterized in a related copyright litigation as a person "who by reason of his remarkable exploits and achievements, primarily in the aviation and motion picture fields, had become quite a public figure" (see *Rosemont Enterprises, Inc. v. Random House, Inc.*, 366 F.2d 303, 305, C.C.A.2nd). . . .

From the opinions in that case it appears that Random House began preparations for its biography in September 1962 and that Hughes, who (p. 309) "has almost an obsession as to his privacy," learned of the project in 1965 resulting in a warning to Random House that he was opposed to the biography and (p. 305) "would make trouble if the book was published." Shortly thereafter, in September 1965, the plaintiff corporation, Rosemont, was organized by close associates of Hughes for the ostensible purpose of preparing an authorized biography of his life. Its subsequent operations, however, indicate that its primary function was to prevent the publication of biographical material which Hughes could not control and, in particular, the Random House biography. An example of its activities in furtherance of such goal was its acquisition on May 20, 1966, of copyrights on a series of articles about Hughes which had appeared in Look Magazine in early 1954, and its institution of the copyright infringement action a scant 6 days thereafter "not with a desire to protect the value of the original writing but to suppress the Random House biography because Hughes wished to prevent its publication." (See *Rosemont Enterprises, Inc. v. Random House, Inc.*, supra, 366 F.2d, concurring opinion at p. 313.)

As Mr. Justice Moore, speaking for the Court, so aptly phrased it, (p. 305) Hughes has "a publicized passion for personal anonymity" and it is his predilection therefor which is at the heart of the present controversy as well as its related litigations.

The complaint in the present action alleges that plaintiff corporation entered into an agreement with Hughes whereby it acquired "the sole and exclusive world-wide rights to exploit commercially in any manner the name, personality, likeness or the life story or incidents in the life of Hughes" and that such exclusive rights "have unique and great commercial value."

Predicated upon its rights under such agreement, plaintiff asserts three causes of action.

The first cause of action alleges that defendants entered into a scheme "to exploit commercially the name, likeness and personality of Hughes without the consent of either Hughes or plaintiff and to capitalize upon the achievements of Hughes and upon his life story or incidents therein" and that in furtherance of said scheme "and solely for the purposes of trade, and . . . creating a profit for themselves" defendants have agreed to write and publish "a book which would not be written or published in order to disseminate newsworthy information but . . . in such manner as to use and exploit commercially the name, likeness and personality of Hughes." Plaintiff further complains that "defendants have not made a *bona fide* effort to assemble facts for the purpose of informing the public as to Hughes or his life story," followed by allegations that defendants have chosen to ignore plaintiff's exclusive rights and are preparing a book for publication and sale to the general public in the immediate future and that any such book "would impair the market for an authoritative biography of Hughes" and would otherwise interfere with and infringe upon the valuable rights plaintiff acquired under its agreement with Hughes and its valuable property interest therein.

The second cause of action charges that defendant's book violates Hughes' right of privacy under Article 5 of the Civil Rights Law with resultant injury to plaintiff's rights.

In the third cause of action a declaratory judgment is sought in the premises.

The precise nature of the first cause of action is somewhat obscure and understandably prompted the District Court Judge in the copyright suit to observe that the issues herein "are not at all clear." Indeed, such first cause of action seems to consist of a combination of diverse allegations relating to several separate and distinct legal concepts which are all woven together into some not easily decipherable hybrid.

Thus the various allegations condemning defendants' publication, at all, of a book about Hughes are on the one hand couched in terms of defendants' scheme "to exploit commercially" for "profit" and "solely for the purposes of trade" which appears to fall within the language of the New York "privacy statute," and on the other hand stress is placed upon the appropriation or infringement of plaintiff's "valuable property interest" of "great commercial value" in its exclusive rights to exploit commercially the name, personality and likeness of Hughes which would have relevance to the separately recognized "right of publicity." (See *Haelan Laboratories v. Topps Chewing Gum,* 202 F.2d 866; Gordon, "Right of Property in Name, Likeness, Personality and History," 55 Northwestern Univ. L.R. 553, at pgs. 569–571.)

To the extent that the first cause of action seeks relief predicated upon either Hughes' "right of privacy" or his "right of publicity" it is fatally defective.

While considerations of social desirability may in the past have prompted a liberal construction of our statutorily derived "right of privacy" despite troublesome confrontations with constitutionally protected areas of speech and press, the permissible limits of such "right of privacy" despite troublesome confrontations with constitutionally protected areas of speech and press, the permissible limits of such "right" have now been clearly and decisively drawn. (See *Time, Inc. v. Hill,* 385 U.S. 374, 87 S.Ct. 534, 17 L.Ed.2d 456.)

A public figure, whether he be such by choice or involuntarily, is subject to the often-searching beam of publicity and, in balance with the legitimate public interest, the law affords his privacy little protection. . . .

That Howard Hughes falls within the category of a public figure is not seriously open to dispute. His actions and dealings have engendered considerable public interest and he has long been a newsworthy personality. . . . Indeed, his standing as a public figure has been admitted by plaintiff's counsel in depositions before trial, and the allegations of the complaint here in issue make his status in that regard clear.

The dominance of the public interest in obtaining information about public figures received early recognition in the construction of the New York privacy statute and publications of factual or biographical information about such persons have usually been held to be outside the protection of the statute. . . . That the New York statute gives a public figure no right to suppress truthful accounts of his life is now settled in the most unequivocal terms. . . .

While plaintiff's brief in the instant case is liberally sprinkled with charges of "plagiarism," and "reckless disregard of the truth," there is not a single showing of any specific misrepresentation of fact or of false or untruthful statements. Instead, plaintiff asserts that it is seeking "relief on account of the *conduct* of defendants and not the *contents* of their book" and it contends that "its position does not depend upon establishing the truth or falsity of any portion of the book" but rather that the protection of the First Amendment is lost when a defendant engages "in flagrant and unreasonable violations of publishing practices and customs normally adhered to by responsible publishers amounting in effect to reckless disregard of the facts." This is accompanied by a broadside of outrage in which defendants are castigated for "publishing as a biography a work based on no real research, no interviews and no *bona fide* investigation," for failing "to meet minimum standards which normally obtain in the . . . preparation of biographies," for using "a totally inexperienced writer" and for otherwise departing from procedures followed in the publishing industry generally and "from what Random House has done in preparing biographies of other public figures."

While plaintiff's condemnation of the literary merit and creative standards used in producing defendants' book might be of interest in a critique of the work appearing in a book review section, such arguments are wholly irrelevant in the present context. . . . If plaintiff had demonstrated material and substantial falsification, then the standard used in compiling the book might be of significance, but only on the issue of defendants' "*knowledge*" or "reckless disregard" of such falsification. . . . Where, however, as is here the case, there is no showing at the outset of any falsity, the question of "knowledge" is never reached, and abstract indictments of defendants' literary standard and esoteric discussions distinguishing "hot news" from other published material are wholly without meaning.

The biography of Howard Hughes, published by defendants herein, irrespective of its literary merit or style . . . falls within those "reports of newsworthy people or events" which are constitutionally protected and which are outside the proscription of the New York "Right of Privacy" statute. The allegation that the book was published for "purposes of trade" and profit does not, as plaintiff seeks to imply, alter its protected status. The publication of a newspaper, magazine, or book which imparts truthful news or other factual information to the public does not fall within "the purposes of trade" contemplated by the New York statute, even though such publication is published and sold for a profit. . . .

The remaining ground on which plaintiff seeks to justify this suit is the assignment to it of Hughes' "right of publicity." This is a right that recognizes the pecuniary value which attaches to the names and pictures of public figures, particularly athletes and entertainers, and the right of such people to this financial benefit. It is not, however, every public use of a prominent person's name that he has a right to exploit financially. It is the unauthorized use in connection with the sale of a commodity for *advertising* purposes which is recognized as an actionable wrong under New York law. The same requirement of commercial use which limits the New York right of privacy inheres in the "right of publicity." . . . The publication of a biography is clearly outside the ambit of the "commercial use" contemplated by the "right of publicity" and such right can have no application to the publication of factual material which is constitutionally protected. Just as a public figure's "right of privacy" must yield to the public interest so too must the "right of publicity" bow where such conflicts with the free dissemination of thoughts, ideas, newsworthy events, and matters of public interest.

Because of such considerations, a public figure can have no exclusive rights to his own life story, and others need no consent or permission of the subject to write a biography of a celebrity. . . .

In addition to the foregoing it must be noted that plaintiff, in any event, has no standing to assert another's right of privacy under Article 5 of the New York Civil Rights Law which is specifically relied upon in its complaint. Plaintiff is alleging an invasion of Hughes' right of privacy, but such right is a purely personal one which may be enforced only by the party himself. . . . Thus, even if this biography infringed any of Hughes' rights, and such is not here the case, plaintiff would have no rights with respect thereto.

Accordingly, the motion is granted dismissing the complaint in its entirety.

Shields v. Gross, 461 N.Y.S.2d 254 (Ct. App. 1983)

SIMONS, J.

The issue on this appeal is whether an infant model may disaffirm a prior unrestricted consent executed on her behalf by her parent and maintain an action pursuant to section 51 of the Civil Rights Law against her photographer for republication of photographs of her. We hold that she may not.

Plaintiff is now a well-known actress. For many years prior to these events she had been a child model and in 1975, when she was 10 years of age, she obtained several modeling jobs with defendant through her agent, the Ford Model Agency. One of the jobs, a series of photographs to be financed by Playboy Press, required plaintiff to pose nude in a bathtub. It was intended that these photos would be used in a publication entitled *Portfolio 8* (later renamed *Sugar and Spice*). Before the photographic sessions, plaintiff's mother and legal guardian, Teri Shields, executed two consents in favor of defendant. After the pictures were taken, they were used not only in *Sugar and Spice* but also, to the knowledge of plaintiff and her mother, in other publications and in a display of larger-than-life photo enlargements in the windows of a store on Fifth Avenue in New York City. Indeed, plaintiff subsequently used the photos in a book that she published about herself and to do so her mother obtained an authorization from defendant to use them. Over the years defendant has also photographed plaintiff for *Penthouse Magazine*, *New York Magazine* and for advertising by the Courtauldts and Avon companies.

In 1980 plaintiff learned that several of the 1975 photographs had appeared in a French magazine called *Photo* and, disturbed by that publication and by information that defendant intended others, she attempted to buy the negatives. In 1981, she commenced this action in tort and contract seeking compensatory and punitive damages and an injunction permanently enjoining defendant from any further use of the photographs. Special Term granted plaintiff a preliminary injunction. Although it determined that as a general proposition consents given by a parent pursuant to section 51 barred the infant's action, it found that plaintiff's claim that the consents were invalid or restricted the use of the photographs by Playboy Press presented questions of fact. After a nonjury trial the court ruled that the consents were unrestricted as to time and use and it therefore dismissed plaintiff's complaint. In doing so, however, it granted plaintiff limited relief. On defendant's stipulation it permanently enjoined defendant from using the photographs in "pornographic magazines or publications whose appeal is of a predominantly prurient nature" and it charged him with the duty of policing their use. . . .

The parties have filed cross appeals. Defendant requests reinstatement of the trial court's judgment. Plaintiff requests, in the alternative, that the order of the Appellate Division be modified by striking the limitation enjoining use only for purposes of advertising and trade, or that the order of the Appellate Division should be affirmed or, failing both of these, that a new trial be granted. Since the Appellate Division accepted the trial court's findings that the consents were valid and unrestricted as to time and use, we are presented with only a narrow issue of law concerning the legal effect to be given to the parent's consents.

Historically, New York common law did not recognize a cause of action for invasion of privacy (*Arrington v. New York Times Co.*, 55 N.Y.2d 433, 449 N.Y.S.2d 941, 434 N.E.2d 1319; *Roberson v. Rochester Folding Box Co.*, 171 N.Y. 538, 64 N.E. 442). In 1909, however, responding to the *Roberson* decision, the Legislature enacted sections 50 and 51 of the Civil Rights Law. Section 50 is penal and makes it a misdemeanor to use a living person's name, portrait or picture for advertising purposes without prior "written consent." Section 51 is remedial and creates a related civil cause of action on behalf of the injured party permitting relief by injunction or damages. . . . Section 51 of the statute states that the prior "written consent" which will bar the civil action is to be as "above provided," referring to section 50, and section 50, in turn, provides that: "A person, firm or corporation that uses for advertising purposes, or for the purposes of trade, the name, portrait or picture of any living person *without having first obtained the written consent of such*

person, or if a minor of his or her parent or guardian, is guilty of a misdemeanor" (emphasis added).

Thus, whereas in *Roberson*, the infant plaintiff had no cause of action against the advertiser under the common law for using her pictures, the new statute gives a cause of action to those similarly situated unless they have executed a consent or release in writing to the advertiser before use of the photographs. The statute acts to restrict an advertiser's prior unrestrained common-law right to use another's photograph until written consent is obtained. Once written consent is obtained, however, the photograph may be published as permitted by its terms (see *Welch v. Mr. Christmas*, 57 N.Y.2d 143, 454 N.Y.S.2d 971, 440 N.E.2d 1317).

Concededly, at common law an infant could disaffirm his written consent. . . . Notwithstanding these rules, it is clear that the Legislature may abrogate an infant's common-law right to disaffirm . . . or, conversely, it may confer upon infants the right to make binding contracts. . . . Where a statute expressly permits a certain class of agreements to be made by infants, that settles the question and makes the agreement valid and enforceable. That is precisely what happened here. The Legislature, by adopting section 51, created a new cause of action and it provided in the statute itself the method for obtaining an infant's consent to avoid liability. Construing the statute strictly, as we must since it is in derogation of the common law . . . the parent's consent is binding on the infant and no words prohibiting disaffirmance are necessary to effectuate the legislative intent. Inasmuch as the consents in this case complied with the statutory requirements, they were valid and may not be disaffirmed. . . .

Nor do we believe that the consents may be considered void because the parties failed to comply with the provisions of section 3–105 of the General Obligations Law requiring prior court approval of infants' contracts. By its terms, section 3–105 applies only to performing artists, such as actors, musicians, dancers and professional athletes; moreover, it is apparent by comparing other statutes with it that the Legislature knowingly has differentiated between child performers and child models. . . . Furthermore, section 3–105 was not designed to expand the rights of infants to disaffirm their contracts, as the concurring Justice at the Appellate Division would apply it, but to provide assurance to those required to deal with infants that the infants would not later disaffirm executory contracts to the adult contracting party's disadvantage. . . . Sections 50 and 51 as we interpret them serve the same purpose, to bring certainty to an important industry which necessarily uses minors for its work. This same need for certainty was the impetus behind not only section 3–105 but the various other sections of the General Obligations Law which prohibit disaffirmance of an infant's contract.

Realistically, the procedures of prior court approval set forth in section 3–105, while entirely appropriate and necessary for performing artists and professional athletes, are impractical for a child model who, whether employed regularly or sporadically, works from session to session, sometimes for many different photographers. Moreover, they work for fees which are relatively modest when compared to those received by actors or professional athletes who may be employed by one employer at considerably greater remuneration for a statutorily permissible three-year term. Indeed, the fee in this case was $450, hardly sufficient to warrant the elaborate court proceedings required by section 3–105 or to necessitate a court's determination of what part should be set aside and preserved for the infant's future needs. Nor do we think court approval necessary under the circumstances existing in the normal child model's career. Given the nature of the employment, it is entirely reasonable for the Legislature to substitute the parents' judgment and approval of what is best for their child for that of a court.

It should be noted that plaintiff did not contend that the photographs were obscene or pornographic. Her only complaint was that she was embarrassed because "they [the photographs] are not me now." The trial court specifically found that the photographs were not pornographic and it enjoined use of them in pornographic publications. Thus, there is no need to discuss the unenforceability of certain contracts which violate public policy (see, e.g., Penal Law, § 235.00 *et seq.*) or to equate an infant's common-law right to disaffirm with that principle, as the dissent apparently does.

Finally, it is claimed that the application of the statute as we interpret it may result in unanticipated and untoward consequences. If that be so, there is an obvious remedy. A parent who wishes to limit the publicity and exposure of her child need only limit the use authorized in the consent, for a defendant's immunity from a claim for invasion of privacy is no broader than the consent executed to him. . . .

The order of the Appellate Division should be modified by striking the further injunction against use of the photographs for uses of advertising and trade, and as so modified, the order should be affirmed.

JASEN, J. (DISSENTING)

Since I believe that the interests of society and this State in protecting its children must be placed above any concern for trade or commercialism, I am compelled to dissent. The State has the right and indeed the obligation to afford extraordinary protection to minors.

At the outset, it should be made clear that this case does not involve the undoing of a written consent given by a mother to invade her infant daughter's privacy so as to affect *prior* benefits derived by a person relying on the validity of the consent pursuant to sections 50 and 51 of the Civil Rights Law. Rather, what is involved is the right of an infant, now 17 years of age, to disaffirm her mother's consent with respect to *future use* of a nude photograph taken of her at age 10.

The majority holds, as a matter of law, not only in this case but as to all present and future consents executed by parents on behalf of children pursuant to sections 50 and 51 of the Civil Rights Law, that once a parent consents to the invasion of privacy of a child, the child is forever bound by that consent and may never disaffirm the continued invasion of his or her privacy, even where the continued invasion of the child's privacy may cause the child enormous embarrassment, distress and humiliation.

I find this difficult to accept as a rational rule of law, particularly so when one considers that it has long been the rule in this State that a minor enjoys an almost absolute right to disaffirm a contract entered into either by the minor or by the minor's parent on behalf of the minor. . . .

Understandably, such a broad right has evolved as a result of the State's policy to provide children with as much protection as possible against being taken advantage of or exploited by adults. . . .

Can there be any question that the State has a compelling interest in protecting children? Indeed, the most priceless possessions we have in the Nation are our children. Recognizing this compelling interest in children, the State has assumed the role of *parens patriae*, undertaking with that role the responsibility of protecting children from their own inexperience. Acting in that capacity, the State has put the interests of minors above that of adults, organizations or businesses. . . . Thus, I am persuaded that, in this case, 17-year-old Brooke Shields should be afforded the right to disaffirm her mother's consent to use a photograph of her in the nude, taken when she was 10 years old, unless it can be said, as the majority holds, that the Legislature intended to abrogate that right when it enacted sections 50 and 51 of the Civil Rights Law. . . . Apparently, in order to alleviate litigation over whether or not consent had been given, the Legislature required that such consent be in writing and, if the person was a minor, that the parent sign the consent form. There is no indication that by requiring consent from the minor's parents, the Legislature intended in any way to abrogate that minor's right to disaffirm a contract at some future date. Indeed, the requirement of parental consent, like the broad right to disaffirm a contract, was granted in order to afford the minor as much protection against exploitation as possible. The assumption, of course, was that a parent would protect the child's interests. But if that assumption proves invalid, as may well be the case if a minor upon reaching the age of maturity realizes that the parent, too, has been exploiting him or her or had failed to adequately guard his or her interest by giving consent for pictures which caused humiliation, embarrassment and distress, then the child should be able to cure the problem by disaffirming the parent's consent. To say, as does the majority, that the

mother could have limited her consent avoids the issue. If the parent has failed to put any restrictions on the consent, as occurred in this case, and has thus failed to protect the child's future interests, I see no reason why the child must continue to bear the burden imposed by her mother's bad judgment. This means the child is forever bound by its parent's decisions, even if those decisions turn out to have been exploitative of the child and detrimental to the child's best interests.

Furthermore, nothing compels the majority's conclusion that the right to disaffirm a contract was eliminated when the Legislature created a new cause of action for invasion of privacy merely because that statute provided safeguards for the child's privacy by giving the parent the right to grant or withhold consent. When both rights are viewed, as I believe they must be, as protection for the child, logic and policy compels the conclusion that the two rights should exist coextensively. The requirement that a parent consent before the child's privacy can be invaded by commercial interests establishes the parent as the first guardian of the child's interest. But the State retains its long-standing role of *parens patriae* so that if the parent fails to protect the child's interests, the State will intervene and do so. One means of doing so is to allow the child to exercise its right to disaffirm if the child concludes that its parent improvidently consented to the invasion of the child's privacy interests. Given the strong policy concern of the State in the child's best interests, I can only conclude that the Legislature did not intend to abrogate the child's common-law right to disaffirm a contract when it required, by statute, the additional protection of written, parental consent prior to any commercial use of the child's image. . . .

Cohen v. Herbal Concepts, Inc., 482 N.Y.S.2d 457 (Ct. App. 1984)

SIMONS, J.

Plaintiffs bring this action pursuant to section 51 of the Civil Rights Law seeking damages from defendants for publishing photographs of them for advertising purposes. It is conceded for purposes of this appeal that plaintiffs are the persons shown in the photographs and that defendants used the photographs as claimed without their consent. The legal issue submitted is whether a photograph of the nude plaintiffs, mother and child, which shows their bodies full length as viewed from a position behind and to the right of them, and which does not show their faces, reveals sufficiently identifiable likenesses to withstand defendants' motions for summary judgment. We hold that it does.

The action arises from these facts.

On the July 4th weekend in 1977, plaintiffs were visiting friends in Woodstock, New York, and Susan Cohen and her four-year-old daughter, Samantha, went bathing in a stream located on their friends' private property. Without their consent, defendant James Krieger took photographs of plaintiffs and subsequently sold them to defendant Herbal Concepts, Inc., a seller and advertiser of consumer products. Herbal Concepts used one of the photographs in an advertisement for Au Naturel, a product designed to help women eliminate body cellulite, those "fatty lumps and bumps that won't go away." The advertisement appeared in two editions of *House and Garden*, which is published by defendant Conde Nast Publications, Inc., and in single editions of *House Beautiful* and *Cosmopolitan*, which are published by defendant Hearst Corporation. Ira Cohen subsequently recognized his wife and daughter in the advertisements while reading one of the magazines and this action followed.

Plaintiffs Susan and Samantha Cohen alleged causes of action seeking compensatory and exemplary damages based upon violations of section 51 of the Civil Rights Law. . . .

Special Term dismissed the privacy actions because it concluded "the identities of the plaintiffs cannot be determined from the picture." Although the Appellate Division Justices were unanimous for reversal, they differed in their reasons for doing so. Two Justices held that section 51 requires only an identifiable likeness capable of being recognized by others, not an identifiable facial representation. They thus concluded that the identification of plaintiffs was a question for the jury. Two other Justices concurred, stating that in their view it was sufficient that the picture was of the plaintiffs and that plaintiffs could identify it as such. Justice Asch

agreed with Special Term that plaintiffs' privacy causes of action lacked merit because neither person in the advertisement was capable of being identified. He concurred in the result, however, after finding that plaintiffs possessed a valid claim for unjust enrichment.

The history of New York's privacy statute has been recited before and need not be repeated here. . . .

The statute is designed to protect a person's identity, not merely a property interest in his or her "name," "portrait" or "picture," and thus it implicitly requires that plaintiff be capable of identification from the objectionable material itself. . . . That is not to say that the action may only be maintained when plaintiff's face is visible in the advertising copy. Presumably, by using the term "portrait" the Legislature intended a representation which includes a facial reproduction, either artistically or by photograph, but if we are to give effect to all parts of the statute, it applies also to the improper use of a "picture" of plaintiff which does not show the face. Manifestly, there can be no appropriation of plaintiff's identity for commercial purposes if he or she is not recognizable from the picture and a privacy action could not be sustained, for example, because of the nonconsensual use of a photograph of a hand or a foot without identifying features. But assuming that the photograph depicts plaintiff, whether it presents a recognizable likeness is generally a jury question unless plaintiff cannot be identified because of the limited subject matter revealed in the photograph or the quality of the image. Before a jury may be permitted to decide the issue, to survive a motion for summary judgment, plaintiff must satisfy the court that the person in the photograph is capable of being identified from the advertisement alone and that plaintiff has been so identified.

The sufficiency of plaintiff's evidence for purposes of the motion will necessarily depend upon the court's determination of the quality and quantity of the identifiable characteristics displayed in the advertisement and this will require an assessment of the clarity of the photograph, the extent to which identifying features are visible, and the distinctiveness of those features. This picture depicts two nude persons, a woman and a child, standing in water a few inches deep. The picture quality is good and there are no obstructions to block the view of the subjects. The woman is carrying a small unidentified object in her left hand and is leading the child with her right hand. Neither person's face is visible but the backs and right sides of both mother and child are clearly presented and the mother's right breast can be seen. The identifying features of the subjects include their hair, bone structure, body contours and stature and their posture. Considering these factors, we conclude that a jury could find that someone familiar with the persons in the photograph could identify them by looking at the advertisement. Although we do not rely on the fact, it is also reasonable to assume that just as something in the advertising copy may aid recognition . . . identifiability may be enhanced also in a photograph depicting two persons because observers may associate the two and thus more easily identify them when they are seen together.

The plaintiffs also submitted evidence that they were identified as the persons in defendants' advertisement by Ira Cohen's affidavit in which he stated that while leafing through one of defendants' magazines he "recognized [his] wife and daughter immediately." That was prima facie sufficient (see Richardson, Evidence [10th ed.], § 364, subd. [a]).

Defendants contend Mr. Cohen's affidavit is not probative on the issue of identification because he was present when the photograph was taken, as indeed he was. He was not only present, he was incensed by the photographer's intrusion and chased him away. Essentially, defendants' contention is that Mr. Cohen's identification is tainted by this independent knowledge that plaintiffs were photographed by defendant Krieger while bathing. Although Mr. Cohen's presence when the photograph was taken may have increased his ability to identify his wife and child, the motion court or the jury at trial could conclude that he also recognized them from the photograph and his presence when it was taken, standing alone, does not disqualify him from offering evidence that he did so. The cases cited by defendants on the point are neither controlling nor persuasive. In *Branson v. Fawcett Pub.*, 124

F. Supp. 429, and *Brauer v. Globe Newspaper Co.*, 351 Mass. 53, 217 N.E.2d 736, the courts found the witnesses in question were incapable of identifying the plaintiffs absent independent knowledge of the photographing because neither photograph contained sufficient identifying characteristics of plaintiffs. In *Branson* the plaintiff was not visible at all, and in *Brauer* the photograph depicted only one ear and the partial outline of the back of a boy's head.

Finally, defendants rely on three cases involving books, plays, and motion pictures in support of their motion for summary judgment. They, too, are readily distinguishable. In both *Wojtowicz v. Delacorte Press* . . . 374 N.E.2d 129, and *Toscani v. Hersey*, 271 App. Div. 445, 65 N.Y.S.2d 814, defendants had not violated the statute because neither plaintiffs' names nor their pictures were published. In *Allen v. Gordon*, 86 A.D.2d 514, 446 N.Y.S.2d 48, affd. 56 N.Y.2d 780, 452 N.Y.S.2d 25, 437 N.E.2d 284, *supra*, the only similarities between the plaintiff and the fictional character in the book were that both had the name "Dr. Allen" and both practiced psychiatry in Manhattan. The record demonstrated that these similarities were mere coincidence and that defendant's fictional portrayal of "Dr. Allen" did not identify plaintiff and thus violate his right of privacy. In this case, the similarity of the details between plaintiffs and the persons appearing in the photograph is complete because concededly plaintiffs were the persons in the picture, not fictional characters. The only question was whether the details were sufficiently identifiable so that plaintiffs could be recognized. . . .

10.20   Right of Publicity

The right of publicity embodies the concept that a person's name, likeness, and other personal characteristics are a type of property. Publicity rights are invoked to prevent the commercial exploitation of that valuable property by others. What constitutes one's name and likeness may be straightforward, but "other personal characteristics" raises amorphous possibilities not immediately fathomable.

Jurisdictions approach rights of publicity in a multitude of ways; the first task is to identify to what extent, if at all, a right of publicity is recognized separate and apart from a right of privacy. These inquiries are pursued in Section 10.21. One differentiation between publicity and privacy is that publicity, as a property right, is freely assignable and descendible. Not all jurisdictions recognize the descendibility of publicity rights, and those that do may limit the length of time the rights continue after death of the celebrity. These problems are examined extensively in Sections 10.21–2, 10.21–3, and 10.22.

The most perplexing problems concern the reach of publicity rights. Do they extend to protecting slogans about a person, and to guarding against degrading cartoon depictions, false stories designed to titillate the public, and even pictures of the equipment a celebrity uses in his or her work? These are the meat of Section 10.23.

10.21   Recognition of the Right

Since New York and California laws are important to the entertainment business and to the celebrities living or working in those states, Sections 10.21–1 and 10.21–2 examine each state's approach to a right of publicity. As will be seen, the approaches are substantially divergent.

The concerns about publicity rights are, of course, not limited to New York and California. Significant litigation has occurred in other states as well. Often courts had no binding precedent to guide them. The resulting "judge-made" law in the various states understandably drew substantial criticism. In several states, legislatures intervened. Examples of legislative actions over the past few years are introduced for comparative purposes in Section 10.21–3.

10.21–1   New York Approach to Publicity

In *Haelan Laboratories v. Topps Chewing Gum*, 202 F.2d 866 (2d Cir. 1953), a U.S. Court of Appeals under the *Erie* doctrine declared New York to have a common law right of publicity separate and distinct from the privacy protections of the New York Civil Rights Law. In later cases, lower New York courts adhered to the *Haelan* precedent (see, for example, *Hicks v. Casablanca Records*, discussed in Section 10.30).

This changed abruptly in 1984 with the following case, *Stephano v. News Group Publications*. The highest court in New York addressed the issue of whether there was in New York a right of publicity separate and distinct from the statutory right of privacy.

Stephano v. New Group Publications, Inc., 485 N.Y.S.2d 220 (Ct. App. 1984)

WACHTLER, J.

. . . In the summer of 1981 the plaintiff agreed to model for an article on men's fall fashions. The photographic session took place on August 11, 1981. The defendant used two of the photographs taken during that session to illustrate an article entitled "Classic Mixes," which appeared under the heading "Fall Fashions" in the September 7, 1981 issue of *New York* magazine. Another photograph taken during the session was used, a week earlier, in the August 31, 1981 issue of *New York* magazine, in a column entitled "Best Bets." That column, a regular feature in the magazine, contains information about new and unusual products and services available in the metropolitan area. One of the items included in the August 31 column was a bomber jacket modeled by the plaintiff. The text above the picture states: "Yes Giorgio—From Giorgio Armani. Based on his now classic turn on the bomber jacket, this cotton-twill version with 'fun fur' collar features the same cut at a far lower price—about $225. It'll be available in the stores next week—Henry Post Bomber Jacket/Barney's, Bergdorf Goodman, Bloomingdales'."

It is the plaintiff's contention that he agreed to model for one article only—the September 7, 1981 article on Fall Fashions—and that the defendant violated his rights by publishing his photograph in the August 31 "Best Bets" column. The complaint alleges two causes of action. First the plaintiff claims that the defendant violated his civil rights by using his photograph for trade or advertising purposes without his consent. In his second cause of action the plaintiff claims that the defendant's conduct "invaded plaintiff's right of publicity." On each cause of action the plaintiff seeks $350,000 in compensatory damages and an equal amount in exemplary damages.

The defendant's answer asserts several affirmative defenses. The primary defense is that the photograph and article relating to it involve matters of legitimate public interest and concern and thus do not violate the plaintiff's rights under the Civil Rights Law (§§ 50, 51), or any common-law right of publicity. The defendant also urged that the second cause of action, for invasion of the plaintiff's right of publicity, does not set forth a claim "separate and distinct" from the first cause of action.

On May 4, 1982 the plaintiff filed a note of issue and statement of readiness indicating that he waived his right to discovery proceedings, that there are no outstanding requests for discovery, and that the case was ready for trial. At the defendant's request, however, the parties stipulated that the note of issue would be withdrawn to afford the defendant an opportunity to move for summary judgment. In the motion for summary judgment the defendant urged that the complaint should be dismissed because the plaintiff's photograph was not published for trade or advertising purposes.

In support of the motion the defendant submitted affidavits by two of the editors involved in the publication of the "Best Bets" column of August 31, 1981. The affidavits state that the column is a regular news feature of the editorial portion of the magazine, designed to provide readers with information, sometimes including prices, concerning interesting products and services in the New York metropolitan area. They state that such information is provided solely for newsworthy purposes—"advertising concerns" play no part in deciding what to include in "Best Bets" and the magazine receives no payment for any item mentioned in the column. They further state that the item concerning the bomber jacket was included in the August 31 "Best Bets" column because the fashion editor suggested that it would be of interest to readers of *New York* magazine.

The plaintiff's affidavit in opposition to the motion stated: "While it may be that a party whose service or product is included in 'Best Bets' does not pay a direct advertising fee to be included, the benefits to the magazine are obtained in an indirect manner. Stores, designers, and retailers featured there have all advertised in *New York* magazine at other times and places, and giving them this 'breakout' feature in the 'Best Bets' column acts as barter for such advertising at another time and place." The plaintiff further stated that the designer and the stores mentioned in the August 31 column had previously advertised in *New York* magazine and observed that "the publicity benefits in the column to the designer and retail outlets mentioned are evident from a fair reading of the column."

The trial court granted summary judgment to the defendant concluding, on the basis of the exhibits submitted, that the bomber jacket item was a "newsworthy observation" and was not published for advertising or trade purposes within the contemplation of the statute. The court also held that the inclusion of information concerning the availability of the jacket at certain stores, which currently advertised in the magazine, was not sufficient to sustain the claim that the item had been published for trade or advertising purposes "without a further showing of benefit to defendant."

The Appellate Division reversed and denied the defendant's motion for summary judgment. The majority observed that the September 7 article was published for trade purposes because it was included to increase circulation. Finding that the "form and presentation" of both articles were identical the majority held that a reasonable person could conclude that the August 31 article was also used for trade purposes. . . . One Justice dissented for essentially the same reasons as those stated by the trial court. We now reverse.

Section 50 of the Civil Rights Law prohibits the use of "the name, portrait or picture of any living person" for advertising or trade purposes without the person's consent and declares a violation of the statute to be a misdemeanor. Section 51 of the statute provides civil remedies, including injunctive relief, compensatory damages and, if the defendant acted knowingly, exemplary damages. . . .

Section 51 of the Civil Rights Law has been applied in cases . . . where the picture of a person who has apparently never sought publicity has been used without his or her consent for trade or advertising purposes. . . . In such cases it has been noted that the statute serves "to protect the sentiments, thoughts and feelings of an individual." . . .

This history has led some courts to conclude that the statutory right to privacy is limited to the type of case which originally prompted its enactment and thus would not preclude the recognition in this State of a common-law "right of publicity" in cases where the defendant has exploited, without consent, and usually without payment, the name, picture, or portrait of an individual who has consciously sought to establish a publicity value for his personality (see, e.g., *Haelan Labs. v. Topps Chewing Gum*, 202 F.2d 866, 868 (2d Cir. 1953), cert. den. 346 U.S. 816, 74 S.Ct. 26, 98 L.Ed. 343; *Factors Etc. v. Pro Arts*, 579 F.2d 215 (2d Cir. 1978), cert. den. 440 U.S. 908, 99 S.Ct. 1215, 59 L.Ed.2d 455; but also see *Brinkley v. Casablancas*, 80 A.D.2d 428, 438 N.Y.S.2d 1004). The statute, however, is not limited to situations where the defendant's conduct has caused distress to a person who wishes to lead a private life free of all commercial publicity.

By its terms the statute applies to any use of a person's picture or portrait for advertising or trade purposes whenever the defendant has not obtained the person's written consent to do so. It would therefore apply, and recently has been held to apply, in cases where the plaintiff generally seeks publicity, or uses his name, portrait, or picture, for commercial purposes but has not given written consent for a particular use. . . .

Thus where the written consent to use the plaintiff's name or picture for advertising or trade purposes has expired . . . or the defendant has otherwise exceeded the limitations of the consent the plaintiff may seek damages or other relief under the statute, even though he might properly sue for breach of contract. The right which the statute permits the plaintiff to vindicate in such a case may, perhaps, more accurately be described as a right of publicity. . . . In this respect the statute parallels the common-law right of privacy which generally provides remedies for any commercialization of the individual's personality without his consent. . . . Since the "right of publicity" is encompassed under the Civil Rights Law as an aspect of the right of privacy, which, as noted, is exclusively statutory in this State, the plaintiff cannot claim an independent common-law right of publicity.

The only question then is whether the defendant used the plaintiff's picture for trade or advertising purposes within the meaning of the statute when it published his picture in the "Best Bets" column without his consent.

The statute does not define trade or advertising purposes. However, the courts have consistently held, from the time of its enactment, that these terms should not be construed to apply to publications concerning newsworthy events or matters of public interest. . . . The exception reflects Federal and State constitutional concerns for free dissemination of news and other matters of interest to the public. . . .

The newsworthiness exception applies not only to reports of political happenings and social trends . . . but also to news stories and articles of consumer interest including developments in the fashion world. . . . Nevertheless, the plaintiff contends that the photograph in this case did not depict a newsworthy event because it is a posed picture of a professional model taken at a photographic session staged by the defendant. However, the event or matter of public interest which the defendant seeks to convey is not the model's performance, but the availability of the clothing item displayed. A fashion display is, of necessity, posed and arranged. Obviously the picture of the jacket does not lose its newsworthiness simply because the defendant chose to employ a person to model it in a controlled or contrived setting. . . .

The fact that the defendant may have included this item in its column solely or primarily to increase the circulation of its magazine and therefore its profits, as the Appellate Division suggested, does not mean that the defendant has used the plaintiff's picture for trade purposes within the meaning of the statute. Indeed, most publications seek to increase their circulation and also their profits. It is the content of the article and not the defendant's motive or primary motive to increase circulation which determines whether it is a newsworthy item, as opposed to a trade usage, under the Civil Rights Law. . . . It is settled that a " 'picture illustrating an article on a matter of public interest is not considered used for the purposes of trade or advertising within the prohibition of the statute . . . unless it has no real relationship to the article . . . or unless the article is an advertisement in disguise.' " . . . A contrary rule would unreasonably and unrealistically limit the exception to nonprofit or purely altruistic organizations which are not the only, or even the primary, source of information concerning newsworthy events and matters of public interest.

The plaintiff's primary contention is that his picture was used for advertising purposes within the meaning of the statute. Although the article was not presented to the public as an advertisement, and was published in a column generally devoted to newsworthy items . . . the plaintiff claims that it is in fact an advertisement in disguise. In addition, although the defendant has submitted affidavits that the article was published solely as a matter of public interest, without any consideration for advertising concerns, and that the magazine received no payment for including the item in its "Best Bets" column, the plaintiff nevertheless contends that he has presented sufficient facts to require a trial on the issue.

The facts on which the plaintiff relies are entirely circumstantial. He does not claim to have personal knowledge, or direct proof, that this particular article was actually published by the defendant for advertisement purposes. The circumstances on which he bases his claim are (1) the fact that the news column contains information normally included in an advertisement identifying the designer of the jacket, the approximate price, and three places where the jacket may be purchased, and (2) the fact that some or all of those stores mentioned in the article had previously advertised products in the magazine. Those circumstances are not enough to raise a jury question as to whether the article was published for advertising purposes.

The plaintiff does not dispute the fact that the information provided in the article is of legitimate reader interest. Indeed, similar information is frequently provided in reviews or news announcements of books, movies, shows or other new products including fashions. . . . Nor does the plaintiff contend that it is uncommon for commercial publishers to print legitimate news items or reviews concerning products by persons or firms who have previously advertised in the publisher's newspaper or magazine. In short, the plaintiff has not presented any facts which would set this particular article apart from the numerous other legitimate news items concerning new products. He offers only his speculative belief that in this case the information on the jacket was included in the defendant's column for advertising purposes or perhaps, more vaguely, to promote additional advertising. That, in our view, is insufficient to defeat the defendant's motion for summary judgment. . . .

Finally, it should be emphasized that we do not mean to suggest that a publisher who has employed a professional model to pose for pictures to be used in an article may avoid the agreed fee, or otherwise ignore contractual arrangements, if the model's pictures are used to illustrate a newsworthy article or one involving matters of public interest. Although the complaint alludes to an agreement between the parties, the plaintiff has not sought to enforce a contract or recover damages for a breach. Since the plaintiff chose to frame his complaint entirely in terms of rights covered by the Civil Rights Law, which we have concluded is not applicable in this case, the complaint should be dismissed. . . .

10.21–2   California Approach to Publicity

California courts flirted with notions of the right to publicity in such well-known cases as

Lugosi v. Universal Pictures, 603 P.2d 425 (Cal. 1979), and *Gugliemi v. Spelling-Goldberg,* 603 P.2d 860 (Cal. 1979). The decisions created confusion as to whether in fact California law recognized a right of publicity separate from a right of privacy. The issue was resolved through legislative intervention by the following enactments. (Section 990 was added to the California Civil Code and § 3344, as it appears below, indicates amendments to the Civil Code.)

§ 990. *Deceased personality's name, voice, signature, photograph or likeness; unauthorized use; damages and profits from use; persons entitled to exercise rights; successors in interest or licensees; registration of claim; uses not requiring consent*

(a) Any person who uses a deceased personality's name, voice, signature, photograph, or likeness, in any manner, on or in products, merchandise, or goods, or for purposes of advertising or selling, or soliciting purchases of, products, merchandise, goods, or services, without prior consent from the person or persons specified in subdivision (c), shall be liable for any damages sustained by the person or persons injured as a result thereof. In addition, in any action brought under this section, the person who violated the section shall be liable to the injured party or parties in an amount equal to the greater of seven hundred fifty dollars ($750) or the actual damages suffered by the injured party or parties, as a result of the unauthorized use, and any profits from the unauthorized use that are attributable to the use and are not taken into account in computing the actual damages. In establishing these profits, the injured party or parties shall be required to present proof only of the gross revenue attributable to the use and the person who violated the section is required to prove his or her deductible expenses. Punitive damages may also be awarded to the injured party or parties. The prevailing party or parties in any action under this section shall also be entitled to attorneys' fees and costs.

(b) The rights recognized under this section are property rights, freely transferable, in whole or in part, by contract, or by means of trust or testamentary documents, whether the transfer occurs before the death of the deceased personality, by the deceased personality or his or her transferees, or, after the death of the deceased personality, by the person or persons in whom such rights vest under this section or the transferees of that person or persons.

(c) The consent required by this section shall be exercisable by the person or persons to whom such right of consent (or portion thereof) has been transferred in accordance with subdivision(b), or if no such transfer has occurred, then by the person or persons to whom such right of consent (or portion thereof) has passed in accordance with subdivision (d).

(d) Subject to subdivisions (b) and (c), after the death of any person, the rights under this section shall belong to the following person or persons and may be exercised, on behalf of and for the benefit of all of those persons, by those persons who, in the aggregate, are entitled to more than a one-half interest in such rights:

(1) The entire interest in those rights belong to the surviving spouse of the deceased personality unless there are any surviving children or grandchildren of the deceased personality, in which case one-half of the entire interest in those rights belong to the surviving spouse.

(2) The entire interest in those rights belong to the surviving children of the deceased personality and to the surviving children of any dead child of the deceased personality unless the deceased personality has a surviving spouse, in which case the ownership of a one-half interest in rights is divided among the surviving children and grandchildren.

(3) If there is no surviving spouse, and no surviving children or grandchildren, then the entire interest in those rights belong to the surviving parent or parents of the deceased personality.

(4) The rights of the deceased personality's children and grandchildren are in all cases

divided among them and exercisable on a per stirpes basis according to the number of the deceased personality's children represented; the share of the children of a dead child of a deceased personality can be exercised only by the action of a majority of them. For the purposes of this section, "per stirpes" is defined as it is defined in Section 240 of the Probate Code.

(e) If any deceased personality does not transfer his or her rights under this section by contract, or by means of a trust or testamentary document, and there are no surviving persons as described in subdivision (d), then the rights set forth in subdivision (a) shall terminate.

(f)(1) A successor-in-interest to the rights of a deceased personality under this section or a licensee thereof may not recover damages for a use prohibited by this section that occurs before the successor-in-interest or licensee registers a claim of the rights under paragraph (2).

(2) Any person claiming to be a successor-in-interest to the rights of a deceased personality under this section or a licensee thereof may register that claim with the Secretary of State on a form prescribed by the Secretary of State and upon payment of a fee of ten dollars ($10). The form shall be verified and shall include the name and date of death of the deceased personality, the name and address of the claimant, the basis of the claim, and the rights claimed.

(3) Upon receipt and after filing of any document under this section, the Secretary of State may microfilm or reproduce by other techniques any of the filings or documents and destroy the original filing or document. The microfilm or other reproduction of any document under the provision of this section shall be admissible in any court of law. The microfilm or other reproduction of any document may be destroyed by the Secretary of State 50 years after the death of the personality named therein.

(4) Claims registered under this subdivision shall be public records.

(g) No action shall be brought under this section by reason of any use of a deceased personality's name, voice, signature, photograph, or likeness occurring after the expiration of 50 years from the death of the deceased personality.

(h) As used in this section, "deceased personality" means any natural person whose name, voice, signature, photograph, or likeness has commercial value at the time of his or her death, whether or not during the lifetime of that natural person the person used his or her name, voice, signature, photograph, or likeness on or in products, merchandise or goods, or for purposes of advertising or selling, or solicitation of purchase of, products, merchandise, goods or service. A "deceased personality" shall include, without limitation, any such natural person who has died within 50 years prior to January 1, 1985.

(i) As used in this section, "photograph" means any photograph or photographic reproduction, still or moving, or any videotape or live television transmission, of any person, such that the deceased personality is readily identifiable. A deceased personality shall be deemed to be readily identifiable from a photograph when one who views the photograph with the naked eye can reasonably determine who the person depicted in the photograph is.

(j) For purposes of this section, a use of a name, voice, signature, photograph, or likeness in connection with any news, public affairs, or sports broadcast or account, or any political campaign, shall not constitute a use for which consent is required under subdivision (a).

(k) The use of a name, voice, signature, photograph, or likeness in a commercial medium shall not constitute a use for which consent is required under subdivision (a) solely because the material containing such use is commercially sponsored or contains paid advertising. Rather it shall be a question of fact whether or not the use of the deceased personality's name, voice, signature, photograph, or likeness was so directly connected with the commercial sponsorship or with the paid advertising as to constitute a use for which consent is required under subdivision (a).

(l) Nothing in this section shall apply to the

owners or employees of any medium used for advertising, including, but not limited to, newspapers, magazines, radio and television networks and stations, cable television systems, billboards, and transit ads, by whom any advertisement or solicitation in violation of this section is published or disseminated, unless it is established that such owners or employees had knowledge of the unauthorized use of the deceased personality's name, voice, signature, photograph, or likeness as prohibited by this section.

(m) The remedies provided for in this section are cumulative and shall be in addition to any others provided for by law.

(n) This section shall not apply to the use of a deceased personality's name, voice, signature, photograph, or likeness, in any of the following instances:

(1) A play, book, magazine, newspaper, musical composition, film, radio or television program, other than an advertisement or commercial announcement not exempt under paragraph (4).

(2) Material that is of political or newsworthy value.

(3) Single and original works of fine art.

(4) An advertisement or commercial announcement for a use permitted by paragraph (1), (2), or (3).

§ 3344. [Use of Name or Photograph Without Consent for Advertising]
(Italics indicates recent amendments.)

(a) Any person who knowingly uses another: name, voice, signature, photograph, or likeness, in any manner, on or in products, merchandise, or goods, or for purposes of advertising or selling *or soliciting purchases of* products, merchandise, goods or services, without such person's prior consent, or, in the case of a minor, the prior consent of his parent or legal guardian, shall be liable for any damages sustained by the person or persons injured as a result thereof. In addition, in any action brought under this section, the person who violated the section shall be liable to the injured party or parties in an amount equal to the greater of seven hundred fifty dollars

($750) *or the actual damages suffered by him or her as a result of the unauthorized use, and any profits from the unauthorized use that are attributable to the use and are not taken into account in computing the actual damages.* In establishing such profits, the injured party or parties are required to present proof only of the gross revenue attributable to such use, and the person who violated this section is required to prove his or her deductible expenses. Punitive damages may also be awarded to the injured party or parties. *The prevailing party in any action under this section shall also be entitled to attorney's fees and costs.*

(b) As used in this section, "photograph" means any photograph or photographic reproduction, still or moving, or any videotape or live television transmission, of any person, such that the person is readily identifiable.

(1) A person shall be deemed to be readily identifiable from a photograph when one who views the photograph with the naked eye can reasonably determine that the person depicted in the photograph is the same person who is complaining of its unauthorized use.

(2) If the photograph includes more than one person so identifiable, then the person or persons complaining of the use shall be represented as individuals rather than solely as members of a definable group represented in the photograph. A definable group includes, but is not limited to, the following examples: a crowd at any sporting event, a crowd in any street or public building, the audience at any theatrical or stage production, a glee club, or a baseball team.

(3) A person or persons shall be considered to be represented as members of a definable group if they are represented in the photograph solely as a result of being present at the time the photograph was taken and have not been singled out as individuals in any manner.

(c) Where a photograph or likeness of an employee of the person using the photograph or likeness appearing in the advertisement or other publication prepared by or in behalf of the user is only incidental, and not essential, to the purpose of the publication in which it appears, there shall arise a rebuttable presumption affecting the burden of producing evidence that the failure to obtain the consent of the employee was not a knowing use of the employee's photograph or likeness.

(d) For purposes of this section, a use of a name, voice, signature, photograph, or likeness in connection with any news, public affairs, or sports broadcast, or likeness in connection with any news, public affairs, or sports broadcast or account, or any political campaign, shall not constitute a use for which consent is required under subdivision (a).

(e) The use of a name, voice, signature, photograph, or likeness in a commercial medium shall not constitute a use for which consent is required under subdivision (a) solely because the material containing such use is commercially sponsored or contains paid advertising. Rather it shall be a question of fact whether or not the use of the person's name, voice, signature, photograph, or likeness was so directly connected with the commercial sponsorship or with the paid advertising as to constitute a use for which consent is required under subdivision (a).

(f) Nothing in this section shall apply to the owners or employees of any medium used for advertising, including, but not limited to, newspapers, magazines, radio and television networks and stations, cable television systems, billboards, and transit ads, by whom any advertisement or solicitation in violation of this section is published or disseminated, unless it is established that such owners or employees had knowledge of the unauthorized use of the person's name, voice, signature, photograph, or likeness as prohibited by this section.

(g) The remedies provided for in this section are cumulative and shall be in addition to any others provided for by law.

NOTE ————————————————

1. For a discussion of the recently enacted Section 990, see Rhode, "Dracula: Still Undead," 5 *California Lawyer* 51 (April 1985).

10.21–3 Recent Statutory Enactments on Right of Publicity

Several states beyond New York and California were faced with lawsuits alleging rights of publicity. Uncertain and confusing decisions were too often the result. As in California, several state legislatures enacted statutes designed to resolve the issues.

In the three examples which follow (Tennessee, Kentucky, and Florida), the only conclusion to be reached is that there is no uniform approach to publicity rights. Of particular note are each state's provisions concerning who can own the right of publicity and how long the right continues after the death of the person who originates the publicity rights.

Tennessee, Senate Bill No. 1566 (Effective June 5, 1984)

SECTION 1. This act shall be known and may be cited as "The Personal Rights Protection Act of 1984."

SECTION 2. As used in this act, unless the context otherwise requires:

(1) "Definable group" means an assemblage of individuals existing or brought together with or without interrelation, orderly form or arrangement, including but not limited to, a crowd at any sporting event, a crowd in any street or public building, the audience at any theatrical or stage production, a glee club, or a baseball team.

(2) "Individual" means human being, living or dead.

(3) "Likeness" means the use of an image of an individual for commercial purposes.

(4) "Person" means any firm, association, partnership, corporation, joint stock company, syndicate, receiver, common law trust, conservator, statutory trust or any other concern by whatever name known or however organized, formed or created, and includes not-for-profit corporations, associations, educational and religious institutions, political parties, community, civic or other organizations.

(5) "Photograph" means any photograph or photographic reproduction, still or moving, or any videotape or live television transmission, of any individual, so that the individual is readily identifiable.

SECTION 3. (a) Every individual has a property right in the use of his name, photograph or likeness in any medium in any manner.

(b) The individual rights provided for in subsection (a) shall constitute property rights and shall be freely assignable and licensable, and shall not expire upon the death of the individual so protected, whether or not such rights were commerciallly exploited by the individual during the individual's lifetime, but shall be descendible to the executors, assigns, heirs, or devisees of the individual so protected by this act.

SECTION 4. (a) The rights provided for in this act shall be deemed exclusive to the individual, subject to the assignment or licensing of such trademarks as provided in Section 3, during such individual's lifetime and to the executors, heirs, assigns or devisees for a period of ten (10) years after the death of the individual.

(b) Commercial exploitation of the property right by an executor, assignee, heir, or devisee if the individual is deceased shall maintain the right as his exclusive property until such right is terminated as provided in this subsection.

The exclusive right to commercial exploitation of the property rights is terminated by proof of the non-use of the name, likeness, or image of any individual for commercial purposes by an executor, assignee, heir or devisee to such use for a period of two (2) years subsequent to the initial ten (10) year period following the individual's death.

SECTION 5. (a) Any person who knowingly uses or infringes upon the use of another individual's name, photograph, or likeness in any medium, in any manner directed to any person other than such individual, as an item of commerce for purposes of advertising products, merchandise, goods or services, or for purposes of fund raising, solicitation of donations, purchases of products, merchandise, goods or services, without such individual's prior consent, or, in the case of a minor, the prior consent of his parent or legal guardian, or in the case of a deceased individual, the consent of the executor or administrator, heirs or devisees of such deceased individual, shall be liable to a civil action.

(b) It shall be no defense to the unauthorized use defined in subsection (a) that the photograph includes more than one (1) individual so identifiable; provided that the individual or individuals complaining of the use shall be represented as individuals per se rather than solely as members of a definable group represented in the photograph.

SECTION 6. (a) The chancery and circuit court having jurisdiction for any action arising pursuant to this act may grant injunctions on such terms as it may deem reasonable to prevent or restrain the unauthorized use of an individual's name, photograph or likeness.

(b) At any time while an action under this act is pending, the court may order the impounding, on such terms as it may deem reasonable, of all materials or any part thereof claimed to have been made or used in violation of the individual's rights, and such court may enjoin the use of all plates, molds, matrices, masters, tapes, film negatives, or other articles by means of which such materials may be reproduced.

(c) As part of a final judgment or decree, the court may order the destruction or other reasonable disposition of all materials found to have been made or used in violation of the individual's rights, and of all plates, molds, matrices, masters, tapes, film negatives, or other articles by means of which such materials may be reproduced.

(d) An individual is entitled to recover the actual damages suffered as a result of the knowing use or infringement of such individual's rights and any profits that are attributable to such use or infringement which are not taken into account in computing the actual damages. Profit or lack thereof by the unauthorized use or infringement of an individual's rights shall not be a criteria of determining liability.

(e) The remedies provided for in this section are cumulative and shall be in addition to any others provided for by law.

SECTION 7. (a) It shall be deemed a fair use and no violation of an individual's rights shall be found, for purposes of this act, if the use of a name, photograph or likeness is in connection with any news, public affairs, or sports broadcast or account.

(b) The use of a name, photograph or likeness in a commercial medium shall not constitute a use for purposes of advertising or solicitation solely because the material containing such use is commercially sponsored or contains paid advertising. Rather it shall be a question of fact whether or not the use of the complainant individual's name, photograph or likeness was so directly connected with the commercial sponsorship or with the paid advertising as to constitute a use for purposes of advertising or solicitation.

(c) Nothing in this section shall apply to the owners or employees of any medium used for advertising, including, but not limited to, newspapers, magazines, radio and television stations, billboards, and transit ads, who have published or disseminated any advertisement or solicitation in violation of this act unless it is established that such owners or employees had knowledge of the unauthorized use of the individual's name, photograph, or likeness as prohibited by this section.

SECTION 8. This act shall apply to any individual otherwise entitled to the protection afforded under Tennessee Code Annotated, Sections 47-25-422 through 47-25-435.

SECTION 9. If any provision of this act or the application thereof to any person or circumstance is held invalid, such invalidity shall not affect other provisions or applications of the act which can be given effect without the invalid provision or application, and to that end the provisions of this act are declared to be severable.

SECTION 10. This act shall take effect on becoming a law, the public welfare requiring it.

Kentucky, House Bill No. 926
(CHAPTER 263)

AN ACT relating to commercial rights to use the names and likenesses of public figures.

Be it enacted by the General Assembly of the Commonwealth of Kentucky:

SECTION 1. A NEW SECTION OF KRS CHAPTER 391 IS CREATED TO READ AS FOLLOWS:

(1) The general assembly recognizes that a person has property rights in his name and likeness which are entitled to protection from commercial exploitation. The general assembly further recognizes that although the traditional right of privacy terminates upon death of the person asserting it, the right of publicity, which is a right of protection from appropriation of some element of an individual's personality for commercial exploitation, does not terminate upon death.

(2) The name or likeness of a person who is a public figure shall not be used for commercial profit for a period of fifty (50) years from the date of his death without the written consent of the executor or administrator of his estate.

Approved April 6, 1984

Florida, Senate Bill No. 494
(CHAPTER 67-57)

AN ACT relating to unauthorized publication for commercial purposes; amending chapter 540 by adding sections 540.08, 540.09, and 540.10, Florida Statutes; prohibiting the unauthorized publication of natural person's name, picture or other likeness; authorizing action to enjoin such unauthorized publication; authorizing action to recover damages; providing limited exemptions from such liability; prohibiting any actions for violations relating to publication of personal likeness after the expiration of forty (40) years; imposing liability for unauthorized publication of pictures or photographs of areas for admittance to which a fee is charged; providing limited exemptions from liability; exempting news media making unauthorized publications from relief except injunctions against future publication; preserving remedies at common law; providing effective date.

Be It Enacted by the Legislature of the State of Florida:

Section 1. Sections 540.08, 540.09, and 540.10 are added to chapter 540, Florida Statutes, to read:

540.08 *Unauthorized publication of name or likeness.—*

(1) No person shall publish, print, display or otherwise publicly use for purposes of trade or for any commercial or advertising purpose the name, portrait, photograph or other likeness of any natural person without the express written or oral consent to such use given by:

(a) Such person; or

(b) Any other person, firm or corporation authorized in writing by such person to license the commercial use of his name or likeness; or

(c) If such person is deceased, any person, firm or corporation authorized in writing to license the commercial use of his name or likeness, or if no person, firm or corporation is so authorized, then by any one from among a class composed of his surviving spouse and surviving children.

(2) In the event the consent required in subsection (1) is not obtained, the person whose name, portrait, photograph, or other likeness is so used, or any person, firm or corporation authorized by such person in writing to license the commercial use of his name or likeness, or, if the person whose likeness is used is deceased, any person, firm or corporation having the right to give such consents, as provided hereinabove, may bring an action to enjoin such unauthorized publication, printing, display or other public use, and to recover damages for any loss or injury sustained by reason thereof, including an amount which would have been a reasonable royalty, and punitive or exemplary damages.

(3) The provisions of this section shall not apply to:

(a) The publication, printing, display or use of the name or likeness of any person in any newspaper, magazine, book, news broadcast or telecast or other news medium or publication as part of any bona fide news report or presentation having a current and legitimate public interest and where such name or likeness is not used for advertising purposes;

(b) The use of such name, portrait, photograph or other likeness in connection with the resale or other distribution of literary, musical or artistic productions or other articles of merchandise or property where such person has consented to the use of his name, portrait, photograph or likeness on or in connection with the initial sale or distribution thereof; or

(c) Any photograph of a person solely as a member of the public and where such person is not named or otherwise identified in or in connection with the use of such photograph.

(4) No action shall be brought under this section by reason of any publication, printing, display or other public use of the name or likeness of a person occurring after the expiration of forty (40) years from and after the death of such person.

(5) As used in this section, a person's "surviving spouse" is the person's surviving spouse under the law of his domicile at the time of his death, whether or not the spouse has later remarried; and a person's "children" are his immediate offspring and any children legally adopted by him. Any consent provided for in subsection (1) shall be given on behalf of a minor by the guardian of his person or by either parent.

(6) The remedies provided for in this section shall be in addition to and not in limitation of the remedies and rights of any person under the common law against the invasion of his privacy.

540.09 *Unauthorized publication of photographs or pictures of areas to which admission is charged.—*

(1) Any person who shall sell any photograph, drawing or other visual representation of any area, building or structure, the entry or admittance to which is subject to an admission charge or fee, or of any real or personal property located therein, or who shall use any such photograph, drawing or other visual representation in connection with the sale or advertising of any other product, property or service,

without the express written or oral consent of the owner or operator of the area, building, structure, or other property so depicted, shall be liable to such owner or operator for any loss, damage or injury sustained by reason thereof, including an amount which would have been a reasonable royalty, and for punitive or exemplary damages, and such unauthorized sale or use may be enjoined.

(2) The provisions of this section shall not apply to:

(a) Photographs, drawings or other visual representations in any newspaper, magazine, book, news broadcast or telecast or other news medium or publication as part of any bona fide news report or presentation having a current and legitimate public interest and where such photographs, drawings or other visual representations are not used for advertising purposes; or

(b) Photographs, drawings or other visual representations in which the depiction of such property is incidental to the principal subject or subjects thereof and not calculated or likely to lead the viewer to associate such property with the sale, offering for sale or advertising of any property, product or service.

(3) The remedies provided for in this section shall be in addition to and not in limitation of the remedies and rights of any person under the common law against the unauthorized sale or use for purposes of trade or advertising of photographs, drawings or other visual representations of his property.

540.10 *Exemption from liability of news media.*—No relief may be obtained under sections 540.08 or 540.09 Florida Statutes, against any broadcaster, publisher or distributor broadcasting, publishing or distributing paid advertising matter by radio or television or in a newspaper, magazine or similar periodical without knowledge or notice that any consent required by sections 540.08 or 540.09 Florida Statutes, in connection with such advertising matter has not been obtained, except an injunction against the presentation of such advertising matter in future broadcasts or in future issues of such newspaper, magazine or similar periodical.

Section 2. This act shall take effect July 1, 1967.

Became a law without the Governor's approval.

Filed in Office Secretary of State May 18, 1967.

10.22   Descendibility of the Right

Earlier reference (see Section 10.21–2) was made to *Lugosi v. Universal Pictures*. This case was the first to examine extensively the issue of descendibility of the right of publicity — that is, the continued existence of the right beyond the life of the person from whom the right originally arises. Other notable cases considering descendibility include *Price v. Hal Roach Studios*, 400 F. Supp. 836 (S.D.N.Y. 1975), which held for the descendibility of the right, and *Memphis Development Foundation v. Factors, Etc.*, 616 F.2d 956 (6th Cir. 1979), which held against. As the prior sections underscore (see Sections 10.21–2 and 10.21–3), much of the uncertainty has been resolved by statutory enactments.

Even so, problems remain. In the two opinions which follow in *Southeast Bank, N.A. v. Lawrence*, the determination of which state law applies was critical. In *Reeves v. United Artists*, the question of whether publicity is subsumed under privacy in Ohio was still the critical issue. In sum, despite progress in determining whether a right of publicity is descendible, not all questions have been resolved.

Southeast Bank, N.A. v. Lawrence, 483 N.Y.S.2d 218 (Sup. Ct. 1984)

Ross, J.

Can the representative of the estate of a deceased public figure assert the right of publicity after his death? This novel issue is presented to us on this appeal.

Thomas Lanier Williams (Williams), better

known as Tennessee Williams, died on February 25, 1983, in New York City. His will was filed in the Circuit Court of Monroe County, Florida, on March 1, 1983, and, pursuant to the terms of that will, the Southeast Bank, N.A. (Southeast), located in Miami, Florida, was named the Personal Representative of the Estate, and appears as the plaintiff in this matter.

During his lifetime, Williams wrote twenty-four full length plays, some of which are among the most popular and critically acclaimed plays in the history of American drama. Some of his best known works include: *The Glass Menagerie, A Streetcar Named Desire, Summer and Smoke, The Rose Tattoo, Camino Real, Cat on a Hot Tin Roof,* and *The Night of the Iguana*. Williams won two Pulitzer prizes, as well as many other honors, including three New York Drama Critics' Circle Awards, the Antoinette Perry Award and a Presidential Medal of Freedom. He has been called one of the world's most noted playwrights.

According to Williams' agent, International Creative Management of New York City, which represented him for over forty years, Williams jealously protected the proprietary rights to the use of his name and to his works. During his lifetime, Williams maintained complete artistic control of the production of his plays. This absolute control by Williams over the content of his work product did not terminate with his death, since, through provisions of his will, he assured that, even after his demise, nobody would be permitted to tamper with his scripts. Thus, Article VIII of Williams' will, in pertinent part, reads:

> It is my wish that no play which I shall have written shall, for the purpose of presenting it as a first-class attraction on the English-speaking stage, be changed in any manner, whether such change shall be by way of completing it, or adding to it, or deleting from it, or in any other way revising it, except for the customary type of stage directions.

Moreover, even though Williams actively promoted himself as a famous person, he was very selective about lending his name to promote causes or artistic projects of others, in view of his desire to prevent the dilution of his world-wide reputation for excellence in his chosen field. Williams refused to associate his name with anything that he did not affirmatively support.

In the light of the record before us, we conclude that the name Tennessee Williams is synonymous with theatrical excellence.

A Senior Trust Officer of Southeast states, in an affidavit, that since Williams' death his estate has received numerous requests for permission to utilize the name "Tennessee Williams," in connection with the production of various dramatic festivals and other such events. However, the Estate, in conformity with Williams' practice of rejecting most of these types of requests when he was alive, has not approved any of them to date. In fact, the Estate has only permitted properly licensed productions of Williams' works and that action has resulted in substantial revenue being realized by the Estate.

At or about February 1984, Southeast learned that the owner of a theater, located at 359 West 48th Street, in Manhattan, intended to rename that theater the "TENNESSEE WILLIAMS." Heretofore, this theater had been called the "Playhouse."

The owner of the subject theater is Jarick Productions, Ltd. (Jarick), which is a New York corporation, and the principals of Jarick are Jack and Richard Lawrence, who are residents of New York State. Jack Lawrence is the President of Jarick, and by his own admission, is known as a composer and lyricist of musical compositions. Furthermore, Jack Lawrence concedes that he has never sought permission from anyone to use the name of "Tennessee Williams." Our examination of the record indicates that Southeast has no affiliation with Jarick and, in addition, will have no control over the activities that will take place at the subject theater. Accordingly, it is fair to conclude that Southeast will be unable to ensure that the quality of the productions presented there meet the standard set by "Tennessee Williams." Obviously, such lack of control can result in diminishing the value of the Williams name.

Jarick claims that the reason they chose to use the Williams name is "to honor the memory and contributions of one of America's greatest playwrights." Southeast disagrees, and contends that Jarick's real purpose is "to trade . . . upon the popularity, good will and high standards of dramatic excellence created by the efforts and achievements of Tennessee Williams."

Within days of learning of Jarick's plans, counsel for Southeast wrote a letter, dated February 10, 1984, to Jack Lawrence advising him that the Williams Estate did not give its consent to Jarick's "use of Tennessee Williams' name;" and, demanded "that you cease and desist from any attempt to appropriate Tennessee Williams' name, or otherwise impair the rights of his Estate." Jack Lawrence acknowledges that he received this letter, but he never replied to Southeast. Thereafter, Southeast was informed that Jarick was proceeding with the renovation of the theater; had erected a marquee identifying the theater as the "TENNESSEE WILLIAMS," and planned to commence rehearsals and a publicity campaign concerning a musical production scheduled to open in March 1984.

On February 24, 1984, plaintiff Southeast commenced the instant action against defendants Jarick and the Lawrences, by the service of a summons and complaint on the defendants, as well as an order to show cause, which brought on plaintiff's motion for a preliminary injunction. The complaint, in substance, seeks permanent injunctive relief against defendants' use of the "Tennessee Williams" name in violation of the Estate's common law right of publicity. . . . Defendants take the position that there is no common law descendible right of publicity in New York. During the period that the motion and the cross-motion were awaiting determination, each side deposed the other.

Ultimately, in the instant order on appeal, Special Term granted plaintiff's motion for a preliminary injunction and denied defendants' cross-motion, upon the basis that plaintiff had met the requirements for preliminary injunctive relief . . . in that the plaintiff demonstrated that it has no adequate legal remedy; that it has a reasonable likelihood of succeeding on the merits in establishing that the defendants had violated its common law right of publicity; that it will suffer irreparable injury if an injunction is not granted and that a balancing of the equities favors plaintiff's position. . . .

It appears that the first mention of the term "right of publicity" occurred more than thirty years ago, in *Haelan Laboratories, Inc. v. Topps Chewing Gum, Inc.*, 202 F.2d 866, 868 (2nd Cir.), *cert. denied*, 346 U.S. 816, 74 S.Ct. 26, 98 L.Ed. 343. The *Haelan* case involved the right of a chewing gum manufacturer, who had obtained the sole right to reproduce a photograph of a baseball player, to stop a business rival from using photographs of the player involved. In deciding this case, the Federal Court stated it would apply New York Law, and, that New York, aside from the statutory right of privacy, recognized a "right of publicity."

The Second Circuit stated, in pertinent part, at page 868 of *Haelan*, cited *supra*, that:

> We think that, in addition to and independent of that right of privacy (which in New York derives from statute), a man has a right in the publicity value of his photograph, *i.e.*, the right to grant the exclusive privilege of publishing his picture. . . .

After making the comments, set forth *supra*, the *Haelan* Court significantly stated: "We think the New York decisions recognize such a right [of publicity]." . . .

Surely, when the right of publicity applies to a public figure's photograph, even more so it would apply, in the instant case, to a public figure's name. We take judicial notice of the fact that "Tennessee Williams" name is far better known than his photograph. . . .

[T]he *Haelan* Court cited the case of *Madison Square Garden Corp. v. Universal Pictures Co.*, 255 App. Div. 459, 7 N.Y.S.2d 845 (First Judicial Department), as an example of a New York Court decision that recognizes the right of publicity. In the *Madison Square Garden Corp. (Garden)* case, the owner of the Garden brought an action against defendants, the motion picture producers and distributors, for distributing a moving picture that purported to show, *inter alia*, the New York Ranger's Hockey team (a team controlled by plaintiff) in a hockey game. The *Garden* case was unanimously decided by our Court and this Court wrote, in pertinent part, at pages 464–466, 7 N.Y.S.2d 845:

> Plaintiff had built up a valuable business licensing the use of genuine photographs taken in the Garden in feature moving pictures, and from that business had derived substantial revenue. That business had been created by the expenditure on plaintiff's part of large sums of money and of effort and skill in the management of its enterprise. ...

The plaintiff clearly had a *property right* in its good name, its reputation, its good will built up at considerable expense, and its business in licensing genuine moving picture photographs to be used in feature films from which it had derived a substantial revenue. (emphasis added) . . .

Some cases have held that, in order for the right of publicity to descend, the celebrity must have exploited that right during his or her lifetime (*Groucho Marx Productions v. Day and Night Co.*, 689 F.2d 317, 322 [2d Cir.]). In this case the Court interpreted California law. If we apply this test to the instant case, we find, based upon the evidence, that "Tennessee Williams" met that test by promoting himself in a number of ways. In 1975 he published an autobiography entitled *Memoirs*; in 1978 he authorized a book of photographs and memorabilia entitled *The World of Tennessee Williams*; and, in January 1980, Williams actively supported and encouraged the Florida Keys Community College to establish the Tennessee Williams Fine Arts Center.

Although we find that Williams exploited his right of publicity when he was alive, we hold that there was no prerequisite for Williams to have exercised this right when he was alive, "in order to protect it from use by others or to preserve any potential right of [Williams'] heirs" (*Price v. Hal Roach Studios, Inc.*, 400 F. Supp. 836, 846 [S.D.N.Y.]) [material in brackets added]. In this case the Court interpreted New York law. . . .

There can be no dispute that "Tennessee Williams" had a valuable property right in his name. In considering whether this right of publicity, survived his death, "there appears to be no logical reason to terminate this right upon death of the person protected. It is for this reason, presumably that this publicity right has been deemed a 'property right' " (*Price v. Hal Roach Studios, Inc.*, cited *supra*, at page 844).

A number of courts have recognized the common law right of publicity. The benefit to a holder of this right "stems from a person's ability to control its use" (*Price v. Hal Roach Studios, Inc.*, cited *supra*, at page 843).

In fact, some states, such as Florida, Oklahoma and Utah, enacted the right of publicity into statutory law. Nevertheless, our analysis of the legal authorities convinces us that there is a common law right of publicity in New York, and, that it is a property right, and, as such is descendible.

Our examination of the deposition of defendant Jack Lawrence leads us to the inevitable conclusion that defendant Jarick's choice of Williams' name for its theater was not for the purpose of honoring him, but rather it was for the purpose of deriving financial benefit from the use of such an illustrious name. In passing, we note that in the case of other theaters in New York City, which are named after well-known theatrical personalities, such as the Ethel Barrymore, Helen Hayes and Eugene O'Neill, prior permission was obtained from the appropriate party before the theater was so named.

In view of our finding that "Tennessee Williams" right of publicity survived his death, we agree with Special Term's grant of plaintiff's motion for a preliminary injunction. . . .

SANDLER, J. (CONCURRING)
In sustaining the order of Special Term granting plaintiff's motion for a preliminary injunction, the Court's opinion relies in large part upon a group of Federal court decisions which, commencing with *Haelan Laboratories v. Topps Chewing Gum*, 202 F.2d 866, cert. den. 346 U.S. 816, 74 S.Ct. 26, 98 L.Ed. 343, have concluded that New York would recognize, separate and apart from the right to privacy embodied in Civil Rights Law Sections 50 and 51, a right of publicity, and one that under appropriate circumstances would be descendible. . . .

In the absence of any authoritative New York decision clearly to the contrary, it seems to me appropriate to give persuasive weight to this carefully considered body of opinions. The basic principles set forth in them seem to me clearly sound, notwithstanding the obvious and serious problem presented in determining the duration in individual situations of the right of publicity after the death of the person whose right has been infringed.

The critical question before us is whether the right of publicity as it has been developed is so closely related to the right sought to be protected in Civil Rights Law Sections 50 and 51, that those sections should be deemed to preclude the acceptance of this separate common law right. As to this issue, I acknowledge some uncertainty as to whether the statutory sections, which in terms prohibit the commercial or trade exploitation without consent of a person's name, picture or portrait, are correctly construed to permit a separate and distinct common law cause of action on behalf of those whose name and picture have an established commercial value. . . .

[I]t seems to me clear that if the decision of the Court of Appeals in *Roberson v. Rochester Folding Box Co.*, 171 N.Y. 538, 64 N.E. 442, had not been responded to by the enactment of Civil Rights Law Sections 50 and 51, and that a similar unconsented to use of the Williams name had been undertaken during his lifetime, the Courts of this State would never have concluded that the *Roberson* decision precluded granting relief against this type of name misappropriation. Since the statutory sections were enacted to address the problem presented in the *Roberson* decision, it would be anomalous to conclude that they precluded relief in a situation which surely would have been deemed appropriate for relief in the courts if these remedial statutory sections had not been adopted.

Southeast Bank, N.A. v. Lawrence, 498 N.Y.S.2d 775 (Ct. App. 1985)

. . . Plaintiff, a Florida-based bank acting as personal representative of the estate of the late playwright Tennessee Williams, a Florida domiciliary at the time of his death, commenced this action to enjoin defendants, the owners of a theatre located on West 48th Street in Manhattan, from renaming the theatre the "Tennessee Williams." In its complaint, plaintiff alleges, among other things, that the renaming of the theatre without its consent violates the decedent's descendible right of publicity.

Special Term granted plaintiff's motion for a preliminary injunction and denied defendant's cross motion to dismiss the complaint. That order has been affirmed by the Appellate Division, First Department, which granted leave to appeal on a certified question. We now reverse.

The parties have assumed that the substantive law of New York is dispositive of the appeal and have addressed Florida law only tangentially.

Both Special Term and the Appellate Division decided the case under what they believed to be New York law. In doing so, all have overlooked the applicable choice of law principle followed by both New York and Florida, that questions concerning personal property rights are to be determined by reference to the substantive law of the decedent's domicile. . . . For choice of law purposes, at least, rights of publicity constitute personality. . . .

Under Florida law (Fla.Stats.Ann. § 540.08), only one to whom a license has been issued during decedent's lifetime and the decedent's surviving spouse and children possess a descendible right of publicity, which is extremely limited and which Florida courts have refused to extend beyond the contours of the statute. . . . Since Tennessee Williams did not have a surviving spouse or child and did not issue a license during his lifetime, plaintiff possesses no enforceable property right. In light of this holding, we do not pass upon the question of whether a common-law descendible right of publicity exists in this State. . . .

Reeves v. United Artists Corp., 765 F.2d 79 (6th Cir. 1985)

PER CURIAM

. . . Plaintiff Louise Reeves is the widow of J.R. Jimmy Reeves, who was a professional boxer during the period from 1939 to 1946. One of Jimmy Reeves' fights was against Jake LaMotta in the old Cleveland Arena on September 24, 1941. This fight was re-created and included immediately after the opening scenes of the motion picture *Raging Bull*, a biographical account of the life of boxer Jake LaMotta, who was portrayed by Robert DeNiro. The dramatized fight scene comprised approximately two minutes of the movie *Raging Bull*, which was produced by defendant United Artists Corporation.

Plaintiff Louise Reeves, Administratrix of the Estate of J.R. Jimmy Reeves, commenced an action for damages against defendant United Artists Corporation and several others for appropriating the name, identity, likeness, character, ability, achievement and performance of J.R. Jimmy Reeves. The district court found that Ohio recognizes the right of publicity which protects against the appropriation or unauthorized use of the name or likeness of another. The district court, however, dismissed the complaint, with prejudice, holding that the right to publicity is not descendible under Ohio law. *Reeves v. United Artists*, 572 F. Supp. 1231 (N.D.Ohio 1983).

Plaintiff Louise Reeves appeals from the order of the district court asserting that Ohio recognizes the right of publicity to one's name, identity and likeness and such right is descendible under Ohio law. Defendant United Artists asserts that the right of publicity is a personal right which is not descendible under Ohio law to the heirs of a deceased person. Alternatively, United Artists claims that the First Amendment precludes a cause of action for appropriation of the right of publicity where a person is the subject of a historical or biographical work.

Zacchini v. Scripps-Howard Broadcasting Co., 47 Ohio St.2d 224, 351 N.E.2d 454 (1976), *rev'd on other grounds*, 433 U.S. 562, 97 S.Ct. 2849, 53 L.Ed.2d 965 (1977), stands for the proposition that Ohio recognizes the right of publicity as a part of that state's common law. . . .

The Ohio Supreme Court did not reach the issue of whether the right of publicity is descendible since the plaintiff there brought suit during his lifetime, but the syllabus clearly indicates the Ohio Supreme Court's recognition of that right as a part of its law concerning the invasion of privacy. Regardless of how other states might consider it, we are convinced that the district judge properly concluded that the right of publicity is part of Ohio's law of invasion of privacy. It is unquestioned and indeed recognized by all parties to this litigation that actions for invasion of privacy in Ohio are not descendible and lapse upon death. . . . Since we have held that the right of publicity is not descendible under Ohio law, we need not and do not reach the difficult First Amendment issues. . . .

10.23   Types of Protections

Courts continue to probe how far a right of publicity extends. Cases in this section illustrate examples of various courts' handiwork. This is not to suggest that all jurisdictions, if faced with similar issues, would extend publicity rights as far as these cases do. Even so, the rationales of the following cases raise intriguing questions as to the reach of a celebrity's *persona*.

In *Carson v. Here's Johnny Portable Toilets*, Johnny Carson alleged that the famous "Here's Johnny" introduction he receives at the start of his show was a protectable right under the concept of a right of publicity. In *Eastwood v. Superior Court L.A. County*, well-known actor (now mayor) Clint Eastwood joined a parade of stars who have at one time or another waged suit against the *National Enquirer*. Eastwood was upset at an *Enquirer* article placing him as the fulcrum in a love triangle that he asserted was patently false. The court's opinion in large part turned on whether a calculated falsehood removed the story from a "public interest" piece and turned it into out-and-out commercial exploitation.

The likeness portrayed in *Ali v. Playgirl* was a drawing of a nude boxer, identified as "Mystery Man," but referred to in verse attending the drawing as "the Greatest." Muhammed Ali in his typical modesty claimed he was the mystery man portrayed and that both his rights of privacy and publicity were violated.

In *Motschenbacher v. R.J. Reynolds Tobacco*, a photograph was used in advertising that plaintiff claimed invaded his rights of privacy and publicity. The photograph did not identify the plaintiff personally; instead, the alleged infringement was that his race car was identifiable, even though the photo had been doctored to alter the appearance of the car.

Carson v. Here's Johnny Portable Toilets Inc., 698 F.2d 831 (6th Cir. 1983)

BROWN, J.

This case involves claims of unfair competition and invasion of the right of privacy and the right of publicity arising from appellee's adoption of a phrase generally associated with a popular entertainer.

Appellant, John W. Carson (Carson), is the host and star of "The Tonight Show," a well-known television program broadcast five nights a week by the National Broadcasting Company. Carson also appears as an entertainer in night clubs and theaters around the country. From the time he began hosting "The Tonight Show" in 1962, he has been introduced on the show each night with the phrase "Here's Johnny." This method of introduction was first used for Carson in 1957 when he hosted a daily television program for the American Broadcasting Company. The phrase "Here's Johnny" is generally associated with Carson by a substantial segment of the television viewing public. In 1967, Carson first authorized use of this phrase by an outside business venture, permitting it to be used by a chain of restaurants called "Here's Johnny Restaurants."

Appellant Johnny Carson Apparel, Inc. (Apparel), formed in 1970, manufactures and markets men's clothing to retail stores. Carson, the president of Apparel and owner of 20% of its stock, has licensed Apparel to use his name and picture, which appear on virtually all of Apparel's products and promotional material. Apparel has also used, with Carson's consent, the phrase "Here's Johnny" on labels for clothing and in advertising campaigns. In 1977, Apparel granted a license to Marcy Laboratories to use "Here's Johnny" as the name of a line of men's toiletries. The phrase "Here's Johnny" has never been registered by appellants as a trademark or service mark.

Appellee, Here's Johnny Portable Toilets, Inc., is a Michigan corporation engaged in the business of renting and selling "Here's Johnny" portable toilets. Appellee's founder was aware at the time he formed the corporation that "Here's Johnny" was the introductory slogan for Carson on "The Tonight Show." He indicated that he coupled the phrase with a second one, "The World's Foremost Commodian," to make "a good play on a phrase." . . .

The appellants . . . claim that the appellee's use of the phrase "Here's Johnny" violates the common law right of privacy and right of publicity. The confusion in this area of the law requires a brief analysis of the relationship between these two rights.

In an influential article, Dean Prosser delineated four distinct types of the right of privacy: (1) intrusion upon one's seclusion or solitude, (2) public disclosure of embarrassing private facts, (3) publicity which places one in a false light, and (4) appropriation of one's name or likeness for the defendant's advantage. Prosser, *Privacy*, 48 Calif.L.Rev. 383, 389 (1960). This fourth type has become known as the "right of publicity." . . .

Dean Prosser's analysis has been a source of some confusion in the law. His first three types of the right of privacy generally protect the right "to be let alone," while the right of publicity protects the celebrity's pecuniary interest in the commercial exploitation of his identity. . . . Thus, the right of privacy and the right of publicity protect fundamentally different interests and must be analyzed separately.

We do not believe that Carson's claim that his right of privacy has been invaded is supported by the law or the facts. Apparently, the gist of this claim is that Carson is embarrassed by and considers it odious to be associated with the appellee's product. Clearly, the association does not appeal to Carson's sense of humor. But the facts here presented do not, it appears to us, amount to an invasion of any of the interests protected by the right of privacy. In any event, our disposition of the claim of an invasion of the right of publicity makes it unnecessary for us to accept or reject the claim of an invasion of the right of privacy.

The right of publicity has developed to protect the commercial interest of celebrities in their identities. The theory of the right is that a celebrity's identity can be valuable in the promotion of products, and the celebrity has an interest that may be protected from the unauthorized commercial exploitation of that identity. . . .

The district court dismissed appellants' claim based on the right of publicity because appellee does not use Carson's name or likeness. 498 F. Supp. at 77. It held that it "would not be prudent to allow recovery for a right of publicity claim which does not more specifically identify Johnny Carson." 498 F. Supp. at 78. We believe that, on the contrary, the district court's conception of the right of publicity is too narrow. The right of publicity, as we have stated, is that a celebrity has a protected pecuniary interest in the commercial exploitation of his identity. If the celebrity's identity is commercially exploited, there has been an invasion of his right whether or not his "name or likeness" is used. Carson's identity may be exploited even if his name, John W. Carson, or his picture is not used.

In *Motschenbacher v. R.J. Reynolds Tobacco Co.*, 498 F.2d 821 (9th Cir. 1974), the court held that the unauthorized use of a picture of a distinctive race car of a well known professional race car driver, whose name or likeness were not used, violated his right of publicity. In this connection, the court said:

> We turn now to the question of "identifiability." Clearly, if the district court correctly determined as a matter of law that plaintiff is not identifiable in the commercial, then in no sense has plaintiff's identity been misappropriated nor his interest violated.
>
> Having viewed a film of the commercial, we agree with the district court that the "likeness" of plaintiff is itself unrecognizable; however, the court's further conclusion of law to the effect that the driver is not identifiable as plaintiff is erroneous in that it wholly fails to attribute proper significance to the distinctive decorations appearing on the car. As pointed out earlier, these markings were not only peculiar to the plaintiff's cars but they caused some persons to think the car in question was plaintiff's and to infer that the person driving the car was the plaintiff.

Id. at 826–827 (footnote omitted). . . .

In *Hirsch v. S.C. Johnson & Son, Inc.*, 90 Wis.2d 379, 280 N.W.2d 129 (1979), the court held that use by defendant of the name "Crazylegs" on a shaving gel for women violated plaintiff's right of publicity. Plaintiff, Elroy Hirsch, a famous football player, had been known by this nickname. The court said:

> The fact that the name, "Crazylegs," used by Johnson, was a nickname rather than Hirsch's actual name does not preclude a cause of action. All that is required is that the name clearly identify the wronged person. In the instant case, it is not disputed at this juncture of the case that the nickname identified the plaintiff Hirsch. It is argued that there were others who were known by the same

name. This, however, does not vitiate the existence of a cause of action. It may, however, if sufficient proof were adduced, affect the quantum of damages should the jury impose liability or it might preclude liability altogether. Prosser points out "that a stage or other fictitious name can be so identified with the plaintiff that he is entitled to protection against its use." 49 Cal.L.Rev., *supra* at 404. He writes that it would be absurd to say that Samuel L. Clemens would have a cause of action if that name had been used in advertising, but he would not have one for the use of "Mark Twain." If a fictitious name is used in a context which tends to indicate that the name is that of the plaintiff, the factual case for identity is strengthened. Prosser, *supra* at 403.

280 N.W.3d at 137.

In this case, Earl Braxton, president and owner of Here's Johnny Portable Toilets, Inc., admitted that he knew that the phrase "Here's Johnny" had been used for years to introduce Carson. . . . That the "Here's Johnny" name was selected by Braxton because of its identification with Carson was the clear inference from Braxton's testimony irrespective of such admission in the opening statement.

We therefore conclude that, applying the correct legal standards, appellants are entitled to judgment. The proof showed without question that appellee had appropriated Carson's identity in connection with its corporate name and its product.

Although this opinion holds only that Carson's right of publicity was invaded because appellee intentionally appropriated his identity for commercial exploitation, the dissent, relying on its interpretation of the authorities and relying on policy and constitutional arguments, would hold that there was no invasion here. We do not believe that the dissent can withstand fair analysis.

The dissent contends that the authorities hold that the right of publicity is invaded only if there has been an appropriation of the celebrity's "name, likeness, achievements, identifying characteristics or actual performances." After so conceding that the right is at least this broad, the dissent then attempts to show that the authorities upon which the majority opinion relies are explainable as involving an appropriation of one or more of these attributes. . . . The dissent explains

588   *Law and Business of the Entertainment Industries*

Hirsch, supra, by pointing out that there the use of the appellation "Crazylegs" by the defendant was in a "context" that suggested a reference to Hirsch and that therefore Hirsch was identified by such use. Here, the dissent states, there is no evidence of the use of "Here's Johnny" in such a suggestive "context." Putting aside the fact that appellee also used the phrase "The World's Foremost Commodian," we fail to see why "context" evidence is necessary where appellee's president admitted that it adopted the name "Here's Johnny" because it identified appellant Carson. We do not understand appellee to even contend that it did not successfully accomplish its intended purpose of appropriating his identity. . . .

It should be obvious from the majority opinion and the dissent that a celebrity's identity may be appropriated in various ways. It is our view that, under the existing authorities, a celebrity's legal right of publicity is invaded whenever his identity is intentionally appropriated for commercial purposes. We simply disagree that the authorities limit the right of publicity as contended by the dissent. It is not fatal to appellant's claim that appellee did not use his "name." Indeed, there would have been no violation of his right of publicity even if appellee had used his name, such as "J. William Carson Portable Toilet" or the "John William Carson Portable Toilet" or the "J.W. Carson Portable Toilet." The reason is that, though literally using appellant's "name," the appellee would not have appropriated Carson's identity as a celebrity. Here there was an appropriation of Carson's identity without using his "name." . . .

KENNEDY, J. (DISSENTING)

I respectfully dissent from that part of the majority's opinion which holds that appellee's use of the phrase "Here's Johnny" violates appellant Johnny Carson's common law right of publicity. While I agree that an individual's identity may be impermissibly exploited, I do not believe that the common law right of publicity may be extended beyond an individual's name, likeness, achievements, identifying characteristics or actual performances, to include phrases or other things which are merely associated with the individual, as is the phrase "Here's Johnny." The majority's

extension of the right of publicity to include phrases or other things which are merely associated with the individual permits a popular entertainer or public figure, by associating himself or herself with a common phrase, to remove those words from the public domain.

The phrase "Here's Johnny" is merely associated with Johnny Carson, the host and star of "The Tonight Show" broadcast by the National Broadcasting Company. Since 1962, the opening format of "The Tonight Show," after the theme music is played, is to introduce Johnny Carson with the phrase "Here's Johnny." The words are spoken by an announcer, generally Ed McMahon, in a drawn out and distinctive manner. Immediately after the phrase "Here's Johnny" is spoken, Johnny Carson appears to begin the program. This method of introduction was first used by Johnny Carson in 1957 when he hosted a daily television show for the American Broadcasting Company. This case is not transformed into a "name" case simply because the diminutive form of John W. Carson's given name and the first name of his full stage name, Johnny Carson, appears in it. The first name is so common, in light of the millions of persons named John, Johnny or Jonathan that no doubt inhabit this world, that alone, it is meaningless or ambiguous at best in identifying Johnny Carson, the celebrity. In addition, the phrase containing Johnny Carson's first stage name was certainly selected for its value as a double entendre. Appellee manufactures portable toilets. The value of the phrase to appellee's product is in the risqué meaning of "john" as a toilet or bathroom. For this reason, too, this is not a "name" case.

Appellee has stipulated that the phrase "Here's Johnny" is associated with Johnny Carson and that absent this association, he would not have chosen to use it for his product and corporation, Here's Johnny Portable Toilets, Inc. I do not consider it relevant that appellee intentionally chose to incorporate into the name of his corporation and product a phrase that is merely associated with Johnny Carson. What is not protected by law is not taken from public use. Research reveals no case in which the right of publicity has been extended to phrases or other things which are merely associated with an individual and are not part of his name, likeness, achievements, identifying characteristics or actual performances. Both the policies behind the right of publicity and countervailing interests and considerations indicate that such an extension should not be made. . . .

The three primary policy considerations behind the right of publicity are succinctly stated in Hoffman, *Limitations on the Right of Publicity*, 28 *Bull. Copr. Soc'y*, 111, 116–22 (1980). First, "the right of publicity vindicates the economic interests of celebrities, enabling those whose achievements have imbued their identities with pecuniary value to profit from their fame." . . . Second, the right of publicity fosters "the production of intellectual and creative works by providing the financial incentive for individuals to expend the time and resources necessary to produce them." . . . Third, "[t]he right of publicity serves both individual and societal interests by preventing what our legal tradition regards as wrongful conduct: unjust enrichment and deceptive trade practices." . . .

None of the above-mentioned policy arguments supports the extension of the right of publicity to phrases or other things which are merely associated with an individual. First, the majority is awarding Johnny Carson a windfall, rather than vindicating his economic interests, by protecting the phrase "Here's Johnny" which is merely associated with him. In *Zacchini*, the Supreme Court stated that a mechanism to vindicate an individual's economic rights is indicated where the appropriated thing is "the product of . . . [the individual's] own talents and energy, the end result of much time, effort and expense." *Zacchini, supra*, 433 U.S. at 575, 97 S.Ct. at 2857. There is nothing in the record to suggest that "Here's Johnny" has any nexus to Johnny Carson other than being the introduction to his personal appearances. The phrase is not part of an identity that he created. In its content "Here's Johnny" is a very simple and common introduction. The content of the phrase neither originated with Johnny Carson nor is it confined to the world of entertainment. The phrase is not said by Johnny Carson, but said of him. Its association with him is derived, in large part, by the context in which it is said—generally by Ed McMahon in

a drawn out and distinctive voice after the theme music to "The Tonight Show" is played, and immediately prior to Johnny Carson's own entrance. Appellee's use of the content "Here's Johnny," in light of its value as a double entendre, written on its product and corporate name, and therefore outside of the context in which it is associated with Johnny Carson, does little to rob Johnny Carson of something which is unique to him or a product of his own efforts.

The second policy goal of fostering the production of creative and intellectual works is not met by the majority's rule because in awarding publicity rights in a phrase neither created by him nor performed by him, economic reward and protection is divorced from personal incentive to produce on the part of the protected and benefited individual. Johnny Carson is simply reaping the rewards of the time, effort and work product of others.

Third, the majority's extension of the right of publicity to include the phrase "Here's Johnny" which is merely associated with Johnny Carson is not needed to provide alternatives to existing legal avenues for redressing wrongful conduct. The existence of a cause of action under section 43(a) of the Lanham Act, 15 U.S.C.A. § 1125(a) (1976) and Michigan common law does much to undercut the need for policing against unfair competition through an additional legal remedy such as the right of publicity. The majority has concluded, and I concur, that the District Court was warranted in finding that there was not a reasonable likelihood that members of the public would be confused by appellee's use of the "Here's Johnny" trademark on a product as dissimilar to those licensed by Johnny Carson as portable toilets. In this case, this eliminates the argument of wrongdoing. Moreover, the majority's extension of the right of publicity to phrases and other things merely associated with an individual is not conditioned upon wrongdoing and would apply with equal force in the case of an unknowing user. With respect to unjust enrichment, because a celebrity such as Johnny Carson is himself enriched by phrases and other things associated with him in which he has made no personal investment of time, money or effort, another user of such a phrase or thing may be enriched somewhat by such use, but this enrichment is not at Johnny Carson's expense. The policies behind the right of publicity are not furthered by the majority's holding in this case. . . .

Protection under the right of publicity confers a monopoly on the protected individual that is potentially broader, offers fewer protections and potentially competes with federal statutory monopolies. As an essential part of three federal monopoly rights, copyright, trademark and patents, notice to the public is required in the form of filing with the appropriate governmental office and use of an appropriate mark. This apprises members of the public of the nature and extent of what is being removed from the public domain and subject to claims of infringement. The right of publicity provides limited notice to the public of the extent of the monopoly right to be asserted, if one is to be asserted at all. As the right of privacy is expanded beyond protections of name, likeness and actual performances, which provide relatively objective notice to the public of the extent of an individual's rights, to more subjective attributes such as achievements and identifying characteristics, the public's ability to be on notice of a common law monopoly right, if one is even asserted by a given famous individual, is severely diminished. Protecting phrases and other things merely associated with an individual provides virtually no notice to the public at all of what is claimed to be protected. By ensuring the invocation of the adjudicative process whenever the commercial use of a phrase or other associated thing is considered to have been wrongfully appropriated, the public is left to act at their peril. The result is a chilling effect on commercial innovation and opportunity. . . .

NOTE _____

1. In *Carson v. Here's Johnny Portable Toilets, Inc.*, the U.S. Court of Appeals (in a part of the opinion omitted in the foregoing report) upheld the district court's finding that Johnny Carson did not have a cause of action against the defendant under a claim of violation of Section 43(a) of the Lanham Act, 15 U.S.C. § 1125(a) (1976). Discussion of Lanham Act claims, including a further note on *Carson*, can be found in Section 10.40 of this chapter.

Eastwood v. Superior Court of L.A. County, 198 Cal. Rptr. 342 (Ct. App. 1983)

THOMPSON, J.

In this proceeding in mandate, we inquire into the propriety of the respondent court's ruling sustaining without leave to amend the general demurrer of the real party in interest, National Enquirer, Inc. (Enquirer), to the second cause of action of the complaint of petitioner, Clint Eastwood (Eastwood), for commercial appropriation of the right of publicity. We consider whether the unauthorized use of a celebrity's name, photograph, or likeness on the cover of a publication and in related telecast advertisements, in connection with a published nondefamatory article, which is false but presented as true, constitutes an actionable infringement of that person's right of publicity under both the common law and Civil Code section 3344, subdivision (a). We have determined that such use constitutes commercial exploitation and is not privileged or protected by constitutional considerations or expressly exempted as a news account under Civil Code section 3344, subdivision (d). Accordingly, we have concluded that the respondent court improperly sustained the general demurrer to the second cause of action without leave to amend. . . .

Eastwood, a well-known motion picture actor, filed a complaint containing two causes of action against the Enquirer. The gist of the first cause of action is for false light invasion of privacy. The second cause of action is for invasion of privacy through the commercial appropriation of name, photograph and likeness under both the common law and Civil Code section 3344.

The following pertinent facts emerge from the allegations of the first cause of action. The Enquirer publishes a weekly newspaper known as the *National Enquirer* which enjoys wide circulation and is read by a great number of people. In its April 13, 1982, edition of the *National Enquirer*, the Enquirer published a 600-word article about Eastwood's romantic involvement with two other celebrities, singer Tanya Tucker and actress Sondra Locke. On the cover of this edition appeared the pictures of Eastwood and Tucker above the caption "Clint Eastwood in Love Triangle with Tanya Tucker."

The article is headlined "Clint Eastwood in Love Triangle" and appears on page 48 of this edition. Eastwood alleges the article is false and in this regard alleges:

(a) The offending article falsely states that Eastwood "loves" Tucker and that Tucker means a lot to him.

(b) The offending article falsely states that Eastwood was, in late February 1982, swept off his feet and immediately smitten by Tucker; that Tucker makes his head spin; that Tucker used her charms to get what she wanted from Eastwood; and that Eastwood now daydreams about their supposedly enchanted evenings together.

(c) The offending article falsely states that Eastwood and Tucker, in late February 1982, shared 10 fun-filled romantic evenings together; were constantly, during that period, in each other's arms; publicly "cuddled" and publicly gazed romantically at one another; and publicly kissed and hugged.

(d) The offending article falsely states that Eastwood is locked in a romantic triangle involving Tucker and Sondra Locke (Locke); is torn between Locke and Tucker; can't decide between Locke and Tucker; is involved in a romantic tug-of-war involving Locke and Tucker; that Locke and Tucker are dueling over him; that Tucker is battling Locke for his affections; and that when he is with Locke, Tucker is constantly on his mind.

(e) The offending article falsely states that, in or about late February of 1982, there were serious problems in Eastwood's relationship with Locke; that he and Locke at that time had a huge argument over marriage; that he and Locke had a nasty fight; and that Locke stormed out of his presence.

(f) The offending article falsely states that after his supposed romantic interlude with Tucker, Locke camped at his doorstep and, while on hands and knees, begged Eastwood to "keep her," vowing that she wouldn't pressure him into marriage; but that Eastwood acted oblivious to her pleas.

Eastwood further asserts that Enquirer "published the offending article maliciously, willfully and wrongfully, with the intent to injure and disgrace Eastwood, either knowing that the statements therein contained were false or with reckless disregard of . . . their . . . falsity." Enquirer used Eastwood's name and photograph without his consent or permission. As a consequence thereof, Eastwood alleges that he has suffered mental anguish and emotional distress and seeks both compensatory and punitive damages.

The second cause of action of the complaint incorporates all the allegations of the first cause of action concerning the status of Enquirer and the falsity of the article. It does not, however, incorporate the allegation that the article was published with knowledge or in reckless disregard of its falsity.

Additionally, Eastwood alleges that the Enquirer made a telecast advertisement in which it featured Eastwood's name and photograph and mentioned prominently the subject article. Moreover, Eastwood alleges that the telecast advertisements as well as the cover of the April 13 publication were calculated to promote the sales of the Enquirer. Eastwood asserts that the unauthorized use of his name and photograph has damaged him in his right to control the commercial exploitation of his name, photograph and likeness, in addition to injuring his feelings and privacy. Eastwood seeks damages under both the common law and Civil Code section 3344.

Enquirer did not challenge the legal sufficiency of the first cause of action for invasion of privacy by placing Eastwood in a false light in the public eye.

Enquirer demurred to the second cause of action for invasion of privacy through appropriation of name, photograph and likeness on the basis it failed to state a cause of action on two grounds: (1) Eastwood's name and photograph were not used to imply an endorsement of the Enquirer; and (2) Eastwood's name and photograph were used in connection with a news account. . . .

This petition poses two basic issues: (1) Has Eastwood stated a cause of action for commercial appropriation of the right of publicity under either the common law or Civil Code section 3344? (2) Is the conduct of the Enquirer privileged so as not to constitute an infringement of Eastwood's right of publicity? . . .

California has long recognized a common law right of privacy . . . which provides protection against four distinct categories of invasion. . . . These four distinct torts identified by Dean Prosser and grouped under the privacy rubric are: (1)

intrusion upon the plaintiff's seclusion or solitude, or into his private affairs; (2) public disclosure of embarrassing private facts about the plaintiff; (3) publicity which places the plaintiff in a false light in the public eye; and (4) appropriation, for the defendant's advantage, of the plaintiff's name or likeness. . . .

Moreover, the fourth category of invasion of privacy, namely, appropriation, "has been *complemented* legislatively by Civil Code section 3344, adopted in 1971." . . .

Civil Code section 3344, subdivision (a), provides in pertinent part as follows: "Any person who knowingly uses another's name, photograph, or likeness, in any manner, for purposes of advertising products, merchandise, goods, or services, or for purposes of solicitation of purchases of products . . . without such person's prior consent . . . shall be liable for any damages sustained by the person . . . injured as a result thereof."

Eastwood has framed his complaint against Enquirer on the third and fourth branches of the right of privacy. His first cause of action, which is not at issue here, rests on the theory that the subject publication placed him in a false light in the public eye. The focus of this tort is the falsity of the published article. His second cause of action, which is at issue here, rests on alternative theories. One is the common law action of commercial appropriation. The other is the statutory remedy provided in Civil Code section 3344, subdivision (a), for the knowing use, without consent, of another's name, photograph or likeness for the purposes of advertising or solicitation of purchases. . . .

Enquirer argues . . . that the failure of Eastwood to allege the appearance of an "endorsement" of the Enquirer is fatal to stating a cause of action for commercial appropriation.

California law has not imposed any requirement that the unauthorized use or publication of a person's name or picture be suggestive of an endorsement or association with the injured person. . . .

[T]he appearance of an "endorsement" is not the *sine qua non* of a claim for commercial appropriation. Thus, in *Stilson v. Reader's Digest Assn., Inc.* (1972) 28 Cal. App.3d 270, 104 Cal. Rptr. 581, the allegedly wrongful use involved a magazine's inclusion of individuals' names in letters soliciting participation in a sweepstake designed to promote subscription. The letters stated that the recipient and other named individuals had been chosen to receive "lucky numbers." No statement or implication that these individuals had consented to promote the magazine was made or implied. Assessing the legal significance of this promotional endeavor, the court stated that "[t]he unauthorized use of one's name for commercial exploitation is actionable." (*Id.*, at p. 273, 104 Cal. Rptr. 581).

Further, Enquirer contends that under *Lugosi* an appropriation of name and likeness for commercial purposes can only be shown by Eastwood, if their use has impressed the Enquirer with a secondary meaning. We disagree.

In *Lugosi v. Universal Pictures*, which involved an action by the heirs of Bela Lugosi for commercial appropriation of his right of publicity, our Supreme Court held that the right of publicity, which is the legally protected interest a person has to control the commercial exploitation of his name, photograph or likeness, is not descendible and expires upon the death of the person so protected. (25 Cal.3d at pp. 819, 824, 160 Cal. Rptr. 323, 603 P.2d 425; see *Guglielmi v. Spelling-Goldberg Productions* (1979) 25 Cal.3d 860, 861, 160 Cal. Rptr. 352, 603 P.2d 454.) Contrary to the Enquirer's position that the impression of a secondary meaning is a prerequisite to a claim for commercial appropriation, *Lugosi* recognized that the right of publicity includes not only the power to control the exploitation of one's personality through licensing agreements, but also the right to obtain relief, both injunctive and/or for damages, when a third party appropriates one's name and likeness for commercial purposes without permission. . . .

Furthermore, to illustrate the import of *Lugosi*, we offer the following example: Henry Ford, during his lifetime, could have given a license to General Motors to use his name to endorse a "Buick" automobile. This would have constituted an assignment of his right of publicity. However, this assignment would have expired upon the death of Henry Ford and his name would have been in the marketplace for anyone to use. . . . On the other hand, if Henry

Ford had used his name as the name for a particular automobile so that his name acquired a secondary meaning, i.e., the use of the name "Ford" meant a particular automobile, it would be protectable as property under the law of unfair competition. . . . Notwithstanding these contrasting uses, Henry Ford could elect not to exercise his right of publicity and "protect it from invasion by others by a suit for injunction and/or damages." . . .

Moreover, apart from its inconsistency with the common law, Enquirer's suggested limitation of the scope of actionable commercial appropriation is at odds with the clear language of Civil Code section 3344. The statute imposes liability on a person "who knowingly uses another name, photograph, or likeness, *in any manner.* . . ." This broad language does not admit of the Enquirer's suggested limitation.

We therefore find that Enquirer's argument is without merit.

Turning to whether the Enquirer has commercially exploited Eastwood's name, photograph or likeness, we note that one of the primary purposes of advertising is to motivate a decision to purchase a particular product or service.

The first step toward selling a product or service is to attract the consumers' attention. Because of a celebrity's audience appeal, people respond almost automatically to a celebrity's name or picture. Here, the Enquirer used Eastwood's personality and fame on the cover of the subject publication and in related telecast advertisements. To the extent their use attracted the readers' attention, the Enquirer gained a commercial advantage. Furthermore, the Enquirer used Eastwood's personality in the context of an alleged news account, entitled "Clint Eastwood in Love Triangle with Tanya Tucker" to generate maximum curiosity and the necessary motivation to purchase the newspaper.

Moreover, the use of Eastwood's personality in the context of a news account, allegedly false but presented as true, provided the Enquirer with a ready-made "scoop"—a commercial advantage over its competitors which it would otherwise not have.

Absent a constitutional or statutory proscription, we find that Eastwood can show that such use is a subterfuge or cover-up for commercial exploitation. . . .

Enquirer argues that Eastwood's second cause of action fails to state an actionable claim under California law because the use of his name and photograph in the telecast advertisements, the cover page, and the story is expressly exempted from liability as a news account under the provisions of Civil Code section 3344, subdivision (d).

Civil Code section 3344, subdivision (d) provides inter alia that "[f]or purposes of this section, a use of a name, photograph or likeness in connection with any news . . . shall not constitute a use for purposes of advertising or solicitation."

While the issue raised by the Enquirer's argument solely involves the statutory remedy of Civil Code section 3344, subdivision (a), its resolution will necessarily determine Eastwood's ability to maintain a cause of action for commercial appropriation under the common law. The reason is that implicit in this issue are major constitutional questions which we must confront and determine. Publication of matters in the public interest, which rests on the right of the public to know, and the freedom of the press to tell it, cannot ordinarily be actionable. . . .

Hence we are called upon to determine the boundaries of Eastwood's ability to control the commercial exploitation of his personality in the publication field. This determination will necessitate a weighing of the private interest of the right of publicity against matters of public interest calling for constitutional protection, and a consideration of the character of these competing interests.

Freedom of the press is constitutionally guaranteed, and the publication of daily news is an acceptable and necessary function in the life of the community. . . . The scope of the privilege extends to almost all reporting of recent events even though it involves the publication of a purely private person's name or likeness. . . .

Yet absolute protection of the press in the case at bench requires a total sacrifice of the competing interest of Eastwood in controlling the commercial exploitation of his personality. Often considerable money, time and energy are needed to develop the ability in a person's name or likeness to attract attention and evoke a desired response in a particular consumer market. . . . Thus, a proper accommodation between these competing concerns must be defined, since "the rights guaranteed by the First Amendment do not require total abrogation of the right to privacy" . . .

Ordinarily, only two branches of the law of privacy, namely, public disclosure and false light, create tension with the First Amendment, because of their intrusion on the dissemination of information to the public. . . . Normally, in a commercial appropriation case involving the right of publicity, the only question is who gets to do the publishing, since the celebrity is primarily concerned with whether he gets the commercial benefit of such publication. . . .

All fiction is false in the literal sense that it is imagined rather than actual. However, works of fiction are constitutionally protected in the same manner as topical news stories. . . .

Therefore, since Eastwood asserts that the alleged news account is entirely false, and is a cover-up or subterfuge for commercial appropriation of his name and likeness, we must consider First Amendment limitations.

We have no doubt that the subject of the Enquirer article—the purported romantic involvements of Eastwood with other celebrities—is a matter of public concern, which would generally preclude the imposition of liability. . . . However, Eastwood argues that the article, and thereby the related advertisements, are not entitled to either constitutional protection or exemption from liability as a news account because the article is a calculated falsehood.

Since *New York Times v. Sullivan* (1964) 376 U.S. 254, 279–280, 84 S.Ct. 710, 725–26, 11 L.Ed.2d 686, it is clear that the First Amendment generally precludes the imposition of liability upon a publisher for its expressive activities, except upon a finding of fault. Thus, our analysis must determine whether Eastwood has alleged the kinds of fault and the appropriate standard that may constitutionally warrant liability in this case. . . .

In actions where the fault involves defamatory statements, the cases have focused on the status of plaintiff to determine the standard of fault necessary to impose liability on a media defendant. For example, in the case of a public official

or public figure, the Supreme Court established the rule that a plaintiff may not recover except upon showing that the defendant published defamatory statements with *actual malice* (hereafter "scienter"), i.e., either with knowledge of their falsity or with reckless disregard for the truth. . . . However, in defamation actions brought by private individuals, the Supreme Court has allowed any appropriate standard of fault less than scienter to be used, short of liability without fault. . . . Thus, a private-party plaintiff may sue for negligent publication of defamatory falsehoods. . . .

Similarly, in privacy actions involving deliberate fictionalization presented as truth, the cases have focused on the materials published to determine the standard of fault required to impose liability on a publisher. For example, where the materials published, although assertedly private and nondefamatory, are matters of public interest, the target of the publication must prove knowing or reckless falsehood. . . .

Moreover, the standard of scienter, whether in a defamation or privacy case, reflects the Supreme Court's recognition that while a calculated falsehood has no constitutional value, such statements are inevitable in the continuing debate on public issues and thus, the fruitful exercise of the freedoms of speech and press requires "breathing space" for speech that matters. . . .

Accordingly, we conclude whether the focus is on the status of Eastwood, or upon the materials published in the Enquirer article, scienter of the alleged calculated falsehood is the proper standard of fault to impose liability on the Enquirer, contrary to the position of Eastwood, that calculated falsehood alone is enough.

Enquirer contends, however, that it is the manifest character of the article which is determinative as to whether it is news under section 3344, subdivision (d). Enquirer argues that the statute, by its terms, refers only to generic categories; it does not distinguish between news accounts that are true or false. Thus, whether an article is a news account does not turn on the truth or falsity of its content. We disagree.

The spacious interest in an unfettered press is not without limitation. This privilege is subject to the qualification that it shall not be so exercised as to abuse the rights of individuals. Hence, in defamation cases, the concern is with defamatory lies masquerading as truth. . . . Similarly, in privacy cases, the concern is with nondefamatory lies masquerading as truth. . . . Accordingly, we do not believe that the Legislature intended to provide an exemption from liability for a knowing or reckless falsehood under the canopy of "news." We therefore hold that Civil Code section 3344, subdivision (d), as it pertains to news, does not provide an exemption for a knowing or reckless falsehood.

Moreover, wherever the line in a particular situation is to be drawn between news accounts that are protected and those that are not, we are quite sure that the First Amendment does not immunize Enquirer when the entire article is allegedly false. . . .

Finally, Enquirer contends that falsity is the predicate, not for commercial appropriation, but for false light claims. We disagree.

As noted earlier, all fiction is literally false, but enjoys constitutional protection.

However, the deliberate fictionalization of Eastwood's personality constitutes commercial exploitation, and becomes actionable when it is presented to the reader as if true with the requisite scienter. . . .

Here, Eastwood failed to incorporate from his first cause of action that the article was published with knowledge or in reckless disregard of its falsity. Accordingly, we find that such failure renders the second cause of action insufficient to make the Enquirer's expressive conduct actionable under the common law or Civil Code section 3344, subdivision (a).

Manifestly, such defect is capable of being cured by amendment. . . .

Let a peremptory writ of mandamus issue requiring the respondent court to set aside its order sustaining the demurrer to Eastwood's second cause of action without leave to amend, and to grant Eastwood leave to amend his second cause of action.

NOTE ———————————————

1. In *Clark v. Celeb Publishing, Inc.*, 530 F. Supp. 979 (S.D.N.Y. 1981), the plaintiff, a model and actress, brough suit against *Celeb Magazine* after her photo-

graphs appeared on the magazine's cover and in advertisements for the publication. *Celeb* had not obtained releases for use of the photograph, and the plaintiff had never consented to any use.

The U.S. District Court in New York applied California law on the grounds that the plaintiff was a California resident, that California had a greater interest in compensating residents for injuries of this type, and that California was the state of "greatest injury." The court held that plaintiff had an actionable tort under a right of privacy under California law.

As to damages, the court applied California Civil Code, §3333, which provides that for "the breach of an obligation not arising from contract, the measure of damages . . . is the amount which will compensate for all the detriment proximately caused thereby, whether it could have been anticipated or not." Damages were divided into three categories: emotional suffering, money not paid for use of photographs, and economic injury suffered as a result of the unauthorized publications. Punitive damages for intentional disregard of plaintiff's rights were also awarded.

Under the above rationale, the court awarded $25,000 for mental anguish, $6,750 for compensation for the photographs, based on a reasonable modeling fee, $7,000 for economic loss resulting from lessened ability to sell her likeness elsewhere, and $25,000 for malice in intentionally publishing a photo without permission.

Ali v. Playgirl, Inc., 447 F. Supp. 723 (S.D.N.Y. 1978)

GAGLIARDI, J.

Plaintiff Muhammad Ali, a citizen of Illinois and until recently the heavyweight boxing champion of the world, has brought this diversity action for injunctive relief and damages against defendants Playgirl, Inc., a California corporation, Independent News Company ("Independent"), a New York corporation, and Tony Yamada, a California citizen, for their alleged unauthorized printing, publication and distribution of an objectionable portrait of Ali in the February 1978 issue of Playgirl Magazine ("Playgirl"), a monthly magazine published by Playgirl, Inc., and distributed in New York State by Independent. The portrait complained of depicts a nude black man seated in the corner of a boxing ring and is claimed to be unmistakably recognizable as plaintiff Ali. Alleging that the publication of this picture constitutes, *inter alia*, a violation of his rights under

Section 51 of the New York Civil Rights Law (McKinney 1976) and of his related common law "right of publicity," Ali now moves for a preliminary injunction pursuant to Rule 65, Fed.R.Civ.P., directing defendants Playgirl, Inc. and Independent to cease distribution and dissemination of the February 1978 issue of Playgirl Magazine, to withdraw that issue from circulation and recover possession of all copies presently offered for sale, and to surrender to plaintiff any printing plates or devices used to reproduce the portrait complained of. For the reasons which follow and to the extent indicated below, plaintiff's motion for a preliminary injunction is granted. . . .

This court concludes that plaintiff has satisfied the standard established in this Circuit for determining whether a preliminary injunction should issue. *Sonesta International Hotels v. Wellington Associates*, 483 F.2d 247 (2d Cir. 1973). The familiar alternative test formula is that

> a preliminary injunction should issue only upon a clear showing of either (1) probable success on the merits *and* possible irreparable injury, *or* (2) sufficiently serious questions going to the merits to make them a fair ground for litigation *and* a balance of hardships tipping decidedly toward the party requesting the preliminary relief.

Id. at 250 (emphasis in original) . . .

In determining the issues of probable success on the merits or sufficiently serious questions going to the merits of this action, it is agreed that this court must look to the substantive law of New York. *Erie Railroad Co.* v. *Tompkins*, 304 U.S. 64, 58 S.Ct. 817, 82 L.Ed. 1188 (1938). To be considered are plaintiff's claims that his statutory "right of privacy" under Sec. 51 of the New York Civil Rights Law and his common law "right of publicity" have been violated.

Section 51 of the New York Civil Rights Law provides in pertinent part:

> Any person whose name, portrait or picture is used within this state for . . . the purposes of trade without the written consent [of that person] may maintain an equitable action . . . against the person, firm or corporation so using his name, portrait or picture, to prevent and restrain the use thereof; and may also sue and recover damages for any injury sustained by reason of such use . . .

Defendants do not, and indeed cannot, seriously dispute the assertion that the offensive drawing is in fact Ali's "portrait or picture." This phrase, as used in sec. 51, is not restricted to photographs . . . but generally comprises those representations which are recognizable as likenesses of the complaining individual. . . . Even a cursory inspection of the picture which is the subject of this action strongly suggests that the facial characteristics of the black male portrayed are those of Muhammad Ali. The cheekbones, broad nose and widest brown eyes, together with the distinctive smile and close cropped black hair are recognizable as the features of the plaintiff, one of the most widely known athletes of our time. In addition, the figure depicted is seated on a stool in the corner of a boxing ring with both hands taped and outstretched resting on the ropes on either side. Although the picture is captioned "Mystery Man," the identification of the individual as Ali is further implied by an accompanying verse which refers to the figure as "the Greatest." This court may take judicial notice that plaintiff Ali has regularly claimed that appellation for himself and that his efforts to identify himself in the public mind as "the Greatest" have been so successful that he is regularly identified as such in the news media.

It is also clear that the picture has been used for the "purpose of trade" within the meaning of sec. 51. In this regard it is the established law of New York that the unauthorized use of an individual's picture is not for a "trade purpose," and thus not violative of sec. 51, if it is "in connection with an item of news or one that is newsworthy." . . .

In the instant case there is no such informational or newsworthy dimension to defendants' unauthorized use of Ali's likeness. Instead, the picture is a dramatization, an illustration falling somewhere between representational art and cartoon, and is accompanied by a plainly fictional and allegedly libellous bit of doggerel. Defendants cannot be said to have presented "the unembroidered dissemination of facts" or "the unvarnished, unfictionalized truth." . . . The nude portrait was clearly included in the magazine solely "for purposes of trade—e.g., merely to attract attention." . . .

Finally, defendants concede that Ali did not consent to the inclusion of his likeness in the February 1978 Playgirl Magazine (Tr. 2). Defendants contend, however, that even if their use of Ali's likeness is determined to be unauthorized and for trade purposes within the meaning of sec. 51, the statutory right of privacy does not extend to protect "someone such as an athlete . . . who chooses to bring himself to public notice, who chooses, indeed, as clearly as the plaintiff here does to rather stridently seek out publicity" (Tr. 5). Defendants are plainly in error in disputing liability on the basis of Ali's status as a public personality. Such a contention

> confuses the fact that projection into the public arena may make for newsworthiness of one's activities, and all the hazards of publicity thus entailed, with the quite different and independent right to have one's personality, even if newsworthy, free from commercial exploitation at the hands of another. . . . That [plaintiff] may have voluntarily on occasion surrendered [his] privacy, for a price or gratuitously, does not forever forfeit for anyone's commercial profit so much of [his] privacy as [he] has not relinquished. [citations omitted]

Booth v. Curtis Publishing Co., 15 A.D.2d 343, 351–52, 223 N.Y.S.2d 737, 745 (1st Dept.), aff'd, 11 N.Y.2d 907, 228 N.Y.S.2d 468, 183 N.E.2d 812 (1962). . . .

Accordingly, this court is satisfied that plaintiff Ali has established probable success on the merits of his claimed violation of privacy under sec. 51 of the New York Civil Rights Law.

The foregoing discussion also establishes the likelihood that plaintiff will prevail on his claim that his right of publicity has been violated by the publication of the offensive portrait. This Circuit has long held that New York recognizes the common law property right of publicity in addition to, and distinct from, the statutory right under sec. 51. *Haelan Laboratories, Inc.* v. *Topps Chewing Gum, Inc.*, 202 F.2d 866, 868 (2d Cir.), *cert. denied*, 345 U.S. 816, 74 S.Ct. 26, 98 L.Ed. 343 (1953). . . .

It must be noted, however, that the courts of New York do not regularly distinguish between the proprietary right of publicity, discussed *infra*, and the sec. 51 right of privacy. The latter has been characterized as establishing and limiting the right of a person "to be left alone" and protecting "the sentiments, thoughts and feelings of an individual . . . from [unwanted] commercial exploitation," *Flores* v. *Mosler Safe Co., supra*, 7

N.Y.2d at 280, 196 N.Y.S.2d at 977–78, 164 N.E.2d at 855, but numerous cases blend the concepts together and expressly recognize a right of recovery under sec. 51 for violations of an individual's property interest in his likeness or reputation. . . .

The distinctive aspect of the common law right of publicity is that it recognizes the commercial value of the picture or representation of a prominent person or performer, and protects his proprietary interest in the profitability of his public reputation or "persona." . . . As held by this Circuit, New York State recognizes that, independent of his sec. 51 rights, "a man has a right in the publicity value of his photograph, i.e., the right to grant the exclusive privilege of publishing his picture." . . .

Accordingly, this right of publicity is usually asserted only if the plaintiff has "achieved in some degree a celebrated status." *Price* v. *Hal Roach Studios, Inc., supra*, 400 F. Supp. at 847, quoting Gordon, *Right of Property in Name, Likeness, Personality and History*, 55 NW. U.L.Rev. 553, 607 (1960). In the instant case, it is undisputed that plaintiff Ali has achieved such a "celebrated status" and it is clear to this court that he has established a valuable interest in his name and his likeness. . . .

It is established that plaintiff must make a showing of irreparable injury. . . .

As has been noted, in the course of his public career plaintiff has established a commercially valuable propietary interest in his likeness and reputation, analogous to the goodwill accumulated in the name of a successful business entity. To the extent that defendants are unlawfully appropriating this valuable commodity for themselves, proof of damages or unjust enrichment may be extremely difficult. . . .

In virtually identical circumstances it has been observed that "a celebrity's property interest in his name and likeness is unique, and therefore there is no serious question as to the propriety of injunctive relief." *Uhlaender* v. *Henricksen, supra*, 316 F. Supp. at 1283. Furthermore, defendants appear not only to be usurping plaintiff's valuable right of publicity for themselves but may well be inflicting damage upon his marketable reputation. As described previously, the "likeness" of Ali which has been published is a full frontal nude drawing, not merely a sketch or photograph of him as he appears in public. Damages from such evident abuse of plaintiff's property right in his public reputation are plainly difficult to measure by monetary standards. . . .

Motschenbacher v. R.J. Reynolds Tobacco Co., 498 F.2d 821 (9th Cir. 1974)

KOELSCH, J.

Lothar Motschenbacher appeals from the district court's order granting summary judgment in favor of defendants in his suit seeking injunctive relief and damages for the alleged misappropriation of his name, likeness, personality, and endorsement in nationally televised advertising for Winston cigarettes. . . .

The "facts" on which the district court rendered summary judgment are substantially as follows: Plaintiff Motschenbacher is a professional driver of racing cars, internationally known and recognized in racing circles and by racing fans. He derives part of his income from manufacturers of commercial products who pay him for endorsing their products.

During the relevant time span, plaintiff has consistently "individualized" his cars to set them apart from those of other drivers and to make them more readily identifiable as his own. Since 1966, each of his cars has displayed a distinctive narrow white pinstripe appearing on no other car. This decoration has adorned the leading edges of the cars' bodies, which have uniformly been solid red. In addition, the white background for his racing number "11" has always been oval, in contrast to the circular backgrounds of all other cars.

In 1970, defendants, R.J. Reynolds Tobacco Company and William Esty Company, produced and caused to be televised a commercial which utilized a "stock" color photograph depicting several racing cars on a racetrack. Plaintiff's car appears in the foreground, and although plaintiff is the driver, his facial features are not visible.

In producing the commercial, defendants altered the photograph: they changed the numbers on all racing cars depicted, transforming plain-

tiff's number "11" into "71"; they "attached" a wing-like device known as a "spoiler" to plaintiff's car; they added the word "Winston," the name of their product, to that spoiler and removed advertisements for other products from the spoilers of other cars. However, they made no other changes, and the white pinstriping, the oval medallion, and the red color of plaintiff's car were retained. They then made a motion picture from the altered photograph, adding a series of comic strip-type "balloons" containing written messages of an advertising nature; one such balloon message, appearing to emanate from plaintiff, was: "Did you know that Winston tastes good, like a cigarette should?" They also added a sound track consisting in part of voices coordinated with, and echoing, the written messages. The commercial was subsequently broadcast nationally on network television and in color.

Several of plaintiff's affiants who had seen the commercial on television had immediately recognized plaintiff's car and had inferred that it was sponsored by Winston cigarettes.

On these facts the district court, characterizing plaintiff's action as one "for damages for invasion of privacy," granted summary judgment for defendants, finding as a matter of law that

. . . [t]he driver of car No. 71 in the commercial (which was plaintiff's car No. 11 prior to said change of number and design) is anonymous: that is, (a) the person who is driving said car is unrecognizable and unidentified, and (b) a reasonable inference could not be drawn that he is, or could reasonably be understood to be, plaintiff, Lothar Motschenbacher, or any other driver or person. . . .

Since the Winston commercial was broadcast on television throughout the United States, our initial inquiry in determining the correct legal standards to be applied on the motion for summary judgment is directed at the proper choice of law. In a diversity case, a federal court must follow the substantive law of the state in which it sits. . . .

In California, as in the vast majority of jurisdictions, the invasion of an individual's right of privacy is an actionable tort. . . .

California courts have observed that "[t]he gist of the cause of action in a privacy case is not injury to the character or reputation, but a direct wrong of a personal character resulting in injury to the feelings without regard to any effect which the publication may have on the property, business, pecuniary interest, or the standing of the individual in the community." . . .

It is true that the injury suffered from an appropriation of the attributes of one's identity may be "mental and subjective"—in the nature of humiliation, embarrassment, and outrage. . . . However, where the identity appropriated has a commercial value, the injury may be largely, or even wholly of an economic or material nature. Such is the nature of the injury alleged by plaintiff. . . .

We turn now to the question of "identifiability." Clearly, if the district court correctly determined as a matter of law that plaintiff is not identifiable in the commercial, then in no sense has plaintiff's identity been misappropriated nor his interest violated.

Having viewed a film of the commercial, we agree with the district court that the "likeness" of plaintiff is itself unrecognizable; however, the court's further conclusion of law to the effect that the driver is not identifiable as plaintiff is erroneous in that it wholly fails to attribute proper significance to the distinctive decoration appearing on the car. As pointed out earlier, these markings were not only peculiar to the plaintiff's cars but they caused some persons to think the car in question was plaintiff's and to infer that the person driving the car was the plaintiff.

Defendant's reliance on *Branson* v. *Fawcett Publications, Inc.*, 124 F. Supp. 429 (E.D. Ill. 1954), is misplaced. In *Branson*, a part-time racing driver brought suit for invasion of privacy when a photograph of his overturned racing car was printed in a magazine without his consent. In ruling that "the photograph . . . does not identify the plaintiff to the public or any member thereof," 124 F. Supp. at 433, the court said:

> [T]he automobile is pointed upward in the air and the picture shows primarily the bottom of the racer. The backdrop of the picture is not distinguishable. No likeness, face, image, form or silhouette of the plaintiff or of any person is shown. From all that appears from the picture itself, there is no one in the car. Moreover, no identifying marks or numbers on the car appear. . . . Plaintiff does not even assert

that the car he was driving was the same color as that which appears in the colored reproduction. 124 F. Supp. at 432.

But in this case, the car under consideration clearly has a driver and displays several uniquely distinguishing features.

The judgment is vacated and the cause is remanded for further proceedings.

10.30 Privacy/Publicity Versus the First Amendment

First Amendment freedoms of speech and press restrict a state's ability to enforce publicity and privacy rights that interfere with legitimate reporting of the news and matters of public interest. This leaves open for dispute just what is a legitimate news story, as opposed to a charade of some sort that attempts to cloak itself with First Amendment protections.

In the preceding section, the court in the dispute between Clint Eastwood and the *National Enquirer* brushed aside the *Enquirer*'s attempts to assert First Amendment protections. The court assumed, for purposes of the appeal, that the *Enquirer*'s story was concocted without factual basis and thus was not news.

The reasoning of the court in *Eastwood* should be compared with the several aspects of the "news" function explored in this section. The cases range widely. In *Bernstein v. NBC* and *Leopold v. Levin*, people were thrust into the public light, voluntarily or not, who years later sought to prevent further publication about their earlier exploits. Another situation (*Hicks v. Casablanca Records*) concerns the fictionalized treatment of a person's life or activities (see also Section 10.50 for discussion of this issue with respect to intentional falsification and libel). Is there free license to alter the facts about real lives for the purposes of dramatic impact? As cases in this section and in Section 10.50 suggest, the answer is far from clear.

Other cases considered here involve a television station filming a performer's entire act (Zacchini, the human cannonball) and reporting it as news *(Zacchini v. Scripps-Howard)*; a magazine taking a photo of a celebrity, used in an earlier news feature, and reprinting the photo in an advertisement for the magazine *(Namath v. Sports Illustrated)*; and a comedian entering the political arena (as a joke?), only to find an enterprising company has printed political posters of the comedian and is selling them *(Paulsen v. Personality Posters, Inc.)*.

Definitions of news, public interest, and public figures have no easy, quick, or finite resolutions, but definitions must be made. Where there is money to be made through news and public interest stories (and other trappings), people will attempt to package and disseminate; and the subjects of the "reporting" will protest.

Bernstein v. National Broadcasting Co., 129 F. Supp. 817 (D.C. 1955)

KEECH, J.

. . . Both actions arise from the same undisputed facts. In 1919 plaintiff, Charles S. Bernstein was convicted of bank robbery in Minnesota and sentenced to imprisonment for forty years. After serving nine years, he was paroled and pardoned. In 1933 in the District of Columbia, plaintiff under the name Charles Harris, was tried and convicted of first-degree murder and sentenced to death by electrocution. In 1934 the conviction was affirmed, *Harris v. U.S.* 63 App.D.C. 232, 71 F.2d 532, and a petition for certiorari denied by the Supreme Court, 293 U.S. 581, 55 S.Ct. 94, 79 L.Ed. 678. Through the efforts of a number of interested persons and committees working in plaintiff's behalf, and partly as the result of the work of Martha Strayer, a reporter on the *Washington Daily News*, in 1935 the death sentence was commuted to life imprisonment. In 1940, after plaintiff had served five years at various federal institutions, he received a conditional release from his life sentence, and in 1945 a Presidential pardon.

Plaintiff alleges that, "Commencing in 1940, and thereafter, . . . [he] was no longer in the public eye; . . . lived an exemplary, virtuous, honorable, righteous, quiet and private life, free from the prying curiosity which accompanies either fame or notoriety; . . . shunned and avoided notoriety and publicity; . . . never exhibited or sought to exploit his name, personality or the incidents of his past life for money, profit, or commercial gain; . . . assumed a place in society, knew many people and made many friends who were not aware of the incidents of his earlier life."

Plaintiff's deposition shows that from the time of the trial until 1940, when plaintiff secured conditional release, his story was given much publicity by the newspapers and others working on his behalf. Subsequent to his release in 1940, he obtained government employment in the District of Columbia, holding various positions and attaining Civil Service Grade CAF-11. In 1945, this employment ended, and thereafter, from 1945 to 1951, he lived in Front Royal, Virginia, operating a "resort lodge." In February 1953, some time after the filing of these actions, plaintiff again secured government employment in the District, rooming in Washington but still maintaining his family home in Front Royal, Virginia.

In 1936 or 1937 a detective story magazine carried an article on plaintiff's case. In 1948 a radio program told plaintiff's story, using Martha Strayer's name, in a fictionalized version, but so similar to the facts that plaintiff and several others identified the story as his.

On January 18, 1952, the defendant NBC telecast "live" over 39 stations in its network a television program prepared by Prockter Television Enterprises, Inc., sponsored by American Cigarette & Cigar Company and advertising Pall Mall cigarettes, entitled "The Big Story." This program, classified by the Federal Communications Commission as a network commercial entertainment program, was a fictionalized dramatization based on the plaintiff's conviction and pardon, and lauding the efforts of Miss Strayer, the Daily News reporter, toward securing commutation of plaintiff's sentence. The same program was telecast over twelve other NBC network stations by means of a kineoscope recording on January 29, 31, February 1, 2, 3, and 8, 1952. The only true names used were those of Martha Strayer, the *Washington Daily News*, the President of the United States, and the District of Columbia. Over forty-three of the NBC stations telecasting "The Big Story," it was announced a week prior to the telecast here involved, that the following week's program would tell the true story of how Martha Strayer fought to save the life of an innocent man convicted of murder. On January 7, 1952, NBC issued a press release concerning the program. Neither the television announcement nor press release mentioned plaintiff's name.

Plaintiff alleges that, although his true name was not used in the telecast, the actor who portrayed him resembled him physically and plaintiff's words and actions were reproduced both visually and aurally, creating a portrayal of plaintiff recognizable to him and to his friends and acquaintances, and clearly identifying plaintiff in the public mind. . . .

Plaintiff alleges that the telecast of this program constituted "a willful and malicious invasion of . . . [his] right of privacy as recognized by the laws of New York, Ohio, Illinois, California, Connecticut, Massachusetts, Rhode Island, Pennsylvania, Delaware, Maryland, Virginia, Wisconsin, Alabama, Tennessee, Iowa, Minnesota, Washington, Texas, Michigan, Missouri, Florida, Utah, Georgia, West Virginia, Kentucky, Nebraska, New Jersey, and Indiana," and the District of Columbia. . . .

Defendant in its motion for summary judgment contends that neither of the complaints states a cause of action upon which relief may be granted. . . .

The telecast here involved was one of a series of similar dramatizations, commending the accomplishments of newspaper reporters in bringing criminals to justice or in securing the release of innocent persons convicted of crime. In each of the programs the actual name of the reporter and his paper were used, but the names of other persons portrayed were changed, and the incidents were fictionalized for dramatic effect.

On this particular program, the man convicted of crime was called Dave Crouch and the murdered man Woody Benson. Benson, a gambler running a game in Alexandria, was shot as he walked along the sidewalk in the District of Columbia, by a man riding in a car. Crouch was arrested while asleep on a bench in a bus terminal in Washington. He was inadequately defended at his trial by a Mr. Kendall, an inexperienced court-assigned counsel, who did not call as an alibi witness Crouch's "common-law wife," Helen Slezak, with whom Crouch had spent the day of the murder in New York. Mr. Kendall showed lack of confidence in the success of the defense, in view of Crouch's previous conviction in Minnesota of which he was innocent and for which he had been pardoned. At the trial, the court admitted a detective's statement as to Crouch's Minnesota conviction, omitting any reference to the pardon. Kendall did not call Helen as a witness, on the ground that the "blue ribbon jury," "all respectable property owners," might be prejudiced against a common-law wife, although Dave explained to him that were not legally married because Helen's husband would not give her a divorce. Crouch was convicted on the testimony of a Mrs. Hedlund, a garrulous middle-aged woman, who positively identified him as the murderer whom she had seen, as he fired the shot, when she looked from the window of her upstairs apartment. After conviction, Crouch was pictured as desperately playing solitaire in his cell and checking off on a calendar the days leading up to his execution, whenever Miss Strayer called upon him there.

Martha Strayer was portrayed as interesting a Mr. Burbage, an attorney of thirty-five years' experience in the Department of Justice, in attempting to have Crouch's sentence commuted, and herself discovering that Mrs. Hedlund could not have seen the murderer from her window, which would have been obscured at the time of the crime by leafed-out branches of a tree. Miss Strayer's newspaper stories were credited with bringing into her office a Mrs. Watson, a theretofore unknown eyewitness, who had clearly seen the crime and testified that the murderer was not Dave Crouch. The program represented Miss Strayer as the person whose faith in the innocence of Crouch and investigations and newspaper articles arousing public opinion resulted in saving Crouch the very day before the execution. In the final scene of the program, Crouch was shown with Mr. Burbage thanking Miss Strayer in her office, following his release from "Lewisburg Prison."

The record in the actual criminal case and the pleadings and deposition of plaintiff in this case reveal: The plaintiff, as Charles Harris, was convicted of first-degree murder in connection with the shooting of Milton White Henry, a Washington gambler, on April 21, 1932, in the District of Columbia. About 6 a.m., while Henry, in his car, was stopped behind a milk wagon in the narrow street in front of his apartment, he was killed by a man who alighted from a Hudson automobile, shot him, and then jumped on the running board of the Hudson, which sped away. Harris was arrested in Philadelphia, while looking in a store window, accompanied by his "wife." At the trial, he was identified as the murderer by a Mr. Rhodes, an attorney with the Federal Trade Commission, who testified that he had seen Harris at the time of the shooting from the window of his apartment and heard Harris tell the driver of the Hudson to "keep moving" and "step on it." Mr. Rhodes testified that the trees in front of his apartment were in bud at the time and "might have been forming leaves," but that he had an unobstructed view of the shooting. The driver of a laundry truck testified that on the day before the crime he had passed by the scene of the murder on three different delivery trips and, five different times, had seen the same car, identified as that driven by the men who committed the murder, with the same two men in it, and that the defendant was one of them.

At the trial Harris was represented by two attorneys of his own selection, one of whom had eight years' experience in the District of Columbia and a largely criminal practice. Plaintiff did not take the stand in his own behalf, but defense witnesses testified that he was in New York at the crucial time. The woman with whom Harris was living in New York was not called as a witness because counsel "didn't want to besmirch her character." Harris and the woman were not legally married because he had a living wife, and the woman's name did not in any way resemble "Helen Slezak." On appeal, Harris was represented by different counsel, one of whom, Mr. Burkinshaw, had had about two or three years' experience with the Department of Justice.

After affirmance of the conviction, new evidence was submitted to the Department of Justice in the form of affidavits from the Department of Agriculture and the Weather Bureau that the trees in front of Mr. Rhodes' apartment would have been fully leafed out at the time of the crime and the testimony of an eyewitness who came forward after the trial, a lady who, after viewing Harris at the Jail, stated he was not the man who did the shooting. Miss Strayer did interview Harris at the Jail on a number of occasions and discussed his case with him, but always in the Superintendent's office or in the "rotunda," not in Harris' cell. Harris did not play solitaire in his cell, as prisoners were not permitted to have cards. He spent a great deal of time reading history, philosophy, and psychology. He did not cross the days off a calendar prior to the execution date, which was postponed eight times by the court. The death sentence was stayed by warrant of reprieve signed by the President four days before the date fixed for electrocution. During the two years he was confined in the "death row" at the District Jail awaiting execution, plaintiff did undergo great mental and emotional strain. The plaintiff, after his release from Leavenworth, went to see Miss Strayer in her office to thank her for her part in securing his release, but he is not sure whether his attorney accompanied him.

Plaintiff alleges that the actor who portrayed Dave Crouch resembled him physically, as he appeared at the time of his trial. For the purpose of this motion, the court will assume that this resemblance exists.

Thus, the points of similarity between the plaintiff's life and the television story of Dave Crouch are reduced to: a conviction in the District of Columbia of first-degree murder in connection with the shooting of a gambler in Washington; failure to call a "common-law wife" as an alibi witness; Miss Strayer's effective interest in proving the defendant's innocence; securing of other counsel after the trial; emotional turmoil of the convicted man while awaiting execution; additional evidence as to the leaves in front of an eyewitness' apartment window; another eyewitness coming forward, after affirmance of the conviction, to state that defendant was not the murderer; thanking of Miss Strayer by the defendant after his release; and a physical resemblance between the actor and the plaintiff as he was twenty years ago.

Plaintiff concedes that there was nothing defamatory of him in the telecast and bases his entire complaint on the alleged invasion of his privacy. . . .

Counsel further concedes that plaintiff's conviction and commutation of sentence, when they occurred, were matters in the public domain, and that a dramatization at that time based on the facts and containing nothing defamatory, similar to the program in question would not have been an invasion of plaintiff's privacy. It is contended, however, that by reason of the lapse of time since plaintiff's release in 1940 and the non-public character of his activities since that date, his life has regained its private character. . . .

As to . . . whether a public person may, by the passage of time in private life, re-acquire a right of privacy as to his past life, there is a divergence of opinion.

The Restatement of the Law of Torts, § 867, summarizes the right of privacy very generally, stating: "A person who unreasonably and seriously interferes with another's interest in not having his affairs known to others or his likeness exhibited to the public is liable to the other."

The Restatement then notes that the protection accorded one's privacy is relative to the custom of the time and place and to the habits and occupation of the plaintiff, and that one must expect the ordinary incidents of community life of which he is a part. It points out that public figures must pay the price of unwelcome publicity and that those who unwillingly come into the public eye in connection with a criminal prosecution, innocent or guilty, are objects of legitimate public interest during a period of time after their conduct or misfortune has brought them to the public attention, and that "until they have reverted to the lawful and unexciting life led by the great bulk of the community, they are subject to the privilege which publishers have to satisfy the

curiosity of the public as to their leaders, heroes, villains and victims."

Several cases have been cited to the court which have dealt with the question whether time brings protection to a former public figure. Two in particular, which reach opposite conclusions, are relevant to the problem. In *Sidis v. F. R. Pub. Corp.*, 2 Cir., 113 F.2d 806, 809, 138 A.L.R. 15, certiorari denied, 1940, 311 U.S. 711, 61 S.Ct. 393, 85 L.Ed. 462, a former child prodigy, who had sought oblivion for many years, loathing public attention, claimed an invasion of his right of privacy by an unvarnished factual account in *The New Yorker* magazine of his life (using his name), including the many years which he had lived out of the public eye and touching on many personal details. It was there held by the federal court sitting in New York (a jurisdiction which has rejected the right of privacy as unrecognized at common law and has strictly interpreted its statute affording limited protection) that, although the plaintiff had dropped out of sight after 1910, "his subsequent history, containing as it did the answer to the question of whether or not he had fulfilled his early promise, was still a matter of public concern," and that *The New Yorker* sketch of the life of such an unusual personality possessed considerable popular news interest. . . .

In *Melvin v. Reid*, 1931, 112 Cal.App. 285, 297 P. 91, 93, a reformed prostitute who had been tried and acquitted on a murder charge, sued for invasion of her privacy by a motion picture based on the facts of her past life, disclosing her former occupation, and using her true maiden name. After stating that the right of privacy does not exist as to public persons, in the dissemination of news and news events, in the discussion of events of the life of a person in whom the public has a rightful interest, or where the information would be of public benefit, and concluding that the mere use in the motion picture of incidents from the life of plaintiff, taken from the public records, was not actionable, the court said:

One of the major objectives of society as it is now constituted, and of the administration of our penal system, is the rehabilitation of the fallen and the reformation of the criminal. Under these theories of sociology, it is our object to lift up and sustain the unfortunate rather than tear him down. Where a person has by his own efforts rehabilitated himself, we, as right-thinking members of society, should permit him to continue in the path of rectitude rather than throw him back into a life of shame or crime. Even the thief on the cross was permitted to repent during the hours of his final agony.

We believe that the publication by respondents of the unsavory incidents in the past life of appellant after she had reformed, *coupled with her true name*, was not justified by any standard of morals or ethics known to us, and was a direct invasion of her inalienable right guaranteed to her by our [California] Constitution, to pursue and obtain happiness. (Emphasis supplied.)

It should be noted that in each of these cases the complainant was identified by name in the publication by defendant, as the plaintiff in this case was not in the telecast. . . . This court agrees that we are not so uncivilized that the law permits, in the name of public interest, the unlimited and unwarranted revival by publication of a rehabilitated wrongdoer's past mistakes in such a manner as to identify him in his private setting with the old crime and hold him up to public scorn. Persons formerly public, however, cannot be protected against disclosure and re-disclosure of known facts through the reading of old newspaper accounts and other publications, oral repetition of facts by those familiar with them, or reprinting of known facts of general interest, in a reasonable manner and for a legitimate purpose. . . .

Public interest must be balanced against the individual's rights. Though fairness and decency dictate that some boundary be fixed beyond which persons may not go in pointing the finger of shame at those who have erred and repented, reasonable freedom of speech and press must be accorded and the fact of social intercourse must be recognized. Public identification of the present person with past facts, however, would constitute a new disclosure and, if unwarranted, would infringe upon an existing privacy. Thus, it would appear that the protection which time may bring to a formerly public figure is not against repetition of the facts which are already public property, but against unreasonable public identification of him in his present setting with the earlier incident.

Determination of this question is not, how-ever, essential to disposition of the present motion. Assuming *arguendo* that at the time of the telecast plaintiff had regained a private status carrying with it legal protection from republication of the facts of his past life, the complaints, as supplemented by plaintiff's deposition and the various admissions, stipulations, and answers to interrogatories by the respective parties, do not state a valid cause of action. . . .

In the two jurisdictions which might be deemed the place of plaintiff's injury and therefore held to govern his right of action, are Virginia and the District of Columbia.

The Virginia Code, 1950 ed., Vol. 2, provides:

§ 8–650. Unauthorized use of the name or picture of any person. A person, firm, or corporation that knowingly uses for advertising purposes, or for the purposes of trade, the name, portrait, or picture of any person resident in the State, without having first obtained the written consent of such person, or if dead, of his surviving consort, or if none, his next of kin, or, if a minor, of his or her parent or guardian, as well as that of such minor, shall be deemed guilty of a misdemeanor and be fined not less than fifty nor more than one thousand dollars. Any person whose name, portrait, or picture is used within this State for advertising purposes or for the purposes of trade, without such written consent first obtained or the surviving consort or next of kin, as the case may be, may maintain a suit in equity against the person, firm, or corporation so using such person's name, portrait, or picture to prevent and restrain the use thereof; and may also sue and recover damages for any injuries sustained by reason of such use. And if the defendant shall have knowingly used such person's name, portrait, or picture in such manner as is forbidden or declared to be unlawful by this chapter, the jury, in its discretion, may award exemplary damages. (Code 1919, § 5782.)

No reported Virginia cases interpreting this statute have been cited to the court, nor has the court found any. It is apparent from a reading of § 8–650 that the right of action accorded is limited. The statute is modeled on the New York law. . . .

Suffice it to say, the New York statute has been given a strict construction. Publication of "biographical narratives of a man's life when it is of legitimate public interest, and "travel stories, stories of distant places, tales of historic personages and events, the reproduction of items of past news, and surveys of social conditions' " are generally considered beyond the purview of the statute. This principle has been extended to the newsreel, the radio, and television.

It is patent that the television program here involved does not fall within the language or purpose of § 8–650 of the Virginia Code.

Whether a right of action for invasion of privacy exists in the District of Columbia has not been authoritatively determined. . . . Judge Pine, . . . in *Elmhurst v. Shoreham Hotel, D.C.* D.C.1945, 58 F. Supp. 484, held that the tort of invasion of the right of privacy was unknown at common law and therefore could not be recognized in the District of Columbia, by reason of § 49–301 of the District of Columbia Code, 1951 Ed., 31 Stat. 1189, which continued in effect in the District the common law, both civil and criminal, in force in Maryland in 1801, except insofar as it is inconsistent with or replaced by subsequent legislation of Congress. The Court of Appeals affirmed the Elmhurst decision . . . but that Court specifically left undecided whether an action for invasion of privacy can be maintained in the District of Columbia. . . .

Whether the right to protection of one's privacy be viewed as stemming from natural law, as a constitutional right, or as a right which was afforded protection under the common law, though not by name, § 49–301 of the District Code does not preclude recognition in the District of Columbia of a common-law action for invasion of privacy.

What are the elements of such a common law action? Invasion of privacy has been summarized in the exhaustive annotation appearing at 138 A.L.R. 22, at 25 (supplemented at 168 A.L.R. 446 and 14 A.L.R.2d 750) as:

> The *unwarranted* appropriation or exploitation of one's personality, the publicising of one's private affairs with which the public has no *legitimate* concern, or the *wrongful* intrusion into one's private activities, in such manner as to outrage or cause mental suffering, shame, or humiliation to a person of ordinary sensibilities. (Emphasis supplied.)

Under this definition, which embodies the minimum requirements of the many cases there noted, the essential elements of an action for invasion of privacy would be: (1) private affairs in which the public has no legitimate concern; (2) publication of such affairs; (3) unwarranted publication, that is, absence of any waiver or privilege authorizing it; and (4) publication such as would cause mental suffering, shame, or humiliation to a person of ordinary sensibilities. As to the first element, the "private" affairs should be at least currently unknown to the public; and as to the second element, publication would necessarily include identification of the facts disclosed with the complainant. The third element, a mixed question of fact and law, and the fourth element, a fact question for the jury, need not be reached if either of the first two elements is not present.

On the undisputed facts disclosed by the various pleadings and admissions before the court on this motion, it is clear that the first two essential elements of a cause of action are lacking in the case at bar.

(1) The plaintiff's affairs were not private and were known to the public. His case had been given considerable publicity from the time of his trial in 1932 until his conditional release from imprisonment in 1940. . . .

(2) The admitted facts show there was no publication by defendant of the program as the plaintiff's prior history. Not only was there no identification of plaintiff by name in either the telecast or defendant's advertisements thereof, but he was doubly insulated from identification by designation of the television character as "Dave Crouch" and his own trial as "Charles Harris." Except to one already familiar with the facts or one who had stumbled on the reported court decision or the old newspaper items, there was nothing to link Charles Harris with any Charles Bernstein, much less plaintiff. To one who viewed the telecast not already aware of plaintiff's past or Miss Strayer's connection with him, the only link between Dave Crouch and Charles S. Bernstein of Front Royal, Virginia, and the District of Columbia was the alleged physical resemblance of the actor to the Charles Bernstein of *twenty years before*. This is too tenuous a thread on which to permit a jury to hang identification, with consequent liability for invasion of privacy.

Plaintiff argues there were three categories of

people as to whom there was identification: first, those who knew about the incidents of plaintiff's past life; second, those who remembered the newspaper articles twenty years before and were able to connect them with the broadcast; and third, those who did not know of Mr. Bernstein's past life but, as the result of the telecast, learned about it "because they were told by other people."

As to persons who already knew the facts of plaintiff's life there was no invasion of plaintiff's privacy by defendant. Although the telecast may have revived their memories, it revealed nothing they did not already know. The gist of an action for invasion of privacy is a wrongful disclosure *by the defendant*. The identification of plaintiff to viewers of the telecast was not by act of the defendant, but by use of their own thought processes. If these people were so thoughtless as to harass plaintiff with calls, as he contends, such harassment was the product of their own deduction and lack of tact and consideration for plaintiff. Persons who recalled the newspaper articles and connected them with plaintiff are indistinguishable from the first group, for the identification to them was through their own mental operations.

As to the third category, those who did not know of Mr. Bernstein's past life but, as the result of the telecast, learned about it "because they were told by other people," counsel for plaintiff very frankly admitted, "We are right in the open spaces." He cited in support of his position a number of cases holding that the author of a defamation is responsible for its repetition by another if the defamation is uttered or published under such circumstances as to time, place, and condition that a repetition or secondary publication is the natural and probable consequence of the original defamation, and for the damage resulting therefrom. The rule varies in different jurisdictions. . . .

But in defamation, there can, of course, be no repetition of a defamatory statement unless the statement is first made. Hence, none of the cited cases deal with an attempt to remedy the absence of proof of publication by defendant, an essential element, by proof of repetition of the statement by third persons. Similarly, in invasion of privacy, where defendant has published facts in such a way that there has been no disclosure to persons not already aware of them, proof of disclosure or identification by third persons to others who lacked prior knowledge cannot be used as a substitute for proof of original disclosure by defendant. . . .

(3) Plaintiff argues that privilege as to one publication or consent to disclosure for one purpose does not constitute privilege or waiver of privacy as to all publications, citing a number of cases, and therefore the fact that the public records were privileged or that plaintiff may have approved the newspaper campaign on his behalf from 1934 to 1940 and not objected to the magazine article of 1936 or 1937 or the radio program of 1948, did not authorize the telecast. Plaintiff further argues that prior wrongful publications cannot make a further wrongful publication legal.

Both general statements are correct. . . .

Privilege or waiver as to a prior disclosure is relevant, therefore, insofar as it relates to the issue whether there was a limited disclosure for a particular purpose or whether the facts became public property. The same is true of any prior disclosure which was not consented to and not privileged. Certain affairs of the individual are inherently private, and wrongful publication of them could not authorize subsequent publicity. In the final analysis, whether disclosed facts are to be held public property depends upon a weighing of all the factors in favor of the free circulation of information against the individual's desire to avoid notoriety. . . . Plaintiff, having conceded that the story of his conviction and pardon were public property at the time they occurred, argues that since the matter had lain dormant from 1940 until 1952, a period of twelve years, it had become "stale news." In view of the radio publication in 1948, plaintiff's affairs had, on his own admission, been out of the public eye only since 1948 or for four years preceding the defendant's telecast. Plaintiff's counsel did not attempt to draw a line as to when matters of current interest become "stale news." Although news value is one of the bases for the privilege to publish, this court prefers the broader test of "public or general interest," advocated by Warren and Brandeis. . . . This court holds, as a matter of law, that a criminal proceeding widely publicized for a period of at least eight years and containing elements of decided popular appeal does not lose its general public interest in a period of four years or even twelve years; . . . hence, republication in a reasonable manner was privileged. . . .

The program of January 18, 1952, although sponsored commercially, was one of general interest. It did not single out plaintiff to expose him to public scorn, but was one of a series of television plays devoted to retelling in fictionalized form the stories of newspaper reporters who had done excellent work in promoting justice. . . . "The Big Story" program was of current public value in demonstrating how an alert reporter, who has an interest in seeing the right prevail, may help an innocent man escape the unhappy consequences of a wrongful conviction, and perhaps might inspire some other reporter to greater efforts or some young person to embrace a newspaper career. There was a careful and honest attempt to conceal the identity of all persons save the reporter, and the facts of the case were sufficiently changed to avoid duplication of the actual proceeding. That the concealment of plaintiff's identity was accomplished is attested by plaintiff's own allegations showing that only those who knew the story recognized it. The convicted man was shown as an entirely sympathetic character, innocent, wrongfully accused, inadequately defended, convicted on flimsy evidence, and saved from a gross miscarriage of justice in the nick of time. The picture painted was more favorable than the facts of record. If plaintiff had wished to publicize his innocence to those who knew of his conviction but had never heard of his pardon, he could have chosen no more effective means than a popular nation-wide television network program.

If anyone's sensibilities should have been wounded by the play, it was the judge, the detectives, and the trial counsel, whose parts were given such unsympathetic treatment as to be defamatory, had there been identification. The whole atmosphere of the trial, as portrayed in the telecast, was not such as to inspire viewers with confidence in the administration of justice in the District of Columbia. . . .

The court holds, as a matter of law, that the facts in this case present no actionable invasion of plaintiff's privacy by defendant. . . .

Leopold v. Levin, 259 N.E.2d 250 (Ill. 1970)

WARD, J.

Nathan F. Leopold, Jr., the plaintiff, brought an action in the circuit court of Cook County, which was in the nature of a suit alleging a violation of the right of privacy. The defendants included: the author, publishers and several local distributors of a novel and a play, entitled *Compulsion*, and the producer, distributor and Chicago area exhibitors of a related motion picture of the same name. . . .

In 1924, Richard Loeb, who is deceased, and Nathan F. Leopold, Jr., the plaintiff, pleaded guilty to the murder and kidnapping for ransom of a 14-year-old boy, Bobby Franks. Following a presentence proceeding, each was given consecutive prison sentences of life and 99 years. The luridness of the crime, the background of the defendants, their representation by the most prominent criminal advocate of the day, the "trial," and its denouement attracted international notoriety. Public interest in the crime and its principals did not wane with the passage of time and the case became an historical *cause célèbre*.

The novel *Compulsion* was first published in hardcover in October 1956. The author was the defendant Meyer Levin, who had been a fellow student of Loeb and Leopold and who had served as a reporter for a Chicago newspaper at the time of the crime. All concerned in this appeal agree that the basic framework of the novel, as well as of the subsequently produced movie, was factually provided by the kidnapping and murder of Bobby Franks, the events leading to the apprehension of Leopold and Loeb, and their prosecution. However, as the author himself, in the foreword of the book, wrote: "Though the action is taken from reality, it must be recognized that thoughts and emotions described in the characters come from within the author, as he imagines them to belong to the personages in the case he has chosen." And, "I follow known events. Some scenes are, however, total interpolations, and some of my personages have no correspondence to persons in the case in question. This will be recognized as the method of the historical novel. I suppose *Compulsion* may be called a contemporary historical novel or a documentary novel, as distinguished from a *roman à clef*. [That is, a novel drawing upon actual occurrences or real persons under the guise of fiction."]

Neither the name of Loeb or Leopold appear in the foreword, and fictitious names are used in the novel itself for all persons who may have been involved in the case. However, the names of Loeb and the plaintiff were used in advertising the novel. Illustrative of this, on the paper jacket to the hardcover edition it was said: "This book is a novel suggested by what is possibly the most famous and certainly one of the most shocking crimes ever committed in America—the Leopold-Loeb murder case." On the page preceding the title page of the paperback edition of *Compulsion*, which was first published in 1958, the following appeared: "In his novel based upon the Leopold-Loeb case, Meyer Levin seeks to discover the psychological motivation behind this monstrous deed." The back cover of the paperback noted that " 'Compulsion' is a spellbinding fictionalized account of one of the most famous and shocking crimes of our age—the Leopold-Loeb murder case."

The case had been of interest to other authors. For example, in 1957, a novel, *Nothing But the Night*, by James Yaffe was published. It bore a fictionalized resemblance to the Leopold-Loeb case, but had a different locale and no reference was apparently made in the advertising of it to the actual case. In the same year a factual account of the life and crimes of Leopold and Loeb by Maureen McKerman, entitled, *The Amazing Crime and Trial of Leopold and Loeb* was published and widely advertised. In 1957, too, an account of the kidnapping, murder and prosecution written by the plaintiff for compensation appeared in serialized form for several weeks in a Chicago newspaper. Story captions included: "Leopold Tells Own Story—How It Felt To Be A Killer"; "Leopold Arrested; Time For Him To Use Alibi"; "Darrow Makes Masterful Plea For Understanding." He was granted parole in 1958 and that year his autobiographical story, *Life Plus 99 Years*, which included a description of his detec-

tion and prosecution and their personal consequences, was published. It was given extensive publicity.

The motion picture *Compulsion* was released in April 1959. Several major characters in the film, including the one corresponding to the appellant, were styled to resemble actual persons in the case. Fictitious names were used, though, and no photographs of the appellant or any other person connected with the case appeared in the movie or in any material used to promote the film. The promotional material did refer to the crime. In a brochure prepared for movie exhibitors, entitled "Vital Statistics," 20th century-Fox Film Corporation, a defendant, outlined the likenesses and differences between the movie and the actual events, and declared: "It should be made clear emphatically that *Compulsion* is not an effort to reproduce the crime of Leopold and Loeb, nor their trial. The screenplay was taken from a recognized work of fiction 'suggested' by the Leopold-Loeb case, but neither the author of the book nor the producer of the film has attempted anything but to tell a dramatic story. . . . The picture is in no way a documentary and its makers have attempted only to translate the book into terms of good dramaturgy." One motion picture exhibitor, the Woods Theatre in Chicago, owned by a defendant here, in advertising the movie used a photographic enlargement of the back cover of the paperback book edition of *Compulsion* in which the plaintiff's name was used, as has been described. It displayed also a blow-up or enlargement of portions of reviews given the movie in which the plaintiff's name had been mentioned. His name also was introduced during personal, radio and television interviews in various cities by certain of the defendants in the course of their promotion of the motion picture.

The plaintiff acknowledges that a documentary account of the Leopold-Loeb case would be a constitutionally protected expression, since the subject events are matters of public record. Also constitutionally protected, the plaintiff continues, would be a completely fictional work inspired by the case if matters such as the locale would be changed and if there would be no promotional identification with the plaintiff. Leopold's claim is that the constitutional assurances of free speech and press do not permit an invasion of his privacy through the exploitation of his name, likeness and personality for commercial gain in "knowingly fictionalized accounts" of his private life and through the appropriation of his name and likeness in the advertising materials. Denying him redress would deprive him, he argues, of his right to pursue and obtain happiness guaranteed by section 1 of article II of the constitution of Illinois, S.H.A. . . .

We agree that there should be recognition of a right of privacy, a right many years ago described in a limited fashion by Judge Cooley with utter simplicity as the right "to be let alone." Privacy is one of the sensitive and necessary human values and undeniably there are circumstances under which it should enjoy the protection of law. However, we must hold here that the plaintiff did not have a legally protected right of privacy. Considerations which in our judgment require this conclusion include: the liberty of expression constitutionally assured in a matter of public interest, as the one here; the enduring public attention to the plaintiff's crime and prosecution, which remain an American *cause celèbre;* and the plaintiff's consequent and continuing status as a public figure.

It has been expressly recognized by the Supreme Court that books, as well as newspapers and magazines, are normally a form of expression protected by the first amendment and that their protection is not affected by the circumstances that the publications are sold for profit. . . . It is urged that motion pictures do not fall within the First Amendment's aegis because their production, distribution, and exhibition is a large-scale business conducted for private profit. We cannot agree. That books, newspapers, and magazines are published and sold for profit does not prevent them from being a form of expression whose liberty is safeguarded by the First Amendment. We fail to see why operation for profit should have any different effect in the case of motion pictures. . . . For the foregoing reasons, we conclude that expression by means of motion pictures is included within the free speech and free press guaranty of the First and Fourteenth Amendments.

In *Time, Inc. v. Hill,* the Supreme Court for the first time had occasion to consider directly the effect of the constitutional guarantees for speech and press upon the rights of privacy. There, as will be seen, the right of privacy when involved with the publication of a matter of public interest was viewed narrowly and cautiously by the court. That decisional attitude toward publication is consistent with other first amendment holdings of the court in recent years, especially in the areas of libel and obscenity, where the announced objective was to insure "uninhibited, robust and wide-open" discussion of legitimate public issues or to protect published materials unless they are "utterly without redeeming social value." . . .

It is of importance here, too, that the plaintiff became and remained a public figure because of his criminal conduct in 1924. No right of privacy attached to matters associated with his participation in that completely publicized crime. . . . The circumstances of the crime and the prosecution etched a deep public impression which the passing of time did not extinguish. A strong curiosity and social and news interest in the crime, the prosecution, and Leopold remained. . . . It is of some relevance, too, in this consideration, that the plaintiff himself certainly did not appear to seek retirement from public attention. The publication of the autobiographical story and other writings and his providing interviews unquestionably contributed to the continuing public interest in him and the crime. . . .

A carefully narrowed argument of the plaintiff appears to be that the defendants through "knowingly fictionalized accounts" caused the public to identify the plaintiff with inventions or fictionalized episodes in the book and motion picture which were so offensive and unwarranted as to "outrage the community's notions of decency." . . . However, the core of the novel and film and their dominating subjects were a part of the plaintiff's life which he had caused to be placed in public view. The novel and film were derived from the notorious crime, a matter of public record and interest, in which the plaintiff had been a central figure. Further, as the trial court appeared to do, we consider that the fictionalized aspects of the book and motion picture were reasonably comparable to, or conceivable from facts of record from which they were drawn, or minor in offensiveness when viewed in the light of such facts. *Sidis*, upon which the plaintiff bottomed this argument of outraging "the community's notions of decency," involved the publishing of a "profile" of a one-time prodigy. A magazine article disclosed his undistinguished achievement as an adult and described some of his eccentricities. The court held the publication proper but in a dictum observed: "Revelations may be so intimate and so unwarranted in view of the victim's position as to outrage the community's notions of decency." Even if one were to accept the validity of the dictum for the purpose of discussing it, the genesis of the fictionalized episodes in *Compulsion*, as we have observed, can be traced in a substantial way to the exposed conduct of Leopold. Argument that the community's notions of decency were outraged here must be regarded as fanciful.

The contention that a right of privacy was violated by an appropriation, without consent, of the plaintiff's name and likeness for the commercial gain of the defendants through their advertisements must also fail. . . . The reference to the plaintiff in the advertising material concerned the notorious crime to which he had pleaded guilty. His participation was a matter of public and, even, of historical record. That conduct was without benefit of privacy.

We consider that *Time, Inc. v. Hill*, 385 U.S. 374, 87 S.Ct. 534, 17 L.Ed.2d 456, to which reference has been made, does not support the plaintiff's positions. *Hill* and his family had been held in their home as hostages for 19 hours by escaped convicts. Their captors did not mistreat them in any way. After the incident Hill moved to another State and discouraged all attempts to keep his family in public view. A book and later a play partly drawn, it would appear, from the incident were published and *Life* magazine carried an article about the play. In the play the author had some members of the captive family subjected to violence and a daughter to verbal abuse. *Life's* article allegedly gave the false impression that the play did reflect what had happened to the Hill family. The Supreme Court held that the constitutional protections of free speech and press prevented Hill's recovering under the New York privacy statute because of this false report of a matter of public interest, unless upon remand of the case there was a showing that the magazine had published the report with knowledge of its falsity or in reckless disregard of the truth. It is clear that *Time, Inc.* involved a situation essentially dissimilar from the one here. The case involved what was claimed to be a false but purportedly factual account of the Hill incident. Here, the motion picture, play and novel, while "suggested" by the crime of the plaintiff, were evidently fictional and dramatized materials and they were not represented to be otherwise. They were substantially creative works of fiction and would not be subject to the "knowing or reckless falsity" or actual malice standards discussed in *Time, Inc. v. Hill*, where the court considered an untrue but supposedly factual magazine account. . . .

We conclude that the judgment of the circuit court of Cook County which vacated the summary judgment for the plaintiff on the issue of liability and granted summary judgment and judgment on the pleadings in favor of the defendants was proper. Accordingly, the judgment is affirmed. . . .

NOTES_____

1. The facts in *Wojtowicz v. Delacorte Press*, 403 N.Y.S.2d 218 (1978), grew out of a notorious Brooklyn bank robbery which originally was covered extensively in the newspapers and by a later feature in *Life Magazine*. The *Life* story ultimately became the matrix for the film *Dog Day Afternoon* and for books based on the screenplay. The opening scene of the movie announced the story as true and gave the date of the robbery and the fact that it had taken place in Brooklyn. However, while *Life* had mentioned the names of the wife and children of one of the robbers, the film did not use the real names of either the robbers or their relatives. The "wife," mentioned in *Life*, was a minor character in the film, and the children were mentioned only incidentally.

The court rejected the wife and children's claims of invasion of privacy. The court held that no rights of privacy in New York existed apart from Civil Rights Law, §§ 50 and 51, and since the plaintiffs' names and likenesses were not used, no causes of action existed.

(Reserved for further consideration were plaintiffs' claims for defamation.)

2. In *Meeropol v. Nizer*, 560 F.2d 1061 (2d Cir.

1977), the court reached the same result as in *Wojto-wicz*, above, rejecting a suit by the sons of Julius and Ethel Rosenberg, where the biography in question did not refer to the sons by their present names or provide a factual link to their adoptive family.

Hicks v. Casablanca Records, 464 F. Supp. 426 (S.D.N.Y. 1978)

[Agatha Christie's heirs sought to prevent the sale of a book and also the distribution of the film version of the book, both entitled *Agatha*, which were fictional accounts of Ms. Christie's activities during a well-publicized eleven-day disappearance in 1926. Both the book and film were clearly stated to be fiction, although based loosely on the true incident.

The court began its analysis by determining that New York recognizes a right of publicity (see the note at the end of the case report for discussion of this point). The court also determined that Ms. Christie's normal professional activities, in which her name was at all times used prominently in connection with her books and plays (and the film versions thereof), were sufficiently exploitive to create descendible rights. The court then considered whether Ms. Christie's right of publicity extended to protecting against fictionalized accounts of an episode in her life.]

PIERCE, J.

. . . Here, the Court is faced with the novel and rather complex question of "whether the right of publicity attaches where the name or likeness is used in connection with a book or movie?" The question is novel in view of the fact that more so than posters, bubble gum cards, or some other such "merchandise," books and movies are vehicles through which ideas and opinions are disseminated and, as such, have enjoyed certain constitutional protections, not generally accorded "merchandise." . . . [I]n search of guidance to resolve the question presented herein, the Court has looked to cases involving the right of privacy pursuant to sec. 51 of the New York Civil Rights Act (McKinney 1976). While the right of publicity is not statutory, nevertheless both the rights of privacy and publicity are intertwined due to the similarity between the nature of the interests

protected by each . . . [citing *Spahn v. Julian Messner, Inc.*, 23 A.D.2d 216] this Court finds that the same privileges and exemptions "engrafted" upon the privacy statute [i.e., matters of news, history, biography, and other factual subjects of public interest] are engrafted upon the right of publicity.

In addressing defendants' argument that the book *Agatha* is a biography protected under *Spahn*, this Court, while noting that the affidavit of the author of the book details her investigation with respect to the "facts" surrounding the disappearance, finds the book to be fiction, not biography. Indeed, defendant Ballantine Books' use of the word "novel" on the cover of the book, as well as the notable absence of any cited source or reference material therein, belie its contention that the book is a biography. Moreover, the only "facts" contained in the book appear to be the names of Mrs. Christie, her husband, her daughter, and Ms. Neely; and that Mrs. Christie disappeared for eleven days. The remainder is mainly conjecture, surmise, and fiction. Accordingly, the Court finds that the defendants cannot avail themselves of the biography privilege in connection with the book or movie. Further, since the book and the movie treat these few scant facts about the disappearance of Mrs. Christie as mere appendages to the main body of their fictional accounts, neither can be considered privileged as "fair comment" . . . or as "newsworthy" . . . or historical. . . .

Thus finding none of the *Spahn* privileges available to the defendants herein, the Court must next inquire as to whether the movie or the novel, as fictionalizations, are entitled to any constitutional protection. In so doing, it is noted that other courts, in addressing the scope of first amendment protections of speech, have engaged in a balancing test between society's interest in the speech for which protection is sought and the societal, commercial or governmental interest seeking to restrain such speech. . . . And unless there appears to be some countervailing legal or policy reason, courts have found the exercise of the right of speech to be protected. . . .

Here, this Court is of the opinion that the interests in the speech sought to be protected, i.e., the movie and the novel, should be protected and that there are no countervailing legal or policy grounds against such protection. . . .

In support of this position, resort is again made to cases in the privacy field, of which two are found to be particularly relevant: *Spahn*, cited supra, and *University of Notre Dame du Lac v. Twentieth Century Fox Film Corp.*, 22 A.D.2d 452, 256 N.Y.S.2d 301 (1965), *aff'd upon the opinion of the Appellate Division*, 15 N.Y.2d 940, 259 N.Y.S.2d 832, 207 N.E.2d 508(1965) [hereinafter cited as *Notre Dame*]. . . .

In applying the holdings of these two cases to those at bar, it would appear that the later decided *Spahn* case—which curiously did not cite *Notre Dame*—would dictate the result herein. However, upon closer scrutiny of *Spahn*, this Court is of the opinion that the *Spahn* holding should be limited to its facts, and that the result here should follow the holding in the *Notre Dame* case. . . . In essence, the Court in *Spahn* stressed the fact that the lower court had found that the defendant had engaged in deliberate falsifications of the circumstances surrounding the life of plaintiff and that such falsifications, which the reader might accept as true, were capable of presenting plaintiff in a false light. . . . Thus, the Court of Appeals in *Spahn* balanced the plaintiff's privacy rights against the first amendment protection of fictionalization *qua* falsification and, after finding there to be no such protection, held for the plaintiff. . . . See, also, *Time, Inc. v. Hill*, 385 U.S. 374, 87 S.Ct. 534, 17 L.Ed.2d 456(1967). Conversely, in the *Notre Dame* case, the Appellate Division, as affirmed by the New York Court of Appeals, found that the defendant had not represented the events in the movie to be true and that a viewer of the film would certainly know that the circumstances involved therein were fictitious; thus, the finding for the defendants.

It is clear from the review of these two cases that the absence of presence of deliberate falsifications or an attempt by a defendant to present the disputed events as true, determines whether the scales in this balancing process shall tip in favor of or against protection of the speech at issue. Since the cases at bar are more factually similar to the *Notre Dame* case, *i.e.*, there were no deliberate falsifications alleged by plaintiffs,

and the reader of the novel in the book case by the presence of the word "novel" would know that the work was fictitious, this Court finds that the first amendment protection usually accorded novels and movies outweighs whatever publicity rights the plaintiffs may possess and for this reason their complaints must be dismissed.

Accordingly, the Court finds that the right of publicity does not attach here, where a fictionalized account of an event in the life of a public figure is depicted in a novel or movie, and in such novel or movie it is evident to the public that the events so depicted are fictitious.

Plaintiffs also claim unfair competition pursuant to 15 U.S.C. sec.1125(a) (1976). "To constitute an actionable tort under the statute, plaintiff must allege: (1) that 'goods or services' are involved, (2) that interstate commerce is affected, and (3) that there is a false designation of origin or a false description or representation." *CBS Inc. v. Springboard Int'l Records*, 429 F. Supp. 563,566 (S.D.N.Y. 1976). That the first two elements of the tort are present in the instant action is undisputed. Defendants do however dispute the presence of the third. "The gist of the action under this section is a use of the mark or tradename in interstate commerce which is likely to cause confusion or to deceive purchasers as to the source of origin of the goods." *Mortellito v. Nina of California, Inc.* 335 F. Supp. 1294 (S.D.N.Y. 1972).

Plaintiffs allege in both cases that the defendants' use of the name "Agatha" and "Agatha Christie" would cause confusion in the minds of the public in general, and Agatha Christie readers in particular, to the effect that the movie and novel were authorized or even written by Mrs. Christie. This Court does not agree. . . .

Accordingly, plaintiffs' motion for a preliminary injunction . . . is denied for failure to establish likelihood of success on the merits. . . . [Defendants'] motions to dismiss are granted. . . .

NOTE

1. The foregoing decision in *Hicks v. Casablanca Records* was issued by a U.S. district court interpreting New York law before the New York Court of Appeals' later decision in *Stephano v. News Group Publications, Inc.* (see Section 10.21–1). Conse-

quently, the court's finding in *Hicks* that New York law recognizes a common law right of publicity that is separate from the statutory right of privacy cannot be sustained. However, the analysis in *Hicks* concerning rights of publicity and privacy as they conflict with rights to produce fiction dealing with a real person is still relevant and important to the central inquiry of this section. In addition, the court's rationale should be compared with the findings in *Spahn v. Julian Messner* (see Section 10.50). The *Hicks* court attempts to distinguish the facts in *Spahn* but does so unconvincingly.

Namath v. Sports Illustrated, 371 N.Y.S.2d 10 (App. Div. 1975)

CAPPAZOLI, J.

Plaintiff sought substantial compensatory and punitive damages by reason of defendants' publication and use of plaintiff's photograph without his consent. That photograph, which was originally used by defendants, without objection from plaintiff, in conjunction with a news article published by them on the 1969 Super Bowl Game, was used in advertisements promoting subscriptions to their magazine, *Sports Illustrated*.

The use of plaintiff's photograph was merely incidental advertising of defendants' magazine in which plaintiff had earlier been properly and fairly depicted and, hence, it was not violative of the Civil Rights Law (*Booth v. Curtis Publishing Co.*, 15 A.D.2d 343, 223 N.Y.S.2d 737, aff'd, 11 N.Y.2d 907, 228 N.Y.S.2d 468, 182 N.E.2d 812).

Certainly, defendants' subsequent republication of plaintiff's picture was "in motivation, sheer advertising and solicitation. This alone is not determinative of the question so long as the law accords an exempt status to incidental advertising of the news medium itself." (*Booth v. Curtis Publishing Co., supra*, p. 349, 223 N.Y.S.2d p. 744.) Again, it was stated, at 15 A.D.2d p. 350, 223 N.Y.S.2d p. 744 of the cited case, as follows:

> Consequently, it suffices here that so long as the reproduction was used to illustrate the quality and content of the periodical in which it originally appeared, the statute was not violated, albeit the reproduction appeared in other media for purposes of advertising the periodical.

Contrary to the dissent, we deem the cited case to be dispositive hereof. The language from the Namath advertisements, relied upon in the dissent, does not indicate plaintiff's endorsement of the magazine *Sports Illustrated*. Had that been the situation, a completely different issue would have been presented. Rather, that language merely indicates, to the readers of those advertisements, the general nature of the contents of what is likely to be included in future issues of the magazine. . . .

KUPFERMAN, J. (DISSENTING)

It is undisputed that one Joseph W. Namath is an outstanding sports figure, redoubtable on the football field. Among other things, as the star quarterback of the New York Jets, he led his team to victory on January 12, 1969 in the Super Bowl in Miami.

This feat and the story of the game and its star were heralded with illustrative photographs in the January 20, 1969 issue of *Sports Illustrated*, conceded to be an outstanding magazine published by Time Incorporated and devoted, as its name implies, to the activities for which it is famous. Of course, this was not the first nor the last time that *Sports Illustrated* featured Mr. Namath and properly so.

The legal problem involves the use of one of his action photos from the January 20, 1969 issue in subsequent advertisements in other magazines as promotional material for the sale of subscriptions to *Sports Illustrated*.

Plaintiff contends that the use was commercial in violation of his right of privacy under sections 50 and 51 of the Civil Rights Law. . . . Further, that because he was in the business of endorsing products and selling the use of his name and likeness, it interfered with this right to such sale, sometimes known as the right of publicity. *Haelan Laboratories v. Topps Chewing Gum*, 202 F.2d 866 (2nd Cir. 1953). Defendants contend there is an attempt to invade their constitutional rights under the First and Fourteenth Amendments by the maintenance of this action and that, in any event, the advertisements were meant to show "the nature, quality and content" of the magazine and not to trade on the plaintiff's name and likeness.

Initially, we are met with the determination in a similar case, *Booth v. Curtis Publishing Co.*, 15

A.D.2d 343, 223 N.Y.S.2d 737 (1st Dept.) *aff'd without op.*, 11 N.Y.2d 907, 228 N.Y.S.2d 468, 182 N.E.2d 812 (1962) relied on by Baer, J., in his opinion at Special Term dismissing the complaint.

The plaintiff was Shirley Booth, the well-known actress, photographed at a resort in the West Indies, up to her neck in the water and wearing an interesting chapeau, which photo appeared in *Holiday Magazine* along with photographs of other prominent guests. This photo was then used as a substantial part of an advertisement for *Holiday*.

Mr. Justice Breitel (now Chief Judge Breitel) wrote:

> Consequently, it suffices here that so long as the reproduction was used to illustrate the quality and content of the periodical in which it originally appeared, the statute was not violated, albeit the reproduction appeared in other media for purposes of advertising the periodical. [15 A.D.2d at p. 350, 223 N.Y.S.2d at p. 744]

However, the situation is one of degree. A comparison of the Booth and Namath photographs and advertising copy shows that in the Booth case, her name is in exceedingly small print, and it is the type of photograph itself which attracted attention. In the Namath advertisement, we find, in addition to the outstanding photograph, in *Cosmopolitan Magazine* (for women) the heading "The Man You Love Loves Joe Namath," and in Life, the heading "How to get Close to Joe Namath." There seems to be trading on the name of the personality involved in the defendants' advertisements. . . .

The complaint should not have been dismissed as a matter of law.

Zacchini v. Scripps-Howard Broadcasting Co., 433 U.S. 562 (1977)

JUSTICE WHITE delivered the opinion of the Court. Petitioner, Hugo Zacchini, is an entertainer. He performs a "human cannonball" act in which he is shot from a cannon into a net some 200 feet away. Each performance occupies some 15 seconds. In August and September 1972, petitioner was engaged to perform his act on a regular basis at the Geauga County Fair in Burton, Ohio. He per-

formed in a fenced area, surrounded by grandstands, at the fair grounds. Members of the public attending the fair were not charged a separate admission fee to observe his act.

On August 30, a freelance reporter for Scripps-Howard Broadcasting Co., the operator of a television broadcasting station and respondent in this case, attended the fair. He carried a small movie camera. Petitioner noticed the reporter and asked him not to film the performance. The reporter did not do so on that day; but on the instructions of the producer of respondent's daily newscast, he returned the following day and videotaped the entire act. This film clip, approximately 15 seconds in length, was shown on the 11 o'clock news program that night, together with favorable commentary.

Petitioner then brought this action for damages, alleging that he is "engaged in the entertainment business," that the act he performs is one "invented by his father and . . . performed only by his family for the last fifty years," that respondent "showed and commercialized the film of his act without consent," and that such conduct was an "unlawful appropriation of plaintiff's professional property." . . . Respondent answered and moved for summary judgment, which was granted by the trial court.

The Court of Appeals of Ohio reversed. The majority held that petitioner's complaint stated a cause of action for conversion and for infringement of a common-law copyright, and one judge concurred in the judgment on the ground that the complaint stated a cause of action for appropriation of petitioner's "right of publicity" in the filming of his act. All three judges agreed that the First Amendment did not privilege the press to show the entire performance on a news program without compensating petitioner for any financial injury he could prove at trial.

Like the concurring judge in the Court of Appeals, the Supreme Court of Ohio rested petitioner's cause of action under state law on his "right to publicity value of his performance." 47 Ohio St. 2d 224, 351 N.E. 2d 454, 455 (1976). The opinion syllabus, to which we are to look for the rule of law used to decide the case, declared first that one may not use for his own benefit the name or likeness of another, whether or not the use or benefit is a commercial one, and second that respondent would be liable for the appropriation, over petitioner's objection and in the absence of license or privilege, of petitioner's right to the publicity value of his performance. *Ibid.* The court nevertheless gave judgment for respondent because, in the words of the syllabus:

> A TV station has a privilege to report in its newscasts matters of legitimate public interest which would otherwise be protected by an individual's right of publicity, unless the actual intent of the TV station was to appropriate the benefit of the publicity of some nonprivileged private use, or unless the actual intent was to injure the individual. *Ibid.*

We granted certiorari, 429 U.S. 1037 (1977), to consider an issue unresolved by this Court: whether the First and Fourteenth Amendments immunized respondent from damages for its alleged infringement of petitioner's state-law "right of publicity." Pet. for Cert. 2. Insofar as the Ohio Supreme Court held that the First and Fourteenth Amendments of the United States Constitution required judgment for respondent, we reverse the judgment of that court. . . .

The Ohio Supreme Court held that respondent is constitutionally privileged to include in its newscasts matters of public interest that would otherwise be protected by the right of publicity, absent an intent to injure or to appropriate for some nonprivileged purpose. If under this standard respondent had merely reported that petitioner was performing at the fair and described or commented on his act, with or without showing his picture on television, we would have a very different case. But petitioner is not contending that his appearance at the fair and his performance could not be reported by the press as newsworthy items. His complaint is that respondent filmed his entire act and displayed that film on television for the public to see and enjoy. This, he claimed, was an appropriation of his professional property. The Ohio Supreme Court agreed that petitioner had "a right of publicity" that gave him "personal control over commercial display and exploitation of his personality and the exercise of his talents." This right of "exclusive control over the publicity given to his performances" was said to be such a "valuable part of the benefit which may be attained by his talents and efforts"

that it was entitled to legal protection. It was also observed, or at least expressly assumed, that petitioner had not abandoned his rights by performing under the circumstances present at the Geauga County Fair Grounds.

The Ohio Supreme Court nevertheless held that the challenged invasion was privileged, saying that the press "must be accorded broad latitude in its choice of how much it presents of each story or incident, and of the emphasis to be given to such presentation. No fixed standard which would bar the press from reporting or depicting either an entire occurrence or an entire discrete part of a public performance can be formulated which would not unduly restrict the 'breathing room' in reporting which freedom of the press requires." 47 Ohio St. 2d, at 235, 351 N.E. 2d, at 461. Under this view, respondent was thus constitutionally free to film and display petitioner's entire act.

The Ohio Supreme Court relied heavily on *Time, Inc. v. Hill*, 385 U.S. 374 (1967), but that case does not mandate a media privilege to televise a performer's entire act without his consent. Involved in *Time, Inc. v. Hill* was a claim under the New York "Right to Privacy" statute that *Life Magazine*, in the course of reviewing a new play, had connected the play with a long-past incident involving petitioner and his family and had falsely described their experience and conduct at that time. The complaint sought damages for humiliation and suffering flowing from these nondefamatory falsehoods that allegedly invaded Hill's privacy. The Court held, however, that the opening of a new play linked to an actual incident was a matter of public interest and that Hill could not recover without showing that the *Life* report was knowingly false or was published with reckless disregard for the truth—the same rigorous standard that had been applied in *New York Times Co. v. Sullivan*, 376 U.S. 254 (1964).

Time, Inc. v. Hill, which was hotly contested and decided by a divided Court, involved an entirely different tort from the "right of publicity" recognized by the Ohio Supreme Court. As the opinion reveals in *Time, Inc. v. Hill*, the Court was steeped in the literature of privacy law and was aware of the developing distinctions and nuances in this branch of the law. The court, for example, cited W. Prosser, *Law of Torts* 831–832 (3d ed. 1964), and the same author's well-known article, "Privacy," 48 Calif. L. Rev. 383 (1960), both of which divided privacy into four distinct branches. The Court was aware that it was adjudicating a "false light" privacy case involving a matter of public interest, not a case involving "intrusion," 385 U.S., at 384–385, n. 9, "appropriation" of a name or likeness for the purposes of trade, *id.*, at 381, or "private details" about a non-newsworthy person or event, *id.*, at 383 no. 7. It is also abundantly clear that *Time, Inc. v. Hill* did not involve a performer, a person with a name having commercial value, or any claim to a "right of publicity." This discrete kind of "appropriation" case was plainly identified in the literature cited by the Court and had been adjudicated in the reported cases.

The differences between these two torts are important. First, the State's interests in providing a cause of action in each instance are different. "The interest protected" in permitting recovery for placing the plaintiff in a false light "is clearly that of reputation, with the same overtones of mental distress as in defamation." Prosser, *supra*, 48 Calif. L. Rev., at 400. By contrast, the State's interest in permitting a "right of publicity" is in protecting the proprietary interest of the individual in his act in part to encourage such entertainment. As we later note, the State's interest is closely analogous to the goals of patent and copyright law, focusing on the right of the individual to reap the reward of his endeavors and having little to do with protecting feelings or reputation. Second, the two torts differ in the degree to which they intrude on dissemination of information to the public. In "false light" cases the only way to protect the interests involved is to attempt to minimize publication of the damaging matter, while in "right of publicity" cases the only question is who gets to do the publishing. An entertainer such as petitioner usually has no objection to the widespread publication of his act as long as he gets the commercial benefit of such publication. Indeed, in the present case petitioner did not seek to enjoin the broadcast of his act; he simply sought compensation for the broadcast in the form of damages. . . .

The broadcast of a film of petitioner's entire act poses a substantial threat to the economic value of that performance. As the Ohio court recognized, this act is the product of petitioner's own talents and energy, the end result of much time, effort, and expense. Much of its economic value lies in the "right of exclusive control over the publicity given to its performance"; if the public can see the act free on television, it will be less willing to pay to see it at the fair. The effect of a public broadcast of the performance is similar to preventing petitioner from charging an admission fee. "The rationale for [protecting the right of publicity] is the straightforward one of preventing unjust enrichment by the theft of goodwill. No social purpose is served by having the defendant get free some aspect of the plaintiff that would have market value and for which he would normally pay." Kalven, "Privacy in Tort Law—Were Warren and Brandeis Wrong?" 31 Law & Contemp. Prob. 326, 331 (1966). Moreover, the broadcast of petitioner's entire performance, unlike the unauthorized use of another's name for purposes of trade or the incidental use of a name or picture by the press, goes to the heart of petitioner's ability to earn a living as an entertainer. Thus, in this case, Ohio has recognized what may be the strongest case for a "right of publicity"—involving, not the appropriation of an entertainer's reputation to enhance the attractiveness of a commercial product, but the appropriation of the very activity by which the entertainer acquired his reputation in the first place.

Of course, Ohio's decision to protect petitioner's right of publicity here rests on more than a desire to compensate the performer for the time and effort invested in his act; the protection provides an economic incentive for him to make the investment required to produce a performance of interest to the public. This same consideration underlies the patent and copyright laws long enforced by this Court. . . . The laws perhaps regard the "reward to the owner [as] a secondary consideration," *United States v. Paramount Pictures*, 334 U.S. 131, 158 (1948), but they were "intended definitely to grant valuable, enforceable right" in order to afford greater encouragement to the production of works of benefit to the public, *Washingtonian Publishing Co. v. Pearson*, 306 U.S. 30, 36 (1939). The Constitution does not prevent Ohio from making a similar choice here in deciding to protect the entertainer's incentive in order to encourage the production of this type of work. Cf. *Goldstein v. California*, 412 U.S. 546 (1973). . . .

There is no doubt that entertainment, as well as news, enjoys First Amendment protection. It is also true that entertainment itself can be important news. *Time, Inc. v. Hill*. But it is important to note that neither the public nor respondent will be deprived of the benefit of petitioner's performance as long as his commercial stake in his act is appropriately recognized. Petitioner does not seek to enjoin the broadcast of his performance; he simply wants to be paid for it. . . .

We conclude that although the State of Ohio may as a matter of its own law privilege the press in the circumstances of this case, the First and Fourteenth Amendments do not require it to do so. *Reversed*.

JUSTICE POWELL, with whom Justice Brennan and Justice Marshall join, dissenting
Disclaiming any attempt to do more than decide the narrow case before us, the Court reverses the decision of the Supreme Court of Ohio based on repeated incantation of a single formula: "a performer's entire act." The holding today is summed up in one sentence:

> Wherever the line in particular situations is to be drawn between media reports that are protected and those that are not, we are quite sure that the First and Fourteenth Amendments do not immunize the media when they broadcast a performer's entire act without his consent.

I doubt that this formula provides a standard clear enough even for resolution of this case. In any event, I am not persuaded that the Court's opinion is appropriately sensitive to the First Amendment values at stake, and I therefore dissent.

Although the Court would draw no distinction, . . . I do not view respondent's action as comparable to unauthorized commercial broadcasts of sporting events, theatrical performances, and the like where the broadcaster keeps the profits. There is no suggestion here that respondent made any such use of the film. Instead, it simply reported on what petitioner concedes to be a newsworthy event, in a way hardly surprising for a television station—means of film coverage. The report was part of an ordinary daily news program, consuming a total of 15 seconds. It is a routine example of the press' fulfilling the informing function so vital to our system.

The Court's holding that the station's ordinary news report may give rise to substantial liability has disturbing implications, for the decision could lead to a degree of media self-censorship. Cf. *Smith v. California*, 361 U.S. 147, 150–154 (1959). Hereafter, whenever a television news editor is unsure whether certain film footage received from a camera crew might be held to portray an "entire act," he may decline coverage—even of clearly newsworthy events—or confine the broadcast to watered-down verbal reporting, perhaps with an occasional still picture. The public is then the loser. This is hardly the kind of news reportage that the First Amendment is meant to foster. . . .

In my view the First Amendment commands a different analytical starting point from the one selected by the Court. Rather than begin with a quantitative analysis of the performer's behavior—is this or is this not his entire act?—we should direct initial attention to the actions of the news media: what use did the station make of the film footage? When a film is used, as here, for a routine portion of a regular news program, I would hold that the First Amendment protects the station from a "right of publicity" or "appropriation" suit, absent a strong showing by the plaintiff that the news broadcast was a subterfuge or cover for private or commercial exploitation. . . . Since the film clip here was undeniably treated as news and since there is no claim that the use was subterfuge, respondent's actions were constitutionally privileged. I would affirm.

Justice Stevens filed a separate dissenting opinion.

Paulsen v. Personality Posters, Inc., 299 N.Y.S.2d 501 (Sup. Ct. N.Y. Co. 1968)

FRANK, J.
The plaintiff, Pat Paulsen, a well-known television performer and comedian, moves for a pre-

liminary injunction to enjoin defendant, Personality Posters, Inc., "from marketing, selling and otherwise dealing in a commercial poster embodying a photograph of the Plaintiff which poster was derived from an unpublished photograph of the Plaintiff which is owned by the Plaintiff." Defendant corporation is in the business of marketing posters of various personalities throughout the United States.

The photograph involved indeed bespeaks the nature of plaintiff's occupation louder than the proverbial "thousand words." A soulfully expressioned plaintiff attired in beruffled cap and prim frock, in a style which might best be characterized as "latter-day Edna May Oliver," is shown holding an unlit candle in one hand while his other arm cradles a rubber tire which is hoisted onto his right shoulder. A contemporary touch is added by a banner draped across plaintiff's chest, in the manner, if not with the style, of a beauty pageant contestant, which bears the legend "1968." The complained-of posters, distributed and marketed by defendant, are nothing more than enlargements, some 30 × 40 inches in size, of the aforedescribed photograph, with the addition of the words "FOR PRESIDENT" at the bottom in 2½″ letters.

It is undisputed that the original photograph was sent to defendant corporation in late 1967 by plaintiff's agent, Ken Kragen. The parties differ sharply, however, as to the basis on which the picture was submitted. Kragen asserts that he spoke with a representative of the defendant corporation toward the end of 1967 about the possibility of using the photograph for a New Year's poster and inquired whether defendant would be interested in a license agreement for such purpose. According to Kragen, the photograph was sent, at the request of defendant's representative, for inspection in connection with such proposal and with the clear understanding that defendant "would be able to use the photograph only in connection with a license agreement with royalties going to our client" and that defendant subsequently rejected such offer. Defendant's president, on the other hand, contends that the photograph was sent, unsolicited, by plaintiff's agent from whom several phone calls were thereafter received urging that defendant

undertake distribution of the picture in poster form in aid of a publicity campaign being carried on in behalf of plaintiff. Defendant flatly denies that any limitation whatsoever was placed on the time or manner in which such distribution was to be made, and states that such matters were left solely to its discretion, and that the photograph was submitted to it with full authorization for unlimited publication and distribution. Defendant further asserts that it frequently receives photographs for proposed poster distribution from press agents seeking publicity for their clients and that the submission of plaintiff's photograph was in accordance with this customary practice.

Whatever the circumstances surrounding the receipt of the photograph, it is conceded that defendant made no use thereof until July 1968 at which time it began marketing and circulating the posters in issue. It is clear that the decision to distribute the posters at that time was directly related to the interest engendered by plaintiff's current comedy routine which is based upon his entry into the presidential race as the "Put-On Presidential Candidate of 1968" under the banner of the STAG Party. Satirical or otherwise, plaintiff's aspirations and his provocative comments on various current issues have been aired with regularity on the nationally televised highly popular "Smothers' Brothers" program. In addition, plaintiff's candidacy has been the subject of comment by other communications media, including a lengthy front page news article in the *Wall Street Journal* (August 15, 1968), he has received several votes in recent primary elections, and he has participated in various activities traditionally associated with political campaigning.

In conjunction with his comedy routine and presidential candidacy, plaintiff has undertaken an extensive merchandising program whereby he has granted an exclusive license to a California company in connection with all campaign buttons, stickers and posters relating to the "Pat Paulsen for President" campaign, and it is alleged that defendant's distribution of the posters has infringed upon and interfered with such license arrangement. While defendant's vice-president, in response to a complaint by plaintiff's attorney, indicated in a letter dated July 23, 1968 that distribution of defendant's Paulsen posters would be discontinued, the moving papers allege that "Personality Posters continued and continues to this day its national sales distribution and marketing of the infringing poster."

The application for injunctive relief is predicated upon the following: (1) an alleged invasion of plaintiff's right of privacy in violation of Section 51 of the Civil Rights Law, and (2) an alleged violation of and infringement upon plaintiff's common law copyright in the photograph which is embodied in the complained-of posters. . . .

Where the unauthorized use of name or picture has been purely for "advertising purposes," in the sense of promoting the sale of a collateral product, stringent enforcement of the statutory prohibition has presented comparatively little difficulty and relief from such "commercial exploitation" has been liberally granted even to those who might be characterized "public figures." . . . A far more restrictive treatment, however, has been accorded the proscription against use "for the purposes of trade," particularly where the use has been in furtherance of the business of a communications medium. Consonant with constitutional considerations, it has consistently been emphasized that the statute was not intended to limit activities involving the dissemination of news or information concerning matters of public interest and that such activities are privileged and do not fall within "the purposes of trade" contemplated by Section 51, notwithstanding that they are also carried on for a profit. . . .

Thus, it was early held that newspapers, magazines, and newsreels are exempt from the statutory injunction when using a name or picture in connection with an item of news or one that is newsworthy and such privileged status has also been extended to other communications media including books, comic books, radio, television and motion pictures. . . . Indeed, it is clear that any format of "the written word or picture," including posters and handbills . . . will be similarly exempted in conjunction with the dissemination of news or public interest presentations. . . .

The scope of the subject matter which may be considered of "public interest" or "newsworthy" has been defined in most liberal and far reaching terms. The privilege of enlightening the public is by no means limited to dissemination of news in the sense of current events but extends far beyond to include all types of factual, educational and historical data, or even entertainment and amusement, concerning interesting phases of human activity. . . .

A logical corollary of the privileged status occupied by the newsworthy is "the rule that a public figure, whether he be such by choice or involuntarily, is subject to the often searching beam of publicity and that, in balance with the legitimate public interest, the law affords his privacy little protection." . . . Such maxim is a realistic recognition that a public figure or personality, by the very nature and character of such status, evokes public interest in his doings and that his activities are generally speaking always "news." . . .

In the instant case, plaintiff is concededly a well-known public personality by professional choice. As such, his affairs would ordinarily engender considerable public interest and, indeed, as an entertainer he actively seeks to promote and stimulate such public attention to enhance his professional standing. In pursuit of such attention he has projected himself into the national political scene, a sphere which is itself always "newsworthy" and which propels into such category all, irrespective of prior status, who aspire to participate therein. It is, moreover, an arena whose participants have traditionally been the fairest of all game for unbridled, unrestrained public comment and criticism ranging from the ridiculous to the scurrilous. Limitations upon the permissible in political expression are almost non-existent. It is the strength of our political system that it can survive and flourish in such matrix, where the sensibilities of the participants must bow to the superior public interest in completely unfettered and unabridged free discussion of whatever persuasion, merit or style. "The risk of this exposure is an essential incident of life in a society which places a primary value on freedom of speech and of press." . . .

It is apparently plaintiff's position that since "he is only kidding" and his presidential activities are really only a "publicity stunt" they fall outside the scope of constitutionally protected matters of public interest. Such premise is wholly untenable. When a well-known entertainer enters the presidential ring, tongue in cheek or otherwise, it is clearly newsworthy and of public interest. A poster which portrays plaintiff in that role, and reflects the spirit in which he approaches said role, is a form of public interest presentation to which protection must be extended. That the format may deviate from traditional patterns of political commentary, or that to some it may appear more entertaining than informing, would not alter its protected status. It is not for this or any court to pass value judgments predicated upon ephemeral subjective considerations which would serve to stifle free expression. . . . Thus, whether the poster involved be considered as a significant satirical commentary upon the current presidential contest, or merely as a humorous presentation of a well-known entertainer's publicity gambit, or in any other light, be it social criticism or pure entertainment, it is sufficiently relevant to a matter of public interest to be a form of expression which is constitutionally protected. . . .

Of course, it is clear that while plaintiff is ostensibly seeking redress for an alleged "violation of his privacy," it is not his privacy at all that concerns him. Privacy in its usual sense is hardly the goal of an entertainer or performer. What such a figure really seeks is a type of relief which will enable him to garner financial benefits from the pecuniary value which attaches to his name and picture. While such concept, which is termed the "right of publicity," has been accorded some limited recognition . . . the courts of this state have evidenced no inclination to adopt or follow such construction within the context of Section 51. On the contrary, it has been made clear that the purpose of the statute is to redress injury for invasions of a "person's right to be let alone," with recovery being grounded on the mental strain, distress, humiliation and disturbance of the peace of mind suffered by such person, hardly what plaintiff here seeks, and that the statute was *not* enacted to fill gaps in the copyright law or to afford substitute relief for breaches of contract or violations of various other species of property rights. . . .

Moreover, even where the "right of publicity" is recognized, it does not invest a prominent person with the right to exploit financially every public use of name or picture. What is made actionable is the unauthorized use for advertising purposes in connection with the sale of a commodity. . . . The "right of publicity," therefore, like that of "privacy" is at best a limited one, within the context of an advertising use, and would be held to have no application where the use of name or picture, as is here the case, is in connection with a matter of public interest. That such use is constitutionally protected and must supersede any private pecuniary considerations is conceded even by those who urge more widespread recognition of a distinct property right of publicity. . . .

Thus, in the present case, where the poster in question appears privileged by virtue of its public interest character, plaintiff has failed to establish any clear legal or factual right, whether viewed within the context of either "right of privacy" or "right of publicity," which would warrant the granting of the preliminary injunction sought. . . .

We turn now to plaintiff's second basis for injunctive relief, a violation of the common-law copyright which he alleges he had in the original photograph which was sent to defendant.

A common-law copyright entitles the proprietor of an intellectual or artistic production to the absolute and exclusive use thereof prior to its publication, and to the right of first publication of the work. . . . Such copyright terminates, however, upon the owner's assent to general publication of such work. . . . While submission of the work to a particular person, or selected group of persons, for a limited purpose, and without right of diffusion, reproduction, distribution or sale, would be considered a "limited publication" which would not result in loss of the common-law copyright . . . there is sharp disagreement between the parties herein as to whether the photograph was sent to defendant for a limited purpose or whether, as defendant claims, it was a completely unrestricted and unlimited submission for purposes of general publication, which would have resulted in a loss of any common-law copyright, which plaintiff may have had in the work. . . . Since such sharp factual dispute on the issue of publication must be resolved at a trial and precludes the granting of the preliminary injunctive relief sought . . . it becomes unnecessary to consider, at this juncture, whether the moving papers sufficiently establish that plaintiff in fact possessed a common-law copyright in the photograph in issue.

While plaintiff's papers stress the need for immediate relief by reason of the proximity of the forthcoming presidential election, such urgency is more apparent than real. He faces no irreparable injury. The entire thrust of his claim, whether founded on "privacy" or "common-law copyright," is the *financial* loss which he has allegedly suffered, and will continue to suffer, by reason of defendant's activities. If plaintiff should ultimately prove to be entitled to a recovery, under either of his causes of action, monetary damages will be available to him and will serve to fully and adequately compensate him. . . .

Upon all of the foregoing, the motion for a temporary injunction is in all respects denied.

10.40 Misappropriation and Unfair Competition

Two lengthy opinions are examined in this section. They are particularly instructive on how celebrities may look beyond rights of privacy and publicity to assert other legal bases for their complaints about invasion of their personal rights.

In *Allen v. National Video*, Woody Allen complained about a look-alike used in the defendants' advertising. Although Allen charged invasion of privacy and violation of his right of publicity, an additional key complaint in the court's opinion was the allegation that the ads constituted a false designation of origin.

In *Estate of Elvis Presley v. Russen*, a production called "The Big El Show" capitalized on the lingering fame and commercial value of the late Elvis Presley. Presley's estate alleged the production invaded rights of publicity, common law unfair competition,

common law trademark and, as in *Allen*, a false designation of the origins of the show.

The false designation claims in both cases were based on § 43 of the federal Lanham Act, encoded in 15 U.S.C. § 1125. This important provision reads as follows:

§ *1125. False designations of origin and false descriptions forbidden*

(a) Any person who shall affix, apply, or annex, or use in connection with any goods or services, or any container or containers for goods, a false designation of origin, or any false description or representation, including words or other symbols tending falsely to describe or represent the same, and shall cause such goods or services to enter into commerce, and any person who shall with knowledge of the falsity of such designation of origin or description or representation cause or procure the same to be transported or used in commerce or deliver the same to any carrier to be transported or used, shall be liable to a civil action by any person doing business in the locality falsely indicated as that of origin or in the region in which said locality is situated, or by any person who believes that he is or is likely to be damaged by the use of any such false description or representation.

Allen v. National Video, Inc., 610 F. Supp. 612 (S.D.N.Y. 1985)

MOTLEY, J.

. . . This case arises because plaintiff, to paraphrase Groucho Marx, wouldn't belong to any video club that would have him as a member. More precisely, plaintiff sues over an advertisement for defendant National Video (National) in which defendant Boroff, allegedly masquerading as plaintiff, portrays a satisfied holder of National's movie rental V.I.P. Card. Plaintiff asserts that the advertisement appropriates his face and implies his endorsement, and that it therefore violates his statutory right to privacy, his right to publicity, and the federal Lanham Act's prohibition of misleading advertising. Plaintiff, basing jurisdiction on diversity of citizenship, seeks an injunction against Boroff and defendant Smith,

Boroff's agent, and damages against all defendants.

Defendants, while conceding that Boroff looks remarkably like plaintiff, deny that the advertisement appropriates plaintiff's likeness or that it poses a likelihood of consumer confusion . . .

The following facts are not in dispute. Plaintiff Woody Allen is a film director, writer, actor, and comedian. Among the films plaintiff has directed are *Annie Hall*, which won several Academy Awards, *Manhattan, Bananas, Sleeper, Broadway Danny Rose*, and, most recently, *The Purple Rose of Cairo*. In addition to being a critically successful artist, plaintiff has for more than 15 years been a major international celebrity. Although he has not often lent his name to commercial endeavors other than his own projects, plaintiff's many years in show business have made his name and his face familiar to millions of people. This familiarity, and plaintiff's reputation for artistic integrity, have significant, exploitable, commercial value.

The present action arises from an advertisement, placed by National to promote its nationally franchised video rental chain, containing a photograph of defendant Boroff taken on September 2, 1983. The photograph portrays a customer in a National video store, an individual in his forties, wtih a high forehead, tousled hair, and heavy black glasses. The customer's elbow is on the counter, and his face, bearing an expression at once quizzical and somewhat smug, is leaning on his hand. It is not disputed that, in general, the physical features and pose are characteristic of plaintiff.

The staging of the photograph also evokes association with plaintiff. Sitting on the counter are videotape cassettes of *Annie Hall* and *Bananas*, two of plaintiff's best known films, as well as *Casablanca* and *The Maltese Falcon*. The latter two are Humphrey Bogart films of the 1940's associated with plaintiff primarily because of his play and film *Play It Again, Sam*, in which the spirit of Bogart appears to the character played by Allen and offers him romantic advice. In addition, the title *Play It Again, Sam* is a famous, although inaccurate, quotation from *Casablanca*.

The individual in the advertisement is holding up a National Video V.I.P. Card, which apparently entitles the bearer to favorable terms on movie rentals. The woman behind the counter is smiling at the customer and appears to be gasping in exaggerated excitement at the presence of a celebrity.

The photograph was used in an advertisement which appeared in the March 1984 issue of *Video Review*, a magazine published in New York and distributed in the Southern District, and in the April 1984 issue of *Take One*, an in-house publication which National distributes to its franchisers across the country. The headline on the advertisement reads "Become a V.I.P. at National Video. We'll Make You Feel Like a Star." The copy goes on to explain that holders of the V.I.P. card receive "hassle-free movie renting" and "special savings" and concludes that "you don't need a famous face to be treated to some pretty famous service."

The same photograph and headline were also used on countercards distributed to National's franchisees. Although the advertisement that ran in *Video Review* contained a disclaimer in small print reading "Celebrity double provided by Ron Smith's Celebrity Look-Alike's, Los Angeles, Calif.," no such disclaimer appeared in the other versions of the advertisements.

None of the defendants deny that the advertisements in question were designed, placed, and authorized by defendant National, that defendant Boroff was selected and posed as he was to capitalize on his resemblance to plaintiff and to attract the attention of movie watchers, that defendants Boroff and Smith were aware of this purpose in agreeing to supply Boroff's services, and that in fact Smith and Boroff have on other occasions offered the servcies of Boroff, a Los Angeles-based actor and director, as a look-alike for plaintiff. Moreover, defendants do not dispute that the photograph in question was used for commercial purposes, and that plaintiff did not give his consent to the use of the photograph.

Plaintiff maintains that these undisputed facts require the court to enter summary judgment for him on his right to privacy, right of publicity, and Lanham Act claims, he urges the court to find, as a matter of law, that defendants used his picture or portrait for commercial purposes without his permission, and that the advertisements were materially misleading and likely to result in consumer confusion as to his endorsement of National's services.

Defendants insist that other disputed facts require denial of plaintiff's motion. Although defendants concede that they sought to evoke by reference plaintiff's general persona, they strenuously deny that they intended to imply that the person in the photograph was actually plaintiff or that plaintiff endorsed National. Defendants offer their own interpretation of the advertisement to support their assertion that the photograph does not depict plaintiff. According to defendants, the idea of the advertisement is that even people who are *not* stars are *treated* like stars at National Video. They insist that the advertisement depicts a "Woody Allen fan," so dedicated that he has adopted his idol's appearance and mannerisms, who is able to live out his fantasy by receiving star treatment at National Video. The knowing viewer is supposed to be amused that the counter person actually believes that the customer is Woody Allen.

Defendants urge that this interpretation cannot be rejected as a matter of law, and that if defendant Boroff merely appeared as someone who looks like Woody Allen, but not as Woody Allen himself, then plaintiff's rights were not violated. Defendants further seek summary judgment against plaintiff on the basis that plaintiff has offered no actual evidence that anyone was actually deceived into thinking that the photograph was of him. In addition, defendants Smith and Boroff seek summary judgment on the basis that they did not "use" the picture in New York, as required under the privacy statute, because the photo session took place in Oregon and they had no control over the design of the advertisement or its placement. Smith and Boroff further urge that they never misrepresented Boroff as plaintiff, that they had insisted that National include a disclaimer in all advertisements using the photo, and that they are therefore guilty of no wrongful conduct and cannot be held liable for the misdeeds of National.

Plaintiff rejects defendants' explanation of the advertisement as fanciful and asserts that since all defendants knowingly participated in creating a photograph that amounts to a portrait of plaintiff to be used for advertising in a national magazine, they are all jointly and severally liable for violating plaintiff's rights.

In addition to the issues outlined above, defendants Smith and Boroff seek indemnity from defendant National, which itself contests the form and content of its contract with Smith and Boroff. It is not disputed that in preparation for the photo session in Oregon, Smith and Boroff sent to National a printed form contract which, *inter alia*, permitted the photographs produced to be used "one or two times" in *Video Review* magazine, prohibited National from representing that Boroff was really Woody Allen, required a disclaimer such as was used in one of the advertisements, and bound National to "forever indemnify and hold harmless and compensate completely" Smith and Boroff for any civil liability resulting from the use of the lookalike's picture.

The contract was delivered to National with defendant Smith's signature, and a blank space for National's representative to sign. It is not disputed that no one ever signed the contract for National. Moreover, National insists that its president, Ron Berger, was unhappy with the indemnification terms, and instructed National's staff designer to work out an oral contract simply to pay Smith and Boroff $2,000 for a one day photo session, with no other strings attached. It is not disputed, however, that this dissatisfaction was never specifically conveyed to Smith and Boroff, and that the written contract was never specifically disavowed; the parties simply proceeded with the photo session.

Smith and Boroff maintain that National adopted the written contract through its performance of the terms and its failure specifically to reject it, and that National should therefore be required to indemnify them for any liability in this case. Further, Smith and Boroff insist that National breached the contract by failing to include a disclaimer in some versions of the advertisement, and by using the photograph in media not authorized by the contract, and that these unauthorized uses of Boroff's photograph for commercial purposes violate Boroff's privacy rights under New York law.

National maintains that only an oral agreement, established in telephone conversations and in person at the photo session, governs the relationship of the parties. Although National does not dispute that it knew that a disclaimer had to be included in all uses of the advertisement, it maintains that an invoice sent by Smith and Boroff with the contract and bearing the words "MODEL RELEASE NOT VALID UNTIL THIS INVOICE IS PAID" operated as a general model release once the $2,000 was paid, defeating Smith and Boroff's contractual claims. At least, argues National, material issues of fact exist regarding the contract which necessitate the denial of summary judgment to Smith and Boroff.

Privacy and Publicity Claims

Plaintiff's right to privacy claim, upon which the parties have focused in this litigation is based on sections 50 and 51 of the New York Civil Rights Law. These narrowly drawn provisions were enacted in the early years of the century when recognition of the novel right was controversial. Although the court concludes that a more appropriate remedy for plaintiff is provided by the Lanham Act, it includes the following discussion for its value in framing the unusual questions presented in this case. . . .

The right to privacy recognized by the Civil Rights law has been strictly construed, both because it is in derogation of New York common law . . . and because of potential conflict with the First Amendment, particularly where public figures are involved. . . . To make out a violation, a plaintiff must satisfy three distinct elements: (1) use of his or her name, portrait, or picture, (2) for commercial or trade purposes, (3) without written permission. Merely suggesting certain characteristics of the plaintiff, without literally using his or her name, portrait, or picture, is not actionable under the statute. . . .

In addition to the statutory right to privacy, plaintiff in this case argues that defendants have violated his "right of publicity," an analogous right recognized in the common law of many jurisdictions. Indeed, until recently, some federal courts assumed that the New York courts would recognize such a common law right independent of that protected by the Civil Rights Law. . . .

The New York Court of Appeals, however, recently has held that no separate common law cause of action to vindicate the right of publicity exists in New York. *Stephano v. News Group Publications, Inc.*, 64 N.Y.2d 174, 485 N.Y.S.2d 220 (1984). The court held, in essence, that the "right of publicity" was merely a misnomer for the privacy interest protected by the Civil Rights Law, as applied to public figures. . . .

This court must also follow *Stephano,* and will treat plaintiff's causes of action for privacy and publicity together under the general rubric of privacy. In this connection, the court notes that the only element under the pre-*Stephano* cases which would distinguish the two theories—the requirement that plaintiff have cultivated a valuable property interest in his public image—is without question satisfied in this case.

In examining the undisputed facts of this case with reference to plaintiff's summary judgment motion, it is immediately clear that two of the three prongs of the Civil Rights Law are satisfied. First, there is no question that the photograph said to be of plaintiff was used for commercial purposes, since it appeared in a magazine advertisement soliciting business for National Video franchises. Second, defendants do not dispute that plaintiff never gave his consent to the use of the photograph, either orally or in writing. It therefore appears that the only element of plaintiff's case over which there is any serious dispute is whether the photograph is a "portrait or picture" of plaintiff.

Plaintiff argues that Boroff's physical resemblance to him, when viewed in conjunction with the undeniable attempt to evoke plaintiff's image through the selection of props and poses, makes the photograph in question a "portrait or picture" of plaintiff as a matter of law. Plaintiff notes that it is not necessary that all persons seeing the photograph actually identify him, only that he be *identifiable* from the photograph. . . . Plaintiff contends that it is beyond cavil that some people will recognize him in this photograph. The cited cases, however, involved photographs which were not disputed to be of the plaintiffs; the only question was whether the pictures were too old or too obscure to be recognizable. They do not help us answer the more basic question of whether the photograph in the case at bar is, in fact, a "picture" or "portrait" of plaintiff.

More helpful are a line of cases holding that any recognizable likeness, not just an actual photograph may qualify as a "portrait or picture." . . .

Therefore, if defendants had used, for example, a clearly recognizable painting or cartoon of plaintiff, it would certainly constitute a "portrait or picture" within the meaning of the statute. The case of a look-alike, however, is more problematic. A painting, drawing or manikin has no existence other than as a representation of something or someone; if the subject is recognizable, then the work is a "portrait." Defendant Boroff, however, is not a manikin. He is a person with a right to his own identity and his own face. Plaintiff's privacy claim therefore requires the court to answer the almost metaphysical question of when one person's face, presented in a certain context, becomes, as a matter of law, the face of another.

This question is not merely theoretical. The use in an advertisement of a drawing, which *has* no other purpose than to represent its subject, must give rise to a cause of action under the Civil Rights Law, because it raises the obvious implication that its subject has endorsed or is otherwise involved with the product being advertised. There is no question that this amounts to an appropriation of another's likeness for commercial advantage.

A living and breathing actor, however, has the right to exploit his or her own face for commercial gain. This right is itself protected by the Civil Rights Law. The privacy law does not prohibit one from evoking certain aspects of another's personality . . . but it does prohibit one from actually representing oneself as another person. . . . The look-alike situation falls somewhere in between and therefore presents a difficult question.

The court is aware of only one case on point. In *Onassis v. Christian Dior N.Y. Inc.*, 122 Misc.2d 603, 472 N.Y.S.2d 254 (S. Ct. N.Y. Co. 1983), plaintiff Jacqueline Kennedy Onassis won an injunction against an advertisement featuring a model who was made up to look like her. The advertisement was part of a series, which ap-

peared for several weeks in major fashion and news magazines, featuring a trio of risque sophisticates known as "The Diors." The advertisements followed the developing relationship (and stunning Christian Dior wardrobes) of the imaginary menage a trois, including, in one week's installment, the marriage of two of the trio in a stylish, "legendary private affair." *Onassis*, 472 N.Y.S. 2d at 257. Appearing among the guests at the soiree, which was portrayed in one large photograph, were several actual celebrities—actress Ruth Gordon, television personality Gene Shalit, and actress/model Shari Belafonte—and a Jacqueline Onassis double provided, as in this case, by Ron Smith's Celebrity Look-Alikes. . . .

The *Onassis* court found that the advertisement violated plaintiff's rights under section 51 of the Civil Rights Law. The court held that an exact duplication of plaintiff was not necessary to make out a cause of action under the statute, so long as the overall impression created clearly was that plaintiff had herself appeared in the advertisement. . . .

The "illusion" created in *Onassis* was that plaintiff had actually appeared in the advertisement. Therefore, the court's holding was consistant with the long-standing requirement under section 51 that the commercial use complained of amount to a "portrait or picture" of an individual, not merely the suggestion of some aspect of a person's public persona. In other words, in the context of the advertisement, the look-alike's face was, as a matter of law, a portrait of Jacqueline Onassis. Important to the court's holding was the unusually realistic tone of the advertisement . . .

The question of whether a photograph presents a recognizable likeness of a person is ordinarily one for the jury. . . . When, as in *Onassis*, the look-alike seems indistinguishable from the real person and the context of the advertisement clearly implies that he or she is the real celebrity, a court may hold as a matter of law that the look-alike's face is a "portrait or picture" of plaintiff. *Onassis* presented an unusual factual setting, in which the mixture of fantasy and reality suggested almost unavoidably the actual presence of the real-life celebrity. In order for the court to reach the same conclusion in the present case, it must conclude on the undisputed facts that the photograph in question similarly creates, as a matter of law, the illusion of Woody Allen's actual presence in the advertisement.

It is not disputed here that in this photograph defendant Boroff is meant to look like Woody Allen. The pose, expression, and props all support the suggestion. However, the question before the court is not whether some, or even most, people will be *reminded* of plaintiff when they see this advertisement. In order to find that the photograph contains plaintiff's "portrait or picture," the court would have to conclude that most persons who could identify an actual photograph of plaintiff would be likely to think that this was actually his picture. This standard is necessary since we deal not with the question of whether an undisputed picture of plaintiff is recognizable to some, but whether an undisputed picture of defendant Boroff should be regarded, as a matter of law, to *be* a portrait or picture of plaintiff.

The court notes several factors that might militate against summary adjudication of this question. First, there are several physical differences between plaintiff's face and that of defendant Boroff. Defendant's photo shows larger eyebrows, a wider face, and more uneven complexion than plaintiff's, and somewhat different glasses than plaintiff generally wears.

Moreover, the hair style and expression, while characteristic of the endearing "schlemiel" embodied by plaintiff in his earlier comic works, are out of step with plaintiff's post-"Annie Hall" appearance and the serious image and somber mien that he has projected in recent years. While this distinction would be of no moment if defendants had appropriated an actual photograph of plaintiff from 15 years ago such as those submitted by plaintiff for comparison . . . it is relevant to the question of whether the audience of movie watchers at whom this advertisement was aimed would conclude that plaintiff had actually appeared in the 1984 advertisement.

Finally, unlike in *Onassis*, where no other plausible interpretation was offered for the presence of the Jacqueline Onassis figure behind the real Ruth Gordon, et al., here defendants argue for a view of the advertisement consistent with the presence of a look-alike who is not thought to

be Woody Allen himself. The court has some doubts as to the ultimate pursuasiveness of this interpretation. We are unable to conclude, however, that no reasonable jury could find that others would so interpret the advertisement, or at least recognize it to contain a look-alike, particularly in light of the distinctions noted above. Therefore, while the court finds that the advertisement at bar clearly makes *reference* to plaintiff, it hesitates to conclude that the photograph is, as a matter of law, plaintiff's portrait or picture.

The foregoing discussion may be helpful in focusing the novel questions presented by this case. The court feels, however, that the facts before it are better addressed in the context of an alleged Lanham Act violation. The substantive standard of likelihood of confusion provided by the Lanham Act, discussed below, seems more appropriate than the somewhat strained construction required here under section 51. . . .

Therefore, the court finds it unnecessary to resolve plaintiff's privacy claim. Defendants' motion for summary judgment on the privacy claim therefore also need not be reached, except to the extent that similar counterarguments are offered in the context of the Lanham Act discussion below.

Lanham Act Claim

Plaintiff seeks summary judgment on his claim under section 43(a) of the federal Lanham Act, 15 U.S.C. section 1125(a) (West 1982) ("the Act"), which prohibits false descriptions of products or their origins. The Act is more than a mere codification of common law trademark infringement. Its purpose is "the protection of consumers and competitors from a wide variety of misrepresentations of products and services in commerce. In enacting the section, Congress in effect created a new federal statutory tort. The section is clearly remedial and should be broadly construed." . . .

The Act has therefore been held to apply to situations that would not qualify formally as trademark infringement, but that involve unfair competitive practices resulting in actual or potential deception. . . . To make out a cause of action under the Act, plaintiff must establish three elements: (1) involvement of goods or services, (2) effect on interstate commerce, and (3) a false designation of origin or false description of the goods or services. . . .

Application of the act is limited, however, to potential deception which threatens economic interests analogous to those protected by trademark law. . . . One such interest is that of the public to be free from harmful deception. Another interest, which provides plaintiff here with standing, is that of the "trademark" holder in the value of his distinctive mark. . . .

A celebrity has a similar commercial investment in the "drawing power" of his or her name and face in endorsing products and in marketing a career. The celebrity's investment depends upon the goodwill of the public, and infringement of the celebrity's rights also implicates the public's interest in being free from deception when it relies on a public figure's endorsement in an advertisement. The underlying purposes of the Lanham Act therefore appear to be implicated in cases of misrepresentations regarding the endorsement of goods and services.

The Act's prohibitions, in fact, have been held to apply to misleading statements that a product or service has been endorsed by a public figure. In *Geisel v. Poynter Products, Inc.* 283 F. Supp. 261 (S.D.N.Y. 1968), plaintiff, the well-known children's book author and artist known as "Dr. Seuss," sought to enjoin the use of his distinctive pseudonym in connection with dolls based on his characters. The court held that "a 'false representation,' whether express or implied, that a product was authorized or approved by a particular person is actionable under [the Act]." . . . The court further held that liability attached not just for descriptions that are literally false, but for those that create a "false impression." *Geisel*, 283 F. Supp. at 267. "The plaintiff is not required to prove actual palming off. A showing of the likelihood of consumer confusion as to the source of the goods is sufficient." *Id.* (citation omitted). Finally, the court held that a showing of actual consumer deception was not required in order to justify injunctive relief under the Act, so long as a "tendency to deceive" was demonstrated. *Id.* at 268.

In *Cher v. Forum International, Ltd.*, 213 USPQ 96 (C.D. Cal 1982), plaintiff, a popular singer and actress, brought a similar Lanham Act claim. Plaintiff sued when an interview she had granted to US magazine was sold to *Forum* magazine, a publication of Penthouse International. *Forum* published the interview and advertised it widely, falsely implying that plaintiff read and endorsed *Forum* and had granted the magazine an exclusive interview. *Id.* at 99–100. The court held that the Act "extends to misrepresentations in advertising as well as labelling of products and services in commerce," *id.* at 102, and noted that no finding of an actual trademark is required under the Act. *Id.* "The Lanham Act proscribes any false designation or representation in connection with any goods or services in interstate commerce," a standard which plaintiff Cher had met. *Id.*

Geisel and *Cher* suggest that the unauthorized use of a person's name or photograph in a manner that creates the false impression that the party has endorsed a product or service in interstate commerce violates the Lanham Act. Application of this standard to the case at bar, however, is complicated by defendants' use of a look-alike for plaintiff, rather than plaintiff's actual photograph, as in *Cher*, or pseudonym, as in *Geisel*. Unlike the state law privacy claim discussed in the foregoing section, the plaintiff's Lanham Act theory does not require the court to find that defendant Boroff's photograph is, as a matter of law, plaintiff's "portrait or picture." The court must nevertheless decide whether defendant's advertisement creates the likelihood of consumer confusion over whether plaintiff endorsed or was otherwise involved with National Video's goods and services. . . .

This inquiry requires the court to consider whether the look-alike employed is sufficiently *similar* to plaintiff to create such a likelihood—an inquiry much like that made in cases involving similar, but not identical, trademarks. The court therefore finds it helpful, in applying the likelihood of confusion standard to the facts of this case, to refer to traditional trademark analysis.

Reference to this analysis is justified since the likelihood of confusion standard is applied to a wide variety of trademark and trademark-related causes of action. The standard is "the heart of a successful claim" under both the Lanham Act and common law trademark infringement. . . . Other cases have held that the standard is applied in state law unfair competition cases as well as in trademark cases. . . .

In *Standard and Poor's,* the Second Circuit suggested six factors for a court to consider in deciding the issue of likelihood of confusion: (1) the strength of plaintiff's marks and name; (2) the similarity of plaintiff's and defendant's marks; (3) the proximity of plaintiff's and defendant's products; (4) evidence of actual confusion as to source or sponsorship; (5) sophistication of the defendant's audience; and (6) defendant's good or bad faith 683 F.2d at 708, 216 USPQ at 843. . . .

The first factor outlined in *Standard and Poor's,* the strength of plaintiff's mark, concerns the extent to which plaintiff has developed a favorable association for his mark in the public's mind. . . . There is no dispute that plaintiff's name and likeness are well-known to the public, and that he has built up a considerable investment in his unique, positive public image. Plaintiff's "mark," to analogize from trademark law, is a strong one.

The similarity of the "marks"—i.e., the similarity of plaintiff to defendant Boroff—is the question posed by the second *Standard and Poor's* factor, and has already been addressed above. While the court was unable to hold that defendant Boroff's photograph was as a matter of law plaintiff's portrait or picture, the resemblance between the two is strong and not disputed.

Under the third factor, proximity of the products, the court notes that while plaintiff does not own a video rental chain, he is involved in producing and distributing his own motion pictures, and he is strongly identified with movies in the public mind. The audience at which National Video's advertisement was aimed—movie watchers—is therefore the same audience to which plaintiff's own commercial efforts are directed. There is no requirement under the Act that plaintiff and defendant actually be in competition. . . .

The court has declined to rely on plaintiff's proffered consumer survey, and plaintiff has submitted no other evidence of actual confusion. Under the fourth *Standard and Poor's* factor,

such evidence, although highly probative of likelihood of confusion, is not required. . . .

The sophistication of the relevant consuming public is measured under the fifth factor. The average reader of *Video Review* or customer of National Video is likely to be comparatively sophisticated about movies, such that a good number of them arguably would realize that plaintiff did not actually appear in the photograph. This is relevant to the question of whether the advertisement contained plaintiff's "portrait or picture." However, given the close resemblance between defendant Boroff's photograph and plaintiff, there is no reason to believe that the audience's relative sophistication eliminates all likelihood of confusion; at a cursory glance, many consumers, even sophisticated ones, are likely to be confused.

The final factor is the good or bad faith of defendants. While plaintiff has not established that defendants acted intentionally to fool people into thinking that plaintiff actually appeared in the advertisement, defendants admit that they designed the advertisement intentionally to evoke an association with plaintiff. They must therefore at least have been aware of the risk of consumer confusion, which militates against a finding that their motives were completely innocent. Defendants may not have intended to imply that plaintiff actually endorsed their product, but they happily risked creating that impression in an attempt to gain commercial advantage through reference to plaintiff's public image. The failure of defendant National to include any disclaimer on all but one of the uses of the photograph also supports a finding of, at best, dubious motives.

A review of all these factors leads the court to the inescapable conclusion that defendants' use of Boroff's photograph in their advertisement creates a likelihood of consumer confusion over plaintiff's endorsement or involvement. In reaching this conclusion, the court notes several distinctions between plaintiff's Lanham Act and privacy claims which make this case more appropriate for resolution under the Lanham Act.

First and most important, the likelihood of confusion standard applied herein is broader than the strict "portrait or picture" standard under the Civil Rights Law. Evocation of plaintiff's general persona is not enough to make out a violation of section 51, but it may create a likelihood of confusion under the Lanham Act. . . .

Second, the likelihood of confusion standard is easier to satisfy on the facts of this case. Enough people may realize that the figure in the photograph is defendant Boroff to negate the conclusion that it amounts to a "portrait or picture" of plaintiff as a matter of law. All that is necessary to recover under the Act, however, is that a *likelihood* of confusion exist. While defendants, as noted above, have urged an interpretation of the advertisement which might defeat a finding of "portrait or picture," the court finds that no such explanation can remove the likelihood of confusion on the part of "any appreciable number of ordinarily prudent" consumers. . . .

Third, although the question of identifiability under the Civil Rights Law is generally one of fact for the jury, the likelihood of confusion standard may be applied by the court. While confusing similarity is technically a question of fact, it has sometimes been regarded as "one for the court to decide through its own analysis, comparison, and judgment." . . . It has therefore been held to be appropriate for summary adjudication. . . .

In seeking to forestall summary judgment, defendants Smith and Boroff maintain that the disclaimer which they insisted be included in the advertisement would have avoided consumer confusion. The court disagrees. Even with regard to the one version of the advertisement in which the requisite disclaimer was included, there exists a likelihood of consumer confusion. The disclaimer, in tiny print at the bottom of the page, is unlikely to be noticed by most readers as they are leafing through the magazine. Moreover, the disclaimer says only that a celebrity double is being used, which does not in and of itself necessarily dispel the impression that plaintiff is somehow involved with National's products or services. To be effective a disclaimer would have to be bolder and make clear that plaintiff in no way endorses National, its products, or it services. . . .

Smith and Boroff also argue that they lacked sufficient control over the design of the advertisement and its placement to be jointly and severally liable to plaintiff along with National. This con-

tention, too, is without merit. There is no dispute that defendants all knowingly agreed to include Boroff in the advertisement as a look-alike for plaintiff and that the pose and props in the photograph were intended in create an association with plaintiff. Defendants Smith and Boroff will not now be heard to plead ignorance when they intentionally created at least the risk of confusion.

The court concludes, on the undisputed facts before it, that a likelihood of consumer confusion exists in this case as a matter of law. Plaintiff's motion for summary judgment on his Lanham Act claim therefore is granted against all defendants. The motion of defendants Smith and Boroff for summary judgment is denied.

Having established a likelihood of consumer confusion, plaintiff is entitled to injunctive relief under the Act. . . .

Defendants have argued that any injunction against them must be limited in geographical scope to New York State. While such a limitation might be required for an injunction under the New York Civil Rights Law, given the differences in privacy law among different jurisdictions, an injunction under the Lanham Act need not be so limited. Plaintiff enjoys a nationwide reputation and defendants advertised a nationally franchised business through a national magazine. The harm sought to be prevented is clearly not limited to the New York area, and the injunction must therefore be national in scope.

Plaintiff seeks an injunction preventing defendants from presenting defendant Boroff as plaintiff in advertising. Defendant Boroff argues that any such injunction would interfere impermissibly with his ability to earn a living and his First Amendment rights.

As defendants correctly point out, the scope of injunctions against misleading commercial speech should be limited to that necessary to avoid consumer confusion. For this reason, disclaimers are favored over outright bans. . . . The court has already found, however, that the disclaimer appended to one of the advertisements before the court was inadequate as a matter of law to dispel a likelihood of consumer confusion. Nevertheless, the court hesitates sweepingly to enjoin defendant Boroff from ever appearing as a look-alike for plaintiff, since that could interfere with his ability to make money and express himself in settings were there is no likelihood of consumer confusion.

What plaintiff legitimately seeks to prevent is not simply defendant Boroff dressing up as plaintiff, but defendant *passing himself off* as plaintiff or an authorized surrogate. Therefore, defendant must be enjoined from appearing in advertising that creates the likelihood that a reasonable person might believe that he was really plaintiff or that plaintiff had approved of his appearance. . . . Defendant may satisfy the injunction by ceasing his work as a Woody Allen look-alike, but he may also satisfy it by simply refusing to collaborate with those advertisers, such as National Video in this case, who recklessly skirt the edge of misrepresentation. Defendant may sell his services as a look-alike in any setting where the overall context makes it completely clear that he *is* a look-alike and that plaintiff has nothing to do with the project—whether that is accomplished through a bold and unequivocal disclaimer, the staging of the photograph, or the accompanying advertising copy. This injunction applies as well to defendant Smith in his role as agent for Boroff. . . .

Difficult questions of law and fact are presented by plaintiff's claim that the photograph of defendant Boroff used in defendant National Video's advertisements constitutes a "portrait or picture" of Woody Allen, entitling him to relief under New York's privacy statute. The court concludes that this case is more properly regarded as one for unfair competition under the Lanham Act, and that plaintiff may gain full relief on this theory. There is no question that the advertisement in question creates at least a likelihood of consumer confusion as to whether plaintiff endorses National Video. Plaintiff therefore is entitled to summary judgment on his Lanham Act claim and an injunction against such potentially confusing use of defendant's photograph. . . .

Estate of Elvis Presley v. Russen, 513 F. Supp. 1339 (D.N.J. 1981)

BROTMAN, J.

During his lifetime, Elvis Presley established himself as one of the legends in the entertainment business. On August 16, 1977, Elvis Presley died, but his legend and worldwide popularity have survived. As Presley's popularity has subsisted and even grown, so has the capacity for generating financial rewards and legal disputes. Although the present case is another in this line, it presents questions not previously addressed. As a general proposition, this case is concerned with the rights and limitations of one who promotes and presents a theatrical production designed to imitate or simulate a stage performance of Elvis Presley.

This action is currently before the court on a motion by plaintiff, the Estate of Elvis Presley, for a preliminary injunction pursuant to Rule 65 of the Federal Rules of Civil Procedure. It seeks a preliminary injunction restraining defendant, Rob Russen, d/b/a/ THE BIG EL SHOW (hereafter Russen), or anyone acting or purporting to act in his or its behalf or in collaboration with it from using the name and service mark THE BIG EL SHOW and design, the image of likeness or persona of Elvis Presley or any equivalent, the names Elvis, Elvis Presley, Elvis in Concert, The King, and TCB or any equivalent or similar names on any goods, in any promotional materials, in any advertising or in connection with the offering or rendering of any musical services.

Plaintiff instituted suit on April 9, 1980 for federal law unfair competition (false designation of origin under § 43(a) of the Lanham Trademark Act, 15 U.S.C. § 1125(a)), common law unfair competition, common law trademark infringement, and infringement of the right of publicity. . . .

Every Finding of Fact that may be a Conclusion of Law is adopted as such; and every Conclusion of Law that may be a Finding of Fact is adopted as such.

Findings of Fact

Plaintiff . . .

3. During his career, Elvis Presley established himself as one of the premier musical talents and entertainers in the United States, Europe and other areas of the world. He was the major force behind the American Rock and Roll movement,

and his influence and popularity has continued to this day. During Presley's legendary career, his talents were showcased in many ways. He performed in concert, setting attendance records and selling out houses in Las Vegas and other cities in which his tour appeared. He starred in numerous motion pictures including one entitled *Viva Las Vegas,* which is also the name of the movie's title song which Presley sang. He made records which sold over one million copies and appeared on television programs and in television specials made from his tour program. . . .

4. The Elvis Presley tours were billed as "Elvis in Concert," and his nightclub performances were billed as the Elvis Presley show, while Elvis Presley shows in Las Vegas were billed simply as "Elvis." Most of Elvis Presley's record albums used the name ELVIS on the cover as part of the title. One of his albums was entitled ELVIS IN CONCERT. . . .

5. Elvis Presley adopted the initials TCB along with a lightning bolt design to identify entertainment services provided by him. This insignia appeared on letterheads, jackets for personnel associated with the show, a ring worn by Presley while performing, and tails of Presley's airplanes. Also, Presley's band was identified as the TCB band. . . .

6. Elvis Presley's nickname was "THE KING." . . .

7. Although Elvis Presley exhibited a range of talents and degrees of change in his personality and physical make-up during his professional career, he, in association with his personal manager, Thomas A. (Col.) Parker, developed a certain, characteristic performing style, particularly as to his live stage shows. His voice, delivery, mannerisms (such as his hips and legs gyrations), appearance and dress (especially a certain type of jumpsuit and a ring), and actions accompanying a performance (such as handing out scarves to the audience), all contributed to this Elvis Presley style of performance. . . .

8. One particular image or picture of Presley became closely associated with and identifiable of the entertainment provided by Elvis Presley. This image (hereafter referred to as the "Elvis pose") consisted of a picture or representation of Elvis Presley dressed in one of his characteristic

jumpsuits with a microphone in his hand and apparently singing. . . .

9. Elvis Presley exploited his name, likeness, and various images during his lifetime through records, photographs, posters, merchandise, movies, and personal appearances. . . .

25. Elvis Presley's popularity did not cease upon his death. His records and tapes are still sold in considerable dollar and unit amounts and Elvis Presley movies are still shown in theaters and on television. Elvis Presley merchandise is still in demand and sold. Also, many people travel to Memphis, Tennessee to visit Presley's gravesite and to see Graceland Mansion, his former home. The extent of Presley's continued popularity and the value and goodwill associated with him and his performances on, for example, record, film, and tape, is evidenced by the over seven (7) million dollars in royalty and licensing payments which Presley's estate received in the first two years of its existence. . . .

28. The Estate has entered into a license agreement for the use of the logo TCB and the lightning bolt design to identify a band composed of the members of Elvis Presley's back-up band. The Estate receives royalties. . . .

32. THE BIG EL SHOW is a stage production patterned after an actual Elvis Presley stage show, albeit on a lesser scale, and featuring an individual who impersonates the late Elvis Presley by performing in the style of Presley. The performer wears the same style and design of clothing and jewelry as did Presley, hands out to the audience scarves as did Presley, sings songs made popular by Presley, wears his hair in the same style as Presley, and imitates the singing voice, distinctive poses, and body movements made famous by Presley. . . .

33. Russen charges customers to view performances of THE BIG EL SHOW or alternatively charges fees to those in whose rooms or auditoriums THE BIG EL SHOW is performed who in turn charge customers to view THE BIG EL SHOW. . . .

34. THE BIG EL SHOW production runs for approximately ninety minutes. The show opens with the theme from the movie *2001—A Space Odyssey* which Elvis Presley also used to open his stage shows. (Exhibit D to Defendant's Answer;

Jarvis Testimony, Tr. p. 62.) The production centers on Larry Seth, "Big El," doing his Elvis Presley impersonation and features musicians called the TCB Band. The TCB Band was also the name of Elvis Presley's band; however THE BIG EL SHOW TCB Band does not consist of musicians from Presley's band. . . .

35. From the inception of THE BIG EL SHOW, the star was Larry Seth. Seth, who is under a long-term contract with THE BIG EL SHOW, recently "retired" from the show; but he may return. (Russen Affidavit; *see* Russen Deposition, p. 171.) THE BIG EL SHOW has continued its performances by using replacements for Seth. . . .

37. Russen has advertised the production as THE BIG EL SHOW and displayed a photograph of the star, Larry Seth, or an artist's rendering of Seth dressed and posed as if in performance. The advertisements make such statements as "Reflections on a Legend . . . A Tribute to Elvis Presley," "Looks and Sounds LIKE THE KING," "12 piece Las Vegas show band." . . .

38. Although the various pictures and artist's rendering associated with THE BIG EL SHOW are photographs of Larry Seth, or based on such photographs . . . a reasonable viewer upon seeing the pictures alone would likely believe the individual portrayed to be Elvis Presley. Even with a side-to-side comparison of photographs of Larry Seth as Big El and of certain photographs of Elvis Presley, it is difficult, although not impossible, to discern any difference.

39. On October 18, 1978, Russen applied to the United States Patent and Trademark Office to register the name THE BIG EL SHOW and the design feature, of that name, *i.e.*, an artist's rendition of Larry Seth as Big El, as a service mark. . . . Plaintiff did prepare and timely file its Notice of Opposition in the United States Patent and Trademark Office to contest the defendant's right to register the mark. . . . The proceeding before the Trademark Trial and Appeal Board has been stayed by the Board pending the results in the suit before this court.

40. Russen has produced or had produced for him records of THE BIG EL SHOW (including two albums and three 45 RPMs). . . .

41. In addition to selling records at perfor-

mances of THE BIG EL SHOW, Russen sold Big El pendants and a button with the picture of Larry Seth as Big El. . . .

Discussion and Conclusions of Law

I. *Standing*

[Omitted]

II. *Laches and Acquiescence*

[Omitted]

III. *Preliminary Injunction Standards*

To prevail on a motion for a preliminary injunction, the moving party must show that it has a reasonable likelihood of eventual success in the litigation, that it will be irreparably injured *pendente lite* if relief is not granted, that a balance of equities favor the plaintiff, and that the public interest considerations support the preliminary injunction's issuance. . . .

A. Likelihood of Success on the Merits

1. Right of Publicity

The plaintiff has asserted that the defendant's production, THE BIG EL SHOW, infringes on the right of publicity which plaintiff inherited from Elvis Presley. . . .

In the present case, we are faced with the following issues: a. Does a right of publicity and the concomitant cause of action for its infringement exist at common law in New Jersey; if so, does this right descend to the estate at the death of the individual? b. Assuming the existence and inheritability of a right of publicity, does the presentation of THE BIG EL SHOW infringe upon the plaintiff's right of publicity?

a. Right of Publicity in New Jersey

Although the courts in New Jersey have not used the term "right of publicity," they have recognized and supported an individual's right to prevent the unauthorized, commercial appropriation of his name or likeness. In the early and widely cited case of *Edison v. Edison Polyform Mfg. Co.*, 73 N.J.Eq. 136, 67 A. 392 (1907), Thomas Edison sought to enjoin a company which sold medicinal preparations from using the name Edison as part of its corporate title or in connection with its business and from using his name, picture, or endorsement on the label of defendant's product or as part of the defendant's advertising. In granting the requested relief, the court concluded that:

> If a man's name be his own property, as no less an authority than the United States Supreme Court says it is . . . it is difficult to understand why the peculiar cast of one's features is not also one's property, and why its pecuniary value, if it has one, does not belong to its owner rather than to the person seeking to make an unauthorized use of it. . . .

In following the approach taken by pre-1968 cases evaluating New Jersey law, we conclude that, today, a New Jersey court would allow a cause of action for infringement of a right of publicity. In addition, this right, having been characterized by New Jersey courts as a property right, rather than as a right personal to and attached to the individual, is capable of being disassociated from the individual and transferred by him for commercial purposes. We thus determine that during his life Elvis Presley owned a property right in his name and likeness which he could license or assign for his commercial benefit.

In deciding whether this right of publicity survived Presley's death, we are persuaded by the approach of other courts which have found the right of publicity to be a property right. These courts have concluded that the right, having been exercised during the individual's life and thus having attained a concrete form, should descend at the death of the individual "like any other intangible property right." *Factors Etc., Inc. v. Creative Card Co.*, 444 F. Supp. 279, 284 (S.D.N.Y. 1977). . . .

b. *Theatrical Imitations and the Right of Publicity*

Having found that New Jersey supports a common law right of publicity, we turn our attention to a resolution of whether this right of publicity provides protection against the defendant's promotion and presentation of THE BIG EL SHOW. In deciding this issue, the circumstances and nature of defendant's activity, as well as the scope of the right of publicity, are to be considered. In a recent law journal article, the authors conducted an extensive and thorough analysis of the cases

and theories bearing on media portrayals, *i.e.*, the portrayal of a real person by a news or entertainment media production. Felcher & Rubin, Privacy, Publicity, and the Portrayal of Real People by the Media, [hereinafter "Portrayal"] 88 Yale L.J. 1577, 1596 (1979). They concluded that "[t]he primary social policy that determines the legal protection afforded to media portrayals is based on the First Amendment guarantee of free speech and press." *Id.* at 1596. Thus, the purpose of the portrayal in question must be examined to determine if it predominantly serves a social function valued by the protection of free speech. If the portrayal mainly serves the purpose of contributing information, which is not false or defamatory, to the public debate of political or social issues or of providing the free expression of creative talent which contributes to society's cultural enrichment, then the portrayal generally will be immune from liability. If, however, the portrayal functions primarily as a means of commercial exploitation, then such immunity will not be granted. *See generally* Portrayal, *supra*, at 1596–99.

The idea that the scope of the right of publicity should be measured or balanced against societal interests in free expression has been recognized and discussed in the case law and by other legal commentators. In general, in determining whether a plaintiff's right of publicity can be invoked to prevent a defendant's activity, the courts have divided along the lines set out above. In cases finding the expression to be protected, the defendant's activity has consisted of the dissemination of such information as "thoughts, ideas, newsworthy events, . . . matters of public interest," . . . and fictionalizations. The importance of protecting fictionalizations and related efforts as against rights of publicity was explained by Chief Justice Bird of the California Supreme Court:

> Contemporary events, symbols and people are regularly used in fictional works. Fiction writers may be able to more persuasively, more accurately express themselves by weaving into the tale persons or events familiar to their readers. The choice is theirs. No author should be forced into creating mythological worlds or characters wholly divorced from reality. The right of publicity derived from public prominence does not confer a shield to ward

off caricature, parody and satire. Rather, prominence invites creative comment.
Guglielmi, 25 Cal.3d at 869, 160 Cal. Rptr. at 358, 603 P.2d at 460 (Bird, C.J. concurring).

On the other hand, most of those cases finding that the right of publicity, or its equivalence, prevails have involved the use of a famous name or likeness predominantly in connection with the sale of consumer merchandise or "solely 'for purposes of trade—*e.g.*, merely to attract attention.' " [without being artistic, informational or newsworthy]. . . . In these cases, it seems clear that the name or likeness of the public figure is being used predominantly for commercial exploitation, and thus is subject to the right of publicity. . . .

In the present case, the defendant's expressive activity, THE BIG EL SHOW production, does not fall clearly on either side. Based on the current state of the record, the production can be described as a live theatrical presentation or concert designed to imitate a performance of the late Elvis Presley. The show stars an individual who closely resembles Presley and who imitates the appearance, dress, and characteristic performing style of Elvis Presley. The defendant has made no showing, nor attempted to show, that the production is intended to or acts as a parody, burlesque, satire, or criticism of Elvis Presley. As a matter of fact, the show is billed as "A TRIBUTE TO ELVIS PRESLEY." In essence, we confront the question of whether the use of the likeness of a famous deceased entertainer in a performance mainly designed to imitate that famous entertainer's own past stage performances is to be considered primarily as a commercial appropriation by the imitator or show's producer of the famous entertainer's likeness or as a valuable contribution of information or culture. After careful consideration of the activity, we have decided that although THE BIG EL SHOW contains an informational and entertainment element, the show serves primarily to commercially exploit the likeness of Elvis Presley without contributing anything of substantial value to society. In making this decision, the court recognizes that certain factors distinguish this situation from the pure commercial use of a picture of Elvis Presley to advertise a product. In the first place, the de-

fendant uses Presley's likeness in an entertainment form and, as a general proposition, "entertainment . . . enjoys First Amendment protection." . . . However, entertainment that is merely a copy or imitation, even if skillfully and accurately carried out, does not really have its own creative component and does not have a significant value as pure entertainment. . . .

In the second place, the production does provide information in that it illustrates a performance of a legendary figure in the entertainment industry. Because of Presley's immense contribution to rock 'n roll, examples of him performing can be considered of public interest. However, in comparison to a biographical film or play of Elvis Presley or a production tracing the role of Elvis Presley in the development of rock 'n roll, the information about Presley which THE BIG EL SHOW provides is of limited value.

This recognition that defendant's production has some value does not diminish our conclusion that the primary purpose of defendant's activity is to appropriate the commercial value of the likeness of Elvis Presley. Our decision receives support from two recent cases. In *Price v. Worldivision Enterprises, Inc.*, 455 F. Supp. 252 (S.D.N.Y. 1978), *aff'd without opinion*, 603 F.2d 214 (2nd Cir. 1979), the court found that the protection of the right of publicity could be invoked by the widows and beneficiaries, respectively, of Oliver Hardy and Stanley Laurel to enjoin the production or distribution of a television series entitled "Stan 'n Ollie," wherein two actors would portray the comedians Laurel and Hardy. Although the facts bearing on the content of the program are not entirely clear, it appears that the show was to be based on old Laurel and Hardy routines which the comedy team performed during the careers and was not a biographical portrayal of the lives of the two men. In this regard, the court can be deemed to have decided that an inherited "right of publicity" can be invoked to protect against the unauthorized use of the name or likeness of a famous entertainer, who is deceased, in connection with in imitation, for commercial benefit, of a performance of that famous entertainer. . . .

We thus find that the plaintiff has demonstrated a likelihood of success on the merits of its right of publicity claim with respect to the defendant's live stage production. In addition, we find this likelihood of success as to the defendant's unauthorized use of Elvis Presley's likeness on the cover or label of any records or on any pendants which are sold or distributed by the defendant. . . .

2. *Common Law Trademark or Service Mark Infringement*

Since the plaintiff does not assert any Federal or State of New Jersey trademark or service mark registrations, any trademark or service mark infringement claims are governed by the common law, which provided the basis for and essentially parallels the protection provided by the Federal or State statutory schemes. . . . In order to prevail on a statutory or common law trademark or service mark infringment claim, the plaintiff must establish that the names or symbols are valid, legally protectible trademarks or service marks; that they are owned by the plaintiff; and that the defendant's subsequent use of the same or similar marks to identify goods or services is infringing, *i.e.*, is likely to create confusion as to the origin of the goods or services. . . .

Plaintiff asserts that Elvis Presley, during his lifetime, created and owned valid trademarks or, more specifically, service marks for musical entertainment services in the names of ELVIS, ELVIS PRESLEY, and THE KING, the phrase ELVIS (or ELVIS PRESLEY) IN CONCERT, the logo composed of the letters TCB and lightning bolt design, and the likeness of Elvis Presley, and that these marks were all legally protectible. After Presley's death the rights in these marks were acquired by the plaintiff, which is entrusted with the preservation and management of the property and rights of the decedent, Elvis Presley, for the benefit of Presley's heirs. The plaintiff points out that, in the fulfillment of its obligations, it has entered into a number of agreements licensing the use of the marks in various ways, including records, movies, merchandise and television performances of Presley, and that the licenses have continued to promote these trademarks and service marks. Thus, the plaintiff claims that since the service marks or trademarks are property rights and have continued to be

used to identify the musical entertainment services of Presley, these marks have been inherited by and continue to exist in the plaintiff estate. Finally, the plaintiff argues that the defendant's uses of the name THE BIG EL SHOW, the logo composed of THE BIG EL SHOW name and the likeness ostensibly of Larry Seth as he appears in THE BIG EL SHOW, the term THE KING, the initials TCB with or without a lightning bolt, and all likenesses of Elvis Presley (whether or not they are really of Larry Seth as he appears or appeared in THE BIG EL SHOW) to identify his production, constitute infringements of plaintiff's marks.

Each of plaintiff's points will be evaluated in seriatim in the context of the requirements for an infringement claim.

a. *Validity of Marks*

A service mark is defined as "a word, name, symbol, device or any combination thereof adopted and used in the sale or advertising of services to identify the service of the entity and distinguish them from the services of others." *Caesars World, Inc.*, 490 F. Supp. at 822; 15 U.S.C. § 1127; N.J.S.A. 56:3–13.1(B). *See generally* 3 Callmann, "common law rights are acquired in a service mark by adopting and using the mark in connection with services rendered. [citations omitted]." *Caesars World, Inc.*, 490 F. Supp. at 822. Since the plaintiff is principally claiming, at the present time, that its marks identify Elvis Presley entertainment services, we will focus on the validity of the names and symbols as service marks. However, it should be noted that these marks also might be trademarks which identify goods, *id.*, or particular products licensed by the marks' owner. . . .

(1). *Names*

The plaintiff claims that the names ELVIS, ELVIS IN CONCERT, ELVIS PRESLEY, and THE KING are valid and protectible service marks. Our review of the record indicates that the first three names have not been used only to identify a particular individual, Elvis Presley. Rather they have been used in advertising, such as for performances, concerts, and on records, to identify a service. They have appeared in close association with a clear reference (*i.e.*, IN CON-

CERT or SHOW) to entertainment services of Presley. Thus, they have attained service mark status. . . .

With respect to the name THE KING, the plaintiff has not established this name as a valid service mark. The record reveals that Elvis Presley's nickname was The King. However, plaintiff has not presented sufficient evidence as to how the name was used to identify services . . . and thus to function as a service mark. Of course, the plaintiff is not precluded from establishing the term THE KING as a valid service mark by presenting appropriate evidence at trial.

(2). *Logo*

The plaintiff has presented sufficient evidence, for the purposes of a preliminary injunction, of connection with Presley entertainment services or business to establish the logo composed of the initials TCB with or without the lightning bolt design as a service mark. For example, the logo was used on Presley's letterhead and on business cards. . . .

(3). *Likeness and Image*

The plaintiff asserts that the likeness and image of Elvis Presley serves as a service mark; however, the available evidence does not support such a broad position. Rather, the record only supports a conclusion that a picture or illustration of Elvis Presley dressed in one of his characteristic jumpsuits and holding a microphone in a singing pose is likely to be found to function as a service mark. This particular image (hereinafter referred to as the "Elvis Pose") has appeared in promotional and advertising material for concerts and on record albums. Thus, even though the "Elvis Pose" identifies the individual performer, we find it also has been used in the advertising and sale of Elvis Presley entertainment services to identify those services. . . . The court recognizes that the "Elvis Pose" has appeared in somewhat different forms; for example, the color of the outfit or the direction of the face has been altered. We do not find such changes to be determinative. . . .

b. *Protectibility*

The requirements for a valid trademark or service mark to be considered protectible under the common law or the Lanham Act depend on the characteristics of the marks themselves. Inherently distinctive trademarks or service marks, such as fanciful or arbitrary or non-descriptive, but suggestive, words and symbols, gain protected status upon their first adoption and use; while non-inherently distinctive marks only achieve protection if the mark is shown to have secondary meaning. . . . A trademark or service mark attains secondary meaning if the consuming public has come to recognize the mark not only as an identification of the goods or services but as a symbol indicating that the goods or services emanate from a single source, even though the identity of that source may in fact be unknown. . . .

Of the five names or symbols found to be valid service marks, the three containing the personal names (surname or first name) of Elvis Presley will be considered as non-inherently distinctive terms. The evidence sufficiently shows that these marks have been used for a long period of time through various promotions and uses, such as in advertising and on records (as well as in connection with certain licensed products), and have acquired a secondary meaning associated with Elvis Presley entertainment services as distinct from other entertainment services. . . .

The mark composed of the TCB and lightning bolt logo can be characterized as inherently distinctive since it is unique and arbitrary. . . . In the alternative, we also find that there is sufficient evidence of use of the mark in association with Elvis Presley entertainment services to show that the mark has acquired a secondary meaning of identifying the source of Presley entertainment services. Thus, the logo is protectible.

Finally, we find that there is sufficient evidence in the record for us to conclude that the particular "Elvis Pose" service mark, although perhaps a descriptive mark in that it illustrates the service, has acquired secondary meaning through its use in advertising and promoting of the entertainment services of Elvis Presley (as well as in identifying licensed products). . . .

c. *Ownership*

Trademarks and service marks are in the nature of property rights. . . . They "can be alienated like any piece of property," . . . however, "unlike patents and copyrights, [they] have no existence independent of the article, service or business in connection with which the mark is used. . . . We find that after Presley's death, the rights to use the service marks and trademarks identifying the entertainment services of Elvis Presley and the merchandise licensed by him passed to Presley's legal representative as a part of the assets of his estate. . . . Thus, as long as these marks continue to be used to identify Elvis Presley entertainment services, which are still available in such forms as records, video tapes, movies, and television performances, the marks will continue to exist and will not be considered abandoned. . . .

Although the record does not provide extensive evidence of the plaintiff's use of the five service marks (or trademarks), we conclude that the evidence is sufficient, for the preliminary injunction motion, to find that plaintiff still owns and properly uses the marks. For example, the plaintiff has licensed the use of the TCB logo to identify Presley's former back up band. The fact that the band previously performed with Presley is significant since there is a connection to Presley's entertainment services. The plaintiff also continues to receive royalties from licensing agreements wherein the licenses advertise and promote the service marks or trademarks to identify Elvis Presley records, movies, merchandise and television performances. In this regard, it should be re-emphasized that the "Elvis Pose" identified earlier is the only specific image of Elvis Presley for which there is sufficient evidence in the record to qualify as a service mark or trademark.

d. *Likelihood of Confusion*

The plaintiff claims that the defendant's uses in connection with THE BIG EL SHOW production of: the initials TCB with and without a lightning bolt, any artist's renderings or pictures, purportedly of Larry Seth as he appears in THE BIG EL SHOW, which resemble Elvis Presley, the name THE BIG EL SHOW, the logo composed of the names THE BIG EL SHOW and the artist's rendering, and the term THE KING, constitute infringements of plaintiff's service marks. Because we find that the term THE

KING, unlike the other items, has not been used by the defendant as a mark to identify his entertainment service, we will not consider this term in the infringement claim.

The test for infringement of common law service marks or trademarks, which is the same as for statutorily registered marks, *See House of Westmore*, 151 F.2d at 265, is whether the defendant has made a subsequent unauthorized use of marks, which are the same or similar to those marks used by the plaintiff, in the sale or advertising of his goods or services to identify those goods or services; and the defendant's use creates a likelihood of confusion or deception as to the source of those goods or services. . . .

The facts that Elvis Presley has died and that it is undisputed that almost no one would expect to see Elvis Presley performing live in THE BIG EL SHOW does not preclude a finding of infringement. The likelihood of confusion test refers to source, and, thus, may be satisfied if the plaintiff proves that consumers viewing the defendant's marks are likely to believe that plaintiff sponsored THE BIG EL SHOW production or licensed defendant to use the marks in connection with the show or was in some other way associated or affiliated with the production. . . .

The determination of likelihood of confusion necessitates our weighing various factors including, but not necessarily limited to, the strength of the plaintiff's mark, the degree of similarity between the marks, the intent of the defendant in adopting the allegedly infringing mark, the similarity of products or services involved, trade channels, manners of marketing and predominant purchasers, and the evidence of actual confusion. . . . By applying these factors in light of our earlier findings of fact and discussions about plaintiff's marks, we have reached certain conclusions based on general comparisons applicable to all of the marks and on specific comparisons of each mark.

(1). *Strength of Plaintiff's Marks*

The strength or weakness of plaintiff's marks is an important consideration. In general, "strong marks are given . . . protection over a wide range of related products [or services] and variations on appearance of the mark [while weak marks are given a narrow range of protection both as to products for services] and as to visual variations." . . . "The term 'strength' as applied to trademarks refers to the distinctiveness of the mark, or more precisely, its tendency to identify the goods sold under the mark as emanating from a particular, although possibly anonymous, source. . . . In view of our earlier discussion concerning the protectibility of plaintiff's marks, it is not necessary to conduct an extensive inquiry. For the purposes of this motion we find that plaintiff's service marks (ELVIS, ELVIS PRESLEY, ELVIS IN CONCERT, TCB with the lightning bolt and, to a lesser degree, without the lightning bolt, and the "Elvis Pose") have acquired great distinctiveness, in the eyes of the public and strongly identify Elvis Presley entertainment services and the source, although not necessarily known by name, of those services. . . . However, we do consider the TCB logo to be somewhat weaker than the others since it has received less public exposure.

(2). *Similarity of the Marks*

It is well-recognized that the greater the similarity between plaintiff's and defendant's marks the greater the likelihood of confusion. . . . An evaluation of similarity generally entails a comparison with respect to similarity of appearance, pronunciation, and meaning. . . . In the present case, appearance is the most dominant element, and similarity of appearance is determined "on the basis of the total effect of the designation, rather than on a comparison of individual features." Restatement of Torts § 729, comment b (1938). Using these general guidelines, we reach the following conclusions.

The defendant's first mark can be considered the initials TCB. The defendant's logo of TCB with the lightning bolt, and, to a slightly lesser degree, without the lightning bolt, is essentially identical to plaintiff's corresponding mark.

The second of the defendant's marks can be characterized as any of the artist's renderings or pictures, which are purportedly of the performer Larry Seth as he appears in THE BIG EL SHOW, standing alone without being part of THE BIG EL SHOW logo. . . . We find that such pictures are highly similar to the image of Elvis Presley portrayed in the "Elvis Pose." The use of an artist's rendering or sketch rather than a photograph does not diminish the resemblance.

The third mark, the name THE BIG EL SHOW, which is the name of defendant's production, is not as similar to one of the plaintiff's marks as the first two are. The plaintiff's marks ELVIS and ELVIS IN CONCERT provide the closest bases for comparison. Using the factors of appearance and pronunciation, we find that there is some similarity between plaintiff's marks and defendant's mark but the extent of similarity is less than for the first two marks. The resemblance results because the EL in THE BIG EL SHOW is the first two letters of Elvis, and it sounds similar, and the defendant's EL appears in the same type of blocked, capital letters as does plaintiff's ELVIS.

The fourth mark in question, and perhaps the most important, is the defendant's logo composed of the words THE BIG EL SHOW and the artist's rendering. . . . Considering the total effect conveyed by this mark, we find there is a high degree of similarity with plaintiff's "Elvis Pose" and a slightly lower degree of similarity with the names ELVIS and ELVIS IN CONCERT. . . . The connection in defendant's logo of the name THE BIG EL SHOW with the picture that looks like Elvis Presley results in the letters EL being more suggestive in meaning of the marks ELVIS and ELVIS PRESLEY.

(3). *Defendant's Intent*

Although the intent of the defendant in adopting a mark is only one of the factors, . . . if a plaintiff can demonstrate that a defendant adopted a mark with the intent of obtaining unfair commercial advantage from the reputation of the plaintiff, then "that fact alone 'may be sufficient to justify the inference that there is confusing similarity.' Restatement of Torts § 729, comment f (1938)." . . .

Because of the nature of the defendant's service, the defendant's intent as specifically related to his marks is interwoven with his intent as to the origin and presentation of the production. We have no doubt that a reason for Russen's starting his show was to capitalize on the popularity of Elvis Presley. It is also quite apparent that the show, the service in question, was designed to simulate or imitate a performance by Elvis Presley. The available evidence bearing on the defendant's reasons for adopting his marks must be considered in light of the nature of the production. It is possible that producer Russen adopted his marks in order to tell the public something about the production and to promote the show. On the other hand, such marks could have been designed mainly to deceive the public and to trade on the good will associated with plaintiff's marks.

Because the record contains a relative paucity of information bearing on defendant's intent, it is difficult to draw many strong conclusions. Based on our review, we make the following observations as to intent. Russen was well aware of Presley's TCB mark and adopted the same mark because of its connection to the Elvis Presley organization. . . . He stated that he got the idea to use TCB as the name of his band because it is the name of Elvis Presley's fan clubs and serves as Presley's motto. We find that the use of TCB in connection with defendant's production was totally unnecessary and was done only to benefit from the good will which attached to Presley and his performances and organization.

As to the name THE BIG EL SHOW and the artist's rendering or picture of the performer Larry Seth as he appears in the show, we are unable to conclude that the defendant adopted these marks *mainly* to "bask in the reflected popularity" generated by plaintiff's marks. . . . The defendant indicated that the name, THE BIG EL SHOW, was thought up by Larry Seth, the star of the production, and agreed to by the defendant Russen. The defendant also indicated that the artist's rendering or pictures were all of Larry Seth as the BIG EL. The plaintiff has not offered any other evidence, beyond the marks themselves, to prove improper motive. We conclude that there is insufficient evidence that the defendant adopted the name or used the pictures predominantly for the purpose of misleading or deceiving the public rather than for suggesting the nature of THE BIG EL SHOW production.

(4). *Similarity of Services*

. . . In the present case, the services of the plaintiff and of the defendant cannot be considered identical, but they are very similar. In general terms, each party's services can be described as musical entertainment provided by one singer or performer with instrumental or vocal background provided by others. There is some difference in the forms of presentation, since plaintiff's entertainment is provided mainly in the forms of records, film, video tape, and audio tape, while defendant's entertainment mainly appears as live, stage productions. The defendant, however, has also produced records, albeit in limited numbers, of THE BIG EL SHOW. In addition, both parties have engaged in forms of licensing or sublicensing their marks to appear on such merchandise as photographs, pendants, and buttons.

A more specific reason for finding strong similarity is that both parties' entertainment services involve Elvis Presley. The plaintiff provides actual performances of Presley, while the defendant provides an imitation of an Elvis Presley performance. The fact that the plaintiff does not provide live stage performances of Presley, admittedly an impossibility due to Presley's current state, makes identical services virtually impossible and does lessen the similarity somewhat. In any event, direct competition or identity of services or products is not required to prove likelihood of confusion. . . .

(5). *Similarity of Channels of Trade, Manners of Marketing, and Predominant Purchasers*

Similarities of channels of trade, manners of marketing, and predominant purchasers of plaintiff's and defendant's services, as well as licensed goods increase the possibilities of confusion. . . . The evidence in the record bearing on these factors is sketchy. By drawing some reasonable inferences from the available information and speculating on certain points, we have concluded that there is some similarity between the trade channels and marketing campaigns and that there is more similarity between the purchasers of the two services.

The enterprises of Presley, and more recently of plaintiff, have been national, including the

New Jersey, Pennsylvania region, and international in scope and distribution. Since Presley's death, his performances as embodied in records and tapes have continued to be sold in major retail outlets. In addition, plaintiff's licenses and sublicensees have conducted marketing campaigns in order to sell a variety of merchandise. Plaintiff has also indicated that a movie about Presley has been filmed and will be released; however, the evidence does not reveal how much of the actual Presley performances will be included in the movie or when and where the movie will be exhibited. Plaintiff has not provided any other evidence that it is currently presenting any entertainment services in theaters or nightclubs. Plaintiff, however, has introduced a license agreement allowing Presley's former band to use the TCB logo on a record and in association with personal appearances.

The defendant's show has had a much smaller and more localized market. Although THE BIG EL SHOW has appeared in different American towns and cities, including Las Vegas, it basically has been localized in the Northeast generally and the New Jersey-Pennsylvania region specifically. The performances usually have been presented in smaller nightclubs, although there was an engagement at a Las Vegas hotel, and the show has been advertised on a local basis.

One particularly important aspect of the defendant's advertising is the emphasis placed on the disputed marks in the records, ads, and promotional materials themselves. The picture or artist's rendering, which we have already found to have an extremely close resemblance to plaintiff's mark, is highlighted along with the name THE BIG EL SHOW, except on one of the album covers which only has a sketch of the performer. The name and the written material, such as "A TRIBUTE TO ELVIS PRESLEY," does suggest the production is a type of simulation or imitation intended to honor Presley, but does not reveal the name of the star or any information as to the producer or sponsor of the show. In essence, there is nothing to negate the reasonable impression that the artist's rendering or picture is of Elvis Presley. . . .

The similarity between the predominant purchasers is greater than that between the marketing campaigns and trade channels. Because defendant's enterprise, THE BIG EL SHOW, is a stylized imitation of an Elvis Presley performance, it seems likely that it would appeal to many of the same members of the public who are interested in and patronize plaintiff's entertainment services. These purchasers could be called members of the Elvis Presley consuming public. . . .

(6). *Actual Confusion*

Plaintiff has not presented any evidence of actual confusion by members of the consuming public. Plaintiff has not shown, for example by survey evidence, that people seeing THE BIG EL SHOW or advertisements for it thought the production was associated with the plaintiff or with Elvis Presley entertainment services. Although a showing of actual confusion could be significant, such evidence is not necessary to a finding of likelihood of confusion. . . .

(7). *Likelihood of Confusion—Conclusion*

. . . analysis of likelihood of confusion can be a complex process because of the variety of factors to be considered and because of the subjective and conjectural nature inherent in the process. In formulating our final conclusions we have used the perspective of the "ordinary purchaser" as our guide in balancing the extent and strength of the similarities against those of the dissimilarities. Based both on our evaluations of defendant's marks in light of the multiple factors and on our general sense impressions we have reached the following conclusions. The defendant's uses of both the initials TCB with or without the lightning bolt and of any artist's rendering or picture which resembles the "Elvis Pose," alone or as part of THE BIG EL SHOW logo, as service marks or trademarks to identify the defendant's production, records, or merchandise create a likelihood of confusion as to source or sponsorship. Although our analysis of the various factors provides ample support for our conclusion, we are especially persuaded by the strength of plaintiff's marks in the entertainment industry and the virtual equivalence of these two marks of the defendant with the corresponding marks of the plaintiff.

In making our decision, it is not necessary to conclude that the public be led to believe that defendant's show is composed of actual Elvis Presley performances or is produced by the plaintiff. It is not even necessary that the public know who the plaintiff is. What is required and what we find is that the ordinary purchaser generally familiar with plaintiff's marks is likely to believe that defendant's show is somehow related to, associated with, or sponsored by the same people or entity that provides the actual Elvis Presley entertainment services identified by its own marks. It is not at all unreasonable for the public to believe that this entity, which is the plaintiff, the Estate of Elvis Presley, has decided to license or sponsor a form of entertainment closely related to its other entertainment services. The public, realizing that an actual Elvis Presley live stage show is now impossible, might assume that the plaintiff's only alternative in order to enter this specific area of the entertainment field was to produce or sponsor an imitation of a real Elvis Presley performance, perhaps by using members of the actual Presley performing troupe or production staff or by supplying costumes or other official Presley items. It is also highly possible that consumers seeing the defendant's TCB logo or the advertisements highlighting the likeness of Elvis Presley might believe that the show is a multimedia presentation and incorporates films or recordings of actual Elvis Presley performances.

Our decisions with respect to the name THE BIG EL SHOW alone and in association with any pictures or artist's renderings resembling the "Elvis Pose" are closer. After careful consideration of the various factors, we have concluded that the use of the name THE BIG EL SHOW by itself does not create a likelihood of confusion, but its use as part of the logo or in connection with misleading pictures does create such confusion.

By attaching the artist's rendering to the name THE BIG EL SHOW to form the logo, the defendant has gone beyond allowable bounds. The likelihood of confusion associated with the artist's rendering is not sufficiently diminished by the use of the name with it. The picture, which certainly appears to be of Elvis Presley, provides the major triggering mechanism for the appeal to the public. . . .

Thus, based on the current state of the record, we have found a likelihood of confusion with respect to the defendant's marks of TCB with or without the lightning bolt, any artist's renderings or pictures which resemble the "Elvis Pose," and the logo. The plaintiff has established the likelihood of its ultimate success on the merits of its infringement claims as to these marks. The plaintiff has not established the same likelihood as to the defendant's use of THE BIG EL SHOW, alone, as the name or mark for its production.

(3). *Common Law Unfair Competition*

Plaintiff has alleged that the defendant's use of the names THE BIG EL SHOW, THE BIG EL SHOW IN CONCERT, THE KING, TCB (with or without the lightning bolt), the pictures resembling Elvis Presley and the presentation of the production imitating an Elvis Presley performance itself constitute common law unfair competition. Plaintiff claims that defendant's show, in combination with his advertising and promotion, should give rise to legal restraints because the defendant has "by unfair means usurped[ed] the goodwill and distinctive attributes of the business so constructed by [plaintiff]." *House of Westmore, Inc. v. Denney*, 151 F.2d 261, 265 (3rd Cir. 1945).

The claim of common law unfair competition, which is governed in this case by New Jersey law, covers a broader spectrum of behavior than trademark or service mark infringement. "In fact the common law of trademarks is but a part of the broader law of unfair competition." . . . Unfair competition "may be distinguished from infringement in that it does not involve the violation of the exclusive right to use a word, mark or symbol, but rather involves any violation of a right arising from the operation of an established business." . . . The focus in trademark litigation is on whether an alleged symbol or name functions to identify and distinguish one's goods or services and whether the usage by another of the same or similar mark is likely to confuse customers. Under unfair competition, the focus, generally, is on the buyer's likely confusion between two products or services based on an examination of everything that is likely to have an impact upon the purchaser. 1 McCarthy, Trademarks and Unfair Competition § 2:2 (1973). Many types of behavior are capable of constituting unfair competition. . . . One common form of unfair competition is closely linked to an action for trademark infringement and involves the use of the same or similar name, or symbols of a competitor or non-competitor. . . .

In light of our earlier discussion, in the service mark infringement context, of the likelihood of confusion as to the names and symbols used by the defendant, it is unnecessary for an extended analysis here. It is generally acknowledged that the same facts supporting a suit for trademark or service mark infringement will support a suit for unfair competition. . . . Thus, our earlier decisions regarding likelihood of confusion and probable success on the merits also hold for the unfair competition claims. Because there are fewer restrictions for a showing of unfair competition and more leeway in the exercise of our equitable powers, we conclude that our findings of likelihood of confusion are even stronger. . . . Therefore, even assuming the names ELVIS, ELVIS PRESLEY, and ELVIS IN CONCERT, the TCB logo, and the "Elvis Pose" have not functioned as service marks, the current uses by the defendant of THE BIG EL SHOW logo (words and Presley likeness), the pictures resembling Presley, and the initials TCB in his advertising and business and promotional materials are still likely to deceive the public as to the origin or sponsorship of the show itself.

As to the defendant's uses of the name THE BIG EL SHOW, without any accompanying photographs or artist's renderings, and the term THE KING, we still do not find a likelihood of confusion or deception. The plaintiff has not made a sufficient showing of unfair practices or other circumstances to convince us that the defendant's proper use of these two items constitutes unfair competition.

In addition to its claims against the defendant's use of certain names or symbols in its business, advertising, or promotional materials, the plaintiff argues that the defendant's production, itself, constitutes unfair competition. The plaintiff asserts that the packaging together of the image, dress, and style of Elvis Presley into an hour and one-half production designed to simulate an actual Elvis Presley production results in unfair competition since the audience viewing the performance is necessarily deceived into believing it is dealing with a service of the Estate of Elvis Presley. Plaintiff mainly relies on a type of unfair competition known as "unreasonable" or unprivileged imitation. . . .

Upon reviewing the record we find that the plaintiff has not presented sufficient evidence, such as eyewitness accounts, films, or video tapes, to show that the defendant's entire production is such a duplication of plaintiff's services that members of the public likely would be deceived into believing the production originated with the plaintiff. Even assuming the defendant's production is shown to have a striking resemblance to an Elvis Presley concert, as embodied in a form such as film or video tape, this resemblance by itself, and without other evidence tending to show a deception of the public as to the origin of the production, probably would not constitute unfair competition in the same manner as a striking resemblance to a distinctive trade or business dress would. Unlike an outside appearance of a store, the presentation of the defendant's production, itself, which occurs in a theater or club, cannot act to mislead customers into attending a performance of the defendant's show in the mistaken belief that it is associated with the plaintiff. Rather, the defendant's advertising and promotional materials for the show function to induce and attract potential customers in a manner similar to a building design or a package for a product. . . .

In any event, even assuming the similarity in shows should be considered, we are convinced that the doctrine of unfair competition was not designed to attach strict liability to a good faith and non-confusing imitation of an entertainment service, such as a concert by a famous performer like Presley, particularly where the original performer is no longer living. . . .

In deciding whether the defendant's activities constitute unfair competition, we must go beyond the question of whether THE BIG EL SHOW production is similar to an actual Elvis Presley performance as recorded on film, video tape, records, etc. Rather, our analysis must focus on the totality of the factors bearing on whether the defendant by his activities in the marketplace has attempted to deceive or confuse the public into believing THE BIG EL SHOW is connected with the actual Elvis Presley performances or sponsored by the same people, Elvis Presley's estate or its licensees, who have been presenting actual Elvis Presley entertainment services. . . . After considering those circumstances in light of our earlier findings as to likelihood of confusion, we conclude that the plaintiff has adequately demonstrated a likelihood of success on the merits as to part of its unfair competition claim. The plaintiff has made a sufficient showing of the deceptive impact of the defendant's advertising and promotional materials and other communication to the public but has not made such a showing with respect to the nature or composition of the defendant's show, itself.

4. *Section 43(a) of the Lanham Act*

The plaintiff argues that the defendant has violated § 43(a) of the Lanham Act, 15 U.S.C. § 1125(a), by his use of the name THE BIG EL SHOW, the initials TCB, the phrase THE BIG EL SHOW IN CONCERT, the picture or artist's rendering which looks like Elvis Presley, and the logo composed of the name and artist's rendering. The plaintiff also claims that the defendant has violated § 43(a) by his complete adoption of the performance style, accouterment and songs made famous by Presley, and by his advertising of "A Tribute to Elvis Presley."

Section 43(a) of the Lanham Act ("Act"), 15 U.S.C. § 1125(a), created a "distinct federal statutory tort," *Franklin Mint, Inc. v. Franklin Mint, Ltd.*, 331 F. Supp. 827, 831 (E.D. Pa. 1971), "designed to afford broad protection against various forms of unfair competition and false advertising." . . .

Although § 43(a) may proscribe competitive torts not covered by trademark infringement law or common law unfair competition, *S K & F, Co.*, 625 F.2d at 1065, as a general rule, the same facts which would support an action for trademark (or service mark) infringement or common law unfair competition (facts indicating a likelihood of confusion as to source or sponsorship of goods or services) would support an action for unfair competitive practices under § 43(a). . . . Because we have already addressed the strength or secondary meaning and the concomitant likelihood of confusion as to each of the names or symbols, as well as to the production itself, we do not find it necessary to conduct a similar examination here. Those conclusions as to likelihood of success on the merits are sufficient to suggest that a similar result is likely for the § 43(a) claims.

As noted, one of the purposes of § 43(a), as distinguished from the common law of unfair competition, is to protect "consumers as well as commercial interests from the effects of false advertising." 2 McCarthy, Trademarks and Unfair Competition, *supra*, § 27:2 at 246. In view of the qualifications attached to our unfair competition decision, we will address some comments to the permissible scope of the defendant's advertising for the stage production. . . .

Assuming arguendo defendant's presentation of a stage show imitating an actual Elvis Presley performance were permissible, defendant would be allowed to use a name and advertising material which suggests something about the production's content. However, the success of the production or service should depend on the quality of the production, itself, and not on the ability of the defendant to deceive the public and to benefit unfairly from the goodwill attached to plaintiff's entertainment services of actual Elvis Presley performances. The defendant would have to make clear in all communications (including, but not limited to, advertising and promotional materials, theater programs or playbills, and record covers) to the consuming public that his production is not affiliated with, sponsored by, or in any other way connected with the same people who provide actual Elvis Presley entertainment services. In this respect, the defendant's current advertisements and promotional materials . . . as well as the album covers . . . and labels on the 45 RPM records . . . are not adequate. They highlight those items, THE BIG EL SHOW logo and pictures or artist's renderings which appear to be of Elvis Presley, which we already have concluded are likely to cause confusion. The use by the defendant only of phrases such as "REFLECTIONS ON A LEGEND . . . A TRIBUTE TO ELVIS PRESLEY," "Looks and Sounds like

The KING," and "LIVE ON STAGE" does not diminish the confusion engendered by the use of the logo or artist's renderings to identify the production. In order to reduce this confusion, the defendant's representations and communications to the consuming public should incorporate in some manner the following ideas: that the production, or recording of the production, is a stage show, called THE BIG EL SHOW, which stars Larry Seth (or whoever is currently starring); that THE BIG EL SHOW is an attempted imitation of a performance or stage show of the late Elvis Presley; who the producer of THE BIG EL SHOW and of the record is; that neither THE BIG EL SHOW nor any recording is authorized or sponsored or licensed by the Estate of Elvis Presley; and that no one involved in the production of actual Elvis Presley performances or films or records is involved in THE BIG EL SHOW or the records of the show. In addition, in order to properly apprise potential customers that the star of THE BIG EL SHOW actually looks like Elvis Presley, the defendant should be able to use properly identified and legally obtained photographs of Elvis Presley to compare with photographs of the star of THE BIG EL SHOW.

B. *Irreparable Injury*

Having found that the plaintiff is likely to succeed on the merits as to certain claims, we must next examine the second requirement for a plaintiff seeking a preliminary injunction. The plaintiff must demonstrate that irreparable injury will result if an injunction is not granted *pendente lite*.

1. *Right of Publicity*

Although the plaintiff has shown a likelihood of success on the merits of its right of publicity claim, the plaintiff has not made a sufficient showing that irreparable injury will result if the defendant's production is not preliminarily enjoined. In making this decision, we note that we are treating a right of publicity claim different than a service mark infringement or unfair competition claim. Because the doctrine of the right of publicity emphasizes the protection of the commercial value of the celebrity's name or likeness, the plaintiff must demonstrate sufficiently

that the defendant's use of the name and likeness of the celebrity has or is likely to result in an identifiable economic loss: In contrast, in the context of the service mark infringement, unfair competition, and § 43(a) of the Lanham Act claims, we found that irreparable injury could result even in the absence of economic harm per se. One reason for this difference in approach stems from the public deception which is part of the latter three causes of action, but not part of the right of publicity claim. As a result of such public deception or confusion as to source, the plaintiff is being harmed. The plaintiff is being unfairly compelled to place the control of the good will attached to its entertainment services in the hands of the defendant.

In addition, and perhaps even more importantly, the close relationship in this case between the right of publicity and the societal considerations of free expression supports the position that the plaintiff in seeking relief for an infringement of its rights of publicity should demonstrate an identifiable economic harm. As we noted earlier, the defendant's activity when viewed simply as a skilled, good faith imitation of an Elvis Presley performance, *i.e.*, without the elements leading to a likelihood of confusion, is, in some measure, consistent with the goals of freedom of expression. Thus, before the harsh step of barring defendant's activity is undertaken, the plaintiff should have to make a showing of immediate, irreparable harm to the commercial value of the right of publicity and should not be able to rely on an intangible potentiality.

In light of these comments, we find that the plaintiff has not made a sufficient showing that the presentation of this particular production, THE BIG EL SHOW, has resulted in any loss of commercial benefits to the plaintiff or will result in an irreparable commercial harm in the near future. . . .

The considerations preventing the issuance of a preliminary injunction as to the show do not sufficiently apply to the sale of pendants or records even though the sales are limited. Since the plaintiff, through its licensing programs, also engages in the sale of such items, this situation is similar to that in *Factors Etc., Inc. v. Pro Arts,*

Inc., 579 F.2d 215 (2nd Cir. 1978), *cert. denied*, 440 U.S. 908, 99 S.Ct. 1215, 59 L.Ed.2d 455 (1979) and *Factors Etc., Inc. v. Creative Card Co.*, 444 F. Supp. 279 (S.D.N.Y. 1977), where irreparable harm was found. We find that irreparable injury would result from the continued sale and distribution of pendants displaying Elvis Presley's likeness or of records whose covers or labels display pictures or artist's renderings which are or appear to be of Elvis Presley.

2. *Service Mark Infringement, Common Law Unfair Competition, and § 43(a) of the Lanham Act*

As a general proposition, in the contexts of service mark (or trademark) infringement and unfair competition, including § 43(a) of the Lanham Act, the plaintiff who demonstrates a likelihood of confusion as to source, and thus, likelihood of success on the merits, will have formed a strong basis for showing irreparable injury. . . . This results because:

> A plaintiff who has demonstrated service mark infringement and unfair competition faces the probability of lost trade and appropriation of its goodwill. The damages in such a case are by their very nature irreparable and not susceptible of adequate measurement. . . . Plaintiff's lack of ability to control the nature and quality of services provided under an infringing service mark, even if defendant matches the high quality of plaintiff's services, constitutes irreparable injury. . . .

Fotomat Corp. v. Photo Drive-Thru, Inc., 425 F. Supp. 696, 711 (D.N.J. 1977). . . .

In the present case, the plaintiff's service marks are widely known and represent high quality entertainment services and substantial goodwill. The plaintiff has a significant stake in continuing to ensure that the services or products identified by these marks maintain these standards. If the defendant were allowed to continue to use those names or symbols (THE BIG EL SHOW logo, the initials TCB with or without a lightning bolt, and pictures or artist's renderings which closely resemble Elvis Presley) previously found to engender confusion as to source, the plaintiff would be harmed seriously by the deprivation of its ability to control the nature and quality of a service which the public believes it provides. . . . In addition, the plaintiff has a right to be protected from the probable damage to its goodwill if the purchasing public believes that the plaintiff has sponsored or helped produce THE BIG EL SHOW and is dissatisfied with the show. Such a loss of intangible value cannot be accurately measured and compensated in damages.

C. *The Balance of Equities*

Recognizing our earlier conclusions as to likelihood of success on the merits and irreparable injury, we find that the hardships to the defendant in complying with a preliminary injunction would not outweigh the harm to the plaintiff resulting from a failure to grant a preliminary injunction. Since the preliminary injunction would not prevent the defendant from using the name THE BIG EL SHOW or from presenting the production itself, the harm to the defendant should not be significant. This conclusion actually is supported by the defendant's own arguments as to the equities. The defendant claims only two equitable considerations: that THE BIG EL SHOW is his and his family's major source of income and that THE BIG EL SHOW has generated its own goodwill with the public. Although we feel the defendant has not made an adequate showing of both of these claims, it is not necessary to consider this in our decision. Since our preliminary injunction would not stop the production or the use of the name THE BIG EL SHOW, the defendant's main concerns are alleviated. The defendant has not indicated that changing the advertising and promotional material and the logo or discontinuing the use of TCB will cause any real financial damage or have any other adverse impact. The effect of an injunction on defendant's sales of records also would not have any significant financial impact because of the limited number of records and extent of distribution. Finally, any loss in trade to the defendant should be due only to the fact that the defendant will no longer be using confusion to trade on the goodwill and reputation of the plaintiff. Any expenses incurred by the defendant in complying with the preliminary injunction could be easily calculated and adequately compensated by an award of monetary damages if the defendant ultimately prevails. . . .

IV. *Conclusion*

In accordance with the reasons set forth herein, a preliminary injunction will be entered as reflected in the attached order.

Order

This matter having been brought before the court on the 29th day of October, 1980; and

The court having considered the testimony, briefs, proposed findings of fact and conclusions of law, exhibits, affidavits, depositions and oral argument; and

For the reasons stated in the court's opinion filed this day,

It is on this 16th day of April, 1980 ORDERED that the defendant Rob Russen, d/b/a THE BIG EL SHOW, his agents, servants, employees and attorneys and all persons in active concert and participation with him or acting on his behalf are restrained and enjoined, pending final determination of this action, from the following:

1. Using the initials TCB (whether in capital letters or lower case letters) alone or in combination with a lightning bolt design, in connection with any advertising, promotional materials, or business material, including letterheads and business cards, or on any covers or labels of records, or on any merchandise, or to refer to any band or orchestra, or in any manner whatsoever to refer to a concert or musical event or entertainment service not conducted or sponsored or licensed by plaintiff or under its authority;

2. Using any pictures, sketches, artist's renderings (or any other such forms) of Elvis Presley or which appear to be of or resemble the "Elvis Pose" as described or which are likely to lead persons into the mistaken belief that it is of Elvis Presley, in any advertising, promotional materials, or business materials or in any other notices or communications to identify an entertainment service or business, or on any record cover or label, or on any product, in any manner tending to deceive the purchasing public into the belief that the services or products provided by the defendant are sponsored or licensed by, or in any other way connected with the plaintiff;

3. Using any future advertisements or promotional materials, including but not limited to posters, newspaper advertisements, playbills, brochures, photograph albums, for the defendant's production of THE BIG EL SHOW which are not consistent with the general guidelines set forth in the opinion this date;

4. Using THE BIG EL SHOW logo or mark . . . which is composed of the name THE BIG EL SHOW and the artist's sketch which closely resembles the "Elvis Pose," in connection with any advertising, promotional materials, or business material, including letterheads and business cards, or on any covers or labels of records, or on any merchandise, or to refer to any band or orchestra, or in any manner whatsoever to refer to a concert or musical event or entertainment service not conducted or sponsored or licensed by plaintiff or under its authority;

5. Further distribution or sale of any copies of records (33 RPMs, LPs, or 45 RPMs, singles), including those designated as Exhibits P 14, 15, 19, which album covers or labels display an actual picture or artist's sketch of Elvis Presley or a picture, artist's rendering, or sketch closely resembling and appearing to be of Elvis Presley; and shall neither transfer nor remove from the jurisdiction any such records;

6. Further distribution or sale of any pendants or merchandise displaying an actual picture or sketch of Elvis Presley or a picture, artist's rendering, or sketch closely resembling and appearing to be of Elvis Presley; and shall neither transfer nor remove from the jurisdiction any such pendants or merchandise;

7. Committing any other acts calculated or likely to lead persons to the mistaken belief that any event or service produced, provided, or presented by defendant emanates from plaintiff or is sponsored, approved, licensed, or supervised by plaintiff, or is in any other way connected with plaintiff; and

8. Infringing on any of plaintiff's service marks set forth in the opinion this date. . . .

NOTES

1. *NFL v. Wichita Falls Sportswear, Inc.*, 532 F. Supp. 651 (W.D. Wash. 1982) discusses extensively the Lanham Act implications of the unauthorized use of NFL team colors, jersey designs, etc.

2. In *Apple Corps Limited v. Leber*, 12 Media L. Rep. 2280 (1986), the producers of "Beatlemania," a stage musical featuring look-alikes performing songs from the Beatles' catalog, were held to have misappropriated the personae of the group, causing audiences to "fall prey to the illusion that they were actually viewing the Beatles in performance."

10.50   Falsification and Libel

Libel covers a wide variety of situations bearing on the rights of celebrities in the entertainment fields. The focus of this section is more narrow. The concern is with avowed works of fiction and claims by individuals that they are characters in these works and are portrayed falsely. The cases which follow should be compared with *Hicks v. Casablanca Records*, the fictionalization of events in the life of Agatha Christie (see Section 10.30).

In *Spahn v. Julian Messner*, ex-major league pitcher Warren Spahn was the central character in a children's biography. Spahn alleged that events were described that never occurred, conversations reported that never happened, and that the only true-to-life aspect of the book was use of his name. The case was in the courts for a long time, making one venture to the U.S. Supreme Court that resulted in a remand and a shift in the New York court's grounds for granting Spahn relief.

Another work of fiction, the source of the complaint in *Bindrim v. Mitchell*, did not identify the plaintiff by name. He contended nevertheless that he was identifiable by the descriptions of him and his "Nude Marathon." Defendant had attended one of plaintiff's marathons, had agreed in the contract admitting her to the encounter sessions that she would not write about her experiences, but had done so anyway. The *Bindrim* result, finding liability, has caused consternation in publishing circles as to potential liability for

fictional works. Thus, the case remains as an important everyday concern for creative artists and those who deal in fictionalized treatments of real events.

Spahn v. Julian Messner, Inc., 260 N.Y.S.2d 451 (1st Dept. 1965)

BREITEL, J.
Plaintiff, a well-known baseball pitcher, obtained compensatory damages of $10,000 and an injunction, after trial without a jury, for invasion of his right of privacy under sections 50 and 51 of the Civil Rights Law. The invasion consisted of an unauthorized fictionalized biography of plaintiff published for a juvenile readership. Defendants' publisher and author appeal. They argue that the publication was privileged and one not for "advertising purposes or the purposes of trade" and therefore without the statute. Plaintiff cross-appeals on the ground of the inadequacy of the compensatory damages and from the denial of exemplary damages and interest on the damage award.

The only significant issue is whether the publication was privileged or exempt. On the damage issues there is insufficient reason to disturb the conclusions of the trial court. Compensation was properly limited to modest proportions because the offending book was a laudatory one and plaintiff had long permitted widespread exploitation of his baseball feats and fame. Exemplary damages were properly denied, at least in the exercise of discretion, because there was no reason to doubt defendants' sincerity of belief that they were privileged in their activities on the ground that the published work was a purported biography and that a biography for juveniles required special treatment. Nor is plaintiff entitled to interest on the award since it does not compensate for an external economic interest. . . . Because it is concluded that the publication was not privileged or exempt, the award for compensatory damages should be affirmed, and therefore the entire judgment should be affirmed as should the order denying the motion for exemplary damages and interest on the award. . . .

The statute, corrective of the common law in

this State, has had a long history and has been the subject of extensive judicial elaboration. . . . Although the statute makes no express provision therefor, the courts have engrafted upon it certain privileged uses or exemptions. Generally, the privileged uses are concerned with leaving untrammeled matters of news, history, biography, and other factual subjects of public interest despite the necessary references to the names, portraits, identities, or histories of living persons. . . .

Plaintiff is concededly a public figure in the sports world and therefore it is not disputed that he and his personal history are subject to public exposure in the news, literature, and public commentaries, whether or not such exposure is for profit. The question in this case arises because the book concerning plaintiff, although a purported biography, has been fictionalized, concededly, in order to make it suitable for a juvenile readership. Plaintiff therefore argues that the publication is not privileged and is not exempted from the statute. Defendants stress that a biography for a juvenile readership must be fictionalized and dramatized if it is in fact to be read widely.

Thus it is conceded that use was made of imaginary incidents, manufactured dialogue and a manipulated chronology. In short, defendants made no effort and had no intention to follow the facts concerning plaintiff's life, except in broad outline and to the extent that the facts readily supplied a dramatic portrayal attractive to the juvenile reader. This liberty, for example, was exercised with respect to plaintiff's childhood, his relationship with his father, the courtship of his wife, important events during their marriage, and his military experience.

In *Koussevitzky v. Allen, Towne & Heath*, a leading case, it was held that the statute was not applicable to a biography. It was also held that the infiltration of inaccuracies did not defeat the privilege, and that for defamatory inaccuracies plaintiff would be left to his remedy under the general law of defamation. Mr. Justice Shientag, in his discussion, emphasized the necessity to avoid hampering freedom of speech and of the press. He also pointed out that "all publications" are produced presumably for profit and with a

view to increasing circulation, and that such a profit motive did not destroy the privilege. At the same time, however, he pointed out: "The right of privacy statute does not apply to an unauthorized biography of a public figure unless the biography is fictional or novelized in character" (188 Misc. at p. 484, 68 N.Y.S. 2d at p. 783).

The distinction between an intentionally fictionalized treatment and a straight factual treatment (subject to inadvertent or superficial inaccuracies) was the basis for this Court's holding in *Youssoupoff v. Columbia Broadcasting System* (19 A.D.2d 865, 244 N.Y.S.2d 1). This appears both from the memorandum of the majority and the concurring opinion of Mr. Justice Steuer, joined in by Mr. Justice Eager. The distinction was again one of the bases for this Court's holding in *Hill v. Hayes* (18 A.D.2d 485, 240 N.Y.S.2d 286, affd. on the maj. and conc. ops. below, 15 N.Y.2d 986, 260 N.Y.S.2d 7, 207 N.E.2d 604), in which Mr. Justice Stevens stressed the fictionalization and dramatization of an actual event as a factor contributing to the negation of any privilege or exemption from the statute. . . .

The distinction or rule is a sound one and it dictates affirmance of the judgment in favor of plaintiff. Notably, the statute makes no provision for any privileged uses or exemptions. Whatever privileges or exemptions have been developed in the decisional law rest on strong policy considerations and, perhaps to some extent, on constitutional guarantees of free speech and of the press. Privileges or exemptions should not be facilely extended judicially except out of the necessities of the strongest public policy or by reason of constitutional mandates. Any extension beyond is in the province of the Legislature.

It may well be, as defendants urged and, perhaps, proved, that juvenile biography requires the fillip of dramatization, imagined dialogue, manipulated chronologies, and fictionalization of events. If so, the publication of juvenile biographies of living persons, even if public figures, may only be effected with the written consent of such persons. And if it also be true, as defendants suggest, that such persons use the consent as a lever for obtaining a price for it, then it is no more than charging a price for taking liberties, otherwise unwarranted, with one's personal history.

The consent and the price can be avoided by writing strictly factual biographies or by confining unauthorized biographies to those of deceased historic persons.

Actually, there is not only a matter of price involved. It is true, as it ought to be, that a public figure is subject to being exposed in a factual biography, even one which contains inadvertent or superficial inaccuracies. But surely, he should not be exposed, without his control, to biographies not limited substantially to the truth.

The fact that the fictionalized treatment is laudatory is immaterial, except perhaps as it may influence the assessment of damages, for three reasons. In the first place, a laudatory treatment may make one appear more ridiculous than a factual one, at least to those who know enough of the truth. In the second place, one may have strong feelings about not being portrayed in any exaggerated light. Lastly, there may be serious difficulties in determining what is laudatory. So long as it is not the truth, the subject of the distorted biography ought to have the right to permit or prevent its being published.

In short, the statute prohibits invasions of privacy for purposes of advertising or trade. Book publication is a trade like any other, except that its intellectual value to society is uniquely great and vital to civilization. To the extent that freedom of the press in the ultimate interest of the public's right to factual knowledge protects the publication of the factual and historical, the publication is exempt from the proscriptions of the statute. . . . If the publication, however, by intention, purport, or format, is neither factual nor historical, the statute applies, and if the subject is a living person his written consent must be obtained.

To be sure, there may be difficulties in many cases in separating the fictionalized work from the factual work, especially if the factual work has been liberally reconstructed from available evidence, but in this case there is no such difficulty. Instead, there was unabashed fictionalization, using some factual background and the identity of plaintiff only because otherwise there would be no interest in the purchase of the book.

In the ultimate result, the publisher of the distorted biography is in no inescapable quandary. All he need do is obtain the written consent of the living person whose personal life he wishes to distort and exploit. Nor will the children who read suffer unduly if the biographies purveyed for their reading are restricted to the duller factual ones or only to the livelier ones for which the subjects, if living, have given their written consents. In any event, the deprivation to the writer, the publisher, and the children is small as compared with subjecting the public figure to the uncontrolled distortion of his personality and history, short only of defamation or an actually intentional injury to his reputation. . . .

NOTE ————————————————

1. The next step in the *Spahn* litigation was appeal by the defendants to the United States Supreme Court. In a brief per curiam note, the Court held: "The judgment is vacated and the case is remanded to the Court of Appeals of New York for further consideration in light of *Time, Inc. v. Hill*, 385 U.S. 374." See 387 U.S. 239 (1967). What follows is the court of appeals reaction to the decision of the Supreme Court.

Spahn v. Julian Messner, Inc., 233 N.E.2d 840 (N.Y. Ct. Apps. 1967)

KEATING, J.

Again before us is this appeal by the defendant—author, Milton Shapiro, and his publisher, the defendant Julian Messner, Inc., from an order of the Appellate Division (First Department) unanimously affirming a judgment of the Supreme Court (Markowitz, J.) enjoining the publication and dissemination of the book *The Warren Spahn Story* and awarding the plaintiff $10,000 in damages.

On July 7, 1967, in conformance with the mandate of the Supreme Court of the United States, we vacated our prior order of affirmance (18 N.Y. 2d 324, 274 N.Y.S. 2d 877, 221 N.E. 2d 543) and ordered that the case be sent down for reargument in light of *Time, Inc. v. Hill*, 385 U.S. 374, 87 S.Ct. 534, 17 L.Ed. 2d 456.

Upon reconsideration of the appeal, we adhere to our original determination and again affirm the order appealed from. . . .

The remand of this appeal by the Supreme Court gives us an opportunity to construe the statute so as to preserve its constitutionality *(People v. Epton,* 19 N.Y.2d 496, cert. den. 281 N.Y.S. 2d 9, 227 N.E.2d 829) and to review the appeal in light of the standards set forth in *New York Times Co. v. Sullivan (supra)* and *Time, Inc. v. Hill,* 385 U.S. 374, 87 S.Ct. 534, 17 L.Ed. 2d 456 *(supra).*

We hold in conformity with our policy of construing sections 50 and 51 so as to fully protect free speech, that, before recovery by a public figure may be had for an unauthorized presentation of his life, it must be shown, in addition to the other requirements of the statute, that the presentation is infected with material and substantial falsification and that the work was published with knowledge of such falsification or with a reckless disregard for the truth.

An examination of the undisputed findings of fact below as well as the defendants' own admission that "[i]n writing this biography, the author used the literary techniques of invented dialogue, imaginary incidents, and attributed thoughts and feelings" (brief for appellants, p. 10) clearly indicates that the test of *New York Times Co. v. Sullivan* (supra) and *Time, Inc. v. Hill (supra)* has been met here.

The Trial Judge found gross errors of fact and "all-pervasive distortions, inaccuracies, invented dialogue, and the narration of happenings out of context" (43 Misc. 2d 219, 230, 250 N.Y.S. 2d 529, 541). These findings were unanimously affirmed by the Appellate Division. The court wrote: "[I]t is conceded that use was made of imaginary incidents, manufactured dialogue and a manipulated chronology. In short, defendants made no effort and had no intention to follow the facts concerning plaintiff's life, except in broad outline and to the extent that the facts readily supply a dramatic portrayal attractive to the juvenile reader. This liberty . . . was exercised with respect to plaintiff's childhood, his relationship with his father, the courtship of his wife, important events during their marriage, and his military experience." (23 A.D. 2d 216, 219, 260 N.Y.S. 2d 451, 454.)

Exactly how it may be argued that the "all-pervasive" use of imaginary incidents—incidents which the author knew did not take place— invented dialogue—dialogue which the author knew had never occurred—and attributed thoughts and feelings—thoughts and feelings which were likewise the figment of the author's imagination—can be said not to constitute knowing falsity is not made clear by the defendants. Indeed, the arguments made here are, in essence, not a denial of knowing falsity but a justification for it.

Thus the defendants argue that the literary techniques used in the instant biography are customary for children's books. To quote from their brief (p. 11): "The use of manufactured dialogue was characterized as 'mandatory' by a noted critic, teacher, and author of children's books. She explained that the dialogue is 'created, and based on probable facts and possible dialogue, which the biographer, through his association with his subject, through the vast amount of research that is necessary, can assume might have happened. It's not a falsification in that sense of the word at all.' Basically a juvenile biography 'has to be a lively story to catch a youngster away from television and all other distractions. . . . You cannot make it straight narrative. It can't list a great many facts or details which you can find in an encyclopedia or *Who's Who.'* "

Even if we were to accept this explanation as a defense to this kind of action (cf. note, 67 Col. L. Rev. 926, 942), the defendants could not succeed here. The author of *The Warren Spahn Story* had virtually no association with the subject. He admitted that he never interviewed Mr. Spahn, any member of his family, or any baseball player who knew Spahn. Moreover, the author did not even attempt to obtain information from the Milwaukee Braves, the team for which Mr. Spahn toiled for almost two decades. The extent of Mr. Shapiro's "vast amount of research" in the case at bar amounted, primarily, to nothing more than newspaper and magazine clippings, the authenticity of which the author rarely, if ever, attempted to check out.

To hold that this research effort entitles the defendants to publish the kind of knowing fictionalization presented here would amount to granting a literary license which is not only unnecessary to the protection of free speech but destructive of an individual's right—albeit a limited one in the case of a public figure—to be free of the commercial exploitation of his name and personality. . . .

For the reasons stated the order appealed from should be affirmed, with costs.

BERGAN, JUDGE (DISSENTING)
Had the Supreme Court agreed with our decision at 18 N.Y.2d 324, 274 N.Y.S. 2d 877, 221 N.E. 2d 543, upholding the constitutional validity of sections 50 and 51 of the Civil Rights Law as applied to Spahn's case, it would normally have affirmed in due course. Instead, it remanded the case back here for further consideration in view of *Time, Inc. v. Hill*, 385 U.S. 374, 87 S.Ct. 534, 17 L.Ed. 2d 456.

This seems to imply that on the present record the court disagrees with our earlier determination to sustain the statute against the argument of defendants that, as invoked by Spahn, it invades the constitutionally protected freedom of the press.

Of course, the converse is also true, that the court could have reversed on the present record if it could see that the case could not be reexamined according to different criteria. But it could not necessarily see that and would then leave it open to the State court to re-examine.

Therefore, one alternative open to us is to remit the case to the trial court to examine and decide the right of plaintiff to recover on showing "calculated falsehood" against which "the constitutional guarantees can tolerate sanctions" (*Hill*, p. 389, 87 S.Ct. p. 543); or a " 'reckless disregard of the truth' " (id., p. 390, 87 S.Ct. p. 543) which is treated similarly. . . .

These specific criteria were neither pleaded nor established on this record which essentially rests on an asserted violation of the statute by an actionable invasion of privacy in fictionalized biographical material relating to plaintiff.

The theory of the case, as presented, was that fictionalization relating to plaintiff's life was itself actionable under the statute as the New York courts have construed it. . . .

The case was not based, therefore, on a consideration of "reckless disregard of the truth" or "calculated falsehood" in the sense the Supreme Court used these terms. If, upon reexamination

it were found that the material complained of was merely "innocent or negligent" in writing and publication, it would seem then to be necessary to give judgment for defendants (*Hill*, 385 U.S. p. 389, 87 S.Ct. p. 543). There seems to be no suggestion that the publication would be proved on a further examination to be more than that.

Even though the fictionalized parts were literally not true, the writer seems to have regarded the fiction as consistent with Spahn's life and possible or even likely. As to certain dialogue complained of, for example, both sides stipulated in the record that it "was written by the author to interpret what he thought the facts were."

The direction of movement of the cases interpreting the constitutionally shielded freedom of the press suggests that the protection to defendants should now be more broadly based than either the narrow grounds that would rest on the *Hill* criteria, or those laid down by our prior decisions. It does not seem probable, reading *Hill* and *New York Times* together, that fiction alone concerning a public figure, actionable under the New York statute as construed, is any longer actionable.

Spahn is a public figure by his own choice. He is not a public official coming literally within *New York Times* or *Garrison*, but the right to print and publish material about a public figure rests on similar policy considerations even though they are not chosen at elections after public debate on their merits. A vast area of public discussion would be closed off if the press could speak much less freely of public figures than of public officials.

At least no good reason exists for imposing sharp discrimination. The material complained of here is not much more a "purely private defamation" than writing false statements about State officers (*Garrison, supra*, 379 U.S. p. 76, 85 S.Ct. p. 216). Therefore, it should be held that as to a public figure willingly playing that role, the New York privacy statute gives no protection against fictionalization not shown to hurt him and not shown designed to hurt him. . . .

NOTE ————————————————

1. The foregoing decision was not quite the end of the protracted *Spahn* litigation. The final gasp came

with the defendants once again filing notice of appeal with the U.S. Supreme Court. The appeal was docketed but then dismissed. See 393 U.S. 1046 (1967). Evidently, the defendants moved the dismissal.

Bindrim v. Mitchell, 155 Cal. Rptr. 29 (Ct. App. 1979)

KINGSLEY, J.

This is an appeal taken by Doubleday and Gwen Davis Mitchell from a judgment for damages in favor of plaintiff-respondent Paul Bindrim, Ph.D. The jury returned verdicts on the libel counts against Doubleday and Mitchell and on the contract count against Mitchell.

The court denied defendants' motion for judgment NOV and granted a new trial subject to the condition that new trial would be denied if plaintiff would consent to (1) a reduction of the libel verdict against Mitchell from $38,000 to $25,000; (2) a striking of the $25,000 punitive damage award against Doubleday on the libel count; and (3) a striking of the $12,000 damage award on the contract court against Mitchell.

Plaintiff consented without prejudice on these issues in any appeal to be taken from the judgment. Defendants appealed and plaintiff crossappealed from the judgment reducing the original jury verdict.

Plaintiff is a licensed clinical psychologist and defendant is an author. Plaintiff used the so-called "Nude Marathon" in group therapy as a means of helping people to shed their psychological inhibitions with the removal of their clothes.

Defendant Mitchell had written a successful best seller in 1969 and had set out to write a novel about women of the leisure class. Mitchell attempted to register in plaintiff's nude therapy but he told her he would not permit her to do so if she was going to write about it in a novel. Plaintiff said she was attending the marathon solely for therapeutic reasons and had no intention of writing about the nude marathon. Plaintiff brought to Mitchell's attention paragraph B of the written contract which reads as follows: 'The participant agrees that he will not take photographs, write articles, or in any manner disclose who has attended the workshop or what has transpired. If he fails to do so he releases all parties from this contract, but remains legally liable for damages sustained by the leaders and participants."

Mitchell reassured plaintiff again she would not write about the session, she paid her money and the next day she executed the agreement and attended the nude marathon.

Mitchell entered into a contract with Doubleday two months later and was to receive $150,000 advance royalties for her novel.

Mitchell met Eleanor Hoover for lunch and said she was worried because she had signed a contract and painted a devastating portrait of Bindrim.

Mitchell told Doubleday executive McCormick that she had attended a marathon session and it was quite a psychological jolt. The novel was published under the name *Touching* and it depicted a nude encounter session in Southern California led by "Dr. Simon Herford."

Plaintiff first saw the book after its publication and his attorneys sent letters to Doubleday and Mitchell. Nine months later the New American Library published the book in paperback.

The parallel between the actual nude marathon sessions and the sessions in the book *Touching* was shown to the jury by means of the tape recordings Bindrim had taken of the actual sessions. Plaintiff complains in particular about a portrayed session in which he tried to encourage a minister to get his wife to attend the nude marathon. Plaintiff alleges he was libeled by the passage below:

[Excerpts from "Touching," Pages 126–127]

The minister was telling us how the experience had gotten him further back to God.

And all the time he was getting closer to God, he was being moved further away from his wife, who didn't understand, she didn't understand at all. She didn't realize what was coming out of the sensitivity training sessions he was conducting in the church.

He felt, he, more than felt, he knew, that if she didn't begin coming to the nude marathons and try to grasp what it was all about, the marriage would be over.

"You better bring her to the next marathon," Simon said.

"I've been trying," said the minister. "I only pray she comes."

"You better do better than pray," said Simon. "You better grab her . . . and drag her here."

"I can only try."

"You can do more than try. You can grab her by the cunt.

"A man with that kind of power, whether it comes from God or from his own manly strength, strength he doesn't know he has, can drag his wife here by the fucking cunt.

"I know," Alex said softly. "I know."

[Transcript of actual session]

"I've come a little way."

"I'd like to know about your wife. She hasn't been to a marathon?"

"No."

"Isn't interested? Has no need?"

"I don't—she did finally say that she would like to go to a standard sensitivity training session somewhere. She would be—I can't imagine her in a nude marathon. She can't imagine it."

"Why?"

"Neither could I when I first came.

"Yeh. She might. I don't know."

"It certainly would be a good idea for two reasons: one, the minor one is that you are involved here, and if she were in the same thing, and you could come to some of the couple ones, it would be helpful to you. But more than that, almost a definite recipe for breaking up a marriage is for one person to go into growth groups and sense change and grow. . . ."

"I know that."

"Boy they sure don't want that, and once they're clear they don't need that mate any more, and they are not very patient."

"But it is true, the more I get open the more the walls are built between us. And it's becoming a fairly intelligent place, a fairly open place, doing moderate sensitivity eyeballing stuff with the kids. I use some of these techniques teaching out [sic] class work."

"Becoming more involved?"

"Yeh, involved at the same time that I am more separated from. It's a paradox again, isn't it?"

"Mmm."

Plaintiff asserts that he was libeled by the suggestion that he used obscene language which he did not in fact use. Plaintiff also alleges various other libels due to Mitchell's inaccurate portrayal of what actually happened at the marathon. Plaintiff alleges that he was injured in his profession and expert testimony was introduced showing that Mitchell's portrayal of plaintiff was injurious

and that plaintiff was identified by certain colleagues as the character in the book, Simon Herford.

I

Defendants first allege that they were entitled to judgment on the ground that there was no showing of "actual malice" by defendants.

As a public figure, plaintiff is precluded from recovering damages for a defamatory falsehood relating to him, unless he proved that the statement was made with "actual malice," that is, that it was made with knowledge that it is false or with reckless disregard of whether it was false or not. . . .

There is clear and convincing evidence to support the jury's finding that defendant Mitchell entertained actual malice, and that defendant Doubleday had actual malice when it permitted the paperback printing of *Touching* although there was no actual malice on the part of Doubleday in its original printing of the hardback edition.

Mitchell's reckless disregard for the truth was apparent from her knowledge of the truth of what transpired at the encounter, and the literary portrayals of that encounter. Since she attended sessions, there can be no suggestion that she did not know the true facts. Since "actual malice" concentrates solely on defendants' attitude toward the truth or falsity of the material published . . . and not on malicious motives, certainly defendant Mitchell was in a position to know the truth or falsity of her own material, and the jury was entitled to find that her publication was in reckless disregard of that truth or with actual knowledge of falsity.

However, plaintiff failed to prove by clear and convincing evidence that the original hardback publication by Doubleday was made with knowledge of falsity or in reckless disregard of falsity. McCormick of Doubleday cautioned plaintiff that the characters must be totally fictitious and Mitchell assured McCormick that the characters in *Touching* were incapable of being identified as real persons. McCormick arranged to have the manuscript read by an editor knowledgeable in the field of libel. The cases are clear that reckless conduct is not measured by whether a reasonably prudent person would have published or would have investigated before publishing. There must be sufficient evidence to permit the conclusion that defendant in fact entertained serious doubts as to the truth of his publication. . . .

Plaintiff suggests that, since the book did not involve "hot news," Doubleday had a duty to investigate the content for truth. Courts have required investigation as to truth or falsity of statements which were not hot news . . . but those cases involved factual stories about actual people. In the case at bar, Doubleday had been assured by Mitchell that no actual, identifiable person was involved and that all the characters were fictitious in the novel. Where the publication comes from a known reliable source and there is nothing in the circumstances to suggest inaccuracy, there is no duty to investigate. . . . There was nothing in the record to sugggest that, prior to the hardback printing, defendant Doubleday in fact entertained serious doubts as to the truth or falsity of the publication, and investigatory failure alone is insufficient to find actual malice.

However, prior to the paperback printing there were surrounding circumstances to suggest inaccuracy, such that at that point Doubleday had a duty to investigate. Plaintiff did show that Doubleday sold the rights to the New American Library after receiving a letter from plaintiff's attorney explaining that plaintiff was Herford and the inscription in the paperback said, "This is an authorized edition published by Doubleday and Company." Although, after the receipt of the plaintiff's attorney's letter, Doubleday again inquired of Mitchell as to whether plaintiff was the character in the book, the jury was entitled to find that Mitchell's assurance to Doubleday was not sufficient to insulate Doubleday from liability and that Doubleday had some further duty to investigate. The jury could have inferred that at that point Doubleday either had serious doubts, or should have had serious doubts, as to the possibility that plaintiff was defamed by *Touching* and that at that point Doubleday had some duty to investigate.

II

For similar reasons, the award for punitive damages against Doubleday may stand. A public figure in a defamation case may be awarded punitive damages when there is "actual malice" under the *New York Times* standard . . . and, as we have said above, actual malice was established for Doubleday. . . .

III

Appellants claim that, even if there are untrue statements, there is no showing that plaintiff was identified as the character, Simon Herford, in the novel *Touching*.

Appellants allege that plaintiff failed to show he was identifiable as Simon Herford, relying on the fact that the character in *Touching* was described in the book as a "fat Santa Claus type with long white hair, white sideburns, a cherubic rosy face and rosy forearms" and that Bindrim was clean shaven and had short hair. Defendants rely in part on *Wheeler v. Dell Publishing Co.* (7th Cir. 1962) 300 F.2d 372, which involved an alleged libel caused by a fictional account of an actual murder trial. The *Wheeler* court said (at p. 376): "In our opinion, any reasonable person who read the book and was in a position to identify Hazel Wheeler with Janice Quill would more likely conclude that the author created the latter in an ugly way so that none would identify her with Hazel Wheeler. It is important to note that while the trial and locale might suggest Hazel Wheeler to those who knew the Chenoweth family, suggestion is not identification. In *Levey [Levey v. Warner Bros. Pictures* (S.D.N.Y. 1944) 57 F. Supp. 40] the court said those who had seen her act may have been reminded of her by songs and scenes, but would not reasonably identify her." However, in *Wheeler* the court found that no one who knew the real widow could possibly identify her with the character in the novel. In the case at bar, the only differences between plaintiff and the Herford character in *Touching* were physical appearance and that Herford was a psychiatrist rather than psychologist. Otherwise, the character Simon Herford was very similar to the actual plaintiff. We cannot say, as did the court in

Wheeler, that no one who knew plaintiff Bindrim could reasonably identify him with the fictional character. Plaintiff was identified as Herford by several witnesses and plaintiff's own tape recordings of the marathon sessions show that the novel was based substantially on plaintiff's conduct in the nude marathon.

Defendant also relies on *Middlebrooks v. Curtis Publishing Co.* (4th Cir. 1969) 413 F.2d 141, where the marked dissimilarities between the fictional character and the plaintiff supported the court's finding against the reasonableness of identification. In *Middlebrooks,* there was a difference in age, an absence from the locale at the time of the episode, and a difference in employment of the fictional character and plaintiff; nor did the story parallel the plaintiff's life in any significant manner. In the case at bar, apart from some of those episodes allegedly constituting the libelous matter itself, and apart from the physical difference and the fact that plaintiff had a Ph.D., and not an M.D., the similarities between Herford and Bindrim are clear, and the transcripts of the actual encounter weekend show a close parallel between the narrative of plaintiff's novel and the actual real life events. . . .

IV

However, even though there was clear and convincing evidence to support the finding of "actual malice," and even though there was support for finding that plaintiff is identified as the character in Mitchell's novel, there still can be no recovery by plaintiff if the statements in *Touching* were not libelous. . . . There can be no libel predicated on an opinion. The publication must contain a false statement of fact. . . .

Plaintiff alleges that the book as a whole was libelous and that the book contained several false statements of fact. Plaintiff relies in part on the above quoted conversation between plaintiff and the minister as one libelous statement of fact. Plaintiff also argues that a particular incident in the book is libelous. That incident depicts an encounter group patient as so distressed upon leaving from the weekend therapy that she is killed when her car crashes. Plaintiff also com-

plains of an incident in the book where he is depicted as "pressing," "clutching," and "ripping" a patient's cheeks and "stabbing against a pubic bone." Plaintiff complains, too, of being depicted as having said to a female patient, "Drop it, bitch." . . .

Our inquiry then, is directed to whether or not any of these incidents can be considered false statements of fact. It is clear from the transcript of the actual encounter weekend proceeding that some of the incidents portrayed by Mitchell are false: i.e., substantially inaccurate description of what actually happened. It is also clear that some of these portrayals cast plaintiff in a disparaging light since they portray his language and conduct as crude, aggressive, and unprofessional. . . .

The courts have set guidelines in determining what is fact and what is opinion. One guideline is that an alleged defamatory statement may constitute a fact in one context and an opinion in another and content of the communication is taken as a whole. In certain settings fiery rhetoric and hyperbolic statements of fact may well assume the character of opinion. . . . Where the statements are unambiguously fact or opinion, . . . the court determines as a matter of law whether the statements are fact or opinion. However, where the alleged defamatory remarks could be determined either as fact or opinion, and the court cannot say as a matter of law that the statements were not understood as fact, there is a triable issue of fact for the jury. . . .

If viewed as a case involving an issue of "opinion," those cases, and other cases involving that issue, make it clear that, since there was evidence that people had identified plaintiff with the Dr. Herford of the book, the jury's finding against defendants is conclusive on that issue.

However, as we have indicated above, we regard the case at bench as involving a different issue. Defendants contend that the fact that the book was labeled as being a "novel" bars any claim that the writer or publisher could be found to have implied that the characters in the book were factual representations not of the fictional characters but of an actual nonfictional person. That contention, thus broadly stated, is unsupported by the cases. . . . The test is whether a reasonable person, reading the book, would understand that the fictional character therein pictured was, in actual fact, the plaintiff acting as described. . . . Each case must stand on its own facts. . . .

Whether a reader, identifying plaintiff with the "Dr. Herford" of the book, would regard the passages herein complained of as mere fictional embroidering or as reporting actual language and conduct, was for the jury. Its verdict adverse to the defendants cannot be overturned by this court.

V

Defendants raise the question of whether there is "publication" for libel where the communication is to only one person or a small group of persons rather than to the public at large. . . . Publication for purposes of defamation is sufficient when the publication is to only one person other than the person defamed. . . . Therefore, it is irrelevant whether all readers realized plaintiff and Herford were identical. . . .

The Cross-Appeal

Bindrim contends that the trial court erred in striking the damage award on the contract count. We are aware of no authority that a professional person can, by contract or otherwise, prevent one of his patients from reporting the treatment that patient received. Since the whole theory of plaintiff's therapy was that of group encounter, what Mitchell saw done to and by other members of the group was part of her own treatment. She was free to report what went on. The limits to her right to report were those involved in the libel counts. Plaintiff has no separate cause of action for the mere reporting.

In addition, although plaintiff testified in broad language that he had been damaged by the publication of the book, it is not clear how much, if any, of that damage flowed from the inaccuracies in the book as distinguished from the fact that his encounter therapy had been given publicity. On this record, we cannot say that the trial court erred. . . .

The judgment, as modified on the motion for a new trial, is further modified as follows:

(1) By substituting for separate judgments against defendants Mitchell and Doubleday a joint and several judgment against both of said defendants in the amount of $50,000; and

(2) By including in said judgment a separate judgment against Doubleday of $25,000 for punitive damages.

Otherwise the judgment is affirmed. Neither party shall recover costs on appeal.

JEFFERSON, J. (CONCURRING)

Although I agree with the majority opinion authored by Justice Kingsley, I am writing a separate concurring opinion in order to comment upon the dissenting opinion. The dissent erroneously describes the majority holding as creating a cause of action for libel out of a work of fiction that attacks the techniques of "nude encounter therapy." Because of this misconception with respect to the majority's holding, the dissent reaches the conclusion that the majority's view "poses a grave threat to any future work of fiction which explores the effect of techniques claimed to have curative value."

Had the defendant author of the work of fiction limited her novel to a truthful or fictional description of the techniques employed in nude encounter therapy, I would agree with the dissent that plaintiff had no cause of action for defamation. But here we have a description of a therapist as using insulting and vulgar language of the rankest sort in addressing his patients. Apparently the dissent does not consider that such language is capable of being considered defamatory of plaintiff in his professional role of a therapist practicing nude encounter therapy. The vulgarity purportedly used by the therapist in the novel would necessarily be considered by numerous persons as completely unprofessional and defamatory if used by a professional therapist such as the plaintiff. I fail to see how any jury or any court could consider such crude vulgarity as *not* defaming a professional therapist to whom such vulgarity was attributed in the practice of his profession. I need not repeat this language here at it is set forth in the majority opinion. . . .

The dissent concludes that the "average reader" would not have considered plaintiff defamed as a professional therapist who used the crude and vulgar language. But the dissent does not tell us what constitutes an "average reader." I assume that novels are read by the learned, the not so learned, and persons in all walks of life. It is my view that any reader of the novel, whether familiar with a professional therapist's practices or not, might well conclude that a therapist described in the novel was a lewd and dissolute character in the practice of his profession. . . .

The dissent sees in the majority opinion a branding of a novel as libelous because it is critical of an occupational practice. This is a distortion of the majority's position. The position of the majority is simply to refuse to permit a writer and publisher to libel a person and hide under the banner of having written only fictional material. . . .

FILES, J. (DISSENTING)

This novel, which is presented to its readers as a work of fiction, contains a portrayal of nude encounter therapy, and its tragic effect upon an apparently happy and well-adjusted woman who subjected herself to it. Plaintiff is a practitioner of this kind of therapy. His grievance, as described in his testimony and in his briefs on appeal, is provoked by that institutional criticism. Plaintiff's "concession" that he is a public figure appears to be a tactic to enhance his argument that any unflattering portrayal of this kind of therapy defames him.

The decision of the majority upholding a substantial award of damages against the author and publisher poses a grave threat to any future work of fiction which explores the effect of techniques claimed to have curative value. . . .

The complaint in this action quotes verbatim the portions of the defendant's novel which are alleged to be libelous. No explanatory matter or special damages are alleged. The only arguably defamatory matter I can find in that complaint is in the passages which portray the fictional therapist using coarse, vulgar and insulting language in

addressing his patients. Some of the therapeutic techniques described in the quoted passages may seem bizarre, but a court cannot assume that such conduct is so inappropriate that a reputable therapist would be defamed if that technique were imputed to him. The alleged defamation therefore is limited to the imputation of vulgar speech and insulting manners.

The defendants asked the trial court to give an instruction to the jury identifying the matter which it could consider as defamatory. The trial court refused. Instead, the court sent the case to the jury without distinction between actionable defamation and constitutionally protected criticism. In addition, the trial court's instructions authorized the jury to award special damages for loss of income which could have resulted from the lawful expression of opinion. . . .

Defendants' novel describes a fictitious therapist who is conspicuously different from plaintiff in name, physical appearance, age, personality and profession.

Indeed the fictitious Dr. Herford has none of the characteristics of plaintiff except that Dr. Herford practices nude encounter therapy. Only three witnesses, other than plaintiff himself, testified that they "recognized" plaintiff as the fictitious Dr. Herford. All three of those witnesses had participated in or observed one of plaintiff's nude marathons. The only characteristic mentioned by any of the three witnesses as identifying plaintiff was the therapy practiced.

Plaintiff was cross-examined in detail about what he saw that identified him in the novel. Every answer he gave on this subject referred to how the fictitious Dr. Herford dealt with his patients.

Plaintiff has no monopoly upon the encounter therapy which he calls "nude marathon." Witnesses testified without contradiction that other professionals use something of this kind. There does not appear to be any reason why anyone could not conduct a "marathon" using the style if not the full substance of plaintiff's practices.

Plaintiff's brief discusses the therapeutic practices of the fictitious Dr. Herford in two categories: Those practices which are similar to plaintiff's technique are classifed as identifying. Those which are unlike plaintiff's are called libelous because they are false. Plaintiff has thus resurrected the spurious logic which Professor Kalven found in the position of the plaintiff in *New York Times v. Sullivan, supra,* 376 U.S. 254. Kalven wrote: "There is revealed here a new technique by which defamation might be endlessly manufactured. First, it is argued that, contrary to all appearances, a statement referred to the plaintiff; then, that it falsely ascribed to the plaintiff something that he did not do, which should be rather easy to prove about a statement that did not refer to plaintiff in the first place. . . ." Kalven, *The New York Times Case: A Note on "The Central Meaning of the First Amendment,"* 1964 Sup. Ct. Rev. 191, 199.

Even if we accept the plaintiff's thesis that criticism of nude encounter therapy may be interpreted as libel of one practitioner, the evidence does not support a finding in favor of plaintiff.

Whether or not a publication to the general public is defamatory is "whether in the mind of the average reader the publication, considered as a whole, could reasonably be considered as defamatory." . . .

The majority opinion contains this juxtaposition of ideas: "Secondly, defendants' [proposed] instructions that the jury must find that a substantial segment of the public did, in fact, believe that Dr. Simon Herford was, in fact, Paul Bindrim was properly refused. For the tort of defamation, publication to one other person is sufficient, *ante.*"

The first sentence refers to the question whether the publication was defamatory of plaintiff. The second refers to whether the defamatory matter was published. The former is an issue in this case. The latter is not. Of course, a publication to one person may constitute actionable libel. But this has no bearing on the principle that the allegedly libelous effect of a publication to the public generally is to be tested by the impression made on the average reader. . . .

The only instruction given the jury on the issue of identification stated that plaintiff had the burden of proving "That a third person read the statement and reasonably understood the defamatory meaning and that the statement applied to plaintiff."

That instruction was erroneous and prejudicial in that it only required proof that one "third person" understood the defamatory meaning.

The word "applied" was most unfortunate in the context of this instruction. The novel was about nude encounter therapy. Plaintiff practiced nude encounter therapy. Of course the novel "applied to plaintiff," particularly insofar as it exposed what may result from such therapy. This instruction invited the jury to find that plaintiff was libeled by criticism of the kind of therapy he practiced. The effect is to mulct the defendants for the exercise of their First Amendment right to comment on the nude marathon. . . .

The majority opinion adopts the position that actual malice may be inferred from the fact that the book was "false." That inference is permissible against a defendant who has purported to state the truth. But when the publication purports to be fiction, it is absurd to infer malice because the fiction is false. . . .

The majority opinion seems to say malice is proved by Doubleday's continuing to publish the novel after receiving a letter from an attorney (not plaintiff's present attorney) which demanded that Doubleday discontinue publication "for the reasons stated in" a letter addressed to Gwen Davis. An examination of the latter demonstrates the fallacy of that inference.

The letter to Davis [Mitchell] asserted that the book violated a confidential relationship, invaded plaintiff's privacy, libelled him and violated a "common law copyright" by "using the unpublished words" of plaintiff. It added "From your said [television] appearances, as well as from the book, it is unmistakable that the 'Simon Herford' mentioned in your book refers to my client." . . .

The letters did not assert that any statement of purported fact in the book was false. The only allegation of falsity was this: "In these [television] appearances you stated, directly or indirectly, that nude encounter workshops, similar to the one you attended, are harmful. The truth is that those attending my client's workshops derive substantial benefit from their attendance at such workshops."

These letters gave Doubleday no factual information which would indicate that the book libelled plaintiff. . . .

From an analytical standpoint, the chief vice of the majority opinion is that it brands a novel as libelous because it is "false," i.e., fiction; and infers "actual malice" from the fact that the author and publisher knew it was not a true representation of plaintiff. From a constitutional standpoint the vice is the chilling effect upon the publisher of any novel critical of any occupational practice, inviting litigation on the theory "when you criticize my occupation, you libel me."

I would reverse the judgment.

TABLE OF CASES

*Asterisk indicates text of case given.

661

INDEX

677